# VERDI AND
# HIS MAJOR CONTEMPORARIES

GARLAND REFERENCE LIBRARY
OF THE HUMANITIES
(VOL. 1016)

ANNALS OF ITALIAN OPERA

# VERDI AND
# HIS MAJOR CONTEMPORARIES
## *A Selected Chronology of*
## *Performances with Casts*

Thomas G. Kaufman

with the research
assistance of
Marion Kaufman

foreword by
William Ashbrook

GARLAND PUBLISHING, INC. • NEW YORK & LONDON
1990

Annals of Opera Vol. 1

Library of Congress Cataloging-in-Publication Data

Kaufman, Thomas G.
   Verdi and his major contemporaries : a selected chronology of
performances with casts / Thomas G. Kaufman with the research
assistance of Marion Kaufman ; foreword by William Ashbrook.
      p. cm. — (Annals of Italian opera) (Garland reference
library of the humanities ; vol. 1016)
   Includes bibliographical references and index.
   ISBN 0-8240-4106-2 (alk. paper)
   1. Opera—19th century—Performances—Bibliography. 2. Opera—
Italy—19th century—Bibliography. 3. Verdi, Giuseppe, 1813–1901—
Performances—Bibliography. I. Kaufman, Marion. II. Title.
III. Series. IV. Series: Garland reference library of the
humanities ; vol. 1016
ML128.O4K4   1990
792.5'0945'0934—dc20                                        90-3549
                                                               CIP
                                                               MN

Printed on acid-free, 250-year-life paper
Manufactured in the United States of America

To
Marion

# CONTENTS

Advisory Board    viii
Foreword, by William Ashbrook    ix
Preface    xi
Acknowledgments    xxiii

Giuseppe Apolloni    1
Luigi Arditi    11
Arrigo Boito    13
Giovanni Bottesini    27
Alfredo Catalani    31
Franco Faccio    45
Antonio Carlos Gomes    47
Filippo Marchetti    61
Saverio Mercadante    77
Emanuele Muzio    109
Otto Nicolai    111
Giovanni Pacini    117
Carlo Pedrotti    155
Achille Peri    169
Errico Petrella    179
Amilcare Ponchielli    221
Federico Ricci    247
Giuseppe Verdi    263

Miscellaneous and Multiple Composers    565

Bibliography    581
Index    589

FOREWORD

One of the great distortions perpetrated by some critics and musicologists has been a narrow-minded emphasis on great composers and masterpieces to the exclusion of background figures and lesser works. When I was young this distortion even extended to the point of regarding the whole field of opera, allowing at most for a scant handful of "exceptions", to be on a much lower level than what used to be referred to as "absolute" music. Such a limited vision makes it difficult, if not impossible, to assess correctly the position of a composer, especially those like Verdi and Wagner, given to perpetrating mystifications and their own distortions about what might have influenced them. There is an imperative need, as my friend John Deathridge likes to put it, "to see the real nineteenth century".

One can scarcely exaggerate the importance of the musical press--a nineteenth century invention, by the way--in affording us a day-by-day, season-by-season impression of where certain operas were given and by whom they were performed. Recently the work of amassing the evidence has been vastly eased by the proliferation of detailed theater histories and *croni-storie* and the reprinting of some of the original journals themselves, to say nothing of their circulation in the convenience of microfilm or microfiche.

The present volume takes the vital next step in affording a basis for the interpretation of this evidence by collecting in a logical and certainly convenient way an ample sampling. This sampling involves the selected works of a representative cross section of Italian opera composers who were roughly contemporary to Verdi. This evidence reveals not only the dispersal of an individual work, but it further allows an impression of the quite extraordinary vogues of such forgotten operas as Apolloni's *L'Ebreo* (1855) and Gomes' *Il Guarany* (1870). It also details the erstwhile popularity of many other works such as Mercadante's *Leonora* (1845), Pacini's *Bondelmonte* (1845), Marchetti's *Ruy Blas* (1870) and Ponchielli's *I Promessi Sposi* (1856) which are yet to be revived in the postwar explosion of interest in the ottocento, and which certainly seem to be deserving of such attention.

To one like myself, who is fascinated by the careers of opera singers, what and where they sang, the information provided by naming the principal mem-bers of the introductory casts in each theater is also very welcome. One wishes that an index of singers had been possible, but I fully understand the reasons for its absence at this time. These cast lists also provide some details of the careers of many of the most important nineteenth century conductors, most of whom have been even more shadowy figures than the singers.

Another fascinating aspect of this volume is the role of touring companies in disseminating opera to what at first glance may seem to be remote and unlikely places.

I do not know anybody better equipped to present this material to the public than Tom Kaufman, whom I have known for a good many years now. He possesses the requisite combination of a wide ranging background impelled by curiosity and fueled by persistence that makes possible as reliable a compilation of selected performance history as we are apt to get. As he is the first to admit, there is more potential information than any single person could cover, let alone absorb, in a multiplicity of lifetimes. I can think of no one with wider experience than his to serve him when it comes to selecting which composers to include and deciding which of their works gives the clearest representative impression of their career and potential influence. Certainly, a broad cross section of the operas of Verdi's leading contem-poraries affords a less distorted view of Verdi's real achievements than we receive if we regard him as an isolated peak rather than as the highpoint in a fascinating mountain range.

We can only hope that other volumes in the series will become available in due season. The necessary information is more elusive from the first decades of the nineteenth century than for the more thoroughly covered second half, but the effort required to produce a volume similar to this one on Rossini, Donizetti and Bellini amid a representative selection of their contemporaries would be more than repaid in appreciation. And may this volume prove an inspiration to succeeding generations of researchers to undertake the task of making available for interpretation more and more areas of performance history.

Terre Haute, Ind.                                                William Ashbrook
December 1989

PREFACE

I did not know it at the time, but this book was born one evening about 40 years ago when I was listening to a radio broadcast of opera excerpts. The announcer played "Suoni la tromba" from Bellini's *I Puritani*, and the marvelous melody new to me took me by storm. It taught me that the works then in the repertory did not have a monopoly on good music, and started me on a lifetime of exploring less familiar works. Ever since, forgotten operas, not only by *bel canto* composers but also by Verdi and his contemporaries in Italy, France and Germany have been of particular interest.

One thing led to another, and I soon found myself writing liner notes for a private label recording of the 1954 Florence production of Donizetti's *Don Sebastiano*. Loewenberg's *Annals of Opera* states that its last previous production was in Rome in 1911. I thought it likely that the great baritone Mattia Battistini sang in the production, but was unable to confirm this with the literature then available. A similar problem came up with liner notes for Mercadante's *Orazi e Curiazi*. Loewenberg said nothing about a production in Vienna, and while he did list one for St. Petersburg, he gave no date. Manferrari mentioned a Vienna staging, and the decision to include it in my essay turned out to be a mistake. Additional research showed that the performance was a figment of somebody's imagination.

This provided the impulse to start preparing little lists of the performance histories with casts of many operas of the period, only to find out that very few of the major theaters of the nineteenth century were documented in the form of published annals. The project was by now too far advanced to let a small detail like that get in the way, and I soon started putting together my own cast lists for these theaters. I needed them to prepare chronologies of the careers of many great singers and to prepare the performance histories of operas.

I discussed the idea of eventually publishing such a study with Don White, of Opera Rara, an organization dedicated to reviving and recording long-forgotten nineteenth century operas, and with a special interest in the performance histories of these works. He was both enthusiastic and helpful, to the extent that this project would not have been possible without his encouragement. He called to my attention such theatrical or musical newspapers as the *Allgemeine Musikalische Zeitung*, while a reference in Harold Rosenthal's *The Mapleson Memoirs* suggested the *Gazzetta Musicale di Milano*. Professor Martin Chusid of the Institute for Verdi Studies told me about *Teatri, Arte e Letteratura*. I soon learned of the existence of many other similar theatrical journals, and with the help of the Biblioteca Nazionale Braidense in Milan, and their photographer, Otello Magnani, I started to amass a collection of these newspapers on microfilm.

Another friend told me about the interlibrary loan system, and I was extremely fortunate to enjoy the help and friendship of Ms. Janet Bone, Interlibrary Loan Librarian, of the Morris County Free Library. Not only did she supply me with countless books, but she also introduced me to what was to be the greatest source of all: A little volume entitled *Newspapers in Microform* which listed all the papers by country and city which were held by U.S. or Canadian libraries. We were both amazed at how many were available on interlibrary loan. Soon, working mainly from these theatrical newspapers and the available political newspapers from many major cities, the rough city chronologies began to take shape. They have become a formidable reference tool--not only for such renowned theaters as the Italien in Paris, the Imperial in St. Petersburg, the first Teatro Colón in Buenos Aires, the Liceo in Barcelona and the Real in Madrid, but even for such less obvious places as the various theaters in Sydney, the Tacon in Havana, the Naum in Constantinople and the Khedivial in Cairo.

During this time I learned that touring companies also visited cities not normally associated with operatic performances, like Calcutta, Shanghai, Manila and Batavia. The latter seemed to be of particular interest because it seemed to be the most remote place to enjoy regular seasons of Italian opera. These presented greater obstacles and would not have been possible without the help of Josie Cook of the Drew University Library, and the fact that the Center for Research Libraries in Chicago will order back issues of newspapers to which they are currently subscribing for patrons affiliated with a member library. Batavia proved to be the most difficult of all, and required a special visit to the Royal Library in Den Haag. It turned up some unexpected findings, e.g., *Aida* was given in far away Batavia six years before Manchester and 10 years before Glasgow. *La Gioconda* was given there 70 years before being heard in Paris (and that performance only a radio broadcast), while the same composer's *I Promessi Sposi*, given in the Javan capital in 1885, is yet to be performed in either that city or London. Calcutta is equally interesting. It actually heard *La Forza del Destino* before it was given in Naples. Adelaide, Australia was apparently the last city to hear Donizetti's *Roberto Devereux* in the nineteenth century, while Los Angeles had that distinction as far as *Anna Bolena* was concerned.

Another city that required a special effort was Dunedin in southern New Zealand. It was of particular importance for two reasons: The New Zealand premieres of many operas took place in Dunedin, rather than in Auckland or Wellington, and it seems to be the southernmost city to have had regular seasons of opera. It may even be the southernmost city to have ever heard operatic performances, although it seems likely that at one time or another a touring company visited Bahia Blanca in Argentina.

I also had the good fortune of being introduced to Dr. Susana Salgado of Montevideo, who was working on a book on the Teatro Solis in that city; Juan Dzazopulos of Santiago, Chile, who had compiled extensive chronicles of the Teatro Municipal; and to Jenny Dawson who had prepared a similar list for performances in Brisbane. Dr. Alison Gyger put her extensive research on Australian performances at my disposal, as did Professor Jerzy Got-Spiegel for Lemberg (Lwov), Dr. Antonio Defraia for Cagliari and John O'Leary for Cork, Ireland.

I encountered many problems in compiling this list, and in order to present the data in an intelligible and concise manner, I had to make many compromises. While I tried to be as consistent as possible, I decided that it would be better to adjust the format to the needs of each particular opera, rather than to try to adjust the facts so that they would conform to one generalized format. Some of these problems and their solutions are discussed below:

1.    Gaps.

There are still many gaps at the time of writing. Most important for performances in Italian are some key seasons in Lima, nearly all the seasons in Quito, Guyaquil, and the Argentine and Mexican provinces, as well as many Spanish provincial centers. Rosario and Cordoba in Argentina, and Cadiz, Malaga, Valencia, Bilbao, and Seville in Spain, had frequent and significant seasons often with star singers, and sometimes featuring long forgotten operas. Seville, for instance, was apparently the only city to give *Stiffelio* and *Aroldo* in the same season during the nineteenth century, an interesting fact discovered by Francisco Segalarva Cabella of Malaga. Virtually nothing has been published on these, and newspapers are almost totally inaccessible at this time. Other gaps include lesser cities (and sometimes the capitals) in Balkan and other eastern European countries, smaller cities in southern Italy and Sicily, the former French North Africa, Viet Nam, and other smaller states.

It must therefore be recognized that what is being presented here is far from a finished document. In addition to these gaps for which information is now totally lacking, there are also a few gaps, especially for postwar performances, which could have been filled had more time been available. But publishers have deadlines to meet, so it was decided to go to press now with whatever data are available and to fill in as many gaps as possible in a later edition. This seems to be the logical approach, since, by its very nature, it is doubtful that this study can ever be finished. There will always be another city, theater, opera, or composer that should have been included, another theatrical journal examined, or another singer identified.

2.  Conductors.

Today's opera audiences are accustomed to a stand-up conductor who shares equal billing with the singers. It was not always so, especially in Italy during the early part of the nineteenth century. In the days of Donizetti and Bellini the stand-up conductor with a baton did not exist, at least in Italy. Instead, a member of the orchestra, frequently, but not necessarily, the first violin, was also its leader during the performance, while it was another maestro who had already prepared the orchestra and singers. The latter usually sat at the "cembalo." Their designation in libretti was often *maestro al cembalo, direttore dell'opera* and *primo violino, direttore dell'orchestra*. They were usually engaged for the season and often stayed in the same city for many years. They were far less famous than the singers, and up to the mid-1850s were rarely mentioned in reviews, although they might well be identified in the prospectus for the season. This practice changed slowly and at a different rate in different cities. If the designations in libretti can be taken literally, the first Italian theater to use a stand-up conductor was probably the Teatro della Pergola in Florence in 1836[1]. Other cities started to change over gradually in the late 1850s, and it is likely that the changeover was complete by the early 1870s. As a result, the conductors can often not be identified for earlier productions, although they are generally available for the later works. No attempt was made to differentiate between first violins and true stand-up conductors.

3.  Singer's names.

These presented two special problems:

a. Married women singers: Many singers continued to sing under their maiden names after marriage, many others did not. Sometimes they used hyphenated names, sometimes these names were reversed. Unfortunately, the literature is inconsistent in this regard, and it is possible for the same artist to be referred to by any number of names. Thus, Angiolina Ortolani-Tiberini, a great singer and the wife of Mario Tiberini, may show up as Ortolani, or Tiberini, or Ortolani-Tiberini, or even Tiberini-Ortolani. Tiberini may have been her second husband, since she is also sometimes referred to as Ortolani-Wallandris. To confuse matters even more, there is

---

[1]. A libretto for the Spring 1836 production of Donizetti's *Belisario* cited by Marcello de Angelis: *La Musica del Granduca* (Florence, 1978) lists Nicola Petrini Zamboni as *capo e dir. d'orch.*; Andrea Nencini as *maestro e dir. dell'opera* and Alamanno Biagi as *primo violino*. This does not necessarily prove the point--the *capo e dir. d'orchestra* may well have been a "*super*" *primo violino* waving his bow while there frequently were several *primo violinos*. But it does serve as a strong indication of change, especially when one considers that Petrini-Zamboni had come from Paris where it is likely that they already had stand-up conductors. (London is known to have had them, and Paris is generally considered as being either even with, or even slightly ahead of London at that time.)

also an Antonietta Ortolani-Brignole. But not all singers used such hyphenated names. Giuditta Pasta sang under her husband's name, and to refer to her as G. Negri-Pasta would be confusing. Adelina Patti apparently always used her maiden name, and it would make no sense to refer to her as Patti-Nicolini, even while she was married to him. Josephine Wilmot sang as Wilmot for a number of years, then after marriage, became Giuseppina Medori and sang under that name, a name under which she became quite famous. Such problems can also occur with male singers. Thus, Ernest Nicolas became Ernesto Nicolini. Also, in many cases given names and nicknames were used interchangeably. For example, Angiolina Tagliavia married a baritone named Cerne and went from her full maiden name to a much simpler, but hardly recognizable Lina Cerne.

b. Spellings: Because of careless reporting or typesetting, the spelling of the names of many singers was, to say the least, inconsistent in the nineteenth century. Thus, Enrico Barbaccini has been spelled Barbacini with one c just as often as with two c's, even in the same source, sometimes on the same page. In the same way, Vicentelli could be Vincentelli, Dalla Costa could be Della Costa, Giordani and Giordano are used almost interchangeably as are De Ruggerio and de Ruggero. It is sometimes impossible to determine which is the correct one. Furthermore, Spanish sources frequently changed the spelling of Italian names, often doubling single consonants (Grisi could become Grissi) and disposing of double consonants (Pretti could become Preti).

In order to be as consistent as possible, but without causing confusion, the following conventions have been used.

a.  Famous artists are listed under the names by which they were best known: A. Patti, G. Grisi, F. Persiani, P. Viardot, M. Malibran, E. Nicolini, Mario (no initial), G. Medori, M. Gazzaniga (no need for -Malaspina), A. Ortolani-Tiberini, etc.

b.  Married artists are listed using hyphenated names: C. Barili-Patti, C. Barili-Thorn, L. Ruggero-Antonioli, etc.

c.  Reasonable but consistent (as far as possible) spellings are used for those singers where the absolute correct spelling is uncertain: C. Baucardé (he is also spelled as Beaucardé or as Baucardè), E. Barbacini, C. Vincentelli, etc.

4.  Arrangement of entries.

Depending on their success, individual operas could range anywhere from one staging to thousands. Thus it was possible to identify only 24 productions of *Alzira*, while it could be estimated that a repertory opera such as *Il Trovatore* or *Aida* probably had 10,000 to 25,000. (For purposes of this study the term "production" refers to a decision to perform--thus if a touring company gave a work in 20 different cities, even with the same cast, it is regarded as 20 different productions, and, provided that the information is available and all the cities important enough, this results in 20 entries). Therefore, an *Alzira* is listed complete (or, rather, as complete as possible), but for *Il Trovatore* only city and opera house premieres are given. Also many operas such as *I Lombardi* or *Luisa Miller* had three distinct careers: A period of great popularity during the mid-nineteenth century when they were performed very frequently, occasional performances in the twentieth century up to 1945, and a new career after that. It was decided to break down the listings into these three time frames for those works where three distinct careers could be identified. It might be best to tabulate the type of treatment given each Verdi opera below:

| Opera | Nineteenth Century | Early Twentieth Century | Post-World War II |
|---|---|---|---|
| *Oberto* | Complete | Complete | Complete |
| *Un Giorno di Regno* | Complete | Complete* | Complete |
| *Nabucco* | Premieres | Selected** | Selected |
| *I Lombardi* | Selected | Complete | Selected |
| *Ernani* | Premieres | Selected | Selected |
| *I Due Foscari* | Selected | Complete | Complete |
| *Giovanna d'Arco* | Complete | Complete* | Complete |
| *Alzira* | Complete | Complete | Complete |
| *Attila* | Selected | Complete | Complete |
| *Macbeth* | Premieres | Complete** | Premieres |
| *I Masnadieri* | Selected | Complete | Complete |
| *Jérusalem* | Selected | Complete*** | Complete |
| *La Battaglia di Legnano* | Complete | Complete | Complete |
| *Luisa Miller* | Premieres | Complete | Complete |
| *Il Corsaro* | Complete | Complete* | Complete |
| *Stiffelio* | Complete | Complete | Complete |
| *Rigoletto* | Premieres | N.A.**** | N.A. |
| *Il Trovatore* | Premieres | N.A. | N.A. |
| *La Traviata* | Premieres | N.A. | N.A. |
| *Les Vêpres Siciliennes* | Complete | Complete** | Complete |
| *Simon Boccanegra* | Complete | Complete** | Selected |
| *Aroldo* | Complete | Complete | Complete |
| *Un Ballo in Maschera* | Premieres | N.A. | N.A. |
| *La Forza del Destino* | Premieres | N.A. | N.A. |
| *Don Carlos* | Complete | Complete** | Selected |
| *Aida* | Premieres | N.A. | N.A. |
| *Otello* | Premieres | N.A. | N.A. |
| *Falstaff* | Premieres | N.A. | N.A. |

\* No performances traced. It is doubtful if there were any between 1900 and 1945.

\*\* Too little is known about the prewar revival of Verdi operas in Germany to do justice to the listings of *Nabucco*, *Macbeth*, *I Vespri Siciliani*, *Simon Boccanegra* and *Don Carlos*.

\*\*\* Only one performance traced, but too little information is available on French opera houses to be certain of this point. It would not be surprising if *Jérusalem* were actually performed frequently in France during this period.

\*\*\*\* N.A. indicates that separate entries for the twentieth century would not be applicable since the opera was always in the repertory.

5.  <u>Importance of information</u>.

Since it would have been impossible and redundant to include all available performance data on the operas of this period in one volume, a decision had to be made regarding the type of data of the greatest interest and value. On this basis, it was felt that the following priorities could be established:

a.  World premieres, with dates and casts of the operas by the most important and most interesting composers of the period. Even here, some significant names had to be excluded or limited to their most successful operas. These are composers like Antonio Cagnoni, essentially because the data available at this time are too fragmentary; Lauro Rossi, for the same reason and because he might fit in better in the bel canto period (which will be covered by a future volume); Giuseppe Libani, because successful as his *Il Conte Verde* was, he had a very short career, dying prematurely before the age of 40; Alessandro Nini because he seems less important than other composers with complete listings; Giuseppe Sanelli, Stefano Gobati, Salvatore Auteri-Manzocchi, and more for similar reasons. On the other hand, even though their works were generally less successful than those of some of the previously mentioned composers, Emanuele Muzio, Luigi Arditi and Franco Faccio are all included because of their importance in the musical life of the nineteenth century in general, and to the career of Giuseppe Verdi in particular. Also, the earlier operas of Pacini and Mercadante have had to be remanded to an earlier volume, and, while Federico Ricci's operas were included, full performance histories of his joint works with his brother Luigi will be included in a later volume (premiere casts of these have been included under multicomposer operas). In the case of Otto von Nicolai, only his Italian operas are included here. It may seem inconsistent to have included Nicolai's *Il Templario*, but not Michael Balfe's *Il Talismano*, the reason being that the Balfe work is more English (it was written to an English text which was translated into Italian) than the Nicolai (composed in Italy to an Italian text) is German.

b.  Dates and casts of the local premieres of repertory operas in as many key operatic centers, cities, and countries as reasonable. Country premieres can be a problem, especially since they did not always take place in the principal city of the country involved. Thus, some operas were given in Nice before Paris, in Odessa before St. Petersburg, or in Adelaide before Sydney or Melbourne. In this regard, the first ever operatic season in New Zealand took place in Dunedin in 1864.

c.  "Complete" performance histories of genuine rarities, especially operas already revived in the postwar period or likely to be revived. This goal leads to many new problems in that some works which today would be considered as genuine rarities were actually repertory operas in the nineteenth century. An excellent example is Apolloni's *Ebreo*, for which it has been possible to identify close to 250 actual productions. To list all of these with full casts, even if they could all be located, would have had limited interest and would take away from more essential information. So a compromise was necessary.

In selecting the works to be listed complete, various other choices had to be made. Thus, it was felt that the operas of Mercadante, Pacini, and Ponchielli would be more interesting than the *buffo* works of Pedrotti or even Petrella. Therefore it was decided to limit the extent of the listings of certain Pedrotti comic operas, although his major *opera seria*, *Isabella d'Aragona*, is listed as complete as possible.

d.  Selected key productions of typical operas of special interest. While a complete list of the productions of, for instance, Verdi's *Otello* would sound fascinating, it would be unworkable. The problems are many: for one thing, most productions were in minor cities with lesser casts. So why not list productions either with major singers or in major cities/opera houses? Even this would not be feasible--many are already listed elsewhere, and those that are not listed, e.g., in Vienna, Paris, Dresden, or Berlin would take years of additional research to identify. Complete chronologies of the Opéra in Paris, The Hofoper in Vienna, or that in Berlin are theoretically possible, and it is to be hoped that some enterprising soul will undertake these projects with a view to eventually publishing the results. Perhaps such a project is already under way. But other key cities, such as Dresden, are not possible because the records were destroyed by the war, and newspapers are not available at this time.

6.  Order of Listings.

Loewenberg's lists are arranged chronologically, both as far as the operas are concerned and also for the entries for each opera. This is fine when there are relatively few entries, but when there are as many, e.g., *Il Trovatore*, a researcher seems more likely to want to look up its premiere in, say Dallas, than its first ten productions. So it was decided to organize the individual entries by country. This immediately causes a new problem--does one list the once German city of Breslau (which has now become Wroclaw in Poland) under Germany or Poland? Is Lemberg/Lwov Austrian, Polish, or Russian? Is Fiume Hungarian, Italian, or Jugoslav? The most logical approach seems to be to follow the boundaries in existence between the two world wars with two exceptions: Some of the cities in Dalmatia (Zara is the best example) are listed under Jugoslavia because they are contiguous with that country while Fiume is listed under Italy because it was essentially Italian during its operatic heyday, and Vilnius is listed under Lithuania because its cultural (and operatic) connotations are with that country. It is also likely that, if Lithuania is given its freedom, Vilnius will remain as its capital. Hong Kong is listed separately, and Belfast is listed under Great Britain. Also, while Loewenberg frequently had separate entries for islands (Corsica, Corfu, Sicily, etc.), this policy also results in inconsistencies. Therefore, they are all included under France, Greece, Italy, etc. Hawaii and Puerto Rico will, however, have separate listings.

On the other hand, cities in countries that have become independent after World War II are listed as being in the newly independent country. Thus, one should look for Jerusalem under Israel rather than Palestine and for Batavia under Indonesia rather than Dutch Indies. Yet the name of the city would not have been changed. St. Petersburg, Constantinople, and Batavia can all be found under their nineteenth century names.

7.  Indices.

Much information on singers and conductors that has never been published elsewhere has been included here. As a result, an index arranged by singers would certainly seem to be desirable. Yet it was decided not to include one at this time. There are many reasons for this:

a.  The information on singers that is actually included would be too fragmentary to be of any real value to individuals researching a given singer.

b.  This series is intended as a research tool in the study of composers and their operas rather than singers. Since the arrangement is by composers, operas are indexed.

c.  It is not always possible to identify a singer in a satisfactory manner. For example there are any number of baritones usually just identified in the literature as Morelli. These include Filippo Morelli Ponti, Antonio Morelli, Cesare Morelli-Condolmieri and Vincenzo Morelli Bartolami. There was also a bass who sang in Paris in the 1830s and 1840s named Giovanni Morelli and another one by the same name who sang in Naples in the 1860s. While it is likely that all the Morellis listed for the mid-nineteenth century were one or another of these, not all have been correctly identified and could not be correctly indexed.

d.  A complete index of singers is planned for the entire series when it is finished.

e.  An index by country, city, and theater that has also been recommended is unnecessary, since the listings are already arranged alphabetically by country and city, and scanning them for entries for a city or theater of particular interest is a relatively easy matter.

8.  Corrections of previously published data.

Some of the dates given in this study differ from those previously published, especially by Loewenberg in his *Annals of Opera*. Desirable as this might seem, it would not have been feasible to footnote all of these corrections to Loewenberg and other well known sources--it would have added significantly to the length of this volume and would have delayed publication. However the basis of changes to Loewenberg have already been published as they apply to Donizetti's *Don Sebastiano*.[2] The sources for the corrections to other operas would be comparable. In a few select cases, usually when they apply to world premieres, the sources are footnoted.

9.  Errors.

It is the goal of every author to achieve an error-free book. Regretfully, this rarely happens, and much as I would like to be an exception, I doubt if I could come near this goal. The reasons for

---

[2]. See Kaufman, Thomas G.: *A Bibliography of Opera House Annals*. Journal 5, Donizetti Society, London, 1984, pp. 320-321.

errors are many. For one thing, it is absolutely impossible to check every source--the fact that a cast is listed in a libretto or newspaper advertisement does not mean that it did not change, or that if it did, the reviewer was aware of the change. Thus, many errors may well be the type that has been handed down by one source to another, and not caught at this point. I am also convinced that I have added many of my own, especially in copying down dates or casts from the printed page to my PC. I can only hope that, in providing such a massive amount of facts I can be forgiven for a small amount of errors that thorough checking did not pick up. I would certainly be grateful if anybody who spots errors, be they of omission or commission, or who knows additional sources or has additional dates and casts, were to bring them to my attention.

10. <u>Language</u>.

Every effort has been made to identify both the local premiere in the vernacular and that in Italian. It should be noted that, on many occasions where Loewenberg might indicate a production in the vernacular, that might only be partly true. The chorus and local singers probably did sing in their native tongue, but in most cases the Italian guests sang in Italian. Productions in mixed languages were very common in the nineteenth and early twentieth centuries, especially in Central and Eastern Europe.

11. <u>Theaters</u>.

The name of the theater is given wherever possible, which is almost always the case. However, a consistent treatment is impossible when, as so often happened, theaters changed their names. In some cases, these changes are fairly well known, for example, the Costanzi in Rome later became the Teatro Reale dell'Opera and finally the Teatro dell'Opera. In other cases these changes are less well known, and thus harder to follow. Thus, the principal theater in Parma was the Nuovo Ducale for 20 years before it became the Regio. It would have seemed to be wrong to refer to the Costanzi as the Teatro dell'Opera, while to have called the Nuovo Ducale by that name would be confusing. Therefore each theater was handled on an individual basis.

The decision whether or not to translate a foreign name was handled the same way. It seems simpler to refer to the Národni Divadla in Prague as the "National", while it would have been ludicrous to translate the San Carlo in Naples or the Sao Carlos in Lisbon into the Saint Charles. Also, and again in the interest of simplicity the term theater was usually omitted. In a few cases, the abbreviation Th. was placed before the word Royal to distinguish a house named Theater Royal from another named Royal Theater.

12. <u>Alternate title of operas</u>.

As a general rule, no attempt was made to indicate whether an opera was given under its original title, or under an alternate title with the names of the characters also changed. To have attempted to do so would have resulted in a great deal of confusion--i.e., should one list a local premiere of Verdi's *I Vespri Siciliani* both under that title and such alternate titles as *Giovanna de Guzman* or *Batilde di Turenna*? This might have been both possible and interesting in this instance, but then, what about performances of *Un Ballo in Maschera* given under that title but with the action reverting to Stockholm and the names of the characters to the original Gustavus III, Anckarstroem, etc.? In the interest of simplicity, it seemed best to leave well enough alone where these alternate titles are well known. On the other hand, they are indicated in a few special cases where the alternate title is not well known, and where it seemed advisable to indicate the fact that both works are one and the same opera.

13. <u>Definitions of terms</u>.

OTHER PREMIERES:     Only local premieres will be listed.

OTHER PRODUCTIONS:   A reasonably complete list.

PRODUCTION:         A decision to stage an opera in a given city or season. The word production, as used in this context, does not imply that it is a new production in the now accepted sense.

PROJECTED:          In a few cases, a production of particular interest is included even if it has only been announced at the time of writing.

SELECTED            A selection of other important productions is pro-
PRODUCTIONS:       vided.

14. <u>Guide to listings</u>.

The opera is listed first, using capital letters, followed by the composer's classification, usually from the libretto. This is of importance in that it identifies the type of opera involved, although if there is a difference between a "*melodramma tragico*" and a "*tragedia lirica*," I do not know what it is. This is followed by the number of acts, if known. The next line gives the city, theater, and date of the premiere. The librettist is given on the third line, followed by the cast of the world premiere. The letters in parentheses after each character's name serve to identify the role sung by each singer in the lists of other premieres or other productions. Finally, the conductor is given, if known. Occasionally, when it is known that the composer acted as the musical director, this is also indicated.

15. <u>Commonly used abbreviations</u>.

| | |
|---|---|
| Ac.: Academy | L. A.: Los Angeles |
| Ant.: Antiguo | Let.: Lettisch |
| Apr.: April | Libr.: Library |
| Aug.: August | Lith.: Lithuanian |
| Ave.: Avenue | Mar.: March |
| Bar.: baritone | Mez.: mezzo soprano or contralto |
| Buf.: buffo | Mus.: Music |
| Bulg.: Bulgarian | Norw.: Norwegian |
| Carn.: Carnival | Nov.: November |
| Croat.: Croatian | Oct.: October |
| d.: des | Op.: Opera |
| Dan.: Danish | Pol.: Polish |
| Dec.: December | Port.: Portuguese |
| Dut.: Dutch | Rum.: Rumanian |
| Eng.: English | Russ.: Russian |
| Feb.: February | Sec.: Secondary role |
| Fed.: Federation | Sep.: September |
| Fest.: Festival | Slov.: Slovenian |
| Fin.: Finnish | Sop.: soprano |
| Flem.: Flemish | Sp.: Spanish |
| Fr.: French | Str.: Street |
| Ger.: German | Swed.: Swedish |
| Heb.: Hebrew | T.: Theater |
| Hung.: Hungarian | Ten.: tenor |
| Kor.: Korean | Th.: Theater |
| It.: Italian | v.: voer |
| Jan.: January | |

Finally, a word about the goals of this study. Obviously, its paramount purpose is to provide useful information. The secondary purpose is to arouse interest in the forgotten operas of the period, a subject always dear to my heart. There are many such works which once were quite successful, often more so than some of the less familiar Verdi operas, and, while now forgotten, would certainly merit revival. Prominent in this list are such works as Pacini's *Bondelmonte*, *Lorenzino de Medici* and *Fidanzata Corsa*, Mercadante's *Elena da Feltre* and *Leonora*, Achille Peri's *Vittor Pisani*, Carlo Pedrotti's *Isabella d'Aragona*, Errico Petrella's *Marco Visconti* and *I Promessi Sposi*, Marchetti's *Ruy Blas* as well as Amilcare Ponchielli's *Marion Delorme*, *Il Figliuol Prodigo* and *I Promessi Sposi*.

ACKNOWLEDGMENTS

By its very nature, this book would not have been possible without the assistance of many other individuals, whom I will never be able to thank sufficiently. This list includes people of various backgrounds: musicologists, academics, book and libretto collectors, archivists and librarians.

I would like to start by expressing my deep gratitude to the members of the advisory board (listed on page viii) for their support, encouragement and interest. I am also grateful to the invaluable assistance of my editor at Garland Publishing, Ms. Marie Ellen Larcada, and to the other members of the Garland Staff, particularly Mr. Leo Balk for his valuable ideas and for his help in the early stages of the book, and Mr. Douglas Goertzen for the marvelous job he did as a proofreader.

Then I would like to express my appreciation to Mrs. Sally Amato, to Prof. Eduardo Arnosi, to Mr. Luis Arrones, to Prof. William Ashbrook for furnishing the foreword, and for providing specialized information on Boito, to Mr. S. Benaroyo for his help with performances in Israel, to Prof. John Black for providing crucial cast details on the absolute premieres of many of the operas listed here, and for checking the sections on Pedrotti and Petrella, to Mrs. Vera Brodsky Lawrence, to Ambassador Dudley Cheke, to Prof. Martin Chusid of the American Institute of Verdi Studies for vital data from their libretto collection and for assistance with nineteenth century conductors, to Prof. Jeremy Commons, to Prof. Marcello Conati, to Ms. Jenny Dawson for sharing her lists of performances in Brisbane, to Dr. Antonino Defraia for his help in locating rare Italian books and in providing details on performances in Cagliari, to Mr. Roberto Di Nobile Terré for his help on Rosario, to Mr. Juan Dzazopulos for looking up invaluable data on performances in Santiago, to Prof. Andrew Farkas for working with me on many aspects of the book, and especially his help on Budapest, to M. Georges Farret, to Mr. Dennis Foreman for telling me about Era, a veritable gold mine of information, to maestro Alfredo Giovine for his help and encouragement through the years, to Prof. Jerzy Got-Spiegel for his help on Lwov, to Prof. Giorgio Gualerzi, to Dr. Alison Gyger for her help with performances in Melbourne and Sidney, to Mr. Lewis Hall, to Prof. Michael Henstock, to Mr. Giovanni Idonea, to Prof. Harlan Jenkins, to Mrs. Clarissa Lablache Cheer, to maestro Gianni Legger, to Mr. Lim Lai for providing me with detailed information on performances in Germany, Central Europe and elsewhere based on his incredible library, as well as for telling me about many books whose existence I would have otherwise totally ignored, to Fulvio Lo Presti for his help on Apolloni, to Mr. Larry Lustig of the Record Collector, to Mr. Carlo Marinelli for providing invaluable data on twentieth century performances in Italy, to Mr. Antonio Massissimo for his valuable help on performances in Spain, to Mr. Charles Mintzer who was always willing to share his profound knowledge of singers and their careers, to Dr. Mario Moreau for his help with Portuguese performances, to Mr. John O'Leary for his help on Cork, to Mr. Roger Pines for his help on performances by the Dallas Opera, to Dr. Katherine Preston, to Mr. Andrew Porter, to Mrs. Maria F. Rich of the Central Opera Service for providing details of some recent New York performances of operatic rarities, to Mr. Jesse Rosenthal, to Dr. Susana Salgado-Morassi for giving me access to her fabulous chronology of the Teatro Solis in Montevideo, to Mr. Francisco Segalarva Cabella for his help on Seville, to M. Sergio Segalini, to Mr. William Seward, to Ms. Charlotte Shockley, archivist of the Cincinnati Opera, to Prof. Adrienne Simpson, to Mrs. Regina Sokol, to Mr. Marius Sotropa, to the late Mr. Oscar Strona for his help on the theaters in Turin and for sending me his chronology of the Teatro Dal Verme in Milan, to Dr. Ruffo Titta, to Mr. Robert Tuggle of the Metropolitan Opera Archives, to Prof. Gaspare Nello Vetro for his help on Bottesini, to Prof. Alexander Weatherson for sharing his encyclopaedic knowledge of the ottocento and for checking the sections on Pacini and Federico Ricci, to Mrs. Sylvia Weiss-

Schwarz, and to Mr. Don White of Opera Rara both for inspiring this book and for sharing details from his fabulous libretto collection, and to Prof. Larry Wolz for his help on early performances in Texas. I would also like to apologize to anyone whose name was inadvertently omitted.

Equally important are the invaluable contributions made by individual librarians including Ms. Janet Bone, Mrs. Ruth Schultz and Mrs. Susan Rowe of the Morris County Free Library, Mrs. Josepha Cooke of the Drew University Library, and Ms. Linda Naru of the Center for Research Libraries who helped me locate many of the books, newspapers and periodicals which were essential to compiling this volume. Also deserving of special thanks are Mr. Donald Wisdom of the Newspapers and Periodicals Division of the Library of Congress and his staff, the staffs of countless university libraries, prominent among them being Princeton, Rutgers, Cornell, Duke, Harvard, Yale, and the following state universities: Illinois, Indiana, Kentucky, Massachusetts, Michigan, Missouri, North Carolina, Oregon, Texas, and Virginia. Libraries and librarians abroad were equally helpful, especially Mr. Roger Dixon of the Central Library in Belfast, Ms. Val Laing of the City Library in Dunedin, N. Z., Ms. Flavia Tibaldi of the Istituto Italiano di Cultura in Cairo, Egypt, the Newspaper Section of the British Library in Colindale, the City Library in Birmingham, England, Mrs. Eerden and her staff in the Newspaper Section of the Royal Library in Den Haag, The Netherlands, Ms. Charlotte Bonello of the Opéra de Nice, Ms. Geneviève Lièvre of the Opéra de Lyon and Ms. Rita Ineichem of the Geneva opera.

And finally, I am indebted to my wife, Marion, without whose patience, assistance (especially with research) and encouragement this or any other project would have been impossible.


Boonton, N. J.
May 1990

Verdi and
His Major Contemporaries

GIUSEPPE  APOLLONI

1. ADELCHI-*Melodramma tragico* in five acts
Vicenza-Teatro Eretenio-Aug. 16, 1852
Libretto by Giovanni Battista Nicolini

| | |
|---|---|
| Gisla (G.) | Emilia Scotta sop. |
| Ermengarda (E.) | Giovannina Casali Campagna mez. |
| Adelchi (A.) | Giovanni De Vecchi ten. |
| Carlo Magno (C.) | Ruggero Pizzigati bar. |
| Desiderio (D.) | Marco Ghini bass |
| Gilda | Luigia Morselli sec. |
| Svarto | Antonio Rossetti sec. |

OTHER PRODUCTIONS

ITALY

| | | | | |
|---|---|---|---|---|
| Treviso | Onigo | Nov. | 1852 | E. Scotta (G.) C. Negrini (A.) R. Pizzigati (C.) |
| Venice | La Fenice | Dec. 26, 1856 | | L. Bendazzi-Secchi (G.) P. Corvetti (E.) C. Negrini (A.) L. Giraldoni (C.) G. Echeverria (D.) C. E. Bosoni cond. |

2. L'EBREO-*Melodramma tragico* in a prologue and three acts
Venice-Teatro La Fenice-Jan. 23, 1855
Libretto by Antonio Boni

| | |
|---|---|
| Leila (L.) | Marianna Barbieri-Nini sop. |
| Adel-Musa (A.) | Carlo Negrini ten. |
| Issachar (I.) | Giovanni Corsi bar. |
| Ferdinando Re di Aragona (F.) | Cesare Nanni bass |
| Isabella | Luigia Morselli sec. |
| Boabdil el Chic | Felice Peranzoni sec. |
| Gran Giudice | Salvatore Poggiali ten. |
| | |
| Conductor | Carlo Ercole Bosoni |
| Director | Giuseppe Apolloni |

OTHER PREMIERES

ARGENTINA

| | | | | |
|---|---|---|---|---|
| Buenos Aires | Ant. Colón | Oct. 13, 1868 | | A. Pasi (L.) L. Lelmi (A.) A. M. Celestino (I.) G. Segri-Segarra (F.) V. Fumi cond. |

AUSTRALIA

| | | | | |
|---|---|---|---|---|
| Adelaide | Th. Royal | July 16, 1873 | | M. Zenoni (L.) F. Rosnati (A.) F. Coliva (I.) E. Dondi (F.) A. Zelman cond. |
| Melbourne | Prince of Wales | Mar. 13, 1873 | | M. Zenoni (L.) F. Rosnati (A.) F. Coliva (I.) E. Dondi (F.) A. Zelman cond. |

Sydney        Victoria     Sep. 22, 1873 M. Zenoni (L.) F. Rosnati (A.) F.
                                         Coliva (I.) E. Dondi (F.) A. Zelman
                                         cond.


BRAZIL
Rio de        Lirico       July 29, 1856 E. Julienne-Dejean (L.) E. Tamber-
  Janeiro       Fluminense               lick (A.) L. Walter (I.) G. Capurri
                                         (F.)


CHILE
Santiago      Municipal    Sep. 25, 1864 C. Manzini (L.) E. Ballerini (A.) G.
                                         Bertolini (I.) P. De Antoni (F.)


Valparaiso    Victoria     Nov. 17, 1864 C. Manzini (L.) E. Ballerini (A.) G.
                                         Bertolini (I.) P. De Antoni (F.)


CUBA
Havana        Villanueva   Feb.  4, 1868 C. Poch (L.) Bichielli (A.) V. Cot-
                                         tone (I.) P. Medini (F.)


EGYPT
Alexandria    Rossini      Apr.     1864 E. Leonpietra (L.) G. Gambetti (A.)
                                         I. Viganotti (I.) P. Poli-Lenzi (F.)


FRANCE
Ajaccio       San          Autumn   1864 G. Ottonelli-Bresciani (L.) A. Bo-
                Gabriele                 etti (A.) A. Pantaleoni (I.) G.
                                         Corregioli (F.)


Nice          Regio        Nov. 28? 1865 L. Kapp-Young (L.) A. Prudenza (A.)
                                         V. Orlandi (I.) E. Rossi-Galli (F.)


GREECE
Athens        Royal        Dec.     1862 A. Murio-Celli (L.) L. Guglielmini
                                         (A.) A. Garcia (I.)


Corfu         San Giacomo Jan.      1857 I. Galletti-Gianoli (L.) P. Bignardi
                                         (A.) M. Servi (I.)


ITALY
Alessandria   Municipale   Nov.  7, 1855 F. Gordosa (L.) C. Liverani (A.) L.
                                         Giraldoni (I.)


Ancona        Muse         Dec. 25, 1863 A. Bianchi (L.) G. Ugolini (A.) L.
                                         Spellini (I.) E. Rossi-Galli (F.)


Arezzo        Petrarca     Dec. 25, 1872 C. Bacchiani (L.) A. Falciai (A.) F.
                                         Zucchi (I.)


Ascoli        Ventidio     Autumn   1860 F. Capuani (L.) E. Concordia (A.) A.
  Piceno        Basso                    Mazzanti (I.) P. Medini (F.)


Badia         Sociale      Aug.     1868 T. Cotta-Morandini (L.) G. Vanzan
  Polesine                               (A.) A. Grandi (I.)


Bari          Piccinni     Autumn   1856 L. Stramesi (L.)


Bergamo       Sociale      Dec. 26? 1855 C. Crémont (L.) G. Sinico (A.) A.
                                         Carapia (I.)


Bologna       Comunale     Dec. 29, 1855 A. Corbari (L.) T. Palmieri (A.) P.
                                         Gorin (I.)

| Brescia | Grande | Dec. 26? | 1860 | A. Bazzurri (L.) G. Gambetti (A.) A. Grandi (I.) C. Moretti (F.) |
|---|---|---|---|---|
| Cagliari | Civico | Feb. 4, | 1860 | S. Norsa (L.) F. Astor (A.) P. Bonora (I.) |
| Catania | Comunale | Jan. 9, | 1864 | V. Pozzi Brazanti (L.) G. Valentini Cristiani (A.) G. Ferri (I.) C. Gianola (F.) |
| Cento | Comunale | Aug. | 1862 | L. Ponti dall'Armi (L.) F. Patierno (A.) E. Mari-Cornia (I.) L. Sarti cond. |
| Cesena | Comunale | Aug. 11, | 1861 | C. Noel-Guidi (L.) A. Prudenza (A.) V. Orlandi (I.) F. Marinozzi (F.) R. Sarti cond. |
| Chieti | Marrucino | June? | 1864 | E. Pezzoli (L.) F. Rosnati (A.) D. Baldassari (I.) V. Giacomelli (F.) V. Boccabianca cond. |
| Cremona | Concordia | Dec. 26, | 1855 | V. Viola (L.) A. Bozzetti (A.) G. Mancusi (I.) A. Marzorati cond. |
| Fano | Fortuna | Dec. 26? | 1864 | V. Potentini (L.) G. Ugolini (A.) F. Archinti (I.) |
| Fermo | Aquila | Aug. | 1863 | I. Edelvira (L.) E. Barbacini (A.) G. Giotti (I.) E. Rossi-Galli (F.) E. Neri cond. |
| Ferrara | Comunale | Dec. 26, | 1857 | G. Naglia (L.) G. B. Milesi (A.) A. Carapia (I.) L. Venerandi (F.) |
| Fiume | Civico | Mar. 18, | 1858 | M. Zenoni (L.) A. Dall'Armi (A.) C. Fabbricatore (I.) G. De Dominicis (F.) |
| Florence | Pagliano | Nov. | 1856 | M. Barbieri-Nini (L.) P. Mongini (A.) F. Cresci (I.) G. B. Cornago (F.) |
| Forli | Comunale | Nov.? | 1861 | L. Ponti dall'Armi (L.) A. Dall'Armi (A.) G. Giori (I.) M. Ghini (F.) |
| Genoa | Carlo Felice | Nov. 20, | 1855 | L. Bendazzi-Secchi (L.) G. Bettini (A.) G. Ferri (I.) B. Laura (F.) A. Mariani cond. |
| Gorizia | Sociale | Mar. 10? | 1881 | R. Fiorentini-Marangoni (L.) G. De Sanctis (A.) I. De Anna (I.) |
| Guastallo | Sociale | Autumn | 1862 | F. Salvini-Donatelli (L.) G. Ortolani (A.) V. Prattico (I.) |
| Iesi | Concordia | Sep. | 1863 | A. Angelini-Cantalamessa (L.) G. Ortolani (A.) G. Cantù (I.) |
| Imola | Comunale | July 13, | 1862 | L. Ponti dall'Armi (L.) F. Patierno (A.) E. Mari-Cornia (I.) Fitrani (F.) |

Livorno        Avvalorati  Mar.       1869 A.  Giannetti  (L.)  P.  Tagliazucchi
                                            (A.) A.  Borella  (I.)

Lucca          Pantera     Dec. 26? 1864 E.  Concordia  (A.)

Macerata       Condomini   Aug. 30, 1856 N.  De Roissi  (L.)  A.  Prudenza  (A.)
                                            V.  Morelli-Bartolami  (I.)  N.  Conte-
                                            dini  (F.)

Mantua         Sociale     Apr. 28, 1855 M.  Barbieri-Nini  (L.)  A.  Agresti
                                            (A.) G.  Fiori  (I.)  C.  Nanni  (F.)

Messina        Vittorio    Dec. 19, 1863 C.  Cattinari  (L.)  A.  Zenari  (A.)  D.
               Emanuele                     Del Negro  (I.)  C.  Lazzaro  (F.)

Milan          La Scala    Dec. 26, 1855 M.  Barbieri-Nini  (L.)  L.  Graziani
                                            (A.) L.  Giraldoni  (I.)  C.  Nanni  (F.)

Modena         Comunale    Dec. 26, 1858 G.  Ottonelli-Bresciani  (L.)  T.  Pal-
                                            mieri  (A.)  G.  Giori  (I.)  L.  Veneran-
                                            di  (F.)  A.  Sighicelli  cond.

Naples         San Carlo   Feb. 13, 1856 G.  Beltramelli  (L.)  L.  Stefani  (A.)
                                            F.  Colini  (I.)  M.  Arati  (F.)  A.  Fa-
                                            relli  cond.

Novara         Nuovo       Jan.       1860 E.  Leonpietra  (L.)  L.  Vistarini  (A.)
                                            A.  D'Ettore  (I.)

Padua          Nuovo       June 12, 1856 M.  Barbieri-Nini  (L.)  L.  Graziani
                                            (A.) G.  B.  Bencich  (I.)  B.  Cervini
                                            (F.)

Palermo        Bellini     Dec.       1864 T.  Stolz  (L.)  G.  Musiani  (A.)  E.
                                            Storti  (I.)  L.  Ruiz  (F.)

Parma          Regio       Mar. 31, 1861 T.  Cotta-Morandini  (L.)  G.  Valentini
                                            Cristiani  (A.)  A.  Grandi  (I.)  A.
                                            Formis  (F.)  G.  C.  Ferrarini  cond.

Pavia          Civico      Carn. 1861-62 C.  Mongini-Stecchi  (L.)

Perugia        Morlacchi   Carn. 1860-61

Pesaro         Rossini     Sep. 22, 1856 N.  De Roissi  (L.)  A.  Prudenza  (A.)
                                            V.  Morelli-Bartolami  (I.)  N.  Conte-
                                            dini  (F.)

Piacenza       Comunale    Dec. 26? 1859 F.  Gordosa  (L.)  A.  Dall'Armi  (A.)  P.
                                            Gorin  (I.)  G.  Jona  cond.

Pisa           Verdi       Jan. 10, 1869 A.  Contarini  (L.)  L.  Gulli  (A.)  C.
                                            Sacchetti  (I.)  P.  Mattioli  Alessan-
                                            drini  (F.)  L.  Quercioli  cond.

Prato          Metastasio  Dec. 26, 1870 B.  D'Aponte  (L.)  F.  De Ruggero  (A.)
                                            A.  Barbieri  (I.)  A.  Nuti  cond.

Ravenna        Alighieri   May   3, 1857 F.  Gordosa  (L.)  L.  Graziani  (A.)  F.
                                            Coliva  (I.)  B.  Cervini  (F.)  E.  Van-
                                            nuccini  cond.

Reggio Emilia Comunale    Apr. 26, 1856 M. Barbieri-Nini (L.) L. Graziani
                                        (A.) F. Steller (I.) P. Milesi (F.)
                                        G. Tebaldi cond. A. Peri dir.

              Municipale   Dec. 25, 1871 O. Pierangeli (L.) F. Cesari (A.) A.
                                        De Magnani (I.) N. Giommi (F.) G.
                                        Tebaldi cond.

Rimini        Nuovo        Jan.     1862 R. Gianfredi (L.) G. Capponi (A.)

Rome          Argentina    Nov. 19, 1855 A. Basseggio (L.) G. Musiani (A.) F.
                                        Cresci (I.) R. Laterza (F.) E. An-
                                        gelini cond.

Rovigo        Sociale      Oct. 18, 1855 F. Salvini-Donatelli (L.) L. Grazi-
                                        ani (A.) P. Giorgi-Cervini (I.) B.
                                        Cervini (F.)

Savona        Chiabrera    Dec. 25, 1868 F. Scheggi (L.) F. Tavella (A.) L.
                                        Spellini (I.)

Siena         Rinnovati    Dec. 26, 1871 B. D'Aponte (L.)

Sinigaglia    Comunale     Dec. 26, 1868 M. Bruccioni (L.) G. Mastroeni-Ali/
                                        E. Concordia (A.) F. Serafini (I.)
                                        N. Adoni (F.) V. Tabellini cond.

Spoleto       Nobile       Dec. 26? 1859 T. Armellini (L.) A. Jacucci (A.) V.
                                        Quintili-Leoni (I.)

Terni         Nobile       Apr. 30, 1857 L. Chiaromonte (L.) G. Musiani (A.)
                                        P. Baraldi (I.)

Trento        Sociale      May  30, 1858 S. De Montelio (L.) G. Musiani (A.)
                                        L. Giraldoni (I.) P. Milesi (F.) G.
                                        Anzoletti cond. G. Apolloni dir.

Treviso       Societa      Oct.  6, 1855 M. Barbieri-Nini (L.) A. Agresti G.
                                        Corsi (I.) C. Nanni (F.)

Trieste       Grande       Sep. 22, 1855 C. Cattinari (L.) C. Negrini (A.) G.
                                        Guicciardi (I.) G. B. Cornago (F.)
                                        G. A. Scaramelli cond.

Turin         Carignano    Oct.     1859 L. Ponti dall'Armi (L.) A. Dall'Armi
                                        (A.) E. Storti (I.) G. Capponi (F.)

              Regio        Mar. 15, 1868 R. Fiorentini-Marangoni (L.) G. Cap-
                                        poni (A.) G. Valle (I.) A. Fiorini
                                        (F.) F. Bianchi cond.

Udine         Minerva      Nov.?    1863 M. Pirola (L.) A. Mazzanti (I.)

Varese        Sociale      Sep. 28, 1864 G. Naglia (L.) F. Toni-Nazzari (A.)
                                        G. Cantù (I.) L. Vecchi (F.)

Venice        San          Apr. 25, 1856 I. Galletti-Gianoli (L.) Mariotti
              Benedetto                  (A.) G. B. Bencich (I.) A. Biacchi
                                        (F.)

              Goldoni      Dec.     1875 E. Malvezzi (L.) S. Malvezzi (A.) I.
                                        De Anna (I.)

Vercelli      Civico       Dec. 26, 1859 A. Bazzurri (L.) G. Gambetti (A.)
                                        Costanti (I.) G. Marchisio (F.)

Verona        Nuovo        Sep.  6, 1855 M. Piccolomini (L.) G. Fraschini
                                        (A.) L. Giraldoni (I.)

              Filarmonico Sep.     1855 M. Piccolomini (L.) G. Fraschini
                                        (A.) L. Giraldoni (I.)

Vicenza       Eretenio     July 28, 1855 M. Piccolomini (L.) G. Fraschini
                                        (A.) L. Giraldoni (I.) B. Cervini
                                        (F.)

Viterbo       Unione       Aug. 1   1857 F. Capuani (L.) G. Musiani (A.) P.
                                        Baraldi (I.) Sozzi (F.)

JUGOSLAVIA
Ljubljana     Stanovskem   July     1865 M. Armandi (L.) F. Rosnati (A.) G
                                        Giori (I.) G. Galvani (F.)

Split                      Apr.?    1865 V. Falconi (L.) F. Tournerie (I.)

Zagreb        National     June  7, 1865 M. Armandi (L.) F. Rosnati (A.) G.
                                        Giori (I.) G. Galvani (F.)

Zara          Nobile       May?     1861 G. Naglia (L.) G. Verati (A.) P.
                                        D'Ettore (I.) E. Daneri (F.)

MALTA
La Valletta   Manoel       Oct.     1856 G. Elena (L.) P. Stecchi (A.) A. Ca-
                                        rapia (I.)

MEXICO
Mexico City   Nacional     Jan. 29, 1884 M. Peri (L.) F. Giannini (A.) T.
                                        Wilmant (I.)

NEW ZEALAND
Dunedin       Queen's      Feb.  3, 1873 M. Zenoni (L.) F. Rosnati (A.) F.
                                        Coliva (I.) E. Dondi (F.) A. Zelman
                                        cond.

PHILIPPINES
Manila        Arroceros    May 18,  1871 E. Leonpietra (L.) Lendinara (A.) A.
                                        Grandi (I.) N. Pozzi (F.) R. Stefani
                                        cond.

PORTUGAL
Lisbon        Sao Carlos   Mar. 26, 1856 M. Spezia-Aldighieri (L.) C. Braham
                                        (A.) O.  Bartolini (I.)  A. M. Ce-
                                        lestino (F.)  P. A. Coppola cond.

Oporto        Sao Joao     Apr.  4, 1857 Almonti (L.) M. Viani (A.) E. Corti
                                        (I.) E. Manfredi (F.)

PUERTO RICO
Ponce         La Perla              1877 E. Petrilli (I.)

ROMANIA
Bucharest     Nacional     Dec.?    1865 T. Pozzi-Brazanti (L.) F. Pozzo (A.)
                                        F. Steller (I.)

Galati                     Nov. 22? 1868 V. Potentini (L.) S. Perozzi (A.) E.
                                        Corti (I.)

Iasi				Teatrul			Nov.	1,	1860	R. Gianfredi (L.) A. Zenari (A.) E. Storti (I.) G. Segri-Segarra (F.)

RUSSIA
Odessa			Municipal		Summer		1858	V. Pozzi-Montegazza (L.) A. Pozzolini (A.) G. Marra (I.)

SPAIN
Barcelona		Liceo			Oct.	6,	1855	E. Julienne-Dejean (L.) G. De Vecchi (A.) G. Fiorio (I.) A. Rodas (F.)

Bilbao			Viejo			Feb.			1863	A. Bazzurri (L.) A. Zenari (A.) F. Bachi-Perego (I.)

Granada			Isabel la		Apr.			1865	L. Ponti dall'Armi (L.) A. Dall'Armi
				Catolica							(A.) P. Baraldi (I.)

Jerez							Oct.			1864	L. Arancio-Guerrini (L.) F. Pozzo (A.) F. Bachi-Perego (I.) Prosperi (F.)

Palma de		Princesa		Feb.?		1858	M. Pirola (L.) F. Pozzo (A.) D. Dal
Mallorca									Negro (I.) P. Sottovia (F.)

San Lucar de					July?			1864	L. Ponti dall'Armi (L.) A. Dall'Armi
Barromeda									(A.) C. Buti (I.) P. Nolasco-Llorens (F.)

Seville			San			June			1864	L. Ponti dall'Armi (L.) A. Dall'Armi
				Fernando							(A.) C. Buti (I.) P. Nolasco-Llorens (F.) D. Antonietti cond.

Valencia		Principal		June			1858	M. Barbieri-Nini (L.) A. Agresti (A.) G. B. Bencich (I.) C. Nanni (F.)

TUNISIA
Tunis			Cringa			Dec. 20?	1887	Calvi (L.) J. Manfrini (A.) Calvi (I.)

TURKEY
Constan-		Naum			Nov. 30,	1858	L. Chiaromonte (L.) G. Piccinnini
tinople									(A.) F. Coliva (I.) Calcaterra (F.)

Smyrna			Cammarano		Oct. 17,	1864	C. Rosavalle (L.) F. Rosnati (A.) Carnelli/Orsini (I.)

URUGUAY
Montevideo		Solis			May	1,	1861	C. Manzini (L.) E. Ballerini (A.) G. Bertolini (I.) P. De Antoni (F.) A. Ferrari cond.

IMPORTANT REVIVALS-NINETEENTH CENTURY

ITALY
Cagliari		Civico			Oct. 10,	1868	C. Rosavalle (L.) A. Masini (A.) A. Pifferi (I.) G. Sampieri (F.)

Florence		Pagliano		Apr. 29?	1868	G. Monti (L.) G. Valentini Cristiani (A.) S. Sparapani (F.)

Modena          Comunale     June       1864 A. Bertucci-Ortolani (L.) G. Ortola-
                                              ni (A.) F. Coliva (I.) C. Zucchelli
                                              (F.) A. Sighicelli cond.

Naples          San Carlo    Oct.  7, 1856 V. Viola (L.) E. Naudin (A.) F. Co-
                                              lini (I.) M. Arati (F.) A. Farelli
                                              cond.

Palermo         Bellini      Jan. 18, 1869 C. Mongini-Stecchi (L.) G. Ugolini
                                              (A.) E. Storti (I.) C. Zucchelli
                                              (F.)

                             Feb.      1873 E. Ciuti (L.) V. Belardi (A.) A.
                                              Burgio (I.) A. Augier (F.)

Rome            Argentina    Apr. 20, 1872 T. Cotta-Morandini (L.) G. Vanzan
                                              (A.) Caravatti (I.)

                             June  4, 1876 I. Negrini (L.) F. Giannini (A.)
                                              Ciotti (I.)

                Alibert      June 30, 1861 L. Ponti dall'Armi (L.) A. Dall'Armi
                                              (A.) E. Storti (I.) G. Marchetti
                                              (F.)

Trieste         Grande       Dec. 26? 1856 R. Gianfredi (L.) V. Sarti (A.) P.
                                              G. Pacini (I.) G. Segri-Segarra (F.)
                                              G. A. Scaramelli cond.

                             Oct.  3, 1858 E. Julienne-Dejean (L.) G. Musiani
                                              (A.) G. Guicciardi (I.) C. Dalla
                                              Costa (F.) G. A. Scaramelli cond.

                             Feb. 20, 1869 A. Contarini (L.) A. Celada (A.) G.
                                              Spallazzi (I.) A. Cremaschi cond.

                             Dec. 26? 1880 R. Fiorentini-Marangoni (L.) G. De
                                              Sanctis-Marianecci (A.) F. De Magis
                                              (I.) G. Zavaglio cond.

Turin           Nazionale    Sep.       1862 L. Ruggero-Antonioli (L.) P. Chiesi
                                              (A.) F. Varesi (I.) N. Rebottaro
                                              (F.)

Vicenza         Eretenio     Jan. 31, 1878 B. Remondini (L.) P. Augusti (A.) S.
                                              Caltagirone (I.) R. Drigo cond.

PORTUGAL
Lisbon          Sao Carlos   Dec.       1862 L. Perelli (L.) M. Neri (A.) V. Or-
                                              landi (I.) A. M. Celestino (F.)

SPAIN
Barcelona       Liceo        Autumn     1857 M. Barbieri-Nini (L.) A. Agresti
                                              (A.) G. B. Bencich (I.)


OTHER PRODUCTIONS-1900-1945

ARGENTINA
Buenos Aires    San Martin   Feb.  6, 1905

EGYPT
Alexandria      Alhambra     Apr. 18, 1908 A. Alloro (L.) Lanzerotti (A.) B.
                                              Challis (I.) A. Sabellico (F.)

Cairo        Abbas       Mar.      1908 A. Alloro (L.) A. Gamba (A.) B.
                                        Challis (I.) A. Sabellico (F.)

ITALY
Fiume        Civico      Mar.      1901 L. Gabbi (L.) A. Gamba (A.) G. Albi-
                                        nolo (I.) L. Rossatto (F.)

Prato        Metastasio  Carn. 1904-05 A. Baccini (L.) A. Spolverini (A.)
                                        R. De Franceschi (I.) O. Dorval (F.)
                                        U. Fratti cond.

Rome         Adriano     July  1? 1905 A. De Revers (L.) A. Cecchi (A.) R.
                                        Billi (I.) E. Borucchia (F.)

Rovigo       Sociale     Apr. 15, 1900 M. Pizzigalli (L.) A. Gamba (A.) F.
                                        Fazzini (I.) A. Brondi (F.) D. Varo-
                                        la cond.

Trieste      Anfiteatro  July  8, 1905 G. Fabris (L.) G. Doni (A.) E. De
                                        Franceschi (I.) Franchi (F.)

Venice       Malibran    May   4, 1901 L. Gabbi (L.) A. Gamba (A.) Barettin
                                        (I.) F. Fabbri-Boesmi (F.) A. Doni-
                                        zetti cond.

Vicenza      Eretenio    May  17, 1922 G. Russ (L.) A. Dolci (A.) E. Moli-
                                        nari (I.)

MALTA
La Valletta  Reale       Feb. 14, 1906 G. Fabris (L.) F. Granados (A.) R.
                                        De Franceschi (I.) A. Carnevali (F.)
                                        N. Guerrera cond.

URUGUAY
Montevideo   Solis       Apr. 21, 1911 L. Gaudiero (L.) P. Novi (A.) S.
                                        Arrighetti (I.) A. Padovani cond.

OTHER PRODUCTIONS-POST-WORLD WAR II

FRANCE
Montpelier   Opéra       July 31, 1990 S. Alaimo (I.) (Projected)

ITALY
Savona       Chiabrera   Oct. 29, 1989 F. Costa (L.) D. Di Domenico (A.) S.
                                        Alaimo (I.) A. Caforio (F.) M. De
                                        Bernart cond.

San Remo     Casino      Nov.  3, 1989 F. Costa (L.) D. Di Domenico (A.) S.
                                        Alaimo (I.) A. Caforio (F.) M. De
                                        Bernart cond.

3. PIETRO D'ABANO-*Melodramma serio* in three acts
Venice-Teatro la Fenice-Mar. 8, 1856
Libretto by Antonio Boni

| | |
|---|---|
| Luisa | Adelaide Cortesi sop. |
| Arnoldo | Emilio Pancani ten. |
| Pietro d'Abano | Francesco Cresci bar. |
| Pietro da Reggio | Giovanni Battista Cornago bass |
| Maria | Carolina Zambelli sec. |
| Lando | Marco Ghini bass |
| Lucio | Antonio Galletti bass |
| | |
| Conductor | Carlo Ercole Bosoni |
| Director | Giuseppe Apolloni |

4. IL CONTE DI KÖNIGSMARCK-*Melodramma serio* in a prologue and three acts
Florence-Teatro della Pergola-Mar. 17, 1866
Librettist unknown

| | |
|---|---|
| Elisabetta (E.) | Maria Palmieri sop. |
| Carlo (C.) | Marietta De Marini mez. |
| Filippo (F.) | Lodovico Graziani ten. |
| Ernesto (Er.) | Achille de Bassini bar. |
| Sofia | Estella Bennati sec. |
| Conte di Groote | Pietro Grassi sec. |
| Barone | Fortunato Cherubini bass |
| | |
| Director | Giuseppe Apolloni |

OTHER PRODUCTIONS

ITALY
Vicenza        Eretenio     Aug. 28? 1867 M. Siebs (E.) A. Baldi (C.) G. Va-
                                         lentini Cristiani (F.) V. Quintili-
                                         Leoni (Er.)

5. GUSTAVO WASA-*Opera seria* in two acts
Trieste-Teatro Grande-Nov. 16, 1872
Libretto by Ulisse Poggi

| | |
|---|---|
| Edvige (E.) | Emma Wiziak sop. |
| Gustavo (G.) | Giuseppe Capponi ten. |
| Arnoldo (A.) | Adriano Pantaleoni bar. |
| Cristierno (C.) | Ormondo Maini bass |
| Un Frate | Paride Povoleri bar. |
| Un Popolano | Carlo Fiorini sec. |
| | |
| Conductor | Antonio Cremaschi |
| Director | Giuseppe Apolloni |

OTHER PRODUCTIONS

ITALY
Vicenza        Eretenio     Jan. 3, 1876 E. Rastelli (E.) M. Benfratelli (G.)
                                         A. Pantaleoni (A.) T. Costa (C.) R.
                                         Kuon cond. G. Apolloni dir.

# LUIGI ARDITI

1. I BRIGANTI-*Farsa* in one act
Milan-Conservatory-Feb. 19, 1841
Librettist unknown[1]

2. GULNARA-*Drama lirico* in two acts
Havana-Teatro Tacon-Feb. 4, 1848
Libretto by Rafael María Mendive (in Spanish)

| | |
|---|---|
| Gulnara | Fortunato Tedesco sop. |
| Conrado | Giovanni Severi ten. |
| Seyde | Luigi Vita bar. |
| | |
| Conductor | Luigi Arditi |
| Director | Giovanni Bottesini |

3. LA SPIA-*Opera seria* in three acts
New York City-Academy of Music-Mar. 24, 1856
Libretto by Filippo Manetta

| | |
|---|---|
| Francesca | Elise Hensler sop. |
| Maria | Anna de la Grange sop. |
| Harvey Birch | Pasquale Brignoli ten. |
| Carlo Dunwoodie | Filippo Morelli-Ponti bar. |
| Wharton | Alessandro Gasparoni bass |
| Lawton | Louis Quinto ten. |
| Sigrevus | William Müller bar. |
| Betta | Morra sec. |
| | |
| Conductor | Luigi Arditi |
| Director | Luigi Arditi and/or Giovanni Bottesini |

---

1. The singers, not further identified as to role, first name or register were all students at the Conservatory. Only their last names are known: Hetznecker, Mazocchi, Gandini and Lorini.

ARRIGO BOITO

1. MEFISTOFELE-*Opera ballo* in a prologue, three acts, and an epilogue
Teatro alla Scala-Mar. 5, 1868
Libretto by Arrigo Boito

| | |
|---|---|
| Margherita (M.) | Melania Reboux sop. |
| Elena (E.) | Melania Reboux sop. |
| Faust (F.) | Girolamo Spallazzi bar. |
| Mefistofele (Me.) | Marcel Junca bass |
| Marta (Ma.) | Guglielmina Flory mez. |
| Pantalis (P.) | Guglielmina Flory mez. |
| Wagner | |
| Nereo | |
| | |
| Conductor | Arrigo Boito |
| Director | Arrigo Boito |

Revised-Bologna-Teatro Comunale-Oct. 4, 1875

| | |
|---|---|
| Margherita (M.) | Erminia Borghi-Mamo sop. |
| Elena (E.) | Erminia Borghi-Mamo sop. |
| Faust (F.) | Italo Campanini ten. |
| Mefistofele (Me.) | Romano Nannetti bass |
| Marta (Ma.) | Antonietta Mazzucco mez. |
| Pantalis (P.) | Antonietta Mazzucco mez. |
| Wagner | Luigi Caserini ten. |
| Nereo | Luigi Caserini ten. |
| | |
| Conductor | Emilio Usiglio |
| Director | Arrigo Boito |

Revised-Venice-Teatro Rossini-May 13, 1876

| | |
|---|---|
| Margherita (M.) | Erminia Borghi-Mamo sop. |
| Elena (E.) | Erminia Borghi-Mamo sop. |
| Faust (F.) | Enrico Barbacini ten. |
| Mefistofele (Me.) | Romano Nannetti bass |
| Marta (Ma.) | Antonietta Mazzucco mez. |
| Pantalis (P.) | Antonietta Mazzucco mez. |
| Wagner | Giovanni De Filippis ten. |
| Nereo | Giovanni De Filippis ten. |
| | |
| Conductor | Franco Faccio |
| Director | Arrigo Boito |

OTHER PREMIERES

ARGENTINA
Buenos Aires  Ant. Colón  July 22, 1881  E. Borghi-Mamo (M. E.) F. Tamagno
(F.) A. Castelmary (Me.) N. Bassi
cond.

Colón  July 12, 1908  M. Farneti (M. E.) A. Bassi (F.) F.
Chaliapin (Me.) L. Mancinelli cond.

AUSTRALIA
Sydney  Radio  Oct. 10, 1933  F. Izal (Me.)

Teachers  June 21, 1974  J. Barber (M.) D. Dehn (E.) R. Rams-
Fed. Hall  den (F.) V. Laptev (Me.) K. Webber
cond.

AUSTRIA
Vienna          Hofoper      Mar. 18, 1882 P. Lucca (M.) M. Küpfer-Berger (E.)
                                           R. Papier (P.) G. Müller (F.) H. Von
                                           Rokitansky (Me.) (in Ger.)

                             May   5, 1884 E. Turolla (M. E.) F. Valero (F.) A.
                                           Castelmary (Me.) O. Bimboni cond.
                                           (in It.)

BELGIUM
Brussels        Monnaie      Jan. 19, 1883 Duvivier (M.) Jourdain (F.) L. Gres-
                                           se (Me.) J. Dupont cond. A. Boito
                                           dir. (in Fr.)

                Galeries     Aug.  4? 1905 A. Agostinelli (M.) F. Carpi (F.) F.
                                           Vecchioni (Me.) (in It.)

                Monnaie      May  10, 1910 E. De Lys (M. E.) D. Smirnoff (F.)
                                           F. Chaliapin (Me.) L. Jehin cond.
                                           (in It.)

Ghent           Grand        Oct.  6? 1908 A. De Roma (M. E.) G. Malferrari
                                           (F.) A. Sabellico (Me.) G. Wehils
                                           cond.

Liége           Grand        July  6? 1905 A. Agostinelli (M. E.) F. Carpi (F.)
                                           F. Vecchioni (Me.)

BRAZIL
Rio de          Pedro II     Sep. 26, 1881 E. Borghi-Mamo (M. E.) F. Tamagno
 Janeiro                                   (F.) A. Castelmary (Me.) N. Bassi
                                           cond.

                Municipal    July 30, 1910 C. Gagliardi (M.) F. Constantino
                                           (F.) C. Walter (Me.) A. Padovani
                                           cond.

Sao Paulo       Sao José     Nov. 24, 1881 E. Borghi-Mamo (M. E.) F. Tamagno
                                           (F.) A. Castelmary (Me.) N. Bassi
                                           cond.

                Municipal    Oct.  5, 1913 M. Farneti (M.) E. Rakowska (E.) E.
                                           Perea (F.) G. Cirino (Me.)

CANADA
Toronto         Grand Opera Mar. 22, 1881 O. Torriani (M. E.) G. Perugini (F.)
                                           G. Conly (Me.) S. Behrens cond. (in
                                           Eng.)

CHILE
Santiago        Municipal    Aug. 14, 1895 P. Roluti-Salto (M. E.) E. Salto
                                           (F.) A. Sabellico (Me.)

Valparaiso      Victoria     Nov. 14, 1895 A. Gini-Pizzorni (M. E.) P. Ferrari
                                           (F.) A. Sabellico (Me.)

COLOMBIA
Bogota          Colón        Nov. 21, 1922 L. Taylor (M.) E. Carrara (E.) J.
                                           Palet (F.) V. Bettoni (Me.) G. So-
                                           riente cond.

CUBA
Havana          Tacon        Dec. 11, 1893 A. Lantes (M.) G. Moretti (F.) A.
                                           Tamburlini (Me.)

CZECHOSLOVAKIA
Prague          Deutsches     Feb. 19, 1881 A. Stoll (F.) (in Ger.)

                National      Dec.  9, 1885 M. Sittová (M.) C. Raverta (F.) F.
                                            Hynek (in Czech)

DENMARK
Copenhagen      Royal         Jan. 20, 1885 Schroder (M.) Keller (E.) Jerndorff
                                            (F.) Lange (M.) (in Dan.)

EGYPT
Alexandria      Zizinia       Oct.     1887 E. Vottero (M.) L. Laspiur (F.) G.
                                            Scarneo (Me.)

Cairo           Khedivial     Dec. 27, 1897 V. Mendioroz (M. E.) G. Borgatti
                                            (F.) G. De Grazia (Me.)

FINLAND
Helsinki        Alexanders    Nov. 28, 1898 L. Sangiorgio (M.) L. Bovero (F.) E.
                                            Gandolfi (Me.) Cooper cond.

                Feb.  2, 1933 (in Fin.)

FRANCE
Marseille       Grand         Feb. 28, 1902 H. Therry (M. E.) E. Scaremberg (F.)
                                            Sentein (Me.) (in Fr.)

Nantes          Apr. 23, 1887 (in Fr.)

Paris           Opéra         May   9, 1912 A. Agostinelli (M.) E. Druetti (E.)
                                            D. Smirnoff (F.) F. Chaliapin (Me.)
                                            T. Serafin cond. (in It.)

                Lyrique       Dec. 25, 1919 (in Fr.)

GERMANY
Berlin          Königliches Apr.  5, 1907 R. Storchio (M.) Z. Brozia (E.) L.
                                            Sobinoff (F.) F. Chaliapin (Me.) L.
                                            Jehin cond. (in It.)

Cologne         Stadt         Feb. 24, 1881 L. Friedmann (M.) von Sigelli (F.)
                                            C. Baumann (Me.) (in Ger.)

Dresden         Staatsoper    May  29, 1987 J. Przestrzelski (F.) R. Tesarowicz
                                            (Me.) (By the company of the Teatr
                                            Wielki, Lodz)

Hamburg         Stadt         Feb. 26, 1881 R. Sucher (M.) H. Winkelmann (F.) E.
                                            Gura (Me.) (in Ger.)

GREAT BRITAIN
Birmingham      Th. Royal     Oct. 16, 1884 M. Roze (M. E.) B. M'Guckin (F.) W.
                                            Ludwig (Me.) E. Goossens cond. (in
                                            Eng.)

Bristol         Prince's      Sep. 12, 1884 M. Roze (M. E.) B. M'Guckin (F.)

Cardiff         New           May   6, 1957 S. de la Motte (M.) J. Barker (E.)
                                            A. Hallett (F.) R. Herincx (Me.) W.
                                            Braithwaite cond.

Edinburgh       Royal         Nov. 21, 1884 M. Roze (M. E.) B. M'Guckin (F.) W.
                Lyceum                       Ludwig (Me.) E. Goossens cond. (in
                                            Eng.)

Glasgow      Th. Royal    Nov. 28, 1884 M. Roze (M. E.) B. M'Guckin (F.) W.
                                        Ludwig (Me.) (in Eng.)

Liverpool    Royal Court Jan.  8, 1885 M. Roze (M. E.) B. M'Guckin (F.) W.
                                        Ludwig (Me.) (In Eng.)

London       Her          July  6, 1880 C. Nilsson (M. E.)  Z. Trebelli (Ma.
             Majesty's                  P.) I. Campanini (F.) R. Nannetti
                                        (Me.) L. Arditi cond. (in Ital.)

             Covent       May  15, 1884 E. Albani (M. E.)  G. Tremelli  (Ma.
             Garden                     P.) W. Mierzwinski (F.) P. Gailhard
                                        (Me.) E. Bevignani cond.

Manchester   Th. Royal    Mar.  6, 1885 M. Roze (M. E.) B. M'Guckin (F.) W.
                                        Ludwig (Me.) E. Goossens cond. (in
                                        Eng.)

Newcastle    Tyne         Nov. 12, 1884 M. Roze (M. E.) B. M'Guckin (F.) W.
                                        Ludwig (Me.) E. Goossens cond. (in
                                        Eng.)

GREECE
Athens                    Jan.     1899 (First production traced)

Corfu        San Giacomo Feb.?    1894 C. Zucchi-Ferrigno (M.) Breccia (F.)
                                        Villani (Me.) (First production tra-
                                        ced)

HUNGARY
Budapest     Nemzeti      Apr. 24, 1882 V. Bartolucci (M.)  Beerman  (E.) G.
             Szinház                    Perotti (F.) D. Ney (Me.) (in Hung.)

             Operaház     June  7, 1885 E. Turolla (M.)

IRELAND
Dublin       Gaiety       Aug. 21, 1884 M. Roze (M. E.) B. M'Guckin (F.) W.
                                        Ludwig (Me.) E. Goossens cond. (in
                                        Eng.)

ITALY
Ancona       Muse         Aug. 30, 1877 M. Mariani-Masi (M. E.) G. Vanzan
                                        (F.) R. Nannetti (Me.) L. Mancinelli
                                        cond.

Bari         Piccinni     Dec. 25, 1888 M. Pizzagalli (M.) E. Cuttica (F.)
                                        C. Bedogni (Me.) C. Lovati-Cazzu-
                                        lani cond.

Bergamo      Donizetti    Aug. 20, 1887 I. Mayer (M.) F. Cardinali (F.) P.
                                        Wulmann (Me.) G. Cimini cond.

Bologna      Comunale     Nov. 10, 1881 E. Theodorini (M. E.) O. Nouvelli
                                        (F.) F. Vecchioni (Me.) L. Manci-
                                        nelli cond.

Brescia      Grande       Aug. 10, 1878 E. Borghi-Mamo (M. E.) I. Campanini
                                        (F.) A. Vidal (Me.) F. Faccio cond.

Cagliari     Civico       Dec. 25, 1895 G. Morgantini (M. E.) F. Carnevalini
                                        (Ma. P.) G. Pagliano (F.) G. Beltra-
                                        mo (Me.) G. Buzenac cond.

| Catania | Bellini | Mar. 12, 1892 | C. Ferrani (M. E.) F. Vignas (F.) A. Tamburlini (Me.) G. Pomè Penna cond. |
|---------|---------|---------------|--------------------------------------------------------------------------|
| Chieti | Marrucino | May  4, 1886 | V. Mendioroz (M. E.) D. Del Papa (F.) A. Sillich (Me.) C. Lovati Cazzulani cond. |
| Cremona | Concordia | Sep.  9, 1886 | V. Mendioroz (M. E.) E. Puerari (F.) R. Ercolani (Me.) D. Acerbi cond. |
| Ferrara | Comunale | Dec. 23? 1883 | I. Mayer (M. E.) D. Del Papa (F.) |
| Fiume | Civico | Apr. 28? 1887 | A. Busi (M.) O. Emiliani (F.) A. Sillich (Me.) V. Podesti cond. |
| Florence | Pergola | Mar.?     1884 | N. Bulicioff (M. E.) F. Marconi (F.) A. Castelmary (Me.) M. Mancinelli cond. |
| Genoa | Carlo Felice | Mar.  8, 1879 | A. Garbini (M.) C. Carpi (F.) A. Castelmary (Me.) G. Rossi cond. |
| Livorno | Rossini? | Mar. 13? 1887 | I. Mayer (M.) O. Emiliani (F.) G. Monti (Me.) |
| Lucca | Giglio | Sep.  5, 1888 | M. Borelli (M. E.) E. De Marchi (F.) R. Ercolani (Me.) G. Pomè Penna cond. |
| Lugo | Rossini | Sep. 10, 1886 | E. Turolla (M. E.) S. Bellincioni (Ma. P.) O. Nouvelli (F.) O. Maini (Me.) |
| Mantua | Sociale | Spring    1884 | G. Rey (M.) E. Puerari (F.) A. Castelmary (Me.) E. Usiglio cond. |
| Messina | Vittorio Emanuele | Jan.  5, 1887 | A. Soffriti (M. E.) F. Cardinali (F.) G. Pomè-Penna cond. |
| Milan | La Scala | May 25, 1881 | M. Mariani-Masi (M. E.) F. Marconi (F.) R. Nannetti (Me.) F. Faccio cond. A. Boito dir. |
| Modena | Comunale | Dec. 25? 1882 | N. Bulicioff (M. E.) P. Alberti (F.) E. Jorda (Me.) L. Mancinelli cond. |
| Naples | San Carlo | Mar. 19, 1884 | E. Turolla (M. E.) E. Barbacini (F.) O. Maini (Me.) R. Kuon cond. |
| Padua | Concordi | Carn. 1880-81 | C. Bernau (M.) L. Filippi-Bresciani (F.) A. Parboni (Me.) A. Pomè cond. |
| Palermo | Politeama | May 19? 1886 | M. Borelli (M. E.) F. Cardinali (F.) E. Lorrain (Me.) F. Nicolao cond. |
|  | Massimo | Mar. 18, 1911 | M. Llacer (M. E.) A. Rocca (F.) A. Masini-Pieralli (Me.) L. Mugnone cond. |
| Parma | Regio | Dec. 25, 1886 | T. Singer (M. E.) E. Puerari (F.) G. Monti (Me.) P. Ferrari cond. |

Piacenza        Municipale  Dec. 26, 1888 M. Rodrigues (M. E.) A. D'Enrici
                                          (F.) P. De Bengardi (Me.) P. Bandini
                                          cond.

Pisa            Verdi       Mar.  1, 1885 E. Frandin (M.) M. Paolicchi (E.) G.
                                          Moretti (F.) G. Monti (Me.) E. Usi-
                                          glio cond.

Ravenna         Alighieri   May  14, 1881 E. Theodorini (M. E.) L. Filippi-
                                          Bresciani (F.) L. Cherubini (Me.) E.
                                          Bernardi cond.

Reggio Emilia Municipale    Dec. 25, 1888 N. Bulicioff (M. E.) O. Novelli (F.)
                                          A. Tamburlini (Me.) M. Bavagnoli
                                          cond.

Rome            Apollo      Apr.  4, 1877 M. Mariani-Masi (M. E.) E. Barbaci-
                                          ni (F.) A. Parboni (Me.) L. Manci-
                                          nelli cond. A. Boito dir.

                Costanzi    Oct. 29, 1887 V. Ferni-Germano (M. E.) E. De Mar-
                                          chi (F.) O. Maini (Me.) E. Maschero-
                                          ni cond.

Rovigo          Sociale     Oct.  5, 1910 C. Toschi (M. E.) E. Gherlinzoni
                                          (F.) P. Ludikar (Me.) T. Serafin
                                          cond.

Trento          Sociale     June  5, 1886 O. Guercia (M. E.) F. Percuopo (F.)
                                          V. Salmasi (Me.)

Treviso         Sociale     Oct. 17, 1880 L. Vanda-Müller (M. E.) E. Mozzi
                                          (F.) G. Mirabella (Me.) G. Gialdini
                                          cond.

Trieste         Comunale    Sep. 25, 1877 A. Fossa (M. E.) E. Barbacini (F.)
                                          E. Dondi (Me.) F. Faccio cond.

Turin           Regio       Dec. 26, 1876 R. Pantaleoni (M. E.) A. Rossetti
                                          (F.) A. Castelmary (Me.) C. Pedrotti
                                          cond.

Udine           Sociale     Aug.  9? 1886 F. Toresella (M. E.) G. Moretti (F.)
                                          R. Ercolani (Me.) G. Gialdini cond.

Venice          La Fenice   Mar.  8, 1879 A. Fossa (M. E.) G. Ortisi (F.) F.
                                          Novara (Me.) F. Magi cond.

Verona          Filarmonico Feb.  2, 1878 E. Tati (M. E.) T. Villa (F.) A.
                                          Alsina (Me.) A. Pomè cond.

                Arena       July 27, 1920 B. Scacciati (M.) L. Barla Ricci
                                          (E.) A. Pertile (F.) N. De Angelis
                                          (Me.) P. Fabbroni cond.

Vicenza         Eretenio    Feb. 25? 1888 V. Mendioroz (M. E.) E. Mozzi (F.)
                                          E. Serbolini (Me.) D. Acerbi cond.

JUGOSLAVIA
Ljubljana       National    Dec. 20, 1922

Zagreb          National    Apr. 13, 1901 A. Alloro (M.) E. Cammarota (F.) E.
                                          Aschenbrenner (M.) N. Faller cond.

LATVIA
Riga            National     Sep. 27, 1929 (in Let.)

MALTA
La Valletta     Real         Mar. 25, 1886 C. Bevilacqua (M.) L. Bellò (F.) E.
                                            Dondi (Me.) Ronzani cond.

MEXICO
Mexico City     Nacional     Nov. 14, 1888 A. Gini-Pizzorni (M. E.) C. Pizzorni
                                            (F.) R. Villani (Me.) G. Golisciani
                                            cond.

MONACO
Monte Carlo     Salle        Feb. 23, 1895 M. De Nuovina (M. E.) E. Gibert (F.)
                Garnier                     A. Gresse (M.) L. Jehin cond.

NETHERLANDS
Amsterdam       Palais v.    Oct. 11, 1897 L. Gilboni (M.) (In It.)
                Volksvligt

Den Haag        Gebouw v.    Oct.  8, 1897 L. Gilboni (M.)  P. Lombardi (F.) L.
                Kunst                       Lucenti (Me.) (in It.)

Rotterdam       Groote       Oct. 16, 1897 L. Gilboni (M.) (in It.)

NORWAY
Oslo            Royal        May  14, 1893 (in Norw.)

PANAMA
Panama City     Nacional     Sep. 16, 1922 L. Taylor (M.) O. Carrara (E.) J.
                                            Palet (F.) V. Bettoni (Me.)

PERU
Lima            Municipal    Nov. 18, 1909 Cavalli (M.) G. Dimitrescu (F.) G.
                                            Sorgi (Me.) Bonazzi cond.[2]

POLAND
Lodz            Wielki       June 23, 1984 D. Ambroziak (M.) E. Ardam (H.) T.
                                            Kopacki (F.) R. Tesarowicz (Me.)

Warsaw          Wielki       Dec. 19, 1880 T. Singer (M. E.) T. Bertini (F.) A.
                                            Castelmary (Me.) C. Trombini cond.
                                            (in It.)

PORTUGAL
Lisbon          Sao Carlos   Feb. 24, 1881 E. Borghi-Mamo (M. E.) G. Fancelli
                                            (F.) R. Nannetti (Me.) R. Kuon cond.

Oporto          Sao Joao     Jan. 19? 1896 D. Barberini (M.) B. Lucignani (F.)
                                            (First production traced)

PUERTO RICO
San Juan        Municipal    Mar. 16, 1918 E. Mason (M.) J. Palet (F.) L. Nico-
                                            letti-Kormann (Me.)

ROMANIA
Bucharest       Nacional     Nov. 16, 1891 A. Gini-Pizzorni (M.) C. Pizzorni
                                            (F.) R. Ercolani (Me.) (in It.)

---

[2]. First complete performance traced in Lima. Two acts had been given on Oct. 15, 1898.

RUSSIA
Kharkov         Municipal   Feb.  7? 1886 E. Sonchi (M.) O. Cappelletti (F.)
                                          G. Belletti (Me.)

Moscow          Bolshoi     Mar. 22, 1882 M. L. Durand (M. E.) F. Marconi (F.)
                                          E. Bevignani cond.

Odessa          Municipal   Nov. 23? 1885 E. Ciuti (M.) F. Cardinali (F.) V.
                                          Salmasi (Me.)

St.             Imperial    Jan. 24, 1881 C. Salla (M.) A. Masini (F.) J. Bou-
 Petersburg                               hy (Me.) (in It.)

                            Jan. 14? 1887 M. Mei (M.) N. Figner (F.) (in Rus.)

SPAIN
Barcelona       Liceo       Dec.  1, 1880 V. Ferni (M. E.) E. Barbacini (F.)
                                          O. Maini (Me.) F. Faccio cond.

Bilbao          Arriaga     May?     1901 J. Palet (F.)

Madrid          Real        Jan. 28, 1883 E. Theodorini (M. E.) A. Masini (F.)
                                          R. Nannetti (Me.) J. Goula cond.

Seville         San         Apr. 16, 1907 O. Petrella (M.) A. Giorgini (F.) L.
                Fernando                  Rossatto (Me.)

Valencia        Principal   Feb.  1, 1885 M. Ricci (M.) E. Treves (Ma.) O.
                                          Cappelletti (F.) E. Dondi (Me.)

SWEDEN
Stockholm       Royal       Feb. 26, 1883 S. Ek (M.) A. M. Javette (E.) A. Öd-
                                          mann (F.) A. Lange (Me.) (in Swed.)

SWITZERLAND
Geneva          Grand       Sep. 14, 1988 D. Soviero (M.) M. J. Johinson (E.)
                                          A. Cupido (F.) S. Ramey (Me.) G.
                                          Patané cond.

Lugano          Apollo      Mar. 29, 1924 R. Bardelli (M.) A. Laskowa (E.) G.
                                          Melnick (Me.)

Zürich          Stadt       June 24, 1926 M. De Voltri (M.) I. Abry (E.) E. De
                                          Muro Lomanto (F.) F. Autori (Me.) A.
                                          Lucon cond. (in It.)

TURKEY
Constan-        Varieties   May 10, 1907 G. Fabris (M.) E. Mancini (F.) F.
 tinople                                 Vecchioni (Me.) (First production
                                         traced)

UNITED STATES
Atlanta         Auditorium  Apr. 24, 1925 F. Alda (M.) F. Peralta (E.) M. Tel-
                                          va (P.) G. Lauri-Volpi (F.) F. Cha-
                                          liapin (Me.) T. Serafin cond.

Baltimore       Ac. of Mus. Jan. 22, 1881 A. Valleria (M. E.) A. L. Cary (Ma.
                                          P.) I. Campanini (F.) F. Novara
                                          (Me.) L. Arditi cond. (in It.)

                            Feb. 21, 1881 M. Roze (M. E.) G. Perugini (F.) G.
                                          Conly (Me.) (in Eng.)

| | | | |
|---|---|---|---|
| Boston | Globe | Nov. 16, 1880 | M. Roze (M. E.) G. Perugini (F.) G. Conly (Me.) (in Eng.) |
| | Boston Th. | Dec. 29, 1880 | A. Valleria (M. E.) A. L. Cary (Ma. P.) I. Campanini (F.) F. Novara (Me.) L. Arditi cond. |
| | Opera | Feb. 18, 1910 | F. Alda (M.) C. Boninsegna (E.) F. Constantino (F.) J. Mardones (Me.) A. Conti cond. |
| Brooklyn | Ac. of Mus. | Dec. 9, 1880 | A. Valleria (M. E.) A. L. Cary (Ma. P.) 1. Campanini (F.) F. Novara (Me.) L. Arditi cond. |
| Chicago | Haverly's | Dec. 10, 1880 | M. Roze (M. E.) G. Perugini (F.) G. Conly (Me.) (in Eng.) |
| | | Feb. 2, 1881 | A. Valleria (M. E.) A. L. Cary (Ma. P.) I. Campanini (F.) F. Novara (Me.) L. Arditi cond. (in It.) |
| | Auditorium | Dec. 19, 1922 | E. Mason (M.) G. Holst (E.) A. Minghetti (F.) F. Chaliapin (Me.) G. Polacco cond. |
| Cincinatti | Pike's | Dec. 29, 1880 | M. Roze (M. E.) G. Perugini (F.) G. Conly (Me.) (in Eng.) |
| | Music Hall | Feb. 23, 1881 | A. Valleria (M. E.) A. L. Cary (Ma. P.) I. Campanini (F.) F. Novara (Me.) L. Arditi cond. (in It.) |
| | Opera | July 9, 1922 | E. Amsden (M. E.) G. Agostini (F.) I. Picchi (Me.) R. Lyford cond. |
| Cleveland | Ac. of Mus. | Apr. 30, 1881 | O. Torriani (M. E.) A. Byron (F.) G. Conly (Me.) (in Eng.) |
| Dallas | Coliseum | Mar. 1, 1924 | E. Mason (M.) M. Sharlow (E.) F. Lamont (F.) F. Chaliapin (Me.) |
| Detroit | Whitney's | Mar. 28, 1881 | O. Torriani (M. E.) L. Annandale (Ma. P.) A. Byron (F.) G. Conly (Me.) S. Behrens cond. |
| Galveston | Tremont | Feb. 3, 1881 | M. Roze (M. E.) G. Perugini (F.) G. Conly (Me.) (in Eng.) |
| Houston | Gray's | Feb. 5, 1881 | O. Torriani (M. E.) G. Perugini (F.) G. Conly (Me.) (in Eng.) |
| Indianapolis | Dickson's | Dec. 20, 1880 | M. Roze (M. E.) G. Perugini (F.) G. Conly (Me.) (in Eng.) |
| Kansas City | Coates | Feb. 12, 1881 | M. Roze (M. E.) G. Perugini (F.) G. Conly (Me.) (in Eng.) |
| Los Angeles | Auditorium | Mar. 4, 1924 | E. Mason (M.) M. Sharlow (E.) F. Lamont (F.) F. Chaliapin (Me.) G. Polacco cond. |

Louisville       Op. House     Dec. 23, 1880 M. Roze (M. E.) G. Perugini (F.) G.
                                             Conly (Me.) S. Behrens cond. (in
                                             Eng.)

Memphis          Leubrie's     Jan. 13, 1881 O. Torriani (M. E.) L. Annandale
                                             (Ma. P.) G. Perugini (F.) G. Conly
                                             (Me.) (in Eng.)

Miami            Opera         Feb. 11, 1980 C. Neblett (M. E.) E. Mauro (F.) J.
                                             Diaz (Me.) E. Buckley cond.

Milwaukee        Op. House     Apr.  9, 1881 O. Torriani (M. E.) A. Byron (F.) G.
                                             Conly (Me.) (in Eng.)

New Orleans      St. Charles   Jan. 19, 1881 M. Roze (M. E.) G. Perugini (F.) G.
                                             Conly (Me.) (in Eng.)

New York         Ac. of Mus.   Nov. 24, 1880 A. Valleria (M. E.) A. L. Cary (Ma.
                                             P.) I. Campanini (F.) F. Novara
                                             (Me.) L. Arditi cond.

                 Fifth Ave.    Feb. 28, 1881 M. Roze (M. E.) L. Annandale (Ma.
                                             P.) G. Perugini (F.) G. Conly (Me.)
                                             (in Eng.)

                 Metro-        Dec.  5, 1883 C. Nilsson (M. E.) Z. Trebelli (Ma.
                 politan                     P.) I. Campanini (F.) G. Mirabella
                                             (Me.) C. Campanini cond.

Philadelphia     Chestnut      Nov. 27, 1880 M. Roze (M. E.) L. Annandale (Ma.
                 Street                      P.) G. Perugini (F.) G. Conly (Me.)
                                             (in Eng.)

                 Ac. of Mus.   Jan. 12, 1881 A. Valleria (M. E.) A. L. Cary (Ma.
                                             P.) I. Campanini (F.) F. Novara
                                             (Me.) L. Arditi cond. (in It.)

Pittsburgh       Libr. Hall    Feb. 17, 1881 O. Torriani (M. E.) G. Perugini (F.)
                                             G. Conly (Me.) S. Behrens cond. (in
                                             Eng.)

St. Louis        Grand O. H.   Jan.  5, 1881 M. Roze (M. E.) G. Perugini (F.) G.
                                             Conly (Me.) (in Eng.)

San Francisco Grand           Feb. 21, 1890 E. Albani (M. E.) O. Synnerberg (Ma.
                                             P.) F. Tamagno (F.) A. Castelmary
                                             and F. Novara (Me.) L. Arditi cond.

                 Opera         Oct.  1, 1923 B. Saroya (M. E.) B. Gigli (F.) A.
                                             Didur (Me.) G. Merola cond.

URUGUAY
Montevideo       Solis         Aug. 30, 1884 E. Theodorini (M. E.) F. Tamagno
                                             (F.) N. Bassi cond.

VENEZUELA
Caracas          Municipal     Jan. 14, 1892

2. NERONE-*Opera* in four acts
Milan-Teatro alla Scala-May 1, 1924
Libretto by Arrigo Boito

| | |
|---|---|
| Asteria (A.) | Rosa Raisa sop. |
| Rubria (R.) | Luisa Bertana mez. |
| Nerone (N.) | Aureliano Pertile ten. |
| Fanuèl (F.) | Carlo Galeffi bar. |
| Simon Mago (S.) | Marcel Journet bass |
| Tigellino (T.) | Ezio Pinza bass |
| Perside | Mita Vasari sec. |
| Cerinto | Maria Doria sec. |
| Gobrias | Giuseppe Nessi ten. |
| Dositèo | Carlo Walter bar. |
| Il Tempiere | Emilio Venturini ten. |
| Primo Viandante | Alfredo Tedeschi ten. |
| Secondo Viandante | Giuseppe Menni ten. |
| Lo Schiavo Ammonitore | Aristide Baracchi bar. |

Conductor                                                 Arturo Toscanini

OTHER PRODUCTIONS

ARGENTINA
Buenos Aires   Colón        May  22, 1926 C. Muzio/G. Arangi-Lombardi (A.) L.
                                          Bertana (R.) A. Pertile/A. Trantoul
                                          (N.) B. Franci (F.) C. Formichi (S.)
                                          E. Pinza (T.) G. Marinuzzi cond.

BRAZIL
Rio de         Lirico       Aug. 27, 1926 G. Arangi-Lombardi (A.)  L. Bertana
 Janeiro                                  (R.) A. Pertile (N.) B. Franci (F.)
                                          E. Pinza (T.) G. Marinuzzi cond.

CHILE
Santiago       Municipal    Aug. 27, 1930 F. Campiña (A.) M. Capuana (R.) J.
                                          De Gaviria (N.) C. Morelli (F.) U.
                                          Di lelio (S.)

EGYPT
Alexandria     Mohamad Aly Mar. 15, 1928 I. Pacetti (A.) M. Capuana (R.) N.
                                          Fusati (N.) C. Morelli (F.) A. Ri-
                                          ghetti (S.)

Cairo          Khedivial    Feb. 22, 1928 I. Pacetti (A.) M. Capuana (R.) N.
                                          Fusati (N.) C. Morelli (F.) A. Ri-
                                          ghetti (S.)

GERMANY
Stuttgart      Opernhaus    May   5, 1928 (in Ger.)

ITALY
Bari           Petruzzelli Feb. 12, 1930 D. De Martis (A.) V. De Kristoff
                                          (R.) G. Taccani (N.) L. Borgonovo
                                          (F.) A. Mongelli (S.) C. Ulivi (T.)
                                          P. Fabbroni cond.

Bologna        Comunale     Oct. 12, 1924 M. Carena (A.) L. Bertana (R.) A.
                                          Pertile (N.) B. Franci (F.) M. Jour-
                                          net (S.) F. Autori (T.) A. Tosca-
                                          nini cond.

Florence     Politeama    May  19? 1928 D. De Martis (A.) B. Siberi (R.) G.
                                        Taccani (N.) A. Beuf (F.) C. Maugeri
                                        (S.) G. Vaghi (T.) F. Ghione cond.

Genoa        Carlo        Jan. 31, 1928 E. Barrigar (A.) B. Siberi (R.) G.
             Felice                     Taccani (N.) E. Molinari (F.) A.
                                        Beuf (S.) G. Vaghi (T.) G. Bavag-
                                        noli cond.

Milan        La Scala     Nov. 15, 1924 M. Carena/R. Raisa (A.) L. Bertana
                                        (R.) A. Pertile (N.) B. Franci (F.)
                                        M. Journet (S.) F. Autori (T.) A.
                                        Toscanini cond.

                          Mar. 31, 1926 R. Raisa (A.) L. Bertana (R.) A.
                                        Pertile (N.) B. Franci (F.) M. Jour-
                                        net (S.) F. Autori (T.) A. Toscanini
                                        cond.

                          Apr. 27, 1927 B. Scacciati (A.) L. Bertana/M. Ca-
                                        puana (R.) V. Trantoul (N.) B. Fran-
                                        ci/C. Sarobe (F.) M. Journet (S.) S.
                                        Baccaloni (T.) A. Toscanini cond.

                          Jan.  1, 1928 B. Scacciati (A.) L. Bertana (R.) V.
                                        Trantoul (N.) C. Galeffi (F.) E. Fa-
                                        ticanti (S.) S. Baccaloni (T.) A.
                                        Toscanini/A. Votto cond.

                          Apr. 20, 1931 M. Carena (A.) E. Stignani (R.) F.
                                        Lo Giudice (N.) C. Galeffi (F.) E.
                                        Faticanti (S.) S. Baccaloni (T.) F.
                                        Calusio cond.

                          Apr. 12, 1939 G. Cigna (A.) E. Stignani/E. Nicolai
                                        (R.) G. Voyer (N.) A. Sved (F.) T.
                                        Pasero (S.) D. Baronti (T.) G. Mari-
                                        nuzzi cond.

Naples       San Carlo    Apr.  4, 1927 E. Barrigar (A.) M. Capuana/B. Sibe-
                                        ri (R.) F. Lo Giudice (N.) L. Monte-
                                        santo (F.) E. Molinari (S.) C. Sabat
                                        (T.) E. Vitale cond.

                          Nov. 30, 1957 A. De Cavalieri (A.) A. Lazzarini
                                        (R.) M. Picchi (N.) G. Guelfi (F.)
                                        M. Petri (S.) F. Mazzoli (T.) F.
                                        Capuana cond.

Palermo      Massimo      Mar. 23, 1929 D. De Martis (A.) B. Siberi (R.) M.
                                        Salazar (N.) E. Faticanti (F.) E.
                                        Grandini (S.) A. Vela (T.) A. Votto
                                        cond.

Pisa         Verdi        Mar.  7, 1929 F. Campiña (A.) B. Castagna (R.) J.
                                        De Gaviria (N.) A. Beuf (F.) M. An-
                                        dreoli (S.) R. Morisani (T.) U. Ben-
                                        venuti Giusti cond.

Rome         Reale        Feb. 27, 1928 B. Scacciati/ E. Barrigar (A.) L.
                                        Bertana (R.) G. Lauri-Volpi/F. Lo
                                        Giudice (N.) B. Franci (F.) C. Mau-
                                        geri/E. Faticanti (S.) E. Dominici
                                        (T.) G. Marinuzzi cond.

|         | Opera     | Dec. 10, 1945 | G. Di Giulio (A.) E. Stignani (R.) A. Pertile (N.) B. Franci (F.) G. Flamini (S.) G. Tomei (T.) G. Santini cond. |

               July 1, 1950   M. Laszlo (A.) D. Minarchi (R.) A. Annaloro (N.) C. Tagliabue (F.) A. Mongelli (S.) G. Tomei (T.) G. Santini cond.

   Sala RAI     Sep. 11, 1938   S. Roman (A.) E. Stignani (R.) O. Vidal (N.) E. Manacchini (F.) E. Molinari (S.) A. Votto cond.

               Oct. 10, 1942   M. Pedrini (A.) E. Stignani (R.) A. Pertile (N.) C. Galeffi (F.) G. Flamini (S.) G. Santini cond.

Turin    Regio       Mar. 21, 1925   M. Carena (A.) L. Bertana (R.) A. Pertile (N.) C. Sarobe (F.) M. Journet (S.) E. Dominici (T.) A. Toscanini cond.

               Jan. 22, 1927   D. De Martis (A.) L. Bertana (R.) A. Pertile (N.) C. Sarobe (F.) M. Journet/E. Faticanti (S.) E. Dominici (T.) G. Marinuzzi cond.

   Sala RAI     Aug. 23, 1975   I. Ligabue (A.) R. Baldani (R.) B. Prevedi (N.) A. Cassis (F.) A. Ferrin (S.) A. Zerbini (T.) G. Gavazzeni cond.

Udine    Castello    July 28, 1928   E. Barrigar (A.) L. Abbrescia (R.) M. Salazar (N.) E. Grandini (F.) A. Righetti (S.) E. Dominici (T.) A. Votto cond.

Verona   Arena       July 24, 1926   E. Barrigar (A.) M. Capuana (R.) F. Lo Giudice (N.) L. Montesanto (F.) E. Molinari (S.) E. Dominici (T.) G. Bavagnoli cond.

SWEDEN
Stockholm  Royal       Apr. 9, 1926   G. Ljundberg (A.) G. Palson-Wettergren (R.) O. Ralf (N.) E. Larson (F.) J. Herou (S.) A. Wallgren (T.) G. Bergman cond. (in Swed.)

UNITED STATES
New York  Carnegie  Apr. 12, 1982   R. Andrade (A.) K. Takacz (R.) K. Cigoj (N.) P. Elvira (F.) J. Morris (S.) E. Queler cond.
         Hall

   Amato Op.   May 14, 1983   D. Lancman/L. Dolce/B. Djupedal/M. Kimball/M. Wilson (A.) J. Franklin/K. Enders/H. Johnsson/L. A. Dunton/F. Schopick (R.) J. Engdahl/A. Fischer/T. Cipolla/D. Sher (N.) J. Pariso/T. Holley/N. Banny (F.) M. Frescoln/R. De la Garza/F. Morsell/P. Cokorinos (S.) A. Amato cond.

## GIOVANNI BOTTESINI

1. COLON EN CUBA-*Ode sinfonica* in one act
Havana-Teatro Tacon-Jan. 31, 1848
Libretto by Ramón de Palma (in Spanish)

| | |
|---|---|
| Ixalagua | Luigia Caranti-Vita sop. |
| Colón | Luigi Vita bar. |
| Lincayum | Pietro Novelli bass |
| | |
| Conductor | Luigi Arditi |
| Director | Giovanni Bottesini |

2. L'ASSEDIO DI FIRENZE-*Opera seria* in three acts
Paris-Théâtre Italien-Feb. 21, 1856
Libretto by Carlo Corghi

| | |
|---|---|
| Maria de'Ricci (M.) | Rosina Penco sop. |
| Lodovico Martelli (L.) | Mario ten. |
| Giovanni Bandino (G.) | Francesco Graziani bar. |
| Michelangelo Buonarotti (B.) | Gian Francesco Angelini bass |
| Dante da Castiglione (D.) | bass |
| Ginevra | sec. |
| Bertino Aldobrandi | ten. |
| Filiberto di Chalons | bass |
| Moreno | bass |
| | |
| Conductor | Giovanni Bottesini |
| Director | Giovanni Bottesini |

Revised-Milan-Teatro alla Scala-Sep. 5, 1860

| | |
|---|---|
| Maria de'Ricci (M.) | Claudina Fiorentini sop. |
| Lodovico (L.) | Giovanni Valentini-Cristiani ten. |
| Giovanni (G.) | Antonio Cotogni bar. |
| Michelangelo Buonarotti (B.) | Cesare Dalla Costa bass |
| Dante da Castiglione | Luigi Alessandrini bass |
| Ginevra | Linda Fiorio mez. |
| Bertino Aldobrandi | Alessandro Manetta ten. |
| Filiberto di Chalons | Vincenzo Paraboschi bass |
| Moreno | Francesco Lodetti bass |
| | |
| Conductor | Eugenio Cavallini |
| Director | Giovanni Bottesini |

OTHER PRODUCTIONS

ITALY
Florence    Pagliano    Apr. 27, 1861 C. Fiorentini (M.) G. Tombesi (L.)
V. Orlandi (G.) H. von Rokitansky
(B.) C. Zuchelli (D.)

3. IL DIAVOLO DELLA NOTTE-*Melodramma semiserio* in four acts
Milan-Teatro Santa Radegonda-Dec. 18, 1858
Libretto by Luigi Scalchi

| | |
|---|---|
| Valeria | Zenobia Papini sop. |
| Clarissa | Eugenia Tebaldi mez. |
| Signor di Candal | Alberto Bozzetti ten. |
| Duca di Turenna | Giuseppe Altini bar. |
| Cavalier Narciso | Alessandro Bottero buf. |
| Luisa | Emilia Biaggini sop. |
| Germano | Alessandro Trabattoni bass |
| | |
| Director | Giovanni Bottesini |

4. MARION DELORME-*Opera seria* in three acts
Palermo-Teatro Bellini-Jan. 10, 1862
Libretto by Antonio Ghislanzoni

| | |
|---|---|
| Marion De Lorme (M.) | Claudina Fiorentini sop. |
| Didier (D.) | Achille Malagola ten. |
| Marchese Saverny (S.) | Giovanni Cima bar. |
| Laffemas (L.) | Alessandro Lanzoni bass |
| Comte de Villac | |
| Brichanteau | |
| Marquis de Nangis | |
| | |
| Conductor | Agostino Lo Casto |
| Director | Giovanni Bottesini |

OTHER PRODUCTIONS

SPAIN
Barcelona    Liceo    Dec. 17, 1864 C. Fiorentini (M.) J. Morini (D.) L.
Colonnese (S.) S. L. Bouché (L.)

5. UN AMOUR EN BAVIERE-*Opéra comique* in two acts
Composed circa 1867-Unperformed

6. VINCIGUERRA IL BANDITO-*Operette bouffe* in one act
Monte Carlo-Salle du Casino-Feb. 22, 1870
Libretto by Eugéne Hugot and Paul Renard (in French)

| | |
|---|---|
| Beatrice (B.) | Julia Baron sop. |
| Marinetta (M.) | Alphonsine mez. |
| Vinciguerra (V.) | Hyacinthe ten. |
| Saint-Urf (S.) | Deschamps bar. |
| Un Gendarme | |

OTHER PRODUCTIONS

FRANCE
Paris          Palais        Apr. 14, 1870 J. Baron (B.) I. Peyron (M.)  Luguet
               Royal                       (V.) Deschamps (S.)

ITALY
Milan          Santa         May  22, 1875 I. Manzoni (B.) Cavalleri (M.) Caro-
               Radegonda                   selli (V.) Ciceri (S.) (in It.)


7. ALI BABA-*Opera comica* in four acts
London-Lyceum Theatre-Jan. 17, 1871
Libretto by Emilio Taddei


Delia                                      Maria Calisto Piccioli sop.
Nadir                                      Girolamo Piccioli ten.
Orsocane                                   Torelli bar.
Aboul Hassan                               Rocca bass
Ali Baba                                   Maurizio Borella buf.
Morgiana                                   Faullo sec.
Thamar                                     Seneca bass
Faor                                       Ponti ten.
Calaf                                      Francesco Fallar bass

Conductor                                  Giovanni Bottesini/Tito Mattei

OTHER PRODUCTIONS

GREAT BRITAIN
London         Garrick       July 26, 1924

ITALY
Genoa          Paganini      June  8, 1920 By a company of marionettes.[3]

SPAIN
Barcelona      Español       July 18, 1872 (in Span.)


8.  CEDAR-*Opera fantastica* in a prologue and three acts
Composed circa 1880-Unperformed


9. ERO E LEANDRO-*Tragedia lirica* in three acts
Turin-Teatro Regio-Jan. 11, 1879
Libretto by Arrigo Boito (as Tobia Gorrio)

Ero (E)                                    Abigaille Bruschi-Chiatti sop.
Leandro (L.)                               Enrico Barbacini ten.
Ariofarne (A.)                             Gaetano Roveri bass

Conductor                                  Carlo Pedrotti

---

[3]. This is not necessarily the first performance of the opera for the puppet theatre. Nor was it the last since, according to Vetro's *Giovanni Bottesini*, it was a part of the repertoire of such a company throughout the 1930s.

OTHER PRODUCTIONS

ARGENTINA
Buenos Aires  Opera        Aug.  1, 1879  E. Ciuti (E.) R. Stagno (L.) L. Mil-
                                          ler (A.) G. Bottesini cond.
CHILE
Santiago      Municipal    Oct. 24, 1884  A. Gabbi (E.) C. Bulterini (L.) E.
                                          Marcassa (A.)

FRANCE
Aix les Bains Cercle       Sep.     1883  C. Smeroschi (E.) L. Signoretti (L.)
                                          P. Purarelli (A.)

ITALY
Milan         Manzoni      Apr. 30, 1883  M. Ricci (E.) E. Mozzi (L.) A. Sil-
                                          lich (A.) R. Drigo cond.

Naples        San Carlo    Apr.  4, 1880  F. Rubini-Scalisi (E.) G. Capponi
                                          (L.) G. Mirabella (A.) C. Scalisi
                                          cond.

Rome          Apollo       Feb. 22, 1880  E. Turolla (E.) R. Stagno (L.) R.
                                          Nannetti (A.) L. Mancinelli cond.

Turin         Carignano    Oct.     1890  A. Busi (E.) E. Cuttica (L.) A.
                                          Tamburlini (A.) V. Podesti cond.


10. LA REGINA DEL NEPAL-*Opera seria* in two acts
Turin-Teatro Regio-Dec. 26, 1880
Libretto by Tommasi da Scaccia

| | |
|---|---|
| Mirtza | Emma Turolla sop. |
| Nekir | Palmira Rambelli mez. |
| Elbis | Antonio Patierno ten. |
| Simar | Mattia Battistini bar. |
| Giamshid | Francesco Navarrini bass |
| | |
| Conductor | Carlo Pedrotti |


11. NERINA-*Idillo* in one act
Naples-Teatro del Palazzo del Duca di Bivona-Dec. 20, 1882
Libretto by the Duke Proto di Maddaloni


12. LA FIGLIA DELL'ANGELO o AZAELE-*Melodramma fantastico* in a prologue and
three acts
Composed circa 1885-Unperformed
Libretto by Ernesto Palermi


13. BABELE-*Melodramma umoristico* in three acts
Period of composition unknown-Unperformed
Libretto by Ernesto Palermi

ALFREDO CATALANI

1. LA FALCE-*Operetta* in a prologue and one act
Milan-Teatro del Conservatorio-July 19, 1875
Libretto by Arrigo Boito

Zohra (Z.)                                              Itala Giorgio sop.
Un Falciatore (F.)                                     Pietro Reslieri ten.

OTHER PRODUCTIONS

ARGENTINA
Buenos Aires                          1932

ITALY
Cremona        Ponchielli   Sep. 28, 1895 D. Farini (Z.) A. De Rubeis (F.)

Lucca          Giglio       Sep. 25, 1987 M. Noto (Z.) M. Frusoni (F.) G. Zani
                                          cond.

Milan          Sala RAI     Feb.  7, 1970 A. Cannarile (Z.) L. Infantino (F.)
                                          F. Scaglia cond.

Rome           Costanzi     Apr. 27, 1911 S. Kruszelnicka/E. Figoriti (Z.) U.
                                          Macnez (F.) G. Zuccani cond.

UNITED STATES
Newport        Festival     July 27, 1974
               Field


2. ELDA-*Dramma fantastico* in four acts
Turin-Teatro Regio-Jan. 31, 1880
Libretto by Carlo d'Ormeville

Elda (E.)                                              Adele Garbini sop.
Ulla (U.)                                              Nadia Bulicioff sop.
Sveno (S.)                                            Enrico Barbacini ten.
Magno (M.)                                             Santo Athos bar.
Re di Leira (L.)                                  Edouard de Reszke bass
Vilberga                                              Lucia Barovetti sec.
Luitlando                                                    Not named
Un Cavaliere                                     Argimiro Bertocchi ten.
Valdemaro                                                   Not named

Conductor                                              Carlo Pedrotti

OTHER PRODUCTIONS

POLAND
Warsaw         Letni        Aug. 21, 1882

3. DEJANICE-*Dramma lirico* in four acts
Milan-Teatro alla Scala-Mar. 17, 1883
Libretto by A. Zanardini

| | |
|---|---|
| Dejanice (D.) | Emma Turolla sop. |
| Argelia (Ar.) | Lena Bordato sop. |
| Admeto (A.) | Edmond Vergnet ten. |
| Dardano (Da.) | Giovanni Bianchi bar. |
| Labdaco (L.) | Francesco Vecchioni bass |

Conductor                                                                  Franco Faccio

OTHER PRODUCTIONS-PRE-WORLD WAR II

CZECHOSLOVAKIA
Prague         Ständisches Nov. 26, 1886 (in Ger.)

EGYPT
Alexandria     Alhambra     Mar.?    1924 S. Caceffo (A.)

Cairo          Khedivial    Feb.  1? 1924 E. Mazzoleni (D.) S. Caceffo (A.) A.
                                          Beuf (Da.)

FRANCE
Nice           Municipal    Feb. 20? 1886 M. Peri (D.) L. Parodi (A.) T. Wil-
                                          mant (Da.)

ITALY
Bari           Petruzzelli Feb. 28, 1924 L. Barla-Ricci (D.) T. Camgati (Ar.)
                                          V. Fullin (A.) C. Del Corso (Da.) A.
                                          Marone (L.) E. Mascheroni cond.

Bologna        Comunale    Dec. 25, 1920 A. Concato (D.) R. Bardelli (Ar.) N.
                                          Piccaluga (A.) B. Franci (Da.) L.
                                          Donaggio (L.) A. Guarnieri cond.

Brescia        Grande      Jan.  6, 1923 E. Mazzoleni (D.) E. Bragiotti (Ar.)
                                          J. De Gaviria (A.) M. Basiola (Da.)
                                          N. Marotta (L.) G. Podestà cond.

Catania        Bellini     Apr.  4, 1925 N. Svilarova (D.) J. Frenkel (Ar.)
                                          S. Caceffo (A.) A. Perrone (Da.) N.
                                          Marotta (L.) G. Armani/Serussi cond.

Cremona        Ponchielli  Feb. 23, 1924 M. Llacer (D.) E. Braggiotti (Ar.)
                                          G. Abate cond.

Faenza         Comunale    June 16? 1920 A. Concato (D.) N. Piccaluga (A.) M.
                                          Stabile (Da.) J. Torres de Luna (L.)
                                          A. Guarnieri cond.

Ferrara        Comunale    Feb.     1922 T. Dal Monte (Ar.)

Genoa          Politeama   Oct. 29, 1920 T. Burchi (D.) R. Bardelli (Ar.) L.
                                          Abrate (A.) C. Togliani (Da.) A.
                                          Galli (L.) P. La Rotella cond.

Mantua         Sociale     Dec. 26? 1928 F. Campigna (D.) R. Bardelli (Ar.)
                                          J. De Gaviria (A.) E. Spada (L.) G.
                                          Neri cond.

Milan          Dal Verme   Mar.  2, 1921 E. Mazzoleni (D.) M. De Voltri (Ar.)
                                          L. Abrate (A.) E. Roggio (Da.) F.
                                          Autori (L.) A. Ferrari cond.

Modena          Municipale  Dec. 26? 1923 M. Llacer (D.) E. Braggiotti (Ar.)
                                          F. Merli (A.) R. Borella (Da.) P. La
                                          Rotella cond.

Palermo         Massimo     Mar. 12, 1925 E. Mazzoleni (D.) D. Fiumana (Ar.)
                                          S. Caceffo (A.) A. Reali (Da.) S.
                                          Baccaloni (L.) A. Lucon cond.

Parma           Regio       Dec. 20, 1921 F. Campigna (D.) O. Perugini (Ar.)
                                          F. Merli/L. Abrate (A.) G. Noto (D.)
                                          B. Carmassi (C.) G. Armani cond.

Ravenna         Alighieri   May  10, 1924 1. Viganò (D.) E. Bragiotti (Ar.) F.
                                          Merli (A.) G. Lulli (Da.) N. Marotta
                                          (L.) F. Ghione cond.

Reggio Emilia Municipale    Dec. 23, 1920 I. Abry (D.) E. Bragiotti (Ar.) A.
                                          Lolla (A.) G. Inghilleri (Da.) I.
                                          Vittorio (L.) G. Neri cond.

Rome            Sala RAI    June 18, 1932 M.   Serra-Massara  (D.)   G.  Caputo
                                          (Ar.)  A. Facchini  (A.)  V.  Sensi
                                          (Da.) P. Prodi (L.) R. Santarelli
                                          cond.

Trieste         Grande      Jan. 31, 1925 G. De Zorzi (D.) G. Chiaia (A.) D.
                                          Menotti (Da.) S. Persichetti (L.) G.
                                          Neri cond.

Turin           Regio       Oct. 21, 1884 R. Pantaleoni (D.) G. Bellincioni
                                          (Ar.) W. Mierzwinski (A.) D. Menotti
                                          (Da.) F. Vecchioni (L.) F. Faccio
                                          cond.

                            Feb. 11, 1920 E. Mazzoleni (D.) T. Dal Monte (Ar.)
                                          G. Taccani (A.) E. Faticanti (Da.)
                                          L. Donaggio (L.) E. Panizza cond.

Verona          Filarmonico Mar.     1921 F. Merli (A.) M. Stabile (Da.) A.
                                          Guarnieri cond.

MALTA
La Valletta     Reale       Jan. 23, 1924 M. Baldini (D.) O. Poletti (Ar.) F.
                                          Battaglia (A.) F. Izal (Da.) G. Ma-
                                          sini (L.) Cantoni cond.

OTHER PRODUCTIONS-POST-WORLD WAR II

ITALY
Lucca           Giglio      Sep.  6, 1985 C. Basto (D.) M. L. Garbato (Ar.) O.
                                          Garaventa (A.) R. Massis (Da.) C.
                                          Zardo (L.) J. L. Koenig cond.

4. EDMEA-*Dramma lirico* in three acts
Milan-Teatro alla Scala-Feb. 27, 1886
Libretto by Antonio Ghislanzoni

Edmea (E.)                                          Virginia Ferni-Germano sop.
Oberto (O.)                                                   Gaetano Ortisi ten.
Ulmo (U.)                                              Francesco Pozzi bar.
Il Barone di Waldeck (B.)                          Tito Scipione Terzi bar.
Il Conte di Leitmeritz (C.)                         Napoleone Limonta bass
Fritz                                                                    Paroli ten.

Conductor                                                        Franco Faccio


OTHER PRODUCTIONS

CHILE
Santiago       Municipale   Oct.   1, 1889 L. Drog (E.) R. Grani (O.) V. Blasi
                                           (U.)

ITALY
Brescia        Grande       Carn. 1898-99 L. Peri-Di Stefani (E.) A. Barbaini
                                          (O.) F. M. Bonini (U.) L. Nicoletti-
                                          Kormann (C.) A. Jacchia cond.

Conegliano                  Sep. 14? 1888 A. Busi (E.) G. Bayo (O.)

Ferrara        Comunale     Jan. 24? 1899 Merolla (E.) F. Constantino (O.) R.
                                          Angelini-Fornari (U.)

Fiume          Civico       Oct. 27? 1889 A. Busi (E.) E. Giannini-Griffini
                                          (O.) A. Pini-Corsi (U.) Travaglini
                                          (C.)

Genoa          Carlo        Jan.   5, 1889 A. Busi (E.) L. Fagotti (O.) F. Poz-
               Felice                      zi (U.) U. Peroni (B.) V. Arimondi
                                           (C.) G. Cimini cond.

Lucca          Giglio       Sep. 18, 1989 M. Noto (E.) M. Frusoni (O.) M.
                                          Chingari (U.) G. Del Vivo (C.)

Modena         Municipale   Jan. 24? 1914 E. Medugno (E.) E. Inchausti (O.) E.
                                          Vaghi (U.) F. Fabbri-Boesmi (C.)

Padua          Verdi        June 12? 1887 V. Ferni-Germano (E.) A. Brasi (O.)
                                          G. Vaselli (U.) R. Drigo cond.

Rome           Argentina    Apr. 30, 1888 V. Ferni-Germano (E.) E. De Marchi
                                          (O.) V. Blasi (U.) C. De Probizi
                                          (B.) P. Wulmann (C.) E. Mascheroni
                                          cond.

Trieste        Grande       Feb. 16, 1887 V. Ferni-Germano (E.) G. Moretti
                                          (O.) G. Balisardi (C.) V. Podesti
                                          cond.

Turin          Carignano    Nov.   5, 1886 V. Ferni-Germano (E.) N. Figner (O.)
                                           S. Sparapani (U.) E. Borucchia (C.)
                                           A. Toscanini cond.

               Regio        Jan. 16, 1910 M. Farneti/M. Roggero (E.) L. Zino-
                                          vieff (O.) O. Benedetti (U.) G.
                                          Quinzi-Tapergi (C.) T. Serafin cond.

Venice        La Fenice    Feb. 17. 1887 A. Busi (E.) L. Fagotti (0.) G. Va-
                                         selli (U.) B. Galeazzi (B.) V. Ari-
                                         mondi (C.) A. Pomè cond.

MEXICO
Mexico City   Nacional     Nov. 16. 1895 L. Drog (E.) F. Baldini (0.) P. Lom-
                                         bardi (C.) L. Angelini (U.)

RUSSIA
Moscow                     June  1, 1901

St.           Panaieff     Mar. 26, 1888 V. Ferni-Germano  (E.)  L.  Fagotti
  Petersburg                             (0.) L. Lalloni (U.) P. Povoleri
                                         (C.)


5. LORELEY-*Azione romantica* in three acts[4]
Turin-Teatro Regio-Feb. 16, 1890
Libretto by Carlo d'Ormeville and Angelo Zanardini

Loreley (L.)                             Virginia Ferni-Germano sop.
Anna (A.)                                 Leonora Dexter sop.
Walter (W.)                               Eugenio Durot ten.
Hermann (H.)                       Enrico Stinco-Palermini bar.
Rodolfo (R.)                             Natale Pozzi bass

Conductor                                Edoardo Mascheroni

OTHER PREMIERES

ARGENTINA
Buenos Aires  Opera        July 23, 1905 R. Giachetti (L.) A. Zepilli (A.) G.
                                         Zenatello (W.) F. M. Bonini (H.) C.
                                         Thos (R.) L. Mugnone cond.

              Colón         June 10, 1913 S. Kruszelnicka (L.) I. M. Ferraris
                                         (A.) R. Grassi (W.) R. Stracciari
                                         (G.) A. Galli (R.) A. Guarnieri
                                         cond.

BRAZIL
Rio de        Lyrico       June  4, 1910 E. Tecchi  (L.) E. Allegri  (A.)  G.
  Janeiro                                Krismer (W.) G. Viglione-Borghese
                                         (H.) A. Dadò (R.)

              Municipal    June 16, 1920 O. Nieto (L.) A. Giacomucci (A.) B.
                                         Gigli (W.) V. Damiani (H.) T. Denta-
                                         le (R.) E. Vitale cond.

Sao Paulo     Politeama    July  9, 1910 T. Poli-Randaccio  (L.)  E. Allegri
                                         (A.) G. Krismer  (W.)  F. Federici
                                         (H.) A. Dadò (R.) G. Polacco cond.

              Municipal    Oct. 24, 1923 C. Muzio (L.) B. Dragoni (A.) A.
                                         Pertile (W.) J. Segura-Tallien (W.)
                                         M. Fiore (R.) G. Marinuzzi cond.

---

[4]. *Loreley* is an extensive revision of the earlier *Elda*.

CHILE
Santiago      Municipal     Oct.   7, 1908 L. Siebanech (L.) I. Cristalli (W.)
                                           A. Costa (H.) G. Armani cond.

Valparaiso    Victoria      Oct.  12, 1908 L. Siebanach (L.) M. Almansi (A.) I.
                                           Cristalli (W.) A. Costa (H.) M. Fi-
                                           ore (R.) G. Armani cond.

EGYPT
Alexandria    Zizinia       Feb.  16, 1907 M. Grisi (L.) G. Finzi-Magrini (A.)
                                           A. Marcolin (W.)

Cairo         Khedivial     Jan.  22? 1910 L. Crestani (L.) I. Ferraris (A.) A.
                                           Cecchi (W.) E. De Marco (H.) G. Ar-
                                           mani cond.

GREAT BRITAIN
London        Covent        July 12, 1907 M. Scalar (L.) S. Kurz (A.) A. Bassi
              Garden                       (W.) G. M. Sammarco (H.) M. Journet
                                           (R.) C. Campanini cond.

ITALY
Ancona        Muse          Apr.   7, 1915 E. Mangili (L.) E. Cesa Bianchi (W.)
                                           E. Faticanti (H.) V. Podesti cond.

Bari          Petrucelli    Feb.   8, 1919 E. Mangili (L.) I. Mion (A.) F. De
                                           Serbini (W.) A. Romboli (H.) C.
                                           Scattola (R.) P. La Rotella cond.

Bergamo       Donizetti     Apr.   8, 1917 F. Solari (L.) I. Mion (A.) A. Dolci
                                           (W.) G. Noto (H.) C. Scattola (R.)
                                           F. Del Cupolo cond.

Bologna       Comunale      Dec.   1, 1914 M. Llacer (L.) L. Lauri (A.) I.
                                           Cristalli (W.) E. Badini (H.) L.
                                           Manfrini (R.) R. Ferrari cond.

Brescia       Grande        Jan.      1910 F. Solari (L.) D. Domar (A.) G. Gau-
                                           denzi (W.) G. Giardini (H.) G. Bardi
                                           (R.) G. Neri cond.

Cagliari      Politeama     Apr.      1922

Catania       Bellini       Mar.  31, 1910 T. Poli-Randaccio (L.) L. Simeoli
                                           (A.) A. Cecchi (W.) A. Passuello
                                           (H.) S. Mossocci (R.) G. Zinetti
                                           cond.

Chieti        Marrucino     May    7, 1911 F. Solari (L.) R. Andreini (W.) O.
                                           Mieli (H.) S. Becucci (R.) E. Romani
                                           cond.

Cremona       Ponchielli    Dec.  26? 1908 O. Petrella (L.) A. Marcolin (W.)

Florence      Verdi         Dec.   1, 1910 E. Burzio (L.) E. Garbin (W.) F. M.
                                           Bonini (H.)

Forli         Comunale      May?      1921 A. M. Turchetti (L.) L. Bragiotti
                                           (A.) I. Voltolini (W.) G. Vanelli
                                           (H.) V. Cassia (R.) G. Armani cond.

Genoa         Carlo         Feb.  18, 1892 C. Ferrani (L.) A. Occhiolini (A.)
              Felice                       V. Ghilardini (W.) V. Brombara (H.)
                                           C. Fiegna (R.) A. Toscanini cond.

Lucca           Giglio      Sep. 10? 1919 F. Solari (L.) E. Marchini (A.) G.
                                          Krismer (W.) E. Mascheroni cond.

Lugo            Rossini     Sep.?    1913 E. Laudan (L.) A. Rebaud (A.) E.
                                          Cunego (W.) G. Azzolini (H.) T.
                                          Montico (R.) G. Armani cond.

Mantua          Sociale     Dec. 26? 1911 C. Pasini (L.) M. Benincori (A.) E.
                                          Garbin (W.) C. Scafa (H.) G. Cac-
                                          cialli (R.) E. Tango cond.

Messina         Vittorio    Feb.  7, 1906 E. Pucci (L.) E. Garagnani (A.) V.
                Emanuele                   Coppola (W.) G. Bellantoni (H.) S.
                                           Carobbi (R.) G. Polacco cond.

Milan           La Scala    Jan. 24, 1894 C. Bonaplata-Bau (L.) E. Sampero
                                          (A.) E. Bertran (W.) T. Wilmant (H.)
                                          E. Brancaleoni (R.)

Modena          Municipale  Dec. 26, 1908 T. Burchi (L.) G. Agostini (W.) V.
                                          Ardito (H.) R. Moranzoni cond.

Naples          San Carlo   Jan. 28, 1910 S. Kruszelnicka (L.) G. Tandi (A.)
                                          I. Cristalli (W.) B. Dadone (H.) B.
                                          Berardi (R.) C. Campanini cond.

Padua           Verdi       Dec. 26, 1898 N. Barbareschi (L.) E. Ghilardini
                                          (W.) A. Anceschi (H.) G. Mansueto
                                          (R.)

Palermo         Politeama   Jan. 12, 1893 M. D'Arneiro (L.) G. Apostolu (W.)
                                          A. Toscanini cond.

                Massimo     May  12, 1906 E. Pucci (L.) L. Simeoli (A.) E. Le-
                                          liva (W.) T. Quercia (H.) G. Ran-
                                          chetti (R.) E. Mascheroni cond.

Parma           Regio       Sep. 24, 1907 E. Mazzoleni (L.) A. Zeppilli (A.)
                                          I. Cristalli (W.) N. Rapisardi (H.)
                                          G. Mansueto (R.) C. Campanini cond.

Piacenza        Municipale  Jan. 16? 1914 S. F. Solari (L.) W. Ferrario (A.)
                                          R. Andreini (W.) A. Armentano (H.)
                                          L. Ferroni (R.) U. Tansini cond.

Pisa            Verdi       Mar.  9, 1909 A. Alloro (L.) G. Tandi (A.) A. Cec-
                                          chi (W.) M. Aineto (H.) L. Contini
                                          (R.) V. Landini cond.

Ravenna         Alighieri   May  10, 1919 A. Concato (L.) N. Zonghi (A.) G.
                                          Merli (W.) E. Roggio (H.) A. Corbet-
                                          ta (R.) A. Guarnieri cond.

Reggio Emilia Municipale  Jan. 19, 1911 E. Landau (L.) A. Sanipoli (A.) G.
                                          Agostini (W.) S. Avezzano (H.) P.
                                          Gramigni (R.) G. Podestà cond.

Rome            Costanzi    Mar. 16, 1906 M. Farneti (L.) M. Benincori (A.) A.
                                          Marcolin (W.) F. Cigada (H.) B. Be-
                                          rardi (R.) R. Ferrari cond.

Trento          Sociale     Jan. 22, 1910 O. Petrella (L.) E. Silva (A.) A.
                                          Marcolin (W.) L. Silvetti (H.) A.
                                          Venturini (R.)

Trieste        Grande      Jan.  3, 1909 L. Crestani (L.) J. Palet (W.) V.
                                        Bettoni (R.)

Venice         La Fenice   Nov. 18, 1920 N. Borina (L.) M. Colombara (A.) L.
                                         Marini (W.) F. Dizal (H.) F. Toledo
                                         (R.) A. Guarnieri cond.

Verona         Filarmonico Mar.  3? 1914 L. Crestani (L.) G. Beninqui (A.) L.
                                         Botta (W.) V. Guicciardi (H.)

               Arena       Aug.  1, 1935 G. Cigna (L.) L. Albanese (A.) F.
                                         Merli (W.) C. Tagliabue (H.) D. Ba-
                                         ronti (R.) G. Marinuzzi cond.

Vicenza        Eretenio    Sep.     1920 A. Conti (L.) I. Cristalli (W.)

MALTA
La Valletta    Reale              1918-19

MEXICO
Mexico City    Iris        Jan. 24, 1926 A. Conti (L.) G. Picco cond.

NETHERLANDS
Amsterdam      Stads       Nov.  6, 1933 G. Cigna (L.) G. Bentonelli (W.) S.
                                         Marchi (H.) M. Parenti cond.

Den Haag                   Nov.  1, 1933 G. Cigna (L.) G. Bentonelli (W.) S.
                                         Marchi (H.) M. Parenti cond.

PORTUGAL
Lisbon         Coliseo     Jan. 29, 1916 S. Kruszelnicka (L.) A. Gargiulo
                                         (A.) G. Tincani (W.) M. Zuffo (H.)

Oporto         Sao Joao    Dec. 30, 1906 E. Corsi (L.) A. Angioletti (W.)

RUSSIA
Odessa         Municipal   Feb.?     1901 V. Mendioroz (L.) G. Apostolu (W.)
                                          F. M. Bonini (H.)

SPAIN
Madrid         Real        Mar. 25, 1916 M. Llacer (L.) J. Palet (W.) L. Al-
                                         movodar (H.) C. Del Pozo (R.) E. Pa-
                                         nizza cond.

UNITED STATES
Atlanta        Auditorium  Apr. 26, 1922 C. Muzio (L.) R. Delaunois (A.) B.
                                         Gigli (W.) G. Danise (H.) G. Martino
                                         (R.) R. Moranzoni cond.

Chicago        Auditorium  Jan. 17, 1919 A. Fitziu (L.) F. Macbeth (A.) A.
                                         Dolci (W.) G. Rimini (H.) V. Lazzari
                                         (R.) G. Polacco cond.

New York       Lexington   Feb. 13, 1919 A. Fitziu (L.) F. Macbeth (A.) A.
                                         Dolci (W.) G. Rimini (H.) V. Lazzari
                                         (R.) G. Polacco cond.

               Metro-      Mar.  4, 1922 C. Muzio (L.) M. Sundelius (A.) B.
               politan                   Gigli (W.) G. Danise (H.) J. Mardo-
                                         nes (R.) R. Moranzoni cond.

Philadelphia   Metro-      Dec. 26, 1922 F. Alda (L.) M. Sundelius (A.) E.
               politan                   Johnson (W.) G. Danise (H.) J. Mar-
                                         dones (R.) R. Moranzoni cond.

URUGUAY
Montevideo     Solis          Aug. 31, 1905 G. Russ (L.) G. Anselmi (W.) F. M.
                                            Bonini (H.)

SELECTED PRODUCTIONS-POST-WORLD WAR II

ITALY
Lucca          Giglio         Sep. 15, 1954 A. De Cavalieri (L.) A. Beltrami
                                            (A.) C. Bergonzi (W.) C. Tagliabue
                                            (H.) G. Tozzi (R.) F. Capuana cond.

                              Sep. 19, 1982 M. Colalillo (L.) M. L. Garbato (A.)
                                            P. Visconti (W.) A. Cassis (H.) G.
                                            Monici (R.) N. Annovazzi cond.

Milan          Sala RAI       Dec. 15, 1954 A. De Cavalieri (L.) R. Gigli (A.)
                                            K. Neate (W.) P. Guelfi (H.) A. Co-
                                            lella (R.) A. Simonetto cond.

               La Scala       Feb. 22, 1968 E. Suliotis (L.) R. Talarico (A.) G.
                                            Cecchele (W.) P. Cappuccilli (H.) G.
                                            Gavazzeni cond.

Rome           Sala RAI       Sep. 23, 1948 A. Guerrini (L.) E. Rizzieri (A.) M.
                                            Filipeschi (W.) P. Sopranzi (H.) A.
                                            Colella (R.) O. De Fabritiis cond.

                              July 23, 1963 G. Frazzoni (L.) D. Carral (A.) L.
                                            Infantino (W.) P. Guelfi (H.) L.
                                            Monreale (R.) A. La Rosa Parodi
                                            cond.

               Caracalla      July 27, 1955 A. De Cavalieri (L.) A. Beltrami
                                            (A.) R. Turrini (W.) P. Silveri (H.)
                                            F. Ghione cond.

6. LA WALLY-*Opera seria* in four acts
Milan-Teatro alla Scala-Jan. 20, 1892
Libretto by Luigi Illica

Wally (W.)                                   Hericlea Darclée sop.
Walter (Wa.)                                 Adelina Stehle sop.
Afra (A.)                                 Virginia Guerrini mez.
Giuseppe Hagenbach (H.)                      Manuel Suagnes ten.
Vincenzo Gellner (G.)                        Arturo Pessina bar.
Stromminger (S.)                         Ettore Brancaleoni bass
Il Pedone                                  Pietro Cesari bass

Conductor                                Edoardo Mascheroni

OTHER PREMIERES-PRE-WORLD WAR II

ARGENTINA
Buenos Aires   Opera          July 28, 1904 M. Farneti (W.) E. Garbin (H.) P.
                                            Amato (G.) R. Ercolani (S.) A. Tos-
                                            canini cond.

|          | Colón      | June 28, 1909 | H. Darclée (W.) G. Grazioli (Wa.) E. Lucci (A.) I. Cristalli (H.) E. Giraldoni (G.) G. Mansueto (S.) G. Barone cond. |
| Rosario  | Colón      | May 22, 1911  | T. Desana (W.) G. Valls (H.) G. Abate cond. |

**BRAZIL**
Rio de Janeiro  Sao Pedro   Oct. 8, 1908   A. De Revers (W.) C. Sainescu (Wa.) R. Sangiorgi (H.) G. Puliti (G.) Benedetti (S.)

          Municipal   July 17, 1912  E. Cervi-Caroli (W.) A. Galli-Curci (Wa.) G. Flory (A.) L. Marini (H.) E. Faticanti (G.) G. Cirino (S.) G. Marinuzzi cond.

Sao Paulo   Santana     Oct. 27, 1908  A. De Revers (W.) C. Sainescu (W.) D. Tanfani (A.) R. Sangiorgi (H.) G. Puliti (G.) Benedetti (S.) Frattini cond.

            Municipal   Aug. 5, 1912   E. Cervi-Caroli (W.) A. Galli-Curci (Wa.) G. Flory (A.) L. Marini (H.) E. Faticanti (G.) G. Cirino (S.) G. Marinuzzi cond.

**CHILE**
Santiago    Municipal   Sep. 27, 1910  C. Gagliardi (W.) G. De Tura (H.) C. Galeffi (G.)

**EGYPT**
Cairo       Khedivial   Feb. 8, 1906   G. Russ (W.) J. Palet (H.) P. Amato (G.)

**GERMANY**
Hamburg     Stadt       Feb. 16, 1893  K. Klafsky (W.) G. Seidel (H.) F. H. Lissmann (G.) (in Ger.)

**GREAT BRITAIN**
Manchester  Gaiety      Mar. 27, 1919  E. Morden (W.) J. Gibson (Wa.) J. Pegg (H.) J. Olivere (G.) J. C. Brewer (S.) (in Eng.)

**IRELAND**
Dublin      Gaiety      Feb. 28, 1919  E. Morden (W.) J. Gibson (Wa.) J. Pegg (H.) J. Olivere (G.) J. C. Browner (S.) C. Hawley cond. (in Eng.)

**ITALY**
Ancona      Muse        Apr. 19, 1915  B. Lenzi (W.) L. Marini (H.) E. Molinari (G.) E. Mascheroni cond.

Bari        Petrucelli  Jan. 28, 1920  B. Scacciati (W.) D. Seghizzi (Wa.) M. Golinelli (A.) C. Broccardi (H.) M. Dragone (G.) A. Galli (S.) E. Mascheroni cond.

Bergamo      Donizetti   Feb. 16? 1913 G. Baldassare-Tedeschi (W.) G. Mi-
                                       cheli (H.) R. Meroni (G.) G. Armani
                                       cond.

Bologna      Comunale    Nov.  5, 1908 E. Druetti (W.) P. Zweifel (Wa.) M.
                                       Vaccari (A.) R. Grassi (H.) D. Vig-
                                       lione-Borghese (G.) S. Cirotto (S.)
                                       E. Vitale cond.

Brescia      Grande      Feb.  6? 1909 O. Del Signore (W.) P. Zweifel (Wa.)
                                       N. Del Ry (H.) E. De Marco (G.) G.
                                       Neri cond.

Cagliari     Civico      Dec. 25, 1909 N. Casini (W.) A. Ramazzini (H.) E.
                                       Omoldi (G.) S. Massoni (S.)

Catania      Bellini     Apr. 13, 1912 V. D'Ornelli (W.) A. Santoro (Wa.)
                                       V. Paganelli (A.) G. Tommasini (H.)
                                       J. Segura-Tallien (G.) L. Ferroni
                                       (S.) F. Russo cond.

Chieti       Maruccino   May 10, 1910 E. Racanelli (W.) R. Andreini (H.)
                                       S. Vinci (G.) U. Canetti (S.) F. Del
                                       Cupolo cond.

Cremona      Ponchielli  Feb. 14, 1906 M. De Macchi (Wa.) P. Zweifel (Wa.)
                                       N. Lollini (A.) A. Cecchi (H.) G. La
                                       Puma (G.) A. Masini-Pieralli (S.) V.
                                       Mingardi cond.

Florence     Verdi       Carn. 1910-11 E. Bianchini-Cappelli (W.) M. Massa
                                       (H.) D. Viglione-Borghese (G.)

Forli        Comunale    May  24, 1919 A. Minotti (W.) M. Guardiola (A.) E.
                                       Cunego (H.) E. Fregosi (G.) G. Cian-
                                       caleoni (S.) A. Gallo cond.

Genoa        Carlo       Oct. 17, 1892 H. Darclée (W.) R. Pinkert (Wa.) E.
             Felice                    Bertrau (H.) L. Fumagalli (G.) V.
                                       Arimondi (S.) A. Toscanini cond.

Livorno      Goldoni     Dec. 20, 1909 T. Desana (W.) C. Carlini (H.) S.
                                       Arrighetti (G.) P. Bellucci cond.

Lucca        Giglio      Sep.  4? 1892 L. Gilboni (W.) C. Lanfredi (H.) M.
                                       Ancona (G.) A. Toscanini cond.

Lugo         Rossini     Sep.?    1914 E. Cervi-Caroli (W.) A. Santoro
                                       (Wa.) A. Poggi (A.) G. Taccani (H.)
                                       E. Bione (G.) S. Beccucci (S.) G.
                                       Armani cond.

Mantua       Sociale     Carn. 1909-10 V. Ardito (G.) W. Aldovrandi cond.

Messina      Vittorio    Dec.  7, 1895 L. Sangiorgio (W.) J. Escursell (H.)
             Emanuele                  Puiggener (G.) M. Spoto (S.) A. Bovi
                                       cond.

Modena       Municipale  Dec. 24? 1909 J. Caracciolo (W.) A. Fazzino (H.)
                                       J. Segura-Tallien (G.) R. Moranzoni
                                       cond.

Naples        San Carlo    Feb.  3, 1907 M. Farneti (W.) T. Ippolito (W.) G.
                                         Zoffoli (A.) R. Grassi (H.) E. Moreo
                                         (G.) P. Wulmann (S.) L. Mugnone
                                         cond.

Padua         Verdi        Jan. 12? 1915 F. Solari (W.)

Palermo       Massimo      Apr.  9, 1907 M. Farneti (W.) E. Allegri (Wa.) A.
                                         Marcello (A.) F. Giraud (H.) E. nani
                                         (G.) R. Galli (S.) T. Serafin cond.

Parma         Regio        Jan. 26, 1907 L. Crestani (W.) M. Longari (A.) J.
                                         Garcia (H.) D. Viglione-Borghese
                                         (G.) I. Cesari (S.) G. A. Fano cond.

Pavia         Fraschini    Jan. 29? 1914 G. Baldassare-Tedeschi (W.) G. Gior-
                                         gi (H.)

Pesaro        Rossini      Feb. 27? 1919 E. Cunego (H.)

Piacenza      Municipale   Jan.  7? 1911 E. Cervi-Caroli (W.) T. Alasia (A.)
                                         N. Fusati (H.) A. Neumacher (G.) V.
                                         Bettoni (S.) A. Dall'Acqua cond.

Pisa          Verdi        Mar.  4, 1910 J. Caracciolo (W.) M. Favilli (A.)
                                         A. Quadri (H.) A. Pacini (G.) E.
                                         Vannuccini (S.) U. Tansini cond.

Ravenna       Alighieri    May   8, 1909 A. Ricci (W.) G. Basti (W.) T. Stup-
                                         pazoni (A.) F. Fazzini (H.) A. Rom-
                                         boli (G.) S. Cirotto (S.) A. Guar-
                                         nieri cond.

Reggio Emilia Municipale   Jan.?    1909 E. Bossetti (W.) V. Bitonto (Wa.) S.
                                         Parisotto (A.) J. Garcia (H.) E. Mo-
                                         reo (G.) C. Preve (S.) P. Duffau
                                         cond.

Rome          Costanzi     Dec.  7, 1899 E. Carelli (W.) C. Rommel (Wa.) A.
                                         Ponzano (A.) L. Innocenti (H.) E.
                                         Moreo (G.) R. Galli (S.) L. Mugnone
                                         cond.

Rovigo        Sociale      Oct.  2, 1909 C. White/L. Crestani (W.) R. Bracci
                                         (H.) E. Lavarello (G.) A. Orlandi
                                         (S.) F. Del Cupolo cond.

Trieste       Grande       Feb.  2, 1906 H. Darclée (W.) E. Ceresoli (A.) F.
                                         Giraud (H.) V. Ardito (G.) M. Spoto
                                         (S.) T. Serafin cond.

Turin         Regio        Jan. 14, 1894 E. Petri (W.) E. Cisterna (Wa.) C.
                                         Zawner (A.) L. Iribarne (H.) E. Si-
                                         vori (G.) V. Salmasi (S.) A. Conti
                                         cond.

Venice        La Fenice    Feb. 17, 1906 C. Pasini (W.) S. Ronconi (A.) F.
                                         Fassino (H.) E. Nani (G.) N. Franchi
                                         (S.) G. Sturani cond.

Verona        Filarmonico  Dec. 23? 1920 C. Toschi (W.) L. Marini (H.) O.
                                         Anselmi cond.

Vicenza          Eretenio     Jan.?     1908 E.  Morando  (W.)  G.  Tasca  (H.)  P.
                                             Grillo (G.) F. Del Cupolo cond.

JUGOSLAVIA
Ljubljana        National     Mar. 30, 1926

MALTA
La Valletta      Reale        Oct. 30, 1908 A.  Botti  (W.)  L.  Tomezzoli  (A.)  O.
                                             Morando  (H.)  R.  Constantino  (G.)
                                             Poggi cond.

MEXICO
Mexico City      Arbeu        Mar. 17, 1920 C.  Melis  (W.)  H.  Lazaro (H.)  G.  Da-
                                             nise (G.) I. Picchi (S.) A. Padovani
                                             cond.

NETHERLANDS
Amsterdam        Palais v.    Feb.  3, 1914 E.  Cottino  (W.)  J.  Nadal  (H.)  L.
                 Volksvligt                  Mazzoleni (G.) F. Guerrieri cond.

Den Haag                      Feb.  7, 1914 E.  Cottino  (W.)  J.  Nadal  (H.)  L.
                                             Mazzoleni (G.) F. Guerrieri cond.

Rotterdam        Groote       Feb.  8, 1914 E.  Cottino  (W.)  J.  Nadal  (H.)  L.
                                             Mazzoleni (G.) F. Guerrieri cond.

POLAND
Warsaw           Wielki       Jan.  1? 1914 E. Cervi-Caroli (W.) P. Cimini cond.

PORTUGAL
Lisbon           Sao Carlos   Jan. 29, 1910 M.  De Lerma  (W.)  G.  Giorgi (H.)  C.
                                             Galeffi (G.)

ROMANIA
Bucharest        Nacional     Feb.  7, 1924 A.  Rodrigo  (W.)  Caravia  (H.)  J.
                                             Athanasiu (G.) Massini cond.

SPAIN
Barcelona        Liceo        Jan.  3, 1911 L.  Crestani  (W.)  M.  Benincori  (A.)
                                             M.  Massa  (H.)  E.  De Marco  (G.)  A.
                                             Brondi (S.)

Madrid           Real         Dec. 15, 1910 C.  Gagliardi  (W.)  R.  Grassi  (H.)  B.
                                             Challis (G.) Giral (S.)

UNITED STATES
New York         Metro-       Jan.  6, 1909 E.  Destinn  (W.)  I.  L'Huillier (Wa.)
                 politan                     M.  Ranzenberg  (A.)  R.  Martin (H.)  P.
                                             Amato (G.) G. Rossi (S.) A. Toscani-
                                             ni cond.

URUGUAY
Montevideo       Solis        Aug. 24, 1904 M.  Farneti  (W.)  E.  Garbin  (H.)  P.
                                             Amato (G.) R. Ercolani (S.) A. Tos-
                                             canini cond.

OTHER PRODUCTIONS-POST-WORLD WAR II

ARGENTINA
Buenos Aires     Colón        Sep. 18, 1981 C.  Neblett  (W.)  M.  Anselmi  (A.)  E.
                                             Mauro  (H.)  G.  Mastromei  (G.)  M.
                                             Veltri cond.

AUSTRIA
Bregenz        Fest-        July 20, 1990 M. Zampieri  (W.)  M. Sylvester (H.)
               spielhaus                  (Projected)

GERMANY
Bremen         Goetheplatz Nov. 24, 1985 K.  Ciesinski  (W.)  J.  Bruggemann
                                         (Wa.) M. Zamfir (H.) G. Dolter (G.)
                                         P. Steinberg cond.

IRELAND
Wexford        Th. Royal    Oct.    1985 J. Ligi (W.) S. J. Langton (Wa.) J.
                                         Bailey (A.) Y. Marusin/L. Bakst (H.)
                                         L. Videnov (G.) J. O'Flynn (S.) A.
                                         Rosen cond.

ITALY
Lucca          Giglio       Sep. 14, 1954 M. Caniglia (W.) R. Scotto (Wa.) M.
                                         Picchi (G.) A. Protti (P.) F. Capua-
                                         na cond.

Milan          dell'Arte    Apr. 19, 1952 A. Guerrini (W.) D. Gatta (Wa.) L.
                                         Danieli (A.) K. Neate (H.) G. Taddei
                                         (G.) D. Caselli (S.) F. Previtali
                                         cond.

               La Scala     Dec.  7, 1953 R. Tebaldi (W.) R. Scotto (Wa.) J.
                                         Gardino (A.) M. Del Monaco/M. Ortica
                                         (H.) G. G. Guelfi (G.) G. Tozzi (S.)
                                         C. M. Giulini cond.

Modena         Municipale   Dec.    1975 R. Kabaivanska (W.) N. Martinucci
                                         (H.) A. Protti (G.) G. Vaghi (S.)

Naples         San Carlo    Feb.  7, 1954 R. Tebaldi (W.) R. Turrini (H.) C.
                                         Tagliabue (G.) A. Cassinelli (S.) G.
                                         Santini cond.

Rome           Sala RAI     Oct. 29, 1960 R. Tebaldi (W.) P. Perotti (Wa.) J.
                                         Gardino (A.) G. Prandelli (H.) D.
                                         Dondi (G.) S. Maionica (S.) A. Basi-
                                         le cond.

Trieste        Grande       Carn. 1949-50 F. Sacchi (W.) V. Campagnano (H.) L.
                                         Donaggio (G.) U. Berrettoni cond.

                            Mar.  6, 1972 R. Kabaivanska (Wa.) A. Zambon (H.)
                                         S. Carroli (G.) R. Gavazzeni cond.

UNITED STATES
New York       Carnegie     Mar.  6, 1968 R. Tebaldi (W.)  C. Bergonzi (H.) P.
               Hall                       Glossop (G.) F. Corena (S.) F. Cleva
                                         cond.

                            Apr. 17, 1990 A. Millo (W.) K. Johannson (H.) J.
                                         Rawnsley (G.) E. Queler cond.

Sarasota       Opera        Mar.  5, 1989 S. Sundine (W.) P. Johnson (Wa.) R.
                                         Locke (H.) C. Serrano (G.) V. De
                                         Renzi cond.

FRANCO FACCIO

1. I PROFUGI FIAMMINGHI-*Melodramma* in three acts
Milan-Teatro alla Scala-Nov. 11, 1863
Libretto by Emilio Praga

| | | |
|---|---|---|
| Margherita | Elena Corani | sop. |
| Ida | Maria Palmieri | sop. |
| Ruggero | Antonio Prudenza | ten. |
| Conte Bergh | Antonio Cotogni | bar. |
| Velasco | Giovanni Capponi | bass |
| Marta | Elisa Repetto | sec. |
| Diego | Giacomo Redaelli | ten. |
| Il Cavaliere di Nua | Luigi Alessandrini | bass |

2. AMLETO-*Tragedia lirica* in four acts
Genoa-Teatro Carlo Felice-May 30, 1865
Libretto by Arrigo Boito

| | | |
|---|---|---|
| Ofelia | Angiolina Ortolani-Tiberini | sop. |
| Geltrude | Elena Corani | sop. |
| Amleto | Mario Tiberini | ten. |
| Claudio | Antonio Cotogni | bar. |
| Lo Spettro | Eraclito Bagagiolo | bass |

Revised-Milan-Teatro alla Scala-Feb. 9, 1871

| | | |
|---|---|---|
| Ofelia | Virginia Pozzi-Brazanti | sop. |
| Geltrude | Marietta Bulli-Paoli | sop. |
| Amleto | Mario Tiberini | ten. |
| Claudio | Zenone Bertolasi | bar. |
| Lo Spettro | Ormondo Maini | bass |
| Primo Cantore | Ferdinanda Cappelli | sec. |
| Secondo Cantore | Fausto Mola | bar. |
| Terzo Cantore | Luigi Manfredi | ten. |
| Laerte | Luigi Manfredi | ten. |
| Orazio | Augusto Gabrieli | sec. |
| Polonio | Angelo De Giuli | bass |
| Marcello | Fausto Mola | bar. |
| Primo Becchino | Fausto Mola | bar. |

## ANTONIO CARLOS GOMES

1. A NOITE DO CASTELO-*Opera* in three acts
Rio de Janeiro-Teatro Lirico Fluminense-Sep. 4, 1861
Libretto by Antônio José Fernandes dos Reis (in Portuguese)

| | |
|---|---|
| Leonor (L.) | Luisa Amat sop. |
| Inêz (I.) | Guillemet sop. |
| Henrique (H.) | Andrea Marchetti ten. |
| Fernando (F.) | Luigi Marina bar. |
| Conte Orlando (O.) | Eduardo Medina Ribas bass |
| Raimundo | Heliodoro Maria da Trindade bass |
| A Pagem | Unknown |
| Roberto | Unknown |
| | |
| Conductor | Julio José Nunes |
| Director | Antonio Carlos Gomes |

OTHER PRODUCTIONS

BRAZIL

| | | | |
|---|---|---|---|
| Campinas | | Sep. 14, 1978 | N. de Castro Tank (L.) L. Pessagno (I.) L. Tenaglia (H.) A. Acosta (F.) J. Dainese (O.) B. Juarez cond. |
| Rio de Janeiro | Lirico Fluminense | June 9, 1863 | L. Amat (L.) Guillemet (I.) A. M. Celestino (F.) A. Rossi Castagnola (F.) |

2. JOANA DE FLANDRES-*Opera*
Rio de Janeiro-Teatro Lirico Fluminense-Sep. 15, 1863
Libretto by Salvador de Mendonça (in Portuguese)

| | |
|---|---|
| | Teresa Bayetti sop. |
| | Luisa Amat sop. |
| | Giuseppe Mazzi ten. |
| | Luigi Walter bar. |
| | Achille Rossi Castagnola bass |
| | Giuseppe Cervini sec. |
| | |
| Conductor | Carlo Ercole Bosoni |
| Director | Antonio Carlos Gomes |

3. IL GUARANY-*Opera ballo* in four acts
Milan-Teatro alla Scala-Mar. 19, 1870
Libretto by Antonio Scalvini

| | |
|---|---|
| Cecilia (C.) | Marie Sasse sop. |
| Pery (P.) | Giuseppe Villani ten. |
| Gonzales (G.) | Enrico Storti bar. |
| Il Cacico (Ca.) | Victor Maurel bar. |
| Don Antonio (A.) | Theodore Coulon bass |
| Don Alvaro | Giuseppe Masato sec. |
| Ruy Bento | Annibale Michelini sec. |
| Alonso | Severino Mazzo sec. |
| Pedro | Not named |
| | |
| Conductor | Eugenio Terziani |
| Director | Antonio Carlos Gomes |

OTHER PREMIERES-NINETEENTH CENTURY

ARGENTINA
Buenos Aires   Ant. Colón   June 27, 1874 M.   Mariani-Masi   (C.)   C.   Bulterini
(P.) G. Toledo (G.) M. Junca (Ca.)
O. Bimboni cond.

AUSTRALIA
Melbourne   Her   Nov. 17, 1888 R. Aimo (C.) Venturi (P.)   G. Pimaz-
Majesty's   zoni (G.) G. Verdi (Ca.) R. Mancini
(A.)

BRAZIL
Rio de   Lirico   Dec.   2, 1870 G. Gasc (C.) L. Lelmi (P.) D. Orlan-
Janeiro   Fluminense   dini (G.) C. Marziali (Ca.) J. Ordi-
nas (A.)

Pedro II   Oct.   1, 1877 L.   Vanda-Miller (C.) L.   Bolis (P.)
G.   Mendioroz   (G.)   A.   Castelmary
(Ca.) L. Lombardelli (A.)

Sao Paulo   Sao José   Oct. 23, 1880 M. L. Durand (C.) C. Bulterini (P.)
E.   Storti   (G.)   E.   Dondi   (Ca.)   P.
Povoleri (A.)

CHILE
Santiago   Municipal   Sep.   7, 1881 A. Alhaiza (C.) T. Bertini (P.) L.
Lalloni (G.) A. Buzzi (Ca.) E. Con-
trucci cond.

Valparaiso   Victoria   Oct. 24, 1893 M. De Nunzio (C.) A. Baggetto (P.)
A. Dorini (G.) G. Wanrell (Ca.)

COLOMBIA
Bogota   Municipal   July 21, 1890 E. Guardenti (P.) A. Ferri (G.)

CUBA
Havana   Peyret   Dec. 17, 1878 A. Urban (C.) L. Vanzetti (P.) M.
Ciapini (G.) A. Souvestre (Ca.) G.
Maffei (A.)

EGYPT
Alexandria   Zizinia   Jan. 22, 1896 L. Gabbi (C.) F. Avedano (P.) A.
Alberti (G.)

FRANCE
Nice            Municipal    Feb. 20, 1880 A. Gabbi (C.) V. Deviliers (P.) V.
                                           De Pasqualis (G.) A. Buzzi (Ca.)

GREAT BRITAIN
London          Covent       July 13, 1872 M. Sessi (C.) E. Nicolini (P.) A.
                Garden                     Cotogni (G.) J. B. Fauré (Ca.) A.
                                           Vianesi cond.

GREECE
Athens          Olimpo       June  8, 1883 V. Di Giovanni (C.) G. De Sanctis-
                                           Marianecci (P.) R. De Giorgi (G.) F.
                                           Micci-Labruna cond.

Corfu           San Giacomo Nov.      1877 M. Boschetta (C.) A. Byron (P.) R.
                                           De Giorgi (G.) E. Fucili (Ca.) G. B.
                                           Del Fabbro (A.) F. Sangiorgi cond.

INDONESIA
Batavia         T. Batavie   Feb. 23, 1885 M. Erba (C.) G. Jenuschi (P.) U.
                                           Forapan (G.) G. Bergamaschi (Ca.) C.
                                           Prò (A.)

ITALY
Alessandria     Municipale   Oct.      1878 E. Angeli-Barbieri (C.) L. Giraud
                                           (P.) E. Barbieri (G.) G. Bolzoni
                                           cond.

Ancona          Muse         Feb. 27? 1886 E. Milanesi (C.) L. Gasparini (P.)
                                           L. Garbini (G.) Amadei cond.

Ascoli          Ventidio     Nov.      1876 Garulli (C.) A. Byron (P.)
 Piceno         Basso

Cagliari        Civico       Oct. 23, 1875 C. De Sanctis (C.) P. Petrovich (P.)
                                           S. Orsi (G.) G. Narberti (Ca.)

Catania         Comunale     Dec. 28, 1872 A. Pascalis (C.) E. Bonacich (P.) I.
                                           Viganotti (G.) F. Trapani-Bono (Ca.)
                                           C. Scalisi cond.

Ferrara         Comunale     Apr. 20, 1872 A. Pascalis (C.) C. Bulterini (P.)
                                           T. Sterbini (G.) G. Bergamaschi
                                           (Ca.)

Fiume           Civico       Apr. 22, 1876 F. Vogri (C.) F. Patierno (P.) A.
                                           Carboni (G.) A. Tamburlini (Ca.)

Florence        Pergola      Oct.      1871 M. Lotti della Santa (C.) L. Bolis
                                           (P.) E. Storti (G.) G. Cima (Ca.)

Genoa           Carlo        Feb. 17, 1872 A. Pascalis (C.) J. Gayarre (P.) E.
                Felice                     Manfredi (G.) S. Cesarò (C.)

Lucca           Giglio       Aug. 30, 1876 A. Conti-Foroni (C.) C. Vincentelli
                                           (P.) Z. Bertolasi (G.) P. Povoleri
                                           (Ca.)

Lugo            Rossini      Aug.      1873 R. Pantaleoni (C.) F. Patierno (P.)
                                           G. Tagliapietra (G.) E. Gasperini
                                           (Ca.) C. Dall'Argine cond.

Mantua        Sociale      Jan.          1876 E. Ciuti (C.) G. Ortisi (P.) I. Vi-
                                              ganotti (G.) M. Junca (Ca.) G. Alsi-
                                              na (A.) C. Lovati-Cazzulani cond.

Naples        San Carlo    Jan. 24, 1877 G. Giovannoni-Zacchi (C.) C. Bulte-
                                              rini (P.) V. Cottone (G.) G. Bellet-
                                              ti (Ca.) A. Buzzi (A.) P. Serrao
                                              cond.

Palermo       Bellini      Jan.          1873 M. Pascal Damiani (C.) V. Belardi
                                              (P.) A. De Antoni (G.) L. Alfano
                                              cond.

Reggio Emilia Municipale   Dec. 25, 1878 G. Caruzzi-Bedogni (C.) E. Arrighi
                                              Misseri (P.) A. Parolini (G.) G.
                                              Galeazzi cond.

Rome          Apollo       Nov.  1, 1871 E. Wiziak (C.) J. Gayarre (P.) A.
                                              Pantaleoni (G.) F. Raguer (Ca.) R.
                                              Nannetti (A.) E. Terziani cond.

Siena         Rinnovati    Dec. 30? 1885 O. De Newosky (C.) A. Volebele (P.)
                                              V. Brombara (C.)

Sinigaglia    Comunale     Fiera         1878 A. Spaak (C.) A. Byron (P.) E. Po-
                                              gliani (G.) A. Morelli (Ca.) A.
                                              Fiorini (A.) G. Galeazzi cond.

Treviso       Comunale     Oct.  5, 1872 A. Pascalis (C.) G. Villani (P.) S.
                                              Orsi (G.) P. Milesi (Ca.) G. Rossi
                                              cond.

Trieste       Grande       Sep. 29, 1872 E. Wiziak (C.) G. Capponi (P.) A.
                                              Pantaleoni (G.) A. Cremaschi cond.

Turin         Regio        Dec. 28, 1872 V. Potentini (C.) G. Capponi (P.) A.
                                              Pantaleoni (G.) E. Gasperini (Ca.)
                                              E. Barberat (A.) C. Pedrotti cond.

Venice        La Fenice    Dec. 26, 1874 J. De Reszke (C.) F. Tamagno (P.) G.
                                              Belletti (G.) G. Carbone (Ca.) G.
                                              Capponi (A.) R. Kuon cond.

Verona        Filarmonico  Feb.  2? 1880 M. Andreeff (C.) V. Clodio (P.) E.
                                              Carnili (G.) U. Giannelli cond.

Vicenza       Eretenio     Aug.  1, 1872 A. Pascalis (C.) E. Barbacini (P.)
                                              G. Rota (G.) A. Castelmary (Ca.)

JUGOSLAVIA
Zagreb        National     Apr. 21, 1883 A. Passetti (P.)


MALTA
La Valletta   Real         Oct. 21, 1879


MEXICO
Mexico City   Nacional     Dec. 22, 1883 M. Peri (C.) F. Giannini (P.) T.
                                              Wilmant (G.) E. Serbolini (Ca.)

PHILIPPINES
Manila        Del Tondo    Feb. 26, 1887 E. Ancarani (C.) A. Castelli (P.) G.
                                              Ciocci (G.) E. Villelmi (Ca.) G.
                                              Tondo cond.

POLAND
Warsaw          Wielki      Feb. 11, 1876 C. De Cepeda (C.) F. Cazaux (P.) L.
                                          Del Fabbro (G.) C. Trombini cond.

PORTUGAL
Lisbon          Sao Carlos  Mar. 31, 1880 E. Borghi-Mamo (C.) F. Tamagno (P.)
                                          F. Pandolfini (G.)

RUSSIA
Moscow          Bolshoi     Feb.  8, 1879 E. Volpini (C.) A. Marin (P.) M. Pa-
                                          dilla (G.) J. Ordinas (A.) E. Bevi-
                                          gnani cond.

St.             Imperial    Feb. 12, 1879 L. Harris (C.) A. Masini (P.) A. Co-
 Petersburg                               togni (G.) V. Maurel (Ca.) E. Gas-
                                          perini (A.) J. Goula cond.

SPAIN
Barcelona       Liceo       Mar.  7, 1876 A. Urban (C.) F. Tamagno (P.) G.
                                          Mendioroz (G.) A. Rodas (Ca.)

Madrid          Real        Oct. 28, 1880 A. Garbini (C.) G. Ortisi (P.) N.
                                          Verger (G.) A. Vidal (Ca.)

TURKEY
Constan-        Concordia   May  17, 1884 C. Bevilacqua (C.) A. Brunetti (P.)
 tinople                                  R. De Giorgio (G.) C. De Jorio (Ca.)
                                          F. Micci-Labruna cond.

UNITED STATES
New York        Star        Nov.  3, 1884 M. Peri (C.) F. Giannini (P.) T.
                                          Wilmant (G.) E. Serbolini (Ca.) L.
                                          Logheder cond.

San Francisco Grand         Aug. 27, 1884 M. Peri (C.) F. Giannini (P.) T.
                                          Wilmant (G.) E. Serbolini (Ca.)

URUGUAY
Montevideo      Solis       July  7, 1876 P. Missorta (C.) G. Toressi (P.) A.
                                          Mazzoli (G.) E. Dondi (Ca.) G.
                                          Tansini (A.)

VENEZUELA
Caracas         Municipal   Jan. 22, 1890 A. Martinez (C.) G. Procacci (P.) E.
                                          De Bernis (G.) E. Cherubini (Ca.)

SELECTED PRODUCTIONS-TWENTIETH CENTURY

BRAZIL
Rio de          Lirico      Sep. 25, 1902 H. Darclée (C.) G. Zenatello (P.) A.
 Janeiro                                  Anceschi (G.)

                            Oct. 29, 1903 H. Darclée (C.) A. Gamba (P.) S.
                                          Vinci (G.) G. Mansueto (Ca.)

                            Sep.  7, 1904 Fontes (C.) G. Zenatello (P.) F. M.
                                          Bonini (G.)

                Municipal   Aug.  3, 1914 Silva (C.) J. Palet (P.) G. Danise
                                          (G.)

                            Sep. 27, 1919 Z. Amaro (C.) G. Taccani (P.) L.
                                          Montesanto (G.)

                            Sep.  7, 1922 M. Ross (C.) M. Fleta (P.) L. Montesanto (G.)

                            Aug. 20, 1936 B. Sayao (C.) G. Thill (P.) A. Borgioli (G.) G. Vaghi (Ca.) U. Berettoni cond.

                            Sep.  7, 1949 M. Sa Earp (C.) M. Del Monaco (P.) J. Villa (G.) N. Rossi-Lemeni (Ca.) T. Serafin cond.

|  | Apollo | May 27, 1916 M. Clasenti (C.) M. Salazar (P.) F. Federici (G.) |

Sao Paulo    Politeama   Nov. 13, 1902 P. Zweifel (C.) G. Zenatello (P.) A. Anceschi (G.) L. Nicoletti Kormann (Ca.)

               Santana     Oct.  7, 1903 H. Darclée (C.) A. Gamba (P.) S. Vinci (G.) G. Mansueto (Ca.)

               Municipal   Oct. 10, 1919 Z. Amaro (C.) G. Taccani (P.) L. Montesanto (G.) N. De Angelis (Ca.)

                            Oct. 24, 1922 M. Ross (C.) M. Fleta (P.) L. Montesanto (G.) G. Cirino (Ca.)

                            Sep. 17? 1936 B. Sayao (C.) G. Thill (P.) A. Borgioli (G.) G. Vaghi (Ca.) U. Berettoni cond.

                            Sep. 30, 1949 M. Sa Earp (C.) M. Del Monaco (P.) P. Fortes (G.) N. Rossi-Lemeni (Ca.) T. Serafin cond.

## ITALY
Genoa          Politeama   Sep. 12, 1917 A. Minotti (C.) G. Campioni (P.) F. M. Bonini (G.) J. Fernandez/V. Bettoni (C.) F. Del Cupolo cond.

Milan          Lirico       Oct. 21, 1936 L. Pagliughi (C.) L. Marletta (P.) G. Fregosi (G.) A. Righetti (Ca.) D. Caselli (A.) U. Benvenuti Giusti cond.

Modena        Municipale  Jan. 31? 1905 E. Bel Sorel (C.) P. Venerandi (P.)

Naples        San Carlo   Jan. 28, 1937 A. Archi (C.) F. Tafuro (P.) L. Montesanto (G.) T. Pasero (Ca.) A. Righetti/ M. Sassanelli (A.) F. Vitale cond.

                            Apr.  2, 1971 N. De Castro Tank/D. Pieranti (C.) A. Assis Pacheco (P.) A. Ramus (G.) B. Da Silva (Ca.) P. Adonis Gonzales (A.) A. Belardi cond.

Palermo       Biondo      Dec. 25, 1913 M. Comida (C.) G. Di Bernardo (P.) G. Lazzarini (G.) L. Lucenti (A.) E. Romano cond.

## UNITED STATES
New York     Carnegie    May  6, 1901 M. Arnold cond.
               Lyceum

4. FOSCA-*Melodramma* in four acts
Milan-Teatro alla Scala-Feb. 16, 1873
Libretto by Antonio Ghislanzoni

| | |
|---|---|
| Fosca (F.) | Gabriella Krauss sop. |
| Delia (D.) | Cristina Lamare sop. |
| Paolo (P.) | Carlo Bulterini ten. |
| Cambro (C.) | Victor Maurel bar. |
| Gajolo (G.) | Ormondo Maini bass |
| Doge di Venezia | Giovanni Tanzio bass |
| Michele Giotta | Angelo De Giuli bass |
| | |
| Conductor | Franco Faccio |
| Director | Antonio Carlos Gomes |

OTHER PRODUCTIONS

ARGENTINA
Buenos Aires   Ant. Colón   July  7, 1877 A. Fricci (F.) A. D'Alberti (D.) L.
                                          Bolis (P.) G. Mendioroz (C.) A. Cas-
                                          telmary (G.) N. Bassi cond.

BRAZIL
Rio de         Pedro II     July 27, 1877 A. Fricci (F.) A. D'Alberti (D.) L.
 Janeiro                                  Bolis (P.) G. Mendioroz (C.) A. Cas-
                                          telmary (G.) N. Bassi cond.

Revised-Milan-Teatro alla Scala-Feb. 7, 1878

| | |
|---|---|
| Fosca (F.) | Amalia Fossa sop. |
| Delia (D.) | Adele Garbini sop. |
| Paolo (P.) | Francesco Tamagno ten. |
| Cambro (C.) | Gustavo Moriami bar. |
| Gajolo (G.) | Ormondo Maini bass |
| Doge di Venezia | Ettore Marcassa bass |
| Michele Giotta | Carlo Moretti bass |
| | |
| Conductor | Franco Faccio |
| Director | Antonio Carlos Gomes |

OTHER PRODUCTIONS-FIRST REVISION

BRAZIL
Rio de         Pedro II     Oct.  6, 1880 M. L. Durand  (F.)  A. Adini (D.) C.
 Janeiro                                  Bulterini (P.) S. Athos-Caldani (C.)
                                          P. Povoleri (G.)

Sao Paulo      Sao José     Nov.  1, 1880 M. L. Durand (F.) A. Adini (D.) C.
                                          Bulterini (P.) S. Athos-Caldani (C.)
                                          P. Povoleri (G.)

ITALY
Modena         Municipale   Feb. 10? 1889 V. Damerini (F.) L. Gabbi (D.) F.
                                          Gambarelli (P.) A. Pessina (C.) V.
                                          Salmasi (G.) E. Usiglio cond.

Revised-Milan-Teatro dal Verme-Oct. 26, 1890

| | |
|---|---|
| Fosca (F.) | Virginia Damerini sop. |
| Delia (D.) | Maria Roussel Giraud sop. |
| Paolo (P.) | Leopoldo Signoretti ten. |
| Cambro (C.) | Carlo Bacchetta bar. |
| Gajolo (G.) | Enrico Serbolini bass |
| Doge di Venezia | Raffaele Terzi bass |
| Michele Giotta | |


Conductor                                                        Arnaldo Conti
Director                                              Antonio Carlos Gomes

OTHER PRODUCTIONS-SECOND REVISION

BRAZIL
Rio de      Lirico      Oct.  6, 1896 C. Zucchi-Ferrigno (F.) A. Bonner
Janeiro                               (D.) G. Vilalta (P.) A. Arcangeli
                                      (C.) D. Rotoli (G.) M. Bavagnoli
                                      cond.

            Municipal   Aug.  7, 1935 C. Gomes (F.) N. Ferrari (D.) E. Re-
                                      is e Silva (P.) G. Danise (C.) G.
                                      Lansky (G.) A. Padovani cond.

                        Nov. 15, 1940 C. Gomes (F.) E. Reis e Silva (P.)

                        May  10, 1950 M. H. Martins (F.) A. Colósimo (P.)

                        Oct. 17, 1952 A. Pacheco (P.)

                        Oct. 31, 1962 I. Miccolis (F.)

                        Apr.  9, 1965 I. Miccolis (F.) A. Pacheco (P.)

Sao Paulo   Sao José    Jan.  9, 1897 A. Stinco-Palermini (F.) A. Bonner
                                      (D.) G. Vilalta (P.) A. Arcangeli
                                      (C.) D. Rotoli (G.) M. Bavagnoli
                                      cond.

            Santana     Dec.     1933 E. Piave (F.) D. Solima (D.) A. De
                                      Angelis (P.) E. Rigazzi (C.) G. Zon-
                                      zini (G.)

            Municipal   Sep. 14, 1966 I. Miccolis (F.) A. Ayres (D.) S.
                                      Albertini (P.) C. Mascitti (C.) M.
                                      Rinaudo (G.)

MALTA
La Valletta  Real       Oct. 31, 1899 Bida (D.) Vanutelli (P.) O. Marini
                                      (C.)

5. SALVATOR ROSA-*Dramma lirico* in four acts
Genoa-Teatro Carlo Felice-Mar. 22, 1874
Libretto by Antonio Ghislanzoni

| | |
|---|---|
| Isabella (I.) | Romilda Pantaleoni sop. |
| Genariello (G.) | Clelia Blenio mez. |
| Salvator Rosa (S.) | Salvatore Anastasi ten. |
| Masaniello (M.) | Leone Giraldoni bar. |
| Il Duca d'Arcos (D.) | Marcel Junca bass |
| Il Conte di Badajoz | ten. |
| Fernandez | ten. |
| Corcelli | bass |
| Bianca | sec. |

| | |
|---|---|
| Conductor | Giovanni Rossi |
| Director | Antonio Carlos Gomes |

OTHER PRODUCTIONS-NINETEENTH CENTURY

ARGENTINA
Buenos Aires   Odeon       Mar. 30, 1897 A. Bonner (G.) G. Villalta (S.) A.
                                         Arcangeli (M.) D. Rotoli (D.)

BRAZIL
Bahia          Sao Joao    June 10, 1880 F. Savio (I.) Orlandini (G.) L. Gi-
                                         raud (S.) A. Putó (M.) R. Mailini
                                         (D.) E. Bernardi cond. A. C. Gomes
                                         dir.

Rio de         Sao Pedro   Sep. 28, 1876 P. Missorta (I.) M. Andreeff (G.) G.
Janeiro                                  Toressi (S.) A. Mazzoli (M.) E. Don-
                                         di (D.)

               Pedro II    Aug.  7, 1880 M. L. Durand (I.) A. Adini (G.) C.
                                         Bulterini (S.) S. Athos-Caldani (M.)
                                         E. Dondi (D.)

                           July 28, 1886 N. Bulicioff (I.) I. Mayer (G.) C.
                                         Callioni (S.) P. Lhérie (M.) G. Ro-
                                         veri (D.) A. Toscanini cond.

               Apollo      Nov. 14, 1896 E. Bassi (I.) A. Bonner (G.) G. Vil-
                                         lalta (S.) A. Arcangeli (M.) D. Ro-
                                         toli (D.)

Sao Paulo      Sao José    Feb. 14, 1883 S. Springer (I.) A. Rebottaro (G.)
                                         P. Setragni (S.) G. Dominici (M.) O.
                                         Tanti (D.)

                           June 20, 1886 N. Bulicioff (I.) I. Meyer (G.) C.
                                         Callioni (S.) P. Lhérie (M.) G. Ro-
                                         veri (D.)

                           Nov. 28, 1896 E. Bassi (I.) A. Bonner (G.) G. Vil-
                                         lalta (S.) A. Arcangeli (M.) D. Ro-
                                         toli (D.) M. Bavagnoli cond.

GREECE
Athens                     Mar.    1880 A. Colombo (I.) Balma (G.) A. Stucci
                                        (S.) A. Prous (M.) Marini (D.)

Corfu          San Giacomo Nov.    1879 G. Caruzzi-Bedogni/A. Colombo (I.)
                                        A. Stucci (S.) Ciolli/A. Prous (M.)
                                        Marini (D.)

ITALY

| | | | | |
|---|---|---|---|---|
| Alessandria | Municipale | Oct. 17? | 1881 | A. Contarini (I.) C. Sartori (G.) G. Santinelli (S.) G. Marabini (M.) F. Bachi-Perego (D.) |
| Ancona | Vittorio Emanuele | Apr. | 1877 | C. De Witten (I.) M. Milani-Vela (G.) G. Santinelli (S.) G. Valle (M.) G. Alsina (D.) M. Vela cond. A. C. Gomes dir. |
| Bergamo | Riccardi | Aug. 15, | 1876 | M. Mantilla (I.) E. Carpi (G.) A. Rossetti (S.) G. Valle (M.) I. Sbordoni (D.) Giovannini cond. A. C. Gomes dir. |
| Brescia | Grande | Dec. 26, | 1877 | R. Aimo (I.) E. Averso (G.) D. Casartelli (S.) V. De Pasqualis (M.) |
| Cagliari | Civico | Jan. 19, | 1887 | L. Rabuffini (I.) V. Ghilardini (S.) U. Franceschi (M.) G. Rubele (D.) Brunetti cond. |
| Como | Sociale | Feb. | 1878 | L. Stefanini (I.) I. D'Avanzo (S.) |
| Cremona | Concordia | Dec. 26, | 1883 | R. Fiorentini-Marangoni (I.) A. Boffa (G.) A. Brunetti (S.) N. Zardo (M.) |
| Cuneo | Civico | Dec. 26, | 1876 | |
| Florence | Pagliano | Oct. 5, | 1878 | P. Missorta (I.) A. Bonner (G.) A. Byron (S.) S. Athos-Caldani (M.) A. Furlan (D.) |
| Genoa | Carlo Felice | Jan. 27, | 1875 | A. Urban (I.) C. Blenio (G.) A. Celada (S.) M. Ciapini (M.) M. Junca (D.) G. Rossi cond. |
| Lecce | Sociale | Feb. | 1886 | E. Giunti-Barbera (I.) D. Del Papa (S.) |
| Milan | La Scala | Sep. 10, | 1874 | E. Wiziak (I.) C. Blenio (G.) I. D'Avanzo (S.) A. Parboni (M.) E. Bagagiolo (D.) |
| Modena | Municipale | Carn. | 1875-76 | P. Missorta (I.) I. De Sassi (G.) A. Rossetti (S.) E. Vanden (M.) C.Morroto (D.) S. Favi cond. |
| Novara | | Dec. 26, | 1880 | I. Giovane (I.) F. Tancioni (G.) G. Santinelli (S.) G. Tagliapietra (M.) C. Ulloa (D.) O. Bimboni cond. |
| Padua | Concordi | Dec. 26, | 1876 | C. Bossi (I.) A. Castelli/E. Baldanza (S.) T. Noto (M.) |
| | | Dec. 26, | 1883 | E. Dotti (I.) I. Cristino (G.) G. Ferrari (S.) E. Pelz (M.) R. Ercolani (D.) Grisanti cond. |
| Palermo | Bellini | Jan. 14, | 1884 | A. Bianchi-Montaldo (I.) N. Pedemonti (G.) G. Vanzan (S.) F. Laban (M.) L. Visconti (D.) F. Nicolao cond. |

Parma          Regio         Feb. 16, 1882 R. Pantaleoni (I.) O. Bazzani (G.)
                                           E. Mozzi (S.) E. Sivori (M.) C. Bo-
                                           logna (D.) P. Ferrari cond.

Pavia          Fraschini     Dec. 26, 1876 C. De Witten (I.)

Piacenza       Municipale    Dec. 26, 1874 P. Missorta (I.) M. Boy-Gibert (G.)
                                           A. Castelli (S.) A. Alvari (M.) I.
                                           Sbordoni (D.) A. Giovannini cond.

Ravenna        Alighieri     Jan.  2, 1876 C. De Witten (I.) G. Colucci (S.) V.
                                           Quintili-Leoni (M.) A. Furlan (D.)
                                           A. Moreschi cond.

Reggio Emilia Municipale     Dec. 25, 1887 M. Mei-Figner (I.) E. Brambilla (G.)
                                           N. Figner (S.) E. Rubirato (M.) E.
                                           Borucchia (D.) M. Bavagnoli cond.

Rome           Argentina     Oct. 10, 1878 M. Stolzmann (I.) E. Ocampo (G.) A.
                                           Rossetti (S.) G. Palou (M.) A. Pinto
                                           (D.)

Sassari        Civico        Dec. 26? 1883 L. Cerne (I.)

Trento         Sociale       Sep.     1875 R. Pantaleoni (I.) C. Blenio (G.) G.
                                           Ortisi (S.) M. Ciapini (M.) I. Sbor-
                                           doni (D.) A. C. Gomes dir.

Treviso        Comunale      Oct.     1882 Morotto (I.) M. Peri (G.) G. Santi-
                                           nelli (S.) A. Parboni (M.) A. Fra-
                                           delloni (D.) E. Usiglio cond.

Trieste        Grande        Sep. 28, 1874 G. Giovannoni-Zacchi (I.) C. Caveda-
                                           ni (G.) F. Patierno (S.) G. Aldighi-
                                           eri (M.) G. Atry (D.) E. Bernardi
                                           cond.

Turin          Regio         Feb. 21, 1875 T. Singer (I.) F. Patierno (S.) G.
                                           Moriami (M.) E. Barberat (D.) C. Pe-
                                           drotti cond.

Verona         Ristori       Oct. 22? 1881 C. Carolli (I.) G. Bellincioni (G.)
                                           C. Pizzorni (S.) G. Campanari (M.)
                                           V. Coda (D.) Furlotti cond.

Vicenza        Eretenio      Jan.?    1877 M. Mantilla (I.) M. Milani-Vela (G.)
                                           E. Ronconi (S.) E. Vanden (M.) R.
                                           Drigo cond.

MALTA
La Valletta    Real          Oct. 15, 1878 T. Vicari (I.) F. Prevost (G.) E.
                                           Baldanza (S.) T. Noto (M.) F. Nava-
                                           rini (D.)

TURKEY
Constan-       Concordia     Mar. 21, 1885 C. Caroli (I.) N. Molinari (G.) A.
 tinople                                   Byron (S.) A. Alberti (M.) G. Scar-
                                           neo (D.)

OTHER PRODUCTIONS-TWENTIETH CENTURY

BRAZIL
| | | | |
|---|---|---|---|
| Rio de Janeiro | Lyrico | Sep. 7, 1905 | M. De Lerma (I.) A. Campagnoli (G.) A. Bassi (S.) A. Magini-Coletti (M.) G. Mansueto (D.) |
| | Municipal | Sep. 27, 1920 | H. Iracema (I.) M. Antonia (G.) F. Merli (S.) C. Galeffi (M.) V. Lazzari (D.) T. Serafin cond. |
| | | Aug. 4, 1926 | B. Scacciati (I.) F. Merli (S.) C. Galeffi (M.) N. De Angelis (D.) E. Vitale cond. |
| | | Sep. 25, 1946 | E. Reis e Silva (S.) |
| Sao Paulo | Sao José | Apr. 17, 1917 | C. Badessi (I.) V. Cacioppo (G.) N. Del Ry (S.) E. De Franceschi (M.) M. Pinheiro (D.) A. De Angelis cond. |
| | Municipal | Aug. 24, 1926 | B. Scacciati (I.) E. Marchini (G.) F. Merli (S.) C. Galeffi (M.) N. De Angelis (D.) |
| | | Sep. 11, 1977 | N. Carini (I.) R. Staeke (G.) B. Maresca (S.) P. Fortes (M.) E. Costa (D.) S. Blech cond. |

ITALY
| | | | |
|---|---|---|---|
| Genoa | Politeama | Nov. 4, 1902 | O. Popovic (I.) I. Longone (G.) B. Lucignani (S.) G. Polese (M.) E. Ciccolini (D.) E. Perosio cond. |
| Rome | Quirino | Oct. 27, 1903 | G. Frampolesi (I.) O. Delle Fornaci (S.) Fari (M.) G. Cirino (D.) R. Mazzoni cond. |

MALTA
| | | | |
|---|---|---|---|
| La Valletta | Reale | Apr. 21? 1902 | M. Passeri (I.) Piacentini (G.) G. Tricario (S.) V. Pozzi-Camola (M.) Boella (D.) A. Siragusa cond. |

6. MARIA TUDOR-*Dramma lirico* in four acts
Milan-Teatro alla Scala-Mar. 27, 18792
Libretto by Emilio Praga

| | |
|---|---|
| Maria Tudor (M.) | Anna D'Angeri sop. |
| Giovanna (G.) | Emma Turolla sop. |
| Fabiano Fabiani (F.) | Francesco Tamagno ten. |
| Gil di Tarragona (T.) | Giuseppe Kaschmann bar. |
| Gilberto (Gi.) | Edouard De Reszke bass |
| Lord Montagu | Argimiro Bertocchi ten. |
| Lord Clinton | Ermengildo De Serini bass |
| Un Paggio | Emilia Galli sec. |
| Un Araldo | Proto Capelli ten. |
| | |
| Conductor | Franco Faccio |
| Director | Antonio Carlos Gomes |

OTHER PRODUCTIONS

BRAZIL
| Rio de Janeiro | Municipal | Aug. 15, 1934 | C. Gomes (M.)  A. de Souza (G.)  E. Reis e Silva (F.) A. Lima (T.) |
| Sao Paulo | Municipal | Oct. 6, 1943 | N. Greco (M.) J. Fonseca (G.) R. Miranda (F.) P. Ansaldi (T.) A. Basso (Gi.) E. De Guarnieri cond. |
|  |  | Dec. 17, 1978 | M. Veleris (M.) A. Cantelli (G.) E. Alvares (F.) F. Teixera (T.) W. Carrara (Gi.) M. Perusso cond. |

7. LO SCHIAVO-*Dramma lirico* in four acts
Rio de Janeiro-Teatro Dom Pedro II-Sep. 27, 1889
Libretto by Rodolfo Paravicini and Alfredo Tarnay

| Ilara (I.) | Maria Peri sop. |
| Condesssa de Boissy (B.) | Marie Van Cauteren sop. |
| Americo (A.) | Franco Cardinali ten. |
| Iberê (Ib.) | Innocenzio De Anna bar. |
| Conde Rodrigo (R.) | Enrico Serbolini bass |
| Goitacà | bass |
| Gianfèra | bar. |
| Lion | bass |
|  |  |
| Conductor | Riccardo Bonicioli |
| Director | Antonio Carlos Gomes |

OTHER PRODUCTIONS

BRAZIL[5]
| Rio de Janeiro | Lyrico | Aug. 13, 1894 | Cruz (I.) A. Occhiolini (B.)  E. De Marchi (A.) E. Camera (Ib.) Rossi (R.) |
|  |  | Sep. 13, 1898 | A. Stinco-Palermini (I.) M. Vendrell (B.) G. Betti (A.) L. Bellagamba (Ib.) A. Didur (R.) |
|  | Municipal | Sep. 21, 1917 | T. Burchi (I.) N. Vallin (B.) C. Hacket (A.) E. De Franceschi (Ib.) |
|  |  | July 29, 1921 | R. Raisa (I.) T. Dal Monte (C.) A. Minghetti (A.) G. Rimini (Ib.) |
|  |  | Sep. 3, 1936 | G. Cigna (I.) M. Sa Earp (C.) A. Marcato (A.) A. Borgioli (Ib.) A. Questa cond. |
| Sao Paulo | Sao José | Nov. 9, 1889 | M. Peri (I.) M. Van Cauteren (B.) F. Cardinali (A.) I. De Anna (Ib.) |

---

5. *Lo Schiavo* became essentially a repertory opera in Brazil starting in 1936. Therefore only selected productions in that country are included.

| | | | |
|---|---|---|---|
| | Santana | Oct. 31, 1901 | A. Stinco-Palermini (I.) L. Cassandro (C.) L. Innocenti (A.) V. Ardito (Ib.) A. Didur (R.) O. Anselmi cond. |
| | Municipal | Oct. 7, 1917 | T. Burchi (I.) A. Giacomucci (C.) C. Hacket (A.) E. De Franceschi (Ib.) |
| | | Aug. 19, 1921 | R. Raisa (I.) T. Dal Monte (C.) A. Minghetti (A.) G. Rimini (Ib.) |
| | | Sep. 20? 1936 | G. Cigna (I.) M. Sa Earp (C.) A. Marcato (A.) A. Borgioli (Ib.) A. Questa cond. |

UNITED STATES
New York    Amato    Sep. 10, 1988    L. Dolce/E. Nadir (I.) J. Stellato/ M. Maguire (C.) V. Titone/J. Landers (A.) J. Pariso/G. Maldonado (Ib.) A. Amato cond.


8. CONDOR-*Azione lirica* in four acts
Milan-Teatro alla Scala-Feb. 21, 1891
Libretto by Mario Canti

Odalea (O.)                          Ericlea Darclée sop.
Adin (A.)                           Adriana Stehle sop.
Zuleida (Z.)      Erina Borlinetto/Andreina Mazzoli-Orsini mez.
Condor (C.)       Giambattista De Negri/Federigo Corrado ten.
Almazor (Al.)       Francesco Navarini/Ettore Borucchia bass
Il Mufti                             Pio Marini bass

Conductor                          Leopoldo Mugnone
Director                          Antonio Carlos Gomes

OTHER PRODUCTIONS

BRAZIL
Rio de      Lyrico      Aug. 18, 1891    E. Theodorini (O.) A. Stehle (A.) E.
 Janeiro                                 Borlinetto (Z.) G. Gabrielescu (C.)
                                         A. Silvestri (Al.)

            Municipal   July 23, 1920    Z. Amaro (O.) A. Ottein (A.) A. Gramegna (Z.) B. De Muro (C.) M. Pinheiro (Al.) E. Vitale cond.

Sao Paulo   Municipal   Aug. 12, 1920    Z. Amaro (O.) A. Ottein (A.) A. Gramegna (Z.) B. De Muro (C.) M. Pinheiro (Al.) E. Vitale cond.

ITALY
Genoa       Carlo       Jan. 26, 1893    M. Pizzagalli (O.) C. Spaziani (A.)
            Felice                       M. Franchini (Z.) E. Galli (C.) L. Lucenti (Al.) G. Pomè Penna cond.

# FILIPPO MARCHETTI

1. GENTILE DA VARANO-*Opera semiseria* in three acts
Turin-Teatro Nazionale-Jan. 30, 1856[6]
Libretto by Raffaele Marchetti

| | |
|---|---|
| Adelina (A.) | Luigia Stramesi sop. |
| Gentile da Varano (G.) | Luigi Caserini ten. |
| Suppo, Conte d'Altino (S.) | Giuseppe Altini bar. |
| Monaldo, Conte di Corvenale (M.) | Giuseppe Rava bass |

Director                                        Filippo Marchetti

OTHER PRODUCTIONS

ITALY
Camerino       Fenice       Jan. 28, 1857 V. Rupini (A.) L. Mencarelli (G.) A.
                                          Olivari (M.) F. Marchetti dir.


2. LA DEMENTE-*Dramma lirico* in three acts
Turin-Teatro Carignano-Nov. 27, 1856
Libretto by Giuseppe Checchetelli

| | |
|---|---|
| Adina di Senlis (A.) | Virginia Boccabadati sop. |
| Luisa di Guisa (L.) | Angelica Montigny mez. |
| Raligo (R.) | Vincenzo Sarti ten. |
| Claudio (C.) | Enrico Delle Sedie bar. |
| Damville (D.) | Cesare Dalla Costa bass |
| Maria Stuarda | Maria Majotti sop. |
| Roberto | Fiorentino Viotti ten. |
| Remigio | Camillo Ferrara bass |

Director                                        Filippo Marchetti

OTHER PRODUCTIONS

ITALY
Iesi          Concordia    Sep. 22, 1858 L. Chiaromonte (A.) A. Pagnoni (R.)
                                          A. Carboni (C.)

Rome          Argentina    Nov.  7, 1857 L. Ponti dall'Armi (A.) P. Corvetti
                                          (L.) V. Sarti (R.) A. Morelli (C.)
                                          C. Nanni (D.) E. Angelini cond.


3. IL PARIA-*Opera seria*
Composed 1859-unperformed
Libretto by Giuseppe Checchetelli

---

[6]. Corrects Grove. See *Il Trovatore*, Turin, Feb. 2, 1856, p. 1.

4. ROMEO E GIULIETTA-*Dramma lirico* in four acts
Trieste-Teatro Grande-Oct. 25, 1865
Libretto by Marcelliano Marcello

| | |
|---|---|
| Giulietta (G.) | Angiolina Ortolani-Tiberini sop. |
| Romeo (R.) | Mario Tiberini ten. |
| Paride (P.) | Leone Giraldoni bar. |
| Frate Lorenzo (L.) | Paolo Medini bass |
| Tebaldo | Ignazio Cancelli ten. |
| Marta | Angelina Zamboni sec. |
| Baldassare | Not named |
| Cappellio | Giovanni Casenato sec. |
| | |
| Conductor | Antonio Cremaschi |
| Director | Filippo Marchetti |

OTHER PRODUCTIONS

ITALY
Milan        Carcano      Dec.      1867 E. Wiziak (G.) G. Artoni (R.) F.
                                    Amodio (P.) P. Poli-Lenzi (L.) E.
                                    Bernardi cond.

Revised-Venice-Teatro La Fenice-Mar. 10, 1872

| | |
|---|---|
| Giulietta (G.) | Angelica Moro sop. |
| Romeo (R.) | Leon Achard ten. |
| Paride (P.) | Luigi Colonnese bar. |
| Frate Lorenzo (L.) | Carlo Zuchelli bass |
| Tebaldo | Arcangelo Cruciani ten. |
| Marta | Olimpia Rossi Bartoli sec. |
| Baldassare | Giovanni Coletti sec. |
| Capellio | Gustavo Panizza sec. |
| | |
| Conductor | Clemente Castagneri |
| Director | Filippo Marchetti |

OTHER PRODUCTIONS

ITALY
Brescia      Grande       Jan.      1873 G. Fabbri-Santini (G.) A. Brunetti
                                    (R.) S. Orsi (P.) R. Blossi (L.)

                          Dec. 26? 1882 A. Tartaglia (G.) G. Procacci (R.)
                                    N. Gamberini (P.) E. Vanden (L.)

Carpi        Comunale     Aug. 16? 1872 P. Missorta (G.) A. Lamponi (R.) S.
                                    Orsi (P.) E. Manfredi (L.)

Cuneo        Civico       Dec. 26? 1874 M. Ricci (G.)

Genoa        Paganini     Dec.  5, 1872 A. Spaak (G.) T. Karl (R.) G. Balsa-
                                    mo (P.) L. Zimelli (L.) C. Corradi
                                    cond.

             Nazionale    Dec. 23, 1873 S. Lezi (G.) G. Ortisi (R.) A. Medi-
                                    ni (P.) A. De Santis (L.) R. Rasori
                                    cond.

Parma        Regio        Dec. 28, 1872 L. Pitarch (G.) U. Forapan (R.) L.
                                    Brignole (P.) L. Viviani (L.) G.
                                    Rossi cond.

Piacenza        Municipale    Jan.?       1877 F. Visconti (G.) G. Marini (R.) M.
                                               Bolini (P.) G. Bolzoni cond.

Rome            Apollo        Apr. 10,    1876 L. Vanda-Miller (G.) I. Campanini
                                               (R.) A. Brogi (P.) R. D'Ottavi (L.)
                                               E. Terziani cond.

Udine           Sociale       Aug.        1872 E. Wiziak (G.) C. Bulterini (R.) G.
                                               Del Puente (P.) R. Nannetti (L.) E.
                                               Bernardi cond. F. Marchetti dir.


5. RUY BLAS-*Dramma lirico* in four acts
Milan-Teatro alla Scala-Apr. 3, 1869
Libretto by Carlo D'Ormeville

Maria de Neubourg (M.)                                    Ida Benza sop.
Casilda (C.)                                          Carmelita Poch mez.
Ruy Blas (R.)                                          Mario Tiberini ten.
Don Sallustio De Bazan (S.)                            Giacomo Rota bar.
Don Guritano (G.)                                   Salvatore Cesarò bass
Donna Giovanna de la Cueva                               Ester Neri sec.
Don Pedro de Guevarra                               Giacomo Redaelli ten.
Don Fernando de Cordova                           Luigi Alessandrini bass
Don Manuel Arias                               Vincenzo Paraboschi ten.
Un Usciere                                      Francesco Fumagalli ten.

Conductor                                            Eugenio Terziani
Director                                             Filippo Marchetti

OTHER PREMIERES

ARGENTINA
Buenos Aires    Ant. Colón    June 10, 1872 E. Saurel (M.) M. Calisto Piccioli
                                               (C.) G. Piccioli (R.) G. Tagliapie-
                                               tra (S.) D. Dal Negro (G.) E. Raini-
                                               eri cond.

AUSTRALIA
Adelaide        Th. Royal     May  8, 1877 A. Guadagnini (M.) M. Venosta (C.)
                                               P. Paladini (R.) C. Orlandini (S.)
                                               G. Cesari (G.) P. Giorza cond.

Melbourne       Th. Royal     Feb. 17, 1877 A. Guadagnini (M.) M. Venosta (C.)
                                               P. Paladini (R.) C. Orlandini (S.)
                                               G. Cesari (G.) P. Giorza cond.

Sydney          Th. Royal     Dec. 9, 1876 A. Guadagnini (M.) M. Venosta (C.)
                                               P. Paladini (R.) C. Orlandini (S.)
                                               G. Cesari (G.) P. Giorza cond.

BRAZIL
Rio de          Lirico        Aug. 9, 1873 P. Missorta (M.) E. Cortesi (C.) G.
  Janeiro         Fluminense                   Toressi (R.) G. Spallazzi (S.) G.
                                               Wagner (G.)

Sao Paulo       Sao José      Nov. 1, 1879 A. Conti-Foroni (M.) R. Vercolini-
                                               Tay (C.) F. Giannini (R.) V. Cottone
                                               (S.) G. Mirabella (G.)

CHILE
Santiago        Municipal     Nov. 19, 1873 L. Corsi (M.) S. Lorini (C.) L. Lel-
                                            mi (R.) E. Carnili (S.) D. Dal Negro
                                            (G.)

Valparaiso      Victoria      Feb. 24, 1874 L. Corsi (M.) S. Lorini (C.) L. Lel-
                                            mi (R.) E. Carnili (S.) D. Dal Negro
                                            (G.)

CHINA
Shanghai        Lyceum        Jan. 17, 1880 R. Genolini (M.) Mancini (C.) E.
                                            Sbriscia (R.) G. Bergamaschi (S.) A.
                                            Bagagiolo (G.)

CUBA
Havana          Tacon         Feb.  7, 1873 M. Bulli-Paoli (M.) E. Palermi (R.)
                                            F. Bacchi-Perego (S.)

CZECHOSLOVAKIA
Prague          Provisional Oct. 25, 1881 (in Czech)

EGYPT
Alexandria      Apollo        May?     1877

Cairo           Khedivial     Jan. 12? 1873 E. Parepa-Rosa (M.) L. Corsi (C.) C.
                                            Carpi (R.) V. Cottone (S.)

FINLAND
Helsinki        Societets     Dec. 30, 1896 E. Bruno (M.) Shaw (C.) O. Delle
                                            Fornaci (R.) G. Pimazzoni (S.) E.
                                            Gandolfi (G.)

FRANCE
Aix les Bains Cercle          Oct.  5, 1884 O. Litvinoff (M.) A. De Andrade (R.)
                                            G. Vaselli (S.) A. Buzzi (G.)

Nice            Municipal     Nov. 14, 1872 C. Scarati-Bresciani (M.) E. Treves
                                            (C.) T. Villa (R.) P. Silenzi (S.)
                                            G. Manfredi (G.)

GERMANY
Berlin          Victoria      Mar.  8, 1882 E. Turolla (M.) G. Pasqua (C.) A.
                                            Corsi (R.) E. De Bernis (S.) W. Sei-
                                            demann (G.) G. Gialdini cond. (in
                                            It.)

Dresden         Hoftheater    Sep.  6, 1879 M. Sembrich (M.) L. Reuther (C.) L.
                                            Riese (R.) P. Bulls (S.) E. Decarli
                                            (G.) Wüllner cond. (in Ger.)

GREAT BRITAIN
Belfast         Th. Royal     Sep.  9, 1886 M. Roze (M.) M. Burton (C.) V. Smith
                                            (R.) L. Crotty (S.) H. Pope (G.) E.
                                            Goossens cond. (in Eng.)

Birmingham      Th. Royal     Sep. 30, 1886 M. Roze (M.) M. Burton (C.) V. Smith
                                            (R.) L. Crotty (S.) H. Pope (G.) E.
                                            Goossens cond. (in Eng.)

Edinburgh       Th. Royal     Mar. 12, 1878 A. Eyre (M.) Parodi (C.) F. Runcio
                                            (R.) G. Del Puente (S.) (in It.)

                Royal         Nov. 10, 1886 M. Roze (M.) V. Smith (R.) L. Crotty
                Lyceum                       (S.) H. Pope (G.) (in Eng.)

Glasgow          Th. Royal     Mar.  7, 1878  A. Eyre (M.) F. Runcio (R.) G. Del
                                              Puente (S.) (in It.)

                 Grand         Nov. 17, 1886  M. Roze (M.) M. Burton (C.) V. Smith
                                              (R.) L. Crotty (S.) H. Pope (G.) (in
                                              Eng.)

Liverpool        Royal         Apr.  9, 1878  A. Eyre (M.) F. Runcio (R.) G. Del
                 Alexandra                    Puente (S.) (in It.)

                 Royal Court   Feb.  4, 1886  M. Roze (M.) M. Burton (C.) V. Smith
                                              (R.) L. Crotty (S.) E. Goossens
                                              cond. (in Eng.)

London           Albert Hall   July 23, 1875  Performance by amateurs

                 Her           Nov. 24, 1877  C. Salla (M.) A. De Belocca (C.) G.
                 Majesty's                     Fancelli (R.) G. Del Puente (S.)
                                              Ghilberti (G.) G. Li Calsi cond. (in
                                              It.)

Manchester       Queen's       Apr.  2, 1878  A. Eyre (M.) Parodi (C.) F. Runcio
                                              (R.) G. Del Puente (S.) Corelli (G.)

GREECE
Athens           Falero        June     1875  O. Pierangeli (M.) G. Prandi (C.)
                                              Criticos (R.) A. Navary (S.) G. Tan-
                                              sini (G.)

Corfu            San Giacomo   Nov.     1872  Dondini   (M.) Jannuzzi (C.)   Ambo-
                                              netti (R.) Morelli (S.) N. Contedini
                                              (G.)

GUATEMALA
Guatemala        Colón                  1876  V. Potentini (M.)
  City

HONG KONG
Hong Kong        Th. Royal     Dec.  2, 1879  R. Genolini (M.) Mancini (C.) E.
                                              Sbriscia (R.) G. Bergamaschi (S.) A.
                                              Bagagiolo (G.)

INDIA
Calcutta         It. Opera     Mar. 14, 1874  A. Giannetti (M.) T. Riboldi (C.) G.
                                              Ferrari (R.) A. Grandi (S.) C. Melzi
                                              (G.) A. Melchiorri cond.

INDONESIA
Batavia          T. Batavie    Aug. 30, 1880  R. Genolini (M.) F. Boganini (R.) G.
                                              Bergamaschi (S.) A. Bagagiolo (G.)

Soerebaya        Theatre       Dec. 27, 1887  M. Balzofiore (M.) L. Balzofiore
                                              (R.) A. Falciai (S.)

IRELAND
Dublin           Gaiety        Aug. 22, 1887  M. Roze (M.) M. Burton (C.) V. Smith
                                              (R.) L. Crotty (S.) M. Eugene (G.)
                                              E. Goossens cond. (in Eng.)

ITALY
Alessandria      Municipale    Oct. 12, 1872  E. Robiati (M.) Rizzi (C.) G. Vil-
                                              lena (R.) F. Tirini (S.)

Ancona        Muse        May        1871 L. Tencajoli (M.) I. Campanini (R.)
                                           G. Cima (S.) L. Miller (G.)

Ascoli        Ventidio    Nov.   4? 1871 V. Pozzi-Brazanti (M.) Marini (C.)
Piceno        Basso                      G. Zaccometti (R.) E. Fagotti (S.)
                                         Angelini cond.

Bari          Piccinni    Dec. 26? 1873 C. De Witten (M.) P. Bignardi (R.)
                                        A. Faentini-Galassi (S.)

Bergamo       Sociale     Dec. 26, 1871 L. Ferretti (M.) A. Papi (C.) A.
                                        Bertocchi (R.) D. Majocchi (S.) G.
                                        Bozzelli cond.

              Riccardi    Aug.?     1877 A. Spack (M.) M. Pansera Comello
                                         (C.) V. Clodio (R.) G. Vasselli (S.)
                                         R. Kuon cond.

Bologna       Comunale    Apr. 12, 1871 E. Ciuti (M.) L. Corsi (C.) G.
                                        Zaccometti (R.) P. Silenzi (S.) R.
                                        Nannetti (G.) C. Berardi cond.

Brescia       Grande      Jan.      1872 E. Robiati (M.) A. Boetti (R.) E.
                                         Storti-Gaggi (S.) R. Marconi (G.) N.
                                         Kyntherland cond.

Cagliari      Civico      Jan.      1873 Bertolotti-Mattioli (M.) Bezzi (C.)
                                         E. Sbriscia (R.) N. Fallica (S.)

Catania       Comunale    Dec. 26, 1871 N. Favi Gallo (M.) C. Ghiotti (C.)
                                        L. Gulli (R.) S. Cappelli (S.) E.
                                        Daneri (G.)

Cento         Comunale    Aug.?     1872 R. Pantaleoni (M.) S. Lezi (C.) A.
                                         Oliva-Pavani (R.) D. Squarcia (S.)
                                         Frontoni (G.)

Cremona       Concordia   Aug. 15, 1871 L. Pitarch (M.) I. Cristofani (C.)
                                        J. Gayarre (R.) A. Pantaleoni (S.)
                                        E. Gasperini (G.) G. Bignami cond.

Fermo         Aquila      Sep.      1872 G. Ronzi-Checchi (M.) R. Vercolini-
                                         Tay (C.) A. Celada (R.) E. Fagotti
                                         (S.) G. Marchetti (G.) F. Cellini
                                         cond.

Ferrara       Comunale    Feb. 17, 1872 F. Pernini (M.) A. Innocenti (C.) L.
                                        Dal Passo (R.) D. Cabella (S.) G.
                                        Forti (G.) R. Sarti cond.

Fiume         Civico      Apr.      1872 V. Pozzi-Brazanti (M.) L. Dal Passo
                                         (R.) G. Toledo (S.)

Florence      Pagliano    Nov.      1869 I. Benza (M.) O. Papini (C.) G. Zac-
                                         cometti (R.) G. Valle (S.)

              Pergola     Nov.      1870 A. Bianchi-Montaldo (M.) O. Papini
                                         (C.) C. Bulterini (R.) P. Silenzi
                                         (S.) G. Maffei (G.)

Genoa         Carlo       Dec. 29, 1870 C. Briol (M.) C. Dory (C.) V. Carpi
              Felice                    (R.) A. Pantaleoni (S.) L. Miller
                                        (G.)

Livorno        Avvalorati   Dec. 26? 1870 L. Pitarch (M.) A. Celada (R.) F.
                                          Trapani-Buono (S.)

Lucca          Giglio       Aug. 10, 1870 C. Castelli (M.) Redi (C.) C. Bulte-
                                          rini (R.) V. Cottone (S.) A. Fradel-
                                          loni (G.)

Lugo           Rossini      Aug. 29, 1871 C. Castelli (M.) C. Dory (C.) C.
                                          Bulterini (R.) A. Mazzoli (S.) C.
                                          Morotto (G.) O. Nicchi cond.

Mantua         Sociale      Dec. 26, 1870 E. Ciuti (M.) C. Massaro (C.) F.
                                          Steger (R.) G. Cima (S.)

Messina        Vittorio     Dec.  4, 1871 G. Ronzi-Checchi (M.) G. Sani (R.)
               Emanuele                   M. Ciapini (S.)

Modena         Comunale     Apr. 13, 1872 C. De Giuli-Borsi (M.) I. Cristofani
                                          (C.) A. Masini (R.) P. Silenzi (S.)
                                          P. Povoleri (G.) G. Colbrand cond.

Naples         San Carlo    Apr. 23, 1871 G. Krauss (M.) E. Saurel (C.) C.
                                          Vincentelli (R.) G. Mendioroz (S.)
                                          O. Lari (G.) G. Moretti cond. F.
                                          Marchetti dir.

Novara                      Dec. 25? 1872 E. Robiati (M.) Preda (C.) Mariani
                                          (R.) A. Navary (S.) A. Polli (G.)

Padua          Nuovo        July     1870 I. Benza (M.) O. Papini (C.) G. Za-
                                          cometti (R.) G. Rota (S.) L. Vecchi
                                          (G.) E. Terziani cond. F. Marchetti
                                          dir.

Palermo        Bellini      Feb. 16, 1871 E. Pascalis (M.) E. Rossi (C.) G.
                                          Valentini-Cristiani (R.) F. Bellini
                                          (S.) A. Garcia (G.) L. Alfano cond.

Parma          Regio        Mar. 22, 1871 E. Ciuti (M.) J. Bay (C.) J. Gayarre
                                          (R.) D. Cesari (S.) G. Morotto (G.)
                                          G. C. Ferrarini cond.

Pavia          Fraschini    Dec. 28, 1872 R. Genolini (M.) E. Stoika (C.) G.
                                          De Antoni (R.) D. Cesari (S.)

Perugia        Verzaro      Oct. 31? 1873 A. Guadagnini (M.) G. Curiel (R.) L.
                                          Borgioli (S.)

Piacenza       Municipale   Dec. 26, 1871 L. Mosconi (M.) A. Verati (C.) M.
                                          Neri (R.) G. Cesari (S.) G. B. Del
                                          Fabbro (G.) P. Montaguti cond.

Pisa           Verdi        Mar.  3, 1873 C. De Witten (M.) G. Rizzini (C.) P.
                                          Paladini (R.) F. Tirini (S.) V.
                                          Gentili (G.) L. Quercioli cond.

Ravenna        Alighieri    June  8, 1871 A. Bianchi-Montaldo (M.) L. Corsi
                                          (C.) I. Campanini (R.) A. Pantaleoni
                                          (S.) A. Fradelloni (G.) E. Usiglio
                                          cond.

Reggio Emilia  Municipale   Dec. 25, 1875 L. Bellini (M.) M. Bianchi-Fiorio
                                          (C.) G. De Antoni (R.) G. Carbone
                                          (S.) S. Mazza (G.) G. Grisanti cond.

Rovereto      Sociale     Nov.      1871 E. Berini (M.) I. Cristofani (C.) A.
                                         Masini (R.) A. Mazzoli (S.) O. Maini
                                         (G.)

Rovigo        Sociale     Oct.      1872 A. Bianchi-Montaldo (M.) M. Verati
                                         (C.) A. Lamponi (R.) A. Burgio (S.)
                                         A. Frontoni (G.) R. Drigo cond.

Sanseverino               June      1871 R. Pantaleoni (M.) G. Zaccometti
                                         (R.) P. Silenzi (S.) R. Nannetti
                                         (G.) F. Marchetti dir.

Siena         Rinnovati   Dec. 26? 1874 P. Donati (M.) F. Guidotti (C.) E.
                                         Battistini (R.) Valenti (S.) E. Ba-
                                         gagiolo (G.)

Sinigaglia    Comunale    Carn. 1882-83 A. Busi (M.)

Spoleto       Nuovo       July 29, 1871 G. De Giuli-Borsi (M.) G. Sani (R.)
                                         F. Pandolfini (S.) A. Fradelloni
                                         (G.) E. Terziani cond.

Trento        Sociale     June ?    1878 L. Vanda-Miller (M.) G. Chastel (C.)
                                         V. Clodio (R.) G. Vaselli (S.) I.
                                         Sbordoni (G.)

Treviso       Sociale     Nov.  8, 1871 V. Potentini (M.) C. Coriolano (C.)
                                         C. Vincentelli (R.) A. Rossi Ghelli
                                         (S.) F. Marinozzi (G.) E. Bernardi
                                         cond.

Trieste       Grande      Oct. 19, 1870 I. Benza (M.) G. Capponi (R.) F.
                                         Pandolfini (S.) A. Cremaschi cond.

Turin         Regio       Jan. 24, 1871 I. Benza (M.) L. Corsi (C.) G. Cap-
                                         poni (R.) G. Moriami (S.) H. Brémond
                                         (G.) C. Pedrotti cond.

Udine         Sociale     Aug.      1871 A. Moro (M.) F. Vogri (C.) C. Carpi
                                         (R.) P. Silenzi (S.) C. Zucchelli
                                         (G.)

Venice        La Fenice   Feb.  7, 1871 T. Stolz (M.) A. Contarini (C.) G.
                                         Fancelli (R.) A. Cotogni (S.) R.
                                         Nannetti (G.) C. Castagneri cond.

Verona        Nuovo       Dec. 26, 1871 A. Marvaldi (M.) E. Werner (C.) L.
                                         Maurelli (R.) G. Toledo (S.) S.
                                         Mazza (G.)

Vicenza       Eretenio    Aug.      1871 A. Bianchi-Montaldo (M.) M. Verati
                                         (C.) I. Campanini (R.) V. Maurel
                                         (S.) L. Miller (G.) C. Dell'Argine
                                         cond.

JUGOSLAVIA
Zagreb        National    May  20, 1875 (in Croat.)

Zara          Nuovo       Oct.  2, 1873 I. Kottas (M.) M. Loparco (R.) G.
                                         Tagliapietra (S.) Marconi (G.) (in
                                         It.)

MALTA
La Valletta    Real          Nov.   1? 1871 R. Pantaleoni (M.) C. Cucchi (C.) A.
                                             Oliva-Pavani (R.) F. Proni (S.) A.
                                             Zambellini (G.)

MEXICO
Guadalajara    Degollado     Sep.   1, 1881

Mexico City    Nacional      Oct. 23, 1872 C. Castelli (M.) A. Faentini-Galassi
                                           (C.) F. Pozzo (R.) C. Zucchelli (G.)

PERU
Lima           Principal     Sep.?     1874 C. Carozzi-Zucchi (M.) G. Toressi
                                            (R.) G. Spalazzi (S.) N. Pozzi (G.)

PHILIPPINES
Manila         Circo         Apr. 19, 1875 L. Arancio-Guerrini (M.) A. Pegollo
                                           (C.) R. Celestini (R.) P. Caravatti
                                           (S.) N. Pozzi (G.)

POLAND
Cracow         Imperial      May       1879 C. Bossi (M.) L. Caracciolo (C.) F.
                                            Graziosi (S.)

Lwov           Szarbek       Dec. 14, 1878 C. Bossi (M.) F. Graziosi (S.) (in
                                           It.)

PORTUGAL
Lisbon         Sao Carlos    Feb. 24, 1872 A. Fricci (M.) (C.) C. Carpi (R.) A.
                                           Cotogni (S.) L. Miller (G.)

Oporto         Sao Joao      Nov.      1873 A. Conti-Foroni (M.) Giannoli (C.)
                                            A. Lamponi/D. Belardi (R.) Predeval
                                            (S.) Giannoli (G.)

PUERTO RICO
Ponce          La Perla                1877

San Juan       Municipal     Feb. 22, 1881 C. Bossi (M.) G. Cavalleri (C.) A.
                                           De Sanctis (R.) I. Viganotti (S.) M.
                                           Della Torre (G.) Cipollini cond.

ROMANIA
Bucharest      Nacional      Jan.?     1873 A. Fossa (M.) Ghiotti (C.) F. Steger
                                            (R.) Z. Bertolasi (S.) L. Lombardel-
                                            li (G.)

RUSSIA
Kharkov        Municipal     Jan.?     1885 R. Aimo (M.) Piave (C.) O. Cappelet-
                                            ti (R.) E. Pelz (S.) G. Belletti
                                            (G.)

Moscow         Bolshoi       Nov.   4, 1877 E. Saurel (M.) M. Bianchi-Fiorio
                                            (C.) A. Masini (R.) A. Parboni (S.)
                                            A. Fiorini (G.)

Odessa         Municipal     Nov.      1880 A. Fossa (M.) O. Cappeletti (R.)

St.            Imperial      Nov.   1, 1877 A. D'Angeri (M.) I. Cristofani (C.)
  Petersburg                                I. Campanini (R.) A. Cotogni (S.) F.
                                            Uetam (G.)

Tbilisi      Imperial     Oct. 30, 1876 C. Scarati-Bresciani (M.) C. Dory
                                        (C.) T. Villa (R.) S. Sparapani (S.)
                                        Saccardi (G.)

SPAIN
Barcelona    Novedades    Aug. 28, 1872 C. Carozzi-Zucchi (M.) E. Stoika
                                        (C.) C. Vincentelli (R.) L. Buti
                                        (S.) F. Uetam (G.) J. Goula cond.

             Liceo        Nov.  9, 1872 L. Ponti dall'Armi (M.) M. Bozzetti
                                        (C.) C. Vincentelli (R.) G. Toledo
                                        (S.) N. Bassi cond.

Madrid       Real         Mar. 29, 1873 C. Casanova de Cepeda (M.) E. Bar-
                                        bacini (R.) G. Rota (S.) J. Ordinas
                                    /   (G.) J. Skoczdopole cond.

Seville      San          Apr. 15, 1872 A. Bianchi-Montaldo (M.) L. Corsi
             Fernando                   (C.) J. Gayarre (R.) F. Pandolfini
                                        (S.) F. Brandini (G.) J. Goula cond.

Valencia     Principal    May      1872 E. Spitzer (M.) F. Vogri (C.) G.
                                        Zaccometti (R.) N. Varvaro (S.) G.
                                        Capriles (G.)

SWITZERLAND
Lugano       Sociale      July  7, 1883 Parodi (M.) Taubert (C.) E. Battis-
                                        tini (R.) Garbini (S.)

TUNISIA
Tunis        Cohen        Apr.  2? 1884 Picchi (M.) Palombi (C.) Di Napoli
                                        (R.) Bona (S.)

TURKEY
Constan-     Concordia    Nov. 17, 1875 Pogliani (M.) Ribaldi (C.) M. Lopar-
tinople                                 co (R.) D. Cesari (S.) A. Fradelloni
                                        (G.)

UNITED STATES
Atlanta      De Give's    Feb.  3, 1888 E. Abbott (M.) L. Annandale (C.) A.
                                        Montegriffo (R.) W. Pruett (S.) W.
                                        Broderick (G.) A. Tomasi cond. (in
                                        Eng.)

Boston       Globe        Dec. 24, 1874 V. Potentini (M.) Donadio (C.) C.
                                        Carpi (R.) G. Tagliapietra (S.) A.
                                        Fiorini (G.) E. Muzio cond.

Buffalo      Ac. of Mus.  Apr. 20, 1888 E. Abbott (M.) L. Annandale (C.)

Chicago      McVicker's   Jan. 30, 1875 A. Maresi (M.) Donadio (C.) C. Carpi
                                        (R.) G. Tagliapietra (S.) A. Fiorini
                                        (G.) E. Muzio cond.

             Grand        Apr.  4, 1888 E. Abbott (M.) L. Annandale (C.) F.
                                        Michelena (R.) W. Pruette (S.) A.
                                        Tomasi cond. (in Eng.)

Cincinnati   Grand        Oct. 19, 1887 E. Abbott (M.) L. Annandale (C.) F.
                                        Michelena (R.) W. Pruett (S.) W.
                                        Broderick (G.) A. Tomasi cond. (in
                                        Eng.)

Dallas          Op. House    Jan.  2, 1888  E. Abbott (M.) L. Annandale (C.) F.
                                            Michelena (R.) W. Pruett (S.) W.
                                            Broderick (G.) A. Tomasi cond. (in
                                            Eng.)

Denver                       Dec.  5, 1887  E. Abbott (M.) (in Eng.)

Detroit         Op. House    Apr. 10, 1888  E. Abbott (M.) L. Annandale (C.) F.
                                            Michelena (R.) W. Pruett (S.) W.
                                            Broderick (G.) A. Tomasi cond. (in
                                            Eng.)

Fort Worth      Op. House    Jan.  6, 1888  E. Abbott (M.) L. Annandale (C.) F.
                                            Michelena (R.) W. Pruett (S.) W.
                                            Broderick (G.) A. Tomasi cond. (in
                                            Eng.)

Galveston       Tremont      Jan. 16, 1888  E. Abbott (M.) L. Annandale (C.) F.
                                            Michelena (R.) W. Pruett (S.) W.
                                            Broderick (G.) A. Tomasi cond. (in
                                            Eng.)

Houston         Gray's       Jan. 21, 1888  E. Abbott (M.) L. Annandale (C.) F.
                                            Michelena (R.) W. Pruett (S.) W.
                                            Broderick (G.) A. Tomasi cond. (in
                                            Eng.)

Kansas City     Coates       Nov. 28, 1887  E. Abbott (M.) L. Annandale (C.) F.
                                            Michelena (R.) W. Pruett (S.) W.
                                            Broderick (G.) A. Tomasi cond. (in
                                            Eng.)

Los Angeles     Grand        Dec. 26, 1888  E. Abbott (M.) L. Annandale (C.) F.
                                            Michelena (R.) W. Pruett (S.) W.
                                            Broderick (G.) A. Tomasi cond. (in
                                            Eng.)

Louisville      Macauley's   Oct. 26, 1887  E. Abbott (M.) L. Annandale (C.) F.
                                            Michelena (R.) W. Pruett (S.) W.
                                            Broderick (G.) A. Tomasi cond. (in
                                            Eng.)

Minneapolis     Grand        Nov.  7, 1887  E. Abbott (M.) L. Annandale (C.) F.
                                            Michelena (R.) W. Pruett (S.) W.
                                            Broderick (G.) A. Tomasi cond. (in
                                            Eng.)

New York        Ac. of Mus.  Oct. 14, 1874  V. Potentini (M.) A. L. Cary (C.)
                                            C. Carpi (R.) G. Del Puente (S.) A.
                                            Fiorini (G.) E. Muzio cond.

Omaha                        Nov. 21, 1887  E. Abbott (M.) (in Eng.)

Philadelphia    Ac. of Mus.  Apr. 27, 1888  E. Abbott (M.) L. Annandale (C.) F.
                                            Michelena (R.) W. Pruett (S.) W.
                                            Broderick (G.) A. Tomasi cond. (in
                                            Eng.)

Portland        New Park     Nov. 16, 1888  E. Abbott (M.) L. Annandale (C.) (in
                                            Eng.)

St. Louis       Olympic       Mar. 23, 1888 E. Abbott (M.) L. Annandale (C.) F.
                                            Michelena (R.) W. Pruett (S.) W.
                                            Broderick (G.) A. Tomasi cond. (in
                                            Eng.)

San Antonio     Grand         Jan. 11, 1888 E. Abbott (M.) L. Annandale (C.) F.
                                            Michelena (R.) W. Pruett (S.) W.
                                            Broderick (G.) A. Tomasi cond. (in
                                            Eng.)

San Francisco   Grand         July 19, 1881 A. Bianchi-Montaldo (M.) G. Tiozzo
                                            (C.) G. Roig (R.) A. Parolini (S.)
                                            G. Paoletti (G.) A. Spadina cond.

                California     Aug.  4, 1884 V. Damerini (M.) A. Orlandi (C.) F.
                                            Giannini (R.) T. Wilmant (S.) E.
                                            Serbolini (G.)

                Baldwin       Nov. 21, 1888 E. Abbott (M.) L. Annandale (C.) F.
                                            Michelena (R.) W. Pruett (S.) W.
                                            Broderick (G.) A. Tomasi cond. (in
                                            Eng.)

Washington      National      Mar.  6, 1888 E. Abbott (M.) L. Annandale (C.) F.
                                            Michelena (R.) W. Pruett (S.) W.
                                            Broderick (G.) A. Tomasi cond. (in
                                            Eng.)

URUGUAY
Montevideo      Solis         Sep. 24, 1873 M. Calisto-Piccioli (M.) I. Martinez
                                            de Escalante (C.) G. Piccioli (R.)
                                            A. Rossi-Ghelli (S.) A. Buzzi (G.)

VENEZUELA
Caracas         T. Caracas    Mar. 13, 1878 E. Savelli (M.) G. Torressi (R.) F.
                                            Bertolini (S.)

                Municipal     Jan. 20, 1881 M. Lucchesi (M.) T. Mestres (C.) F.
                                            Giannini (R.) D. Farina (S.) R. Man-
                                            cini (G.) F. Rachelle cond.

OTHER PRODUCTIONS-TWENTIETH CENTURY

ARGENTINA
Buenos Aires    Politeama     July 21, 1900 R. Jacoby (M.) E. Marcomini (C.) E.
                                            Ghilardini (R.) F. M. Bonini (S.)

BRAZIL
Rio de          Fluminense    Dec. 13, 1904 L. Silva (M.) S. Collamarini (C.) G.
Janeiro                                     Doni (R.) S. Vinci (S.) G. Sorgi
                                            (G.)

Sao Paulo       Santana       Dec. 30, 1902 E. Prosnitz (M.) E. Mazzi (C.) O.
                                            Delle Fornaci (R.) S. Vinci (S.) F.
                                            Spangher (G.)

                Politeama     Feb.  1, 1905 L. Silva (M.) S. Collamarini (C.) S.
                                            Vinci (S.)

CHILE
Santiago        Municipal     Sep. 22, 1900 N. Mazzi (M.) M. Pozzi (C.) M. Iz-
                                            quierdo (R.) T. Ruffo (S.) A. Ven-
                                            turini (G.)

| | | | |
|---|---|---|---|
| Valparaiso | Victoria | Oct. 1, 1900 | N. Mazzi (M.) M. Pozzi (C.) M. Izquierdo (R.) T. Ruffo (S.) |

EGYPT
| | | | |
|---|---|---|---|
| Alexandria | Champs Elysées | Sep. 12, 1900 | T. Chelotti (M.) L. Monti-Brunner (C.) G. Perez (R.) |
| | Alhambra | Mar. 12, 1901 | L. De Sirianna (M.) O. Delle Fornaci (R.) E. Pignataro (S.) G. Beltramo (G.) |
| Cairo | Ezbekieh Gardens | May 5, 1900 | T. Chelotti (M.) L. Monti-Brunner (C.) G. Perez (R.) E. Pignataro (S.) |
| | Varieties | Apr. 17, 1901 | L. De Sirianna (M.) O. Delle Fornaci (R.) |

GREECE
| | | | |
|---|---|---|---|
| Athens | Royal | Apr. 15, 1901 | Santamaria (M.) L. Monti-Brunner (C.) G. Mori (R.) G. Schottler (S.) |

IRELAND
| | | | |
|---|---|---|---|
| Cork | Th. Royal | Nov. 12, 1915 | F. Morden (M.) Thomas (C.) H. Thomson (R.) J. Olivere (S.) W. Anderson (G.) (in Eng.) |
| Dublin | Gaiety | Nov. 26, 1915 | F. Morden (M.) Thomas (C.) H. Thomson (R.) J. Olivere (S.) W. Anderson (G.) (in Eng.) |

ITALY
| | | | |
|---|---|---|---|
| Camerino | Marchetti | May 19, 1931 | H. Spani (M.) E. Casazza (C.) J. Palet (R.) F. Valentino (S.) C. Ulivi (G.) S. Gualandi Gamberini cond. |
| Catania | Pacini | May 19, 1902 | T. Chelotti (M.) A. Motta (C.) G. Perez (R.) M. Cavalieri (S.) G. Berenzone (G.) G. Giannetti cond. |
| | Bellini | Dec. 7, 1919 | W. Giovanelli (M.) N. Lollini (C.) C. Folco Bottari (R.) G. Parigi (S.) O. Luppi (G.) L. Mugnone/G. Fratini cond. |
| Genoa | Politeama | Oct. 14, 1903 | E. Morando (M.) A. Tassinari (C.) V. Bieletto (R.) G. La Puma (S.) S. Queirolo (G.) |
| Lecce | Greco | Apr. 16, 1911 | R. Garitano (M.) C. Supervia (C.) B. De Muro (R.) F. Cigada (S.) G. Martino (G.) G. Golisciani cond. |
| | | Apr. 16, 1927 | H. Spani (M.) G. Sani (C.) J. Palet (R.) V. Guicciardi (S.) F. Zaccarini (G.) G. Falconi cond. |
| Milan | Dal Verme | May 15, 1900 | C. Boninsegna (M.) C. Pagnoni (C.) G. Bertini (R.) G. Maggi (S.) C. Thos (G.) Dalli Ponti cond. |
| | | Dec. 26, 1903 | E. Bosetti (M.) A. Iracena (C.) G. Perez (R.) C. Bacchetta (S.) A. Niccolini (G.) R. Bonicioli cond. |

Feb. 15, 1911 Ceclakoff (M.) I. Vannini (C.) G.
Martinelli (R.) S. Vinci (S.) Galli
(G.) Baldi Zenoni cond.

Carcano       Nov. 20, 1900 M. Tozzi Fornari (M.) N. Molinari/I.
Rolla (C.) R. Martelli (R.) E. Moreo
(S.) F. Rusconi (G.) N. Guerrera
cond.

Fossati       Aug. 31, 1901 V. Giorgi (M.) I. Melloni (C.) G.
Damaso (R.) R. Costantini (S.) C.
Baldi (G.) B. Lombardi cond.

Verdi         Dec. 29, 1923 A. Laskova (M.) M. Ceccherini (C.)
V. Fullin (R.) G. Albinolo (S.) G.
Sappa (G.) T. Cremagnini cond.

Palermo    Politeama    Nov. 22, 1903 M. Santoliva Villani (M.) E. Bruno
(C.) A. Cecchi/A. Fassino (R.) A.
Arcangeli (S.) S. Becucci (G.) E.
Panizza cond.

Nov.  3, 1925 E. Franco (M.) E. Carabelli (C.)
Michelon (R.) L. Dimitry (S.) G.
Ranchetti (G.) A. Sigismondo cond.

Biondo        Nov. 22, 1912 L. Micucci (M.) T. Massucci (C.) A.
Tafuro (R.) G. Parigi (S.) C. Meloc-
chi (G.) R. Bianchi cond.

Parma      Reinach      Oct. 22, 1910 A. De Angelis (M.) I. Vannini (C.)
A. Perico (R.) M. Roussel (S.) O.
Banti (G.) G. Podestà cond.

Rome       Adriano      Mar.  9? 1901 L. Rebuffini (M.) C. Pagnoni (C.) G.
Martinez-Patti (R.) G. Bernal (S.)
Boella (G.) A. Siragusa cond.

Sep. 17, 1911 E. Ceccotti (M.) L. Monti Brunner
(C.) E. Ghisletti (R.) V. Romano
(S.) P. Argentini (G.) A. Morelli
cond.

Apr. 24, 1915 M. Rossini (M.) M. Passari (C.) A.
Perico (R.) M. Battistini (S.) V.
Arimondi (G.) G. Zuccani cond.

Quirino       Sep.  3, 1904 I. Giacomelli (M.) I. Barbi (C.) G.
Bertini/O. Delle Fornaci (R.) R.
Caldani (S.) R. Bigiani (G.) E.
Galeazzi cond.

Apr. 24, 1907 A. Barone/A. Jodice/G. Scagliarini
(M.) L. Del Lungo (C.) G. Bambacioni/
O. Delle Fornaci (R.) R. Caldani (S.)
A. Natali (G.) G. Sacconi/F. Guerrie-
ri cond.

Morgana       Oct. 13, 1921 G. Gregori (M.) B. Candioli (C.) A.
Braglia (R.) A. Sabbi (S.) V. Pisto-
lesi (G.) A. Consorti cond.

| | Sala RAI | Sep. 16, 1933 | C. Jacobo (M.) G. Sani (C.) A. Melandri (R.) V. Guicciardi (S.) A. Marone (G.) R. Santarelli cond. |
|---|---|---|---|
| Turin | Vittorio Emanuele | Feb. 2, 1909 | P. Gorianz (M.) M. De Marsan (C.) Baudino (R.) G. Rebonato (S.) Ronconi (G.) G. Puccetti cond. |

MALTA

| La Valletta | Real | Nov. 1902 | Tebro (M.) Budriesi (C.) Conti (R.) F. Cigada (S.) |
|---|---|---|---|
| | | Oct. 30? 1924 | I. Pacetti (M.) Ceccherini (C.) V. Fullin (R.) |

MONACO

| Monte Carlo | Salle Garnier | Mar. 27, 1919 | L. Villani (M.) N. Lollini (C.) U. Lappas (R.) M. Battistini (S.) M. Journet (G.) G. Lauweryns cond. |
|---|---|---|---|

UNITED STATES

| New York | Bel Canto | May 26, 1984 | W. Hill/A. Donaldson (M.) L. Munguia (C.) D. Cobb (R.) H. Macklowski (S.) J. M. Russell (G.) |
|---|---|---|---|

URUGUAY

| Montevideo | Solis | Aug. 15, 1900 | R. Jacoby (M.) V. Ghilardini (R.) F. M. Bonini (S.) A. Donizetti cond. |
|---|---|---|---|

6. GUSTAVO WASA-*Dramma lirico* in four acts
Milan-Teatro alla Scala-Feb. 7, 1875
Libretto by Carlo D'Ormeville

| | |
|---|---|
| Romilia (R.) | Maddalena Mariani-Masi sop. |
| Gustavo Wasa (G.) | Luigi Bolis ten. |
| Osvaldo Ritter (O.) | Adriano Pantaleoni bar. |
| Cristiano II (C.) | Ormondo Maini bass |
| Trolle (T.) | Giovanni Marchetti bass |
| Un Capo di Minatori | Giovanni Battista Cornago bass |
| Un Capitano Danese | Argimiro Bertocchi ten. |
| Un Comandante di Pattugia | Argimiro Bertocchi ten. |
| | |
| Conductor | Franco Faccio |
| Director | Filippo Marchetti |

OTHER PRODUCTIONS

ITALY

| Florence | Pergola | Mar. 18, 1877 | M. L. Durand (R.) C. Carpi (G.) A. Mazzoli (O.) L. Lombardelli (C.) E. Manfredi (T.) T. Mabellini cond. F. Marchetti dir. |
|---|---|---|---|

7. DON GIOVANNI D'AUSTRIA-*Dramma lirico* in four acts
Turin-Teatro Regio-Mar. 11, 1880
Libretto by Carlo D'Ormeville

| | |
|---|---|
| Flora di Sandoval (F.) | Teresa Brambilla-Ponchielli sop. |
| Pablo (P.) | Lena Bordato sop. |
| Don Giovanni (G.) | Edmond Vergnet ten. |
| Filippo II (F.) | Teofilo Manoury bar. |
| Don Quesada (Q.) | Ignazio Viganotti bar. |
| Frate Arsenio (A.) | Edouard De Reszke bass |
| Dorotea | Lucia Baroletti sec. |
| Don Ruy Gomez | Francesco Migliara bass |
| Domingo | Pietro Mascotti sec. |
| Un Monaco | Andrea Zatelli sec. |
| Un Messo | Ferdinando Isoardi ten. |
| | |
| Conductor | Carlo Pedrotti |
| Director | Filippo Marchetti |

OTHER PRODUCTIONS

ITALY
Rome          Costanzi     Dec.  6, 1885 A. Cattaneo (F.) E. Colonnese (P.)
                                        C. Vincentelli (G.) L. Giraldoni
                                        (F.) L. Pignalosa (Q.) P. Wulman
                                        (A.) E. Mascheroni cond.

SAVERIO MERCADANTE

1. LE DUE ILLUSTRI RIVALI-*Melodramma* in three acts
Venice-Teatro La Fenice-Mar. 10, 1838
Libretto by Gaetano Rossi

| | |
|---|---|
| Bianca (B.) | Carolina Ungher sop. |
| Elvira (E.) | Eugenia Tadolini sop. |
| Armando (A.) | Napoleone Moriani ten. |
| Alvaro (Al.) | Achille Balestracci ten. |
| Gusmano (G.) | Ignazio Marini bass |
| Enellina | Fausta Piombanti sop. |
| Inigo | Domenico Raffaelli sec. |

| | |
|---|---|
| Conductor | Gaetano Mares |
| Director | Saverio Mercadante |

OTHER PRODUCTIONS-NINETEENTH CENTURY

ITALY

| | | | | |
|---|---|---|---|---|
| Ancona | Muse | Fiera | 1842 | F. Maray (B.) A. Mattioli (E.) N. Ivanoff (A.) G. Lucchesi (Al.) S. Ronconi (G.) |
| Faenza | Comunale | Fiera | 1842 | F. Maray (B.) A. Mattioli (E.) N. Ivanoff (A.) G. Lucchesi (Al.) S. Ronconi (G.) |
| Florence | Pergola | Mar. 20, 1840 | | C. Ungher (B.) A. Mattioli (E.) N. Ivanoff (A.) S. Ronconi (G.) A. Biagi cond. |
| | | Mar. 29, 1843 | | F. Maray (B.) I. Secci-Corsi (E.) A. Castellan (A.) E. Testa (Al.) C. O. Porto (G.) A. Biagi cond. |
| Livorno | Rossini | Nov. 5, 1842 | | F. Maray (B.) S. Grevedon (E.) A. Castellan (A.) C. O. Porto (G.) |
| Lucca | Giglio | Aug. 16, 1840 | | C. Ungher (B.) G. Strepponi (E.) N. Ivanoff (A.) C. O. Porto (G.) |
| Milan | La Scala | Dec. 26, 1839 | | E. Frezzolini (B.) T. Brambilla (E.) N. Moriani (A.) C. Lonati (Al.) I. Marini (G.) |
| Naples | San Carlo | Feb. 21, 1840 | | M. Palazzesi (B.) A. Granchi (E.) G. Basadonna (A.) P. Gianni (G.) A. Farelli cond. |
| Palermo | Carolino | Jan. 1, 1843 | | A. Rainieri-Marini (B.) T. Merli-Clerici (E.) N. Ivanoff (A.) D. Marchelli (G.) P. Raimondi cond. |
| Sinigaglia | Comunale | Fiera | 1840 | A. Mattioli (B.) G. Strepponi (E.) G. Basadonna (A.) C. O. Porto (G.) |
| Venice | La Fenice | Mar. 12, 1839 | | C. Ungher (B.) G. Strepponi (E.) N. Moriani (A.) A. Balestracci (Al.) I. Marini (G.) |

SPAIN
Barcelona    Principal    Jan. 22, 1846 E. Goggi (B.) C. Cattinari (E.) G.
                                        B. Milesi (A.) F. Martorell (Al.) P.
                                        Novelli (G.)

                          Sep.    1847 A. Rainieri-Marini (B.) C. Cattinari
                                        (E.) E. Tamberlick (A.) C. Scola
                                        (Al.) A. Selva (G.)

OTHER PRODUCTIONS-TWENTIETH CENTURY

ITALY
Venice       La Fenice    Dec.  9, 1970 C. Parada (B.) V. Papantoniou (E.)
                                        A. Liviero (A.) A. Zambon (Al.) G.
                                        Pappas (G.) E. Gracis cond.


2. ELENA DA FELTRE-*Dramma tragico* in three acts
Naples-Teatro San Carlo-Jan. 1, 1839
Libretto by Salvadore Cammarano

Elena (E.)                              Giuseppina Ronzi de Begnis sop.
Ubaldo (U.)                             Adolphe Nourrit ten.
Guido (G.)                              Paolo Barroilhet bar.
Sigifredo (S.)                          Pietro Gianni bass
Imberga                                 Emilia Gandaglia sec.
Boemondo                                Teofilo Rossi ten.
Gualtiero                               Giuseppe Benedetti bass

Conductor                               Giuseppe Festa
Director                                Saverio Mercadante

OTHER PRODUCTIONS

AUSTRIA
Vienna       Kärntnertor May  20, 1840 E. Frezzolini (E.) C. Lonati (U.) C.
                                        Badiali (G.) H. Proch cond.

GREAT BRITAIN
London       Covent       Jan. 15, 1842 A. Kemble (E.)   W.  Harrison (U.)
             Garden                      Stretton (G.) (in Eng.)

             Her          May  31, 1842 E. Frezzolini (E.) C. Guasco (U.) G.
             Majesty's                   Ronconi (G.) M. Costa cond. (in It.)

GREECE
Corfu        San Giacomo Oct.    1842 G. Nerozzi (U.) L. Del Riccio (G.)

ITALY
Ancona       Muse         May  11, 1841 G. Strepponi (E.) G. Roppa (U.) G.
                                        Ronconi (G.)

                          May      1871 L. Tencajoli (E.) I. Campanini (U.)
                                        G. Cima (G.)

Asti         Civico       Spring  1854 M. Villa (E.) L. Bianchi (U.) A.
                                        Grandi (G.)

Bologna      Comunale     Oct.  5, 1839 E. Frezzolini (E.) C. Guasco (U.) O.
                                        Cartagenova (G.)

|         |              |              |        |                                                              |
|---------|--------------|--------------|--------|--------------------------------------------------------------|
|         | Corso        | Nov.         | 1853   | V. Boccabadati (E.) B. Massimiliani (U.) P. Baraldi (G.)      |
| Brescia | Grande       | Aug. 21,     | 1841   | G. Ronzi De Begnis (E.) E. Musich (U.) G. Ronconi (G.)       |
| Chieti  | San Ferdinando | June 28,   | 1846   |                                                              |
| Crema   | Sociale      | Jan. 17,     | 1843   | M. Marchesini (E.) G. Pelosio (U.)                           |
| Cremona | Concordia    | Autumn       | 1839   | F. Forconi (E.) L. Bonfigli (U.) R. Ferlotti (G.)            |
| Fabriano | Camurrio    | Jan.  3,     | 1860   | C. Martelli (E.) F. Piccioni (U.) G. Giori (G.)              |
| Faenza  | Comunale     | June 13,     | 1841   | G. Strepponi (E.) G. Roppa (U.) G. Ronconi (G.)              |
| Ferrara | Comunale     | Feb.         | 1843   | A. Mattioli (E.)                                             |
| Florence | Pergola     | Nov.  3,     | 1840   | C. Ungher (E.) E. Musich (U.) G. Ronconi (G.)                |
| Genoa   | Carlo Felice | May 29,      | 1839   | G. Armenia (E.) G. Zoboli (U.) F. Bottelli (G.) G. Serra cond. |
|         |              | Apr. 10,     | 1841   | D. Dérancourt (E.) C. Manfredi (U.) L. Valli (G.) G. Serra cond. |
| Livorno | Rossini      | Feb. 15,     | 1846   | L. Bassano (E.) G. Lucchesi (U.) L. Rinaldini (G.)           |
| Macerata | Condomini   | Sep. 11,     | 1841   | J. Olivieri (E.) E. Caggiati (U.) D. Cosselli (G.)           |
| Mantua  | Sociale      | Carn.        | 1839-40 | A. Kemble (E.) G. B. Genero (U.) P. Minoja (G.)             |
| Messina | Munizione    | Apr.         | 1843   | A. Rebussini (E.) G. B. Bertolasi (U.) E. Luisia (G.)        |
| Milan   | La Scala     | Aug. 31,     | 1843   | A. Gambaro (E.) L. Ferretti (U.) G. Ferri (G.)               |
| Naples  | San Carlo    | Sep. 26,     | 1839   | M. Palazzesi (E.) G. Basadonna (U.) P. Barroilhet (G.) A. Farelli cond. |
| Novara  | Nuovo        | Feb.         | 1854   | E. Zenoni (E.) G. Ghislanzoni (U.) F. Giorgi (G.)           |
| Padua   | Nuovo        | June 12,     | 1839   | F. Goldberg (E.) G. B. Verger (U.) O. Cartagenova (G.)       |
| Parma   | Regio        | Feb. 13,     | 1841   | O. Malvani (E.) A. De Val (U.) D. Cosselli (G.) N. De Giovanni cond. |
| Pavia   | Condomini    | Dec. 26,     | 1839   | V. Eden (E.) Fillipini (U.) A. De Bassini (G.)              |
| Perugia | Morlacchi    | Aug. 18,     | 1839   | E. Frezzolini (E.) E. Giampietro (U.) F. Varesi (G.)         |

Piacenza        Municipale    Carn. 1844-45 G. Caspani (E.) G. Bianchi (U.) G.
                                            Donelli (G.) G. Jona cond.

Pisa            Ravvivati     June 18, 1839 E. Frezzolini (E.) E. Giampietri
                                            (U.) F. Colini (G.) C. Giacomelli
                                            cond.

Reggio Emilia Comunale        Apr. 30, 1839 E. Frezzolini (E.) C. Guasco (U.) O.
                                            Cartagenova (G.) S. Mercadante dir.
                                            L. Boyer cond.

Sassari         Civico        Nov.    1853 M. Marchesini (E.) G. Ferrari (U.)
                                           G. Ippolito (G.)

Treviso         Onigo         Autumn  1844 L. Matthey (E.) A. Della Cella (U.)
                                           E. Luisia (G.)

Trieste         Grande        Sep. 28, 1844 E. Frezzolini (E.) L. Ferretti (U.)
                                            F. Colini (G.) G. A. Scaramella
                                            cond.

Udine           Nuovo         Sep. 3, 1857 V. Boccabadati (E.) V. Sarti (U.) E.
                                           Delle Sedie (G.)

Venice          Rossini       Apr. 16, 1842 G. Leva (E.) B. Galliani (U.) P. Mi-
                                            noja (G.)

                Apollo        Oct. 25, 1845 M. Cavalli (E.) V. Ferrari-Stella
                                            (U.) L. Rinaldini (G.)

Verona          Filarmonico Feb.     1841 C. Ungher (E.) N. Moriani (U.) G.
                                          Ronconi (G.)

Vicenza         Eretenio      July 30, 1839 L. Boccabadati/G. Ronzi de Begnis
                                            (E.) G. Fraschinni (U.) C. Badiali
                                            (G.)

JUGOSLAVIA
Zara            Nobile        Autumn  1845 E. Zenoni (E.) Mancini (U.) Mercal-
                                           li (G.)

MALTA
La Valletta     Manoel        Spring  1840 Darbois (E.) A. Cristofani (U.) C.
                                           Leonardis (G.)

NETHERLANDS
Amsterdam       Italien       Oct. 27, 1845 M. Tizzoni (E.) R. Castigliano (U.)
                                            G. Mancusi (G.) A. Bregozzo cond.

PORTUGAL
Lisbon          Sao Carlos Apr. 4, 1840 L. Schieroni-Nulli (E.) E. Spech
                                        (U.) R. Ferlotti (G.)

                              Nov. 15, 1841 L. Schieroni-Nulli (E.) L. Ferretti
                                            (U.) G. Nulli (G.)

SPAIN
Barcelona       Principal     May 9, 1840 L. Assandri (E.) A. Piacenti (U.) P.
                                          Balzar (G.)

Madrid          De la Cruz Feb. 12, 1841 L. Franceschini-Rossi (E.) P. Unanue
                                         (U.) G. Miral (G.)

3. IL BRAVO-*Melodramma* in three acts
Milan-Teatro alla Scala-Mar. 9, 1839
Libretto by Gaetano Rossi

| | |
|---|---|
| Violetta (V.) | Eugenia Tadolini sop. |
| Teodora (T.) | Sofia Schoberlechner sop. |
| Il Bravo (B.) | Domenico Donzelli ten. |
| Pisani (P.) | Andrea Castellan ten. |
| Foscari (F.) | Pietro Balzar bass |
| Michelina | Angiolina Villa sop. |
| Un Messo dei Tre | Napoleone Marconi ten. |
| Cappello | Antonio Benciolini bass |
| Luigi | Giovanni Quattrini bass |
| Marco | Eutimio Polonini bass |
| | |
| Conductor | Eugenio Cavallini |
| Director | Saverio Mercadante |

OTHER PRODUCTIONS

ARGENTINA
Buenos Aires  Argentino  May 13, 1854  I. Edelvira (V.) G. Tati (T.) L.
Guglielmini (B.) G. C. Casanova (F.)

AUSTRIA
Vienna  Kärntnertor May 12, 1841  E. Tadolini (V.) S. Schoberlechner
(T.) D. Donzelli (B.) A. Castellan
(P.) R. Ferlotti (F.) H. Proch cond.

Apr. 30, 1842  E. Tadolini (V.) Schrikel/F. Salvi-
ni-Donatelli (T.) D. Donzelli (B.)
A. Castellan (P.) P. Dérivis (F.) H.
Proch cond.

Apr. 26, 1856  L. Bendazzi-Secchi (V.) L. Lesniewska (T.) G. Bettini (B.) A. Bettini
(P.) A. De Bassini (F.)

BRAZIL
Rio de       Lirico      Mar. 21, 1853  A. Candiani (V.) G. Zecchini (T.) A.
Janeiro      Fluminense                 Gentile (B.) D. Labocetta (P.) L. De
Lauro (F.)

CHILE
Santiago  Republica  July 15, 1852  T. Rossi (V.) C. Pantanelli (T.) L.
Cavedagni (B.) J. Ubaldi (P.) G.
Bastoggi (F.)

Oct. 18, 1853  T. Rossi (V.) C. Pantanelli (T.) L.
Cavedagni (B.) J. Ubaldi (P.) G.
Bastoggi (F.)

July 6, 1856  I. Edelvira (V.) G. Amei (T.) L.
Guglielmini (B.) U. Devoti (P.) J.
Casanova (F.)

Valparaiso  Victoria  Feb. 12, 1852  T. Rossi (V.) C. Pantanelli (T.) L.
Cavedagni (B.) J. Ubaldi (P.) G.
Bastoggi (F.)
FRANCE
Nice       Regio      Jan. 20, 1855  S. Cammerer (V.) M. Villa (T.) M.
Sacchero (B.) G. Ferrari (P.) G. B.
Antonucci (F.) G. Bragozzo cond.

Paris            Italien       May  12, 1853 G. Beltramelli (V.) A. De la Grange
                                            (T.) G. Bettini (B.) C. Guidotti
                                            (P.) G. Belletti (F.) C. Castagneri
                                            cond.

GERMANY
Berlin           Hofoper       Oct.  2, 1840 J. Schulze (V.) S. Loewe (T.) K. A.
                                            Bader (B.) E. Mantius (P.) Tschieshe
                                            (F.) (in Ger.)

Hannover         Hoftheater    Oct. 30, 1851 H. Marschner cond. (in Ger.)

1TALY
Alessandria      Municipale    Autumn   1842 J. Olivier (V.) A. De Rieux (T.) R.
                                            Monti (B.) Antonelli (P.) L. Corra-
                                            di-Setti (F.)

                               Nov.     1862 A. Peralta (V.) I. Alba (T.) G.
                                            Pardini (B.)

Bergamo          Sociale       Carn. 1843-44 A. Gambardella (V.) E. Zenoni (T.)
                                            L. Bonfigli/L. Biacchi (B.) E.
                                            Cossetta (P.)

Bologna          Corso         Mar.     1861 A. Frangini (V.) L. Arancio-Guerrini
                                            (T.) E. Barbacini (B.) A. Cruciani
                                            (P.) F. Marinuzzi (F.)

Brescia          Grande        Summer   1839 B. Colleoni-Corti (V.) E. D'Alberti
                                            (T.) D. Donzelli (B.) V. Jacobelli
                                            (P.) P. Balzar (F.)

Cagliari         Civico        Carn. 1846-47 E. Dielitz (V.) Ricca (T.) C. Scola
                                            (B.) G. Carboni (P.) R. Pizzigati
                                            (F.)

Casale           Sociale       Nov. 27, 1861 G. Ugolini (B.)
  Monferrato

Chieti           San           July  6, 1841 M. Rinaldini (B.) F. Venanzi cond.
                 Ferdinando

                               May   6, 1846 G. Montucchielli (V.) A. Calveri
                                            (T.) A. Balestracci (B.) G. Aducci
                                            (P.) C. Busi (F.)

Cremona          Concordia     Autumn   1847 Gius. Brambilla (V.) M. Gazzaniga
                                            (T.) G. Masset (B.)

Ferrara          Comunale      May  21, 1844 L. Schieroni-Nulli (V.) M. Gresti
                                            (T.) D. Donzelli (B.) P. Zilioli
                                            (P.) L. Del Riccio (F.)

Florence         Pergola       Oct. 20, 1841 S. Mequillet (V.) F. Maray (T.) D.
                                            Donzelli (B.) A. Castellan (P.) S.
                                            Ronconi (F.) A. Biagi cond.

                               May  12, 1844 E. Frezzolini (V.) M. Gazzaniga (T.)
                                            A. Poggi (B.) A. Castellan (P.) A.
                                            De Bassini (F.)

                               June  2, 1848 G. Sikorska-Moriani (V.) Mariotti
                                            (T.) N. Moriani (B.) G. Pozzolini
                                            (P.) Gherardini (F.)

|          |                 |           |      |                                                                                                                    |
|----------|-----------------|-----------|------|--------------------------------------------------------------------------------------------------------------------|
|          |                 | Jan. 11,  | 1872 | A. Mattioli (V.) A. Bianchi-Montaldo (T.) G. Villani (B.) G. Galvani (P.) G. Cima (F.)                              |
| Forli    | Comunale        | Spring    | 1840 | A. Del Serre (V.) A. Moltini (T.) D. Donzelli (B.) A. Castellan (P.) Guscetti (F.)                                  |
| Genoa    | Carlo Felice    | May 14,   | 1842 | G. Cavedoni (V.) F. Goldberg (T.) E. Musich (B.) S. Lavia (P.) P. Ambrosini (F.) G. Serra cond.                     |
|          |                 | Jan. 25,  | 1846 | A. Boccabadati (V.) F. Tedesco (T.) L. Bianchi (B.) D. Labocetta (P.) G. Euzet (F.)                                 |
|          | Andrea Doria    | July 13,  | 1862 |                                                                                                                    |
| Gorizia  | Sociale         | Dec. 26,  | 1842 |                                                                                                                    |
|          |                 | Sep.      | 1844 | R. Agostini (V.) T. Rusmini-Solera (T.) G. Santi (B.)                                                               |
| Imola    | Comunale        | Fiera     | 1842 | M. Cavalli (T.) L. Bignami (B.) C. Dossi (F.)                                                                       |
| Lodi     | Sociale         | Dec. 26?  | 1852 | E. D'Alberti (T.) G. Tamaro (B.)                                                                                    |
| Lucca    | Giglio          | Summer    | 1841 | F. Maray (T.) D. Donzelli (B.) A. Castellan (P.) S. Ronconi (F.)                                                    |
| Mantua   | Sociale         | Jan. 30,  | 1846 | L. Assandri (V.) E. Boldrini (T.) A. Poggi (B.) G. Pozzolini (P.) G. Mitrovich (F.)                                 |
| Messina  | Munizione       | Nov. 28,  | 1846 | E. Fioretti (V.) C. Rambur (T.) L. Biacchi (B.)                                                                     |
| Milan    | La Scala        | Dec. 26,  | 1840 | E. Tadolini (V.) A. De Rieux (T.) D. Donzelli (B.) A. Castellan (P.) N. Costantini (F.) E. Cavallini cond.          |
|          |                 | Mar. 11,  | 1846 | R. Basso-Borio (V.) Calcagno/C. Hayes (T.) G. Masset (B.) D. Labocetta (P.) F. Beneventano (F.) E. Cavallini cond.  |
|          |                 | Jan. 15,  | 1851 | L. Lesniewska (V.) A. Falconi (T.) D. Conti (B.) B. Rossi (P.) A. Rivieri (F.) E. Cavallini cond.                   |
|          |                 | Dec. 30,  | 1862 | C. Mongini-Stecchi/P. Colson (V.) R. Devries (T.) G. Landi (B.) G. Galvani (P.) L. Saccomanno (F.)                  |
|          | Manzoni         | Apr. 27,  | 1893 | Bacichi (V.) De Livron (T.) E. Barbacini (B.) Biancardi (P.) V. Villani (F.)                                        |
| Modena   | Comunale        | Oct. 16,  | 1841 | E. Frezzolini (V.) M. Barbieri-Nini (T.) A. Poggi (B.) A. Castellan (P.) V. Meini (F.) A. Sighicelli cond.          |

Naples        San Carlo     Oct. 17, 1840 A. Kemble (V.) F. Maray (T.) D. Re-
                                          ina (B.) G. Fraschini (P.) O. Car-
                                          tagenova (F.) A. Farelli cond.

                            Oct. 13, 1844 E. Tadolini (V.) A. Bishop (T.) D.
                                          Donzelli (B.) G. Fraschini (P.) F.
                                          Coletti (F.) A. Farelli cond.

              Nuovo         Oct. 20, 1840 G. David (V.) A. Gambardella (T.) A.
                                          Furlani (B.) S. Lavia (P.) Ruggero
                                          (F.)

                            Spring   1841 G. David (V.) A. Gambaro (T.) A.
                                          Furlani (B.)

Novara        Nuovo         Jan. 15, 1842 G. Leva (V.) L. Righini (T.) G. B.
                                          Genero (B.) P. Franzi (P.) G. Donel-
                                          li (F.)

                            Jan.     1862 C. Castelli (V.) Bertoletti (T.) E.
                                          Concordia (B.) Vecchi (F.)

Padua         Nuovo         June 29, 1844 M. Gresti (V.) L. Schieroni-Nulli
                                          (T.) G. Fraschini (B.) P. Zilioli
                                          (P.) P. Balzar (F.)

Palermo       Carolino      Dec. 26, 1841 B. Colleoni-Corti (V.) A. Gambardel-
                                          la (T.) F. Borioni (B.) G. Cenni
                                          (P.) P. Balzar (F.)

Parma         Regio         Apr.  5, 1847 C. Rapazzini (V.) C. Vittadini (T.)
                                          G. Masset (B.) R. Castigliano (P.)
                                          L. Caliari (F.) N. De Giovanni cond.

Pavia         Condomini     Carn. 1843-44 R. Agostini (V.) E. Agostini (T.) G.
                                          Olivieri (B.) A. Assandri (P.) A.
                                          Cecconi (F.)

Perugia                     Feb.?    1862

Piacenza      Municipale    Dec. 26, 1842 B. Colleoni-Corti (V.) A. De la
                                          Grange (T.) G. Santi (B.) Dall'Oro
                                          (P.) E. Santi (F.) G. Jona cond.

Reggio di     Borbonico        1846-47 E. Tomassi (V.) E. Corsini (T.) P.
  Calabria                             Cimino (B.) A. Antonelli (P.)

Rome          Apollo        Feb. 18, 1840 S. Mequillet (V.) C. Ungher (T.) D.
                                          Donzelli (B.) A. Castellan (P.) L.
                                          Fornasari (F.) G. C. Ferrarini cond.

Siena         Ravvivati     Summer   1847 E. Zani (V.) E. Parepa (T.) V. Fer-
                                          rari-Stella (B.) E. Concordia (P.)

Sinigaglia    Comunale      July 16, 1843 E. Frezzolini (V.) M. Barbieri-Nini
                                          (T.) A. Poggi (B.) A. Castellan (P.)
                                          C. O. Porto (F.) G. C. Ferrarini
                                          cond.

Spoleto       Nobile        Dec. 26, 1852 E. Fioretti (V.) De Giuli-Ciabò (T.)
                                          Lombardi (B.) Ricci (F.)

Trento        Sociale       June  7, 1845 E. Zani (V.) G. Armenia (T.) L.
                                          Biacchi (B.) G. Antoldi (F.)

| | | | |
|---|---|---|---|
| Treviso | Onigo | Dec. 3, 1843 | M. Belloni (V.) L. Franceschini-Rossi (T.) L. Biacchi (B.) E. Rossi-Guerra (P.) E. Santi (F.) |
| Trieste | Grande | Feb. 19, 1840 | T. Tavola (V.) S. Schoberlechner (T.) A. Poggi (B.) F. Cuturi (P.) R. Ferlotti (F.) A. Scaramelli cond. |
| | | Carn. 1852-53 | A. Corbari (V.) A. Agresti (B.) G. Petrovich (P.) C. Dalla Costa (F.) G. A. Scaramella cond. |
| | Mauroner | Spring 1842 | |
| Turin | Regio | Dec. 25, 1856 | A. Corbari (V.) R. Devries (T.) P. Mongini (B.) L. Stecchi-Bottardi (P.) G. Miral (F.) |
| Udine | Sociale? | July 1844 | A. Giovanelli-Biava (V.) L. Schieroni-Nulli (T.) G. Santi (B.) A. Zuliani (P.) F. Gorin (F.) |
| Venice | Apollo | Nov. 8, 1840 | G. Strepponi (V.) C. Ferlotti (T.) D. Donzelli (B.) A. Castellan (P.) G. Ferri (F.) |
| Verona | Filarmonico | Oct. 1, 1840 | A. Giovanelli-Biava (V.) C. Ferlotti (T.) D. Donzelli (B.) A. Castellan (P.) G. Ferri (F.) |
| | | Jan. 17, 1857 | S. Dottini (V.) C. Carozzi-Zucchi (T.) S. Malvezzi (B.) F. Pozzo (P.) F. Pons (F.) |
| | Nuovo | Sep. 29, 1846 | A. Bosio (V.) R. Basso-Borio (T.) D. Conti (B.) R. Castigliano (P.) G. Corsi (F.) |
| Vicenza | Eretenio | July 18, 1840 | A. Perelli (V.) G. Micciarelli-Sbriscia (T.) A. Poggi (B.) C. Mugnai (P.) G. Antoldi (F.) L. Aliani cond. |
| JUGOSLAVIA Ljubljana | Stanovskem | Apr. 22, 1843 | E. Ranzi (T.) S. Lavia (B.) F. Fallardi (F.) |
| Zagreb | National | Mar. 1843 | E. Ranzi (T.) S. Lavia (B.) F. Fallardi (F.) |
| Zara | Nobile | Oct. 13, 1846 | P. Scotti (V.) Carulli (T.) L. Bottagisi (B.) Zecchini (P.) G. Lovati (F.) |
| MALTA La Valletta | Manoel | 1842 | |
| NETHERLANDS Amsterdam | Italien | Dec. 27, 1843 | F. Salvini-Donatelli (V.) E. Boldrini (T.) A. Brunacci (B.) V. Jacobelli (P.) G. Catalano (F.) C. Pedrotti cond. |

|  |  | Feb. 26, 1845 | A. Bertucca (V.) T. Questa (T.) L. Mei (B.) N. Perelli (P.) G. B. Bencich (F.) C. Pedrotti cond. |
|---|---|---|---|

PERU
Lima           Principal      May  31, 1853  C. Barili-Thorn (V.) T. Cailly (T.)
                                            B. Galliani (B.) D. Lorini (P.) F.
                                            Leonardi (F.)

POLAND
Lwov           Skarbek        Feb.  8, 1851

Warsaw         Wielki         Mar. 17, 1853  J. Dobrski (B.)

PORTUGAL
Lisbon         Sao Carlos     June 29, 1841  L. Boccabadati (V.) A. Boccabadati
                                            (T.) D. Conti (B.) L. Ferretti (P.)
                                            G. Antoldi (F.)

                              Feb. 15, 1842  L. Boccabadati (V.) A. Boccabadati
                                            (T.) D. Conti (B.) L. Ferretti (P.)
                                            G. Antoldi (F.) (Probable cast)

Oporto         Sao Joao       Mar.     1853  L. Giordani (V.) Lainati (T.) L. Ce-
                                            resa (B.) Biscaccia (P.) Lepri (F.)

                              Dec.     1858  G. Borsi de Leurie (V.) R. Feltri-
                                            Spalla (T.) G. De Vecchi (B.) G.
                                            Mazzi (P.) Rossi (F.)

RUSSIA
St.            Imperial       Mar.  7, 1857  F. Maray (V.) M. Lotti della Santa
  Petersburg                                 (T.) G. Bettini (B.) A. Bettini (P.)
                                            A. De Bassini (F.) E. Baveri cond.

SPAIN
Barcelona      Montesion      Oct.  2, 1841  Scannavino (V.) F. Rocca-Alessandri
                                            (T.) B. Galliani (B.) G. Carboni
                                            (P.) E. Polonini (F.)

               Liceo          May  29, 1847  F. Salvini-Donatelli (V.) G. Rossi-
                                            Caccia (T.) C. Liverani (B.) A. Cas-
                                            tellan (P.) G. Ferri (F.)

                              Mar.  6? 1869  G. Giovannoni-Zacchi (V.) L. Rug-
                                            gero-Antonioli (T.) F. Steger (B.)
                                            F. Garibay (P.) D. Squarcia (F.)

               Principal      June  4, 1856  M. Sulzer (V.) S. Peruzzi (T.) G.
                                            Landi (B.) B. Belart (P.) A. Selva
                                            (F.)

Madrid         De la Cruz     Jan. 17, 1846  C. Bertolini-Raffaelli (V.) G. Ros-
                                            setti-Sikorska (T.) N. Moriani (B.)
                                            E. Carrion (P.) G. Ferri (F.)

Zaragozza      Principal          1845-46

TURKEY
Constan-       Naum           Dec. 14, 1853  G. Beltramelli (V.) A. Conti-Foroni
  tinople                                    (T.) C. Liverani (B.) C. Guidotti
                                            (P.) E. Manfredi (F.) V. Fumi cond.

UNITED STATES
Philadelphia             Oct.  2, 1849 Seguin (V.) Richings (B.) (in Eng.)

OTHER PRODUCTIONS-TWENTIETH CENTURY

ITALY
Martina      Festival     July 28, 1990 (Projected)
 Franca

Rome         Opera        Dec. 28, 1976 M. Matsumoto (V.) M. Parazzini/F.
                                        Forgiero (T.) W. Johns/B. Rufo (B.)
                                        A. Savastano/C. Tuand (P.) P. Wash-
                                        ington/A. Tomicich (F.) G. Ferro
                                        cond.

4. LA VESTALE-*Tragedia lirica* in three acts
Naples-Teatro San Carlo-Mar. 10, 1840
Libretto by Salvadore Cammarano

Emilia (E.)                                     Adelina Spech sop.
Giunia (G.)                                     Eloisa Buccini mez.
Decio (D.)                                      Domenico Reina ten.
Publio (P.)                                    Paolo Barroilhet bar.
Metellio (M.)                                     Pietro Gianni bass
La Gran Vestale                                    Anna Salvetti sop.
Licinio                                     Timoleone Barattini ten.
Lucio                                      Giuseppe Benedetti bass

Conductor                                          Antonio Farelli
Director                                       Saverio Mercadante

OTHER PREMIERES

ARGENTINA
Buenos Aires  Argentino    Sep.  2, 1855

              Ant. Colón   July 12, 1873 A. Pozzoni-Anastasi (E.) P. Stoika
                                         (G.) L. Gulli (D.)

AUSTRALIA
Adelaide      Th. Royal    Apr. 21, 1877 A. Guadagnini (E.) M. Venosta (G.)
                                         P. Paladini (D.) G. Gambetti (P.) G.
                                         Cesari (M.) P. Giorza cond.

Sydney        Th. Royal    June 23, 1877 A. Guadagnini (E.) M. Venosta (G.)
                                         P. Paladini (D.) G. Gambetti (P.) G.
                                         Cesari (M.) P. Giorza cond.

AUSTRIA
Vienna        Kärntnertor Apr.  2, 1842 A. Rainieri-Marini (E.) M. Brambilla
                                         (G.) D. Donzelli (D.) F. Varesi (P.)
                                         G. Donatelli (M.) H. Proch cond.

BELGIUM
Antwerp       Royal        Jan.  4, 1852 V. Viola (E.) Semiglia (G.) E. Ar-
                                         Armandi (D.) L. Finocchi (P.)

BRAZIL
Rio de        Sao Pedro    June 19, 1849 A. Candiani (E.) C. Canonero (G.) F.
 Janeiro                                 Tati (D.) F. Massiani (P.) C. Ecker-
                                         lin (M.) J. V. Ribas cond.

CHILE
Santiago        Municipal    May        1868 M. Mollo (E.) E. Ballerini (D.)

Valparaiso      Victoria     Feb.?      1869 M. Mollo (E.)

EGYPT
Alexandria      Europeo      Oct.       1858 R. Pellini (E.) C. Pellini (G.)

FRANCE
Ajaccio         San          Feb.?      1860
                Gabriele

Paris           Italien      Dec. 23, 1841 G. Grisi (E.) E. Albertazzi (G.)
                                           Mario (D.) A. Tamburini (P.) G.
                                           Morelli (M.) T. Tilmant cond.

GERMANY
Berlin          Königstädt-  Nov. 16, 1844 Egnauer/L. Schieroni-Nulli (E.) E.
                liches                      Bendini (G.) F. Borioni (D.) G. Lan-
                                           di (P.)

GREECE
Corfu           San Giacomo  Feb.       1865 V. Falconi (E.) C. Ghedini (G.) L.
                                           Caserini (D.) Coronato (M.)

Zante                        Nov.?      1863 A. Bellati (E.) A. Ponti (D.) A.
                                           Vitti (P.)

ITALY
Alessandria     Civico       Autumn     1841 G. Micciarelli-Sbriscia (E.) B.
                                           Calveri-Winter (D.)

Ancona          Muse         Spring     1845 E. Boldrini (E.) T. Cresci (G.) L.
                                           Bernabei (D.)

Arezzo          Petrarco     Autumn     1844 E. Parepa-Archibugi (E.) G. Dossi
                                           (G.) O. Paglieri (D.) P. Bartolini
                                           (P.)

Bari            Piccinni     June 5, 1869 Gigli (E.) Faina (G.) C. Baroni (D.)
                                           G. Sansone (P.)

Bergamo         Sociale      Carn. 1842-43 L. Matthey (E.) A. Tantalora (G.) A.
                                           Paterni (D.)

Bologna         Comunale     Jan.       1846 A. Masenza (E.) S. Lussanti (G.) V.
                                           Ferrari-Stella (D.) G. Zucchini (P.)
                                           L. Tabellini (M.) G. Manetti cond.

Brescia         Grande       Dec. 26, 1846 A. Ramaccini (E.) R. Lucchini (G.)
                                           E. Antico (D.) L. Caliari (P.) V.
                                           Robaudi (M.)

Cagliari        Civico       Sep.?      1842 E. Bertuzzi (E.) A. Tadini (G.) C.
                                           Mugnai (D.) G. B. Righini (P.)

Catania         Comunale     Carn. 1841-42 T. Casanova (E.) E. Toccagni (G.) A.
                                           Della Cella (D.) D. Marchelli (P.)

Chieti          San          May 28, 1842 A. Fanti (E.) D. Santolini (G.) G.
                Ferdinando                 Costantini (D.) A. Angelini (P.) L.
                                           Alfani (M.)

Cremona      Concordia   Autumn    1841 F. Goldberg (E.) M. Croff (G.) G.
                                        Leonardi (D.) L. Rinaldini (P.)

Cuneo        Civico      Dec. 26? 1847 E. Rossi-Guerra (D.)

Ferrara      Comunale    Spring    1843 T. Tavola (E.) D. Santolini (G.) F.
                                        Borioni (D.)

Fiume        Civico      Apr. 25, 1855 C. Marziali (E.) P. Corvetti (G.) B.
                                        Negri (D.) F. Stella (P.)

Florence     Pergola     Apr.      1841 F. Maray (E.) S. Mequillet (G.) E.
                                        Musich (D.) S. Ronconi (P.) P. Gian-
                                        ni (M.) A. Biagi cond.

Genoa        Carlo       Feb. 6, 1841 A. Rainieri-Marini (E.) M. Croff
             Felice                     (G.) C. Lonati (D.) R. Ferlotti (P.)
                                        G. Serra cond.

Livorno      Rossini     Carn. 1843-44 E. Ercolani (E.) E. d'Angri (G.) G.
                                        Pardini (D.) L. Del Riccio (P.)

Lucca        Giglio      Aug.      1841 F. Maray (E.) D. Donzelli (D.) S.
                                        Ronconi (P.)

Lugo         Rossini     Sep.      1870 M. Majo (E.) O. Beltramelli (G.) V.
                                        Quintili-Leoni (P.)

Mantua       Sociale     Dec. 26? 1846 T. Turola (E.) L. Bernabei (D.)

Messina      Munizione   Carn. 1840-41 L. Schieroni-Nulli (E.) Turchini
                                        (G.) F. Gumirato (D.) L. Giorza (P.)

Milan        La Scala    Aug. 10, 1841 A. Fink-Lohr (E.) M. Brambilla (G.)
                                        C. Guasco (D.) F. Varesi (P.) F.
                                        Leonardi (M.)

Modena       Comunale    Carn. 1842-43 B. Steffenone (E.) A. Fouché (G.) L.
                                        Cuzzani (D.) R. Colmenghi (P.) A.
                                        Sarti (M.) A. Sighicelli cond.

Novara       Antico      Jan. 14, 1871 M. De Zorzi (E.) Casati (G.) E.
                                        Biondini (D.) G. Gambetti (P.) G. B.
                                        Del Fabbro (M.) A. Buzzi cond.

Padua        Nuovo       June 12, 1841 O. Malvani (E.) M. Brambilla (G.) G.
                                        Leonardi (D.) L. Rinaldini (P.)

Palermo      Carolino    Jan. 12, 1841 A. Fink-Lohr (E.) C. Gramaglia (G.)
                                        G. B. Verger (D.) F. Colini (P.) P.
                                        Raimondi cond.

Parma        Regio       Jan. 15, 1842 T. De Giuli-Borsi (E.) M. Croff (G.)
                                        G. B. Montresor (D.) R. Ferlotti
                                        (P.) R. Anconi (M.) N. De Giovanni
                                        cond.

Pavia        Civico      Aug. 13, 1842 Librandi (E.) C. Imola (G.) L. Cuz-
                                        zani (D.) R. Colmenghi (P.)

Perugia      Morlacchi   Jan. 30? 1858 E. Belmonte (E.) L. Ferrari-Stella
                                        (D.) R. Maestri (P.) P. Vannucci
                                        (M.)

Pesaro          Rossini      Feb.?    1865 E. Bedetti (E.) E. Ajroldi (G.) C.
                                           De Marco (D.) C. Sacchetti (P.)

Piacenza        Municipale   Spring   1843 L. Abbadia (E.) C. Imoda (G.) L. Mei
                                           (D.) R. Colmenghi (P.) L. Bianchi
                                           (M.) G. Jona cond.

Reggio Emilia Municipale Dec. 25, 1867 L. Bacarotti (E.) L. Viale (G.) V.
                                           Avoni (D.) S. Rossi-Rumiati (P.) C.
                                           Fiordiponte (M.) G. Tebaldi cond.

Rome            Valle        Sep. 28, 1842 L. Schieroni-Nulli (E.) E. Musich
                                           (D.) F. Varesi (P.)

Rovigo          Sociale      Fiera    1843 E. Hallez (E.) G. B. Milesi (D.) G.
                                           Fiori (P.)

Siena           Rinnovati    Carn. 1845-46 C. Forti-Babacci (E.) C. Soldini
                                           (D.) L. Parmigiani (P.)

Sinigaglia      Comunale     July 17, 1845 C. Gruitz (E.) R. Olivieri (G.) S.
                                           Malvezzi (D.) L. Finocchio (P.) P.
                                           Balzar (M.) N. De Giovanni cond.

Trento          Sociale      June  6, 1846 L. Abbadia (E.) E. Naudin (D.) L.
                                           Caliari (P.)

Treviso         Onigo        Oct.     1841 M. Accorsi (E.) G. Leonardi (D.) L.
                                           Rinaldini (P.)

Trieste         Grande       Jan. 11, 1842 O. Malvani (E.) C. Gramaglia (G.) G.
                                           B. Verger (D.) A. Scaramelli cond.

Turin           Carignano    Oct.  6, 1841 O. Malvani (E.) C. Gramaglia (G.) G.
                                           B. Verger (D.) V. Sermattei (P.)

                Regio        Mar. 10, 1869 A. Pozzoni (E.) D. Garbato (G.) G.
                                           Capponi (D.) F. Bellini (P.) C.
                                           Pedrotti cond.

Venice          Rossini      May   8, 1841 G. Miciarelli-Sbriscia (E.) I. Ber-
                                           trand (G.) G. B. Bertolasi (D.) A.
                                           Superchi (P.)

Vercelli        Civico       Jan. 14, 1845 C. Barili-Thorn (E.) C. Imoda (G.)
                                           A. Della Cella (D.) F. Taffanelli
                                           (P.) De Lorenzi (M.)

Verona          Filarmonico Dec.      1842 T. Tavola (E.) E. Zmyoschi (G.) E.
                                           Caggiati (D.) F. Gorin (P.)

Vicenza         Eretenio     Carn. 1842-43 E. Goggi (E.) A. Poppi (G.) E.
                                           Caggiati (D.) G. Torre (P.)

JUGOSLAVIA
Zara            Nobile       Oct.  7, 1843 A. Mazza (E.) Gerli (G.) P. Cer-
                                           vati (D.) G. Bastoggi (P.) Lodetti
                                           (M.)

MALTA
La Valletta     Manuel       Jan.     1850 C. Rambur (E.) A. Borghi-Mamo (G.)
                                           E. Pancani (D.) E. Crivelli (P.) F.
                                           Leonardi (M.)

MEXICO
Mexico City    Nacional    Nov. 25, 1855 C. Manzini (E.) F. Vestvali (G.) L.
                                         Giannoni (D.) E. Winter (P.) C.
                                         Carroni (M.) J. Winter cond.

PERU
Lima           Principal   July      1869 M. Mollo (E.) Fiorio (G.) G. Lim-
                                          berti (D.) G. Marra (P.) Gennari
                                          (M.)

PORTUGAL
Lisbon         Sao Carlos  July 29, 1842 E. Boldrini (E.) R. Vitali (D.) N.
                                         Costantini (P.) C. Eckerlin (M.)

Oporto         Sao Joao    Jan.?     1843 R. Vitali (E.) C. Eckerlin (M.)

ROMANIA
Bucharest      Nacional    Oct.?     1850 A. Corbari (G.) E. Rossi-Guerra (D.)

Iasi           Teatrul     Feb.  4, 1852 L. Giordano (E.) D. Santolini (G.)
                                         G. B. Milesi (D.) G. Donelli (P.) P.
                                         Tozzoli (M.)

RUSSIA
Odessa         Municipal   Spring    1844

SPAIN
Barcelona      Principal   May   8, 1841 M. Palazzesi (E.) R. Gariboldi-Bassi
                                         (G.) C. Lonati (D.) A. Alba (P.) P.
                                         Novelli (M.)

               Liceo       May   8, 1852 L. Ponti dall'Armi (E.) G. Baldanza
                                         (D.) E. Manfredi (M.)

Madrid         Circo       June 21, 1842 T. Bovay (E.) R. De Bernardi (G.) G.
                                         Olivieri (D.) R. Anconi (P.) P.
                                         Gianni (M.)

               Real        Feb.  2, 1870 C. Ferni (E.) F. Natali-Testa (G.)
                                         E. Tamberlick (D.) D. Squarcia (P.)
                                         G. B. Antonucci (M.) F. A. Barbieri
                                         cond.

Seville        San         Jan.?    1859 S. Peruzzi (E.) G. Landi (D.) D.
               Fernando              Mattioli (P.) A. Selva (M.)

Valencia       Principal   May      1859 S. Peruzzi (E.) A. Corbari (G.) G.
                                         Landi (D.) D. Mattioli (P.) A. Selva
                                         (M.)

TURKEY
Constan-       Naum        Oct. 25, 1852 L. Coradori (E.) C. Ghedini (G.) C.
tinople                                  Liverani (D.) P. Gorin (P.) G. B.
                                         Cornago (M.)

Smyrna         Cammarano   Oct.  3, 1867 Ciccaglia (E.) Ciaramponi (G.) E.
                                         Giusti (D.)

SELECTED REVIVALS-NINETEENTH CENTURY

CHILE
Santiago       Municipal   June     1870 M. Mollo (E.) A. Mazzucco (G.) P.
                                         Baccei (D.)

ITALY
Altamura      Mercadante   Sep. 19? 1895 E. Carelli (E.) E. Riso (G.) Ja-
                                        ricci (D.) Melillo (P.) R. De Falco
                                        (M.)

Bologna       Comunale     Dec. 26, 1849 A. Vianelli (E.) D. Santolini (G.)
                                        A. Giuglini (D.) A. Carapia (P.) F.
                                        Dall'Asta (M.) G. Manetti cond.

                           Nov. 22, 1851 R. Gariboldi-Bassi (E.) C. Ghedini
                                        (G.) G. Fraschini (D.) F. Colini
                                        (P.) G. Mirandola (M.) G. Manetti
                                        cond.

              Corso        Apr.     1862 L. Gavetti-Reggiani (E.) A. Zenari
                                        (D.) A. De Antoni (P.)

Ferrara       Tosi-Borghi  Nov. 16? 1892 E. Ferrari (E.) M. Franchini (G.) E.
                                        Niccoli (D.) G. Borghi (P.) Contini
                                        (M.)

Florence      Pergola      Oct. 30, 1858 C. Carozzi-Zucchi (E.) E. Pancani
                                        (D.) A. Mazzanti (P.) G. Segri-
                                        Segarra (M.)

Genoa         Carlo        Mar. 29, 1842 F. Goldberg (E.) M. Croff (G.) E.
              Felice                    Musich (D.) P. Ambrosini (P.) G.
                                        Serra cond.

                           Jan. 17, 1850 K. Evers (E.) A. Casaloni (G.) L.
                                        Cuzzani (D.) L. Gassier (P.) C.
                                        Fedrighini (M.) G. Serra cond.

                           Feb. 14, 1855 L. Bendazzi-Secchi (E.) C. Ghedini
                                        (G.) G. Landi (D.) F. Colini (P.) A.
                                        Mariani cond.

                           Dec. 25, 1866 P. Vaneri (E.) F. Curti (G.) G. Cap-
                                        poni (D.) E. Dondi (P.) A. Fiorini
                                        (M.) A. Mariani cond.

Milan         La Scala     Jan. 18, 1845 E. D'Angri (E.) Accenti (G.) G. Pog-
                                        gi (D.) A. Alizard (M.) E. Cavallini
                                        cond.

                           Feb. 6, 1855 G. Sanchioli (E.) G. Bregazzi (G.)
                                        G. Sinico (D.) D. Mattioli (P.) F.
                                        Pons (M.) E. Cavallini cond.

              Carcano      Oct. 5, 1850 R. Gariboldi-Bassi (E.) A. Casaloni
                                        (G.) G. Fedor (D.) C. Bartolucci
                                        (P.) F. Pons (M.)

                           Nov.     1866 G. Boema (E.) G. Gavotti (G.) G.
                                        Petrovich (D.) C. Fabbricatore (P.)
                                        G. Norbis (M.)

Naples        San Carlo    June 14, 1840 F. Pixis (E.) E. Buccini (G.) D.
                                        Reina (D.) O. Cartagenova (P.) A.
                                        Farelli cond.

                           June 27, 1841 A. Rainieri-Marini (E.) E. Buccini
                                        (G.) G. Fraschini (D.) F. Colini
                                        (P.) P. Gianni (M.) A. Farelli cond.

July 17, 1845 G. Sanchioli (E.) E. Buccini (G.) G.
Fraschini (D.) G. De Baillou (P.) A.
Farelli cond.

Oct. 28, 1845 R. Gabussi De Bassini (E.) E. Buccini (G.) G. Fraschini (D.) F. Co-
letti (P.) M. Arati (M.) A. Farelli
cond.

Oct. 15, 1851 L. Bendazzi-Secchi (E.) A. Borghi-
Mamo (G.) G. Roppa/G. B. Verger (D.)
A. De Bassini (P.) M. Arati (M.) A.
Farelli cond.

Dec. 29, 1857 E. Fioretti (E.) C. Guarducci (G.)
G. Baldanza (D.) F. Coliva (P.)

Dec. 25, 1866 L. Bendazzi-Secchi (E.) G. Tati (G.)
R. Sirchia/T. Palmieri (D.) L. Colonnese (P.) Emeric/M. Arati (M.)

Feb. 5, 1873 M. Majo (E.) M. De Gourieff (G.) A.
Celada (D.) V. Collini (P.) S. Ce-
sarò (M.) P. Serrao cond.

Palermo      Carolino      Nov. 16, 1842 A. Rainieri-Marini (E.) C. Orlandi
(G.) B. Winter (D.) A. Superchi (P.)
P. Raimondi cond.

Nov. 19, 1844 L. Abbadia (E.) G. B. Milesi (D.) R.
Ferlotti (P.) P. Raimondi cond.

Dec. 5, 1847 G. Sanchioli (E.) A. Orlandi (G.) E.
Musich (D.) L. Corradi-Setti (P.) P.
Raimondi cond.

            Bellini       Apr.?    1871 M. Destin (E.) E. Rossi (G.) G.
Valentini-Cristiani (D.) A. Pifferi
(P.) A. Garcia (M.) L. Alfano cond.

Parma        Regio         May 9, 1843 L. Matthey (E.) A. Fouché (G.) L.
Cuzzani (D.) F. Colini (P.) V. Cas-
pani (M.) N. De Giovanni cond.

Rome         Alibert       Sep. 12, 1843 R. Gabussi De Bassini (E.) F. Borioni (D.) P. Balzar (P.) R. Scalese
(M.)

            Argentina     Oct.     1855 A. Basseggio (E.) G. Miciarelli-
Sbriscia (G.) G. Musiani (D.) F.
Cresci (P.)

Trieste      Grande        Dec. 26, 1854 K. Evers (E.) A. Corbari (G.) C.
Liverani (D.) A. Morelli (P.) N.
Benedetti (M.) G. A. Scaramelli
cond.

Turin        Carignano     Nov. 12, 1850 C. Gruitz (E.) L. Graziani (D.) S.
Scappini (M.)

            Sep.?    1858 E. D'Ania (E.) G. Bregazzi (G.) A.
Cruciani (D.) P. Gorin (P.) H. von
Rokitansky (M.) F. Bianchi cond.

|           | Vittorio<br>Emanuele | Nov. 14, 1863 | T. Stolz (E.)  G. Flory (G.)  G. Va-<br>lentini-Cristiani (D.)  V. Quintili-<br>Leoni (P.) |
|-----------|----------|----------|----------|
| Venice    | San<br>Benedetto | Nov. 29, 1842 | O. Malvani (E.) A. Poppi (G.)  A. De<br>Bassini (P.) |
|           |          | July 25, 1846 | L. Abbadia (E.) E. Naudin (D.) L.<br>Caliari (P.) |
| Verona    | Filarmonico | May  8, 1846 | L. Abbadia (E.) Dogliotti (G.) G.<br>Fedor (D.) L. Caliari (P.) Gionesi<br>(M.) |
|           |          | Sep. 27, 1851 | M. Spezia-Aldighieri (E.) D. Conti<br>(D.) |

PORTUGAL
Lisbon       Sao Carlos   Jan. 16, 1866   A. Borghi-Mamo (E.) G. Tati (G.) P.
                                          Mongini (D.) D. Squarcia (P.) M.
                                          Junca (M.)

SPAIN
Madrid       Real         Mar. 6, 1873    G. Pasqua (E.) C. Mantilla (G.) E.
                                          Barbacini (D.) G. Rota (P.) J. Or-
                                          dinas (M.)

OTHER PRODUCTIONS-TWENTIETH CENTURY

ITALY
Altamura     Mercadante   Dec. 29, 1969   M. Rosati (E.) M. Pirazzini (G.) S.
                                          Puma (D.) G. Guarnera (P.) A. Colel-
                                          la (M.) G. Ruisi cond.

Civitavecchia Fortezza    Aug. 28, 1970   A. Vercelli (E.) M. Pirazzini (G.)
                                          G. Gismondo (D.) G. Guarnera (P.) A.
                                          Colella (M.) G. Ruisi cond.

Pistoia      Lux          Sep. 5, 1970    M. Rosati (E.) M. Pirazzini (G.) G.
                                          Gismondo (D.) G. Guarnera (P.) A.
                                          Colella (M.) V. Machi cond.

JUGOSLAVIA
Split        National     Apr. 4, 1987    D. Vejzovic (E.) P. Romanò (G.) G.
                                          Cecchele (D.) F. Sioli (P.) G.
                                          Boldrini (M.) V. Sutej cond. (in
                                          It.)


5. LA SOLITARIA DELLE ASTURIE-*Melodramma* in five parts
Venice-Teatro La Fenice-Mar. 12, 1840
Libretto by Felice Romani

La Solitaria                                  Amalia Schütz-Oldosi sop.
Elvira                                         Adelaide Moltini sop.
Pelagio                                    Francesco Pedrazzi ten.
Gusmano                                         Pietro Balzar bass
Manuza                                     Augusto Razzanelli sec.

Conductor                                          Gaetano Mares
Director                                      Saverio Mercadante

6. IL PROSCRITTO-*Melodramma tragico* in three acts
Naples-Teatro San Carlo-Jan. 4, 1842
Libretto by Salvadore Cammarano

| | |
|---|---|
| Malvina Douglas (M.) | Antonietta Rainieri-Marini sop. |
| Odoardo Douglas (O.) | Eloisa Buccini mez. |
| Giorgio Argyll (G.) | Giovanni Basadonna ten. |
| Arturo Murray (A.) | Gaetano Fraschini ten. |
| Guglielmo Ruthven (R.) | Pietro Gianni bass |
| Anna Ruthven | Anna Salvetti sop. |
| Clara | Adelaide Gualdi mez. |
| Osvaldo | Teofilo Rossi ten. |
| Un officiale di Cromwell | Giuseppe Benedetti bass |

| | |
|---|---|
| Conductor | Antonio Farelli |
| Director | Saverio Mercadante |

OTHER PRODUCTIONS

ITALY
Naples          San Carlo    May  30, 1842 C. Gruitz (M.) M. Taglioni (O.) G.
                                          Basadonna (G.) G. Fraschini (A.) A.
                                          Farelli cond.


7. IL REGGENTE-*Tragedia lirica* in three acts
Turin-Teatro Regio-Feb. 2, 1843
Libretto by Salvadore Cammarano

| | |
|---|---|
| Amelia (A.) | Ottavia Malvani sop. |
| Meg (Me.) | Isabella Tadini sop. |
| Oscar (O.) | Elisa Bendini mez. |
| Il Conte Murray (M.) | Lorenzo Salvi ten. |
| Hamilton (H.) | Luciano Fornasari bar. |
| Lord Kilkardy | Giuseppe Bruscoli bass |
| Lord Howe | Michele Novaro bass |
| Scoto | Giovanni Battista Boeri ten. |
| Un Servo di Hamilton | Leone Marrani sec. |

| | |
|---|---|
| Conductor | Giovanni Battista Polledro |
| Director | Saverio Mercadante |

OTHER PRODUCTIONS-NINETEENTH CENTURY

GREECE
Corfu          San Giacomo Carn. 1849-50

ITALY
Bergamo        Sociale      Jan. 21, 1845 C. Griffini (A.) E. Gandaglia (Me.)
                                          Volpini (O.) G. Ricci (M.) G. C.
                                          Casanova (H.)

Cagliari       Civico       Dec. 28, 1858 B. Bellocchio (A.) V. Sarti (M.) P.
                                          Nolasco Llorens (H.)

Genoa          Carlo        May  7, 1844 S. Loewe (A.) T. Remorini (Me.) E.
               Felice                     Buccini (O.) G. Roppa (M.) P. Déri-
                                          vis (H.) G. Serra cond.

Milan          Re           Apr. 21, 1851 L. Finetti-Batocchi (A.) O. Mongè
                                          (Me.) R. Pozzi (O.) G. Galvani (M.)
                                          F. Giannini (H.)

Novara        Nuovo        Carn. 1852-53 B. Bellocchio (A.) A. Artioli (O.)
                                         P. Samat (M.) L. Montani (H.)


Padua         Nuovo        July 22, 1843 L. Abbadia (A.) L. Salvi (M.) F.
                                         Colini (H.)


Palermo       Carolino     Apr.  3, 1870 M. Majo (A.) L. Viale (O.) F. Ros-
                                         nati (M.) G. F. Beneventano (H.) L.
                                         Alfano cond.


Parma         Regio        Feb. 13, 1844 B. Colleoni-Corti (A.) R. Lucchini
                                         (O.) G. Lega (Me.) G. B. Milesi (M.)
                                         P. Dérivis (H.) N. De Giovanni cond.


                           Jan. 17, 1845 A. Moltini (A.) T. Ricca (Me.) D.
                                         Santolini (O.) G. Ricci (M.) P. Bal-
                                         zar (H.)


Piacenza      Comunale     Jan.     1850 C. Griffini (A.) O. Mongè (Me.) T.
                                         Palmieri (M.) S. Scappini (H.) G.
                                         Jona cond.


Rome          Apollo       Dec. 26, 1844 O. Malvani (A.) R. Olivieri (Me.) M.
                                         Gori (O.) E. Musich (M.) P. Dérivis
                                         (H.) E. Angelini cond.


Sassari       Civico       Dec. 26, 1847 C. Rota-Galli (A.) G. D'Apice (M.)
                                         G. Zambellini (H.)


Trani         San             1850-51
              Ferdinando


Trapani       San          Dec.     1868 T. Alvisi (A.)
              Ferdinando


Trieste       Grande       Nov. 11, 1843 E. Tadolini (A.) C. Guasco (M.) F.
                                         Varesi (H.)


Turin         Carignano    Nov. 17, 1854 K. Evers (A.) C. Ghedini (O.) V.
                                         Sarti (M.) P. Nolasco Llorens (H.)


MALTA
La Valletta   Manuel          1848-49


PORTUGAL
Lisbon        Sao Carlos   Jan. 10, 1844 G. Rossi-Caccia (A.) L. Flavio (M.)
                                         F. Bottelli (H.)


Oporto        Sao Joao        1844


SPAIN
Barcelona     Principal    June 27, 1844 B. Colleoni-Corti (A.) G. B. Verger
                                         (M.) A. Superchi (H.)


              Liceo        Feb. 25, 1860 C. Carozzi-Zucchi (A.) C. Dory (O.)
                                         T. Palmieri (M.) A. Rodas (H.)

OTHER PRODUCTIONS-TWENTIETH CENTURY

ITALY
Siena        Rinnovati    Sep.  7, 1970  M.  Chiara    (A.)  L.  Vajna  (Me.)  E.
                                         Zilio  (O.)  G.  Merighi  (M.)  L.  Monte-
                                         fusco  (H.)  B.  Martinotti  cond.


8. LEONORA-*Melodramma* in four acts
Naples-Teatro Nuovo-Dec. 5, 1844
Libretto by Marco d'Arienzo

Leonora (L.)                                       Adelaide Rebussini sop.
Oscar Müller (O.)                                     Emanuele Testa ten.
Guglielmo (G.)                                      Domenico Labocetta ten.
Il Barone Lutzow (Lu.)                               Antonio Avignone bar.
Strelitz (S.)                                            Gennaro Luzio buf.
Geltrude                                             Adelaide De Rosa mez.
Giorgio                                                    Luigi Vita bass

Conductor                                                      Andrea Baly
Director                          Errico Petrella and Saverio Mercadante

OTHER PRODUCTIONS

ARGENTINA
Buenos Aires  Argentino   July  6, 1855  I. Edelvira (L.) L. Guglielmini (G.)
                                         Mazzio (Lu.) P. Franchi (S.)

BRAZIL
Rio de       Lirico       May   3, 1853  G. Zecchini  (L.)  D. Labocetta (G.)
  Janeiro      Fluminense                A. Gentile (O.) L. De Lauro (Lu.) E.
                                         Ribas (S.)

DENMARK
Copenhagen   Royal         Mar. 24, 1848  A. Ricci (L.) E. Caggiati (G.) C.
                                         Vajro (Lu.) Gallo (S.) P. Sperati
                                         cond.

FRANCE
Ajaccio      San          Jan.     1858  R. Mori-Spalazzi (L.) F. Cesari (G.)
               Gabriele                  G. Caravaglia (Lu.) C. Baldelli (S.)

Paris        Italien      Jan.  8, 1866  G. Vitali (L.) G. Fraschini (G.) E.
                                         Delle Sedie (Lu.) R. Scalese (S.)

GERMANY
Berlin       Königstädt-  Nov. 13, 1847  G. Fodor (L.) D. Labocetta (G.) Pig-
               liches                    noli (Lu.) E. Luisia (S.)

GREECE
Corfu        San Giacomo Dec.      1846  E. Boldrini (L.) D. Mecksa (G.) G.
                                         De Lorenzi (Lu.) D. Scheggi (S.)

             Feb. 22, 1853  C. Guerra (L.) G. Giorgetti (G.) T.
                                         Pieri (Lu.) D. Scheggi (S.)

ITALY[7]

| Ancona | Muse | Dec. 26, 1846 | M. Cavalli (L.) G. Gamboggi (G.) L. Corradi-Setti (Lu.) G. Cavalli (S.) |

| Bari | Piccinni | May 17, 1855 | A. Ortolani-Brignole (L.) A. Oliva-Pavani (G.) D. Squarcia (Lu.) L. Conti (S.) |

| Bitonto | | Feb.  1858 | M. Mazzoni (L.) P. Sparagano (G.) G. Pisani (Lu.) Benigno (S.) |

| Bologna | Comunale | May 27, 1849 | F. Capuani (L.) E. Naudin (G.) A. Carapia (Lu.) A. Rivarola (S.) G. Manetti cond. |

| Cagliari | Civico | Oct. 11, 1847 | G. Berlam-Massai (L.) Aldini-Mazzi (G.) I. Didier (Lu.) Marconi (S.) |

| | | Jan. 13? 1868 | E. Concordia (G.) C. Baldelli (S.) |

| Catanzaro | Comunale | Oct.  1851 | N. Barbieri-Thiollier (L.) P. De Nobile (G.) L. Vendemmia (Lu.) Leva (S.) |

| Crema | Sociale | Dec. 26, 1847 | Zagnoli (L.) Michel (G.) P. Merigo (S.) |

| Cuneo | Civico | Jan.  1850 | T. Cotta-Morandini (L.) C. Scannavino (G.) G. Vercellini (Lu.) Rocca (S.) |

| Fano | Fortuna | Carn. 1852-53 | S. Zudoli (L.) A. Clerici-Severini (G.) L. Roncagli (Lu.) G. Mellini (S.) |

| Fiume | Civico | Spring  1864 | A. Fumagalli (L.) S. Perozzi (G.) V. Quintili-Leoni (Lu.) A. Fiorini (S.) |

| Florence | Alfieri | May  2, 1847 | Rossi (L.) A. Bettini (G.) D. Scheggi (S.) |

| | Pergola | Dec. 26, 1848 | O. Avenali (L.) G. Pozzolini (G.) |

| | | Jan. 13, 1855 | G. Brambilla (L.) C. Guidotti (G.) C. Everardi (Lu.) F. Frizzi (S.) |

| | Piazza Vecchia | 1851 | Martelli (L.) D. Scheggi (S.) |

| | Nuovo | Feb.  1854 | O. Mongè (L.) F. Cuturi (Lu.) P. Rafaelli (S.) |

| Genoa | Carlo Felice | Sep. 12, 1846 | A. Rebussini (L.) E. Naudin (G.) E. Rossi-Guerra (O.) E. Luisia (Lu.) A. Rovere (S.) G. Serra cond. |

| | | May  1, 1848 | A. Rebussini (L.) G. De Vecchi (G.) L. Ferrario (Lu.) F. Frizzi (S.) G. Serra cond. |

---

[7]. *Leonora* was also given in Molfetta in 1852, at the Teatro Bellini in Naples in 1865 and again in 1867, in Reggio di Calabria in the 1849-50 season, in Sutera in 1854, in Trani during the 1845-46 and 1850-51 seasons and in Salerno during the autumn of 1856.

July 14, 1859 S. Casimir-Ney (L.) G. Mea (G.) A.
Fiorini (Lu.) F. Frizzi (S.) A. Mariani cond.

Apollo        Mar.  7, 1854 F. Scheggi (L.) G. D'Apice (G.) D.
Squarcia (Lu.) G. Scheggi (S.)

Iesi      Concordia   Jan. 14? 1867 M. Mazzoni (L.) Pietroboni (G.) E.
Antico (Lu.) C. Bellincioni (S.)

Livorno   Rossini     Feb.     1848 V. Viola (L.) G. Fedor (G.) L.
Ferrario (Lu.) G. Scheggi (S.)

Nov.     1858 C. Lipparini (L.)

Leopoldo    Oct. 20, 1858 A. Pasi (L.) G. Boy (G.) B. Mazzetti
(S.)

Lucca     Pantera     Feb.     1850 C. Forti-Babacci (L.) G. Pellegrini
(G.) Pelliccio (Lu.) D. Raffaelli
(S.)

Mantua    Sociale     Jan.     1853 C. Lorenzetti (L.) A. Castellan (G.)
D. Mattioli (Lu.) F. Frizzi (S.)

Messina   Sant'       Feb.     1855 C. Lorenzetti (L.)
Elisabetta

Vittorio    Jan.  1, 1861 Z. Papini (L.) V. Graziani (G.)
Emanuele

Milan     Re          July 19, 1845 L. Pozzi (L.) V. Jacobelli (G.) G.
Bastoggi (Lu.) G. Scheggi (S.)

July 17, 1847 A. Rebussini (L.) A. Bettini (G.) O.
Bonafous (Lu.) G. Scheggi (S.)

Canobbiana May   6, 1851 M. Vetturi-Olivi (L.) G. Tamaro (G.)
G. Massiani (Lu.) C. Soares (S.)

Carcano     Aug.  1, 1856 A. Ortolani-Tiberini (L.) A. Biundi
(G.) A. Carapia (Lu.) D. Raffaelli
(S.)

Modena    Comunale    Dec. 26, 1855 C. Lorenzetti (L.) G. Giorgetti (G.)
E. Rossi-Corsi (Lu.) C. Bellincioni
(S.) A. Sighicelli cond.

Naples    Nuovo       Nov.     1845 R. Vigliardi (L.) V. Prattico (G.)
A. Olivari (Lu.) G. Luzio (S.)

Nov. 13, 1849 Z. Papini (L.) G. Bettini (G.) T.
Remorini (O.) V. Orlandi (Lu.) L.
Cammarano (S.)

July 13, 1851 N. Barbieri-Thiollier/C. Martinelli
(L.) A. Pagnoni/G. Bettini (G.) T.
Remorini (O.) R. Mastriani (Lu.) L.
Cammarano (S.)

May 27, 1854 F. Scheggi (L.) D. Squarcia (Lu.) M.
Tiberini (G.) G. Valentini-Cristiani
(O.) L. Conti (S.)

Fondo            Aug. 26, 1846 T. Brambilla (L.) S. Malvezzi (G.)
                               F. Gionfrida (Lu.) G. Luzio (S.)

                 May  12, 1850 F. Maray (L.) C. Miraglia (G.) A. De
                               Bassini (Lu.) Pappone (S.)

                 Aug.  9, 1855 Crespi (L.) P. Cecchi (G.) C. Lauda-
                               no (O.) P. Brayda-Lablache (Lu.) G.
                               Luzio (S.)

San Carlo        Oct. 12, 1846 T. Brambilla (L.) S. Malvezzi (G.)
                               F. Gionfrida (Lu.) G. Luzio (S.) A.
                               Farelli cond.

                 May  31, 1850 F. Maray (L.) C. Miraglia (G.) A. De
                               Bassini (Lu.) G. Luzio (S.) A. Fa-
                               relli cond.

                 Aug. 15, 1855 Crespi  (L.)  C.  Laudano  (G.)  P.
                               Brayda-Lablache (Lu.) G. Luzio (S.)
                               A. Farelli cond.

Sannazaro        Feb.  1, 1876 E. Nascio (L.) V. Montanaro (G.)
                               Polonini (Lu.) A. De Bassini (S.)

Novara      Nuovo            July      1855 E. Kenneth (L.) P. Chiesi (G.) C.
                               Morelli-Condolmieri (Lu.) A. Riva-
                               rola (S.)

Padua       Concordi       Feb.      1855 A.  Alessandri  (L.)  G.  Pellegrini
                               (G.) C. Busi (Lu.) C. Bellincioni
                               (S.)

Palermo     Carolino       Nov. 25, 1846 R. Vigliardi (L.) E. Caggiati (G.)
                               V. Mela (Lu.) G. Zambelli (S.) P.
                               Raimondi cond.

                 Feb. 16, 1859 L. Brenna (L.) P. Stecchi-Bottardi
                               (G.) E. Crivelli (Lu.) F. Frizzi
                               (S.) A. Lo Casto cond.

Parma       Regio         Jan. 23, 1848 V. Bozzi (L.) E. Antico (G.) C.
                               Marié (Lu.) G. Zambelli (S.) N. De
                               Giovanni cond.

Pavia       Civico        Feb. 16, 1847 Pecorini (L.) G. De Vecchi (G.) G.
                               B. Righini (Lu.) L. Silingardi (S.)

Perugia     Morlacchi     Feb. 11, 1852 M. Gresti (L.) A. Oliva-Pavani (G.)
                               A. Ortolani (Lu.) Negri-Lipparini
                               (S.)

Pisa        Ravvivati     Dec. 26, 1850 A. Salati (L.) C. Pellegrini (G.) A.
                               Ortolani (Lu.) G. Scheggi (S.)

            Verdi         Dec. 25, 1868 A. Contarini (L.) L. Gulli (G.) C.
                               Sacchetti (Lu.) P. Mattioli (S.) L.
                               Quercioli cond.

Prato       Metastasio    Jan. 27, 1865 G. Giuria (L.) O. Graziani (G.) O.
                               Paoli (Lu.) F. Becheri (S.)

Sassari     Civico        Feb.      1847 G. Berlam-Massai (L.) F. Gumirato
                               (G.) P. Merigo (S.)

| Siena | Rinnovati | Dec. 26, 1853 | F. Scheggi (L.) L. Caserini (G.) L. Brignole (Lu.) G. Scheggi (S.) |
|---|---|---|---|
| | | Dec. 26, 1864 | A. Luppi (L.) Campanelli (G.) Albieri (Lu.) Del Vivo (S.) |
| Spoleto | Nobile | Dec. 26, 1853 | V. Tilli (L.) S. Perozzi (G.) E. Antico (Lu.) Negri-Lipparini (S.) |
| Treviso | Sociale | June 1856 | Campi (L.) L. Caserini (G.) A. Vitti (Lu.) Finetti (S.) |
| Trieste | Grande | Feb. 6, 1847 | R. Gariboldi-Bassi (L.) G. Fedor (G.) G. De Baillou (Lu.) L. Maggiorotti (S.) G. A. Scaramelli cond. |
| | | Dec. 26, 1856 | C. Carozzi-Zucchi (L.) V. Sarti (G.) P. Baraldi (Lu.) F. Frizzi (S.) G. A. Scaramelli cond. |
| Turin | D'Angennes | June 25, 1845 | G. Ricci (G.) L. Valli (Lu.) Rossi (S.) |
| | Nazionale | Apr. 27, 1855 | R. Vigliardi (L.) G. Petrovich (G.) E. Rossi-Corsi (Lu.) C. Bellincioni (S.) |
| | Rossini | May 1860 | A. Fumagalli (L.) A. Cruciani (G.) L. Ferrario (Lu.) C. Bellincioni (S.) |
| Venice | San Benedetto | Dec. 26, 1856 | E. Fioretti (L.) Generini (G.) G. Sansone (Lu.) C. Bellincioni (S.) |
| | San Samuele | Apr. 1857 | A. Fumagalli (L.) Mariotti (G.) G. Vercellini (Lu.) D. Raffaelli (S.) |
| Verona | Nuovo | Oct. 23, 1852 | V. Boccabadati (L.) M. Neri (G.) F. Mazzoni (Lu.) F. Frizzi (S.) |
| Vicenza | Eretenio | Dec. 26, 1845 | L. Pozzi (L.) A. Della Cella (G.) S. Scappini (Lu.) C. Soares (S.) |
| PORTUGAL Lisbon | Sao Carlos | Apr. 13, 1846 | E. Ranzi (L.) G. B. Severi (G.) L. Salandri (Lu.) J. Catalano (S.) A. L. Miró cond. |
| | | June 18, 1847 | F. Rocca-Alessandri (L.) J. Solieri (G.) I. Patriossi (S.) |
| Oporto | Sao Joao | Jan. 1851 | Bianchi (L.) G. Gamboggi (G.) V. Prattico (Lu.) |
| RUSSIA Odessa | Municipal | June 1851 | G. Brambilla (L.) L. Stecchi Bottardi (G.) A. Ottaviani (Lu.) F. Frizzi (S.) |
| | | June? 1854 | E. Cherubini (L.) J. Solieri (G.) M. Zacchi (Lu.) L. Cammarano (S.) |

SPAIN
Barcelona      Liceo        Aug. 14, 1847 G. Rossi-Caccia (L.) A. Castellan
                                          (G.) G. Ferri (Lu.) F. Salas (S.)


                            Apr.?    1851

                            Feb.     1855 V. Tilli (L.) G. Galvani (G.) Rossi
                                          (Lu.) P. Rafaelli (S.)

Madrid         De la Cruz   June  5, 1847 La Torre (L.) E. Carrion (G.) F. Sa-
                                          las (S.)

                            July  6, 1848 L. Alessandri (L.) E. Carrion (G.)
                                          F. Salas (S.)

TURKEY
Constan-       Naum      ⸺  Mar. 24, 1859 F. Scheggi (L.) Chierici (G.) A.
  tinople                                 Laurence (Lu.) G. Scheggi (S.)




9. IL VASCELLO DI GAMA-*Melodramma* in a prologue and three acts
Naples-Teatro San Carlo-Mar. 6, 1845
Libretto by Salvadore Cammarano

Rosalia (R.)                                    Anna Bishop sop.
Fausto (F.)                              Gaetano Fraschini ten.
Rodrigo (R.)                               Filippo Coletti bar.
Bruno (B.)               Giuseppe Federico Beneventano bar.
Marco (M.)                                   Marco Arati bass
Amalia                                   Anna Salvetti sop.
Un Comandante                             Teofilo Rossi ten.
Un Proscritto                            Pasquale Ceci ten.
Gianni                                   Michele Tucci ten.
Gulludda                          Giuseppe Benedetti bass

Conductor                                  Antonio Farelli
Director                               Saverio Mercadante

OTHER PRODUCTIONS

BRAZIL
Rio de         Sao Pedro   July  9, 1950 I. Edelvira (R.) F. Tati (F.)
  Janeiro

10. ORAZI E CURIAZI-*Tragedia lirica* in three acts
Naples-Teatro San Carlo-Nov. 10, 1846
Libretto by Salvadore Cammarano

| | |
|---|---|
| Camilla (C.) | Erminia Frezzolini sop. |
| Curiazo (Cu.) | Gaetano Fraschini ten. |
| Orazio (O.) | Pietro Balzar bar. |
| Vecchio Orazio (V. O.) | Marco Arati bass |
| Sabina | Anna Salvetti sop. |
| Il Gran Sacerdote | Teofilo Rossi ten. |
| Primo Fratello di Orazio | Vincenzo Capranica sec. |
| Secondo Fratello di Orazio | Nuzzi sec. |
| Primo Fratello di Curiazo | Michele Memmi ten. |
| Secondo Fratello di Curiazo | Michele Tucci ten. |
| | |
| Conductor | Antonio Farelli |
| Director | Saverio Mercadante |

OTHER PRODUCTIONS-NINETEENTH CENTURY

BRAZIL

| | | | |
|---|---|---|---|
| Rio de Janeiro | Lirico Fluminense | Mar. 11, 1856 | E. La Grua (C.) G. Gentile (Cu.) L. Arnaud (O.) C. Capurri (V. O.) |
| | | Dec. 2, 1859 | G. Medori (C.) R. Mirate (Cu.) L. Arnaud (O.) |

HUNGARY

| | | | |
|---|---|---|---|
| Budapest | Nemzeti Szinház | May 13, 1848 | C. Hollósy (C.) Wolf (Cu.) M. Füredy (O.) K. Köszeghi (V. O.) (in Hung.) |

ITALY

| | | | |
|---|---|---|---|
| Bari | Piccinni | Feb. 1856 | A. Ortolani-Brignole (C.) A. Oliva-Pavani (Cu.) D. Squarcia (O.) |
| Bergamo | Sociale | Dec. 26, 1851 | E. Lorenzetti (C.) L. Perozzi (Cu.) P. Gianni (O.) |
| Brescia | Grande | Jan. 1853 | L. Luxor-Pretti (C.) T. Palmieri (Cu.) P. Bonora (O.) A. Morelli (V. O.) |
| Chieti | Marrucino | Spring 1865 | A. Giannetti (C.) G. Scannapiero (Cu.) F. Cecchi (O.) C. Pisani (V. O.) F. Micaldi cond. |
| Cosenza | | Dec. 1859 | N. Rossi (C.) G. De Filippis (Cu.) |
| Florence | Pergola | Mar. 19, 1857 | L. Biscaccianti (C.) A. Salviani (Cu.) R. Ferlotti (O.) L. Domenech (V. O.) |
| Foggia | Dauno | Dec. 1853 | Z. Papini (C.) G. Villani (Cu.) F. Gionfrida (O.) |
| Genoa | Carlo Felice | Feb. 3, 1848 | M. Gazzaniga (C.) L. Ferretti (Cu.) F. Gnone (O.) |
| Lecce | Paisiello | Carn. 1858-59 | |
| Messina | Sant' Elisabetta | Feb. 11, 1852 | C. Forti-Babacci (C.) A. Dall'Armi (Cu.) L. Arnaud (O.) G. B. Antonucci (V. O.) |

| | | | |
|---|---|---|---|
| Milan | La Scala | Dec. 26, 1847 | E. Tadolini (C.) R. Mirate (Cu.) G. Corsi (O.) A. Rodas (V. O.) |
| Naples | Nuovo | June 5, 1854 | Cappelli (C.) G. Villani (Cu.) F. Gionfrida (O.) Biondi (V. O.) |
| | Circo Olimpico | June 11, 1859 | L. Borghi (C.) F. Patierno (Cu.) Seccio (O.) |
| | San Carlo | Mar. 12, 1882 | A. Fossa (C.) G. Sani (Cu.) G. Mirabella (O.) E. Serbolini (V. O.) C. Scalisi cond. |
| Padua | Nuovo | June 12, 1852 | M. Gazzaniga (C.) R. Mirate (Cu.) G. B. Bencich (O.) A. Rodas (V. O.) |
| Palermo | Carolino | Sep. 3, 1850 | E. Scotta (C.) G. Landi (Cu.) F. Cresci (O.) A. Selva (V. O.) P. Raimondi cond. |
| Parma | Regio | Jan. 8, 1848 | G. Bertolotti (C.) G. Roppa (Cu.) C. Marié (O.) G. Setti (V. O.) N. De Giovanni cond. |
| Perugia | Morlacchi | Feb. 1857 | D. De Moro (C.) G. Giorgetti (Cu.) A. Cotogni (O.) C. Zuchelli (V. O.) |
| Reggio di Calabria | Borbonico | Sep. 2, 1857 | L. Giordano (C.) G. Valentini-Cristiani (Cu.) L. Roncagli (O.) |
| Rome | Argentina | Nov. 7, 1847 | V. Boccabadati (C.) L. Bernabei (Cu.) F. Gnone (O.) P. Sottovia (V. O.) |
| Siracusa | | Dec.? 1853 | A. Artioli (C.) S. Fratello (Cu.) A. Burgio (O.) P. Navaro (V. O.) Privitero cond. |
| Trieste | Grande | Nov. 6, 1847 | M. Gazzaniga (C.) L. Ferretti (Cu.) A. Superchi (O.) G. A. Scaramelli cond. S. Mercadante dir. |
| | | Oct. 25, 1850 | M. Gazzaniga (C.) G. Fraschini (Cu.) F. Colini (O.) C. Dalla Costa (V. O.) G. A. Scaramelli cond. |
| Turin | Regio | Feb. 18, 1865 | G. Medori (C.) C. Lefranc (Cu.) C. Boccolini (O.) E. Bagagiolo (V. O.) F. Bianchi cond. |
| Venice | La Fenice | Sep. 6, 1847 | A. De la Grange (C.) R. Mirate (Cu.) A. De Bassini (O.) G. Lodi (V. O.) G. Mares cond. |
| MALTA La Valletta | Manoel | Apr. 16, 1853 | C. Rapazzini (C.) L. Stefani (Cu.) G. Sansoni (O.) |
| PORTUGAL Lisbon | Sao Carlos | Apr. 9, 1849 | M. Gresti (C.) G. Baldanza (Cu.) G. Fiori (O.) N. Benedetti (V. O.) |

RUSSIA
St.            Imperial     Mar.  9, 1850 E. Frezzolini (C.)  I. Gardoni (Cu.)
  Petersburg                              F. Coletti (O.)  J. Tagliafico (V.
                                          O.) E. Baveri cond.

SPAIN
Barcelona      Liceo        Aug. 24, 1848 F. Salvini-Donatelli (C.) G. Roppa
                                          (Cu.) L. Silingardi (O.) G. Mitro-
                                          vich (V. O.)

OTHER PRODUCTIONS-TWENTIETH CENTURY

GREAT BRITAIN
Bristol        Colston      Apr. 23, 1975 J. Price (C.) R. Greager (Cu.) C. Du
               Hall                       Plessis (O.) M. King (V. O.) K.
                                          Montgomery cond.

Exeter         Univ. Hall   Apr. 25, 1975 J. Price (C.) R. Greager (Cu.) C. Du
                                          Plessis (O.) M. King (V. O.) K.
                                          Montgomery cond.

London         Elizabeth    Apr. 27, 1975 J. Price (C.) R. Greager (Cu.) C. Du
               Hall                       Plessis (O.) M. King (V. O.) K.
                                          Montgomery cond.


11. LA SCHIAVA SARACENA-*Melodramma tragico* in four acts
Milan-Teatro alla Scala-Dec. 26, 1848
Libretto by Francesco Maria Piave

Lea (L.)                                    Carlotta Gruitz sop.
Guido (G.)                                   Luigi Ferretti ten.
Ismaella (I.)                              Giovanni Corsi bar.
Goffredo (Go.)              Giovanni Battista Cornago bass
Legato di Roma                            Luigi Sonderegger bass
Pietro l'Eremita                         Francesco Lodetti bass
Boemondo                                 Napoleone Marconi ten.

Conductor                                 Eugenio Cavallini
Director                                  Saverio Mercadante

OTHER PRODUCTIONS

ITALY
Naples         San Carlo    Oct. 29, 1850 E. Tadolini (L.) L. Cuzzani (G.) A.
                                          De Bassini (I.) M. Arati (Go.) A.
                                          Farelli cond.

MALTA
La Valletta    Manuel       Feb.?    1862 A. Bazzurri (L.) G. Gambetti (G.)

12. MEDEA-*Tragedia lirica* in three Acts
Naples-Teatro San Carlo-Mar. 1, 1850
Libretto by Felice Romani and Salvadore Cammarano

| | |
|---|---|
| Medea | Rita Gabussi De Bassini sop. |
| Timante | Gaetano Baldanza ten. |
| Giasone | Achille De Bassini bar. |
| Creonte | Marco Arati bass |
| Creusa | Giuseppina Zecchini sop. |
| Ismene | Anna Salvetti sop. |
| Stenelo | Teofilo Rossi ten. |
| | |
| Conductor | Antonio Farelli |
| Director | Saverio Mercadante |

13. STATIRA-*Tragedia lirica* in three acts
Naples-Teatro San Carlo-Jan. 8, 1853
Libretto by Domenico Bolognese

| | |
|---|---|
| Statira | Teresa de Giuli-Borsi sop. |
| Olimpia | Adelaide Borghi-Mamo mez. |
| Cassandro | Raffaele Mirate ten. |
| Antigono | Gaetano Ferri bar. |
| Gran Sacerdote | Marco Arati bass |
| | |
| Conductor | Antonio Farelli |
| Director | Saverio Mercadante |

14. VIOLETTA-*Melodramma* in four acts
Naples-Teatro Nuovo-Jan. 10, 1853
Libretto by Marco d'Arienzo

| | |
|---|---|
| Violetta (V.) | Lucy Escott sop. |
| Rosalba (R.) | Enrichetta Cherubini sop. |
| Odino (O.) | Luigi Bianchi ten. |
| Giacomo (G.) | Luigi Fioravanti bar. |
| Berardo (B.) | Leopoldo Cammarano buf. |
| Il Landamano | Rafaelle Grandillo bass |
| Fiorina | Carolina Cetronè mez. |
| Un Caporale | Ferdinando Imbimbo bass |
| Un Villano | Not named |
| | |
| Conductor | Michele Di Natale |
| Director | Saverio Mercadante |

OTHER PRODUCTIONS

ITALY
| | | | |
|---|---|---|---|
| Naples | Nuovo | Jan. 1, 1854 | L. Escott (V.) A. Ruggero (R.) M. Tiberini (O.) L. Fioravanti (G.) A. Zoboli (B.) M. Di Natale cond. |
| | Fondo | June 11, 1856 | C. Frassini (V.) E. Cherubini (R.) G. Villani (O.) L. Fioravanti (Gi.) L. Cammarano (B.) A. Farelli cond. |

San Carlo    June 17, 1856 C. Frassini (V.) E. Cherubini (R.)
                           G. Villani (O.) L. Fioravanti (G.)
                           L. Cammarano (B.) A. Farelli cond.


15. PELAGIO-*Tragedia lirica* in four acts
Naples-Teatro San Carlo-Feb. 12, 1857
Libretto by Marco D'Arienzo

Bianca (B.)                                    Fortunato Tedesco mez.
Abdel-Aor (A.)                                 Francesco Graziani ten.
Pelagio (P.)                                      Filippo Coletti bar.
Giralda                                                   Schiavi sop.
Asan                                           Giuseppe Benedetti bass
Aliatar                                            Pasquale Ceci ten.
Mendo de Quexada                                  Giuseppe Monti sec.
Un Gionese                                         Teofilo Rossi ten.

Conductor                                              Antonio Farelli
Director                                            Saverio Mercadante

OTHER PRODUCTIONS

ITALY
Bergamo        Riccardi      Dec. 26, 1863 C. Lavini (B.) E. Mariani (A.) V.
                                           Petrali cond.

Milan          La Scala      Oct.  2, 1858 M. Lafon (B.) V. Sarti (A.) V. Or-
                                           landi (P.)

PORTUGAL
Lisbon         Sao Carlos    Feb.  3, 1858 F. Tedesco (B.) S. Malvezzi (A.) F.
                                           Beneventano (P.)

SPAIN
Barcelona      Liceo         Apr. 15, 1858 E. Masson (B.) A. Agresti (A.) G. B.
                                           Bencich (P.)

16. VIRGINIA-*Tragedia lirica* in three acts
Naples-Teatro San Carlo-Apr. 7, 1866
Libretto by Salvadore Cammarano

| | |
|---|---|
| Virginia (V.) | Marcellina Lotti Della Santa sop. |
| Icilio (I.) | Giorgio Stigelli ten. |
| Appio (A.) | Raffaele Mirate ten. |
| Virginio (Vo.) | Francesco Pandolfini bar. |
| Marco | Marco Arati bass |
| Tullia | Adelaide Morelli sec. |
| Valerio | Michele Memmi ten. |

Conductor                                          Giuseppe Puzone

OTHER PRODUCTIONS

GREAT BRITAIN
Belfast       Whitla Hall Nov. 27, 1976 J. Price (V.) M. Arthur (I.) B. Bottone (A.) C. Du Plessis (Vo.) J. Judd cond.

ITALY
Naples        Bellini     Feb.  6, 1901 T. Chelotti (V.) E. Strada (I.) A. Querzé (A.) C. Montella (Vo.) Scalisi cond.

Rome          Apollo      Mar. 20, 1872 M. Lotti Della Santa (V.) Castelli (I.) I. Campanini (A.) V. Cottone (Vo.) E. Terziani cond.

Turin         Vittorio    Sep. 26, 1877 B. Blume (V.) O. Tasca de Cappello (A.) Priani (Vo.)
              Emanuele

17. CATERINA DEI MEDICI
Incomplete

EMANUELE MUZIO

1. GIOVANNA LA PAZZA-*Opera seria* in three acts
Brussels-Théâtre du Cirque-Apr. 8, 1851
Libretto by L. Silva

| | |
|---|---|
| Giovanna di Castiglia | Giuseppina Medori sop. |
| Aixa | Sofia Vera-Lorini sop. |
| Filippo di Lorena | Giuseppe Lucchesi ten. |
| Aben-Hassan | Filippo Morelli-Ponti bar. |
| Federico | |
| Ferdinando d'Aragona | |
| Alvaro | |
| Una Donzella | |

| | |
|---|---|
| Conductor | Felice Ricci |
| Director | Emanuele Muzio |

Revised-Milan-Teatro Canobbiana-Sep. 6, 1852

| | |
|---|---|
| Giovanna di Castiglia | Carlotta Lorenzetti sop. |
| Aixa | Teresa Bajetti sop. |
| Filippo di Lorena | Marco Viani ten. |
| Aben-Hassan | Giovanni Guicciardi bar. |
| Federico | Giacomo Redaelli ten. |
| Ferdinando d'Aragona | Luigi Alessandrini bass |
| Alvaro | Napoleone Marconi ten. |
| Una Donzella | Felicità Baillou-Hilaret sec. |

| | |
|---|---|
| Conductor | Eugenio Cavallini |
| Director | Emanuele Muzio |

2. CLAUDIA-*Dramma lirico* in three acts
Milan-Teatro Re-Feb. 7, 1853
Libretto by Giulio Carcano

| | |
|---|---|
| Claudia (C.) | Amalia Jacobson sop. |
| Silvio (S.) | Gaspare Gamboggi ten. |
| Remigio (R.) | Luigi Walter bar. |
| Pier d'Asturia (P.) | Giacomo Vercellini bar. |
| Rosa | Regina Cosa sec. |
| Bastiano | Carlo Massera bar. |
| Marta | Claudina Cairoli sec. |

| | |
|---|---|
| Director | Emanuele Muzio |

OTHER PRODUCTIONS

ITALY
| | | |
|---|---|---|
| Milan | Re | Aug. 15? 1855 A. Ravaglia (C.) V. Sarti (S.) F. Coliva (R.) P. Nolasco Llorens (P.) |

3. LE DUE REGINE-*Melodramma tragico* in three acts
Milan-Teatro Canobbiana-May 17, 1856
Libretto by Giovanni Peruzzini

| | |
|---|---|
| Maria Tudor | Letizia Borgognoni sop. |
| Giovanna Grey | Giuditta Beltramelli sop. |
| Lord Ghilfort | Antonio Agresti ten. |
| Il Duca di Suffolk | Mauro Zacchi bar. |
| Il Duca di Northumberland | Luigi Alessandrini bass |
| Lord Surrey | Giuseppe Benzi sec. |
| Elisa | Orsola Bignami sec. |
| | |
| Conductor | Eugenio Cavallini |
| Director | Emanuele Muzio |

4. LA SORRENTINA-*Dramma lirico* in four acts
Bologna-Teatro Comunale-Nov. 14, 1857
Librettist unknown

| | |
|---|---|
| Olimpia | Adelaide Basseggio sop. |
| Elena | Carlina Benedetti mez. |
| Casimiro | Raffaele Mirate ten. |
| Messer Giordano | Luigi Merly bar. |
| Fiordalisa | Luigia Morselli sop. |
| Ansaldo | Giovanni Gambelli ten. |
| Messo | Cesare Bortolotti ten. |
| Duca di Trani | Antonio Dolcibene bass |
| | |
| Conductor | Giuseppe Manelli |
| Director | Emanuele Muzio |

OTTO NICOLAI

1. ENRICO II-*Melodramma serio* in two acts
Trieste-Teatro Grande-Nov. 26, 1839
Libretto by Felice Romani

| | |
|---|---|
| Rosmonda Clifford | Adele Dabedeilhe sop. |
| Leonora di Guienna | Carolina Ungher sop. |
| Enrico II | Napoleone Moriani ten. |
| Clifford | Domenico Cosselli bass |
| Berta | Teresa Strinasacchi sop. |
| Arturo | Giuseppe Torri bar. |
| | |
| Conductor | Alessandro Scaramelli |
| Director | Luigi Ricci and Otto Nicolai |

2. IL TEMPLARIO-*Melodramma serio* in three acts
Turin-Teatro Regio-Feb. 11, 1840
Libretto by Girolamo Maria Marini

| | |
|---|---|
| Rebecca (R.) | Antonietta Rainieri Marini sop. |
| Rowena (Ro.) | Luigia Abbaddia mez. |
| Vilfredo d'Ivanhoe (I.) | Lorenzo Salvi ten. |
| Briano di Bois-Guilbert (B.) | Carlo Badiali bar. |
| Cedrico (C.) | Pio Botticelli bass |
| Luca di Beaumanoir | Eutemio Polonini bass |
| Isacco di York | Achille Bassi ten. |
| Emma | Angela Villa mez. |
| Gualtiero | Antonio Bruni ten. |

OTHER PRODUCTIONS

ARGENTINA
Buenos Aires   Victoria     Sep. 25, 1851 I. Edelvira (R.)

AUSTRIA
Vienna         Kärntnertor May  31, 1841 E. Tadolini (R.) L. Abbadia (Ro.) N.
                                         Moriani (I.) C. Badiali (B.) D. Co-
                                         letti (C.) (in It.)

                            Dec. 20, 1845 W. von Hasseldt-Barth (R.) Hein
                                         (Ro.) J. Erl (I.) E. Leithner (B.)
                                         C. Formes (C.) O. Nicolai cond. (in
                                         Ger.)

BELGIUM
Antverp        Royal        Apr.  1, 1861 Vibert (R.) Michel (Ro.) Koubly (I.)
                                         Peruggi (B.) Ticoulet (C.) (in Fr.)

Brussels       La Monnaie   Mar. 28, 1862 Elmire (R.) Bonnefoy (Ro.) Bertrand
                                         (I.) J. V. Ismael (B.) Périé (C.)
                                         (in Fr.)

BRAZIL
Rio de         Sao Pedro    Nov. 13, 1849 A. Candiani (R.) T. Benedetti (Ro.)
Janeiro                                   F. Tati (I.) F. Massiani (B.) C.
                                         Eckerlin (C.)

**CHILE**

| | | | |
|---|---|---|---|
| Santiago | Principal | July 23, 1850 | C. Pantanelli (R.) A. Pantanelli (Ro.) A. Zambaiti (I.) G. Bastoggi (B.) E. Lanza (C.) R. Pantanelli cond. |
| Valparaiso | Victoria | Feb. 11, 1851 | T. Rossi (R.) G. Ubaldi (Ro.) G. Bastoggi (B.) F. Leonardi (C.) R. Pantanelli cond. |

**DENMARK**

| | | | |
|---|---|---|---|
| Copenhagen | Royal | Apr. 3, 1846 | T. Tavola (R.) F. Leon (Ro.) P. Rossi-Cicerchia (I.) C. Vajro (B.) V. Torre (C.) P. Sperati cond. |

**FRANCE**

| | | | |
|---|---|---|---|
| Bordeaux | Grand | Apr. 1864 | (in Fr.) |
| Nice | Regio | Jan. 21, 1854 | C. Sannazaro (R.) L. Pecis (Ro.) B. Danieli (I.) E. Winter (B.) G. B. Antonucci (C.) G. Bregozzo cond. |
| Paris | Italien | Jan. 28, 1868 | G. Krauss (R.) Simoni (Ro.) E. Nicolini (I.) F. Steller (B.) L. Agnesi (C.) J. Skoczdopole cond. |

**GERMANY**

| | | | |
|---|---|---|---|
| Berlin | Königstädt-liches | Sep. 15, 1844 | L. Schieroni-Nulli (R.) C. Remorini (Ro.) F. Borioni (I.) G. Ramonda (B.) G. Mitrovich (C.) |

**HUNGARY**

| | | | |
|---|---|---|---|
| Budapest | | June 30, 1842 | |

**ITALY[8]**

| | | | |
|---|---|---|---|
| Alessandria | Municipale | Autumn 1843 | T. Tavola (R.) G. Zoboli (I.) V. Meini (B.) R. Luchini (C.) |
| Ancona | Muse | Spring 1843 | R. Gabussi De Bassini (R.) G. Roppa (I.) S. Ronconi (B.) |
| Asti | Civico | June 1843 | G. Montuchielli (R.) Remorini (Ro.) A. Castellan (I.) G. B. Righini (B.) |
| Bergamo | Sociale | Dec. 26? 1841 | C. Griffini (R.) A. Scalese (Ro.) G. Zoboli (I.) O. Bonafous (B.) R. Scalese (C.) |
| Bologna | Comunale | Oct. 14, 1849 | E. Parepa Archibugi (R.) L. Morselli (Ro.) L. Stecchi-Bottardi (I.) R. Pizzigati (B.) L. Canedi (C.) G. Manetti cond. |
| Cagliari | Civico | Dec. 26? 1842 | Librandi (R.) C. Mugnai (I.) G. B. Righini (B.) |
| Como | Sociale | Aug. 1843 | M. Gazzaniga (R.) G. Fedor (I.) E. Luisia (B.) G. Catalano (C.) |

---

8. Other productions include Brescia in the summer of 1842, Casalmonferrato, Chiavari in autumn 1844, Chieti Sept. 25, 1843, Perugia in autumn 1863, possibly Pisa in 1848, Tortona in spring 1843 and Voghera.

| | | | | |
|---|---|---|---|---|
| Cremona | Concordia | Autumn | 1842 | G. Armenia (R.) L. Corradi (Ro.) F. Borioni (I.) A. De Bassini (B.) |
| | | Carn. | 1863-64 | P. Vaneri (R.) Eugedi (Ro.) P. Tagliazucchi (I.) V. Quintili-Leoni (B.) P. Milesi (C.) |
| Cuneo | Civico | Dec. 26, | 1842 | Corini (R.) Remorini (Ro.) Darexy (I.) Colla (B.) |
| Fiume | Civico | Apr. 27, | 1844 | T. Rusmini-Solera (R.) G. Lega (Ro.) C. Miraglia (I.) F. Dall'Asta (B.) S. Demi (C.) |
| Florence | Pergola | Nov.? | 1842 | R. Gabussi De Bassini (R.) E. Buccini (Ro.) N. Ivanoff (B.) S. Ronconi (C.) |
| Forli | Comunale | May 31, | 1843 | R. Gabussi De Bassini (R.) G. Roppa (I.) S. Ronconi (B.) I. Patriossi (C.) |
| Genoa | Carlo Felice | Apr. 20, | 1840 | A. Rainieri-Marini (R.) M. Spinach (Ro.) L. Salvi (I.) V. Negrini (B.) F. Leonardi (C.) G. Serra cond. |
| | | Dec. 26, | 1844 | C. Gramaglia (R.) A. Moltini (Ro.) C. Guasco/G. Gamboggi (I.) N. Costantini (B.) F. Bozzano (C.) G. Serra cond. |
| | | Feb. 8, | 1859 | A. Angiolini (R.) T. Bellocchio (Ro.) A. Agresti (I.) R. Pizzigati (B.) H. von Rokitansky (C.) A. Mariani cond. |
| Livorno | Floridi | Nov. 5, | 1844 | A. Rainieri-Marini (R.) R. Mirate (I.) G. Zucchini (B.) |
| | Avvalorati | Feb. 1, | 1879 | E. Tati (R.) A. Brunetti (I.) I. De Anna (B.) |
| Lugo | Rossini | Sep. 7, | 1844 | A. Rainieri-Marini (R.) R. Mirate (I.) E. Crivelli (B.) L. Tabellini (C.) |
| Mantua | Sociale | Carn. | 1841-42 | A. Moltini (R.) C. Miraglia (I.) L. Valli (B.) A. Benciolini (C.) |
| Messina | Munizione | Oct. | 1842 | A. Dabeldeilhe (R.) A. Rebussini (Ro.) G. B. Bertolasi (I.) E. Luisia (B.) C. Poggiali (C.) |
| Milan | La Scala | Aug. 13, | 1840 | A. Rainieri-Marini (R.) L. Abbadia (Ro.) L. Salvi (I.) R. Ferlotti (B.) R. Scalese (C.) E. Cavallini cond. |
| | | Feb. 5, | 1866 | C. Dory (R.) M. Bouché (Ro.) A. Corsi (I.) C. Santley (B.) E. Bagagiolo (C.) |
| | Carcano | May 12? | 1855 | C. Viale (R.) A. Heller (Ro.) G. Ghislanzoni (I.) A. Ghislanzoni (B.) |

Modena      Comunale    Dec. 26, 1847 M. Gresti (R.) V. Vaccari (Ro.) G.
                                      Gamboggi (I.) G. Zucchini (B.) G.
                                      Lodi (C.) A. Sighicelli cond.

Naples      San Carlo   Sep. 26, 1843 F. Goldberg (R.) C. Gruitz (Ro.) E.
                                      Tamberlick (I.) F. Coletti (B.) M.
                                      Arati (C.) A. Farelli cond.

Padua       Nuovo       July 10, 1842 L. Abbadia (R.) L. Salvi (I.) A. De
                                      Bassini (B.)

Palermo     Carolino    Oct.  4, 1844 L. Abbadia (R.) M. Tizzoni (Ro.) G.
                                      B. Milesi (I.) R. Ferlotti (B.) G.
                                      Catalano (C.) P. Raimondi cond.

Parma       Regio       Feb.  1, 1843 E. Hallez (R.) M. Albizzati (Ro.) G.
                                      Baldanza (I.) L. Valli (B.) C. Fer-
                                      dighini (C.) N. De Giovanni cond.

Pavia       Civico      Apr.     1842 G. Olivieri (I.)

Piacenza    Municipale  Dec. 26? 1841 E. Boldrini (R.) I. Pasini (I.) C.
                                      Capitini (B.) G. Jona cond.

                        Feb.?    1851 I. Secci-Corsi (R.) G. Comolli (I.)
                                      C. Bartolucci (B.) F. Rigo (C.) G.
                                      Jona cond.

Ravenna     Comuni-     May   6, 1843 E. D'Alberti (R.) T. Cresci (Ro.) G.
            tativo                    Pancani (I.) F. Cresci (B.) G. Gus-
                                      cetti (C.) G. Nostini cond.

Rovigo      Sociale     Jan. 16, 1855 M. Winter (R.) P. Scotti (I.) O.
                                      Winter (B.) C. Rossi Martinenghi
                                      (C.) D. Tosarini cond.

Sassari     Civico      Nov.     1845 E. Rossi-Guerra (I.) Battaglini (B.)

Treviso     Onigo       Oct. 15, 1842 E. D'Alberti (R.) G. B. Genero (I.)

Trieste     Grande      Sep. 19, 1840 R. Gabussi de Bassini (R.) N. Mori-
                                      ani (I.) S. Ronconi (B.) S. Panzini
                                      (C.) A. Scaramelli cond.

                        Mar. 11, 1843 L. Abbadia (R.) L. Salvi (I.) R.
                                      Ferlotti (B.) A. Scaramelli cond.

Venice      La Fenice   Dec. 25, 1840 D. Dérancourt (R.) F. Olivier (Ro.)
                                      N. Ivanoff (I.) G. Ronconi (B.) R.
                                      D'Anconi (C.)

Verona      Filarmonico Dec. 26, 1841 R. Gabussi de Bassini (R.) F. Salvi-
                                      ni-Donatelli (Ro.) C. Guasco (I.) A.
                                      Superchi (B.) G. Donatelli (C.)

            Nuovo       Apr. 13, 1850 L. Ponti dall'Armi (R.) E. Berini
                                      (Ro.) T. Palmieri (I.) C. Bartolucci
                                      (B.)

Vicenza     Eretenio    July 22, 1841 R. Gabussi De Bassini (R.) I. Pasini
                                      (I.) O. Cartagenova (B.)

JUGOSLAVIA
Zara            Nobile      Apr. 30, 1842 E. Ranzi (R.) A. Tantalora (Ro.) F.
                                          Personi (I.) G. C. Casanova (B.) F.
                                          Lodetti (C.) L. Garbato cond.

MEXICO
Mexico City     Opera       Apr. 15, 1842

PORTUGAL
Lisbon          Sao Carlos  May  18, 1842 L. Perelli (R.) V. Fasciotti (Ro.)
                                          G. Confortini (I.) N. Constantini
                                          (B.) C. Eckerlin (C.)

ROMANIA
Bucharest       National    Jan.?    1848 C. Griffini (R.) G. B. Montresor
                                          (I.) D. Marchelli (B.) P. Tozzoli
                                          (C.)

RUSSIA
Odessa          Municipal       1850-51

                            Sep. 24, 1851 C. Rambur (R.) G. Brambilla (Ro.) E.
                                          Naudin (I.) S. Ronconi (B.) A. Ber-
                                          lendis (C.)

St.             Imperial    Dec. 29, 1845 P. Viardot (R.) A. Moltini (Ro.) L.
 Petersburg                               Salvi (I.) L. Walter (B.) Petroff
                                          (C.) E. Baveri cond.

                            Nov.  4, 1846 L. Salvi (I.) E. Tamburini (B.) E.
                                          Baveri cond.

SPAIN
Barcelona       Principal   June  8, 1841 M. Palazzesi (R.) R. Gariboldi-Bassi
                                          (Ro.) C. Lonati (I.) A. Alba (B.) P.
                                          Novelli (C.)

                            Aug. 19, 1847 A. Rainieri-Marini (R.) E. Tamber-
                                          lick (I.) E. Barili (B.)

Cadiz           Principal   Feb.?    1847 C. Bertolini-Raffaelli (R.) G. Con-
                                          fortini (I.) V. Sermattei (B.) C. O.
                                          Porto (C.)

Cordoba                     Sep.?    1842 A. Planiol (Ro.)

Granada                     Oct. 31, 1842 C. Di Franco (R.) P. Unanue (I.) J.
                                          Calonge (B.)

Madrid          de la Cruz  Nov. 11, 1841 A. Perelli (R.) Lombia (Ro.) P. Una-
                                          nue (I.) G. Miral (B.)

                            Oct.  5, 1845 C. Bertolini-Raffaelli (R.) J. Chi-
                                          meno (Ro.) R. Mirate (I.) G. Ferri
                                          (B.) G. Becerra (C.)

Malaga          Principal   Apr. 14, 1842 Ceremoli (R.) L. Bonfigli (I.) E.
                                          Crivelli (B.)

Palma de        Comedias    Summer   1844 A. Aguilò (R.) G. B. Bertolasi (I.)
 Mallorca                                 G. Bastoggi (B.)

Seville        San          Dec.  1, 1841  C. Barili-Patti  (R.)  Planiol (Ro.)
               Fernando                     G. Confortini  (I.)  E.  Spech  (B.)
                                            Santarelli (C.)

Zaragozza      Principal    Dec. 14, 1842  Ceremoli  (R.)  A.  Planiol  (Ro.)  L.
                                           Aparicio  (I.)  E.  Crivelli  (B.)  P.
                                           Rodda (C.)

URUGUAY
Montevideo     San Felipe   Apr. 13, 1853  R. Olivieri  (R.)  C.  Lanzani (Ro.)  G.
                                           Dordoni  (I.)  E.  Luisia (B.)  P. Figa-
                                           ri (C.)

3. GILDIPPE E ODOARDO-*Melodramma* in three acts
Genoa-Teatro Carlo Felice-Dec. 26, 1840
Libretto by Temistocle Solera

Gildippe                                Antonietta Rainieri-Marini sop.
Odoardo                                         Catone Lonati ten.
Guido, Signor di Lara                       Raffaele Ferlotti bar.
Idelfonso                                    Annibale Statuti bass
Elvira                                Teresa Gramostini-Saetti sec.

Conductor                                         Giovanni Serra

4. IL PROSCRITTO-*Melodramma tragico* in three acts
Milan-Teatro alla Scala-Mar. 13, 1841
Libretto by Gaetano Rossi

Leonora (L.)                               Erminia Frezzolini sop.
Arturo, Conte di Norton (A.)               Domenico Donzelli ten.
Giorgio (G.)                                Andrea Castellan ten.
Edemondo di Salisbury (E.)                    Filippo Coletti bass
Irene                                  Felicità De Baillou Hilaret sop.
Riccardo di Somerset                          Gaetano Rossi bass
Williams                                   Napoleone Marconi ten.

Conductor                                      Eugenio Cavallini

OTHER PRODUCTIONS

AUSTRIA
Vienna         Kärntnertor  Feb.  3, 1844  W. von Hasseldt-Barth (L.)  J.  Erl
                                           (A.)  J.  Pfister (G.)  J.  Staudigl
                                           (E.)  O. Nicolai cond. (in Ger.)

               Oct.  9, 1857  L. Dustmann-Meyer (L.)  Meyer (A.)  G.
                                           Walther  (G.)  C.  Schmid  (E.)  (in
                                           Ger.)

GERMANY
Berlin         Hofoper      Nov. 19, 1849 (in Ger.)

GIOVANNI PACINI

1. FURIO CAMILLO-*Melodramma tragico* in three acts
Rome-Teatro di Apollo-Dec. 26, 1839
Libretto by Giacomo Ferretti

Emilia   (E.)
Camillo  (C.)                                    Carolina Ungher sop.
Lucio    (L.)                                    Domenico Donzelli ten.
Brenno   (B.)                                    Luciano Fornasari bar.
Valeria                                          Cleto Capitini bass
Manlio                                           Adelaide Gualdi mez.
Ponzio                                           Gaetano Coccetti bass
                                                 Pietro Gasperini ten.

Conductor                                        Cesare Ferrarini
Director                               Luigi Orsini and Giovanni Pacini

OTHER PRODUCTIONS

ITALY
Naples        San Carlo    Feb. 16, 1841  F. Maray (E.) D. Reina (C.) P. Gian-
                                          ni (L.) G. Benedetti (B.) A. Farelli
                                          cond.


2. SAFFO-*Tragedia lirica* in three parts
Naples-Teatro San Carlo-Nov. 29, 1840
Libretto by Salvadore Cammarano[9]

Saffo    (S.)
Climene  (C.)                                    Francilla Pixis sop.
Faone    (F.)                                    Eloisa Buccini sop.
Alcandro (A.)                                    Gaetano Fraschini ten.
Dirce                                            Orazio Cartagenova bar.
Ippia                                            Anna Salvetti sop.
Lisimacco                                        Teofilo Rossi ten.
                                                 Giuseppe Benedetti bass

Conductor                                        Antonio Farelli
Director                                         Giovanni Pacini

OTHER PREMIERES

ARGENTINA
Buenos Aires  Argentino   Sep. 15, 1854  I.  Edelvira (S.) G.  Tati (C.) L.
                                         Guglielmini (F.) G. C. Casanova (A.)
                                         J. V. Rivas cond.

              Ant. Colón  Aug. 11, 1857  E.  La Grua (S.) A.  Fusoni (C.) G.
                                         Ubaldi (F.) G. C. Casanova (A.) C.
                                         Castagneri cond.

---

[9]. Although it has been generally neglected in the past decade (only three revivals in the 1980s), *Saffo* was one of the most successful operas of the mid-nineteenth century. This popularity did not manifest itself in northern Europe. The opera had only one production each in London (in English!) and Berlin, two each in Paris and Vienna, and four in St. Petersburg and was apparently never given in Sweden. Its performance history in Meditteranean countries outside Italy is a totally different matter. Thus it had some 20 productions in Barcelona, 15 in Madrid, 13 in Lisbon and at least 10 in Seville.

AUSTRALIA
Adelaide        Th. Royal     Mar. 22, 1872 M. Zenoni (S.) E. Polli (C.) F.
                                            Rosnati (F.) F. Coliva (A.) A. Mar-
                                            zorati cond.

Melbourne       Princess      July 12, 1871 M. Zenoni (S.) E. Polli (C.) F.
                                            Rosnati (F.) F. Coliva (A.) A. Mar-
                                            zorati cond.

Sydney          Prince        Sep. 19, 1871 M. Zenoni (S.) E. Polli (C.) F.
                of Wales                    Rosnati (F.) F. Coliva (A.) A. Mar-
                                            zorati cond.

AUSTRIA
Vienna          Kärntnertor   June  2, 1842 A. Rainieri-Marini (S.) M. Brambilla
                                            (C.) A. Castellan (F.) C. Badiali
                                            (A.) H. Proch cond.

BRAZIL
Rio de          Sao Pedro     Oct.  4, 1845 A. Candiani (C.) M. Deperini (C.) A.
Janeiro                                     Graziani (F.) A. Fiorito (A.) J. V.
                                            Rivas cond.

CHILE
Santiago        Republica     Aug.  3, 1852 T. Rossi (S.) A. Pantanelli (C.) G.
                                            Bastoggi (A.)

Valparaiso      Victoria      Mar. 28, 1854 T. Rossi (S.) A. Pantanelli (C.) L.
                                            Cavedagni (F.) G. Bastoggi (A.)

CUBA
Havana          Tacon         Dec. 22, 1846 F. Tedesco (S.) S. Marini (C.) L.
                                            Arditi cond.

DENMARK
Copenhagen      Royal         Nov.  3, 1844 D. Dérancourt (S.) I. Bertrand (C.)
                                            G. Baldanza (F.) N. Torre (A.) P.
                                            Sperati cond.

FRANCE
Nice            Regio         Mar.     1854 C. Sannazaro (S.) L. Pecis (C.) B.
                                            Danieli (F.) E. Winter (A.)

Paris           Italien       Mar. 15, 1842 G. Grisi (S.) E. Albertazzi (C.)
                                            Mario (F.) A. Tamburini (A.) T. Til-
                                            mant cond.

GERMANY
Berlin          Königstädt-   Mar. 22, 1845 L. Schieroni-Nulli (S.) E. Bendini
                liches                      (C.) G. Landi (F.) G. Mitrovich (A.)

GREAT BRITAIN
London          Drury Lane    Apr.  1, 1843 C. Novello (S.) M. Shaw (C.) Allen
                                            (F.) Phillips (A.) (in Eng.)

GREECE
Athens          Royal         Feb.?    1851 E. Bruni (S.)

Corfu           San Giacomo Sep. 30, 1843 C. Cuzzani (S.) C. Costa (C.) M.
                                            Forti (F.) L. Pellegrini (A.)

INDIA
Calcutta      Opera House  Feb. 22, 1875 R. Genolini (S.) De Dominicis (C.)
                                         L. Gallo (F.) F. Trapani-Buono (A.)
                                         W. Mack cond.

ITALY
Alessandria   Civico       Nov.?    1843 T. Tavola (S.) R. Lucchini (C.) G.
                                         Zoboli (F.) V. Meini (A.)

Ancona        Muse         Apr. 19, 1843 R. Gabussi De Bassini (S.) E. Buc-
                                         cini (C.) G. Roppa (F.) S. Ronconi
                                         (A.)

Ascoli        Ventidio     Nov.  3? 1873 G. Galassi (S.) Tamanti (C.) A. Ma-
Piceno        Basso                      rubini (F.) A. Faentini-Galassi (A.)

Bergamo       Sociale      Dec. 26? 1842 E. D'Alberti (S.) A. Tantalora (C.)
                                         A. Paterni (F.) G. Giordani (A.)

              Riccardi     Aug.?    1868 G. Borsi de Leurie (S.) C. De Ros-
                                         selli (C.) E. Ronconi (F.) G. Della
                                         Baratta cond.

Bologna       Comunale     Oct.  3, 1842 E. Hallez (S.) M. Alboni (C.) G.
                                         Roppa (F.) P. Balzar (A.) G. Manetti
                                         cond.

Brescia       Grande       Dec. 26, 1844 F. Tedesco (S.) T. Fasciotti (C.) C.
                                         Della Longa (F.) A. Alba (A.)

Cagliari      Civico       Dec. 26, 1846 E. Dielitz (S.) C. Vietti (C.) C.
                                         Scola (F.) R. Pizzigati (A.)

Catania       Comunale     Mar.     1846 F. Maray (S.) C. Martelli (C.) E.
                                         Marcucci (F.) P. Bartolini (A.) M.
                                         Pappalardo cond.

Chieti        San          May  28, 1842 A. Fanti (S.) D. Santolini (C.) G.
              Fernando                   Costantini (F.)

Cremona       Concordia    Dec. 26, 1844 M. Corridori (S.) A. Pardini (C.) E.
                                         Naudin (F.) E. Luisia (A.)

Fermo         Aquila       Aug. 14, 1842 C. Novello (S.) D. Santolini (C.) G.
                                         B. Genero (F.) G. Zucchini (A.) G.
                                         C. Ferrarini cond.

Ferrara       Comunale     Apr.  2, 1842 R. Gabussi De Bassini (S.) R. Luc-
                                         chini (C.) L. Bonfigli (F.) P. Bot-
                                         ticelli (A.)

Fiume         Civico       Apr.  2, 1850 L. Ruggero-Antonioli (S.) A. Ruggero
                                         (C.) L. Guglielmini (F.) G. Sacconi
                                         (A.)

Florence      Pergola      Apr. 17, 1842 T. Brambilla (S.) E. Buccini (C.) G.
                                         Roppa (F.) D. Cosselli (A.) A. Biagi
                                         cond.

Forli         Comunale     Apr.?    1843 R. Gabussi De Bassini (S.) E. Bucci-
                                         ni (C.) G. Roppa (F.) S. Ronconi
                                         (A.)

| | | | |
|---|---|---|---|
| Genoa | Carlo Felice | Jan. 29, 1842 | G. Strepponi (S.) C. Imoda (C.) N. Ivanoff (F.) N. Costantini (A.) G. Serra cond. |
| Livorno | Rossini | Feb. 1843 | C. Bertolini-Raffaelli (S.) E. Buccini (C.) G. Zoboli (F.) M. Alberti (A.) |
| Lucca | Giglio | Sep. 21, 1842 | R. Gabussi De Bassini (S.) E. Buccini (C.) N. Ivanoff (F.) S. Ronconi (A.) |
| Lugo | Rossini | Aug. 1842 | D. Dérancourt (S.) I. Bertrand (C.) G. Baldanza (F.) C. Capitini (A.) |
| Mantua | Sociale | Carn. 1842-43 | G. Bortolotti (S.) D. Santolini (C.) A. Deval (F.) D. Cosselli (A.) |
| Messina | Munizione | Oct. 24, 1841 | A. Tramontani (S.) L. De Baillou (C.) A. Pompejano (F.) G. De Baillou (A.) |
| Milan | La Scala | Jan. 6, 1842 | L. Abbadia (S.) M. Brambilla (C.) L. Salvi (F.) F. Varesi (A.) E. Cavallini cond. |
| Modena | Comunale | Feb. 13, 1847 | E. Scotta (S.) A. Borghi-Mamo (C.) G. Baldanza (F.) A. Morelli (A.) A. Sighicelli cond. |
| Padua | Nuovissimo | Spring 1842 | E. Parepa-Archibugi (S.) C. Costa (C.) G. Baldanza (F.) L. Caliari (A.) |
| | Nuovo | July 11, 1847 | G. Medori (S.) D. Santolini (C.) D. Labocetta (F.) P. Dérivis (A.) |
| Palermo | Carolino | Mar. 3, 1842 | R. Gabussi De Bassini (S.) F. Borioni (F.) A. De Bassini (A.) P. Raimondi cond. |
| Parma | Regio | Dec. 26, 1842 | E. Hallez (S.) R. Lucchini (C.) G. Baldanza (F.) L. Valli (A.) N. De Giovanni cond. |
| Piacenza | Municipale | Spring 1842 | E. D'Alberti (S.) M. Azon (C.) F. Pedrazzi (F.) L. Valli (A.) G. Jona cond. |
| Pisa | Ravvivati | Dec. 26, 1843 | T. Brambilla (S.) E. Buccini (C.) A. Castellan (F.) L. Salandri (A.) |
| Ravenna | Comunitativo | May 21, 1842 | G. Bortolotti (S.) T. Paradisi (C.) L. Biacchi (F.) V. Sermattei (A.) |
| Reggio Emilia | Comunale | May 24, 1842 | S. Schoberlechner (S.) I. Bertrand (C.) F. Regoli (F.) A. Superchi (A.) L. Boyer cond. |
| Rome | Valle | Nov. 20, 1841 | M. Albini (S.) M. Taglioni (C.) E. Marcucci (F.) P. Balzar (A.) |
| | Apollo | Jan. 27, 1842 | F. Maray (S.) D. Santolini (C.) A. Poggi (F.) C. Badiali (A.) |

| Siena | Rinnovati | July 16, 1843 | C. Bertolini-Raffaelli (S.) E. Buccini (C.) L. Corelli (F.) L. Salandri (A.) |
|---|---|---|---|
| Sinigaglia | La Fenice | Aug.      1855 | R. Donzelli (S.) G. Brambilla-Marulli (C.) L. Stefani (F.) G. Fiori (A.) F. Bianchi cond. |
| Spoleto | Nobile | Dec. 26? 1846 | S. Zudoli (S.) C. Croci (C.) C. Mancini (F.) G. Staffolini (A.) |
| Trento | Sociale | June 11, 1844 | E. D'Alberti (S.) L. Viale (C.) A. Balestracci (F.) E. Santi (A.) |
| Treviso | Onigo | Nov. 6, 1842 | E. D'Alberti (S.) G. B. Genero (F.) O. Bonafous (A.) |
| Trieste | Grande | Sep. 11, 1841 | D. Dérancourt (S.) M. Shaw (C.) L. Salvi (F.) C. Badiali (A.) A. Scaramelli cond. |
| Turin | Regio | Mar. 29, 1842 | D. Dérancourt (S.) M. Shaw (C.) L. Salvi (F.) F. Colini (A.) |
| Venice | La Fenice | Dec. 26, 1841 | F. Goldberg (S.) I. Bertrand (C.) A. Deval (F.) F. Coletti (A.) |
| Verona | Filarmonico | Jan.?    1842 | R. Gabussi De Bassini (S.) A. Poppi (C.) C. Guasco (F.) A. Superchi (A.) |
| Vicenza | Eretenio | Aug. 19, 1841 | R. Gabussi De Bassini (S.) R. Lucchini (C.) I. Pasini (F.) O. Cargenova (A.) |
| JUGOSLAVIA Zara | Nobile | Jan. 25, 1845 | G. Sarasin (S.) E. Malvasi (C.) A. Cosma (F.) P. Botticelli (A.) |
| MALTA La Valletta | Manoel | Nov.?    1848 | A. Borghi-Mamo (C.) (First production traced) |
| MEXICO Mexico City | Nacional | Dec. 8, 1857 | A. Cortesi (S.) E. Tomassi (C.) L. Stefani (F.) A. Ottaviani (A.) C. Fattori cond.[10] |
| NETHERLANDS Amsterdam | Italien | Nov. 13, 1843 | E. Boldrini (S.) L. Mascheroni (C.) A. Brunacci (F.) G. Corsi (A.) C. Pedrotti cond. |
| NEW ZEALAND Auckland | Prince of Wales | Nov. 23, 1871 | M. Zenoni (S.) E. Polli (C.) F. Rosnati (F.) F. Coliva (A.) A. Marzorati cond. |
| Dunedin | Princess | Jan. 29, 1872 | M. Zenoni (S.) E. Polli (C.) F. Rosnati (F.) F. Coliva (A.) G. Bartolometti cond. |

---

10. The company toured Mexico during 1858, and is known to have presented *Saffo* in Vera Cruz, Guanajato and Guadalajara that year.

POLAND
Warsaw          Wielki        Jan. 18, 1870 C. Marchisio (S.) B. Marchisio (C.)
                                           T. De Azula (F.) G. Rota (A.)

PORTUGAL
Lisbon          Sao Carlos    Mar. 23, 1843 E. Boldrini (S.) V. Fasciotti (C.)
                                           L. Ferretti (F.) N. Costantini (A.)

Oporto          Sao Joao      May  27, 1845 F. Rocca-Alessandri (S.) A. Campos
                                           (C.) G. Confortini (F.) L. Montemer-
                                           li (A.)

PUERTO RICO
San Juan        Municipal     Mar. 31, 1887 M. Bulli-Paoli (S.) G. Tiozzo (C.)
                                           F. Migliori (F.) F. Cavazza (A.) G.
                                           Lorini cond.

ROMANIA
Bucharest       Nacional      Nov. 25, 1850 R. Olivieri (S.) A. Corbari (C.) E.
                                           Rossi-Guerra (F.) G. Marini (A.)

RUSSIA
Kharkov         Municipal     Spring   1869 L. Ponti dall'Armi (S.) G. Giotti
                                           (A.)

Kiev            Imperial      Feb. 13, 1886 E. Dotti (S.) Cavalleri (C.) V. Bac-
                                           ci (F.) G. Pimazzoni (A.)

Moscow          Bolshoi       Sep. 30, 1869 C. Marchisio (S.) B. Marchisio (C.)
                                           E. Carrion (F.) G. Rota (A.)

Odessa          Municipal     Spring   1844 I. Secci-Corsi (S.) Z. Sbriscia (C.)
                                           R. Vitali (F.) G. Marini (A.)

St.             Imperial      Nov. 18, 1854 F. Tedesco (S.) M. Bourdet (C.) E.
 Petersburg                                Tamberlick (F.) A. De Bassini (A.)
                                           E. Baveri cond.

SPAIN
Barcelona       Principal     Nov. 14, 1842 G. Brambilla (S.) R. Gariboldi-Bassi
                                           (C.) J. Gomez (F.) I. Marini (A.)

                Liceo         May  26, 1849 C. Gruitz (S.) C. Más-Porcell (C.)
                                           G. Fedor (F.) A. Rodas (A.)

Cadiz           Principal     Summer   1843

Madrid          Circo         Aug.  9, 1842 R. Basso-Borio (S.) L. De Bezzi (F.)
                                           R. Anconi (A.)

                Real          Feb. 12, 1853 C. Novello (S.) E. d'Angri (C.) G.
                                           Roppa (F.) F. Coletti (A.) J. Skocz-
                                           dopole cond.

Seville                       Autumn   1843

Valencia        Principal     Spring   1844 Mugnoz (S.)

Valladolid      Calderon      Mar. 17, 1844 C. Más-Porcell (S.) A. Aguilò (C.)
                                           F. Porcell (F.) G. Gerli (A.)

Zaragozza       Principal     Nov. 21, 1844 C. Más-Porcell (S.) A. Aguilò (C.)
                                           F. Porcell (F.) G. Gerli (A.)

| | | | |
|---|---|---|---|
| **TURKEY** | | | |
| Constan-<br>tinople | Naum | Apr. 21, 1846 | E. Cominotti (S.)  C. Morandi  (C.)<br>Lanzoni (F.) A. Avignone (A.) |
| **UNITED STATES** | | | |
| Boston | Atheneum | May  4, 1847 | F. Tedesco (S.)  S. Marini  (C.) L.<br>Perozzi (F.) L. Battaglini (A.) L.<br>Arditi cond. |
| Chicago | Crosby's | Nov. 27, 1865 | M. Gazzaniga (S.) R.  Cash-Pollini<br>(C.) G. Musiani (F.) F. Brandini<br>(A.) |
| Cincinnati | Mozart Hall | Jan.  2, 1866 | M. Gazzaniga (S.) R.  Cash-Pollini<br>(C.) G. Musiani (F.) F. Brandini<br>(A.) |
| Louisville | Theatre | Dec. 26, 1865 | M. Gazzaniga (S.) R.  Cash-Pollini<br>(C.) G. Musiani (F.) |
| New York | Park | June 14, 1847 | F. Tedesco (S.)  S. Marini  (C.) L.<br>Perozzi (F.) L. Battaglini (A.) L.<br>Arditi cond. |
| | Ac. of Mus. | June 21, 1858 | M. Gazzaniga (S.) A. Phillips (C.)<br>P. Brignoli (F.) L. Gassier (A.) |
| Philadelphia | Walnut St. | July 12, 1847 | F. Tedesco (S.)  S. Marini  (C.) L.<br>Perozzi (F.) L. Battaglini (A.) L.<br>Arditi cond. |
| | Ac. of Mus. | Dec. 15, 1859 | M. Gazzaniga (S.) A. Patti-Strakosch<br>(C.) P. Brignoli (F.) G. Ferri (A.) |
| St. Louis | De Bar's | Dec. 16, 1865 | M. Gazzaniga (S.) R.  Cash-Pollini<br>(C.) G. Musiani (F.) F. Brandini<br>(A.) |
| **URUGUAY** | | | |
| Montevideo | San Felipe | June 25, 1854 | R. Olivieri (S.) C. Canonero (C.) E.<br>Rossi-Guerra (F.) E. Luisia (A.) |
| | Solis | Sep. 14, 1857 | E. La Grua (S.) A. Casaloni (C.) G.<br>Ubaldi (F.) G. Cima (A.) |

SELECTED REVIVALS-NINETEENTH CENTURY

| | | | |
|---|---|---|---|
| **AUSTRIA** | | | |
| Vienna | Kärntnertor | May 28, 1864 | C. Barbot (S.) D. Artôt (C.) G.<br>Pardini (F.) L. Saccomanno (A.) |
| **FRANCE** | | | |
| Nice | Cercle Med. | Autumn  1881 | A. Urban (S.) M. Mei-Figner (C.) E.<br>Vanden (A.) |
| Paris | Italien | Nov. 28, 1866 | E. La Grua (S.) F. Llanes (C.) E.<br>Nicolini (F.) F. Cresci (A.) J.<br>Scozdopole cond. |
| **ITALY** | | | |
| Milan | La Scala | Oct. 29, 1844 | R. Gabussi De Bassini (S.) E. D'An-<br>gri (C.) C. Guasco (F.) A. Alba (A.)<br>E. Cavallini cond. |

Feb. 20, 1878 A. Urban (S.) G. Faentini-Galassi/C.
Ferni (C.) G. Sani (F.) A. Faentini-
Galassi/Z. Bertolasi (A.)

Naples      San Carlo   Oct. 30, 1841 E. Hallez (S.) E. Buccini/M. Taglioni (C.) G. Fraschini (F.) P. Bar-
roilhet (A.) A. Farelli cond.

Aug.  7, 1842 A. Rainieri-Marini (S.) M. Taglioni
(C.) G. Fraschini (F.) F. Coletti
(A.) A. Farelli cond.

June 11, 1843 F. Goldberg (S.) M. Taglioni (C.) G.
Fraschini (F.) F. Coletti (A.) A.
Farelli cond.

July 12, 1845 Lebrun (S.) E. Buccini (C.) G. Fraschini (F.) F. Coletti/G. de Baillou
(A.) A. Farelli cond.

Oct. 21, 1849 M. Gazzaniga (S.) L. Salandri (C.)
S. Malvezzi (F.) F. Varesi (A.)

Nov. 12, 1851 A. Cortesi (S.) A. Borghi-Mamo (C.)
G. Roppa (F.) A. De Bassini (A.) A.
Farelli cond.

Dec. 15, 1852 S. Peruzzi (S.) A. Borghi-Mamo (C.)
E. Pancani (F.) F. Monari (A.) A.
Farelli cond.

Dec. 25, 1855 G. Beltramelli (S.) E. Paganini (C.)
L. Stefani (F.) A. Morelli (A.) A.
Farelli cond.

July 25, 1860 S. Vera-Lorini (S.) C. Dory (C.) R.
Bertolini (F.) A. Capurro (A.) A.
Farelli cond.

Mar. 20, 1861 M. Spezia-Aldighieri (S.) G. Tati
(C.) C. Lefranc (F.) G. Aldighieri
(A.)

Jan. 28, 1880 A. Urban (S.) A. Armandi (C.) E. Engel (F.) G. Aldighieri (A.) G. Dell'
Orefice cond.

Rome        Argentina   Sep. 28, 1846 L. Abbadia (S.) M. Alboni (C.) E.
Pancani (F.) L. Valli (A.)

Nov. 23, 1880 A. Urban (S.) T. Vigna (C.) G. Ferrari (F.) E. Pogliani (A.)

Apollo      Jan. 15, 1867 C. Marchisio (S.) B. Marchisio (C.)
F. Patierno (F.) A. Carboni (A.) E.
Angelini cond.

Turin       Regio       Mar.  4, 1871 M. Biancolini (S.) L. Corsi (C.) G.
Pardini (F.) A. Mazzoli (A.) C. Pe-
drotti cond.

PORTUGAL
Lisbon      Sao Carlos  Oct. 18, 1864 A. Borghi-Mamo (S.) G. Tati (C.) R.
Stagno (F.) D. Squarcia (A.)

Oct.  8, 1867  C. Marchisio (S.) B. Marchisio (C.)
               E. Naudin (F.) J. Petit (A.)

RUSSIA
St.            Imperial    Nov. 18, 1865  C. Barbot (S.)  C. Nantier-Didiée
Petersburg                                (C.) O. Tasca di Capello (F.) F.
                                          Graziani (A.)

                           Jan.  9, 1867  C. Barbot (S.)  C. Nantier-Didiée
                                          (C.) O. Tasca di Capello (F.) F.
                                          Graziani (A.)

                           Nov.  3, 1869  C. Marchisio (S.) B. Marchisio (C.)
                                          G. Capponi (F.) F. Steller (A.)

SPAIN
Barcelona      Liceo       Jan.     1860  C. Carozzi-Zucchi (S.) C. Dory (C.)
                                          T. Palmieri (F.) A. Rodas (A.)

                           Apr. 11, 1863  C. Barbot (S.) E. Grossi (C.) G. Mu-
                                          siani (F.) F. Graziani (A.)

                           Aug.     1863  A. Borghi-Mamo (S.) M. Mallknecht
                                          (C.) E. Irfrè (F.) G. Ferri (A.)

                           Oct.     1863  E. La Grua (S.) E. Grossi (C.) C.
                                          Fabbris (F.) F. Cresci (A.)

                           May  14, 1871  G. Demi (S.) A. Bianco (C.) C. Bul-
                                          terini (F.) A. Rodas (A.)

                           June  9, 1872  C. Ferni (S.) T. Ferni (C.) A. Aram-
                                          buro (F.) L. Giraldoni (A.)

                           Dec.     1872  C. Ferni (S.) T. Ferni (C.) G. Aram-
                                          buro (F.) L. Giraldoni (A.)

                           Apr.     1874  I. Galletti-Gianoli (S.) E. Treves
                                          (C.) Sigelli (F.) V. Quintili-Leoni
                                          (A.)

                           Nov.     1875  A. Urban (S.) F. Llanes (C.) F. Ta-
                                          magno (F.) G. Mendioroz (A.)

                           Mar.     1881  A. Urban (S.) G. Celega (C.) L.
                                          Abrugnedo (F.) L. Giraldoni (A.)

Cadiz          Principal   July     1870  C. Ferni (S.) E. Tamberlick (F.) L.
                                          Giraldoni (A.)

Madrid         Real        Nov.  2, 1887  E. Tetrazzini (S.) G. Fabbri (C.) L.
                                          Signoretti (F.) R. Blanchart (A.)

UNITED STATES
New York       Castle      Aug. 31, 1847  F. Tedesco (S.)  S. Marini (C.) L.
               Garden                     Perozzi (F.) L. Battaglini (A.) L.
                                          Arditi cond.

                           Aug. 24, 1850  F. Tedesco (S.) C. Vietti (C.) D.
                                          Lorini (F.) L. Vita (A.) L. Arditi
                                          cond.

               Ac. of Mus. June  3, 1859  A. Cortesi (S.) A. Patti-Strakosch
                                          (C.) P. Brignoli (F.)

Feb. 17, 1860 M. Gazzaniga (S.) A. Patti-Strakosch (C.) P. Brignoli (F.)

May 11, 1866 M. Gazzaniga (S.) R. Cash-Pollini
(C.) G. Musiani (A.)

OTHER PRODUCTIONS-1900-1945

ITALY
Catania      Del Popolo  Aug. 30, 1939 M. Carbone (S.) I. Colasanti (C.) F.
Tasso (F.) G. Inghilleri (A.) A.
Votto cond.

Florence     Politeama   Apr.     1911 H. Darclée (S.) F. Anitua (C.) A.
Scampini (F.) G. Bellantoni (A.)

Milan        La Scala    Jan. 20, 1911 E. Burzio (S.) F. Anitua (C.) A.
Scampini (F.) G. Bellantoni (A.) T.
Serafin cond.

Palermo      Biondo      Dec. 2, 1909 A. Alloro (S.) E. Gherlinzoni (F.)
M. Aineto (A.) G. Abbate cond.

Rome         Costanzi    Oct. 28, 1911 H. Darclée (S.) F. Anitua (C.) F.
Castellani (F.) G. Bellantoni (A.)
E. Tango cond.

OTHER PRODUCTIONS-POST-WORLD WAR II

ITALY
Catania      Bellini     Feb. 24, 1983 A. Negri (S.) A. Parutto (C.) P.
Visconti (F.) G. Floresta (A.) C.
Franci cond.

Naples       San Carlo   Apr. 1, 1967 L. Gencer (S.) F. Mattiucci (C.) T.
Del Bianco (F.) L. Quilico (A.) F.
Capuana cond.

SPAIN
Barcelona    Liceo       June 21, 1987 M. Caballé (S.) P. Malakova (C.) A.
Ordonez (F.) E. Serra (A.) M. Ramin
cond.

UNITED STATES
New York     Town Hall   Feb. 7, 1982 L. Alba (S.) B. Berini (C.) L. Bartolini (F.) L. Quilico (A.) R. Kapp
cond.

3. L'UOMO DEL MISTERO-*Melodramma semiserio* in three parts
Naples-Teatro Nuovo-Nov. 9, 1841
Libretto by Domenico Andreotti

| | |
|---|---|
| Isabella (I.) | Giuseppina David sop. |
| Earclif (E.) | Adelaide Gambaro sop. |
| Mauley (M.) | Timoleone Barattini ten. |
| Tom (T.) | Raffaele Casaccia bar. |
| Langley (L.) | Luigi Fioravanti buf. |
| Ellieslaw (El.) | Giuseppe Lodi bass |
| Ratcliffe | Michele Tucci sec. |
| | |
| Conductor | Gaetano Coccia |
| Director | Giovanni Pacini |

OTHER PRODUCTIONS

ITALY

| | | | |
|---|---|---|---|
| Naples | Nuovo | Oct. 26, 1842 | G. David (I.) Lucia (E.) T. Barattini (M.) R. Casaccia (T.) G. Fioravanti (L.) G. Lodi (El.) G. Coccia cond. |
| Rome | Argentina | Feb.? 1847 | M. Cioffi (I.) C. Laudano (M.) |
| Turin | Sutera | Spring 1845 | E. Sara (I.) C. Biscottini-Fiorio (E.) G. Cortopassi (M.) A. Rivarola (T.) A. Orlandi (L.) L. Walter (El.) |

4. IL DUCA D'ALBA-*Tragedia lirica* in two acts
Venice-Teatro la Fenice-Feb. 26, 1842
Libretto by Francesco Maria Piave and Giovanni Peruzzini

| | |
|---|---|
| Margarita (M.) | Fanny Goldberg sop. |
| Elvira (E.) | Ida Bertrand mez. |
| Egmondo (Eg.) | Napoleone Moriani ten. |
| Il Duca d'Alba (D.) | Filippo Coletti bar. |
| Ines | Teresa Cucchi sop. |
| Giovanni di Vargas | Gaetano Salani sec. |
| Arnoldo | Antonio Zanchi sec. |
| Diego | Giuseppe Bianchi ten. |
| | |
| Conductor | Gaetano Mares |
| Director | Giovanni Pacini |

OTHER PRODUCTIONS

ITALY

| | | | |
|---|---|---|---|
| Naples | San Carlo | Nov. 4, 1842 | S. Loewe (M.) C. Gruitz (E.) G. Fraschini (Eg.) F. Coletti (D.) A. Farelli cond. (as Adolfo di Warbel) |

5. LA FIDANZATA CORSA-*Melodramma tragico* in three acts
Naples-Teatro San Carlo-Dec. 10, 1842
Libretto by Salvadore Cammarano

| | |
|---|---|
| Rosa (R.) | Eugenia Tadolini sop. |
| Alberto (A.) | Giovanni Basadonna ten. |
| Ettore (E.) | Gaetano Fraschini ten. |
| Pietro (P.) | Filippo Coletti bar. |
| Guido Tobianchi (G.) | Marco Arati bass |
| Giacinta | Anna Salvetti sop. |
| Alessio | Teofilo Rossi ten. |
| Leone | Giuseppe Benedetti bass |
| | |
| Conductor | Antonio Farelli |
| Director | Giovanni Pacini |

OTHER PRODUCTIONS

ARGENTINA
Buenos Aires   Argentino   Feb. 17, 1854 I. Edelvira (R.) L. Guglielmini (A.)
                                         G. Dordoni (E.) G. C. Casanova (P.)
                                         J. V. Rivas cond.

BRAZIL
Rio de         Sao Pedro   Dec.  2, 1850 I. Edelvira (R.) F. Tati (A.) C. Ca-
  Janeiro                                purri (P.)

               Lirico      Nov. 13, 1855 A.  Charton-Demeur  (R.)  A. Gentili
                 Fluminense               (A.) Dufresne (E.) L. Walter (P.)

FRANCE
Paris          Italien     Nov. 17, 1846 F. Persiani (R.) Mario (A.) Cellini
                                         (E.)  F.  Coletti  (P.)  T.  Tilmant
                                         cond.

ITALY
Ancona         Muse        Jan. 18, 1853 A.  Angelini-Cantalamessa  (R.)  L.
                                         Bernabei (A.)

Aquila         Municipale       1848

Avelino                    July      1847 Z.  Papini  (R.)  C.  Ballestra (A.)
                                         Monti (E.) Schifini (P.)

Barletta       Ettore      Feb. 16, 1856 M.  Armandi  (R.)  G.  Colla  (E.)
                 Fieramosca

Caltagirone                Carn. 1858-59

Catania        Comunale    Sep.      1846 C. Lusignani (R.) F. Wenzel (A.) L.
                                         Scopa (E.) C. Busi (P.)

                           Apr.  1, 1871 E. Domasi (R.) G. Tombesi (A.) G.
                                         Toressi (E.) F. Amodio (P.) R. Spe-
                                         dalieri cond.

Catanzaro      Comunale    Jan.      1847 Z. Papini (R.) R. D'Andrea (A.) T.
                                         Schifini (P.)

Chieti         San         June 17, 1844 E. Parepa-Archibugi (R.)
                 Ferdinando

| Cosenza | | Spring | 1847 | Delfanti (R.) A. Agresti (A.) Zury (P.) |
|---|---|---|---|---|
| Florence | Pergola | Mar. 10, | 1844 | T. Brambilla (R.) G. Roppa (A.) A. Castellan (E.) A. De Bassini (P.) A. Biagi cond. |
| Foggia | Ferdinando | July 4, | 1847 | E. Bruni (R.) C. Fabbricatore (A.) F. De Ruggero (E.) L. Finocchi (P.) |
| Lucca | Giglio | Sep. | 1844 | T. De Giuli-Borsi (R.) G. Roppa (A.) F. Cimino (E.) A. De Bassini (P.) |
| Messina | Munizione | Oct. | 1843 | G. Armenia (R.) G. B. Genero (A.) A. Agresti/Sorino (E.) S. Scappini (P.) |
| Milan | La Scala | Dec. 30? | 1845 | A. Bishop (R.) E. D'Angri (A.) E. Musich (E.) G. Euzet (P.) E. Cavallini cond. |
| Naples | San Carlo | June 27, | 1843 | A. Bishop (R.) E. Tamberlick (A.) G. Fraschini (E.) F. Coletti (P.) M. Arati (G.) A. Farelli cond. |
| | | Mar. 23, | 1845 | A. Bishop (R.) Valgy (A.) G. Fraschini (E.) F. Coletti (P.) M. Arati (G.) A. Farelli cond. |
| | | June 1, | 1845 | A. Bishop (R.) J. B. Bordas (A.) G. Fraschini (E.) F. Coletti (P.) M. Arati (G.) A. Farelli cond. |
| | | Nov. 11, | 1866 | L. Bendazzi-Secchi (R.) G. Stigelli (A.) R. Bertolini (E.) L. Colonnese (P.) M. Arati (G.) |
| | Nuovo | Feb. 2, | 1850 | Z. Papini (R.) T. Remorini (A.) Fischetti (E.) V. Orlandi (P.) Pisani (G.) |
| Palermo | Carolino | Oct. 28, | 1843 | G. Bortolotti (R.) G. Pancani (A.) L. Mei (E.) L. Valli (P.) P. Raimondi cond. |
| | | Feb. 21, | 1846 | M. Gazzaniga (R.) L. Bonfigli (A.) A. Castellan (E.) L. Valli (P.) P. Raimondi cond. |
| Reggio di Calabria | Borbonico | Dec. | 1844 | E. Bruni (R.) De Rossi (A.) Varial (E.) G. De Baillou (P.) |
| Rome | Alibert | Autumn | 1843 | I. Ober-Rossi (R.) F. Borioni (A.) L. Donati (E.) P. Balzar (P.) |
| Trani | San Ferdinando | Mar.? | 1865 | L. Banti (R.) |
| Venice | La Fenice | Jan. 9, | 1844 | I. Ober-Rossi (R.) C. Vietti (A.) G. Bettini (E.) A. Latour (P.) |
| Vicenza | Eretenio | Aug.? | 1845 | T. De Giuli-Borsi (R.) L. Cuzzani (A.) R. Colmenghi (P.) |

MALTA
La Valletta    Manoel      May       1845  C.  Ferrarini-Baschieri   (R.)   Carli
                                           (A.)  M.  Forti  (E.)  L.  Del  Riccio
                                           (P.)

PORTUGAL
Lisbon         Sao Carlos  Mar. 12,  1848  T.  Bovay  (R.)  G.  Baldanza  (A.)  A.
                                           Volpini  (E.)  R.  Pizzigati  (P.)

RUSSIA
Odessa         Municipal   June?     1845  A.  Scalese  (R.)

SPAIN
Barcelona      Principal   Aug. 18,  1848  C.  Rovelli  (R.)  E.  Tamberlick  (A.)
                                           J.  Gomez  (E.)  P.  Dérivis  (P.)

URUGUAY
Montevideo     Teatro      Oct. 12,  1853  I.  Edelvira  (R.)  L.  Guglielmini  (A.)
                                           G.  Bordoni  (E.)  L.  Contini  (P.)  F.
                                           Tati  (G.)  J.  V.  Ribas  cond.

6. MARIA, REGINA D'INGHILTERRA-*Tragedia lirica* in three acts
Palermo-Teatro Carolino-Feb. 11, 1843
Libretto by Leopoldo Tarantini

| | |
|---|---|
| Maria (M.) | Antonietta Rainieri-Marini sop. |
| Clotilde Talbot(C.) | Teresa Merli-Clerici sop. |
| Riccardo Fenimoore (R.) | Nicola Ivanoff ten. |
| Ernesto Malcom (E.) | Antonio Superchi bar. |
| Gualtiero Churcill (G.) | Antonio Benciolini bass |
| Un Paggio | Carlotta Orlandi Benanti mez. |
| Il Custode della torre | Giovanni d'Ippolito ten. |
| | |
| Conductor | Pietro Raimondi |
| Director | Giovanni Pacini |

OTHER PRODUCTIONS-NINETEENTH CENTURY

ITALY
Genoa      Carlo       Feb.  1,  1844  A.  Rainieri-Marini  (M.)  T.  Merli-
           Felice                      Clerici  (C.)  F.  Borioni  (R.)  R.  Col-
                                       menghi  (E.)

Messina    Sant'       Dec.  1,  1853  E.  Nostini-Rossi  (M.)  M.  L.  D'Andrea
           Elisabetta                  (C.)  C.  Braham  (R.)  Rossi  (E.)  R.
                                       Laterza  (G.)  A.  Laudamo  cond.

Milan      La Scala    Dec. 26,  1843  A.  Moltini  (M.)  L.  Pozzi  (C.)  N.
                                       Ivanoff  (R.)  R.  Ferlotti  (E.)  A.
                                       Benciolini  (G.)  E.  Cavallini  cond.

Palermo    Carolino    Oct. 30,  1852  E.  Marcolini  (M.)  N.  De  Roissi  (C.)
                                       N.  Ivanoff  (R.)  F.  Colini  (E.)  A.  Lo
                                       Casto  cond.  G.  Pacini  dir.

Turin      Carignano   Oct. 21,  1843  L.  Abbadia  (M.)  G.  Caremoli-Crivelli
                                       (C.)  R.  Mirate  (R.)  E.  Crivelli  (E.)

MALTA
La Valletta    Manuel       Oct.  1, 1857 M. Whitty (M.) L. Stramesi (C.) A.
                                         Oliva-Pavani (R.) L. Rossi (E.) P.
                                         Varvaro (G.)

PORTUGAL
Lisbon        Sao Carlos   Oct. 29, 1853 A. Castellan (M.) A. Anglés-Fortuni
                                         (C.) C. Miraglia (R.) O. Bartolini
                                         (E.) G. Gasparini (G.)

SPAIN
Barcelona     Principal    Oct.  7, 1845 C. Di Franco (M.) T. Merli-Clerici
                                         (C.) J. Solieri (R.) M. Assoni (E.)

OTHER PRODUCTIONS-TWENTIETH CENTURY

GREAT BRITAIN
London        Camden       Mar. 26, 1983 P. Walker (M.) M. Hill Smith (C.) K.
              Festival                   Lewis (R.) C. Blades (E.) A. Vassi-
                                         lev (G.) D. Parry cond.


7. MEDEA-*Tragedia lirica* in three acts
Palermo-Teatro Carolino-Nov. 28, 1843
Libretto by Benedetto Castiglia

Medea (M.)                              Geltrude Bortolotti sop.
Giasone (G.)                            Giovanni Pancani ten.
Creonte (C.)                                Luigi Valli bar.
Calcante (Ca.)                           Secondo Torre bass
Cassandra                               Giovanna Austin mez.
Licisca                                 Adelaide Orlandi mez.

Conductor                                  Pietro Raimondi
Director                                  Giovanni Pacini

OTHER PRODUCTIONS

ARGENTINA
Buenos Aires  Ant. Colón   June  7, 1865 C. Briol (M.) A. Pozzolini (G.) A.
                                         Celestino (C.) L. Walter (Ca.)

                           Oct.  5, 1866 C. Briol (M.)

CUBA
Havana        Tacon        Jan.  7, 1860 A. Cortesi (M.) G. Musiani (G.) C.
                                         Nanni (Ca.)

HAITI
Port au                    Dec.     1860 A. Cortesi (M.) G. Musiani (G.)
  Prince

ITALY
Ancona        Muse         May   9, 1855 A. Cortesi (M.) E. Pancani (G.) P.
                                         Giorgi-Pacini (C.) G. Pacini dir.

Ascoli        Ventidio     Oct. 29, 1856 G. Sanchioli (M.) A. Prudenza (G.)
  Piceno      Basso                      P. Baraldi (C.) C. Nanni (Ca.)

Bergamo       Sociale      Dec. 26, 1845 L. Schieroni-Nulli (M.) A. Bales-
                                         tracci (G.) G. Nulli (C.)

| Catania | Comunale | Dec.? | 1850 | E. Parepa-Archibugi (M.) A. Silvestroni (G.) F. Cuturi (C.) M. Pappalardo cond. |
|---------|----------|-------|------|---------|
| Chieti | San Ferdinando | June 1, | 1854 | T. Pozzi-Montegazza (M.) V. Ferrari-Stella (G.) A. Vitti (C.) |
| Cosenza | | Nov. | 1858 | C. Marziali (M.) O. Sindaci (G.) G. Viola (C.) |
| Cremona | Concordia | Autumn | 1845 | G. Sanchioli (M.) G. Pancani (G.) F. Taffanelli (C.) |
| Florence | Pergola | June 12, | 1850 | C. Alaimo (M.) L. Graziani (G.) M. Zacchi (C.) |
| | Pagliano | Jan. 20, | 1857 | A. Cortesi (M.) A. Prudenza (G.) F. Giannini (C.) |
| Forli | Comunale | June | 1856 | A. Cortesi (M.) P. Mongini (G.) P. Baraldi (C.) |
| Livorno | Floridi | Mar. 24, | 1852 | C. Alaimo (M.) A. Giuglini (G.) E. Crivelli (C.) |
| | Avvalorati | Oct. | 1857 | G. Sanchioli (M.) G. Ortolani (G.) G. Massiani (C.) F. Pons (Ca.) |
| Macerata | Condomini | Sep. 4, | 1853 | C. Alaimo (M.) C. Conti (G.) E. Barili (C.) |
| Messina | Munizione | Oct. | 1845 | E. D'Alberti (M.) C. Della Longa (G.) G. Corsi (C.) |
| Modena | Comunale | Feb. 20, | 1851 | C. Alaimo (M.) L. Bernabei (G.) M. Zacchi (C.) G. Poggiali (Ca.) A. Sighicelli cond. |
| Naples | San Carlo | Feb. 26, | 1853 | C. Alaimo (M.) E. Pancani (G.) G. Ferri (C.) M. Arati (Ca.) A. Farelli cond. |
| Padua | Nuovo | June 11, | 1854 | C. Alaimo (M.) C. Braham (G.) G. Guicciardi (C.) |
| Palermo | Carolino | Nov. 27, | 1845 | T. Tavola (M.) A. Castellan (G.) A. Zucconi (C.) P. Raimondi cond. |
| Perugia | Pavone | Jan. 28, | 1855 | T. Pozzi-Montegazza (M.) V. Ferrari-Stella (G.) A. Donzelli (C.) |
| Pesaro | Rossini | Jan. 16, | 1853 | T. Pozzi-Montegazza (M.) A. Errani (G.) G. B. Righini (C.) L. Marini (Ca.) A. Marziali cond. |
| Piacenza | Comunale | Jan. 28, | 1851 | I. Secci-Corsi (M.) G. De Vecchi (G.) F. Rigo (C.) G. Jona cond. |
| Ravenna | Alighieri | June 6, | 1852 | A. Cortesi (M.) M. Viani (G.) R. Pizzigati (C.) |
| Rome | Argentina | Oct. 28, | 1856 | A. Cortesi (M.) B. Massimiliani (G.) F. Coliva (C.) E. Angelini cond. G. Pacini dir. |

| | | | |
|---|---|---|---|
| Terni | Comunale | Jan. 17, 1852 | T. Pozzi-Montegazza (M.) L. Bernabei (G.) M. Zacchi (C.) L. Grandassi cond. |
| Trani | San Ferdinando | 1852-53 | |
| Trieste | Grande | Sep. 21, 1845 | S. Loewe (M.) P. Unanue (G.) L. Valli (C.) P. Coronini cond. |
| Turin | Carignano | Aug. 20, 1845 | R. Basso-Borio (M.) S. Malvezzi (G.) R. Pizzigati (C.) |
| Venice | La Fenice | Mar. 9, 1850 | A. Cortesi (M.) R. Mirate (G.) L. Valli (C.) G. Mares cond. |
| Verona | Filarmonico | Mar. 9, 1853 | T. De Giuli-Borsi (M.) S. Malvezzi (G.) R. Pizzigati (C.) |
| Vicenza | Eretenio | Jan. 22, 1845 | T. Tavola (M.) C. Miraglia (G.) F. Gorin (C.) G. Pacini dir. |
| | | Aug. 17, 1856 | A. Cortesi (M.) R. Mirate (G.) F. Cresci (C.) |
| Viterbo | Unione | Fiera 1864 | G. Giovannoni-Zacchi (M.) Piermarini (G.) A. Carboni (C.) |
| **MALTA** La Valletta | Manoel | Dec. 1858 | G. Bonheur (M.) A. Marchetti (G.) C. Bartolucci (C.) |
| **MEXICO** Mexico City | Nacional | Oct. 10, 1858 | A. Cortesi (M.) A. Volpini (G.) A. Ottaviani (C.) C. Nanni (Ca.) A. Barili cond. |
| **RUSSIA** Odessa | Municipal | 1852 | M. Zacchi (C.) |
| **SPAIN** Barcelona | Principal | Oct. 15, 1845 | E. Goggi (M.) G. B. Milesi (G.) A. Superchi (C.) |
| Madrid | Circo | Feb. 27, 1847 | G. Bortolotti (M.) E. Tamberlick (G.) F. Morelli-Ponti (C.) |
| **UNITED STATES** New York | Niblo's Garden | Sep. 27, 1860 | A. Cortesi (M.) G. Musiani (G.) A. Ardavani (C.) |
| **URUGUAY** Montevideo | Solis | Feb. 28, 1866 | C. Briol (M.) L. Lelmi (G.) A. M. Celestino (C.) |
| **VENEZUELA** Caracas | Teatro | Oct. 3, 1861 | A. Cortesi (M.) G. Musiani (G.) F. Amodio (C.) C. Nanni (Ca.) |

8. LUISETTA, o LA CANTATRICE DEL MOLO-*Melodramma giocosa* in two acts
Naples-Teatro Nuovo-Dec. 13, 1843
Libretto by Leopoldo Tarantini

| | |
|---|---|
| Luisetta (L.) | Adele Rebussini sop. |
| Floresca (F.) | Annetta Silvestri mez. |
| Giulio (G.) | Domenico Labocetta ten. |
| Cesare (C.) | Raffaele Casaccia bar. |
| Saltarelli (S.) | Giuseppe Fioravanti buf. |
| Rossetta | Antonietta Carmignani sec. |
| Don Pecchino | Salvatore Perelli bass |
| Poeta | Gaetano De Nicola sec. |
| | |
| Conductor | Gaetano Coccia |
| Director | Giovanni Pacini |

OTHER PRODUCTIONS

ITALY[11]

| Naples | Nuovo | June 16, 1846 | R. Vigliardi (L.) Trotta (G.) R. Casaccia (C.) G. Fioravanti (S.) |
|---|---|---|---|
| | | Apr. 20, 1851 | C. Martinelli (L.) C. D'Amora (F.) T. Remorino (G.) R. Casaccia (C.) G. Fioravanti (S.) M. Di Natale cond. |
| | Bellini | Mar. 14, 1867 | Gigli (L.) Dodoni (G.) |
| Turin | Sutera | Spring 1846 | V. Viola (L.) M. Albizzati (F.) C. Scannavino (G.) F. Frizzi (C.) B. Mazzetti (S.) |

9. L'EBREA-*Dramma lirico* in four acts
Milan-Teatro alla Scala-Feb. 27, 1844
Libretto by Giacomo Sacchèro

| | |
|---|---|
| Rachele (R.) | Antonietta Montenegro sop. |
| Berenice (B.) | Marietta Alboni mez. |
| Manlio (M.) | Nicola Ivanoff ten. |
| Antioco (A.) | Raffaele Ferlotti bar. |
| Eleazaro (E.) | Ignazio Marini bass |
| Ottavia | Teresa Ruggeri sop. |
| Sejano | Luigi Bottagisi ten. |
| Cesennio | Giovanni Battista Acquarone sec. |
| | |
| Conductor | Eugenio Cavallini |
| Director | Giovanni Pacini |

OTHER PRODUCTIONS

SPAIN

| Barcelona | Principal | Nov. 17, 1848 | C. Cattinari (R.) R. Agostini (B.) E. Tamberlick (M.) E. Barili (A.) A. Selva (E.) |
|---|---|---|---|

---

[11]. *Luisetta* was also given in Siracusa in 1854 and again in 1855 as well as Trani during the 1847-48 season.

10. LORENZINO DE'MEDICI-*Tragedia lirica* in two acts and four parts
Venice-Teatro la Fenice-Mar. 4, 1845
Libretto by Francesco Maria Piave

| Luisa Strozzi (L.) | Marianna Barbieri-Nini sop. |
| Lorenzino de'Medici (Lo.) | Andrea Castellan ten. |
| Filippo Strozzi (F.) | Sebastiano Ronconi bar. |
| Alessandro de'Medici (A.) | Giuseppe Miral bass |
| Assunta | Amalia Patriossi sec. |
| Giomo | Francesco Rossi ten. |
| Michele | Ignazio Patriossi bass |

| Conductor | Gaetano Mares |
| Director | Giovanni Pacini |

OTHER PRODUCTIONS

AUSTRIA
Vienna          Kärntnertor May  18, 1859 M. Lafon (L.) G. Musiani/G. Limberti
                                          (Lo.) D. Squarcia (F.) G. F. Angeli-
                                          ni (A.)

ITALY
Ancona          Muse         Dec. 26, 1861 L. Banti (L.) G. Giannini (Lo.) A.
                                           Morelli (F.) G. Capriles (A.)

Ascoli          Ventidio     Oct. 27, 1857 L. Ruggero-Antonioli (L.) G. Limber-
  Piceno        Basso                      ti (Lo.) F. Cresci (F.) G. Capriles
                                           (A.)

Bergamo         Sociale      Jan. 16, 1859 E. Galli (L.) J. Swift (Lo.) D.
                                           Squarcia (F.)

Cagliari        Civico       Feb. 11, 1874

Cesena          Comunale     Aug. 15, 1857 L. Ruggero-Antonioli (L.) G. Limber-
                                           ti (Lo.) F. Cresci (F.) P. Milesi
                                           (A.)

Chieti          San          May  18, 1862
                Ferdinando

Ferrara         Comunale     Jan.     1863 E. Brambilla (L.) A. Di Benedetto
                                           (Lo.) F. Proni (F.) M. Ghini (A.)

Florence        Pergola      Oct. 16, 1845 M. Barbieri-Nini (L.) G. Roppa (Lo.)
                                           S. Ronconi (F.) G. Miral (A.) A.
                                           Biagi cond.

                Pagliano     Dec. 26, 1857 C. Ghirlanda-Tortolini (L.) G. Lim-
                                           berti (Lo.) F. Cresci (F.) G. Miral
                                           (A.)

                Nuovo        May  3, 1873 V. Fiorellini-Balma (L.) G. Balma
                                          (Lo.) A. Borella (F.) G. Belletti
                                          (A.)

Forli           Comunale     Spring  1845 M. Barbieri-Nini (L.) G. Roppa (Lo.)
                                          S. Ronconi (F.) G. Miral (A.)

Jesi            Concordia    Sep.     1845 M. Barbieri-Nini (L.) L. Bernabei
                                          (Lo.) S. Ronconi (F.) L. Della Santa
                                          (A.)

Livorno        Avvalorati   Jan. 29, 1857 L. Ruggero-Antonioli (L.) G. Limber-
                                          ti (Lo.) D. Squarcia (F.) P. Milesi
                                          (A.)

               Leopoldo     Nov. 25, 1866 Gualtieri (L.) G. Firpo (Lo.) F.
                                          Proni (F.) A. Pelletti (A.) V. Gia-
                                          nelli cond.

Lucca          Pantera      Mar.  8, 1857 L. Ruggero-Antonioli (L.) G. Limber-
                                          ti (Lo.) D. Squarcia (F.) P. Milesi
                                          (A.)

Macerata       Condominio   Sep.  2, 1858 F. Scheggi (L.) P. Tagliazucchi
                                          (Lo.) M. Zacchi (F.)

Milan          La Scala     Oct. 22, 1859 E. Galli (L.) G. Ghislanzoni (Lo.)
                                          G. Corsi (F.) G. Echeverria (A.) E.
                                          Cavallini cond.

Modena         Comunale     Jan.  6, 1855 C. Crémont (L.) G. Ortolani (Lo.) A.
                                          Mazzanti (F.) C. Dalla Costa (A.) A.
                                          Sighicelli cond.

Naples         San Carlo    Mar. 20, 1858 E. Fioretti (L.) G. Galvani (Lo.) F.
                                          Coliva (F.) G. B. Antonucci (A.)

Padua          Nuovo        June 12, 1847 M. Barbieri-Nini (L.) G. Roppa (Lo.)
                                          L. Valli (F.) G. Euzet (A.)

Perugia        Morlacchi    Jan.  2, 1858 E. Belmonte (L.) G. Rustichelli
                                          (Lo.) R. Maestri (F.) P. Vannucci
                                          (A.)

Pesaro         Rossini      Jan. 14, 1860 C. Marziali (L.) G. Capponi (Lo.) C.
                                          Boccolini (F.) F. Marinozzi (A.) A.
                                          Marziali cond.

                            Carn. 1860-61 A. Ravaglia (L.) L. Pencarelli (Lo.)
                                          F. Pandolfini (F.) G. Capriles (A.)
                                          E. Vannuccini cond.

Pisa           Ravvivati    Dec. 26, 1860 E. Ghirlanda-Tortolini (L.) P. Chie-
                                          si (Lo.) A. Berlendis (A.)

Prato          Metastasio   Feb. 18, 1873 V. Fiorellini-Balma (L.) G. Balma
                                          (Lo.) G. Stiattesi (F.) A. Pelletti
                                          (A.) A. Borgioli cond.

Reggio Emilia  Comunale     Apr. 25, 1845 M. Barbieri-Nini (L.) G. Roppa (Lo.)
                                          S. Ronconi (F.) G. Miral (A.) G. Pa-
                                          cini dir.

Rome           Apollo       Jan.  3, 1854 M. Barbieri-Nini (L.) B. Massimilia-
                                          ni (Lo.) F. Monari (F.) A. Lanzoni
                                          (A.)

Siena          Rinnovati    July 18, 1858 L. Rugggero-Antonioli (L.) A. Alta-
                                          villa (Lo.) C. Busi (F.) F. Mazzoni
                                          (A.)

Spoleto        Nobile       Jan. 26, 1859 C. Martelli (L.) E. Pizioli (Lo.)

Terni          Comunale     Dec. 26, 1853 C. Crémont (L.) P. Cecchi (Lo.) A.
                                          Vitti (F.) F. Bartolini (A.)

| Trieste | Grande | Feb. 14, 1846 | A. De la Grange (L.) L. Mei (Lo.) V. Caspani (F.) G. A. Scaramelli cond. |
| | | Oct. 7, 1848 | M. Barbieri-Nini (L.) G. Roppa (Lo.) A. De Bassini (F.) G. A. Scaramelli cond. |
| Turin | Carignano | Autumn 1848 | T. Brambilla (L.) G. B. Milesi (Lo.) F. Monari (F.) G. De Baillou (A.) |
| Venice | San Benedetto | Mar. 14, 1859 | E. Galli (L.) A. Oliva-Pavani (Lo.) D. Squarcia (F.) P. Milesi (A.) |
| Vicenza | Eretenio | Aug. 27, 1846 | M. Barbieri-Nini (L.) G. Sinico (Lo.) F. Varesi (F.) S. L. Bouché (A.) |
| SPAIN | | | |
| Barcelona | Liceo | Feb. 24, 1858 | M. Barbieri-Nini (L.) A. Errani (Lo.) G. B. Bencich (F.) C. Nanni (A.) |

11. BONDELMONTE-*Tragedia lirica* in three parts[12]
Florence-Teatro in via della Pergola-June 18, 1845
Libretto by Salvador Cammarano

Beatrice (B.)                      Marietta Gazzaniga sop.
Isaura (I.)                        Clelia Forti-Babacci sop.
Bondelmonte (Bo.)                  Ettore Caggiati ten.
Amedei (A.)                        Cesare Badiali bar.
Bianca Donati                      Faustina Piombanti mez.
Uberti                             Demetrio Masselli bass
Gangalandi                         Giovacchino Lucchesi sec.
Mosca                              Ettore Profili bass
Fifanti                            Giovanni Nottoli sec.

Conductor                                        Alamanno Biagi
Director                                         Giovanni Pacini

OTHER PRODUCTIONS

ARGENTINA
Buenos Aires   Ant. Colón   Oct. 7, 1860   C. Manzini (B.) Ardinti (I.) E. Ballerini (Bo.) G. Bertolini (A.)

                           1861   C. Manzini (B.) E. Ballerini (Bo.) G. Bertolini (A.)[13]

---

12. Although the opera was originally given as *Bondelmonte*, it was most frequently referred to, even by the composer, and given as *Buondelmonte*.

13. This particular company also toured South America during the early 1860s. While little is known about their itinerary beyond their stays in Buenos Aires, Montevideo, Santiago and Valparaiso, it is likely that they also visited other cities such as Rosario and possibly Cordova. If so, *Bondelmonte* was a staple of their repertory and is almost certain to have been given there as well.

BRAZIL
Rio de        San            Nov.  5, 1851 G. Zecchini (B.)  M. Eboli  (I.)  D.
Janeiro       Januario                    Labocetta (Bo.) L. Di Lauro (A.)

              Provisorio     Apr. 14, 1852 G. Zecchini (B.) M. Pinzarone (I.)
                                           D. Labocetta (Bo.) L. Di Lauro (A.)


CHILE
Santiago      Municipal      July 16, 1864 C. Manzini (B.)  I. Vitali (I.)  E.
                                           Ballerini (Bo.) G. Bertolini (A.)

Valparaiso    Victoria       Apr.  7, 1864 C. Manzini (B.)  I. Vitali (I.)  E.
                                           Ballerini (Bo.) G. Bertolini (A.)

                             Jan. 19, 1865 C. Manzini (B.)  I. Vitali (I.)  E.
                                           Ballerini (Bo.) G. Bertolini (A.)


GREECE
Athens        Royal          Oct. 14, 1857 D. De Moro (B.)  Onorii (I.)  P.
                                           Chiesi (Bo.) C. Bartolucci (A.)

Corfu         Nobile         Sep. 14, 1850 F. Rocca-Alessandri (B.) G. Galvani
                                           (Bo.) F. Bartolini (A.)


ITALY[14]
Ancona        Muse           Dec. 30, 1851 G. Mazzoni (B.)  L. Galli (Bo.)  G.
                                           Staffolini (A.)

Bari          Piccinni       Dec.?    1859 C. Peccia (B.)

Bergamo       Sociale        Dec. 26, 1852 C. Moltini (B.)  L. Gavetti-Regnani
                                           (I.) G. De Vecchi (Bo.) R. De Giorgi
                                           (A.)

                             Jan. 18, 1879 Pogliaghi (B.) G. De Filippis (Bo.)
                                           N. Fallica (A.)

Bologna       Comunale       Mar.  9, 1850 F. Capuani (B.)  E. Nostini (I.) M.
                                           Viani (Bo.) G. L. Pellegrini (A.) G.
                                           Manetti cond.

                             June 10, 1857 F. Salvini-Donatelli (B.) E. Tebaldi
                                           (I.) E. Naudin (Bo.) R. Pizzigati
                                           (A.) G. Manetti cond. G. Pacini dir.

              Corso          Mar.  6, 1855 E. Fioretti (B.) A. Molinari (I.) L.
                                           Stefani (Bo.) R. Pizzigati (A.) G.
                                           Manetti cond.

Brescia       Grande         July 23, 1853 M. Barbieri-Nini (B.) A. Ortolani-
                                           Brignole (I.) G. Petrovich (Bo.) F.
                                           Colini (A.)

Caltagirone                  Feb.     1859 L. Giordano (B.) C. Leonardis (I.)
                                           F. Nenci (Bo.) L. Vendemmia (A.)

                             Carn. 1861-62 E. Natali (B.) G. De Filippis (Bo.)
                                           Nascia (A.)

---

14. Other Italian towns to have heard *Bondelmonte* include Arezzo, Aquila (May 1851),
Catanzaro (Autumn 1851), Lanciano (August 1851), Medica (Carnival 1858-59), Siracusa (1850)
and Trani (1847-48).

| | | | |
|---|---|---|---|
| Catania | Comunale | Nov. 20, 1852 | C. Forti-Babacci (B.) A. Remorini (I.) L. Ferrari-Stella (Bo.) P. Giorgi-Pacini (A.) M. Pappalardo cond. |
| | | Jan. 18, 1878 | F. Visconti (B.) A. Brunetti (Bo.) |
| Chieti | San Ferdinando | Apr. 24, 1847 | Zudoli (B.) Silvestrini (Bo.) Sabattini (A.) |
| Città di Castello | | Sep. 1853 | O. Mongé (B.) L. Lelmi (Bo.) F. Monari (A.) |
| Faenza | Comunale | June 19, 1850 | F. Salvini-Donatelli (B.) E. Naudin (Bo.) F. Gnone (A.) |
| Ferrara | Comunale | Apr. 20, 1854 | F. Salvini-Donatelli (B.) Brasini (I.) L. Stefani (Bo.) P. Baraldi (A.) G. C. Ferrarini cond. |
| Fiume | Comunale | Apr. 10? 1881 | B. D'Ariis (B.) E. Baldini (I.) L. Parodi (Bo.) E. Bernardi cond. |
| Florence | Pagliano | Nov. 7, 1855 | G. Zecchini (B.) A. Patriossi (I.) A. Pagnoni (Bo.) S. Ronconi (A.) |
| | | Sep. 7, 1856 | M. Barbieri-Nini (B.) D'Annia (I.) R. Bertolini (Bo.) F. Cresci (A.) |
| | Pergola | Mar. 22, 1859 | E. Julienne-Dejean (B.) G. Villani (Bo.) L. Giraldoni (A.) |
| Foggia | Dauno | May 1860 | C. Peccia (B.) |
| Genoa | Carlo Felice | Apr. 21, 1851 | M. Barbieri-Nini (B.) A. Mattioli (I.) L. Graziani (Bo.) O. Bartolini (A.) G. Serra cond. |
| Livorno | Rossini | Aug. 9, 1846 | M. Gazzaniga (B.) L. Bernabei (Bo.) F. Colini (A.) |
| | | July 29, 1851 | E. Scotta (B.) L. Vasoli (I.) G. Pasi (Bo.) F. Colini (A.) |
| Lucca | Giglio | Aug.? 1850 | M. Barbieri-Nini (B.) E. Naudin (Bo.) F. Varesi (A.) |
| Lugo | Rossini | Aug. 27, 1853 | S. Peruzzi (B.) A. Grandi (I.) L. Stefani (Bo.) L. Storti (A.) P. Montaguti cond. |
| Macerata | Condomini | Jan. 4, 1862 | Faleni (B.) Cesari (Bo.) Santini (A.) |
| Mantua | Sociale | Jan. 1852 | C. Moltini (B.) C. Miraglia (Bo.) D. Celli (A.) |
| | | Apr. 18, 1857 | M. Barbieri-Nini (B.) F. Tagliazucchi (Bo.) G. Marra (A.) |
| Messina | Munizione | Autumn 1849 | G. Zecchini (B.) G. Musiani (Bo.) G. Ortolani (A.) |

| | | | | |
|---|---|---|---|---|
| Milan | La Scala | Oct. 13, 1853 | F. Salvini-Donatelli (B.) Sperati (I.) T. Remorini (Bo.) R. Pizzigati (A.) |
| | Carcano | Sep. 1885 | Pogliaghi (B.) Orlandi (I.) Casartelli (Bo.) I. Viganotti (A.) |
| Modena | Comunale | Feb. 2, 1850 | F. Capuani (B.) E. Nostini (I.) M. Viani (Bo.) A. Ottaviani (A.) A. Sighicelli cond. |
| | | Jan. 13, 1855 | C. Crémont (B.) M. Sola (I.) G. Ortolani (Bo.) A. Mazzanti (A.) A. Sighicelli cond. |
| Naples | Fondo | May 16, 1846 | T. Brambilla (B.) C. Rambur (I.) S. Malvezzi (Bo.) F. Gionfrida (A.) A. Farelli cond. |
| | San Carlo | Oct. 4, 1846 | T. Brambilla (B.) C. Rambur (I.) S. Malvezzi (Bo.) F. Gionfrida (A.) A. Farelli cond. |
| | | Oct. 4, 1847 | T. Brambilla (B.) C. Rambur (I.) S. Malvezzi (Bo.) F. Gionfrida (A.) A. Farelli cond. |
| | | Oct. 19, 1850 | G. Zecchini (B.) M. Riva-Giunti (I.) G. Baldanza (Bo.) F. Gionfrida (A.) A. Farelli cond. |
| Padua | Nuovo | July 7, 1855 | F. Capuani (B.) C. Liverani (Bo.) P. Baraldi (A.) |
| Palermo | Carolino | Dec. 1850 | E. Scotta (B.) D. Nascio (I.) S. Sacchero (Bo.) F. Cresci (A.) P. Raimondi cond. |
| Parma | Regio | May 27, 1855 | A. Angelini-Cantalamessa (B.) I. Sassoreni (I.) A. Pagnoni (Bo.) S. Ronconi (A.) N. De Giovanni cond. |
| Pesaro | Rossini | Dec. 27, 1858 | A. Bertucci (B.) G. Berardinelli (I.) A. Altavilla (Bo.) C. Melzi (A.) A. Marziali cond. |
| Pisa | Ravvivati | Jan. 12, 1857 | V. Campi (B.) P. Giorgi-Pacini (A.) |
| Reggio di Calabria | Borbonico | Carn. 1846-47 | E. Corsini (B.) F. Cimino (Bo.) A. Olivari (A.) |
| | | Jan.? 1854 | A. Pagnoni (Bo.) L. Vendemmia (A.) |
| Reggio Emilia | Comunale | May 28, 1850 | F. Salvini-Donatelli (B.) E. Naudin (Bo.) F. Gnone (A.) |
| Rome | Argentina | Oct. 1852 | M. Barbieri-Nini (B.) F. Scheggi (I.) A. Giuglini (Bo.) G. Corsi (A.) |
| | Apollo | Jan. 1859 | E. Julienne-Dejean (B.) M. Alfieri (I.) G. Villani (Bo.) F. Colini (A.) E. Angelini cond. |

Rovigo          Sociale      Jan. 11, 1857 F. Capuani (B.) G. Zecchini (I.) E.
                                           Ballerini (Bo.) G. B. Bencich (A.)
                                           D. Tosarini cond.

Salerno         La Fiore     Jan.     1857 M. Armandi (B.) G. D'Apice (Bo.) L.
                                           Roncagli (A.)

                             June?    1859 E. Natali (B.) Perroulez (A.)

Sinigaglia      Comunale     July 26, 1850 M. Barbieri-Nini (B.) E. Naudin
                                           (Bo.) F. Colini (A.) G. Pacini dir.

Spoleto         Nobile       Dec. 26, 1855 I. Galletti-Gianoli (B.) V. Lepo-
                                           relli (I.) V. Tesi (Bo.) L. Banti
                                           (A.)

Trapani         San          Nov.     1850 E. Zani (B.) C. Siesta-Izzo (I.) L.
                Ferdinando                 Stefani (Bo.) Anito (A.)

Trento          Sociale      June 13, 1858 S. De Montelio (B.) G. Musiani (Bo.)
                                           L. Giraldoni (A.)

Treviso         Onigo        Nov. 10, 1855 M. Barbieri-Nini (B.) L. Chiaromonte
                                           (I.) A. Agresti (Bo.) G. Corsi (A.)
                                           G. C. Ferrarini cond.

Trieste         Grande       Sep. 24, 1853 M. Barbieri-Nini (B.) L. Graziani
                                           (Bo.) F. Coletti (A.) G. A. Scara-
                                           melli cond.

                             Mar. 28, 1860 I. Galletti-Gianoli (B.) G. Tombesi
                                           (Bo.) F. Monari (A.) G. A. Scaramel-
                                           li cond.

Turin           Regio        Jan.  8, 1853 M. Barbieri-Nini (B.) R. Pasta-An-
                                           glois (I.) C. Miraglia (Bo.) E. Cri-
                                           velli (A.) G. Ghebart cond.

Venice          La Fenice    Dec. 26, 1852 F. Salvini-Donatelli (B.) M. De
                                           Gianni Vivez (I.) L. Graziani (Bo.)
                                           F. Varesi (A.) G. Mares cond.

                Apollo       Feb.  1, 1854 T. Brambilla (B.) A. Oliva-Pavani
                                           (Bo.) S. Ronconi (A.)

                San Samuele Dec.  1, 1855 M. Barbieri-Nini (B.) L. Chiaromonte
                                           (I.) A. Agresti (Bo.) G. Corsi (A.)

Verona          Filarmonico Mar.  7, 1852 E. Scotta (B.) R. Mirate (Bo.) F.
                                           Varesi (A.)

Vicenza         Eretenio     July     1852 E. Scotta (B.) G. De Vecchi (Bo.) R.
                                           Pizzigati (A.)

MALTA
La Valletta     Manoel            1848-49

MEXICO
Mexico City     Nazional     Aug. 12, 1865 L. Stefani (Bo.) A. Ottaviani (A.)

RUSSIA
Odessa          Municipal    Dec.     1851 T. Brambilla (B.) C. Rambur (I.) E.
                                           Naudin (Bo.) S. Ronconi (A.)

|           |           | June 21, 1852 | T. Brambilla (B.) V. Tilli (I.) E. Naudin (Bo.) S. Ronconi (A.) |
|-----------|-----------|---------------|---|
|           |           | Nov. 5, 1854 | F. Gordosa (B.) T. Palmieri (Bo.) R. Ferlotti (A.) |
| SPAIN Barcelona | Liceo | Apr. 8, 1855 | N. Barbieri-Thiollier (B.) C. Ballestra (Bo.) F. Varesi (A.) |
|           |           | Oct. 1, 1857 | M. Barbieri-Nini (B.) A. Agresti (Bo.) G. B. Bencich (A.) |
| Granada   |           | Spring 1858 | M. Barbieri-Nini (B.) A. Agresti (Bo.) G. B. Bencich (A.) |
| Malaga    | Principal | Spring 1858 | M. Barbieri-Nini (B.) A. Agresti (Bo.) G. B. Bencich (A.) |
| Valencia  | Principal | Spring 1858 | M. Barbieri-Nini (B.) A. Agresti (Bo.) G. B. Bencich (A.) |
| URUGUAY Montevideo | Solis | Oct. 4, 1861 | C. Manzini (B.) E. Buil (I.) E. Ballerini (Bo.) G. Bertolini (A.) |
|           |           | Dec. 20, 1867 | C. Briol (B.) L. Lelmi (Bo.) E. Bonetti (A.) |

12. STELLA DI NAPOLI-*Dramma lirico* in three parts
Naples-Teatro San Carlo-Dec. 11, 1845
Libretto by Salvadore Cammarano

| | |
|---|---|
| Stella (S.) | Eugenia Tadolini sop. |
| Olimpia (O.) | Eloisa Buccini mez. |
| Armando (A.) | Gaetano Fraschini ten. |
| Gianni (G.) | Filippo Coletti bar. |
| Generale D'Aubigni | Marco Arati bass |
| Marta | Anna Salvetti sop. |
| Clodoveo | Teofilo Rossi ten. |
| Alberto | Giuseppe Benedetti bass |
| Conductor | Antonio Farelli |
| Director | Giovanni Pacini |

OTHER PRODUCTIONS

| GREECE Corfu | San Giacomo | Jan. 6, 1855 | L. Gavetti-Reggiani (S.) A. Agostini (O.) P. Chiesi (A.) C. Morelli-Condolmieri (G.) R. Sarti cond. |
|---|---|---|---|
| ITALY Bari | Provisorio | Jan. 1852 | Cioffi (S.) |
| Bergamo | Sociale | Feb. 1860 | G. Guerrabella (S.) Zamboni (O.) G. Petrovich (A.) F. Bertolini (G.) |
| Chieti | San Ferdinando | Spring 1853 | M. Mari (S.) A. Ferlotti (O.) G. Banti (A.) E. Delle Sedie (G.) |

| Cuneo | Sociale | Dec. 26, 1846 | M. Zagnoli (S.) Z. Sbriscia (O.) L. Lattuada (A.) L. Pellegrini (G.) |
|-------|---------|---------------|---|
| Fermo | Aquila | Aug.    1857 | I. Galletti-Gianoli (S.) P. Chiesi (A.) F. Coliva (G.) |
| Foligno | Apollo | Jan. 1, 1859 | Ercolani (S.) Uberti (O.) Tesi (A.) E. Salvi (G.) |
| Pavia | Fraschini | Mar. 4, 1856 | L. Gavetti-Reggiani (S.) L. Corbari (O.) R. Bertolini (A.) C. Bartolucci (G.) |
| Perugia | Morlacchi | Jan.    1856 | A. Mollo (S.) E. Conrani (O.) R. Dei (A.) Cavalieri (G.) |
| Rome | Argentina | Oct. 31, 1858 | I. Galletti-Gianoli (S.) M. Talvo (O.) G. Valentini-Cristiani (A.) E. Delle Sedie (G.) |
| Terni | Comunale | Jan. 25, 1852 | E. De Vrient (S.) De Cruz (O.) F. De Ruggero (A.) C. Fabbricatore (G.) |
| Trani | San Ferdinando | Nov. 4, 1852 | N. Barbieri-Thiollier (S.) |
| MALTA La Valletta | Manoel | 1848-49 | A. Borghi-Mamo (O.) |

13. LA REGINA DI CIPRO-*Dramma lirico* in four acts
Turin-Teatro Regio-Feb. 7, 1846
Libretto by Francesco Guidi

Caterina (C.)
Gerardo (G.)
Mocenigo (M.)
Andrea Cornaro (A.)
Adele
Marco
Giacomo di Lusignano

Erminia Frezzolini sop.
Luigi Ferretti ten.
Cesare Badiali bar.
Stanislao Demi bass
Marietta Laghi sop.
Giovanni Battista Boeri ten.
Francesco Lodetti bass

Conductor
Director

Giuseppe Ghebart
Giovanni Pacini

OTHER PRODUCTIONS

ARGENTINA
Buenos Aires   Argentino   July 26, 1854   I. Edelvira (C.) L. Guglielmini (G.)
                                           J. V. Rivas cond.

BRAZIL
Rio de         Sao Pedro   Oct.  7, 1850   I. Edelvira (C.) F. Tati (G.) C. Ca-
Janeiro                                    purri (M.)

               Provisorio  Apr. 17, 1852   G. Zecchini (C.) D. Labocetta (G.)
                                           L. De Lauro (M.)

                           Nov. 16, 1852   G. Zecchini (C.) D. Labocetta (G.)
                                           L. De Lauro (M.)

|  |  |  |  |
|---|---|---|---|
|  |  | Mar. 17, 1853 | G. Zecchini (C.) D. Labocetta (G.) L. De Lauro (M.) |
|  | Lirico Fluminense | Oct. 2, 1856 | E. Julienne-Dejean (C.) E. Tamberlick (G.) L. Walter (M.) |
|  |  | July 1857 | E. Julienne-Dejean (C.) G. Reina (M.) A. Susini (A.) |
|  |  | May 5, 1859 | A. De La Grange (C.) G. Comolli (G.) G. Arnaud (M.) A. Didot (A.) |
| **ITALY** Bergamo | Societa | Jan. 19, 1856 | C. Crémont (C.) G. Sinico (G.) F. Furga (M.) C. Castelli (A.) |
| Ferrara | Comunale | Apr. 26, 1846 | E. Frezzolini (C.) C. Guasco (G.) C. Badiali (M.) |
| Fiume | Civico | Spring 1860 | M. Pirola (C.) G. Petrovich (G.) G. Giotti (M.) |
| Modena | Comunale | Dec. 27, 1851 | M. Gresti (C.) G. Comolli (G.) D. Mattioli (M.) A. Sighicelli cond. |
| Naples | San Carlo | Oct. 10, 1846 | E. Frezzolini (C.) G. Fraschini (G.) P. Balzar (M.) A. Farelli cond. |
| Novara | Nuovo | Dec. 26, 1862 | T. Pozzi-Montegazza (C.) E. Mariani (G.) F. Brandini (M.) G. Cazzani (A.) |
| Padua | Concordi | Summer 1846 | A. De la Grange (C.) F. Borioni (G.) F. Morelli-Ponti (M.) |
| Sinigaglia | Comunale | Aug. 2, 1846 | G. Medori (C.) G. Fraschini (G.) F. Coletti (M.) |
| Trieste | Mauroner | Aug. 1864 | G. Cantù (M.) |
| Venice | Apollo | Dec. 26, 1859 | |
| **PORTUGAL** Lisbon | Sao Carlo | Jan. 22, 1848 | T. Bovay (C.) G. Baldanza (G.) R. Pizzigati (M.) |

14. MEROPE-*Tragedia lirica* in three acts
Naples-Teatro San Carlo-Nov. 25, 1847
Libretto by Salvadore Cammarano

| | |
|---|---|
| Merope (M.) | Marianna Barbieri-Nini sop. |
| Egisto (E.) | Gaetano Fraschini ten. |
| Polifonte (P.) | Francesco Gionfrida bar. |
| Polidoro (Pd.) | Marco Arati bass |
| Ismene | Anna Salvetti sop. |
| Ipparco | Giuseppe Ceci ten. |
| | |
| Conductor | Antonio Farelli |
| Director | Giovanni Pacini |

OTHER PRODUCTIONS

BRAZIL

| Rio de Janeiro | Provisorio | Mar. 14, 1854 | G. Zecchini (M.) A. Gentile (E.) F. Tati (P.) H. Whitworth (Pd.) |

ITALY

| Barletta | Ettore Fieramosca | Nov. | 1852 | |
| Catania | Comunale | Feb.? | 1852 | |
| Catanzaro | Comunale | | 1854 | |
| Trapani | San Ferdinando | Feb. | 1854 | Ricci (P.) |

MALTA

| La Valletta | Reale | Dec. | 1866 | C. Rosavalle (M.) E. Serazzi (E.) A. Burgio (P.) R. Laterza (Pd.) D. Amore cond. |

15. ESTER D'ENGADDI-*Dramma tragico* in three acts
Turin-Teatro Regio-Feb. 1, 1848
Libretto by Francesco Guidi

| Ester (E.) | Eugenia Garcia sop. |
| Azaria (A.) | Giuseppe Sinico ten. |
| Jefte (J.) | Prosper Dérivis bass |
| Eleazaro | Cesare Ferri bass |
| Sommo Sacerdote | Francesco Leonardi bass |
| Sara | Marietta Boeri sop. |

| Conductor | Giuseppe Ghebart |
| Director | Giovanni Pacini |

OTHER PRODUCTIONS

ITALY

| Florence | Pergola | Feb. | 1851 | F. Capuani (E.) G. Musiani (A.) G. Fiori (J.) |

16. ALLAN CAMERON-*Melodramma* in four acts
Venice-Teatro La Fenice-Mar. 21, 1848
Libretto by Francesco Maria Piave

| Editta (E.) | Anna De la Grange sop. |
| Charles II (C.) | Domenico Conti ten. |
| Allan Cameron (A.) | Felice Varesi bar. |
| Evano | Angelo Zuliani ten. |
| Malvina | Maria Zambelli De Rosa sec. |
| Gionata | Eugenio Monzani sec. |

| Conductor | Gaetano Mares |
| Director | Giovanni Pacini |

OTHER PRODUCTIONS

ITALY
Modena          Comunale    July 12, 1851 F. Salvini-Donatelli (E.) R. Mirate
                                         (C.) R. Ferlotti (A.)

Venice          La Fenice   Jan. 11, 1851 T. Brambilla (E.) R. Mirate (C.) F.
                                         Varesi (A.) G. Mares cond.

Verona          Filarmonico Feb.?    1854 F. Salvini-Donatelli (E.) G. Bettini
                                         (C.) L. Della Santa (A.)


16A. L'ORFANA SVIZZERA[15]


17. ZAFFIRA o LA RICONCILIAZIONE-*Melodramma lirico* in three acts
Naples-Teatro Nuovo-Nov. 14, 1851
Libretto by Andrea De Leone

| | |
|---|---|
| Zaffira | Rachele Gianfredi sop. |
| Ghita | Carolina D'Amora mez. |
| Armando | Tancredi Remorini ten. |
| Duca Gualtiero | Raffaele Mastriani bar. |
| Gillotto | Raffaele Casaccia buf. |
| Gennaro | Raffaele Grandillo bass |
| Un Assessore | Ferdinando Imbimbo bass |
| | |
| Conductor | Michele Di Natale |
| Director | Giovanni Pacini |


18. MALVINA DI SCOZIA-*Tragedia lirica* in three acts
Naples-Teatro San Carlo-Dec. 27, 1851
Libretto by Salvadore Cammarano

| | |
|---|---|
| Malvina (M.) | Adelaide Cortesi sop. |
| Morna (Mo.) | Adelaide Borghi-Mamo mez. |
| Wortimer (W.) | Corrado Laudano ten. |
| Arturo (A.) | Achille De Bassini bar. |
| Malcom (Ma.) | Marco Arati bass |
| Edvige | Anna Salvetti sop. |
| Rodwaldo | Giuseppe Benedetti bass |
| | |
| Conductor | Antonio Farelli |
| Director | Giovanni Pacini |

---

[15]. There is no evidence that this opera, frequently attributed to Pacini, and reported as having been given in Naples during the spring of 1848, was ever performed. It is not listed by Florimo and a thorough examination of the *Programma Giornaliera*, Naples for 1848 has shown no indication of a production.

OTHER PRODUCTIONS

BRAZIL
Rio de        Lirico       Sep.  7, 1860  G. Medori (M.) S. Tosi (Mo.)
  Janeiro       Fluminense

MALTA
La Valletta   Manuel       Jan.    1862 A.  Bazzurri  (M.)  L.  Caracciollo
                                         (Mo.) T. Sterbini (A.)


19. L'ASSEDIO DI LEIDA-*Opera seria*
Composed circa 1852-Unperformed
Libretto by Francesco Maria Piave


20. RODRIGO DI VALENZA-*Opera seria*
Composed for Palermo circa 1852-Unperformed


21. IL CID-*Tragedia lirica* in three acts
Milan-Teatro alla Scala-Mar. 12, 1853
Libretto by Achille de Lauzières

| | |
|---|---|
| Climene | Marietta Gazzaniga sop. |
| Rodrigo | Carlo Negrini ten. |
| Diego | Giovanni Corsi bar. |
| Fernando I | Agostino Rodas bass |
| Edita | Orsolina Bignami sec. |
| Alonzo | Giacomo Redaelli ten. |
| Gomez | Luigi Alessandrini bass |
| | |
| Conductor | Eugenio Cavallini |
| Director | Giovanni Pacini |


22. ROMILDA DI PROVENZA-*Tragedia lirica* in three acts
Naples-Teatro San Carlo-Dec. 8, 1853
Libretto by Gaetano Micci

| | |
|---|---|
| Romilda | Teresa De Giuli-Borsi sop. |
| Odetta | Adelaide Borghi-Mamo mez. |
| Carlo di Lorgues | Gaetano Fraschini ten. |
| Ubaldo | Gaetano Ferri bar. |
| Arturo di Berre | Marco Arati bass |
| Ida | Anna Salvetti sop. |
| Artos | Giuseppe Benedetti bass |
| | |
| Conductor | Antonio Farelli |
| Director | Giovanni Pacini |

23. LA DONNA DELLE ISOLE-*Opera seria*
Composed for Venice in 1853-Unperformed


24. LA PUNIZIONE-*Melodramma* in three acts[16]
Venice-Teatro La Fenice-Mar. 8, 1854
Libretto by Cesare Perini

| | |
|---|---|
| Lidia (L.) | Augusta Albertini sop. |
| Arminio (A.) | Raffaele Mirate ten. |
| Rodrigo (R.) | Giovannni Battista Bencich bar. |
| Maser (M.) | Marco Ghini bass |
| Amalia | Luigia Morselli sec. |
| Brenno | Angelo Zuliani ten. |
| Paolo | Placido Meneguzzi bass |
| Montosino | G. Rossetti bass |
| | |
| Director | Giovanni Pacini |


OTHER PRODUCTIONS

ITALY
| | | | |
|---|---|---|---|
| Bologna | Comunale | Oct. 21, 1858 | A. Fricci (L.) G. Limberti (A.) L. Walter (R.) A. Biacchi (M.) G. C. Ferrarini cond. G. Pacini dir. (as Lidia di Bruxelles) |
| Rome | Apollo | Feb. 1857 | A. Albertini (L.) C. Baucardé (A.) G. Ferri (R.) C. Bossi (M.) E. Angelini cond. |


25. MARGHERITA PUSTERLA-*Melodramma* in two acts
Naples-Teatro San Carlo-Feb. 25, 1856
Libretto by Domenico Bolognese

| | |
|---|---|
| Margherita Pusterla | Giuseppina Medori sop. |
| Alpinolo | Ester Paganini mez. |
| Francisco Pusterla | Raffaele Mirate ten. |
| Lucchino | Filippo Coletti bar. |
| Ramengo | Marco Arati bass |
| | |
| Conductor | Antonio Farelli |
| Director | Giovanni Pacini |

---

16. There is every indication that this opera was originally composed for Palermo (as *Lidia di Brabante)* in the spring of 1853 but not performed. Leone does not list *Lidia di Brabante* in his books on the history of opera in Palermo, nor is a performance mentioned in the Italian theatrical press.

25A. I PORTOGHESI NEL BRASILE[17]

26. IL SALTIMBANCO-*Dramma lirico* in three acts
Rome-Teatro Argentina-May 24, 1858
Libretto by Giuseppe Checchetelli

| | |
|---|---|
| Lena (L.) | Elena Kenneth sop. |
| Alfredo di Blangy (B.) | Remigio Bertolini ten. |
| Guglielmo Belfegor (Be.) | Ottavio Bartolini bar. |
| Arnoldo/Rolando (A.) | Stefano Santucci bass |
| Duca d'Almonte | Giuseppe Bazzoli ten. |
| Geltrude | Carolina de Caroli sop. |
| Linda | Teodolinda Rotolini sec. |
| Scudiere | Luigi Rossi sec. |
| | |
| Conductor | Emilio Angelini |
| Director | Giovanni Pacini |

OTHER PRODUCTIONS

ARGENTINA
Buenos Aires  Ant. Colón  Nov.  7, 1866 C. Briol (L.) L. Lelmi (B.) A. Ce-
                                        lestino (Be.)

GREECE
Corfu         San Giacomo Oct.?    1861 Martini (L.) Ciarlini (B.) Mottino/
                                        A. Vitti (Be.)

ITALY
Ascoli        Ventidio    Nov.     1858 L. Ponti dall'Armi (L.) A. Pagnoni
  Piceno      Basso                     (B.) M. Zacchi (Be.)

Florence      Pergola     Jan.  6, 1859 F. Salvini-Donatelli (L.) P. Bignar-
                                        di (B.) A. Rossi-Ghelli (Be.) B.
                                        Cervini (A.) G. Pacini dir.

              Lent               1859 E. Julienne-Dejean (L.) G. Villani
                                        (B.) L. Giraldoni (Be.) G. Segri-
                                        Segarra (A.)

Naples        San Carlo   Mar. 27, 1859 G. Medori (L.) F. Prudenza (B.) F.
                                        Coletti (Be.) G. B. Antonucci (A.)
                                        A. Farelli cond.

Palermo       Carolino    Apr.  9, 1859 I. Alba (L.) A. Salviani (B.) E.
                                        Crivelli (Be.) F. Rinaldi (A.) A. Lo
                                        Casto cond.

Parma         Regio       Feb. 23, 1859 C. Carozzi-Zucchi (L.) G. Musiani
                                        (B.) E. Fagotti (Be.) G. Capriles
                                        (A.) G. C. Ferrarini cond. G. Pacini
                                        dir.

---

17. There is no evidence that this opera, frequently attributed to Pacini, and reported
as being given in Rio de Janeiro in 1856, was ever performed. It is not listed by De Andrade
in his *Francisco Manuel da Silva e seu tempo* and a thorough examination of the *Jornal do
Comercio*, Rio de Janeiro has shown no indication of a production.

Reggio Emilia Municipale  Jan. 23, 1859 A. Jackson (L.) L. Ceresa (B.) A.
                                       Grandi (Be.) M. Ghini (A.) G. Tebal-
                                       di cond.

Treviso       Societa     Oct. 30, 1858 L. Lesniewska (L.) E. Naudin (B.) L.
                                       Merly (Be.) R. Laterza (A.) N. Bassi
                                       cond. G. Pacini dir.

Turin         Regio       Jan. 26, 1859 L. Lesniewska (L.) R. Bertolini (B.)
                                       G. Ferri (Be.) G. Echeverria (A.) N.
                                       Bassi cond. G. Pacini dir.

Venice        La Fenice   Mar. 10, 1859 M. Lafon/A. Jackson (L.) V. Sarti
                                       (B.) G. Guicciardi (Be.) C. Della
                                       Costa (A.) C. E. Bosoni cond. G.
                                       Pacini dir.

Viterbo       Unione      Aug. 31, 1858 L. Ponti dall'Armi (L.) A. Dall'Armi
                                       (B.) F. Giannini (Be.) Fossati (A.)
                                       G. Pacini dir.

MALTA
La Valletta   Manoel      Feb.     1860 A. Moro (L.) G. Piccinnini (B.)

PERU
Lima          Principal   May?     1860 O. Sconcia (L.) A. Rossi-Ghelli
                                       (Be.)

PORTUGAL
Oporto        Sao Joao    Oct.     1859 E. Hensler (L.) M. Neri (B.) G. Man-
                                       cusi (Be.) P. Nolasco-Llorens (A.)

RUSSIA
Odessa        Municipal   Winter?  1864 C. Noel-Guidi (L.) A. Gottardi (B.)
                                       V. Morelli-Bartolami (Be.) G. B.
                                       Cornago (A.)

SPAIN
Barcelona     Liceo       Mar. 24, 1859 A. Ortolani-Tiberini (L.) M. Tiber-
                                       ini (B.) G. F. Beneventano (Be.) A.
                                       Rodas (A.)

Cadiz         Principal   Dec.?    1859 C. Ghirlanda-Tortolini (L.) L. Stec-
                                       chi-Bottardi (B.) P. Giorgi-Pacini
                                       (Be.) A. Selva (A.)

Madrid        Real        Mar. 21, 1859 E. Kenneth (L.) A. Luise (B.) O.
                                       Bartolini (Be.) P. Nolasco-Llorens
                                       (A.) J. Skoczdopole cond.

                          Oct. 26, 1865 A. States (L.) G. Fancelli (B.) L.
                                       Merly (Be.) N. Contedini (A.) J.
                                       Skoczdopole cond.

TURKEY
Constan-      Naum        Apr.     1860 C. Rovelli (L.) A. Zennari (B.) C.
tinople                                Visai (Be.) O. Lari (A.)

27. GIANNI DI NISIDA-*Dramma lirico* in four acts
Rome-Teatro Apollo-Oct. 29, 1860
Libretto by Giuseppe Checchetelli

| | |
|---|---|
| Chiara Montalto (C.) | Luigia Ponti dall'Armi sop. |
| Bionda (B.) | Eufemia Barlani-Dini mez. |
| Gianni di Nisida (G.) | Geremia Bettini ten. |
| Roberto (R.) | Davide Squarcia bar. |
| Michele Vertunno (M.) | Raffaele Laterza bass |
| Giamir | Caterina De Caroli sop. |
| Marco | Giuseppe Bazzoli ten. |
| Giacomo | Cesare Bossi bass |
| Ramadà | Giovanni Bernardoni bass |
| | |
| Conductor | Emilio Angelini |
| Director | Giovanni Pacini |

OTHER PRODUCTIONS

ITALY

| | | | |
|---|---|---|---|
| Florence | Pergola | Dec. 26, 1861 | L. Ponti dall'Armi (C.) E. Barlani-Dini (B.) P. Bignardi (G.) I. Viganotti (R.) P. Medini (M.) |
| Lugo | Rossini | Aug. 29, 1861 | L. Ponti dall'Armi (C.) E. Barlani-Dini (B.) E. Barbacini (G.) V. Collini (R.) P. Medini (M.) M. Parma cond. |
| Rome | Apollo | Apr. 13, 1861 | L. Ponti dall'Armi (C.) G. Tati (B.) P. Bignardi (G.) L. Buti (R.) N. Benedetti (M.) E. Angelini cond. |

28. IL MULATTIERE DI TOLEDO-*Commedia lirica* in five acts
Rome-Teatro Apollo-May 25, 1861
Libretto by Giuseppe Cencetti

| | |
|---|---|
| Elvira | Luigia Ponti dall'Armi sop. |
| Carmine | Giuseppina Tati mez. |
| Don Sancio | Pietro Bignardi ten. |
| Don Pedro | Ludovico Buti bar. |
| Don Cesare | Luigi Fioravanti buf. |
| Geltrude | Caterina De Caroli sop. |
| Capitano | Luigi Fossi ten. |
| Alfonso | Giacomo Castelli bass |
| Paolo | Filippo Vitalini sec. |
| Don Sallustio | Pietro Cassani ten. |
| | |
| Conductor | Emilio Angelini |
| Director | Giovanni Pacini |

29. BELFEGOR-*Melodramma fantastico* in a prologue and four parts
Florence-Teatro in via della Pergola-Dec. 1, 1861
Libretto by Antonio Lanari

| | |
|---|---|
| Virginia | Marcellina Lotti della Santa sop. |
| Fernando | Ernesto Nicolini ten. |
| Belfegor | Ludovico Buti bar. |
| Plutone | Vito Orlandi bass |
| Pedrillo | Filippo Catani buf. |
| Ines | sop. |
| Un Servo | ten. |
| Alonso | bass |
| | |
| Conductor | Luigi Vannuccini |
| Director | Giovanni Pacini |

30. CARMELITA-*Opera seria*
Composed for La Scala in Milan in 1863-Unperformed
Libretto by Francesco Maria Piave

31. DON DIEGO DI MENDOZA-*Opera fantastica* in three acts
Venice-Teatro La Fenice-Jan. 12, 1867
Libretto by Francesco Maria Piave

| | |
|---|---|
| Mariquita | Angela Ortolani-Tiberini sop. |
| Paquita | Elvira Stecchi sop. |
| Don Diego | Mario Tiberini ten. |
| Don Enrico | Giuseppe Federico Beneventano bar. |
| Il Malgenio di Mendoza | Paolo Poli-Lenzi bass |
| Donna Vittoria | Clotilde Mainetti sec. |
| Don Cristoval | Antonio Galletti ten. |
| Don Sandoval D'Oviedo | Augusto Pelletti sec. |
| Francesco | Francesco Rebussini sec. |
| | |
| Conductor | Emanuele Muzio |
| Director | Giovanni Pacini |

32. BERTA DI VARNOL-*Dramma lirico* in a prologue and three acts
Naples-Teatro San Carlo-Apr. 6, 1867
Libretto by Francesco Maria Piave

| | |
|---|---|
| Berta | Luigia Bendazzi-Secchi sop. |
| Irene | Giuseppina Tati mez. |
| Corrado | Giorgio Stigelli ten. |
| Ottone | Luigi Colonnese bar. |
| Pietro l'Eremita | Marco Arati bass |
| Marsa | Carolina Cetrone mez. |
| Gualtiero | Enrico Guarnieri sec. |
| Mattia | Antonio Donadio sec. |
| Verner | Giuseppe Benedetti bass |
| Eino | Pasquale De Marinis sec. |
| | |
| Director | Giovanni Pacini |

33. NICOLO DE'LAPI-*Melodramma tragico* in three acts
Florence-Teatro Pagliano-Oct. 29, 1873
Libretto by Cesare Perini[18]

| | |
|---|---|
| Lisa (L.) | Giuditta Ronzi-Checchi sop. |
| Lamberto (La.) | Paolo Augusti ten. |
| Nicolo (N.) | Luigi Merly bar. |
| Troilo (T.) | Alessandro Silvestri bass |
| Averado | Clemente Scannavino ten. |
| Vieri | Federico Becheri bass |
| Bindo | Pietro Lybert ten. |
| Fede | Bianca Cortesi Dell'Ozzi sec. |
| Un Monaco | Fortunato Cherubini bass |
| | |
| Conductor | Teodulo Mabellini |

OTHER PRODUCTIONS

ITALY

| | | | |
|---|---|---|---|
| Arezzo | Petrarca | Jan. 5, 1887 | Florenza (L.) Maestrani (La.) Alberti (N.) R. Mancini (T.) |
| Florence | Principe Umberto | July 8, 1879 | V. Crespi (L.) V. Clodio (La.) L. Merly (N.) T. Mabellini cond. |
| Livorno | Rossini | Nov. 9, 1879 | V. Crespi (L.) V. Clodio (La.) E. Carnili (N.) |

---

18. It is very likely that *Nicolo de'Lapi* is merely a "rifacimento" of the earlier *La Punizione*, which deals with essentially the same plot, although the plot in the original work had been transposed to Brussels. *Nicolo de'Lapi* had been expressly composed for Rio in 1855, but was never performed there. This contention is based on the following considerations: (a) The libretto is identical for Acts I and III, (b) It seems improbable that Pacini would have composed new music to the same text for a premiere in such a remote and then unimportant city, and (c) this possibility is brought out, but not stated as fact in a review of the premiere of *Nicolo de'Lapi* in the Nov. 1, 1873 issue of *Il Sistro*, Florence, p. 161.

Parma          Regio        Jan. 24, 1880  I.  Martinez  de  Escalante  (L.)  L.
                                          Giraud  (La.)  E.  Carnili  (N.)  L.
                                          Contini (T.) A. Gianelli cond.

Verona         Filarmonico Jan. 19? 1881 R. Caponetti (L.) De Angelis (La.)
                                          E. Carnili (N.) A. Gianelli cond.

CARLO PEDROTTI

1. LINA-*Dramma semiserio* in two acts
Verona-Teatro Filarmonico-May 2, 1840
Libretto by Marcelliano Marcello

Lina                                    Josephine De Mery sop.
Imero                                   Prospero Ferrari ten.
Raimondo                                Eugenio Linari-Bellini bar.


2. CLARA DI MAILAND-*Opera seria* in three acts
Composed circa 1840 Probably unperformed
Librettist unknown


3. MATILDE-*Melodramma* in three acts
Composed circa 1840-41 Probably unperformed
Librettist unknown


4. LA FIGLIA DELL'ARCIERE-*Melodramma serio* in two acts
Amsterdam-Théâtre Italien-Feb. 29, 1844
Libretto by Felice Romani

Adelia (A.)                             Fanny Salvini-Donatelli sop.
Oliviero (O.)                           Angelo Brunacci ten.
Arnoldo (A.)                            Antonio Avignone bar.
Odetta
Carlo
Comino
Un Scudiere

Conductor                                            Carlo Pedrotti
Director                                             Carlo Pedrotti

OTHER PRODUCTIONS

NETHERLANDS
Utrecht                 Mar. 22, 1844 F. Salvini-Donatelli (A.) A. Brunac-
                        ci (O.) A. Avignone (A.)

5. ROMEA DI MONTFORT-*Melodramma* in four parts
Verona-Teatro Filarmonico-Feb. 19, 1846
Libretto by Gaetano Rossi

| | |
|---|---|
| Romea di Montfort (R.) | Carlotta Vittadini sop. |
| Terigi, Conte di Chatillon (T.) | Alberto Bozzetti ten. |
| Lotario, Duca di Montfort (L.) | Felice Varesi bar. |
| Roberto di Versac (V.) | Luigi Sonderegger bass |
| Ferrante d'Alby | G. Perelli ten. |
| Loride | Marietta Perelli sop. |

Director                                    Carlo Pedrotti

OTHER PRODUCTIONS

ITALY
Piacenza      Municipale  May   6, 1846 R. Basso-Borio (R.) D. Mecksa (T.)
                                       F. Varesi (L.) G. Jona cond. C. Pe-
                                       drotti dir.


6. FIORINA o LA FANCIULLA DI GLARIS-*Melodramma semiserio* in two acts
Verona-Teatro Nuovo-Nov. 22, 1851
Libretto by Benedetto Serenelli

| | |
|---|---|
| Fiorina (F.) | Aurora Valesi sop. |
| Rodingo (R.) | Paolo Scotti ten. |
| Ermanno (Er.) | Lorenzo Montani bar. |
| Giuliano (G.) | Giovanni Zucchini buf. |
| Eugenio (E.) | ten. |
| Giannetta | |
| Un Giocatore | |

Conductor                                    Luigi Dorigo
Director                                    Carlo Pedrotti

OTHER PRODUCTIONS

AUSTRIA
Vienna        Kärntnertor June  3, 1859 E. Fioretti (F.) E. Carrion (R.) D.
                                       Squarcia (Er.) G. Zucchini (G.)

BRAZIL
Rio de        Lirico      June 15, 1857 L. Lelmi (R.)
  Janeiro     Fluminense

FRANCE
Paris         Italien     Dec.  8, 1855 R. Penco (F.) E. Carrion (R.) C.
                                       Everardi (Er.) G. Zucchini (G.) G.
                                       Bottesini cond.

GREECE
Corfu         San Giacomo Sep.?   1862 R. De Baillou (F.)

                          Nov. 27? 1892 A. De Paoli (F.) S. Mastrobuono (R.)

ITALY
Alessandria   Municipale  Carn. 1860-61 Brema (F.) Mottino (Er.) C. Bellin-
                                       cioni (G.)

Bassano                   Feb.    1857 Campi (F.) Grossi (R.)

| | | | | |
|---|---|---|---|---|
| Bergamo | Sociale | Jan.? | 1866 | V. Potentini (F.) |
| Bologna | Comunale | Jan. 29, | 1852 | A. Giovanelli-Biava (F.) P. Scotti (R.) P. Zilioli (E.) C. Morelli-Condolmieri (Er.) G. Zucchini (G.) G. Manetti cond. C. Pedrotti dir. |
| | Contavalli | May | 1867 | C. Flavis (F.) G. Guidi (R.) E. Topai (G.) |
| Brescia | Grande | Dec. 26, | 1853 | V. Pozzi-Brazanti (F.) A. Bozetti (R.) |
| Cagliari | Civico | Feb. | 1857 | P. Dompieri (F.) C. Scannavino (R.) |
| Catania | Comunale | Jan. | 1864 | Tamburini (F.) N. Andreef (R.) G. Cantù (Er.) |
| Ceneda | | Aug. | 1856 | M. Plodowska (F.) A. Luise (R.) D. Dal Negro (Er.) G. Zambelli (G.) |
| Crema | Sociale | Jan. | 1855 | B. Bellocchio (F.) G. Piccinnini (R.) |
| Cremona | Concordia | May 10, | 1856 | A. Altavilla (R.) G. Bergamaschi (Er.) A. Marzorati cond. |
| Florence | Nuovo | July 17, | 1853 | C. Crémont (F.) L. Donati (R.) P. Mattioli-Alessandrini (G.) |
| Genoa | Carlo Felice | Oct. 20, | 1852 | A. Rebussini (F.) T. Palmieri (R.) G. Righetti (Er.) E. Rossi-Corsi (G.) A. Mariani cond. |
| | Paganini | Apr. 16, | 1855 | L. Ruggero-Antonioli (F.) V. Sarti (R.) E. Fagotti (Er.) G. Zucchini (G.) |
| | | Nov. 17, | 1860 | T. Pozzi (F.) G. Tombesi (R.) A. Vitti (Er.) F. Catani (G.) |
| Lodi | Sociale | Jan? | 1857 | S. Specchi (F.) G. Dordoni (R.) |
| Mantua | Sociale | Dec. 26? | 1852 | C. Lorenzetti (F.) A. Castellan (R.) D. Mattioli (Er.) F. Frizzi (G.) |
| Milan | Canobbiana | Sep. 14, | 1852 | A. Conti-Foroni (F.) E. Carrion (R.) A. Padovani-Polli (Er.) M. Borella (G.) |
| | | Sep. 18, | 1854 | V. Viola (F.) E. Carrion (R.) A. Benciolini (Er.) G. Zucchini (G.) |
| Modena | Goldoni | May | 1882 | C. Flavis (F.) E. Marchi (R.) A. Gnaccarini (Er.) G. Bergami (G.) G. Trebbi cond. |
| Novara | Nuovo | Autumn | 1855 | C. Crémont (F.) V. Sarti (R.) C. Bellincioni (G.) |
| Padua | Nuovo | Nov. 10, | 1852 | G. Leva (F.) V. Sarti (R.) A. Morelli (Er.) G. Zucchini (G.) |

Parma          Regio        Jan.   5, 1861 A. Tagliana (F.) A. Campanelli (R.)
                                           G. Romanelli (Er.) F. Catani (G.) G.
                                           C. Ferrarini cond.

Piacenza       Municipale   Spring   1856 V. Luzzi (F.) C. Conti (R.) E. For-
                                           tuna (Er.) B. Mazzetti (G.) G. Jona
                                           cond.

                            Spring   1873 N. Gnone (R.) E. Boselli (Er.) F.
                                           Catani (G.) P. Montaguti cond.

Reggio Emilia Comunale       Dec. 26, 1855 T. Ballerini-Mistrali (F.) P. Stec-
                                           chi (R.) G. Zambellini (Er.) O. Bo-
                                           nafous (G.) G. Tebaldi cond.

Rome           Argentina    Carn. 1863-64 G. Giovannoni-Zacchi (F.) P. Stecchi
                                           (R.) F. Tournerie (Er.) G. Zucchini
                                           (G.) F. Ammirato cond.

Trento         Sociale      Mar.     1855 B. Bellocchio (F.) P. Scotti (R.) G.
                                           Colombo (Er.) Rocca (G.)

Treviso        Onigo        Apr.?    1856 Campi (F.) L. Caserini (R.) Righi
                                           (Er.) Menin (G.)

Trieste        Grande       Dec. 26, 1852 A. Corbari (F.) A. Agresti (R.) G.
                                           Paletta (E.) A. Ottaviani (Er.) M.
                                           Borella (G.) G. A. Scaramelli cond.

Udine                       Nov.     1856 M. Pirola (F.) P. Chiesi (R.)

Venice         Apollo       Apr. 21, 1852 A. Conti-Foroni (F.) M. Neri (R.)
                                           Ajani (Er.) C. Bellincioni (G.)

               San          Dec. 26, 1852 A. Conti-Foroni (F.) V. Sarti (R.)
               Benedetto                   A. Morelli (Er.) G. Zucchini (G.)

Verona         Nuovo        Apr.     1857 C. Mongini-Stecchi (F.) G. Tombesi
                                           (R.) F. Giannini (Er.) G. Zucchini
                                           (G.)

Vicenza        Eretenio     Dec.?    1854 A. Rossetti (F.) E. Armandi (R.) T.
                                           Consoli (Er.) G. Zambelli (G.)

Voghera                     Autumn   1858

JUGOSLAVIA
Zara           Nobile       Jan. 12, 1854 P. Prinetti (F.) F. De Ruggero (R.)
                                           A. Balderi (Er.) E. Topai (G.)

MALTA
La Valletta    Manoel       Oct.     1863

POLAND
Warsaw         Wielki       Dec. 13, 1853 M. Spezia-Aldighieri (F.) F. Ciaffei
                                           (R.) L. Buti (Er.) G. Zucchini (G.)

                            Sep. 28, 1856 C. Valori (F.) F. Ciaffei L. Buti
                                           (Er.)

PORTUGAL
Lisbon         Sao Carlos   Mar. 11, 1863 L. Perelli (F.) M. Neri (R.) V.
                                           Orlandi (Er.) P. A. Coppolla cond.

RUSSIA
St.          Imperial    Dec. 17, 1866 L. Perelli (F.) E. Calzolari (R.) S.
Petersburg                             Malvezzi (E.) C. Everardi (Er.) L.
                                       Fioravanti (G.) E. Baveri cond.

SPAIN
Barcelona    Liceo       June 13, 1856 C. Crescimano (F.) G. De Vecchi (R.)
                                       D. Mattioli (Er.)

Palma di     Coliseo     Feb.?    1857 A. Luise (R.) G. Colombo (Er.)
Mallorca

TURKEY
Constan-     Naum        Nov.     1856 A. Murio-Celli (F.) B. Danieli (R.)
tinople                                D. Dal Negro (Er.) O. Bonafous (G.)
                                       L. Arditi cond.


7. IL PERUCCHIERE DELLA REGGENZA-*Melodramma comico* in three acts
Verona-Teatro Nuovo-May 5, 1852
Libretto by Gaetano Rossi

Mina (M.)                              Adele Rebussini sop.
Armando (A.)                             Mariano Neri ten.
Pietro il Grande (P.)                  Giovanni Sansoni bar.
Floridor (F.)                          Giovanni Zucchini buf.
Sofia                                   Luigia Morselli mez.
La Rose                             Salvatore Poggiali ten.
Pouskin                                      Baroni bass
Uficiale                                   Barbieri bass

Conductor                                  Luigi Dorigo
Director                                  Carlo Pedrotti

OTHER PRODUCTIONS

ITALY
Venice       San         Jan.  5, 1853 R. Donzelli (M.) V. Sarti (A.) A.
             Benedetto                 Morelli (P.) G. Zucchini (F.)


8. GELMINA o COL FUOCO NON SI SCHERZA-*Melodramma semiserio* in three acts
Milan-Teatro alla Scala-Nov. 3, 1853
Libretto by Giovanni Peruzzini

Gelmina                             Fanny Salvini-Donatelli sop.
Bianca                                   Fanny Gordosa sop.
Rodolfo                                   Luigi Stefani ten.
Il Duca di Bracciano                    Giacomo Arnaud bar.
Il Marchese di Valrosa                  Maurizio Borella buf.
La Marchesa                             Orsolina Bignami sec.
Un Paggio                              Stefano Morzenti ten.
Ruggeri                               Giacomo Redaelli ten.

Conductor                              Eugenio Cavallini
Director                                Carlo Pedrotti

9. GENOVEFFA DEL BRABANTE-*Melodramma* in three acts
Milan-Teatro alla Scala-Mar. 20, 1854
Libretto by Gaetano Rossi

| | |
|---|---|
| Genoveffa | Rosalia Gariboldi-Bassi sop. |
| Enrico duca del Brabante | Emanuele Carrion ten. |
| Arturo conte d'Hainaut | Giovanni Guicciardi bar. |
| Vander | Hyppolite Brémont bass |
| Margherita | Orsolina Bignami sec. |
| Ubaldo | Giacomo Redaelli ten. |
| Roberto | Antonio Benciolini bass |
| | |
| Conductor | Eugenio Cavallini |
| Director | Carlo Pedrotti |

10. TUTTI IN MASCHERA-*Comedia lirica* in three acts
Verona-Teatro Nuovo-Nov. 4, 1856
Libretto by Marcelliano Marcello

| | |
|---|---|
| Vittoria (V.) | Laura Ruggero-Antonioli sop. |
| Dorotea (D.) | Adele Ruggero mez. |
| Emilio (E.) | Giovanni Petrovich ten. |
| Abdala (A.) | Davide Squarcia bar. |
| Martello (M.) | Bisi bass |
| Don Gregorio (G.) | Pietro Mattioli Alessandrini buf. |
| Lisetta | sec. |
| | |
| Conductor | Luigi Dorigo |
| Director | Carlo Pedrotti |

SELECTED PRODUCTIONS-NINETEENTH CENTURY

AUSTRALIA
Adelaide       Th. Royal     Apr. 13, 1877 M.  Caranti-Vita  (V.)  P.  Paladini
                                           (E.) A. Tessada (G.) P. Giorza cond.

Melbourne      Th. Royal     Mar. 15, 1877 M.  Caranti-Vita  (V.)  P.  Paladini
                                           (E.) G. Gambetti (A.) A. Tessada
                                           (G.) P. Giorza cond.

Sydney         Th. Royal     June  7, 1877 M.  Caranti-Vita  (V.)  P.  Paladini
                                           (E.) G. Gambetti (A.) A. Tessada
                                           (G.) P. Giorza cond.

AUSTRIA
Vienna         Kärntnertor May 18, 1865 E.  Volpini  (V.)  Fabbrini  (D.)  C.
                                        Guidotti (E.) C. Boccolini (A.) L.
                                        Fioravanti (G.)

CHINA
Shanghai       Lyceum       Jan.  3, 1882 Pinelli  (V.)  A.  Silini  (D.)  L.
                                          Vanzetti (E.) G. Ciocci (A.) E.
                                          Corti (G.)

FRANCE
Nice           Municipal    Dec.    1862 V. Pozzi-Brazanti (V.) A. Corsi (E.)
                                         G. Giotti (A.) S. Ronconi (G.)

GREECE
Corfu          San Giacomo Oct.      1875 M.  Milani-Vela  (V.)  Mercanti  (D.)
                                          Baghi  (E.)  G.  Bergamaschi  (A.)  O.
                                          Bonafous  (G.)

HONG KONG
Hong Kong      Th. Royal    Mar. 14, 1882 Pinelli   (V.)   A.   Silini   (D.)   L.
                                          Vanzetti  (E.)  G.  Ciocci  (A.)  E.
                                          Corti  (G.)

INDIA
Bombay         Grant Road   Nov. 19, 1864 M.  Bozetti  (V.)  A.  Mazzucco  (D.)  A.
                                          Bozetti  (E.)  S.  Orsi  (A.)  E.  Papini
                                          (G.)

Calcutta       Royal        Nov.  6, 1866 Longhena  (V.)  Fiorio  (D.)  A.  Rinal-
                                          dini  (E.)  Villani  (A.)  S.  Grandi
                                          (G.)

ITALY
Alessandria    Municipale   Dec. 26? 1862 P.  Tacchinardi  (V.)  N.  Baldassari
                                          (E.)  C.  Lenghi  (A.)  P.  Prette  (G.)

Bergamo        Sociale      Carn. 1864-65 A.  Cesarini  (V.)

Bologna        Comunale     Jan. 31, 1860 A.  Fumagalli  (V.)  A.  Cravero Turolla
                                          (D.)  F.  De Ruggero  (E.)  G.  Altini
                                          (A.)  L.  Parmeggiani  (M.)  L.  Fiora-
                                          vanti  (G.)  C.  Verardi cond.

Cremona        Concordia    June  4, 1864 C.  Ghirlanda-Tortolini  (V.)  G.  Spa-
                                          lazzi  (E.)  P.  Mattioli-Alessandrini
                                          (G.)

Florence       Pagliano     Jan. 17, 1862 A.  Moro  (V.)  L.  De Fanti  (D.)  A.
                                          Campanelli  (E.)  F.  Bellini  (A.)  P.
                                          Mattioli Alessandrini  (G.)

Genoa          Gustavo      Sep. 19, 1857 N.  Barbieri-Thiollier  (V.)  E.  Pasi
               Modena                     (E.)  F.  Giannini  (A.)  L.  Fioravanti
                                          (G.)  A.  Mariani cond.

               Carlo        Oct. 21, 1857 N.  Barbieri-Thiollier  (V.)  E.  Pasi
               Felice                     (E.)  F.  Giannini  (A.)  L.  Fioravanti
                                          (G.)  A.  Mariani cond.

Milan          Santa        Mar.  5, 1859 A.  Moro  (V.)  Zaviska  (D.)  G.  Altini
               Radegonda                  (A.)  M.  Borella  (G.)

               Canobbiana   Apr. 20, 1861 V.  Pozzi-Brazanti  (V.)  T.  Alvisi
                                          (D.)  C.  Vincentelli  (E.)  A.  Cotogni
                                          (A.)  P.  Mattioli-Alessandrini  (G.)

Modena         Aliprandi    Nov.  5, 1864 A.  Cesarini  (V.)  P.  Bovi  (E.)  F.
                                          Mottino  (A.)  L.  Galli  (G.)

Padua          Concordia    Lent     1866 A.  Giannetti  (V.)  V.  Sabatini  (E.)
                                          F.  Tournerie  (A.)  P.  Prette  (G.)

Palermo        Bellini      Mar. 10, 1867 Franzini  (V.)  L.  De Fanti  (D.)  G.
                                          Sbriglia  (E.)  F.  Coliva  (A.)  S.  Ron-
                                          coni  (G.)  L.  Alfano cond.

Garibaldi    Jan.      1881 M. Balzofiore (V.) S. Carlone (D.)
                            L. Balzofiore (E.) M. Guidi (A.) A.
                            Florio (G.) E. Sarria cond.

Parma        Regio     Apr. 25, 1859 L. Ruggero-Antonioli (V.) A. Ruggero
                            (D.) G. Petrovich (E.) L. Ferrario
                            (A.) C. Bellincioni (G.) G. C. Fer-
                            rarini cond.

             Nov.   4, 1865 A. Fumagalli (V.) E. Brunacci (D.)
                            G. Balma (E.) S. Orsi (A.) P. Prette
                            (G.)

Piacenza     Municipale Aug. 12? 1863 R. De Baillou (V.) L. Vistarini (E.)
                            P. Garcia (A.) C. Bellincioni (G.)
                            G. Jona cond.

Pesaro       Rossini   Carn. 1871-72 T. Rastelli (V.) A. Zanardi-Landi
                            (E.) E. De Leva (G.) G. Grilli cond.

Pisa         Ravvivati Mar. 16, 1867

Reggio Emilia Municipale Jan. 25, 1862 G. Amey (V.) E. Mussi (D.) L. Stec-
                            chi-Bottardi (E.) F. Tournerie (A.)
                            L. Fagnoni (M.) L. Galli (G.) G.
                            Tebaldi cond.

Sinigaglia   Comunale  Carn. 1871-72

Trieste      Grande    Jan.   8, 1861 V. Pozzi-Brazanti (V.) L. Stecchi-
                            Bottardi (E.) A. Cotogni (A.) L.
                            Fioravanti (G.) G. A. Scaramelli
                            cond.

             Carn. 1863-64 A. Tagliana (V.) M. Allievi (D.) C.
                            Guidotti (E.) G. Reduzzi (M.) G.
                            Ciampi (G.) A. Cremaschi cond.

Turin        D'Angennes Apr.    1857 V. Pozzi-Brazanti (V.) G. Stigelli
                            (E.) D. Squarcia (A.) P. Mattioli-
                            Alessandrini (G.)

Varese       Sociale   Autumn 1858 E. Crivelli (A.) P. Mattioli-Ales-
                            sandrini (G.)

Venice       Apollo    Dec.      1862 Angeleri (V.) L. Caserini (E.) M.
                            Borella (G.)

JUGOSLAVIA
Zara         Nobile    Oct. 30? 1867 A. Acconci (E.) D. Dal Negro (A.)

MALTA
La Valletta  Manoel    Dec.      1861 A. Fumagalli (V.) Righi (E.) T.
                            Sterbini (A.)

PHILIPPINES
Manila       Español   Dec. 14, 1875 Bellot (V.) Polli (D.) A. Zanardi-
                            Landi (E.) S. Rossi-Romiati (A.) G.
                            Marchisio (G.) Zavaglio cond.

ROMANIA
Bucharest    Nacional  Feb.      1866 V. Pozzi-Brazanti (V.) A. Minetti
                            (E.) D. Dal Negro (A.) M. Borella
                            (G.)

RUSSIA
Odessa          Municipal    Feb.      1861 I. Edelvira (V.) E. Irfré (E.) M.
                                            Padilla (A.) E. Topai (G.)

SPAIN
Barcelona       Circo        Apr. 22, 1863 A. Gottardi (E.) P. Mattioli-Ales-
                                            sandrini (G.)

                Liceo        Jan. 14, 1871 A. Minetti (E.) G. Spallazzi (A.) P.
                                            Mattioli-Alessandrini (G.)

TURKEY
Constan-        Naum         Oct.      1862 G. Giovannoni-Zacchi (V.) C. Bellin-
  tinople                                   cioni (G.)

OTHER PRODUCTIONS-TWENTIETH CENTURY

ITALY
Florence        Nazionale    Mar. 24, 1930 D. Fiumana (V.) R. Brunetto (D.) A.
                                            Spigolon (E.) G. Cassoli (A.) C. Pa-
                                            terna (G.) U. Mugnai cond.

Genoa           Politeama    Oct. 31, 1903 P. Zweifel (V.) L. Battaglini cond.

Milan           Fossati      Sep.  1, 1905 L. Cortesi (V.) E. Daelli (D.) A.
                                            Gilberti/E. Bottolini (E.) N. Fos-
                                            setta (A.) P. Cesari/C. Rossi (G.)
                                            E. Romano cond.

                Eden         July 30, 1921 C. Zappa (V.) E. Castellazzi (E.) T.
                                            Luci (A.) C. Paterna (G.) E. Dal
                                            Monte cond.

                Diana        Aug.  2, 1921 C. Zappa (V.) E. Castellazzi (E.) T.
                                            Luci (A.) C. Paterna (G.) E. Dal
                                            Monte cond.

Turin           Sala RAI     June 16, 1935 I. Brunazzi (V.) V. Palombini (D.)
                                            L. Fort (E.) E. Ghirardini (A.) E.
                                            Badini (G.) A. Sabino cond.


11. ISABELLA D'ARAGONA-*Dramma lirico* in three acts
Turin-Teatro Vittorio Emanuele-Feb. 7, 1859 (Inauguration of the theatre)
Libretto by Marcelliano Marcello

Isabella d'Aragona (I.)                          Antonietta Fricci sop.
Antoniello Caracciolo (A.)                         Emilio Naudin ten.
Rocco Del Pizzo (R.)                          Enrico Delle Sedie bar.
Fra Donato (D.)                                   Giorgio Atry bass
Raimondo Caracciolo                           Antonio Cavalieri bass
Esmeralda                                        Claudina Tosi sec.
Leonora                                               Not named
Un Nobile Calabrese                                  Not named
Un Servo                                             Not named

Conductor                                        Francesco Bianchi
Director                                            Carlo Pedrotti

OTHER PRODUCTIONS

GREECE
Corfu          San Giacomo Nov.  1, 1869 Bedetti (I.) Ferrer (A.) Torriani
                                         (R.)

ITALY
Amelia                      Summer    1870 E. Grilli (I.) T. Lucidi (A.) R.
                                          Mancini (R.) Conti (D.)

Asti           Alfieri      Autumn    1860 A. Fricci (I.) E. Barbacini (A.) V.
                                          Orlandi (R.) G. Atry (D.) G. Cotti
                                          cond.

Belluno                     Summer    1871 C. Scarati-Bresciani (I.) G. Chiesi-
                                          Moj (A.) A. Souvestre (R.)

Bergamo        Sociale      Jan.?     1873 Marizzani (I.) Gruppello (A.) Azza-
                                          lini (R.) E. De Serini (D.)

Brescia        Grande       Dec. 26, 1865 G. Stella (I.) G. Vizzani (A.) G.
                                          Cantù (R.)

                            Jan.      1875 S. Lezi (I.) F. Bellotti (A.)

Cagliari       Civico       Dec. 31, 1871 C. Poloni-Coppa (I.) E. Sbriscia
                                          (A.) N. Fallica (R.)

Cento          Comunale     Aug. 15, 1861 L. Giraldoni (R.) H. von Rokitansky
                                          (D.) C. Pedrotti cond.

Como           Sociale      Carn. 1879-80 D. Casartelli (A.) E. De Bernis (R.)

Crema          Sociale      Dec. 25, 1868

Cremona        Concordia    Jan.  1, 1870 G. Caruzzi-Bedogni (I.) L. Gulli
                                          (A.) E. Carneli (R.)

Cuneo          Civico       Dec. 26? 1863 C. Marazzini (I.) S. Perozzi (A.) E.
                                          Bonetti (R.)

Faenza         Comunale     June 18? 1862 M. Zenoni (I.) R. Bertolini (A.) E.
                                          Storti (R.) M. Ghini (D.)

Ferrara        Comunale     Apr.      1862 M. Zenoni (I.) R. Bertolini (A.) E.
                                          Storti (R.)

                            Dec. 26, 1868 E. Grilli (I.) C. Baroni (A.) F. Ar-
                                          chinti (R.)

Genoa          Nazionale    Oct. 12, 1872 I. Gerli (I.)

Lucca          Pantera      Dec. 26, 1870 G. Boema (I.) C. Baroni (A.) L.
                                          Spellini (R.) N. Rebottaro (D.)

Milan          Canobbiana   Sep. 14, 1864 E. Demi (I.) G. De Antoni (A.) A.
                                          Cotogni (R.) E. Daneri (D.)

Modena         Comunale     Dec. 28, 1861 C. Lanzi (I.) E. Nicolini (A.) A.
                                          Carboni (R.) D. Dal Negro (D.)

Naples         Fondo        June      1870 Contarini (I.) L. Bolis (A.) A.
                                          Souvestre (R.) P. Serrao cond.

| | | | | |
|---|---|---|---|---|
| Novara | | Feb. | 1867 | E. Palmana (I.) P. Chiesi (A.) Lenghi (R.) |
| Novi Ligure | | Nov.? | 1870 | C. Marazzani (I.) Morini (A.) Novari (R.) |
| Parma | Regio | Jan. 3, | 1863 | M. Zenoni (I.) G. Ugolini (A.) A. De Antoni (R.) E. Bagagiolo (D.) G. C. Ferrarini cond. |
| Pavia | Fraschini | Jan. 1, | 1870 | C. Rubini-Tisci (I.) G. Artoni (A.) F. Tirini (R.) A. De Giuli (D.) |
| | | Jan. 18? | 1887 | I. Zeffirini (I.) V. Parboni (R.) |
| Perugia | Morlacchi | Dec. 26, | 1865 | F. Gordosa (I.) L. Bolis (A.) F. Archinti (R.) |
| Pesaro | Rossini | Dec. 26, | 1863 | S. Della Valle (I.) T. Villa (A.) G. Rota (R.) A. Ciccognani (D.) G. Banchi cond. |
| Piacenza | Municipale | Summer | 1860 | V. Pozzi-Brazanti (I.) A. Malagola (A.) C. Visai (R.) G. Capponi (D.) G. Jona cond. |
| Reggio Emilia | Municipale | Dec. 26, | 1869 | G. Boema (I.) F. De Ruggero (A.) E. Campobello (R.) G. Perkins (D.) G. Tebaldi cond. A. Peri dir. |
| Rimini | Nuovo | July | 1862 | M. Zenoni (I.) R. Bertolini (A.) M. Ghini (D.) |
| Rome | Apollo | Nov. 20, | 1861 | T. De Giuli-Borsi (I.) V. Sarti (A.) E. Storti (R.) G. Marchetti (D.) E. Terziani cond. |
| Rovigo | Sociale | Oct. 14, | 1875 | V. Garulli (I.) I. D'Avanzo (A.) E. Utto (R.) A. Buzzi (D.) L. Cherubini cond. |
| Sassari | Civico | Nov. | 1864 | R. Vielli-Villa (I.) T. Villa (A.) N. Fallica (R.) |
| Savona | Chiabrera | Jan. 17, | 1872 | I. D'Este (I.) Ghislanzoni (R.) |
| Spoleto | Nuovo | Carn. | 1862-63 | |
| Trieste | Grande | Oct. 8, | 1859 | C. Marchisio (I.) E. Carrion (A.) D. Squarcia (R.) A. Lanzoni (D.) G. A. Scaramelli cond. |
| Turin | Vittorio Emanuele | June 10, | 1862 | F. Salvini-Donatelli (I.) F. Patierno (A.) E. Crivelli (R.) |
| Vercelli | Civico | Dec. 26, | 1862 | |
| Vigevano | Cagnoni | Oct. 4, | 1879 | A. Fidi-Azzolini (I.) Milani (A.) Bellati (R.) Rinaldi (D.) |
| Voghera | Nuovo | Oct. | 1863 | E. Lombardi (I.) Bertolotti (A.) Calderoni (R.) |

12. GUERRA IN QUATTRO-*Opera buffa* in three acts
Milan-Teatro Canobbiana-May 25, 1861
Libretto by Marcelliano Marcello

| | |
|---|---|
| Angelica | Virginia Pozzi-Brazanti sop. |
| Orsola | Linda Fiorio mez. |
| Gabriele | Carlo Vincentelli ten. |
| Candido | Antonio Cotogni bar. |
| Don Prosdocimo Bonafede | Pietro Mattioli-Alessandrini buf. |
| Don Torribio | Giacomo Redaelli ten. |
| Il Conte Gemignano | Luigi Alessandrini bass |
| Un Caporale | Not named |
| | |
| Conductor | Eugenio Cavallini |
| Director | Carlo Pedrotti |

Revised-Trieste-Teatro Grande-Feb. 22, 1862

| | |
|---|---|
| Angelica (A.) | Ida Pelegatti Visconti sop. |
| Orsola (O.) | Marietta Allievi mez. |
| Gabriele (G.) | Enrico Barbacini ten. |
| Candido (C.) | Cesare Boccolini bar. |
| Don Prosdocimo Bonafede (P.) | Luigi Fioravanti buf. |
| Conte Gemignano | A. Cravero Turolla bass |
| Un Notajo | Salvatore Poggiali ten. |
| Un Caporale | Giovanni Schiavi bass |
| | |
| Conductor | Giuseppe Alessandro Scaramella |
| Director | Carlo Pedrotti |

OTHER PRODUCTIONS

FRANCE
Nice          Municipal    Jan.        1864 E. Varesi (A.) V. Cantoni (G.) F.
                                        Varesi (C.) S. Ronconi (P.)

ITALY
Genoa         Paganini     Sep. 27, 1862 I. Pelegatti-Visconti (A.) G. Colom-
                                        bo (G.) G. Verati (C.) L. Fioravanti
                                        (P.)

Parma         Regio        Apr. 20, 1862 V. Pozzi-Brazanti (A.) M. Allievi
                                        (O.) L. Stecchi-Bottardi (G.) G.
                                        Marra (C.) L. Fioravanti (P.) G. C.
                                        Ferrarini cond.

13. MAZEPPA-*Melodramma tragico* in four acts
Bologna-Teatro Comunale-Dec. 3, 1861
Libretto by Achille de Lauzières

| | |
|---|---|
| Maria (M.) | Caroline Barbot sop. |
| Corrado Bogdan (C.) | Remigio Bertolini ten. |
| Mazeppa (Ma.) | Leone Giraldoni bar. |
| Natalia | Teresa Colzi sop. |
| Ellina | Geltrude Paolinelli sec. |
| Orlik | Gaetano Scardovi ten. |
| Roberto Voinarowski | Carlo Trivero bass |
| | |
| Conductor | Angelo Mariani |
| Director | Carlo Pedrotti |

OTHER PRODUCTIONS

ITALY
Venice      Rossini      Feb. 28, 1866 M. Spezia-Aldighieri (M.) F. Patier-
                          no (C.) G. Aldighieri (Ma.)

14. MARION DE LORME-*Dramma lirico* in four acts
Trieste-Teatro Grande-Nov. 16, 1865
Libretto by Marcelliano Marcello

| | |
|---|---|
| Marion de Lorme | Maria Spezia Aldighieri sop. |
| Arturo de Gassé | Giovannina Bonafi-Lucas sop. |
| Renato | Giuseppe Villani ten. |
| Saverny | Gottardo Aldighieri bar. |
| Il Grazioso | Sebastiano Ronconi bar. |
| Laffemas | Paolo Medini bass |
| Rosa | Eloisa Bellio sop. |
| Villac | Ignazio Cancelli sec. |
| L'Angely | Giovanni Schiavi bass |
| Il Banditore | Pietro Cosmi sec. |
| | |
| Conductor | Antonio Cremaschi |
| Director | Carlo Pedrotti |

15. LA VERGINE DI KERMO-*Opera seria* in three acts
Cremona-Teatro Concordia-Feb. 16, 1870
Libretto by Francesco Guidi

This opera, sometimes attributed to Pedrotti, is a pasticcio of pieces
composed by the following: Antonio Cagnoni, Francesco Cortesi, Fiori, Jacopo
Foroni, Ruggero Manna, Alberto Mazzucato, Giovanni Pacini, Carlo Pedrotti,
Amilcare Ponchielli, Federico Ricci and Lauro Rossi. Please refer to the
section on operas by multiple composers for further details.

16. IL FAVORITO-*Tragedia lirica* in three acts
Turin-Teatro Regio-Mar. 15, 1870
Libretto by Gualfardo Bercanovich

| | |
|---|---|
| Elena | Teresa Stolz sop. |
| Olga | Albina Contarini sop. |
| Boscaris | Carlo Carpi ten. |
| Obolenski | Antonio Cotogni bar. |
| Belski | Luigi Vecchi bass |
| Beatrice | Angelica Zamboni sec. |
| Blaskoff | Carlo Trivero bass |
| | |
| Conductor | Carlo Pedrotti |
| Director | Carlo Pedrotti |

17. OLEMA LA SCHIAVA-*Melodramma* in four acts
Modena-Teatro Municipale-May 4, 1872
Libretto by Francesco Maria Piave

| | |
|---|---|
| Olema (O.) | Isabella Galletti-Gianoli mez. |
| Giovanna (G.) | Gemma Tiozzo mez. |
| Don Filippo d'Austria (F.) | Angelo Masini ten. |
| Ben Zagal (B.) | Pietro Silenzi bar. |
| Ximene (X.) | Lodovico Viviani bass |
| Egmont | |
| Don Ruiz | |

OTHER PRODUCTIONS

ITALY
Milan          Dal Verme    June 19, 1873 I. Galletti-Gianoli (O.) T. Ferni
                            (G.) P. Augusti (F.) G. Aldighieri
                            (B.) L. Lombardelli (X.)

## ACHILLE PERI

1. UNA VISITA A BEDLAM-*Melodramma semiserio* in two acts
Turin-Teatro d'Angennes-June 2, 1839[19]
Libretto by Giuseppe Arnaud

| | |
|---|---|
| Amalia | Rita Gabussi de Bassini sop. |
| Alfredo | Andrea Castellan ten. |
| Barone di S. Elmo | Raffaele Scalese buf. |
| Crescendo | Vincenzo Galli buf. |
| Tom | Eutimio Polonini bass |
| Anna | Amalia Sacchi sop. |


2. IL SOLITARIO-*Melodramma* in three acts
Reggio Emilia-Teatro Comunale-May 29, 1841
Libretto by G. Bassi

| | |
|---|---|
| Elodia | Eugenia D'Alberti sop. |
| Il Solitario | Lorenzo Biacchi ten. |
| Erberto | Gaetano De Baillou bar. |
| Romilda | Luigia De Baillou sop. |
| Gherardo | Domenico Rossi ten. |
| Anselmo | Francesco Perdagnesi bass |
| | |
| Conductor | Luigi Boyer |
| Director | Achille Peri |


3. ESTER D'ENGADDI-*Dramma tragico* in three acts
Parma-Teatro Regio-Feb. 19, 1843
Libretto by Salvadore Cammarano

| | |
|---|---|
| Ester (E.) | Emilia Tosi sop. |
| Azaria (A.) | Gaetano Baldanza ten. |
| Ruben (R.) | Luigi Valli bar. |
| Jefte (J.) | Camillo Fedrighini bass |
| Rebecca | Teresa Biaggi sec. |
| Eleazaro | Gaetano Salani bar. |
| Natan | Felice Rossi ten. |
| | |
| Conductor | Nicola De Giovanni |
| Director | Achille Peri |

OTHER PRODUCTIONS

ITALY
Reggio Emilia Comunale    Feb. 17, 1846 A. Dall'Argine (E.) G. Comassi (A.)
                          G. Fiori (R.) F. Dall'Asta (J.) G.
                          Tebaldi cond. A. Peri dir.

---

[19]. *Una Visita a Bedlam* was originally composed for Marseille but not given there.

Verona         Filarmonico Carn. 1843-44 L. Matthey (E.) R. Vitali (A.) F.
                                           Colini (R.)G. Dal Pesce (J.) C. Sam-
                                           pietro cond. A. Peri dir.


4. DIRCE-*Tragedia lirica* in three acts
Reggio Emilia-Teatro Comunale-May 20, 1843
Libretto by Pietro Martini

Dirce (D.)                                          Fanny Maray sop.
Linceo (L.)                                     Napoleone Moriani ten.
Aristodemo (A.)                                    Gaetano Ferri bar.
Cleomene (C.)                                     Antonio Cotturi bass
Argia                                            Elettra Manetti sec.


Conductor                                             Luigi Boyer
Director                                              Achille Peri

OTHER PRODUCTIONS

ITALY
Florence       Pergola       Feb. 10, 1844 M. Barbieri-Nini (D.) E. Musich (L.)
                                           G. Miral (A.) I. Patriossi (C.)


Livorno        Avvalorati    Autumn  1843 C. Bertolini-Rafaelli (D.) E. Musich
                                           (L.) L. Salandri (A.)


Lugo           Rossini       Sep.?   1846 E. Boldrini (D.) E. Musich (L.) N.
                                           Constantini (A.)




5. TANCREDA-*Dramma lirico* in three acts
Genoa-Teatro Carlo Felice-Dec. 26, 1847
Libretto by Francesco Guidi

Tancreda (T.)                                  Marietta Gazzaniga sop.
Eudo (E.)                                         Luigi Ferretti ten.
Alzor (A.)                                     Francesco Gnone bar.
Adalberto (Al.)                                Giovanni Garibaldi bar.
Lionello                                       Timoleone Barattini ten.
Osmano                                         Giuseppe Righetti bass


Conductor                                         Giovanni Serra
Director                                           Achille Peri

OTHER PRODUCTIONS

ITALY
Bologna        Comunale      Dec. 26, 1854 A. Ortolani-Brignole (T.) L. Fer-
                                           retti (E.) G. Reina (A.) A. Ortolani
                                           (Al.) G. Manetti cond.


Cuneo                        Dec. 26, 1868 G. Giorgetti (E.)


Genoa          Carlo         May 15, 1850 C. Gruitz (T.) R. Mirate (E.) L.
               Felice                      Gassier (A.)

| Parma | Regio | Mar. | 3, 1852 | M. Gazzaniga (T.) L. Ferretti (E.) G. Guicciardi (A.) F. Lodetti (Al.) |
|---|---|---|---|---|

Persiceto                    Sep.      1854    T. Pozzi-Montegazza (T.) L. Ferretti
                                               (E.) E. Antico (A.)

Reggio Emilia Comunale       Feb.   7, 1854    T. Pozzi-Montegazza (T.) L. Ferretti
                                               (E.) E. Delle Sedie (A.) G. Tebaldi
                                               cond. A. Peri dir.

              Municipale      Feb.   6, 1868    L. Bacarotti (T.) V. Avoni (E.) S.
                                               Rossi-Rumiati (A.) A. Del Monte
                                               (Al.) G. Tebaldi cond. A. Peri dir.


6. ORFANO E DIAVOLO-*Melodramma comico-fantastico* in three acts
Reggio Emilia-Teatro Comunale-Dec. 27, 1854
Libretto by Carlo Grisanti

| Casilda | Virginia Ugolini sop. |
|---|---|
| Maria Teresa | Carolina Stanghi mez. |
| Raffaele | Remigio Bertolini ten. |
| Carlo Broschi | Massimiliano Severi bar. |
| Ferdinando VI | Luigi Venerandi bass |
| Gil-Vergas | Angelo Del Monte bass |
| Il Conte di Medrano | Eugenio Manzini ten. |

| Conductor | Giuseppe Tebaldi |
|---|---|
| Director | Achille Peri |

Revised (billed as a premiere)-Modena-Teatro Municipale-Jan. 25, 1871

| Casilda | Angiolina D'Alberti sop. |
|---|---|
| La Regina | Beatrice Cosmelli sop. |
| Raffaele D'Estuniga | Augusto Rampini Boncori ten. |
| Carlo Broschi | Ignazio Viganotti bar. |
| Ferdinando VI | Raimondo Buffagni bass |
| Il Conte di Medrano | Carlo Righi ten. |
| Gil Vergas | Ernesto Enrici Maurizi bass |

| Conductor | Venceslao Zawerthal |
|---|---|
| Director | Achille Peri |


7. I FIDANZATI-*Opera* in three acts
Genoa-Teatro Carlo Felice-Feb. 7, 1856
Libretto by Francesco Maria Piave

| Sara (S.) | Luigia Bendazzi-Secchi sop. |
|---|---|
| Asfene (A.) | Antonietta Melada mez. |
| Ismaele (I.) | Geremia Bettini ten. |
| Manasse (M.) | Gaetano Ferri bar. |
| Mambre | ten. |
| Giobbe | |
| Arasse | bass |
| Nemrod | bass |
| Nitocri | bass |

| Conductor | Angelo Mariani |
|---|---|
| Director | Achille Peri |

OTHER PRODUCTIONS

ITALY
Bologna        Comunale    Jan. 26, 1862 A. Pasi (S.) A. Martoni (A.) A. Mi-
                                         netti (I.) V. Panerai (M.) N. Bassi
                                         cond.

Mantua         Sociale     Mar.     1867 V. Pozzi-Brazanti (S.) E. Flori (A.)
                                         G. Verati (I.) G. Moriami (M.)


8. VITTOR PISANI-*Melodramma* in three acts
Reggio Emilia-Teatro Municipale-Apr. 21, 1857
Libretto by Francesco Maria Piave

| | |
|---|---|
| Maria Pisani (M.) | Luigia Bendazzi-Secchi sop. |
| Pietro (P.) | Pietro Mongini ten. |
| Vittor Pisani (V.) | Leone Giraldoni bar. |
| Antonio Barbo (A.) | Giovanni Battista Cornago bass |
| Andrea Contarini | Marco Ghini bass |
| Alba | Anna Gresti sop. |
| Nicolo'Memo | Salvatore Poggialo ten. |
| Messer Grande | Eugenio Manzini ten. |
| | |
| Conductor | Giuseppe Tebaldi |
| Director | Achille Peri |

OTHER PRODUCTIONS

FRANCE
Ajaccio        San         Oct.     1863 E. Berti (M.) F. Rosnati (P.)
               Gabriele

GREECE
Corfu          San Giacomo Jan.     1861 A. Argentini-Cantalamessa (M.) G.
                                         Giorgetti (P.) F. Proni (V.)

ITALY[20]
Ascoli         Ventidio    Nov.     1861 N. Rossi (M.) E. Pizioli (P.) C.
Piceno         Basso                     Boccolini (V.)

Asti           Alfieri     Oct. 15, 1862 G. Borsi de Leurie (M.) G. Valentini
                                         Cristiani (P.) A. De Antoni (V.) E.
                                         Bagagiolo (A.) G. Cotti cond.

Bari           Piccinni    Nov.?    1869 Innocenti (M.) T. Lucidi (P.) G.
                                         Sansone (V.)

                           Mar. 30? 1881 M. Van (M.) F. Rosnati (P.) C. Cos-
                                         tello (V.)

Bassano                    Sep.     1869 G. Borsi De Leurie (M.) Bernabini
                                         (P.) I. Viganotti (V.)

---

[20]. Other stagings of *Vittor Pisani* in Italy include Alessandria in 1863, Brescia in
1878-79, Crema in 1879 and Imola in 1861.

Bergamo        Riccardi     Jan.      1862 G. Naglia (M.) A. Dell'Armi (P.) E.
                                           Antico (V.) F. Zanchi cond.

Bologna        Comunale     Oct.   8, 1859 I. Galletti-Gianoli (M.) G. Bettini
                                           (P.) M. Zacchi (V.) G. B. Cornago
                                           (A.) E. Vannuccini cond. A. Peri
                                           dir.

               Contavalli   Nov.      1862 A. Di Benedetto (P.)

Brescia        Grande       Aug.      1860 I. Galletti-Gianili (M.) G. Tombesi
                                           (P.) M. Zacchi (V.) G. B. Cornago
                                           (A.)

Carpi          Comunale     Aug. 15? 1867 A. Bianchi (M.) R. Bertolini (P.) A.
                                           Mazzoli (V.) A. Rossi (A.) A. Peri
                                           dir.

Castiglione    Sociale      Sep.      1862 S. Casimir-Ney (M.) G. Gambetti (P.)
d. Stiviere                                G. Giotti (V.)

Cesena         Comunale     Aug. 11, 1860 L. Ponti dall'Armi (M.) P. Bignardi
                                           (P.) A. Mazzanti (V.) P. Medini (A.)
                                           R. Sarti cond.

Chieti         Maruccino    Apr.   5? 1866 G. Ottonelli-Bresciani (M.) G. Bac-
                                           hetti (P.) E. Antico (V.) A. De
                                           Giulio (A.) C. Biacchi cond.

Como           Sociale      Jan.      1862 L. Tencajoli (M.) Bertani (V.)

Cuneo          Civico       Dec. 26, 1866 A. Contarini (M.) E. Pizioli (P.)
                                           Grimelli (V.)

Fano           Fortuna      Jan.      1865 V. Potentini (M.) G. Ugolini (P.) F.
                                           Archinti (V.)

Ferrara        Comunale     May  17, 1859 I. Galletti-Gianoli (M.) B. Massimi-
                                           liani (P.) C. Massera (V.) S. Scap-
                                           pini (A.)

                            Dec. 25, 1863 A. Winans (M.) G. Giorgetti/G. Orto-
                                           lani (P.) E. Crivelli (V.)

Fiume          Civicco      May       1868 L. Baratti (M.) M. Neri (P.) A. Car-
                                           boni (V.) G. Vecchi (A.)

Florence       Pergola      Mar.   7, 1860 R. Laborde (M.) G. Bettini (P.) An-
                                           fossi (V.) C. Bossi (A.)

Foligno        Apollo       Jan.      1863 A. Ortolani-Bertucci (M.) G. Ortola-
                                           ni (P.) F. Sutter (V.)

Forli          Comunale     Apr.      1863 G. Vitali (M.) V. Sarti (P.) D.
                                           Squarcia (V.)

Genoa          Paganini     Nov. 14, 1860 T. Pozzi (M.) G. Tombesi (P.)

Lodi           Sociale      Dec. 26, 1862 M. Fabbri (M.) M. Urio (P.) C. Fab-
                                           bricatore (V.)

Mantua         Sociale      Feb.      1863 V. Falconi (M.) F. De Ruggero (P.)
                                           I. Viganotti (V.) E. Dondi (A.)

Milan        La Scala    Oct.   4, 1860 I. Galletti-Gianoli (M.) G. Valen-
                                        tini-Cristiani (P.) A. Cotogni (V.)
                                        C. Dalla Costa (A.)

             Carcano     Jan.      1863 M. Anselmi (M.) G. Cantù (V.)

             Ciniselli   May       1870 M. Bozzetti (M.) Davini (P.) Torri-
                                        ani (V.)

             Castelli    Oct.      1875 V. Passigli (M.) O. Cappelletti (P.)
                                        G. Valcheri (V.) R. Kuon cond.

Mirandola                Sep.      1862 A. Bazzurri (M.) A. Di Benedetto
                                        (P.) L. Rossi de Ruggiero (V.) E.
                                        Rossi-Galli (A.)

Modena       Aliprandi   Mar.      1869 Z. Bellusi (M.) A. Crespolani/S.
                                        Crespada (P.) A. Fellini/P. Rinaldi
                                        (V.) A. Ferrari cond.

Molfetta                 Oct.  31, 1868 G. Fabris-Santini (M.) F. De Rug-
                                        gero (P.) Bozelli (V.) Calò (A.)

Monza        Sociale     Oct.  11, 1887 A. Filibert (M.) C. Bianco (P.) G.
                                        Perez (V.) Guarnieri cond.

Novara                   Dec.  26? 1863 L. Zacconi (M.) E. Palermi (P.) C.
                                        Massera (V.) G. Colli (A.)

Padua        Nuovo       June  27, 1857 A. Basseggio (M.) P. Mongini (P.) G.
                                        Guicciardi (V.) C. Dalla Costa (A.)

Palermo      Carolino    Mar.   7, 1860 L. Bendazzi-Secchi (M.) V. Sarti
                                        (P.) G. B. Bencich (V.) A. Lanzoni
                                        (A.) A. Lo Casto cond.

Parma        Regio       Jan.  29, 1862 G. Borsi de Leurie (M.) R. Bertolini
                                        (P.) E. Storti (V.) G. B. Cornago
                                        (A.) G. C. Ferrarini cond.

Perugia                  Dec.  26? 1864 N. Dunord (M.) S. Cerbara (P.) L.
                                        Spellini (V.)

Piacenza     Municipale  Autumn   1879 E. Ferri (M.)

Pisa         Verdi       Jan.  25, 1873 C. De Witten (M.) P. Paladini (P.)
                                        F. Tirini (V.) V. Gentili (A.)

Pistoia      Manzoni     Jan.  26? 1888 M. Mori (M.) C. Jorio (A.)

Prato        Metastasio  Jan.      1864 G. Modiano (M.) L. Coy (P.) L. Maz-
                                        zoni Osti (V.) F. Becheri (A.) A.
                                        Borgioli cond.

Ravenna      Alighieri   May       1861 L. Bendazzi-Secchi (M.) V. Sarti
                                        (P.) R. Pizzigati (V.) P. Medini
                                        (A.)

Rimini       Nuovo       Jan.      1869 E. Sgargi (M.) L. Abrugnedo (P.) D.
                                        Cesari (V.) N. Contedini (A.)

Rome         Apollo      Dec.  26, 1859 L. Lesniewska (M.) G. Bettini (P.)
                                        F. Coletti (V.) R. Laterza (A.) E.
                                        Angelini cond.

|  |  |  |  |  |
|---|---|---|---|---|
|  | Politeama | July | 1873 | E. Fabbris-Santini (M.) L. Del Passo (P.) L. Brignole (V.) Manni (A.) |
| San Severino |  | June? | 1867 | E. Sgargi (M.) C. Carpi (P.) A. Carboni (V.) G. Capriles (A.) |
| Savona | Chiabrera | Dec. 26, | 1872 |  |
| Sinigaglia | Comunale | Dec. 26, | 1871 | E. Gulli (M.) L. Giuggiolini (P.) E. Fucili (V.) V. Gentili (A.) |
| Spoleto | Nobile | Carn. | 1860-61 | A. Pasi (M.) A. Acconci (P.) G. Sacconi (V.) |
| Trieste | Grande | Jan. 30, | 1866 | L. Tencajoli (M.) T. De Azula (P.) E. Storti-Gaggi (V.) A. Fiorini (A.) A. Cremaschi cond. |
| Udine | Minerva | July | 1868 | L. Banti (M.) R. Bertolini (P.) A. Laurence (V.) F. Fiorani (A.) |
| Varese | Sociale | Sep. 28, | 1861 | L. Gavetti-Reggiani (M.) Massini (P.) C. Massera (V.) C. Moretti (A.) |
| Venice | Apollo | May 20, | 1868 | E. Wiziak (M.) G. Zacometti (P.) V. Orlandi (V.) |
| Vercelli | Civico | Jan. | 1861 |  |
| Verona | Ristori | Apr. | 1863 | L. Tencajoli (M.) F. Rosnati (P.) Florenza (V.) |
| Vicenza | Eretenio | Dec. 25, | 1871 |  |
| Viterbo | Unione | July | 1867 | Armellini (M.) Pinzi (P.) S. Sparapani (V.) |
| Voghera | Nuovo | Oct. | 1862 | A. Jackson (M.) |
| JUGOSLAVIA Zara | Nobile | Apr. | 1861 | G. Naglia (M.) G. Verati (P.) P. D'Ettore (V.) |
| PORTUGAL Oporto | Sao Joao | Mar. | 1861 | I. Paul-Donati (M.) P. Tagliazucchi (P.) V. Prattico (V.) Marcucci (A.) |
| ROMANIA Bucharest | Nacional | Feb. 15? | 1871 | L. Ponti dall'Armi (M.) F. Patierno (P.) S. Sparapani (V.) T. Costa (A.) |
| RUSSIA Kharkov | Municipal | Apr.? | 1865 | C. Noel-Guidi (M.) |
| Odessa | Municipal | Feb.? | 1865 | C. Noel-Guidi (M.) A. Agresti (P.) Corona (V.) P. Poli-Lenzi (A.) |
|  |  | Nov. | 1868 | A. Bianchi-Montaldo (M.) P. Bignardi (P.) O. Maini (A.) |
| SPAIN Barcelona | Principal | Mar. 2, | 1859 | A. Basseggio (M.) S. Malvezzi (P.) G. Aldighieri (V.) |

Palma di      Princesa    Sep.?    1866 G. Naglia (M.)  A. Agresti  (P.)  V.
Mallorca                             Prattico (V.) A. Rodas (A.) J. Goula
                                     cond.

Valencia      Principal   Nov.  6? 1865 G. Marziali-Passerini (M.) A. Oliva-
                                     Pavani (P.) N. Varvaro (V.) O. Maini
                                     (A.)


9. GIUDITTA-*Melodramma biblico* in three acts
Milan-Teatro alla Scala-Mar. 26, 1860
Libretto by Marcelliano Marcello

Giuditta (G.)                                Sofia Vera-Lorini sop.
Abramia (A.)                                 Teresina Mistrali sop.
Gionata (Gi.)                                   Emilio Pancani ten.
Oloferne (O.)                                 Giovanni Corsi bar.
Eliachimo (E.)                             Cesare Dalla Costa bass
Arzaele                                    Fanny Sidri Baragli mez.
Vagao                                     Clemente Scannavino ten.
Eleazaro                                       Marco Ghini bass

Conductor                                     Eugenio Cavallini
Director                                         Achille Peri

OTHER PRODUCTIONS

CUBA
Havana        Tacon       Feb.  8, 1863 G. Medori (G.) H. Sulzer (A.) F.
                                     Mazzoleni (Gi.) F. Bellini (O.)

ITALY
Cuneo         Civico      Feb.  8, 1868 V. Tilli (G.) C. Baroni (Gi.) A.
                                     Borzelli (O.) L. Rossi cond.

Ferrara       Comunale    Apr. 27, 1865 G. Beltramelli (G.) O. Beltramelli
                                     (A.) S. Perozzi (Gi.) V. Quintili-
                                     Leoni (O.)

Florence      Pagliano    Sep.?    1861 S. Vera-Lorini (G.) F. Mazzoleni
                                     (Gi.) G. Aldighieri (O.) A. Garcia
                                     (E.)

Lucca         Giglio      Aug. 22, 1868 M. Spezia-Aldighieri (G.) P. Augusti
                                     (Gi.) G. Aldighieri (O.)

Milan         La Scala    Sep. 24, 1862 M. Gazzaniga (G.) Morini (Gi.) L.
                                     Colonnese (O.) A. Fiorini (E.) E.
                                     Cavallini cond.

              Dal Verme   May       1873 M. Spezia-Aldighieri (G.) G. Tombe-
                                     si/G. Ortisi (Gi.) G. Aldighieri
                                     (O.) L. Lombardelli (E.) R. Kuon
                                     cond.

Piacenza      Municipale  Dec. 26? 1860 E. Weisser (G.) A. Malagola (Gi.) A.
                                     Mazzanti (O.) O. Maini (E.) G. Jona
                                     cond.

Reggio Emilia Municipale  Apr. 28, 1860 E. Julienne-Dejean (G.) G. Bettini
(Gi.) G. B. Bencich (O.) C. Dalla
Costa (E.) A. Peri dir.

Trieste       Grande      Sep. 23, 1865 M. Spezia-Aldighieri (G.) G. Villani
(Gi.) G. Aldighieri (O.) P. Medini
(E.) A. Cremaschi cond.

              Armonia     Nov. 14, 1868 M. Spezia-Aldighieri (G.) P. Augusti
(Gi.) G. Aldighieri (O.)

SPAIN
Barcelona     Liceo       Nov.  5, 1862 S. Vera-Lorini (G.) G. Musiani (Gi.)
F. Cresci (O.) C. Dalla Costa (E.)
J. B. Dalmau cond.

Madrid        Real        Nov. 20, 1861 E. Julienne-Dejean (G.) G. Bettini
(Gi.) F. Coletti (O.) S. L. Bouché
(E.) J. Skoczdopole cond.

Malaga        Principe    Dec.     1866 M. Spezia-Aldighieri (G.) G. Aldi-
              Alfonso                   ghieri (O.) A. Garcia (E.)

Valencia      Principal   May      1866 M. Spezia-Aldighieri (G.) A. Oliva-
Pavani (Gi.) G. Aldighieri (O.) O.
Maini (E.)

UNITED STATES
Boston        Boston Th.  Jan. 25, 1864 G. Medori (G.) H. Sulzer (A.) F.
Mazzoleni (Gi.) D. Bellini (O.) A.
Biacchi (E.)

New York      Ac. of Mus. Nov. 11, 1863 G. Medori (G.) H. Sulzer (A.) F.
Mazzoleni (Gi.) D. Bellini (O.) A.
Biacchi (E.)


10. L'ESPIAZIONE-*Opera* in four acts
Milan-Teatro alla Scala-Feb. 7, 1861
Libretto by Temistocle Solera

Nella                                      Adelaide Borghi-Mamo mez.
Gino dei Marchesi Corsini                      Mario Tiberini ten.
Bernardo                          Giuseppe Federico Beneventano bar.
Il Cavaliere degli Altoviti                Raffaele Laterza bass
Giulia                                     Teresina Mistrali sec.

Conductor                                      Eugenio Cavallini
Director                                          Achille Peri

11. RIENZI-*Libretto* in three epochs
Milan-Teatro alla Scala-Dec. 26, 1862
Libretto by Francesco Maria Piave

| | |
|---|---|
| Giulia Raselli | Adelaide Borghi-Mamo mez. |
| Rienzi | Carlo Negrini ten. |
| Don Egidio Albornozzo | Giovanni Guicciardi bar. |
| Fra Gualtiero di Monreale | Hyppolyte Brémond bass |
| Benedetta | Linda Fiorio mez. |
| Savelli | Giacomo Redaelli ten. |
| Cecco del Vecchio | Luigi Alessandrini bass |
| Rodolfo di Sassonia | Vincenzo Paraboschi ten. |
| Un Araldo | Gaetano Archinti sec. |
| Un Auditore | Antonio Rera sec. |
| | |
| Conductor | Eugenio Cavallini |
| Director | Achille Peri |

ERRICO PETRELLA

1. IL DIAVOLO COLOR DI ROSA-*Opera buffa* in two acts[21]
Naples-Teatro La Fenice-Dec. 31, 1828
Libretto by Andrea Leone Tottola


2. IL GIORNO DELLE NOZZE ovvero PULCINELLA MARITO E NON MARITO-*Commedia per musica* in two acts
Naples-Teatro Nuovo-Jan. 28, 1830
Libretto by Andrea Leone Tottola

| | |
|---|---|
| Romilda | De Mattei |
| Giulietta | Bartoccini |
| Giocondo | Auriemma ten. |
| Il Conte Alfonso | De Ninnis |
| Ambrogio | Gaetano De Nicola buf. |
| Colandica | Tauro |
| Ersinda | Bini |
| Marcone | Nadauro |
| Pulcinella | Barbiere |
| | |
| Conductor | Gennaro Pepe |


3. LO SCROCCONE-*Opera buffa*
Naples-Teatro Nuovo-Feb. 8, 1834
Libretto believed to be by Giovanni Peruzzini

| | |
|---|---|
| Donna Elisa | Teresa Tavola sop. |
| Donna Checchina | Francesca Checcherini sop. |
| Olimpia | Marianna Checcherini mez. |
| Don Marco | De Nicola buf. |
| Don Federico | De Rosa |
| Don Saverio | Carlo Casaccia bass |
| Don Scolastico | Giuseppe Fioravanti bass |
| Minicone | Giuseppe Papi |
| Milon | Costantini |
| Rita | Grossi |
| Pascariello | Nadauro |
| | |
| Conductor | Gennaro Pepe |


4. LA CIMODOCEA-*Opera seria*
Composed for Naples (Teatro San Carlo) circa 1834-Unperformed

---

21. *Il Diavolo Color di Rosa* was in the repertory of various minor Neapolitan theatres through 1832, being given some 50 times at the Teatro La Fenice, once at the Teatro San Ferdinando and eight times at the Teatro Partenope.

5. I PIRATI SPAGNUOLI-*Melodramma* in two acts[22]
Naples-Teatro Nuovo-May 13, 1838
Libretto by Emanuele Bidera

Chiara Rover (C.)                                    Marietta Riva sop.
Ottavio Gomez (O.)                                   Raffaele Mirate ten.
Pedro (P.)                                           Antonio Sparalik bar.
L'Alcade (A.)                                        Giuseppe Fioravanti bass
Rodrigo                                              Michele Tomeo sec.
Rosa                                                 Amalia Tucci sec.

OTHER PRODUCTIONS

ITALY
Chieti          San             June 16, 1841
                Ferdinando

Naples          Partenope       Oct. 26, 1839

                Nuovo           1840

Revised-Naples-Teatro Nuovo-July 16, 1856

Chiara Rover (C.)                                    Zenobia Papini sop.
Ottavio Gomez (O.)                              Antonio Di Benedetto ten.
Pedro (P.)                                        Alessandro Zoboli bass
L'Alcade (A.)                                    Giuseppe Fioravanti bass

Conductor                                            Michele Di Natale
Director                                             Errico Petrella

OTHER PRODUCTIONS

ITALY
Campobasso                      Dec.     1859

Foggia          Ferdinando      May   12, 1860

Palermo         Garibaldi       Nov.     1872 M. Del Buono-Corona (C.)

Reggio di        Borbonico      Jan.?    1862
 Calabria


6. LE MINIERE DI FREINBERG-*Melodramma* in two acts
Naples-Teatro Nuovo-Feb. 16, 1843
Libretto by Emanuele Bidera

Vilelmina (V.)                                       Giuseppina David sop.
Angiolina (A.)                                        Luisa Luciani mez.
Carlo Revel (C.)                                   Domenico Labocetta ten.
Roberto (R.)                                         Luigi Fioravanti bass
Don Fabrizio  (F.)                                 Raffaele Casaccia bar.
Errico Dreier (E.)                                   Giuseppe Lodi bass
Luigi                                                Michele Tucci sec.

Conductor
Director                                             Errico Petrella

---

[22]. The first performances of *I Pirati Spagnuoli* appear to have been given as *I Due Pirati*.

OTHER PRODUCTIONS

ITALY
Naples        Nuovo        Nov. 27, 1843 G. Medori (V.) L. Luciani (A.) D.
                                        Labocetta (C.) L. Fioravanti (R.) R.
                                        Casaccia (F.) D. Coletti (E.)

Revised-Naples-Teatro Nuovo-May 29, 1853

| | |
|---|---|
| Vilelmina (V.) | Lucy Escott sop. |
| Angiolina (A.) | Marianna Eboli mez. |
| Carlo Revel (C.) | Mario Tiberini ten. |
| Roberto (R.) | Alessandro Zoboli bass |
| Don Fabrizio (F.) | Luigi Fioravanti buf. |
| Errico Dreier (E.) | Sebastiano Giordano bass |
| Guglielmo | Raffaele Grandillo bass |
| Luigi | Ferdinando Imbimbo bass |

| | |
|---|---|
| Conductor | Michele di Natale |
| Director | Errico Petrella |

OTHER PRODUCTIONS[23]

ITALY
Naples        Nuovo        Oct. 19, 1855 Z. Papini (V.) P. Brayda-Lablache
                                        (R.)

Turin         Rossini      Feb.  1856 L. Perelli (V.) A. Zennari (C.)


7. LE PRECAUZIONI ovvero IL CARNEVALE DI VENEZIA-*Commedia* in three acts
Naples-Teatro Nuovo-May 11, 1851[24]
Libretto by Marco D'Arienzo

| | |
|---|---|
| Albina (A.) | Clotilde Martinelli sop. |
| Romilla (R.) | Carolina D'Amora mez. |
| Mimosa (M.) | Chiara Gualdi mez. |
| Oreste (O.) | Tancredi Remorini ten. |
| Pilade (P.) | Leopoldo Cammarano bar. |
| Cola (C.) | Pasquale Savoja buf. |
| Conte Bietola (B.) | Giuseppe Fioravanti bass |
| Muzio (Mu.) | Raffaele Casaccia buf. |
| Truffaldino (T.) | Valentino Fioravanti bass |
| Zanni | Raffaele Grandillo bass |

| | |
|---|---|
| Conductor | Michele Di Natale |
| Director | Giuseppe Staffa |

SELECTED PRODUCTIONS-NINETEENTH CENTURY

EGYPT
Cairo         Francais      Oct. 30, 1872 L. Corsi (A.) I. Corsi (O.) G.
                                        Bottesini cond.

---

[23]. The opera was also given in Rome, but no further details are available at this time.

[24]. This is the correct date. See *Programma Giornaliera*, Naples, May 11, 1851, announcing the first performance, and May 12, 1851, announcing the second performance.

FRANCE
Nice            Municipal    Oct. 10, 1873 O. Trebbi (A.) Polonini (P.) G.
                                         Bragozzo cond.

GREAT BRITAIN
London          Lyceum       Mar. 23, 1871 Colombo (A.) M. Veralli (M.) Fabbri
                                         (O.)

GREECE
Patras                       Jan.     1875 Maris-Concetti (A.) Trinci (C.) Pa-
                                         nari (Mu.)

ITALY[25]
Asti            Alfieri      Apr.     1863 E. De Baillou (A.) P. Prette (Mu.)
                                         E. Petrella dir.

Bari            Piccinni     Dec. 26? 1870

Bergamo         Sociale      Dec. 26, 1875

Bologna         Comunale     Dec. 26, 1859 A. Fumagalli (A.) A. Borelli Cecconi
                                         (O.) G. Altini (P.) L. Fioravanti
                                         (C.) L. Parmeggiani (B.) S. Demi
                                         (Mu.)

                Contavalli   Mar. 16, 1867 A. Giannetti (A.)

Brescia         Grande       Jan. 15, 1859

Cagliari        Civico       Mar. 11, 1873 O. Trebbi (A.) T. Parasini (O.) V.
                                         Fioravanti (C.) P. Prette (Mu.)

Chieti          Marrucino    Summer   1859 C. Marziali (A.)

Como            Sociale      Jan.     1870 A. Fumagalli (A.) J. Gayarre (O.)

Florence        Pagliano     Aug. 30, 1866 V. Sabatini (O.) M. Borella (C.) V.
                                         Fioravanti (Mu.)

                Nazionale    Nov.     1866 E. Bedetti (A.) G. Marchisio (C.)

Genoa           Carlo        Nov. 30, 1853 C. Marziali (A.)  A. Errani (O.) O.
                Felice                   Bonafous (P.)

                             Oct. 23, 1862 I. Pelagatti-Visconti (A.) L. Stec-
                                         chi-Bottardi (O.)

                             Oct. 15, 1863 G. Giovannoni-Zacchi (A.) L. Casari-
                                         ni (O.)

                Nazionale    Dec. 19, 1870 M. Dérivis (A.) V. Fioravanti (C.)
                                         A. Bottero (Mu.)

Iesi            Concordia    Dec. 26, 1865 A. Giannetti (A.) A. Vicini (O.) P.
                                         Prette (C.) C. Castelli (Mu.)

Imola           Comunale     Mar. 1? 1870

Livorno         Leopoldo     Oct.     1858 A. Pasi (A.) Faleni (R.) G. Boy (O.)

---

[25]. Le Precauzioni was particularly popular in Italy for many years. Only a small fraction of its many productions are listed here.

Lucca          Pantera      Dec. 31, 1866

Macerata                    Jan.    1865 C. Castelli (A.)

Milan          Santa        Feb. 15, 1858 C. Marziali (A.)
               Radegonda

Modena         Aliprandi    Oct. 31, 1863 E. De Baillou (A.) B. Bernabei (R.)
                                          L. Lazzeri (M.) A. Vicini (O.) L.
                                          Ferrario (P.) O. Papini (C.) R. Buf-
                                          fagni (B.) E. Menici (Mu.) P. Manni
                                          cond.

                            May  20, 1865 M. Villa (A.) F. Gavirati (R.) A.
                                          Rasori (M.) G. Savelli (O.) D. Bal-
                                          dassari (P.) L. Massa (C.) G. Norbis
                                          (B.) P. Prette (Mu.) L. Adani cond.

                            Feb. 20, 1875 Irma De Sassi (A.) V. Zenobbi Fri-
                                          giotti (R.) Irene De Sassi (M.) E.
                                          Camero (O.) A. Borella (P.) G. Fri-
                                          giotti (C.) F. Migliara (Mu.) S.
                                          Favi cond.

Naples         Nuovo        July 23, 1853

                            July 18, 1854

                            July  2, 1859 L. Zacconi (A.) M. Alfieri (R.) C.
                                          Gualdi (M.) C. Gennari (O.) A. Zo-
                                          boli (P.) P. Savoja (C.) V. Fiora-
                                          vanti (Mu.)

               Bellini      Feb.  6, 1868

Padua          Concordia    Feb. 24? 1866 A. Giannetti (A.) V. Sabatini (O.)
                                          F. Tournerie (P.) P. Prette (C.) C.
                                          Castelli (Mu.)

Palermo        Garibaldi    Nov.    1870 A. De Ruvo (A.) A. Martino (R.) A.
                                          Biondi (M.) G. Quaranta (O.) R. De
                                          Giorgi (C.) F. Imbimbo (Mu.) A.
                                          Pancrazy cond.

Parma          Regio        Oct. 21, 1865 A. Fumagalli (A.) A. Simonetti (O.)
                                          S. Orsi (P.) P. Prette (C.) C. Cas-
                                          telli (Mu.) G. C. Ferrarini cond.

Pavia          Condominio   June?   1867 M. Armandi (A.) L. Vistarini (O.) P.
                                          Prette (C.) Polonini (Mu.)

                            Nov.    1872 Irma De Sassi (A.) A. Medini (P.) R.
                                          Grandillo (C.) F. Migliara (Mu.)

Piacenza       Municipale   Aug.  8, 1862 E. Rossetti-Grassi (A.) S. Corbaro
                                          (O.) M. Grassi (P.) G. Jona cond.

                            Mar. 12, 1865 M. Villa (A.) F. Piana (O.) P. Pret-
                                          te (C.)

Ravenna        Alighieri    Dec. 25, 1866 L. Lazzari (A.) G. Pasi (O.) F.
                                          Brandini (P.) G. Marchisio (C.) C.
                                          Castelli (Mu.) S. Montanari cond.

| | | | |
|---|---|---|---|
| Rimini | Nuovo | Dec. 26? 1870 | A. Giannetti (A.) |
| Rovigo | Sociale | Jan. 22, 1871 | C. Miles (A.) C. Bellincioni (C.) |
| Sassari | Civico | Nov.     1869 | E. Martini (A.) |
| Savona | Chiabrera | Dec. 26, 1872 | |
| Sinigaglia | Comunale | Summer   1869 | A. Vinea-Paoletti (A.) L. Paoletti (O.) |
| Terni | Comunale | Feb.     1868 | C. Bellincioni (C.) |
| Treviso | Garibaldi | May 15, 1869 | P. Setragni (O.) Ciceri (P.) |
| Trieste | Grande | Mar. 22, 1862 | G. Giovannoni-Zacchi (A.) C. Bocco-lini (P.) C. Bellincioni (C.) L. Fioravanti (Mu.) A. Cremaschi cond. |
| | Mauroner | Apr.  2? 1866 | A. Giannetti (A.) V. Sabatini (O.) F. Tournerie (P.) P. Prette (C.) C. Castelli (Mu.) |
| Turin | Nazionale | Summer   1860 | I. Paul Donati (A.) |
| | Vittorio Emanuele | Oct.     1862 | |
| Udine | Minerva | Apr.     1866 | A. Giannetti (A.) V. Sabatini (O.) F. Tournerie (P.) P. Prette (C.) C. Castelli (Mu.) |
| Varese | Sociale | Oct. 27, 1881 | |
| Venice | San Samuele | Jan.     1867 | Lomi (A.) Piazza (O.) Colein (P.) V. Fioravanti (C.) Baldassari (Mu.) |
| Vercelli | | Dec. 26, 1865 | Fabbri (O.) |
| Verona | Nuovo | May      1858 | |
| | | Autumn   1870 | M. Bozzetti (A.) V. Fioravanti (C.) |
| Vicenza | Eretenio | Jan.     1869 | L. Sainz (A.) |
| MALTA La Valletta | Manoel | Jan. 29, 1855 | E. Storti (P.) |
| MEXICO Mexico City | Nacional | July 13, 1890 | (in Sp.) |
| RUSSIA Odessa | Municipale | Oct. 19, 1870 | E. Cortesi (A.) A. Vicini (O.) S. Orsi (P.) G. Zambellini (Mu.) L. Conti (C.) |
| St. Petersburg | Imperial | Jan. 18, 1883 | E. Repetto-Trisolini (A.) C. Baldel-li (C.) |
| SPAIN Barcelona | Circo | Apr. 11, 1863 | |
| Madrid | Zarzuela | Oct. 16, 1869 | |

UNITED STATES

| | | | |
|---|---|---|---|
| Atlanta | De Give's | Feb. 4, 1888 | E. Abbott (A.) |

Boston      Selwyn      Dec. 19, 1867 M. Hauck (A.) A. Ronconi (R.) F. Na-
                        tali-Testa (M.) R. Baragli (O.) G.
                        Ronconi (C.) F. Bellini (Mu.) N. Ba-
                        rili (B.)

Brooklyn    Ac. of Mus. Apr. 11, 1867 C. L. Kellogg (A.) F. Natali-Testa
                        (M.) R. Baragli (O.) G. Ronconi (C.)

Chicago     Grand       Apr. 4, 1888 E. Abbott (A.) L. Annandale (M.) F.
                        Michelena (O.) A. Montegriffo (B.)
                        W. Pruette (P.) W. Allen (C.) W.
                        Broderick (Mu.)

Cincinnati  Grand       Oct. 22, 1887 E. Abbott (A.)

Cleveland   Op. House   Apr. 23, 1887 E. Abbott (A.)

Dallas      Op. House   Jan. 3, 1888 E. Abbott (A.) L. Annandale (M.) F.
                        Michelena (O.) A. Montegriffo (B.)
                        W. Pruette (P.) W. Broderick (Mu.)
                        A. Tomasi cond.

Denver                  Dec. 6, 1887 E. Abbott (A.)

Detroit     Op. House   Apr. 15, 1887 E. Abbott (A.) H. Bertram (R.) L.
                        Annandale (M.) W. Pruette (P.)

            Apr. 9, 1888 E. Abbott (A.) H. Bertram (R.) L.
                        Annandale (M.) F. Michelena (O.) W.
                        Pruette (P.) W. Broderick (Mu.)

Indianapolis Dickson's  Apr. 2, 1887 E. Abbott (A.)

Kansas City Coates      Nov. 29, 1887 E. Abbott (A.)

Los Angeles Grand       Jan. 8, 1887 E. Abbott (A.)

Louisville  Macauley's  Oct. 27, 1887 E. Abbott (A.) L. Annandale (M.) F.
                        Michelena (O.) A. Montegriffo (B.)
                        W. Pruette (P.) W. Broderick (Mu.)
                        (in Eng.)

            Apr. 6, 1889 E. Abbott (A.)

Minneapolis Grand       Nov. 10, 1887 E. Abbott (A.)

New York    Ac. of Mus. Apr. 3, 1867 C. L. Kellogg (A.) F. Natali-Testa
                        (M.) R. Baragli (O.) G. Ronconi (C.)

            Pike's      Feb. 28, 1868 M. Hauck (A.) A. Ronconi (R.) F.
                        Natali-Testa (M.) E. Testa (O.) F.
                        Bellini (Mu.) G. Ronconi (C.)

Omaha                   Dec. 16? 1886 E. Abbott (A.)

Philadelphia Ac. of Mus. Jan. 10, 1868 M. Hauck (A.) R. Baragli (O.) F.
                        Bellini (Mu.) G. Ronconi (C.)

Portland    New Market  Feb. 5, 1887 E. Abbott (A.)

|            | New Park      | Nov. 13, 1888 E. Abbott (A.) L. Annandale (M.) F. Michelena (O.) W. Pruette (P.) W. Broderick (Mu.) |

St. Louis      Olympic        Mar. 22, 1888 E. Abbott (A.)

Salt Lake      Salt Lake      Mar.  5, 1887 E. Abbott (A.)
City           Theatre

San Antonio    Grand          Dec. 24, 1886 E. Abbott (A.) L. Annandale (M.) F. Michelena (O.)

                              Jan. 12, 1888 E. Abbott (A.) L. Annandale (M.) F. Michelena (O.) W. Pruette (P.) W. Broderick (Mu.) A. Tomasi cond. (in Eng.)

San Francisco Baldwin         Jan. 12, 1887 E. Abbott (A.) (in Eng.)

Washington     National       May   6, 1887 E. Abbott (A.) (in Eng.)

                              Mar.  8, 1888 E. Abbott (A.)

OTHER PRODUCTIONS-TWENTIETH CENTURY

ITALY
Rome           Quirino        Sep.  4, 1915 N. Marmora (A.) T. Menarin Barbieri (M.) I. Ferrero (R.) G. Favi (O.) O. Galleotti (P.) C. Di Cola (C.) A. Sabbi (Mu.) G. Zuccani cond.

               Argentina      July 16, 1924 T. Poggetti (A.) R. Farina (O.) C. Di Cola (C.) S. Baccaloni (Mu.) F. Mercolini cond.

               Eliseo         Aug.  2, 1924 T. Poggetti (A.) A. M. Bertolasi (M.) R. Farina (O.) C. Di Cola (C.) S. Baccalloni (Mu.) F. Mercolini cond.

8. ELENA DI TOLOSA-*Dramma lirico* in three epochs
Naples-Teatro del Fondo-Aug. 12, 1852
Libretto by Domenico Bolognese

| Elena (E.)      | Rosina Penco sop.        |
| Arturo (A.)     | Emilio Pancani ten.      |
| Lambert (L.)    | Francesco Cresci bar.    |
| Il Barone (B.)  | Marco Arati bass         |
| Andrea (An.)    | Gennaro Luzio buf.       |
| Gino            | Giuseppe Benedetti bass  |

| Conductor | Antonio Farelli  |
| Director  | Errico Petrella  |

OTHER PRODUCTIONS

GREECE
Corfu          San Giacomo Jan.     1864 G. Naglia (E.)

ITALY[26]

| Bari | Piccinni | Oct. 11, 1854 | E. Scotta (E.) Bruno (A.) D. Squarcia (L.) |
|------|----------|---------------|---------------------------------------------|
| Cagliari | Civico | Feb. 1862 | |
| Catania | Comunale | Dec. 30, 1856 | E. Boncinelli (E.) C. Giuliani (A.) L. Banti (L.) |
| Florence | Pergola | Feb. 2, 1858 | F. Scheggi (E.) D. Lorini (A.) E. Storti (L.) Cairione (An.) |
| Messina | Sant' Elisabetta | Mar. 17, 1857 | Menici (E.) G. Valentini-Cristiani (A.) R. Mastriani (L.) G. Scheggi (An.) A. Laudamo cond. |
| Milan | Canobbiana | Apr. 9, 1856 | L. Chiaromonte (E.) A. Agresti (A.) G. Corsi (L.) |
| | Santa Radegonda | June 1858 | P. Scotti (E.) |
| Naples | San Carlo | Aug. 21, 1852 | R. Penco (E.) E. Pancani (A.) F. Cresci (L.) M. Arati (B.) G. Luzio (An.) A. Farelli cond. |
| | | June 4, 1854 | N. De Roissi (E.) E. Pancani (A.) P. Giorgi-Pacini/L. Walter (L.) M. Arati (B.) G. Luzio (An.) A. Farelli cond. |
| | Fondo | June 3, 1854 | N. De Roissi (E.) E. Pancani (A.) P. Giorgi-Pacini (L.) M. Arati (B.) G. Luzio (An.) A. Farelli cond. |
| | Nuovo | Aug. 20 1853 | L. Escott (E.) G. Valentini-Cristiani (A.) R. Mastriani (L.) R. Grandillo (B.) L. Fioravanti (An.) M. Di Natale cond. |
| | San Ferdinando | Nov. 23, 1853 | L. Escott (E.) G. Valentini-Cristiani (A.) R. Mastriani (L.) R. Grandillo (B.) L. Fioravanti (An.) M. Di Natale cond. |
| | | Feb. 1855 | P. Scotti (E.) T. Palmieri (A.) D. Squarcia (L.) |
| | Circo Nazionale | Mar.? 1882 | A. Cattaneo (E.) L. Parodi (A.) A. Pini-Corsi (L.) Frigiotti (An.) L. Mugnone cond. |
| Palermo | Carolino | Dec. 25, 1857 | A. Molinari/I. Paul-Donati (E.) G. Villani (A.) S. Ronconi (L.) R. Giacomelli (An.) A. Lo Casto cond. |
| Perugia | Pavone | Dec. 29, 1858 | E. Lipparini (E.) Serafini (A.) G. Sacconi (L.) L. Manari (An.) |

---

[26]. *Elena di Tolosa* was also given in Barletta in 1856, in Capua on Jan. 17, 1858, in Catanzaro in 1855, in Chieti in 1854, in Lanciano during the autumn of 1857, at the Teatro Mercadante in Naples in Nov. 1871, at the Teatro Garibaldi in Palermo in Feb. 1882, and in Vasto in the carnival season of 1857-58.

Reggio di      Borbonico    Dec.?    1856 M. Naselli (E.)  G.  Valentini-Cris-
  Calabria                             stiani (A.) F. Tournerie (L.) P. De
                                       Biase (B.)

Rome           Argentina    Dec. 26? 1853 C.  Crespolani  (E.)  V.  Ferrari-
                                       Stella (A.) C. Busi (L.) G. Fossati
                                       (B.) A. Rivarola (An.)

Rovigo         Sociale      Feb. 11, 1855 M. Winter (E.) P. Scotti (A.) O.
                                       Winter (L.) P. Tosarini cond.

Trieste        Grande       Carn. 1853-54 M. Vetturi-Olivi (E.) L. Stecchi-
                                       Bottardi (A.) L. Giraldoni (L.) R.
                                       Scalese (An.) G. A. Scaramelli cond.

Turin          Gerbino      July     1864 F. Scheggi (E.) T. Villa (A.) Mazzo-
                                       ni-Osti (L.) G. Zambelli/G. Marchi-
                                       sio (An.)

MALTA
La Valletta    Manoel       Mar.?    1855

                            Jan.?    1866 E. Natali (E.) G. De Filippis (A.)
                                       A. Parboni (L.) L. Conti (An.)


9. MARCO VISCONTI-*Melodramma tragico* in three acts
Naples-Teatro San Carlo-Feb. 9, 1854
Libretto by Domenico Bolognese

Bice (B.)                                        Rosina Penco sop.
Tremacoldo (T.)                          Adelaide Borghi-Mamo mez.
Ottorino (O.)                              Gaetano Fraschini ten.
Marco Visconti (M.)                            Gaetano Ferri bar.
Conte del Balzo (C.)                            Marco Arati bass
Laura                                          Anna Salvetti sop.
Lodrisio Visconti                          Corrado Laudano ten.

Conductor                                      Antonio Farelli
Director                                       Errico Petrella

OTHER PRODUCTIONS-NINETEENTH CENTURY

ARGENTINA
Buenos Aires   Victoria     Apr. 27, 1859 T. Bayetti (B.) A. Casaloni (T.) F.
                                       Cima (M.) C. Castagneri cond.

AUSTRIA
Vienna         Kärntnertor May 13, 1855 G. Medori (B.) A. Borghi-Mamo (T.)
                                       G. Bettini (O.) G. Ferri (M.) G. F.
                                       Angelini (C.)

BRAZIL
Rio de         Lirico       Apr. 25, 1860 G. Medori (B.) S. Tosi (T.) R. Mira-
  Janeiro      Fluminense              te (O.) É. Mary (M.) G. Echeverria
                                       (C.)

CUBA
Havana         Tacon        Jan. 25, 1861 M. Lotti della Santa (B.) F. Cresci
                                       (M.)

GREECE
Corfu          San Giacomo  Sep.      1857 T. Pozzi-Montegazza (B.) D. Santo-
                                           lini (T.) G. Petrovich (O.) Ramoni
                                           (M.) B. Cervini (C.)

ITALY[27]
Alessandria    Civico       Oct.  8, 1870 G. Borsi de Leurie (B.) Ammorini
                                           (T.) L. Filippi-Bresciani (O.) Cap-
                                           pelli (M.) C. Morroto (C.) G. Zabag-
                                           lio cond.

Ancona         Muse         Apr. 30, 1859 A. Albertini (B.) G. Sanchioli (T.)
                                           G. Villani (O.) O. Bartolini (M.) G.
                                           B. Cornago (C.)

Asti           Alfieri      Oct.?    1879 A. Marubini (O.) G. Mirsky (M.)

Bari           Piccinni     Dec.     1856 G. Borsi de Leurie (B.) Lety (T.) G.
                                           Ghislanzoni (O.) V. Prattico (M.) F.
                                           Gionfrida (C.)

Brescia        Grande       Aug.  1, 1858 F. Gordosa (B.) L. Viale (T.) G. Mu-
                                           siani (O.) V. Prattico (M.) N. Bene-
                                           detti (C.)

                            Feb.  6, 1870 E. Corani (B.) L. Berini (T.) P. Ta-
                                           gliazucchi (O.) A. Burgio (M.) E.
                                           Bernardi cond.

Cagliari       Civico       Dec. 26, 1861 A.  Massimiliani-Ferraris  (B.)  E.
                                           Biondini (O.) V. Quintili-Leoni (M.)
                                           N. Rebottaro (C.)

                            Nov.     1872 Coriolano (B.)  Locatelli  (T.)  E.
                                           Sbriscia (O.) N. Fallica (M.)

Catania        Comunale     Mar.  5, 1857 O. Prata (B.) M. Berti (T.) R. Bet-
                                           tazzi (O.) L. Banti (M.) M. Pappa-
                                           lardo cond.

                            Feb. 19, 1859 C. Schenardi (B.) Schiavoni (T.) A.
                                           Di Benedetto (O.)  T.  Sterbini/C.
                                           Lazzari (M.) M. Pappalardo cond.

Chieti         San          June 13, 1857 M. Armandi (B.) G. Giovannoni-Zacchi
               Ferdinando                 (T.) V. Ferrari-Stella (O.) L. Ron-
                                           cagli (M.)

Como           Sociale      Sep.  7, 1875 F. Meyer (B.) Galliani (T.) G. De
                                           Sanctis-Marianecci (O.)  E.  Corti
                                           (M.)

Cremona        Concordia    Dec. 26? 1860 A. Moro (B.) G. De Antoni (O.) V.
                                           Collini (V.)

               Ricci        Aug.     1877 Bardelli (B.) Bellariva (T.) G. Cal-
                                           dani-Kuon (O.) G. Mirski (M.) M. Ve-
                                           la cond.

---

[27]. Other productions of *Marco Visconti* include Aci Reale in 1858, Arezzo in 1876,
Caltagirone and Capua in 1858, Casalmonferrato in 1868, Codogno in 1873, Cosenza in 1860,
Cuneo in 1877, Fano in 1875, Lanciano in 1858, Marsala in 1857, Rimini in 1880, Salerno in
1873, San Severo in 1857 and Velletri in 1867.

| | | | |
|---|---|---|---|
| Ferrara | Comunale | Apr. 23, 1861 | G. Borsi de Leurie (B.) R. Feltri-Spalla (T.) A. Pagnoni (O.) G. Reina (M.) E. Rossi-Galli (C.) |
| Fiume | Civico | Mar. 18, 1874 | E. Ciuti (B.) Piccoli (T.) A. Byron (O.) G. Morelli-Machi (M.) I. Sbordoni (C.) |
| Florence | Nuovo | Sep. 18, 1866 | A. Pasi (B.) L. Caracciollo (T.) S. Perozzi (O.) G. Guicciardi (M.) |
| | Pagliano | July 5, 1885 | L. Stefanini (B.) Bourmann (T.) G. Procacci (O.) S. Sparapani (C.) |
| Foggia | Dauno | Feb. 1857 | L. Giordano (B.) M. Mollo (T.) E. Concordia (O.) A. Capurro (M.) |
| Foligno | Apollo | Dec. 26? 1866 | M. Gualtieri (B.) L. Cencetti (O.) |
| Genoa | Carlo Felice | Apr. 15, 1854 | R. Penco (B.) C. Biscottini-Fiorio (T.) E. Carrion (O.) L. Della Santa (M.) G. F. Angelini (C.) A. Mariani cond. |
| | | Dec. 26, 1862 | E. Berini (B.) S. Tosi (T.) G. Gambetti (O.) E. Storti (M.) A. Mariani cond. |
| | Andrea Doria | June 21, 1858 | N. De Roissi (B.) S. Ciaschetti (T.) G. Petrovich (O.) Capurro (M.) G. De Dominicis (C.) |
| | Genovese | Mar. 1, 1890 | C. Carpi/M. Nicolini (B.) E. Bobbio (T.) D. Puppo (O.) G. M. Sammarco (M.) A. Gorè cond. |
| Iesi | Concordia | Sep. 1, 1858 | L. Chiaromonte (B.) Morea (T.) A. Pagnoni (O.) A. Carboni (M.) Paolicchi (C.) |
| Lanciano | | Sep. 1858 | Cappelli (B.) |
| Lecce | Paisiello | May 1857 | G. Morghen (M.) |
| Livorno | Avvalorati | Jan.? 1860 | A. Fricci (B.) Guidantoni (T.) A. Prudenza (O.) F. Cresci (M.) |
| Lucca | Pantera | Dec. 26, 1875 | Angeli (B.) A. Marubini (O.) A. Marescalchi (M.) Panari (C.) |
| Mantua | Sociale | Dec. 26, 1858 | C. Cattinari (B.) A. Ansaldi (T.) A. Dall'Armi (O.) G. B. Bencich (M.) |
| Messina | Sant' Elisabetta | Dec. 12, 1857 | V. Lorini (B.) P. Tagliazucchi (O.) A. Morelli (M.) Giovannoni (C.) A. Laudamo cond. |
| Milan | La Scala | Dec. 26, 1854 | A. Albertini (B.) M. De Gianni-Vivez (T.) R. Mirate (O.) G. Ferri (M.) G. Echeverria (C.) E. Cavallini cond. |
| | Castelli | Oct. 31, 1874 | E. Ciuti (B.) E. Treves (T.) G. De Sanctis-Marianecci (O.) V. Quintili-Leoni (M.) |

Naples        San Carlo   Dec. 25, 1854 G. Medori (B.) E. Carrion (O.) F.
                                        Coletti (M.) M. Arati (C.) A.
                                        Farelli cond.

                          June  9, 1859 G. Borsi de Leurie (B.) G. Giovan-
                                        noni-Zacchi (T.) A. Pagnoni (O.) M.
                                        Zacchi (M.) M. Arati (C.) A. Farelli
                                        cond.

                          Aug. 20, 1859 G. Borsi de Leurie (B.) A. Pagnoni
                                        (O.) M. Zacchi (M.) M. Arati (C.) A.
                                        Farelli cond.

              Nuovo       Apr. 19, 1856 Z. Papini (B.) S. Marini-Testa (T.)
                                        A. Di Benedetto (O.) I. Canedi (M.)
                                        Brutti (C.)

Padua         Nuovo       June     1867 A. Pozzoni-Anastasi (B.) G. De
                                        Marini (T.) C. Bulterini (O.) T.
                                        Sterbini (M.)

Palermo       Carolino    Oct.  6, 1855 M. Anselmi (B.) M. Gastaldi (T.) G.
                                        Gamboggi (O.) R. Pizzigati (M.) F.
                                        Pons (C.) A. Lo Casto cond.

Parma         Regio       Dec. 24, 1871 L. Corsi (B.) R. Foa (T.) C. Baroni/
                                        A. Gottardi (O.) S. Otto (M.) F.
                                        Becheri (C.) G. Rossi cond.

Pavia         Condomini   Dec. 26? 1861 C. Mongini-Stecchi (B.) A. Pozzolini
                                        (O.) F. Biondini (M.) N. Contedini
                                        (C.)

Perugia       Morlacchi   Jan. 24, 1866 F. Gordosa (B.) A. Falconi (T.) L.
                                        Bolis (O.) F. Archinti (M.) G. Marè
                                        (C.) Corticelli cond.

Pesaro        Rossini     Feb.     1862 A. Jackson (B.) M. Mallknecht (T.)
                                        L. Ceresa (O.)

Prato         Metastasio  Carn. 1897-98 M. Socci (B.) E. Zobil (O.) P.
                                        Scamuzzi (M.) G. Cacialli (C.) E.
                                        Contrucci cond.

Reggio di     Borbonico   Oct.  4, 1856 M. Naselli (B.) O. De Mattia (T.) G.
  Calabria                              Valentini-Cristiani (O.) Varani (M.)

Rome          Apollo      Jan. 13, 1855 R. Penco (B.) Z. Sbriscia (T.) A.
                                        Agresti (O.) G. B. Bencich (M.) G.
                                        F. Angelini (C.) E. Angelini cond.

              Argentina   Oct.  1, 1864 A. Mori (B.) Z. Trebelli (T.) O.
                                        Tasca Di Cappellio (O.) E. Storti
                                        (M.) E. Rossi-Galli (C.)

              Politeama   July 22, 1872 E. Ciuti (B.) Colarieti (T.) L.
                                        Gulli (O.) M. Ciapini (M.)

                          May      1880 M. Pisani (B.)

              Uberto I    Apr. 29, 1886

Salerno       La Fiore    Autumn   1857 E. Natale-Sbriglia (B.) F. Ricci
                                        (T.) R. Mastriani (M.)

Sassari        Civico      Oct.        1862 A. Poppi (B.) Bovi (O.) Ruggiero
                                            (M.)

Savona         Chiabrera   Dec. 26? 1874 C. Dory (B.)

Siracusa                   Jan.        1858 M. Guccini (B.) Rossi-Bagnoli (T.)
                                            G. Morghen (M.) Mariani (C.)

Spoleto        Nobile      Dec. 26? 1884 R. Rinaldini (B.) E. Grassi (O.)

Terni          Comunale    Jan.        1862 M. Neri (M.)

Trapani        San         Nov.?       1856 M. Gresti (B.)  S. Marini-Testa (T.)
               Ferdinando                   A. Miserocchi (O.) R. Giacomelli
                                            (M.)

Trieste        Grande      Oct. 11, 1854 F. Salvini-Donatelli (B.) A. Borghi-
                                            Vietti (T.) R. Mirate (O.) G. Ferri
                                            (M.) N. Benedetti (C.) G. A. Scara-
                                            melli cond.

Turin          Regio       Feb.  3, 1855 F. Salvini-Donatelli (B.) C. Guer-
                                            rini (T.) G. Bettini (O.) L. Della
                                            Santa (M.) G. C. Nerini (C.)

               Balbo       Apr. 15, 1875 I. Gerli (B.) Franco (O.)

Venice         La Fenice   Dec. 26, 1854 M. Barbieri-Nini (B.) A. Borghi-Vi-
                                            etti (T.) C. Negrini (O.) G. Corsi
                                            (M.) C. Nanni (C.)

Vercelli       Civico      Dec. 26, 1881 Ilari (B.) Polli (M.) L. Cromberg
                                            (C.)

Verona         Ristori     Mar.?       1875 Piccioli (B.) C. Dory (T.) Verdini
                                            (O.) Otto (M.) Sampieri (C.)

Vicenza        Eretenio    Aug.        1854 M. Lotti della Santa (B.) T. Chini
                                            (T.) G. Galvani (O.) G. B. Bencich
                                            (M.) G. B. Cornago (C.)

Viterbo        Unione      Sep.        1862 Martelli (B.)

                           Aug.?       1864 G. Giovannoni-Zacchi (B.) E. Pierac-
                                            cini (O.) A. Carboni (M.)

MALTA
La Valletta    Manoel      Oct. 15, 1859 T.  Cotta-Morandini  (B.)  Zangheri
                                            (T.) V. Montanaro (O.) T. Sterbini
                                            (M.) L. Del Riccio (C.)

               Nov.        1861 A.  Fumagalli  (B.)  L.  Carraciollo
                                            (T.) G. Gambetti (O.) T. Sterbini
                                            (M.) L. Del Riccio (C.)

               Nov.        1878 Vicari (B.) G. Ravogli (T.) E. Sbri-
                                            scia (O.) T. Noto (M.)

MEXICO
Mexico City    Nacional    Feb. 17, 1859 E. Tomassi (B.) E. Volpini (T.) A.
                                            Volpini (O.) A. Ottaviani (M.)

               Aug. 29, 1861 G. Sbriglia (O.)

PORTUGAL
Lisbon          Sao Carlos    Jan.  6, 1856 M. Spezia-Aldighieri (B.) Valli (T.)
                                            A. Volpini (A.) O. Bartolini (M.)

                              Feb. 20, 1859 F. Gordosa (B.) Sylvia (T.) R. Mira-
                                            te (O.) F. Cresci (M.)

Oporto          Sao Joao      Feb.     1856 B. Danieli (O.) Rossi (M.)

SPAIN
Barcelona       Principal     Nov. 27, 1855 M. Sulzer (B.) H. Sulzer (T.) B.
                                            Belart (O.) E. Fagotti (M.) G. Car-
                                            bonell (C.)

Madrid          Real          Jan.  9, 1855 M. Spezia-Aldighieri (B.) C. Nan-
                                            tier-Didiée (T.) A. Prudenza (O.)
                                            E. Crivelli (M.) G. De Baillou (C.)
                                            J. Skoczdopole cond.

Palma di        Principal     Oct.     1858 M. Roffi (B.) E. Schiapié (T.) P.
Mallorca                                    Stecchi (O.) A. Carapia (M.) G. Dal-
                                            besio (C.)

Zaragozza       Principal     Autumn   1860 T. Cotta-Morandini (B.) Poma (T.) G.
                                            De Vecchi (O.) A. D'Ettore (M.) E.
                                            Calcaterra (C.)

TURKEY
Constan-        Naum          Nov.?    1859 M. Zenoni (B.) S. Ciaschetti (T.) A.
tinople                                     Zennari (O.) C. Visai (M.)

URUGUAY
Montevideo      Solis         Sep.  3, 1859 C. Cailly (B.) A. Casaloni (T.) L.
                                            Lelmi (O.) G. Cima (M.) L. Scarabel-
                                            li (C.) C. Castagneri cond.

OTHER PRODUCTIONS-TWENTIETH CENTURY

ITALY
Rome            Argentina     Mar. 14, 1900 M. Passeri (B.) M. Verger (T.) E.
                                            Strada (O.) E. Pignataro (M.) R.
                                            Matteini (C.) C. Sebastiani cond.


10. L'ASSEDIO DI LEIDA-*Melodramma tragico* in a prologue and three acts
Milan-Teatro alla Scala-Mar. 4, 1856
Libretto by Domenico Bolognese

Elnava (E.)                              Enrichetta Weisser sop.
Armando (A.)                             Ludovico Graziani ten.
Valdes (V.)                              Giovanni Corsi bar.
Giovanni (G.)                            Cesare Nanni bass
Anna                                     Orsola Bignami sec.
Diego de Guibo                           Luigi Alessandrini bass
Ramiro                                   Francesco Lodetti bass
Inigo                                    Giacomo Redaelli ten.

Conductor                                Eugenio Cavallini
Director                                 Errico Petrella

OTHER PRODUCTIONS

GREECE
Corfu          San Giacomo Jan.  9, 1871 De Ficarra (E.) G. Toledo (V.)

ITALY
Alessandria    Civico      Oct.?     1856 E. Weisser (E.) A. Pagnoni/G. Sti-
                                          gelli (A.) F. Gnone (V.) A. Garcia
                                          (G.)

Bari           Piccinni    Jan.      1858 M. Anselmi (E.) G. Ricci (A.) G.
                                          Sansone (V.) F. Gionfrida (G.)

                           Feb.?     1860 C. De Vero (E.) V. Sabatini (A.) G.
                                          Sansone (V.)

Brescia        Grande      June      1856 G. Beltramelli (E.) A. Agresti (A.)
                                          G. Corsi (V.) G. Segri-Segarra (G.)
                                          Conti cond.

                           Dec. 26,  1874 S. Lezi (E.) Ballotti (A.)

Cagliari       Civico      Jan.?     1860 P. Bonora (V.) De Dei (G.)

Caltanisetta               Feb.      1859 Castellani (E.) Fiore (A.) Ruggeri
                                          (V.) D'Angiolo (G.)

Catania        Comunale    Dec.      1857 E. Sutton (E.) M. Stile (A.) T.
                                          Durante (V.) C. Formilli (G.) M.
                                          Pappalardo cond.

Catanzaro      Comunale    Nov.?     1858 E. Natali (E.) T. Palmieri (A.) L.
                                          Roncagli (V.)

Chieti         San         Apr. 22,  1858 L. Giordano (E.) G. De Fillipis (A.)
               Ferdinando            P. Bonora (V.) P. Vannucci (G.)

Cosenza                    Apr. 24,  1859 M. Armandi (E.) Sindaci (A.) L. Ron-
                                          cagli (V.)

Crema          Sociale     Feb. 27?  1889 A. Agresti (E.)

Cremona        Concordia   Feb.      1857 E. Weisser (E.) R. Bertolini (A.) F.
                                          Coliva (V.) A. Garcia (G.)

Cuneo          Civico      Dec. 26,  1857 E. Ballerini (E.) E. Giusti (A.) A.
                                          Cotogni (V.) Melia (G.)

Foggia         Dauno       May       1857 L. Giordano (E.)

Gallipoli                  Dec. 26?  1861 E. Schenardi (E.) G. Serri-Chiesi
                                          (A.) L. Roncagli (V.)

Genoa          Carlo       Mar. 20,  1866 M. Siebs (E.) V. Sarti (A.) L. Brig-
               Felice                nole (V.) P. Milesi (G.)

Lecce          Paisiello   Aug.?     1858 Volpari (E.) Bettini (A.) L. Ronca-
                                          gli (V.)

Livorno        Floridi     Summer    1857 E. Kenneth (E.) R. Bertolini (A.) O.
                                          Bartolini (V.) R. Laterza (G.)

Lodi           Sociale     Sep.      1870 E. Ciuti (E.) A. Lamponi (A.) Cap-
                                          pelli (V.) E. Bernardi cond.

| Messina | Sant'<br>Elisabetta | Nov. 15, 1856 | F. Scheggi (E.) G. Musiani (A.) E. Storti (V.) G. Capriles (G.) A. Laudamo cond. |
|---|---|---|---|
| Milan | Canobbiana | Mar. 26, 1856 | E. Weisser (E.) A. Agresti (A.) G. Corsi (V.) C. Nanni (G.) |
| | Carcano | Feb. 25, 1858 | A. Moro (E.) V. Prattico (V.) |
| | La Scala | Oct. 6, 1866 | M. Majo (E.) C. Bulterini (A.) G. Moriami (V.) E. Rossi-Galli (G.) |
| Modena | Comunale | Dec. 26, 1857 | E. Weisser (E.) A. Prudenza (A.) F. Massiani (V.) C. Zucchelli (G.) A. Sighicelli cond. |
| Naples | San Carlo | Nov. 18, 1856 | V. Viola (E.) L. Graziani (A.) F. Coletti (V.) M. Arati (G.) A. Farelli cond. |
| | | May 9, 1858 | A. Angelini-Cantalamessa (E.) A. Prudenza (A.) G. Sansone (V.) M. Arati (G.) A. Farelli cond. |
| | Nuovo | Nov. 11, 1856 | Z. Papini (E.) G. Tombesi (A.) I. Canedi (V.) Glover (G.) M. Di Natale cond. |
| Perugia | Morlacchi | Jan.? 1867 | |
| Pistoia | Risvegliati | Dec. 25, 1872 | |
| Palermo | Carolino | Feb. 1858 | I. Paul-Donati (E.) G. Villani (A.) E. Fagotti (V.) A. Lo Casto cond. |
| Rome | Apollo | Dec. 27, 1856 | A. Albertini (E.) C. Baucardé (A.) G. Ferri (V.) E. Angelini cond. |
| San Severo | | May 12, 1857 | Rossi (E.) Colli (A.) Mascia (V.) |
| Sassari | Civico | Dec. 26? 1857 | G. Hüber (E.) B. Negri (A.) A. Pellegrini (V.) |
| Trani | San Ferdinando | Jan.? 1865 | L. Banti (E.) Parisot (A.) R. Mastriani (V.) |
| Trapani | San Ferdinando | Dec.? 1859 | C. Bulletti (E.) S. Cerbara (A.) E. Petrilli (V.) G. Perrella (G.) |
| Turin | Vittorio Emanuele | Oct. 5, 1872 | G. Caruzzi-Bedogni (E.) M. Benfratelli (A.) L. Lalloni (V.) D. Cesari (G.) |
| MALTA<br>La Valletta | Manoel | Oct. 17, 1857 | L. Perelli (E.) T. Palmieri (A.) L. Brignole (V.) |
| PORTUGAL<br>Lisbon | Sao Carlos | Sep. 16, 1856 | M. Bernardi (E.) C. Vincentelli (A.) F. Monari (V.) A. M. Celestino (G.) |

SPAIN
Barcelona      Liceo        Oct.  1, 1859 C. Carozzi-Zucchi (E.) G. Limberti
                                          (A.) F. Bellini (V.) A. Rodas (G.)

TURKEY
Constan-       Naum         Feb. 27, 1861 T. Stolz (E.) L. Bianchi (A.) F. Co-
tinople                                   Coliva (V.) A. Fiorini (G.) C. Gua-
                                          telli cond.


11. JONE o L'ULTIMO GIORNO DI POMPEI-*Dramma lirico* in four acts
Milan-Teatro alla Scala-Jan. 26, 1858
Libretto by Giovanni Peruzzini

Jone (J.)                                        Augusta Albertini sop.
Nidia (N.)                                        Carmelita Poch mez.
Glauco (G.)                                         Carlo Negrini ten.
Arbace (A.)                                     Giovanni Guicciardi bar.
Burbo (B.)                                        Annibale Biacchi bass
Sallustio                                    Giuseppe Bernasconi bass
Dirce                                               Linda Fiorio sec.
Claudio

Conductor                                         Eugenio Cavallini
Director                                          Errico Petrella

OTHER PREMIERES

ARGENTINA
Buenos Aires   Ant. Colón   July 21, 1864 C. Briol (J.) M. Mollo (N.) L. Lelmi
                                          (G.) A. Celestino (A.) L. Walter
                                          (B.) F. Nicolai cond.

AUSTRALIA
Melbourne      Th. Royal    Aug.  1, 1870 L. Baratti (J.) L. Chambers (N.) M.
                                          Neri (G.) L. Contini (A.) E. Dondi
                                          (B.) A. Marzorati cond.

Sydney         Prince       Nov.  5, 1870 L. Baratti (J.) L. Chambers (N.) M.
               of Wales                   Neri (G.) L. Contini (A.) E. Dondi
                                          (B.) A. Marzorati cond.

AUSTRIA
Vienna         Th. an       July 31, 1871 G. Caruzzi-Bedogni (J.) E. Galimber-
               der Wien                   ti (N.) F. Patierno (G.) F. Bertoli-
                                          ni (A.) P. Milesi (B.)

BRAZIL
Rio de         Lirico       Oct. 12, 1865 C. Briol (J.) Mariotti (N.) L. Lelmi
Janeiro        Fluminense                 (G.) A. Celestino (A.) L. Walter
                                          (B.)

Sao Paulo      San José     Oct. 26, 1879 A. Garbini (J.) R. Vercolini-Tay
                                          (N.) F. Giannini (G.) V. Cottone
                                          (A.) G. Mirabella (B.)

CHILE
Santiago       Municipal    July    1869 A. Pezzoli (J.) M. Pagani (N.) E.
                                          Ballerini (G.) C. Marziali (A.) Be-
                                          retta (B.)

Valparaiso  Victoria  Jan.  9, 1870 A. Pezzoli (J.) De Carotti (N.) E. Ballerini (G.) C. Marziali (A.) Beretta (B.)

COLOMBIA
Bogota  Teatro  Apr.  6, 1874

CUBA
Havana  Nacional  Jan. 10, 1863 G. Medori (J.) H. Sulzer (N.) F. Mazzoleni (G.) F. Bellini (A.) A. Biacchi (B.)

EGYPT
Alexandria  Rossini  Feb. 28, 1866 T. De Giuli-Borsi (J.) M. Mallknecht (N.) E. Barbacini (G.) E. Mari-Cornia (A.)

Cairo  Khedivial  Jan.?  1877 L. Vanda-Miller (J.) F. Patierno (G.) V. Maurel (A.) P. Medini (B.)

FRANCE
Ajaccio  San  Autumn  1868
  Gabriele

Nice  Regio  Oct. 18, 1862 M. Mollo (J.) M. Nerasi (N.) A. Oliva-Pavani (G.) G. Giotti (A.) P. De Antoni (B.) G. Bregazzi cond.

  Municipal  Mar.?  1887 E. Tetrazzini (J.) Falconis (N.) A. Garulli (G.) C. Campanini cond.

GIBRALTAR
Gibraltar  Jan.  1873

GREECE
Athens  Nov. 15, 1868 Fiorenzoli (J.) Burattini (N.) T. Lucidi (G.) Brambilla (A.) N. Rebottaro (B.)

Corfu  San Giacomo Oct.  1863 G. Naglia (J.) Mea (G.) E. Storti Gaggi (A.)

INDIA
Calcutta  Op. House  Mar. 16, 1872 E. Bosisio (J.) T. Riboldi (N.) G. Artoni (G.) Ghiotti (A.) Vecchi (B.)

INDONESIA
Batavia  T. Batavie  Dec. 10, 1884 E. Jenuschi (J.) V. Falchero-Corsi (N.) C. Ferrari (G.) U. Forapan (A.) C. Prò (B.)

Soerebaya  Theatre  Sep. 13, 1889 M. Balzofiore (J.) L. Balzofiore (G.) A. Falciai (A.)

ITALY
Alessandria  Municipale  Oct. 18, 1868 E. Fiorentini (J.) Bellindio (N.) T. De Azula (G.) Z. Bertolasi (A.)

Ancona  Muse  Jan.?  1864 A. Pasi (J.) G. Ugolini (G.)

Ascoli  Ventidio  Oct. 30, 1867 G. Baratti (J.) G. Ugolini (G.) D.
 Piceno  Basso  Mazzoli (A.)

Bari  Piccinni  Nov.  1866

| Bergamo | Riccardi | Jan. 29, 1871 | C. Bolla (J.) F. Toni-Nazari (G.) F. Sutter (A.) L. Lombardelli (B.) G. Zavaglio cond. |
| Bologna | Comunale | Oct. 4, 1865 | M. De Zorzi (J.) A. Heller (N.) E. Loris (G.) G. Cantù (A.) E. Manfredi (B.) A. Mariani cond. |
| Brescia | Grande | Aug.? 1865 | A. Pozzoni-Anastasi (J.) S. Polli (N.) C. Bulterini (G.) V. Quintili-Leoni (A.) E. Daneri (B.) |
| Cagliari | Civico | Oct. 7, 1865 | F. Rosnati (G.) E. Anselmi (B.) |
| Cento | Comunale | Aug. 27, 1864 | G. Ronzi-Checchi (J.) E. Barbacini (G.) E. Masi (A.) A. Fiorini (B.) |
| Chieti | Maruccino | Spring 1860 | |
| Cremona | Concordia | Autumn 1863 | |
| Fermo | Aquila | Dec. 26? 1866 | A. Callery (J.) R. Pala (N.) M. Urio (G.) G. Murri (A.) C. Morroto (B.) |
| Ferrara | Comunale | Dec. 26, 1865 | C. Fiorentini (J.) G. Ugolini (G.) Giannoli (A.) |
| Fiume | Comunale | Mar. 1866 | L. Banti (J.) G. Ugolini (G.) G. Cantù (A.) E. Gasperini (B) |
| Florence | Pergola | Oct. 23, 1862 | G. Mora (J.) Censi (N.) G. Landi (G.) F. Coliva (A.) Kandratieff (B.) |
| Forli | Comunale | Apr. 1870 | |
| Genoa | Carlo Felice | Apr. 25, 1859 | L. Lesniewska (J.) M. De Gianni-Vivez (N.) C. Negrini (G.) A. Rossi-Ghelli (A.) C. Dalla Costa (B.) |
| Livorno | Avvalorati | Apr. 26? 1868 | T. Isturiz (J.) C. Dory (N.) G. Ugolini (G.) A. Souvestre (A.) D. Prosperi (B.) U. Gianelli cond. |
| Lucca | Pantera? | Carn. 1862-63 | Bellini (J.) A. Pozzolini (G.) M. Severi (A.) G. C. Nerini (B.) |
| Lugo | Rossini | Sep. 22, 1871 | C. Castelli (J.) C. Dory (N.) C. Bulterini (G.) A. Parboni (B.) |
| Mantua | Sociale | Dec. 25, 1867 | M. De Zorzi (J.) R. Ajraghi (N.) L. Ceresa (G.) L. Spellini (A.) A. De Giuli (B.) |
| Messina | Vittorio Emanuele | Nov. 23, 1864 | A. Pasi (J.) Cavetti (N.) C. Bulterini (G.) G. F. Beneventano (A.) G. Benedetti (B.) |
| Modena | Comunale | May 14, 1862 | A. Moro (J.) S. Marini Testa (N.) C. Negrini (G.) L. Colonnese (A.) G. B. Cornago (B.) A. Sighicelli cond. |
| Naples | San Carlo | Nov. 9, 1858 | G. Medori (J.) Ruta (N.) C. Negrini (G.) F. Coletti (A.) G. B. Antonucci (B.) |

Novara                        Dec. 25? 1865 M. Armandi (J.) Giuissani (N.) Bac-
                                            chetti (G.) L. Spellini (A.)

Padua            Nuovo        July 10, 1858 L. Bendazzi-Secchi (J.) A. Heller
                                            (N.) C. Negrini (G.) G. Corsi (A.)
                                            A. Selva (B.)

Palermo          Bellini      Mar. 22, 1863 E. Poinsot (J.) E. Barbacini (G.) G.
                                            Aldighieri (A.) M. Junca (B.) A. Lo
                                            Casto cond.

Parma            Regio         Feb. 22, 1868 L. Banti (J.) V. Ferrini (N.) M.
                                            Neri (G.) A. Carboni (A.) A. Fron-
                                            toni (B.) G. C. Ferrarini cond.

Pavia            Condominio  Dec. 26? 1868 G. Caruzzi-Bedogni (J.) Trucco (N.)
                                            A. Grandi (A.)

Pesaro           Rossini       Dec. 26, 1870 E. Sgargi (J.) Micheli (N.) Scipioni
                                            (G.) A. Carboni (A.) C. Ferrara (B.)
                                            Grilli cond.

Piacenza         Municipale  Summer   1858 A. Pomè (J.) L. Berini (N.) E. Con-
                                            cordia (G.) U. Brambilla (A.) S. Ge-
                                            rini (B.) P. Montaguti cond.

Pisa             Ravvivati     Dec. 12, 1866 R. Gabussi De Bassini (J.) E. Ajrol-
                                            di (N.) G. Musiani (G.) G. Gambetti
                                            (A.) C. Agrolli (B.) L. Quercioli
                                            cond.

Ravenna          Alighieri     Dec. 30, 1866 A. Pasi (J.) L. Viale (N.) G. Gam-
                                            betti (G.) A. Sauvestre (A.) G.
                                            Marchetti (B.)

Reggio Emilia Municipale  Dec. 25, 1874 M. L. Swift (J.) G. Iones (N.) V.
                                            Matteucci (G.) S. Cappelli (A.) F.
                                            Novara (B.) G. Grisanti cond.

Rome             Argentina     May  20, 1863 P. Colson (J.) A. Zamboni (N.) C.
                                            Negrini (G.) F. Pandolfini (A.) R.
                                            Laterza (B.) E. Angelini cond.

Rovigo           Sociale       Oct. 17, 1869 P. Missorta (J.) A. Gottardi (G.) F.
                                            Tirini (A.) M. Severi (B.)

Savona           Chiabrera     Dec. 26? 1870 A. Schwarz (J.) Basso (N.) O. Mari-
                                            ani (G.) P. Caravatti (A.) D. Ben-
                                            ferreri (B.)

Siena            Rinnovati     Dec. 26, 1870

Spoleto          Nuovo         Aug.     1864 A. Pasi (J.) E. Ajroldi (N.) G. Vil-
                                            lani (G.) V. Quintili-Leoni (A.) E.
                                            Rossi-Galli (B.)

Trento           Sociale       June     1870 A. Bianchi-Montaldo (J.) G. Lemaire
                                            (N.) F. Patierno (G.) G. Valle (A.)

Treviso          Comunale      Nov.  9, 1870 L. Tencajoli (J.) E. Treves (N.) F.
                                            Steger (G.) G. Cima (A.) P. Dérivis
                                            (B.) E. Terziani cond.

| | | | |
|---|---|---|---|
| Trieste | Grande | Nov. 13, 1862 | L. Bendazzi-Secchi (J.) G. Flory (N.) C. Negrini (G.) D. Squarcia (A.) H. Brémond (B.) A. Cremaschi cond. |
| Turin | Regio | Jan. 31, 1863 | L. Bendazzi-Secchi (J.) G. Fleury (N.) G. Villani (G.) L. Colonnese (A.) R. Laterza (B.) F. Bianchi cond. E. Petrella dir. |
| Venice | Rossini | Nov. 19, 1870 | C. Noel-Guidi (J.) Luini (N.) A. Boetti (G.) A. Parboni (A.) L. Lombardelli (B.) |
| | La Fenice | Jan. 16, 1872 | A. Schwarz (J.) E. Treves (N.) M. Toressi (G.) L. Colonnese (A.) C. Zucchelli (B.) C. Castagneri cond. |
| Verona | Ristori | Oct.? 1863 | L. Baratti (J.) F. Toni-Nazzari (G.) N. Fallica (A.) |
| Vicenza | Eretenio | Dec. 26, 1869 | A. Schwarz (J.) O. Mariani (G.) F. Serafini (A.) R. Buffagni (B.) Manzato cond. |
| **JUGOSLAVIA** Zagreb | National | May 1869 | L. Papini (J.) L. Chambers (N.) L. Abrugnedo (G.) G. Del Puente (A.) G. Kaschmann (B.) |
| Zara | Nuovo | Oct. 12, 1867 | Sternini (J.) T. Miserocchi (G.) D. Dal Negro (A.) C. Morroto (B.) |
| **MALTA** La Valletta | Manoel | Oct.? 1860 | E. Brambilla (J.) A. Oliva-Pavani (G.) T. Sterbini (A.) |
| **MEXICO** Guadalajara | Degollado | Feb. 15, 1872 | I. Visconti (J.) Mendoza (N.) G. Verati (G.) A. Ottaviani (A.) |
| Mexico City | Nacional | Oct. 28, 1865 | I. Alba (J.) H. Sulzer (N.) G. Tombesi (G.) M. Padilla (A.) G. B. Cornago (B.) |
| **PERU** Lima | Principal | Aug. 8, 1871 | M. Bulli-Paoli (J.) Cuzzeri (N.) T. De Azula (G.) C. Lenghi (A.) A. Buzzi (B.) C. Lietti cond. |
| **PHILIPPINES** Manila | Del Tondo | Dec. 18, 1886 | E. Ancarani (J.) A. Silini (N.) Castelli (G.) G. Ciocci (A.) E. Villelmi (B.) |
| **PORTUGAL** Lisbon | Sao Carlos | Dec. 15, 1869 | C. Poch (J.) E. Fossa (N.) G. Ugolini (G.) L. Merly (A.) G. Marchetti (B.) P. A. Coppolla cond. |
| Oporto | Sao Joao | Feb. 13, 1871 | B. Blume (J.) L. Berini (N.) P. Bignardi (G.) A. Parboni (A.) E. Rossi-Galli (B.) |

PUERTO RICO
Ponce            La Perla      Nov.  3, 1883  E. Tetrazzini (J.) P. Rambelli (N.)
                                              A. Patierno (G.) V. Quintili-Leoni
                                              (A.)

San Juan         Municipal     Feb. 23, 1888  I. Zeffirini (J.) L. Bellò (G.) L.
                                              Valentini (A.) G. Lorini cond.

ROMANIA
Bucharest        Nacional      Feb.?    1868  A. Moro (J.) Gaggiotti (N.) E.
                                              Harvin (G.) F. Archinti (A.)

Craiova          Theodorini    Dec.  2, 1871  E. Sgargi (J.) B. Malvezzi (N.) S.
                                              Malvezzi (G.) Boschini (A.) A. Vitti
                                              (B.)

RUSSIA
Odessa           Municipal     Feb.     1867  L. Ponti dall'Armi (J.) Polacchi
                                              (N.) G. Zaccometti (G.) L. Rossi de
                                              Ruggero (A.) O. Maini (B.)

Tbilisi          Imperial      Dec. 14, 1875  A. Conti-Foroni (J.) G. Tiozzo (N.)
                                              G. Villena (G.) E. Carnili (A.)

SPAIN
Barcelona        Liceo         Oct.  3, 1863  P. Colson (J.) E. Presli (N.) C. Ne-
                                              grini (G.) L. Rossi de Ruggero (A.)
                                              A. Selva (B.) G. Bottesini cond.

Cadiz            Principal     Feb.  5, 1873  V. Tilli (J.) Corsi (N.) G. Zacco-
                                              metti (G.) F. Amodio (A.) F. Uetam
                                              (B.)

Madrid           Principe      May  16, 1872  E. Wijiak (J.) E. Barlani-Dini (N.)
                 Alfonso                       F. Steger (G.) A. Faentini-Galassi
                                              (A.) G. David (B.) E. Terziani cond.

Palma di         Principal     Spring   1874  V. Tilli (J.) F. Llanes (N.) R. Pe-
  Mallorca                                    trovich (G.)

Seville          San           Oct.     1867  C. Marziali-Passerini (J.) C. Mar-
                 Fernando                      telli (N.) G. Landi (G.) F. Coliva
                                              (A.)

Valencia         Principal     Apr. 23? 1868  C. Lanzi (J.) A. Oliva-Pavani (G.)
                                              F. Amodio (A.) H. Brémond (B.)

Zaragozza        Principal     Mar. 23, 1884  C. Castiglioni (J.) Paolicchi (N.)
                                              A. Ottaviani (G.) A. Gnaccarini (A.)
                                              I. Sbordoni (B.)

TUNISIA
Tunis            Cohen         May?     1880

TURKEY
Constan-         Naum          Oct. 17, 1863  L. Tencajoli (J.) G. Zaccometti (G.)
  tinople                                     Grossi (A.) Vecchi (B.)

Smyrna           Cammarano     Oct.     1866  F. Scheggi (J.) Assi (N.) E. Concor-
                                              dia (G.) S. Orsi (A.) N. Savoldelli
                                              (B.)

UNITED STATES
Baltimore      Concordia    Dec. 20, 1865 E. Bosisio (J.) A. Phillips (N.) F.
                                          Mazzoleni (G.) D. Bellini (A.) G. B.
                                          Antonucci (B.)

Boston         Boston Th.   Jan.  4, 1864 G. Medori (J.) H. Sulzer (N.) F.
                                          Mazzoleni (G.) D. Bellini (A.) A.
                                          Biacchi (B.)

Mobile         Mobile Th.   Mar.  2, 1867 C. Cattinari (J.) A. Boetti (G.) A.
                                          Strozzi (A.)

New Orleans    Opéra        Feb.  8, 1867 C. Cattinari (J.) De Gebele (N.) A.
                                          Boetti (G.) A. Strozzi (A.)

New York       Ac. of Mus.  Apr.  6, 1863 G. Medori (J.) H. Sulzer (N.) F.
                                          Mazzoleni (G.) D. Bellini (A.) A.
                                          Biacchi (B.)

Philadelphia   Ac. of Mus.  Dec.  2, 1863 G. Medori (J.) H. Sulzer (N.) F.
                                          Mazzoleni (G.) D. Bellini (A.) A.
                                          Biacchi (B.)

San Francisco  Maguire's    July 10, 1867 E. Brambilla (J.) S. Bonheur (N.) G.
                                          Limberti (G.) G. Mancusi (A.) S.
                                          Milleri (B.) G. T. Evans cond.

Washington     Grover's     Dec. 26, 1865 E. Bosisio (J.) A. Phillips (N.) F.
                                          Mazzoleni (G.) D. Bellini (A.) G. B.
                                          Antonucci (B.)

URUGUAY
Montevideo     Solis        Jan. 10, 1866 C. Briol (J.) R. Mariotti (N.) L.
                                          Lelmi (G.) A. M. Celestino (A.) G.
                                          C. Nerini (B.)

VENEZUELA
Caracas        T. Caracas   Apr. 12, 1874 M. Majo (J.) L. Caracciolo (N.) F.
                                          Mazzoleni (G.) A. Strozzi (A.)

               Municipal    Feb. 26, 1881 M. Lucchesi (J.) T. Mestres (N.) F.
                                          Giannini (G.) F. Farina (A.) G.
                                          Sampieri (B.) F. Rachelle cond.

SELECTED REVIVALS-NINETEENTH CENTURY

ITALY
Bologna        Comunale     Oct. 30, 1883 A. Bianchi-Montaldo (J.) G. Levi
                                          (N.) G. Caldani-Kuon (G.) S. Calta-
                                          girone (A.) C. Bedogni (B.) L. Man-
                                          cinelli cond.

Florence       Pergola      Oct. 27, 1870 A. Bianchi-Montaldo (J.) F. Mariani
                                          De Angelis (N.) C. Bulterini (G.) P.
                                          Silenzi (A.) G. Maffei (B.)

Milan          La Scala     Dec. 26, 1861 P. Colson (J.) M. Talvò (N.) C. Ne-
                                          grini (G.) G. F. Beneventano/L. Co-
                                          lonnese (A.) G. Atry (B.)

Naples         San Carlo    Feb.  9, 1861 G. Medori (J.) C. Weber (N.) C. Ne-
                                          grini (G.) F. Coletti (A.) M. Arati
                                          (B.)

                        Oct. 24, 1868 M. Lotti Della Santa (J.) F. Rubini
                                      (N.) F. Mazzoleni (G.) F. Coletti/V.
                                      Quintili-Leoni (A.) M. Arati (B.)

Rome        Argentina   May  20, 1863 P. Colson (J.) A. Zamboni (N.) C.
                                      Negrini (G.) F. Pandolfini (A.) R.
                                      Laterza (B.) E. Angelini cond.

                        Apr. 20, 1864 G. Beltrami-Mariangeli (J.) G. Flory
                                      (N.) C. Negrini (G.) G. Cima (A.) C.
                                      Della Costa (B.) E. Angelini cond.

            Apollo      Jan. 19, 1864 E. Poinsot (J.) E. Grossi (N.) E.
                                      Barbacini (G.) G. Cima (A.) H. Bré-
                                      mond (B.) E. Angelini cond.

                        Dec. 26, 1868 T. Stolz (J.) C. Dory (N.) G. Zaco-
                                      metti (G.) T. Sterbini (A.) G.
                                      Capponi (B.) E. Angelini cond.

                        Dec. 26, 1870 A. Bianchi-Montaldo (J.) G. Galassi/
                                      F. Mariani De Angelis (N.) C. Bulte-
                                      rini (G.) G. Sani/G. Valle (A.) P.
                                      Milesi (B.) R. Kuon cond.

Turin       Regio       Feb. 15, 1868 E. Galli-Altini (J.) R. Vercolini-
                                      Tay (N.) G. Piccioli (G.) L. Brig-
                                      nole (A.) G. Galvani (B.)

SPAIN
Barcelona   Liceo       Mar. 13, 1872 C. Briol (J.) F. Llanes (N.) F.
                                      Steger (G.) L. Merly (A.) A. Rodas
                                      (B.)

                        Oct. 13, 1877 A. Bianchi-Montaldo (J.) C. Prandi
                                      (N.) C. Bulterini (G.) M. Ciapini
                                      (A.) R. D'Ottavi (B.)

                        Mar. 29? 1879 A. Bianchi-Montaldo (J.) C. Bulteri-
                                      ni (G.) G. Moriami (A.) G. Mirabella
                                      (B.)

UNITED STATES
New York    Ac. of Mus. Oct. 14, 1863 G. Medori (J.) H. Sulzer (N.) F.
                                      Mazzoleni (G.) D. Bellini (A.) A.
                                      Biacchi (B.)

                        Oct.  2, 1865 E. Bosisio (J.) A. Phillips (N.) F.
                                      Mazzoleni (G.) D. Bellini (A.) A.
                                      Biacchi/G. B. Antonucci (B.)

                        Oct. 18, 1886 A. Bianchi-Montaldo (J.) C. Prandi
                                      (N.) F. Giannini (G.) E. Pogliani
                                      (A.) A. Pinto (B.) O. Bimboni cond.

San Francisco Alhambra  July  9, 1899

OTHER PRODUCTIONS-TWENTIETH CENTURY

ITALY
Catania     Bellini     June  8, 1909 B. Cocchi (J.) M. Favilli (N.) F.
                                      Castellani (G.) E. De Marco (A.) A.
                                      Giudice (B.) G. Frattini cond.

Lucca          Giglio        Dec. 29? 1904 M. Bruschi (J.)

Messina        Mastroieni    Jan. 28, 1915 G. Piccoletti (J.) T. Masucci (N.)
                             A. Maurini (G.) L. Ferraioli (B.) G.
                             Soriente cond.

Naples         Bellini       Jan. 12? 1912 M. Rossini (J.) A. Colombini (N.) O.
                             Rosati (G.) Caldini (A.)

                             Sep. 27? 1913 C. Forni (J.) V. Gallmary (N.) L.
                             Siroli (G.) Viggiani (A.)

Padua          Rotonda       Aug. 29? 1904 A. De Angelis (J.) N. Molinari (N.)
                             G. Cesarini (G.)

Palermo        Biondo        May  22, 1909 B. Cocchi (J.) M. Favilli (N.) F.
                             Castellani (G.) E. De Marco (A.) E.
                             Gorelli (B.) G. Frattini cond.

                             Oct. 29, 1909 R. Garitano (J.) A. Brunamonti (N.)
                             F. Castellani (G.) G. Comune (A.) E.
                             Cassia (B.) G. Abbate cond.

               Politeama     Nov. 25, 1914 E. Galleazzi (J.) T. Alasia (N.) I.
                             Righi-Briani (G.) E. Faticanti (A.)
                             G. Bardi (B.) P. La Rotella cond.

                             Nov. 27, 1924 A. Rossi-Oliver (J.) L. Salvatori
                             (N.) F. Castellani (G.) C. Morini
                             (A.) E. Fumagalli (B.) A. Sigismondo
                             cond.

Rome           Morgana       Apr.  7, 1922 E. Facondini Loppi (J.) L. Warko
                             (N.) F. Castellani (G.) L. Siravo
                             (A.) C. Ulivi (B.) A. Consorti cond.

Taranto                      May      1916 A. De Angelis (J.) L. Starace (N.)
                             O. Rosati (G.) G. Noto (A.) De Falco
                             (B.)

VENEZUELA
Caracas        Municipal     Jan. 30, 1981 A. Negri (J.) S. Silva (N.) B.
                             Sebastian (G.) G. Mastromei (A.) L.
                             Lebherz (B.) E. Müller cond.

12. IL DUCA DI SCILLA-*Dramma lirico* in four acts
Milan-Teatro alla Scala-Mar. 24, 1859
Libretto by  Giovanni Peruzzini and L. Fortis

Mirta (M.)                                          Carlotta Marchisio sop.
Giulia (G.)                                         Barbara Marchisio mez.
Baldo (B.)                                          Emilio Pancani ten.
Manuello (Ma.)                                      Luigi Merly bar.
Petraccio (P.)                                      Raffaele Laterza bass
Editta                                              Linda Fiorio sec.
Conte di Montefiore                                 Giacomo Redaelli ten.
Gisca                                               Giuseppe Bernasconi bass
Gennaro                                             Luigi Alessandrini bass

Conductor                                           Eugenio Cavallini
Director                                            Errico Petrella

OTHER PRODUCTIONS

ITALY
Naples         San Carlo    Mar. 28, 1860 B. Steffenone (M.) E. Paganini (G.)
                                          C. Negrini (B.) G. Guicciardi (Ma.)
                                          P. Brignole (P.)


13. MOROSINA o L'ULTIMO DE'FALIERI-*Melodramma tragico* in three acts
Naples-Teatro San Carlo-Jan. 6, 1860
Libretto by Domenico Bolognese

Morosina Morosini (M.)                              Balbina Steffenone sop.
Alba (A.)                                  Ginevra Giovannoni Zacchi sop.
Galieno (G.)                                        Carlo Negrini ten.
Giovanni Orseolo (O.)                      Giovanni Guicciardi bar.
Amelia                                              Gaetana Garito sec.
Una Zingarella                             Teresa Nocciuoli sec.
Spolatro                                            Luigi Brignole bar.
Il Doge                                    Giuseppe Benedetti bass
Jacopo                                              Luigi Bisaccia ten.

Director                                            Errico Petrella


OTHER PRODUCTIONS

ITALY
Bari           Piccinni     Jan.      1864 A.  Angelini-Cantalamessa  (M.)   E.
                                           Concordia (G.) G. Reina (O.)

Cagliari       Civico       Dec. 25, 1868 C. Rosavalle (M.) B. Capozzi (A.) A.
                                           Masini (G.) A. Pifferi (O.)

Milan          La Scala     Mar. 23, 1862 S. Vera-Lorini (M.) M. Talvò (A.) C.
                                           Negrini (G.) L. Colonnese (O.)

MALTA
La Valletta    Manoel       Apr.      1863 V.  Tilli  (M.)  E.  Serazzi (G.)  T.
                                           Sterbini (O.)

14. IL FOLLETTO DI GRESY-*Commedia lirica* in three acts
Naples-Teatro del Fondo-Aug. 28, 1860
Libretto by Domenico Bolognese

| | |
|---|---|
| Silvia (S.) | Sofia Vera-Lorini sop. |
| Duchessa | Carolina Cetronè mez. |
| Cav. Eugenio (E.) | Remigio Bertolini ten. |
| Riccardo (R.) | Giovanni Guicciardi bar. |
| Conte Orazio (O.) | Rafaelle Scalese buf. |
| Una Dama | Gaetana Garito sec. |
| Il Duca | Luigi Bisaccia ten. |
| Un Ufficiale | Giuseppe Benedetti bass |

Director                                          Errico Petrella

OTHER PRODUCTIONS

ITALY

| | | | |
|---|---|---|---|
| Alessandria | Civico | Dec. 26, 1867 | Amaldi (S.) |
| | | Dec. 26, 1872 | Amaldi (S.) Borelli (R.) P. Prette (O.) |
| Florence | Nazionale | Sep. 14, 1866 | E. Ridolfi (S.) E. Sbriscia (E.) E. Papini (O.) |
| Forli | Comunale | Dec. 25, 1867 | E. Ridolfi (S.) Gurini (E.) |
| Genoa | Andrea Doria | July 1865 | T. Pozzi (S.) Banni (E.) A. Padovani (R.) A. Bottero (O.) |
| | Carlo Felice | Nov. 17, 1868 | C. Facccio (S.) A. Celada (E.) A. Parboni (R.) A. Fiorini (O.) |
| Livorno | Rossini | Nov. 6, 1867 | A. Montebello (S.) P. Ronzi (E.) I. Viganotti (R.) E. Ricci (O.) |
| Milan | Santa Radegonda | Jan. 18, 1863 | T. Pozzi (S.) P. Stecchi (E.) F. Archinti (R.) A. Bottero (O.) |
| | Carcano | Nov. 5, 1863 | T. Pozzi (S.) L. Bolis (E.) F. Archinti (R.) A. Bottero (O.) |
| Naples | San Carlo | Sep. 7, 1860 | S. Vera-Lorini (S.) R. Bertolini (E.) L. Brignole (R.) R. Scalese (O.) A. Farelli cond. |
| | | Dec. 14, 1860 | S. Vera-Lorini (S.) R. Bertolini (E.) L. Brignole (R.) R. Scalese (O.) |
| Pavia | Condominio | Feb. 1865 | T. Pozzi (S.) F. Righi-Gurini (E.) C. Massera (R.) A. Bottero (O.) |
| Ravenna | Alighieri | Jan. 19, 1867 | L. Lazzari (S.) G. Pasi (E.) F. Brandini (R.) G. Marchisio (O.) |
| Rome | Argentina | Dec. 26, 1864 | C. Mongini-Stecchi (S.) C. Guidotti (E.) L. Brignole (R.) F. Catani (O.) R. Kuon cond. |
| Savona | Chiabrera | Dec.? 1879 | |

| Trieste | Grande | Mar. 15, 1866 E. Sorandi (S.) A. Zamboni (E.) E. Storti-Gaggi (R.) S. Ronconi (O.) A. Cremaschi cond. |
|---|---|---|
| Turin | Vittorio Emanuele | Nov. 26, 1870 E. Ciuti (S.) |
| | Balbo | Dec. 18, 1872 A. Rizzi (S.) L. Baldelli (O.) |
| MALTA La Valletta | Manoel | Oct.? 1863 E. Bosisio (S.) E. Serazzi (E.) F. Brandini (R.) L. Conti (O.) |
| | | Oct. 1864 E. Bosisio (S.) E. Serazzi (E.) F. Brandini (R.) |
| | Reale | Feb.? 1889 M. Roussel-Giraud (S.) N. Muller (E.) |

15. VIRGINIA-*Tragedia lirica* in three acts
Naples-Teatro San Carlo-July 23, 1861
Libretto by Domenico Bolognese

| | |
|---|---|
| Virginia | Isabella Galletti-Gianoli sop. |
| Icilio | Carlo Negrini ten. |
| Virginio | Filippo Coletti bar. |
| Appio | Marco Arati bass |
| Clelia | Carolina Cetronè mez. |
| Claudio | Luigi Bisaccia ten. |
| Decio | Pasquale Ceci ten. |
| Il Duce | Antonio Donadio bass |
| Conductor | |
| Director | Errico Petrella |

16. LA CONTESSA D'AMALFI-*Dramma lirico* in four acts
Turin-Teatro Regio-Mar. 8, 1864
Libretto by Giovanni Peruzzini

| | |
|---|---|
| Leonora (L.) | Luigia Bendazzi-Secchi sop. |
| Tilde (T.) | Benedettina Grosso sop. |
| Egidio (E.) | Ludovico Graziani ten. |
| Duca Carnioli (C.) | Luigi Colonnese bar. |
| Sertorio (S.) | Marcel Junca bass |
| Berta | Luigia Marenco sec. |
| Il Conte di Lara | Luigi Manfredi ten. |
| Conductor | Francesco Bianchi |
| Director | Errico Petrella |

OTHER PRODUCTIONS

ARGENTINA
Buenos Aires   Colon      June 29, 1872 E. Saurel (L.) L. Lelmi (E.) G. Ta-
                                    gliapietra (C.)

BRAZIL
Rio de       Lyrico       Oct. 30, 1873 P. Missorta (L.) E. Cortesi (T.) M.
  Janeiro    Fluminense                 Toressi (E.) G. Spalazzi (C.)

CHILE
Santiago     Municipal    July     1870 M. Mollo (L.) P. Baccei (E.)

FRANCE
Ajaccio      San          Nov.?    1878 De Clans (L.)
             Gabriele

Nice         Municipal    Feb.?    1870 L. Varesi (L.) E. Berini (T.) C.
                                        Vincentelli (E.) F. Cresci (C.) G.
                                        Bregozzo cond.

GREECE
Athens       Falero?      Aug.?    1876 Avagnini (L.) Caselli (T.) Avagnini
                                        (E.) A. Navary (C.) R. Mancini (S.)

Corfu        San Giacomo Nov.      1867 V. Potentini (L.) M. Urio (E.)

ITALY[28]
Alessandria  Civico       Oct.     1869 I. Pelegatti-Visconti (L.) Rovilli
                                        (T.) Marelli (E.) E. Fagotti (C.)
                                        Ruiz (S.) G. Zavaglio cond.

Ancona       Muse         Apr. 30, 1866 V. Saurel (L.) E. Pizioli (E.) Paoli
                                        (C.)

Ascoli       Ventidio     Nov.     1871 V. Pozzi-Brazanti (L.)  G. Zacometti
  Piceno     Basso                      (E.) E. Fagotti (C.)

Bergamo      Riccardi     Mar. 10, 1867 L. Mosconi (L.) G.  Petrovich (E.)
                                        G. Massera (C.) G. Della Baratta
                                        cond.

Bologna      Contavalli   May?     1873 I. Biron/L. Bordato (L.) E. Jenus-
                                        chi (E.) N. Gullo (E.) N. Giommi
                                        (C.) N. Pozzi (S.)

Brescia      Grande       Dec. 26? 1866 G. Ferrari (L.) C. Amaldi (T.) L.
                                        Marelli (E.) D. Cesari (C.) N.
                                        Contedini (S.)

Cagliari     Civico       Nov. 21, 1868 C. Rosavalle (L.) B. Capozzi (T.) A.
                                        Masini (E.) A. Pifferi (C.)

Carpi        Comunale     Aug. 23, 1868 G. Caruzzi-Bedogni (L.) P. Cecchi/V.
                                        Belardi (E.) G. Spallazzi (C.)

---

28. *La Contessa d'Amalfi* was quite popular in Italy during the last quarter of the 19th century. Other productions include Aci Reale in Jan. 1873, Bari in 1887, Bergamo in Jan. 1878, Camerino in 1873, Cesena in 1868, Chiavari in 1873, Civitavecchia in 1869, Codogno in 1870, Como in 1882, Empoli in 1880, Este in 1877, Foggia in 1888, Forli in 1874, Fossano in 1870, the Teatro Andrea Podesta in Genoa in 1898, Guastalla in 1875, Lecce and Livorno in 1873, Novara in 1868, Novi Ligure in 1869, Osimo in 1873, Ostiglia in 1881, Pinerolo in 1877, Pistoia in 1866, Reggio Calabria in 1873, Rieti in 1869, the Politeama in Rome in 1872, Saluzzo in 1871 and 1882, Savigliano in 1876, Stradella in 1874, Terni in 1865, Tortona in 1872, the Teatro Alfieri in Turin in 1872 and 1878, Vercelli in 1869 and 1880, Vicenza in 1873, Viterbo in 1869, Voghera in 1871 and Volterra in 1889.

| Casal-monferrato | Sociale | Nov. 15, 1873 | G. Caruzzi-Bedogni (L.) M. Milani-Vela (T.) M. Vidal (E.) F. Graziosi (C.) |
|---|---|---|---|
| Catania | Comunale | Apr. 1875 | B. Capozzi (L.) G. Frapolli (E.) |
| Cento | Comunale | Aug. 1869 | M. Calisto' (L.) P. Missorta (T.) A. Gottardi (E.) A. Moragas (C.) M. Severi (S.) |
| Chieti | Maruccino | Apr. 18, 1868 | L. Mattei Casanova (L.) G. Firpo (E.) C. Sacchetti (C.) |
| Como | Sociale | Dec. 26, 1870 | I. De Howe (L.) N. Marzy (T.) F. Mancio (E.) N. Azzaliai (C.) A. Savoldelli (S.) G. B. Caldera cond. |
| Cremona | Concordia | Sep. 2? 1868 | A. Moro (L.) L. Ferrari (T.) F. Pozzo (E.) F. Amodio (C.) E. Bagagiolo (S.) |
| Fermo | Aquila | Dec. 26? 1873 | V. Arnoldi (L.) C. Prampolini (T.) P. Mameco (C.) |
| Ferrara | Comunale | Jan. 3, 1867 | Ferrucci (L.) E. Campagnoli (T.) Colombini (E.) A. Albieri (C.) F. Rigo (S.) |
| Fiume | Civico | Mar. 1867 | V. Saurel (L.) E. Pizioli (T.) G. Gambetti (E.) G. Valle (C.) G. Segri-Segarra (S.) |
| Florence | Pergola | Dec. 26, 1864 | A. Ortolani-Tiberini (L.) M. Tiberini (E.) L. Giraldoni (C.) |
| | Pagliano | Jan. 1869 | C. Castelli (L.) F. Meyer (T.) F. Pozzo (E.) G. Cima (C.) |
| Genoa | Carlo Felice | Feb. 6, 1870 | G. Marziali-Passarini (L.) B. Cosmelli (T.) E. Barbacini (E.) A. Pantaleoni (C.) S. Cesarò (S.) |
| | | Jan. 27, 1872 | L. Perelli (L.) L. Corsi (T.) G. Vanzan (E.) S. Orsi (C.) A. Fradelloni (S.) |
| | | Jan. 12, 1884 | E. Tati (L.) C. Gallioni (E.) |
| | Andrea Doria | Nov. 6, 1870 | O. Torriani (L.) Riccia (T.) P. Ronzi (E.) D. Cesari (C.) |
| | Nazionale | May 1, 1873 | I. Kottas (L.) B. Dani (T.) |
| | Politeama | Aug. 5, 1876 | I. Giorgi (L.) R. Robiati (T.) L. Dal Passo (E.) G. Dominici (C.) A. Padovani (S.) |
| | Margherita | Apr. 13, 1887 | I. Biliotti (L.) R. Bareggi (T.) A. D'Enrici (E.) R. Dolcibene (C.) A. Canessa (S.) |
| La Spezia | Civico | Feb. 1869 | B. D'Aponte (L.) A. Cortesi (T.) Cingolani (E.) A. Borella (C.) Becheri (S.) |

La Contessa d'Amalfi

| Livorno | Floridi | June | 1867 | G. Borsi de Leurie (L.) B. D'Aponte (T.) A. Zenari (E.) G. Moriami (C.) E. Rossi-Galli (S.) |
|---|---|---|---|---|
| | Rossini | Nov. | 1867 | Montebello (L.) P. Ronzi (E.) I. Viganotti (C.) E. Gasperini (S.) |
| Lucca | Giglio | Sep. 12, | 1866 | Corradi (L.) A. Corsi (E.) Gianoli (C.) Becheri (S.) |
| Lugo | Rossini | Spring | 1879 | C. Brini (L.) |
| Macerata | | Sep. 20, | 1865 | G. Borsi de Leurie (L.) F. Patierno (E.) G. Cima (C.) |
| Messina | Vittorio Emanuele | Apr. 2, | 1867 | C. Noel-Guidi (L.) Riccopieri F. Zucchi (E.) A. Laurence (C.) C. Lazzaro (S.) |
| Milan | La Scala | Dec. 26, | 1864 | M. Lotti della Santa (L.) P. Colson (T.) E. Carrion (E.) O. Bartolini (C.) P. Medini (S.) |
| | Re | May 15, | 1869 | Manini (L.) Blasco (T.) T. Karl (E.) Manini (C.) Bosco (S.) |
| | Santa Radegonda | Feb. | 1871 | Da Maestri (L.) K. Scott (T.) P. Se-Setragni (E.) Manini (C.) A. Pomè cond. |
| Modena | Goldoni | Summer | 1869 | C. Ziska (L.) E. Boracchi (T.) T. Karl (E.) U. Brambilla (C.) R. Buffagni (S.) P. Manni cond. |
| | Comunale | Dec. 25, | 1870 | A. D'Alberti (L.) B. Cosmelli (T.) A. Rampini-Boncore (E.) E. Storti-Gaggi/F. Proni/I. Viganotti (C.) R. Buffagni (S.) V. Zawerthal cond. |
| Naples | San Carlo | Dec. 15, | 1867 | A. Pozzoni-Anastasi (L.) T. Palmieri (E.) L. Colonnese (C.) C. Zucchelli (S.) |
| | Bellini | Apr. 26? | 1888 | L. Cerne (L.) P. Pellagalli-Rossetti (E.) E. Cerne (C.) |
| Padua | Concordi | Dec. 26? | 1866 | A. Contarini (L.) M. Pagani (T.) L. Bolis (E.) Z. Bertolasi (C.) E. Gasperini (S.) |
| Palermo | Bellini | Feb. | 1869 | C. Mongini-Stecchi (L.) G. Ugolini (E.) A. Pantaleoni (C.) C. Zucchelli (S.) L. Alfano cond. |
| Parma | Regio | Feb. 5, | 1870 | E. Ciuti (L.) L. Marenco-Corsi (T.) E. Serazzi/P. Cecchi (E.) A. Grandi (C.) R. Mailini (S.) G. C. Ferrarini cond. |
| | | Mar. 5, | 1871 | E. Ciuti (L.) J. Bay (T.) A. Rampini Boncori (E.) D. Cesari (C.) C. Morroto (S.) G. C. Ferrarini cond. |

| Pavia | Condominio | Oct. 7, 1868 | G. Caruzzi-Bedogni (L.) Boracchi (T.) A. Lamponi (E.) A. Moragas (C.) G. B. Del Fabbro (S.) |
|---|---|---|---|
| Perugia | | Apr.? 1865 | A. Carruzzi (L.) Castelli (E.) Villani (C.) |
| Pesaro | Rossini | Dec. 26, 1868 | E. Biscaccianti (L.) A. Mugnoz (T.) E. Ronconi (E.) A. Albieri (C.) G. Capriles (S.) |
| Piacenza | Municipale | Carn. 1869-70 | C. Ferlotti (L.) A. Boetti (E.) G. Valle (C.) A. Mazzucato cond. |
| | | Autumn 1878 | L. Mosconi (L.) F. Boganini (E.) T. Piroli cond. |
| Prato | Metastasio | Jan.? 1867 | C. Ghirlanda-Tortolini (L.) M. Bracci (T.) L. Dainelli (E.) A. Graziani (C.) F. Panari (S.) A. Nuti cond. |
| Ravenna | Alighieri | Dec. 25, 1868 | G. Beltramini (L.) D. Crosio (T.) G. Marelli (E.) G. Giotti (C.) A. Calzelli (S.) |
| Reggio Emilia | Municipale | Jan. 20, 1872 | E. Campagnoli (L.) O. Pierangeli (T.) S. Cerbara (E.) U. Brambilla (C.) N. Giommi (S.) A. Peri dir. G. Tebaldi cond. |
| Rimini | Nuovo | Dec. 26, 1867 | V. Pozzi-Brazanti (L.) G. Petrovich (E.) Previdal (C.) |
| Rome | Argentina | Apr. 1870 | E. Wiziak (L.) G. Perotti (E.) S. Sparapani (C.) C. Zuchelli (S.) |
| Savona | Chiabrera | Carn. 1867-68 | G. Caruzzi-Bedogni (L.) Bolzoni cond. E. Petrella dir. |
| Siena | Rinnovati | Jan. 1869 | Eboli (L.) Spagnoli (T.) Alegiani (E.) P. Povoleri (S.) |
| Spoleto | Nuovo | Jan. 1869 | B. D'Aponte (L.) E. Cortesi (T.) Cingolani (E.) |
| Trento | Sociale | June 1879 | A. Fidi-Azzolini (L.) D. Casartelli (E.) Z. Bertolasi (C.) I. Sbordoni (S.) |
| Treviso | Societa | Oct. 1867 | E. Berini (L.) P. Dompieri (T.) G. Valentini-Cristiani (E.) G. Cima (C.) G. B. Cornago (S.) |
| Trieste | Grande | Apr. 7, 1867 | G. Ferrari (L.) M. Allievi (T.) G. Marelli (E.) I. Viganotti (C.) C. Zucchelli (S.) A. Cremaschi cond. |
| | | Dec. 26? 1867 | V. Saurel (L.) V. Belardi (E.) A. Borella (C.) N. Contedini (S.) A. Cremaschi cond. |
| | | Feb. 1877 | E. Wiziak (L.) O. Cappelletti (E.) L. Giraldoni (C.) G. Galvani (S.) G. Gialdini cond. |

Turin        Vittorio      Oct.        1864 M. Palmieri/L. Bendazzi-Secchi (L.)
             Emanuele                        Ferrari (T.) G. Zacometti (E.) G.
                                             Cima (C.) E. Bagagiolo (S.)

                           Jan.        1869 O. Torriani (L.) G. Petrovich (E.)
                                             J. Da Veiga (C.) Pisani (S.)

                           Nov.        1870 E. Ciuti (L.) Aime (T.) Fabbri (E.)
                                             Manini (C.) Cesari (S.)

                           Oct. 20, 1875 V. Crespi (L.) Grosso (T.) Marini
                                             (E.) G. Cima (C.) A. Furlan (S.)

             Balbo         May    2, 1868 V. Potentini (L.) Bodio (T.) A. Lam-
                                             poni (E.) Mazzoli (C.) C. Trivero
                                             (S.)

                           July 30, 1879 A. Bonner (L.) Levi (T.) G. Gozzoli-
                                             ni (E.) A. Navary (C.) A. Bagagiolo
                                             (S.)

Udine        Minerva       Apr. 13, 1873 Capozzi (L.) Cesari (E.)

Venice       Apollo        Nov.        1868 O. Torriani (L.) Bolis (T.) L. Bolis
                                             (E.) A. Grandi (C.) A. Balderi (S.)

                           Feb.        1873 V. Pozzi-Ferrari (L.) A. Franchini
                                             (E.) D. Squarcia (C.)

Verona       Filarmonico   Jan. 11, 1868 G. Stella (L.) A. Contarini (T.) P.
                                             Baccei (E.) I. Viganotti/G. Valle
                                             (C.) C. Dalla Costa (S.)

Vicenza      Eretenio      Jan.  9, 1868 C. Ghirlanda-Tortolini (L.) P. Bozzo
                                             (T.) A. Lamponi (E.) Conti Marroni
                                             (S.)

MALTA
La Valletta  Reale         Oct.  2, 1871 E. Ciuti (L.) Cucchi (T.) E. Serazzi
                                             (E.) E. Carnilli (C.) G. Wagner (S.)

                           Feb. 22, 1875 Bergamini-Paolicchi (L.) Conti (T.)
                                             E. Serazzi (E.) Paolicchi (C.) G.
                                             Zambellini (S.)

                           Jan.        1878

                           Apr.        1879

MEXICO
Guadalajara  Degollado     Nov. 26, 1881 A. Peralta (L.) L. Giraud (E.)[29]

Mexico City  Nacional      Oct.  3, 1872 C. Castelli (L.) M. Beluta (T.) I.
                                             D'Avanzo (E.) F. Bertolini (C.) C.
                                             Zuchelli (S.)

---

29. Angelica Peralta and her company toured throughout Mexico during the period from 1881-1883 or 1884 with La Contessa d'Amalfi as part of their repertory. They are known to have given this opera in Queretaro in Oct. 1883 and in San Luis Potosi in Nov. of that year, but it is likely that it was given in many other cities as well.

PORTUGAL
Oporto          Sao Joao      Feb.        1873 E. Tagliana (L.) Dario-Maggi (T.) A.
                                               Marubini (E.) E. Masi (C.) L. Conti
                                               (S.) Maggi cond.

ROMANIA
Iasi            Teatro        Mar. 22, 1873 V. Falchero-Corsi (L.)

RUSSIA
Kishinev                      Oct.        1872 V.  Falchero-Corsi  (L.)  Bertocchi
                                               (E.) Dominici (S.)

Odessa          Municipal     Jan.        1865 T. De Giuli-Borsi (L.) A. Gottardi
                                               (E.) L. Vendemmia (C.) P. Poli-Lenzi
                                               (S.)

                              Oct. 28, 1870 E. Wiziak (L.) Bernardoni (T.) F.
                                               Pozzo (E.) S. Orsi (C.) G. Zambelli-
                                               ni (S.)

                              June        1872 V. Falchero-Corsi (L.)

Tbilisi         Imperial            1871-72 I. D'Avanzo (E.)

SPAIN
Barcelona       Liceo         Mar. 21, 1874 G. De Giuli-Borsi (L.) E. Lasauca
                                               (T.) C. Carpi (E.) V. Quintili-Leoni
                                               (C.) A. Rodas (S.)

Valencia        Principal     Nov.  2? 1867 C. Lanzi (L.) Sabatini (T.) C. Carpi
                                               (E.) Fellini (C.)

SWITZERLAND
Lugano          Sociale       Sep.        1875

URUGUAY
Montevideo      Solis         Aug. 24, 1872 M. Mollo (L.) Estagel (T.) P. Setra-
                                               gni (E.) L. Mazzoni-Osti (C.) A.
                                               Buzzi (S.)

OTHER PRODUCTIONS-TWENTIETH CENTURY

ITALY
Palermo         Biondo        Oct. 28, 1910 C. Rubini (L.) M. Comida (T.) E.
                                               Pazzi (E.) G. Rimini (C.) R. De Fal-
                                               co (S.) E. Granelli cond.

17. CELINDA-*Melodramma tragico* in three acts
Naples-Teatro San Carlo-Mar. 11, 1865
Libretto by Domenico Bolognese

Celinda (C.)                                          Emma La Grua sop.
Rodrigo (R.)                                          Rafaelle Mirate ten.
Arnaldo (A.)                                          Achille de Bassini bar.
Duca di Altamira (D.)                                 Giovanni Morelli bass
Palmita                                               Carolina Cetronè mez.
Gusman                                                Luigi Bisaccia bar.
Inigo                                                 Antonio Donadio bass
Diego                                                 Michele Memmi ten.

Conductor
Director                                              Errico Petrella

OTHER PRODUCTIONS

ITALY
Brescia        Grande      Feb.  8, 1868 G. Boema (C.) G. Valentini-Cristiani
                                         (R.) D. Dal Negro (A.) F. Tirini
                                         (D.)

Ferrara        Comunale    May      1870 E. Bosisio (C.) G. Fancelli (R.) Z.
                                         Bertolasi (A.) O. Maini (D.) R. Sar-
                                         ti cond. E. Petrella dir.

Fiume          Civico      Apr.     1870 G. Boema (C.) L. Gulli (R.) G. Valle
                                         (A.)

Florence       Nuovo       Spring   1877

Genoa          Politeama   June  1, 1871 A. Urban (C.) L. Filippi-Bresciani
                                         (R.) F. Cresci (A.) G. Bregozzo
                                         cond.

Mantua         Sociale     Dec. 31, 1868 G. Borsi de Leurie (C.) F. Patierno
                                         (R.) V. Prattico (A.)

Padua          Concordia   Jan.     1871 R. Fiorentini-Morangoni (C.) V. Be-
                                         lardi (R.) L. Lalloni (A.) G. Cesari
                                         (D.) R. Drigo cond.

Rimini         Nuovo       Dec. 26, 1868 E. Sgargi (C.) L. Abrugnedo (R.) D.
                                         Cesari (A.) N. Contedini (D.)

Rome           Argentina   June 16, 1865 E. Demi (C.) C. Bulterini (R.) L.
                                         Colonnese (A.) E. Rossi-Galli (D.)

Turin          Regio       Feb. 28, 1866 E. Berini (C.) C. Vincentelli (R.)
                                         A. Cotogni (A.) C. Trivero (D.) F.
                                         Bianchi cond.

                           Mar. 27, 1875 G. Scarati-Bresciani (C.) L. Filippi
                                         Bresciani (R.) L. Borgioli (A.) A.
                                         Tamburlini (D.) C. Pedrotti cond.

MALTA
La Valletta    Manoel      Oct. 17, 1867 Magni   (C.) A. Celada (R.) Cappelli
                                         (A.)

18. CATERINA HOWARD-*Tragedia lirica* in three acts
Rome-Teatro Apollo-Feb. 7, 1866
Libretto by Giuseppe Cencetti

| | |
|---|---|
| Caterina (C.) | Angiolina Ortolani-Tiberini sop. |
| Etevoldo (E.) | Mario Tiberini ten. |
| Enrico VIII (H.) | Francesco Pandolfini bar. |
| Kennedy | Francesca Quadri sop. |
| Paggio | Pietro Cassani ten. |
| Sir Tommasso | Giovanni Bernardoni bass |
| Flemmingh | Albino Felici bass |

| | |
|---|---|
| Conductor | Emilio Angelini |
| Director | Errico Petrella |

OTHER PRODUCTIONS

ITALY

| | | | |
|---|---|---|---|
| Brescia | Grande | Aug. 8, 1868 | M. Siebs (C.) G. Valentini-Cristiani (E.) V. Quintili-Leoni (H.) E. Petrella dir. |
| Turin | Alfieri | Aug. 1878 | E. Giunti-Barbera (C.) A. Franco (E.) E. Masi (H.) |

19. GIOVANNA II DI NAPOLI-*Dramma lirico* in a prologue and three acts
Naples-Teatro San Carlo-Feb. 27, 1869
Libretto by Antonio Ghislanzoni

| | |
|---|---|
| Giovanna (G.) | Marcellina Lotti-Della Santa sop. |
| Matilde (M.) | Nicolina Favi-Gallo mez. |
| Lorenzo (L.) | Giovanni Zacometti ten. |
| Aniello (A.) | Vicenzo Quintili-Leoni bar. |
| Marino (Ma.) | Enrico Rossi-Galli bass |
| Marta | Adelaide Morelli sec. |
| Fabrizio | Antonio Donadio sec. |
| Sforza | Giovanni Morelli bar. |

| | |
|---|---|
| Conductor | Paolo Serrao |
| Director | Errico Petrella |

OTHER PRODUCTIONS

ITALY

| | | | |
|---|---|---|---|
| Cuneo | Civico | Dec. 26, 1880 | L. Stefanini (G.) |
| Fermo | Aquila | Aug. 31, 1872 | G. Ronzi-Checchi (G.) R. Vercolini-Tay (M.) A. Celada (L.) E. Fagotti (A.) G. Marchetti (Ma.) F. Cellini cond. E. Petrella dir. |
| Fiume | Civico | May 22, 1873 | L. Arancio-Guerrini (G.) Rivoli (M.) A. Lamponi (L.) L. Borgioli (A.) C. Melzi (Ma.) |
| Florence | Pergola | Dec. 26, 1869 | G. Giovannoni-Zacchi (G.) G. Perotti (L.) S. Sparapani (A.) A. Fiorini (Ma.) |

Milan          La Scala      Aug. 23, 1873 A. Conti-Foroni (G.) G. Pasqua (M.)
                                           A. Celada (L.) A. Burgio (A.) A. Pa-
                                           dovani (Ma.)

Modena         Comunale      Dec. 25, 1872 L. Mosconi (G.) I. Augustini (M.) A.
                                           Lamponi (L.) G. Giotti (A.) R. Buf-
                                           fagni/C. Orlandini (Ma.) A. Moreschi
                                           cond.

Sassari        Civico        Jan. 26, 1876 Gabrielli  (G.)  Pocchini  (M.)  F.
                                           Torres-Bini  (L.)  D.  Belardi  (A.)
                                           Leonardi (Ma.)

Savigliano                   Nov. 20? 1887 E. Callery-Viviani (G.) Ruano (M.)
                                           Mari (L.) Bucci (A.) Greco (Ma.) Sa-
                                           racini cond.

Siena          Rinnovati     Dec. 26, 1875 Bonal (G.) Parodi (M.) Marasini (L.)
                                           N. Fallica (A.) Banchi (Ma.)

Turin          Regio         Dec. 25, 1869 T. Stolz (G.) A. Contarini (M.) G.
                                           Fancelli (L.) A. Cotogni (A.) C.
                                           Melzi (Ma.) G. B. Polledro cond.


20. I PROMESSI SPOSI-*Melodramma* in three acts
Lecco-Teatro Sociale-Oct. 2, 1869
Libretto by Antonio Ghislanzoni

Lucia (L.)                                          Emma Wiziak sop.
Agnese (A.)                                      Marietta Pavoni sop.
Perpetua (P.)                              Enrichetta Bernardoni mez.
Renzo (R.)                                      Carlo Vincentelli ten.
Don Rodrigo (D. R.)                                Gaetano Giori bar.
Padre Cristoforo (P. C.)                        Salvatore Cesarò bass
Don Abbondio (Ab.)                                   Luigi Rocco buf.
Innominato

Conductor                                                    Rivetta
Director                                            Errico Petrella

OTHER PRODUCTIONS

ARGENTINA
Buenos Aires   Opera         Dec. 25, 1878 L. Avalli (L.) L. Lelmi (R.)

GREECE
Corfu          San Giacomo Nov.     1882

INDIA
Calcutta       Op. House     Mar.  8, 1878 B. Capozzi (L.) A. Orlandi (A.) L.
                                           Colombana (R.) A. Navarry (D. R.) M.
                                           Della Torre (P. C.)

ITALY[30]

| | | | |
|---|---|---|---|
| Alessandria | Municipale | Oct. 14, 1871 | L. Corsi (L.) Bianchi (A.) Magi (P.) Piazza (R.) Corsi (D. R.) Melzi (P. C.) E. Bianchi cond. |
| Brescia | Guillaume | Oct. 29, 1887 | A. Stecchi (L.) A. Chiaveri (A.) C. Perelli/N. Lorenzini (R.) A. Prandi (D. R.) Casanova (F. C.) Q. Merly (Ab.) G. Premoli cond. |
| Genoa | Politeama | June 4, 1870 | N. Favi-Gallo (L.) B. Da Ponte (A.) D. Garbato (P.) C. Vicentelli (R.) E. Mari (D. R.) E. Rossi-Galli (P. C.) L. Rocco (Ab.) G. Bossola cond. E. Petrella dir. (Inauguration of the theater) |
| | | Aug. 1, 1877 | G. De Senespleda (L.) M. Bianchi-Florio (P.) E. Vicini (R.) M. Ciapini (D. R.) G. Ghia (P. C.) G. Marchisio (Ab.) |
| | | Dec. 8, 1883 | T. Gastaldi (L.) I. Castellani (P.) A. Savignoni (D. R.) E. Borucchia (P. C.) |
| | | Mar. 24, 1888 | P. Marilli (L.) S. Mastrobuono (R.) G. Sansone (D. R.) Gutierrez (P. C.) |
| | | Oct. 12, 1892 | O. Litvinova (L.) Z. Monteiro (P.) C. Lanfredi (R.) G. Bianchi (D. R.) A. Monchero (P. C.) F. Carbonetti (Ab.) |
| | Paganini | Nov. 15, 1871 | A. Brambilla (L.) D. Garbato (P.) G. Firpo (R.) A. Burgio (D. R.) A. Tessada (P. C.) C. Zucchelli (Ab.) |
| | | Oct. 30, 1886 | I. Cristino (L.) G. Levi (P.) N. Gnone (R.) L. Pignalosa (D. R.) A. Gellini (P. C.) F. Carbonetti (Ab.) |
| | Nazionale | Jan. 20, 1874 | S. Lezi (L.) E. Polli (P.) L. Da Ponte (A.) G. Ortisi (R.) A. Medini (D. R.) A. De Santis (P. C.) L. Galli (Ab.) Rubini cond. |
| Livorno | Rossini | Nov. 8, 1873 | Rosetti (L.) Bernardoni (P.) A. Rampini-Boncori (R.) A. Borella (D. R.) A. Zezevich (P. C.) |
| Lodi | Piontelli | Oct. 12, 1874 | V. Crespi (L.) C. Vincentelli (R.) Marenco cond. |
| Longiano | Petrella | July 24, 1870 | E. Ciuti (L.) R. Pala-Graziosi (A.) Valtorta (P.) T. Karl (R.) F. Graziosi (D. R.) S. Cesarò (P. C.) G. Marchisio (Ab.) E. Petrella dir. (Inauguration of the theater) |

---

[30]. There were many other productions of Petrella's opera, including Alessandria in Nov. 1883, Livorno in Dec. 1883, the Teatro Bellini in Naples in 1882, Novi in 1878, Porto Maurizio in 1876, Saluzzo in 1880, Verona in the carnival season of 1888-89 and Voghera in 1878.

| | | | |
|---|---|---|---|
| Mantua | Andreani | Sep. 15, 1883 | A. Rizzato (L.) C. Desvignes (P.) E. Lorini (R.) |
| Messina | Vittoria Emanuele | Dec. 21, 1879 | A. Fidi-Azzolini (L.)  A. De Bassini (R.) |
| Milan | Carcano | May       1871 | M. Dérivis (L.) Garbato (P.) T. Karl (R.) L. Giraldoni (D. R.) S. Cesarò (P. C.) F. Catani (Ab.) E. Petrella dir. |
| | | Oct.      1873 | I. Cristino (L.) De Fanti (P.) C. Vincentelli (R.) L. Giraldoni (D. R.) A. Furlan (P. C.) G. Marchisio (Ab.) E. Bernardi cond. |
| | Dal Verme | Sep. 17, 1883 | Zucchini (L.) P. Pelagalli-Rossetti (R.) A. Pessina (D. R.) A. Abramoff (P. C.) |
| Modena | Aliprandi | Apr. 18, 1874 | B. Cosmelli (L.) M. Rovaglia Porati (P.) E. Galli (A.) G. Piccioli (R.) P. Cabella (D. R.) A. De Santis (P. C.) L. Galli (Ab.) A. Tomasi cond. |
| Naples | San Carlo | Apr. 23, 1873 | B. Blume (L.) G. Tati (P.) A. Celada (R.) T. Sterbini (D. R.) S. Cesarò (P. C.) A. De Bassini (Ab.) |
| Rome | Apollo | Nov. 30, 1871 | E. Wiziak (L.) G. Tiozzo (P.) G. Somigli (A.) J. Gayarre (R.) A. Pantaleoni (D. R.) R. Nannetti (P. C.) F. Catani (Ab.) E. Terziani cond. |
| | Argentina | May 29, 1877 | L. Brignole (D. R.) |
| Sassari | Civico | Nov.      1876 | Portas (L.) Leliva (P.) Braghi (D. R.) Sampieri (P. C.) |
| Trieste | Grande | Mar. 4, 1880 | R. Caponetti (L.) E. Vicini (R.) M. Bolini (D. R.) F. Navarini (P. C.) E. Dalmau cond. |
| Turin | Carignano | Nov.      1869 | A. Peralta (L.) R. Pala-Graziosi (P.) V. Montanaro (R.) F. Graziosi (D. R.) C. Zuchelli (P. C.) A. Bottero (Ab.) Bertuzzi cond. |
| | Balbo | May 22, 1874 | B. D'Aponte (L.) Giordano (R.) F. Graziosi (D. R.) A. Furlan (P. C.) |
| | Vittorio Emanuele | Oct. 30? 1888 | Ferretti (L.) |
| Venice | Rossini | Dec. 26, 1883 | G. Procacci (R.) Polli (D. R.) R. Bracale cond. |

## OTHER PRODUCTIONS-TWENTIETH CENTURY

ITALY
| | | | |
|---|---|---|---|
| Genoa | Carlo Felice | Mar. 8, 1913 | M. Crosa (L.) D. Frau (P.) H. Lazaro (R.) |
| | Paganini | June 10, 1920 | By a company of marionettes |

Naples          San Carlo      Mar.  5, 1950 M. Pobbe (L.) G. Sani (P.) T. Des-
                                             tito (A.) F. Albanese (R.) P. Guelfi
                                             (D. R.) M. Petri (P. C.) V. De Ta-
                                             ranto (Ab.) G. Santini cond.


21. MANFREDO-*Dramma lirico* in a prologue and three acts
Naples-Teatro San Carlo-Mar. 24, 1872
Libretto by Giorgio Tomasso Cimino

Lina (L.)                                          Gabriella Krauss sop.
Ranuccio (R.)                                      Enrico Barbacini ten.
Manfredo (M.)                                   Gottardo Aldighieri bar.
Cencio (C.)                              Gian Francesco Angelini bass
Il Duca                                              Marco Arati bass
Duchessa                                        Carolina Cetronè mez.
Un Pellegrino                                     Salvatore Mele ten.
Uno Scudiero                                      Luigi Bisaccia ten.
Un Armigero                                       Michele Memmi ten.


Conductor                                          Giovanni Moretti
Director                                           Errico Petrella

OTHER PRODUCTIONS

ITALY
Genoa           Carlo          Dec. 26, 1872 R. Pantaleoni (L.) O. Tasca de Cap-
                Felice                       pellio (R.) A. Parboni (M.) L. Vec-
                                             chi (C.)

Rome            Apollo         Feb. 15, 1873 E. Wiziak (L.) J. Gayarre (R.) G.
                                             Aldighieri (M.) G. David (C.) E.
                                             Terziani cond.


22. BIANCA ORSINI-*Melodramma* in four acts
Naples-Teatro San Carlo-Apr. 4, 1874
Libretto by Giorgio Tomasso Cimino

Bianca Orsini                                      Gabriella Krauss sop.
Adriano                                            Enrico Barbacini ten.
Aldo                                              Luigi Colonnese bar.
Fra Felice                                           Giorgio Atry bass
Giulio Orsini                                      Paride Povoleri bass
Viandante                                          Salvatore Mele ten.


Conductor                                             Paolo Serrao
Director                                           Errico Petrella

23. DIANA ovvero LA FATA DI POZZUOLI-*Opera buffa* in three acts
Composed circa 1876-Unperformed
Libretto by Raffaele d'Ambra

AMILCARE PONCHIELLI

1. I PROMESSI SPOSI-*Melodramma* in four parts
Cremona-Teatro della Concordia-Sept. 17, 1856
Librettists unknown

| | |
|---|---|
| Luisa | Luigia Ponti Dall'Armi sop. |
| La Signora di Monza | Annetta Heller mez. |
| Renzo | Agostino Dall'Armi ten. |
| Don Rodrigo | Giuseppe Voto Orlandi bar. |
| Eremito | Cesare Nanni bass |
| Innominato | Salvatore de Angelis ten. |
| | |
| Conductor | Achille Marzorati |

Revised-Milan-Teatro dal Verme-Dec. 4, 1872
Libretto by Emilio Praga

| | |
|---|---|
| Lucia (L.) | Teresina Brambilla-Ponchielli sop. |
| La Signora di Monza (M.) | Eufemia Barlani-Dini mez. |
| Renzo (R.) | Pietro Fabbri ten. |
| Don Rodrigo (D. R.) | Augusto Brogi bar. |
| Fra Cristoforo (C.) | Marcel Junca bass |
| Innominato | Eugenio Manfredi bass |
| Cardinale | Luigi Calcaterra bass |
| Griso | Erfi sec. |
| Nibbio | Saccardi sec. |
| | |
| Conductor | Roberto Kuon |
| Director | Amilcare Ponchielli |

OTHER PRODUCTIONS-NINETEENTH CENTURY

AUSTRALIA
| Adelaide | Th. Royal | Aug. | 2, 1887 | L. Cerne (L.) G. Cavalleri (M.) G. Santinelli (R.) G. Pimazzoni (D. R.) A. Buzzi (C.) R. Hazon cond. |
|---|---|---|---|---|
| Brisbane | Th. Royal | June | 6, 1887 | L. Cerne (L.) G. Cavalleri (M.) G. Santinelli (R.) G. Pimazzoni (D. R.) A. Buzzi (C.) R. Hazon cond. |
| Melbourne | Th. Royal | Feb. | 10, 1887 | L. Cerne (L.) G. Cavalleri (M.) G. Santinelli (R.) G. Pimazzoni (D. R.) A. Buzzi (C.) R. Hazon cond. |
| Sydney | Th. Royal | May | 2, 1887 | L. Cerne (L.) G. Cavalleri (M.) G. Santinelli (R.) G. Pimazzoni (D. R.) A. Buzzi (C.) R. Hazon cond. |

CHILE
| Santiago | Municipal | Aug. | 1, 1888 | A. Turconi-Bruni (L.) A. Mazzoli-Orsini (M.) R. Grani (R.) F. Bartolomasi (D. R.) V. Salmasi (C.) A. Padovani cond. |
|---|---|---|---|---|

GREAT BRITAIN[31]
| Belfast | Th. Royal | May | 5, 1881 | J. Gaylord (L.) J. Yorke (M.) B. M'Guckin (R.) L. Crotty (D. R.) Pyatt (C.) (In Eng.) |
|---|---|---|---|---|

---

[31]. Loewenberg lists a revival in Glasgow during the summer of 1932. An examination of the *Glasgow Herald* from May through October of that year shows no evidence of such a production.

Birmingham     Th. Royal     Apr.  7, 1881 J. Gaylord (L.) J. Yorke (M.) B.
                                           M'Guckin (R.) L. Crotty (D. R.)
                                           Pyatt (C.) (In Eng.)

Bristol        Th. Royal     Apr. 27, 1881 J. Gaylord (L.) J. Yorke (M.) B.
                                           M'Guckin (R.) L. Crotty (D. R.)
                                           Pyatt (C.) (In Eng.)

Edinburgh      Th. Royal     Mar. 23, 1881 J. Gaylord (L.) J. Yorke (M.) B.
                                           M'Guckin (R.) L. Crotty (D. R.)
                                           Pyatt (C.) (In Eng.)

Newcastle      Th. Royal     Mar. 30, 1881 J. Gaylord (L.) J. Yorke (M.) B.
                                           M'Guckin (R.) L. Crotty (D.R.)
                                           Pyatt (C.) (in Eng.)

GREECE
Corfu          San Giacomo Oct. 26? 1875 Severni/M. Milani-Vela (L.) L. Co-
                                         lombana (R.) G. Bergamaschi (D. R.)
                                         C. Prò (C.) M. Vela cond.

INDONESIA
Batavia        Th. Batavie Mar. 16, 1885 M. Erba (L.) Musini (M.) Boschetti
                                         (R.) U. Forapan (D. R.) C. Pró (C.)

IRELAND
Dublin         Gaiety        May 16, 1881 J. Gaylord (L.) J. Yorke (M.) B.
                                          M'Guckin (R.) L. Crotty (D. R.)
                                          Pyatt (C.) (in Eng.)

ITALY[32]
Alessandria    Politeama     Oct. 22? 1882 E. Russell (L.) T. Mestres (M.) A.
                                           Brunetti (R.) Salvi (D. R.) L.
                                           Cromberg (C.)

Ancona         Muse          Feb.  5, 1876 N. Pedemonti (L.) Forty (M.) P.
                                           Bignardi (R.) Giannini (D. R.)

Bergamo        Sociale       Dec. 26, 1873 E. Albini (M.) G. Piccioli (R.) V.
                                           De Pasqualis (D. R.) G. Calcaterra
                                           (C.)

Bologna        Brunetti      Nov.  1, 1880 L. Negroni (L.) Borghi (M.) F. Va-
                                           lero (R.) Trabadello (D. R.) C. Ul-
                                           loa (C.)

Brescia        Grande        Dec. 25, 1873 C. Lanzi (L.) L. De Fanti (M.) L.
                                           Maurelli (R.) E. Corti (D. R.) C.
                                           Morotto (C.)

Cagliari       Civico        Feb.  8, 1876 A. Guadagnini (L.) A. De Bassini
                                           (R.) A. Borella (D. R.) G. Narberti
                                           (C.)

                             Jan. 11, 1891 Feliciani (L.) Garbarini (M.) Bra-
                                           bosti (R.) Portos (D. R.) Bellusi
                                           (C.)

---

32. Other productions include Ancona in 1881, Cagliari in 1891, Casalmonferrato in 1878,
Codogno in 1875, Correggio in 1873, Crema in 1877, Faenza in 1886, Lodi in 1881, Novara in
1875, Pistoia in 1884, Savigliano in 1886, Soresina in 1889, and Tortona in 1886.

| Catania | Nazionale | Dec. 25, 1894 | E. De Cesare (L.) A. Budriesi (M.) P. Gherardi (R.) E. Bucalo (D. R.) C. Gagliardi (C.) |
|---------|-----------|---------------|---|
| Cento | Comunale | Sep. 2? 1873 | T. Bellariva (L.) G. Tiozzo (M.) G. Piazza (R.) Z. Bertolasi (D. R.) L. Lombardelli (C.) |
| Cesena | Comunale | Feb. 16, 1884 | G. Musiani (L.) G. Sommelius (M.) C. Elias (R.) A. d'Andrade (D. R.) O. Bottero (C.) |
| Como | Sociale | Dec. 26, 1874 | C. Marco (L.) Lenzi (M.) A. Adama (R.) G. Tagliapietra/V. De Pasqualis (D. R.) |
| Cremona | Concordia | Nov. 11, 1873 | T. Brambilla-Ponchielli (L.) T. Ferini (M.) E. Palermi (R.) A. Parboni (D. R.) G. Atry (C.) C. Trombini cond. A. Ponchielli dir. |
|  |  | Jan. 26, 1884 | R. Fiorentini-Marangoni (L.) A. Boffa (M.) A. Brunetti (R.) F. Scurani (D. R.) A. Dadò (C.) A. Panizza cond. |
| Ferrara | Comunale | Jan. 22, 1874 | I. Cristino (L.) M. Venosta (M.) U. Forapan (R.) E. Fucili (D. R.) R. Sarti cond. |
| Fiume | Comunale | Nov. 18, 1887 | T. Brambilla-Ponchielli (L.) I. Sambo (M.) F. Gambarelli (R.) F. Bartolomasi (D. R.) L. Rossato (C.) |
| Florence | Pergola | Mar. 7, 1883 | T. Brambilla-Ponchielli (L.) D. Del Papa (R.) A. Brogi (D. R.) L. Visconti (C.) |
| Forli | Comunale | Jan.? 1879 | L. Mosconi (L.) G. Cavalleri (M.) G. Gozzolini (R.) C. Marziali (D. R.) |
| Genoa | Carlo Felice | Dec. 27, 1873 | R. Pantaleoni (L.) G. Tiozzo (M.) L. Filippi Bresciani (R.) D. Squarcia (D. R.) G. Galvani (C.) G. Rossi cond. |
| Lecco | Sociale | Oct. 8? 1882 | A. Martinez (L.) V. Donati (M.) A. Passetti (R.) D. Farina (D. R.) O. Bottero (C.) A. Ponchielli dir. |
| Livorno | Rossini | Nov. 15, 1882 | T. Brambilla-Ponchielli (L.) Marini (M.) F. d'Andrade (R.) A. Magini-Coletti (D. R.) L. Donati (C.) |
| Mantua | Sociale | Jan. 22, 1879 | L. Allegri (L.) G. Cariol/L. Maurelli (R.) G. Camoletti (D. R.) F. Roncaglia cond. |
| Messina | Vittorio Emanuele | Dec. 21, 1879 | A. Fidi-Azzolini (L.) M. Zanon (M.) L. Cherubini (C.) |

Milan          Dal Verme    Apr. 19, 1873 Moreno (L.) E. Barlani-Dini (M.) A.
                                          Byron (R.) Barré (D. R.) G. Atry
                                          (C.) R. Kuon cond. A. Ponchielli
                                          dir.[33]

                            Oct. 26, 1873 T. Brambilla-Ponchielli (L.) R.
                                          Gianfredi (M.) E. Palermi (R.) A.
                                          Parboni (D. R.) L. Vecchi (C.) R.
                                          Kuon cond.[34]

                            Sep. 3, 1877 L. Bordato (L.) P. Rambelli (M.) L.
                                          Maurelli (R.) E. Masi (D. R.)   C.
                                          Ulloa (C.) E. Bernardi cond.

                            Oct. 9, 1878 M. Lodi (L.) P. Rambelli (M.) L.
                                          Maurelli (R.) A. Brogi (D. R.) C.
                                          Ulloa (C.) E. Bernardi cond.

                            Dec. 12, 1882 A. Cobianchi (L.) M. Peri (M.) V.
                                          Bacci (R.) V. Carpi (D. R.) V. Sal-
                                          masi (C.) Rivetti cond.

                            Nov. 2, 1888 E. Boronat (L.) T. Carotini (M.) A.
                                          A. Baroncelli (R.) L. Pignalosa (D.
                                          R.) L. Rossato (C.) A. Toscanini
                                          cond.

                            Jan. 1, 1894 G. Piccoletti (L.) C. Sartori (M.)
                                          G. Cokinis (R.) A. Arcangeli (D. R.)
                                          A. Silvestri (C.) S. Boscarini cond.

               La Scala     Oct. 11, 1874 M. Mantilla (L.) G. Tiozzo (M.) I.
                                          D'Avanzo (R.) A. Parboni (D. R.) E.
                                          Bagagiolo (C.) F. Faccio cond.

               Castelli     Oct. 16, 1875 S. Bordato (L.) Berio (M.) G. Carri-
                                          on (R.) V. De Pasqualis (D. R.) C.
                                          Ulloa (C.) R. Kuon cond.

               Carcano      Oct. 16, 1884 A. Turconi-Bruni (L.) E. Borlinetto
                                          (M.) A. Baroncelli (R.) C. Bachetta
                                          (D. R.) G. Pomè-Penna cond.

Monza          Sociale      Oct.    1875 E. Brambilla-Vidal (L.) V. Deliliers
                                          (R.) E. Masi (D. R.) Franceschi (C.)
                                          E. Bernardi cond.

Padua          Nuovo        July 5, 1873 M. Mariani-Masi (L.) V. Bracciolini
                                          (M.) J. Gayarre (R.) Z. Bertolasi
                                          (D. R.) O. Maini (C.) R. Drigo cond.
                                          A. Ponchielli dir.

               Verdi        Jan. 16? 1897 A. Barone (L.) I. Sambo (M.) F. Per-
                                          cuopo (R.) F. Corradetti (D. R.) G.
                                          Wanrell (C.)

---

[33]. Ponchielli added some numbers to the earlier revision at the same theatre.

[34]. This production involved still more changes and is believed to be the definitive
edition of the opera.

Palermo        Bellini      Feb. 27, 1875 T. Brambilla-Ponchielli (L.) E. Tre-
                                          ves (M.) E. Barbacini (R.) L. Giral-
                                          doni (D. R.) L. Vecchi (C.) L. Alfa-
                                          no cond.

Pavia          Civico       Dec. 25, 1873 M. L. Mayer (L.) L. Bagenova (M.) L.
                                          Gallo (R.) L. Magnani (D. R.) N. Re-
                                          bottaro (C.) Ramperti cond.

Pesaro         Rossini      Dec. 26? 1876 E. Brambilla-Vidal (L.) V. Bartoluc-
                                          ci (M.) C. Sarti (R.) A. Marescalchi
                                          (D. R.) A. Frontoni (C.) A. Mandelli
                                          cond.

Piacenza       Municipale   Dec. 26? 1873 B. Capozzi (L.) G. Celega (M.) A.
                                          Rampini-Bocori (R.) V. Quintili-
                                          Leoni (D. R.) G. Tansini (C.) A.
                                          Giovannini cond.

Pisa           Verdi        Dec. 26, 1875 A. Marzi (L.) T. Scarlatti Macaferri
                                          (M.) U. Candio (R.) E. Masi (D. R.)
                                          A. Mancini Silvani (C.) L. Quercioli
                                          cond.

Prato          Metastasio   Carn. 1892-93 A. Barone (L.) T. Marchi (M.) A.
                                          Rosenoer (R.) L. D'Andrea (D. R.) G.
                                          Salvi (C.) A. Nuti cond.

Ravenna        Mariani      Nov.  5, 1890 A. Valentini (L.) F. Pagano (R.) A.
                                          Putò (D. R.) I. Sbordoni (C.)

Reggio Emilia Municipale   Dec. 25, 1884 G. Monsour (L.) M. Zanon (M.) L.
                                          Fagotti (R.) S. Carobbi (D. R.) A.
                                          Martelli (C.) M. Bavagnoli cond.

Rimini         Vittorio     Dec. 26? 1875 S. Bordato (L.) A. Cobianchi (M.) V.
               Emanuele                   Sarti (R.) A. Pifferi (D. R.)

Savona         Chiabrera    Dec. 26? 1882 C. Buratti (L.) T. Lopresti (M.) G.
                                          Migliori (R.) A. De Vaschetti (C.)
                                          T. S. Terzi (D. R.) F. Rossetti
                                          cond.

Spoleto        Nuovo        Aug.    1873 G. Giovannoni-Zacchi (L.) E. Bernar-
                                          doni (M.) L. Filippi-Bresciani (R.)
                                          G. Toledo (D. R.)

Trieste        Grande       Mar.  8, 1876 I. Kottas (L.) G. Levi (M.) F. Pozzo
                                          (R.) A. Faentini-Galassi (D. R.) C.
                                          Melzi (C.) G. Gialdini cond.

Turin          Vittorio     Sep. 27, 1873 E. Ciuti (L.) A. Cellini-Azzoni (M.)
               Emanuele                   G. Piazza (R.) A. Brogi (D. R.) P.
                                          Milesi (C.) Foschini cond.

Udine                       Mar.    1883 Porto (L.) G. Levi (M.) Pagano (R.)
                                          L. Russo (D. R.)

Varese         Sociale      Sep.    1882 A. Turconi-Bruni (L.) B. D'Ariis
                                          (M.) A. Carnelli (R.) G. Claus (D.
                                          R.) A. Curti (C.)

Venice        Rossini      Jan. 20, 1883 T. Brambilla-Ponchielli (L.) M. L.
                                         Paolicchi (M.) A. De Bassini (R.) M.
                                         Ciapini (D. R.) G. Tansini (C.)

                           Nov. 18, 1886 T.  Brambilla-Ponchielli  (L.)  G.
                                         Zeppilli-Villani (M.) R. Grani (R.)
                                         G. Bianchi (D. R.) Acerbi cond.

Vercelli      Civico       Dec. 26, 1873 A. Fidi-Azzolini (L.) M. De Gourieff
                                         (M.) G. Giacomini (R.) N. Azzolini
                                         (D. R.) L. Beretta (C.) A. Panizza
                                         cond.

                           Dec. 26, 1887 C. Ferrani (L.) Moreschi (M.) N.
                                         Müller (R.) T. Maestrani (D. R.)
                                         Morreale cond.

Verona        Nuovo        Jan.     1874 G. Avigliana (L.) G. Preda (M.) P.
                                         Fabbri (R.) S. Cappelli (D. R.) A.
                                         Furlan (C.) A. Palminteri cond.

Vicenza       Eretenio     Dec. 27? 1884 Paltrinieri  (L.)  Crippa  (M.)  B.
                                         Lucignani (R.) T. S. Terzi (D. R.)
                                         L. Donati (C.)

MALTA
La Valletta   Reale        Oct. 14, 1876 Raimondi  (L.)  Gasparini-Putò  (M.)
                                         Santa Croce (R.) A. Putò (D. R.) F.
                                         Brandini (C.)

POLAND
Warsaw        Wielki       Nov.     1884 E. Russel (L.)

PORTUGAL
Lisbon        Sao Carlos   June  8, 1876 (Performed by amateurs)

              Coliseo      Mar. 16, 1885 (Performed by amateurs)

SPAIN
Barcelona     Novedades    Aug.  7, 1875 M. Mantilla (L.) E. Pascalis (M.)
                                         Ferrari (R.) A. Parboni (D. R.) A.
                                         Buzzi (C.) G. Gialdini cond.

OTHER PRODUCTIONS-TWENTIETH CENTURY

ITALY
Cremona       Politeama    Nov.?    1906 S. Aifos (L.) M. Grisi (M.) G. Arma-
              Verdi                      nini (R.) G. Falconi/Annibale Pon-
                                         chielli cond.

Milan         Dal Verme    Feb. 14, 1912 C. Muzio (L.) Aversano (M.) A. Rocca
                                         (R.) D. Zani (D. R.) V. Bettoni (C.)

Rome          Quirino      Nov. 13, 1905 E. Welkos (L.) I. Bellabarba (M.) T.
                                         Venturini (R.) A. Sabbi (D. R.) A.
                                         Natili (C.) P. Bellucci cond.

2. BERTRANDO DA BORNIO
Composed in 1858-Unperformed

3. LA SAVOIARDA-*Dramma lirico* in three acts
Cremona-Teatro della Concordia-Jan. 19, 1861
Libretto by Francesco Guidi

| Lina | Angelica Moro sop. |
| La Contessa Lina | Virginia Vender sec. |
| Gualtiero | Giorgio De Antoni ten. |
| Carlo | Celestino Viotti bar. |
| Rodolfo | Virgilio Collini bass |

Conductor

Revised as LINA-*Dramma lirico* in three acts
Milan-Teatro dal Verme-Nov. 17, 1877
Libretto by Francesco Guidi and Carlo D'Ormeville

| Lina (L.) | Teresina Brambilla-Ponchielli sop. |
| La Contessa Lina (C. L.) | Margherita Riccardi mez. |
| Gualtiero (G.) | Carlo Vincentelli ten. |
| Rodolfo (R.) | Zenone Bertolasi bar. |
| Carlo (C.) | Luigi Vannini bass |

| Conductor | Gialdino Gialdini |
| Director | Amilcare Ponchielli |

OTHER PRODUCTIONS

ITALY
Cremona      Ponchielli   Jan. 31, 1912 I. Quaiatti (L.) A. Ponzano (C. L.)
                           G. Tomassini (G.) U. Micheli (R.) U.
                           Malfatti (C.) A. Vigna cond.


4. RODERICO RE DEI GOTI-*Opera seria* in a prologue and three acts
Piacenza-Teatro Municipale-Dec. 26, 1863
Libretto by Francesco Guidi

| Florina (F.) | Fanny Scheggi sop. |
| Irene (I.) | Emanuela Florenza-Glori mez. |
| Roderico (R.) | Filippo Patierno ten. |
| Il Conte Giuliano (G.) | Giovanni Zucchi bar. |
| Munuza (M.) | Agostino Doblez bass |

Conductor                              Giuseppe Jona

OTHER PRODUCTIONS

ITALY
Milan        Carcano     Jan. 28, 1888 T. Brambilla-Ponchielli (F.) G. Lam-
                           berti (I.) V. Maina (R.) C. Bacchet-
                           ta (G.) A. Gautiero (M.) C. Rossi
                           cond.


5. LA STELLA DEL MONTE
Unperformed
Libretto by Temistocle Solera

6. IL PARLATORE ETERNO-*Scherzo comico* in one act
Lecco-Teatro Sociale-Oct. 18, 1873
Libretto by Antonio Ghislanzoni

Lelio (L.)                                            Ignazio Viganotti bar.

Conductor
Director                                              Amilcare Ponchielli

OTHER PRODUCTIONS

ITALY
Cremona        Ricci        Nov. 16, 1878 A. Pini-Corsi (L.) L. Logheder cond.

Genoa          Politeama    Dec. 5, 1892 A. Pini-Corsi (L.)

UNITED STATES
New York       After        June  8, 1979 R. Andrews (L.) G. Stramer cond. (in
               Dinner Op.                Eng.)


7. I LITUANI-*Dramma lirico* in a prologue and three acts
Milan-Teatro alla Scala-Mar. 7, 1874
Libretto by Antonio Ghislanzoni

Aldona (A.)                                   Antonietta Fricci sop.
Wilnio                                        Maria Luisa Durand sop.
Walter/Corrado Wallenrod (C.)                     Luigi Bolis ten.
Arnoldo (Ar.)                             Francesco Pandolfini bar.
Albano (Al.)                                      Jules Petit bass
Vitoldo                                      Antonio Padovani bass
A Herald                                          Luigi Turco bass

Conductor                                         Franco Faccio
Director                                      Amilcare Ponchielli

Revised-Milan-Teatro alla Scala-Mar. 6, 1875

Aldona (A.)                                  Maddalena Mariani-Masi sop.
Walter/Corrado Wallenrod (C.)                     Luigi Bolis ten.
Arnoldo (Ar.)                                 Adriano Pantaleoni bar.
Albano (Al.)                                      Ormondo Maini bass
Vitoldo                           Giovanni Battista Del Fabbro bass

Conductor                                         Franco Faccio
Director                                      Amilcare Ponchielli


OTHER PRODUCTIONS

ARGENTINA
Buenos Aires  Politeama    June 26, 1889 E. Tetrazzini (A.) F. Signorini (C.)
                                         R. Blanchart (Ar.) G. Rossi (Al.) A.
                                         Conti cond.

ITALY
Brescia       Grande       Aug. 12, 1886 M. Borelli (A.) G. Ortisi (C.) E.
                                         Dufriche (Ar.) A. Silvestri (Al.) F.
                                         Faccio cond.

Cremona      Concordia   Sep.  5, 1876 M. Mariani-Masi (A.) L. Bolis (C.)
                                       F. Pandolfini (Ar.) O. Maini (Al.)
                                       F. Faccio cond.

             Ponchielli  Feb.  5? 1901 R. Calligaris-Marty (A.) E. Ghilar-
                                       dini (C.) T. S. Terzi (Ar.) C. Preve
                                       (Al.) V. Mingardi cond.

                         Feb. 12, 1984 F. Garbi (A.) D. Antonioli (C.) G.
                                       Mastromei (Ar.) C. Zardo (Al.) E.
                                       Müller cond.

Milan        Dal Verme   Nov. 13, 1886 A. Gabbi (A.) L. Signoretti (C.) P.
                                       Lhérie (Ar.) A. Sillich (Al.) F.
                                       Faccio cond.

             La Scala    Apr.  5, 1903 E. Bianchini-Cappelli (A.) M. Mari-
                                       acher (C.) R. Blanchart (Ar.) O.
                                       Luppi (Al.) A. Toscanini cond.

Rome         Apollo      Feb.  2, 1887 M. Borelli (A.) F. Marconi (C.) G.
                                       Devoyod (Ar.) F. Vecchioni (Al.) E.
                                       Mascheroni cond.

Trieste      Grande      Nov. 18, 1875 M. Marioni (A.) F. Patierno (C.) A.
                                       Pantaleoni (Ar.) O. Maini (Al.) F.
                                       Faccio cond. A. Ponchielli dir.

Turin        Regio       Jan.  8, 1887 A. Gabbi (A.) F. D'Andrade (C.) G.
                                       Kaschmann (Ar.) G. Tansini (Al.) G.
                                       Bolzoni cond.

             Sala RAI    May   6, 1979 Y. Hayashi (A.) O. Garaventa (C.) A.
                                       Cassis (Ar.) C. De Bortoli (Al.) T.
                                       Guschlbauer cond.

RUSSIA
St.          Imperial    Nov. 20, 1884 M. L. Durand (A.) F. Marconi (C.) A.
 Petersburg                            Cotogni (Ar.) F. Uetam (Al.) E. Be-
                                       vignani cond. (as Aldona)
UNITED STATES
Chicago      Auditorium  July  1, 1983 (in Lith.)

URUGUAY
Montevideo   Solis       Aug. 18, 1888 R. Pantaleoni (A.) F. Cardinali (C.)
                                       D. Menotti (Ar.) F. Vecchioni (Al.)
                                       A. Conti cond.

             Cibils      Aug.     1889 E. Tetrazzini (A.) F. Signorini (C.)
                                       R. Blanchart (Ar.) C. Campanini
                                       cond.

8. LA GIOCONDA-*Melodramma* in four acts
Milan-Teatro alla Scala-Apr. 8, 1876
Libretto by Arrigo Boito (As Tobia Gorrio)

| | |
|---|---|
| La Gioconda (G.) | Maddalena Mariani-Masi sop. |
| Laura (L.) | Marietta Biancolini mez. |
| La Cieca (C.) | Eufemia Barlani-Dini mez. |
| Enzo Grimaldo (E.) | Julian Gayarre ten. |
| Barnaba (B.) | Gottardo Aldighieri bar. |
| Alvise Badoero (A.) | Ormondo Maini bass |
| Isepo | Amodeo Grazzi ten. |
| Zuane | Giovanni Battista Cornago bass |
| Un Cantore | Giovanni Battista Cornago bass |
| Un Pilota | Not named |
| | |
| Conductor | Franco Faccio |
| Director | Amilcare Ponchielli |

Revised-Venice-Teatro Rossini-Oct. 18, 1876

| | |
|---|---|
| La Gioconda (G.) | Maddalena Mariani-Masi sop. |
| Laura (L.) | Eulalia Kadmina mez. |
| La Cieca (C.) | Amelia Sbolgi mez. |
| Enzo Grimaldo (E.) | Enrico Barbacini ten. |
| Barnaba (B.) | Giuseppe Kaschmann bar. |
| Alvise Badoero (A.) | Ormondo Maini bass |
| Zuane | Leoni Abulcher bass |
| Un Cantore | Leoni Abulcher bass |
| | |
| Conductor | Franco Faccio |
| Director | Amilcare Ponchielli |

OTHER PRODUCTIONS-FIRST REVISION

ITALY
Genoa        Politeama     Nov. 27, 1879 M. Mariani-Masi (G.) F. Mariani De
                                        Angelis (L.) G. Celega (C.) F. Mar-
                                        coni (E.) G. Moriami (B.) E. De Res-
                                        zke (A.) G. Gialdini cond.

Rome         Apollo        Jan. 23, 1877 M. Mariani-Masi (G.) F. von Edels-
                                        berg (L.) A. Sbolgi (C.) E. Barbac-
                                        cini (E.) A. Parboni (B.) L. Müller
                                        (A.) L. Mancinelli cond. A. Ponchi-
                                        elli dir.

Revised-Milan-Teatro alla Scala-Feb. 12, 1880

| | |
|---|---|
| La Gioconda (G.) | Maddalena Mariani-Masi sop. |
| Laura (L.) | Helen Leavington mez. |
| La Cieca (C.) | Elvira Demi mez. |
| Enzo Grimaldo (E.) | Francesco Marconi ten. |
| Barnaba (B.) | Gustavo Moriami bar. |
| Alvise Badoero (A.) | Juan Ordinas bass |
| Zuane | Ermengildo De Serini bass |
| Un Cantore | Ermengildo De Serini bass |
| Isepo | Proto Capelli ten. |
| Un Pilota | Luigi Turco bass |
| | |
| Conductor | Franco Faccio |
| Director | .Amilcare Ponchielli |

OTHER PREMIERES-SECOND REVISION

ARGENTINA
Buenos Aires  Ant. Colón  June 28, 1884  E.  Theodorini  (G.)  M.  Mey-Figner (L.) G. Ravogli (C.) F. Tamagno (E.) A. Verdini (B.) A. Tamburlini (A.) N. Bassi cond.

Colón  June 24, 1908  A. Pinto (G.) T. Ferraris (L.) G. Fabbri (C.) M. Polverosi (E.) T. Ruffo (B.) V. Arimondi (A.) A. Vigna cond.

Cordoba  Progresso  June  1887  C. Bevilacqua (G.) Zani (L.) M. Massimi (E.) Bonfanti (B.) Notargiacomo (A.)

La Plata  Olimpo  May 26, 1887  G. Bellincioni (G.) E. Mantelli (L.) R. Stagno (E.) S. Sparapani (B.) L. Viviani (A.) G. Pomè-Penna cond.

Rosario  Olimpo  Mar.?  1886

AUSTRALIA
Melbourne  Th. Royal  Nov.  5, 1887  E. Ciuti (G.) G. Cavalieri (L.) F. Simonsen (C.) P. Lazzarini (E.) G. Pimazzoni (B.) A. Buzzi (A.) R. Hazon cond.

Sydney  Her Majesty's  Jan.  4, 1902  L. De Benedetto (G.) E. Marcomini (L.) V. Larizza (E.) I. Bozzoli (B.) B. Travaglini (A.) R. Hazon cond.

AUSTRIA
Vienna  Hofoper  Apr. 29, 1884  R. Pantaleoni (G.) G. De Giuli-Borsi (L.) L. Meislinger (C.) F. Valero (E.) E. Dufriche (B.) A. Pinto (A.) O. Bimboni cond. (in It.)

Feb. 17, 1885  P. Lucca (G.) (in Ger.)

BELGIUM
Brussels  Monnaie  Dec. 28, 1887  Pother (G.) F. Litvinne (L.) Martini (C.) P. Engel (E.) Seguin (B.) Vinche (A.) (First time in French)

Ghent  Grand  Jan.  6, 1909  M. Alexina (G.) R. Galan (L.) E. Ventura (E.) G. Hernandez (B.) A. Sabellico (A.) M. Wehils cond. (in It.)

BRAZIL
Rio de Janeiro  Pedro II  Aug. 10, 1885  E. Borghi-Mamo (G.) A. Stahl (L.) F. Marconi (E.) A. Brogi (B.) A. Tamburlini (A.) N. Bassi cond.

Municipal  July 26, 1911  C. Boninsegna (G.) L. Hotkowska (L.) I. Cristalli (E.) C. Galeffi (B.) G. Mansueto (A.) P. Mascagni cond.

Sao Paulo  San José  June  8, 1886  N. Bulicioff G.) M. Mei-Figner (L.) E. Mantelli (C.) N. Figner (E.) P. Lhérie (B.) G. Roveri (A.)

Municipal     July 29, 1920 Z. Amaro (G.) E. Casazza (L.) A.
                            Gramegna (C.) B. Gigli (E.) J. Segu-
                            ra-Tallien (B.) M. Pinheiro (A.) E.
                            Vitale cond.

BULGARIA
Sofia         Luxembourg          1895 G. Badarocco (E.) (in It.)

CANADA
Montreal      His          Nov. 17, 1913 M. Rappold (G.) M. Claessens (L.) R.
              Majesty's                  Olitzka (C.) G. Farmo (E.) J. Segu-
                                         ra-Tallien (B.) G. Martino (A.)

Toronto       Alexandra    Jan. 26, 1914 M. Rappold (G.) M. Claessens (L.) R.
                                         Olitzka (C.) G. Farmo (E.) J. Segu-
                                         ra-Tallien (B.) N. Cervi (A.)

CHILE
Santiago      Municipal    Oct. 17, 1882 C. Scarati-Bresciani (G.) E. Guar-
                                         denti (E.)

Valparaiso    Victoria     Dec. 22, 1887 T. Singer (G.) E. Borlinetto (L.) L.
                                         Caracciolo (C.) G. Moretti (E.) D.
                                         Menotti (B.) A. Monchero (A.)

CHINA
Shanghai      Victoria     Jan. 22, 1915 F. Impallomeni (G.) T. Visoni (L.)
                                         L. Da Gradi (E.) V. Scamuzzi (B.) A.
                                         Mauceri (A.) G. Gonsalez cond.

COLOMBIA
Bogota        Municipal    Sep. 27, 1891 R. Aimo (G.) A. Ravagli (E.) A.
                                         Alberti (B.) E. Fucili (A.) A.
                                         Azzali cond.

CUBA
Havana        Tacon        Jan.  8? 1886 A. Gini-Pizzorni (G.) E. Bassi (L.)
                                         G. Tiozzo (C.) C. Pizzorni (E.) E.
                                         Pogliani (B.) R. Mancini (A.) V.
                                         D'Alessio cond.

CZECHOSLOVAKIA
Prague        Ständisches Dec.    1884 (in Ger.)

EGYPT
Alexandria    Politeama    Oct. 12, 1887 Monti (G.) E. Matteuzzi (L.) A. Ba-
              Egiziano                   roncelli (E.) E. Massini (B.) F.
                                         Zavaschi (A.) F. Micci-Labruna cond.

              Zizinia       May     1894 L. Rebuffini (G.) G. Zeppilli-Vil-
                                         lani (L.) A. Nava (C.) G. Laura (E.)
                                         E. Massini (B.) A. Dadò (A.)

Cairo         Ezbekieh     Nov.  9, 1895 E. Bianchini-Cappelli (G.) M. Panta-
              Gardens                    nelli (L.) E. Caruso (E.) V. Ferra-
                                         guti (B.) A. Sarmiento cond.

              Khedivial    Dec. 13, 1898 M. D'Arneiro (G.) E. Leonardi (L.)
                                         A. Borda (C.) G. Cremonini (E.) G.
                                         Kaschmann (B.) G. Tansini (A.)

FINLAND
Helsinki          Societets      Jan. 12, 1897 A. Bruno (G.) Shaw (L.) G. Cokinis
                                               (E.) G. Pimazzoni (B.) L. Ferraioli
                                               (A.) Spatzek cond.

FRANCE
Marseille         Gymnase        Oct.  1, 1898 Costa (G.) M. Pozzi (L.) Pozzano
                                               (C.) G. Rambaldi (E.) Benedetti (B.)
                                               F. Vecchioni (A.) Pennati-Malvezzi
                                               cond. (in It.)

                  Opéra          Oct. 26, 1967 R. Crespin (G.) M. Vilma (L.) C.
                                               Smith (C.) C. Cossuta (E.) G. Mas-
                                               tromei (B.) P. Clabassi (A.) N.
                                               Santi cond.

Nice              Municipal      Dec. 29, 1886 E. Tetrazzini (G.) V. Falconis (L.)
                                               C. Bacchiani (C.) O. Nouvelli (E.)
                                               T. Wilmant (B.) V. Salmasi (A.) C.
                                               Campanini cond. (in It.)

Paris             Radio ORTF     Apr. 17, 1987 G. Savova (G.) C. Ciurca (L.) J.
                                               Rappé (C.) L. Bartolini (E.) V. Sar-
                                               dinero (B.) L. Roni (A.) G. Masini
                                               cond.

Rouen             des Arts       Mar. 14, 1895 Illy (B.) (in Fr.)

GERMANY
Berlin            Hofoper        Oct. 23, 1889 B. Pierson (G.) I. Hiedler (L.) G.
                                               Staudigl (C.) N. Rothmühl (E.) P.
                                               Bulss (B.) R. Biberti (A.) Kahl
                                               cond. (in Ger.)

                  Deutsche       Mar.  1, 1974 L. Rysanek (G.) E. Randova (L.) Fr.
                                               Tagliavini (E.) K. Paskalis (B.) G.
                                               Patané cond. (in It.)

Breslau           Stadt          Mar.?    1896 (in Ger.)

Cologne           Opernhaus      Oct. 27, 1907 A. Guszalewicz (G.) Dalossy (L.)
                                               Rohr (C.) Batz (E.) Liszewski (B.)
                                               Wiedemann (A.) D'Arnals cond. (in
                                               Ger.)

Frankfurt         Opernhaus      Mar.  6, 1888 M. Schröder-Hanfstängl (G.) K. Weber
                                               (L.) A. Luger (C.) de Grach (E.) G.
                                               W. Heine (B.) C. Baumann (A.) (in
                                               Ger.)

Hamburg           Stadt          Sep. 28, 1888 K. Klafsky (G.) Goetz (L.) E. Schu-
                                               mann-Heink (C.) H. Bötel (E.) R.
                                               Ritter (B.) H. Wiegand (A.) (in
                                               Ger.)

Wiesbaden         Königliches May  5, 1884 Baumgärtner (G.) Blum (B.) Reiss
                                               cond. (First time in German)

GREAT BRITAIN
Edinburgh         Royal          Mar. 13, 1903 B. Marchesi (G.) A. Hickisch (L.) M.
                  Lyceum                        Alexander (C.) J. O'Mara (E.) G. Fox
                                               (B.) C. Magrath (A.) R. Eckhold
                                               cond. (in Eng.)

Hull            Th. Royal   Jan.  8, 1903 F.  Moody  (G.)  A.  Hickisch  (L.)  M.
                                           Alexander  (C.)  J.  O'Mara  (E.)  C.
                                           Magrath  (B.)  (First time in English)

Liverpool       Shakespeare Apr.  2, 1903 B.  Marchesi  (G.)  A.  Hickisch  (L.)  J.
                                           O'Mara  (E.)  G.  Fox  (B.)  C.  Magrath
                                           (A.)  R.  Eckold cond.  (in Eng.)

London          Covent      May  31, 1883 M.  L.  Durand  (G.)  A.  Stahl  (L.)  G.
                Garden                     Tremelli  (C.)  F.  Marconi  (E.)  A.
                                           Cotogni  (B.)  E.  De Reszke  (A.)  E.
                                           Bevignani cond.  (in It.)

                Kennington  May   6, 1903 B.  Marchesi  (G.)  A.  Hickisch  (L.)  M.
                                           Alexander  (C.)  J.  O'Mara  (E.)  G.  Fox
                                           (B.)  C.  Magrath  (A.)  R.  Eckhold
                                           cond.  (in Eng.)

Newcastle       Tyne        Mar.  5, 1903 B.  Marchesi  (G.)  A.  Hickisch  (L.)  M.
                                           Alexander  (C.)  J.  O'Mara  (E.)  G.  Fox
                                           (B.)  C.  Magrath  (A.)  (in Eng.)

GREECE
Athens          Royal       Mar. 21, 1891 Paganelli  (G.)  G.  Procacci  (E.)  G.
                                           Pimazzoni  (B.)

Corfu           San Giacomo Nov. 23? 1887 Angelini  (G.)  G.  Lucazewska  (L.)  A.
                                           Stucci  (E.)  V.  Ferraguti  (B.)  A.
                                           Bettarini  (A.)

GUATEMALA
Guatemala       Nacional    Jan. 11? 1890 A.  Bourmann  (G.)  L.  Cavallini  (L.
City                                       C.)  G.  Martinez-Patti  (E.)  G.  Caru-
                                           son  (B.)  C.  De Probizzi  (A.)  A.  Dis-
                                           conzi cond.

HUNGARY
Budapest        Nemzeti     Dec.  8, 1883 E.  Turolla  (G.)  V.  Bartolucci  (L.)
                Szinház                    Saxlein  (C.)  G.  Perotti  (E.)  F.  Láng
                                           (B.)  D.  Ney  (A.)

                Operaház    Dec. 18, 1884 E.  Turolla  (G.)  G.  Perotti  (E.)

INDIA
Bombay          Excelsior   Apr. 23, 1916 A.  De Revers  (G.)  T.  Visoni  (L.)  N.
                                           Russ  (C.)  B.  Capelli  (E.)  I.  Belloni
                                           (B.)  G.  Cacciali  (A.)  G.  Gonsalez
                                           cond.

Calcutta        Grand Op.   Feb.  1, 1916 A.  De Revers  (G.)  T.  Visoni  (L.)  N.
                                           Russ  (C.)  B.  Capelli  (E.)  E.  Filip-
                                           pini  (B.)  G.  Cacciali  (A.)  G.  Gonsa-
                                           lez cond.

INDONESIA
Batavia         Stads       July  2, 1915 F.  Impallomeni  (G.)  T.  Visoni  (L.)
                                           L.  Da Gradi  (E.)  V.  Scamuzzi  (C.)  A.
                                           Mauceri  (A.)

IRELAND
Cork            Th. Royal   Jan. 29, 1903 F.  Moody  (G.)  A.  Hickisch  (L.)  M.
                                           Alexander  (C.)  J.  O'Mara  (E.)  G.  Fox
                                           (B.)  C.  Magrath  (A.)  (in Eng.)

| | | | |
|---|---|---|---|
| Dublin | Th. Royal | Apr. 15, 1903 | B. Marchesi (G.) A. Hickisch (L.) M. Alexander (C.) J. O'Mara (E.) G. Fox (B.) C. Magrath (A.) R. Eckhold cond. (in Eng.) |
| Wexford | Th. Royal | Oct. 27, 1963 | E. Tarrés (G.) G. Lane (L.) A. Reynolds (C.) G. Gismondo (E.) L. Puglisi (B.) F. Ventriglia (A.) G. Staern cond. (in It.) |

ISRAEL

| | | | |
|---|---|---|---|
| Tel Aviv | National | Jan.? 1968 | M. Candida (G.) L. Shani (L.) E. Kochanov (C.) J. Lloveras (E.) R. Novello (B.) S. Ronly-Riklis cond. |

ITALY

| | | | |
|---|---|---|---|
| Alessandria | Politeama | Sep. 1883 | R. Pantaleoni (G.) F. Mariani De Angelis (L.) E. Durot (E.) O. Beltrami (B.) G. Jeronim (A.) E. Usiglio cond. |
| Ancona | Muse | Sep. 18, 1887 | A. Cataneo (G.) E. Locatelli (L.) E. Guarnieri (C.) A. Anton (E.) T. S. Terzi (B.) G. Rossi (A.) R. Ferrari cond. |
| Ascoli Piceno | Ventidio Basso | Nov. 1883 | M. Mariani-Masi (G.) F. Mariani De Angelis (L.) G. Oselio (C.) L. Signoretti (E.) G. Moriami (B.) E. Corti (A.) Galeazzi cond. |
| Bari | Piccinni | Feb. 6, 1889 | T. Singer (G.) A. Belloni (L.) E. Riso (C.) E. Cuttica (E.) L. Pignalosa (B.) C. Bedogni (A.) C. Lovati-Cazzolani cond. |
| | Petruzzelli | Feb. 9, 1905 | O. Petrella (G.) F. Fassini (L.) R. Alvarez (C.) G. Giorgi (E.) O. Beltrami (B.) O. Carozzi (A.) O. Anselmi cond. |
| Bergamo | Donizetti | Aug. 28, 1886 | P. Rossini (G.) P. Roluti (L.) E. Guarnieri (C.) E. De Marchi (E.) O. Beltrami (B.) F. Graziosi (A.) G. Cimini cond. |
| Bologna | Comunale | Oct. 8, 1882 | M. Mariani-Masi (G.) F. Mariani De Angelis (L.) Z. Cortini (C.) G. Frapolli (E.) T. Wilmant (B.) A. Tamburlini (A.) L. Mancinelli cond. |
| Brescia | Grande | Aug. 11, 1883 | E. Theodorini (G.) F. Mariani De Angelis (L.) Z. Cortini (C.) G. Ortisi (E.) G. Moriami (B.) L. Visconti (A.) F. Faccio cond. |
| Cagliari | Civico | Dec. 26? 1892 | C. Joanna (G.) C. Boasso (L.) E. Niccoli (E.) V. Ferraguti (B.) L. Ferraioli (A.) A. Vigna cond. |
| Catania | Bellini | July 14, 1890 | N. Bulicioff (G.) G. Zeppilli-Villani (L.) E. Rossi (C.) F. Cardinali (E.) E. Camera (B.) G. Rossi (A.) C. Rossi cond. |

| Chieti | Marruccino | Apr. 22, 1885 | M. Herz (G.) A. Bourmann (L.) E. Locatelli (C.) C. Callioni (E.) O. Beltrami (B.) E. Brancaleoni (A.) G. Bolzoni cond. |
|---|---|---|---|
| Cremona | Concordia | Sep. 4, 1880 | M. Mariani-Masi (G.) F. Mariani De Angelis (L.) T. Vigna (C.) F. Marconi (E.) G. Mariani (B.) G. Gialdini cond. |
| Fermo | Aquila | Aug. 14, 1927 | G. Arangi-Lombardi (G.) M. Capuana (L.) F. Franchi (C.) F. Jagel (E.) V. Damiani (B.) C. Zambelli (A.) G. Santini cond. |
| Ferrara | Comunale | Dec. 26, 1884 | Razzani (G.) I. Castellani (L.) E. Metellio (E.) A. Pessina (B.) C. Campanini cond. |
| Fiume | Civico | Oct. 22? 1885 | M. Borelli (G.) C. Sartori (L.) T. Bertini (E.) G. Caruson (B.) |
| Florence | Pagliano | May 19, 1880 | M. Mariani-Masi (G.) F. Mariani De Angelis (L.) T. Vigna (C.) F. Marconi (E.) G. Moriami (B.) E. Barberat (A.) F. Faccio cond. |
| Forli | Comunale | Aug. 29, 1882 | R. Pantaleoni (G.) V. Stracca (L.) E. Treves (C.) E. Durot (E.) O. Beltrami (B.) G. Jeronim (A.) E. Usiglio cond. |
| Genoa | Carlo Felice | Mar. 23, 1884 | A. Conti-Foroni (G.) G. Savelli (L.) E. Borlinetto (C.) L. Filippi Bresciani (E.) S. Athos (B.) G. Monti (A.) N. Bassi cond. |
| Livorno | Goldoni | Mar. 20? 1886 | G. Savelli (G.) P. Roluti (L.) E. Guardenti (E.) S. Terzi (B.) P. De Bengardi (A.) R. Ferrari cond. |
| Lodi | Sociale | Sep. 8, 1883 | M. Mariani-Masi (G.) G. Savelli (L.) G. Oselio (C.) E. Puerari (E.) G. Moriami (B.) G. Gialdini cond. |
| Lucca | Giglio | Aug. 3, 1887 | N. Bulicioff (G.) E. Steinbach (L.) G. Levi (C.) C. Callioni (E.) F. Pozzi (B.) P. De Bengardi (A.) G. Gialdini cond. |
| Lugo | Rossini | Sep. 8, 1884 | M. Borelli (G.) E. Savelli (L.) G. Oseglio (C.) T. Bertini (E.) S. Sparapani (B.) V. Salmasi (A.) E. Usiglio cond. |
| Mantua | Sociale | Sep. 14, 1882 | M. Mariani-Masi (G.) F. Mariani De Angelis (L.) E. Tosi (C.) A. Petrovich (E.) T. Wilmant (B.) A. Leoni (A.) G. Gialdini cond. |
| Messina | Vittorio Emanuele | Feb. 11, 1886 | P. Rossini (G.) A. Aimery (L.) E. Rossi (C.) G. Procacci (E.) O. Beltrami (B.) V. Coda (A.) G. Rossi cond. |

Modena        Comunale     Dec. 26, 1883 G. Rey (G.) A. Leoni (L.) A. Del
                                         Bruno (C.) V. Papeschi (E.) A. Ver-
                                         dini (B.) G. Belletti (A.) V. For-
                                         nari cond.

Naples        San Carlo    Apr. 1, 1881 M. Mariani-Masi (G.) F. Mariani De
                                         Angelis (L.) H. Leavington (C.) G.
                                         Sani (E.) Z. Bertolasi (B.) G.
                                         Mirabella (A.) C. Scalisi cond.

Novara        Coccia       Jan. 15? 1890 O. Bazzani (G.) E. Treves (L.) G.
                                         Cremonini (E.) G. Salassa (B.) Cor-
                                         si (A.) Boscarini cond.

Padua         Verdi        July    1884 F. Copca (G.) A. Stahl (L.) G. Cele-
                                         ga (C.) G. Sani (E.) D. Menotti (B.)
                                         F. Navarini (A.) R. Drigo cond.

Palermo       Bellini      Apr. 24, 1884 M. Mariani-Masi (G.) F. Mariani De
                                         Angelis (L.) G. Oselio (C.) F. Car-
                                         dinali (E.) O. Beltrami (B.) L. Vis-
                                         conti (A.) F. Nicolao cond.

              Massimo      May  29, 1897 M. Borelli (G.) E. Borlinetto (L.)
                                         M. Paolicchi-Mugnone (C.) E. Caruso
                                         (E.) T. S. Terzi (B.) P. Wulmann
                                         (A.) L. Mugnone cond.

Parma         Regio        Dec. 26, 1885 A. Cattaneo (G.) M. Mei-Figner (L.)
                                         E. Guarnieri (C.) N. Figner (E.) D.
                                         Menotti (B.) L. Contini (A.) N.
                                         Bassi cond.

Piacenza      Municipale   Dec. 27? 1885 T. Brambilla-Ponchielli (G.) C. Bac-
                                         chiani (L.) T. Carotini (C.) E.
                                         Guardenti (E.) N. Zardo (B.) L. No-
                                         targiacomo (A.) N. Guerrera cond.

Pisa          Verdi        Mar. 14, 1884 G. Rey (G.) G. Sommelius (L.) A. Del
                                         Bruno (C.) G. Frapolli (E.) A. Ver-
                                         dini (B.) A. Curti (A.) V. Fornari
                                         cond.

Ravenna       Alighieri    Jan. 16? 1886 G. Savelli (G.) P. Roluti (L.) A. B.
                                         Baldi (C.) V. Grilli (E.) T. S. Ter-
                                         zi (B.) E. Serbolini (A.) R. Ferrari
                                         cond.

Reggio Emilia Municipale   Dec. 25, 1886 T. Brambilla-Ponchielli (G.) M. Za-
                                         non (L.) E. Guarnieri (C.) E. Rubi-
                                         rato (B.) E. Borucchia (A.) M. Bava-
                                         gnoli cond.

Rome          Apollo       Mar. 25, 1886 M. L. Durand (G.) M. Duvivier (L.)
                                         G. Oselio (C.) E. Barbacini (E.) G.
                                         Vaselli (B.) O. Maini (A.) E. Mas-
                                         cheroni cond.

              Costanzi     May  25, 1886 R. Pantaleoni (G.) A. Stahl (L.) A.
                                         Boriani (C.) G. Ortisi (E.) E. Du-
                                         friche (B.) F. Navarini (A.) F.
                                         Faccio cond.

Rovigo        Sociale      Oct. 11? 1885 M. Herz (G.) G. Oselio (L.) E. Mon-
                                        temerli (C.) C. Callioni (E.) A.
                                        Verdini (B.) G. Tansini (A.) G. Bol-
                                        zoni cond.

Siena         Rinnovati    Dec. 24? 1897 V. Petrilli-Sulli (G.) T. Alasia
                                        (L.) M. Bodini (C.) Sarcoli (E.) F.
                                        Cattadori (B.) A. Brondi (A.)

Trento        Sociale      June 4, 1887 L. Mayer (G.) C. Sartori (L.) L.
                                        Flotow (C.) F. Gambarelli (E.) A.
                                        Pantaleoni (B.) O. Bottero (A.)

Treviso       Sociale      Oct. 15, 1881 R. Pantaleoni (G.) E. Ziffer (L.) G.
                                        Casaglia (C.) L. Bellò (E.) T. Wil-
                                        mant (B.) I. Sbordoni (A.) C.
                                        Lovati-Cazzulani cond.

Trieste       Grande       Mar. 9, 1887 F. Copca (G.) F. Mariani De Angelis
                                        (L.) E. Montemerli (C.) A. Brasi
                                        (E.) A. Pessina (B.) G. Balisardi
                                        (A.) V. Podesti cond.

Turin         Regio        Dec. 24, 1881 M. Mariani-Masi (G.) F. Mariani De
                                        Angelis (L.) Z. Cortini (C.) G. Or-
                                        tisi (E.) T. Wilmant (B.) E. Cheru-
                                        bini (A.) C. Pedrotti cond.

Udine         Sociale      Mar. 7, 1885 L. Peydro (G.) E. Borlinetto (L.) L.
                                        Martinetti (C.) C. Callioni (E.) A.
                                        Pantaleoni (B.) G. Tansini (A.) R.
                                        Kuon cond.

Venice        La Fenice    Jan. 11, 1885 A. Conti Foroni (G.) E. Leonardi
                                        (L.) M. Petich (C.) A. Garulli (E.)
                                        E. Sivori (B.) P. De Bengardi (A.)
                                        E. Usiglio cond.

Verona        Filarmonico  Dec. 25? 1883 F. Copca (G.) G. Levi (L.) E. Parsi
                                        (C.) E. Durot (E.) O. Beltrami (B.)
                                        G. Jeromin (A.) E. Usiglio cond.

              Arena        July 29, 1925 G. Arangi-Lombardi (G.) I. Minghini-
                                        Cattaneo (L.) F. Franchi (C.) V.
                                        Lois (E.) B. Franci (B.) G. Tomei
                                        (A.) S. Failoni cond.

Vicenza       Eretenio     Dec. 27, 1885 E. Tivoli (G.) C. Sartori (L.) E.
                                        Montemerli (C.) C. Callioni (E.) A.
                                        Pessina (B.) R. D'Ottavi (A.) C.
                                        Conti cond.

JAMAICA
Kingston      Th. Royal    Aug. 4, 1900 N. Barbareschi (G.) A. Turconi-Bruni
                                        (L.) V. E. Castellano (E.) L. Bella-
                                        gamba (B.) L. Lucenti (A.)

JAPAN
Tokyo         Imperial     Mar. 16, 1925 A. Laskova (G.) Minotti (L.) F. Cor-
                                        betta (E.) V. Scamuzzi (B.) Milocchi
                                        (A.)

JUGOSLAVIA
Ljubljana     National     June 4, 1938 (in Slov.)

Zagreb National May 18, 1884 E. De Rüti (G.) D. Del Papa (E.) (in Croat.)

Zara Nobile Sep. 1888 E. Ancarani (G.) A. Belloni (L.) G. Rizzini (E.) N. Melossi (B.) A. Gautiero (A.)

LATVIA
Riga Municipal 1893 (in Ger.)

May 22? 1900 F. Percuopo (E.) G. Pimazzoni (B.) N. Giommi (A.) (in It.)

National Nov. 15, 1928 (in Let.)

LITHUANIA
Kaunas National May 2, 1929 (in Lith.)

Vilnius Municipal Mar.? 1897 G. Pimazzoni (B.) L. Ferraioli (A.)

MALTA
La Valletta Real Nov. 6, 1886 L. Stefanini (G.) I. Castellani (L.) A. Parmigiani (C.) G. Procacci (E.) V. Blasi (B.) V. Coda (A.) C. Ronzani cond.

MEXICO
Mexico City Nacional Oct. 14, 1885 A. Gini-Pizzorni (G.) E. Bassi (L.) G. Tiozzo (C.) C. Pizzorni (E.) E. Pogliani (B.) R. Mancini (A.) V. D'Alessio cond.

MONACO
Monte Carlo Salle Jan. 12, 1895 A. Gini-Pizzorni (G.) M. Giudice
Garnier (L.) Broemsen (C.) G. Cremonini (E.) G. Caruson (B.) G. Tansini (A.) L. Jehin cond.

NETHERLANDS
Amsterdam Palais v. Oct. 3, 1897 L. Gilboni (G.) I. Sambo (L.) P.
Volksvligt Lombardi (E.) G. Lunardi (B.) F. Spangher (A.)

Den Haag Gebouw v. Sep. 28, 1897 L. Gilboni (G.) I. Sambo (L.) P.
Kunst Lombardi (E.) G. Lunardi (B.) F. Spangher (A.)

Rotterdam Groote Oct. 1? 1897 L. Gilboni (G.) I. Sambo (L.) P. Lombardi (E.) G. Lunardi (B.) F. Spangher (A.) E. Natale cond.

PANAMA
Panama City Nacional Nov. 19, 1908 L. De Benedetto (G.) R. Pezzati (L.) E. Battain (E.) G. Pimazzoni (B.) N. Cervi (A.)

PERU
Lima Principal Jan. 1, 1898 B. Barducci (G.) C. Prandi (L.) E. Nerozzi (C.) J. Badarocco (E.) J. Ferrari (B.) J. Travaglini (A.) H. Barducci cond.

PHILIPPINES
Manila          Circo        Mar. 29, 1894 M. Balzofiore (G.) L. Cavallini (L.)
                Zorilla                    U. Francesconi (E.) U. Ciabò (B.) N.
                                           Giommi (A.)


POLAND
Lwov            Municipal    Mar. 22? 1890 Pawlikoff (G.) Heller (L.) Franklin
                                           (C.) F. Percuoco (E.) A. Putò (B.)
                                           G. Jeronim (A.)


Warsaw          Wielki       Jan.  3, 1885


PORTUGAL
Lisbon          Sao Carlos   Feb. 18, 1886 E. Borghi-Mamo (G.) G. Novelli (L.)
                                           E. Borlinetto (C.) A. De Bassini
                                           (E.) A. Cotogni (B.) A. Pinto (A.)
                                           M. Mancinelli cond.


Oporto          Sao Joao     Feb. 27, 1889 L. Peydro (G.) C. Mas (L.) G. Masin
                                           (E.) P. Ughetto (B.) A. Pinto (A.)


PUERTO RICO
Ponce           La Perla     Apr.  5? 1915

San Juan        Municipal    Dec. 20, 1910 A. De Revers (G.) R. Alvarez (L.) G.
                                           De Martin (C.) G. Di Bernardo (E.)
                                           V. Barettoni (B.) F. Rusconi (A.) G.
                                           Pucetti cond.


ROMANIA
Bucharest       Nacional     Nov. 29, 1889 A. Cattaneo (G.) S. Bellincioni (L.)
                                           A. Belloni (C.) B. Lucignani (E.) T.
                                           S. Terzi (B.) A. Silvestri (A.) F.
                                           Spetrino cond.

Galati                       Jan. 20? 1880 O. De Newosky (G.) Monti (L.) M.
                                           Pantanelli (C.) Di Napoli (E.) E.
                                           Massini (B.) F. Zavaschi (A.)


RUSSIA
Kharkov         Municipal    May  26? 1887 R. Calligaris-Marty (G.) T. Lubato-
                                           vich (L.) L. Ottaviani (E.) M. Polli
                                           (B.) V. Salmasi (A.) Truffi cond.

Kiev            Imperial     Dec. 24, 1885 E. Dotti (G.) V. Bacci (E.) G. Pi-
                                           mazzoni (B.)

Moscow          Bolshoi      Mar. 25, 1883 M. L. Durand (G.) Hermann (L.) G.
                                           Tremelli (C.) F. Marconi (E.) G. Va-
                                           selli (B.) A. Pinto (A.)

Odessa          Municipal    Sep. 15, 1885 Q. Lorenzini-Gianoli (G.) S. Kram-
                                           berger (L.)  P. Lazzarini (E.) N.
                                           Zardo (B.) V. Salmasi (A.) G. Pomè-
                                           Penna cond.

St.             Imperial     Jan. 30  1883 M. L. Durand (G.) Hermann (L.) A.
Petersburg                                 Stahl (C.) F. Marconi (E.) A. Coto-
                                           gni (B.) P. Povoleri (A.) E. Bevi-
                                           gnani cond.


                             Feb.     1888 (in Russ.)

SINGAPORE
Singapore    Victoria    Nov.  3, 1915  A. De Revers (G.) T. Visoni (L.) N. Russ (C.) B. Capelli (E.) E. Filippini (B.)

SOUTH AFRICA
Capetown    Opera House Mar. 18, 1895  E. Ancarani (G.) T. Alasia (L.) L. Rossi (C.) A. Mauri (E.) M. De Padova (B.) A. Gautiero (A.)

Johannesburg  Amphi-    May  4, 1895  E. Ancarani (G.) T. Alasia (L.) L. theatre                    Rossi (C.) V. Maina (E.) M. De Padova (B.) A. Gautiero (A.)

SPAIN
Alicante    Principal  Feb. 10? 1895  M. Kupfer-Berger (G.)

Barcelona   Liceo     Feb. 26, 1883  M. Mariani-Masi (G.) G. Novelli (L.) E. Treves (C.) G. Sani (E.) S. Athos (B.) A. Vianesi cond.

Bilbao     Arriaga   May 31, 1890  M. Borelli (G.) G. Pasqua (L.) Bustos (C.) G. Moretti (E.) L. Pignalosa (B.) E. Borucchia (A.)

Cordoba    Gran     May 20, 1891  G. Pasqua (L.) G. Gabrielescu (E.) Capitan                 P. Lhérie (B.) P. Urrutia cond.

Madrid     Real      Feb.  7, 1884  E. Theodorini (G.) A. Mazzoli-Orsini (L.) A. Borghi (C.) A. Masini (E.) G. Bianchi (B.) F. Vecchioni (A.) J. Goula cond.

Malaga     Cervantes  May  2, 1891  M. Kupfer-Berger (G.) G. Pasqua (L.) G. Gabrielescu (E.) P. Lhérie (B.) R. Ercolani (A.) P. Urrutia cond.

Palma di   Principal  May 21, 1891  M. Rodriguez (G.) V. Guerrini (L.) Mallorca                   T. Carotini (C.) R. Grani (E.) E. Laban (B.) L. Visconti (A.) E. Mascheroni cond.

Seville    San      May 17, 1889  G. Bellincioni (G.) A. Del Bruno Fernando             (L.) E. Treves (C.) E. Giannini-Griffoni (E.) D. Menotti (B.) N. Serra (A.) J. Tolosa cond.

Valencia   Principal  Feb.  7? 1890  M. Borelli (G.) A. Del Bruno (L.) E. De Marchi (C.) E. Laban (B.) J. Goula cond.

SWEDEN
Stockholm  Royal     Mar. 10, 1892  C. Östberg (G.) D. Edling (L.) S. Wolf (C.) A. Ödmann (E.) O. Johanson (B.) A. Sellergren (A.) (in Swed.)

SWITZERLAND
Berne      Stadt     May  9, 1986  G. Savova (G.) M. L. Nave (L.) M. Cioromila (C.) A. Filistad (E.) A. Zanazzo (A.) P. Olmi cond.

Geneva    Grand     Apr.  3, 1902  Marcillac (C.) Annibale Ponchielli cond. (in Fr.)

Dec.  6, 1979 M. Caballe (G.) M. L. Nave (L.) J.
                            Carreras (E.) M. Manuguerra (B.) B.
                            Giaiotti (A.) J. Lopez-Cobos cond.
                            (in It.)

Lugano       Apollo       May   3? 1906 I. Citti-Lippi (G.) G. Trapani (L.)
                            M. Bodini (C.) E. Mancini (E.) G.
                            Nistri (B.) E. Garavaglia (A.) C.
                            Cavalieri cond.

Zürich       Stadt        June 22, 1920 G. Russ (G.) V. Devries (L.) L. Dos-
                            tel (C.) P. Gubellini (E.) L. Almo-
                            vodar (B.) F. Autori (A.) G. Falconi
                            cond. (in Ital.)

TURKEY
Constan-     Petit        Jan. 24, 1888 E. Boschetti (G.) F. Riolo (L.)
tinople      Champs                    Croscignano (C.) G. Russitano (E.)
                            F. Talamanca (B.) N. Giommi (A.)

Smyrna       Alhambra     Apr. 17, 1884 A. Giannetti (G.) C. Bacchiani (L.)
                            A. Brunetti (E.) R. De Giorgio (B.)
                            F. Micci-Labruna cond.

UNITED STATES
Baltimore    Lyric        Jan.  6, 1908 L. Nordica (G.) M. Claessens (L.) R.
                            Olitzka (C.) F. Constantino (E.) R.
                            Blanchart (B.) A. Perello de Seguro-
                            la (A.)

Boston       Boston Th.   Jan.  1, 1884 C. Nilsson (G.) E. Fursch-Madi (L.)
                            S. Scalchi (C.) R. Stagno (E.) G.
                            Del Puente (B.) F. Novara (A.) A.
                            Vianesi cond.

Chicago      Auditorium   Jan. 28, 1884 C. Nilsson (G.) E. Fursch-Madi (L.)
                            S. Scalchi (C.) R. Stagno (E.) G.
                            Del Puente (B.) F. Novara (A.) A.
                            Vianesi cond.

             Lyric        Nov.  1, 1957 E. Farrell (G.) G. Simionato (L.) I.
                            Kramarich (C.) R. Tucker (E.) A.
                            Protti (B.) W. Wildermann (A.) T.
                            Serafin cond.

Cincinnati   Music Hall   Feb. 14, 1884 C. Nilsson (G.) E. Fursch-Madi (L.)
                            S. Scalchi (C.) I. Campanini (E.) G.
                            Del Puente (B.) F. Novara (A.) A.
                            Vianesi cond.

             Opera        June 24, 1923 E. de Lys (G.) H. Wakefield (L.) A.
                            Klinova (C.) L. Tomarchio (E.) M.
                            Valle (B.) I. Picchi (A.) R. Lyford
                            cond.

Cleveland    Keith's      Feb.  3, 1914 M. Rappold (G.) M. Claessens (L.) R.
                            Olitzka (C.) G. Farmo (E.) J. Segu-
                            ra-Tallien (B.)

Dallas       Coliseum     Feb. 10, 1914 M. Rappold (G.) M. Claessens (L.) R.
                            Olitzka (C.) G. Farmo (E.) G. Mar-
                            tino (A.)

Denver      Broadway    Feb. 7, 1910 E. Bosetti (G.) D. Frau (L.) A. Maurini (E.) G. Maggi (B.)

Detroit      Washington   Feb. 6, 1914 M. Rappold (G.) M. Claessens (L.) R.
Olitzka (C.) G. Farmo (E.) J. Segu-
ra-Tallien (B.) G. Martino (A.)

Houston      Auditorium   Feb. 13, 1914 M. Rappold (G.) M. Claessens (L.) R.
Olitzka (C.) G. Farmo (E.) J. Segu-
ra-Tallien (B.) G. Martino (A.)

Los Angeles   Theatre     Oct. 12, 1897 N. Mazzi (G.) A. Fanton (L.) G. Agostini (E.) C. Cioni (B.) L. Sco-
lari (A.)

Minneapolis   Metro-      Jan. 11, 1917 M. Kaestner (G.) M. Correno (L.) S.
politan                  De Mette (C.) E. Salazar (E.) P. De
Biasi (A.)

New Orleans   Orleans     Jan. 26, 1907 L. Nordica (G.) I. Monti-Baldini
(L.) E. Borlinetto (C.) F. Constan-
tino (E.) R. Angelini-Fornari (B.)
A. Perello de Segurola (A.)

New York     Metro-      Dec. 20, 1883 C. Nilsson (G.) E. Fursch-Madi (L.)
politan                  S. Scalchi (C.) R. Stagno (E.) G.
Del Puente (B.) F. Novara (A.) A.
Vianesi cond.

           Century     Sep. 23, 1913 L. Ewell (G.) M. Jordan (L.) G.
Bergman (E.) L. Kreidler (B.) A.
Kaufman (A.) (in Eng.)

Philadelphia Ac. of Mus. Jan. 18, 1884 C. Nilsson (G.) E. Fursch-Madi (L.)
S. Scalchi (C.) V. Capoul (E.) G.
Del Puente (B.) F. Novara (A.) A.
Vianesi cond.

St. Louis     Olympic     Feb. 8, 1884 C. Nilsson (G.) L. Lablache (L.) S.
Scalchi (C.) R. Stagno (E.) G. Del
Puente (B.) F. Novara (A.) C. Campa-
nini cond.

San Francisco California   Nov. 2, 1897 N. Mazzi (G.) A. Fanton (L.) G. Agostini (E.) C. Cioni (B.)

           Opera      Sep. 30, 1947 S. Roman (G.) B. Thebom (L.) M. Har-
shaw (C.) K. Baum (E.) L. Warren
(B.) N. Moscona (A.) R. Marzollo
cond.

Washington    National    Feb. 27, 1884 C. Nilsson (G.) E. Fursch-Madi (L.)
S. Scalchi (C.) I. Campanini (E.) G.
Del Puente (B.) F. Novara (A.) A.
Vianesi cond.

URUGUAY
Montevideo    Solis      Aug. 24, 1884 E. Theodorini (G.) M. Mei-Figner
(L.) S. Ravogli (C.) F. Tamagno (E.)
A. Verdini (B.) A. Tamburlini (A.)
N. Bassi cond.

VENEZUELA
Caracas      Municipal   Jan.? 1890 C. Jodici (G.) O. Guercia (L.)

9. IL FIGLIUOL PRODIGO-*Melodramma* in four acts
Milan-Teatro alla Scala-Dec. 26, 1880
Libretto by A. Zanardini

Jeftele (J.)                                 Maria d'Angeri sop.
Nefte (N.)                                Bianca Maria Prasini mez.
Azaele (A.)                                 Francesco Tamagno ten.
Amenofi (Am.)                               Federico Salvati bar.
Ruben (R.)                                 Edouard De Reszke bass


Conductor                                       Franco Faccio
Director                                     Amilcare Ponchielli

OTHER PRODUCTIONS

ARGENTINA
Buenos Aires    Opera        May  22, 1897 C. Bonaplata-Bau (J.) V. Guerrini
                                          (N.) M. Mariacher (A.) A. Scotti
                                          (Am.) G. Rossi (R.) E. Mascheroni
                                          cond.


ITALY
Cremona         Concordia    Sep. 14, 1892 C. Bonaplata-Bau (J.) V. Guerrini
                                          (N.) E. Durot (A.) A. Pessina (Am.)
                                          G. Rossi (R.) E. Mascheroni cond.


                Ponchielli   Jan. 29, 1921 T. Milanesi (J.) M. Lampaggi (N.) F.
                                          Bottaro (A.) G. Morellato (Am.)


                Piazza       July  1, 1934 G. Arangi-Lombardi (J.) E. Nicola
                del Comune                (N.) F. Merli (A.) M. Basiola (Am.)
                                          T. Pasero (R.) T. Serafin cond.

Florence        Pergola      Jan. 22, 1919 T. Milanesi (J.) De Vries (N.) P.
                                          Zeni (A.) F. Bonini (Am.)


                             Jan. 24? 1920 T. Milanesi (J.) P. Zeni (A.) F.
                                          Bonini (Am.) E. Vannuccini (R.)

Milan           La Scala     Mar. 31, 1892 C. Bonaplata-Bau (J.) V. Guerrini
                                          (N.) M. Mariacher (A.) A. Pessina
                                          (Am.) G. Rossi (R.)


                             Dec. 26, 1934 G. Cigna (J.) E. Stignani (N.) A.
                                          Melandri (A.) C. Tagliabue (Am.) T.
                                          Pasero (R.) V. De Sabata cond.


                Arena        June 21, 1921 W. Giovanelli (J.) R. Brunetto (N.)
                                          S. Montelauri (A.) A. Pilotto (Am.)
                                          G. Nicolesco (R.) P. Fabbroni/R.
                                          Selvaggi cond.


Turin           Regio        Dec. 27, 1883 M. Mariani-Masi (J.) F. Mariani De
                                          Angelis (N.) G. Sani (A.) G. B. Va-
                                          selli (Am.) A. Tamburlini (R.) A.
                                          Pomè cond. A. Ponchielli dir.


                Sala RAI     July 26, 1931 E. Maroli (J.) R. Toniolo (N.) A.
                                          Ferrara (A.) G. Noto (Am.) E. Spada
                                          (R.) A. Pedrollo cond.

Verona        Arena        July 31, 1919 T. Milanesi/B. Cocchi (J.) I. Berga-
                                        masco/V. De Cristoff (N.) P. Zeni/A.
                                        Perico (A.) F. Bonini/G. Morellato
                                        (Am.) O. Luppi/A. Alfieri (R.) E.
                                        Panizza cond.


10. MARION DELORME-*Melodramma* in four acts
Milan-Teatro alla Scala-Mar. 17, 1885
Libretto by Enrico Golisciani

Marion (M.)                                    Romilda Pantaleoni sop.
Lelio (L.)                                        Adele Borghi mez.
Didier (D.)                                   Francesco Tamagno ten.
Marchese Saverny (S.)                            Augusto Brogi bar.
Laffemas (La.)                                Angelo Tamburlini bass
Brichanteau                                   Angelo Fiorentini ten.
Gasse/Un Carceriere                          Napoleone Limonta bass
Un Capitano/Un Banditore                         Carlo Moretti bass


Conductor                                          Franco Faccio
Director                                       Amilcare Ponchielli

Revised-Brescia-Teatro Grande-Aug. 9, 1885

Marion (M.)                                    Romilda Pantaleoni sop.
Lelio (L.)                                        Adele Borghi mez.
Didier (D.)                                    Enrico Puerari ten.
Marchese Saverny (S.)                            Paolo Lhérie bar.
Laffemas (La.)                                Francesco Navarini bass


Conductor                                          Franco Faccio
Director                                       Amilcare Ponchielli

OTHER PRODUCTIONS

BRAZIL
Rio de        Pedro II     July  5, 1886 M. Mei-Figner (M.) E. Mantelli (L.)
  Janeiro                                 N. Figner (D.) P. Lhérie (S.) G. Ro-
                                          veri (La.) A. Toscanini cond.

Sao Paulo     San José     May   4, 1886 M. Mei-Figner (M.) E. Mantelli (L.)
                                          N. Figner (D.) P. Lhérie (S.) G. Ro-
                                          veri (La.)

ITALY
Cremona       Concordia    Feb.  8, 1896 I. Ricetti/S. Kruszelnicka (M.) M.
                                          Svetandé (L.) P. Zeni (D.) P.
                                          Giacomollo (S.) A. Perello de
                                          Segurola (La.) A. Gianoli cond.

Milan         Lirico       Apr. 15, 1919 E. Burzio (M.) A. Ponzano (L.) A.
                                          Paoli (D.) G. Bellantoni (S.) O.
                                          Luppi (La.) G. Armani cond.

Parma         Regio        Mar. 13, 1886 A. Cattaneo (M.) E. Guarnieri (L.)
                                          N. Figner (D.) D. Menotti (S.) L.
                                          Contini (La.) N. Bassi cond.

Rome          Costanzi     June 24, 1886 R. Pantaleoni (M.) A. Boriani (L.)
                                         G. Ortisi (D.) E. Dufriche (S.) F.
                                         Navarini (La.) F. Faccio cond.

Venice        La Fenice    Jan. 27, 1886 V. Damerini (M.) M. Zanon (L.) B.
                                         Lucignani (D.) E. Dufriche (S.) G.
                                         Roveri (La.) R. Drigo cond.


11. I MORI DI VALENZA-*Dramma lirico* in four acts
Monte Carlo-Salle Garnier-Mar. 17, 1914
Libretto by Antonio Ghislanzoni
Completed by Arturo Cadore

Eléma (E.)                                      Lydia Lipkowska sop.
Carmine (C.)                                   Jacqueline Royer mez.
Fernando d'Albayda (F.)                     Giovanni Martinelli ten.
Alberigo Delascar (A.)                        George Baklanoff bar.
Filippo III (Fi.)                              Robert Marvini bass
Il Duca di Lerma                                          Etex ten.
Don Giovanni d'Aguilar                        Pierre Clauzure bass
A Moor                                        Bindo Gasparini ten.
A Servant                                             Sorret ten.

Conductor                                       Alexandre Pomé
Director                                         Arturo Cadore


OTHER PRODUCTIONS

ITALY
Milan         Arena        July 19, 1914 G. Russ (E.) M. Passari (C.) G. De
                                         Tura (F.) G. Segura-Tallien (A.) E.
                                         Molinari (Fi.) A. Guarnieri cond. A.
                                         Cadore dir.

FEDERICO RICCI

1. MONSIEUR DE CHALUMEAUX-*Melodramma comico* in two acts
Venice-Teatro San Benedetto-June 14, 1835
Libretto by Giacopo Ferretti

Adele (A.)                                    Rosa Bottrigari sop.
Belfiore (B.)                                      Fabbio Dei ten.
Il Duca Giocondo di Villard (G.)         Giovanni Cavaceppi bass
Mons. de Chalumeaux (C.)                     Vincenzo Galli buf.
Tibbury                                    Giuseppe Grazioli bass
Isabella                                     Marietta Bramati sec.
Conte Gustavo                                Lorenzo Lombardi sec.


OTHER PRODUCTIONS

ITALY

| | | | |
|---|---|---|---|
| Florence | Pergola | Dec. 26, 1835 | C. Barili-Patti (A.) S. Patti (B.) C. Leoni (G.) V. Galli (C.) N. Petrini-Zamboni cond. |
| Genoa | Carlo Felice | Oct. 26, 1836 | R. Bottrigari (A.) G. Cappelli (B.) M. Alberti (G.) V. Graziani (C.) |
| Milan | La Scala | Jan. 22, 1839 | M. Brambilla (A.) G. Roppa (B.) C. Badiali (G.) V. Galli (C.) E. Cavallini cond. |
| Trieste | Grande | Dec. 26, 1835 | R. Bottrigari (A.) G. B. Genero (B.) G. Cavaceppi (G.) V. Cavisago (C.) A. Scaramelli cond. |
| Turin | Sutera | Dec. 26? 1838 | E. Hallez (A.) L. Alberti (B.) Quattrini (G.) L. Profeti (C.) |
| Venice | San Benedetto | June 14, 1837 | Berti (A.) A. Balestracci (B.) P. Novelli (G.) R. Scalese (C.) |

SPAIN

| | | | |
|---|---|---|---|
| Madrid | Principe | Oct. 30, 1837 | E. D'Alberti (A.) A. Arrigotti (B.) G. Cavaceppi (G.) |


2. LA PRIGIONE DI EDIMBURGO-*Melodramma semiserio* in three acts
Trieste-Teatro Grande-Mar. 13, 1838
Libretto by Gaetano Rossi

Giovanna (G.)                          Rita Gabussi De Bassini sop.
Ida (I.)                                  Giuseppina Armenia sop.
Giorgio (Gi.)                               Lorenzo Bonfigli ten.
Tom (T.)                                   Giuseppe Scheggi buf.
Il Duca D'Argil (D.)                         Lorenzo Biondi bass
Fanny                                       Marietta Biondi sec.
Patrizio                               Antonio Benciolini bass

Conductor                                Alessandro Scaramelli
Director                                        Federico Ricci

OTHER PRODUCTIONS

ARGENTINA
Buenos Aires  Victoria      Oct.  7, 1853 R.  Olivieri  (G.)  E.  Rossi-Guerra
                                             (Gi.)

AUSTRIA
Vienna        Kärntnertor Apr.  2, 1840 R.  Gabussi De Bassini (G.) L. Abba-
                                         dia (I.) G. Roppa (Gi.) G. Frezzoli-
                                         ni (T.)

BRAZIL
Rio de        Sao Pedro     May   3, 1847 A.  Tassini Mugnai (G.) N. Barbieri-
Janeiro                                   Thiollier (I.) C. Mugnai (Gi.) F.
                                          Massiani (T.)

                            June 30, 1848 A.  Candiani (G.) C. Merea (I.) F.
                                          Tati (Gi.) F. Massiani (T.)

CHILE
Santiago      Republica     Apr. 17, 1855 R.  Olivieri (G.) E.  Rossi-Guerra
                                             (Gi.)

Valparaiso    Victoria      Jan. 10, 1856 R.  Olivieri (G.) E.  Rossi-Guerra
                                             (Gi.)

CZECHOSLOVAKIA
Prague                      Apr.  5, 1843 (in It.)

DENMARK
Copenhagen    Royal         Apr. 13, 1842 F.  Forconi (G) A. Rivolta (I.) F.
                                          Ciaffei (Gi.) C. Rocca (T.) P. Spe-
                                          rati cond.

FRANCE
Nice          Regio         Nov. 22, 1840 M.  Franceschini-Garis (G.) M. Gazza-
                                          niga (I.) P. Ferrari (Gi.) C. Rocca
                                          (T.)

GERMANY
Hamburg       Stadt         Apr. 27, 1842 (in Ger.)

HUNGARY
Budapest                    Oct. 15, 1842 (in Ger.)

ITALY
Alessandria   Municipale    Carn. 1839-40 C.  Marzia (G.) G. Scavarda (Gi.) G.
                                          Saunier (T.) G. Del Pesce (D.)

Ancona        Muse          Jan. 20, 1844 C.  Cosentino (G.) Cusati (I.) C.
                                          Soldini (Gi.)

Ascoli        Ventidio      Carn. 1850-51 A.  Angelini-Cantalamessa (G.) Asdru-
Piceno        Basso                       bali (I.) V. Montanari (Gi.)

Bologna       Comunale      Apr.  6, 1839 A.  Manzocchi (G.) E. Manzocchi (I.)
                                          A. Dagnini (Gi.) G. Cavalli (T.) F.
                                          Razzanelli (D.)

Brescia       Grande        Dec. 26? 1839 C.  Vittadini (G.) T. Pusterla (I.)
                                          E. Bonfigli (Gi.) V. Galli (T.) R.
                                          Anconi (D.)

Cagliari      Civico        Carn. 1839-40 A.  Pompejano (Gi.)

| | | | |
|---|---|---|---|
| Chieti | San Fernando | May 27, 1843 | G. Nerozzi (Gi.) L. Rinaldini (T.) F. Venanzi cond. |
| Como | Sociale | Aug. 31, 1844 | A. Gambaro (G.) C. Rapazzini (I.) S. Benedetti (Gi.) G. Catalano (T.) |
| Crema | Sociale | Carn. 1839-40 | C. Steyer (G.) A. Casilieri (I.) G. B. Bertolasi (Gi.) P. Zambelli (T.) |
| Cremona | Concordia | Carn. 1839-40 | L. Schieroni-Nulli (G.) E. Turpini (I.) G. B. Milesi (Gi.) F. Facchini (T.) F. Rossi (D.) |
| Ferrara | Comunale | Aug. 25, 1845 | S. Marini-Testa (G.) M. Forti (Gi.) G. Fiori (T.) |
| Florence | Pergola | Nov. 22, 1838 | D. Dérancourt (G.) F. Pixis (I.) F. L. Morini (Gi.) G. Scheggi (T.) |
| | | Spring 1839 | D. Dérancourt (G.) E. Tadolini (I.) A. De Val (Gi.) C. Cambiaggio (T.) |
| | | Sep. 1840 | I. Secci-Corsi (I.) F. L. Morini (Gi.) G. Scheggi (T.) |
| | Alfieri | Summer 1839 | T. Cresci (G.) I. Secci-Corsi (I.) F. L. Morini (Gi.) G. Scheggi (T.) |
| | | July 1850 | G. Borsi de Leurie (G.) |
| Genoa | Carlo Felice | Oct. 9, 1839 | C. Steyer (G.) L. Giannoni (I.) A. Dagnini (Gi.) N. Fontana (T.) G. Serra cond. |
| | | Sep. 18, 1841 | T. Merli-Clerici (G.) L. Serati (I.) L. Donati (Gi.) V. Galli (T.) G. Bonazzi (D.) G. Serra cond. |
| | | Nov. 11, 1843 | C. Griffini (G.) A. Tirelli (I.) E. Caggiati (Gi.) G. Scheggi (T.) G. Serra cond. |
| | | Oct. 17, 1846 | G. Pecorini (G.) T. Paradisi (I.) E. Rossi-Guerra (Gi.) F. Frizzi (T.) G. Serra cond. |
| | | Oct. 19, 1854 | G. Borsi de Leurie (G.) M. Bottaro (I.) L. Stecchi-Bottardi (Gi.) F. Frizzi (T.) G. Garibaldi (D.) A. Mariani cond. |
| | | Sep. 30, 1865 | L. De Fanti (G.) E. Presly (I.) L. Stecchi-Bottardi (Gi.) F. Frizzi (T.) |
| | Paganini | Nov. 9, 1857 | A. Ravaglia (G.) E. Pasi (Gi.) M. Borella (T.) |
| Livorno | Avvalorati | Spring 1839 | I. Secci-Corsi (I.) F. L. Morini (Gi.) G. Scheggi (T.) A. Superchi (D.) |

| | Floridi | Spring | 1841 | F. Scheggi (G.) I. Secci-Corsi (I.) G. Luchessi (Gi) G. Scheggi (T.) F. Linari-Bellini (D.) |
|---|---|---|---|---|
| Lucca | Pantera | Dec. 26? | 1838 | A. Mazza (G.) M. Barbieri-Nini (I.) F. L. Morini (Gi.) G. Luzio (T.) G. Scheggi (D.) F. Ricci dir. |
| | Giglio | Jan. | 1845 | F. Ciaffei (Gi.) |
| Milan | La Scala | Oct. 16, | 1838 | S. Schoberlechner (G.) E. Tadolini (I.) D. Conti (Gi.) R. Scalese (T.) E. Polonini (D.) |
| | Re | Carn. | 1841-42 | T. Tavola (G.) E. Caggiati (Gi.) G. Zucchini (T.) |
| | Carcano | Aug. 6, | 1859 | |
| Modena | Comunale | Dec. 26, | 1841 | C. Soret (G.) I. Secci-Corsi (I.) R. Gamberini (Gi.) N. Fontana (T.) F. Razzanelli (D.) A. Sighicelli cond. |
| Naples | Fondo | Aug. 3, | 1839 | F. Pixis (G.) A. Granchi (I.) G. Basadonna (Gi.) F. Salvetti (T.) G. Benedetti (D.) |
| | Nuovo | Oct. 12, | 1844 | A. Rebussini (G.) L. Caranti-Vita (I.) Cenno (Gi.) L. Vita (T.) |
| Padua | Nuovissimo | Dec. 26? | 1840 | A. Rebussini (G.) T. Pusterla (I.) F. Tati (Gi.) G. Rebussini (T.) |
| | | Feb.? | 1844 | R. Mazzarelli (G.) G. Santi (Gi.) E. Luisia (T.) |
| Palermo | Carolino | Dec. | 1840 | F. Pixis (G.) E. Benzoni (I.) P. Rossi-Cicercia (Gi.) F. Colini (T.) B. De Ninnnis (D.) P. Raimondi cond. |
| | | Feb. 12, | 1844 | R. Gabussi De Bassini (G.) G. Austin (I.) L. Mei (Gi.) S. Torre (D.) P. Raimondi cond. |
| | | Feb. 12, | 1852 | S. Peruzzi (G.) P. Dompieri (I.) L. Stefani (Gi.) F. Rinaldi (T.) A. Selva (D.) P. Raimondi cond. |
| Parma | Regio | Dec. 28, | 1839 | R. Lugani-Notary (G.) E. Gebaur (I.) P. Ferrari (Gi.) F. Lauretti (T.) E. Mazzotti (D.) N. De Giovanni cond. |
| Pavia | Civico | Jan. | 1842 | T. Biaggi (G.) T. Fasciotti (I.) L. Paulin (Gi.) G. Fiori (T.) |
| Piacenza | Municipale | Carn. | 1843-44 | T. Tavola (G.) A. Balestracci (Gi.) |
| Pisa | Ravvivati | Dec. 26, | 1839 | T. Cresci (G.) I. Secci-Corsi (I.) F. L. Morini (Gi.) G. Scheggi (T.) A. Superchi (D.) |
| | | Feb. 10, | 1847 | |

Feb.?     1851  A. Salati (G.) E. Pellegrini (Gi.)
                G. Scheggi (T.) A. Ortolani (D.)

Ravenna          Comuni-      Dec. 26, 1846  A. Masaenza (G.) G. Brun (I.) G.
                 tativo                      Cortopassi (Gi.) G. Nostini cond.

Reggio Emilia Comunale        Jan. 18, 1845  C. Pastori (G.) C. Sordelli (I.) L.
                                             Tomassoni (Gi.) L. Cammarano (T.) L.
                                             Boyer cond.

Rome             Valle        Feb.?     1839  F. Forconi (G.) A. Viale (I.) G. Ba-
                                              sadonna (Gi.) C. Cambiaggio (T.)

                 Argentina    June      1840  T. Cresci (G.) I. Secci-Corsi (I.)
                                              F. L. Morini (Gi.) G. Scheggi (T.)
                                              G. Romanelli (D.)

Rovigo           Sociale      Carn. 1845-46  M. Arigotti (G.) G. Mercuriali (Gi.)
                                             V. Cavisago (T.)

Siena            Rinnovati    Aug.      1840

                              Jan.      1863  Albertoni (G.) Regan (I.) Severini
                                              (Gi.)

Trieste          Grande       Carn. 1840-41  F. Goldberg (G.) R. Scalese (T.) G.
                                             Amadio (Gi.) A. Scaramelli cond.

Turin            D'Angennes   May       1839  R. Gabussi De Bassini (G.) A. Cas-
                                              tellan (Gi.) V. Galli (T.) E. Polo-
                                              nini (D.)

                 Carignano    Nov.      1839  R. Gabussi De Bassini (G.) T. Bram-
                                              billa (I.)

Venice           San          May 25, 1839  A. Castellan (G.) A. Dabedeilhe (I.)
                 Benedetto                   Asti (Gi.) N. Fontana (T.)

Verona           Filarmonico May        1840  J. De Mery (G.) A. Venier (I.) P.
                                              Ferrari (Gi.) N. Fontana (T.)

Vigevano                      Feb.      1841

Vicenza          Berico       May 14, 1850  M. Anselmi (G.) G. Mora (Gi.) R.
                                            Gallo-Tomba (D.)

MALTA
La Valletta      Manoel                 1841

MEXICO
Mexico City      Opera        Jan. 14, 1842

                              May 22, 1842

POLAND
Warsaw           Wielki       Oct.  5, 1844

PORTUGAL
Lisbon           Sao Carlos   Feb. 12, 1841  C. Barili-Patti (G.) L. Ferretti
                                             (Gi.) L. Fornasari (T.)

                              June?     1842  L. Perelli (G.) L. Ferretti (Gi.) V.
                                              Galli (T.)

Oporto        Sao Joao    Feb.?    1843 C. Ferlotti (G.) F. Vitali (Gi.) F.
                                        Galli (T.)

RUSSIA
Odessa        Municipal   Autumn?  1841

SPAIN
Barcelona     Principal   July 24, 1840 T. Tavola (G.) L. Assandri (l.) A.
                                        Piacenti (Gi.) F. Regini (T.) S.
                                        Demi (D.) M. A. Rachel cond.

Cadiz         Principal   June     1841 L. Maggiorotti (T.)

Granada                   Oct. 18, 1842

Madrid        Principe    Aug. 28, 1840 R. Mazzarelli (G.) J. Lombia (l.) M.
                                        Ojeda (Gi.)

              De la Cruz  June 29, 1841 R. Mazzarelli (G.) J. Lombia (l.) M.
                                        Ojeda (Gi.)

Malaga        Principal   Apr.     1842 L. Aparicio (Gi.)

Palma de      Comedias    Jan.  1, 1851 G. B. Bertolasi (Gi.) J. Calonge
Mallorca                                (T.)

SWITZERLAND
Lugano        Sociale     Oct.     1855

URUGUAY
Montevideo    San Felipe  Mar. 11, 1853 R. Olivieri (G.) A. Ghioni (I.) E.
                                        Rossi-Guerra (Gi.) G. Olivieri (T.)
                                        P. Figari (D.)

              Sep.  7, 1854 R. Olivieri (G.) G. Amei (I.) E.
                                        Rossi-Guerra (Gi.) G. Olivieri (T.)
                                        G. Pruzzo (D.)


3. UN DUELLO SOTTO RICHELIEU-*Melodramma* in two acts
Milan-Teatro alla Scala-Aug. 17, 1839
Libretto by F. Dall'Ongaro, Antonio Somma and Antonio Gazzoletti

Maria Di Rohan                              Adelina Salvi Spech sop.
Armando Di Gondi                            Marietta Brambilla mez.
Il Conte di Chalais                            Lorenzo Salvi ten.
Il Duca di Chèvreuse                          Ignazio Marini bass
La Regina                                  Marietta Sacchi sec.
Il Re                                       Antonio Dal Vivo bar.
Gianni                                    Francesco Regini bass
Corso                                     Napoleone Marconi ten.

Conductor                                   Eugenio Cavallini
Director                                     Federico Ricci

4. LUIGI ROLLA-*Melodramma tragico* in three acts
Florence-Teatro in via della Pergola-Mar. 30, 1841
Libretto by Salvadore Cammarano

| | |
|---|---|
| Eleonora (E.) | Giuseppina Strepponi sop. |
| Stefano (S.) | Irene Secci-Corsi mez. |
| Luigi Rolla (L.) | Napoleone Moriani ten. |
| Il Marchese Appiani (A.) | Sebastiano Ronconi bar. |
| Ginevra | Faustina Piombanti mez. |
| Micheleangelo | Giuseppe Bertini bass |
| Andrea Costa | Ettore Profili bass |
| Un Familiare di Appiani | Demetrio Masselli bass |
| | |
| Conductor | Alamanno Biagi |
| Director | Federico Ricci |

OTHER PRODUCTIONS

DENMARK
Copenhagen    Royal        Dec. 10, 1848 G. Pecorini (E.) A. Ricci (S.) A.
                                        Castellan (L.) S. Scappini (A.)

GERMANY
Dresden       Hoftheater   Aug. 24, 1843 N. Moriani (L.)

HUNGARY
Budapest                   Sep.     1843 N. Moriani (L.)

ITALY
Bergamo       Riccardi     Sep.  3, 1846 E. Scotta (E.) A. Ricci (S.) N. Mo-
                                        riani (L.) G. F. Beneventano (A.) M.
                                        Bonesi cond.

Conegliano                 Sep. 17? 1876 C. Castelli (E.) N. Pedemonti (S.)
                                        F. Pozzo (L.) V. De Pasqualis (A.)
                                        E. Bernardi cond. F. Ricci dir.

Faenza        Comunale     Summer   1847 G. Sikorska-Moriani (E.) N. Moriani
                                        (L.) F. Gnone (A.)

Florence      Pergola      Apr. 18, 1876 A. Ortolani-Tiberini (E.) S. Barton
                                        (S.) M. Tiberini (L.) E. Storti-
                                        Gaggi (A.) M. Mancinelli cond. F.
                                        Ricci dir.

Livorno       Rossini      Jan. 31, 1853 G. Sikorska-Moriani (E.) G. Bregazzi
                                        (S.) N. Moriani (L.) F. Giorgi (A.)

Milan         Carcano      Apr. 26, 1847 G. Sikorska-Moriani (E.) Bertucci
                                        (S.) N. Moriani (L.) Morino (A.) A.
                                        Mariani cond.

Udine                      Oct.?    1878 C. Castelli (E.) F. Pozzo (L.)

Venice        Apollo       Nov.     1846 G. Sikorska-Moriani (E.) R. Lucchini
                                        (S.) N. Moriani (L.) G. Zucchini
                                        (A.)

Verona        Filarmonico  Jan. 16, 1847 E. Garcia (E.) L. Abbadia (S.) D.
                                        Conti (L.) G. Zucconi (A.)

              Ristori      Nov.     1878 C. Castelli (E.) Chiappa (S.) F.
                                        Pozzo (L.) L. Borgioli (A.)

POLAND
Warsaw       Wielki     Aug.  9, 1851 M. Sulzer (E.) H. Sulzer (S.) J.
                                      Dobrski (L.) M. Assoni (A.)

PORTUGAL
Lisbon       Sao Carlos May  13, 1855 M. Sulzer (E.) H. Sulzer (S.) B.
                                      Belart (L.) A. M. Celestino (A.)

Oporto       Sao Joao   Mar.     1856

RUSSIA
St.          Imperial   Dec. 23, 1864 E. Fioretti (E.) M. Bernardi (S.) A.
Petersburg                            Giuglini (L.) F. Graziani (A.) E.
                                      Baveri cond.

SPAIN
Madrid       De la Cruz Jan. 25, 1845 A. Tirelli (E.) J. Chimeno (S.) N.
                                      Moriani (L.)

             Mar. 21, 1846 G. Sikorska-Moriani (E.) J. Chimeno
                                      (S.) N. Moriani (L.)


5. CORRADO DI ALTAMURA-*Dramma lirico* in a prologue and two acts
Milan-Teatro alla Scala-Nov. 16, 1841
Libretto by Giacomo Sacchèro

Delizia (D.)                         Luigia Abbadia sop.
Guiscardo Bonello (G.)               Marietta Brambilla mez.
Roggero (R.)                         Carlo Guasco ten.
Corrado d'Altamura (C.)              Felice Varesi bar.
Margarita                   Felicità Baillou-Hilaret sec.
Isabella                             Teresa Ruggeri sop.
Il Marchese Albarosa                 Napoleone Marconi ten.
Giffredo                             Gaetano Rossi bass

Conductor                            Eugenio Cavallini
Director                             Federico Ricci

OTHER PRODUCTIONS

ARGENTINA
Buenos Aires Colón      May 12, 1860 A. De la Grange (D.) A. Casaloni
                                      (G.) L. Lelmi (R.) G. Cima (C.)

AUSTRIA
Vienna       Kärntnertor Apr. 21, 1842 O. Malvani (D.) M. Brambilla (G.) N.
                                      Moriani (R.) F. Varesi (C.) H. Proch
                                      cond.

             Apr. 17, 1843 P. Viardot (D.) M. Alboni (G.) C.
                                      Guasco (R.) F. Varesi (C.)

CHILE
Santiago     Principal  Sep. 10, 1850 T. Rossi (D.) C. Pantanelli (G.) A.
                                      Zambaiti (R.) G. Bastoggi (R.) R.
                                      Pantanelli cond.

CUBA
Havana       Tacon      Feb.  9, 1847 F. Tedesco (D.) S. Marini-Testa (G.)
                                      N. Perelli (R.) L. Arditi cond.

Nov. 18, 1847 F. Tedesco (D.) L. Perozzi (G.) G.
Severi (R.) L. Arditi cond.

Jan. 15, 1861 I. Natali (D.) F. ,Natali-Testa (G.)
E. Pancani (R.) F. Cresci (C.) L.
Gottschalk cond.

CZECHOSLOVAKIA
Olmutz                              1845

DENMARK
Copenhagen      Royal       Nov. 28, 1845 T. Tavola (D.) E. Bendini (G.) C.
Pagliani (R.) V. Piberi (C.) P. Spe-
rati cond.

FRANCE
Paris           Italien     Mar. 15, 1844 G. Grisi (D.) M. Brambilla (G.)
Mario (R.) G. Ronconi (C.) T. Til-
mant cond.

Feb. 8, 1845 G. Grisi (D.) M. Brambilla (G.)
Mario (R.) G. Ronconi (C.) T. Til-
mant cond.

GREAT BRITAIN
London          Her         Aug. 10, 1844 G. Grisi (D.) Favanti (G.) Mario
Majesty's                  (R.) L. Fornasari (C.) M. Costa
cond.

GREECE
Athens          Royal       Autumn   1855 D. Svazzo (D.) Mazza (G.) M. Neri
(R.)

HUNGARY
Budapest        Stadt       Aug. 26, 1844 (in Ger.)

ITALY
Alessandria     Municipale  Oct. 20, 1842 A. De Rieux (D.) Costa (G.) R. Monti
(R.) L. Corradi-Setti (C.)

Sep.     1847 R. Gariboldi-Bassi (D.) C. Imoda
(G.) D. Mecksa (R.) G. Donelli (C.)

Ancona          Muse        Dec. 26, 1862 L. Zacconi (D.) C. Bennini (G.) A.
Pozzolini (R.) F. Bonetti (C.)

Bergamo         Riccardi    Sep. 6, 1842 E. Frezzolini (D.) C. Griffini (G.)
L. Salvi (R.) R. Ferlotti (C.) M.
Bonesi cond.

Cagliari        Civico      Oct. 23, 1858 T. Alvisi (D.) C. Alberti (G.) P.
Samat (R.) F. Ceccarelli (C.)

Casal-          Sociale     Jan. 25, 1854 A. Botta (D.) Farré (G.) Bandinelli
monferrato                 (R.) Castelli (C.)

Crema           Sociale     Mar.     1870 Panzetti (D.)

Cuneo           Sociale     Carn. 1846-47 M. Zagnoli (D.) Z. Sbriscia (G.) L.
Bottagisi (R.) Pellegrini (C.)

Ferrara         Comunale    Jan.?    1849 R. Mori-Spallazzi (D.) G. Gamboggi
(R.) A. Carapia (C.)

| | | | | |
|---|---|---|---|---|
| Florence | Pergola | Autumn | 1848 | E. Goggi (D.) G. Pozzolini (R.) R. Ferlotti (C.) |
| | | Spring | 1849 | |
| Genoa | Carlo Felice | Apr. 16, | 1842 | F. Goldberg (D.) L. Olivieri (G.) E. Musich (R.) P. Ambrosini (C.) G. Serra cond. |
| | | Feb. 2, | 1862 | E. Poinsot (D.) G. Chiari (G.) E. Armandi (R.) F. Pandolfini (C.) |
| Lucca | Pantera | Feb. | 1870 | Fabris (D.) Ronzi (R.) |
| Mantua | Sociale | Spring | 1846 | E. Dielitz/R. Gariboldi-Bassi (D.) E. Baldanza (R.) |
| Milan | La Scala | Sep. 22, | 1842 | L. Abbadia (D.) E. Bendini (G.) C. Guasco (R.) R. Ferlotti (C.) |
| | Canobbiana | Sep. 15, | 1855 | A. Orecchia (D.) R. Bertolini (R.) E. Delle Sedie (C.) |
| Modena | Comunale | Autumn | 1843 | A. De la Grange (D.) A. Bothe (G.) G. Fodor (R.) A. De Bassini (C.) A. Sighicelli cond. |
| Naples | San Carlo | Oct. 4, | 1850 | K. Evers (D.) C. Croci (G.) E. Baldanza (R.) A. De Bassini (C.) A. Farelli cond. |
| Padua | Concordi | Carn. | 1845-46 | R. Gariboldi-Bassi (D.) C. Imoda (G.) G. Pardini (R.) R. Dal Vivo (C.) |
| Palermo | Carolino | Mar. 7, | 1846 | T. Tavola (D.) A. Orlandi (G.) L. Bonfigli (R.) P. Raimondi cond. |
| Parma | Regio | Apr. 13, | 1857 | M. De Gianni-Vivez (D.) P. Corvetti (G.) V. Sarti (R.) G. B. Bencich (C.) G. Rossi cond. |
| Pavia | Condominio | Dec. 26, | 1843 | C. Griffini (D.) C. Brambilla (G.) G. Ricci (R.) G. Mancusi (C.) |
| Piacenza | Municipale | Carn. | 1843-44 | T. Tavola (D.) A. Fouché (G.) A. Balestracci (R.) G. C. Casanova (C.) G. Jona cond. |
| Ravenna | Comunitativo | May 27, | 1846 | A. Masenza (D.) S. Lussanti (G.) V. Ferrari-Stella (R.) G. Fiori (C.) G. Nostini cond. |
| Rome | Valle | Sep. | 1842 | L. Schieroni-Nulli (D.) Columberti (G.) E. Musich (R.) F. Varesi (C.) |
| Saluzzo | | Jan. | 1854 | A. Dall'Argine (D.) G. Lusagnani-Assoni (G.) G. Mora (R.) A. Grandi (C.) |
| Treviso | Onigo | Autumn | 1847 | L. Ponti dall'Armi (D.) M. Brambilla (G.) E. Caggiati (R.) L. Rinaldini (C.) |

| | | | |
|---|---|---|---|
| Trieste | Grande | Oct. 22, 1842 | E. Frezzolini (D.) L. Salvi (R.) L. Fornasari (C.) A. Scaramelli cond. |
| | | Carn. 1847-48 | L. Ponti dall'Armi (D.) L. Graziani (R.) G. Fiori (C.) G. A. Scaramelli cond. |
| Turin | Regio | Apr. 12, 1842 | S. Loewe (D.) M. Shaw (G.) L. Salvi (R.) F. Colini (C.) |
| | Carignano | Oct. 1862 | P. Colson (D.) G. Zacometti (R.) C. Boccolini (C.) |
| Varese | Sociale | Oct. 1, 1844 | C. Imoda (D.) Corridori (G.) C. Della Longa (R.) Pignoli (C.) |
| Venice | La Fenice | Mar. 12, 1842 | F. Goldberg (D.) I. Bertrand (G.) N. Moriani (R.) F. Coletti (C.) |
| | San Benedetto | Oct. 25, 1842 | |
| Verona | Filarmonico | Autumn 1845 | C. Griffini (D.) A. Tantalora (G.) A. Brunacci (R.) G. B. Bencich (C.) |
| MALTA La Valletta | Manoel | Mar.? 1851 | A. Borghi-Mamo (G.) A. Rossi (C.) |
| NETHERLANDS Amsterdam | Italien | Jan. 25, 1845 | T. Questa (D.) G. Perelli (G.) L. Mei (R.) G. B. Bencich (C.) C. Pe-drotti cond. |
| PORTUGAL Lisbon | Sao Carlos | Feb. 2, 1846 | V. Grimoldi (D.) L. Persolli (G.) G. Severi (R.) L. Salandri (C.) A. L. Miró cond. |
| ROMANIA Bucharest | Nacional | Mar. 1, 1851 | R. Olivieri (D.) C. Parodi (G.) E. Rossi-Guerra (R.) G. Marini (C.) |
| RUSSIA Odessa | Municipal | July 1854 | F. Gordosa (D.) E. Schiapié (G.) |
| SPAIN Barcelona | Principal | May 20, 1843 | E. Goggi (D.) J. Gomez (G.) G. B. Verger (R.) M. Alberti (C.) |
| | | Sep. 18, 1844 | E. Goggi (D.) L. Viale (G.) G. B. Verger (R.) A. Superchi (C.) |
| | Liceo | Nov. 9, 1851 | L. Abbadia (D.) E. Baldanza (R.) To-nelli (C.) |
| La Corugna | Principal | May 2, 1847 | T. Pozzi (D.) Miró (R.) Lambertini (C.) |
| Madrid | Circo | May 24, 1845 | G. Ronconi (D.) Pardini (G.) G. Bet-tini (R.) G. Ronconi (C.) |
| Seville | San Fernando | Spring 1848 | Grimoldi (D.) G. Mancusi (C.) |

TURKEY
Constan-      Naum       Autumn    1849  L. Abbadia (D.)   C. Negrini  (R.) G.
tinople                                  B. Bencich (C.)  A. Mariani cond.

              Nov.    1863  L. Tencajoli (D.)  L. Soroldini (G.)
                            G. Zacometti (R.)  P. Baraldi (C.)

UNITED STATES
Boston        Athenaeum   Oct.  1, 1847  F. Tedesco (D.)  S. Marini-Testa (G.)
                                         L. Arditi cond.

6. VALLOMBRA-*Dramma lirico* in two acts
Milan-Teatro alla Scala-Dec. 26, 1842
Libretto by Giacomo Sacchèro

Vallombra                               Erminia Frezzolini sop.
Gonzalvo                                  Carlo Guasco ten.
Mudarra                                 Achille De Bassini bar.
Gualdo                                    Secondo Torre bass
Il Conte di Gandi                       Napoleone Marconi ten.

Conductor                               Eugenio Cavallini
Director                                Federico Ricci

7. ISABELLA DE'MEDICI-*Opera seria* in three acts
Trieste-Teatro Grande-Mar. 3, 1845
Libretto by Antonio Gazzoletti

Isabella de'Medici                      Teresa De Giuli-Borsi sop.
Adele                                     Virginia Viola sop.
Gualtiero                               Carmelo Della Longa ten.
Paolo Giordano Orsini                     Ignazio Marini bass
Cosimo Ranieri                          Stanislao Demi bass
Lucrezia di Frescobaldi                 Teresa Pusterla sop.
Giovanni Altoviti                         Carlo Crosa ten.
Luca del Prato                          Francesco Corazzari ten.
Ristoro Machiavelli                     Vincenzo Caspani bass

Conductor                               Paolo Coronini
Director                                Federico Ricci

8. ESTELLA-*Melodramma serio* in three acts
Milan-Teatro alla Scala-Feb. 21, 1846
Libretto by Francesco Maria Piave

| | |
|---|---|
| Estella (E.) | Caterina Hayes sop. |
| Don Diego Tellez (D.) | Giuseppe Sinico ten. |
| Don Ferdinando (F.) | Achille de Bassini bar. |
| Don Enrico Paceco (P.) | Giuseppe Federico Beneventano bar. |
| Francesca | Teresa Ruggeri mez. |
| Benedetto | Napoleone Marconi ten. |
| Lelio | Giuseppe Lodi bass |
| | |
| Conductor | Eugenio Cavallini |
| Director | Federico Ricci |

OTHER PRODUCTIONS

AUSTRIA
Vienna        Kärntnertor  Apr. 23, 1847 C. Hayes (E.) R. Mirate (D.) F.
                                         Colini (F.)

BRAZIL
Rio de        Lirico       Aug. 11, 1862 M. De Gianni Vivez (E.) A. Gentili
  Janeiro      Fluminense                 (D.) F. Briani (F.) Fernando (P.)

DENMARK
Copenhagen    Royal        Apr. 15, 1849 G. Pecorini (E.) A. Castellan (D.)
                                         G. Guicciardi (F.) S. Scappini (P.)
                                         P. Sperati cond.

ITALY
Genoa         Carlo        May  8, 1848 T. De Giuli-Borsi (E.) G. Roppa (D.)
              Felice                    F. Gnone (F.) L. Bianchi (P.)

Venice        San          Apr. 1, 1850 G. Pecorini (E.) G. Fraschini (D.)
              Benedetto                  L. Rinaldini (F.)


9. GRISELDA-*Opera seria* in four acts
Venice-Teatro La Fenice-Mar. 13, 1847
Libretto by Francesco Maria Piave

| | |
|---|---|
| Griselda (G.) | Caterina Hayes sop. |
| Persival (P.) | Luigi Ferretti ten. |
| Cedrico (C.) | Cesare Badiali bar. |
| Tristano (T.) | Enrico Crivelli bar. |
| Ginevra | Marietta Zambelli sop. |
| Arturo | Angelo Zuliani ten. |
| Lancellotto | Carlo Crosa ten. |
| | |
| Conductor | Gaetano Mares |
| Director | Federico Ricci |

OTHER PRODUCTIONS

ITALY
Rovigo        Sociale      Oct. 31, 1847 S. Cruvelli (G.) A. Palma (P.) G.
                                         Zucchini (C.) G. Torre (T.) D. Tosa-
                                         rini cond.

SPAIN
Barcelona     Principal    Dec. 19, 1848 Rovelli (G.) E. Tamberlick (P.) R.
                                      Pizzigati (C.) V. Sermattei (T.)

10. I DUE RITRATTI-*Opera comica* in two acts
Venice-Teatro San Benedetto-Nov. 21, 1850
Libretto by Federico Ricci

| | |
|---|---|
| Giulietta | Josephine Gassier sop. |
| Visconte Dumont | Antonio Giuglini ten. |
| Giorgio | Pietro Gorin bar. |
| Martino | Giovanni Zucchini bass |
| Matilde | |
| Rosina | |
| Ambrogio | |

Conductor
Director                                               Federico Ricci

11. IL MARITO E L'AMANTE-*Melodramma comico* in three acts
Vienna-Kärntnertor Theater-June 9, 1852
Libretto by Gaetano Rossi

| | |
|---|---|
| Adele (A.) | Giuseppina Medori sop. |
| Lisetta (L.) | Emilie De Meric mez. |
| Ernesto (E.) | Gaetano Fraschini ten. |
| Belmont (B.) | Achille De Bassini bar. |
| Frontino (F.) | Raffaele Scalese buf. |
| Cloe | Not named |
| Motus | |

OTHER PRODUCTIONS

AUSTRIA
Vienna        Kärntnertor Apr. 24, 1853 G. Medori (A.) E. De Meric (L.) G.
                                        Fraschini (E.) A. De Bassini (B.) R.
                                        Scalese (F.)

FRANCE
Paris         Athénée      Feb. 15, 1872 (in Fr.)

RUSSIA
St.           Imperial     Dec. 2, 1853 G. Medori (A.) E. De Meric (L.) E.
Petersburg                             Tamberlick (E.) A. De Bassini (B.)
                                        L. Lablache (F.) E. Baveri cond.

12. IL PANIERE D'AMORE-*Melodramma comico* in two acts
Vienna-Kärntnertor Theater-May 25, 1853
Libretto by Gaetano Rossi

| | |
|---|---|
| Lucrezia | Giuseppina Medori sop. |
| Isabella | Emilie De Meric mez. |
| Giulio | Gaetano Fraschini ten. |
| Beppo | Achille De Bassini bar. |
| Dottore Tiritofolo | Raffaele Scalese buf. |
| Barnabò | Stanislao Demi bass |

13. UNE FOLIE A ROME-*Opéra bouffe* in three acts
Paris-Théâtre des Fantaisies Parisiennes-Jan. 30, 1869
Libretto by Federico Ricci, translated into French by Victor Wilder

| | |
|---|---|
| Laurence (L.) | Marie Marimon sop. |
| Elvire (E.) | Persini mez. |
| Ninette (N.) | Decroix mez. |
| Maurice (M.) | Leopold Ketten ten. |
| Fabien (F.) | Arsandaux bar. |
| Don Pacifique (P.) | Soto buf. |
| Beppo | |

| | |
|---|---|
| Conductor | Constantin |

Italian version
Genoa-Teatro Nazionale-Apr. 20, 1870

| | |
|---|---|
| Carina (C.) | Felicita Pernini sop. |
| Elisa (E.) | Teresina Pozzi mez. |
| Giannetta (G.) | Adele Berio mez. |
| Riccardo (R.) | Giacomo Piazza ten. |
| Dottore (D.) | Cesare Airoldi bar. |
| Ambrogio (A.) | Alessandro Bottero buf. |
| Enrico | Luigi Torre bass |

OTHER PRODUCTIONS

BELGIUM
| | | | |
|---|---|---|---|
| Antwerp | Royal | Feb. 10, 1870 | M. Hasselmans (L.) Servatius (E.) Bertin (N.) Fabre (M.) Guillemot (F.) (in Fr.) |
| Brussels | La Monnaie | Feb. 11, 1870 | J. Devries (L.) Peschard (E.) Froment (M.) Troy (D.) (in Fr.) |

FRANCE
| | | | |
|---|---|---|---|
| Lyon | Grand | Mar. 17, 1869 | |
| Paris | Athenée | Mar.? 1870 | M. Marimon (L.) |

ITALY
| | | | |
|---|---|---|---|
| Cremona | | Spring 1872 | F. Pernini (C.) G. Petrovich (R.) Migmiara (A.) Bignami cond. |
| Florence | Pergola | Feb. 2, 1871 | F. Pernini (C.) O. Papini (G.) Braccialini (E.) G. Piazza (R.) A. Souvestre (D.) G. Marchisio (A.) |

| Genoa | Nazionale | Mar. 19, 1871 | F. Pernini (C.) T. Pozzi (E.) P. Gaggiotti (G.) T. Parasini (R.) P. Cabella (D.) A. Bottero (A.) E. Bernardi cond. |
| Messina | Vittorio Emanuele | Feb. 5, 1875 | A. Bottero (A.) |
| Milan | Politeama | Aug. 22? 1872 | F. Pernini (C.) Luini (E.) T. Parasini (R.) Baldassari (D.) A. Bottero (A.) |
| Trieste | Comunale | Feb. 26, 1875 | M. Dérivis (C.) T. Parasini (R.) E. Borelli (D.) A. Bottero (A.) E. Bernardi cond. |
| Turin | Carignano | Oct. 22, 1870 | F. Pernini (C.) T. Parasini (R.) Lenghi (D.) A. Bottero (A.) Bertuzzi cond. |
| Venice | Comploy | June 1870 | F. Pernini (C.) T. Pozzi (E.) Zamboni (G.) G. Piazza (R.) C. Airoldi (D.) A. Bottero (A.) |
| SWITZERLAND Geneva | Grand | Jan. 20, 1870 | Arnaud (L.) Leclerc (E.) Arnaud (M.) Reynal (F.) Feitlinger (P.) |

14. LE DOCTEUR ROSE-*Opéra bouffe* in three acts
Paris-Bouffes Parisiens-Feb. 10, 1872
Libretto by Emile de Najac

| Gardinella | Fonti sop. |
| Tonine | Peyron sop. |
| Zéroli | Peschard mez. |
| Coronini | Berthelier |
| Capsulo | Désiré |
| Giacomine | Bonelli |

## GIUSEPPE VERDI

1. OBERTO, CONTE DI SAN BONIFACIO-*Dramma* in two acts
Milan-Teatro alla Scala-Nov. 17, 1839
Libretto by Antonio Piazza and Temistocle Solera

| | |
|---|---|
| Leonora (L.) | Antonietta Rainieri-Marini sop. |
| Cuniza (C.) | Mary Shaw mez. |
| Riccardo (R.) | Lorenzo Salvi ten. |
| Oberto (O.) | Ignazio Marini bass |
| Imelda | Marietta Sacchi mez. |

Conductor                                              Eugenio Cavallini
Director                         Giacomo Panizza, Giuseppe Verdi

OTHER PRODUCTIONS-NINETEENTH CENTURY

ITALY

| Genoa | Carlo Felice | Jan. 9, 1841 | A. Rainieri-Marini (L.) C. Ferlotti (C.) C. Lonati (R.) R. Ferlotti (O.) G. Serra cond. G. Verdi dir. |
|---|---|---|---|
| Milan[35] | La Scala | Oct. 17, 1840 | A. Rainieri-Marini (L.) L. Abbadia (C.) L. Salvi (R.) R. Ferlotti (O.) E. Cavallini cond. G. Verdi dir. |
| Naples | San Carlo | June 2, 1841 | A. Rainieri-Marini (L.) E. Buccini (C.) G. Fraschini (R.) F. Colini (O.) A. Farelli cond. |
| Turin | Regio | Jan. 11, 1840 | A. Rainieri-Marini (L.) L. Abbadia (C.) L. Salvi (R.) C. Badiali (O.) G. B. Polledro cond. |

JUGOSLAVIA

| Zara | Nobile | Dec. 1, 1847 | L. Ruggero-Antonioli (L.) A. Ruggero (C.) L. Guglielmini (R.) |
|---|---|---|---|

MALTA

| La Valletta | Manuel | Mar. 1860 | T. Cotta-Morandini (L.) G. Piccinnini (R.) T. Sterbini (O.) |
|---|---|---|---|

SPAIN

| Barcelona | Principal | Feb. 1, 1842 | M. Palazzesi (L.) R. Gariboldi-Bassi (C.) J. Gomez (R.) I. Marini (O.) |
|---|---|---|---|

OTHER PRODUCTIONS-1900-1945[36]

ARGENTINA

| Buenos Aires | Colón | Nov. 17, 1939 | H. Spani (L.) S. César (C.) D. Mastronardi (R.) M. Urízar (O.) A. De Angelis cond. |
|---|---|---|---|

ITALY

| Busseto | Verdi | July 30, 1939 | G. Di Giulio (L.) I. Colasanti (C.) G. Momo (R.) A. Righetti (O.) A. Lucon cond. |
|---|---|---|---|

---

35. Loewenberg lists a production in Milan on Nov. 17, 1889. This could not be confirmed by an examination of the Milanese theatrical newspapers for the period.

36. Loewenberg lists a production in Chicago in October 1903. This could not be confirmed by an examination of the Chicago newspapers for that month.

Parma            Regio        Sep.  6, 1913 R. Raisa (L.) N. Frascani (C.) I.
                                            Cristalli (R.) A. Masini-Pieralli
                                            (O.) C. Campanini cond.

OTHER PRODUCTIONS-POST-WORLD WAR II

GREAT BRITAIN
London           Collegiate   Feb. 17, 1982 H. Walker (L.) M. King (C.) A. Roden
                                            (R.) N. Welsby (O.) C. Fifield cond.

ITALY
Bologna          Comunale     Jan. 13, 1977 A. Gulin/F. Como (L.) V. Cortez/A.
                                            Stamenova (C.) U. Grilli/G. Cianella
                                            (R.) S. Estes/F. Furlanetto (O.) Z.
                                            Pesko cond.

                              Jan. 23, 1979 M. L. Cioni (L.) S. Mazzieri (C.) U.
                                            Grilli (R.) F. Furlanetto (O.) Z.
                                            Pesko cond.

Milan            La Scala     Feb. 13, 1951 M. Caniglia (L.) E. Stignani (C.) G.
                                            Poggi (R.) T. Pasero/G. Modesti (O.)
                                            F. Capuana cond.

Modena           Municipale   Jan. 15, 1978 A. Gulin (L.) S. Mazzieri (C.) U.
                                            Grilli (R.) S. Estes (O.) Z. Pesko
                                            cond.

Parma            Regio        Jan. 25, 1978 A. Gulin (L.) V. Cortez/S. Mazzieri
                                            (C.) U. Grilli (R.) S. Estes/F.
                                            Furlanetto (O.) Z. Pesko cond.

Reggio Emilia Municipale      Apr.  8, 1978 A. Gulin (L.) U. Grilli (R.) Z.
                                            Pesko cond.

Turin            Sala RAI     Apr. 26, 1951 M. Vitale (L.) E. Nicolai (C.) G.
                                            Bonelli (R.) G. Modesti (O.) A. Si-
                                            monetto cond.

UNITED STATES
New York         Amato Op.    Feb. 18, 1978 P. De Lara (L.) L. A. Dunton (C.) V.
                                            Titone (R.) M. Frescoln (O.) A.
                                            Amato cond.

San Diego        Opera        Mar.  9, 1985 R. Gettler (L.) S. Marsee (C.) C.
                                            Montane (R.) F. Furlanetto (O.) K.
                                            Bakels cond.

2. UN GIORNO DI REGNO-*Melodramma giocosa* in two acts
Milan-Teatro alla Scala-Sep. 5, 1840
Libretto by Felice Romani

| | |
|---|---|
| Marchesa del Poggio (M.) | Antonietta Rainieri-Marini sop. |
| Giulietta (G.) | Luigia Abbadia mez. |
| Edoardo (E.) | Lorenzo Salvi ten. |
| Cavaliere di Belfiore  (B.) | Raffaele Ferlotti bar. |
| Signor La Rocca (T.) | Agostino Rovere buf. |
| Barone di Kelbar (K.) | Raffaele Scalese buf. |
| Conte Ivrea | Giuseppe Vaschetti ten. |
| Delmonte | Napoleone Marconi ten. |

Conductor                                         Eugenio Cavallini
Director           Giacomo Panizza and/or Giuseppe Verdi

OTHER PRODUCTIONS-NINETEENTH CENTURY

ITALY

| Naples | Nuovo | June 11, 1859 | E. De Vrient (M.) L. Zacconi (G.) E. Concordia (E.) I. Canedi (B.) A. Zoboli (T.) P. Savoja (K.) |
|---|---|---|---|
| Rome | Valle | Feb. 9, 1846 | C. Marziali (M.) E. Cherubini (G.) L. Graziani (E.) G. Bastoggi (B.) C. Cambiaggio (K.) Viviani cond. |
| Venice | San Benedetto | Oct. 11, 1845 | C. Marziali (M.) E. Cherubini (G.) L. Graziani (E.) L. Ferrario (B.) C. Cambiaggio (K.) |

OTHER PRODUCTIONS-POST-WORLD WAR II

AUSTRIA

| Bregenz | Korn | July 19, 1974 | M. Rinaldi (M.) E. Zilio (G.) V. Terranova (E.) D. Trimarchi (B.) E. Fissore (T.) G. Taddei (K.) P. Bellugi cond. |
|---|---|---|---|

FRANCE

| Marseille | Chateau de Borely | July 21, 1985 | K. Michalowska (M.) D. Palade (G.) C. Papy (E.) A. Salvadori (B.) L. Masson (T.) J. Brun (K.) A. Cavallaro cond. |
|---|---|---|---|

GREAT BRITAIN

| London | St. Pancras Town Hall | Mar. 21, 1961 | B. Jonic (M.) C. Jolly (G.) A. Hallett (E.) J. Hauxvell (B.) J. Atkins (T.) E. Garrett (K.) H. Ucko cond. |
|---|---|---|---|

ITALY

| Genoa | Politeama | Sep. 12, 1980 | D. Dessi (M.) F. Mattiucci (G.) B. Trotta (E.) S. Alaimo (B.) A. Corbelli (T.) O. Mori (K.) F. M. Martini cond. |
|---|---|---|---|
| Milan | Sala RAI | Jan. 25, 1951 | L. Pagliughi (M.) L. Cozzi (G.) J. Oncina (E.) R. Capecchi (B.) C. Dalamangas (T.) S. Bruscantini (K.) A. Simonetto cond. |

Parma           Regio        Oct. 16, 1963 R. Righetti (M.)  B. M. Casoni (G.)
                                          U. Benelli (E.) G. Fioravanti (B.)
                                          P. Pedani (T.) P. Montarsolo (K.) A.
                                          Zedda cond.

POLAND
Wroclaw                      May  24, 1987 J. Monarcha (B.) A. Wicharek cond.[37]

UNITED STATES
New York        Town Hall    June 18, 1960 L. Caputo (M.) H. Feit (G.) W. Car-
                                          ringer (E.) J. Fiorito (B.) K. Cos-
                                          ta (T.) D. Rosenstein (K.) A. Amato
                                          cond. (in Eng.)

San Diego       Opera        June 20, 1981 A. Saunders (M.) S. Marsee (G.) B.
                                          Reed (E.) J. P. Raftery (B.) J. Bil-
                                          lings (T.) H. Foss (K.) C. Simmons
                                          cond. (in Eng.)

San Francisco   Pocket       June 11, 1989 M. Cope-Hart (M.) H. Axelson (G.) R.
                Opera                     Tate (E.) L. Venza (B.) M. Klebe
                                          (T.) W. Matthes (K.) (in Eng.)


3. NABUCODONOSOR (NABUCCO)-*Dramma lirico* in four parts
Milan-Teatro alla Scala-Mar. 9, 1842
Libretto by Temistocle Solera

Abigaille (A.)                              Giuseppina Strepponi sop.
Fenena (F.)                              Giovannina Bellinzaghi sop.
Ismaele (I.)                                Corrado Miraglia ten.
Nabucco (N.)                                 Giorgio Ronconi bar.
Zaccaria (Z.)                               Prosper Dérivis bass
Anna                                         Teresa Ruggeri sop.
Abdallo                                  Napoleone Marconi ten.
Il Gran Sacerdote                           Gaetano Rossi bass

Conductor                                   Eugenio Cavallini
Director                                     Giuseppe Verdi

OTHER PREMIERES-NINETEENTH CENTURY

ALGERIA
Algiers                      Summer    1845

ARGENTINA
Buenos Aires    Victoria     Aug. 23, 1850 L. Pretti (A.) M. Questa (F.) C.
                                          Rico (I.) J. M. Ramonda (N.) P.
                                          Franchi (Z.) J. V. Rivas cond.

                Ant. Colón   June 20, 1857 E. La Grua (A.)

---

[37]. This production was previously given at Oberhausen.

AUSTRALIA
Melbourne     Th. Royal      Sep.  1, 1860  G. Bianchi (A.) O. Hamilton (F.) E.
                                            Bianchi (I.) E. Coulon (N.) J. Gregg
                                            (Z.)

Sydney        Prince         June 16, 1860  G. Bianchi (A.) O. Hamilton (F.) E.
              of Wales                      Bianchi (l.) E. Coulon (N.) J. Gregg
                                            (Z.)

AUSTRIA
Graz          Stadt          Jan.  8, 1849  (in Ger.)

Linz          Landes         Oct. 31, 1851  (in Ger.)

Vienna        Kärntnertor    Apr.  4, 1843  T. De Giuli-Borsi (A.) F. Salvini-
                                            Donatelli (F.) G. Severi (I.) G.
                                            Ronconi (N.) P. Dérivis (Z.) G.
                                            Verdi dir. (in It.)

                             Jan. 22, 1848  W. von Hasseldt-Barth (A.) L. Lieb-
                                            hardt (F.) Brandes (I.) E. Leithner
                                            (N.) J. Draxler (Z.) (in Ger.)

BELGIUM
Antwerp       Royal          Sep. 21, 1851  V. Viola (A.) Bacci (I.) L. Finocchi
                                            (N.) G. C. Nerini (Z.) L. Di Cepeda
                                            cond. (in It.)

Brussels      Monnaie        Oct. 29, 1848  Julian van Gelder (A.) J. E. Massol
                                            (N.) (in Fr.)

              Cirque         Feb. 11, 1851  G. Medori (A.) G. Lucchesi (I.) F.
                                            Morelli-Ponti (N.) A. Zucconi (Z.)
                                            Felice Ricci cond. E. Muzio dir. (in
                                            It.)

BRAZIL
Rio de        Sao Pedro      Nov. 18, 1848  A. Candiani (A.) G. Sicuro (I.) F.
  Janeiro                                   Massiani (N.) C. Eckerlin (Z.)

Sao Paulo     Provisorio     July 24, 1875  E. Pezzoli (A.) St. Clair (F.) G.
                                            Limberti (I.) Barcena (N.) G. Miran-
                                            dola (Z.)

CHILE
Santiago      Republica      July  6, 1848  C. Pantanelli (A.) G. Bastoggi (N.)
                                            E. Lanza (Z.) R. Pantanelli cond.

              Municipal      Sep. 23, 1857  G. Bastoggi (N.) A. Lanzoni (Z.)

Valparaiso    Victoria       July 11, 1850  L. Micciarelli (A.) J. Ubaldi (I.)
                                            L. Cavedagni (N.) F. Leonardi (Z.)

COLOMBIA
Bogota        Teatro              1858

CUBA
Havana        Tacon          Dec.  4, 1847  F. Tedesco (A.) L. Perozzi (I.) L.
                                            Vita (N.) L. Arditi cond. G. Botte-
                                            sini dir.

Santiago      Principal      Summer   1851  L. Caranti-Vita (A.)

CZECHOSLOVAKIA
Bratislava              Dec.    1846

Prague          Ständiches  Mar.  5, 1849 (in Ger.)

                Provisional Dec.  7, 1868 (in Czech)

DENMARK
Copenhagen      Royal       Dec. 21, 1845 F. Leon (A.) L. Tavola (F.) C. Pag-
                                          liani (I.) E. Mazzotti (N.) N. Torre
                                          (Z.) P. Sperati cond.

FRANCE
Lyon            Grand       July 25, 1853 S. Vera-Lorini (A.) F. Gnone (N.) V.
                                          Caspani (Z.) (in It.)

Marseille       Grand       Aug.  2, 1845 V. Viola (A.) E. Luisia (N.) A. Ali-
                                          zard (Z.) (in It.)

Nice            Regio       Aug. 22, 1846 E. Mascarich (A.) A. Zocchi (I.) L.
                                          Walter (N.) G. B. Antonucci (Z.)

Paris           Italien     Oct. 16, 1845 T. Brambilla (A.) L. Corelli (I.) G.
                                          Ronconi (N.) P. Dérivis (Z.) T. Til-
                                          mant cond. (in It.)

GERMANY
Berlin          Königstädt- Sep. 21, 1844 L.  Schieroni-Nulli  (A.)  A.  Landi
                liches                    (I.) G. Ramonda (N.) G. Mitrovich
                                          (Z.) (in It.)

Cologne         Stadt       Dec.  3, 1847

Darmstadt       Hoftheater  Oct. 20, 1850

Dresden         Hoftheater  Mar. 16, 1851

Frankfurt       Stadt       Dec. 15, 1847 Kern (A.) Fehr (F.) Caspari (I.)
                                          Chrudimsky (N.) Conradi (Z.) (in
                                          Ger.)

Hamburg         Stadt       June 28, 1845 E. D'Alberti (A.) S. Benedetti (I.)
                                          E. Crivelli (N.) G. Mitrovich (Z.)
                                          (in It.)

                            Oct. 29, 1845 (in Ger.)

Hannover        Hofoper     Dec.  9, 1846 (in Ger.)

Leipzig         Stadt       Jan.  5, 1855 (in Ger.)

Mainz           Stadt       Sep. 16, 1847 Dressler-Pollert  (A.)  Rauch  (F.)
                                          Eitel (I.) Dupont (N.) Leser (Z.)
                                          (in Ger.)

Munich          Hoftheater  Oct.  5, 1852 Palm (A.) A. Kindermann (N.) (in
                                          Ger.)

Nürnberg        Stadt       Mar. 20, 1851 (in Ger.)

Stuttgart       Hoftheater  Sep. 27, 1844 (First time in German)

GREAT BRITAIN

London      Her       Mar.  3, 1846  G. Sanchioli (A.) A. Corbari (F.) L.
            Majesty's               Corelli (I.) L. Fornasari (N.) F.
                                      Botelli (Z.) M. Balfe cond.

            Covent    May  30, 1850  A. Castellan (A.) S. Vera-Lorini
            Garden               (F.) E. Tamberlick (I.) G. Ronconi
                                  (N.) J. Tagliafico (Z.) M. Costa
                                  cond.

GREECE

Athens      Royal     Dec.  6, 1851  E. Cominotti (A.) Garofalo (F.)
                                    Scardoni (I.) E. Antico (N.)

Corfu       San Giacomo Sep. 28, 1844  E. Ranzi (A.) C. Parodi (N.) G.
                                    Bianchi (Z.)

HUNGARY

Budapest    Deutsches  Aug. 26, 1846  E. Ercolani (A.) G. Paltrinieri (N.)
                                    G. Reina (Z.) (in It.)

            Nemzeti   Jan.  2, 1847  R. Schodel (A.) M. Füredi (N.) M.
            Szinház              Udvarhelyi (Z.) F. Erkel cond. (in
                                    Hung.)

INDONESIA

Batavia    T. Batavie June 20, 1870  M. Zenoni (A.) Verini (F.) P. Setra-
                                    gni (I.) L. Magnani (N.) E. Gasperi-
                                    ni (Z.)

ITALY

Alessandria Municipale Oct. 25, 1845  G. Strepponi (A.) N. Costantini (N.)

Ancona     Muse     June 14, 1844  T. De Giuli-Borsi (A.) A. Cignozzi
                                    (F.) G. Lucchesi (I.) C. Badiali
                                  (N.) C. O. Porto (Z.) G. C. Ferrari-
                                  ni cond.

Bari       Piccinni  Oct.    1859  C. Peccia (A.) V. Sabatini (I.) E.
                                    Antico (N.)

Bergamo    Sociale   Feb.  3, 1844  A. Gambardella (A.) C. Valtorta (F.)
                                    E. Cossetta (I.) L. Biacchi (N.) G.
                                  Maspes (Z.)

Bologna    Comunale  Oct.  7, 1843  G. Strepponi (A.) A. Ramaccini (F.)
                                    R. Dei (I.) C. Badiali (N.) L. Cali-
                                  iari (Z.) G. Manetti cond.

Brescia    Grande    July 30, 1843  T. De Giuli-Borsi (A.) A. Dall'Ar-
                                    gine (F.) G. Severi (I.) A. De
                                  Bassini (N.) L. Corradi-Setti (Z.)

Cagliari   Civico    Sep.  9, 1843  C. Lusignani (A.) C. Mugnai (I.) E.
                                    Mazzotti (N.)

Catania    Comunale  Nov. 12, 1849  M. Alberti (A.) L. Tonelli (F.) F.
                                  Gionfrida (N.) R. Fischetti Z.) M.
                                Pappalardo cond.

Chieti     San       Apr. 21, 1849  M. Alberti (A.) P. Finocchi (F.) G.
            Ferdinando         Bacci (I.) F. Coliva (N.) L. Finoc-
                                chi (Z.)

Cremona        Concordia      Dec. 26, 1843 G. Caspani (A.) T. Ricca (F.) S. Be-
                                            nedetti (I.) F. Gnone (N.) G. Mitro-
                                            vich (Z.)

Faenza         Comunale       June 13, 1843 D. Dérancourt (A.) A. Ramaccini (F.)
                                            G. Ramoni (I.) C. Badiali (N.) Peri
                                            (Z.) G. Manetti cond.

Fermo          Aquila         Aug. 14, 1844 C. Cuzzani (A.) M. Biondi (F.) R.
                                            Dei (I.) N. Costantini (N.) P. Toz-
                                            zoli (Z.) G. C. Ferrarini cond.

Ferrara        Comunale       Apr. 20, 1844 L. Schieroni-Nulli (A.) E. Manetti
                                            (F.) P. Zilioli (I.) L. Del Riccio
                                            (N.) L. Tabellini (Z.)

Fiume          Civico         Mar. 27, 1852 T. Rupnick (A.) E. Pellegrini (I.)
                                            E. Storti (N.) Mazza cond.

Florence       Pergola        Jan. 11, 1844 M. Barbieri-Nini (A.) A. Cignozzi
                                            (F.) E. Musich (I.) S. Ronconi (N.)
                                            G. Miral (Z.) L. M. Viviani cond.

Forli          Comunale       Apr.     1844 M. Barbieri-Nini (A.) A. Cignozzi
                                            (F.) G. Lucchesi (I.) S. Ronconi
                                            (N.) C. O. Porto (Z.) G. C. Ferrari-
                                            ni cond.

Genoa          Carlo          Apr. 15, 1843 S. Loewe (A.) E. Gamarra (F.) D.
               Felice                       Mecksa (I.) R. Ferlotti (N.) L. Ta-
                                            bellini (Z.) N. Uccelli cond.

Livorno        Rossini        Oct. 19, 1844 M. Gazzaniga (A.) F. Piombanti (F.)
                                            G. Lucchesi (I.) S. Ronconi (N.) G.
                                            Miral (Z.)

Lucca          Giglio         Aug. 10, 1844 T. De Giuli-Borsi (A.) M. Tizzoni
                                            (F.) G. Lucchesi (I.) A. De Bassini
                                            (N.) C. O. Porto (Z.)

Lugo           Rossini        Aug.     1852 L. Finetti-Batocchi (A.) A. Badula-
                                            chi (I.) F. Coliva (N.) P. Montaguti
                                            cond.

Mantua         Sociale        Dec. 26, 1843 T. Pinelli (A.) R. Mori-Spallazzi
                                            (F.) G. Severi (I.) N. Costantini
                                            (N.) G. Fiori (Z.) G. C. Ferrarini
                                            cond.

Messina        Munizione      Carn. 1848-49 C. Worska (A.) E. Sestini (F.) E.
                                            Irfré (I.) L. Biacchi (N.) R.
                                            Laterza (Z.)

Modena         Comunale       Dec. 26, 1843 A. De la Grange (A.) E. Carnio (F.)
                                            G. Fedor (I.) A. De Bassini (N.) L.
                                            Bianchi (Z.) A. Sighicelli cond.

Naples         San Carlo      Mar. 22, 1848 T. Brambilla (A.) C. Rambur (F.) C.
                                            Laudano (I.) R. Ferlotti (N.) F.
                                            Gionfrida (Z.) A. Farelli cond.

Padua          Nuovo          June 10, 1843 E. Hallez (A.) A. Tirelli (F.) E.
                                            Rossi-Guerra (I.) F. Colini (N.) A.
                                            Rodas (Z.)

Palermo | Carolino | Oct. 1, 1852 N. De Roissi (A.) C. Diodati (F.) P.
Mazza (I.) F. Colini (N.) C. Nanni
(Z.) A. Lo Casto cond.

Parma | Regio | Apr. 17, 1843 G. Strepponi (A.) M. Albizzati (F.)
E. Rossi-Guerra (I.) F. Colini (N.)
G. Miral (Z.) N. De Giovanni cond.
G. Verdi dir.

Piacenza | Municipale | May 13, 1843 L. Abbadia (A.) C. Imoda (F.) L. Mei
(I.) R. Colmenghi (N.) L. Bianchi
(Z.) G. Jona cond.

Pisa | Ravvivati | Dec. 26, 1844 C. Bertolini-Raffaelli (A.) F. Piom-
banti (F.) F. Cimino (I.) L. Salan-
dri (N.) G. Miral (Z.) L. Nicolai
cond.

Ravenna | Comuni- tativo | May 1, 1847 C. Ferrarini-Baschieri (A.) G. Gam-
boggi (I.) L. Montemerli (N.) M.
Ghirardini (Z.)

Reggio Emilia Comunale | | Dec. 27, 1845 A. Dall'Argine (A.) A. Errani (I.)
G. Fiori (N.) F. Dall'Asta (Z.) G.
Tebaldi cond.

Rome | Apollo | Feb. 9, 1843 F. Maray (A.) R. Olivieri (F.) P.
Gasparini (I.) F. Varesi (N.) P.
Balzar (Z.) F. Fioravanti cond.

Rovigo | Sociale | Oct. 19, 1844 G. Bortolotti (A.) M. Biondi (F.) R.
Dei (I.) N. Costantini (N.) A. Selva
(Z.) D. Tosarini cond.

Siena | Rinnovati | July 16, 1844 M. Barbieri-Nini (A.) F. Piombanti
(F.) F. Cimino (I.) L. Rinaldini
(N.) G. Miral (Z.)

Sinigaglia | La Fenice | July 17, 1844 G. Micciarelli-Sbriscia (A.) R. Oli-
vieri (F.) C. Mariani (I.) F. Colet-
ti (N.) P. Balzar (Z.) N. De Giovanni cond.

Spoleto | Nobile | Dec. 26, 1850 L. Evangelista (A.) G. Pasi (I.) M.
Severi (N.)

Treviso | Onigo | Oct. 28, 1843 M. Belloni (A.) E. Rossi-Guerra (I.)
L. Biacchi (N.) E. Santi (Z.)

Trieste | Grande | Jan. 11, 1843 L. Abbadia (A.) M. Tizzoni (F.) D.
Mecksa (I.) R. Ferlotti (N.) L. Ta-
bellini (Z.) G. A. Scaramelli cond.

Turin | Carignano | Aug. 20, 1843 L. Abbadia (A.) L. Alloardi (F.) D.
Mecksa (I.) E. Crivelli (N.) F. Rigo
(Z.)

Udine | Sociale | Aug. 1844 F. Gorin (N.)

Venice | La Fenice | Dec. 26, 1842 S. Loewe (A.) A. Granchi (F.) E.
Rossi-Guerra (I.) C. Badiali (N.) G.
Miral (Z.) G. Mares cond.

Verona      Filarmonico Mar.  4, 1846 C. Griffini (A.) F. Varesi (N.) F.
                                      Fonte (Z.)

Vicenza     Eretenio    Dec. 26, 1844 T. Tavola (A.) L. Tavola (F.) C.
                                      Miraglia (I.) L. Rigamonti (N.) A.
                                      Rodas (Z.)

JUGOSLAVIA
Ljubljana   Stanovskem  May   8, 1852 G. Casali-Campagna (A.) E. Pellegri-
                                      ni (I.) E. Storti (N.) E. Topai (Z.)

Zagreb      National    Oct.  1, 1878 E. Giunti-Barbera (A.) G. B. De Ne-
                                      gri (I.) J. Mirsky (N.) Kratochvil
                                      (Z.)

Zara        Nobile      Oct.?    1844 G. Sarasin (A.) A. Cosma (I.)

LATVIA
Riga        Municipal   Oct.     1858 (in Ger.)

MALTA
La Valletta Manoel      Oct.  5, 1844 C. Ferrarini Boschieri (A.) L. Del
                                      Riccio (N.) Anito (Z.)

MEXICO
Mexico City Nacional    Nov. 23, 1856 G. Casali-Campagna (A.) A. Garofali
                                      (F.) E. Bianchi (I.) A. Ottaviani
                                      (N.) E. Linari-Bellini (Z.) C. Fat-
                                      tori cond.

NETHERLANDS
Amsterdam   Italien     Oct. 26, 1844 L. Giordani (A.) G. B. Bencich (N.)

PERU
Lima        Principal   Nov. 18, 1849 L. Micciarelli (A.) L. Cavedagni
                                      (I.) P. Ferretti (N.) Guido (Z.) A.
                                      Neumann cond.

POLAND
Cracow      Imperial    Feb. 22, 1857

Lwov        Szarbek     Nov. 10, 1849 J. Casimir-Ney (A.) Hammermeister
                                      (F.) J. Erl (I.) Wack (N.) (in Ger.)

Warsaw      Wielki      Feb. 25, 1854 M. Spezia-Aldighieri (A.)

PORTUGAL
Lisbon      Sao Carlo   Oct. 29, 1843 J. Olivier (A.) E. Carmini (F.) A.
                                      Picasso (I.) V. Sermattei (N.) G. C.
                                      Casanova (Z.)

Oporto      Sao Joao    Apr. 18, 1844 J. Olivier (A.) A. Picasso (I.) V.
                                      Sermattei (N.) G. C. Casanova (Z.)

ROMANIA
Bucarest    Nacional    Oct.     1847 C. Griffini (A.) D. Marchelli (N.)
                                      P. Tozzoli (Z.)

Iasi        Teatrul     Nov.  2, 1851 L. Caradori (A.) L. Gavetti-Reggiani
                                      (F.) L. Capra (I.) G. Donelli (N.)
                                      P. Dérivis (Z.)

RUSSIA
Odessa      Municipal   Mar.     1847 I. Secci-Corsi (A.) G. Marini (N.)

St.              Imperial      Dec. 27, 1851  G. Medori (A.) E. Tamberlick (I.) G.
 Petersburg                                   Ronconi (N.) K. Formes (Z.) E. Bave-
                                              ri cond.

SPAIN
Barcelona        Principal     May   2, 1844  E. Goggi (A.) A. Superchi (N.) P.
                                              Novelli (Z.)

                 Liceo         May  24, 1851  T. De Giuli-Borsi (A.) G. Valli (N.)
                                              A. Rodas (Z.) J. B. Dalmau cond.

Cadiz            Principal     July     1844  A. Albertini (A.) E. Tamberlick (I.)
                                              V. Sermattei (N.)

Madrid           Circo         Oct. 10, 1844  I. Ober-Rossi (A.) E. Carrion (I.)
                                              G. Euzet (N.) L. Rossi cond.

                 Real          Jan. 27, 1853  F. Capuani (A.) A. Bettini (I.) F.
                                              Coletti (N.) G. Echeverria (Z.) J.
                                              Skoczdopole cond.

Seville          San           May      1846  C. Villò-Ramos  (A.) M. Assoni (N.)
                 Fernando                     Santarelli (Z.)

SWITZERLAND
Lugano           Sociale       Oct.     1852  Tatti (A.) Fracchia (F.) Mauri (I.)
                                              G. B. Righini (N.) Vecchi (Z.)

Zürich           Stadt         Nov. 26, 1851  (in Ger.)

TURKEY
Constan-                       Mar. 18, 1845  E. Cominotti (A.) A. Avignone (N.)
 tinople

UNITED STATES
Boston           Melodeon      June  4, 1848  T. Truffi-Benedetti (A.) S. Benedet-
                                              ti (I.) F. Beneventano (N.) S. Rossi
                                              (Z.)

New York         Astor Place Apr.  4, 1848    T. Truffi-Benedetti (A.) A. Patti-
                                              Strakosch (F.) F. Bailini (I.) F.
                                              Beneventano  (N.) S. Rossi (Z.) M.
                                              Rapetti cond.

San Francisco Metro-           Nov. 30, 1854  M. Bedei (A.) M. S. Voorhees (F.) C.
                politan                       Scola (I.) A. Lanzoni (N.) F. Leo-
                                              nardi (Z.)

URUGUAY
Montevideo       San Felipe    May 16, 1852   I. Edelvira (A.) T. Questa (F.) C.
                                              Rico (I.) F. Tati (N.) A. Chiodini
                                              (Z.)

                 Solis         Oct. 30, 1859  T. Bajetti (A.) G. Cima (N.) C.
                                              Castagneri cond.

VENEZUELA
Caracas          Teatro        Jan.  1, 1855  F. Dragone (N.)

                 Municipal     Jan. 15, 1882  A. Conti-Foroni (A.) I. De Anna (N.)
                                              R. D'Ottavi (Z.) F. Rachelle cond.

SELECTED PRODUCTIONS-1900-1945

ARGENTINA
Buenos Aires   Colón        June 25, 1914  C. Gagliardi (A.) G. Bertazzoli (F.)
                                           L. Botta (I.) C. Galeffi (N.) N. De
                                           Angelis (Z.) T. Serafin cond.

GERMANY
Berlin         Berliner     Apr. 4, 1935   (in Ger.)

Kassel         Staats       Dec. 25, 1939  (in Ger.)

Mannheim       National     Oct. 28, 1928  (in Ger.)

ITALY
Bari           Piccinni     Mar. 16, 1901  I. Paoli (A.) E. Mazzi (F.) A. Gnac-
                                           carini (N.) E. Borucchia (Z.) V.
                                           Lombardi cond.

               Petruzzelli  Mar. 9, 1920   T. Milanesi (A.) M. Zanella (F.) G.
                                           Bellantoni (N.) L. Ferroni (Z.) E.
                                           Mascheroni cond.

Florence       Verdi        Autumn  1913

               Comunale     Apr. 22, 1933  G. Cigna (A.) E. Stignani (F.) A.
                                           Dolci (I.) C. Galeffi (N.) T. Pasero
                                           (Z.) V. Gui cond. (The opening of
                                           the first Maggio Musicale Fiorenti-
                                           no)

Genoa          Paganini     Mar. 23, 1901  A. Antinori (A.) L. Garibaldi (F.)
                                           U. Pittarello (I.) G. Maggi (N.) L.
                                           Sabellico (Z.)

               Carlo        Feb. 6, 1915   C. Gagliardi (A.) I. Vannini (F.) A.
               Felice                      Tocchi (I.) C. Galeffi (N.) N. De
                                           Angelis (Z.) T. Serafin cond.

                            Mar. 2, 1937   C. Jacobo (A.) N. Giani (F.) A. Dol-
                                           ci (I.) B. Franci (N.) G. Vaghi (Z.)
                                           V. Gui cond.

Milan          La Scala     Oct. 1, 1913   C. Gagliardi (A.) L. Garibaldi (F.)
                                           S. Sabatano (I.) C. Galeffi (N.) N.
                                           De Angelis (Z.) L. Mugnone/Dell'Era
                                           cond.

                            Nov. 30, 1913  C. Gagliardi/M. Magagna Lopez (A.)
                                           L. Garibaldi (F.) S. Sabatano (I.)
                                           C. Galeffi (N.) N. De Angelis (Z.)

                            Dec. 26, 1933  G. Cigna (A.) E. Stignani (F.) G.
                                           Voyer (I.) C. Galeffi (N.) T. Pasero
                                           (Z.) V. Gui/Fornarini cond.

Naples         San Carlo    Dec. 14, 1911  J. Capella (A.) N. Lollini (F.) E.
                                           Casolari (I.) E. Faticanti (N.) J.
                                           Torres de Luna (Z.) L. Mugnone cond.

                            Dec. 26, 1936  C. Jacobo (A.) A. Buades/A. Toini
                                           (F.) A. Dolci (I.) B. Franci (N.) A.
                                           Righetti (Z.) A. Guarnieri/A. Sabino
                                           cond.

Padua        Verdi        Oct. 21? 1916 T. Burchi (A.) G. Bellantoni (N.) A.
                                       Masini-Pieralli (Z.)

Parma        Regio        Sep. 10, 1913 G. Russ (A.) N. Frascani (F.) R.
                                       Lassalle (I.) G. Bellantoni (N.) N.
                                       De Angelis (Z.) C. Campanini cond.

Pisa         Verdi        Dec.  1, 1919 G. Russ (A.) L. Ussa (I.) G. Bellan-
                                       toni (N.) G. Mansueto (Z.) A. Scia-
                                       voni cond.

Rome         Costanzi     May  16, 1900 A. Antinori (A.) A. Signoretti (F.)
                                       V. Laraspata (I.) V. Ardito (N.) E
                                       Borucchia (Z.) L. Mugnone cond.

                          June  1, 1916 C. Gagliardi (A.) F. Anitua (F.) S.
                                       Sabatano (I.) C. Galeffi (N.) N. De
                                       Angelis (Z.) L. Mugnone cond.

Trieste      Grande       Carn. 1912-13 M. Magagna Lopez (A.) E. Giunta (I.)
                                       G. Bellantoni (N.) P. Ludikar (Z.)
                                       R. Ferrari cond.

                          Carn. 1922-23 N. Borina (A.) E. Venturini (I.) E.
                                       De Franceschi (N.) A. Righetti (Z.)

Verona       Arena        July 24, 1938 C. Jacobo (A.) E. Stignani (F.) G.
                                       Voyer (I.) C. Tagliabue (N.) T. Pa-
                                       sero (Z.) F. Capuana cond.

NETHERLANDS
Amsterdam    Carré        Nov. 24, 1936 A. Vane (A.) R. Toniolo (F.) G. Voy-
                                       er (I.) C. Galeffi (N.) Melnick (Z.)

Den Haag                  Nov. 19, 1936 A. Vane (A.) R. Toniolo (F.) G. Voy-
                                       er (I.) C. Galeffi (N.) Melnick (Z.)

                          Oct. 28, 1937 C. Jacobo (A.) S. Costa Lo Giudice
                                       (I.) L. Montesanto (N.) A. Longhelli
                                       (Z.) De Vecchi cond.

Rotterdam    Groote       Nov. 25, 1936 A. Vane (A.) R. Toniolo (F.) G. Voy-
                                       er (I.) C. Galeffi (N.) Melnick (Z.)

PORTUGAL
Lisbon       Coliseo      May  23, 1903 R. De Vila (A.) E. Belli (F.) G.
                                       Tanci (I.) A. Modesti (N.) E. Can-
                                       dela (Z.) V. Petri cond.

SELECTED PRODUCTIONS-POST-WORLD WAR II

ARGENTINA
Buenos Aires Colón        Aug. 18, 1972 D. Mastilovic (A.) M. Colalillo (F.)
                                       C. MacNeil (N.) B. Giaiotti (Z.) F.
                                       Previtali cond.

                          Aug.  5, 1988 A. Negri (A.) E. Brex (F.) L. Simo-
                                       nella (I.) L. Miller (N.) N. Mene-
                                       ghetti (Z.) R. Censabella cond.

AUSTRALIA
Sydney                    May  15, 1971 E. Vaughan (E.)

Opera House Sep. 29, 1973 L. Koppel Winther/A. Fischer (A.) B.
                          Furlan (F.) J. Shaw (N.) M. Elder
                          cond.

BELGIUM
Ghent          Grand      Nov. 26, 1965 C. Ferrario (A.) J. Veerbeeck (I.)
                          G. Dubuc (N.)T. Wiersbicki (Z.) J.
                          Mestdagh cond.

BRAZIL
Rio de         Municipal  Aug. 29, 1969 L. Maragliano (A.) D. Lago (F.) P.
Janeiro                   Mirando Ferraro (I.) G. Guelfi (N.)
                          C. Cava (Z.) O. De Fabritiis cond.
                          (By the company of the Teatro San
                          Carlo, Naples)

               Mar. 25, 1982 A. Gomez (A.) E. Jankovic (F.) E.
                          Alvarez (I.) W. Janulako/F. Texeira
                          (N.) W. de Kanel (Z.) R. Gandolfi
                          cond.

CANADA
Edmonton       Opera      May 14, 1981 C. Deutekom (A.) A. Glass (F.) D.
                          Bailey (I.) R. Edwards (N.) D. Ka-
                          vrakos (Z.) I. Pallo cond.

Montreal       Expo 67    Oct. 9, 1967 E. Suliotis (A.) G. Lane (F.) G.
                          Cecchele (I.) G. Guelfi (N.) G. Ga-
                          vazzeni cond. (By the company of La
                          Scala, Milan)

Vancouver      Opera      Oct. 22, 1983 P. Tinsley (A.) D. Jeans (F.) T. Di
                          Paolis (I.) R. Edwards (N.) J. Tom-
                          linson (Z.) A. Campori cond.

Winnipeg                  Apr. 1981 C. Deutekom (A.) A. Glass (F.) D.
                          Bailey (I.) R. Edwards (N.) D. Ka-
                          vrakos (Z.) I. Pallo cond.

CHILE
Santiago       Municipal  July 14, 1981 C. Deutekom (A.) G. Araya (F.) B.
                          Maresca (I.) K. Nurmela (Z.) J.
                          Hines (Z.) M. Veltri cond.

CZECHOSLOVAKIA
Prague         Smetana    1965-1966 M. Subrtrová (A.) E. Zikmondová (F.)
                          A. Svorc (N.) Z. Kroupa (Z.) R. Va-
                          sata cond.

FRANCE
Bordeaux       Grand      Mar. 12, 1976 A. Gulin (A.) R. Penkova (F.) A.
                          Bevacque (I.) G. Mastromei (N.) B.
                          Giaiotti (Z.) M. Plasson cond.

Marseille      Opéra      Mar. 20, 1981 G. Dimitrova (A.) M. Manuguerra (N.)
                          B. Giaiotti (Z.)

Orange                    Aug. 7, 1982 G. Dimitrova (A.) B. Baglioni (F.)
                          N. Todisco (I.) S. Carroli (N.) B.
                          Giaiotti (Z.)

Paris          Opéra      June 30, 1979 G. Bumbry (A.) V. Cortez (F.) C.
                          Cossuta (I.) S. Milnes (N.) R.
                          Raimondi (Z.) N. Santi cond.

Palais      May   5, 1987  G. Dimitrova (A.) C. Cossuta (I.) P.
Omnisports                 Cappuccilli (N.) S. Elenkov (Z.) M.
                           Plasson cond.

Toulouse    Halle       Jan. 20, 1988  G. Dimitrova (A.) C. Ciurca (F.) G.
            aux Grains                 Boyagian/G. Zancanaro (N.) S. Elen-
                                       kov (Z.) S. Cardon cond.

GERMANY
Berlin      Städtische              1954  C. Goltz (A.) M. Rothmüller (N.)

            Deutsche     Feb.  8, 1979  A. Gulin (A.) M. Svetlov (I.) I.
                                        Wixell (N.) B. Rundgren (Z.) J.
                                        Lopez-Cobos cond.

                         Nov. 12, 1987

GREAT BRITAIN
Cardiff     Sophia       Oct.  7, 1952  R. Packer (A.) J. Stevens (F.) R.
            Gardens                     Jackson (N.) H. Alan (Z.) L. Quayle
                                        cond.[38]

Glasgow     Alhambra     Spring?  1959

Leeds       Grand        Mar. 31, 1980  M. Andrew (A.)

London      Sadler's     May   9, 1961  E. Vaughan (A.) G. Dowdle (F.) T.
            Wells                       Ferendinos (I.) B. Drake (N.) H.
                                        Alan (Z.) C. Groves cond.

            Drury Lane   Nov.  3, 1968  E. Suliotis (A.) L. A. Wyckoff (F.)
                                        S. Novoa (I.) P. Cappuccilli (N.) B.
                                        Christoff (Z.) M. Gusella cond.

            Covent       Mar. 27, 1972  E. Suliotis (A.) M. Pellegrini (F.)
            Garden                      E. Mauro (I.) P. Glossop (N.) D.
                                        Ward (Z.) C. Davis cond.

                         Jan.  2, 1973  E. Vaughan (A.) G. Knight (F.) E.
                                        Mauro (I.) P. Glossop (N.) R. Van
                                        Allen (Z.) E. Downes cond.

Manchester  Palace       Mar. 23, 1982  P. Tinsley (A.) R. Ferguson (I.) N.
                                        Bailey (N.) C. Timms cond. (in It.)

HUNGARY
Budapest    Margaret     Aug.  8, 1973  E. Suliotis (A.) A. M. Rota (F.) R.
            Island                      Merolla (I.) G. Taddei (N.) C. Cava
                                        (Z.) F. Previtali cond.

            Erkel        Dec. 18, 1987  M. Sudlik (A.) J. Németh (N.) K. Ko-
            Szinház                     váts (Z.) (in It.)

IRELAND
Dublin      Gaiety       Apr.?   1962

                         Apr.  4, 1972  O. Tanyeri (A.) L. Savoldi (I.) P.
                                        Farres (N.) G. Casarini (Z.) M.
                                        Braggio cond.

---

[38]. *Nabucco* was a repertory opera for the Welsh National Opera from 1952 to 1963, being given every season for these eleven years.

Apr.  8, 1986 R. Bakocevic (A.) L. Montefusco (N.)
G. Veneri cond.

ISRAEL
Tel Aviv      National    Aug.  7, 1958 P. Baird (A.) N. Pincus (F.) J. Ro-
den (I.) E. Hurskell (N.) R. Polani
(Z.) G. Singer cond.

Dec. 23, 1979 C. Minicozzi (A.) J. E. Shertz (F.)
U. Scalavino (I.) R. Novello (N.) T.
Kunii (Z.) G. Singer cond.

ITALY
Bari          Petruzzelli Jan.  4, 1960 S. Dall'Argine (A.) A. Colzani (N.)
B. Giaiotti (Z.) F. Del Cupolo cond.

Feb. 15, 1975 R. Orlandi-Malaspina (A.) G. Mastromei (N.) L. Roni (Z.) O. Ziino cond.

Jan. 12, 1978 A. Gomez (A.) R. Bruson (N.) B.
Christoff (Z.) O. Ziino cond.

Bologna       Comunale    Oct. 22, 1946 M. Pedrini (A.) F. Barbieri (F.) A.
Ziliani (I.) P. Guelfi (N.) T. Pase-
ro (Z.) F. Ghione cond.

Nov. 13, 1957 M. Roberti (A.) L. Danieli (F.) G.
Limarilli (I.) D. Dondi (N.) I. Vin-
co (Z.) F. Capuana cond.

Oct.  8, 1960 L. Maragliano (A.) F. Cossotto (F.)
L. Ottolini (I.)  G. Guelfi (N.) I.
Vinco (Z.) A. Basile cond.

Catania       Comunale    Mar.  8, 1955 M. Pedrini (A.) U. Savarese (N.) M.
Petri (Z.) F. Del Cupolo cond.

Jan. 17, 1968 E. Suliotis (A.) M. Zanasi (N.) R.
Ariè (Z.) V. Gui cond.

Florence      Comunale    Dec. 16, 1954 A. Cerqueti (A.) M. Pirazzini (F.)
F. Albanese (I.) T. Gobbi (N.) B.
Christoff (Z.) T. Serafin cond.

Aug. 26, 1961 M. Parutto (A.) A. M. Rota (F.) L.
Ottolini (I.) E. Bastianini (N.) I.
Vinco (Z.) B. Bartoletti cond.

May   5, 1977 C. Deutekom (A.) S. Corbacho/B. Pecchioli (F.) N. Todisco/V. Bello (I.)
S. Nimsgern/K. Paskalis (N.) B. Gi-
aiotti/A. Ferrin (Z.) R. Muti cond.

Giardino    July  8, 1959 M. Roberti/M. Parullo (A.) M. Piraz-
di Boboli                zini (F.) G. Limarilli (I.) E. Bastianini (N.) P. Washington (Z.) B.
Bartoletti cond.

Genoa         Comunale    Feb. 28, 1956 C. Mancini (A.) A. Colzani (N.) I.
Vinco (Z.) E. Tieri cond.

Macerata      Arena       July 12, 1981 A. Gomez (A.) G. Cecchele (I.) R.
Bruson (N.) N. Ghiuselev (Z.) F. Mo-
linari-Pradelli cond.

Milan        La Scala    Dec. 26, 1946 M. Pedrini/L. Turcano (A.) F. Bar-
                                       bieri (F.) M. Binci (I.) G. Bechi
                                       (N.) C. Siepi (Z.) T. Serafin cond.

                         June  1, 1958 A. Cerqueti/M. Roberti (A.) G. Si-
                                       mionato/F. Cossotto (F.) G. Poggi/A.
                                       Bertocci (I.) E. Bastiannini (N.) C.
                                       Siepi/N. Zaccaria (Z.) A. Votto
                                       cond.

                         Dec.  7, 1966 E. Suliotis (A.) G. Lane (F.) G.
                                       Raimondi (I.) G. G. Guelfi (N.) N.
                                       Ghiaurov (Z.) G. Gavazzeni cond.

                         May  12, 1968 E. Suliotis (A.) G. Lane (F.) G.
                                       Raimondi (I.) G. G. Guelfi/F. Schia-
                                       vi (N.) N. Ghiaurov (Z.) M. Gusella
                                       cond.

                         Dec.  7, 1986 G. Dimitrova (A.) R. Bruson/E. Tuma-
                                       gian (N.) P. Burchuladze (Z.) R.
                                       Muti cond.

Naples       San Carlo   Dec. 20, 1949 M. Callas (A.) A. Pini (F.) G. Si-
                                       nimbergi (I.) G. Bechi (N.) L. Nero-
                                       ni (Z.) V. Gui cond.

                         Dec.  7, 1968 E. Suliotis (A.) F. Rafanelli (F.)
                                       G. Raimondi (I.) G. G. Guelfi (N.)
                                       A. Ferrin (Z.) G. Gavazzeni cond.

Palermo      Massimo     Apr. 15, 1947 L. Turcano (A.) V. Palombini (F.) G.
                                       Poggi (I.) M. Basiola (N.) L. Nero-
                                       ni (Z.) F. Capuana cond.

                         Feb. 16, 1961 M. Parutti (A.) M. Pirazzini (F.) M.
                                       Picchi (I.) E. Bastiannini (N.) I.
                                       Vinco (Z.) V. Gui cond.

                         Jan. 15, 1974 E. Suliotis/G. Dimitrova (A.) F.
                                       Mattiucci (F.) R. Bondino/U. Scala
                                       (I.) C. MacNeil (N.) B. Christoff
                                       (Z.) O. De Fabritiis cond.

Parma        Regio       Dec. 25, 1948 M. Pedrini (A.) P. Guelfi (N.) A.
                                       Mongelli (Z.) O. De Fabritiis cond.

                         Dec. 26, 1958 S. Vartenissian (A.) U. Savarese
                                       (N.) R. Ariè (Z.) V. Bellezza cond.

                         Dec. 26, 1978 A. Gulin (A.) R. Bruson (N.) B.
                                       Giaiotti (Z.) M. Veltri cond.

             Ducale      Jan.  3, 1984 S. Kotlenko (A.) P. Cappuccilli (N.)
                                       N. Ghiuselev (Z.) R. Gandolfi cond.

Ravenna                  Aug.     1979 G. Dimitrova (A.) R. Bruson (N.) B.
                                       Giaiotti (Z.) B. Rigacci cond.

             Rocca Bran- July 29, 1988 L. Roark-Strummer (A.) N. Curiel
             caleone                   (F.) E. Di Cesare (I.) R. Bruson
                                       (N.) S. Elenkov (Z.) R. Gandolfi
                                       cond.

Rome        Sala RAI    Jan. 16, 1951 C. Mancini (A.) G. Gatti (F.) M.
                                       Binci (I.) P. Silveri (N.) A. Cas-
                                       sinelli (Z.) F. Previtali cond.

                         Apr. 10. 1963 F. Assandri Norelli (A.) M. Binci
                                       (I.) G. Ciminelli (N.) S. Pezzetti
                                       (Z.) C. Franci cond.

            Opera        Dec.  8, 1951 M. Caniglia/C. Mancini (A.) M. Pi-
                                       razzini (F.) F. Albanese (I.) G.
                                       Bechi (N.) N. Rossi-Lemeni (Z.) V.
                                       Gui cond.

                         Nov. 16, 1970 E. Suliotis/E. Renzi (A.) F. Mat-
                                       tiucci (F.) A. Mori/A. Galiè (I.) M.
                                       Zanasi/G. Ciminelli (N.) C. Cava
                                       (Z.) V. Gui/M. Gusella cond.

            Caracalla    June 27, 1954 C. Mancini (A.) M. Pirazzini (F.) F.
                                       Albanese (I.) T. Gobbi (N.) B.
                                       Christoff (Z.) G. Santini cond.

                         Aug.  7, 1984 D. Vejzovic (A.) L. Shemciuk (F.) N.
                                       Todisco (I.) S. Carroli (N.) N. Sto-
                                       rojev (Z.) R. Giovaninetti cond.

                         Aug.  4, 1985 D. Vejzovic (A.) E. Jankovic (F.) N.
                                       Todisco (I.) S. Carroli (N.) N. Sto-
                                       rojev (Z.) R. Gandolfi cond.

Trieste     Verdi        Winter   1969 L. Vajna (A.) T. Del Bianco (I.) L.
                                       Montefusco (N.) V. M. Brunetti (Z.)
                                       F. Previtali cond.

                         Oct. 27, 1981 R. Bakocevik (A.)

Turin       Regio        May   5, 1983 O. Stapp (A.) O. Garaventa (I.) K.
                                       Nurmela/R. Bruson (N.) B. Giaiotti
                                       (Z.) M. Arena cond.

Venice      La Fenice    Jan. 12, 1946 M. Pedrini (A.) G. Voyer (I.) G.
                                       Bechi (N.) C. Siepi (Z.) F. Ghione
                                       cond.

                         May 21, 1960 L. Kelston (A.) A. Protti (N.) R.
                                       Ariè (Z.)  T. Serafin cond.

                         Nov. 30, 1972 A. Gulin (A.) M. Pecile (F.) G. Li-
                                       marilli (I.) M. Zanasi (N.) B. Gi-
                                       aiotti (Z.) N. Sanzogno cond.

Verona      Arena        July 26, 1981 G. Dimitrova/O. Stapp (A.) B. Bag-
                                       lioni/G. Dalle Molle (F.) O. Gara-
                                       venta/G. Scano/R. Bondino (I.) R.
                                       Bruson/M. Manuguerra (N.) D. Petkov/
                                       B. Giaiotti (Z.) M. Arena cond.

MEXICO
Mexico City Bellas       Sep. 23, 1969 A. Gulin (A.) B. Berini (F.) A.
            Artes                      Protti (N.) J. Hecht (Z.) L. Herrera
                                       de la Fuente cond.

NETHERLANDS
Amsterdam                Apr. 17, 1961

Scheveningen                Dec. 12, 1972 P. Tinsley (A.) J. Blinkhof (I.) P.
                                          Derksen (N.) H. Smit (Z.) H. Vonk
                                          cond.
POLAND
Lodz            Wielki      May  2, 1983 J. Homik (I.) R. Tesarowicz (Z.) (in
                                          It.)

PORTUGAL
Lisbon          Sao Carlos  Mar. 20, 1966 E. Suliotis (A.) A. Finelli (F.) N.
                                          Tagger (I.) G. Guelfi (N.) P. Wash-
                                          ington (Z.) A. Erede cond.

SOUTH AFRICA
Blomfontein     Sand du     Aug.  1, 1985 M. Napier (A.) D. Domenico (I.) H.
                Plessis                   van Heerden (N.) A. Haller (Z.) G.
                                          Geist cond.

Johannesburg                         1968 R. Bruson (N.)

Pretoria                             1968 R. Bruson (N.)

                State       Mar. 10, 1984 A. Negri (A.) S. Braatvedt (F.) J.
                                          Treleaven (I.) M. Manuguerra (N.) R.
                                          Beukes (Z.) V. Yampolsky cond.

SPAIN
Barcelona       Liceo       Feb.  1, 1970 E. Renzi (A.) J. Carreras (I.) C.
                                          MacNeil (N.) B. Giaiotti (Z.) O. Zi-
                                          ino cond.

                            Feb.  4, 1977 R. Orlandi-Malaspina (A.) M. Aparici
                                          (F.) F. Bordoni (N.) B. Giaiotti
                                          (Z.) D. Belardinelli cond.

                            Mar. 23, 1984 G. Dimitrova (A.) R. Isàs (F.) J.
                                          Ruiz (I.) S. Carroli (N.) Y. Nester-
                                          enko (Z.) R. Gandolfi cond.

Bilbao          Coliseo     Aug. 27, 1955 M. Pedrini (A.) A. Lazzarini (F.) G.
                Alba                      Vertecchi (I.) U. Savarese (N.) I.
                                          Vinco (Z.) M. Parenti cond.

                            Sep. 10, 1960 C. Parada (A.) M. L. Castellano (F.)
                                          L. Ottolini (I.) C. MacNeil (N.) B.
                                          Giaiotti (Z.) R. Frühbeck cond.

                            Sep. 11, 1963 M. De Osma (A.) G. Vighi (F.) A. Lo
                                          Forese (I.) A. Protti (N.) R. Ariè
                                          (Z.) N. Rescigno cond.

                            Sep.  5, 1968 V. Gordoni (A.)  M. Pecile (F.) F.
                                          Hormaeche (I.) P. Cappuccilli (N.)
                                          R. Raimondi (Z.) L. Maggiera cond.

                            Sep.  9, 1973 A. Gulin (A.) A. Stamenova (F.) N.
                                          Todisco (I.) C. MacNeil (N.) P.
                                          Washington (Z.) G. Ruisi cond.

                            Sep. 12, 1983 G. Dimitrova (A.) G. Scano (I.) M.
                                          Manuguerra (N.) K. B. Woon (Z.) U.
                                          R. Laorden cond.

SWITZERLAND
Zürich          Opernhaus     June  5, 1979 O.  Stapp  (A.)  S.  Carroli  (N.)  B.
                                            Giaiotti (Z.) N. Santi cond.

                              June 21, 1980 O.  Stapp  (A.)  S.  Carroli  (N.)  P.
                                            Plishka (Z.) N. Santi cond.

                              Mar. 17, 1982 R. Bakocevik (A.) K. Nurmela (N.) D.
                                            Petkov (Z.) N. Santi cond.

UNITED STATES
Chicago         Lyric         Oct.  4, 1963 D.  Mastilovic (A.) A. M. Rota (F.)
                                            A.  La Morena (I.) T. Gobbi (N.) B.
                                            Christoff (Z.) B. Bartoletti cond.

Newark          State Opera Mar. 18, 1990 S.  Misura  (A.)  S.  Cowan  (N.)  P.
                                            Plishka (Z.) A. Silipigni cond.

New Orleans                   Oct. 19, 1978 R. Hunter (A.) R. De Carlo (F.) S.
                                            Novoa (I.) K. Paskalis (N.) F. Fur-
                                            lanetto (Z.) A. Coppola cond.

New York        Metro-        Oct. 24, 1960 L.  Rysanek  (A.)  R.  Elias  (F.)  E.
                politan                     Fernandi  (I.)  C.  MacNeil  (N.)  C.
                                            Siepi (Z.) T. Schippers cond.

                Carnegie      Oct. 11, 1969 E.  Suliotis  (A.)  L.  Pearl  (F.)  D.
                Hall                        Barioni  (I.)  K.  Paskalis  (N.)  L.
                                            Roni (Z.) C. F. Cillario cond.

                              May 13, 1984 G. Dimitrova (A.) P. Schuman (F.) J.
                                            Pinto (I.) A. Monk (N.) P. Plishka
                                            (Z.) E. Queler cond.

                              Feb. 20, 1989 L. Roark-Strummer (A.) L. d'Intino
                                            (F.) E. Tumagian (N.) P. Burchuladze
                                            (Z.) R. Muti cond.

                City Opera  Sep. 17, 1981 G.  Bumbry  (A.)  J.  Simon  (F.)  R.
                                            Calleo  (I.)  J.  Brocheler  (N.)  J.
                                            Diaz (Z.) I. Pallo cond.

Philadelphia  Ac. of Mus.  Nov. 29, 1960 L.  Rysanek  (A.)  R.  Elias  (F.)  E.
                                            Fernandi  (I.)  C.  MacNeil  (N.)  C.
                                            Siepi (Z.) T. Schippers cond.

                              Nov. 14, 1969 E. Suliotis (A.) R. De Carlo (F.) S.
                                            Novoa  (I.)  P.  Glossop  (N.)  E.
                                            Flagello (Z.) A. Guadagno cond.

San Antonio                   Spring   1960 F. Yeend (A.) G. Valdengo (N.) V.
                                            Alessandro cond.

San Diego       Opera         June 19, 1981 C. Deutekom (A.) K. Nurmela (N.) E.
                                            Flagello (Z.) M. Arena cond.

San Francisco Opera           Oct. 10, 1970 M. Lippert (A.) S. Anderson (F.) R.
                                            Bjoerling (I.) C. MacNeil (N.) G.
                                            Tozzi (Z.) C. F. Cillario cond.

                              June 17, 1982 O.  Stapp/J. Telep-Ehrlich  (A.)  S.
                                            Quittmeyer  (F.)  G.  Greer  (I.)  M.
                                            Manuguerra (N.) P. Plishka (Z.) K.
                                            Adler cond.

4. I LOMBARDI ALLA PRIMA CROCIATA-*Dramma lirico* in four acts
Milan-Teatro alla Scala-Feb. 11, 1843
Libretto by Temistocle Solera

| | |
|---|---|
| Giselda (G.) | Erminia Frezzolini sop. |
| Oronte (O.) | Carlo Guasco ten. |
| Arvino(A.) | Giovanni Severi ten. |
| Pagano/Un Eremita (P.) | Prosper Dérivis bass |
| Viclinda | Teresa Ruggggeri sop. |
| Sofia | Amalia Gandaglia sop. |
| Priore di Milano | Napoleone Marconi ten. |
| Pirro | Gaetano Rossi bass |
| Acciano | Luigi Vajro bass |
| | |
| Conductor | Eugenio Cavallini |
| Director | Giuseppe Verdi |

OTHER PREMIERES-NINETEENTH CENTURY

ARGENTINA
Buenos Aires    Victoria      Apr. 26, 1851 I. Edelvira (G.)   C. Mugnai (O.) J.
                                           M. Ramonda (P.) J. V. Rivas cond.

AUSTRALIA
Adelaide        Th. Royal     Oct. 16, 1874 M. Zenoni (G.)  F. Rosnati (O.) E.
                                           Dondi (P.) A. Zelman cond.

Melbourne       Prince        May  25, 1874 M. Zenoni (G.)  F. Rosnati (O.) E.
                of Wales                   Dondi (P.) A. Zelman cond.

Sydney          Victoria      Aug.  1, 1874 M. Zenoni (G.)  F. Rosnati (O.) E.
                                           Dondi (P.) A. Zelman cond.

AUSTRIA
Graz            Stadt         Dec. 28, 1861 (in Ger.)

Vienna          Kärntnertor May  27, 1846 E. Scotta (G.)  E. Musich (O.) F.
                                           Colini (P.) H. Proch cond.

BRAZIL
Rio de          Sao Pedro     Sep.  7, 1848 C. Merea (G.) G. Sicuro (O.) F. Mas-
 Janeiro                                    siani (P.)

CHILE
Santiago        Republica     June 16, 1852 T. Rossi (G.) J. Ubaldi (O.) F. Leo-
                                           nardi (P.)

Valparaiso      Victoria      Aug.  8, 1850 L. Micciarelli (G.) J. Ubaldi (O.)
                                           F. Leonardi (P.)

CUBA
Havana          Tacon         Dec.  1, 1846 L. Caranti-Vita (G.) G. Severi (O.)
                                           P. Novelli (P.) L. Arditi cond. G.
                                           Bottesini dir.

DENMARK
Copenhagen      Royal         Mar. 26, 1847 A. Bosio (G.) F. Ciaffei (O.) N.
                                           Torre (P.) P. Sperati cond.

EGYPT
Alexandria      Europeo       June?    1844

FRANCE
Nice         Regio        Mar.?   1863 V. Pozzi-Brazanti (G.) A. Corsi (O.)
                                       G. Giotti (P.)

Paris        Italien      Jan. 10, 1863 E. Frezzolini (G.) E. Naudin (O.) O.
                                       Bartolini (P.) V. Bonetti cond.

GERMANY
Berlin       Königstädt-  Aug. 25, 1845 F. Salvini-Donatelli (G.) A. Bozzet-
             liches                    ti (O.) G. Dalbesio (P.)

Darmstadt    Hoftheater   Dec. 16, 1849 (in Ger.)

Hamburg      Stadt        July 10, 1849

GREAT BRITAIN
London       Her          May 12, 1846 G. Grisi (G.) Mario (O.) L. Fornasa-
             Majesty's                 ri (P.) M. Balfe cond.

GREECE
Athens       Royal        Dec.?   1851 E. Cominotti (G.)

Corfu        San Giacomo  Oct. 15, 1851 L. Luxor-Pretti (G.) A. Errani (O.)
                                       L. Busi (P.)

HUNGARY
Budapest     Varietées    Mar. 22, 1870 A. Bianchi-Montaldo (G.) L. Graziani
                                       (O.) P. Medini (P.) (in It.)

ITALY
Alessandria  Municipale   Nov.  6, 1844 V. Boccabadati (G.) E. Musich (O.)
                                       G. Ferri (P.)

Ancona       Muse         Dec. 26, 1847 S. Zudoli (G.) L. Caserini (O.) L.
                                       Roncagli (P.)

Bari         Piccinni     Oct. 15, 1857 M. Anselmi (G.) G. Ricci (O.)

Bergamo      Sociale      Dec. 26, 1844 T. Truffi-Benedetti (G.) G. Ricci
                                       (O.) G. C. Casanova (P.)

             Riccardi     Aug. 11, 1847 B. Colleoni-Corti (G.) R. Mirate
                                       (O.) A. Rodas (P.) M. Bonesi cond.

Bologna      Comunale     Oct. 22, 1845 T. De Giuli-Borsi (G.) A. Poggi (O.)
                                       C. Badiali (P.) G. Manetti cond.

Brescia      Grande       Aug. 24, 1845 E. Scotta (G.) E. Calzolari (O.) G.
                                       F. Beneventano (P.)

Cagliari     Civico       Sep.  6, 1845 E. Fodor-Mainville (G.) O. Fort (O.)
                                       L. Caliari (P.)

Catania      Comunale     Dec. 29 1849 A. Artioli (G.) L. Palmieri (O.) F.
                                       Gionfrida (P.)

Chieti       San          May 11, 1848 A. Artioli (G.) G. Musiani (O.) L.
             Ferdinando                Roncagli (P.)

Cremona      Concordia    Spring  1845 F. Salvini-Donatelli (G.) A. Bozzet-
                                       ti (O.)

Faenza       Comunale     May 29, 1847 G. Rossetti-Sikorska (G.) N. Moriani
                                       (O.) F. Gnone (P.)

| | | | | |
|---|---|---|---|---|
| Ferrara | Comunale | Spring | 1845 | E. Frezzolini (G.) A. Poggi (O.) L. Rinaldini (P.) |
| Fermo | Aquila | August | 1846 | L. Matthey (G.) E. Marcucci (O.) R. Colmenghi (P.) |
| Fiume | Civico | Mar. 6, | 1847 | R. Olivieri (G.) E. Naudin (O.) E. Luisia (P.) |
| Florence | Pergola | Oct. 15, | 1843 | E. Frezzolini (G.) A. Poggi (O.) F. Colini (P.) L. M. Viviani cond. |
| Forli | Comunale | June 14, | 1851 | A. Albertini (G.) S. Malvezzi (O.) F. Varesi (P.) |
| Genoa | Carlo Felice | Jan. 16, | 1844 | A. Boccabadati (G.) F. Borioni (O.) C. O. Porto (P.) N. Uccelli cond. |
| Livorno | Floridi | Apr. 17, | 1844 | A. De la Grange (G.) G. Solieri (O.) G. Zucchini (P.) |
| Lucca | Giglio | Sep. 13, | 1843 | E. Frezzolini (G.) A. Poggi (O.) F. Colini (P.) |
| Lugo | Rossini | Sep. | 1845 | G. Bartolotti (G.) G. Roppa (O.) R. Ferlotti (P.) C. Aria cond. |
| Mantua | Sociale | Carn. | 1845-46 | L. Assandri (G.) E. Naudin (O.) G. Mitrovich (P.) |
| Messina | Munizione | Nov. 6, | 1850 | R. Mori-Spallazzi (G.) A. Bettini (O.) Bianchi (P.) |
| Modena | Comunale | Dec. 27, | 1845 | T. Truffi-Benedetti (G.) D. Lorini (O.) V. Mela (P.) |
| Naples | San Carlo | Oct. 7, | 1848 | M. Gazzaniga (G.) C. Baucardé (O.) A. Rodas (P.) A. Farelli cond. |
| Padua | Nuovo | Oct. | 1853 | A. Rebussini (G.) G. Pellegrini (O.) F. Massiani (P.) |
| Palermo | Carolino | Oct. 1, | 1845 | M. Gazzaniga (G.) A. Castellan (O.) G. Zucconi (P.) P. Raimondi cond. |
| Parma | Regio | Apr. 4, | 1844 | A. Boccabadati (G.) F. Borioni (O.) N. Costantini (P.) N. De Giovanni cond. |
| Piacenza | Municipale | Spring | 1845 | C. Vittadini (G.) V. Ferrari-Stella (O.) L. Caliari (P.) G. Jona cond. |
| Pisa | Ravvivati | Carn. | 1846-47 | A. Rebussini (G.) M. Forti (O.) G. Zucchini (P.) |
| Ravenna | Comuni- tativo | May | 1850 | A. Rebussini (G.) E. Marcucci (O.) G. Nostini cond. |
| Reggio Emilia | Comunale | Apr. 28, | 1847 | M. Gazzaniga (G.) G. Sinico (O.) E. Crivelli (P.) G. Tebaldi cond. |
| Rome | Apollo | Feb. 3, | 1844 | E. Frezzolini (G.) A. Poggi (O.) P. Balzar (P.) E. Angelini cond. |

Sinigaglia    La Fenice    July 29, 1843 E. Frezzolini (G.) A. Poggi (O.) C.
                                         O. Porto (P.) G. C. Ferrarini cond.
                                         G. Verdi dir.

Trento        Sociale      June    1846 A. Bertucca (G.) E. Naudin (O.) L.
                                         Caliari (P.)

Treviso       Sociale      Nov. 23, 1847 L. Ponti dall'Armi (G.) E. Caggiati
                                         (O.) L. Rinaldini (P.)

Trieste       Grande       Oct. 24, 1843 E. Tadolini (G.) C. Guasco (O.) P.
                                         Dérivis (P.) P. Coronini cond.

Turin         Regio        Dec. 26, 1843 E. Tadolini (G.) C. Guasco (O.) F.
                                         Varesi (P.) G. P. Polledro cond.

Udine                      Aug.  2, 1846 E. Parepa-Archibugeri (G.) F. Ciaf-
                                         fei (O.) G. Zucchini (P.)

Venice        La Fenice    Dec. 26, 1843 S. Loewe (G.) D. Conti (O.) A. Su-
                                         perchi (P.) G. Mares cond. G. Verdi
                                         dir.

Verona        Filarmonico  Jan. 18, 1845 S. Loewe (G.) L. Cuzzani (O.) G.
                                         Ferri (P.)

Vicenza       Eretenio     July 22, 1845 T. De Giuli-Borsi (G.) L. Cuzzani
                                         (O.) R. Colmenghi (P.)

MEXICO
Mexico City   Nacional     July 11, 1852 A. Valtellina (P.)

NETHERLANDS
Amsterdam                  Sep. 24, 1895 (in Dut.)

PERU
Lima          Principal    Dec.  8, 1849 M. De Ferretti (G.) E. Pellegrini
                                         (O.) P. Ferretti (P.) A. Neumann
                                         cond.

PHILIPPINES
Manila        Arroceros    Apr. 20, 1871 E. Leonpietra (G.) V. Sabatini (O.)
                                         A. Grandi (P.)

POLAND
Warsaw        Wielki       Mar. 25, 1848 (in Pol.)[39]

                           Oct.  7, 1851 M. Sulzer (G.) J. Dobrsky (O.)
                                         Froschel (P.) (in It.?)

PORTUGAL
Lisbon        Sao Carlos   Mar. 10, 1845 A. Albertini (G.) E. Tamberlick (O.)
                                         E. Santi (P.)

Oporto        Sao Joao     Nov.     1845 F. Rocca-Alessandri (G.) G. Barbieri
                                         (O.)

ROMANIA
Bucharest     Nacional     Oct.     1845 C. Hollósy (G.) V. Jacobelli (O.) E.
                                         Santi (P.)

---

[39]. Given as *Jerozolima*. It is not clear from this title whether the opera was *Jerusalem* or *I Lombardi*.

| Iasi | Teatrul | Oct. 13, 1851 | L. Giordani (G.) G. B. Milesi (O.) P. Dérivis (P.) |
|---|---|---|---|
| **RUSSIA** Moscow | Bolshoi | Sep. 25, 1873 | M. De Zorzi (G.) E. Naudin (O.) G. Rota (P.) E. Bevignani cond. |
| Odessa | Municipal | Apr. 17, 1845 | A. Scalese (G.) R. Vitali (O.) G. Marini (P.) |
| St. Petersburg | Imperial | Nov. 12, 1845 | A. Moltini (G.) L. Salvi (O.) A. Tamburini (P.) E. Baveri cond. |
| **SPAIN** Alicante | Principal | Aug. 2, 1850 | C. Villò-Ramos (G.) E. Carrion (O.) |
| Barcelona | Principal | June 7, 1845 | C. Cattinari (G.) G. B. Milesi (O.) A. Superchi (P.) |
| | Liceo | May 27, 1848 | |
| Cadiz | Principal | Oct. 1845 | G. Caspani (G.) G. Zoboli (O.) V. Sermattei (P.) |
| Madrid | Circo | Dec. 20, 1844 | I. Ober-Rossi (G.) G. Bettini (O.) G. Euzet (P.) L. Rossi cond. |
| | Real | Oct. 1, 1853 | A. Basseggio (G.) S. Malvezzi (O.) G. Echeverria (P.) J. Skoczdopole cond. |
| Malaga | Principal | Apr. 22, 1847 | T. Rusmini-Solera (G.) Carisio (O.) Velasco (P.) |
| Seville | San Fernando | Dec. 25, 1847 | C. Vittadini (G.) G. Solieri (O.) C. O. Porto (P.) |
| Valencia | Principal | Jan.? 1848 | |
| **SWEDEN** Stockholm | Mindre | Feb. 20, 1849 | R. Penco (G.) F. Ciaffei (O.) G. C. Casanova (P.) P. Sperati cond. |
| **TURKEY** Constan- tinople | Naum | Jan. 6, 1851 | M. Lotti della Santa (G.) A. Prudenza (O.) G. Mitorvich (P.) |
| **UNITED STATES** Boston | Athenaeum | May 20, 1847 | L. Caranti-Vita (G.) G. Severi (O.) P. Novelli (P.) L. Arditi cond. |
| New York | Palmo's | Mar. 3, 1847 | C. Barili-Patti (G.) S. Benedetti (O.) G. F. Beneventano (P.) M. Rapetti cond. |
| | Ac. of Mus. | Oct. 22, 1886 | M. Ricci (G.) F. Giannini (O.) A. Pinto (P.) O. Bimboni cond. |
| Philadelphia | Walnut St. | July 17, 1847 | L. Caranti-Vita (G.) L. Perozzi (O.) P. Novelli (P.) L. Arditi cond. |
| San Francisco | Metro- politan | May 1, 1855 | C. Barili-Thorn (G.) C. Scola (O.) A. Lanzoni (P.) |

URUGUAY
Montevideo    San Felipe   Apr. 27, 1853

              Solis        June 20, 1858 T. Bajetti (G.) L. Lelmi (O.) G. C.
                           Casanova (P.) L. Pretti cond.

VENEZUELA
Caracas       T. Caracas   Feb. 27, 1874 M. Majo (G.) F. Mazzoleni (O.) J.
                           Cajano cond.

SELECTED REVIVALS-NINETEENTH CENTURY

AUSTRIA
Vienna        Kärntnertor  Apr. 14, 1847 E. Borghese (G.) R. Mirate (O.) F.
                           Colini (P.)

                           May 16, 1853 G. Medori (G.) R. Mirate (O.) A. De
                           Bassini (P.)

                           Apr.  1, 1865 M. Lotti della Santa (G.) L. Grazia-
                           ni (O.) G. F. Angelini (P.)

GREAT BRITAIN
London        Her          July  6, 1847 A. Castellan (G.) I. Gardoni (O.) F.
              Majesty's    Coletti (P.)

                           Apr. 30, 1867 T. Tietiens (G.) T. Hohler (O.) C.
                           Santley (P.)

ITALY
Florence      Pergola      May 30, 1844 E. Frezzolini (G.) A. Poggi (O.) A.
                           De Bassini (P.)

                           Sep. 19, 1847 A. Basseggio (G.) L. Graziani (O.)
                           G. Belletti (P.)

                           Autumn   1849 T. De Giuli-Borsi (G.) L. Bernabei
                           (O.) L. Maggiorotti (P.)

                           June 22, 1853 E. Frezzolini (G.) Toffanari (O.) E.
                           Barili (P.)

Genoa         Carlo        May 18, 1845 A. Boccabadati (G.) L. Cuzzani (O.)
              Felice       P. Dérivis (P.)

                           May  8, 1847 E. Frezzolini  (G.) E. Musich (O.)
                           L. Corradi-Setti (P.)

                           May 13, 1851 M. Barbieri-Nini (G.) L. Graziani
                           (O.) L. Bouché (P.)

                           Dec. 26, 1858 E. Parepa-Rosa (G.) H. von Rokitan-
                           sky (P.)

                           Apr. 14, 1864 M. Palmieri (G.) T. Palmieri (O.) H.
                           Brémond (P.)

Milan         La Scala     Dec. 26, 1844 E. Frezzolini (G.) A. Poggi (O.) F.
                           Colini (P.) E. Cavallini cond.

                           Mar. 21, 1855 A. Albertini (G.) R. Mirate (O.) G.
                           Echeverria (P.) E. Cavallini cond.

May  1, 1855 F. Cordosa (G.) B. Massimiliani (O.)
             G. Echeverria (P.) E. Cavallini
             cond.

Mar. 19, 1857 A. Basseggio (G.) F. Mazzoleni (O.)
              A. Didot (P.)

Feb. 11, 1860 E. Weisser (G.) E. Nicolini (O.) C.
              Dalla Costa (P.) E. Cavallini cond.

Jan.  2, 1864 M. Palmieri (G.) G. Limberti/R. Ber-
              tolini (O.) G. Capponi (P.)

Naples      San Carlo   June 10, 1849 A. Albertini (G.) C. Baucardé (O.)
                                      A. Selva (P.) A. Farelli cond.

Oct. 22, 1853 T. De Giuli Borsi (G.) G. Fraschini
              (O.) G. Ferri (P.) A. Farelli cond.

Oct.  4, 1854 N. De Roissi (G.) E. Naudin (O.) L.
              Vendemmia/F. Coletti (P.) A. Farelli
              cond.

June 17, 1857 E. Fioretti (G.) F. Prudenza (O.) G.
              B. Antonucci (P.) A. Farelli cond.

Oct. 11, 1857 E. Fioretti (G.) G. Galvani (O.) G.
              B. Antonucci (P.) A. Farelli cond.

Rome        Apollo      Feb. 29, 1848 E. Nissen (G.) N. Ivanoff (O.) G.
                                      Mitrovich (P.) E. Angelini cond.

Dec. 29, 1856 A. Angelini-Cantalamessa (G.) G. Mu-
              siani (O.) P. Giorgi-Pacini (P.) E.
              Angelini cond.

Feb. 15, 1871 A. Bianchi-Montaldo (G.) G. Sani
              (O.) P. Milesi (P.) R. Kuon cond.

Argentina   Apr. 20, 1850 T. De Giuli-Borsi (G.) S. Malvezzi
                          (O.) F. Colini (P.)

Sep. 24, 1859 C. Moltini (G.) V. Sarti (O.) A. De
              Antoni (P.)

Turin       Regio       Mar.  6, 1873 A. Bianchi-Montaldo (G.) L. Filippi-
                                      Bresciani (O.) A. Pifferi (P.) C.
                                      Pedrotti cond.

RUSSIA
St.         Imperial    Dec. 14, 1846 T. De Giuli-Borsi (G.) C. Guasco
Petersburg                            (O.) A. Tamburini (P.) E. Baveri
                                      cond.

Oct. 11, 1847 E. Frezzolini (G.) C. Guasco (O.) F.
              Colini (P.) E. Baveri cond.

Oct.  9, 1850 A. Cortesi (G.) E. Tamberlick (O.)
              F. Coletti (P.) E. Baveri cond.

Feb.     1852 G. Medori (G.) E. Tamberlick (O.) A.
              Tamburini (P.) E. Baveri cond.

Oct. 31, 1855 M. Lotti Della Santa (G.) E. Tamberlick (O.) A. Didot (P.) E. Baveri
cond.

Jan.  9, 1857 M. Lotti Della Santa (G.) E. Calzolari (O.) A. De Bassini (P.) E. Ba-
veri cond.

Sep. 21, 1857 M. Lotti Della Santa (G.) P. Mongini
(O.) A. De Bassini (P.) E. Baveri
cond.

Sep. 20, 1858 M. Lotti Della Santa (G.) P. Mongini
(O.) A. De Bassini (P.) E. Baveri
cond.

Oct. 23, 1863 E. Fioretti (G.) E. Tamberlick (O.)
G. F. Angelini (P.) E. Baveri cond.

Feb. 13, 1867 L. Perelli (G.) E. Tamberlick (O.)
G. F. Angelini (P.)

SPAIN
Barcelona    Liceo         1849-50 C. Gruitz (G.) G. Roppa (O.) A. Rodas (P.)

Dec.   1852 E.  Julienne-Dejean (G.)  E.  Irfré
(O.) E. Manfredi (P.)

Oct. 30, 1868 L. Ruggero-Antonioli (G.) Bichielli/
F. Steger (O.) P. Dérivis (P.) A.
Orsini cond.

Madrid       Real     Nov.  9, 1857 G. Medori (G.) G. Bettini (O.) G.
Echeverria (P.) J. Skoczdopole cond.

Apr. 29, 1876 A. Fossa (G.) E. Tamberlick (O.) J.
Ordinas (P.)

SELECTED PRODUCTIONS-1900-1945

ITALY
Bologna      Comunale   Dec.  4, 1913 E. Mazzoleni (G.) E. Garbin (O.) G.
Cirino (P.) R. Ferrari cond.

Florence     Verdi      Jan. 25, 1902 A. Gabbi (G.) E. Garbin (O.) S.
Cirotto (P.)

Genoa        Politeama   Apr. 28, 1906 I. Fassio (G.) G. Agostini (O.)

Apr. 10, 1918 M. Dorini (G.) U. Lappas (O.) O.
Luppi (P.) A. Ferrari cond.

Milan        Dal Verme   Feb.  5, 1902 I. Paoli (G.) A. Cecchi (O.) L.
Lucenti (P.) G. Falconi cond.

La Scala    Dec.  7, 1930 B. Scacciati (G.) F. Merli (O.) G.
Vaghi (P.) E. Panizza cond.

Modena       Municipale Dec. 23? 1905 F. Solari (G.) O. Frosini (O.) S.
Cirotto (P.) E. Perosio cond.

Palermo      Biondo      Feb. 21, 1919 A.  Brighi  (G.)  Celesia  (O.)  P.
Marucci (P.) R. Giovannelli cond.

Rome          Quirino      Jan. 17, 1905 G. Mancini Frampolesi/A. Mazzarelli/
                                          M.   Sacchi   (G.)   G.   Bambacioni/A.
                                          Rossi (O.) A. Natili (P.) F. Valcel-
                                          li cond.

              Nazionale    Nov. 24, 1915 A. De Angelis (G.) B. Lucignani (O.)
                                          R.  Caldani   (P.)   G.  Scognamiglio
                                          cond.

                           May   4, 1918 M. Viscardi/E. Pucci (G.) F. De An-
                                          gelis (O.)  G. De Grazia/A. Sabelli-
                                          co (P.) G. Soriente cond.

Turin         Vittorio     Jan.  6, 1914 E. Barbieri  (G.)  A. Dolci (O.)  M.
              Emanuele                    Pinheiro (P.) V. Lombardi cond.

              Regio        Dec. 26, 1926 M.  Carena  (G.)  N.  Fusati  (O.)  V.
                                          Zitek (P.) G. Marinuzzi cond.

NETHERLANDS
Amsterdam     Palais v.    Feb. 18, 1914 B. Formen  (G.)   T. Franci  (O.)  M.
              Volksvligt                  Baldelli (P.) F. Guerrieri cond.

Den Haag                   Feb. 27, 1914 B.  Formen  (G.)   T. Franci  (O.)  M.
                                          Baldelli (P.) F. Guerrieri cond.

Rotterdam     Groote       Feb. 22? 1914 B.  Formen  (G.)   T. Franci  (O.)  M.
                                          Baldelli (P.) F. Guerrieri cond.

PORTUGAL
Lisbon        Sao Carlos   Dec. 31, 1903 E.  Bianchini-Cappelli  (G.)  J.  Biel
                                          (O.)  V.  Arimondi  (P.)  V.  Lombardi
                                          cond.

UNITED STATES
Los Angeles   Cline's      Jan. 21, 1915 Rainoldi (G.)  Poggi-Rivera  (O.) I.
              Auditorium                  Picchi (P.)

San Francisco Gaiety       Mar.  2, 1915 Rainoldi  (G.)  E.  De Folco (O.)  I.
                                          Picchi (P.)

OTHER PRODUCTIONS-POST-WORLD WAR II

CANADA
Vancouver     Pacific      Aug. 24, 1986 E. Connell (G.)  V. Luchetti (O.) P.
              Coliseum                    Plishka (P.) G. Gavazzeni cond. (By
                                          the La Scala company of Milan at
                                          Expo '86)

GREAT BRITAIN
Cardiff       New          Autumn   1956

                           Oct.  2, 1959

London        Sadler's     July 16, 1956 R. Raisbeck (G.)  A. Hallett (O.) B.
              Wells                       Drake (P.) W. Braithwaite cond.

                           June 25, 1957 J.  Barker  (G.)  A. Hallett (O.)  B.
                                          Drake (P.) W. Braithwaite cond.

                           May  18, 1962 R. Woodland (G.) W. Midgley (O.) B.
                                          Drake (P.) B. Balkwill cond.

| | Covent<br>Garden | June 9, 1976 | S. Sass (G.) J. Carreras (O.) N.<br>Ghiuselev (P.) L. Gardelli cond. |

Neath          Gwynn Hall    May  5, 1981  L. Walzer (G.) D. Kestel (O.) B.
                                           Kemp (P.) A. James cond.

Swansea        Grand         Apr. 15, 1959

                             Mar.  7, 1963

HUNGARY
Budapest       Erkel         Apr.  7, 1974  S. Sass (G.) L. Gardelli cond.
               Szinház

ITALY
Milan          Sala RAI      Feb. 11, 1951  M. Vitale (G.) G. Gallo (O.) M. Pe-
                                            tri (P.) M. Wolf-Ferrari cond.

               La Scala      Apr. 20, 1984  G. Dimitrova (G.) J. Carreras (O.)
                                            S. Carroli (P.) G. Gavazzeni cond.

                             Jan. 28, 1986  E. Connell (G.) A. Cupido (O.) P.
                                            Burchuladze (P.) T. Fulton cond.

Parma          Regio         Dec. 23, 1973  R. Scotto/G. Trombin (G.) J. Car-
                                            reras (O.) M. Mazzieri (P.) C. F.
                                            Cillario cond.

Rome           Opera         Nov. 20, 1969  R. Scotto (G.) L. Pavarotti (O.) R.
                                            Raimondi (P.) G. Gavazzeni cond.

Turin          Sala RAI      Oct.  6, 1957  M. Laszlò (G.) R. Lagares (O.) P.
                                            Clabassi (P.) F. Vernizzi cond.

Verona         Arena         July 22, 1984  K. Ricciarelli (G.) V. Luchetti (O.)
                                            R. Raimondi (P.) M. Arena cond.

PORTUGAL
Lisbon         Sao Carlos    Nov. 18, 1987  S. Mosca (G.) C. Bergonzi (O.) M.
                                            Pertusi (P.) A. Campori cond.

SPAIN
Bilbao         Coliseo       Mar. 31, 1976  C. Deutekom (G.) J. Carreras (O.) M.
               Alba                         Manuguerra (P.) M. Veltri cond.

SWITZERLAND
Berne          Stadt         Nov. 14, 1954  C. Owen (G.) T. Bitzos (O.) Fehr
                                            (P.)

UNITED STATES
New Orleans    Opera         Dec.  9, 1982  C. Deutekom (G.) C. Bergonzi (O.) F.
                                            Furlanetto (P.) A. Coppola cond.

New York       Carnegie      Dec.  7, 1972  R. Scotto (G.) J. Carreras (O.) P.
               Hall                         Plishka (P.) E. Queler cond.

                             Jan. 19, 1986  A. Millo (G.) C. Bergonzi (O.) P.
                                            Plishka (P.) E. Queler cond.

               City          Apr. 11, 1982  R. Shane/A. Putnam (G.) R. Calleo
               Opera                        (O.) J. Diaz (P.) C. Keene cond.

San Diego      Opera         June 22, 1979  C. Deutekom (G.) C. Bergonzi (O.) P.
                                            Plishka (P.) M. Arena cond.

5. ERNANI-*Dramma lirico* in four acts
Venice-Teatro la Fenice-Mar. 9, 1844
Libretto by Francesco Maria Piave

| | |
|---|---|
| Elvira (E.) | Sofia Loewe sop. |
| Ernani (H.) | Carlo Guasco ten. |
| Don Carlo (C.) | Antonio Superchi bar. |
| Don Ruy Gomez de Silva (S.) | Antonio Selva bass |
| Giovanna | Laura Saini sop. |
| Don Riccardo | Giovanni Lanner ten. |
| Jago | Andrea Bellini bass |

Conductor                                              Gaetano Mares
Director                        Luigi Carcano and Giuseppe Verdi

OTHER PREMIERES

ALGERIA
Algiers                  May  31, 1845 C. Rapazzini (E.) G. Winter (H.)
                                       Pauli (C.) G. Rossi (S.)

ARGENTINA
Buenos Aires  Victoria   July 26, 1849 N. Barbieri-Thiollier (E.) P. Senta-
                                       ti (H.) J. Thiollier (C.) P. Franchi
                                       (S.) C. Wymen cond.

              Ant. Colón June?    1857 S. Vera-Lorini (E.)

AUSTRALIA
Adelaide      Victoria   Mar.  6, 1861 G. Bianchi (E.) E. Bianchi (H.) E.
                                       Grossi (C.) J. Gregg (S.)

Melbourne     Princess   Nov. 22, 1858 M. Carandini (E.) Laglaise (H.) E.
                                       Coulon (C.) Schluter (S.)

Sydney        Prince     Apr. 18, 1857 M. Carandini (E.) Laglaise (H.) E.
              of Wales                 Coulon (C.) F. Howson (S.)

AUSTRIA
Graz          Stadt      Sep.  7, 1847 (in Ger.)

Linz          Landes     Oct. 25, 1848 (in Ger.)

Vienna        Kärntnertor May 30, 1844 E. Tadolini (E.) L. Ferretti (H.) G.
                                       Ronconi (C.) I. Marini (S.) H. Proch
                                       cond. (in It.)

              Mar.  3, 1849 A. Ander (H.) (in Ger.)

BELGIUM
Antwerp       Royal      Sep. 14, 1851 V. Viola (E.) E. Armandi (H.) L.
                                       Finocchi (C.) G. C. Nerini (S.)

Brussels      Monnaie    Dec. 15, 1845 Julien (E.) Laborde (H.) Laurent
                                       (C.) C. H. Zelger (S.) (in Fr.)

              Galeries   Dec. 14, 1848 K. Evers (E.) E. Calzolari (H.) A.
                                       Olivari (C.) A. Zucconi (S.) (in
                                       It.)

Ghent         Grand      Mar. 18, 1863 Mayer-Boulart (E.) Tallon (H.) S.
                                       Carman (C.) T. Coulon (S.)

BRAZIL
Rio de        Sao Pedro    June 16, 1846 M. Marinangeli (E.) G. Marinangeli
Janeiro                                  (H.) F. Massiani (C.) G. Franchi
                                         (S.)

Sao Paulo     Provisorio          1874 E. Pezzoli (E.) G. Limberti (H.) L.
                                       Barcena (C.) G. Mirandola (S.)

CANADA
Montreal      Th. Royal    June 29, 1853 R. Devries (E.) G. Forti (H.) F.
                                         Taffanelli (C.) D. Coletti (S.) L.
                                         Arditi cond.

Quebec        Music Hall   Aug.  2, 1860 C. Ghioni (E.) G. Sbriglia (H.) A.
                                         Ardavani (C.) G. Mirandola (S.)

Toronto       Grand        May  11, 1875 (in Eng.)

CHILE
Santiago      Republica    July 11, 1847 T. Rossi (E.) A. Zambaiti (H.) G.
                                         Bastoggi (C.) R. Pantanelli cond.

              Municipal    Sep. 17, 1857 S. Amic-Gazan (E.) L. Guglielmini
                                         (H.) A. Lanzoni (C.) G. Bastoggi
                                         (S.) (Inauguration of the theatre)

Valparaiso    Victoria     Dec. 24, 1847 T. Rossi (E.) G. Bastoggi (C.)

CHINA
Shanghai      Lyceum       Jan.  5, 1880 R. Genolini (E.) E. Sbriscia (H.) G.
                                         Bergamaschi (C.) A. Bagagiolo (S.)

COLOMBIA
Bogota        Teatro       Aug.     1858 R. Olivieri (E.) E. Rossi-Guerra
                                         (H.) E. Luisia (C.) G. Mirandola
                                         (S.)

CUBA
Havana        Tacon        Nov. 18, 1846 F. Tedesco (E.) N. Perelli (H.) L.
                                         Vita (C.) L. Battaglini (S.)

Santiago      Principal    Summer   1851 L. Caranti-Vita (E.) A. Arnoldi (H.)
                                         A. Gasparoni (S.)

CZECHOSLOVAKIA
Bratislava                 Dec.     1846 M. L. Ruggeri (E.) Lanner (H.) G.
                                         Reina (C.) O. Bonafous (S.)

Brno          Stadt        Aug. 20, 1847

Prague        Ständiches   Dec. 15, 1849 Fehringer (E.) (in Ger.)

              Provisional  Sep. 10, 1865 E. Ehrenberg (E.) J. Schwarz (C.)
                                         (in Czech)

DENMARK
Copenhagen    Royal        Mar.  1, 1846 F. Leon (E.) P. Cicerchia Rossi (H.)
                                         C. Vajro (C.) N. Torre (S.) P. Spe-
                                         rati cond. (in It.)

EGYPT
Cairo         Khedivial    Dec. 11? 1869 E. La Grua (E.) C. Bulterini (H.) C.
                                         Boccolini (C.) E. Rossi-Galli (S.)
                                         G. Bottesini cond.

FINLAND
Helsinki                July 19, 1857 (in Ger.)

                 Jan. 4, 1876 (in Fin.)

         Alexanders Feb. 19, 1881 A. Spaak (E.) A. Brunetti (H.) M. Danisi (C.) A. Fiorini (S.) (in It.)

FRANCE
Lyon         Grand       July ? 1851 V. Viola (E.) A. Giuglini (H.) A. Ghislanzoni (C.) A. Susini (S.) (In It.)

                  Feb. 1861 (in Fr.)

Marseille    Grand       Jan. 1846 (in Fr.)

Nice         Municipal   Sep. 12 1846 E. Mascarich (E.) G. Ricci (H.) L. Walter (C.) G. B. Antonucci (S.)

Paris        Italien     Jan. 6, 1846 T. Brambilla (E.) S. Malvezzi (H.) G. Ronconi (C.) P. Dérivis (S.)

GERMANY
Berlin       Königstädt- Dec. 27, 1845 R. Basso-Borio (E.) L. Tomassoni liches (H.) E. Crivelli (C.) G. Dalbesio (S.)

          Hofoper     May 16, 1859 L. Köster (E.) A. Ander (H.) F. Betz (C.) A. L. Fricke (S.) Taubert cond. (in Ger.)

Braunschweig Hoftheater Apr. 4, 1847

Breslau     Stadt       July 25, 1858 (in Ger.)

Darmstadt   Hoftheater Oct. 10, 1847

Dresden     Hoftheater Mar. 5, 1849 J. Wagner (E.) R. Wagner cond. (in Ger.)

Frankfurt   Stadt       Feb. 12, 1851 E. Capitain (E.) F. Chrudimsky (H.) Clement (C.) Leser (S.) (in Ger.)

                  May 24, 1852 V. Viola (E.) E. Armandi (H.) F. Giannini (C.) A. Zucconi (S.) (in It.)

Hamburg     Stadt       May 1846 F. Salvini-Donatelli (E.) N. Benedetti (H.) E. Crivelli (C.) (in It.)

                  Jan. 20, 1847 (in Ger.)

Hannover    Hoftheater Apr. 15, 1847 (in Ger.)

Leipzig     Stadt       July 4, 1858 (in Ger.)

Mainz       Stadt       Mar. 3, 1853 Beyer (H.) (in Ger.)

Munich      Hoftheater Apr. 13, 1848 (in Ger.)

Nürnberg    Stadt       Nov. 17, 1850 (in Ger.)

Stuttgart   Hoftheater Feb. 21, 1847 (in Ger.)

Weimar          Hoftheater    Sep. 12, 1852 (in Ger.)

GREAT BRITAIN
Birmingham      Th. Royal     Nov. 27, 1886 K. Rolla (E.) F. Runcio (H.) I. De
                                            Anna (C.) A. Abramoff (S.) L. Arditi
                                            cond. (in It.)

Edinburgh       Th. Royal     Jan. 29, 1856 E. Fodor-Mainville (E.) P. Neri-Ba-
                                            raldi (H.) F. Monari (C.) C. H.
                                            Zelger (S.) (in It.)

                Operetta      Feb.  2, 1869 I. Gilliess (E.) H. Bond (H.) H.
                House                        Corri (C.) Ha. Corri (S.) J. W. Pew
                                            cond. (in Eng.)

Glasgow         Royal         Aug. 16, 1869 I. Gilliess (E.) W. Parkinson (H.)
                Alexandra                   H. Corri (C.) Ha. Corri (S.) J. W.
                                            Pew cond. (in Eng.)

                Th. Royal     May  4, 1910 Protti (E.) Barbato (H.) Modesti
                                           (C.) (in It.)

Liverpool       Th. Royal     Sep.  5, 1854 S. Cruvelli (E.) E. Tamberlick (H.)
                                            Fortini (C.) J. Tagliafico (S.)

London          Her           Mar.  8, 1845 R. Basso-Borio (E.) N. Moriani (H.)
                Majesty's                   L. Fornasari (C.) A. Bottelli (S.)
                                            M. Costa cond.

                Covent        July  3, 1847 B. Steffenone (E.) L. Salvi (E.) M.
                Garden                       Alboni (C.) I. Marini (S.) M. Costa
                                            cond.

                Surrey        Nov.  1, 1851 (in Eng.)

Manchester      Th. Royal     Aug. 28, 1854 S. Cruvelli (E.) E. Tamberlick (H.)
                                            Fortini (C.) J. Tagliafico (S.)

GREECE
Athens          Royal         Jan.?    1851 M. Marchesini (E.) D. Mecksa (H.)
                                            Consoli (C.) G. Capriles (S.)

Corfu           San Giacomo Jan.       1845 C. Hollósy (E.) A. Zinghi (H.) R.
                                            Colmenghi (C.) A. Loglio (S.)

GUATEMALA
Guatemala       Carrera       Nov.  8, 1859 C. Cairoli (E.) Guidi (H.) Ungari
City                                        (C.) L. Maggiorotti (S.)

HONG KONG
Hong Kong       Lusitano      May  25, 1867 M. Veralli (E.) A. Errani (H.) G.
                                            Colombo (C.) G. Reina (S.)

HUNGARY
Budapest        Nemzeti       Aug.  6, 1846 E. Ercolani (E.) G. Bianchi (H.) G.
                Szinház                      Paltrinieri (C.) C. Rocca (S.) (in
                                            It.)

                Feb.  3, 1847 C. Hollósy (E.) K. Farkas-Wolf (H.)
                                            M. Füredi (C.) K. Köszeghy (S.) F.
                                            Erkel cond. (in Hung.)

                Operaház      Oct. 30, 1884 I. Reich (E.) G. Perotti (H.) L. von
                                            Bignio (C.) L. Odry (S.) (in Hung.)

INDIA
Bombay       Grant Rd.     Dec. 18, 1878 R. Genolini (E.) L. Coy (H.) G. Ber-
gamaschi (C.) Salvarani (S.)

Calcutta       Town Hall     May    2, 1866 R. Vielli-Villa (E.) T. Villa (H.)
A. Grandi (C.) F. Fiorani (S.)

INDONESIA
Batavia       T. Batavie    Aug. 31, 1865 De Mesmaeckers (E.) J. Moulin (H.)
Lavagne (C.) De Gréef (S.) (in Fr.)

                                        July 12, 1869 R. Vielli-Villa (E.) T. Villa (H.)
L. Magnani (C.) E. Gasperini (S.)
(in It.)

IRELAND
Dublin        Th. Royal     Oct. 30, 1849 Lucombe-Reeves (E.) S. Reeves (H.)
Delavanti (C.) H. Whitworth (S.)
Lavenu cond. (in Eng.)

                                        Feb. 24, 1851 Lucombe-Reeves (E.) S. Reeves (H.)
Mengis (C.) Paltoni (S.) (in It.)

ITALY
Alessandria    Civico       Oct.   5, 1844 A. Boccabadati (E.) E. Musich (H.)
G. Ferri (C.) C. Gazzuoli Boccabada-
ti (S.)

Ancona        Muse         Jan. 17, 1846 G. Montuchielli (E.) G. Nerozzi (H.)
G. Sansoni (C.) G. De Lorenzi (S.)

Bari          Piccinni     Dec.   1, 1855 A. Oliva-Pavani (H.) D. Squarcia
(C.) F. Gionfrida (S.)

Bergamo      Riccardi     Aug. 11, 1844 G. Strepponi (E.) L. Cuzzani (H.) F.
Colini (C.) L. Caliari (S.) M. Bone-
si cond.

Bologna      Comunale    Oct. 19, 1844 S. Loewe (E.) N. Ivanoff (H.) F. Varesi (C.) L. Tabellini (S.) G. Ma-
netti cond.

Brescia      Grande      Aug. 18, 1844 A. Boccabadati (E.) L. Ferretti (H.)
R. Colmenghi (C.) S. Torre (S.)

Cagliari     Civico       Dec. 27, 1845 E. Fodor-Mainville (E.) A. Pompejano
(H.) F. Tati (C.) L. Caliari (S.)

Catania      Comunale    Nov. 11, 1845 F. Maray (E.) E. Marcucci (H.) P.
Bartolini (C.) G. Lauri (S.) M.
Pappalardo cond.

Chieti        Maruccino   Apr. 24, 1848 A. Arcioli (E.) G. Musiani (H.) L.
Roncagli (C.) A. Mauri (S.) G. Libe-
rali cond.

Cremona      Concordia   Sep.   9, 1844 C. Barili-Patti (E.) G. Bettini (H.)
L. Valli (C.) G. De Lorenzi (S.)

Faenza        Comunale    June 30, 1844 G. Leva (E.) F. Ciaffei (H.) F. Colini (C.) L. Della Santa (S.)

Fermo         Aquila      Aug.      1845 R. Gabussi De Bassini (E.) A. Castellan (H.) N. Costantini (C.) S.
Panzini (S.) G. C. Ferrarini cond.

| | | | |
|---|---|---|---|
| Ferrara | Comunale | May 5, 1845 | E. Frezzolini (E.) A. Poggi (H.) L. Rinaldini (C.) G. Bruscoli (S.) |
| Fiume | Civico | Mar. 17, 1846 | C. Lusignani (E.) O. Fort (H.) G. Paltrinieri (C.) G. Paltoni (S.) |
| Florence | Pergola | June 20, 1844 | E. Frezzolini (E.) A. Poggi (H.) A. De Bassini (C.) G. Miral (S.) |
| Genoa | Carlo Felice | June 13, 1844 | S. Loewe (E.) G. Roppa (H.) P. Dérivis (C.) F. Leonardi (S.) G. Serra cond. |
| Jesi | Concordia | Aug. 30, 1845 | M. Barbieri-Nini (E.) L. Bernabei (H.) S. Ronconi (C.) G. Miral (S.) |
| Livorno | Rossini | Aug. 13, 1844 | M. Gazzaniga (E.) G. Pancani (H.) S. Ronconi (C.) L. Salandri (S.) |
| Lucca | Giglio | Aug. 27, 1844 | T. De Giuli-Borsi (E.) G. Roppa (H.) A. De Bassini (C.) C. Porto (S.) |
| Lugo | Rossini | Sep. 11, 1847 | E. Nissen (E.) G. Sinico (H.) G. Fiori (C.) L. Corradi-Setti (S.) |
| Mantua | Sociale | Dec. 26, 1844 | R. Gabussi De Bassini (E.) A. Castellan (H.) A. De Bassini (C.) S. Rosi (S.) G. C. Ferrarini cond. |
| Messina | Munizione | Dec. 9, 1847 | A. Bertucca (E.) A. Pompejano (H.) Poggiali (S.) |
| Milan | La Scala | Sep. 3, 1844 | R. Gabussi De Bassini (E.) C. Guasco (H.) O. Mancusi (C.) I. Marini (S.) E. Cavallini cond. |
| Modena | Comunale | Dec. 26, 1844 | C. Cuzzani (E.) V. Ferrari-Stella (H.) F. Tati (C.) G. Rossi (S.) A. Sighicelli cond. |
| Naples | San Carlo | May 13, 1847 | T. Brambilla (E.) S. Malvezzi (H.) F. Gionfrida (C.) N. Benedetti (S.) A. Farelli cond. |
| Padua | Nuovo | July 14, 1844 | G. Bortolotti (E.) G. Fraschini (H.) F. Varesi (C.) A. Selva (S.) |
| Palermo | Carolino | Dec. 29, 1844 | G. Strepponi (E.) G. B. Milesi (H.) F. Ferlotti (C.) G. Catalano (S.) |
| Parma | Regio | Dec. 26, 1844 | M. Barbieri-Nini (E.) N. Ivanoff (H.) F. Varesi (C.) S. L. Bouché (S.) N. De Giovanni cond. |
| Pavia | Condominio | Dec. 26, 1844 | A. Mairani Poppi (E.) G. Borelli (H.) O. Mancusi (C.) G. Maspes (S.) |
| Piacenza | Municipale | Aug. 9, 1845 | L. Abbadia (E.) A. Brunacci (H.) G. B. Giani (C.) G. B. Acquaroni (S.) G. Jona cond. |
| Pisa | Ravvivati | Dec. 12, 1845 | C. Ferrarini Baschieri (E.) E. Caggiati (H.) F. Cuturi (C.) G. Miral (S.) L. Nicolai cond. |

Verdi

| Ravenna | Comuni-<br>tativo | Apr. 30, 1845 | C. Cuzzani (E.) N. Ivanoff (H.) N. Costantini (C.) C. Crescentini (S.) G. Nostini cond. |
|---|---|---|---|
| Reggio Emilia | Comunale | Oct. 5, 1845 | G. Minozzi (E.) A. Della Cella (H.) L. Pignoli (C.) G. Bruscoli (S.) G. Tebaldi cond. |
| Rome | Argentina | May 29, 1844 | G. Leva (E.) F. Ciaffei (H.) F. Co-lini (C.) L. Della Santa (S.) |
| | Apollo | Dec. 27, 1845 | T. De Giuli-Borsi (E.) N. Ivanoff (H.) F. Colini (C.) A. Zanchi (S.) E. Angelini cond. |
| | Costanzi | Oct. 12, 1882 | E. Colonna (E.) H. Prévost (H.) E. Rubirato (C.) A. Silvestri (S.) M. Mancinelli cond. |
| Rovigo | Sociale | Nov. 12, 1844 | G. Bortolotti (E.) G. Solieri (H.) N. Costantini (C.) A. Selva (S.) D. Tosarini cond. |
| Sinigaglia | Comunale | Aug. 27, 1844 | E. Frezzolini (E.) A. Poggi (H.) P. Balzar (C.) G. Staffolini (S.) |
| Siena | Rinnovati | July 16, 1845 | M. Gazzaniga (E.) E. Caggiati (H.) F. Cuturi (C.) L. Salandri (S.) |
| Spoleto | Nobile | Carn. 1848-49 | |
| Trento | Sociale | May 25, 1845 | G. Armenia (E.) L. Bianchi (H.) G. Antoldi (C.) L. Maggiorotti (S.) |
| Treviso | Onigo | Oct. 26, 1844 | L. Matthey (E.) A. Della Cella (H.) D. Marchelli (C.) G. B. Acquaroni (S.) |
| Trieste | Grande | Oct. 26, 1844 | E. Frezzolini (E.) L. Ferretti (H.) F. Colini (C.) A. Rodas (S.) G. A. Scaramelli cond. |
| Turin | Regio | Dec. 26, 1844 | T. De Giuli-Borsi (E.) L. Ferretti (H.) A. Olivari (C.) I. Marini (S.) |
| Udine | Sociale | July 26, 1845 | G. Armenia (E.) A. Balestracci (H.) G. Antoldi (C.) G. Dal Pesce (S.) |
| Verona | Filarmonico | Dec. 26, 1844 | S. Loewe (E.) L. Cuzzani (H.) G. Ferri (C.) C. Gazzuoli-Boccabadati (S.) C. Sampietro cond. |
| Vicenza | Eretenio | July 13, 1844 | T. Brambilla (E.) G. Bettini (H.) L. Valli (C.) G. Bottura (S.) |

JAPAN

| Tokyo | Imperial | Mar. 11, 1925 | A. Laskova (E.) F. Corbetta (H.) V. Scamuzzi (C.) Milocchi (S.) |
|---|---|---|---|

JUGOSLAVIA

| Ljubljana | Stanowskem | Apr. 23, 1850 | |
|---|---|---|---|
| Zagreb | National | Apr.? 1852 | G. Montuchielli (E.) F. De Ruggero (H.) T. Pieri (C.) G. Gerli (S.) |

Zara          Nobile       Dec.    1846 S. Scotti (E.) A. Cosma (H.) G. Lo-
                                        vati (S.)

LATVIA
Riga          National     Jan. 30, 1931 (in Let.) (Given earlier in German
                                        and probably in Italian)

LITHUANIA
Vilnius       Municipal    Mar.    1898 (in It.) (First production traced)

MALTA
La Valletta   Manoel       Dec.    1846 E. Servoli (E.) L. Ademollo (H.) L.
                                        Del Riccio (C.) C. Leonardis (S.)

MEXICO
Mexico City   Nacional     May 18, 1850 C. Barili-Thorn (E.) A. Arnoldi (H.)
                                        L. Taffanelli (C.) A. Valtellina
                                        (S.) A. Barili cond.

NETHERLANDS
Amsterdam     Italien      Nov.  8, 1845 B. Colleoni-Corti (E.) R. Castig-
                                        liano (H.) G. Mancusi (C.) R. Anconi
                                        (S.)

NEW ZEALAND
Auckland      Prince       Dec.  6, 1864 L. Escott (E.) H. Squires (H.) H.
              of Wales                  Wharton (C.) J. B. Kitts (S.)

Dunedin       Princess     Sep. 15, 1864 L. Escott (E.) H. Squires (H.) H.
                                        Wharton (C.) J. B. Kitts (S.)

NORWAY
Oslo          Royal        Aug.  7, 1849 A. Ricci (E.) E. Caggiati (H.) G.
                                        Guicciardi (C.) G. C. Casanova (S.)
                                        (in It.)

                           Jan.    1876 (in Norw.)

PERU
Lima          Principal    July 20, 1848 L. Micciarelli (E.) E. Pellegrini
                                        (H.) L. Walter (C.) Borsotti (S.)

PHILIPPINES
Manila                     Sep.?   1867 L. De Ponte (E.)

POLAND
Cracow        Imperial     June 11, 1853 (in Ger.)

Lwov          Szarbek      Apr. 18, 1850 Köfer (E.) Eppich (H.) (in Ger.)

                           May  6, 1867 G. Ronzi-Checchi (E.) G. Sbriglia
                                        (H.) V. Cottone (C.) C. Dalla Costa
                                        (S.) (in It.)

Warsaw        Wielki       Aug. 19, 1851 A. Valesi (E.) R. Assoni (C.) (in
                                        It.)

PORTUGAL
Lisbon        Sao Carlos   Jan.  1, 1845 A. Albertini (E.) E. Tamberlick (H.)
                                        V. Sermattei (C.) E. Santi (S.)

Oporto        Sao Joao     May  3, 1845 F. Rocca-Alessandri (E.) G. Confor-
                                        tini (H.) G. Manzocchi (C.) L.
                                        Montemerli (S.)

PUERTO RICO
San Juan                        1852

ROMANIA
Bucharest     Nacional     Nov.  2, 1846  F.  Massimino  (E.)  G.  B.  Montresor
                                          (H.)  E.  Ventura  (C.)  P.  Tozzoli  (S.)
                                          (in It.)

                           Oct.?    1932  J.  Athanasiu  (C.)  (in Rum.)

Iasi          Teatrul     May  11, 1851  L.  Giordano  (E.)  G.  Ricci  (H.)  G.
                                          Donelli  (C.)  P.  Tozzoli  (S.)

RUSSIA
Kharkov       Municipal    Apr.?    1864  C.  Noel-Guidi  (E.)  A.  Gottardi  (H.)
                                          F.  Giannini  (C.)  E.  Manfredi  (S.)

Kiev          Imperial     Nov.?    1863  E.  Martoni  (E.)  V.  Bacci  (H.)  C.
                                          Fabbricatore  (C.)

Moscow        Bolshoi     Sep.  5, 1856  M.  Lotti  Della  Santa  (E.)  E.  Calzo-
                                          lari  (H.)  A.  De  Bassini  (C.)  I.  Ma-
                                          rini  (S.)  E.  Baveri  cond.

Odessa        Municipal    June?    1846

St.           Imperial    Sep. 30, 1846  T.  De  Giuli-Borsi  (E.)  C.  Guasco
  Petersburg                              (H.)  F.  Colini  (C.)  A.  Tamburini
                                          (S.)  E.  Baveri  cond.

Tbilisi       Imperial     Oct.?    1852  Minozzi  (E.)

SOUTH AFRICA
Capetown      Th. Royal   Dec.  3, 1875  A.  Brambilla  (E.)  Greco  (C.)  De  San-
                                          tis  (S.)

Johannesburg  Amphi-      June 13, 1895  E.  Ancarani  (E.)  A.  Mauri  (H.)  M.  Da
              theatre                     Padova  (C.)  D.  Benferreri  (S.)

SPAIN
Barcelona     Nuevo       Apr. 16, 1845  E.  Parepa-Archebugi  (E.)  G.  Solieri
                                          (H.)  M.  Assoni  (C.)  A.  Selva  (S.)

              Liceo       Sep. 24, 1847  F.  Salvini-Donatelli  (E.)  A.  Castel-
                                          lan  (H.)  G.  Ferri  (C.)  S.  L.  Bouché
                                          (S.)

Cadiz         Principal   July 26, 1845  C.  Bertolini-Raffaelli  (E.)  G.  Zobo-
                                          li  (H.)  V.  Sermattei  (C.)  D.  Raffa-
                                          elli  (S.)

Madrid        Circo       Nov. 25, 1844  I.  Ober-Rossi  (E.)  G.  Bettini  (H.)
                                          E.  Spech  (C.)  G.  Euzet  (S.)

              Real        Mar. 13, 1851  E.  Frezzolini  (E.)  G.  Masset  (H.)  P.
                                          Barroilhet  (C.)  K.  Formes  (S.)

Valencia      Principal   Dec.  7, 1845  C.  Villò-Ramos  (E.)  J.  Gomez  (H.)
                                          E.  Santi  (C.)  A.  Santarelli  (S.)

SWEDEN
Stockholm     Mindre      Aug. 23, 1848  R.  Penco  (E.)  F.  Ciaffei  (H.)  L.
                                          Della  Santa  (C.)  G.  C.  Casanova  (S.)
                                          (in It.)

| | | | |
|---|---|---|---|
| Royal | Oct. 3, 1848 | R. Penco (E.) F. Ciaffei (H.) L. Della Santa (C.) G. C. Casanova (S.) |

SWITZERLAND

| | | |
|---|---|---|
| Basel | Stadt | Nov. 2, 1860 Morska (E.) |
| Geneva | Grand | June 20, 1861 (in Ger.) |
| | | Jan. 10, 1865 (in It.) |
| Lugano | Sociale | Oct. 10, 1846 V. Bozzi (E.) S. Borelli (H.) T. Smitter (C.) L. Silingardi (S.) (in It.) |
| Zürich | Stadt | Jan. 17, 1853 (in Ger.) |

TURKEY

| | | |
|---|---|---|
| Constan-tinople | Naum | Feb. 1? 1845 E. Cominotti (E.) A. Piacentini (H.) A. Avignone (C.) Marchesini (S.) |

UNITED STATES

| | | |
|---|---|---|
| Baltimore | Holliday Street | Jan. 23, 1851 T. Truffi-Benedetti (E.) G. Forti (H.) A. Avignone (C.) |
| Boston | Athenaeum | Apr. 23, 1847 F. Tedesco (E.) N. Perelli (H.) L. Vita (C.) P. Novelli (S.) |
| Chicago | Metro-politan | Dec. 6, 1859 T. Parodi (E.) G. Sbriglia (H.) F. Gnone (C.) N. Barili (S.) A. Torriani cond. |
| Cincinnati | Lyceum | July 27, 1853 R. Devries (E.) L. Forti (H.) F. Taffanelli (C.) D. Coletti (S.) L. Arditi cond. |
| Cleveland | Ac. of Mus. | Oct. 31, 1859 T. Parodi (E.) G. Sbriglia (H.) F. Gnone (C.) N. Barili (S.) A. Torriani cond. |
| Dallas | Op. House | Dec. 19, 1889 E. Abbott (E.) (in Eng.) |
| Detroit | Metro-politan | Nov. 24, 1859 T. Parodi (E.) G. Sbriglia (H.) F. Gnone (C.) N. Barili (S.) A. Torriani cond. |
| Houston | Gray's | Jan. 2, 1890 E. Abbott (E.) (in Eng.) |
| Los Angeles | Theatre | Dec. 22, 1890 E. Abbott (E.) (in Eng.) |
| | | Oct. 15, 1897 N. Mazzi (E.) F. Collenz (H.) C. Cioni (C.) F. Scolari (S.) (in It.) |
| Louisville | City Th. | Aug. 9, 1853 R. Devries (E.) G. Forti (H.) F. Taffanelli (C.) D. Coletti (S.) L. Arditi cond. |
| Milwaukee | Music Hall | Oct. 30, 1865 C. Ghioni (E.) A. Macaferri (H.) G. Mancusi (C.) A. Susini (S.) M. Strakosch cond. |
| New Orleans | St. Charles | Mar. 31, 1854 R. Devries (E.) A. Arnoldi (H.) F. Taffanelli (C.) L. Rocco (S.) L. Arditi cond. |

New York      Park          June 14, 1847 F. Tedesco (E.) N. Perelli (H.) L.
                                          Vita (C.) P. Novelli (S.) L. Arditi
                                          cond.

              Ac. of Mus.   May  25, 1855 A. De la Grange (E.) R. Mirate (H.)
                                          F. Morelli-Ponti (C.) I. Marini (S.)
                                          L. Arditi cond.

Philadelphia  Chestnut      July 14, 1847 F. Tedesco (E.) N. Perelli (H.) L.
              Street                      Vita (C.) P. Novelli (S.) L. Arditi
                                          cond.

              Ac. of Mus.   Apr.  8, 1857 M. Gazzaniga (E.) A. Arnoldi (H.·) F.
                                          Amodio (C.) Arnoldi (S.)

Pittsburgh    Atheneum      Nov. 28, 1853 R. Devries (E.) A. Arnoldi (H.) F.
                                          Taffanelli (C.) D. Coletti (S.) L.
                                          Arditi cond.

St. Louis     Varieties     Oct. 14, 1853 R. Devries (E.) A. Arnoldi (H.) F.
                                          Taffanelli (C.) D. Coletti (S.) L.
                                          Arditi cond.

San Francisco Metro-        Nov. 14, 1854 C. Barili-Thorn (E.) C. Scola (H.)
              politan                     A. Lanzoni (C.) F. Leonardi (S.)

Washington    Washington    Mar. 20, 1860 P. Colson (E.) G. Stigelli (H.) G.
                                          Ferri (C.) A. Susini (S.)

URUGUAY
Montevideo    Teatro        Feb. 18, 1852 I. Edelvira (E.)

              Solis         Aug. 25, 1856 S. Vera Lorini (E.) G. Comolli (H.)
                                          G. Cima (C.) F. Tati (S.) L. Pretti
                                          cond.

VENEZUELA
Caracas       T. Caracas    Oct. 22, 1854 C. Saeman (E.) Soler (H.) F. Dra-
                                          gone (C.) V. Caspani (S.)

              Municipal     Feb. 10, 1881 M. Lucchesi (E.) F. Giannini (H.) D.
                                          Farina (C.) R. Mancini (S.) F. Ra-
                                          chelle cond.

SELECTED PRODUCTIONS-1900-1945

ARGENTINA
Buenos Aires  Opera         May  25, 1902 M. De Lerma (E.) J. Biel (H.) M. An-
                                          cona (C.) R. Ercolani (S.)

              Politeama     July  3, 1903 E. Bianchini-Cappelli (E.) A. Fran-
                                          ceschini (H.) G. M. Sammarco (C.) G.
                                          De Grazia (S.)

                            June  7, 1908 M. De Lerma (E.) J. Biel (H.) F. M.
                                          Bonini (C.) G. Mansueto (S.)

AUSTRIA
Vienna        Hofoper       June  3, 1910 E. De Lys (E.) F. Fazzini (H.) M.
                                          Battistini (C.) V. Arimondi (S.) A.
                                          Vigna cond. (in It.)

CHILE
Santiago        Municipal    July 19, 1902 C. Boninsegna (E.) A. Franceschini
                                           (H.) G. Pacini (C.) P. Wulman (S.)
                                           G. Armani cond.

                             Aug. 11, 1903 A. Alloro (E.) C. Cartica (H.) E.
                                           Nani (C.) L. Nicoletti-Kormann (S.)

                             Sep. 14, 1907 G. Russ (E.) P. Schiavazzi (H.) E.
                                           Giraldoni (C.) A. Masini-Pieralli
                                           (S.) G. Armani cond.

                             Oct. 3, 1908 L. Siebanech (E.) A. Franceschini
                                           (H.) P. Amato (C.) A. Masini-Pieral-
                                           li (S.) G. Armani cond.

                             Oct. 4, 1911 C. Boninsegna (E.) G. De Tura (H.)
                                           C. Galeffi (C.) G. Mansueto (S.)

                             Sep. 17, 1917 O. Nieto (E.) A. Scampini (H.) G.
                                           Segura-Tallien (C.) L. Nicoletti-
                                           Kormann (S.)

CZECHOSLOVAKIA
Prague          Neues        May 5, 1901 M. De Macchi (E.) F. Cardinali (H.)
                Deutsches                 V. Brombara (C.) V. Arimondi (S.)

                             May 8, 1909 E. De Lys (E.) C. Barrera (H.) M.
                                          Battistini (C.) V. Arimondi (S.) A.
                                          Vigna cond.

                             May 23, 1910 E. De Lys (E.) F. Fazzini (H.) M.
                                           Battistini (C.) V. Arimondi (S.) A.
                                           Vigna cond.

ITALY
Bergamo         Donizetti    Aug.    1919 G. Russ (E.) C. Maestri (H.) G. Noto
                                          (C.) L. Donaggio (S.) G. Neri cond.

Florence        Pagliano     Dec. 6, 1900 F. Signorini (E.)

                Verdi        May 5, 1904 T. Chelotti (E.) V. Bieletto (H.) M.
                                         Battistini (C.) L. Rossato (S.)

                             Apr. 8, 1930 B. Scacciati (E.) A. Lamperi (H.) G.
                                          Bechi (C.) U. Novelli (S.) G. Mucci
                                          cond.

Milan           Dal Verme    Dec. 29, 1910 L. Ceglokoff (E.) G. Martinelli (H.)
                                           V. Ardito (C.) Montico (S.) Baldi
                                           Zenoni cond.

                             May 16, 1929 M. Carena (E.) G. Martinelli (H.) L.
                                           Montesanto (C.) U. Di Lelio (S.) U.
                                           Benvenuti cond.

                La Scala     Jan. 4, 1917 E. Mazzoleni (E.) N. Fusati (H.) M.
                                          Battistini (C.) G. Mansueto (S.) E.
                                          Panizza cond.

                             Dec. 26, 1935 G. Cigna (E.) F. Merli (H.) A. Bor-
                                           gioli (C.) T. Pasero (S.) G. Mari-
                                           nuzzi cond.

|  |  | Dec. 26, 1941 | C. Castellani (E.) F. Merli (H.) G. Bechi (C.) T. Pasero (S.) G. Marinuzzi cond. |
|---|---|---|---|

Naples    San Carlo    Jan. 30, 1902 M. De Macchi (E.) G. Dimitrescu/B. Lucignani/G. Jarici/A. Maurini (H.) M. Ancona (C.) C. Thos (S.) E. Mascheroni cond.

Mar. 29, 1911 E. Maglinlo (E.) F. Signorini (H.) R. Stracciari (C.) O. Luppi (S.) V. Gui cond.

Palermo    Massimo    Mar. 16, 1915 J. Capella/M. Cantoni (E.) N. Fusati (H.) L. Montesanto (C.) A. Masini-Pieralli/A. Gallo (S.) G. Bavagnoli cond.

Rome    Costanzi    Apr. 9, 1912 J. Capella (E.) A. Scampini (H.) M. Battistini (C.) G. Cirino (S.) E. Vitale cond.

Reale    Feb. 11, 1939 G. Cigna (E.) A. Lamperi/A. Melandri (H.) A. Borgioli (C.) G. Vaghi (S.) T. Serafin cond.

Oct. 17, 1941 G. Gatti/M. Pedrini (E.) F. Beval/G. Momo (H.) C. Tagliabue (C.) A. Beuf/ I. Tajo (S.) G. Baroni cond.

Sala RAI    July 25, 1934 C. Jacobo (E.) G. Breviario (H.) V. Guicciardi (C.) A. Marone (S.) A. Votto cond.

May 26, 1937 G. Gatti (E.) F. Merli (H.) C. Tagliabue (C.) N. Moscona (S.) V. Gui cond.

Dec. 9, 1944 G. Gatti (E.) R. Gigli (H.) G. Bechi (C.) I. Tajo (S.) F. Previtali cond.

Trieste    Verdi    Oct. 20, 1942 C. Castellani (E.) A. Pravadelli (H.) G. Bechi (C.) A. Beuf (S.) A. Narducci cond.

POLAND
Warsaw    Wielki    Jan. 1, 1902 E. Bianchini-Cappelli (E.) F. Constantino (H.) M. Battistini (C.)

Dec. 20, 1902 S. Kruszelnicka (E.) G. Dimitrescu (H.) M. Battistini (C.)

May 2, 1903 I. De Frate (E.) O. Cosentino (H.) G. Kaschmann (C.)

Feb. 16, 1905 E. Corsi (E.) C. Barrera (H.) M. Battistini (C.)

Feb. 6, 1909 M. Battistini (C.)

Feb. 24? 1910 M. Ischierdo (H.) M. Battistini (C.)

RUSSIA
Kharkov        Municipal    Apr. 28? 1902 E.  Adaberto (E.) F. De Grandi (H.)
                                         M. Battistini (C.) F. Vecchioni (S.)

Kiev           Imperial     Apr.  9? 1902 E.  Adaberto (E.) F. Constantino (H.)
                                         M. Battistini (C.) F. Vecchioni (S.)

                            Mar. 20? 1903 E.  Adaberto (E.) F. Cardinali (H.)
                                         M. Battistini (C.) F. Vecchioni (S.)

                            Mar. 10, 1914 C.  Boninsegna (E.) A. Tedeschi (H.)
                                         M. Battistini (C.)

Moscow         Bolshoi      Mar. 12, 1901 M.  De Lerma (E.) L. Longobardi (H.)
                                         M. Battistini (C.) V. Arimondi (S.)

Odessa         Municipal    Mar. 19? 1902 E.  Adaberto (E.) F. Constantino (H.)
                                         M. Battistini (C.) F. Vecchioni (S.)

                            Mar. 15, 1914 C.  Boninsegna (E.) Seliavin (H.) M.
                                         Battistini (C.)

St.            Conser-      Mar. 18, 1901 S.  Kruszelnicka (E.) L. Longobardi
Petersburg     vatoire                   (H.) M. Battistini (C.) V. Arimondi
                                         (S.)

                            Mar.  5, 1902 S.  Kruszelnicka (E.) F. Constantino
                                         (H.) M. Battistini (C.) V. Arimondi
                                         (S.)

                            Feb.  2, 1903 E.  Bianchini-Cappelli (E.) A. Bassi
                                         (H.) G. Kaschmann (C.) V. Arimondi
                                         (S.)

                            Mar.  2, 1909 Pegini (E.) A. Pintucci (H.)  M.
                                         Battistini (C.) F. Navarini (S.)

                            Mar. 21, 1910 T.  Burchi (E.) A. Pintucci (H.) M.
                                         Battistini (C.) G. Mansueto (S.)

                            Jan. 28, 1911 E.  Pucci (E.) A. Pintucci (H.) M.
                                         Battistini (C.) F. Navarini (S.)

               Petit        Mar. 20, 1908 E.  Corsi (E.) A. Pintucci (H.) M.
                                         Battistini (C.) F. Navarini (S.)

               Noriadago    Jan. 28, 1914 C.  Boninsegna (E.) A. Pintucci (H.)
               Doma                      M. Battistini (C.) F. Navarini (S.)

SPAIN
Barcelona      Liceo        Dec.  4, 1906 C.  David (E.) J. Biel (H.) M. Bat-
                                         tistini (C.) F. Navarini (S.)

                            Dec. 14, 1909 M.  Llacer (E.) A. Pintucci (H.) M.
                                         Battistini  (C.) L. Rossato (S.)

                            Dec. 11, 1912 A.  Agostinelli/E. Pucci (E.) L.
                                         Colazza (H.) R. Stracciari/L. Sil-
                                         vetti (C.) E. Sesona (S.)

                            Nov.  8, 1916 O.  Nieto (E.) F. Fazzini (H.) M.
                                         Battistini (C.) A. Masini-Pieralli
                                         (S.)

|          |              | Jan.  6, 1921 | T. Poli-Randaccio (E.) G. Campioni (H.) L. Montesanto (C.) J. Torres de Luna (S.) |

Madrid        Real          Mar.  4, 1916  O. Nieto (E.) E. Cunego (H.) M. Bat-
                                           tistini (C.) G. Mansueto (S.)

UNITED STATES
Atlanta       Auditorium    Apr. 24, 1922  R. Ponselle (E.) G. Martinelli (H.)
                                           G. Danise (C.) J. Mardones (S.) G.
                                           Papi cond.

Brooklyn      Ac. of Mus.   Dec. 25, 1923  R. Ponselle (E.) G. Martinelli (H.)
                                           T. Ruffo (C.) J. Mardones (S.) G.
                                           Papi cond.

New York      Metro-        Jan. 28, 1903  M. Sembrich (E.)  E. De Marchi  (H.)
              politan                      A. Scotti (C.) E. De Reszke (S.) L.
                                           Mancinelli cond.

                            Dec.  8, 1921  R. Ponselle (E.) G. Martinelli (H.)
                                           G. Danise/T. Ruffo (C.) J. Mardones
                                           (S.) G. Papi cond.

                            Dec. 16, 1922  R. Ponselle (E.) G. Martinelli (H.)
                                           T. Ruffo (C.) J. Mardones (S.) G.
                                           Papi cond.

                            Dec. 28, 1923  R. Ponselle (E.) G. Martinelli (H.)
                                           T. Ruffo/G. Danise (C.) J. Mardones
                                           (S.) G. Papi cond.

                            Dec. 17, 1928  R. Ponselle (E.) G. Martinelli/F.
                                           Jagel (H.) T. Ruffo/G. Danise/M. Ba-
                                           siola (C.) E. Pinza (S.) V. Bellezza
                                           cond.

Philadelphia  Metro-        Dec. 13, 1921  R. Ponselle (E.)  G. Martinelli (H.)
              politan                      G. Danise (C.) J. Mardones (S.) G.
                                           papi cond.

                            Dec. 11, 1928  R. Ponselle (E.) G. Martinelli (H.)
                                           G. Danise (C.) E. Pinza (S.) V. Bel-
                                           lezza cond.

SELECTED PRODUCTIONS-POST-WORLD WAR II

AUSTRIA
Bregenz       Fest-         July 21, 1987  A. Millo (E.)  G. Cianella  (H.)  R.
              spielhaus                    Bruson (C.) P. Burchudladze (S.) P.
                                           Steinberg cond.

FRANCE
Marseille     Opéra         Oct. 15, 1976  I. Ligabue/G. Dimitrova (E.) N. To-
                                           disco (H.) F. Bordoni (C.) G. Pappas
                                           (S.) C. F. Cillario cond.

GERMANY
Dresden                     May      1980  S. Murphy (E.) K. Collins (H.) C.
                                           Opthof (C.) R. Van Allen (S.) R.
                                           Armstrong cond.

Hamburg        Stadt        Jan.   6, 1980 G. Bumbry (E.)  C.  Cossuta (H.)  G.
                                           Zancanaro  (C.)  H.  Sotin  (S.)  N.
                                           Santi cond.

                            Mar. 19, 1981 E. Marton (E.)  V.  Moloveanu (H.)  A.
                                           Salvador  (C.)  C.  Siepi/A.  Ferrin
                                           (S.) N. Santi cond.

GREAT BRITAIN
Cardiff        New          Oct. 30, 1979 S. Murphy (E.)  K.  Collins (H.)  C.
                                           Opthof (C.)  R.  Van Allen (S.)

                            Feb. 28, 1980 S. Murphy (E.)  A. van Limpt (H.)  T.
                                           Sharpe (C.)  D.  Gwynne (S.)  A.  Hose
                                           cond.

London         Sadler's     Feb. 28, 1967 P. Tinsley  (E.)  D.  Smith  (H.)  R.
               Wells                        Bickerstaff (C.)  C.  Grant (S.)  B.
                                           Balkwill cond. (in Eng.)

                            Dec.  5, 1967 P. Tinsley (E.)  D.  Pilley (H.)  R.
                                           Bickerstaff (C.)  D.  Garrard (S.)  J.
                                           Baker cond.

               Royal        Oct. 30, 1972 V. Papantoniou (E.) R.  Merolla (H.)
               Fest. Hall                   P. Cappuccilli (C.) N.  Ghiaurov (S.)
                                           R. Giovaninetti cond.

               Dominion     Dec. 13, 1979 S. Murphy (E.)  K.  Collins (H.)  C.
                                           Opthof (C.)  R.  Van Allen (S.)  R.
                                           Armstrong cond.

Manchester     Opera Th.    Dec.  6, 1982 E. Nicholson (E.)  A.  Mee (H.)  K.
                                           Latham (C.)  S.  Richardson (S.)  E.
                                           Downes cond.

HUNGARY
Budapest                    Summer   1967 M. De Osma (E.)  L.  Ottolini (H.)  D.
                                           Dondi (C.)  C.  Cava (S.)  C.  Franci
                                           cond.

               Operaház     Jan. 24, 1980 V. Kincses (E.)  J.  Nagy (H.)  L. Mil-
                                           ler (C.)  K.  Kováts (S.)  L.  Gardelli
                                           cond.

ITALY
Florence       Comunale     June 14, 1957 A. Cerqueti (E.)  M.  Del Monaco (H.)
                                           E. Bastianini (C.)  B.  Christoff (S.)
                                           D. Mitropoulos cond.

                            Jan. 24, 1965 M. Roberti (E.)  U.  Borsò (H.)  M.  Za-
                                           nasi (C.)  P.  Washington (S.)  B.  Ri-
                                           gacci cond.

Genoa          Margherita   Nov. 18, 1974 C. Parada (E.)  C.  Bergonzi/B.  Preve-
                                           di (H.)  M.  Zanasi (C.)  B.  Giaiotti/
                                           M. Rinaudo (S.)  F.  Molinari-Pradelli
                                           cond.

Milan          La Scala     Feb. 25, 1959 M. Roberti/C. Parada (E.)  F.  Corel-
                                           li/P. Mirando-Ferraro (H.)  E.  Bas-
                                           tianini/D. Dondi/C. MacNeil (C.)  N.
                                           Rossi-Lemeni/N.  Zaccaria  (S.)  G.
                                           Gavazzeni cond.

|          |           | Dec.  7, 1969 | R. Kabaivanska (E.) P. Domingo (H.) C. Meliciani (C.) N. Ghiaurov (S.) A. Votto cond. |
|----------|-----------|---------------|---|

Dec.  7, 1982 M. Freni (E.) P. Domingo (H.) R. Bruson (C.) N. Ghiaurov (S.) R. Muti cond.

Sala RAI  Mar. 25, 1969 M. Caballé (E.) B. Prevedi (H.) P. Glossop (C.) B. Christoff (S.) G. Gavazzeni cond.

Modena  Comunale  Jan. 5, 1978 M. Parazzini (E.) N. Todisco (H.) L. Saccomani (C.) C. Cava (S.) G. Neuhold cond.

Naples  San Carlo  Nov. 27, 1960 M. Roberti (E.) M. Del Monaco (H.) E. Bastianini (C.) N. Rossi-Lemeni/ U. Novelli (S.) F. Previtali cond.

Apr. 18, 1982 M. Parazzini (E.) B. Rufo (H.) L. Saccomani (C.) N. Ghiuselev (S.) E. Boncompagni cond.

Palermo  Massimo  Dec. 9, 1965 A. Stella (E.) G. Limarilli (H.) C. MacNeil (C.) R. Ariè (S.) N. Sanzogno cond.

Rome  Sala RAI  June 25, 1950 C. Mancini (E.) G. Penno (H.) G. Taddei (C.) G. Vaghi (S.) F. Previtali cond.

Dec. 25, 1958 C. Araujo (E.) M. Del Monaco (H.) M. Sereni (C.) C. Siepi (S.) F. Previtali cond.

Opera  Feb. 10, 1951 C. Mancini (E.) G. Penno (H.) P. Silveri (C.) B. Christoff (S.) G. Santini cond.

Mar. 22, 1967 A. Stella (E.) M. Del Monaco/R. Orofino (H.) M. Zanasi (C.) R. Ariè/C. Cava (S.) F. Previtali cond.

Apr. 15, 1970 I. Ligabue (E.) A. Mori/R. Bondino (H.) M. Zanasi (C.) C. Cava (S.) F. Previtali cond.

Apr. 11, 1978 A. Gulin/S. Del Grande (E.) G. Casellato-Lamberti/P. Visconti (H.) R. Bruson/L. Montefusco (C.) M. Rinaudo/P. Washington (S.) B. Bartoletti/ M. Rinaldi cond.

Trieste  Verdi  Dec. 26? 1950 A. Guerrini (E.) G. Penno (H.) C. Tagliabue (C.) T. Pasero (S.) A. Votto cond.

Mar. 7, 1970 L. Vajna (E.) R. Bondino (H.) R. Bruson (C.) C. Cava (S.) O. Ziino cond.

Turin          Regio         Feb. 16, 1971 L. Maragliano/C. Parada (E.) F. Labò
                                           (H.) L. Montefusco (C.) B. Giaiotti
                                           (S.) A. Gatto cond.

                             Sep.  9, 1976 R. Orlandi-Malaspina (E.) G. Cecche-
                                           le (H.) A. Salvadori (C.) G. Casari-
                                           ni (S.) F. Molinari-Pradelli cond.

Venice         La Fenice     May 11, 1946 M. Pedrini (E.) G. Momo (H.) C. Ta-
                                           gliabue (C.) C. Siepi (S.) F. Ghione
                                           cond.

                             Dec. 26, 1950 C. Mancini (E.) G. Puma (H.) C. Ta-
                                           gliabue (C.) T. Pasero (S.) A. Votto
                                           cond.

                             Dec.  9, 1967 R. Orlandi-Malaspina (E.) M. Del
                                           Monaco/A. Mori (H.) M. Zanasi (C.)
                                           R. Ariè (S.) N. Sanzogno cond.

Verona         Arena         July 15, 1972 I. Ligabue/V. Gordoni (E.) F. Corel-
                                           li (H.) P. Cappuccilli (C.) R. Rai-
                                           mondi/I. Vinco (S.) O. De Fabritiis
                                           cond.

PORTUGAL
Lisbon         Sao Carlos    Apr.  3, 1970 A. Stella (E.) A. Zambon (H.) F.
                                           Bordoni (C.) A. Ferrin (S.) M.
                                           Wolff-Ferrari cond.

SPAIN
Barcelona      Liceo         Jan. 22, 1972 E. Renzi (E.) G. Cecchele (H.) P.
                                           Glossop (C.) P. Lagger (S.)

                             Dec. 16, 1981 O. Stapp (E.) N. Todisco (H.) P.
                                           Cappuccilli/J. Pons (C.)

Bilbao         Coliseo       Dec. 28, 1983 O. Stapp (E.) N. Todisco (H.) P.
               Alba                        Cappuccilli (C.) G. Surian (S.) U.
                                           R. Laorden cond.

Madrid         Zarzuela      May     1968 A. Stella (E.) A. Mori (H.) M. Petri
                                           (C.) R. Ariè (S.) C. Franci cond.

Valencia       Principal     May 11, 1977 M. Galvany (E.) P. Lavirgen (H.) M.
                                           Manuguerra (C.) D. Petkov (S.) A.
                                           Guadagno cond.

UNITED STATES
Chicago        Lyric         Oct. 24, 1984 G. Bumbry (E.) L. Bartolini (H.) P.
                                           Cappuccilli (C.) N. Ghiaurov (S.) D.
                                           Renzetti cond.

Cincinnati     Music Hall    May 30, 1975 C. Carson (E.) N. Shicoff (H.) C.
                                           MacNeil (C.) B. Giaiotti (S.) J.
                                           Levine cond.

Dallas         Opera         Dec. 18, 1982 G. Dimitrova (E.) C. Bini (H.) M.
                                           Manuguerra (C.) P. Plishka (S.) N.
                                           Rescigno (cond.

Los Angeles    Auditorium    Mar. 14, 1969 L. Price (E.) R. Cioni (H.) P. Glos-
                                           sop (C.) G. Tozzi (S.)

New Orleans                    Oct.  6, 1977 C. Carson (E.) R. Francesconi (H.)
                                           L. Quilico (C.) E. Flagello (S.) K.
                                           Andersson cond.

New York        Metro-         Nov. 23, 1956 Z. Milanov (E.) M. Del Monaco (H.)
                politan                     L. Warren/F. Guarrera (C.) C. Siepi/
                                           G. Tozzi (S.) D. Mitropolous cond.

                               Nov. 14, 1970 M. Arroyo (E.) C. Bergonzi (H.) S.
                                           Milnes (C.) R. Raimondi (S.)

                               Nov. 18, 1983 L. Mitchell/A. Negri (E.) L. Pava-
                                           rotti (H.) S. Milnes/P. Elvira (C.)
                                           R. Raimondi (S.) J. Levine cond.

San Francisco Opera            Sep. 13, 1968 L. Price (E.) R. Cioni (H.) P. Glos-
                                           sop (C.) E. Flagello (S.) G. Patanè
                                           cond.

                               Sep. 15, 1984 M. Caballé (E.) N. Todisco (H.) S.
                                           Milnes (C.) P. Plishka (S.) L. Gar-
                                           delli cond.


6. I DUE FOSCARI-*Tragedia lirica* in three acts
Rome-Teatro Argentina-Nov. 3, 1844
Libretto by Francesco Maria Piave

Lucrezia Contarini (L.)                        Marianna Barbieri-Nini sop.
Jacopo Foscari (J.)                                Giacomo Roppa ten.
Francesco Foscari (F.)                         Achille De Bassini bar.
Jacopo Loredano                                Baldassare Mirri bass
Pisana                                             Giulia Ricci sop.
Barbarigo                                      Atanasio Pozzolini ten.

Conductor
Director                                           Giuseppe Verdi

OTHER PREMIERES

ARGENTINA
Buenos Aires    Victoria       May  25, 1850 L. Pretti (L.) M. Liguori (J.) G.
                                           Ramonda (F.) J. V. Rivas cond.

AUSTRALIA
Melbourne       Haymarket      Feb. 13, 1868 I. Vitali (L.) U. Devoti (J.) G.
                                           Bertolini (F.)

Sydney          Prince         May  20, 1868 I. Vitali (L.) U. Devoti (J.) G.
                of Wales                    Bertolini (F.)

AUSTRIA
Vienna          Kärntnertor Apr.  1, 1845 R. Gabussi De Bassini (L.) E. Calzo-
                                           lari (J.) A. De Bassini (F.)

BELGIUM
Antwerp         Royal          Dec. 18, 1849 A. Lacombe (L.) Tisseyre (J.) Sardou
                                           (F.) (in Fr.)

                               Sep. 28, 1851 V. Viola (L.) A. Macaferri (J.) L.
                                           Finocchi (F.) (in It.)

Brussels        Galeries      Sep.?      1850 M. Clary (L.)

BRAZIL
Rio de          Sao Pedro     Sep. 12, 1849 L. Pretti (L.)   F. Spotorno  (J.) G.
Janeiro                                    Costa (F.)

Sao Paulo       Sao José      Aug. 12, 1884 F. Savio (L.)  T. Dasso (J.)  S. Sof-
                                           fietti (F.)

CHILE
Santiago        Universidad Oct. 1, 1848 T. Rossi (L.)  A. Zambaiti (J.)  G.
                                         Bastoggi (F.)  R. Pantanelli cond.

Valparaiso      Victoria      Mar. 31, 1850 L. Micciarelli (L.)  J. Ubaldi (J.)
                                           F. Leonardi (F.)

COLOMBIA
Bogota          Municipal     Aug. 11, 1893

CUBA
Havana          Tacon         Jan.  2, 1847

Santiago        Principal     Summer    1851 L. Caranti-Vita (L.)  A. Arnoldi (J.)

CZECHOSLOVAKIA
Bratislava                    May       1853 E. Zani (L.)  F. De Ruggero (J.)  A.
                                           Carapia (F.)  (in It.)

EGYPT
Alexandria      Rossini       Autumn    1880

FRANCE
Paris           Italien       Dec. 17, 1846 G. Grisi (L.)  Mario (J.)  F. Coletti
                                           (F.)  T. Tilmant cond.

GERMANY
Weimar          Hoftheater    Apr.  6, 1856 (in Ger.)

GREAT BRITAIN
London          Her           Apr. 10, 1847 A. Montenegro (L.)  G. Fraschini (J.)
                Majesty's                  F. Coletti (F.)  M. Balfe cond.

                Covent        June 19, 1847 G. Grisi (L.)  Mario (J.)  G. Ronconi
                Garden                     (F.)  M. Costa cond.

HUNGARY
Budapest        Nemzeti       Dec.  9, 1850 K. Farkas-Wolf (J.)  G. Reina (F.) K.
                Szinház                    Doppler cond. (in Hung.)

INDIA
Calcutta        Op. House     Dec. 26, 1871 R. Aimo (L.)  G. Artoni (J.)  G. Ghi-
                                           otti (F.)

INDONESIA
Batavia         T. Batavie    July 15, 1870 M. Zenoni (L.)  P. Setragni (J.)  L.
                                           Magnani (F.)

ITALY
Alessandria     Civico        Nov. 15, 1845 G. Leva (L.)  E. Calzolari (J.)  N.
                                           Costantini (F.)

Ancona          Muse          Apr.      1845 E. Boldrini (L.)  L. Bernabei (J.) F.
                                           Cuturi (F.)

| Bari | Piccinni | July | 1855 | E. Zenoni (L.) G. Pasi (J.) D. Squarcia (F.) |
|------|----------|------|------|--------|
| Bergamo | Riccardi | Aug. 25, | 1845 | T. Parodi (L.) P. Unanue (J.) F. Varesi (F.) M. Bonesi cond. |
| Bologna | Comunale | Oct. 2, | 1845 | L. Assandri (L.) S. Ronzi (J.) C. Badiali (F.) G. Manetti cond. |
| Brescia | Grande | Aug. 1, | 1846 | R. Gabussi De Bassini (L.) E. Musich (J.) A. De Bassini (F.) |
| Cagliari | Civico | Sep. | 1846 | E. Dielitz (L.) C. Scola (J.) R. Pizzigati (F.) |
| Catania | Comunale | Jan. 24, | 1846 | A. Mattioli (L.) E. Marcucci (J.) P. Bartolini (F.) M. Pappalardo cond. |
| Chieti | San Ferdinando | June 22, | 1845 | A. Mattioli (L.) E. Marcucci (J.) P. Bartolini (F.) B. Romanini cond. |
| Cremona | Concordia | Autumn | 1845 | G. Sanchioli (L.) G. Pancani (J.) F. Varesi (F.) |
| Faenza | Comunale | Dec. 26, | 1848 | F. Capuani (L.) C. Liverani (J.) M. Zacchi (F.) |
| Fermo | Aquila | Aug. | 1845 | R. Gabussi De Bassini (L.) A. Castellan (J.) N. Costantini (F.) G. C. Ferrarini cond. |
| Ferrara | Comunale | Apr. 10, | 1847 | C. Cuzzani (L.) G. Roppa (J.) G. Corsi (F.) |
| Fiume | Civico | Mar. | 1848 | C. Rapazzini (L.) G. Pavesi (J.) Morino (F.) |
| Florence | Pergola | Jan. 17, | 1845 | G. Bortolotti (L.) G. Sinico (J.) C. Badiali (F.) |
| Forli | Comunale | Apr. | 1845 | M. Barbieri-Nini (L.) G. Roppa (J.) S. Ronconi (F.) |
| Genoa | Carlo Felice | Apr. 12, | 1845 | A. Boccabadati (L.) L. Cuzzani (J.) F. Tafanelli (F.) N. Uccelli cond. |
| Livorno | Rossini | Dec. 26, | 1844 | E. Boldrini (L.) G. Pancani (J.) L. Rinaldini (F.) |
| Lucca | Giglio | Sep. 11, | 1845 | A. Boccabadati (L.) L. Ferretti (J.) F. Colini (F.) |
| Lugo | Rossini | Summer | 1845 | G. Bartolotti (L.) G. Roppa (J.) R. Ferlotti (F.) C. Aria cond. |
| Mantua | Sociale | Spring | 1846 | A. Artioli (L.) C. Miraglia (J.) |
| Messina | Munizione | Dec.? | 1847 | |
| Milan | La Scala | Aug. 26, | 1845 | C. Birch (L.) E. Musich (J.) A. De Bassini (F.) E. Cavallini cond. |
| Modena | Comunale | May 29, | 1847 | E. Garcia (L.) L. Ferretti (J.) C. Badiali (F.) A. Sighicelli cond. |

Naples          San Carlo     Feb.  9, 1845 A. Bishop (L.) G. Fraschini (J.) F.
                                            Coletti (F.) A. Farelli cond.

Padua           Nuovo         June 18, 1850 S. Cruvelli (L.) G. Fraschini (J.)
                                            G. Corsi (F.)

Palermo         Carolino      Oct.  3, 1846 G. Sanchioli (L.) E. Musich (J.) L.
                                            Corradi-Setti (F.) P. Raimondi cond.

Parma           Regio         Mar. 24, 1845 G. Leva (L.) E. Musich (J.) F. Vare-
                                            si (F.) N. De Giovanni cond.

Piacenza        Municipale    Carn. 1845-46 E. Ercolani (L.) O. Paglieri (J.) D.
                                            Coletti (F.) G. Jona cond.

Pisa            Ravvivati     Dec. 28, 1846 A. Moltini (L.) L. Bernabei (J.) G.
                                            Pellegrini (F.)

Ravenna         Comuni-       May      1847 C. Ferrarini-Baschieri (L.)  G. Gam-
                tativo                       boggi (J.) L. Montemerli (F.)

Reggio Emilia   Comunale      May  17, 1845 M. Barbieri-Nini (L.) G. Roppa (J.)
                                            S. Ronconi (F.) L. Boyer cond.

Siena           Rinnovati     July     1846 K. Evers (L.) J. B. Bordas (J.) F.
                                            Gorin (F.)

Sinigaglia      La Fenice     July?    1847 G. Rossetti-Sikorska (L.) N. Moriani
                                            (J.) A. De Bassini (F.)

Spoleto         Nobile        Dec. 26, 1847 A. Artioli (L.) L. Stefani (J.) A.
                                            Sabbatini (F.)

Trento          Sociale       June     1851 Castagnola (L.) T. Palmieri (J.) C.
                                            Bartolucci (F.)

Treviso         Onigo         Spring   1853 Cacciatori  (L.)  F.  Banti  (J.)  E.
                                            Storti (F.)

Trieste         Grande        Dec. 27, 1844 C. Moltini (L.) G. Pardini (J.) G.
                                            Corsi (F.) G. A. Scaramelli cond.

Turin           Carignano     Sep. 27, 1845 E. Boldrini (L.) S. Malvezzi (J.) F.
                                            Gorin (F.)

                Regio         Mar.  6, 1851 C. Gruitz (L.) G. Fraschini (J.) G.
                                            Ferri (F.) G. Ghebart cond.

Udine           Sociale       Aug.  8, 1847 S. Cruvelli (L.) A. Palma (J.) Lova-
                                            ti (F.)

Venice          San           Mar. 30, 1845 G. Bortolotti (L.)  G. Pancani  (J.)
                Benedetto                   C. Badiali (F.) G. Verdi dir.

                La Fenice     Feb. 11, 1847 E. Goggi (L.) L. Ferretti (J.) C.
                                            Badiali (F.) G. Mares cond.

Verona          Filarmonico   Dec. 26? 1845 T. Parodi (L.) A. Bozzetti (J.) F.
                                            Varesi (F.)

Vicenza         Eretenio      July 25, 1847 L. Assandri (L.) C. Miraglia (J.) L.
                                            Corradi-Setti (F.)

JUGOSLAVIA
Ljubljana      Stanowskem   Apr.     1853 E. Zani-Gherardi (L.) G. Aducci (J.)
                                          C. Busi (F.)

Zagreb         National     Apr.?    1852 G. Montuchielli (L.) F. De Ruggero
                                          (J.) T. Pieri (F.)

Zara           Nobile       Apr.?    1857 C. Marziali (L.) G. Petrovich (J.)

MALTA
La Valletta    Manuel       Autumn   1845

NETHERLANDS
Amsterdam      Italien      Nov.  4, 1847 M. Franceschini-Garis (L.) F. Gumi-
                                          rato (J.) F. Fallar (F.)

PERU
Lima           Principal    Nov. 12, 1848 L. Micciarelli (L.) E. Pellegrini
                                          (J.) L. Walter (F.)

PHILIPPINES
Manila         Principe     Autumn   1867 L. De Ponte (L.)
               Alfonso

POLAND
Lwov           Szarbek      May  31, 1856 Schreiber-Kirchberger  (L.)  Barrach
                                          (J.) Köhler (F.)

Warsaw         Wielki       May  24, 1849 (in Pol.)

                            Nov. 27, 1851 M. Sulzer (L.) G. Gamboggi (J.) (in
                                          It.)

PORTUGAL
Lisbon         Sao Carlos   Mar.  5, 1846 E. Ranzi (L.) G. Landi (J.)

Oporto         Sao Joao     Nov.?    1848 C. Belloni (L.) G. De Bezzi (J.) A.
                                          Alba (F.)

ROMANIA
Bucharest      Nacional     Jan. 14, 1850 C. Cuzzani (L.) G. De Vecchi (J.) G.
                                          Marini (F.)

Iasi           Teatrul      May  16, 1851 L. Caradori (L.) G. Pavesi (J.) G.
                                          Donelli (F.)

RUSSIA
Odessa         Municipal    Dec.  6, 1850 A. Basseggio (L.) M. Viani (J.)

St.            Imperial     Jan. 20, 1847 T.  De Giuli-Borsi  (L.)  C.  Guasco
 Petersburg                               (J.) F. Colini (F.) E. Baveri cond.

SPAIN
Barcelona      Principal    July  8, 1845 C. Cattinari (L.) G. B. Milesi (J.)
                                          A. Superchi (F.)

               Liceo        May  12, 1847 F. Salvini-Donatelli (L.) A. Castel-
                                          lan (J.) G. Ferri (F.)

Madrid         Circo        July 22, 1845 I.  Ober-Rossi  (L.)  E.  Tamberlick
                                          (J.) C. Salvatori (F.)

               Real         Mar. 13, 1852 C. Cattinari (L.) G. Sinico (J.) F.
                                          Cresci (F.)

Malaga        Principal   Jan.  9, 1849 T.  Rusmini-Solera  (L.)  G.  Solieri
                                          (J.) G. Assoni (F.)

Seville       San         May?     1846
              Fernando

SWITZERLAND
Lugano        Sociale     Autumn ? 1848

TUNISIA
Tunis         Filarmonico Oct. 29, 1882

TURKEY
Constan-      Naum        Oct. 17, 1846 M. Gresti (L.) A. Zinghi (J.) G. Fi-
tinople                                 ori (F.)

UNITED STATES
Boston        Athenaeum   May  11, 1847 T. Rainieri (L.) N. Perelli (J.) L.
                                        Vita (F.) L. Arditi cond.

New Orleans   Orleans     Mar.  6, 1851 R. Devries (L.) Duluc (J.) Genibrel
                                        (F.) (in Fr.)

              Opera       Jan. 19, 1865 A. Ghioni (L.) A. Macaferri (J.) G.
                                        Marra (F.) (in It.)

New York      Park        June  9, 1847 T. Rainieri (L.) N. Perelli (J.) L.
                                        Vita (F.) L. Arditi cond.

              Ac. of Mus. Apr. 15, 1863 G. Medori (L.) F. Mazzoleni (J.) F.
                                        Bellini (F.) E. Muzio cond.

Philadelphia  Walnut St.  July 19, 1847 T. Rainieri (L.) N. Perelli (J.) L.
                                        Vita (F.) L. Arditi cond.

San           It. Opera   May  26, 1855 C. Barili-Thorn  (L.)  C. Scola (J.)
Francisco                               A. Lanzoni (F.)

URUGUAY
Montevideo    San Felipe  Feb.  6, 1852 I. Edelvira (L.)

SELECTED REVIVALS-NINETEENTH CENTURY

AUSTRIA
Vienna        Kärntnertor May  8, 1851 C. Rapazzini (L.) G. Fraschini (J.)
                                       A. De Bassini (F.)

FRANCE
Paris         Italien     Aug.  1, 1848 M. Clary (L.) J. B. Bordas (J.) For-
                                        tini (F.) T. Tilmant cond.

              Oct. 10, 1848 A. Bosio (L.) J. B. Bordas (J.) F.
                                        Morelli-Ponti (F.) T. Tilmant cond.

              Nov. 17, 1849

              Nov. 11, 1856 C. Cattinari (L.) C. Ballestra (J.)
                                        G. Corsi (F.) G. Bottesini cond.

GREAT BRITAIN
London        Her         Mar. 21, 1848 S. Cruvelli (L.) I. Gardoni (J.) F.
              Majesty's                 Coletti (F.)

Mar. 30, 1849 Julian van Gelder (L.) J. B. Bordas
              (J.) F. Coletti (F.)

May   4, 1850 T. Parodi (L.) C. Baucardé (J.) F.
              Coletti (F.)

ITALY
Milan    La Scala    Oct.  7, 1847 C. Gruitz (L.) E. Musich (J.) G.
                                   Corsi (F.) E. Cavallini cond.

                     Jan.  8, 1849 C. Gruitz (L.) L. Ferretti (J.) G.
                                   Corsi (F.) E. Cavallini cond.

                     Sep.  4, 1858 T. Cotta-Morandini (L.) E. Naudin
                                   (J.) G. Corsi (F.)

Naples   San Carlo   June  3, 1845 A. Bishop (L.) G. Fraschini (J.) F.
                                   Coletti (F.) A. Farelli cond.

                     Feb. 27, 1847 C. Gruitz (L.) S. Malvezzi (J.) F.
                                   Gionfrida (F.) A. Farelli cond.

                     Oct. 10, 1847 C. Rambur (L.) S. Malvezzi (J.) F.
                                   Gionfrida (F.) A. Farelli cond.

                     Aug. 24, 1849 A. Albertini (L.) S. Malvezzi (J.)
                                   A. De Bassini (F.) A. Farelli cond.

                     Feb. 18, 1851 G. Zecchini (L.) G. Fedor (J.) A. De
                                   Bassini (F.) A. Farelli cond.

                     Oct.  4, 1852 S. Peruzzi (L.) E. Pancani (J.) F.
                                   Monari (F.) A. Farelli cond.

                     Mar. 22, 1855 G. Beltramelli (L.) E. Pancani (J.)
                                   F. Coletti (F.) A. Farelli cond.

                     Feb. 13, 1858 R. Gariboldi-Bassi (L.) G. Fraschini
                                   (J.) F. Coletti (F.) A. Farelli
                                   cond.

                     Jan. 25, 1859 G. Medori (L.) F. Prudenza (J.) F.
                                   Coletti (F.) A. Farelli cond.

                     June 13, 1860 L. Ruggero-Antonioli (L.) R. Berto-
                                   lini (J.) G. Guicciardi (F.) A. Fa-
                                   relli cond.

                     Oct. 13, 1860 L. Ruggero-Antonioli (L.) R. Berto-
                                   lini (J.) G. Guicciardi (F.)

                     May   4, 1864 G. Borsi de Leurie (L.) F. Patierno
                                   (J.) A. De Bassini (F.)

Rome     Argentina   Mar. 25, 1845 T. Truffi (L.) R. Mirate (J.) G.
                                   Ferri (F.)

                     May      1852 F. Capuani (L.) G. Landi (J.) F. Co-
                                   letti (F.)

                     Nov. 27, 1870 L. Gulli (J.) V. Quintili-Leoni (F.)

         Apollo      Jan.  7, 1847 A. Montenegro (L.) G. Roppa (J.) F.
                                   Varesi (F.) E. Angelini cond.

Jan.  5, 1850 A. Albertini (L.) E. Naudin (J.) F. Colini (F.) E. Angelini cond.

Feb. 15, 1854 M. Barbieri-Nini (L.) C. Baucardé (J.) F. Coletti (F.) E. Angelini cond.

Apr. 25, 1860 E. Boccherini (L.) C. Negrini (J.) F. Coletti (F.) E. Angelini cond.

Oct. 22, 1873 T. Singer (L.) F. Patierno (J.) F. Bacchi-Perego (F.)

Turin        Regio        Feb. 11, 1860 A. Basseggio (L.) A. Malagola (J.) G. F. Beneventano (F.) F. Bianchi cond.

UNITED STATES
New York     Ac. of Mus. Oct. 27, 1886 G. Valda (L.) E. Salto (J.) E. Pogliani (F.) O. Bimboni cond.

OTHER PRODUCTIONS-1900-1945

GERMANY
Halle                     Feb. 12, 1929 (in Ger.)

ITALY
Rome         Quirino      July  1, 1905 I. Imperiali (L.) G. Gelmore (J.) G. Giani (F.) P. Bellucci cond.

             Aug. 28, 1905 I. Imperiali/E. Ferrari/A. Mazzarelli (L.) G. Davi (J.) R. Caldani/V. Pastorelli (F.) P. Bellucci cond.

MALTA
La Valletta  Real         Dec. 14? 1901 Trapasso (L.) Barbaro (J.) V. Pozzi-Camola (F.)

OTHER PRODUCTIONS-POST-WORLD WAR II

ARGENTINA
Buenos Aires Colón        July 17, 1979 M. Castro-Alberty (L.) G. Casellato-Lamberti (J.) R. Bruson (F.) M. Veltri cond.

BELGIUM
Ghent        Grand        Mar. 12, 1978

CANADA
Hamilton                  Sep. 23, 1989 L. Roark-Strummer (L.) Villa (J.) L. Quilico (F.)

CHILE
Santiago     Municipal    Sep. 16, 1982 M. Castro-Alberty (L.) G. Scano (J.) V. Sardinero (F.) M. Veltri cond.

CZECHOSLOVAKIA
Pilsen                           1972 M. Cihelnikova (L.) K. Vasata cond.

FRANCE
Paris        Radio ORTF   Nov.  8, 1979 Floyd (L.) G. Casellato-Lamberti (J.) De Salas (F.) N. Bonovolonta cond.

GERMANY
Bremerhaven                    Jan.  6, 1990 (in Ger.) Projected

Duisburg        Oper           Oct. 23, 1963 G. de Groot (L.) W. E. Olvis (J.) A.
                am Rhein                     Polakoff (F.) A. Erede cond. (in
                                             Ger.)

Stuttgart       Opernhaus      June 19, 1956 F. Leitner cond. (in Ger.)

GREAT BRITAIN
Cambridge       Arts Th.       July 24, 1973 J. Jacques (L.) S. Kale (J.) C. du
                                             Plessis (F.) I. Kemp cond.

London          Univ. Coll.    Feb.  6, 1963 E. Kenworthy (L.) T. Jenkins (J.) D.
                                             Miller (F.) F. Manton cond.

                BBC            Jan. 11, 1970 P. Tinsley (L.) K. Erwen (J.) T.
                                             Sharpe (F.) M. Dods cond.

                Coliseum       May   4, 1978 L. McDonall (L.) D. Blackwell (J.)
                                             N. Howlett (F.) C. Groves cond. (in
                                             Eng.)

IRELAND
Wexford         Th. Royal      Oct. 26, 1958 M. Angioletti (L.) C. del Monte (J.)
                                             P. Pedani (F.)

ITALY
Bologna         Comunale       Jan.  2, 1967 R. Orlandi-Malaspina (L.) L. Otto-
                                             lini (J.) P. Cappuccilli (F.) F.
                                             Vernizzi cond.

Milan           Sala RAI       Dec.  5, 1951 M. Vitale (L.) C. Bergonzi (J.) G.
                                             Guelfi (F.) C. M. Giulini cond.

                La Scala       Dec. 18, 1979 K. Ricciarelli/Y. Hayashi (L.) G.
                                             Cianella/ B. Rufo (J.) P. Cappuccil-
                                             li/L. Nucci (F.) L. Chailly cond.

                               Jan. 12, 1988 L. Roark-Strummer/M. Guleghina (L.)
                                             A. Cupido/K. Johannson (J.) R. Bru-
                                             son/E. Tumagian (F.) G. Gavazzeni
                                             cond.

Naples          San Carlo      May  16, 1968 M. Pobbe (L.) A. Bottion (J.) P.
                                             Cappucilli (F.) A. Ceccato cond.

Padua           Verdi          Oct.  6, 1972 K. Ricciarelli (L.) G. Scano (J.) P.
                                             Cappuccilli (F.) A. Zedda cond.

Parma           Regio          Dec. 26, 1966 R. Orlandi-Malaspina (L.) L. Otto-
                                             lini (J.) P. Cappuccilli (F.) F.
                                             Vernizzi cond.

                               Jan.  8, 1985 G. Kalinina (L.) V. Luchetti/A. Ele-
                                             na (J.) R. Bruson (F.) H. Soudant
                                             cond.

Rome            Opera          Apr.  3, 1968 L. Maragliano (L.) R. Cioni (J.) M.
                                             Zanasi (F.) B. Bartoletti cond.

                               Dec. 13, 1980 M. Parazzini (L.) C. Bergonzi (J.)
                                             R. Bruson (F.) D. Oren cond.

| | | | |
|---|---|---|---|
| Trieste | Verdi | Dec. 14, 1974 | O. Santunione (L.) B. Rufo (J.) P. Cappuccilli (F.) O. De Fabritiis cond. |
| | | Mar. 26, 1976 | R. Orlandi-Malaspina (L.) N. Todisco (J.) P. Cappuccilli (F.) O. De Fabritiis cond. |
| | | Oct. 20, 1983 | M. Zampieri (L.) B. Rufo (J.) P. Cappuccilli/ J. Pons (F.) D. Oren cond. |
| Turin | Sala RAI | Sep. 21, 1971 | L. Vajna (L.) B. Prevedi (J.) R. Bruson (F.) M. Rinaldi cond. |
| | Regio | Nov. 22, 1984 | D. Vejzovic/ L. Canepa (L.) N. Martinucci/O. Garaventa (J.) R. Bruson/ L. Montefusco (F.) M. Arena cond. |
| Venice | La Fenice | Dec. 26, 1957 | L. Gencer (L.) M. Picchi (J.) G. Guelfi (F.) T. Serafin cond. |
| SPAIN Barcelona | Liceo | Nov. 5, 1977 | R. Orlandi-Malaspina (L.) P. Lavirgen (J.) V. Sardinero (F.) F. Molinari-Pradelli cond. |
| Bilbao | Coliseo Alba | Sep. 4, 1983 | M. Parazzini (L.) G. Scano (J.) S. Cowan (F.) G. Rivoli cond. |
| Oviedo | Campoamor | Sep. 23, 1978 | M. Parazzini (L.) R. Francesconi (J.) V. Sardinero (F.) G. Rivoli cond. |
| UNITED STATES Chicago | Lyric | Sep. 22, 1972 | K. Ricciarelli (L.) Fr. Tagliavini (J.) P. Cappuccilli (F.) B. Bartoletti cond. |
| New York | Metropolitan | July 1, 1968 | L. Maragliano (L.) R. Cioni (J.) M. Zanasi (F.) B. Bartoletti cond. (By the company of the Teatro dell'Opera, Rome) |
| | Carnegie Hall | Nov. 20, 1981 | M. Castro-Alberty (L.) C. Bergonzi (J.) R. Bruson (F.) E. Queler cond. |

7. GIOVANNA D'ARCO-*Dramma lirico* in four acts
Milan-Teatro alla Scala-Feb. 15, 1845
Libretto by Temistocle Solera

| | |
|---|---|
| Giovanna (G.) | Erminia Frezzolini sop. |
| Carlo VII (C.) | Antonio Poggi ten. |
| Giacomo (Gi.) | Filippo Colini bar. |
| Delil | Napoleone Marconi ten. |
| Talbot | Francesco Lodetti bass |
| | |
| Conductor | Eugenio Cavallini |
| Director | Giuseppe Verdi |

OTHER PRODUCTIONS-NINETEENTH CENTURY

ARGENTINA
Buenos Aires  Argentino   Aug. 19, 1854 I. Edelvira (G.) L. Guglielmini (C.)
                                        G. C. Casanova (Gi.) J. V. Rivas
                                        cond.

AUSTRIA
Vienna        Kärntnertor May   2, 1857 M. Lotti della Santa (G.) E. Pancani
                                        (C.) G. Ferri (Gi.) H. Proch cond.

FRANCE
Paris         Italien     Mar. 28, 1868 A. Patti (G.) E. Nicolini (C.) F.
                                        Steller (Gi.) J. Skoczdopole cond.

GREECE
Corfu         Nobile      Sep.  4, 1852 M. Mariotti (G.) G. Giorgetti (C.)
                                        T. Pieri (Gi.)

ITALY
Alessandria   Municipale  Nov.     1864 L. Ruggero-Antonioli (G.) F. Patier-
                                        no (C.) L. Spellini (Gi.)

Ancona        Muse        Spring    1854 E. Scotta (G.) C. Negrini (C.) E.
                                        Crivelli (Gi.)

Arezzo        Petrarca    Carn. 1851-52 M. Armandi (G.) F. De Ruggero (C.)
                                        T. Pieri (Gi.)

Badia         Sociale     Aug.      1857 C. Rapazzini (G.) L. Ceresa (C.) D.
 Polesine                               Dal Negro (Gi.)

Bergamo       Sociale     Jan. 17, 1855 C. Moltini (G.) G. Petrovich (C.) C.
                                        Bartolucci (Gi.)

Bologna       Corso       Apr.      1853 S. Zudoli (G.) G. Comolli (C.) E.
                                        Antico (Gi.)

Brescia       Grande      Spring    1856 E. Schenardi (G.) G. Bazzini (C.) G.
                                        Crotti (Gi.)

Cagliari      Civico      Jan.      1848 L. Matthey (G.) G. Mazza (C.) I. Di-
                                        dier (Gi.)

                          Jan. 18, 1871 C. Poloni-Coppa (G.) F. Tavella (C.)
                                        E. Torriani (Gi.) V. Dessy cond.

Casal-        Municipale  Nov.      1869 V. Tilli (G.) G. De Fillipis (C.)
 Monferrato                             Buongiorno (Gi.)

Catania       Comunale    Jan. 18, 1855 M. Armandi (G.) G. Carpano (C.) I.
                                        Canedi (G.) M. Pappalardo cond.

Cosenza                   Feb.      1859 M. Armandi (G.)

Este          Sociale     Oct.  5, 1847 M. Arrigotti (G.) C. Miraglia (C.)

Ferrara       Comunale    Spring    1858 L. Ponti dall'Armi (G.) V. Orlandi
                                        (Gi.)

                          Dec. 26, 1869 L. Banti (G.) G. Marelli (C.) G.
                                        Parolini (Gi.)

Fiume         Comunale    Spring    1848 C. Rapazzini (G.) G. Pavesi (C.)

|           |              | Mar. 18, 1851 | L. Ruggero-Antonioli (G.) C. Scanna-vino (C.) F. Steller (Gi.) |
|-----------|--------------|---------------|----------------------------------------------------------------|
| Florence  | Pergola      | Apr. 15, 1845 | M. Gazzaniga (G.) E. Caggiati (C.) C. Badiali/L. Salandri (Gi.) |
|           | Politeama    | Aug. 1871     | Mariani (G.) Manfredi (C.) |
| Forli     | Comunale     | Apr. 1862     | S. Casimir-Ney (G.) G. Ortolani (C.) E. Mari-Cornia (Gi.) |
| Genoa     | Carlo Felice | Dec. 26, 1846 | C. Cuzzani (G.) D. Labocetta (C.) S. Ronconi (Gi.) |
| Livorno   | Rossini      | July 18, 1846 | M. Gazzaniga (G.) L. Bernabei (C.) F. Colini (Gi.) |
| Lodi      | Sociale      | Jan. 1858     | T. Cotta-Morandini (G.) A. Marchetti (C.) C. Visai (Gi.) |
| Lucca     | Giglio       | Autumn 1845   | A. Boccabadati (G.) L. Ferretti (C.) F. Colini (Gi.) |
| Lugo      | Rossini      | Aug. 30, 1851 | E. Scotta (G.) G. Musiani (C.) R. Colmenghi (Gi.) |
| Mantua    | Sociale      | Dec. 26, 1847 | C. Gruitz (G.) L. Giannoni (C.) L. Valli (Gi.) G. Luppi cond. |
| Milan     | Carcano      | Spring 1847   | E. Ranzi (G.) A. Volpini (C.) C. Ferri (Gi.) A. Mariani cond. |
|           | Canobbiana   | Apr. 21, 1851 | M. Arrigotti (G.) C. Liverani (C.) G. Fiori (Gi.) |
|           | La Scala     | Feb. 15, 1858 | R. Devries (G.) C. Negrini (C.) A. Morelli (Gi.) E. Cavallini cond. |
|           |              | Sep. 23, 1865 | T. Stolz (G.) T. De Azula (C.) A. De Antoni (Gi.) |
|           | Castelli     | Apr. 1876     | Rastelli (G.) De Angelis (C.) G. Valle (Gi.) E. Bernardi cond. |
| Modena    | Comunale     | Carn. 1869-70 | I. Pelegatti-Visconti (G.) P. Augus-ti (C.) E. Fagotti (Gi.) G. Zavaglio cond. |
| Naples    | San Ferdinando | Carn. 1855  | P. Scotti (G.) G. Lucchesi (C.) A. Capurro (Gi.) |
|           | San Carlo    | Nov. 15, 1855 | G. Beltramelli (G.) L. Stefani (C.) F. Coletti (Gi.) |
| Padua     | Nuovo        | Oct. 30, 1847 | C. Cuzzani (G.) E. Naudin (C.) C. Fallardi (Gi.) |
|           | Concordia    | Spring 1853   | L. Ruggero-Antonioli (G.) G. Tamaro (C.) F. Cuturi (Gi.) |
|           |              | Lent 1858     | S. Peruzzi (G.) L. Ceresa (C.) |
|           |              | Jan. 1869     | M. Savertal (G.) G. Vizzani (C.) G. Del Puente (Gi.) Girardini cond. |

| Palermo | Carolino | Oct. 26, 1847 | E. Ranzi (G.) G. Lucchesi C.) G. B. Bencich (Gi.) P. Raimondi cond. |
|---------|----------|---------------|---------|
| Parma | Regio | Dec. 26, 1858 | C. Carozzi-Zucchi (G.) G. Musiani (C.) E. Fagotti (Gi.) G. C. Ferrarini cond. |
| Pavia | Condomini | Jan. 25, 1858 | E. Villelma/L. Gavetti-Reggiani (G.) L. Ceresa (C.) E. Mari-Cornia (Gi.) |
| Piacenza | Municipale | Carn. 1846-47 | A. Tirelli (G.) A. Volpini (C.) G. Corsi (Gi.) G. Jona cond. |
| Pisa | Ravvivati | Apr. 10, 1851 | E. Zilioli (G.) G. Zoboli (C.) M. Quilici cond. |
| Reggio Emilia | Comunale | Apr. 29, 1855 | N. De Roissi (G.) C. Negrini (C.) G. Guicciardi (Gi.) G. Tebaldi cond. |
| Rome | Argentina | May 5, 1845 | T. Truffi-Benedetti (G.) R. Mirate (C.) G. Ferri (Gi.) E. Angelini cond. |
| | | Oct. 9 1845 | A. Boccabadati (G.) L. Ferretti (C.) A. D'Avila (Gi.) |
| | | Oct. 2, 1847 | A. Boccabadati (G.) L. Bernabei (C.) F. Gnone (Gi.) |
| | Apollo | Jan. 29, 1855 | M. Piccolomini (G.) E. Naudin (C.) G. B. Bencich (Gi.) E. Angelini cond. |
| Sassari | Civico | Nov. 1861 | Cesarini (G.) P. Samat (C.) C. Fabbricatore (Gi.) |
| Siena | Rinnovati | July 1856 | M. Arrigotti (G.) G. Tamaro (C.) F. Massiani (Gi.) |
| Sinigaglia | Comunale | Fiera 1845 | E. Frezzolini (G.) A. Poggi (C.) P. Balzar (Gi.) |
| Spoleto | Nobile | Jan. 24, 1850 | Gamberini (G.) G. Galvani (C.) M. Severi (Gi.) |
| Terni | Comunale | 1849-50 | |
| Treviso | Onigo | Jan. 1854 | L. Donati (G.) E. Pellegrini (C.) E. Rossi-Corsi (Gi.) |
| Trieste | Mauroner | July 14, 1850 | L. Ruggero-Antonioli (G.) L. Guglielmini (C.) G. Sacconi (Gi.) |
| | Grande | Jan. 17, 1852 | R. Penco (G.) G. Mazzi (C.) L. Buti (Gi.) G. A. Scaramelli cond. |
| | | Feb. 9, 1856 | C. Carozzi-Zucchi (G.) V. Sarti (C.) P. Baraldi (Gi.) G. A. Scaramella cond. |
| Turin | Regio | Dec. 27, 1845 | E. Frezzolini/T. Bovay (G.) L. Ferretti (C.) C. Badiali (Gi.) G. Ghebart cond. |

|            | Carignano  | Sep.          | 1859 A. Orecchia (G.) C. Vincentelli (C.) E. Storti (Gi.) |
|------------|------------|---------------|-----------------------------------------------------------|
| Venice     | La Fenice  | Dec. 26,      | 1845 S. Loewe (G.) C. Guasco (C.) N. Costantini (Gi.) G. Mares cond. |
|            |            | Sep. 21,      | 1847 A. De La Grange (G.) R. Mirate (C.) A. De Bassini (Gi.) G. Mares cond. |
|            | Apollo     | Nov.          | 1847 M. Arrigotti (G.) C. Miraglia (C.) T. Smitter (Gi.) |
|            |            | Autumn        | 1850 L. Ruggero-Antonioli (G.) L. Guglielmini (C.) G. Sacconi (Gi.) |
|            | Rossini    | Mar. 11,      | 1865 G. Monti (G.) G. D'Antoni (C.) E. Storti-Gaggi (Gi.) |
| Vercelli   | Civico     | Carn.         | 1849-50 C. Moltini (G.) E. Scotti (C.) R. Rivieri (Gi.) |
| Vicenza    | Eretenio   | Aug.          | 1847 L. Assandri (G.) C. Miraglia (C.) L. Corradi-Setti (Gi.) |
|            |            | Dec. 26,      | 1853 N. Barbieri-Thiollier (G.) E. Concordia (C.) G. Donelli (Gi.) G. Bolelli cond. |

JUGOSLAVIA

| Zara           | Nobile      | Oct. 29,  | 1850 Miller (G.) E. Galli (C.) G. Altini (Gi.) |
|----------------|-------------|-----------|-------------------------------------------------|

MALTA

| La Valletta    | Manoel      | Oct. 2,   | 1852 C. Rapazzini (G.) L. Stefani (C.) Bartolini (Gi.) |
|----------------|-------------|-----------|--------------------------------------------------------|

MEXICO

| Mexico City    | Nacional    | Dec. 23,  | 1857 E. Zilioli-Fattori (G.) A. Volpini (C.) E. Barili (Gi.) C. Fattori cond. |
|----------------|-------------|-----------|-------------------------------------------------------------------------------|

POLAND

| Warsaw         | Wielki      | Dec. 18,  | 1872 M. Mariani-Masi (G.) A. Oliva-Pavani (C.) L. Buti (Gi.) Quattrini cond. |
|----------------|-------------|-----------|------------------------------------------------------------------------------|

PORTUGAL

| Lisbon         | Sao Carlos  | Nov. 10,  | 1847 T. Bovay (G.) A. Volpini (C.) R. Pizzigati (Gi.) |
|----------------|-------------|-----------|-------------------------------------------------------|

| Oporto         | Sao Joao    | Autumn    | 1855 C. Truffi (G.) C. Baldanza (C.) A. Rossi (Gi.) |
|----------------|-------------|-----------|-----------------------------------------------------|

ROMANIA

| Bucharest      | Nacional    | Oct.      | 1850 C. Cuzzani (G.) E. Rossi-Guerra (C.) G. Marini (Gi.) |
|----------------|-------------|-----------|-----------------------------------------------------------|

RUSSIA

| Odessa         | Municipal   | Aug. 8,   | 1851 A. Basseggio (G.) E. Naudin (C.) A. Ottaviani (Gi.) |
|----------------|-------------|-----------|----------------------------------------------------------|

|            |             | Dec.?     | 1860 I. Edelvira (G.) E. Irfré (C.) M. Padilla (Gi.) |

St.              Imperial       Jan. 10, 1850 E. Frezzolini  (G.)  I. Gardoni (C.)
 Petersburg                                   F. Coletti (Gi.) E. Baveri cond.

SPAIN
Barcelona        Liceo          July 28, 1847 F. Salvini-Donatelli  (G.)  A. Cas-
                                              tellan (C.) G. Ferri (Gi.)

                 Principal      Apr.  8, 1858 R. Devries (G.)  C. Negrini (C.)  G.
                                              Guicciardi (Gi.)

Madrid           Circo          Oct. 30, 1846 G. Bortolotti  (G.)  E.  Tamberlick
                                              (C.) R. Ferlotti (Gi.)

                                Apr. 21, 1847 G. Bortolotti (G.) G. B. Milesi (C.)
                                              G. Miral (Gi.)

Palma di         Circulo        Jan.?    1856 Crescimano (G.) M. Severi (Gi.)
 Mallorca        Mallorquin

                 Coliseo        Mar.     1859 M. Roffi (G.)  G. Aducci (C.) A. Ca-
                                              rapia (Gi.)

TURKEY
Constan-         Naum           Oct. 29, 1849 G. Medori (G.)  C. Negrini (C.)  G. B.
 tinople                                      Bencich (Gi.)

OTHER PRODUCTIONS-POST-WORLD WAR II

FRANCE
Paris            Opéra          June 30, 1951 R. Tebaldi  (G.)  G. Penno  (C.)  U.
                                              Savarese (Gi.) G. Santini cond. (By
                                              the company of the Teatro San Carlo,
                                              Naples)

Toulouse         Capitole       Dec.     1963 R. Orlandi-Malaspina (G.) F. Patanè
                                              cond.

GERMANY
Hamburg          Stadt          Oct. 10, 1983 M. Price (G.) V. Moldeveanu (C.) B.
                                              Weikl (Gi.) G. Masini cond.

GREAT BRITAIN
London           Kensington     Nov.  4, 1963 F. Dion (G.) B. Powell (C.)  M. Mau-
                 Town Hall                    rel (Gi.) L. Head cond.

                 Royal Ac.      May  23, 1966 D. Faye-Carr (G.)  G. West  (C.)  A.
                 of Music                     Charles (Gi.) G. Treacher cond.

                 University     Feb. 28, 1989 S. Bisatt (G.)  M. Benedict (C.)  G.
                 College                      Hargreaves (Gi.) C. Fifield cond.

                 Royal          Mar. 16, 1989 M. Price  (G.)  O. Garaventa (C.)  S.
                 Fest. Hall                   Leiferkus (Gi.) R. Bradshaw cond.

Oxford           Playhouse      Feb. 19, 1977 H. Walker (G.) M. Hamilton (C.)  P.
                                              Reynolds (Gi.) D. Arnold cond.

IRELAND
Wexford          Th. Royal      Summer?  1976 E. Maruyama (G.)  C. Rayam (C.)  L.
                                              Miller (Gi.) J. Judd cond.

ITALY
Bologna          Comunale       Nov. 23, 1989 S. Dunn  (G.)  V. La Scola (C.)  R.
                                              Bruson (Gi.)

Brescia        Grande        Nov. 25, 1988 L. Roark-Strummer (G.) B. Beccaria
                                          (C.) A. Noli (Gi.) G. Masini cond.

Milan          Sala RAI      May  26, 1951 R. Tebaldi (G.) C. Bergonzi (C.) R.
                                          Panerai (Gi.) A. Simonetto cond.

               Nuovo         Sep.  9, 1963 R. Orlandi Malaspina (G.) G. Berta-
                                          gna (C.) C. D'Anna (Gi.) C. Camerini
                                          cond.

Naples         San Carlo     Mar. 15, 1951 R. Tebaldi (G.) G. Penno (C.) U.
                                          Savarese (Gi.) G. Santini cond.

Parma          Regio         Feb.  9, 1980 A. Gulin (G.) G. Cecchele (C.) Boy-
                                          agian (Gi.) M. Veltri cond.

Piacenza       Municipale    Feb. 22, 1980 A. Gulin (G.) G. Bavaglio (C.) G.
                                          Boyagian (Gi.) M. Veltri cond.

Rome           Opera         May  15, 1972 K. Ricciarelli/C. Forti (G.) F. Labò
                                          (C.) M. Sereni (Gi.) B. Bartoletti
                                          cond.

Treviso        Sociale       Oct. 21, 1979 M. Zampieri (G.)

Venice         La Fenice     Apr. 22, 1972 K. Ricciarelli (G.) F. Labò (C.) M.
                                          Zanasi (Gi.) C. Franci cond.

Verona         Filarmonico   Apr. 30, 1988 L. Roark-Strummer (G.) B. Beccaria
                                          (C.) A. Noli (Gi.) G. Masini cond.

SWITZERLAND
Zürich         Stadt         Feb.     1984 N. Santi cond.


UNITED STATES
Brooklyn       Ac. of Mus.   May  14, 1976 P. Sellers (G.) A. Inchaustegui (C.)
                                          M. Andoor (Gi.) V. La Selva cond.

New York       Carnegie      Mar.  1, 1966 T. Stratas (G.) A. Mori (C.) S. Mil-
               Hall                        nes (Gi.) C. F. Cillario cond.

San Diego      Opera         June 26, 1980 A. Maliponte (G.) L. Lima (C.) P.
                                          Elvira (Gi.) E. Müller cond.

8. ALZIRA-*Tragedia lirica* in a prologue and two acts
Naples-Teatro San Carlo-Aug. 12, 1845
Libretto by Salvadore Cammarano

Alzira (A.)  
Zamoro (Z.)  
Gusmano (G.)  
Alvaro (Al.)  
Zuma  
Otumbo  
Ovando  
Ataliba  

Eugenia Tadolini sop.  
Gaetano Fraschini ten.  
Filippo Coletti bar.  
Marco Arati bass  
Anna Salvetti mez.  
Teofilo Rossi ten.  
Pasquale Ceci ten.  
Giuseppe Benedetti bass  

Conductor  
Director  

Antonio Farelli  
Giuseppe Verdi  

OTHER PRODUCTIONS-1845-1945

AUSTRIA  
Vienna          Radio          Sep. 18, 1936

CHILE  
Valparaiso      Victoria       Nov. 10, 1850 I. Neumann (A.) L. Cavedagni (Z.) G. Bastoggi (G.) A. Neumann cond.

ITALY  
Ferrara         Comunale       May      1847 C. Cuzzani (A.) G. Roppa (Z.) G. Corsi (G.)

Lugo            Rossini        Sep. 16, 1846 L. Assandri (A.) G. Roppa (Z.) E. Crivelli (G.)

Milan           La Scala       Jan. 16, 1847 E. Tadolini (A.) S. Reeves (Z.) A. De Bassini (G.)

Parma           Regio          Jan. 17, 1846 A. Moltini (A.) G. Roppa (Z.) P. Balzar (G.) L. Bianchi (Al.) N. De Giovanni cond.

Rome            Argentina      Oct. 28, 1845 A. Boccabadati (A.) L. Ferretti (Z.) A. D'Avila (G.)

Turin           Carignano      Sep. 8, 1854 G. Brambilla (A.) V. Sarti (Z.) A. Olivari (G.)

Venice          Apollo         Dec. 4, 1847 M. Arrigotti (A.) C. Miraglia (Z.) T. Smitter (G.)

MALTA  
La Valletta     Manoel         Apr. 5, 1858 L. Perelli (A.) D. Lorini (Z.) L. Rossi (G.)

PERU  
Lima            Principal      Jan. 20, 1850 M. De Ferretti (A.) L. Cavedagni (Z.) P. Ferretti (G.) A. Neumann cond.

PORTUGAL  
Lisbon          Acc. Filar. Mar. 27, 1847 E. dos Santos/M. H. Quintella/M. C. Quintella (A.) J. Solieri (Z.) C. de Cunha (G.)

Sao Carlos   Oct. 29, 1849 M. Gresti  (A.)  G. Baldanza (Z.)  G.
                                     Fiori (G.)

SPAIN
Barcelona      Liceo        Feb.  3, 1849 F. Salvini-Donatelli  (A.)  G. Roppa
                                     (Z.)  G. Ferri (G.)

OTHER PRODUCTIONS-POST-WORLD WAR II

GREAT BRITAIN
London         Collegiate   Feb. 10, 1970 C. Duval  (A.)  G. Wilcock  (Z.)  C.
                                     Bellamy (G.)  G. Badacsonyi cond. (in
                                     Eng.)

ITALY
Modena         Comunale     Feb. 23, 1981 A. Hazzan (A.)  B. Rufo (Z.)  G. Boya-
                                     gian (G.)  E. Schulz cond.

Parma          Regio        Feb. 10, 1981 A. Hazzan (A.)  B. Rufo (Z.)  G. Boya-
                                     gian (G.)  E. Schulz cond.

Reggio Emilia Municipale    Feb. 18, 1981 A. Hazzan (A.)  B. Rufo (Z.)  G. Boya-
                                     gian (G.)  E. Scholz cond.

Rome           Opera        Mar. 16, 1967 V. Zeani  (A.)  G. Cecchele (Z.)  C.
                                     MacNeil (G.)  F. Capuana cond.

Turin          Sala RAI     Jan.  2, 1973 A. Gulin  (A.)  G. Cecchele (Z.)  M.
                                     Sereni (G.)  M. Rinaldi cond.

NETHERLANDS
Amsterdam                   Oct. 11, 1980 C. Deutekom (A.)  A. van Limpt (Z.)
                                     H. Smith (G.)  K. Bakels cond.

UNITED STATES
New York       Carnegie     Jan. 17, 1968 E. Ross (A.)  G. Cecchele  (Z.)  L.
               Hall                  Quilico (G.)  J. Perlea cond.


9. ATTILA-*Dramma lirico* in a prologue and three acts
Venice-Teatro La Fenice-Mar. 17, 1846
Libretto by Temistocle Solera with alterations by Francesco Maria Piave


Odabella (O.)                                  Sofia Loewe sop.
Foresto (F.)                                   Carlo Guasco ten.
Ezio (E.)                                    Natale Costantini bar.
Attila (A.)                                   Ignazio Marini bass
Uldino                                        Ettore Profili ten.
Leone                                    Giuseppe Romanelli bass

Conductor                                       Gaetano Mares
Director                                        Giuseppe Verdi

OTHER PREMIERES-NINETEENTH CENTURY

ARGENTINA
Buenos Aires   Victoria     Sep. 23, 1853 R. Olivieri  (O.)  E. Rossi-Guerra
                                     (F.)  G. Olivieri (E.)  E. Luisia (A.)
                                     P. A. Garcia cond.

|  |  |  |  |
|---|---|---|---|
|  | Ant. Colón | Nov. 1, 1860 | C. Manzini (O.) E. Ballarini (F.) G. Bertolini (E.) P. De Antoni (A.) |
| **AUSTRALIA** Adelaide | Victoria | Feb. 25, 1861 | G. Bianchi (O.) E. Bianchi (F.) J. Gregg (E.) E. Grossi (A.) |
| Melbourne | Th. Royal | Aug. 17, 1860 | G. Bianchi (O.) E. Bianchi (F.) R. Farquharson (E.) J. Gregg (A.) |
| Sydney | Prince of Wales | July 12, 1860 | G. Bianchi (O.) E. Bianchi (F.) E. E. Coulon (E.) E. Grossi (A.) |
| **AUSTRIA** Vienna | Kärntnertor | June 11, 1851 | C. Gruitz (O.) G. Fraschini (F.) G. Ferri (E.) A. Didot (A.) |
| **BELGIUM** Antwerp | Royal | Apr. 30, 1854 | E. Tomassi (O.) M. Forti (F.) A. Ardavani (E.) V. Caspani (A.) C. Castagneri cond. (in It.) |
| Brussels | Monnaie | Dec. 13, 1850 | A. Lacombe (O.) Octave (F.) Martin (E.) S. L. Bouché (A.) (in Fr.) |
| **BRAZIL** Bahia | Publico | Dec. 2, 1855 | G. Montuchielli (O.) L. Lelmi (F.) G. B. Giani (E.) S. Scappini (A.) |
| Rio de Janeiro | Provisorio | Sep. 7, 1853 | A. Jacobson (O.) A. Gentili (F.) F. Tati (E.) H. Whitworth (A.) J. V. Ribas cond. |
|  | Lirico Fluminense | Mar. 25, 1856 | E. La Grua (O.) A. Gentili (F.) L. Walter (E.) A. Susini (A.) |
| **CHILE** Santiago | Principal | Aug. 20, 1850 | C. Pantanelli (O.) A. Zambaiti (F.) G. Bastoggi (E.) E. Lanza (A.) R. Pantanelli cond. |
|  | Municipal | Aug. 6, 1861 | I. Martinez de Escalante (O.) A. Rossi-Ghelli (E.) G. Mirandola (A.) |
| Valparaiso | Victoria | May 9, 1850 | L. Micciarelli (O.) G. Ubaldi (F.) L. Cavedagni (E.) F. Leonardi (A.) |
| **COLOMBIA** Bogota | Teatro | Nov. 1858 | R. Olivieri (O.) E. Rossi-Guerra (F.) E. Luisia (E.) G. Mirandola (A.) |
| **CUBA** Havana | Tacon | Jan. 23, 1848 | F. Tedesco (O.) L. Vita (E.) P. Novelli (A.) L. Arditi cond. |
| Santiago | Principal | Summer 1851 | L. Caranti-Vita (O.) A. Arnoldi (F.) A. Gasparoni (A.) |
| **DENMARK** Copenhagen | Royal | Mar. 7, 1847 | A. Ricci (O.) A Vietti (F.) C. Vajro (E.) N. Torre (A.) P. Sperati cond. (in It.) |

EGYPT
Alexandria      Europeo              1849-50

FRANCE
Nice            Regio        Oct. 15, 1853 L. Pecis (O.) B. Danieli (F.) E.
                                           Winter (E.) G. B. Antonucci (A.) G.
                                           Bragozzo cond.

GERMANY
Stuttgart       Hoftheater   Feb. 12, 1854 (in Ger.)

GREAT BRITAIN
London          Her          Mar. 14, 1848 S. Cruvelli (O.) I. Gardoni (F.) L.
                Majesty's                  Cuzzani (E.) G. Belletti (A.)

GREECE
Athens          Royal        Feb.  5, 1853 L. Finetti-Batocchi (O.) G. Ortolani
                                           (F.) V. Orlandi (E.) A. Casali (A.)

Corfu           San Giacomo Dec.?    1846 E. Boldrini (O.) D. Mecksa (F.) G.
                                           De Lorenzi (E.) S. Demi (A.)

HUNGARY
Budapest        Nemzeti      July 17, 1852 L. Gino (O.) G. Mazzi (F.) E. Longo-
                Szinház                    ni (E.) G. Reina (A.)

INDONESIA
Batavia         T. Batavie   Aug. 15, 1870 M. Zenoni (O.) P. Setragni (F.) L.
                                           Magnani (E.) E. Gasperini (A.)

ITALY
Alessandria     Municipale   Autumn   1846 L. Ponti dall'Armi (O.) G. Sinico
                                           (F.) G. B. Bencich (E.) S. Scappini
                                           (A.)

Ancona          Muse         Spring   1848 M. Gresti (O.)

Bergamo         Riccardi     Aug. 18, 1852 M. Lotti della Santa (O.) G. Musiani
                                           (F.) G. Fiori (E.) G. Dalbesio (A.)
                                           G. Bragozzo cond.

Bologna         Comunale     Oct. 10, 1846 H. Nissen (O.) G. Baldanza (F.) L.
                                           Roncagli (E.) L. Montemerli (A.) G.
                                           Manetti cond.

Brescia         Grande       Aug.     1847 M. Gazzaniga (O.) A. Bozzetti (F.)
                                           G. Corsi (E.) G. Mitrovich (A.)

Cagliari        Civico       Sep. 21, 1847 M. F. Massimino (O.)

Catania         Comunale     Dec. 26, 1855 C. Mauri Ventura (O.) P. Cecchi (F.)
                                           L. Roncagli (E.) P. De Antonis (A.)
                                           M. Pappalardo cond.

Chieti          Marrucino    Apr.     1856 M. Armandi (O.) R. Bettazzi (F.) L.
                                           Roncagli (E.) P. De Antoni (A.) G.
                                           Liberali cond.

Como            Sociale      Carn. 1847-48 L. Abbadia (O.) C. Negrini (F.) G.
                                           Guicciardi (E.) L. Bianchi De Maz-
                                           zoletti (A.)

Cremona        Concordia    Aug. 25? 1846  F. Salvini-Donatelli (O.) A. Castel-
                                           lan (F.) A. Superchi (E.) G. Mitro-
                                           vich (A.)

Fermo          Aquila       Aug. 15, 1847  C. Ferrarini-Baschieri (O.) G. Pan-
                                           cani (F.) L. Rinaldini (E.) M. Ghe-
                                           rardini (A.)

Ferrara        Comunale     May 14, 1848   R. Gariboldi-Bassi (O.) B. Massimi-
                                           liani (F.) F. Massiani (E.) F. Dalla
                                           Costa (A.)

Fiume          Civico       Apr. 3, 1869   Tabacchi (O.) M. Neri (F.) F. Coliva
                                           (E.)

Florence       Pergola      Apr. 16, 1846  M. Barbieri-Nini (O.) L. Bernabei
                                           (F.) F. Gorin (E.) P. Balzar (A.) P.
                                           Romani cond.

Foligno        Apollo       Aug.     1853  M. Cagnolis-Tancioni (O.) L. Toffa-
                                           nari (F.) N. Benedetti (A.)

Forli          Comunale     June 14, 1854  M. Arrigotti (O.) L. Stefani (F.) F.
                                           Coliva (E.) S. Panzini (A.)

Genoa          Carlo        Jan. 9, 1847   M. Gazzaniga (O.) F. Borioni (F.) G.
               Felice                      Ferri (E.) E. Jones (A.) G. Serra
                                           cond.

Livorno        Avvalorati   Sep. 9, 1846   S. Loewe (O.) L. Bernabei (F.) G.
                                           Ferri (E.) F. Cuturi (A.)

Lucca          Giglio       Aug. 21, 1847  E. Tadolini (O.) A. Brunacci (F.) F.
                                           Gorin (E.) N. Benedetti (A.)

Lugo           Rossini      Aug. 28, 1847  H. Nissen (O.) G. Sinico (F.) G.
                                           Fiori (E.) L. Roncagli (A.)

Macerata       Lauro Rossi  Aug. 11, 1852  T. Pozzi-Montegazza (O.) A. Errani
                                           (F.) E. Antico (E.) G. Capriles (A.)

Mantua         Sociale      Spring   1847  M. Barbieri-Nini (O.) L. Graziani
                                           (F.) A. De Bassini (E.) L. Salandri
                                           (A.)

Messina        Munizione    Oct. 9, 1851   C. Forti-Babacci (O.) Giannoni (F.)
                                           G. Arnaud (E.) G. B. Antonucci (A.)

Milan          La Scala     Dec. 26, 1846  E. Tadolini (O.) N. Moriani (F.) A.
                                           De Bassini (E.) I. Marini (A.) E.
                                           Cavallini cond.

Modena         Comunale     June 22, 1850  T. Brambilla (O.) S. Malvezzi (F.)
                                           F. Varesi (E.) S. Panzini (A.) A.
                                           Sighicelli cond.

Naples         San Carlo    Jan. 29, 1848  T. Brambilla (O.) S. Malvezzi (F.)
                                           E. Crivelli (E.) F. Gionfrida (A.)
                                           A. Farelli cond.

Novara         Nuovo        Feb. 13, 1851  A. Ferraris (O.) M. Bernardi (F.) A.
                                           Sabbatini (E.) P. Sottovia (A.)

Padua          Nuovo          June 12, 1850 S. Cruvelli (O.) G. Fraschini (F.)
                                          G. Corsi (E.) G. Mitrovich (A.)

Palermo        Carolino       Nov. 18, 1854 C. Carozzi-Zucchi (O.) L. Graziani
                                          (F.) A. Vitti (E.) A. Garcia (A.) A.
                                          Lo Casto cond.

Parma          Regio          Dec. 26, 1846 M. Barbieri-Nini (O.) A. Poggi (F.)
                                          N. Gnone (E.) G. Mitrovich (A.) N.
                                          De Giovanni cond.

Perugia        Pavone         Oct.     1851 Monti (O.) E. Pellegrini (F.) G.
                                          Staffolini (E.) L. Battaglini (A.)

Pesaro         Rossini        Carn. 1851-52 L. Finetti-Battocchi (O.) E. Concor-
                                          dia (F.) A. Rossi (E.) G. Capriles
                                          (A.) A. Barattini cond.

Piacenza       Municipale     Summer   1847 L. Abbadia (O.) V. Jacobelli (F.) L.
                                          Bianchi-Mazzoletti (E.) A. Ghislan-
                                          zoni (A.) G. Jona cond.

Pisa           Ravvivati      Dec. 26, 1848 E. Parepa-Archibugeri (O.) E. Panca-
                                          ni (F.) F. Cuturi (E.) A. Selva (A.)
                                          C. Giacomelli cond.

Ravenna        Comuni-        Jan. 27, 1852 V. Tilli (O.) L. Lombardi (F.) E.
               tativo                     Storti (E.) P. De Antonis (A.) G.
                                          Nostini cond.

Reggio Emilia  Comunale       May  19, 1846 M. Barbieri-Nini (O.) L. Bernabei
                                          (F.) F. Gorin (E.) P. Balzar (A.) G.
                                          Tebaldi cond.

Rome           Apollo         Dec. 26, 1847 H. Nissenn (O.) N. Ivanoff (F.) A.
                                          Superchi (E.) G. Mitrovich (A.) E.
                                          Angelini cond.

Rovigo         Sociale        Oct. 16, 1847 S. Cruvelli (O.) A. Palma (F.) G.
                                          Zucchini (E.) G. Torre (A.)

Savona         Chiabrera      Oct.  1, 1853 C. Gruitz (O.) C. Negrini (F.) G.
                                          Mancusi (E.) B. Laura (A.) (Inaugu-
                                          ration of the theater)

Siena          Rinnovati      Summer   1849 M. Dille (O.) D. Severini (F.) A.
                                          Sabatini (E.) L. Salandri (A.)

Sinigaglia     Comunale       July 17, 1847 E. Tadolini (O.) L. Graziani (F.) A.
                                          De Bassini (E.) N. Benedetti (A.)

Terni          Comunale       Dec. 27, 1851 T. Pozzi-Montegazza (O.) L. Bernabei
                                          (F.) M. Zacchi (E.) G. F. Angelini
                                          (A.) L. Gradassi cond.

Trento         Sociale        June 29, 1850 E. Cominotti (O.) G. Mazzi (F.) C.
                                          Bartolucci (E.) G. Dalbesio (A.)

Treviso        Onigo          Oct. 15, 1853 G. Sanchioli (O.) R. Mirate (F.) G.
                                          Corsi (E.) G. B. Cornago (A.)

Trieste        Grande         Sep. 28, 1846 M. Barbieri-Nini (O.) N. Ivanoff
                                          (F.) A. De Bassini (E.) A. Zucconi
                                          (A.) G. A. Scaramelli cond.

Turin       Regio        Dec. 26, 1848 M. Gazzaniga (O.) N. Ivanoff (F.) A.
                                       De Bassini (E.) R. Anconi (A.) G.
                                       Ghebart cond.

Udine       Sociale      July 24, 1847 S. Cruvelli (O.) A. Palma (F.)  Lo-
                                       vati (E.) G. B. Antonucci (A.)

Verona      Nuovo        Sep. 12, 1846 R. Basso Borio (O.) R. Castigliano
                                       (F.) G. Corsi (E.) Torre (A.)

            Filarmonico  Dec. 26, 1849 C. Bortolotti (O.) G. B. Milesi (F.)
                                       P. Giani (E.) G. Mitrovich (A.)

Vicenza     Eretenio     July 18, 1846 M. Barbieri-Nini (O.) E. Calzolari
                                       (F.) F. Varesi (E.) S. L. Bouché
                                       (A.)

Viterbo     Del Genio    Aug.  2, 1851 M. Diekl (O.) E. Pellegrini (F.) A.
                                       Vitti (E.) L. Battaglini (A.)

JUGOSLAVIA
Ljubljana   Stanowskem   May   3, 1860 A. Bazurri (O.) G. Gambetti (F.) G.
                                       Bertolini (E.)

Zagreb      National     June  9, 1852 G. Montuchielli (O.) F. Di Ruggero
                                       (F.) T. Pieri (E.) G. Gerli (A.)

Zara        Nobile       Apr.     1858 D. Barberini (O.) G. Giusti (F.) A.
                                       Cotogni (E.) Maccani (A.)

MALTA
La Valletta Manoel       Mar.?    1849 E. Crivelli (E.)

MEXICO
Guadalajara Degollado    Oct.  4, 1866

Mexico City Nacional     Aug. 31, 1854 B. Steffenone (O.) L. Salvi (F.) F.
                                       Beneventano (E.) I. Marini (A.) J.
                                       Nicolao cond.

NORWAY
Oslo        Royal        Oct.  1, 1849 A. Ricci (O.) E. Caggiati (F.) G.
                                       Guicciardi (E.) G. C. Casanova (A.)
                                       P. Sperati cond. (in It.)

PERU
Lima        Principal    Jan. 13, 1850 L. Micciarelli (O.) L. Cavedagni
                                       (F.) F. Leonardi (E.) P. Ferretti
                                       (A.) A. Neumann cond.

POLAND
Warsaw      Wielki       Aug. 21, 1852 (in It.)

PORTUGAL
Lisbon      Sao Carlos   Apr.  5, 1847 F. Rocca Alessandri (O.) G. Solieri
                                       (F.) I. Patriossi (E.) C. O. Porto
                                       (A.)

Oporto      Sao Joao     July ?   1849 M. Gresti (O.) A. Volpini (F.) G.
                                       Fiori (E.) N. Benedetti (A.)

ROMANIA
Bucarest    Nacional     Oct. 15, 1849 C. Cuzzani (O.) G. De Vecchi (F.) G.
                                       Marini (E.) S. Torre (A.)

Iasi          Teatrul      Oct.   7, 1852 G. Brambilla (O.) P. Scotti (F.) G.
                                  Donelli (E.) H. Brémond (A.)

RUSSIA
Odessa        Municipal    Dec. 27, 1849 C. Marziali (O.)

SPAIN
Alicante      Principal    Jan. 18, 1848 Gamarra (O.) L. Aparicio (F.) Agui-
                                  lor (E.) Saez (A.)

Barcelona     Principal    May  15, 1847 C. Bertolini-Raffaelli (O.) E. Tam-
                                  berlick (F.) E. Barili (E.) C. Sal-
                                  vatori (A.)

              Liceo        Sep. 21, 1850 N. De Roissi (O.) C. Baucardé (F.)
                                  L. Valli (E.) A. Rodas (A.)

Bilbao        Viejo        Spring   1858 A. Luise (F.)

Cadiz         Principal    Feb.   5, 1847 C. Bertolini-Raffaelli (O.) G. Zobo-
                                  li (F.) V. Sermattei (E.) C. O. Por-
                                  to (A.)

La Corugna    Principal    Dec.     1862 C. Poch (O.) A. Ponti (F.) N. Fal-
                                  lica (E.) Filibert (A.)

Madrid        Circo        Jan.   5, 1847 G. Bortolotti (O.) E. Tamberlick
                                  (F.) F. Morelli-Ponti (E.) G. Miral
                                  (A.)

              Real         Nov. 15, 1854 M. Spezia-Aldighieri (O.) A. Pruden-
                                  za (F.) G. Guicciardi (E.) P. Via-
                                  letti (A.) J. Skoczdopole cond.

Malaga        Principal    Jan.?    1853 Vianelli (O.) G. Sinico (F.) A.
                                  Gironello (E.) Castillo (A.)

Palma de      Comedias     Oct.     1851 E. Tomassi (O.) E. Irfré (F.) A.
Mallorca                          Ardavani (E.) Fabregua (A.)

Seville       San          Jan. 13, 1848 C. Vittadini (O.) G. Solieri (F.) G.
              Fernando            Mancusi (E.) C. O. Porto (A.)

Valencia      Principal        1847-48

Valladolid    Lope           1858-59 C. Forti-Babacci (O.) M. Viani (F.)
              da Vega             C. Morelli-Condomieri (E.) O. Lari
                                  (A.)

Zaragozza     Principal    Lent     1850 C. Más Porcell (O.) L. Bottagisi
                                  (F.) C. Ferri (E.) Fonti (A.)

TUNISIA
Tunis                      Jan.?    1855

TURKEY
Constan-      Naum         Spring   1849 E. Cominotti (O.) C. Negrini (F.) G.
tinople                           B. Bencich (E.) C. Nanni (A.) A. Ma-
                                  riani cond.

Smyrna        Alhambra     Aug.     1881 Focchi (O.) A. Brunetti (F.) Gambet-
                                  ti (E.) N. Giommi (A.)

UNITED STATES
New York        Niblo's      Apr. 15, 1850 F. Tedesco (O.) D. Lorini (F.) L.
                                           Corradi-Setti (E.) I. Marini (A.) L.
                                           Arditi cond.

San Francisco American        Aug. 18, 1859 G. Bianchi (O.) E. Bianchi (F.) S.
                                           W. Leach (E.) Roncovieri (A.)

URUGUAY
Montevideo      San Felipe   Nov. 13, 1852 R. Olivieri (O.) G. Dordoni (F.) J.
                                           Olivieri (E.) E. Luisia (A.)

                Solis        July 19, 1858 T. Bajetti (O.) L. Lelmi (F.) G. C.
                                           Casanova (E.) G. Bastoggi (A.) L.
                                           Pretti cond.

VENEZUELA
Caracas         Teatro       Aug.  2, 1857 C. Saeman (O.) M. Tiberini (F.) F.
                                           Morelli-Ponti (E.) A. Gasparoni (A.)

SELECTED REVIVALS-NINETEENTH CENTURY

ITALY
Florence        Pergola      Lent     1847 M. Barbieri-Nini (O.) L. Bernabei
                                           (F.) F. Gorin (E.) L. Salandri (A.)

                             May  29, 1859 C. Manzini (O.) A. Agresti (F.) G.
                                           Guicciardi (E.) G. Segri-Segarra
                                           (A.)

Genoa           Carlo        Nov. 23  1850 S. Cruvelli (O.) C. Liverani (F.) F.
                Felice                     Monari (E.) R. Anconi (A.) N. Uccel-
                                           li cond.

                             Apr. 13, 1857 E. Weisser (O.) C. Negrini (F.) P.
                                           G. Pacini (E.) H. Brémond (A.) A.
                                           Mariani cond.

Milan           La Scala     Dec. 26, 1849 S. Cruvelli (O.) E. Musich (F.) N.
                                           Gnone (E.) E. Manfredi (A.)

                             Jan.  1, 1852 M. Lotti della Santa (O.) G. Musiani
                                           (F.) F. Gorin (E.) A. Didot (A.)

                             Nov. 24, 1860 G. Borsi de Leurie (O.) G. Valenti-
                                           ni-Cristiani (F.) A. Cotogni (E.) C.
                                           Dalla Costa (A.)

                             Mar.  2, 1867 T. Cotta Morandini (O.) D. Rosnati/
                                           L. Abrugnedo (F.) T. Sterbini/G.
                                           Cantù (E.) G. Vecchi (A.)

Naples          San Carlo    Oct. 26, 1848 E. Tadolini (O.) S. Malvezzi (F.) R.
                                           Mastriani (E.) A. Rodas (A.) A. Fa-
                                           relli cond.

Trieste         Grande       Carn. 1848-49 S. Cruvelli (O.) G. Alzamora (F.) F.
                                           Cresci (E.) S. Torre (A.) G. A. Sca-
                                           ramelli cond.

                             Dec. 26? 1850 L. Bendazzi-Secchi (O.) L. Graziani
                                           (F.) F. Monari (E.) C. Dalla Costa
                                           (A.) G. A. Scaramelli cond.

|  |  | Jan. | 29, 1855 | V. Rupini (O.) C. Liverani (F.) A. Morelli (E.) N. Benedetti (A.) G. A. Scaramelli cond. |
|--|--|------|----------|------|

Feb.      1865 G. Borsi de Leurie (O.) E. Palermi
               (F.) V. Orlandi (E.) L. Rossi (A.)

MEXICO
Mexico City   Nacional    Jan.      1856 M. Almonti (O.) L. Giannoni (F.) E.
                                         Winter (E.) C. Carroni (A.) J. Win-
                                         ter cond.

                          Nov.   1, 1857 E. Zilioli-Fattori (O.) L. Stefani/
                                         A. Volpini (F.) A. Ottaviani (E.) G.
                                         Gariboldi (A.) C. Fattori cond.

                          Aug.   1, 1861 A. Ottaviani (E.) A. Biacchi (A.) J,
                                         Nicolao cond.

                          Oct.      1865

PORTUGAL
Lisbon        Sao Carlos  Dec. 17, 1847 E. Librandi/T. Bovay (O.) A. Volpini
                                         (F.) R. Pizzigati (E.) F. Sansoni
                                         (A.)

                          Oct. 29, 1848 M. Gresti (O.) A. Volpini (F.) N.
                                         Benedetti (A.)

                          Oct. 24, 1849 M. Gresti (O.) G. Baldanza (F.) G.
                                         Fiori (E.) N. Benedetti (A.)

                          Sep. 16, 1855 A. Carradori (O.) E. Irfré (F.) O.
                                         Bartolini (E.) C. G. Nerini (A.)

                          Oct.  8, 1856 M. Bernardi (O.) L. Saccomano (F.)
                                         F. Monari (E.) P. Nolasco Llorens
                                         (A.)

ROMANIA
Iasi          Teatrul     Oct.      1853 L. Abbadia/L. Gino (O.) A. Prudenza
                                         (F.) V. Sermattei (E.) P. Dérivis
                                         (A.)

                          Nov.      1854 T. Brambilla (O.) A. Pozzolini (F.)
                                         V. Sermattei (E.) G. Mitrovich (A.)

                          Dec.?     1855 C. Mansur (O.) G. Petrovich (F.) F.
                                         Giannini (E.) H. Brémond (A.)

                          Nov.      1860 A. Jackson (O.) A. Zenari (F.) E.
                                         Storti (E.) G. Segri-Segarra (A.)

SPAIN
Barcelona     Liceo       Jan. 25, 1852 L. Abbadia (O.) G. Baldanza (F.)

                          Feb. 13, 1856 M. Bernardi (O.) M. Sacchero (F.) G.
                                         Fiori/D. Mattioli (E.) A. Rodas (A.)

Madrid        Circo       Dec.  8, 1847 A. Bosio (O.) G. B. Milesi (F.) F.
                                         Morelli-Ponti (E.) L. Fornasari (A.)

                          Feb. 16, 1850 T. Rusmini-Solera (O.) G. Alzamora
                                         (F.) G. Mancusi (E.) G. Euzet (A.)

UNITED STATES
San Francisco  Metro-        Sep.    5, 1862 G. Bianchi (O.)   E. Bianchi (F.)   J.
               politan                        Gregg  (E.)   E.  Grossi  (A.)  G.  T.
                                              Evans cond.

                             July 30, 1866 E. Brambilla (O.) E. Bianchi (F.) G.
                                           Mancusi  (E.)  S.  Milleri  (A.)  R.
                                           Herold cond.

                             Nov. 22, 1872 L. Bernardi (O.) P. Baccei (F.) S.
                                           Rossi (E.) F. Rigo (A.) G. T. Evans
                                           cond.


OTHER PRODUCTIONS-1900-1945

EGYPT
Cairo          Varietà       May   17? 1901 L. De Sirianna (O.) O. Delle Fornac-
                                            ci (F.) E. Massini (E.) G. Beltramo
                                            (A.) G. Galletti cond.

ITALY
Lucca          Pantera       Dec. 25? 1900

Naples         Bellini       Jan.     1900 Casale (O.) A. Franceschini (F.) V.
                                           Morghen (E.) Roveri (A.)

Turin          Balbo         Feb. 13, 1912 Baldini (O.) E. Cunego (F.)   Pagli-
                                           olico (E.) Melocchi (A.)

OTHER PRODUCTIONS-POST-WORLD WAR II

ARGENTINA
Buenos Aires   Colón         Aug.    6, 1966 N. Tatum (O.)  C. Cossutta (F.)  P.
                                             Glossop (E.) J. Hines (A.) J. Prit-
                                             chard cond.

AUSTRIA
Graz                         Feb. 26, 1966 A. Bridges (O.) J. M. Perez (F.) R.
                                           Constantin (E.) K. Ohashi (A.) B.
                                           Arnaducci cond. (in Ger.)

Vienna         Staatsoper    Dec. 21, 1980 M. Zampieri (O.) P. Visconti (F.) P.
                                           Cappuccilli (E.) N. Ghiaurov (A.) G.
                                           Sinopoli cond.

                             Feb. 19, 1984 M. Chiara (O.) N. Martinucci (F.) P.
                                           Cappuccilli (E.) N. Ghiaurov (A.) C.
                                           Mackerras cond.

CANADA
Calgary                      Spring   1978 C. Deutekom (O.) R. Bondino (F.) C.
                                           Opthof (E.) J. Hines (A.) A. Guada-
                                           gno cond.

Edmonton       Opera         Apr. 29, 1978 C. Deutekom (O.) R. Bondino (F.) C.
                                           Opthof (E.) J. Hines (A.) A. Guada-
                                           gno cond.

FINLAND
Helsinki                     May      1980 J.  Anvelt  (O.)  H.  Krumm  (F.)  T.
                                           Kuusik (E.) M. Palm (A.)

FRANCE
Marseille      Opéra       Jan. 13, 1978 R. Bakocevic (O.) V. Luchetti (F.)
                                        A. Salvadori (E.) J. Van Dam (A.) M.
                                        Veltri cond.

                           Mar. 14? 1985 L. Strow-Piccolo (O.) B. Prior (F.)
                                        J. Rawnsly (E.) J. Van Dam (A.) A.
                                        Siciliani cond.

Paris          Châtelet    Mar. 14, 1982 M. Zschau (O.) F. Ortiz (F.) J.
                                        Rawnsley (E.) K. Rydl (A.) G. Gel-
                                        metti cond.

GERMANY
Berlin         Deutsche    June  6, 1971 G. Janowitz (O.) Fr. Tagliavini (F.)
                                        I. Wixell (E.) J. Van Dam (A.) G.
                                        Patanè cond. (in It.)

Bremerhaven    Stadt       Oct. 22, 1964 A. Salta (O.) C. Kaiser (F.) J.
                                        Derksen (E.) D. Weller (A.) (in It.)

ITALY
Bologna        Comunale    Feb.  2, 1985 M. Zampieri (O.) V. Luchetti (F.) S.
                                        Carroli (E.) R. Raimondi (A.)

Catania        Massimo     Jan. 13, 1979 O. Stapp (O.) R. Bondino (F.) G.
                                        Floresta (E.) C. Cava (A.)

Florence       Comunale    Dec.  1, 1962 M. Roberti (O.) G. Limarilli (F.) G.
                                        Guelfi (E.) B. Christoff (A.) B.
                                        Bartoletti cond.

                           Dec. 23, 1972 L. Gencer (O.) V. Luchetti (F.) N.
                                        Mittellmann (E.) N. Ghiaurov (A.) R.
                                        Muti cond.

Genoa          Margherita  Feb. 27, 1983 M. Chiara (O.) N. Martinucci (F.) G.
                                        Boyagan/G. Zancanaro (E.) N. Ghiuse-
                                        lev (A.) N. Santi cond.

Milan          La Scala    May 15, 1975 R. Orlandi-Malaspina (O.) V. Luchet-
                                        ti (F.) P. Cappuccilli (E.) N. Ghi-
                                        aurov (A.) G. Patanè cond.

Naples         San Carlo   Dec.  6, 1970 L. Maragliano (O.) B. Prevedi (F.)
                                        G. Guelfi (E.) C. Cava (A.) G. Mag-
                                        giore cond.

                           Feb.  3, 1987 M. Zampieri/J. Omilian (O.) B. Bec-
                                        caria (F.) S. Carroli (E.) N. Ghiu-
                                        selev (A.) G. Masini/G. Maggiore
                                        cond.

Parma          Regio       Jan. 20, 1973 G. Trombin/L. Maragliano (O.) G.
                                        Casellato-Lamberti (F.) L. Saccoma-
                                        ni/G. Lormi (E.) D. Petrov (A.) P.
                                        Maag cond.

                           May 19, 1983 S. Kotlenko (O.) V. Luchetti (F.) G.
                                        Boyagan (E.) N. Ghiuselev (A.)

Rome           Sala RAI    Mar. 29, 1967 M. De Osma (O.) L. Ottolini (F.) D.
                                        Dondi (E.) R. Ariè (A.) F. Previtali
                                        cond.

Dec.  8, 1970 A.  Stella  (O.)  G.  Cecchele  (F.)  G.
G.  Guelfi  (E.)  R.  Raimondi  (A.)  R.
Muti cond.

Opera        June  2, 1981 M.  Parazzini  (O.)  N.  Todisco  (F.)  M.
Manuguerra  (E.)  N.  Ghiuselev  (A.)  B.
Bartoletti cond.

Trieste      Verdi        Nov.  9, 1966 M.  De  Osma  (O.)  R.  Bondino  (F.)  S.
Carroli  (E.)  B.  Christoff  (A.)  O.  De
Fabritiis cond.

Turin        Regio        Dec.  1, 1983 M.  Chiara/D.  Vejzovic  (O.)  V.  Lu-
chetti/A.  Elena  (F.)  S.  Carroli/F.
Sioli  (E.)  N.  Ghiuselev  (A.)  N.
Santi cond.

Venice       La Fenice    Sep. 12, 1951 C.  Mancini  (O.)  G.  Penno  (F.)  G.  G.
Guelfi  (E.)  I.  Tajo  (A.)  C.  M.  Giu-
lini cond.  (Radio broadcast by RAI)

Jan. 10, 1976 M.  Parazzini  (O.)  M.  Ortiz  (F.)  L.
Saccomani  (E.)  B.  Christoff  (A.)

June  6, 1986 L.  Roark-Strummer  (O.)  W.  Donati
(F.)  W.  Stone  (E.)  S.  Ramey  (A.)  G.
Ferro cond.

Jan. 21, 1987 L.  Roark-Strummer  (O.)  V.  Luchetti
(F.)  W.  Stone  (E.)  S.  Ramey  (A.)  G.
Ferro cond.

Verona       Arena        Aug. 22, 1985 M.  Chiara/A.  Manotti  (O.)  V.  Luchetti  (F.)  S.  Carroli  (E.)  Y.  Nester-
enko  (A.)  N.  Santi cond.

JUGOSLAVIA
Belgrade                  Winter? 1987 M.  Stojanovic  (O.)  S.  Sankovic  (E.)
A.  Djokic  (A.)  Zlicar cond.

POLAND
Poznan       State        Mar.   1968 A.  Dankowska  (O.)  M.  Kouba  (F.)  A.
Fechner  (E.)  H.  Lukaszek  (A.)  M.
Lantieri cond.

PORTUGAL
Lisbon       Sao Carlos   Mar.  5, 1985 H.  Krige  (O.)  P.  Iorio  (F.)  M.  Au-
gustini  (E.)  K.  Byung-Woon  (A.)  J.
Neschling cond.

May  14, 1986 E.  Bayan  (O.)  P.  Iorio  (F.)  M.  Augustini  (E.)  S.  Elenkof  (A.)  J.  La-
tham-König cond.

Coliseo      Mar. 10, 1985 H.  Krige  (O.)  P.  Iorio  (F.)  M.  Augustini  (E.)  K.  Byung-Woon  (A.)  J.
Neschling cond.

SOVIET UNION
Ulan-Ude                  1980 L.  Levshenko/  O.  Mironova  (O.)  Y.
Shevshenko/  V.  Balshinimayev  (F.)  V.
Buruev/I  Shobolov  (E.)  L.  Morozovsky
cond.

SPAIN
Barcelona      Liceo        Apr.   1? 1984 G. Dimitrova (O.) N. Todisco (F.) A.
                                            Salvadori (E.) Y. Nesterenko (A.) R.
                                            Abbado cond.

Bilbao         Coliseo      Sep.  11, 1977 R. Orlandi-Malaspina (O.)  N. Marti-
               Alba                         nucci (F.) A. Salvadori (E.) R. Rai-
                                            mondi (A.) G. Rivoli cond.

Madrid         Zarzuela     Feb.  16, 1988 M. Zampieri (O.) M. Malagnini (F.)
                                            J. Rawnsley (E.) Y. Nesterenko (A.)
                                            R. Gandolfi cond.

Oviedo         Campoamor    Sep.  21, 1977 R. Orlandi-Malaspina (O.) N. Marti-
                                            nucci (F.) A. Salvadori (E.) R. Rai-
                                            mondi (A.) G. Rivoli cond.

SWITZERLAND
Zürich         Opernhaus    Feb.   4, 1981 M. Chiara (O.) V. Moldeveanu (F.) G.
                                            Zancanaro (E.) S. Estes/B. Giaiotti
                                            (A.) N. Santi cond.

UNITED STATES
Chicago        Lyric        Oct.  26, 1980 G. Cruz-Romo (O.) V. Luchetti (F.)
                                            S. Carroli (E.) J. Hines/N. Ghiaurov
                                            (A.) B. Bartoletti cond.

Cincinnati     Opera        July  21, 1979 M. Galvany (O.) E. Di Giuseppe (F.)
                                            C. Opthof (E.) J. Diaz (A.) A. Cop-
                                            pola cond.

                            June  28, 1984 M. Galvany (O.) E. Di Giuseppe (F.)
                                            C. Long (E.) J. Diaz (A.) A. Coppola
                                            cond.

Memphis                     Dec.   8, 1979 M. Galvany (O.) H. Theyard (F.) R.
                                            Stenborg (E.) J. Hines (A.)

Newark                      Oct.  20, 1972 L. Gencer (O.) N. Martinucci (F.) C.
                                            Bardelli (E.) J. Hines (A.) A. Sili-
                                            pigni cond.

New York       City Opera   Mar.  13, 1981 M. Zschau/M. Galvany (O.) E. Di Giu-
                                            seppe/J. Evans (F.) R. Fredericks/W.
                                            Justus (E.) S. Ramey (A.) S. Comisi-
                                            ona cond.

                            July  28, 1985 L. Roark-Strummer (O.) J. F. West
                                            (F.) F. Burchinal (E.) S. Ramey (A.)
                                            C. Keene cond.

Philadelphia  Ac. of Mus.  Apr.      1978 G. Cruz-Romo (O.) G. Cecchele (F.)
                                            C. Opthof (E.) J. Hines (A.) I.
                                            Pallo cond.

Tulsa                       Mar.  13, 1982 M. Galvany (O.) C. Bergonzi (F.) A.
                                            Fazah (E.) S. Estes (A.) E. Kohn
                                            cond.

Washington     Kennedy      Dec.   3, 1976 M. Galvany (O.) H. Theyard (F.) A.
               Center                       Salvadori (E.) J. Diaz (A.) A.
                                            Guadagno cond.

10. MACBETH-*Melodramma* in four parts
Florence-Teatro in via della Pergola-Mar. 14, 1847
Libretto by Francesco Maria Piave with changes by Andrea Maffei

| | |
|---|---|
| Lady Macbeth (L.) | Marianna Barbieri-Nini sop. |
| Macduff (Md.) | Angelo Brunacci ten. |
| Macbeth (M.) | Felice Varesi bar. |
| Banquo (B.) | Niccola Benedetti bass |
| Dama di Lady Macbeth | Faustina Piombanti mez. |
| Malcolm | Francesco Rossi ten. |
| Medico | Giuseppe Romanelli bass |
| Sicario | Giuseppe Bertini bass |
| | |
| Conductor | Alamanno Biagi |
| Director | Pietro Romani and Giuseppe Verdi |

Revised-Paris-Théâtre Lyrique-Apr. 21, 1865

| | |
|---|---|
| Lady Macbeth | Inez Rey-Balla sop. |
| Macduff | Jules Sebastien Monjauze ten. |
| Macbeth | Jean Vital Ismael bar. |
| Banquo | Jules Petit bass |
| La Comtesse | Mairot sop. |
| Un Médecin | Guyot bass |
| Un Sicaire | Caillot bar. |
| Un Officier | Troy bar. |
| Premier Phantome | Peront bass |
| Deuxieme Phantome | Gilland ten. |
| Troisieme Phantome | Renaudy sop. |
| | |
| Conductor | |
| Director | Giuseppe Verdi |

OTHER PREMIERES-NINETEENTH CENTURY

ARGENTINA
Buenos Aires  Argentino    Mar. 21, 1854 I.  Edelvira  (L.)  L.  Guglielmini
                                         (Md.) E. M. Rivas (M.) F. Tati (B.)

             Ant. Colón  July?     1857 E. La Grua (L.) G. C. Casanova (M.)

AUSTRALIA
Adelaide     Th. Royal   Apr.  3, 1872 M. Zenoni (L.) L. Coy (Md.) F. Coli-
                                         va (M.) E. Dondi (B.)

Melbourne    Th. Royal   Sep.  8, 1860 G. Bianchi (L.) E. Bianchi (Md.) E.
                                         Coulon (M.) J. Gregg (B.)

Sydney       Prince      July  5, 1860 G. Bianchi (L.) E. Bianchi (Md.) E.
             of Wales                    Coulon (M.) E. Grossi (B.)

AUSTRIA
Graz         Stadt       Sep. 22, 1856 (In Ger.)

Linz         Landes      Mar. 19, 1858 (in Ger.)

Vienna       Kärntnertor Dec. 11, 1849 W. von Hasseldt-Barth (L.) Kreutzer
                                         (Md.) J. Staudigl (M.) (in Ger.)

             Apr. 21, 1851 C. Gruitz (L.) J. B. Bordas (Md.) A.
                           De Bassini (M.) E. Manfredi (B.) H.
                           Proch cond. (In It.)

BRAZIL
Rio de          Lyrico      Mar. 25, 1852 G. Zecchini (L.) Vergini (Md.) L. Di
Janeiro         Fluminense               Lauro (M.)

                Pedro II    Aug. 16, 1877 A. Fricci (L.) F. Ambrosi (Md.) G.
                                          Mendioroz (M.) L. Lombardelli (B.)
                                          N. Bassi cond.


CHILE
Santiago        Republica   June 15, 1855 R. Olivieri (L.)  E. Rossi-Guerra
                                          (Md.) E. Luisia (M.) Bruscoli (B.)

                Municipal   Sep. 29, 1857 1. Edelvira (L.)  L. Guglielmini
                                          (Md.) A. Lanzoni (M.)

Valparaiso      Victoria    Dec. 28, 1855 R. Olivieri (L.)  E. Rossi-Guerra
                                          (Md.) E. Luisia (M.) G. Mirandola
                                          (B.)


COLOMBIA
Bogota          Teatro      Dec.  5, 1858 R. Olivieri (L.)  E. Rossi-Guerra
                                          (Md.) E. Luisia (M.) G. Mirandola
                                          (B.)


CUBA
Havana          Tacon       Dec. 19, 1849 A. Bosio (L.) D. Lorini (Md.) C. Ba-
                                          diali (M.) D. Coletti (B.) L. Arditi
                                          cond.


CZECHOSLOVAKIA
Bratislava                          1856

Brno            Stadt       Dec. 13, 1856

DENMARK
Copenhagen      Royal       Jan. 11, 1854 V. Gazziello-Brambilla (L.) G. Bian-
                                          chi (Md.) G. Reina (M.) G. Mirandola
                                          (B.)


EGYPT
Alexandria      Europeo     Nov.  3, 1858 R. Pellini (L.) A. Marini (Md.) Q.
                                          Fabbricatore (M.)


FRANCE
Nice            Municipal   Dec.     1876 V. Potentini (L.) Bugamini (Md.) F.
                                          Cresci (M.) C. Gianola (B.) (in It.)

Pau                         Spring   1869 Ferlotti (L.) Otto (M.) (in It.)

GERMANY
Berlin          Kroll       Nov. 20, 1878 M. Boy-Gilbert (L.) Bertocchio (Md.)
                                          M. Medica (M.) P. Povoleri (B.) O.
                                          Bimboni cond. (in It.)

Hannover        Hoftheater  Dec. 23, 1850 (in Ger.)


GREAT BRITAIN
Birmingham      Th. Royal   Aug. 27, 1860 Zamboni (L.) Operti (M.) Longhi (B.)

Liverpool       Th. Royal   Oct.  8, 1860 P. Viardot (L.) A. Luise (Md.) G.
                                          Ciampi (M.) F. Fallar (B.) A. Via-
                                          nesi cond.

Manchester    Th. Royal    Oct.  2, 1860 P. Viardot (L.) A. Luise (Md.) G.
                                         Ciampi (M.) E. Cosselli (B.) A.
                                         Vianesi cond.

GREECE
Athens        Royal        Feb.    1856 G. Zecchini (L.)

Corfu         San Giacomo Sep. 15, 1849 G. Leva (L.) G. Donelli (M.) F. Ri-
                                         ghi (B.)

GUATEMALA
Guatemala     Carrera            1867-68
City

HUNGARY
Budapest      Nemzeti      Feb. 26, 1848 R. Schodel (L.) G. Reina (M.)
              Szinház

INDIA
Calcutta      Op. House    Jan. 28, 1869 M. Zenoni (L.) E. Caroselli (Md.) A.
                                         De Antoni (M.) E. Gasperini (B.) A.
                                         melchiori cond.

IRELAND
Dublin        Th. Royal    Mar. 30, 1859 P. Viardot  (L.)  Corsi  (Md.)  F.
                                         Graziani (M.) A. Lanzoni (B.) L.
                                         Arditi cond.

ITALY
Alessandria   Civico       Nov. 14, 1855 F. Gordosa (L.) Ferlotti (Md.) L.
                                         Giraldoni (M.) Gandini (B.)

Ancona        Muse         May   4, 1848 M. Arrigotti (L.) C. Miraglia (Md.)
                                         G. Fiori (M.) E. Manfredi (B.)

Bari          Piccinni     Feb.    1861 L. Finetti-Batocchi (L.) G. Sansoni
                                         (M.)

Bergamo       Riccardi     Aug.  7, 1852 M. Lotti della Santa (L.) G. Musiani
                                         (Md.) G. Fiori (M.) G. Dalbesio (B.)
                                         G. Bragozzo cond.

Bologna       Comunale     Nov.  7, 1849 T.  Bovay  (L.)  L. Stecchi-Bottardi
                                         (Md.)  G.  Ferri  (M.)  F. Dall'Asta
                                         (B.) G. Manetti cond.

Brescia       Grande       Dec. 26, 1848

Cagliari      Civico       Sep.  8, 1858 A. Melada (L.) F. Ceccarelli (M.) G.
                                         Ascani (B.)

Catania       Comunale     Nov. 15, 1853 S. Zudoli (L.) L. Lelmi (Md.) P.
                                         Giorgi-Pacini  (M.)  M.  Pappalardo
                                         cond.

Chieti        Marrucino    May   8, 1863 I. Dordoni (L.) L. Caserini (Md.) F.
                                         Proni (M.) L. Caprile (B.)

Cremona       Concordia    Dec. 27, 1856 E.  Weisser  (L.)  R.  Bertolini (Md.)
                                         F. Coliva (M.) A. Garcia (B.)

Faenza        Comunale     Summer   1852 K. Evers (L.) G. Corsi (M.) C. Nanni
                                         (B.)

Fermo          Aquila        Aug.       1848 M. Gresti (L.) F. Banti (Md.) G.
                                              Fiori (M.) E. Manfredi (B.) F. Cel-
                                              lini cond.

Ferrara        Comunale      Apr. 24, 1852 C. Gruitz (L.) R. Giorgi (Md.) E.
                                              Crivelli (M.) A. Lanzoni (B.)

Fiume          Civico        Apr. 12, 1852 G. Casali-Campagna (L.) E. Pelle-
                                              grini (Md.) E. Storti (M.) E. Topai
                                              (B.)

Forli          Comunale      June 8, 1850 A. Albertini (L.) F. Colini (M.)

Genoa          Carlo         May 13, 1848 T. De Giuli-Borsi (L.) G. Roppa
               Felice                         (Md.) F. Gnone (M.) L. Bianchi (B.)

Livorno        Avvalorati    Oct. 9, 1847 K. Evers (L.) A. Brunacci (Md.) F.
                                              Gorin (M.) N. Benedetti (B.)

Lucca          Giglio        July 29, 1847 E. Tadolini (L.) A. Brunacci (Md.)
                                              F. Gorin (M.) N. Benedetti (B.)

Lugo           Rossini       Sep. 18, 1852 L. Finetti-Batocchi (L.) A. Badaluc-
                                              chi (Md.) F. Coliva (M.) P. Montagu-
                                              ti cond.

Mantua         Sociale       Feb. 18, 1848 C. Gruitz (L.) Mercuriali (Md.) L.
                                              Valli (M.) N. Torre (B.) G. Luppi
                                              cond.

Messina        Sant'         Apr. 2, 1853 A. Boccabadati (L.) M. Russo (Md.)
               Elisabetta                     L. Walter (M.) C. Lazzari (B.) A.
                                              Laudamo cond.

Milan          La Scala      Feb. 24, 1849 C. Gruitz (L.) L. Ferretti (Md.) F.
                                              Gnone (M.) R. Scalese (B.)

                             Jan. 28, 1874 A. Fricci (L.) Cesi (Md.) F. Pandol-
                                              fini (M.) A. Padovani (B.) F. Faccio
                                              cond.[40]

Modena         Comunale      Dec. 26, 1850 C. Alaimo (L.) G. Poggiali (Md.) M.
                                              Zacchi (M.) P. Ferretti (B.) A. Si-
                                              ghicelli cond.

Naples         San Carlo     Jan. 22, 1849 E. Tadolini (L.) A. Agresti (Md.) C.
                                              Badiali (M.) M. Arati (B.)

Novara         Nuovo         Dec. 26, 1855 S. Della Valle (L.) A. Badalucchi
                                              (Md.) C. Busi (M.) P. Nolasco-Llo-
                                              rens (B.)

Padua          Nuovo         July 29, 1847 M. Barbieri-Nini (L.) Lanner (Md.)
                                              F. Colini (M.) G. Euzet (B.)

Palermo        Carolino      Dec. 13, 1852 E. Marcolini (L.) A. Pompeiani (Md.)
                                              E. Barili (M.) C. Nanni (B.) A. Lo
                                              Casto cond.

---

[40]. This is believed to be the Italian premiere of the revised version of *Macbeth*
(*Macbeth* II).

Parma         Regio        Dec. 26, 1849 F. Salvini-Donatelli (L.) A. Bozzet-
                                         ti (Md.) L. Ferrario (M.) F. Goré
                                         (B.) N. De Giovanni cond.

Perugia       Morlacchi    Aug. 13, 1853 L. Finetti-Batocchi (L.) Orlandi
                                         (Md.) A. Morelli (M.) G. Capriles
                                         (B.)

Pesaro        Rossini      Dec. 26, 1857 I. Galletti-Gianoli (L.) A. Svampa
                                         (Md.) G. Fiori (M.) N. Contedini
                                         (B.) G. Altinieri cond.

Piacenza      Comunale     Dec. 26, 1855 M. Arrigotti (L.) B. Negri (Md.) F.
                                         Massiani (M.) L. Bisi (B.) G. Jona
                                         cond.

Pisa          Ravvivati    Dec. 26, 1851 T. Bovay (L.) P. Chiesi (Md.) R.
                                         Pizzigati (M.) A. Lanzoni (B.) C.
                                         Marsili cond.

Ravenna       Alighieri    Apr. 28, 1855 T. De Giuli-Borsi (L.) E. Testa
                                         (Md.) A. Morelli (M.) G. Atry (B.)
                                         L. Vannuccini cond.

Reggio Emilia Comunale     Apr. 23, 1848 R. Gabussi De Bassini (L.) E. Pan-
                                         cani (Md.) A. De Bassini (M.) N. Be-
                                         nedetti (B.) G. Tebaldi cond.

Rome          Argentina    Sep. 12, 1847 A. Boccabadati (L.) G. Lucchesi
                                         (Md.) F. Gnone (M.) P. Sottovia (B.)

Siena         Rinnovati    Carn. 1851-52

Sinigaglia    La Fenice    July 17, 1850 M. Barbieri-Nini (L.) G. Biondi
                                         (Md.) F. Colini (M.) C. Della Costa
                                         (B.)

Spoleto       Nobile       Dec. 28, 1861 V. Censi (L.) F. Mottino (M.)

Trento        Sociale      June  9, 1851 Castagnola (L.) T. Palmieri (Md.) C.
                                         Bartolucci (M.) A. Padovani (B.)

Treviso       Garibaldi    Nov.  7, 1868 F. Scheggi (L.) A. Grandi (M.)

Trieste       Grande       Nov. 15, 1848 M. Barbieri-Nini (L.) G. Pavesi
                                         (Md.) A. De Bassini (M.) A. Giaco-
                                         melli (B.) G. A. Scaramella cond.

Turin         Regio        Dec. 25, 1850 M. Barbieri-Nini (L.) T. Palmieri
                                         (Md.) G. Ferri (M.) L. Vajro (B.) G.
                                         Ghebart cond.

Udine         Sociale      Nov. 11, 1855 A. Murio-Celli (L.) V. Prattico (M.)

Venice        La Fenice    Dec. 26, 1847 A. De la Grange (L.) A. Palma (Md.)
                                         F. Varesi (M.) F. Rigo (B.) G. Mares
                                         cond.

Verona        Filarmonico  Dec. 30, 1847 K. Evers (L.) F. Borioni (Md.) A. De
                                         Bassini (M.)

Vicenza       Eretenio     Jan.     1858 M. Arrigotti (L.) G. Sacconi (M.) R.
                                         Farina (B.)

JUGOSLAVIA
Ljubljana      Stanovskem    May         1852 G.  Casali-Campagna  (L.)  E.  Pelle-
                                              grini  (Md.)  E.  Storti  (M.)  E.  Topai
                                              (B.)

Zagreb         National      Feb.  1,  1853 V.  Gaziello-Brambilla  (L.)  Viotti
                                              (Md.)  Gianni  (M.)  Celli  (B.)

Zara           Nobile        May         1857 C.  Marziali  (L.)  G.  Petrovich  (Md.)
                                              G.  Bertolini  (M.)  F.  Dalla  Costa
                                              (B.)

MALTA
La Valletta    Manoel        Mar.  31,  1849 E.  Servoli  (L.)  L.  Bianchi  (Md.)  E.
                                              Crivelli  (M.)  G.  Poggiali  (B.)

MEXICO
Mexico City    Nacional      Jan.  10,  1857 G.  Casali-Campagna  (L.)  E.  Bianchi
                                              (Md.)  E.  Barili  (M.)  E.  Casali  (B.)
                                              C.  Fattori  cond.

NETHERLANDS
Amsterdam      Stads         Feb.  28,  1860 R.  Devries  (L.)  B.  Danieli  (Md.)  G.
                                              Marra  (M.)  A.  Bianchi  (B.)  N.  Bassi
                                              cond.

NEW ZEALAND
Auckland       Choral Hall   Dec.   4,  1872 M.  Zenoni  (L.)  L.  Coy  (Md.)  F.  Coli-
                                              va  (M.)  E.  Dondi  (B.)  A.  Zelman
                                              cond.

Dunedin        New Queen's   Jan.  28,  1873 M.  Zenoni  (L.)  L.  Coy  (Md.)  F.  Coli-
                                              va  (M.)  E.  Dondi  (B.)  A.  Zelman
                                              cond.

PERU
Lima           Principal     June  1,  1856 R.  Olivieri  (L.)  E.  Rossi-Guerra
                                              (Md.)  A.  Lanzoni  (M.)  G.  Mirandola
                                              (B.)  C.  Lietti  cond.

PHILIPPINES
Manila         Circo         Jan.  17,  1875 L.  Arancio-Guerrini  (L.)  Vistarini
                                              (Md.)  Rossi  (M.)  Garcia  (B.)

POLAND
Warsaw         Wielki        Jan.   1,  1849

PORTUGAL
Lisbon         Sao Carlos    Jan.  13,  1849 M.  Gresti  (L.)  A.  Volpini  (Md.)  G.
                                              Fiori  (M.)  N.  Benedetti  (B.)

Oporto         Sao Joao      July        1849 M.  Gresti  (L.)  A.  Volpini  (Md.)  G.
                                              Fiori  (M.)  N.  Benedetti  (B.)

PUERTO RICO
San Juan       Municipal     June  10,  1877 E.  D'Aponte  (L.)  G.  Mariani  (Md.)  E.
                                              Petrilli  (M.)  M.  Atienza  (B.)  R.
                                              Aruti  cond.

ROMANIA
Bucharest      Nacional      Dec.   5,  1855 A.  Ravaglia  (L.)  D.  Lorini  (Md.)  F.
                                              Coliva  (M.)  Giannelli  (B.)

Iasi            Teatrul      Winter    1856 C. Mansui (L.) G. Petrovich (Md.) F.
                                            Giannini (M.)

Temesvar                     1850-51 (in Ger.)

RUSSIA
Kharkov         Municipale   Spring    1864 C. Noel-Guidi (L.) A. Gottardi (Md.)
                                            F. Giannini (M.) E. Manfredi (B.)

Odessa          Municipal    Nov.      1852 A. Basseggio (L.) G. Volta (Md.) M.
                                            Zacchi (M.) N. Benedetti (B.)

St.             Imperial     Dec. 16, 1854 F. Tedesco (L.) A. Bettini  (Md.) A.
Petersburg                                  De Bassini (M.)

Tbilisi         Imperial     Sep.  1, 1861 T. Stolz (L.) P. Baraldi (M.)

SPAIN
Barcelona       Liceo        July  1, 1848 F. Salvini-Donatelli (L.) A. Bozet-
                                            ti (Md.) G. Ferri (M.) L. Silingardi
                                            (B.)

Cadiz           Principal              1849

Madrid          Circo        Feb. 20, 1848 A. Bosio (L.) E. Calzolari (Md.) F.
                                            Morelli-Ponti (M.)

                Real         Jan.  2, 1852 C. Cattinari (L.) F. Martorell (Md.)
                                            F. Cresci  (M.)  V.  Barba  (B.)  J.
                                            Skoczdopole cond.

Malaga          Principal    Dec.?    1851 V. Sermattei (M.)

Seville         San          Oct. 23, 1851 Bianchi (L.) V. Prattico (M.) (First
                Fernando                    production traced)

Valencia        Principal    Oct.     1848 C. Cattinari (L.) J. Font (Md.) A.
                                            De Gironella (M.) G. Segri-Segarra
                                            (B.)

SWEDEN
Stockholm       Royal        Apr. 29, 1852 Normanni (L.) L. Della Santa (M.)

TURKEY
Constan-        Naum         Oct.  4, 1848 G. Medori (L.) Ademollo (Md.) G. B.
tinople                                     Bencich (M.) C. Nanni (B.) A. Maria-
                                            ni cond.

Smyrna          Cammarano    Nov.     1861 Bresciani (L.) F. Sutter (M.)

UNITED STATES
Boston          Howard       May  28, 1850 A.  Bosio ( L.)  D. Lorini (Md.)  C.
                Atheneum                    Badiali  (M.)  D.  Coletti  (B.)  L.
                                            Arditi cond.

New York        Niblo's      Apr. 24, 1850 A. Bosio (L.) D. Lorini (Md.) C.
                Garden                      Badiali  (M.)  D.  Coletti  (B.)  L.
                                            Arditi cond.

                Ac. of Mus. Oct. 21, 1863 G.  Medori  (L.)  Lotti  (Md.)  D.
                                            Bellini (M.) D. Coletti (B.)

Philadelphia  Ac. of Mus.  Oct. 21, 1863 G.  Medori  (L.)  Lotti  (Md.)  D.
                                        Bellini (M.) D. Coletti (B.)

San Francisco Maguire's    Nov. 11, 1862 G. Bianchi (L.) E. Bianchi (Md.) J.
                                        Gregg (M.) E. Grossi (B.)

URUGUAY
Montevideo    San Felipe   May 12, 1855 S. Vera-Lorini (L.) G. Comolli (Md.)
                                        G. Cima (M.) P. Figari (B.)

              Solis         Apr. 18, 1860 A. De la Grange (L.) G. Arnaud (M.)
                                        P. Figari (B.)

SELECTED PRODUCTIONS-1900-1945

ARGENTINA
Buenos Aires  Colon         June 23, 1939 H. Spani (L.) Mastronardi (Md.) A.
                                        Sved (M.) G. Vaghi (B.)

AUSTRIA
Vienna        Staatsoper    Apr. 28, 1933 G. Ruenger (L.) J. Kalenberg (Md.)
                                        A. Jerger (M.) R. Mayr (B.)

CZECHOSLOVAKIA
Prague        Neues         Nov. 30, 1935 R. Pauly (L.) J. Schwarz (M.)
              Deutsches

GERMANY
Berlin        Stadt         Oct. 13, 1931 S. Onegin (L.) H. Reinmar (M.) (in
                                        Ger.)

                            May 31, 1932 G. Bindernagel (L.) H. Reinmar (M.)
                                        I. Andresen (B.) (In Ger.)

                            Nov. 8, 1933 S. Onegin (L.) H. Reinmar (M.) I.
                                        Andresen (B.) (in Ger.)

Dresden       Staatsoper    Apr. 21, 1928 Burckhardt (L.) Bader (M.) R. Burg
                                        (B.) (in Ger.)

Frankfurt     Opernhaus     Jan. 23, 1932 E. Gentner-Fischer (L.) J. Stern
                                        (M.) H. Seidelmann cond. (in Ger.)

Hamburg       Stadt         Apr. 6, 1933 S. Kalter (L.) M. Ahlersmayer (M.)
                                        H. Marowski (B.) K. Böhm cond.

Munich        National      Dec. 12, 1934 G. Ranczak (L.) R. Gerlach-Rusnak
                                        (Md.) H. Rehkemper (M.) L. Weber
                                        (B.)

GREAT BRITAIN
Glyndebourne  Festival      May 21, 1938 V. Schwarz (L.) D. Lloyd (Md.) F.
                                        Valentino (M.) D. Franklin (B.) F.
                                        Busch cond.

                            June 2, 1939 M. Grandi (L.) D. Lloyd (Md.) F.
                                        Valentino (M.) D. Franklin (B.) F.
                                        Busch cond.

ITALY
Florence      Verdi         Nov. 8, 1904 T. Chelotti (L.) L. Fini (Md.) G.
                                        Pacini (M.)  B. Berardi (B.) T. De
                                        Angelis cond.

Milan          La Scala      Dec. 26, 1938 C. Jacobo (L.) E. Parmegggiani (Md.)
                                           A. Sved (M.) T. Pasero (B.) G. Mari-
                                           nuzzi cond.

Rome           Costanzi      Mar. 11, 1911 C. Gagliardi (L.) G. Sala (Md.) M.
                                           Battistini/G. Kaschmann (M.) G. Man-
                                           sueto (B.) L. Mancinelli/G. Zuccani
                                           cond.

               Reale         Dec. 26, 1932 B. Scacciati (L.) J. De Gaviria/N.
                                           Mazziotti (Md.) B. Franci (M.) G.
                                           Vaghi (B.) A. Guarnieri cond.

Treviso        Sociale       Oct. 30, 1901 R. Calligaris-Marty (L.) C. Spadoni
                                           (Md.) A. Gnaccarini (M.) M. Spoto
                                           (B.) R. Ferrari cond.

PORTUGAL
Lisbon         Sao Carlos    Dec. 17, 1903 E. Bianchini-Cappelli (L.) G. Pacini
                                           (M.) G. Mansueto (B.) V. Lombardi
                                           cond.

                             Feb. 24, 1905 E. Bianchini-Cappelli (L.) A. Arcan-
                                           geli (M.) A. Mariani (B.) V. Lombar-
                                           di cond.

SPAIN
Madrid         Real          Feb.  1, 1905 M. De Lerma (L.) O. Gennari (Md.) G.
                                           Pacini (M.) L. Rossatto (B.) J. To-
                                           losa cond.

Malaga         Cervantes     May      1905 R. De Vila (L.) R. Blanchart (M.) J.
                                           Tolosa cond.

Seville        San           May   6, 1905 R. De Vila (L.) R. Blanchart (M.) J.
               Fernando                    Tolosa cond.

SWEDEN
Stockholm      Royal         Oct. 15, 1921 Aithen (L.) Richter (M.) I.  Andre-
                                           sen (B.) (in Swed.)

SWITZERLAND
Zürich         Stadt         Oct.  7, 1928 E. Delius (L.) H. Depsir (Md.) K.
                                           Schmid-Bloss (M.) W. Hiller (B.) M.
                                           Conrad cond. (in Ger.)

UNITED STATES
New York       44th Str.     Oct. 24, 1941 Kirk  (L.)  Marshall  (Md.)  Walters
                                           (M.) Silva (B.)

OTHER PREMIERES-POST-WORLD WAR II

AUSTRIA
Salzburg       Felsen-       Aug.  7, 1964 G. Bumbry (L.)  E. Lorenzi (Md.)  D.
               reitschule                  Fischer-Dieskau (M.) P. Lagger (B.)
                                           W. Sawallisch cond.

BELGIUM
Brussels       Monnaie       Mar. 13, 1970 N.  Tatum (L.)  N.  Van Way (Md.)  T.
                                           Tipton (M.) F. Voutsinos (B.)

CANADA
Montreal        Her           Jan. 22, 1959 M. Tynes (L.) A. Turp (Md.) W. Chap-
                Majesty's                   man (M.) C. Watson (B.) E. Cooper
                                            cond.

Toronto         Canadian      Sep. 25? 1966 M. Tynes (L.) L. Infantino (Md.) L.
                Opera                       Quilico (M.) O. Hoshuliak (B.) H.
                                            Geiger-Torel cond.

FRANCE
Lyon            Grand         Jan. 19, 1978 J. Barstow (L.) A. Cupido (Md.) M.
                                            Zanasi (M.)

Marseille       Opéra         Mar. 10, 1978 G. Dimitrova (L.) B. Prior (Md.) M.
                                            Manuguerra (M.) P. Thau (B.) M.
                                            Veltri cond.

Paris           Châtelet      Feb. 24, 1982 O. Stapp (L.) M. Frusoni (Md.) K.
                                            Nurmela (M.) H. Dworchak (B.) Ren-
                                            zetti cond.

                Opéra         Sep. 28, 1984 S. Verrett (L.) T. Ichihara (Md.) R.
                                            Bruson (M.) J. Tomlinson (B.) G.
                                            Prêtre cond.

GERMANY
Berlin          Deutsche      Sep. 29, 1963 G. Kuchta (L.) J. King (Md.) W.
                                            Dooley (M.) M. Rossi cond.

Stuttgart       Opernhaus     Sep. 21, 1961 F. Leitner cond.

GREAT BRITAIN
Cardiff         New           Sep. 23, 1963 P. Tinsley (L.) R. Thomas (Md.) R.
                                            Lewis (M.) D. Gwynne (B.) B.
                                            Balkwill cond.

Edinburgh       King's        Aug. 24, 1947 M. Grandi (L.) W. Midgley (Md.) F.
                                            Valentino (M.) I. Tajo (B.) B. Gold-
                                            schmidt cond.

Leeds           Grand         Sep. 17, 1981

London          Covent        Mar. 31, 1960 A. Shuard (L.) A. Turp (Md.) T. Gob-
                Garden                       bi (M.) J. Rouleau (B.)

SPAIN
Bilbao          Coliseo       Sep.  7, 1964 M. Pender (L.) G. Merighi (Md.) M.
                Alba                         Zanasi (M.) B. Giaiotti (B.)

Oviedo          Campoamor     Sep. 19, 1964 M. De Osma (L.) G. Merighi (Md.) M.
                                            Zanasi (M.) B. Giaiotti (B.) M. Wolf
                                            Ferrari cond.

UNITED STATES
Atlanta                       May   7, 1973 G. Bumbry (L.) S. Milnes (M.) R.
                                            Raimondi (B.) F. Molinari-Pradelli
                                            cond.

Chicago         Lyric         Oct.  1, 1969 G. Bumbry (L.) B. Marti (Md.) G. G.
                                            Guelfi (M.) S. Estes (B.) B. Barto-
                                            letti cond.

Cincinnati      Opera        June 23, 1960 M.  Curtis-Verna  (L.)  C.  Anthony
                                           (Md.) F. Guerrera (M.) B. Giaiotti
                                           (B.) F. Cleva cond.

Dallas          Civic Opera Nov. 23, 1966 G.  Jones (L.) Fr. Tagliavini (Md.)
                                           M. Zanasi (M.) N. Zaccaria (B.)

Houston         Opera        Oct.  9, 1973 P. Tinsley (L.)  S.  Novoa (Md.)  G.
                                           Mastromei (M.) J. Morris (B.)

Los Angeles     Music        Dec. 14, 1987 G. Bumbry  (L.)  N. Wilson (Md.)  J.
                Center                     Diaz (M.) M. Talvela (B.) P. Domingo
                                           cond.

Miami           Opera              1977 J. Barstow (L.)  H. Theyard (Md.) S.
                                           Milnes  (M.)  E.  Flagello  (B.)  E.
                                           Buckley cond.

New Orleans     Op. House    Nov.  2, 1967 I. Borkh (L.) C. MacNeil (M.)

New York        Metro-       Feb.  5, 1959 L. Rysanek (L.) C. Bergonzi (Md.) L.
                politan                    Warren (M.) J. Hines (B.) E. Leins-
                                           dorf cond.

San Francisco Opera          Sep. 27, 1955 I. Borkh (L.) W. Fredericks (Md.) R.
                                           Weede (M.) G. Tozzi (B.) F. Cleva
                                           cond.

Washington      Kennedy      Sep. 21, 1973 P. Tinsley (L.) Little (Md.) Sarabia
                Center                     (M.) P. Plishka (B.)


OTHER PRODUCTIONS OF MACBETH I-1969-1981

GREAT BRITAIN
London          Collegiate  Feb. 18, 1976 J.  Jacques (L.)  Blackwell (Md.) J.
                                           Summers (M.) Lawrence (B.) (in Eng.)

                Albert Hall July 25, 1978 R. Hunter (L.) K. Collins (Md.) P.
                                           Glossop (M.) J. Tomlinson (B.)

UNITED STATES
Boston          Shubert      Mar. 31, 1969 Kuhse (L.) Novoa (Md.) K. Paskalis
                                           (M.) S. Estes (B.)

Danville, Ky. Centre         Nov. 11, 1977 A. Hunt (L.) Khanzadian (Md.)  Fazah
                                           (M.) Gaal (B.) (in Eng.)

Louisville      Macauley     Nov.     1977 A. Hunt (L.) Khanzadian (Md.)  Fazah
                                           (M.) Gaal (B.) (in Eng.)

Stony Brook     Fine Arts    Mar. 15, 1981 Fiske (L.)  Manno  (Md.)  Stith (M.)
L. I., N. Y.                               Ramirez (B.)

11. I MASNADIERI-*Melodramma tragico* in four parts
London-Her Majesty's Theatre-July 22, 1847
Libretto by Andrea Maffei

| | |
|---|---|
| Amalia (A.) | Jenny Lind sop. |
| Carlo (C.) | Italo Gardoni ten. |
| Francesco (F.) | Filippo Coletti bar. |
| Massimiliano (M.) | Luigi Lablache bass |
| Arminio | Leone Corelli ten. |
| Moser | Stefano Luciano Bouché bass |
| Rolla | Dal Fiori ten. |
| | |
| Conductor | Giuseppe Verdi |
| Director | Giuseppe Verdi |

OTHER PREMIERES

ARGENTINA
Buenos Aires   Victoria      Sep. 12, 1853 M. Landa (A.) E. Rossi-Guerra (C.)
                                          E. Luisia (F.) P. Franchi (M.)

AUSTRIA
Innsbruck                    Apr. 26, 1854 C. Rota Galli (A.) G. Giorgetti (C.)
                                          C. Bartolucci (F.) D. Celli (M.)

Vienna         Kärntnertor June  3, 1854 G. Medori (A.) R. Mirate (C.) A. De
                                          Bassini (F.) B. Laura (M.)

BELGIUM
Antwerp        Royal         Mar. 29, 1870 Hasselmans (A.) Fabre (C.)   Guille-
                                          mot (F.) Boyer (M.) Brunet cond. (in
                                          Fr.)

Brussels       Cirque        Sep. 14, 1850 G. Medori (A.) G. Mazzi (C.) F. Mo-
                                          relli-Ponti (F.) A. Zucconi (M.)
                                          Felice Ricci cond. E. Muzio dir. (in
                                          It.)

BRAZIL
Rio de         Sao Pedro     Sep.  7, 1849 I. Edelvira (A.) A. Brunacci (C.) G.
 Janeiro                                  Costa (F.) C. Bennati (M.)

CHILE
Santiago       Republica     June 13, 1852 T. Rossi (A.) J. Ubaldi (C.) G. Bas-
                                          toggi (F.) F. Leonardi (M.)

Valparaiso     Victoria      Nov. 20, 1851 T. Rossi (A.) J. Ubaldi (C.) G. Bas-
                                          toggi (F.) F. Leonardi (M.)

COLOMBIA
Bogota         Teatro        Mar. 12, 1858 R. Olivieri (A.) E. Rossi-Guerra
                                          (C.) E. Luisia (F.) G. Mirandola
                                          (M.)

CUBA
Havana         Tacon         Jan. 16, 1855 B. Steffenone (A.) L. Salvi (C.) G.
                                          F. Beneventano (F.) I. Marini (M.)
                                          G. Bottesini cond.

FRANCE
Ajaccio        San           Oct.?   1864 G. Ottonelli-Bresciani (A.) A. Boet-
               Gabriele                   ti (C.)

Lille                        Mar. 24, 1870 (in Fr.)

Nice            Regio         Oct.      1851 V. Gaziello-Brambilla (A.) A. Pozzo-
                                             lini (C.) C. Everardi (F.)

Paris           Athenée       Feb.   3, 1870 M. Marimon (A.) Jourdan (C.) Arsan-
                                             daux (F.) J. Jamet (M.)  Constantin
                                             cond.

GREECE
Athens          Royal         Nov. 18, 1852 G.  Casali-Campagna  (A.)  Ortolani
                                             (C.) V. Orlandi (F.) A. Casali (M.)

Corfu           San Giacomo Nov.      1851 L. Luxor-Pretti (A.) A. Errani (C.)
                                             C. Busi (F.) G. Carbonell (M.)

GUATEMALA
Guatemala                     Dec.?     1871
City

HUNGARY
Budapest        Nemzeti       Aug.   2, 1852 L. Gino (A.) G. Mazzi (C.)  G. Reina
                Szinház                       (F.) P. De Antoni (M.)

ITALY
Alessandria     Municipale    Mar. 11, 1854 F.  Rocca-Alessandri/M.  Ballerini
                                             (A.) Federigo (C.) Sacconi (F.) A.
                                             Garcia (M.)

Ancona          Muse          Spring    1848 M. Arrigotti (A.) C. Miraglia (C.)
                                             G. Fiori (F.) E. Manfredi (M.)

Bari            Piccinni      Nov.?     1863 T. Alvisi (A.) E. Concordia (C.) C.
                                             Bartolucci (F.) E. Anselmi (M.)

Bergamo         Sociale       Dec. 26, 1847 E. Taccani (A.) A. Bozzetti (C.) F.
                                             Monari (F.) G. Galli (M.)

                Riccardi      Aug. 10, 1850 F.  Salvini-Donatelli  (A.)  G.  Fras-
                                             chini (C.) F. Gnone (F.) G. B. Cor-
                                             nago (M.)

Bologna         Comunale      Oct. 14, 1848 A. Albertini (A.) E. Naudin (C.) C.
                                             Badiali (F.) G. B. Antonucci (M.) G.
                                             Manetti cond.

Brescia         Grande        Carn. 1849-50 Caspani (A.) E. Rossi-Guerra (C.) L.
                                             Montani (F.) L. Galli (M.)

Cagliari        Civico        Autumn    1849 R. Olivieri (A.) A. Prudenza (C.) E.
                                             Luisia (F.) L. Bianchi (M.)

Catania         Comunale      Nov. 16, 1851 O. Avenali (A.) A. Silvestroni (C.)
                                             M. Severi (F.) A. De Angelis (M.) M.
                                             Pappalardo cond.

Cesena          Comunale      Dec. 28, 1850 O. Avenali (A.) A. Giuglini (C.) A.
                                             Carapia (F.) F. Dall'Asta (M.) P.
                                             Trentanove cond.

Chieti          Marrucino     June 27, 1861 N. Rossi (A.) V. Leoni (F.) V. Cari-
                                             so (M.)

Como            Sociale       Jan.?     1858 E. Galli (A.) L. Mencarelli (C.) A.
                                             Olivari (F.) P. Llorens (M.)

Crema        Sociale      Dec. 26? 1851 R.  Mori-Spalazzi  (A.)  A.  Assandri
                                       (C.)  Alessandrini  (F.)  E.  Longoni
                                       (M.)

Cremona      Concordia    Dec. 26, 1849 E.  Cominotti  (A.)  G.  Mazzi  (C.)  C.
                                       Bartolucci  (F.)  G.  Dalbesio  (M.)  G.
                                       Cortesi cond.

Faenza       Comunale     Summer   1850 F.  Salvini-Donatelli/A.  Albertini
                                       (A.)  E.  Naudin  (C.)  F.  Gnone  (F.)

Fermo        Aquila       August   1849 L.  Giordano  (A.)  E.  Naudin  (C.)  L.
                                       Canedi  (M.)  G.  C.  Ferrarini cond.

Ferrara      Comunale     Dec. 26, 1848 R.  Mori-Spallazzi  (A.)  G.  Gamboggi
                                       (C.)  A.  Carapia  (F.)  L.  Canedi  (M.)

Fiume        Civico       Spring   1848 C.  Rapazzini  (A.)  G.  Pavesi  (C.)  V.
                                       Morino  (F.)  A.  Bianchi  (M.)

Florence     Pergola      Mar. 18, 1848 C.  Hayes  (A.)

Forli        Comunale     July  2, 1854 M.  Arrigotti  (A.)  L.  Stefani  (C.)  F.
                                       Coliva  (F.)  A.  Biacchi  (M.)

Genoa        Carlo        Jan. 25, 1849 C.  Hayes  (A.)  R.  Mirate  (C.)  F.  Mo-
             Felice               nari  (F.)  L.  Vita  (M.)

Imola        Comunale     Carn. 1860-61 E.  Concordia  (C.)  F.  Tournerie  (F.)
                                       Baccelli  (M.)

Jesi         Concordia    Aug. 28, 1852 A.  Angelini-Cantalamessa  (A.)  M.  Ne-
                                       ri  (C.)  C.  Morelli-Condolmieri  (F.)
                                       Baroncini  (M.)

Livorno      Rossini      Apr. 17, 1854 Ruppini  (A.)  A.  Biundi  (C.)  Sumner
                                       (F.)  C.  Boccolini  (M.)

Lodi         Sociale      Feb. 15, 1851 T.  Pozzi-Montegazza  (A.)  G.  Piccin-
                                       nini  (C.)

Lucca        Giglio       Sep.  3, 1853 E.  Marcolini  (A.)  P.  Cecchi  (C.)
                                       Rossi  (F.)  A.  Balderi  (M.)

Lugo         Rossini      Sep.     1853 S.  Peruzzi  (A.)  L.  Stefani  (C.)  E.
                                       Storti  (F.)  M.  Ghini  (M.)  P.  Monta-
                                       guti cond.

Macerata     Condomini    Carn. 1849-50 L.  Cherubini  (A.)  P.  Stecchi-Bottar-
                                       di  (C.)  L.  Roncagli  (F.)

Mantua       Sociale      Dec. 26? 1850 E.  Cominotti  (A.)  G.  Alzamora  (C.)
                                       E.  Luisia  (F.)  A.  Casali  (M.)  G.
                                       Luppi cond.

Messina      Munizione    Jan.?    1851 Vaselli  (A.)  A.  Bettini  (C.)  V.
                                       Orlandi  (F.)

Milan        Re           Carn. 1848-49 G.  Jotti  (A.)  L.  Ceresa  (C.)  V.  Mo-
                                       rino  (F.)  L.  Bianchi  (M.)

             La Scala     Sep. 20, 1853 F.  Gordosa  (A.)  E.  Irfré/L.  Ceresa
                                       (C.)  C.  Everardi  (F.)  A.  Lanzoni
                                       (M.)  E.  Cavallini cond.

| | | | |
|---|---|---|---|
| Modena | Comunale | Dec. 26, 1848 | A. Albertini (A.) E. Naudin (C.) A. Sabbatini (F.) E. Manfredi (M.) A. Sighicelli cond. |
| Naples | San Carlo | May 15, 1849 | E. Tadolini (A.) C. Baucardé (C.) F. Varesi (F.) A. Selva (M.) |
| Novara | Nuovo | Dec. 26? 1850 | A. Ferraris (A.) M. Bernardi (C.) A. Sabbatini (F.) P. Sottovia (M.) |
| Padua | Nuovo | July 2, 1851 | M. Gazzaniga (A.) C. Negrini (C.) A. Superchi (F.) F. Pons (M.) |
| Palermo | Carolino | Oct. 10, 1851 | S. Peruzzi (A.) L. Stefani (C.) G. Reina (F.) A. Selva (M.) |
| Parma | Regio | Feb. 22, 1848 | G. Bortolotti (A.) G. Roppa (C.) C. Marié (F.) G. Setti (M.) N. De Giovanni cond. |
| Pavia | Condomini | Apr. 26, 1851 | A. Albertini (A.) F. De Ruggero (C.) Lucchi (F.) S. Torre (M.) |
| Perugia | Pavone | Dec. 26, 1852 | Morelli (A.) A. Badalucci (C.) M. Severi (F.) Sassaroli (M.) |
| Pesaro | Rossini | Carn. 1849-50 | C. Steller (A.) E. Marcucci (C.) F. Steller (F.) G. Baroni (M.) |
| Piacenza | Municipale | Jan. 1848 | C. Cuzzani (A.) V. Jacobelli (C.) L. Caliari (F.) G. Jona cond. |
| Pisa | Ravvivati | Mar. 16, 1861 | A. Moro (A.) F. Patierno (C.) F. Massiani (F.) C. Gennari (M.) C. Finci cond. |
| Prato | Metastasio | Dec. 26? 1860 | A. Mattioli (A.) A. Guido (C.) A. Del Vivo (F.) E. Profili (M.) A. Borgioli cond. |
| Ravenna | Comunitativo | Apr. 27, 1850 | A. Rebussini (A.) E. Marcucci (C.) F. Steller (F.) G. Rebussini (M.) G. Nostini cond. |
| Reggio Emilia | Comunale | Dec. 26, 1849 | G. Jotti (A.) G. Mora (C.) E. Ventura (F.) B. Gandini/Cavalieri (M.) G. Tebaldi cond. |
| | Municipale | Jan. 21, 1856 | M. Bozzetti (A.) A. Celada (C.) R. Arrigoni (F.) F. Rigo (M.) G. Tebaldi cond. |
| Rome | Apollo | Feb. 12, 1848 | A. Albertini (A.) N. Ivanoff (C.) C. Badiali (F.) G. Mitrovich (M.) E. Angelini cond. |
| Rovigo | Sociale | Fiera 1852 | A. Moltini (A.) C. Miraglia (C.) F. Coliva (F.) G. Capriles (M.) |
| Savona | Chiabrera | Jan. 1866 | I. Ridolfi (A.) C. Baroni (C.) A. Romanelli (F.) |

Siena          Rinnovati   Aug.      1858 L. Ruggero-Antonioli (A.) A. Alta-
                                          villa (C.) C. Busi (F.) F. Mazzoni
                                          (M.)

Sinigaglia     Comunale    July 21,  1855 R. Donzelli (A.) L. Stefani (C.) G.
                                          Fiori (F.) L. Ruiz (M.)

Spoleto        Nobile      Dec. 26,  1849 C. Gamberini (A.) G. Galvani (C.) M.
                                          Severi (F.) T. Mastripieri (M.)

Trento         Sociale     June 12,  1850 E. Cominotti (A.) G. Mazzi (C.) C.
                                          Bartolucci (F.) G. Dalbesio (M.)

Treviso        Onigo       Oct.      1852 E. Scotta (A.) C. Negrini (C.) R.
                                          Pizzigati (F.) M. Ghini (M.)

               Sociale     Feb.      1876 C. Venanzi (A.) Parmisini (C.) G.
                                          Santini (F.) C. De Probizi (M.) C.
                                          Fontebasso cond.

Trieste        Grande      Dec. 26,  1847 L. Ponti dall'Armi (A.) L. Graziani
                                          (C.) G. Fiori (F.) G. Euzet (M.) G.
                                          A. Scaramelli cond.

Turin          Regio       Jan.  3,  1850 M. Barbieri-Nini (A.) G. Fraschini
                                          (C.) F. Monari (F.) O. Bonafous (M.)
                                          G. Ghebart cond.

Udine          Sociale     Aug. 27,  1853 M. Lotti della Santa (A.) R. Mirate
                                          (C.) G. Corsi (F.) C. Dalla Costa
                                          (M.)

Varese         Sociale     Oct.      1865 C. Marazzini (A.) Soriano (C.) V.
                                          Graziani (F.)

Venice         La Fenice   Dec. 26,  1849 A. Cortesi (A.) R. Mirate (C.) L.
                                          Valli (F.) G. B. Cornago (M.) G.
                                          Mares cond.

Verona         Filarmonico Dec. 26,  1847 C. Hayes (A.) F. Borioni (C.) A. De
                                          Bassini (F.) N. Benedetti (M.)

Vicenza        Berico      Apr. 24,  1850 M. Anselmi (A.) Mora (C.) R. Gallo-
                                          Tomba (M.)

               Eretenio    Sep. 13,  1851 L. Ruggero-Antonioli (A.) R. Mirate
                                          (C.) G. Zambellini (F.) R. Gallo-
                                          Tomba (M.)

JUGOSLAVIA
Zara           Nobile      May   8,  1852 F. Castellani (A.) G. Petrovich (C.)
                                          D. Mattioli (F.) D. Dal Negro (M.)

MALTA
La Valletta    Manoel      Nov.?     1848

MEXICO
Guadalajara    Degollado   Nov. 20,  1873 L. D'Aponte (A.) Tasso (C.) E. Pe-
                                          trilli (F.)

Mexico City    Nacional    Dec.  4,  1856 G. Landi (A.) L. Stefani (C.) A.
                                          Ottaviani (F.) E. Casali (M.) C.
                                          Fattori cond.

PERU
Lima            Principal    May   3, 1853 C. Cailly (A.) D. Lorini (C.) A.
                                           Avignone (F.) F. Leonardi (M.)

PORTUGAL
Lisbon          Sao Carlos   Mar.  8, 1849 M. Gresti (A.) A. Volpini (C.) G.
                                           Fiori (F.) N. Benedetti (M.)

Oporto          Sao Joao     June     1849 M. Gresti (A.) A. Volpini (C.) G.
                                           Fiori (F.) N. Benedetti (M.)

ROMANIA
Bucharest       Nacional     Oct. 23, 1850 R. Olivieri (A.) E. Rossi-Guerra
                                           (C.) G. Parodi (F.) B. Gandini (M.)

Iasi            Teatrul      Nov.  4, 1852 L. Vaschetti (A.) P. Scotti (C.) G.
                                           Donelli (F.) H. Brémond (M.)

RUSSIA
Odessa          Municipal    Jan. 15, 1853 T. Brambilla (A.) E. Naudin (C.) S.
                                           Ronconi (F.) N. Benedetti (M.)

SPAIN
Barcelona       Principal    June  3, 1848 C. Rovelli (A.) E. Tamberlick (C.)
                                           V. Sermattei (F.) P. Dérivis (M.)

Cadiz           Principal    Feb.?    1852 E. Fodor (A.) Alzamora (C.)

Madrid          Museo        Feb. 10, 1849 F. Alessandri (A.) J. Saez (F.) G.
                                           Echeverria (M.) J. Skoczdopole cond.

                Real         Mar. 11, 1854 A. Basseggio (A.) P. Mongini (C.) V.
                                           Orlandi (F.) G. Echeverria (M.) J.
                                           Skoczdopole cond.

Palma di        Princesa     Dec.     1857 M. Pirola (A.) F. Pozzo (C.) D. Dal
  Mallorca                                 Negro (F.) P. Sottovia (M.)

SWITZERLAND
Geneva          Grand        Nov.?    1878 (in Fr.)

Lugano          Sociale      Sep. 29, 1850 G. Jotti (A.) A. Assandri (C.) G.
                                           Zambellini (F.) Vecchi (M.)

TURKEY
Constan-        Naum         Oct. 28, 1852 E. D'Alberti (A.) T. Palmieri (C.)
  tinople                                  C. Bartolucci (F.) Salani (M.)

Smyrna          Cammarano    Nov.  3, 1851 Mariotti (A.) G. Aducci (C.) Ricci
                                           (F.)

UNITED STATES
New York        Winter       May  31, 1860 R. Olivieri (A.) E. Rossi-Guerra
                Garden                     (C.) E. Luisia (F.) G. Mirandola
                                           (M.) M. Maretzek cond.

San Francisco   Metro-       May  29, 1863 G. Bianchi (A.) E. Bianchi (C.) A.
                politan                    Fellini (F.) E. Grossi (M.)

                Maguire's     Aug. 23, 1865 E. Brambilla (A.) G. Sbriglia (C.)
                                           D. Orlandini (F.) G. Fossati (M.)

URUGUAY
Montevideo     San Felipe  Jan. 13, 1853 R.  Olivieri  (A.)  E.  Rossi-Guerra
                                          (C.) E.  Luisia (F.)  P.  Figari (M.)

               Solis       Oct.  4, 1859 C.  Cailly (A.) L.  Lelmi (C.) G.  Cima
                                          (F.)  P.  Figari  (M.)  C.  Castagneri
                                          cond.

SELECTED REVIVALS-NINETEENTH CENTURY

ITALY
Bologna        Comunale    Feb.  6, 1855 A.  Ortolani-Brignoli (A.) L.  Stefani
                                          (C.)  G.  Reina  (F.)  A.  Biacchi (M.)
                                          G.  Manetti cond.

Florence       Pergola     Apr. 20, 1850 V.  Boccabadati (A.) L.  Graziani (C.)
                                          M.  Zacchi (F.)  P.  Mazzarini (M.)

Genoa          Carlo       Feb. 24, 1852 A.  Albertini (A.)  G.  Landi (C.)  G.
               Felice                     B.  Bencich (F.)

                           June  4, 1857 E.  Weisser (A.)  C.  Negrini (C.)  P.
                                          Giorgi Pacini (F.) H.  Brémond (M.)

Milan          La Scala    Sep.  6, 1862 L.  Boschetti  (A.)  C.  Vincentelli
                                          (C.)  L.  Saccomanno  (F.)  C.  Nanni
                                          (M.)

               Carcano     Oct.  8, 1870 J.  Gayarre  (C.)  S.  Rossi-Rumiati
                                          (F.) A.  Buzzi (M.)

Rome           Apollo      Dec. 12, 1854 M.  Piccolomini (A.)  A.  Agresti (C.)
                                          V.  Morelli-Bartolami (F.)  R.  Laterza
                                          (M.)  E.  Angelini cond.

               Argentina   May      1863 P.  Colson (A.)  C.  Negrini (C.)  F.
                                          Pandolfini (F.)  R.  Laterza (M.)  E.
                                          Angelini cond.

Trieste        Grande      Lent     1850 C.  Rapazzini (A.) L.  Graziani (C.)
                                          F.  Cresci (F.)  C.  Dalla Costa (M.)
                                          G.  A.  Scaramelli cond.

                           Sep. 30, 1852 A.  Albertini (A.)  G.  Fraschini (C.)
                                          G.  B.  Bencich (F.) G.  Mitrovich (M.)
                                          G.  A.  Scaramelli cond.

Turin          Regio       Dec. 31, 1862 L.  Boschetti (A.) G.  Tombesi (C.) V.
                                          Collini (F.)  C.  Nanni (M.)  F.  Bian-
                                          chi cond.

MEXICO
Mexico City    Nacional    Nov. 29, 1857 A.  Cortesi (A.) L.  Stefani (C.)  A.
                                          Ottaviani  (F.)  Gariboldi  (M.)  C.
                                          Fattori cond.

                           Oct.     1864

PORTUGAL
Lisbon         Sao Carlos  Nov. 30, 1851 M.  Arrigotti (A.)  E.  Musich (C.)  G.
                                          Mancusi (F.)  F.  Gorin (M.)

                           Oct.  1, 1853 A.  Fortuni  (A.)  J.  Swift  (C.)  O.
                                          Bartolini (F.) A.  Zucconi (M.)

Dec. 14, 1860 E. Hensler (A.) A. Agresti (C.) E.
Fagotti (F.) G. B. Antonucci (M.)

Jan. 22, 1863 L. Perelli (A.) L. Stefani (C.) V.
Orlandi (F.) G. B. Antonucci (M.)

SPAIN
Madrid          Real          Jan. 28, 1860 E. Fioretti (A.) E. Naudin (C.) D.
Squarcia    (F.) E. Manfredi (M.) J.
Skocjdopole cond.


OTHER PRODUCTIONS-1900-1945

GERMANY
Barmen                        Mar. 29, 1928 (in Ger.)

ITALY
Milan           Fossati       Aug. 29, 1903 Magliano-Muccioli (A.) G. Doni (C.)
R. Paglialico (F.) Perini (M.)


OTHER PRODUCTIONS-POST-WORLD WAR II

ARGENTINA
Buenos Aires   Coliseo       Mar. 23, 1979 M. Veleris (A.) D. Ranieri (C.) F.
Barabino (F.) N. Meneghetti (M.) A.
Russo cond.

AUSTRALIA
Sydney         Opera House July  2, 1980 J. Sutherland (A.) D. Smith/Ferris
(C.) Allman/Badcock (F.) Grant (M.)
R. Bonynge cond.

AUSTRIA
Vienna         Volksoper     Mar.    1966 L. Sorell (A.) J. Cox (C.) T. O'Leary (F.) E. Gutstein (M.) A. Quadry
cond.

Oct.    1966 C. Sorell (A.) J. Cox (C.) T. O'Leary (F.) M. Cordes (M.) A. Quadry
cond.

FRANCE
Nancy          Opera         Jan. 23, 1980 G. Dimitrova (A.) N. Todisco (C.) A.
Salvadori  (F.)  L.  Roni  (M.)  D.
Masson cond.

Paris          Châtelet      Feb. 20, 1982 M. Castro-Alberty (A.) O. Garaventa
(C.) A. Salvadori (F.) Bogart (M.)
D. Masson cond.

GERMANY
Mannheim       National      Oct.    1969 Molnar (A.) J. Cox (C.) Davidson
(F.) Dalberg (M.) Eykman cond.

GREAT BRITAIN
Bristol        Hippodrome  Apr. 29, 1977

Cardiff        New           Mar. 29, 1977 S. Murphy (A.) K. Collins (C.) T.
Sharpe (F.) R. Van Allen (M.) R.
Armstrong cond. (in Eng.)

Llandudno      Astra        June 11, 1977 S. Murphy (A.) K. Collins (C.) N.
                            Howlett (F.) W. White (M.) R. Arm-
                            strong cond. (in Eng.)

London         St. Pancras  Mar. 20, 1962 P. Tinsley (A.) E. Byles (C.) N.
                            Miller (F.) G. Morgan (M.) F. Marton
                            cond.

Oxford         New          May  21, 1977

Swansea        Grand        May  14, 1977

ITALY
Catania        Massimo      Dec. 18, 1980 I. Ligabue (A.) G. Casellato-Lam-
                            berti (C.) A. Cassis (F.) C. Cava
                            (M.) G. Gavazzeni cond.

Florence       Comunale     June 18, 1963 M. Roberti (A.) G. Limarilli (C.) M.
                            Zanasi (F.) B. Giaiotti (M.) G.
                            Gavazzeni cond.

Milan          Sala RAI     Mar. 29, 1951 A. Guerrini (A.) R. Lambert (C.) R.
                            Panerai (F.) S. Bruscantini (M.) A.
                            Simonetto cond.

               La Scala     Jan. 28, 1978 A. Maliponte (A.) O. Garaventa (C.)
                            M. Manuguerra (F.) Y. Nesterenko
                            (M.)

                            Sep.     1978 M. Zampieri (A.) O. Garaventa (C.)
                            M. Manuguerra (F.) P. Washington
                            (M.) E. Müller cond.

Montepulciano Policiano     July 31, 1977 M. Zampieri (A.) G. Cianella (C.) L.
                            De Corato (F.) A. Bramante (M.) R.
                            Chailly cond.

Parma          Regio        Dec. 23, 1974 M. Pellegrini/G. Trombin (A.) G.
                            Cecchele/S. D'Amico (C.) L. Saccoma-
                            ni/G. Zancanaro (F.) M. Mazzieri
                            (M.) A. Campori cond.

Piacenza       Municipale   Feb.? 1975 M. Pellegrini (A.) G. Cecchele (C.)
                            G. Zancanaro (F.) M. Mazzieri (M.)
                            A. Campori cond.

Pisa           Verdi        Sep. 27, 1983 A. Maliponte (A.) N. Todisco (C.) V.
                            Sardinero (F.) L. Roni (M.) R. Gan-
                            dolfi cond.

Rome           Opera        Nov. 25, 1972 I. Ligabue (A.) G. Raimondi/G. Cor-
                            radi (C.) R. Bruson (F.) B. Chris-
                            toff (M.) G. Gavazzeni/A. Ventura
                            cond.

Ravenna        Alighieri    Jan. 18, 1975 G. Trombin (A.) G. Cecchele (C.) L.
                            Saccomani (F.) C. De Bortoli (M.)
                            A. Campori cond.

Turin          Sala RAI     May  29, 1971 R. Orlandi-Malaspina (A.) G. Lima-
                            rilli (C.) M. Petri (F.) B. Giaiotti
                            (M.) F. Mannino cond.

SPAIN
Bilbao        Coliseo      Sep. 1, 1976 C. Deutekom (A.) P. Lavirgen (C.) M.
Manuguerra (F.) B. Giaiotti (M.) M.
Veltri cond.

SWITZERLAND
Zürich        Opernhaus    Oct. 21, 1982 C. Deutekom (A.) V. Moldeveanu (C.)
G. Zancanaro (F.) N. Santi cond.

UNITED STATES
New York     Carnegie     Feb. 12, 1975 G. Trombin (A.) W. Lewis (C.) M.
              Hall               Manuguerra (F.) P. Plishka (M.) E.
Queler cond.

San Diego    Opera       June 21, 1984 J. Sutherland (A.) G. Greer (C.) A.
Salvadori (F.) Zanazzo (M.) R.
Bonynge cond.


12. JERUSALEM-*Opéra* in four acts[41]
Paris-Academie Royale de Musique (Opéra)-Nov. 26, 1847
Libretto by Alphonse Royer and Gustave Vaëz

| | |
|---|---|
| Helène (H.) | Julian Van Gelder sop. |
| Gaston (G.) | Gilbert Louis Duprez ten. |
| Roger (R.) | Adolphe Alizard bass |
| Isaure | Muller sop. |
| Raymond | Barbot ten. |
| Un Officier | Koenig ten. |
| Comte de Toulouse | Charles Portehaut bar. |
| Adhemar de Montheil | Hyppolyte Brémond bass |
| Un Soldat | Ferdinand Prevost bass |
| Un Heraut | Mulinier bass |
| L'Emir du Ramla | Guignot bass |

Conductor
Director                               Giuseppe Verdi


OTHER PREMIERES-NINETEENTH CENTURY

ALGERIA
Algiers               Lent     1857 C. Charles (H.) Chambon (G.)

BELGIUM
Antwerp     Royal        Jan. 23, 1849 A. Lacombe (H.) Allard (G.) Malhieu
(R.)

Brussels    Monnaie     July 15, 1848 Julian van Gelder (H.) G. L. Duprez
(G.) C. H. Zelger (R.)

---

41. *Jérusalem* is a fairly extensive revision of *I Lombardi*, adapted to the French language and French tastes. It has an unusual performance history in that it was one of the young Verdi's most popular operas in France and in French language theatres outside France, but was a great rarity in its Italian translation, being unable to supplant the earlier *I Lombardi* in Italy and Italian language houses. To give an idea of the popularity of the French version this was given during at least 8 seasons in Antverp, 15 in Brussels, 18 in Ghent, and 15 in New Orleans. No similar data are available for any French city, but it is safe to assume that its popularity in many French theatres was comparable.

Ghent          Grand        Apr. 12, 1849 Valton (H.) Bourdais (G.) C. H. Zel-
                                          ger (R.)

Liége          Grand        Apr. 19, 1850 Lacombe   (H.)  Octave  (G.)  Depassio
                                          (R.)

CANADA
Montreal       Op. Franc.   Feb.  6, 1896 Essiani   (H.)  Vendivic  (G.)  Preval
                                          (R.)

FRANCE
Lyon           Grand        Mar. 13, 1849 Corneille (H.) Duprat (G.)

Marseille      Grand        Feb. 23, 1849 S. Heinefetter (H.) Mathieu (G.) A.
                                          Didot (R.)

Paris          Opéra        Sep. 11, 1848 Julian van Gelder (H.) G. L. Duprez/
                                          Masset (G.) A. Alizard (R.)

Rouen          des Arts     Nov. 11, 1851 S. Mequillet (H.)

Toulouse       Capitole     Spring   1850 S. Heinefetter (H.)

INDONESIA
Batavia        T. Batavie   Mar. 23, 1866 Mendioroz (H.) Moulin (G.) Lavagne
                                          (R.)

Soerabaya                   Oct. 24, 1864

1TALY
Milan          La Scala     Dec. 26, 1850 M. Gazzaniga (H.) C. Negrini (G.) A.
                                          Didot (R.) E. Cavallini cond. (in
                                          1t.)

Rome           Acc. Filar.  Mar.?    1859 T. Armellini (H.) E. Corsi (G.) A.
                                          De Antoni (R.)

               Apollo       Feb.     1865 L. Bendazzi-Secchi (H.) R. Sirchia
                                          (G.) G. F. Beneventano (R.) E. Ange-
                                          lini cond.

Turin          Regio        Jan.  8, 1851 C. Gruitz (H.) G. Fraschini (G.) G.
                                          Euzet (R.) G. Ghebart cond.

Venice         La Fenice    Jan. 11, 1854 A. Albertini (H.) R. Mirate (G.) P.
                                          Vialetti (R.)

Verona         Nuovo        Nov.     1855 C. Carozzi-Zucchi (H.) A. Vietti/T.
                                          Palmieri (G.) A. Carapia (R.)

Vercelli       Civico       Carn. 1857-58 C. Lendy (H.) V. Tartini (G.) F.
                                          Bellini (R.)

NETHERLANDS
Amsterdam      Francais     May 15, 1851 Stranski  (H.)  Allard  (G.)  Thibaud
                                          (R.) (in Fr.)

PORTUGAL
Lisbon         Sao Carlos   May 30, 1884 Strassi (H.) A. Guille (G.) A. Pon-
                                          sard (R.) G. Lelong cond. (in Fr.)

RUSSIA
St.            Imperial     Feb. 11, 1882 E.  Fursch-Madi  (H.)  E.  Barbacini
Petersburg                                (G.) J. Devoyod (R.) (in It.)

SWITZERLAND
Geneva          Grand        Apr.   9, 1850  E. Poinsot (H.) G. L. Duprez (G.)

TUNISIA
Tunis                        Nov.?     1855

UNITED STATES
Cincinnati      National     July 12, 1860

New Orleans     Orléans      Jan. 24, 1850  R. Devries (H.) Duluc (G.) Bessin
                                            (R.) E. Prévost cond.

St. Louis       Op. House    June 23, 1860


SELECTED REVIVALS-NINETEENTH CENTURY

FRANCE
Paris           Opéra        Sep.   1, 1852  E. Poinsot (H.) Chapuis (G.) De-
                                            passio (R.)

RUSSIA
St.             Imperial     Nov. 19, 1882  Frank-Duvernoy (H.) E. Sylva (G.) J.
 Petersburg                                 Devoyod (R.) R. Drigo cond. (in It.)

OTHER PRODUCTIONS-1900-1945

FRANCE
Nice            Municipal    Jan.   3, 1914  M. Claessens (H.) F. Gautier/ Gail-
                                            lard (G.) Meurisse (R.)

OTHER PRODUCTIONS-POST-WORLD WAR II

FRANCE
Paris           Opéra        Feb. 18, 1984  C. Gasdia (H.) V. Luchetti (G.) S.
                                            Carroli (R.) D. Renzetti cond.

GERMANY
Munich          National     May 14, 1965  L. Gencer (H.) G. Aragall (G.) R.
                                            Raimondi (R.) E. Gracis cond.

Wiesbaden       Staatsoper   May 17, 1965  L. Gencer (H.) G. Aragall (G.) R.
                                            Raimondi (R.) E. Gracis cond.

GREAT BRITAIN
Leeds           Grand        Mar. 31, 1990  J. Cairns (H.) A. Davies (G.) J.
                                            Garcia (R.)   P. Daniel cond. (in
                                            Fr.)

London          BBC          Sep. 25, 1984  J. Anderson (H.) K. Collins (G.)

ITALY
Parma           Regio        Jan.   7, 1986  K. Ricciarelli (H.) V. Luchetti (G.)
                                            C. Siepi (R.) (in Fr.)

Turin           Sala RAI     Dec. 20, 1975  K. Ricciarelli (H.) J. Carreras (G.)
                                            S. Nimsgern (R.) G. Gavazzeni cond.
                                            (in Fr.)

Venice          La Fenice    Sep. 24, 1963  L. Gencer (H.) G. Aragall (G.) G.
                                            Guelfi (R.) G. Gavazzeni cond.

                             June   5, 1964  L. Gencer (H.) G. Aragall (G.) G.
                                            Guelfi (R.) G. Gavazzeni cond.

13. IL CORSARO-*Opera seria* in three acts
Trieste-Teatro Grande-Oct. 25, 1848
Libretto by Francesco Maria Piave

Medora (M.)                          Carolina Rapazzini sop.
Gulnara (G.)                      Marianna Barbieri-Nini sop.
Corrado (C.)                         Gaetano Fraschini ten.
Seid (S.)                           Achille De Bassini bar.
Selimo                              Giovanni Petrovich ten.
Eunuco                            Francesco Cucchiari ten.
Uno Schiavo                       Stefano Albanassich ten.
Giovanni                            Giovanni Volpini ten.

Conductor                 Giuseppe Alessandro Scaramelli
Director                               Luigi Ricci

OTHER PRODUCTIONS-NINETEENTH CENTURY

CHILE
Valparaiso     Victoria     Jan.  1, 1852  I. Neumann (M.) A. Pantanelli (G.)
                                           L. Cavedagni (C.) G. Bastoggi (S.)

ITALY
Cagliari       Civico       Carn. 1849-50  R. Olivieri (G.) A. Prudenza (C.) E.
                                           Luise (S.)

Florence       Borgo-       Sep.    1856  Benedetti (M.) Orlandi (G.) Mari
               gnisanti                    (C.) A. Padovani-Polli (S.)

Lodi           Sociale      Dec. 26? 1860  C. Proche (M.) E. Gruitz (G.) P. Er-
                                           rani (C.) L. Spellini (S.)

Milan          Carcano      Feb.  7, 1852  M. De Gianni-Vivez (M.) G. Leva (G.)
                                           F. Borioni (C.) L. Walter (S.)

                            Mar.  1, 1854  L. Francia (M.) A. Ortolani-Tiberini
                                           (G.) G. De Vecchi (C.) A. Olivari
                                           (S.)

Modena         Comunale     Dec. 26, 1852  G. Borsi de Leurie (M.) C. Sannazaro
                                           (G.) F. Borioni (C.) C. Morelli-Con-
                                           dolmieri (S.) A. Sighicelli cond.

Naples         San Carlo    July  2, 1854  C. Carozzi-Zucchi (M.) N. De Roissi
                                           (G.) E. Pancani (C.) L. Walter (S.)
                                           A. Farelli cond.

Novara         Nuovo        Jan.    1853  E. Baratti (M.) B. Bellocchio (G.)
                                           G. D'Apice (C.) L. Montani (S.)

Piacenza       Comunale     Carn. 1852-53  C. Corbetta (M.) M. Cagnola-Tancioni
                                           (G.) L. Comolli (C.) F. Cuturi (S.)
                                           G. Jona cond.

Turin          Carignano    Sep. 18, 1852  M. De Gianni-Vivez (M.) M. Vetturi-
                                           Olivi (G.) G. De Vecchi (C.) L. Gi-
                                           raldoni (S.)

Venice         La Fenice    Feb. 12, 1853  M. De Gianni-Vivez (M.) F. Salvini-
                                           Donatelli (G.) L. Graziani (C.) F.
                                           Varesi (S.) G. Mares cond.

Vercelli       Civico       Jan. 25, 1853  M. Pinelli (M.) A. Rebussini (G.) M.
                                           Sacchero (C.) L. Rinaldini (S.)

MALTA
La Valletta    Manoel        Mar.      1854 M. Mollo (M.) G. Mora (G.) G. Comol-
                                       li (C.) G. Sansone (S.)

PORTUGAL
Oporto         Sao Joao      Mar.      1864 A. Fabbri (M.) Garulli (G.) G. De
                                       Antoni (C.) A. De Antoni (S.)

SPAIN
Palma de       Princesa      Mar.?     1858 F. Pozzo (C.) (Planned, but not con-
Mallorca                               firmed)


OTHER PRODUCTIONS-POST-WORLD WAR II

GERMANY
Frankfurt      Century       Oct.   2, 1971 K. Ricciarelli (M.) A. Gulin (G.) G.
               Hall                    Casellato-Lamberti (C.) R. Bruson
                                       (S.) J. Lopez-Cobos cond. (By the
                                       company of the Teatro La Fenice, Ve-
                                       nice)

GREAT BRITAIN
London         St. Pancras Mar. 15, 1966 J. Sinclair (M.) P. Tinsley (G.) D.
               Town Hall               Smith (C.) B. Drake (S.) L. Head
                                       cond.

               BBC          Feb. 27, 1971 P. McCarry (M.) P. Tinsley (G.) K.
                                       Erwen (C.) T. Sharpe (S.)

               Bloomsbury   Feb. 23, 1988 C. Bunning (M.) S. McCulloch (G.) W.
                                       Dyer (C.) D. Barrell (S.) C. Fifield
                                       cond.

ITALY
Bussetto       Piazza       July   9, 1988 A. Campori cond.
               Verdi

Parma          Regio        Jan. 22, 1972 K. Ricciarelli (M.) M. A. Rosati
                                       (G.) G. Casselato Lamberti (C.) G.
                                       Lormi (S.) P. Maag cond.

San Remo       Casino       Sep.   9, 1980 M. G. Guida (M.) F. Ferraro (G.) N.
                                       Antinori (C.) S. Sasso (S.) M. Ri-
                                       naldi cond.

Trieste        Verdi        Mar.   8, 1972 K. Ricciarelli (M.) G. Casselato
                                       Lamberti (C.) C. Franci cond.

Venice         Con-         Aug. 31, 1963 M. Battinelli (M.) V. Notardistefani
               servatory              (G.) A. Bottion (C.) S. Carroli (S.)
                                       P. Wollny cond.

               La Fenice    Mar.   2, 1971 V. Papantoniou (M.) A. Gulin (G.) G.
                                       Casellato-Lamberti (C.) R. Bruson/G.
                                       Scandola (S.)

UNITED STATES
New York       Town Hall    Dec. 16, 1981 C. Val-Schmidt (M.) S. Reese (G.) C.
                                       Bergonzi (C.) J. Dietsch (S.) D.
                                       Lawton cond.

San Diego      Opera        June 18, 1982 R. Plowright (M.) J. Anderson (G.)
                                          A. Navarrete (C.) J. P. Raftery (S.)
                                          E. Müller cond.

Stony Brook    Main Th.     Dec. 12, 1981 C. Val-Schmidt (M.) S. Reese (G.) C.
L. I., N. Y.                              Bergonzi (C.) J. Dietsch (S.) D.
                                          Lawton cond.


14. LA BATTAGLIA DI LEGNANO-*Tragedia lirica* in four acts
Rome-Teatro Argentina-Jan. 27, 1849
Libretto by Salvadore Cammarano

Lida (L.)                                      Teresa de Giuli Borsi sop.
Arrigo (A.)                                    Gaetano Fraschini ten.
Rolando (R.)                                   Filippo Colini bar.
Federico Barbarossa (F.)                       Pietro Sottovia bass
Imelda                                         Vincenza Marchesi sop.
Un Scudiero                                    Mariano Conti ten.
Un Araldo                                      Luigi Ferri ten.
Marcovaldo                                     Lodovico Buti bar.
Primo Console                                  Alessandro Lanzoni bass
Secondo Console                                Achille Testi bass
Il Podestà di Como                             Filippo Giannini bass

Conductor                                      Emilio Angelini
Director                                       Giuseppe Verdi

OTHER PRODUCTIONS-NINETEENTH CENTURY

CHILE
Santiago       Municipal    Aug.?    1864 C. Manzini (L.) E. Ballerini (A.) R.
                                          Bertolini (R.) P. De Antoni (F.)

Valparaiso     Victoria     Feb.  5, 1865 C. Manzini (L.) E. Ballerini (A.) R.
                                          Bertolini (R.) P. De Antoni (F.)

GREECE
Corfu          San Giacomo Autumn    1855 C. Rota-Galli (L.) Negri (A.) G.
                                          Marra (R.)

ITALY
Ancona         Muse         May   6, 1849 N. Hoge-Brandini (L.) C. Liverani
                                          (A.) A. Ottaviani (R.)

Bologna        Comunale     Dec. 26, 1860 C. Cattinari (L.) A. Prudenza (A.)
                                          P. Gorin (R.) E. Daneri (F.) A. Ma-
                                          riani cond.

Cagliari       Civico       Nov. 15, 1860 S. Della Valle (L.) G. Marelli (A.)

Chieti         Marrucino    Apr.  4, 1861 N. Rossi (L.) C. Gennari (A.)

Ferrara        Comunale     Jan.     1860 C. Lanzi (L.) G. Ortolani (A.) F.
                                          Proni (R.)

Florence       Pergola      Feb.?    1849 M. Barbieri-Nini (L.) G. Fraschini
                                          (A.) R. Ferlotti (R.)

Genoa          Carlo        June 12, 1850 C. Gruitz (L.) R. Mirate (A.) A.
               Felice                     Ottaviani (R.)

| Macerata | Lauro Rossi | Jan. | 1861 | E. Leonpietra (L.) P. Grilli (A.) V. Leoni (R.) |
|---|---|---|---|---|
| Messina | Vittorio Emanuele | Dec. 26, | 1860 | L. Ruggero-Antonioli (L.) V. Massini (A.) F. Cellini (R.) |
| Milan | Carcano | June 24, | 1859 | A Jackson (L.) E. Barbacini (A.) G. Marra (R.) E. Cavallini cond. |
| | La Scala | Nov. 23, | 1861 | P. Colson (L.) R. Sirchia (A.) G. Marra (R.) F. Taste (F.) E. Cavallini cond. |
| Naples | San Carlo | Jan. 13, | 1861 | C. Weber (L.) C. Negrini (A.) F. Bellini (R.) |
| Parma | Regio | Jan. 26, | 1860 | C. Marchisio (L.) A. Pagnoni (A.) E. Crivelli (R.) C. Boccabadati (F.) G. C. Ferrarini cond. |
| Perugia | Morlacchi | Dec. 26, | 1860 | L. Arancio-Guerrini (L.) A. Di Benedetto (A.) G. Giori (R.) |
| Piacenza | Municipale | Aug. | 1859 | A. Jackson (L.) C. Negrini (A.) G. Marra (R.) G. Moretti (F.) G. Jona cond. |
| Rome | Politeama | Spring | 1874 | C. Noel-Guidi (L.) E. Ronconi (A.) M. Ciapini (R.) |
| Turin | Nazionale | Mar. 30, | 1859 | L. Gavetti-Regnani (L.) G. Boy (A.) A. Olivari (R.) |
| MALTA La Valletta | Manoel | Oct. 30, | 1861 | A. Bazzurri (L.) Mercanti (A.) L. Vendemmia (R.) |
| PERU Lima | Principal | Aug. 7, | 1853 | C. Barili-Thorn (L.) D. Lorini (A.) A. Avignone (R.) F. Leonardi (F.) |
| PORTUGAL Oporto | Sao Joao | Dec.? | 1858 | N. De Roissi (L.) G. De Vecchi (A.) A. Fellini (R.) A. Rossi (F.) |
| RUSSIA Odessa | Municipal | Dec. | 1860 | I. Edelvira (L.) E. Irfré (A.) M. Padilla (R.) |
| URUGUAY Montevideo | Solis | Apr. 6, | 1861 | C. Manzini (L.) E. Ballerini (A.) G. Bertolini (R.) L. Pretti cond. |

OTHER PRODUCTIONS-1900-1945

| ARGENTINA Buenos Aires | Colòn | May 28, | 1916 | R. Raisa (L.) G. Crimi (A.) G. Rimini (R.) G. Mansueto (F.) G. Barone cond. |
|---|---|---|---|---|
| BRAZIL Sao Paulo | Municipal | Sep. 23, | 1916 | R. Raisa (L.) G. Crimi (A.) G. Rimini (R.) G. Mansueto (F.) G. Barone cond. |

ITALY
Florence      Politeama    Jan.      1916 G. Russ (L.) G. Tomassini (A.) E.
                                          Nani (R.)

Milan         La Scala     Jan. 19, 1916 R. Raisa (L.) G. Crimi (A.) G. Dani-
                                          se (R.) G. Cirino (F.) G. Marinuzzi
                                          cond.

Rome          Nazionale    Oct. 13, 1916 I. Sabbatini (L.) F. De Angelis (A.)
                                          R. Rasponi (R.)


OTHER PRODUCTIONS-POST-WORLD WAR II

GREAT BRITAIN
Cardiff       New          Oct.  3, 1960 H. Harper (L.) R. Dowd (A.) R. Lewis
                                          (R.) H. Alan (F.) C. Groves cond.
                                          (in Eng.)

                           Oct.     1961

London        Sadler's     May   8, 1961 H. Harper (L.) R. Dowd (A.) R. Lewis
              Wells                        (R.) H. Alan (F.) C. Groves cond.
                                          (in Eng.)

ITALY
Florence      Pergola      May  10, 1959 L. Gencer (L.) G. Limarilli (A.) G.
                                          Taddei (R.) P. Washington (F.) V.
                                          Gui cond.

Milan         La Scala     Dec.  7, 1961 A. Stella/Mirnenco (L.) F. Corelli/
                                          G. Limarilli (A.) E. Bastianini/D.
                                          Dondi (R.) M. Stefanoni (F.) G. Ga-
                                          vazzeni cond.

              Sala RAI     Dec. 18, 1973 R. Orlandi-Malaspina (L.) G. Cec-
                                          chele (A.) M. Sereni (R.) M. Rinaldi
                                          cond.

Parma         Regio        Oct. 17, 1951 A. Guerrini (L.) G. Penno (A.) U.
                                          Savarese (R.) A. Mongelli (F.) A.
                                          Questa cond.

Rome          Sala RAI     July 22, 1948 C. Mancini (L.) J. Huttunen (A.) M.
                                          Borriello (R.) F. Previtali cond.

                           June 19, 1949 C. Mancini (L.) A. Baldelli (A.) G.
                                          Taddei (R.) F. Previtali cond.

                           Mar. 13, 1951 C. Mancini (L.) A. Berdini (A.) R.
                                          Panerai (R.) F. Previtali cond.

              Opera        Dec.  4, 1983 M. Zampieri (L.) N. Todisco (A.) L.
                                          Miller (R.) F. Ferro cond.

Trieste       Verdi        Mar.  8, 1963 L. Gencer (L.) J. Gibin (A.) U. Sa-
                                          varese (R.) F. Molinari-Pradelli
                                          cond.

Venice        La Fenice    Dec. 26, 1959 L. Gencer (L.) P. Miranda Ferraro
                                          (A.) U. Savarese (R.) F. Capuana
                                          cond.

UNITED STATES
New York        Cooper        Feb. 28, 1976 J. Robinson (L.) R. Van Valkenburg
                Union                       (A.) G. Vorhes (R.) J. Morgan (F.)
                                            A. Amato cond.

                Carnegie      Jan. 12, 1987 A. Millo (L.) M. Malagnini (A.) M.
                Hall                        Manuguerra (R.) E. Queler cond.

Pittsburgh      Heinz Hall    Sep. 20, 1984 J. Anderson (L.) G. Scano (A.) G.
                                            Dolter (R.) R. Cross (F.) T. Alcan-
                                            tara cond.


15. LUISA MILLER-*Melodramma tragico* in three acts
Naples-Teatro San Carlo-Dec. 8, 1849
Libretto by Salvadore Cammarano

Luisa (L.)
Federica (F.)                                   Marietta Gazzaniga sop.
Rodolfo (R.)                                      Teresa Salandri mez.
Miller (M.)                                     Settimio Malvezzi ten.
Il Conte di Walter (W.)                        Achille De Bassini bar.
Wurm (Wu.)                                         Antonio Selva bass
Laura                                              Marco Arati bass
Un Contedino                                      Anna Salvetti sop.
                                                 Teofilo Rossi ten.

Conductor                                          Antonio Farelli
Director                                           Giuseppe Verdi

OTHER PREMIERES-NINETEENTH CENTURY

ARGENTINA
Buenos Aires    Argentino     Jan. 28, 1854 I. Edelvira (L.) G. Tati (F.) L.
                                            Guglielmini (R.) G. C. Casanova (M.)
                                            F. Tati (W.) J. V. Rivas cond.

                Ant. Colón    June 27, 1860 A. De la Grange (L.) L. Lelmi (R.)
                                            G. Cima (M.) A. Didot (W.)

AUSTRALIA
Melbourne       Th. Royal     Nov. 23, 1859 M. Carandini (L.) S. Flower (F.) W.
                                            Sherwin (R.) R. Farquharson (M.) J.
                                            Gregg (W.)

AUSTRIA
Vienna          Kärntnertor   Apr. 20, 1852 A. Albertini (L.) L. Graziani (R.)
                                            A. De Bassini (M.) G. Mitrovich (W.)
                                            H. Proch cond.

BRAZIL
Rio de          Provisorio    May 25, 1853  G. Zecchini (L.) B. Kastrup (F.) A.
Janeiro                                      Gentile (R.) E. Rivas (M.) C. Capur-
                                            ri (W.) J. V. Rivas cond.

Sao Paulo       Sao José      Apr. 1, 1876  A. Cortesi (L.) L. Canepa (F.) L.
                                            Lelmi (R.) G. Spalazzi (M.) G. Mi-
                                            randola (W.)

CHILE
Santiago        Republica     Sep. 22, 1853

Valparaiso    Victoria      Jan. 27, 1857 I.  Edelvira (L.) Dubreuil (F.) L.
                                          Guglielmini (R.) A. Lanzoni (M.) G.
                                          C. Casanova (W.)

COLOMBIA
Bogota        Teatro             1878 L.  D'Aponte (L.) Pocoleri (F.) E.
                                          Petrilli (M.) De Sanctis (W.)

CUBA
Havana        Tacon         Dec.  8, 1854 C.  Manzini (L.) L. Salvi (R.) G. F.
                                          Beneventano (M.) I. Marini (W.) G.
                                          Bottesini cond.

FRANCE
Ajaccio       San           Oct.?    1853 C.  Charles (L.) Lombardi (R.) F.
              Gabriele                    Mazzoni (M.) P. Brayda-Lablache (W.)

Bastia                      Oct. 24, 1857 Stanghi (L.) V. Tesi (R.) F. Mazzoni
                                          (M.)

Nice          Regio         Jan. 20, 1853 Morra (L.) Perez (R.)

Paris         Italien       Dec.  7, 1852 S.  Cruvelli (L.) C. Nantier-Didiée
                                          (F.) G. Bettini (R.) G. Valle (M.)
                                          A. Susini (W.) C. Castagneri cond.

              Opéra         Feb.  2, 1853 A.  Bosio (L.) E. Masson (F.) L.
                                          Guyemard (R.) F. Morelli-Ponti (M.)
                                          L. Merly (W.) (in Fr.)

GERMANY
Hannover      Hoftheater    May  27, 1851 H.  Marschner cond. (in Ger.)

GREAT BRITAIN
London        Sadler's      June  3, 1858 Haigh-Dyer (L.) E. Poma (F.) H.
              Wells                       Haigh (R.) E. Rosenthal (M.) Borrani
                                          (W.)

              Her           June  8, 1858 M.  Piccolomini (L.) M. Alboni (F.)
              Majesty's                   A. Giuglini (R.) F. Beneventano (M.)
                                          F. Vialetti (W.) V. Bonetti cond.
                                          (in It.)

GREECE
Athens        Royal         Nov. 30, 1852 M.  Marinangeli (L.) D. Santolini
                                          (F.) C. Scola (R.) V. Orlandi (M.)
                                          A. Casali (W.)

Corfu         San Giacomo Dec.  9, 1851 L.  Luxor-Pretti (L.) A. Errani (R.)
                                          L. Busi (M.)

HUNGARY
Budapest      Nemzeti       May  30, 1851 J.  Kaiser-Ernst (L.) F. Steger (R.)
              Szinház                     M. Füredi (M.) K. Benza (W.) (in
                                          Hung.)

INDIA
Calcutta      Opera House Feb. 23, 1869 C.  Ghirlanda-Tortolini (L.) A. Maz-
                                          zucco (F.) T. Villa (R.)

ITALY
Alessandria   Civico        Oct. 30, 1851 M.  Gazzaniga (L.) S. Malvezzi (R.)
                                          A. De Bassini (M.) A. Selva (W.)

Ancona        Muse         Dec. 26, 1850 L.  Finetti-Batocchi  (L.)  M.  Neri
                                        (R.)  F. Giannini  (M.)  C.  Boccolini
                                        (W.)

Bari          Piccinni     Feb.?    1857 L.  Stramesi  (L.)

Bergamo       Riccardi     Aug. 12, 1851 M. Gazzaniga (L.) C. Negrini (R.) F.
                                        Gorin (M.)  F. Pons (W.)  G. Vailati
                                        cond.

Bologna       Comunale     Oct. 10, 1850 M.  Barbieri-Nini  (L.)  S.  Malvezzi
                                        (R.)  G. Ferri  (M.)  S. Panzini  (W.)
                                        G. Manetti cond. G. Verdi dir.

Brescia       Grande       July 31, 1852 R. Gariboldi-Bassi (L.) T. Rambosio
                                        (F.) C. Miraglia (R.) P. Gorin (M.)
                                        F. Pons (W.)

Cagliari      Civico       Oct. 20, 1851 M. Marinangeli (L.) D. Mecksa (R.)

Catania       Comunale     Apr.     1851 E. Parepa-Archibugi (L.) A. Silves-
                                        troni (R.) F. Cuturi (M.) G. Patri-
                                        arca (W.) M. Pappalardo cond.

Cesena        Comunale     Aug. 29, 1854 A.  Angelini-Cantalamessa  (L.)  C.
                                        Bernagozzi (F.) C. Liverani (R.) L.
                                        Bianchi (M.) F. Fioravanti (W.) P.
                                        Trentanove cond.

Cremona       Concordia    Feb. 15, 1853 L. Ruggero-Antonioli (L.) P. Neri-
                                        Baraldi (R.) G. Altini (M.) P. No-
                                        lasco Llorens (W.) N. Bassi cond.

Faenza        Comunale     June 15, 1853 A. Anglés-Fortuni (L.) G. Brambilla-
                                        Marulli (F.) L. Graziani (R.) P. Ba-
                                        raldi (M.)

Ferrara       Comunale     Apr. 21, 1851 A. Albertini (L.) L. Rosetti-Bocco-
                                        lini (F.) S. Malvezzi (R.) F. Varesi
                                        (M.) C. Boccolini (W.)

Fermo         Aquila       Aug. 16, 1851 A. Albertini (L.) G. Bregazzi (F.)
                                        G. Galvani (R.) E. Crivelli (M.) C.
                                        Boccolini (W.)

Fiume         Civico       Feb. 26, 1856 C. Mongini-Stecchi (L.) E. Laurelli
                                        (F.) A. Errani (R.) A. Carapia (M.)
                                        G. Zambellini (W.)

Florence      Pergola      Mar. 18, 1851 A. Albertini (L.) G. Bregazzi (F.)
                                        E. Naudin (R.) A. Ottaviani (M.)

Forli         Comunale     June 22, 1850 A. Albertini (L.) T. Chini (F.) E.
                                        Marcucci (R.) F. Colini (M.)

Genoa         Carlo        Dec. 26, 1850 S. Cruvelli (L.) M. Cruvelli (F.) S.
              Felice                     Malvezzi (R.) F. Gnone (M.) S. Pan-
                                        zini (W.)

Livorno       Rossini      July 12, 1851 E. Scotta (L.) A. Vasoli (F.) G. Pa-
                                        si (R.) F. Cresci (M.) A. Lanzoni
                                        (W.)

Lucca          Giglio       Aug. 23, 1851 G. Bortolotti (L.) A. Vasoli (F.) C.
                                          Baucardé (R.) F. Colini (M.) A. Lan-
                                          zoni (W.)

Lugo           Rossini      Aug.?    1850 V. Cherubini (L.) G. Setti (R.) A.
                                          Ottaviani (M.) G. Biserni cond.

Mantua         Sociale      Feb. 18, 1851 E. Cominotti (L.) G. Alzamora (R.)
                                          E. Luisia (M.) A. Casali (W.) G.
                                          Luppi cond.

Messina        Munizione    Oct.     1851 C. Forti-Babacci (L.) Giannoni (R.)
                                          G. Arnaud (M.) G. B. Antonucci (W.)

Milan          Carcano      Sep.  9, 1850 R. Gariboldi-Bassi (L.) A. Casaloni
                                          (F.) G. Fedor (R.) G. Corsi (M.) F.
                                          Pons (W.)

               La Scala     Dec. 26, 1851 C. Gruitz (L.) F. Ferretti (F.) S.
                                          Malvezzi (R.) G. Fiori (M.) A. Didot
                                          (W.) E. Cavallini cond.

Modena         Comunale     May  25, 1850 T. Brambilla (L.) A. Casaloni (F.)
                                          S. Malvezzi (R.) F. Varesi (M.) S.
                                          Panzini (W.) A. Sighicelli cond.

Novara         Nuovo        Nov.     1864 G. Naglia (L.) F. Toni-Nazzari (R.)
                                          G. Cantù (M.) L. Vecchi (W.)

Padua          Nuovo        July 20, 1851 M. Gazzaniga (L.) C. Negrini (R.) A.
                                          Superchi (M.) F. Pons (W.)

Palermo        Carolino     Oct.  2, 1851 F. Salvini-Donatelli (L.) A. Borghi-
                                          Vietti (F.) V. Jacobelli (R.) G.
                                          Corsi (M.) A. Selva (W.) P. Raimondi
                                          cond.

Parma          Regio        Dec. 26, 1850 M. Gresti (L.) C. Ghedini (F.) G. B.
                                          Milesi (R.) A. Superchi (M.) D. Mag-
                                          gi (W.) N. De Giovanni cond.

Perugia        Morlacchi    Carn. 1851-52 C. Cuzzani (L.) A. Oliva-Pavani (R.)
                                          A. Ortolani (M.) G. Mirandola (W.)

Piacenza       Municipale   Dec. 26? 1851 E. Gambardella (L.) B. Bolcioni (R.)
                                          L. Montani (M.) F. Gallo-Tomba (W.)
                                          G. Jona cond.

Pisa           Ravvivati    Dec. 26, 1852 M. Piccolomini (L.) C. Merli (F.) E.
                                          Pasi (R.) F. Graziani (M.) C. Mar-
                                          sili cond.

Ravenna        Comuni-      May   6, 1851 F. Capuani (L.) L. Castagnoli  (F.)
               tativo                     L. Bernabei (R.) M. Zacchi (M.) G.
                                          Nostini cond.

Reggio Emilia Comunale      Apr. 27, 1852 E. Scotta (L.) T. Chini (F.) R. Mi-
                                          rate (R.) F. Varesi (M.) A. Dolci-
                                          bene (W.) G. Tebaldi cond.

Rome           Apollo       Feb.  5, 1850 A. Albertini (L.) Z. Sbriscia (F.)
                                          E. Naudin (R.) F. Colini (M.) L.
                                          Buti (W.) E. Angelini cond.

Rovigo       Sociale     Autumn    1850 L. Cherubini (L.) E. Marcucci (R.)
                                        A. Ottaviani (M.)

Siena        Rinnovati   July 15, 1852 A. Rebussini (L.) A. Giuglini (R.)
                                        E. Barili (M.)

Sinigaglia   La Fenice   July 19, 1852 A. Albertini (L.) G. Bregazzi (F.)
                                        C. Baucardé (R.) G. Ferri (M.) C.
                                        Dalla Costa (W.)

Spoleto      Nobile      Dec. 27, 1851 C. Crespolani (L.) M. Branca (F.) V.
                                        Ferrari-Stella (R.) A. Frontoni (M.)
                                        G. Marchetti (W.)

Trento       Sociale     July  7, 1852 M. Oliva-Venturi (L.) A. Prudenza
                                        (R.) Gianni (M.)

Treviso      Onigo       Oct. 22, 1854 A. Albertini (L.) G. Bregazzi (F.)
                                        C. Baucardé (R.) G. B. Bencich (M.)
                                        G. B. Cornago (W.)

Trieste      Grande      Oct.  5, 1850 M. Gazzaniga (L.) G. Fraschini (R.)
                                        F. Colini (M.) C. Dalla Costa (W.)
                                        G. A. Scaramelli cond.

Turin        Carignano   Aug. 30, 1851 F. Capuani (L.) M. Viani (R.) F.
                                        Cresci (M.)

             Regio       Feb.  1, 1853 A. Albertini (L.) A. Winnen (F.) G.
                                        Fraschini (R.) E. Crivelli (M.) A.
                                        Didot (W.) G. Ghebart cond.

Udine        Sociale     July 19, 1856 M. Gazzaniga (L.) C. Negrini (R.) G.
                                        Guicciardi (M.)

Venice       La Fenice   Dec. 26, 1850 T. Brambilla (L.) A. Casaloni (F.)
                                        R. Mirate (R.) F. Varesi (M.) F.
                                        Pons (W.) G. Mares cond.

Verona       Filarmonico Dec. 26, 1850 R. Gariboldi-Bassi (L.) A. Borghi-
                                        Vietti (F.) G. Stigelli (R.) L.
                                        Biacchi (M.) C. Nanni (W.)

Vicenza      Eretenio    Aug. 22, 1855 M. Piccolomini (L.) G. Fraschini
                                        (R.) L. Giraldoni (M.) B. Cervini
                                        (W.)

JUGOSLAVIA
Zara         Nobile      Apr. 17, 1852 F. Castellani (L.) G. Petrovich (R.)
                                        D. Mattioli (M.) D. Dal Negro (W.)

LITHUANIA
Vilnius                            1873 (in It.)

MALTA
La Valletta  Manoel      Oct.?     1850 E. Gambardella (L.) U. Albiccini
                                        (R.) A. Rossi (M.)

MEXICO
Mexico City  Nacional    Nov. 15, 1855 C. Manzini (L.) F. Vestvali (F.) L.
                                        Giannoni (R.) E. Winter (M.) G.
                                        Winter cond.

PERU
Lima            Principal    Aug. 30, 1856

PHILIPPINES
Manila          Principe     Oct.?     1867 L. Da Ponte (L.)
                Alfonso

PORTUGAL
Lisbon          Sao Carlos   June 22, 1851 L. Bianchi (L.) E. Musich (R.) V.
                                           Prattico (M.) G. B. Cornago (W.)

Oporto          Sao Joao     Feb.?     1851 L. Abbadia (L.) G. Gamboggi (R.) V.
                                           Prattico (M.)

ROMANIA
Bucharest       Nacional     Dec. 12, 1852 P. Corvetti (F.) G. Musiani (R.)

Iasi            Teatrul      Dec.?     1853 M. Anselmi (L.) A. Prudenza (R.) V.
                                           Sermattei (M.) Carbonell (W.)

RUSSIA
Moscow          Bolshoi      Feb. 14, 1874

Odessa          Municipal    July 26, 1851 T. Brambilla (L.) Guerrini (F.) E.
                                           Pancani (R.) S. Ronconi (M.)

St.             Imperial     Jan.  3, 1858 A. Bosio (L.) E. De Meric (F.) P.
Petersburg                                 Mongini (R.) A. De Bassini (M.) C.
                                           Everardi (W.)

SPAIN
Barcelona       Principal    Oct. 25, 1851 L. Abbadia (L.) G. Baldanza (R.) E.
                                           Luisia (M.) E. Manfredi (W.)

                Liceo        Oct. 28, 1851 L. Abbadia (L.) G. Baldanza (R.) E.
                                           Luisia (M.) E. Manfredi (W.)

Madrid          Real         Dec. 11, 1852 F. Capuani (L.) G. Roppa (R.) F. Co-
                                           letti (M.) A. Selva (W.) J. Skoczdo-
                                           pole cond.

Malaga          Principal    Feb. 18, 1852 C. Vittadini (L.) C. Mas Porcell
                                           (F.) E. Testa (R.) V. Sermattei (M.)

Palma di        Coliseo      Jan.?     1856 C. Crescimano (L.) P. Samat (R.) Ca-
Mallorca                                   valetti (M.)

TURKEY
Constan-        Naum         Dec. 16, 1852 C. Rambur (L.) C. Ghedini (F.) A.
tinople                                    Malagola (R.) P. Gorin (M.) Malasco-
                                           ni (W.)

UNITED STATES
Cincinnati      National     Feb. 24, 1854 C. Richings (L.) (in Eng.)

New York        Castle       July 20, 1854 V. Gomez (L.) G. Martini-d'Ormy (F.)
                Garden                     P. Neri-Baraldi (R.) W. Müller (M.)
                                           D. Coletti (W.) M. Maretzek cond.

Philadelphia    Walnut Str.  Oct. 27, 1852 C. Richings (L.) E. Reed (F.) T.
                                           Bishop (R.) P. Richings (M.) P. Rohr
                                           (W.) W. P. Cunnington cond. (in
                                           Eng.)

San Francisco Metro-      May  18, 1863 G. Bianchi (L.) Younker (F.) E.  Bi-
                politan                  anchi (R.) A. Fellini (M.) Roncovie-
                                         covieri (W.)


OTHER PRODUCTIONS-1900-1945

AUSTRIA
Vienna          Akademie   Mar. 14, 1930 (in Ger.)

GERMANY
Berlin          Kroll       Dec. 10, 1927 K. Heidersbach (L.) M. Schutz-Dorn-
                                         berg (F.) H. Kuppinger (R.) I. Gol-
                                         land (M.) M. Abendroth (W.) F. Zweig
                                         cond. (in Ger.)

                            May  14, 1929 (in Ger.)

HUNGARY
Budapest                    Mar.     1929 (in Hung.)

ITALY
Florence        Comunale    Apr. 27, 1937 M. Caniglia (L.) N. Giani (F.) G.
                                         Lauri-Volpi (R.) M. Basiola (M.) T.
                                         Pasero (W.) V. Gui cond.

Milan           La Scala    Jan.  1, 1903 L. Micucci-Betti (L.) A. Giacomini
                                         (F.) M. Mariacher (R.) A. Magini-
                                         Coletti (M.) O. Carozzi (W.) A.
                                         Toscanini cond.

Parma           Regio       Feb.  1, 1941 C. Castellani (L.) M. L. Cova (F.)
                                         A. Pravadelli (R.) E. Mascherini
                                         (M.) L. Meroni (W.) F. Capuana cond.

Rome            Reale       Feb. 26, 1938 M. Caniglia (L.) G. Alfano (F.) G.
                                         Lauri-Volpi (R.) A. Borgioli/G. Ma-
                                         nacchini (M.) G. Vaghi (W.) T. Sera-
                                         fin cond.

Turin           Regio       Jan.  7, 1933 G. Dalla Rizza (L.) N. Covaceva (F.)
                                         F. Merli (R.) C. Galeffi (M.) G. To-
                                         mei (W.) F. Paolantonio cond.

RUSSIA
Leningrad                   May      1936 (in Rus.)

SWITZERLAND
Zürich          Stadt                1938 (in Ger.)

UNITED STATES
New York        Metro-      Dec. 21, 1929 R. Ponselle (L.) M. Telva/ G. Swart-
                politan                  hout (F.) G. Lauri-Volpi (R.) G. De
                                         Luca (M.) T. Pasero (W.) T. Serafin
                                         cond.

                            Dec. 22, 1930 R. Ponselle (L.) M. Telva (F.) G.
                                         Lauri-Volpi (R.) G. De Luca (M.) T.
                                         Pasero (W.) T. Serafin cond.

OTHER PRODUCTIONS-POST-WORLD WAR II

ARGENTINA
Buenos Aires   Colón        May  28, 1968 L. Maragliano (L.) F. Mattiucci (F.)
                                          F. Labò (R.) C. MacNeil (M.) N. Ros-
                                          si Lemeni (W.) B. Bartoletti cond.

AUSTRIA
Innsbruck                   Nov. 14, 1982 L. Karlsson (L.) G. Eckert (F.) K.
                                          Reiem (R.) M. Hechenleitner (M.) P.
                                          Neuner (W.)

Vienna         Staats       Jan. 23, 1974 L. Sukis (L.) C. Ludwig (F.) F. Bo-
                                          nisolli (R.) G. Taddei (M.) B. Giai-
                                          otti (W.) A. Erede cond.

                            May  13, 1983 K. Ricciarelli (L.) J. Carreras (R.)
                                          G. Zancanaro (M.) P. Wimberger (W.)
                                          A. Guadagno cond.

                            Feb. 18, 1986 C. Gasdia (L.) Yachmi/Gall (F.) L.
                                          Pavarotti (R.) R. Bruson/W. Brendel
                                          (M.) P. Burchuladze (W.) A. Guadagno
                                          cond.

BELGIUM
Brussels       Monnaie      Feb. 16, 1982 E. Shade (L.) B. Pecchioli (F.) Fr.
                                          Tagliavini (R.) R. Constantin (M.)
                                          L. Polgar (W.) S. Cambreling cond.

FRANCE
Aix en         Festival     July 26, 1974 Y. Hayashi (L.)  N. Denize (F.)  O.
Provence                                  Garaventa (R.) A. MacLane (M.) J.
                                          Mars (W.)

Lyon           Auditorium   May  10, 1988 J. Anderson (L.) S. Anselmi (F.) T.
                                          Ichihara (R.)  E. Tumagian (M.) P.
                                          Plishka (W.) M. Arena cond.

Montpelier     Opéra        June  5, 1986 O. Liani (L.) A. Cupido (R.) L. Roni
                                          (W.) C. Diedrich cond.

Paris          Opéra        May  30, 1983 K. Ricciarelli/A. Maliponte (L.) De-
                                          nize (F.) L. Pavarotti (R.) P. Cap-
                                          puccilli (M.) Cheek (W.) A. Guadagno
                                          cond.

Strasbourg                  May   9, 1975 A. Riera (L.) N. Denize (F.)

GERMANY
Cologne        Stadt        June 27, 1981 E. Moldoveanu (L.) G. Casellato-
                                          Lamberti (R.) V. Sardinero (M.) A.
                                          Ferrin (W.) N. Santi cond.

Freiburg       Stadt        Winter?  1968 A. Ludwig (L.) M. Hall (F.) P. Gre-
                                          otti (R.) J. Wiles (M.) P. Wimberger
                                          (W.) R. Werner cond.

Hamburg        Stadt        Nov.  8, 1981 K. Ricciarelli/E. Moldoveanu (L.) J.
                                          Carreras/P. Domingo (R.) L. Nucci/V.
                                          Sardinero (M.) R. Raimondi/G. Howell
                                          (W.) G. Sinopoli cond.

Stuttgart      Opernhaus     Oct. 11, 1969 L. Rebmann (L.) I. Piso (R.) T. Tip-
                                          ton (M.) K. Bertram (W.) A. Erede
                                          cond. (in Ger.)

Wiesbaden                    Autumn   1961 L. Rebmann (L.) K. Mietzner (F.) G.
                                          Misske (M.) P. Meven (W.) H. Wessel-
                                          Therhorn cond. (in Ger.)

GREAT BRITAIN
Durham         Caedmon       May   1, 1975 M. Clark (L.)  H. Thompson  (F.)  M.
               Hall                       Hunt (R.) D. Peacock (M.) D. Wea-
                                          therley (W.) A. Fearon cond.

Edinburgh      Festival      Aug. 26, 1963 M. Roberti (L.) A. M. Rota (F.) R.
                                          Cioni (R.) P. Cappuccilli (M.) P.
                                          Washington (W.) A. Erede cond. (By
                                          the company of the Teatro San Carlo,
                                          Naples)

               Church Hill Oct. 15, 1987 R. Cowan (L.) A. Borthwick (R.) A.
                                          Lindsey (M.) N. Mantle cond.

London         Sadler's      Oct.  1, 1953 V. Elliott (L.)  J. Watson  (F.)  O.
               Wells                      Kirkop (R.) J. Hargreaves (M.) D.
                                          Ward (W.) J. Robertson cond. (in
                                          Eng.)

               Covent        June 19, 1978 K. Ricciarelli (L.) E. Connell  (F.)
               Garden                     L. Pavarotti/J. Carreras (R.) L.
                                          Nucci/G. Zancanaro (M.) R. Lloyd
                                          (W.) L. Maazel cond.

               June  7, 1979 K. Ricciarelli (L.) E. Connel (F.)
                                          P. Domingo (R.) R. Bruson (M.) G.
                                          Howell (W.) L. Maazel cond.

               June  8, 1981 K. Ricciarelli (L.) P. Cannan (F.)
                                          C. Bergonzi/J. Carreras (R.) L. Nuc-
                                          ci (M.) G. Howell (W.) P. Steinberg
                                          cond.

IRELAND
Wexford        Th. Royal     Oct. 27, 1970 L. Kelston (L.) B. Greevy (F.) A. Lo
                                          Forese (R.) T. Sharpe (M.) S. Pag-
                                          liuca (W.) M. Fredman cond.

ITALY
Bologna        Comunale      Jan. 14, 1963 M. Roberti (L.) A. M. Rota (F.) R.
                                          Cioni (R.) P. Cappuccilli (M.) P.
                                          Washington (W.) A. Erede cond.

Cagliari       Massimo       Dec.?    1966 L. Malagrida (L.) F. Rafanelli (F.)
                                          A. Bottion (R.) W. Alberti (M.) F.
                                          Davià (W.) P. Bellughi cond.

Florence       Comunale      May   7, 1966 E. Suliotis (L.) G. Lane (F.) E. Tei
                                          (R.) C. MacNeil (M.) C. Cava (W.) N.
                                          Sanzogno cond.

Genoa          Comunale      Sep. 24, 1972 R. Orlandi-Malaspina (L.) C. Bergon-
                                          zi (R.) A. Protti (M.) M. Rinaudo
                                          (W.) G. Patanè cond.

Milan        La Scala     May  15, 1969 L. Maragliano (L.) R. Tucker (R.) P.
                          Washington (W.) F. Molinari-Pradelli
                          cond.

             May  12, 1976 M. Caballé/A. Maliponte (L.) B. Ba-
                          glioni/Iori (F.) L. Pavarotti (R.)
                          P. Cappuccilli/Salvadori (M.) N.
                          Zardo/P. Washington (W.) G.
                          Gavazzeni cond.

Modena       Comunale     Jan.  5, 1976 R. Scotto (L.) L. Bocca (F.) G.
                          Cianella (R.) G. Zancanaro (M.) M.
                          Mazzieri (W.) P. Maag cond.

Naples       San Carlo    Feb. 23, 1963 M. Roberti (L.) A. M. Rota (F.) R.
                          Cioni (R.) G. Guelfi (M.) P. Wash-
                          ington (W.) A. Erede cond.

             Jan.  6, 1979 K. Ricciarelli (L.) M. Parutto (F.)
                          C. Bini (R.) R. Bruson (M.) A. Fer-
                          rin (W.) F. Molinari-Pradelli cond.

Palermo      Massimo      Jan. 14, 1963 A. Stella (L.) O. Dominguez (F.) G.
                          Di Stefano (R.) C. MacNeil (M.) R.
                          Ariè (W.) N. Sanzogno cond.

Parma        Regio        Dec. 26, 1962 M. Roberti (L.) A. M. Rota (F.) R.
                          Cioni (R.) P. Cappuccilli (M.) N.
                          Zaccaria (W.) A. Erede cond.

             Dec. 22, 1975 R. Scotto/M. Zampieri (L.) L. Bocca/
                          I. Iori (F.) G. Cecchele/G. Cianella
                          (R.) R. Bruson/G. Zancanaro (M.) M.
                          Mazzieri/C. De Bortoli (W.) K. I.
                          Kobayashi cond.

Piacenza     Municipale   Jan.? 1976 M. Zampieri (L.) G. Cecchele (R.) R.
                          Bruson (M.) M. Mazzieri (W.) P. Maag
                          cond.

Reggio Emilia Municipale  Jan.  9, 1976 M. Zampieri (L.) L. Bocca (F.) G.
                          Cecchele (R.) R. Bruson (M.) M.
                          Mazzieri (W.) K. I. Kobayashi cond.

Treviso      Comunale     Autumn 1983 Y. Hayashi (L.) V. Bello (R.) E. Pa-
                          doan (M.) B. Martinotti cond.

Trieste      Verdi        Nov. 10, 1965 E. Suliotis (L.) A. Mori (R.) G.
                          Guelfi (M.) F. Capuana cond.

             Apr. 13, 1978 K. Ricciarelli (L.) Fr. Tagliavini
                          (R.) L. Nucci (M.) A. Ferrin (W.) O.
                          De Fabritiis cond.

Turin        Regio        May   5, 1976 K. Ricciarelli (L.) S. Silva (F.) J.
                          Carreras (R.) R. Bruson (M.) C. De
                          Bortoli (W.) F. Previtali cond.

Venice       La Fenice    Feb. 12, 1963 M. Roberti/ M. Angioletti (L.) A. M.
                          Rota (F.) R. Cioni (R.) G. Guelfi
                          (M.) N. Zaccaria (W.) A. Votto cond.

PORTUGAL
Lisbon        Sao Carlos   May   23,  1983  M. Zampieri (L.) M. Castani (F.) B.
                                            Prior (R.) G. Zancanaro (M.) D. Pet-
                                            kov (W.) F. Ferraris cond.

SPAIN
Barcelona     Liceo        Jan.  30,  1972  M. Caballé (L.) J. Blackham (F.) J.
                                            Carreras (R.) P. Glossop (M.) M.
                                            Mazzieri (W.) A. Camozzo cond.

                           Feb.   3,  1983  A. Gulin (L.) S. Mineva (F.) J. Car-
                                            reras (R.) M. Manuguerra (M.)

Bilbao        Coliseo      Sep.  13,  1975  A. Gulin (L.)  F. Cossotto (F.) J.
              Alba                          Carreras (R.) M. Manuguerra (M.) B.
                                            Giaiotti (W.) G. Morelli cond.

                           Sep.         1978  M. Caballé (L.) J. Jori (F.) L. Pa-
                                            varotti (R.) G. Zancanaro (M.) B.
                                            Giaiotti (W.) B. Lauret cond.

Oviedo        Campoamor    Sep.  19,  1975  A. Gulin (L.)  F. Cossotto (F.) J.
                                            Carreras (R.) M. Manuguerra (M.) B.
                                            Giaiotti (W.) G. Morelli cond.

                           Sep.  15,  1978  M. Caballé (L.) J. Jori (F.) L. Pa-
                                            varotti (R.) G. Zancanaro (M.) B.
                                            Giaiotti (W.) B. Lauret cond.

SWITZERLAND
Zürich        Opernhaus    Oct.  24,  1981  E. Moldoveanu (L.) Fr. Tagliavini
                                            (R.) G. Zancanaro (M.) B. Giaiotti
                                            (W.) N. Santi cond.

UNITED STATES
Atlanta                    May    6,  1968  M. Caballé (L.) L. Pearl (F.) R.
                                            Tucker (R.) S. Milnes (M.) G. Tozzi
                                            (W.) F. Cleva cond.

Boston                     Apr.  22,  1968  M. Caballé (L.) L. Pearl (F.) R.
                                            Tucker (R.) S. Milnes (M.) B. Giai-
                                            otti (W.) F. Cleva cond.

Chicago       Lyric        Dec.   7,  1982  E. Shade (L.) D. Curry (F.) G. Cia-
                                            nella (R.) W. Brendel (M.) P. Wash-
                                            ington (W.) M. Gomez-Martinez cond.

Cleveland                  Apr.  29,  1968  M. Caballé (L.) L. Pearl (F.) R.
                                            Tucker (R.) S. Milnes (M.) G. Tozzi
                                            (W.) F. Cleva cond.

Dallas                     June   6,  1968  L. Amara (L.) L. Pearl (F.) R.
                                            Tucker (R.) S. Milnes (M.) B. Giai-
                                            otti (W.) F. Cleva cond.

Detroit                    May   20,  1968  M. Caballé (L.) L. Pearl (F.) R.
                                            Tucker (R.) S. Milnes (M.) B. Giai-
                                            otti (W.) F. Cleva cond.

Minneapolis                May   17,  1968  M. Caballé (L.) L. Pearl (F.) R.
                                            Tucker (R.) S. Milnes (M.) B. Giai-
                                            otti (W.) F. Cleva cond.

| New York | Town Hall | Spring | 1960 | D. Mari (L.) J. Lo Monaco (R.) A. Amato cond. |
| | Carnegie Hall | Jan. 9, | 1963 | D. Mari (L.) M. Dunn (F.) G. Campora (R.) P. Maero (M.) F. Dante (W.) A. Amato cond. |
| | Metro-politan | Feb. 8, | 1968 | M. Caballé (L.) L. Pearl (F.) R. Tucker (R.) S. Milnes (M.) G. Tozzi (W.) T. Schippers cond. |
| | | Nov. 4, | 1971 | A. Maliponte (L.) P. Domingo (R.) M. Sereni (M.) B. Giaiotti (W.) P. Plishka (Wu.) B. Bartoletti cond. |
| | | Nov. 20, | 1978 | K. Ricciarelli/R. Scotto (L.) M. Dunn/J. Kraft (F.) C. Bini/J. Alexander/J. Carreras/P. Domingo (R.) C. MacNeil/M. Serena/S. Milnes (M.) P. Plishka/B. Giaiotti (W.) J. Levine cond. |
| | | Jan. 11, | 1982 | K. Ricciarelli/A. Maliponte (L.) B. Berini (F.) J. Carreras/J. Alexander/L. Pavarotti (R.) L. Nucci/M. Sereni (M.) P. Plishka/D. Kavrakos (W.) N. Santi cond. |
| Philadelphia | | June 1, | 1968 | M. Caballé (L.) L. Pearl (F.) R. Tucker (R.) S. Milnes (M.) B. Giaiotti (W.) F. Cleva cond. |
| | Schubert | Apr. 7, | 1989 | A. Banaudi/L. Rybarska (L.) P. Romano (F.) L. Pavarotti (R.) H. Fu/H. Choi (M.) P. Burchuladze (W.) A. Guadagno cond. |
| San Francisco | Opera | Nov. 13, | 1974 | K. Ricciarelli (L.) H. Tourangeau (F.) L. Pavarotti (R.) L. Quilico (M.) G. Tozzi (W.) J. Lopez-Cobos cond. |
| VENEZUELA Caracas | Municipal | June 1, | 1979 | A. Maliponte (L.) |

16. STIFFELIO-*Melodramma* in three acts
Trieste-Teatro Grande-Nov. 16, 1850
Libretto by Francesco Maria Piave

| Lina (L.) | Marietta Gazzaniga sop. |
| Stiffelio (S.) | Gaetano Fraschini ten. |
| Stankar (St.) | Filippo Colini bar. |
| Dorotea | Amalia Viezzoli De Silvestrini sop. |
| Raffaele | Rainieri Dei ten. |
| Federico | Giovanni Petrovich ten. |
| Jorg | Francesco Reduzzi bass |
| | |
| Conductor | Giuseppe Alessandro Scaramelli |
| Director | Giuseppe Verdi |

OTHER PRODUCTIONS-NINETEENTH CENTURY

ITALY

| | | | |
|---|---|---|---|
| Florence | Pergola | May 30, 1851 | R. Gariboldi-Bassi (L.) G. Baldanza (S.) F. Monari (St.) |
| Naples | San Carlo | Nov. 24, 1855 | G. Medori (L.) R. Mirate (S.) A. Morelli (St.) A. Farelli cond. |
| Palermo | Carolino | Mar. 20, 1855 | M. Lotti Della Santa (L.) L. Graziani (S.) G. Fiori (St.) |
| Rome | Apollo | Feb. 23, 1851 | A. Albertini (L.) E. Naudin (S.) R. Ferlotti (St.) E. Angelini cond. |
| | | Dec. 27, 1851 | R. Gariboldi-Bassi (L.) G. Fraschini (S.) F. Colini (St.) E. Angelini cond. |
| Trieste | Grande | Nov. 6, 1852 | A. Albertini (L.) G. Fraschini (S.) G. B. Bencich (St.) G. A. Scaramelli cond. |
| Venice | La Fenice | Jan. 13, 1852 | K. Evers (L.) L. Graziani (S.) F. Coletti (St.) G. Mares cond. |

PORTUGAL

| | | | |
|---|---|---|---|
| Oporto | Sao Joao | Oct. 22, 1857 | S. Della Valle (L.) F. Mazzoleni (S.) A. Vitti (St.) |

SPAIN

| | | | |
|---|---|---|---|
| Barcelona | Principal | Oct. 20, 1856 | M. Anselmi (L.) G. Landi (S.) E. Fagotti (St.) |
| | Liceo | Nov. 24, 1860 | C. Carozzi-Zucchi (L.) G. Landi (S.) G. B. Bencich (St.) |
| Malaga | Principe Alfonso | Nov. 1862 | A. Albertini (L.) L. Marelli (S.) P. Giorgi Pacini (St.) G. De Paolis cond. |
| Palma de Mallorca | Coliseo | Dec. 1859 | A. Agresti (S.) |
| | Princesa | Dec. 1866 | G. Naglia (L.) A. Agresti (S.) V. Prattico (St.) |
| Seville | San Fernando | Mar. 17, 1859 | S. Peruzzi (L.) G. Landi (S.)[42] |

OTHER PRODUCTIONS-POST-WORLD WAR II

GERMANY

| | | | |
|---|---|---|---|
| Cologne | Stadtoper | Oct. 29, 1972 | S. Mangelsdorff/G. de la Cruz (L.) W. Götz (S.) C. Meghor/W. Janulako (St.) I. Kertész cond. (in Ger.) |

---

[42]. It is interesting to note that both *Stiffelio* and *Aroldo* were given during the same season in the same theatre. This is probably the only time this happened during the nineteenth century.

GREAT BRITAIN
London        University   Feb. 14, 1973 A. Conoley (L.) S. Kale (S.) P. Lyon
              College                    (St.) G. Badacsonyi cond.

ITALY
Naples        San Carlo    Dec. 26, 1972 A. Gulin (L.) M. Del Monaco (S.) G.
                                         Fioravanti (St.) O. De Fabritiis
                                         cond.

Parma         Regio        Dec. 12, 1968 A. Gulin (L.) G. Limarilli/R. Gava-
                                         rini (S.) W. Alberti/V. Martinoiu
                                         (St.) P. Maag cond.

Venice        La Fenice    Dec. 14, 1985 R. Plowright (L.) A. Barasorda (S.)
                                         B. Ellis (St.) E. Inbal cond.

                           May  20, 1988 L. Roark Strummer/J. Omilian (L.) A.
                                         Ordonez (S.) T. Noble (St.) H. Sou-
                                         dant cond.

SWITZERLAND
Berne         Oper         Apr.     1973 H. Döse (L.) P. Bahrig (S.) L. An-
                                         derko (St.) (in Ger.)

UNITED STATES
Boston                     Feb. 15, 1978 A. Moffo/L. Munro (L.) R. Taylor
                                         (S.) B. Ellis (St.) S. Caldwell
                                         cond.

Brooklyn      Ac. of Mus.  June  4, 1976 N. French (L.) R. Taylor (S.) T.
                                         Lambrinos (St.) V. LaSelva cond.

Wilmington    Grand        Nov. 26, 1988


17. RIGOLETTO-*Melodramma serio* in three acts
Venice-Teatro La Fenice-Mar. 11, 1851
Libretto by Francesco Maria Piave

Gilda (G.)                                   Teresina Brambilla sop.
Maddalena (M.)                               Annetta Casaloni mez.
Il Duca di Mantova (D.)                      Raffaele Mirate ten.
Rigoletto (R.)                               Felice Varesi bar.
Sparafucile (S.)                             Feliciano Pons bass
Contessa di Ceprano                          Luigia Morselli mez.
Giovanna                                     Laura Saini mez.
Paggio                                 Annetta Modes Lovati mez.
Matteo Borsa                                 Angelo Zuliani ten.
Usciere di Corte                             Antonio Rizzi ten.
Monterone                                    Paolo Damini bar.
Marullo                                Francesco Kunerth bar.
Ceprano                                      Andrea Bellini bass

Conductor                                       Gaetano Mares
Director                                        Giuseppe Verdi

OTHER PREMIERES

ARGENTINA
Buenos Aires  Argentino    June 16, 1855  I. Edelvira (G.) G. Tati (M.) L.
Guglielmini (D.) G. C. Casanova (R.)
F. Tati (S.) J. V. Rivas cond.

Ant. Colón   May    2, 1857  S. Vera-Lorini (G.) A. Casaloni (M.)
E. Tamberlick (D.) G. Cima (R.)

Colón        June 14, 1908  E. Clasenti (G.) T. Ferraris (M.) A.
Bassi (D.) T. Ruffo (R.) L. Nico-
letti-Kormann (S.) A. Vigna cond.

AUSTRALIA
Adelaide     Th. Royal     Apr. 10, 1872  G. Tamburini-Coy (G.) E. Polli (M.)
D. Rosnati (D.) F. Coliva (R.) E.
Dondi (S.) A. Zelman cond.

Brisbane     Th. Royal     Dec.  8, 1882  M. Boy-Gilbert (G.) E. Fabris (M.)
E. Sbriscia (D.) I. Viganotti (R.)
D. Benferreri (S.)

Melbourne    Th. Royal     Sep. 15, 1860  G. Bianchi (G.) O. Hamilton (M.) E.
Bianchi (D.) E. Coulon (R.) J. Gregg
(S.)

Sydney       Lyceum        Nov. 25, 1861  G. Bianchi (G.) E. Howson (M.) E.
Bianchi (D.) J. Howson (R.) E. Gros-
si (S.)

AUSTRIA
Graz         Stadt         Jan. 18, 1853  (in Ger.)

Linz         Landes        Mar.  5, 1854  (in Ger.)

Vienna       Kärntnertor   May  12, 1852  A. Albertini (G.) L. Graziani (D.)
G. Ferri (R.) H. Proch cond. (in
It.)

Nov. 24, 1860  M. Wildauer (G.) H. Sulzer (M.) A.
Ander (D.) J. N. Beck (R.) C. Mayerhofer (S.) H. Proch cond. (in Ger.)

BELGIUM
Antverp      Royal         Feb. 25, 1864  Bessin-Poouilley (G.) Sapin (D.)
Lèderac (R.) (in Fr.)

Apr. 22, 1869  M. Calisto (G.) K. Morensi (M.) G.
Piccioli (D.) G. Mendioroz (R.) (in
It.)

Brussels     Monnaie       Nov. 29, 1858  Vandenhaute (G.) Meunot (M.) Wicart
(D.) S. Carman (R.) Depoitier (S.)
C. L. Hanssens cond. (in Fr.)

Cirque       Jan. 19, 1866  A. Sarolta (G.) E. Pancani (D.) F.
Cresci (R.) (in It.)

Ghent        Grand         Dec. 10, 1862  Mayer-Boulart (G.) H. Tallon (D.) S.
Carman (R.) T. Coulon (S.) (in Fr.)

Liége        Grand         Feb. 22, 1864

BRAZIL
Rio de        Lirico      Jan. 17, 1856 A. Charton-Demeur (G.) A. Ghioni
Janeiro       Fluminense                 (M.) Dufresne (D.) L. Walter (R.) S.
                                          L. Bouché (S.)

              Municipal   July 21, 1910 G. Bevignani (G.) E. Mazzi (M.) F.
                                         Constantino (D.) C. Galeffi (R.) A.
                                         Padovani cond.

Sao Paulo     Provisorio  Dec.?     1869 E. Bonacich (D.)

              Sao José    Apr. 29, 1876 A. Cortesi (G.) L. Canepa (M.) L.
                                         Lelmi (D.) G. Spalazzi (R.) G. Mi-
                                         randolo (S.)

              Municipal   Sep. 26, 1911 G. Pareto (G.) F. Perini (M.) A.
                                         Bonci (D.) T. Ruffo (R.) P. Ludikar
                                         (S.) E. Vitale cond.

BULGARIA
Sofia         Luxembouurg Aug. 13, 1895 A. Bottero (G.) G. Badarocco (D.)

CANADA
Edmonton      Empress     Jan. 21, 1919 Q. Mario (G.) G. Agostini (D.) M.
                                         Antola (R.)

              Opera       Oct. 16, 1964 C. Vallee (G.) K. Forrest (M.) P.
                                         Lorieau (D.) N. Bisson (R.) L.
                                         Lorieau (S.) J. Letourneau cond.

Montreal      Ac. de Mus. Jan.  6, 1883 E. Abbott (G.) Z. Seguin (M.) (in
                                         Eng.)

                          Sep. 20, 1894 Humphreys (G.) Fleming (M.) A. Mon-
                                         tegriffo (D.) G. Del Puente (R.)
                                         Viviani (S.) (in Ital.)

Toronto       Grand       May   2, 1890 P. L'Allemand (G.) Tomlinson (M.) F.
                                         Baster (D.) W. M. Mertens (R.) (in
                                         Eng.)

Vancouver     Opera House Jan.  5, 1898

              Opera       Mar.  8, 1962 R. Grist (G.) E. Bonazzi (M.) J.
                                         Alexander (D.) N. Bisson (R.) R.
                                         Cross (S.) M. Bernardi cond.

Winnipeg      Princess    Sep. 14, 1883 E. Abbott (G.) Z. Seguin (M.) V. Fa-
                                         brini (D.) G. Tagliapietra (R.) J.
                                         H. Rosewald cond. (in Eng.)

                          Dec. 19, 1916 E. Vaccari (G.) S. De Mette (M.) De
                                         Falco (D.) M. Antola (R.) P. De Bia-
                                         si (S.) (in Ital.)

CHILE
Santiago      Republica   June?     1857 I. Edelvira (G.) U. Devoti (D.) G.
                                         C. Casanova (R.)

              Municipal   Sep. 21, 1857 I. Edelvira (G.) L. Guglielmini (D.)

Valparaiso    Victoria    Feb. 27, 1862 O. Sconcia (G.) I. Martinez de Esca-
                                         lante (M.) B. Danieli (D.) A. Rossi-
                                         Ghelli (R.) G. Mirandola (S.)

CHINA
Shanghai      Lyceum      Jan. 10,  1880 Hirlemann (G.) F. Mancini (M.) E.
                                         Sbriscia (D.) G. Bergamaschi (R.) A.
                                         Bagagiolo (S.)

COLOMBIA
Bogota        Teatro      July 20,  1865 Bellini (G.) A. Bellini (M.) Sindic-
                                         ci (D.) E. Petrilli (R.) E. Bellini
                                         (S.)

CUBA
Havana        Tacon       Aug. 22,  1855 L. Caranti-Vita (G.) M. Tiberini
                                         (D.) L. Vita (R.)

Santiago                  Feb.?     1860

CZECHOSLOVAKIA
Bratislava                          1857

Brno          Stadt       Jan.  8,  1853 T. Titiens (G.) (in Ger.)

Prague        Ständiches  Feb.  5,  1853 L. von Bracht (G.) F. Steger (D.)
                                         Steinecke (R.) K. Schmidt (S.) Mil-
                                         dner cond. (in Ger.)

              Provisional Sep. 10,  1864 E. Ehrenberg (G.) J. Schwarze (R.)
                                         (in Czech)

              Neustädter  Aug. 15? 1882 E. Nevada (G.) A. Aramburo (D.) G.
                                         Vaselli (R.) E. Gasperini (S.) O.
                                         Bimboni cond. (in It.)

DENMARK
Copenhagen    Royal       Mar. 15,  1854 V. Gaziello-Brambilla (G.) A. Remo-
                                         rini (M.) T. Remorini (D.) G. Reina
                                         (R.) G. Mirandola (S.) W. Dahl cond.

                          Sep. 18,  1879 A. Schou (G.) Jastrau (D.) (in Dan.)

EGYPT
Alexandria    Europeo     Nov.      1854 C. Crespolani (G.) L. Rossetti-Boc-
                                         colini (M.) R. Bettazzi (D.) G. Sac-
                                         coni (R.) C. Boccolini (S.) E. Ebano
                                         cond.

Cairo         Khedivial   Nov.  1,  1869 G. Vitali (G.) L. Grossi (M.) E.
                                         Naudin (D.) C. Boccolini (R.) Pado-
                                         vani (S.) E. Muzio cond. (Inaugura-
                                         tion of the theatre)

FINLAND
Helsinki      Alexanders  Nov. 30,  1880 C. Bottarelli (G.) Bettini (M.) A.
                                         Brunetti (D.) M. Danisi (R.) (in
                                         It.)

              National    Apr. 24,  1917 (in Fin.)

FRANCE
Bastia                    Jan.?     1855 C. Cavini (G.) G. Scardovi (D.) E.
                                         Ricci (R.) P. Vannucci (S.)

Lyon          Grand       Jan.      1855 I. Rey-Balla (G.) Bourgeois (M.)
                                         Bovier-Lapierre (D.) J. V. Ismael
                                         (R.) Marthieu (S.)

Marseille      Grand       May  13, 1860 Meillet (G.) Elmire (M.) E. Armandi
                                         (D.) J. V. Ismael (R.) G. Depassio
                                         (S.)

Nice           Regio       Sep. 30, 1854 C. Forti-Babacci (G.) A. Fontanesi
                                         (M.) P. Scotti (D.) G. Marra (R.) S.
                                         Grandi (S.) G. Bregazzo cond.

Paris          Italien     Jan. 19, 1857 E. Frezzolini (G.) M. Alboni (M.)
                                         Mario (D.) G. Corsi (R.) G. F. An-
                                         gelini (S.) G. Bottesini cond.

               Lyrique     Dec. 24, 1863 C. de Maesen (G.) Dubois (M.) J. S.
                                         Monjauze (D.) J. V. Ismael (R.) L.
                                         E. Wartel (S.) (in Fr.)

               Opéra       Feb. 27, 1885 G. Krauss (G.) Richard (M.) Dereims
                                         (D.) J. Lassalle (R.) A. Boudoures-
                                         que (S.) (in Fr.)

Rouen          des Arts    May  13, 1861 (in Fr.)

                           Aug.     1864 M. Marinangeli (G.) B. Danieli (D.)
                                         L. Guadagnini (R.) (in It.)

GERMANY
Berlin         Victoria    Feb.  4, 1860 R. De Ruda (G.) D. Artôt (M.) E.
                                         Carrion (D.) E. Delle Sedie (R.) H.
                                         Brémond (S.) (in It.)

               Hofoper     Nov.  5, 1860 V. Lorini (G.) Z. Trebelli (M.) G.
                                         Galvani (D.) M. Zacchi (R.) (in It.)

                           Mar. 15, 1865 P. Lucca (G.) C. Adams (D.) F. Betz
                                         (R.) (in Ger.)

Braunschweig   Hoftheater  Jan. 25, 1854 (in It.)

Breslau        Stadt       Mar. 15, 1859

Cologne        Stadt       Oct. 30, 1863 (in Ger.)

                           July  4, 1864 G. Vitali (G.) R. Baragli (D.) T.
                                         Sterbini (R.) (in It.)

Darmstadt      Hoftheater  Dec. 30, 1857 (in Ger.)

Dresden        Hoftheater  Apr. 14, 1864 (in It.)

                           Dec.  3, 1874 (in Ger.)

Frankfurt      Stadt       July 24, 1859 Morska (G.) Medal (M.) Brunner (D.)
                                         Pichler (R.) Abiger (S.) (in Ger.)

                           July 19, 1860 (in It.)

Hamburg        Stadt       Sep. 24, 1855 Kreysel (G.) Eppich (D.) Haimer (R.)
                                         (in Ger.)

Hannover       Hoftheater  Feb. 25, 1853 (in Ger.)

Kassel         Hoftheater  Sep. 17, 1871 (in Ger.)

Königsberg     Stadt       Feb. 25, 1859 (in Ger.)

Leipzig        Stadt         Jan. 11, 1871 (in Ger.)

                             May 11, 1872 D. Artôt (G.) L. Marin (D.) M. Pa-
                                          dilla (R.) (in It.)

Mainz          Stadt         Jan. 1, 1862 (in Ger.)

Munich         Hoftheater    Apr. 20, 1854 Rettisch (G.) Brandes (D.) A. Kin-
                                           dermann (S.)

Nürnberg       Stadt         Jan. 25, 1866 (in Ger.)

Stuttgart      Hoftheater    Jan. 30, 1853 (in Ger.)

Weimar         Hoftheater    Jan. 25, 1863 R. von Miller (G.) Meffert (D.) F.
                                           von Milder (R.) (in Ger.)

GREAT BRITAIN
Belfast        Th. Royal     Jan.     1869 (in Eng.)

Birmingham     Prince        Summer   1867 F. Lancia (G.) W. Parkinson (D.) C.
               of Wales                    Durand (R.) (in Eng.)

               Th. Royal     Oct. 19, 1876 A. Valleria (G.) Bignami (M.) L.
                                           Gillandi (D.) G. Del Puente (R.)
                                           Broccolini (S.) G. Li Calsi cond.
                                           (in It.)

Bristol        Th. Royal     Dec. 18, 1875 G. Del Puente (R.)

Edinburgh      Th. Royal     Mar.  5, 1869 J. van Zandt (G.) S. Scalchi (M.)
                                           Chelli (D.) C. Santley (R.) A. Foli
                                           (S.) L. Arditi cond. (in It.)

Glasgow        Th. Royal     Feb. 12, 1869 J. van Zandt (G.) S. Scalchi (M.) C.
                                           Bulterini (D.) C. Santley (R.) A.
                                           Foli (S.) L. Arditi cond.

Leeds          Amphi-        Oct.  4, 1867 F. Lancia (G.) C. Zerbini (M.) W.
               theatre                     Parkinson (D.) C. Durand (R.) G.
                                           Cooke cond. (in Eng.)

                             Mar. 12, 1877 (in It.)

Liverpool      Th. Royal     Aug. 18, 1857 A. Bosio (G.) C. Nantier-Didiée (M.)
                                           P. Neri-Baraldi (D.) G. Ronconi (R.)
                                           J. Tagliafico (S.) A. Mellon cond.

London         Covent        May 14, 1853 A. Bosio (G.) C. Nantier-Didiée (M.)
               Garden                      Mario (D.) G. Ronconi (R.) J. Ta-
                                           gliafico (S.) M. Costa cond. (in
                                           It.)

                             Oct. 20, 1909 B. Miranda (G.) M. Brown (M.) W.
                                           Wheatley (D.) A. Turner (R.) A.
                                           Winckworth (S.) E. Goossens cond.
                                           (in Eng.)

Manchester     Th. Royal     Aug. 24, 1857 A. Bosio (G.) C. Nantier-Didiée (M.)
                                           P. Neri-Baraldi (D.) G. Ronconi (R.)
                                           J. Tagliafico (S.) A. Mellon cond.

Sheffield        Th. Royal     Mar. 18, 1857 R. Isaacs (G.) F. Reeves (M.) E. Ga-
                                             ler (D.) Borrani (R.) (First time in
                                             English)

GREECE
Athens           Royal         Oct. 28, 1853 A. Angelini-Cantalamessa (G.) G. Or-
                                             tolani (D.) C. Morelli-Condolmieri
                                             (R.) G. Capriles (S.) F. Zecchini
                                             cond.

Corfu            San Giacomo Dec. 25, 1852 M. Mariotti (G.) T. Bruno (M.) G.
                                             Giorgetti (D.) T. Pieri (R.) O. Lari
                                             (S.) Romanini cond.

GUATEMALA
Guatemala        Carrera       Feb.?    1861 C. Cairoli (G.) A. Macaferri (D.) D.
City                                         Lorini (R.)

HAWAI
Honolulu         Royal         Mar.  3, 1913 R. Vicarino (G.) F. Pineschi (M.) G.
                 Hawaian                     Agostini (D.) M. Giovacchini (R.)

HONG KONG
Hong Kong        Lusitano      June 12, 1867 M. Bouché (G.) M. Veralli (M.) P.
                                             Errani (D.) G. Colombo (R.) G. Reina
                                             (S.)

HUNGARY
Budapest         Nemzeti       Dec. 18, 1852 L. Gino (G.) P. Korcsek (M.) G. Maz-
                 Szinház                     zi (D.) M. Füredi (R.) K. Köszeghy
                                             (S.) F. Erkel cond. (in Hung.)

                               July  7, 1857 G. Medori (G.) E. Carrion (D.) A. De
                                             Bassini (R.) (in It.)[43]

                 Operaház      July 16, 1885 H. Bély (G.) G. Perotti (D.) J. Man-
                                             heit (R.) (in Hung.)

INDIA
Bombay           Grant Rd.     Jan. 26, 1866 A. Jackson (G.) M. Veralli (M.) P.
                                             Errani (D.) G. Colombo (R.) N. Re-
                                             bottaro (S.)

Calcutta         Opera House Jan. 21, 1868 R. Vielli-Villa (G.) A. Mazzucco
                                             (M.) T. Villa (D.) A. Grandi (R.) A.
                                             Melchiori cond.

INDONESIA
Batavia          T. Batavie    June 14, 1869 C. Ghirlanda-Tortolini (G.) G. Fer-
                                             rari-Pocoleri (M.) T. Villa (D.) L.
                                             Magnani (R.) E. Gasperini (S.)

IRELAND
Cork             Th. Royal     Dec. 26, 1867 F. Lancia (G.) C. Zerbini (M.) W.
                                             Parkinson (D.) C. Durand (R.) (in
                                             Eng.)

                               Apr. 24, 1877 E. Howson (G.) G. Vizzani (D.) (in
                                             It.)

---

   43. Conati lists a performance in Italian on or about Mar. 10, 1855 which could not be
confirmed.

Dublin       Th. Royal   Aug.  4, 1857 A. Bosio (G.) C. Nantier-Didiée (M.)
                                       P. Neri-Baraldi (D.) G. Ronconi (R.)
                                       J. Tagliafico (S.) A. Mellon cond.

ISRAEL
Jerusalem                Oct. 30, 1923 (in Heb.)

Tel Aviv     Habimah     Sep. 27, 1949 (in Heb.)

ITALY
Alessandria  Municipale  Oct.  7, 1854 G. Beltramelli (G.)  P. Duclout (M.)
                                       A. Agresti (D.) D. Mattioli (R.) F.
                                       Pons (S.)

Ancona       Muse        Apr. 19, 1854 E. Scotta (G.) A. Agostini (M.) C.
                                       Negrini (D.) E. Crivelli (R.) F.
                                       Varani (S.) G. Banchi cond.

Ascoli       Ventidio    Oct. 20? 1852 K. Evers (G.)  L. Rossetti-Boccolini
Piceno       Basso                     (M.) F. Varesi (R.) A. Dolcibene
                                       (S.)

Bari         Piccinni    Apr.  6, 1854 M. Zenoni (G.) A. Oliva-Pavani (D.)
                                       G. Sansone (R.)

             Petruzzelli Mar.  6, 1906 B. Morello (G.) G. Giaconia  (M.) I.
                                       Cristalli (D.) O. Benedetti (R.) N.
                                       De Angelis (S.) G. Polacco cond.

Bergamo      Riccardi    Sep.  3, 1851 M. Gazzaniga (G.) C. Semiglia (M.)
                                       C. Negrini (D.) F. Gorin (R.) F.
                                       Pons (S.)

Bologna      Comunale    Dec. 26, 1852 V. Boccabadati (G.) I. Secci-Corsi
                                       (M.) A. Giuglini (D.) F. Massiani
                                       (R.) F. Dall'Asta (S.) G. Manetti
                                       cond.

Brescia      Grande      Aug.  6, 1853 A. Ortolani-Brignoli (G.) T. Rambo-
                                       sio (M.) L. Graziani (D.) F. Colini
                                       (R.) F. Dalla Costa (S.)

Busseto      Verdi       Aug. 15, 1868 E. Berini (G.) P. Gaggiotti (M.) A.
                                       Prudenza (D.) Z. Bertolasi (R.) C.
                                       Zucchelli  (S.)  G.  Bassoli  cond.
                                       (Inauguration of the theatre)

Cagliari     Civico      Sep. 30, 1856 G. Sperati-Coscia (G.) M. Zai (M.)
                                       C. Scannavino (D.) C. Melzi (R.) G.
                                       Marchisio (S.)

Carpi        Comunale    Aug. 11, 1861 E. Fioretti (G.) G. Flori (M.) P.
                                       Mongini (D.) G. Guicciardi (R.) G.
                                       Capponi (S.) G. Bustini cond. (In-
                                       auguration of the theatre)

Catania      Comunale    Mar.?    1853 E. Lipparini (G.) A. Remorini (M.)
                                       L. Ferrari-Stella (D.) P. Giorgi-
                                       Pacini (R.) A. Zoboli (S.) M. Pappa-
                                       lardo cond.

             Bellini     May  25, 1897 A. Campagnoli (G.) M. Zivener (M.)
                                       S. Panbianchi (D.) A. Modesti (R.)
                                       E. Ciccolini (S.) O. Anselmi cond.

| Chieti | San Ferdinando | Apr. 21, 1855 | A. Mollo (G.) L. Bernabei (D.) E. Ricci (R.) |
|--------|----------------|---------------|---------------------------------------------|
| Cremona | Concordia | Dec. 31, 1853 | A. Rebussini (G.) A. Zamperini (M.) E. Pellegrini (D.) F. Massiani (R.) F. Dalla Costa (S.) |
| Faenza | Comunale | July 24, 1852 | K. Evers (G.) I. Ferlotti (M.) S. Malvezzi (D.) G. Corsi (R.) C. Nanni (S.) G. Manetti cond. |
| Fermo | Aquila | Aug. 14, 1853 | T. Brambilla (G.) L. Rossetti (M.) G. Pardini (D.) F. Giannini (R.) G. De Lorenzi (S.) A. Marziali cond. |
| Ferrara | Comunale | Apr. 18, 1853 | V. Boccabadati (G.) I. Secci-Corsi (M.) P. Mongini (D.) F. Coliva (R.) P. Baroncini (S.) G. C. Ferrarini cond. |
| Fiume | Civico | Oct. 1852 | M. Sulzer (G.) H. Sulzer (M.) G. Petrovich (D.) A. Ottaviani (R.) |
| Florence | Pergola | Mar. 21, 1852 | A. Albertini (G.) G. Bregazzi (M.) G. Landi (D.) F. Gorin (R.) G. Euzet (S.) A. Biagi cond. |
| Forli | Comunale | July 6, 1853 | C. Alaimo (G.) C. Croci (M.) G. Landi (D.) G. B. Bencich (R.) F. Varani (S.) L. Viviani cond. |
| Genoa | Carlo Felice | Dec. 25, 1852 | E. Scotta (G.) C. Biscottini-Fiorio (M.) P. Mongini (D.) F. Cresci (R.) G. Carbonell (S.) A. Mariani cond. |
| Livorno | Floridi | Aug. 4, 1852 | T. De Giuli-Borsi (G.) I. Secci-Corsi (M.) C. Baucardé (D.) G. Ferri (R.) C. Dalla Costa (S.) L. Vannuccini cond. |
| Lucca | Giglio | Sep. 11, 1852 | E. Marcolini (G.) C. Merli (M.) P. Cecchi (D.) A. Rossi (R.) A. Balderi (S.) L. Vannuccini cond. |
| Lugo | Rossini | Sep.? 1856 | G. Beltramelli (G.) A. Agostini (M.) C. Liverani (D.) P. Baraldi (R.) |
| Mantua | Sociale | Mar. 28, 1853 | R. Gariboldi-Bassi (G.) T. Chini (M.) B. Massimiliani (D.) F. Massiani (R.) F. Dalla Costa (S.) |
| Messina | Sant' Elisabetta | Nov. 12, 1853 | M. Arrigotti (G.) L. Schieroni-Nulli (M.) G. Fedor (D.) L. Walter (R.) Lazzari (S.) |
| Milan | La Scala | Jan. 18, 1853 | A. Anglés-Fortuni (G.) G. Brambilla-Marulli (M.) E. Carrion (D.) G. Corsi (R.) A. Rodas (S.) E. Cavallini cond. |
| Modena | Comunale | Apr. 3, 1853 | M. Lotti della Santa (G.) G. Brambilla-Marulli (M.) L. Graziani (D.) F. Cresci (R.) P. Vialetti (S.) A. Sighicelli cond. |

Verdi

| | | | |
|---|---|---|---|
| Naples | Nuovo | Oct. 1, 1853 | L. Escott (G.) C. Cetroné (M.) G. Piccinnini (D.) R. Mastriani (R.) A. Zoboli (S.) M. Di Natale cond. |
| | San Carlo | Mar. 1, 1855 | G. Medori (G.) M. Zenoni (M.) E. Carrion (D.) F. Coletti (R.) M. Arati (S.) A. Farelli cond. |
| Novara | Coccia | Nov. 7, 1855 | C. Crémont (G.) R. Pozzi (M.) V. Sarti (D.) F. Steller (R.) G. Gazzone (S.) A. Cremaschi cond. |
| Padua | Nuovo | June 26, 1852 | M. Gazzaniga (G.) R. Mirate (D.) G. B. Bencich (R.) A. Rodas (S.) |
| Palermo | Carolino | Feb. 22, 1853 | N. De Roissi (G.) A. Orlandi (M.) A. Dall'Armi (D.) F. Colini (R.) C. Nanni (S.) A. Lo Casto cond. |
| | Massimo | Apr. 2, 1901 | R. Pinkert (G.) G. Giaconia (M.) G. Anselmi (D.) G. M. Sammarco (R.) G. Tisci-Rubini (S.) R. Ferrari cond. |
| Parma | Regio | Dec. 26, 1852 | L. Bendazzi-Secchi (G.) R. Luchini (M.) B. Massimiliani (D.) G. Fiori (R.) L. Bianchi (S.) N. De Giovanni cond. |
| Pavia | Condominio | Apr. 14, 1855 | C. Mongini-Stecchi (G.) T. Ghini (M.) G. Giorgetti (D.) F. Massiani (R.) B. Cervini (S.) |
| Perugia | Morlacchi | July 28, 1855 | T. De Giuli-Borsi (G.) I. Secci-Corsi (M.) G. Bettini (D.) G. Corsi (R.) G. F. Angelini (S.) N. De Giovanni cond. |
| Piacenza | Municipale | Dec. 26, 1853 | T. Pozzi-Montegazza (G.) T. Ghini (M.) A. Errani (D.) G. Zambellini (R.) G. Marchisio (S.) G. Jona cond. |
| Pisa | Ravvivati | Dec. 26? 1853 | E. Scotta (G.) P. Neri-Baraldi (D.) E. Fagotti (R.) L. Vannuccini cond. |
| Ravenna | Alighieri | Apr. 23, 1853 | A. Albertini (G.) G. Bregazzi (M.) P. Neri-Baraldi (D.) R. Ferlotti (R.) P. Sottovia (S.) G. Nostini cond. |
| Reggio Emilia | Comunale | Apr. 26, 1854 | V. Boccabadati (G.) C. Guerrini (M.) C. Baucardé (D.) G. Fiori (R.) M. Ghini (S.) G. Tebaldi cond. |
| Rome | Argentina | Sep. 27, 1851 | K. Evers (G.) C. Biscottini-Fiorio (M.) C. Baucardé (D.) F. Coletti (R.) N. Benedetti (S.) E. Terziani cond. |
| | Costanzi | Nov. 19, 1881 | G. Gargano (G.) T. Scarlatti-Macaferri (M.) R. Stagno (D.) S. Athos-Caldani (R.) L. Fradelloni (S.) A. Pomé cond. |

Rovigo          Sociale      Oct. 15, 1853 E.  Scotta (G.)  T.  Ghini  (M.)  G.
                                          Landi (D.) G. Fiori (R.) A. Dolci-
                                          bene (S.) D. Tosarini cond.

Siena           Rinnovati    July 20? 1853 V. Boccabadati (G.) B. Massimiliani
                                          (D.) F. Cresci (R.)

Sinigaglia      Comunale     July 17, 1852 F. Salvini-Donatelli (G.) H. Sulzer
                                          (M.) L. Graziani (D.) F. Varesi (R.)
                                          G. Mitrovich (S.) G. C. Ferrarini
                                          cond.

Spoleto         Nobile       Dec. 26? 1856 F. Massimiliani (G.) A. Gresti (M.)
                                          O. Graziani (D.) D. Bertani (R.)

Trento          Sociale      May  28, 1853 S. Peruzzi (G.) C. Guerrini (M.) B.
                                          Massimiliani (D.) F. Varesi (R.) A.
                                          Dolcibene (S.)

Treviso         Onigo        Sep. 23, 1851 M. Gresti (G.) T. Ghini (M.) E. Mar-
                                          cucci (D.) F. Varesi (R.) A. Dolci-
                                          bene (S.) G. Mares cond.

Trieste         Grande       Nov. 15, 1851 A. Albertini (G.) L. Rossetti (M.)
                                          S. Malvezzi (D.) G. Ferri (R.) C.
                                          Nanni (S.) G. A. Scaramelli cond.

Turin           Regio        Feb. 17, 1852 T. De Giuli-Borsi (G.) O. Mongé (M.)
                                          C. Baucardé (D.) G. Ferri (R.) G. B.
                                          Cornago (S.) G. Ghebart cond.

Udine           Sociale      July 23, 1853 M. Lotti della Santa (G.) T. Ghini
                                          (M.) R. Mirate (D.) G. Corsi (R.) C.
                                          Dalla Costa (S.)

Urbino          Raffaele     Aug. 20, 1853 N. Barbieri-Thiollier (G.) C. Croci
                Sanzio                     (M.) G. Landi (D.) G. B. Bencich
                                          (R.) F. Varani (S.)

Verona          Filarmonico Dec. 26, 1851 E. Scotta (G.) T. Ghini (M.) R. Mi-
                                          rate (D.) F. Varesi (R.) A. Dolci-
                                          bene (S.)

Vicenza         Eretenio     Jan. 19, 1853 L. Bianchi (G.) C. Rosati (M.) L.
                                          Ferrari-Stella (D.) F. Coliva (R.)
                                          A. Escudier (S.)

Viterbo         Unione       Aug.  4, 1855 V. Boccabadati (G.) Z. Sbriscia (M.)
                                          E. Naudin (D.) F. Colini (R.) R. La-
                                          terza (S.) (Inauguration of the
                                          theatre)

JAPAN
Tokyo           Imperial     Sep. 24, 1921 Kasanskaya (G.) (in Rus.)

                             Jan. 27, 1923 (in It.)

JUGOSLAVIA
Belgrade        National     July  6, 1912 L. Pieroni (G.) A. De Roma (M.) O.
                                          Santarelli (D.) O. Mieli (R.) A.
                                          Mauceri (S.) Giovanelli cond. (in
                                          It.)

|             |              | Feb.  | 9, 1921 | S. Drauselj (G.) V. Turinski (D.) G. Jurjenev (R.) (in Serb.) |
|-------------|--------------|-------|---------|---|
| Ljubljana   | Stanovskem   | Dec. 16, 1855 | | |
| Zagreb      | National     | May   | 1858 | A. Fumagalli (G.) A. Marchetti (D.) Cellini (R.) (in It.) |
|             |              | Dec. 13, 1873 | | (in Croat.) |
| Zara        | Nobile       | Oct. 28, 1854 | | A. Boccabadati (G.) Manzoni (M.) C. Scannavino (D.) R. Colmenghi (R.) Ragosini (S.) (in It.) |
| LATVIA      |              |       |         | |
| Riga        | Municipal    | July  | 1861 | R. Laborde (G.) R. Baragli (D.) F. Briani (R.) (in It.) |
|             | National     | Mar. 2, 1920 | | B. Valle cond. (in Let.) |
| LITHUANIA   |              |       |         | |
| Kaunas      | Imperial     | Dec. 13? 1906 | | G. Wermez (G.) Balboni (D.) E. Pignataro (R.) (in It.) |
|             | National     | Nov. 3, 1921 | | (in Lith.) |
| Vilnius     | Municipal    | Mar. 7, 1898 | | S. Aifos (G.) Pagnoni (M.) Massimi (D.) (in It.) |
| MALTA       |              |       |         | |
| La Valletta | Manuel       | Jan. 8, 1853 | | C. Rapazzini (G.) Bodino (M.) L. Stefani (D.) G. Sansone (R.) L. Del Riccio (S.) |
| MEXICO      |              |       |         | |
| Guadalajara | Degollado    | May ? | 1858 | A. Cortesi (G.) G. Casali-Campagna (M.) E. Bianchi (D.) A. Ottaviani (R.) C. Fattori cond. |
| Mexico City | Nacional     | Nov. 7, 1856 | | G. Landi (G.) L. Stefani (D.) E. Barili (R.) E. Casali (S.) C. Fattori cond. |
| Vera Cruz   | Principal    | Mar.? | 1858 | A. Cortesi (G.) A. Volpini (D.) A. Ottaviani (R.) C. Fattori cond. |
| MONACO      |              |       |         | |
| Monte Carlo | Salle Garnier | Jan. 29, 1881 | | A. Patti (G.) E. Stuarda (M.) E. Nicolini (D.) Berardi (R.) Ampici (S.) R. Accursi cond. |
| NETHERLANDS |              |       |         | |
| Amsterdam   | Stadt        | Nov. 13, 1860 | | N. De Roissi (G.) Baldi (M.) A. Dall'Armi (D.) E. Crivelli (R.) G. Capponi (S.) N. Bassi cond. (in It.) |
| NEW ZEALAND |              |       |         | |
| Auckland    | His Majesty's | Jan. 5, 1916 | | E. Gonsalez (G.) N. Russ (M.) V. Lois (D.) L. Filippini (R.) G. Cacciali (S.) G. Gonsalez cond. |
| Dunedin     | Princess     | Sep. 16, 1864 | | L. Escott (G.) H. Squires (D.) H. Wharton (R.) |

Wellington     Grand        Dec. 15, 1916 E. Gonsalez (G.) N. Russ (M.)

NORWAY
Oslo           Christiana   June  8, 1868 M. Calisto (G.) Thoresen (M.) G.
                                           Bentami (D.) A. Pantaleoni (S.)

PERU
Lima           Principal    Aug.?    1863 O. Sconcia (G.) R. De Filatoff (M.)
                                           B. Massimiliani (D.) A. Rossi-Ghelli
                                           (R.) Lari (S.)

PHILIPPINES
Manila         Principe     Nov.?    1867 L. De Ponte (G.)
               Alfonso

POLAND
Cracow         Imperial     Dec.  3, 1856 (in Ger.)

Lwov           Szarbek      Sep.  3, 1853 Schreiber-Kirchberger (G.) Haimer
                                           (R.) (in Ger.)

Warsaw         Wielki       Nov.  8, 1853 M. Spezia-Aldighieri (G.) F. Ciaffei
                                           (D.) L. Buti (R.) (in It.)

PORTUGAL
Lisbon         Sao Carlos   Jan. 29, 1854 A. Anglés-Fortuni (G.) C. Miraglia
                                           (D.) O. Bartolini (R.) L. Bianchi
                                           (S.)

Oporto         Sao Joao     Nov.     1853 L. Giordani (G.) 1. Alba (M.) Bi-
                                           saccia (D.) C. Bartolucci (R.)

ROMANIA
Bucharest      Nacional     Mar.     1854 E. Kenneth (G.) Turina (M.) G. Musi-
                                           ani (D.) F. Giannini (R.) G. Segri-
                                           Segarra (S.)

Iasi           Teatrul      Mar. 26, 1854 L. Gino (G.) A. Prudenza (D.) V.
                                           Sermattei (R.)

RUSSIA
Kharkov        Municipal    May?     1864 C. Noel-Guidi G.) A. Gottardi (D.)
                                           F. Giannini (R.) (in It.)

Moscow         Bolshoi      Sep. 27, 1856 A. Bosio (G.) E. De Meric (M.) G.
                                           Bettini (D.) A. De Bassini (R.) E.
                                           Baveri cond. (in It.)

Odessa         Municipal    June?    1854 F. Gordosa (G.) E. Schiapié (M.) T.
                                           Palmieri (D.) R. Ferlotti (R.) (in
                                           It.)

St.            Imperial     Feb. 12, 1853 F. Maray (G.) E. De Meric (M.) Mario
Petersburg                                 (D.) G. Ronconi (R.) J. Tagliafico
                                           (S.) E. Baveri cond. (in It.)

                            Nov. 18, 1878 (in Rus.)

Tbilisi        Imperial     Jan.?    1854 M. Roffi (G.) A. Vasoli (M.) P. Fis-
                                           chietti (D.) G. Ramoni (R.) P. Vichi
                                           (S.) G. Barberi cond. (in It.)

SINGAPORE
Singapore      Town Hall    Aug.  7, 1880 M. Milani-Vela (G.) F. Boganini (D.)
                                           G. Bergamaschi (R.) M. Vela cond.

SOUTH AFRICA
Capetown      Th. Royal    May    5, 1876  A. Brambilla (G.) Neri (M.) Cosmi
                                           (D.) Greco (R.) De Santis (S.)

Johannesburg  Amphi-       May   30, 1895  A. Scalera (G.) L. Rossi (D.) M. De
              theatre                      Padova (R.) A. Gautiero (S.) Peri-
                                           gozza cond.

SPAIN
Alicante      Principal    May   11, 1859  F. Pozzo (D.) L. Walter (R.)

Barcelona     Liceo        Dec.   3, 1853  A. Corbari (G.) A. Aguilò (M.) E.
                                           Irfré (D.) A. Superchi (R.) A. Rodas
                                           (S.)

Cadiz         Principal    Apr.      1853  M. Sulzer (G.) H. Sulzer (M.) B. Be-
                                           lart (D.) A. Superchi (R.) V. Barba
                                           (S.)

Granada       Principal    June?     1853  M. Sulzer (G.) H. Sulzer (M.) B. Be-
                                           lart (D.) A. Superchi (R.) A. Rodas
                                           (S.)

Madrid        Real         Oct. 18, 1853   A. Basseggio (G.) C. Biscottini-
                                           Florio (M.) P. Mongini (D.) F. Va-
                                           resi (R.) G. De Baillou (S.) J.
                                           Skoczdopole cond.

Malaga        Liceo        Oct. 25, 1853   R. Giordano (G.) D. Bertani (R.)

Palma de      Coliseo      Autumn    1855  C. Crescimano (G.)
Mallorca

Seville       San          May   21, 1853  J. Gassier (G.) G. Sinico (D.) L.
              Fernando                     Gassier (R.)

Valencia      Principal    June      1854  C. Villò-Ramos (G.) S. Malvezzi (D.)
                                           F. Varesi (R.) G. De Baillou (S.)

Valladolid    Lope         May   24, 1859  C. Forti-Babacci (G.) I. Vitali (M.)
              da Vega                      M. Viani (D.) C. Morelli-Condolmieri
                                           (S.)

SWEDEN
Gotheborg                  Apr.      1868  (in It.)

Stockholm     Royal        June   3, 1861  F. Andrée (G.) G. Lublin (M.) W. D.
                                           Richard (D.) G. Sandström (R.) A.
                                           Willman (S.) (in Swed.)

              Mindre       Oct. 23, 1868   Z. Dalti (G.) A. L. Cary (M.) G.
                                           Bentami (D.) G. Mendioroz (R.) T.
                                           Coulon (S.) (in It.)

SWITZERLAND
Basel         Stadt        Jan. 31, 1861   (in Ger.)

                           June   9, 1926  M. Gentile (G.) E. De Muro Lomanto
                                           (D.) C. Morelli (R.) F. Autori (S.)
                                           A. Lucon cond. (In It.)

Geneva        Grand        Mar. 21, 1862   Alrit (G.) Alary-Peytavit (D.) Ramo-
                                           nat (R.) (in Fr.)

Lugano          Sociale       Sep. 27, 1870 Coriolano (G.) Badalucchi (D.) Sac-
                                            chetti (R.)

Zürich          Stadt         Mar.  2, 1863 R. de Ruda (G.) Götte (D.) Rosner
                                            (R.) (in Ger.)

                              May  29, 1916 G. Finzi-Magrini (G.) R. Ciaroff
                                            (D.) E. Giraldoni (R.) G. Armani
                                            cond. (in It.)

TURKEY
Constan-        Naum          Feb. 14, 1854 G. Beltramelli (G.) G. Bregazzi (M.)
tinople                                     C. Liverani (D.) D. Mattioli (R.) E.
                                            Manfredi (S.)

UNITED STATES
Baltimore       Holliday      Dec. 21, 1860 P. Colson (G.) A. Phillips (M.) G.
                Street                       Sbriglia (D.) F. Gnone (R.) N.
                                            Barili (S.)

Boston          Boston Th.    June  8, 1855 A. Bertucca (G.) F. Vestvali (M.) B.
                                            Bolcioni (D.) A. Amodio (R.)

Brooklyn        Ac. of Mus.   Mar.  5, 1861 C. L. Kellogg (G.) G. Stigelli (D.)
                                            G. Ferri (R.) E. Muzio cond.

Chicago         McVicker's    Feb. 26, 1859 C. De Wildhorst (G.) A. Patti-Stra-
                                            kosch (M.) H. Squires (D.) E. Barili
                                            (R.) M. Strakosch cond.

                Auditorium    Nov. 25, 1891 E. Albani (G.) S. Scalchi (M.) F.
                                            Valero (D.) E. Camera (R.) J. Vin-
                                            che (S.)

                Lyric         Nov. 12, 1955 T. Stich-Randall (G.) M. Dunn (M.)
                                            J. Bjoerling (D.) T. Gobbi (R.) W.
                                            Wildermann (S.) N. Rescigno cond.

Cincinatti      Pike's        Sep.  2, 1859 James (G.) G. Sbriglia (D.) F. Gnone
                                            (R.) N. Barili (S.) A. Torriani
                                            cond.

                Opera         July  4, 1921 M. Passmore (G.) E. de Sellem (M.)
                                            S. Sciaretti (D.) M. Valle (R.) P.
                                            Quintana (S.) R. Lyford cond.

Dallas          Op. House     Jan. 26, 1910 I. De Frate (G.) Bugamelli (M.) J.
                                            Nadal (D.) Maggi (R.) V. Viola (S.)
                                            F. Guerrieri cond.

                Opera         Nov.  5, 1966 M. Rinaldi (G.) B. Casoni (M.) C.
                                            Bergonzi (D.) P. Glossop (R.) N.
                                            Zaccaria (S.) N. Rescigno cond.

Detroit         Whitney's     Mar.  2, 1881 A. Valleria (G.) I. Campanini (D.)
                                            A. Faentini-Galassi (R.) L. Arditi
                                            cond.

Houston         Prince        Nov.  4, 1914 Vergeri (G.) Ceccotti (D.) M. Antola
                                            (R.) (First production traced)

                Grand Opera   Nov. 17, 1958 P. Stark (G.) F. Junger (M.) J.
                                            Alexander (D.) C. MacNeil (R.) N.
                                            Treigle (S.) W. Herbert cond.

Los Angeles   Grand        Feb. 10, 1885  E. Abbott (G.) (in Eng.)

              Theater      Oct. 19, 1897  C. Vicini (G.) A. Franco (M.) G.
                                          Agostini (D.) C. Cioni (R.) (in It.)

New Orleans   Crisp's      May  22, 1857  L. Caranti-Vita (G.) F. Vestvali
              Gaiety                      (M.) M. Tiberini (D.) L. Corradi-
                                          Setti (R.) (in It.)

              Opéra        Mar. 19, 1860  St. Urbain (G.) Mathieu (D.) Melchi-
                                          sédec (R.) (in Fr.)

New York      Ac. of Mus.  Feb. 19, 1855  A. Bertucca (G.) A. Patti-Strakosch
                                          (M.) B. Bolcioni (D.) E. Barili (R.)
                                          L. Rocco (S.) M. Maretzek cond.

                           Jan. 27, 1874  J. Van Zandt (G.) Z. Seguin (M.) J.
                                          Maas (D.) G. F. Hall (R.) H. Peakes
                                          (S.) F. Howson cond. (in Eng.)

              Stadt        Dec. 14, 1870  C. Bernard (D.) E. Vierling (R.) (in
                                          Ger.)

              Metro-       Nov. 16, 1883  M. Sembrich (G.) S. Scalchi (M.) R.
              politan                     Stagno (D.) L. Guadagnini (R.) F.
                                          Novara (S.) A. Vianesi cond.

Philadelphia  Ac. of Mus.  Jan. 25, 1858  A. De la Grange (G.) E. D'Angri (M.)
                                          P. Bignardi (D.) F. Taffanelli (R.)

                           Feb.  3, 1874  J. Van Zandt (G.) Z. Seguin (M.) J.
                                          Maas (D.) G. F. Hall (R.) (in Eng.)

St. Louis     Theater      Feb. 16, 1859  C. De Wildhorst (G.) A. Patti-Stra-
                                          kosch (M.) H. Squires (D.) E. Barili
                                          (R.)

San Francisco Maguire's    July  1, 1860  L. Escott (G.) Schwegerie (M.) H.
                                          Squires (D.) F. Lyster (R.) J. De
                                          Hage (S.)

              Opera        Oct.  8, 1923  Q. Mario (G.) D. Fernanda (M.) B.
                                          Gigli (D.) G. De Luca (R.) A. Didur
                                          (S.) G. Merola cond.

Washington    National     Jan.     1874  J. Van Zandt (G.) Z. Seguin (M.) J.
                                          Maas (D.) G. F. Hall (R.) H. Peakes
                                          (S.) (in Eng.) (First production
                                          traced)

URUGUAY
Montevideo    San Felipe   Aug. 18, 1855  S. Vera-Lorini (G.) B. Tati (M.) G.
                                          Comolli (D.) G. Cima (R.)

              Solis        Sep.  7, 1856  S. Vera-Lorini (G.) B. Tati (M.) G.
                                          Comolli (D.) G. Cima (R.)

VENEZUELA
Caracas       Teatro       June 15, 1858  A. Natali (G.) L. Giannoni (D.) F.
                                          Morelli-Ponti (R.)

              Municipale   Feb. 13, 1881  B. D'Aponte (G.) T. Mestres (M.) V.
                                          Grilli (D.) D. Farina (R.) G. Sam-
                                          pieri (S.) F. Rachelle cond.

18. IL TROVATORE-*Dramma* in four acts
Rome-Teatro Apollo-Jan. 19, 1853
Libretto by Salvadore Cammarano

| | |
|---|---|
| Leonora (L.) | Rosina Penco sop. |
| Azucena (A.) | Emilia Goggi mez. |
| Manrico (M.) | Carlo Baucardé ten. |
| Conte De Luna (D. L.) | Giovanni Guicciardi bar. |
| Ferrando (F.) | Arcangelo Balderi bass |
| Inez | Francesca Quadri sop. |
| Ruiz | Giuseppe Bazzoli ten. |
| Un Vecchio Zingaro | Raffaele Marconi bass |
| Un Messo | Luigi Fani ten. |
| | |
| Conductor | Emilio Angelini |
| Director | Giuseppe Verdi |

OTHER PREMIERES

ARGENTINA
Buenos Aires  Argentino    Jan.  4, 1855 I. Edelvira  (L.) M. Eboli  (A.)  L.
                                         Guglielmini  (M.) J. Casanova  (D.
                                         L.) J. V. Rivas cond.

              Ant. Colón  Apr. 29, 1857 S. Vera-Lorini  (L.) A.  Casaloni
                                         (A.) E. Tamberlick (M.) G. Cima (D.
                                         L.)

              Colón       Aug.  6, 1908 L. Crestani (L.) M. Verger (A.) A.
                                         Paoli (M.) G. Bellantoni (D. L.) B.
                                         Berardi (F.) A. Vigna cond.

AUSTRALIA
Adelaide      Victoria    Feb. 20, 1861 G.  Bianchi  (L.)   Harland  (A.) E.
                                         Bianchi  (M.) J. Gregg  (D.  L.) E.
                                         Grossi (F.) (in It.)

Brisbane      Mason's     July  8, 1865 L. Escott  (L.)  G. Hodson (A.) H.
                                         Squires (M.) H. Wharton (D. L.) (in
                                         It.)

Melbourne     Princess    Oct. 21, 1858 Carandini  (L.) J. Harland  (A.) La-
                                         glaise  (M.) E. Coulon  (D.  L.) (in
                                         It.)

Sydney        Prince      June 25, 1859 Carandini  (L.)  S.  Flower (A.)  W.
              of Wales                   Sherwin  (M.)  J. Gregg  (D. L.)  F.
                                         Howson (F.) (in  It.)

AUSTRIA
Graz          Stadt       Sep. 29, 1855 (in Ger.)

Linz          Landes      Oct. 12, 1857 (in Ger.)

Vienna        Kärntnertor May 11, 1854 L. Bendazzi-Secchi  (L.) E. De Meric
                                         (A.) G.  Bettini  (M.) G. Ferri  (D.
                                         L.) B.  Laura  (F.) K.  Eckert cond.
                                         (in It.)

              Dec. 20, 1859 R. Czillag  (L.) H. Sulzer  (A.)  G.
                                         Walter (M.) F. Hrabanek (D. L.) K.
                                         Mayerhofer  (F.) (in Ger.)

              Josephstadt Oct.  9, 1857 (in Ger.)

Hofoper        Sep. 21, 1869 L. Hahn (L.) E. Gindele (A.) G. Mül-
                             ler (M.) L. von Bignio (D. L.) (in
                             Ger.)

BELGIUM
Antwerp        Royal        Mar. 28, 1859 Roziès (L.) Renonville (A.) Jouard
                             (M.) Comte-Borchard (D. L.) Arnoldi
                             (F.) (in Fr.)

               Apr. 27, 1862 P. Vaneri (L.) A. Phillips (A.) G.
                             Galvani (M.) M. Zacchi (D. L.) L.
                             Agnesi (F.) (in It.)

Brussels       Monnaie      May 20, 1856 Vandenhaute (L.) Wicart (M.) S. Car-
                             man (D. L.) (in Fr.)

               Cirque       Apr. 14, 1860 V. Lorini (L.) C. Vietti (A.) G.
                             Galvani (M.) D. Squarcia (D. L.) (in
                             It.)

Ghent          Grand        Mar. 7, 1860 Isnard (L.) Hilaire (A.) Tallon (M.)
                             Bussine (D. L.) Zelger (F.) (in Fr.)

Liège          Grand        Apr. 24, 1859 Neulat-Chambon (L.) Ravisy (M.)
                             Bryon-Dongeval (D. L.) (in Fr.)

BRAZIL
Rio de         Fluminense   Sep. 7, 1854 A. Charton-Demeur (L.) A. Casaloni
Janeiro                      (A.) D. Labocetta (M.) G. Arnaud (D.
                             L.) S. L. Bouché (F.)

               Pedro II     July 1, 1871 G. Gasc (L.) I. Martinez de Esca-
                             lante (A.) L. Lelmi (M.) A. Celes-
                             tino (D. L.) J. Ordinas (F.)

               Municipal    Aug. 1, 1910 C. Gagliardi (L.) A. Luglia (A.)
                             G. De Tura (M.) C. Galeffi (D. L.)
                             A. Rossi (F.) A. Padovani cond.

Sao Paulo      Provisorio   Autumn 1874 E. Pezzoli (L.) M. Polonio (A.) G.
                             Limberti (M.) L. Barcena (D. L.) G.
                             Mirandola (F.) G. Giraudon cond.

               Municipal    Oct. 4, 1923 C. Muzio (L.) L. Bertana (A.) J.
                             O'Sullivan (M.) C. Galeffi (D. L.)
                             M. Fiore (F.) V. Bellezza cond.

BULGARIA
Sofia          Luxembourg   Aug. 12, 1895 Bottero (L.) (in It.)

               National     Jan. 17, 1914 (in Bulg.)

CANADA
Edmonton       Empire       Jan. 22, 1919 E. Wentworth (L.) D. Fernanda (M.)
                             G. Agostini (M.) J. Royer (D. L.) N.
                             Cervi (F.)

               Opera        Nov. 20, 1970 C. Carson (L.) L. Chookasian (A.) B.
                             Marti (M.) E. Sordello (D. L.) L.
                             Lishner (F.) R. Karp cond.

Montreal       Th. Royal    Oct. 19, 1858 A. Milner (L.) Holman (A.) Miranda
                             (M.) Guilmette (D. L.) (in Eng.)

|  | Nord-<br>heimer's | July 18, 1859 | C. Alaimo (L.) T. Parodi (A.) G.<br>Sbriglia (M.) F. Gnone (D. L.) N.<br>Barili (F.) A. Torriani cond. (in<br>It.) |
|---|---|---|---|
| Quebec | Music Hall | July 23, 1859 | C. Alaimo (L.) T. Parodi (A.) G.<br>Sbriglia (M.) F. Gnone (D. L.) N.<br>Barili (F.) A. Torriani cond. (in<br>It.) |
| Toronto | Royal<br>Lyceum | June 20, 1859 | A. Milner (L.) (in Eng.) |
|  |  | Aug. 4, 1859 | C. Alaimo (L.) T. Parodi (A.) G.<br>Sbriglia (M.) F. Gnone (D. L.) N.<br>Barili (F.) A. Torriani cond. (in<br>It.) |
| Vancouver | Opera House | Feb. 10, 1891 | Meislinger (L.) P. Clarke (M.) Stor-<br>mont (D. L.) (in Eng.) |
|  | Opera | Feb. 17, 1966 | E. Ross (L.) M. Horne (A.) B. Dal<br>Ponte (M.) C. Ludgin (D. L.) L.<br>Lishner (F.) H. Lewis cond. |
| Winnipeg | Princess | Sep. 15, 1883 | J. Rosenwald (L.) Seguin (A.) V.<br>Fabrini (M.) G. Tagliapietra (D. L.)<br>W. Broderick (F.) (In Eng.) |
| CHILE<br>Santiago | Republica | June 22, 1856 | I. Edelvira (L.) Amei (A.) L. Gu-<br>glielmini (M.) G. C. Casanova (D.<br>L.) |
|  | Municipal | Oct. 1857 | I. Edelvira (L.) S. Amic-Gazan (A.)<br>L. Guglielmini (M.) |
| Valparaiso | Victoria | Feb. 8, 1856 | M. de Ferretti (L.) R. Olivieri (A.)<br>E. Rossi-Guerra (M.) P. Ferretti (D.<br>L.) G. Mirandola (F.) |
| CHINA<br>Shanghai | Lyceum | Dec. 1879 | R. Genolini (L.) F. Mancini (A.) E.<br>Sbriscia (M.) G. Bergamaschi (D. L.)<br>A. Bagagiolo (F.) |
| COLOMBIA<br>Bogota | Teatro | 1858 | E. Rossi-Guerra (M.) |
| Medellin |  | Sep. 1893 | A. Conti-Foroni (L.) Sarruggia (A.)<br>Nicoli (M.) Bartolomasi (D. L.) |
| CUBA<br>Havana | Tacon | Aug. 11, 1855 | L. Caranti de Vita (L.) M. Caccia-<br>tori (A.) M. Tiberini (M.) L. Vita<br>(D. L.) |
| Santiago |  | Jan. 1858 | T. Parodi (L.) L. Vita (A.) A.<br>Macaferri (M.) |
| CZECHOSLOVAKIA<br>Bratislava |  | Oct. 18, 1855 | (in Ger.) |
| Brno |  | Aug. 1855 | (in Ger.) |

Prague      Ständisches July 19, 1856 Rotter (L.) Gunther (A.) F. Steger (M.) (in Ger.)

           Provisional June 30, 1861 E. Ehrenberg (L.) (in Czech)

                       July 3, 1864 C. Marchisio (L.) B. Marchisio (A.) A. Minetti (M.) M. Zacchi (D. L.) (in It.)

           National Apr. 29, 1885 E. Ehrenberg (L.)

DENMARK
Copenhagen     Royal Sep. 10, 1865 Michaeli (L.) Bournonville (A.) Jastrau (M.) Hansen (D. L.) (in Dan.)

           Casino Jan. 25, 1866 Sonnieri (L.) K. Morensi (A.) N. Andreef (M.) Giori (D. L.) (in Ital.)

EGYPT
Alexandria     Europeo Mar. ? 1855 C. Crespolani (L.) L. Rossetti-Boccolini (A.) R. Bettazzi (M.) G. Sacconi (D. L.) C. Boccolini (F.) E. Ebano cond.

Cairo                   Oct. 1863 E. Cortesi (L.) Cruciani (M.) Bentivoglio (D. L.)

           Khedivial Nov. 8? 1869 B. Merson-Ferrucci (L.) E. Grossi (A.) C. Bulterini (M.) O. Bartolini (D. L.) E. Muzio cond.

FINLAND
Helsinki                 July 6, 1862 (in Swed.)

           Arkadia Nov. 25, 1870 I. Basilier (L.) G. Fogelberg (M.) (in Fin.)

           Alexanders Dec. 4, 1880 A. Spaak (L.) Bettini (A.) A. Brunetti (M.) M. Danisi (D. L.) (in It.)

FRANCE
Bordeaux     Grand Apr. 27, 1858 Laget-Planterre (L.) Cornelis (A.) Koubly (M.) (in Fr.)

Lyon         Grand Apr. 2, 1857 S. Cruvelli (L.) Geisner (A.) Renard (M.) Vigourel (D. L.) (in Fr.)

Marseille     Grand Feb. 22, 1856 I. Rey-Balla (L.) Saunier (A.) Mathieu (M.) J. V. Ismael (D. L.) (in Fr.)

                  Oct. 1856 A. Charton-Demeur (L.) E. Armandi (M.) (in It.)

Nice         Regio Sep. 30, 1855 E. Kenneth (L.) E. Schiapié (A.) P. Chiesi (M.) G. Reina (D. L.) (in It.)

Paris        Italien Dec. 23, 1854 E. Frezzolini (L.) A. Borghi-Mamo (A.) C. Baucardé (M.) F. Graziani (D. L.) L. Gassier (F.) V. Bonetti cond. G. Verdi dir. (in It.)

|              |            |                |                                                                                                                                      |
|--------------|------------|----------------|--------------------------------------------------------------------------------------------------------------------------------------|
|              | Opéra      | Jan. 12, 1857  | P. Gueymard-Lauters (L.) A. Borghi-Mamo (A.) L. Gueymard (M.) M. Bonnehée (D. L.) P. Dérivis (F.) N. Girard cond. G. Verdi dir. (in Fr.) |
| Rouen        | des Arts   | Apr. 4, 1859   | Charry (L.) Micheau (A.) Ecarlat (M.)                                                                                                 |
| Toulouse     | Capitole   | Dec. 22, 1858  | Guesmard (L.) Bovier-Lapierre (M.)                                                                                                    |

GERMANY

|             |            |               |                                                                                                                          |
|-------------|------------|---------------|--------------------------------------------------------------------------------------------------------------------------|
| Berlin      | Hofoper    | Mar. 24, 1857 | L. Köster (L.) J. Wagner (A.) T. Formes (M.) J. Krause (D. L.) A. L. Fricke (F.) (in Ger.)                                |
|             | Victoria   | Mar. 10, 1860 | D. Artôt (L.) L. Abbadia (A.) E. Carrion (M.) E. Delle Sedie (D. L.) (in It.)                                             |
|             | Deutsche   | Oct. 22, 1964 | L. Price (L.) A. Lazzarini (A.) B. Prevedi (M.) G. Guelfi (D. L.) N. Zaccaria (F.) H. von Karajan cond. (in It.)          |
| Braunschweig | Hoftheater | Apr. 20, 1855 |                                                                                                                          |
| Breslau     | Stadt      | Mar. 5, 1858  | Palm-Spatzer (L.) Mik (A.) Herrmann (M.) Rieger (D. L.) (in Ger.)                                                         |
|             |            | May      1861 | V. Lorini (L.) Z. Tremelli (A.) G. Galvani (M.) M. Zacchi (D. L.) L. Orsini cond. (in It.)                                |
| Cologne     | Stadt      | Nov. 1, 1862  | (in Ger.)                                                                                                                |
|             |            | June 26, 1864 | G. Vitali (L.) E. De Meric (A.) R. Baragli (M.) T. Sterbini (D. L.) (in It.)                                              |
| Darmstadt   | Hoftheater | Dec. 2, 1855  | (in Ger.)                                                                                                                |
| Dresden     | Hoftheater | July 26, 1860 | J. Casimir-Ney (L.) J. Michalesi (A.) L. Schnorr von Carolsfeld (M.) Hardtmuth (D. L.) (in Ger.)                          |
|             |            | June     1861 | V. Lorini (L.) Z. Trebelli (A.) G. Galvani (M.) M. Zacchi (D. L.) (in It.)                                                |
| Frankfurt   | Stadt      | Feb. 4, 1858  | E. Capitain (L.) Kessenheimer (A.) F. Eppich (M.) Pichler (D. L.) Stern (F.) (in Ger.)                                    |
|             |            | June 29, 1860 | V. Lorini (L.) C. Pico-Vietti (A.) G. Galvani (M.) D. Squarcia (D. L.) L. Orsini cond. (in It.)                           |
| Hamburg     | Stadt      | Dec. 25, 1856 | (in Ger.)                                                                                                                |
|             |            | Nov.     1857 | M. Piccolomini (L.) A. Giuglini (M.) G. Aldighieri (D. L.) (in It.)                                                       |
| Hannover    | Hoftheater | Feb. 12, 1858 | Nottes (L.) Stögel (A.) A. Niemann (M.) Rudolf (D. L.) (in Ger.)                                                          |

Verdi 403

| Karlsruhe | Hoftheater | Oct. 15, 1857 (in Ger.) |
| Kassel | Hoftheater | Sep. 2, 1867 (in Ger.) |
| Königsberg | Stadt | Aug. 18, 1860 (in Ger.) |

Nov.    1861 C. Marchisio (L.) B. Marchisio (A.) E. Pancani (M.) (in It.)

Leipzig    Stadt    May 9, 1861 V. Lorini (L.) Z. Trebelli (A.) G. Galvani (M.) M. Zacchi (D. L.) (in It.)

May 29, 1862 Weidemann (D. L.) (in Ger.)

Mainz    Stadt    Sep. 3, 1857 Neumüller (L.) Bywater (A.) Messert (M.) Boschi (D. L.) R. Genée cond. (in Ger.)

Munich    Hoftheater    Sep. 15, 1859 F. Schwarzbach (L.) A. Stöger (A.) M. Grill (M.) A. Kindermann (D. L.)

Nürnberg    Stadt    Feb. 3, 1859 (in Ger.)

Stuttgart    Hoftheater    Oct. 12, 1856 Mayerhofer (L.) Lechinger (A.) Sontheim (M.) J. B. Pischek (D. L.)

Weimar    Hoftheater    Apr. 13, 1857 (in Ger.)

GREAT BRITAIN
Belfast    Th. Royal    Oct. 20, 1856 L. Escott (L.) Haigh-Dyer (A.) A. Braham (M.) C. Durand (D. L.) J. H. Tully cond. (in Eng.)

Birmingham    Th. Royal    Dec. 9, 1856 R. Isaacs (L.) F. Reeves (A.) E. Galer (M.) Borrani (D. L.) (in Eng.)

Mar. 12, 1857 G. Grisi (L.) Amadei (A.) A. Volpini (M.) D. Lorini (D. L.) (in It.)

Bristol    Th. Royal    Sep. 16? 1856 R. Isaacs (L.) F. Reeves (A.) E. Galer (M.) Borrani (D. L.) (in Eng.)

Nov. 27, 1857 L. Gassier (L.) Borchhardt (A.) S. Reeves (M.) (in It.)

Edinburgh    Th. Royal    Jan. 21, 1856 E. Fodor-Mainville (L.) Wideman (A.) P. Neri-Baraldi (M.) F. Monari (D. L.) C. H. Zelger (F.) (in It.)

Sep. 29, 1856 L. Escott (L.) F. Huddart (A.) A. Braham (M.) C. Durand (D. L.) (in Eng.)

Glasgow    Th. Royal    Mar. 4, 1856 E. Fodor-Mainville (L.) Wideman (A.) P. Neri-Baraldi (M.) F. Monari (D. L.) C. Boccolini (F.) (in It.)

Sep. 15, 1856 L. Escott (L.) F. Huddart (A.) A. Braham (M.) C. Durand (D. L.) J. H. Tully cond. (in Eng.)

Liverpool     Th. Royal    Aug. 14, 1855 A. Bosio (L.) P. Viardot (A.) E.
                                         Tamberlick (M.) F. Graziani (D. L.)
                                         E. Polonini (F.) A. Mellon cond. (in
                                         It.)

London        Covent       May 10, 1855 J. Casimir-Ney (L.) P. Viardot (A.)
              Garden                    E. Tamberlick (M.) F. Graziani (D.
                                        L.) J. Tagliafico (F.) M. Costa
                                        cond.

              Drury Lane   Mar. 24, 1856 L. Escott (L.) F. Huddart (A.) A.
                                         Braham (M.) H. Drayton (D. L.) R.
                                         Farquharson (F.) (in Eng.)

Manchester    Th. Royal    Aug. 23, 1855 A. Bosio (L.) P. Viardot (A.) E.
                                         Tamberlick (M.) F. Graziani (D. L.)
                                         E. Polonini (F.) A. Mellon cond. (in
                                         It.)

                           Aug. 11, 1856 L. Escott (L.) F. Huddart (A.) A.
                                         Braham (M.) C. Durand (D. L.) J. H.
                                         Tully cond. (in Eng.)

Newcastle     Th. Royal    Nov. 28? 1856 R. Isaacs (L.) F. Reeves (A.) E.
                                         Galer (M.) (in Eng.)

GREECE
Athens        Royal        Feb.    1854 A. Angelini-Cantalamessa (L.) C.
                                        Guerrini (A.) G. Ortolani (M.) C.
                                        Morelli-Condolmieri (D. L.) Giordani
                                        (F.)

Corfu         San Giacomo Sep. 6, 1853 T. Truffi-Benedetti (L.) E. Della
                                       Porta (A.) R. Bettazzi (M.) M. Seve-
                                       ri (D. L.) L. Ruiz (F.) R. Santi
                                       cond.

GUATEMALA
Guatemala     Carrera      Feb. 5, 1860 C. Cairoli (L.) Zenon (A.) E. Gui-
City                                    di (M.) Ungari (D. L.) L. Maggio-
                                        rotti (F.)

HAWAII
Honolulu      Royal        Mar. 4, 1913 E. Adaberto (L.) B. Fox (A.) E. Fol-
              Hawaiian                  co (M.) F. Nicoletti (D. L.)

HONG KONG
Hong Kong     Lusitano     Apr. 5, 1867 M. Bouché (L.) M. Veralli (A.) E.
                                        Pizzioli (M.) G. Colombo (D. L.) G.
                                        Reina (F.)

HUNGARY
Budapest      Nemzeti      Oct. 31, 1854 L. Lesniewska (L.) R. Bovya (A.) G.
              Szinház                    Mazzi (M.) M. Füredy (D. L.) K. Kös-
                                         zeghi (F.) (in Hung.)

                           July    1857 G. Medori (L.) G. Brambilla-Marulli
                                        (A.) G. Bettini (M.) A. De Bassini
                                        (D. L.) (in It.)

              Operaház     Dec. 7, 1884 E. Turolla (L.) V. Bartolucci (A.)
                                        Z. Hajos (M.) L. von Bignio (D. L.)
                                        (in Hung.)

Verdi

INDIA
Bombay Grant Rd. Nov. 2, 1864 A. Jackson (L.) A. Mazzucco (A.) E.
Giusti (M.) E. Corti (D. L.) F. Fi-
orani (F.)

Calcutta Town Hall Apr. 25, 1866 R. Vielli-Villa (L.) Fiorio (A.) T.
Villa (M.) A. Grandi (D. L.) F. Fio-
rani (F.)

INDONESIA
Batavia T. Batavie Sep. 29, 1865 De Mesmaecker (L.) Mendioroz (A.) J.
Moulin (M.) Lavagne (D. L.) De Gréef
(F.) (in Fr.)

June 11, 1869 R. Vielli-Villa (L.) G. Ferrari-Po-
coleri (A.) P. Errani (M.) L. Magna-
ni (D. L.) E. Gasperini (F.) (in
It.)

IRELAND
Cork Th. Royal Nov. 26, 1856 L. Escott (L.) Haigh-Dyer (A.) A.
Braham (M.) C. Durand (D. L.) J. H.
Tully cond. (in Eng.)

Apr. 17? 1857 C. Hayes (L.) Corelli (A.) A. Volpini (M.) C. Badiali (D. L.) (in
It.)

Dublin Th. Royal Sep. 3, 1855 F. Maray (L.) P. Viardot (A.) E.
Tamberlick (M.) F. Graziani (D. L.)
E. Polonini (F.) A. Mellon cond. (in
It.)

Nov. 10, 1856 L. Escott (L.) Haigh-Dyer (A.) A.
Braham (M.) C. Durand (D. L.) J. H.
Tully cond. (in Eng.)

ISRAEL
Jerusalem Dec. 21, 1924 (in Heb.)

Tel Aviv National July 1973 G. Cruz-Romo (L.) M. Dunn (A.) R.
Tucker (M.) S. Nimsgern (D. L.) Z.
Mehta cond.

ITALY
Alessandria Municipale Nov. 5, 1854 G. Beltramelli (L.) P. Duclout (A.)
A. Agresti (M.) D. Mattioli (D. L.)
F. Pons (F.)

Ancona Muse Apr. 24, 1853 F. Salvini-Donatelli (L.) E. Morel-
li-Montalti (A.) G. Pardini (M.) R.
Pizzigati (D. L.) S. Panzini (F.)

Ascoli Ventidio Nov. 1853 C. Alaimo (L.) L. Rossetti-Boccolini
Piceno Basso (A.) A. Agresti (M.) G. B. Bencich
(D. L.) C. Boccolini (F.)

Bari Piccinni Oct. 15, 1854 A. Basseggio (L.) C. Lusignani (A.)
B. Massimiliani (M.) G. Sansone (D.
L.) Tucci (F.)

Petruzzelli Mar. 18, 1903 C. Boninsegna (L.) R. Casini (A.) C.
Cartica (M.) E. Moreo (D. L.) E.
Ciccolini (F.) V. Lombardi cond.

| | | | |
|---|---|---|---|
| Bergamo | Riccardi | Aug. 6, 1853 | M. Gazzaniga (L.) C. Lorenzetti (A.) G. Fraschini (M.) R. Pizzigati (D. L.) B. Gandini (F.) |
| Bologna | Corso | Oct. 5, 1853 | V. Boccabadati (L.) I. Secci-Corsi (A.) P. Neri-Baraldi (M.) P. Baraldi (D. L.) G. F. Angelini (F.) G. Manetti cond. |
| | Comunale | Oct. 23, 1855 | A. Albertini (L.) G. Brambilla-Marulli (A.) C. Baucardé (M.) E. Crivelli (D. L.) L. Ruiz (F.) |
| Brescia | Grande | Aug. 1, 1854 | F. Salvini-Donatelli (L.) M. De Gianni-Vivez (A.) G. Bettini (M.) G. Ferri (D. L.) C. Dalla Costa (F.) |
| Cagliari | Civico | Sep. 8, 1855 | G. Huber (L.) G. Assoni (A.) G. Aducci (M.) F. Mazzoni (D. L.) |
| Catania | Comunale | Jan. 1854 | C. Forti-Babacci (L.) C. Lusignani (A.) P. Soderini (M.) P. Giorgi-Pacini (D. L.) N. Contedini (F.) M. Pappalardo cond. |
| | Bellini | Mar. 4, 1903 | E. Regini (L.) G. Lucacevska (A.) F. Nieddu (M.) P. Amato (D. L.) M. Fiore (F.) A. Doncich cond. |
| Chieti | San Fernando | Apr. 22, 1854 | T. Pozzi-Montegazza (L.) C. Angelici (A.) V. Ferrari-Stella (M.) A. Vitti (D. L.) L. Bigazzi (F.) |
| Como | Sociale | Carn. 1854-55 | D. Demoro (L.) P. Corvetti (A.) V. Sarti (M.) F. Steller (D. L.) |
| Cremona | Concordia | Dec. 26, 1854 | C. Marziali (L.) R. Luccini (A.) G. Ghislanzoni (M.) A. Olivari (D. L.) B. Tovajera (F.) A. Marzorati cond. |
| Faenza | Comunale | June 28, 1853 | A. Anglés-Fortuni (L.) G. Brambilla-Marulli (A.) L. Graziani (M.) P. Baraldi (D. L.) G. Mirandola (F.) |
| Fermo | Aquila | Sep. 3, 1853 | T. Brambilla (L.) L. Rossetti-Boccolini (A.) G. Pardini (M.) F. Giannini (D. L.) G. De Lorenzi (F.) A. Marziali cond. |
| Ferrara | Comunale | May 11, 1853 | V. Boccabadati (L.) I. Secci-Corsi (A.) P. Mongini (M.) F. Coliva (D. L.) P. Baroncini (F.) |
| Fiume | Civico | Mar. 10, 1855 | C. Marziali (L.) G. Jotti-Negri (A.) B. Negri (M.) F. Steller (D. L.) |
| Florence | Pergola | Oct. 4, 1853 | A. Albertini (L.) E. Goggi (A.) C. Baucardé (M.) F. Graziani (D. L.) A. Baccelli (F.) |
| Forli | Comunale | June 18, 1853 | C. Alaimo (L.) C. Croci (A.) G. Landi (M.) G. B. Bencich (D. L.) F. Varani (F.) |

Genoa       Carlo        Dec. 26, 1853  F. Salvini-Donatelli (L.) M. L. Fer-
            Felice                      ravilla (A.) L. Graziani (M.) F.
                                        Cresci (D. L.) A. Mariani cond.

Livorno     Floridi      Aug. 16, 1853  R. Penco (L.) G. Brambilla-Marulli
                                        (A.) C. Baucardé (M.) F. Coletti (D.
                                        L.) G. F. Angelini (F.)

Lucca       Giglio       Aug. 15, 1854  A. Albertini (L.) C. Biscotini-Fio-
                                        rio (A.) A. Giuglini (M.) A. Otta-
                                        viani (D. L.) G. Atry (F.) E. Vannu-
                                        cini cond.

Lugo        Rossini      Aug. 29, 1854  C. Crémont (L.) C. Guercini (A.) P.
                                        Cecchi (M.) E. Delle Sedie (D. L.)
                                        P. Montaguti cond.

Macerata    Condomini    Aug. 13, 1854  V. Boccabadati (L.) E. Ribiska (A.)
                                        G. Ortolani (M.) F. Coliva (D. L.)
                                        N. Contedini (F.)

Mantua      Sociale      Dec. 26, 1853  F. Capuani (L.) P. Duclout (A.) A.
                                        Giuglini (M.) F. Coliva (D. L.) R.
                                        Anconi (F.) G. Luppi cond.

Messina     Sant'        Nov. 21, 1853  G. Borsi de Leurie (L.) L. Schieroni
            Elisabetta                  Nulli (A.) B. Bolcioni (M.) G. B.
                                        Righini (D. L.)

Milan       La Scala     Sep. 15, 1853  R. Gariboldi-Bassi (L.) F. Vestvali
                                        (A.) G. Bettini (M.) L. Giraldoni
                                        (D. L.) C. G. Nerini (F.) E. Caval-
                                        lini cond.

Modena      Comunale     Dec. 26, 1853  V. Boccabadati (L.) A. Winnen (A.)
                                        G. Tamaro (M.) P. Baraldi (D. L.) F.
                                        Varani (F.) A. Sighicelli cond.

Naples      San Carlo    Oct.  6, 1853  R. Penco (L.) A. Borghi-Mamo (A.) G.
                                        Fraschini (M.) G. Ferri (D. L.) M.
                                        Arati (F.) A. Farelli cond.[44]

Novara      Nuovo        Dec. 26? 1854  G. Borsi de Leurie (L.) S. Tosi (A.)
                                        L. Caserini (M.) A. Grandi (D. L.)

Padua       Nuovo        June 25, 1853  T. De Giuli-Borsi (L.) M. De Gianni-
                                        Vivez (A.) S. Malvezzi (M.) A. De
                                        Bassini (D. L.) C. Nanni (F.) Spada
                                        cond.

Palermo     Carolino     Oct. 11, 1853  M. Piccolomini (L.) M. Gastaldi (A.)
                                        G. Pardini (M.) F. Colini (D. L.) A.
                                        Lo Casto cond.

Parma       Regio        Feb.  4, 1854  L. Bendazzi-Secchi (L.) G. Sanchioli
                                        (A.) G. Galvani (M.) R. Pizzigati
                                        (D. L.) G. B. Cornago (F.) N. De
                                        Giovanni cond.

---

[44]. The first two acts were performed on Oct. 4, 1854.

| Perugia | Civico | Dec. 26, 1854 | T. Pozzi-Montegazza (L.) A. Crescimbene (A.) V. Ferrari-Stella (M.) A. Donzelli (D. L.) |
|---|---|---|---|
| Pesaro | Rossini | Jan.     1855 | V. Boccabadati (L.) I. Secci-Corsi (A.) G. Roppa (M.) P. Baraldi (D. L.) S. Panzini (F.) A. Marziali cond. |
| Piacenza | Municipale | Dec. 26? 1854 | E. Marcolini (L.) A. Diamonti (A.) B. Negri (M.) V. Prattico (D. L.) C. Caron (F.) G. Jona cond. |
| Pisa | Ravvivati | Dec. 26, 1854 | C. Frassini (L.) C. Mansui (A.) G. Forti (M.) P. Giorgi-Pacini (D. L.) G. De Dominicis (F.) M. Tilli cond. |
| Ravenna | Alighieri | May 6, 1854 | M. Lotti Della Santa (L.) I. Secci-Corsi (A.) G. Pardini (M.) G. B. Bencich (D. L.) V. Ghiberti (F.) G. Nostini cond. |
| Reggio Emilia | Comunale | May 19, 1853 | M. Piccolomini (L.) M. De Gianni-Vivez (A.) S. Malvezzi (M.) G. B. Bencich (D. L.) F. Mazzoni (F.) G. Tebaldi cond. |
| Rimini | Comunale | Jan. 18, 1854 | M. Armandi (L.) M. Franchini-Marazzoni (A.) C. Conti (M.) G. Staffolini (D. L.) G. Muratori cond. |
| Rome | Costanzi | Dec. 22, 1880 | O. Picconi-Pierangeli (L.) I. Galletti-Gianoli (A.) A. Rossetti (M.) E. Ciolli (D. L.) G. Fagioli (F.) G. Rossi cond. |
| Rovigo | Sociale | Oct. 29, 1853 | E. Scotta (L.) M. De Gianni-Vivez (A.) G. Landi (M.) G. Fiori (D. L.) A. Dolcibene (F.) D. Tosarini cond. |
| Siena | Rinnovati | July 25, 1855 | A. Angelini-Cantalamessa (L.) C. Cruci (A.) A. Pagnoni (M.) S. Ronconi (D. L.) G. Atry (F.) |
| Sinigaglia | Comunale | July 19, 1854 | R. Gariboldi-Bassi (L.) A. Borghi-Vietti (A.) E. Carrion (M.) A. De Bassini (D. L.) N. Benedetti (F.) F. Bianchi cond. |
| Spoleto | Nobile | Dec. 26, 1854 | M. Mollo (L.) Lattanzi (A.) L. Ferrari-Stella (M.) A. Cotogni (D. L.) G. Galli (F.) |
| Trento | Sociale | June 21, 1854 | A. Cortesi (L.) G. Brambilla-Marulli (A.) A. Agresti (M.) G. Altini (D. L.) A. Dolcibene (F.) |
| Treviso | Sociale | Oct. 8, 1854 | A. Albertini (L.) G. Bregazzi (A.) C. Baucardé (M.) G. B. Bencich (D. L.) G. B. Cornago (F.) |
| Trieste | Grande | Oct. 22, 1853 | M. Barbieri-Nini (L.) A. Winnen (A.) L. Graziani (M.) F. Coletti (D. L.) C. Dalla Costa (F.) |

Turin        Regio        Mar. 11, 1854 C. Alaimo (L.) E. Goggi (A.) C. Bau-
                                        cardé (M.) G. Fiori (D. L.) G. F.
                                        Angelini (F.) G. Ghebart cond.

Udine        Sociale      July 24, 1854 M. Piccolomini (L.) I. Secci-Corsi
                                        (A.) C. Baucardé (M.) F. Cresci (D.
                                        L.) F. Pons (F.)

Urbino       Raffaele     Sep.  6, 1853 N. Barbieri-Thiollier (L.) C. Cruci
             Sanzio                     (A.) G. Landi (M.) G. B. Bencich (D.
                                        L.) F. Varani (F.) G. Muratori cond.

Venice       La Fenice    Dec. 26, 1853 A. Albertini (L.) I. Secci-Corsi
                                        (A.) R. Mirate (M.) G. B. Bencich
                                        (D. L.) P. Vialetti (F.) G. Mares
                                        cond.

Verona       Filarmonico Dec. 26, 1853 M. Lotti Della Santa (L.) M. De
                                        Gianni-Vivez (A.) G. Bettini (M.) L.
                                        Della Santa (D. L.) C. Fedrighini
                                        (F.)

             Arena        July 28, 1926 V. Manna (L.) I. Minghini-Cattaneo
                                        (A.) J. O'Sullivan (M.) A. Borgioli
                                        (D. L.) E. Dominici (F.) G. Bavagno-
                                        li cond.

Vicenza      Eretenio     July  9, 1853 F. Salvini-Donatelli (L.) A. Winnen
                                        (A.) E. Carrion (M.) G. Fiori (D.
                                        L.) M. Ghini (F.)

Viterbo      Del Genio    Aug.  7, 1854 E. Schenardi (L.) Durante (A.) B.
                                        Bolcioni (M.) T. Durante (D. L.)

JAPAN
Tokyo        Imperial     Sep. 25, 1921 Marcia (in Rus.)

                          Feb.  3, 1923 (in It.)

JUGOSLAVIA
Belgrade     National     June     1911 Friziero (L.) Sala (M.) A. Mascarag-
                                        na (D. L.) Lizza (F.) B. Mari cond.
                                        (in It.)

Ljubljana    Stanovskem   Apr. 18, 1860 A. Bazzurri (L.) Fantozzi (A.) G.
                                        Gambetti (M.) Bertolini (D. L.) (in
                                        It.)

Zagreb       National     Apr.     1858 A. Fumagalli (A.) A. Marchetti (M.)
                                        Cellini (D. L.) (in It.)

Zara         Nobile       Nov.     1855 M. Plodowska (L.) G. D'Apice (M.)
                                        (in It.)

LATVIA
Riga         Municipal    Jan. 22, 1859 (in Ger.)

                          June?    1861 R. Laborde (L.) R. Baragli (M.) F.
                                        Briani (D. L.) (in It.)

             National     Oct. 24, 1928 T. Reiters cond. (in Let.)

LITHUANIA
Kaunas       Imperial     Dec. 12? 1906 G. Procacci (M.) (in It.)

|          | National  | Nov. 14, 1929 (in Lith.) |
|----------|-----------|--------------------------|

| Vilna    | Municipal | Mar.     1886 (in It.)    |

MALTA
La Valletta   Manoel      Oct.  1, 1853 G. Morra (L.) C. Rapazzini (A.) G.
                                        Comolli (M.) G. Sansone (D. L.) L.
                                        Del Riccio (F.)

MEXICO
Guadalajara   Degollado   Sep. 18, 1866 I. Alba (L.) H. Sulzer (A.) G. Tom-
                                        besi (M.)

Mexico City   Nacional    Jan. 27, 1856 M. Almonti (L.) F. Vestvali (A.) L.
                                        Ceresa (M.) E. Winter (D. L.) C.
                                        Carroni (F.) G. Winter cond.

MONACO
Monte Carlo   Salle       Feb.  9, 1884 C. Salla (L.)  G. Novelli  (A.)  E.
              Garnier                   Vergnet (M.) F. Pandolfini (D. L.)
                                        A. Castelmary (F.)

NETHERLANDS
Amsterdam     Stads       Sep. 30, 1858 Bauer (L.) Tobisch (A.) Solano (M.)
                                        (in Ger.)

                          Oct. 25, 1859 R. Devries (L.) G. Brambilla-Marulli
                                        (A.) B. Danieli (M.) G. Marra (D.
                                        L.) A. Fossati (F.) N. Bassi cond.
                                        (in It.)

Den Haag      Royal       Feb.     1857 Laurent (L.) Chenest (M.) Ribes (D.
                                        L.) (in Fr.)

                          Nov. 19, 1859 R. Devries (L.) G. Brambilla-Marulli
                                        (A.) B. Danieli (M.) G. Marra (D.
                                        L.) A. Fossati (F.) N. Bassi cond.
                                        (in It.)

Rotterdam                 Nov. 18, 1859 R. Devries (L.) G. Brambilla-Marulli
                                        (A.) B. Danieli (M.) G. Marra (D.
                                        L.) A. Fossati (F.) N. Bassi cond.
                                        (in It.)

NEW ZEALAND
Auckland      Prince      Nov. 19, 1864 L. Escott (L.)  G. Hodson (A.) H.
              of Wales                  Squires (M.) H. Wharton (D. L.) J.
                                        B. Kitts (F.)

Dunedin       Princess    Aug. 31, 1864 L. Escott (L.)  G. Hodson (A.) H.
                                        Squires (M.) H. Wharton (D. L.) J.
                                        B. Kitts (F.)

Wellington    Old Fellows Dec. 23, 1864 L. Escott (L.)  G. Hodson (A.) H.
              Hall                      Squires (M.) H. Wharton (D. L.) J.
                                        B. Kitts (F.)

NORWAY
Oslo          Christiana  July  8, 1861 (in Swed.)

                          Apr. 24, 1868 M. Calisto (L.) A. L. Cary (A.) G.
                                        Bentami (M.) A. Pantaleoni (D. L.)
                                        G. B. Cornago (F.) (in It.)

**PERU**

| Lima | Principal | June 8, 1856 | T. Bayetti (L.) R. Olivieri (A.) E. Rossi-Guerra (M.) A. Lanzoni (D. L.) G. Mirandola (F.) |

**PHILIPPINES**

| Manila | | Sep.? 1867 | L. De Ponte (L.) M. Veralli (A.) E. Pizzioli (M.) G. Reina (F.) |

**POLAND**

| Cracow | Imperial | Feb. 2, 1857 | T. Biegl (L.) V. Bühner (A.) B. Biegl (M.) Minetti (D. L.) (in Ger.) |
| | | May 18? 1867 | G. Ronzi-Checchi (L.) R. Cash-Pollini (A.) G. Sbriglia (M.) V. Cottone (D. L.) C. Dalla Costa (F.) (in It.) |

| Lwov | Szarbek | Oct. 29, 1857 | Schreiber-Kirchberger (L.) B. Moser (A.) Barrach (M.) K. Moser (D. L.) Kunz (F.) (in Ger.) |
| | | Aug. 1862 | E. Volpini (L.) A. Phillips (A.) G. Tombesi (M.) M. Zacchi (D. L.) (in It.) |
| | | July 29, 1872 | (in Pol.) |

| Warsaw | Wielki | July 29, 1854 | A. Ortolani-Brignoli (L.) Bussek (A.) F. Ciaffei (M.) L. Buti (D. L.) (in It.) |

**PORTUGAL**

| Lisbon | Sao Carlos | Apr. 17, 1854 | A. Castellan (L.) E. Agostini (A.) C. Miraglia (M.) O. Bartolini (D. L.) L. Biacchi (F.) |

| Oporto | Sao Joao | Mar. 20, 1854 | L. Ponti dall'Armi (L.) E. Poma (A.) A. Dall'Armi (M.) P. Gorin (D. L.) D. Cervini (F.) |

**PUERTO RICO**

| San Juan | Municipal | 1855 | |

**ROMANIA**

| Bucharest | Nacional | Feb. 1855 | T. Truffi-Benedetti (L.) J. Lemaire (A.) E. Irfré (M.) G. Mancusi (D. L.) |

| Iasi | Teatrul | Dec.? 1854 | T. Brambilla (L.) Bodino (A.) |

| Temesvar | | Jan. 9, 1855 | (First time in German) |

**RUSSIA**

| Kharkov | Municipal | Spring 1864 | C. Noel-Guidi (L.) A. Casaloni (A.) A. Gottardi (M.) |

| Kiev | Imperial | Jan.? 1864 | E. Martoni (L.) P. Baccei (M.) C. Fabbricatore (D. L.) |

| Moscow | Bolshoi | Sep. 12, 1856 | A. Bosio (L.) E. De Meric (A.) G. Bettini (M.) O. Bartolini (D. L.) E. Baveri cond. |

| | | | |
|---|---|---|---|
| Odessa | Municipal | June 24, 1854 | F. Gordosa (L.) M. L. Ferravilla (A.) T. Palmieri (M.) M. Zacchi (D. L.) L. Ruiz (F.) |
| St. Petersburg | Imperial | Nov. 29, 1855 | A. Bosio (L.) E. De Meric (A.) E. Tamberlick (M.) A. De Bassini (D. L.) J. Tagliafico (F.) E. Baveri cond. |
| | | Dec. 22, 1859 | (in Rus.) |
| Tbilisi | Imperial | Oct. 1857 | L. Ferrari (L.) V. Massini (M.) |
| SOUTH AFRICA Capetown | Mutual Hall | Sep. 7, 1869 | Hirst (L.) Leffier (A.) Miranda (M.) Harper (D. L.) (in Eng.) |
| | Th. Royal | Nov. 15, 1875 | A. Brambilla (L.) Neri (A.) P. Setragni (M.) Greco (D. L.) (in It.) |
| Johannesburg | Th. Royal | Sep. 2, 1889 | De Bremont (L.) B. Fenton (A.) V. Reid (M.) G. Verdi (D. L.) H. Harper (F.) (in Eng.) |
| | Amphitheatre | May 27, 1895 | E. Ancarani (L.) T. Alasia (A.) V. Maina (M.) M. De Padova (D. L.) D. Benferreri (F.) (in It.) |
| SPAIN Alicante | Principal | Mar. 24, 1859 | F. Pozzo (M.) L. Walter (D. L.) |
| Barcelona | Liceo | May 20, 1854 | A. Corbari (L.) E. D'Angri (A.) E. Irfré (M.) A. Superchi (D. L.) A. Rodas (F.) |
| Bilbao | Viejo | Apr. 1858 | C. Forti-Babacci (L.) L. Corbari (A.) A. Luise (M.) C. Morelli-Condolmieri (D. L.) |
| Cadiz | Principal | Aug. 1854 | M. Sulzer (L.) H. Sulzer (A.) B. Belart (M.) A. Celestino (D. L.) L. Silingardi (F.) |
| Madrid | Real | Feb. 16, 1854 | M. Gazzaniga (L.) C. Biscotini-Fiorio (A.) S. Malvezzi (M.) F. Varesi (D. L.) G. Baillou (F.) J. Skoczdopole cond. |
| Malaga | Principal | Summer 1854 | M. Sulzer (L.) H. Sulzer (A.) |
| Palma de Mallorca | Coliseo | Oct. 10, 1855 | C. Crescimano (L.) Campos (A.) M. Severi (D. L.) |
| Seville | San Fernando | June 7, 1855 | M. Spezia-Aldighieri (L.) Pinelli (A.) A. Volpini (M.) M. Assoni (D. L.) |
| Valencia | Principal | June 4? 1854 | M. Gazzaniga (L.) G. Mora (A.) S. Malvezzi (M.) M. Assoni (D. L.) G. Echeverria (F.) |
| Valladolid | Lope da Vega | Mar. 3, 1859 | C. Forti-Babacci (L.) I. Vitali (A.) M. Viani (M.) C. Morelli-Condolmieri (D. L.) O. Lari (F.) |

Zaragozza       Principal    July?    1855 M. Gazzaniga (L.) Campos (A.) S.
                                           Malvezzi (M.) A. Rossi (D. L.)

SWEDEN
Stockholm       Royal        May  31, 1860 F. Andrée (L.) G. Lublin (A.) W. D.
                                           Richard (M.) G. Sandström (D. L.) A.
                                           Willman (F.) (in Swed.)

                Mindre       Oct. 31, 1868 E. Tomassi (L.) A. L. Cary (A.) G.
                                           Bentami (M.) G. Mendioroz (D. L.) E.
                                           Coulon (F.) (in It.)

SWITZERLAND
Basel           Stadt        Jan. 20, 1860 (in Ger.)

Geneva          Grand        May  16, 1861 (in Ger.)

                             Feb. 21, 1862 (in Fr.)

                             June     1865 F. Scheggi (L.) A. Boetti (M.) M.
                                           Padilla (D. L.) (in It.)

Lugano          Sociale      Oct.     1857 L. Viale (L.) G. Cella-Crotti (A.)
                                           F. Albesani (M.) G. Crotti (D. L.)

Zürich          Stadt        Oct. 19, 1859 (in Ger.)

TURKEY
Constan-        Naum         Nov.  4, 1853 A. Conti-Foroni (L.) G. Bregazzi
 tinople                                   (A.) C. Liverani (M.) D. Mattioli
                                           (D. L.) E. Manfredi (F.) V. Fumi
                                           cond.

UNITED STATES
Atlanta         Bell John-   Oct. 18, 1866 A. Ghioni (L.) A. Patti-Strakosch
                son Hall                   (A.)

Baltimore       Holliday     Oct. 23, 1858 T. Parodi (L.) A. Patti-Strakosch
                Street                      (A.) P. Brignoli (M.) A. Amodio (D.
                                           L.) N. Barili (F.)

Boston          Boston Th.   May  28, 1855 B. Steffenone (L.) F. Vestvali (A.)
                                           P. Brignoli (M.) A. Amodio (D. L.)
                                           N. Barili (F.)

Brooklyn        Ac. of Mus.  Jan. 30, 1861 I. Hinckley (L.) A. Phillips (A.) P.
                                           Brignoli (M.) G. Ferri (D. L.) D.
                                           Coletti (F.) E. Muzio cond.

Buffalo         Saint        Aug. 10, 1859 C. Alaimo (L.) T. Parodi (A.) G.
                James Hall                 Sbriglia (M.) F. Gnone (D. L.) N.
                                           Barili (F.) A. Torriani cond.

Charleston      Charleston   Jan. 27, 1858 R. Durand (L.) G. King (A.) G. Hod-
                Theatre                    son (M.) F. Lyster (D. L.) (in Eng.)

                             Feb. 27, 1860 C. Alaimo (L.) T. Parodi (A.) G.
                                           Sbriglia (M.) F. Gnone (D. L.) A.
                                           Torriani cond. (in It.)

Chicago         McVicker's   Oct.  8, 1858 R. Durand (L.) A. King (A.) G. Hod-
                                           son (M.) F. Lyster (D. L.) (in Eng.)

                       Feb. 28, 1859 T. Parodi (L.) A. Patti-Strakosch
                                     (A.) P. Brignoli (M.) A. Amodio (D.
                                     L.) (in It.)

           Auditorium  Dec. 13, 1889 G. Valda (L.) G. Fabbri (A.) F. Ta-
                                     magno (M.) G. Del Puente (D. L.) A.
                                     De Vaschetti (F.) L. Arditi cond.

           Lyric       Nov.  5, 1955 M. Callas (L.) E. Stignani (A.) J.
                                     Bjoerling (M.) E. Bastiannini (D.
                                     L.) N. Rescigno cond.

Cincinnati Wood's      July  6, 1857 L. Caranti-Vita (L.) F. Vestvali
                                     (A.) A. Macaferri (M.) L. Corradi-
                                     Setti (D. L.) F. Mancini (F.)

           Opera       July 24, 1921 J. Barondess (L.) H. Wakefield (A.)
                                     R. Boscacci (M.) G. Evans (D. L.) L.
                                     Wilson (F.) R. Lyford cond.

Cleveland  Ac. of Mus. Nov.  3, 1859 C. Alaimo (L.) T. Parodi (A.) G.
                                     Sbriglia (M.) F. Gnone (D. L.) N.
                                     Barili (F.) A. Torriani cond.

Dallas     Op. House   Nov. 24, 1880 Zelna (L.) M. Phillips (A.) G.
                                     Baldanza (M.) G. Tagliapietra (D.
                                     L.) (in It.)

           Opera       Dec. 13, 1984 S. Evstatieva (L.) B. Berini (A.) G.
                                     Giacomini (M.) M. Manuguerra (D. L.)
                                     F. Ventriglia (F.) N. Rescigno cond.

Denver                 Mar.  1, 1890 L. Nordica (L.) H. Synnerberg (A.)
                                     F. Tamagno (M.) G. Del Puente (D.
                                     L.) L. Arditi cond.

Detroit    Metro-      Nov. 26, 1859 C. Alaimo (L.) T. Parodi (A.) G.
           politan                   Sbriglia (M.) F. Gnone (D. L.)

Houston    Theatre     Apr. 12, 1867

           Grand Opera Nov. 29, 1962 E. Ross (L.) I. Kramarich (A.) F.
                                     Labo (M.) E. Sordello (D. L.) J.
                                     Hecht (F.) W. Herbert cond.

Kansas City Coates     Mar.  1, 1879 (in Eng.)

Los Angeles Grand      Feb.  7, 1885 L. Bellini (L.) L. Annandale (A.)
                                     Fabrini (M.) (in Eng.)

           Theater     Oct. 16, 1897 N. Mazzi (L.) A. Fanton (A.) F. Col-
                                     lenz (M.) Francesconi (D. L.)

Memphis    Crisp's     June 25, 1858 R. Durand (L.) A. King (A.) G. Hod-
                                     son (M.) F. Lyster (D. L.) (in Eng.)

Nashville  Crisp's     Jan. 18, 1860 C. Alaimo (L.) T. Parodi (A.) G.
                                     Sbriglia (M.) F. Gnone (D. L.) N.
                                     Barili (F.) A. Torriani cond.

New Orleans Orleans    Apr. 13, 1857 P. Colson (L.) Bourgeois (A.) Dela-
                                     grave (M.) Magne (D. L.) (in Fr.)

               Crisp's      Apr. 15, 1857 L. Caranti-Vita (L.) C. Vita (A.) A.
                                              Macaferri (M.) Viera (D. L.) F. Man-
                                              cini (F.) (in It.)

New York      Ac. of Mus. May   2, 1855 B. Steffenone (L.) F. Vestvali (A.)
                                              P. Brignoli (M.) A. Amodio (D. L.)
                                              L. Rocco (F.) M. Maretzek cond. (in
                                            It.)

               Burton's     Oct.  4, 1858 L. Escott (L.) H. Squires (M.) (in
                                            Eng.)

               Metro-       Oct. 26, 1883 A. Valleria (L.) Z. Trebelli (A.) R.
               politan                 Stagno (M.) G. Kaschmann (D. L.) A.
                                            Augier (F.) A. Vianesi cond.

Philadelphia Walnut St.  Jan. 14, 1856 A. De la Grange (L.) C. Nantier-
                                            Didiée (A.) P. Brignoli (M.) A.
                                            Amodio (D. L.) M. Maretzek cond.

               Ac. of Mus. Feb. 25, 1857 M. Gazzaniga (L.) Z. Aldini (A.) P.
                                            Brignoli (M.) A. Amodio (D. L.)

Pittsburgh   Atheneum   July 22, 1857 L. Caranti-Vita (L.) C. Vita (A.) A.
                                            Macaferri (M.) L. Corradi-Setti (D.
                                            L.) F. Mancini (F.)

St. Louis    Varieties   June 15, 1857 L. Caranti-Vita (L.) F. Vestvali
                                            (A.) A. Macaferri (M.) L. Corradi-
                                            Setti (D. L.) F. Mancini (F.)

San Francisco Maguire's  May   5, 1859 G. Bianchi (L.) Feret (A.) E. Bian-
                                            chi (M.) Leach (D. L.) Roncovieri
                                            (F.)

               Auditorium Oct.  6, 1926 C. Muzio (L.) K. Meisle (A.) A.
                                              Lindi (M.) R. Bonelli (D. L.)

Washington  National    Jan.  9, 1856 A. De la Grange (L.) C. Nantier-
                                            Didiée (A.) P. Brignoli (M.) A. Amo-
                                            dio (D. L.) M. Maretzek cond.

URUGUAY
Montevideo  San Felipe Apr. 14, 1855 S. Vera-Lorini (L.) B. Tati (A.) G.
                                            Comolli (M.) G. Cima (D. L.) P. Fi-
                                            gari (F.)

               Solis        Oct. 18, 1856 S. Vera-Lorini (L.) G. Tati (A.) G.
                                              Comolli (M.) G. Cima (D. L.) F. Tati
                                            (F.) L. Pretti cond.

VENEZUELA
Caracas     Teatro     Aug. 13, 1857 C. Saeman (L.) Z. Aldini (A.) M. Ti-
                                            berini (M.) F. Morelli-Ponti (D. L.)
                                            A. Gasparoni (F.)

               Municipal  Jan.  4, 1881 M. Lucchesi (L.) T. Mestres (A.) F.
                                            Giannini (M.) D. Farina (D. L.) R.
                                            Mancini (F.) F. Rachelle cond.

19. LA TRAVIATA-*Melodramma* in three acts
Venice-Teatro La Fenice-Mar. 6, 1853
Libretto by Francesco Maria Piave

| | |
|---|---|
| Violetta (V.) | Fanny Salvini-Donatelli sop. |
| Alfredo Germont (A.) | Lodovico Graziani ten. |
| Giorgio Germont (G.) | Felice Varesi bar. |
| Flora | Speranza Giuseppini mez. |
| Annina | Carlotta Berini sop. |
| Gastone | Angelo Zuliani ten. |
| Giuseppe | G. Borsato ten. |
| Barone Douphol | Francesco Dragone bar. |
| Marchese D'Obigny | Arnaldo Silvestri bass |
| Dottore Grenvil | Andrea Bellini bass |
| Domestico di Flora | G. Tona bass |
| Comissionario | Antonio Mazzini bass |
| | |
| Conductor | Gaetano Mares |
| Director | Giuseppe Verdi |

Revised-Venice-Teatro San Benedetto-May 6, 1854

| | |
|---|---|
| Violetta (V.) | Maria Spezia-Aldighieri sop. |
| Alfredo Germont (A.) | Giovanni Landi ten. |
| Giorgio Germont (G.) | Filippo Coletti bar. |
| Flora | Luigia Morselli mez. |
| Annina | Laura Saini sop. |
| Gastone (Ga.) | Antonio Galetti ten. |
| Giuseppe | Placido Meneguzzi ten. |
| Dottore Grenvil | Andrea Bellini bass |
| | |
| Conductor | |
| Director | Giuseppe Verdi |

OTHER PREMIERES

ARGENTINA
| | | | |
|---|---|---|---|
| Buenos Aires | Victoria | June 10, 1856 | S. Vera-Lorini (V.) G. Comolli (A.) G. Cima (G.) L. Pretti cond. |
| | Ant. Colón | Apr. 25, 1857 | S. Vera-Lorini (V.) E. Tamberlick (A.) G. Cima (G.) |
| | Colón | May 24, 1910 | R. Storchio (V.) A. Pintucci (A.) G. De Luca (G.) E. Vitale cond. |

AUSTRALIA
| | | | |
|---|---|---|---|
| Adelaide | Victoria | Mar. 13, 1861 | G. Bianchi (V.) E. Bianchi (A.) J. Gregg (G.) (in It.) |
| Brisbane | Mason's | July 11, 1865 | L. Escott (V.) H. Squires (A.) H. Wharton (G.) |
| Melbourne | Royal | Jan. 23, 1860 | G. Bianchi (V.) E. Bianchi (A.) R. Farquharson (G.) |
| Sydney | Prince of Wales | June 5, 1860 | G. Bianchi (V.) E. Bianchi (A.) E. Coulon (G.) |

AUSTRIA
| | | | |
|---|---|---|---|
| Graz | Stadt | July 21, 1858 | Hartmann (V.) (in Ger.) |
| Linz | Landes | Jan. 24, 1864 | (in Ger.) |

Vienna           Kärntnertor May   4, 1855 L. Bendazzi-Secchi (V.) E. Carrion
                                            (A.) G. Ferri (G.) (in It.)

                 Hofoper      Mar. 11, 1876 P. Lucca (V.) V. Capoul (A.) A.
                                            Strozzi (G.) (in It.)

                              Feb.  5, 1879 K. Schuch-Proska (V.) G. Müller (A.)
                                            L. von Bignio (G.) (in Ger.)

BELGIUM
Antwerp          Royal        Mar. 29, 1864 M. Guerra (V.) G. Musiani (A.) M.
                                            Zacchi (G.) (in It.)

Brussels         Cirque       Mar.  6, 1861 M. Brunetti (V.) Z. Trebelli (Ga.)[45]
                                            G. Galvani (A.) M. Zacchi (G.) L.
                                            Orsini cond. (in It.)

                 Monnaie      Oct. 20, 1865 D. Artôt (V.) Jourdan (A.) Monnier
                                            (G.) (in Fr.)

Ghent            Grand        Apr.  3, 1864 M. Guerra (V.) G. Musiani (A.) M.
                                            Zacchi (G.) (in It.)

Liège            Grand        Dec.  7, 1868 (in Fr.)

BRAZIL
Rio de           Fluminense   Dec. 15, 1855 A. Charton-Demeur (V.) G. Gentile
Janeiro                                     (A.) L. Walter (G.)

                 Pedro II     Oct. 19, 1871 A. Pasi (V.) E. Ballarini (A.) C.
                                            Marziali (G.)

                 Municipal    July 29, 1910 G. Bellincioni (V.) P. Schiavazzi
                                            (A.) A. Anceschi (G.) A. Padovani
                                            cond.

Sao Paulo        Provisorio   Nov.     1869 E. Bonacich (A.)

                 San José     Apr. 15, 1876 A. Cortesi (V.) L. Lelmi (A.) G.
                                            Spalazzi (G.) J. Mirandola cond.

                 Municipal    Aug.  1, 1912 R. Storchio (V.), M. Polverosi (A.)
                                            R. Stracciari (G.) G. Marinuzzi
                                            cond.

BULGARIA
Sofia            Luxembourg        1895 G. Badarocco (A.)

                 National     Feb. 10, 1910 (in Bulg.)

CANADA[46]
Edmonton         Opera        Oct.  5, 1965 M. Di Gerlando (V.) P. Duval (A.) G.
                                            Williams (G.) B. Priestman cond.

---

45. The star of the Merelli company which toured Northern and Central Europe during the
1860s was Zelia Trebelli. In order to be able to include her in their production of *La
Traviata* the role of Gastone was expanded. This version was also heard in Berlin, Leipzig, and
Frankfurt.

46. The productions listed for Edmonton and Vancouver are the first by the resident opera
company. It is very likely that the work had already been given by touring companies, but no
details are available at this time.

Montreal      Nordheimer  July 11, 1859  C. Alaimo  (V.)  G. Sbriglia (A.)  F.
                                         Gnone (G.)  A. Torriani cond.

Toronto       Royal       Aug.  2, 1859  T. Parodi (V.)  G. Sbriglia (A.)  F.
              Lyceum                     Gnone (G.)  A. Torriani cond.

Vancouver     Opera       May   4, 1961  B. Bower  (V.)  F. Poretta  (A.)  I.
                                         Gorin (G.)  O. W. Mueller cond.

Victoria      Victoria    Feb.  8, 1887  E. Abbott (V.)  F. Michelena (A.)  W.
              Theatre                    Pruette (G.)  (in Eng.)

Winnipeg      Walker      Dec. 23, 1918  A. Homer  (V.)  R. Boscacci  (A.)  J.
                                         Royer (G.)

CHILE
Santiago      Republica   June 25, 1857  I. Edelvira (V.)  L. Guglielmini (A.)
                                         G. Bastoggi (G.)

              Municipal   Sep. 22, 1857  I. Edelvira (V.)  L. Guglielmini (A.)
                                         A. Lanzoni (G.)

Valparaiso    Victoria    Feb. 11, 1858  I. Edelvira (V.)  L. Guglielmini (A.)
                                         A. Lanzoni (G.)

CHINA
Shanghai      Lyceum      Jan. 19, 1880  R. Genolini (V.)  E. Sbriscia (A.)  G.
                                         Bergamaschi (G.)

COLOMBIA
Bogota        Teatro      Aug. 28, 1864  A. Mazetti (V.)  E. Rossi-Guerra (A.)
                                         E. Luisia (G.)

CUBA
Havana        Tacon       Dec. 31, 1856  A. De la Grange (V.)  P. Brignoli
                                         (A.)  A. Amodio  (G.)  M. Maretzek
                                         cond.

Santiago                  Jan.    1858   A. Macaferri (A.)

CZECHOSLOVAKIA
Brno                      Sep. 13, 1862  (in Ger.)

Prague        Ständisches June 28, 1862  D. Artôt (V.)  Bachmann (A.)  Hardt-
                                         muth (G.)  (in Ger.)

                          July 24, 1862  E. Volpini (V.)  G. Tombesi (A.)  M.
                                         Zacchi (G.)  (in It.)

              Provisional June 13, 1868  (in Czech)

DENMARK
Copenhagen    Casino      Feb.  9, 1866  J. Van Zandt (V.)  N. Andreef (A.)  G.
                                         Giori (G.)  (in It.)

              Royal       Nov. 29, 1887  E. Dons (V.)  A. Ödman (A.)  N. J. Si-
                                         monsen (G.)  (in Dan.)

EGYPT
Alexandria    Europeo     Oct. 15, 1856  C. Crescimano  (V.)  G. Ricci  (A.)
                                         Francolini (G.)

Cairo         Khedivial   Nov.    1869   A. Sarolta (V.)  E. Naudin (A.)  C.
                                         Boccolini (G.)

FINLAND
Helsinki       Suomalainen Aug. 21, 1876 I. Basilier (V.) Nauratil (A.) Ackte
                                        (G.) (in Fin.)

               Nya         Mar. 12, 1879 Engdahl (V.) Berthman (A.) Bentzen
                                        (G.) (in Swed.)

               Alexanders  Mar. 30, 1882 Marco (V.) (in It.)

FRANCE
Lille                      Nov. 26, 1861 (First time in Fr.)

Lyon           Grand       May   6, 1862 Van den Heuven (V.) Achard (A.) (in
                                        Fr.)

Marseille      Grand       Jan.     1865 D. Calderon (V.) V. Montanari (A.)
                                        L. Guadagnini (G.) (in It.)

Nice           Regio       Dec. 11, 1856 C. Sannazaro (V.) G. Pasi (A.) F.
                                        Briani (G.) (in It.)

Paris          Italien     Dec.  6, 1856 M. Piccolomini (V.) Mario (A.) F.
                                        Graziani (G.) G. Bottesini cond.

               Lyrique     Oct. 27, 1864 C. Nilsson (V.) Monjauze (A.)  Lutz
                                        (G.) Deloffre cond. (in Fr.)

               Opéra       Dec. 24, 1926 F. Heldy (V.) G. Thill (A.) E. Rou-
                                        ard (G.) H. Busser cond. (in Fr.)

Rouen          des Arts    Aug. 30, 1864 M. Marinangeli (V.) B. Danieli (A.)
                                        L. Guadagnini (G.) (in It.)

               Apr.  5, 1869 (in Fr.)

GERMANY
Baden-Baden    Kursaal     Aug. 19, 1865 C. Castelli (V.) E. Nicolini (A.) E.
                                        Delle Sedie (G.) (in It.)

Berlin         Victoria    Nov. 10, 1860 A. De la Grange (V.) B. Danieli (A.)
                                        E. Delle Sedie (G.) (in It.)

               Hofoper     Dec. 13, 1860 M. Brunetti (V.) Z. Trebelli (Ga.)
                                        G. Galvani (A.) M. Zacchi (G.) (in
                                        It.)

Braunschweig   Hoftheater  May 17, 1858 (in Ger.)

Breslau        Stadt       May?     1869 L. Artôt (V.) L. Riese (A.) E. Gura
                                        (G.) (in Ger.)

Darmstadt      Hoftheater  Jan.  8, 1865 (in Ger.)

Dresden        Hofoper     Nov. 11, 1875 C. Proska (V.) E. von Schuch cond.

Frankfurt      Stadt       July 15, 1861 D. Calderon (V.) B. Marchisio (Ga.)
                                        G. Galvani (A.) M. Zacchi (G.) (in
                                        It.)

               Nov.  6, 1865 I. Fabbri (V.) G. Müller (A.) Pich-
                                        ler (G.) (in Ger.)

Hamburg        Stadt       Nov. 10, 1857 (in Ger.)

Hannover        Hofoper      Nov.  9, 1892 (in Ger.)

Kassel          Hoftheater   Nov. 19, 1905 (in Ger.)

Leipzig         Stadt        May  13, 1861 D. Calderon (V.) Z. Trebelli (Ga.)
                                           G. Galvani (A.) M. Zacchi (G.) (in
                                           It.)

                             May   9, 1882 (in Ger.)

Mainz           Hoftheater   Mar.  2, 1887 (in Ger.)

Munich                       July?    1863 A. Altavilla (A.) (in It.)

                Hoftheater   Apr. 27, 1883 (in Ger.)

Nürnberg        Stadt            1873-74 (in Ger.)

Stuttgart       Hoftheater   Jan. 24, 1866 (in Ger.)

Weimar          Hoftheater   Mar. 17, 1898 (in Ger.)

GREAT BRITAIN
Birmingham      Th. Royal    Aug. 25, 1856 M. Piccolomini (V.) C. Braham (A.)
                                           G. F. Beneventano (G.) (in It.)

Bristol         Th. Royal    Aug. 21, 1857 M. Piccolomini (V.) A. Giuglini (A.)
                                           G. F. Beneventano (G.)

Edinburgh       Th. Royal    Feb. 25, 1857 J. Gassier (V.) A. Volpini (A.) D.
                                           Lorini (G.)

Glasgow         Th. Royal    Feb. 20, 1857 J. Gassier (V.) A. Volpini (A.) D.
                                           Lorini (G.)

Leeds           Princess     Apr. 17, 1857 L. Escott (V.) H. Haigh (A.) C.
                                           Durand (G.) J. H. Tully cond. (in
                                           Eng.)

                             Aug. 23, 1859 M. Piccolomini (V.) B. Belart (A.)
                                           G. Aldighieri (G.) (in It.)

Liverpool       Th. Royal    Oct. 21, 1856 M. Piccolomini (V.) C. Braham (A.)
                                           G. Belletti (G.) (in It.)

London          Her          May  24, 1856 M. Piccolomini (V.) E. Calzolari
                Majesty's                  (A.) G. F. Beneventano (G.) V. Bo-
                                           netti cond.

                Covent       May  16, 1857 A. Bosio (V.) Mario (A.) F. Graziani
                Garden                     (G.) M. Costa cond.

                Surrey       June  8, 1857 L. Escott (V.) H. Haigh (A.) C. Du-
                                           rand (G.) J. H. Tully cond. (in
                                           Eng.)

Manchester      Th. Royal    Sep.  8, 1856 M. Piccolomini (V.) C. Braham (A.)
                                           G. F. Beneventano (G.) (in It.)

                             Sep.  3, 1857 L. Escott (V.) C. Durand (G.) (in
                                           Eng.)

GREECE
Athens        Royal        Oct. 31, 1857 T. Gori (V.) D. Chiesi (A.) O. Bar-
                                        tolucci (G.)

Corfu         San Giacomo Oct. 29, 1855 D. Demoro (V.) G. Pasi (A.) A. Vitti
                                        (G.)

GUATEMALA
Guatemala     Carreras     Nov. 25, 1859 C. Cairoli (V.) E. Guidi (A.) Ungari
City                                     (G.)

HAWAII
Honolulu      Royal        Mar. 10, 1913 R. Vicarino (V.)  E.  Folco (A.)  F.
              Hawaiian                   Nicoletti (G.)

HONG KONG
Hong Kong     Lusitano     Apr. 16, 1867 M. Bouche (V.) P. Errani (A.) G. Co-
                                         lombo (G.)

HUNGARY
Budapest      Nemzeti      Nov. 10, 1857 C. Hollósy (V.)  Jekelfalusy (A.) M.
              Szinház                    Füredy (G.) (in Hung.)

              May?         1869 A. Pozzoni-Anastasi (V.) S. Anastasi
                                (A.) F. Pandolfini (G.) (in It.)

              Operaház     Oct. 18, 1884 I.  Reich  (V.)  Gassi  (A.)  L.  von
                                         Bignio (G.) (in Hung.)

INDIA
Bombay        Grant Road  Dec.  3, 1864 E.  Puerari  (V.)  E.  Giusti  (A.)  E.
                                        Corti (G.)

Calcutta      Town Hall   May      1866 R.  Vielli-Villa  (V.)  T.  Villa  (A.)
                                        A. Grandi (G.)

INDONESIA
Batavia       T. Batavie June 21, 1869 C. Ghirlanda-Tortolini (V.) T. Villa
                                       (A.) L. Magnani (G.) (in It.)

IRELAND
Dublin        Th. Royal   Oct. 14, 1856 M.  Piccolomini  (V.)  C.  Braham  (A.)
                                        G. Belletti (G.) (in It.)

ISRAEL
Jerusalem                 Aug. 19, 1923 Muste (V.) Kund (A.) Hermelach (G.)
                                        (in Heb.)

Tel Aviv                          1946 E. de Phillipe (V.) A. Feldmann (A.)
                                       P. Gorin (G.) (in Heb.)

ITALY
Alessandria   Municipale  Oct.      1855 F.  Gordosa  (V.)  C.  Liverani  (A.)  L.
                                         Giraldoni (G.)

Ancona        Muse        Apr. 14, 1855 A.  Cortesi  (V.)  E.  Pancani  (A.)  P.
                                        Giorgi-Pacini (G.)

Ascoli        Ventidio    Nov. 14, 1855 R.  Gianfredi  (V.)  A.  Dall'Armi  (A.)
Piceno        Basso                     A. Ottaviani (G.)

Bari          Piccinni    Dec. 26, 1855 A.  Ortolani-Brignole  (V.)  A.  Oliva-
                                        Pavani (A.) D. Squarcia (G.)

|  |  |  |  |
|---|---|---|---|
|  | Petruzzelli | Dec. 25, 1903 | E. Clasenti (V.) G. Genzardi (A.) S. Vinci (G.) |
| Bergamo | Sociale | Dec. 26, 1854 | A. Moltini (V.) G. Petrovich (A.) C. Bartolucci (G.) |
| Bologna | Comunale | Nov. 20, 1855 | A. Albertini (V.) C. Baucardé (A.) E. Crivelli (G.) |
| Brescia | Grande | Dec. 26, 1856 | G. Brambilla (V.) G. Petrovich (A.) C. Morelli-Condolmieri (G.) |
| Cagliari | Civico | Sep. 8, 1857 | L. Borgognoni (V.) A. Zennari (A.) P. D'Ettore (G.) |
| Catania | Comunale | Jan. 3, 1856 | C. Martinelli (V.) P. Cecchi (A.) L. Roncagli (G.) M. Pappalardo cond. |
|  | Bellini | June 8, 1893 | G. Gargano (V.) P. Lazzarini (A.) E. Stinco-Palermini (G.) G. Pomé-Penna cond. |
| Chieti | Maruccino | Apr. 29, 1856 | M. Armandi (V.) R. Bettazzi (A.) L. Roncagli (G.) G. Liberali cond. |
| Cremona | Concordia | Sep. 16, 1856 | L. Ponti dall'Armi (V.) A. Dall'Armi (A.) G. Orlandi (G.) |
| Faenza | Comunale | June? 1855 | A. Cortesi (V.) E. Pancani (A.) A. Ottaviani (G.) |
| Fermo | Aquila | Aug.? 1856 | F. Salvini-Donatelli (V.) B. Massimiliani (A.) R. Pizzigati (G.) A. Marziali cond. |
| Ferrara | Comunale | May 1857 | R. Gianfredi (V.) C. Liverani (A.) F. Massiani (G.) |
| Fiume | Civico | Mar. 1857 | V. Boccabadati (V.) A. Pagnoni (A.) G. Orlandi (G.) |
| Florence | Pergola | Sep. 20, 1854 | A. Cortesi (V.) G. Fraschini (A.) P. Baraldi (G.) |
| Forli | Comunale | May? 1855 | V. Boccabadati (V.) A. Agresti (A.) G. Fiori (G.) |
| Genoa | Carlo Felice | Jan. 18, 1855 | L. Bendazzi-Secchi (V.) G. Landi (A.) F. Colini (G.) A. Mariani cond. |
| Livorno | Floridi | Oct. 14, 1855 | A. Cortesi (V.) E. Pancani (A.) G. B. Bencich (G.) |
| Lucca | Giglio | Sep. 18, 1856 | R. Gianfredi (V.) S. Malvezzi (A.) E. Storti (G.) |
| Lugo | Rossini | Aug.? 1856 | G. Beltrameli (V.) C. Liverani (A.) P. Baraldi (G.) |
| Mantua | Sociale | Dec. 26? 1855 | F. Gordosa (V.) A. Malagola (A.) E. Delle Sedie (G.) |
| Messina | Sant' Elisabetta | Mar. 5, 1856 | A. Argentini-Cantalamessa (V.) G. Pardini (A.) R. Mastriani (G.) |

Verdi

| Milan | Canobbiana | Sep. 10, 1856 | M. Spezia-Aldighieri (V.) E. Pancani (A.) L. Giraldoni (G.) |
|---|---|---|---|
| | La Scala | Dec. 29, 1860 | E. Weisser (V.) E. Nicolini (A.) M. Zacchi (G.) E. Cavallini cond. |
| Modena | Comunale | Apr. 15, 1855 | V. Boccabadati (V.) G. Landi (A.) F. Coletti (G.) A. Sighicelli cond. |
| Naples | San Carlo | Jan. 28, 1855 | G. Beltramelli (V.) E. Carrion (A.) L. Giraldoni (G.) A. Farelli cond. |
| Padua | Nuovo | June 12, 1857 | A. Basseggio (V.) A. Pagnoni (A.) G. Guicciardi (G.) |
| Palermo | Carolino | Feb. 28, 1856 | A. Basseggio (V.) E. Naudin (A.) L. Pignolo (G.) A. Lo Casto cond. |
| | Massimo | Feb. 17, 1898 | G. Gargano (V.) C. Lanfredi (A.) S. Carobbi (G.) A. Palmintieri cond. |
| Parma | Regio | Jan. 10, 1855 | A. Cortesi (V.) G. Pardini (A.) A. Ottaviani (G.) N. De Giovanni cond. |
| Pavia | Condomini | Dec. 26, 1856 | V. De Martini (V.) E. Giusti (A.) A. Rossi (G.) |
| Perugia | Verzaro | Aug. 15, 1856 | A. Angelini-Cantalamessa (V.) L. Mencarelli (A.) A. Morelli (G.) |
| Pesaro | Rossini | Dec. 26? 1855 | F. Capuani (V.) G. Ortolani (A.) A. Fellini (G.) G. Francalucci cond. |
| Pisa | Ravvivati | Dec. 28, 1854 | C. Frassi (V.) G. Forti (A.) P. Giorgi-Pacini (G.) C. Marsili cond. |
| Ravenna | Alighieri | May 18, 1856 | A. Basseggio (V.) B. Massimiliani (A.) G. Guicciardi (G.) |
| Reggio Emilia | Municipale | Jan. 12, 1858 | G. Beltramini (V.) G. Piccinnini (A.) T. Consoli (G.) G. Tebaldi cond. A. Peri dir. |
| Rome | Apollo | Dec. 30, 1854 | R. Penco (V.) E. Naudin (A.) G. B. Bencich (G.) E. Angelini cond. |
| | Costanzi | Dec. 21, 1881 | G. Gargano (V.) A. Rossetti (A.) A. Souvestre (G.) G. Mililotti cond. |
| Rovigo | Sociale | Oct. 17, 1854 | V. Boccabadati (V.) A. Giuglini (A.) A. Ottaviani (G.) D. Tosarini cond. |
| Siena | Rinnovati | Feb. 14, 1856 | M. Piccolomini (V.) A. Prudenza (A.) S. Ronconi (G.) |
| Sinigaglia | Comunale | July 18, 1857 | F. Salvini-Donatelli (V.) S. Malvezzi (A.) F. Coliva (G.) |
| Spoleto | Nobile | Dec. 26, 1857 | M. Mollo (V.) E. Biondini (A.) G. Orsini (G.) |
| Trento | Sociale | June 1856 | R. Gianfredi (V.) C. Negrini (A.) L. Giraldoni (G.) |

Treviso        Societa       Oct. 11, 1856 T. De Giuli-Borsi (V.) A. Giuglini
                                           (A.) P. Giorgi-Pacini (G.)

Trieste        Grande        Sep. 17, 1856 M. Gazzaniga (V.) C. Negrini (A.) G.
                                           Guicciardi (G.) G. A. Scaramelli
                                           cond.

Turin          Carignano     Oct. 9, 1855 M. Piccolomini (V.) B. Massimiliani
                                          (A.) F. Colini (G.)

               Regio         Apr. 2, 1860 F. Gordosa (V.) M. Tiberini (A.) G.
                                          F. Beneventano (G.)

Udine          Sociale       July    1860 V. Boccabadati (V.) V. Sarti (A.) E.
                                          Delle Sedie (G.)

Verona         Filarmonico Dec. 26, 1854 C. Alaimo (V.) A. Giuglini (A.) F.
                                         Cresci (G.)

Vicenza        Eretenio      Dec. 26? 1866 A. Heller (V.) L. Vistarini (A.) G.
                                           Valle (G.)

Viterbo        Unione        Aug.    1857 F. Capuani (V.) G. Musiani (A.) P.
                                          Baraldi (G.)

JAPAN
Tokyo          Imperial      Sep. 9, 1919 Osipova (V.) Preobajenki (A.) Gor-
                                          denko (G.) (in Rus.)

                             Jan. 21, 1923 (in It.)

Yokohama       Gaiety        Sep. 17, 1919 (in Rus.)

JUGOSLAVIA
Belgrade       National      June    1911 Placucci (V.) Pluchino (A.) A. Mas-
                                          caragna (G.) (in It.)

Ljubljana      National      Dec. 10, 1898

Zagreb         National      May     1858 C. Crescimano (V.) A. Marchetti (A.)
                                          V. Collini (G.)

Zara           Nobile        Apr.?   1858 D. Barberini (V.) E. Giusti (A.) A.
                                          Cotogni (G.)

LATVIA
Riga           Municipal     May     1900 F. Percuopo (A.) Pompa (G.) (in It.)
                                          (First production traced)

               National      Jan. 17, 1920 B. Valle cond. (in Let.)

LITHUANIA
Kaunas         Imperial      Dec. 16, 1906 G. Wermez (V.) A. Balboni (A.) L.
                                           Fillipini (G.)

               National      Dec. 31, 1920 (in Lith.)

Vilnius        Municipal     Mar. 8, 1898 S. Aifos (V.) M. Massimi (A.) Bon-
                                          fanti (G.) (in It.)

MALTA
La Valletta    Manoel        Oct. 2, 1855 E. Parepa (V.) F. Tamaro (A.) E.
                                          Storti (G.)

MEXICO
Guadalajara    Degollado                  1858 A. Cortesi (V.)

Mexico City    Nacional        Dec. 23, 1856 G. Landi  (V.)  L.  Stefani  (A.)  A.
                                            Ottaviani (G.) C. Fattori cond.

MONACO
Monte Carlo    Salle           Jan. 22, 1881 A. Patti  (V.) E. Nicolini  (A.)  B.
               Garnier                       Berardi (G.) R. Accursi cond.

NETHERLANDS
Amsterdam      Stads           Apr. 24, 1860 L. Ponti dall'Armi (V.) B. Danieli
                                            (A.) G. Marra (G.) N. Bassi cond.

NEW ZEALAND
Auckland       Prince          Nov. 28, 1864 L. Escott  (V.)  H. Squires (A.)  H.
               of Wales                      Wharton (G.)

Dunedin        Princess        Sep.  7, 1864 L. Escott  (V.)  H. Squires (A.)  H.
                                            Wharton (G.)

Wellington     Th. Royal       Feb. 27, 1880 G. Tamburini-Coy (V.) L. Coy (A.) G.
                                            Verdi (G.)

NORWAY
Oslo           Christiana      May   5, 1868 M. Calisto (V.) G. Bentami (A.) A.
                                            Pantaleoni (G.) (in It.)

                               Oct.  3, 1888 (in Norw.)

PANAMA
Panama City    Nacional        Nov. 24, 1908 C. Tamanti-Zavaschi (V.)

PERU
Lima           Principal       Dec. 12, 1857 I. Edelvira (V.) L. Guglielmini (A.)
                                            A. Lanzoni (G.)

PHILIPPINES
Manila                         Nov.?    1867 L. De Ponte (V.) E. Pizzioli (A.) G.
                                            Reina (G.)

POLAND
Cracow         Imperial        July  4, 1866 Clement (A.) Tillmetz (G.) (in Ger.)

Lvov           Szarbek         Aug.     1862 E. Volpini (V.) M. Zacchi (G.) (in
                                            It.)

Warsaw         Wielki          Apr. 27, 1856 E. Berini  (V.)  F.  Ciaffei (A.)  L.
                                            Buti (G.) (in It.)

PORTUGAL
Lisbon         Sao Carlos      Oct. 29, 1855 M. Spezia-Aldighieri (V.) A. Volpini
                                            (A.) O. Bartolini (G.)

Oporto         Sao Joao        Feb.     1855 L. Ponti dall'Armi (V.) G. Dall'Armi
                                            (A.) F. Gnone (G.)

ROMANIA
Bucharest      Nacional        Dec.?    1856 L. Ponti dall'Armi (V.) G. Dall'Armi
                                            A. Vitti (G.) (in It.)

Iasi           Teatrul         Feb.?    1857 R. Gariboldi-Bassi (V.) G. De Vecchi
                                            (A.) C. Busi (G.)

RUSSIA
Kharkov        Municipal    May?       1864 Sermattei (V.) A. Gottardi (A.) F.
                                            Giannini (G.)

Kiev           Imperial     Dec.?      1865 A. D'Alberti (V.) P. Cecchi (A.) C.
                                            Fabbricatore (G.)

Moscow         Bolshoi      Oct.  1, 1856 A. Bosio (V.) E. Calzolari (A.) A.
                                            De Bassini (G.) E. Baveri cond.

Odessa         Municipal    Jan.?      1858 C. Mongini-Stecchi (V.) A. Pozzolini
                                            (A.)

St.            Imperial     Nov.  1, 1856 A. Bosio (V.) E. Calzolari (A.) O.
Petersburg                                  Bartolini (G.) E. Baveri cond.

                            May   8, 1868 (in Rus.)

Tbilisi        Imperial     Nov. 30, 1858 Ramoni (V.) F. Briani (A.)

SOUTH AFRICA
Capetown       Th. Royal    Feb. 26, 1876 A. Brambilla (V.) Cosmi (A.) Greco
                                            (G.) (in It.)

Johannesburg   Amphi-       June 11, 1895 E. Ancarani (V.) V. Maina (A.) M. De
               theatre                      Padova (G.) Perigozzo cond. (in It.)

SPAIN
Alicante       Principal    Apr. 13, 1859 F. Pozzo (A.) L. Walter (G.)

Barcelona      Liceo        Oct. 25, 1855 E. Julienne-Dejean (V.) G. De Vecchi
                                            (A.) G. Fiori (G.)

Bilbao         Viejo        Mar.?      1858 C. Forti-Babacci (V.) Berti (A.) C.
                                            Morelli-Condolmieri (G.)

Cadiz          Principal    Apr.?      1855 M. Spezia-Aldighieri (V.) A. Pruden-
                                            za (A.) E. Crivelli (G.)

Madrid         Real         Feb.  1, 1855 M. Spezia-Aldighieri (V.) S. Malvez-
                                            zi (A.) G. Guicciardi (G.) J. Skocz-
                                            dopole cond.

Seville        San          June  8, 1858 A. Ortolani-Brignole (V.) F. Mazzo-
               Fernando                     leni (A.) A. M. Celestino (G.)

Valencia       Principal    Sep.?      1855 M. Gazzaniga (V.) S. Malvezzi (A.)

Valladolid     Lope         Jan. 15, 1859 C. Forti-Babacci (V.) M. Viani (A.)
               de Vega                      C. Morelli-Condolmieri (G.)

SWEDEN
Gotheborg                   Apr.       1868 M. Calisto (V.) G. Bentami (A.) A.
                                            Pantaleoni (G.) (in It.)

Stockholm      Royal        Feb. 21, 1868 E. Sorandi (V.) F. Ambrosi (A.) G.
                                            Sandström (G.)

               Mindre       Nov. 18, 1868 Z. Dalti (V.) G. Bentami (A.) G.
                                            Mendioroz (G.)

SWITZERLAND
Basel          Stadt        May   1, 1863 A. Leona (V.) A. Altavilla (A.) Bor-
                                            ghese (G.) (in It.)

                              Mar.  18, 1887 (in Ger.)

Geneva        Grand         Oct.      1865 A. Winans (V.) (in Fr.)

                              Mar.      1870 (In It.)

Lugano        Sociale       Oct.      1861 Mazzoni (V.) (in It.)

Zürich        Stadt         Nov. 22, 1877 (in Ger.)

TURKEY
Constan-      Naum          Nov. 27, 1856 F. Salvini-Donatelli (V.) A. Mala-
  tinople                                 gola (A.) G. Fiori (G.) L. Arditi
                                          cond.

UNITED STATES
Baltimore     Holliday      Mar. 15, 1860 P. Colson (V.)  G. Stigelli (A.)  A.
              Street                      Amodio (G.)

Boston        Boston Th.    June  8, 1857 M. Gazzaniga (V.) P. Brignoli (A.)
                                          A. Amodio (G.)

Brooklyn      Ac. of Mus.   Feb.  8, 1862 C. L. Kellogg (V.) P. Brignoli (A.)

Buffalo       St. James     Aug.  8, 1859 C. Alaimo (V.) G. Sbriglia (A.) F.
                                          Gnone (G.) A. Torriani cond.

Charleston    New Th.       Feb. 21, 1860 C. Alaimo (V.) G. Sbriglia (A.) F.
                                          Gnone (G.) A. Torriani cond.

Chicago       McVicker's    Feb. 23, 1859 P. Colson (V.) P. Brignoli (A.) A.
                                          Amodio (G.) M. Strakosch cond.

              Auditorium    Dec. 24, 1889 A. Patti (V.) L. Ravelli (A.) A.
                                          Marescalchi (G.) R. Sapio cond.

              Lyric         Nov.  8, 1854 M. Callas (V.) L. Simoneau (A.) T.
                                          Gobbi (G.) N. Rescigno cond.

Cincinnati    Wood's        July 15, 1857 C. Cairoli (V.) A. Macaferri (A.) L.
                                          Corradi-Setti (G.)

              Opera         July  9, 1923 E. De Lys (V.) L. Tomarchio (A.) M.
                                          Valle (G.) R. Lyford cond.

Dallas        Op. House     Feb. 28, 1885 E. Abbott (V.) (in Eng.)

              Opera         Oct. 31, 1958 M. Callas (V.) N. Filacuridi (A.) G.
                                          taddei (G.) N. Rescigno cond.

Denver                      Sep.      1881 E. Abbott (V.) (In Eng.)

                            Mar.  1, 1884 A. Patti (V.) E. Vicini (A.) A. Ga-
                                          lassi (G.) (in It.) L. Arditi cond.

Detroit       Metro-        Nov. 25, 1859 C. Alaimo (V.)  G. Sbriglia (A.)  F.
              politan                     Gnone (G.) A. Torriani cond.

Houston       Theatre       Apr. 11, 1867

              Grand Opera   Feb.  7, 1957 K. Fitzpatrick (V.) D. Poleri (A.)
                                          P. Maero (G.) W. Herbert cond.

Los Angeles   Grand        Feb.  4, 1885 E.  Abbott  (V.)  W.  Castle  (A.)  G.
                                          Tagliapietra (G.) (in Eng.)

              Theatre      Oct. 30, 1897 C.  Vicini (V.) G. Agostini (A.) (in
                                          It.)

Louisville    Theatre      Jan. 27, 1859 C. De Wildhorst (V.) H. Squires (A.)
                                          A. Amodio (G.) M. Strakosch cond.

Milwaukee                           1861 (in Ger.)

              Music Hall   May 14, 1866 A. Ghioni (V.) B. Massimiliani (A.)
                                          F. Bellini (G.)

Nashville     Crisp's      Jan. 21, 1860 C. Alaimo (V.) G. Sbriglia (A.) F.
                                          Gnone (G.) A. Torriani cond.

New Orleans   Crisp's      Apr. 22, 1857 G. Landi (V.) M. Tiberini (A.) Vier-
                                          ri (G.) (in It.)

              Opera        Dec. 23, 1865 A.  Ghioni  (V.)  A.  Errani (A.)   G.
                                          Mancusi (G.) (in It.)

                           Jan. 28, 1869 (in Fr.)

New York      Ac. of Mus. Dec.  3, 1856 A.  De  la  Grange  (V.)  P.  Brignoli
                                          (A.)  A.  Amodio  (G.)  M.  Maretzek
                                          cond.

              Metro-       Nov.  5, 1883 M. Sembrich (V.)  V. Capoul (A.)  G.
              politan                     Del Puente (G.) A. Vianesi cond.

Philadelphia  Ac. of Mus. Mar. 13, 1857 M. Gazzaniga (V.) P. Brignoli (A.)
                                          A. Amodio (G.)

Pittsburgh    National     Apr. 16, 1859 P.  Colson (V.)  H.  Squires (A.)  A.
                                          Amodio (G.) M. Strakosch cond.

St. Louis     Theatre      Feb.  4, 1859 P.  Colson (V.)  H.  Squires (A.)  A.
                                          Amodio (G.) M. Strakosch cond.

San Francisco American     Aug. 13, 1859 G. Bianchi (V.) E. Bianchi (A.) S.
                                          W. Leach (G.)

              Auditorium   Oct.  4, 1924 C. Muzio (V.) T. Schipa (A.) G. De
                                          Luca (G.) G. Merola cond.

Washington    Theatre      Apr. 13, 1858 M. Gazzaniga (V.) P. Brignoli (A.)
                                          A. Gasparoni (G.)

              National     Dec. 14, 1868 A. De la Grange (V.) A. Boetti (A.)

URUGUAY
Montevideo    San Felipe   May 10, 1856 S. Vera-Lorini (V.) G. Comolli (A.)
                                          G. Cima (G.) L. Pretti cond.

              Solis        Sep.  2, 1856 S. Vera-Lorini (V.) G. Comolli (A.)
                                          G. Cima (G.) L. Pretti cond.

VENEZUELA
Caracas       Teatro       Dec. 19, 1860

              Municipal    Jan. 29, 1881 M. Lucchesi (V.) F. Giannini (A.) D.
                                          Farina (G.) F. Rachelle cond.

20.  LES VEPRES SICILIENNES-*Opéra* in five acts
Paris-Académie Impériale de Musique (Opéra)-June 13, 1855
Libretto by Eugène Scribe and Charles Duveyrier

| | |
|---|---|
| Hélène (E.) | Sofia Cruvelli sop. |
| Henri (A.) | Louis Guyemard ten. |
| Guy de Montfort (G.) | Marc Bonnehée bar. |
| Jean Procida (P.) | Louis-Henri Obin bass |
| Ninetta | Sannnier mez. |
| Danieli | Boulo ten. |
| Thibaut | Aimès ten. |
| Mainfroid | König ten. |
| Béthune | Theodore Coulon bass |
| Robert | Marié bar. |
| Vaudemont | Guignot bass |

Conductor
Director                                              Giuseppe Verdi

OTHER PRODUCTIONS-NINETEENTH CENTURY

ARGENTINA
Buenos Aires   Ant. Colon   May  23, 1862  T. Parodi (E.) L. Mazzi (A.) L. Walter (G.) A. Chiodini (P.) V. Fumi
cond.

May  14, 1874  M. Mariani-Masi (E.) C. Bulterini
(A.) L. Colonnese (G.) M. Junca (P.)

Opera        July 25, 1891  L. Gabbi (E.) M. Mariacher (A.) A.
Scotti (G.) E. Serbolini (P.) M.
Mancinelli cond.

July  2, 1892  C. Bordalba (E.) M. Mariacher (A.)
A. Scotti (G.) R. Ercolani (P.)

AUSTRALIA
Adelaide       Th. Royal    Oct. 23, 1874  M. Palmieri (E.) D. Rosnati (A.) F.
Coliva (G.) E. Dondi (P.) A. Zelman
cond.

Melbourne      Th. Royal    July 14, 1870  L. Baratti (E.) M. Neri (A.) L. Con-
tini (G.) E. Dondi (P.) A. Marzorati
cond.

Princess     Mar.  8, 1872  A. States (E.) P. Cecchi (A.) G. Orlandini (G.) A. Susini (P.)

Sydney         Prince       May  12, 1870  L. Baratti (E.) M. Neri (A.) L. Con-
of Wales                      tini (G.) E. Dondi (P.) A. Marzorati
cond.

Oct. 28, 1870  L. Baratti (E.) M. Neri (A.) L. Con-
tini (G.) E. Dondi (P.) A. Marzorati
cond.

Victoria     Aug.  7, 1874  M. Palmieri (E.) A. Beaumont (A.) F.
Coliva (G.) E. Dondi (P.) A. Zelman
cond.

AUSTRIA
Vienna         Kärntnertor Nov. 19, 1857  T. Tietiens (E.) A. Ander (A.) J. N.
Beck (G.) J. Draxler (P.)

Oct. 23, 1858 T. Tietiens (E.) F. Steger (A.) J.
N. Beck (G.) J. Draxier (P.)

Hofoper        Nov. 23, 1878

BELGIUM
Brussels       Monnaie      Nov. 18, 1856 Vandenhaute (E.) Wicart (A.) S. Carman (G.) Depoitier (P.)

BRAZIL
Rio de         Pedro II     Aug. 25, 1871 A. Pasi (E.) L. Lelmi (A.) C. Mar-
Janeiro                                   ziali (G.) J. Ordinas (P.)

Sao Paulo      Sao José     Sep. 14, 1892 C. Bordalba (E.) M. Mariacher (A.)
A. Scotti (G.) R. Ercolani (P.)

CHILE
Santiago       Municipal    Oct. 24? 1857 I. Edelvira (E.) L. Guglielmini (A.)
A. Lanzoni (G.) G. Bastoggi (P.)

CUBA
Havana         Tacon        Mar.  6, 1862 E. Kenneth (E.) G. Tombesi (A.) G.
Ferri (G.) G. B. Antonucci (P.)

FRANCE
Bordeaux       Grand        Mar.     1882

Marseille      Grand        May  26, 1868 M. Lafon (E.) Michot (A.) J. V. Ismael (G.) P. Dérivis (P.)

Nice           Municipal    Jan. 21? 1877 V. Potentini (E.) M. Neri (A.) Cappelli (G.) (in It.)

Paris          Opéra        Sep.     1855 S. Cruvelli/Moreau-Sainti (E.) L.
Guyemard (A.) M. Bonnehée (G.) L. H.
Obin (P.)

Oct.?    1856 G. Medori/Moreau-Sainti (E.) L.
Guyemard (A.) M. Bonnehée (G.) L. H.
Obin (P.)

May      1859 C. Barbot (E.) L. Guyemard (A.) M.
Bonnehée (G.) L. H. Obin (P.)

July 20, 1863 M. Sasse (E.) P. F. Villaret (A.) M.
Bonnehée (G.) L. H. Obin (P.)

Sep. 21, 1863 M. Sasse (E.) P. F. Villaret (A.)
Caron (G.) L. H. Obin (P.)

Sep.     1864 M. Sasse (E.) Warot (A.) M. Bonnehée
(G.) L. H. Obin (P.)

GERMANY
Darmstadt      Hoftheater   Mar. 14, 1857 Nimbs (E.) Grille (A.) K. Becker
(G.) F. Dalle Aste (P.) (in Ger.)

Sep. 12, 1887 (in Ger.)

Hamburg        Stadtoper    Oct. 14, 1857 (in Ger.)

Königsberg     Stadt        Feb.?    1870 (in Ger.)

GREAT BRITAIN
London          Drury Lane   July 27, 1859 T. Tietiens (E.) P. Mongini (A.) E.
                                           Fagotti (G.) P. Vialetti (P.) L. Ar-
                                           diti cond.

GREECE
Corfu           San Giacomo Oct.   1860 A. Angelini-Cantalamessa  (E.)  G.
                                        Giorgetti (A.) F. Proni (G.) F.
                                        Fiorani (P.)

HUNGARY
Budapest        Nemzeti      Oct.  7, 1856 J. Kaiser-Ernst (E.) J. Ellinger
                Szinház                    (A.) M. Füredy (G.) K. Köszeghi (P.)
                                           F. Erkel cond. (in Hung.)

ITALY
Alessandria     Municipale   Oct.    1879

Ancona          Muse         May  20, 1856 M. Gazzaniga (E.) P. Mongini (A.) P.
                                           Gorin (G.) F. Pons (P.)

Bari            Piccinni     Feb.    1867 A. Pasi (E.) G. Ugolini (A.) G. San-
                                          sone (G.) Maccani (P.)

Bergamo         Riccardi     Aug. 14, 1870 L. Bendazzi-Secchi (E.) G. De Antoni
                                           (A.) F. Graziosi (G.) G. Vecchi (P.)

Bologna         Comunale     Oct.  2, 1856 L. Bendazzi-Secchi (E.) R. Mirate
                                           (A.) G. B. Bencich (G.) R. Laterza
                                           (P.) G. Manetti cond.

Brescia         Grande       Aug.  7, 1869 L. Bendazzi-Secchi (E.) G. Fancelli/
                                           M. Neri (A.) G. Rota (G.) P. Medini
                                           (P.)

Cagliari        Civico       Feb. 21? 1867 L. Banti (E.)

Carpi           Comunale     Aug.    1869 Z. Papini (E.) G. Toressi (A.) G.
                                          Del Puente (G.) C. Zucchelli (P.)

Casalmon-       Municipale   Oct. 29, 1865 C. Cattinari (E.) M. Neri (A.) I.
  ferrato                                  Viganotti (G.) P. Dérivis (P.)

Chieti          San          Apr. 30, 1859 C. Marziali (E.) U. Albicini (A.) C.
                Ferdinando                 Boccolini (G.)

Cremona         Concordia    Jan. 11, 1873 M. De Zorzi (E.) A. Da Ponti (A.) T.
                                           Noto (G.) G. Marchetti (P.) G. Bi-
                                           gnami cond. A. Ponchielli dir.

Ferrara         Comunale     Apr.    1864 P. Colson (E.) P. Bignardi (A.) D.
                                          Dal Negro (G.) A. Fiorini (P.) R.
                                          Sarti cond.

Fiume           Civico       Mar. 14, 1868 L. Banti (E.) M. Neri (A.) A. Carbo-
                                           ni (G.) G. Vecchi (P.)

Florence        Pagliano     Apr. 15, 1856 A. Albertini (E.) C. Baucardé (A.)
                                           P. Giorgi-Pacini (G.) G. B. Antonuc-
                                           ci (P.)

                             Oct.  4, 1856 M. Barbieri-Nini (E.) P. Mongini
                                           (A.) F. Cresci (G.) G. B. Cornago
                                           (P.) E. Vannuccini cond.

|          |                   | Oct.         | 1872    | L. Bendazzi-Secchi (E.) G. Vanzan (A.) V. Quintili-Leoni (G.) A. Fiorini (P.) |
|          |                   | Nov. 15,     | 1890    | R. Calligaris-Marty (E.) G. Sani (A.) S. Carobbi (G.) |
|          | Pergola           | Sep. 19,     | 1857    | A. Albertini (E.) C. Baucardé (A.) G. Guicciardi (G.) G. Segri-Segarra (P.) |
|          | Lent              |              | 1864    | C. Fiorentini (E.) G. Stigelli (A.) G. Cima (G.) C. Dalla Costa (P.) |
| Genoa    | Carlo Felice      | May 22,      | 1856    | C. Goldberg-Strozzi (E.) A. Giuglini (A.) F. Cresci (G.) G. B. Cornago (P.) A. Mariani cond. |
|          |                   | Mar. 28,     | 1864    | C. Carozzi-Zucchi (E.) E. Carrion (A.) A. Cotogni (G.) H. Brémond (P.) A. Mariani cond. |
|          |                   | Dec. 26,     | 1868    | L. Bendazzi-Secchi (E.) S. Malvezzi (A.) F. Pandolfini (G.) G. Capponi (P.) A. Mariani cond. |
| Livorno  | Floridi           | Aug. 10,     | 1856    | R. Penco (E.) S. Malvezzi (A.) Quercia (G.) L. Domenech (P.) |
| Lucca    | Giglio            | Aug.         | 1872    | V. Potentini (E.) G. Vanzan (A.) G. Cima (G.) E. Rossi-Galli (P.) |
| Lugo     | Rossini           | Aug.?        | 1865    | L. Bendazzi-Secchi (E.) P. Bignardi (A.) A. Cotogni (G.) F. Rigo (P.) Centolani cond. |
| Mantua   | Sociale           | Carn.        | 1873-74 | C. Carozzi-Zucchi (E.) G. Cima (G.) |
| Messina  | Vittorio Emanuele | Jan. 30,     | 1865    | A. Pasi (E.) C. Bulterini (A.) A. Carbone (G.) G. Benedetti (P.) |
| Milan    | La Scala          | Feb. 4,      | 1856    | M. Barbieri-Nini (E.) L. Graziani (A.) L. Giraldoni (G.) C. Nanni (P.) E. Cavallini cond. |
|          |                   | Dec. 26,     | 1857    | A. Albertini (E.) C. Negrini (A.) G. Guicciardi (G.) A. Biacchi (P.) E. Cavallini cond. |
|          |                   | Feb. 7,      | 1864    | M. Lotti della Santa (E.) E. Carrion (A.) O. Bartolini (G.) S. Cesarò (P.) |
|          |                   | Dec. 26,     | 1875    | M. Mariani-Masi (E.) L. Bolis (A.) G. Aldighieri (G.) O. Maini/G. Marchetti (P.) |
| Modena   | Comunale          | Dec. 29,     | 1860    | M. Talvò (E.) G. Villani (A.) F. Bachi-Perego (G.) N. Contedini (P.) A. Sighicelli cond. |
|          |                   | Dec. 25,     | 1879    | N. Bonal/V. Crespi (E.) F. Bellotti (A.) A. Medini (G.) L. Vierzbicki (P.) M. Vela cond. |

| Naples | Nuovo | June 6, 1857 | Z. Papini (E.) E. Concordia (A.) I. Canedi (G.) Aversa (P.) M. Di Natale cond. |
|---|---|---|---|
| | San Carlo | Sep. 5, 1857 | V. Viola (E.) A. Prudenza (A.) F. Coletti (G.) G. B. Antonucci (P.) A. Farelli cond. |
| | | Dec. 25, 1857 | R. Penco (E.) G. Fraschini (A.) F. Coletti (G.) M. Arati (P.) A. Farelli cond. |
| | | Aug. 6, 1859 | L. Bendazzi-Secchi/L. Lesniewska (E.) F. Mazzoleni (A.) F. Coletti/G. Guicciardi (G.) M. Arati/G. Atry (P.) A. Farelli cond. |
| | | Jan. 17, 1866 | M. Lotti della Santa (E.) G. Stigelli (A.) L. Colonnese (G.) H. Brémond (P.) |
| | | Jan. 6, 1898 | L. Pagin/L. Montuschi (E.) G. Peirani (A.) E. Giraldoni (G.) N. Serra (P.) E. Vitale cond. |
| Padua | Nuovo | July 5, 1856 | M. Barbieri-Nini (E.) L. Graziani (A.) G. B. Bencich (G.) B. Cervini (P.) |
| | Concordi | Jan. 1870 | R. Costa-Giani (E.) G. Vanzan (P.) A. Pifferi (G.) |
| Palermo | Carolino | Oct. 3, 1856 | F. Gordosa (E.) C. Miraglia (A.) R. Pizzigati (G.) G. B. Antonucci (P.) A. Lo Casto cond. |
| | Bellini | Jan. 1861 | A. Ortolani-Brignole (E.) F. Mazzoleni (A.) R. Pizzigati (G.) S. Cesarò (P.) A. Lo Casto cond. |
| | | Mar. 1863 | E. Poinsot (E.) E. Barbacini (A.) G. Aldighieri (G.) F. Rinaldi (P.) A. Lo Casto cond. |
| | | Dec. 26, 1865 | T. Stolz (E.) C. Bulterini (A.) G. Guicciardi (G.) G. Capponi (P.) L. De Carlo cond. |
| | | Dec. 29, 1874 | T. Brambilla-Ponchielli (E.) E. Barbacini (A.) L. Giraldoni (G.) L. Vecchi (P.) L. Alfano cond. |
| | Politeama | Dec. 26, 1893 | R. Calligaris-Marty (E.) B. Lucignani (A.) I. Tabuyo/G. Pacini (G.) E. Serbolini (P.) G. Gialdini cond. |
| Parma | Regio | Dec. 26, 1855 | C. Goldberg-Strossi (E.) A. Giuglini (A.) F. Cresci (G.) G. Atry (P.) N. De Giovanni cond. |
| | | Dec. 25, 1867 | L. Banti (E.) M. Neri (A.) A. Carboni (G.) A. Frontoni (P.) G. C. Ferrarini cond. |

Pavia          Fraschini   Dec. 31, 1871 V. Saurel (E.) A. Ponti (A.) A.
                                         Pifferi (G.)

Perugia        Verzaro     Dec. 26, 1870 C. De Witten (E.) L. Donati (A.) F.
                                         Zucchi (G.) Gianoli (P.)

Piacenza       Municipale  Dec. 26? 1870 M. Savertal (E.) F. Cesari (A.) E.
                                         Corti (G.) C. Morroto (P.) P. Monta-
                                         guti cond.

Pisa           Verdi       Jan. 5, 1874 O. Picconi Pierangeli (E.) M. Neri
                                         (A.) A. Pogliano (G.) N. Pozzi (P.)
                                         L. Quercioli cond.

Ravenna        Alighieri   May 4, 1861 L. Bendazzi-Secchi (E.) V. Sarti
                                         (A.) R. Pizzigati (G.) P. Medini
                                         (P.) A. Moreschi cond.

Reggio Emilia Municipale  May 15, 1864 E. Corani (E.) P. Tasca de Cappello
                                         (A.) G. Guicciardi (G.) P. Medini
                                         (P.) G. Tebaldi cond.

Rimini         Nuovo       June     1863 L. Bendazzi-Secchi (E.) G. Villani
                                         (A.) C. Boccolini (G.) Rossi (P.)

Rome           Argentina   Apr. 6, 1856 T. De Giuli-Borsi (E.) G. Fraschini
                                         (A.) F. Coletti (G.) R. Laterza (P.)

               Jan.        1891 R. Calligaris-Marty (E.) G. Sani
                                         (A.) A. Scotti (G.) G. Notargiacomo
                                         (P.) E. Usiglio cond.

               Apollo      Dec. 26, 1858 L. Ponti dall'Armi (E.) G. Fraschini
                                         (A.) L. Giraldoni (G.) G. Segri-
                                         Segarra (P.) E. Angelini cond.

               Jan. 27, 1872 M. Lotti della Santa (E.) I. Campa-
                                         nini (A.) V. Cottone (G.) L. Vecchi
                                         (P.) E. Terziani cond.

               Politeama   July 5, 1873 C. Noel-Guidi (E.) A. Franchini (A.)
                                         S. Orsi (G.)

Rovigo         Sociale     Oct. 10, 1858 A. Albertini (E.) C. Baucardé (A.)
                                         L. Giraldoni (G.) G. Atry (P.)

Sinigaglia     Comunale    Fiera    1862 M. Lotti della Santa (E.) V. Sarti
                                         (A.) A. Cotogni (G.) H. Brémond (P.)

Terni          Nobile      Dec.     1864 E. Pezzoli (E.)

Trani          San         Apr.?    1865 L. Banti (E.) Massini (A.) R. Mas-
               Ferdinando                triani (G.)

Trento         Sociale     June 1, 1873 F. Vogry (E.) G. De Antoni (A.) A.
                                         Burgio (G.) Bastiannini (P.)

Trieste        Grande      Oct. 25, 1856 M. Gazzaniga (E.) C. Negrini (A.) G.
                                         Guicciardi (G.) B. Laura (P.) G. A.
                                         Scaramelli cond.

               Sep. 21? 1862 L. Bendazzi-Secchi (E.) C. Negrini
                                         (A.) D. Squarcia (G.) H. Brémond
                                         (P.) A. Cremaschi cond.

Feb. 9, 1873 L. Bendazzi-Secchi (E.) G. Vanzan
(A.) G. Valle (G.) G. C. Nerini (P.)
A. Cremaschi cond.

Turin        Regio        Jan. 5, 1856 M. Gazzaniga (E.) G. Fraschini (A.)
E. Crivelli (G.) G. Echeverria (P.)
G. C. Ferrarini cond.

Dec. 25, 1862 L. Bendazzi-Secchi (E.) A. Agresti
(A.) L. Colonnese (G.) R. Laterza
(P.) F. Bianchi cond.

Mar. 7, 1891 V. Damerini (E.) M. Mariacher (A.)
A. Pessina (G.) E. Serbolini (P.) G.
Cimini cond.

Carignano    Sep.?    1861 G. Beltramelli (E.) G. Limberti (A.)
A. Carboni (G.) A. Lanzoni (P.)

Balbo        Apr. 2, 1872 G. Boema (E.) A. Franchini (A.) Cabella (G.) Monti (P.) Simondi cond.

Udine                     July 27, 1858 A. Albertini (E.) C. Baucardé (A.)
L. Giraldoni (G.) G. Atry (P.)

Varese       Sociale      Sep. 28, 1869 V. Saurel (E.) R. Bertolini (A.) U.
Brambilla (G.) R. Buffagni (P.)

Venice       La Fenice    Feb. 16, 1856 L. Lesniewska (E.) E. Pancani (A.)
G. Guicciardi (G.) G. B. Cornago
(P.) C. E. Bosoni cond.

Nov. 4, 1856 A. Albertini (E.) S. Malvezzi (A.)
G. Ferri (G.) G. Echeverria (P.) C.
E. Bosoni cond.

Mar. 13, 1880 G. De Giuli-Borsi (E.) G. Ferrari
(A.) G. Vaselli (G.) A. Silvestri
(P.) M. Mancinelli cond.

Apollo       Autumn   1858 A. Albertini (E.) C. Baucardé (A.)
L. Giraldoni (G.)

Verona       Filarmonico Feb. 26, 1856 A. Albertini (E.) C. Baucardé (A.)
G. B. Bencich (G.) L. Ruiz (P.)

Jan.?    1868 A. Contarini (E.)

Vicenza      Eretenio     Jan.?    1882 F. Savio/F. Conti (E.) A. Conti
cond.

MALTA
La Valletta  Manoel       May 2, 1857 G. Elena (E.) A. Oliva-Pavani (A.)
G. Spallazzi (G.) L. Rossi (P.)

MEXICO
Mexico City  Nacional     Nov. 27, 1864 M. Sulzer (E.) F. Mazzoleni (A.) A.
Ottaviani (G.) A. Biacchi (P.) J.
Nunò cond.

POLAND
Warsaw       Wielki       Dec. 23, 1873 M. Lotti della Santa (E.) A. Oliva-
Pavani (A.) E. Storti (G.) R. Nan-
netti (P.)

PORTUGAL
Lisbon        Sao Carlos   Mar. 12, 1857 T. De Giuli-Borsi (E.) P. Neri-Ba-
                           raldi (A.) G. F. Beneventano (G.) P.
                           Nolasco-Llorens (P.)

                           Feb. 27, 1858 F. Tedesco (E.) S. Malvezzi (A.) G.
                           F. Beneventano (G.) S. L. Bouché
                           (P.)

                           Mar. 17, 1860 F. Tedesco (E.) G. Fraschini (A.) O.
                           Bartolini (G.) G. B. Antonucci (P.)

                           Oct.  2, 1861 L. Bendazzi-Secchi (E.) G. Fraschini
                           (A.) G. Guicciardi (G.) C. Dalla
                           Costa (P.)

                           Dec. 10, 1862 M. Lotti della Santa (E.) P. Mongini
                           (A.) G. F. Beneventano (G.) G. B.
                           Antonucci (P.)

                           Dec.  7, 1863 F. Tedesco (E.) P. Mongini (A.) F.
                           Pandolfini (G.) P. Medini (P.)

                           Dec. 30, 1870 M. Lotti della Santa (E.) G. Ugolini
                           (A.) T. Sterbini (G.) J. Petit (P.)

Oporto        Sao Joao     Apr. 23, 1857 A. Ortolani-Brignole (E.) F. Mazzo-
                           leni (A.) A. Vitti (G.) E. Manfredi
                           (P.)

                           Autumn   1863 I. Alba (E.) G. De Antoni (A.) A. De
                           Antoni (G.)

ROMANIA
Bucharest     Nacional     Oct.?    1861 C. Cattinari (E.) F. Steger (A.) G.
                           Reina (G.) P. Nolasco-Llorens (P.)

                           Winter?  1870 A. Bianchi-Montaldo (E.) F. Patierno
                           (A.) P. Milesi (P.)

                           Feb. 11? 1872 A. Fossa (E.) F. Patierno (A.) L.
                           Rossi de Ruggero (G.) P. Milesi (P.)

Iasi          Teatrul      Mar.?    1874

RUSSIA
Astrakhan                  Sep.?    1874 E. Grilli (E.)

Odessa        Municipal    Dec.     1859 G. Beltramelli (E.) E. Irfré (A.) G.
                           Colombo (G.) G. Mitrovich (P.)

                           Aug.?    1860 I. Edelvira (E.) E. Irfré (A.) M.
                           Padilla (G.) G. Mitorovich (P.)

                           Autumn?  1863 C. Noel-Guidi (E.) S. Gottardi (A.)
                           V. Morellli-Bartolani (G.) G. B.
                           Cornago (P.)

                           Dec.     1865 B. Steffenone (E.) G. Ortolani (A.)
                           O. Bartolini (G.) Marinozzi (P.)

Mar. 12, 1869 A. Bianchi-Montaldo (E.) P. Bignardi
(A.) F. Bachi-Perego (G.) O. Maini
(P.)

St.            Imperial    Dec.  5, 1857 M. Lotti della Santa (E.) P. Mongini
Petersburg                              (A.) A. De Bassini (G.) C. Everardi
                                        (P.) E. Baveri cond.

               Oct.  1, 1858 M. Lotti della Santa (E.) P. Mongini
                             (A.) A. De Bassini (G.) C. Everardi
                             (P.) E. Baveri cond.

SPAIN
Alicante       Principal    Apr.  2, 1862 C. Poch (E.) G. De Antoni (A.)

Barcelona      Liceo        Oct.  4, 1856 C. Goldberg-Strozzi (E.) A. Agresti
                                          (A.) D. Mattioli (G.) A. Rodas (P.)

               Jan.?        1858 E. Masson (E.) A. Agresti (A.) G. B.
                                 Bencich (G.) C. Nanni (P.)

               Oct. 16, 1869 L. Bendazzi-Secchi (E.) A. Prudenza
                             (A.) V. Quintili-Leoni (G.) G. Cap-
                             poni (P.)

Cadiz          Principal    Oct.   1861 C. Poch (E.) G. De Antoni (A.) Con-
                                        stantini (G.) A. Rodas (P.)

Granada        Principal    May    1863 L. Ponti dall'Armi (E.) A. Dall'Armi
                                        (A.) P. Giorgi-Pacini (G.) Ruiz (P.)

Madrid         Real         Dec. 22, 1856 R. Penco (E.) G. Fraschini (A.) A.
                                          Rossi-Ghelli (G.) P. Vialetti (P.)
                                          J. Skoczdopole cond.

               Oct.  2, 1860 E. Julienne-Dejean (E.) G. Fraschini
                             (A.) L. Giraldoni (G.) S. L. Bouché
                             (P.) J. Skoczdopole cond.

               Feb. 21, 1862 E. Julienne-Dejean (E.) G. Villani
                             (A.) F. Coletti (G.) S. L. Bouché
                             (P.) J. Skoczdopole cond.

               Jan.  9, 1867 M. Lotti della Santa (E.) G. Frasc-
                             hini (A.) A. De Bassini (G.) P. Me-
                             dini (P.) V. Bonetti cond.

               Nov. 26, 1873 A. Fossa (E.) G. Ugolini (A.) C.
                             Boccolini (G.) J. Ordinas (P.) J.
                             Skoczdopole cond.

Seville        San          May    1861 C. Poch (E.) C. Baucardé (A.) P.
               Fernando                 Giorgi-Pacini (G.) A. Selva (P.)

               June  6, 1866 L. Ponti dall'Armi (E.) P. Bignardi
                             (A.) F. Bachi-Perego (G.) M. Junca
                             (P.)

TURKEY
Constan-       Naum         Dec.? 1859 C. Rovelli/G. Beltramelli (E.) A.
tinople                                Zennari (A.) S. Binaghi (G.) G. B.
                                       Cornago (P.)

|  |  | Oct. | 1860 | T. Stolz (E.) M. Neri (A.) F. Monari (G.) A. Fiorini (P.) |
|--|--|--|--|--|

Oct. 1864 R. Gianfredi (E.) R. Bertolini (A.) E. Mari-Cornia (G.) L. Vecchi (P.)

UNITED STATES

Baltimore    Holliday      Mar. 17, 1860 P. Colson (E.) G. Stigelli (A.) G.
             Street                      Ferri (G.) M. Junca (P.) E. Muzio
                                         cond.

             Dec. 18, 1860 P. Colson (E.) P. Brignoli (A.) G.
                           Ferri (G.) A. Susini (P.) E. Muzio
                           cond.

             May  4, 1863 S. Vera-Lorini (E.) P. Brignoli (A.)
                          A. Amodio (G.) A. Susini (P.)

             Concordia     Dec. 21, 1868 A. States (E.) P. Brignoli (A.) D.
                                         Orlandini (G.) G. B. Antonucci (P.)

Boston       Boston Th.    Jan.  2, 1860 P. Colson (E.) P. Brignoli (A.) G.
                                         Ferri (G.) M. Junca (P.) E. Muzio
                                         cond.

             Mar. 11, 1863 S. Vera-Lorini (E.) P. Brignoli (A.)
                           Dubreuil (G.) A. Susini (P.)

             Jan. 14, 1869 A. States (E.) P. Brignoli (A.) D.
                           Orlandini (G.) G. B. Antonucci (P.)

Brooklyn     Ac. of Mus.   Jan. 28, 1861 P. Colson (E.) P. Brignoli (A.) G.
                                         Ferri (G.) A. Susini (P.)

Chicago      McVicker's    June 27, 1863 S. Vera-Lorini (E.) P. Brignoli (A.)
                                         A. Amodio (G.) A. Susini (P.) E.
                                         Muzio cond.

             Crosby's      Oct.  7, 1868 A. States (E.) P. Brignoli (A.) D.
                                         Orlandini (G.) G. B. Antonucci (P.)

Cincinnati   Pike's        June  3, 1863 S. Vera-Lorini (E.) P. Brignoli (A.)
                                         A. Amodio (G.) A. Susini (P.)

             Mozart Hall   Nov.  9, 1868 A. States (E.) P. Brignoli (A.) D.
                                         Orlandini (G.) G. B. Antonucci (P.)

New York     Ac. of Mus.   Nov.  7, 1859 P. Colson (E.) P. Brignoli (A.) G.
                                         Ferri (G.) M. Junca (P.) E. Muzio
                                         cond.

             Sep. 18, 1860 P. Colson (E.) G. Stigelli (A.) G.
                           Ferri (G.) A. Susini (P.)

             Jan.  7, 1863 V. Whiting-Lorini (E.) P. Brignoli
                           (A.) A. Amodio (G.) A. Susini (P.)

             Nov. 20, 1868 A. States (E.) P. Brignoli (A.) D.
                           Orlandini (G.) G. B. Antonucci (P.)

             May 19, 1871 A. States (E.) G. Villani (A.) D.
                          Orlandini (G.) A. Susini (P.)

Philadelphia  Ac. of Mus.  Dec.  7, 1859  P. Colson (E.) P. Brignoli (A.) G.
                                          Ferri (G.) M. Junca (P.) E. Muzio
                                          cond.

                           Mar. 10, 1860  P. Colson (E.) G. Stigelli (A.) G.
                                          Ferri (G.) M. Junca (P.) E. Muzio
                                          cond.

                           Dec. 23, 1862  S. Vera-Lorini (E.) P. Brignoli (A.)
                                          A. Amodio (G.) A. Susini (P.)

                           Dec.  2, 1868  A. States (E.) P. Brignoli (A.) D.
                                          Orlandini (G.) G. B. Antonucci (P.)

St. Louis     De Bar's     Oct. 26, 1868  A. States (E.) P. Brignoli (A.) D.
                                          Orlandini (G.) G. B. Antonucci (P.)

San Francisco Metro-       Aug. 10, 1871  A. States (E.) P. Cecchi (A.) D.
              politan                     Orlandini (G.) A. Susini (P.)

URUGUAY
Montevideo    Solis        Sep.  3, 1862  T. Parodi (E.) G. Mazzi (A.) L. Wal-
                                          ter (G.) A. Rossi-Ghelli (P.) W.
                                          Fumi cond.


OTHER PRODUCTIONS-1900-1945

GERMANY
Berlin        Staatsoper   June  5, 1932  H. Konetzni (E.) H. Rosswaenge (A.)
                                          H. Schlussnuss (G.) E. List (P.) E.
                                          Kleiber cond. (in Ger.)

                           June  5, 1933  H. Konetzni (E.) H. Rosswaenge (A.)
                                          H. Schlussnuss (G.) E. List (P.) E.
                                          Kleiber cond. (in Ger.)

Hamburg       Stadt        Apr. 14, 1901  (in Ger.)

Stuttgart     Opernhaus    Nov. 23, 1929  (in Ger.)

ITALY
Genoa         Carlo        Dec. 26, 1939  C. Jacobo/B. Scacciati (E.) G. Oli-
              Felice                      vato (A.) A. Borgioli (G.) T. Pasero
                                          (P.) V. Gui/V. Marini cond.

Milan         La Scala     Feb. 21, 1909  E. Mazzoleni (E.) A. Bassi (A.) R.
                                          Stracciari (G.) N. De Angelis (P.)
                                          E. Vitale cond.

Palermo       Massimo      Mar. 31, 1937  G. Arangi-Lombardi (E.) F. Lo Giudi-
                                          ce (A.) V. Guicciardi (G.) G. Vaghi
                                          (P.) F. Capuana cond.

Parma         Regio        Dec. 25, 1902  C. Boninsegna (E.) F. Signorini (A.)
                                          M. Aineto (G.) M. Riera (P.) A. Con-
                                          ti cond.

Rome          Sala RAI     May  28, 1939  G. Gatti (E.) G. Olivato (A.) G. Vi-
                                          viani (G.) T. Pasero (P.) F. Previ-
                                          tali cond.

          Reale          Oct.  3, 1940 M. Pedrini (E.) P. Civil (A.) C. Ta-
                                      gliabue (G.) T. Pasero (P.) T. Sera-
                                      fin cond.

Turin         Sala RAI        Aug. 18, 1932 V. Amerighi-Rutili (E.) A. Ferrara
                                      (A.) C. Tagliabue (G.) F. Zaccarini
                                      (P.) U. Tansini cond.

MALTA
La Valletta   Reale          Dec.      1938

PORTUGAL
Lisbon        Sao Carlos     Jan. 13, 1904 E. Bianchini-Cappelli/G. Russ (E.)
                                      O. Cosentino (A.) L. Giraldoni/G.
                                      Pacini (G.) G. Mansueto (P.) V. Lom-
                                      bardi cond.

              Jan.  4, 1905 R. Calligaris-Marty (E.) M. Mari-
                                      acher (A.) A. Arcangeli (G.) A. Ma-
                                      riani (P.) V. Lombardi cond.

SWITZERLAND
Basel         Stadt          Sep.  1, 1932


SELECTED PRODUCTIONS-POST-WORLD WAR II

ARGENTINA
Buenos Aires  Colon          July 24, 1970 M. Arroyo (E.) P. Lavirgen (A.) S.
                                      Milnes (G.) B. Giaiotti (P.) F. Mo-
                                      linari-Pradelli cond.

AUSTRIA
Graz          Stadt          1958-1959 M. Kouba (E.) G. Fourié (A.) G. Sou-
                                      cek (G.) A. Fenyves (P.) G. Cerny
                                      cond.

CZECHOSLOVAKIA
Ostrava                      1961 E. Gebauerová (E.) J. Zahradnicek
                                      (A.) F. Vajnar cond.

FRANCE
Paris         Opéra          Apr.  9, 1974 M. Arroyo (E.) P. Domingo (A.) D.
                                      Ohanesian/P. Glossop (G.) R. Soyer
                                      (P.) N. Santi cond. (in It.)

              1975 C. Deutekom (E.) F. Bonisolli (A.)
                                      P. Glossop (G.) R. Raimondi (P.) (in
                                      It.)

GERMANY
Berlin        Städtische     1960 H. Hillebrecht (E.) R. Schock (A.)
                                      R. Polke (G.) P. Roth-Ehrang (P.) R.
                                      Kraus cond. (in Ger.)

              Deutsche       Feb. 21, 1977 A. Gulin (E.) V. Luchetti (A.) R.
                                      Kerns (G.) H. Stamm (P.) J. Lopez-
                                      Cobos cond. (in It.)

Bonn          Apr. 12, 1987 O. Stapp (E.) G. Cianella (A.) J.
                                      Pons (G.) L. Roni (P.) U. Weder
                                      cond.

Cologne        Stadt         Dec.  8, 1970 M. Stojanovic (E.) R. Ilosfalvy (A.)
                                           W. Janulako (G.) G. Kuscheff (P.) N.
                                           Santi cond. (in Ger.)

Hamburg        Stadt         May   4, 1969 F. Weathers (E.) W. Ochman (A.) D.
                                           Ohanesian (G.) H. Sotin (P.) N.
                                           Santi cond. (in It.)

                             Sep. 10, 1979 C. Deutekom/M. Arroyo (E.) W. Och-
                                           man/G. Casellato-Lamberti (A.) K.
                                           Paskalis/S. Carroli (G.) P. Plish-
                                           ka/H. Sotin (P.) N. Santi cond.

                             Aug.  9, 1980 M. Arroyo (E.) V. Moldoveanu (A.) M.
                                           Manuguerra (G.) H. Stamm (P.) N.
                                           Santi cond.

Munich         National      July 24, 1969 H. Hillebrecht (E.) R. Ilosfalvy
                                           (A.) T. Tipton (G.) F. Crass (P.) N.
                                           Santi cond. (In Ger.)

GREAT BRITAIN
Cardiff        New           Nov.  1, 1954 R. Packer (E.) B. Powell (A.) R.
                                           Jones (G.) H. Alan (P.) F. Berend
                                           cond.

                             Sep.     1955

London         Opera Club    May  28, 1954 E. Wiener (E.) R. Gandy (A.) T. Mant
                                           (G.) Gowing (P.) A. Dempster cond.

               Sadler's      July 12, 1955 R. Packer (E.) B. Powell (A.)
               Wells

               Albert Hall   Aug. 19, 1969 J. Brumaire (E.) J. Bonhomme (A.) H.
                                           Peyrottes (G.) A. Baran (P.) M.
                                           Rossi cond. (in Fr.)

               Camden        Mar. 25, 1977 M. Haggart (E.) A. de Peyer (A.) W.
               Town Hall                   Elvin (G.) J. Tomlinson (P.) J.
                                           Matheson cond. (in Fr.)

               Coliseum      Apr. 19, 1984 R. Plowright (E.) K. Collins (A.) N.
                                           Howlett (G.) R. Van Allen (P.) M.
                                           Elder cond. (in Eng.)

Oxford         Town Hall     Dec.  4, 1963 C. Hunter (E.) B. Powell (A.) N.
                                           Taylor (G.) J. Byrt cond.

Swansea        Grand         Apr. 25, 1955 V. Tausky cond.

ITALY
Florence       Comunale      May  26, 1951 M. Callas (E.) G. Kokolios (A.) E.
                                           Mascherini (G.) B. Christoff (P.) E.
                                           Kleiber cond.

                             May  13, 1978 R. Scotto (E.) V. Luchetti (A.) R.
                                           Bruson (G.) R. Raimondi (P.) R. Muti
                                           cond.

Milan          La Scala      Dec.  7, 1951 M. Callas (E.) E. Conley (A.) E.
                                           Mascherini (G.) B. Christoff/G. Mo-
                                           desti (P.) V. De Sabata/A. Quadri
                                           cond.

Dec.  7, 1970 R. Scotto/L. Gencer (E.) G. Raimondi
(A.) P. Cappuccilli/L. Saccomanno
(G.) R. Raimondi/P. Washington (P.)
G. Gavazzeni cond.

Dec.  7, 1989 C. Studer (E.) C. Merritt (A.) G.
Zancanaro (G.) F. Furlanetto (P.) R.
Muti cond.

Naples      San Carlo    Jan. 16, 1955 A. De Cavalieri (E.) M. Filipeschi
(A.) G. Guelfi (G.) G. Neri (P.) T.
Serafin cond.

Palermo     Massimo      Jan. 18, 1957 A. Stella/M. Roberti (E.) M. Filipeschi (A.) G. Taddei (G.) B. Ladysz
(P.) T. Serafin/C. Martinez cond.

Rome        Opera        Apr.  3, 1956 A. Stella (E.) R. Turrini (A.) G.
Guelfi (G.) G. Neri (P.) G. Santini
cond.

            Dec.  5, 1964 L. Gencer (E.) G. Limarilli/G. Ca-
sellato (A.) G. Guelfi (G.) N. Rossi
Lemeni (P.) G. Gavazzeni cond.

            Sala RAI     Dec.  5, 1970 M. Arroyo (E.) G. Cecchele (A.) S.
Milnes (G.) B. Giaiotti (P.) T.
Schippers cond.

Trieste     Verdi        Nov.  4, 1968 F. Cavalli (E.) R. Bondino (A.) A.
Boyer (G.) R. Ariè (P.) O. De Fa-
britiis cond.

Turin       Regio        Apr. 10, 1973 R. Kabaivanska (E.) G. Raimondi/D.
Antonioli (A.) L. Montefusco (G.) B.
Giaiotti (P.) F. Vernizzi cond.

SPAIN
Barcelona   Liceo        Dec. 28, 1974 M. Caballé (E.) P. Domingo (A.) F.
Bordoni (G.) J. Diaz (P.) E. Queler
cond.

Bilbao      Coliseo      Sep.  3, 1975 R. Scotto (E.) Fr. Tagliavini (A.)
            Alba                       M. Manuguerra (G.) B. Giaotti (P.)
M. Veltri cond.

Oviedo      Campoamor    Sep. 15, 1975 R. Scotto (E.) Fr. Tagliavini (A.)
M. Manuguerra (G.) B. Giaotti (P.)
M. Veltri cond.

SWITZERLAND
Geneva      Grand        June 16, 1985 O. Stapp (E.) G. Cianella (A.) L.
Saccomani (G.) R. Lloyd (P.) D. Ren-
zetti cond.

Zürich      Opernhaus    Sep. 25, 1971 E. Illes (E.) S. di Amorim (A.) K.
Nurmela (G.) A. Neagu (P.) N. Santi
cond.

UNITED STATES
Atlanta     Civic        May   6, 1974 C. Deutekom (E.) Fr. Tagliavini (A.)
            Center                     C. MacNeil (G.) P. Plishka (P.) R.
Woitach cond.

| Boston | Auditorium | Apr. 23, 1974 | C. Deutekom (E.) Fr. Tagliavini (A.) C. MacNeil (G.) P. Plishka (P.) R. Woitach cond. |
| Cleveland | Auditorium | Sep. 17, 1974 | C. Deutekom (E.) W. Lewis (A.) S. Milnes (G.) P. Plishka (P.) J. Levine cond. |
| Detroit | Masonic Temple | May 1, 1974 | C. Deutekom (E.) Fr. Tagliavini (A.) C. MacNeil (G.) P. Plishka (P.) R. Woitach cond. |
| Minneapolis | Auditorium | May 20, 1974 | C. Deutekom (E.) W. Lewis (A.) C. MacNeil (G.) P. Plishka (P.) R. Woitach cond. |
| New York | Philhar- monic Hall | Jan. 13, 1964 | I. Jordan (E.) E. Ruhl (A.) G. Taddei (G.) N. Moscona (P.) T. Scherman cond. |
| | Metro- politan | Jan. 31, 1974 | M. Caballé/C. Deutekom (E.) N. Gedda/Fr. Tagliavini (A.) S. Milnes/C. MacNeil (G.) J. Diaz/P. Plishka (P.) J. Levine cond. |
| | | Sep. 23, 1974 | C. Deutekom/M. Niska/R. Scotto (E.) P. Domingo/W. Lewis/W. Ochman (A.) S. Milnes/L. Shadur (G.) P. Plishka/J. Morris (P.) J. Levine cond. |
| | | Mar. 17, 1982 | R. Scotto (E.) W. Ochman/V. Moldeveanu (A.) P. Elvira (G.) R. Raimondi/F. Furlanetto (P.) J. Levine/T. Fulton cond. |
| | Carnegie Hall | Jan. 16, 1990 | S. Dunn (E.) R. Brubaker and A. Glassmann (A.) R. Bruson (G.) P. Plishka (P.) E. Queler cond. |
| Newport | Festival Field | Aug. 23, 1967 | V. Zeani (E.) E. Fernandi (A.) K. Paskalis (G.) B. Giaiotti (P.)[47] |

---

21. SIMON BOCCANEGRA-*Melodramma* in a prologue and three acts
Venice-Teatro La Fenice-Mar. 12, 1857
Libretto by Francesco Maria Piave with changes by Giuseppe Montanelli

| | |
|---|---|
| Amelia/Maria Boccanegra (A.) | Luisa Bendazzi-Secchi sop. |
| Gabriele Adorno (G.) | Carlo Negrini ten. |
| Simon Boccanegra (S.) | Leone Giraldoni bar. |
| Fiesco (F.) | Giuseppe Echeverria bass |
| Paolo (P.) | Giacomo Vercellini bar. |
| Pietro (Pi.) | Andrea Bellini bar. |
| | |
| Conductor | Emanuele Muzio |
| Director | Giuseppe Verdi |

---

[47]. A shortened version in concert form by the Metropolitan Opera Company.

OTHER PRODUCTIONS-ORIGINAL VERSION-NINETEENTH CENTURY

ARGENTINA
Buenos Aires  Ant. Colón  June 29, 1862 G. Altieri (A.) G. Mazzi (G.) L.
                                        Walter (S.) A. Rossi-Ghelli (F.) W.
                                        Fumi cond.

EGYPT
Alexandria    Rossini     Dec.      1880 R. Aimo (A.) Castelli (G.) L. Rossi
                                        de Ruggero (S.) N. Giommi (F.) F.
                                        Micci-Labruna cond.

GREECE
Corfu         San Giacomo Nov. 1, 1870 R. De Ficarra (A.) G. Scannapiero
                                        (G.) F. Serafini (S.) M. Schiavone
                                        (F.) N. Palumbo cond.

ITALY
Bari          Piccinni    Mar.?    1862 I. Morazzoni-Dordoni (A.) Massini
                                        (G.) G. Sansone (S.)

Bologna       Comunale    Oct. 15, 1861 C. Barbot (A.) R. Bertolini (G.) L.
                                        Giraldoni (S.) H. Von Rokitansky
                                        (F.) A. Mariani cond.

Catania       Comunale    Jan. 20, 1859 E. Schenardi (A.) A. Di Benedetto
                                        (G.) T. Sterbini (S.) F. Varani (F.)
                                        M. Pappalardo cond.

Catanzaro     Comunale    Dec.?    1859 V. Luzzi-Pieralli (A.) G. Palmieri
                                        (G.) G. Morelli (S.) M. Brunetti
                                        (F.)

Florence      Pergola     Oct. 23, 1857 A. Albertini (A.) C. Baucardé (G.)
                                        G. Guicciardi (S.) G. Segri-Segarra
                                        (F.)

Foggia        Dauno       Apr.?    1860 M. Armandi (A.) G. Zacometti (G.) L.
                                        Roncagli (S.)

                          May ?    1861 E. Sutton-Ruta (A.) A. Miserocchi
                                        (G.) G. Morelli (S.) Brutti (F.)

Genoa         Carlo       Dec. 26, 1859 L. Ponti dall'Armi (A.) C. Vincen-
              Felice                    telli (G.) A. Mazzanti (S.) E. Cal-
                                        caterra (F.) A. Mariani cond.

Girgenti                  Nov.     1863

Lucera                    Autumn   1860 E. Schenardi (A.)

Messina       Vittorio    Jan. 17, 1860 L. Ruggero-Antonioli (A.) R. Berto-
              Emanuele                  lini (G.) L. Rossi (S.)

Milano        La Scala    Jan. 24, 1859 L. Bendazzi-Secchi (A.) E. Pancani
                                        (G.) S. Ronconi (S.) R. Laterza (F.)
                                        E. Cavallini cond.

Naples        San Carlo   Nov. 28, 1858 E. Fioretti (A.) G. Fraschini/F.
                                        Mazzoleni (G.) F. Coletti (S.) G. B.
                                        Antonucci (F.) A. Farelli cond.

                          Nov. 5, 1864 L. Perelli (A.) R. Sirchia (G.) A.
                                        De Bassini (S.) G. Atry (F.)

|              | Nuovo        | Jan.?     | 1860 |                                                                                              |
|--------------|--------------|-----------|------|----------------------------------------------------------------------------------------------|
| Palermo      | Carolino     | Dec. 25,  | 1859 | L. Bendazzi-Secchi (A.) V. Sarti (G.) G. B. Bencich (S.) A. Lanzoni (F.) A. Lo Casto cond.    |
|              |              | Dec.      | 1862 | E. Poinsot (A.) V. Sarti (G.) G. Aldighieri (S.) M. Junca (F.) A. Lo Casto cond.              |
| Reggio Emilia | Municipale  | June 9,   | 1857 | L. Bendazzi-Secchi (A.) P. Mongini (G.) L. Giraldoni (S.) G. B. Cornago (F.) G. Tebaldi cond. |
| Rome         | Apollo       | Dec. 26,  | 1857 | L. Chiaromonte (A.) G. Musiani (G.) L. Giraldoni (S.) R. Laterza (F.) E. Angelini cond.       |
|              |              | Apr. 12,  | 1860 | E. Boccherini (A.) C. Negrini (G.) F. Coletti (S.) R. Laterza (F.) E. Angelini cond.          |
| Trapani      | San Ferdinando | Nov.?   | 1859 | C. Bulletti (A.) S. Cerbara (G.) E. Petrilli (S.) G. Perella (F.)                             |
| Turin        | Regio        | Dec. 25,  | 1864 | M. Palmieri (A.) L. Graziani (G.) C. Boccolini (S.) C. Dalla Costa (F.) F. Bianchi cond.      |

MALTA

| La Valletta  | Manoel       | Feb.      | 1859 | G. Bonheur (A.) T. Miserocchi (G.) A. Vitti (S.)                                              |

PORTUGAL

| Lisbon       | Sao Carlos   | Oct. 29,  | 1861 | L. Bendazzi-Secchi (A.) G. Fraschini (G.) G. Guicciardi (S.) C. Dalla Costa (F.)              |
| Oporto       | Sao Joao     | May 14,   | 1858 | S. Della Valle (A.) F. Mazzoleni (G.) A. Vitti (S.) E. Manfredi (F.)                          |

SPAIN

| Barcelona    | Liceo        | Dec. 31,  | 1862 | S. Vera-Lorini (A.) G. Musiani (G.) F. Cresci (S.) C. Dalla Costa (F.)                        |
| Madrid       | Real         | Jan. 7,   | 1861 | A. Sarolta (A.) G. Fraschini (G.) L. Giraldoni (S.) S. L. Bouché (F.) J. Skoczdopole cond.    |

URUGUAY

| Montevideo   | Solis        | Aug. 6,   | 1862 | G. Altieri (A.) G. Mazzi (G.) L. Walter (S.) A. Rossi-Ghelli (F.)                             |


OTHER PRODUCTIONS-ORIGINAL VERSION-TWENTIETH CENTURY

GREAT BRITAIN

| London       | BBC          | Aug.      | 1975 | J. Ligi (A.) A. Turp (G.) S. Bruscantini (S.) G. Howell (F.) J. Matheson cond.                |

Revised-Milan-Teatro alla Scala-Mar. 24, 1881
Libretto by Francesco Maria Piave with revisions by Arrigo Boito


Amelia/Maria Boccanegra (A.)                          Anna D'Angeri sop.
Gabriele Adorno (G.)                              Francesco Tamagno ten.
Simon Boccanegra (S.)                                 Victor Maurel bar.
Fiesco (F.)                                       Edouard De Reszke bass
Paolo (P.)                                           Federico Salvati bar.
Pietro (Pi.)                                          Giovanni Bianco bar.
Un Capitano dei Balestrieri                         Angelo Fiorentini ten.
Un Ancella di Amelia                                 Fernanda Capelli sop.

Conductor                                                   Franco Faccio
Director                                                   Giuseppe Verdi


OTHER PRODUCTIONS-REVISED VERSION-PRE-WORLD WAR I

ARGENTINA
Buenos Aires   Opera        Aug. 18, 1889 I. Ricetti (A.) G. B. De Negri (G.)
                                          M. Battistini (S.) P. Wulmann (F.)
                                          M. Mancinelli cond.


AUSTRIA
Vienna         Hofoper      Nov. 18, 1882 A. Materna (A.) J. N. Beck (S.) H.
                                          von Rokitansky (F.) (in Ger.)

EGYPT[48]
Alexandria     Alhambra     Nov. 25, 1904


Cairo          Ezbekieh     Oct. 20, 1904
               Gardens


FRANCE
Paris          Gaité        Nov. 27, 1883 F. Devries/O. Litvinoff (A.) O. Nou-
                                          velli (G.) V. Maurel (S.) E. De
                                          Reszke (F.) F. Faccio cond.


ITALY
Alessandria    Municipale   Nov.     1884 A. Gini (A.) G. B. De Negri (G.) E.
                                          Sivori (S.) V. Salmasi (F.) E. Usig-
                                          lio cond.


Genoa          Carlo        Jan.  9, 1892 C. Ferrani (A.) F. Vignas (G.) R.
               Felice                     Blanchart (S.) C. Fiegna (F.) A.
                                          Toscanini cond.


Mantua         Sociale      Jan. 19? 1891 R. Giovannoni-Zacchi (A.) G. Ortisi
                                          (G.) E. Camera (S.) C. Fiegna (F.)


Messina        Vittorio     Feb.  3, 1892 A. Agresti (A.) G. Ortisi (G.) E.
               Emanuele                   Barbieri (S.) A. Sabellico (F.) C.
                                          Vallini cond.


Milan          La Scala     Mar. 21, 1882 M. Borelli (A.) W. Mierzwinski (G.)
                                          V. Maurel (S.) R. Nannetti (F.)


_____

   [48]. The two Egyptian productions listed below were announced in the *Egyptian Gazette*,
Cairo and Alexandria, but the performances were not reviewed.

                              Jan. 15, 1890 A. Cattaneo (A.) G. B. De Negri/F.
                                            Cardinali (G.) M. Battistini (S.) F.
                                            Navarini (F.)

                              Dec. 21, 1910 A. Agostinelli (A.) A. Scampini (G.)
                                            M. Battistini/E. Giraldoni (S.) G.
                                            Cirino (F.)

Modena        Comunale        Carn. 1888-89 L. Gabbi (A.) F. Gambarelli (G.) A.
                                            Pessina (S.) G. Balisardi/V. Salmasi
                                            (F.) E. Usiglio cond.

Naples        San Carlo       Apr.  8, 1883 F. Rubini-Scalisi (A.) F. Cardinali
                                            (G.) G. Kaschmann/L. Giraldoni (S.)
                                            A. Marescalchi (F.) C. Scalisi cond.

Palermo       Massimo         Jan. 14, 1909 E. Ruszkowska (A.) N. Fusati/G. Zam-
                                            pieri (G.) C. Galeffi (S.) A. Ric-
                                            ceri (F.) G. Marinuzzi cond.

Rome          Costanzi        May  17, 1892 H. Darclée (A.) G. B. De Negri (G.)
                                            M. Battistini (S.) L. Broglio (F.)
                                            E. Mascheroni cond.

Treviso       Sociale         Oct. 18, 1884 A. Garbini (A.) G. B. De Negri (G.)
                                            E. Sivori (S.) V. Salmasi (F.) E.
                                            Usiglio cond.

Trieste       Grande          Feb. 24, 1891 V. Mendioroz (A.) E. De Marchi (G.)
                                            E. Camera (S.) A. Sillich (F.) M.
                                            Bavagnoli cond.

Turin         Regio           Jan. 24, 1883 M. Borelli (A.) G. Ortisi (G.) D.
                                            Menotti (S.) A. Tamburlini (F.) G.
                                            Gialdini cond.

                              Sep. 21, 1899 A. Antinori (A.) O. Cosentino (G.)
                                            E. Giraldoni (S.) G. Rossi (F.) A.
                                            Conti cond.

Venice        La Fenice       Feb.  7, 1885 B. Pierson (A.) G. B. De Negri (G.)
                                            E. Sivori (S.) V. Salmasi (F.) E.
                                            Usiglio cond.

PORTUGAL
Lisbon        Sao Carlos      Mar. 23, 1887 E. Bendazzi-Garulli (A.) B. Lucigna-
                                            ni (G.) E. Dufriche (S.) A. Vidal
                                            (F.) M. Mancinelli cond.

SPAIN
Madrid        Real            Nov. 22, 1890 V. Mendioroz (A.) B. Lucignani (G.)
                                            M. Battistini (S.) F. Uetam (F.)

TURKEY
Constan-      Concordia       Aug. 25, 1884 A. Giannetti (A.) A. Brunetti (G.)
  tinople                                   R. De Giorgio (S.) A. Lanzoni (F.)
                                            F. Micci Labruna cond.

URUGUAY
Montevideo    Solis           Sep.  3, 1889 I. Ricetti (A.) G. B. De Negri (G.)
                                            M. Battistini (S.) P. Wulmann (F.)
                                            M. Mancinelli cond.

448                                                    Simon Boccanegra

OTHER PRODUCTIONS-1914-1945

ARGENTINA
Buenos Aires    Colón      June  6, 1935 A. Helm-Spisá/H. Spani (A.) K. von
                                        Pataky (G.) C. Galeffi (S.) G. Vaghi
                                        (F.) E. Panizza cond.

                           July 12, 1942 Z. Milanov/D. Rigal (A.) F. Jagel
                                        (G.) L. Warren (S.) G. Vaghi (F.) E.
                                        Panizza cond.

AUSTRIA
Vienna          Staatsoper Jan. 12, 1930 M. Nemeth (A.) K. von Pataky (G.) W.
                                        Rode (S.) J. von Manowarda (F.)

BRAZIL
Rio de          Municipal  Aug.     1942 F. Kirk (A.) F. Jagel (G.) L. Warren
Janeiro                                 (S.) D. Baronti (F.) F. Calusio
                                        cond.

                           Aug.     1943 F. Kirk (A.) F. Jagel (G.) L. Warren
                                        (S.) G. Vaghi (F.) E. De Guarnieri
                                        cond.

CZECHOSLOVAKIA
Bratislava      National   Jan. 30, 1932 (in Czech)

Prague          Neues      Nov. 23, 1930 L. Kruse (A.) Helm (G.) Boeck (S.)
                Deutsches               Andersen (F.) G. Széll cond. (in
                                        Ger.)

GERMANY
Berlin          Stadtoper  Feb.  8, 1930 B. Malkin (A.) K. M. Oehmann (G.) H.
                                        Reinmar (S.) L. Hoffman (F.) F.
                                        Stiedry cond. (in Ger.)

Cologne         Opernhaus  Feb. 23, 1932 Schramm-Tschörner (A.) Gillmann (G.)
                                        Treskow (S.) L. Weber (F.) H. Jalo-
                                        wetz cond. (in Ger.)

Frankfurt       Opernhaus  Nov. 26, 1930 V. Ursuleac (A.) J. Gläser (G.) J.
                                        Stern (S.) H. Erl (F.) (in Ger.)

Hamburg         Stadtoper  Sep. 10, 1931 M. Geister (A.) C. Günther (G.) J.
                                        Groenen (S.) H. Marowski (F.) (in
                                        Ger.)

Munich          National   Sep.  1, 1940 K. Kronenberg (S.) (in Ger.)

Stuttgart       Opernhaus  Oct.  8, 1932 (in Ger.)

HUNGARY
Budapest        Operaház   June 11, 1937 M. Rigó (A.) J. Halmos (G.) I. Palló
                                        (S.) M. Székely (F.) Failoni cond.
                                        (in Hung.)

ITALY
Bologna         Comunale   Nov. 16, 1938 I. Pacetti/M. Pedrini (M.) P. Civil
                                        (G.) A. Borgioli (S.) G. Vaghi (F.)
                                        G. Marinuzzi cond.

Florence        Comunale   Apr. 28, 1938 M. Caniglia (A.) P. Civil (G.) A.
                                        Sved (S.) T. Pasero (F.) V. Gui
                                        cond.

| | | | |
|---|---|---|---|
| Genoa | Carlo Felice | Dec. 26, 1931 | M. Carena (A.) A. Bagnariol (G.) C. Galeffi (S.) L. Donaggio (F.) G. Bavagnoli cond. |
| Milan | La Scala | Mar. 12, 1933 | M. Caniglia (A.) A. Bagnariol (G.) C. Galeffi (S.) N. De Angelis (F.) V. Gui cond. |
| Naples | San Carlo | Jan. 23, 1930 | A. Concato (A.) A. Bagnariol (G.) B. Franci (S.) A. Righetti (F.) E. Vitale cond. |
| Rome | Reale | Mar. 3, 1934 | I. Pacetti (A.) F. Merli (G.) C. Galeffi (S.) G. Vaghi (F.) G. Marinuzzi cond. |
| | | Nov. 1, 1941 | J. Magnoni/V. Passerini (A.) P. Civil (G.) B. Franci/T. Gobbi (S.) T. Pasero/I. Tajo (F.) V. Bellezza cond. |

JUGOSLAVIA

| | | | |
|---|---|---|---|
| Zagreb | National | May 14, 1931 | Z. Milanov (A.) |

SWITZERLAND

| | | | |
|---|---|---|---|
| Basel | Stadt | Sep. 3, 1931 | |

UNITED STATES

| | | | |
|---|---|---|---|
| Los Angeles | Auditorium | Nov. 3, 1941 | S. Roman (A.) F. Jagel (G.) L. Tibbett (S.) E. Pinza (F.) G. Papi cond. |
| New York | Metropolitan | Jan. 28, 1932 | M. Müller (A.) G. Martinelli (G.) L. Tibbett (S.) E. Pinza/T. Pasero (F.) T. Serafin cond. |
| | | Nov. 21, 1932 | M. Müller (A.) G. Martinelli (G.) L. Tibbett (S.) E. Pinza/T. Pasero (F.) T. Serafin cond. |
| | | Jan. 5, 1934 | M. Müller (A.) G. Martinelli (G.) L. Tibbett (S.) E. Pinza (F.) T. Serafin cond. |
| | | Jan. 11, 1935 | E. Rethberg (A.) G. Martinelli (G.) L. Tibbett (S.) E. Pinza (F.) E. Panizza cond. |
| | | Jan. 13, 1939 | M. Caniglia/E. Rethberg (A.) G. Martinelli (G.) L. Tibbett (S.) E. Pinza (F.) E. Panizza cond. |
| | | Nov. 27, 1939 | E. Rethberg/I. Jessner (A.) G. Martinelli/F. Jagel (G.) L. Tibbett (S.) E. Pinza (F.) E. Panizza cond. |
| Philadelphia | | Feb. 16, 1932 | M. Müller (A.) G. Martinelli (G.) L. Tibbett (S.) E. Pinza (F.) T. Serafin cond. |
| | | Dec. 13, 1932 | M. Müller (A.) G. Martinelli (G.) L. Tibbett (S.) T. Pasero (F.) T. Serafin cond. |

San Francisco Opera       Nov.  1, 1941 S. Roman (A.) F. Jagel (G.) L. Tib-
                                        bett (S.) E. Pinza (F.) F. Leinsdorf
                                        cond.


SELECTED PRODUCTIONS-POST-WORLD WAR II

ARGENTINA
Buenos Aires  Colón        June 21, 1946 D. Rigal/M. Rinaldi (A.) A. Vela
                                        (G.) L. Warren (S.) G. Vaghi (F.) E.
                                        Panizza cond.

                           Aug. 20, 1961 F. Cavalli (A.) F. Labò (G.) G. Tad-
                                        dei/A. Mattiello (S.) P. Clabassi/
                                        J. Algorta (F.)

                           June 26, 1964 L. Gencer (A.) C. Cossutta (G.) C.
                                        MacNeil (S.) W. Wildermann (F.) B.
                                        Bartoletti cond.

                           Apr.  5, 1966 N. Carini (A.) E. Sarramida (G.) A.
                                        Mattiello (S.) V. de Narké (F.) A.
                                        Tauriello cond.

                           Aug. 29, 1967 I. Ligabue (A.) C. Cossutta (G.) C.
                                        MacNeil (S.) W. Wildermann (F.) E.
                                        Previtali cond.

                           Apr. 15, 1983 M. Chiara (A.) G. Pastine (G.) G.
                                        Mastromei (S.) N. Ghiuselev (F.) A.
                                        Tauriello cond.

AUSTRALIA
Sydney       Opera House Aug. 13, 1975 J. Carden/D. Cambridge (A.) Byers/R.
                                        Donald (G.) R. Allman/J. Shaw (S.)
                                        Warren-Smith/Shanks (F.) E. Downes
                                        cond.

                           July?    1976 K. Te Kanawa (A.) J. Shaw (S.)

AUSTRIA
Salzburg     Felsen-       Aug.  9, 1961 L. Gencer (A.) G. Zampieri (G.) T.
             reitschule                 Gobbi (S.) G. Tozzi (F.) G. Gavaz-
                                        zeni cond.

             Fest-         Oct. 17, 1981 M. Gessendorf (A.) P. Visconti (G.)
             spielhaus                  G. Sarabia (S.) K. Rydl (F.) R. Wei-
                                        kert cond.

Vienna       Staatsoper    Mar. 28, 1969 G. Janowitz (A.) C. Cossutta (G.) E.
                                        Wächter (S.) N. Ghiaurov (F.) J.
                                        Krips cond. (in It.)

                           Autumn   1969 E. Vaughan (A.) G. Zampieri (G.) G.
                                        Taddei (S.) R. Raimondi (F.)

                           Mar. 22, 1984 K. Ricciarelli/M. Freni (A.) V. Lu-
                                        chetti/J. Carreras/Fr. Tagliavini
                                        (G.) R. Bruson (S.) R. Raimondi/K.
                                        Rydl (F.) C. Abbado cond.

BELGIUM
Brussels      Monnaie      Nov.      1976 M. Zampieri (A.) B. Sebastian/G.
                                          Caseiiato-Lamberti (G.) P. Cappuc-
                                          cilli (S.) O. De Fabrittis cond. (By
                                          the company of the Teatro Regio,
                                          Parma)

                           Oct. 19, 1982 E. Shade (A.) G. Casselato-Lamberti
                                          (G.) J. Van Dam (S.) P. Thau (F.) S.
                                          Cambreling cond.

Ghent                      Nov. 22, 1963 G. Bruninx (A.) P. Lani (G.) L. Cat-
                                          tin (S.) G. Hoekman (F.) A. Nemeth
                                          cond.

BRAZIL
Rio de        Municipal    Sep.  9, 1954 A. Stella (A.) G. Penno (G.) G. Tad-
Janeiro                                   dei/P. Silveri (S.) G. Neri (F.) O.
                                          De Fabritiis cond.

CANADA
Toronto       Maple Leaf   June  3, 1960 M. Curtis-Verna (A.) R. Tucker (G.)
              Gardens                     A. Colzani (S.) G. Tozzi (F.) N.
                                          Verchi cond.

              O'Keefe      Sep. 19, 1979 P. Wells (A.) C. Bini (G.) L. Quili-
              Center                      lico (S.) D. Garrard (F.) N. Res-
                                          cigno cond.

CHILE
Santiago      Municipal    Sep.      1978 M. Castro-Alberty (A.) C. Bini (G.)
                                          R. Bruson (S.) M. Rinaudo (F.) M.
                                          Veltri cond.

CZECHOSLOVAKIA
Prague        National     Winter   1972 (in Czech)

DENMARK
Copenhagen    Royal        May 10, 1968 L. Koppel/K. Schultz (A.) J. Moul-
                                          sen/O. Jensen (G.) I. Hansen (S.) O.
                                          V. Hansen/ C. Lembek (F.) G. Patanè/
                                          T. Vetö cond. (In Dan.)

FINLAND
Helsinki      National     Feb. 19, 1987

FRANCE
Avignon                    Feb. 26, 1983 G. Dimitrova (A.) B. Prior (G.) R.
                                          Bruson (S.) B. Giaiotti (F.) A.
                                          Guingal cond.

Marseille     Opéra        Dec. 15, 1972 O. Santunione (A.) J. Van Dam (F.)
                                          R. Giovaninetti cond.

Nice          Municipal    Mar.     1979 I. Ligabue (A.) G. Casellato-Lamber-
                                          ti (G.) S. Carroli (S.) B. Giaiotti
                                          (F.) G. Masini cond.

Paris         Opéra        Oct. 25, 1978 K. Ricciarelli (A.) V. Luchetti (G.)
                                          P. Cappuccilli (S.) N. Ghiaurov (F.)
                                          C. Abbado cond.

GERMANY
Berlin          Deutsche      Feb.   5, 1969 G. Janowitz (A.) C. Cossutta (G.) I.
                                              Wixell (S.) M. Talvela (F.) L. Maa-
                                              zel cond. (in It.)

                              Sep.      1969 G. Janowitz (A.) Fr. Tagliavini (G.)
                                              K. Paskalis (S.) M. Talvela (F.) L.
                                              Maazel cond. (in It.)

                              Aug.   5, 1971 M. Chiara (A.) C. Cossutta (G.) I.
                                              Wixell (S.)    M. Talvela (F.) L.
                                              Maazel cond. (in It.)

                              June 30, 1984 M. Zampieri (A.) V. Lucchetti (G.)
                                              R. Bruson (S.) K. Rydl (F.) G. Sino-
                                              poli cond.

Munich          Apot-         Aug.   4, 1966 A. Stella (A.) G. Cecchele (G.) G.
                thekenhof                     Taddei (S.) G. Tozzi (F.) G. Patané
                                              cond.

                National      July 21, 1971 G. Janowitz (A.) R. Ilosfalvy (G.)
                                              E. Wächter (S.) R. Raimondi (F.) C.
                                              Abbado cond.

                              Summer    1974 G. Janowitz (A.) G. Casellato-Lam-
                                              berti (G.) E. Wächter (S.) R. Rai-
                                              mondi (F.) J. Lopez Cobos cond.

                              Feb.   9, 1981 M. Freni/M. Price (A.) V. Luchetti/
                                              C. Cossutta (G.) P. Cappuccilli/R.
                                              Bruson (S.) N. Ghiaurov/R. Lloyd
                                              (F.) R. Chailly/M. Gomez-Martinez
                                              cond.

                              July 30, 1981 M. Freni (A.) V. Luchetti (G.) R.
                                              Bruson (S.) N. Ghiaurov (F.) R.
                                              Chailly cond.

                              Mar. 30, 1984 M. Zampieri (A.) V. Luchetti (G.) W.
                                              Brendel (S.) M. Talvela (F.) G. Pa-
                                              tanè cond.

Stuttgart       Opernhaus     Mar. 21, 1982 M. De Francesca-Cavazza (A.) R.
                                              Bondino (G.) R. Wolansky (S.) R.
                                              Bracht (F.) D. R. Davies cond.

GREAT BRITAIN
Bristol         Hippodrome    May    7, 1971

Cardiff         New           Sep. 21, 1970 J. Barstow (A.) K. Erwen (G.) D.
                                              Bryn-Jones (S.) F. Robinson (F.) (in
                                              Eng.)

                              Apr. 22, 1971 J. Barstow (A.) T. Sharpe (S.) (in
                                              Eng.)

                              Sep. 27, 1974 B. Edwards (A.) K. Collins (G.) E.
                                              Holmes (S.) D. Gwynne (F.) K. Mont-
                                              gomery cond.

Glasgow         Th. Royal     Oct. 14, 1978 G. Cegoléa (A.) A. Cathcart (G.) J.
                                              Derksen (S.) R. Lloyd (F.) H. Lewis
                                              cond.

Glyndebourne Festival    May   28, 1986 C. Vaness (A.) T. Rafalli/M. Malagnani (G.) T. Noble (S.) R. Lloyd (F.) B. Haitink cond.

London    Sadler's Wells    Oct. 27, 1948 J. Gartside (A.) J. Johnston (G.) A. Matters (S.) H. Glynns (F.) M. Mudie cond. (in Eng.)

Covent Garden    Dec. 1, 1965 O. Santunione (A.) R. Cioni (G.) T. Gobbi (S.) J. Rouleau (F.) O. De Fabritiis cond. (in It.)

Nov. 11, 1966 E. Vaughan/O. Santunione (A.) R. Cioni (G.) J. Shaw (S.) D. Ward (F.) E. Downes cond.

May 14, 1969 E. Vaughan (A.) C. Cossutta (G.) P. Glossop (S.) D. Ward (F.) C. Mackerras cond.

Feb. 23, 1972 E. Vaughan (A.) C. Cossutta/E. Mauro (G.) I. Wixell (S.) R. Raimondi (F.) A. Ceccato cond.

Oct. 16, 1973 K. Te Kanawa (A.) E. Mauro (G.) P. Glossop (S.) B. Christoff (F.) J. Matheson cond.

Mar. 4, 1976 M. Freni (A.) V. Luchetti (G.) P. Cappuccilli (S.) R. Raimondi (F.) C. Abbado cond. (By the company of the Teatro alla Scala, Milan)

June 2, 1980 K. Te Kanawa (A.) V. Luchetti (G.) S. Milnes (S.) R. Lloyd (F.) C. Davis cond.

Oct. 20, 1981 L. Mitchell (A.) C. Bini/W. Lewis (G.) S. Milnes (S.) G. Howell (F.) J. Conlon cond.

May 18, 1982 H. Döse (A.) F. Bonisolli (G.) R. Bruson (S.) R. Lloyd (F.) E. Downes cond.

Jan. 14, 1986 K. Te Kanawa (A.) G. Merighi (G.) R. Bruson (S.) R. Lloyd (F.) E. Downes cond.

Manchester    Palace    Nov. 11, 1986

Swansea    Grand    May 12, 1971

ITALY
Bologna    Comunale    Jan. 5, 1966 R. Orlandi-Malaspina (A.) G. Cecchele (G.) P. Glossop (S.) R. Ariè (F.) A. Erede cond.

Feb. 19, 1984 J. Ligi (A.) O. Garaventa (G.) L. Nucci (S.) B. Giaiotti (F.) G. Patanè cond.

Catania    Bellini    Feb. 26, 1959 F. Cavalli (A.) F. Ferrari (G.) T. Gobbi (S.) I. Vinco (F.)

|           |            | Jan. 16, 1973 | M. Sighele (A.) G. Cecchele (G.) M. Zanasi (S.) C. Cava (F.) F. Scaglia cond. |

Florence    Comunale    Dec.  7, 1961  M. Parutto (A.) G. Gibin (G.) M. Zanasi (S.) P. Washington (F.) V. Gui cond.

Genoa       Comunale    Apr. 30, 1952  C. Mancini (A.) M. Picchi (G.) G. Taddei (S.) M. Petri (F.) F. Capuana cond.

                        Apr. 26, 1967  R. Orlandi-Malaspina (A.) A. Mori (G.) A. Colzani (S.) P. Washington (F.) F. Capuana cond.

                        Oct. 21, 1975  R. Orlandi-Malaspina (A.) F. Labò (G.) G. P. Mastromei (S.) R. Ariè (F.) A. Erede cond.

Milan       La Scala    May 10, 1965   G. Tucci (A.) B. Prevedi (G.) G. Guelfi (S.) N. Ghiaurov (F.) G. Gavazzeni cond.

                        Dec.  7, 1971  M. Freni (A.) G. Raimondi (G.) P. Cappuccilli (S.) N. Ghiaurov (F.) C. Abbado cond.

                        Dec. 15, 1973  M. Freni (A.) G. Cecchele (G.) P. Cappuccilli (S.) R. Raimondi (F.) C. Abbado cond.

                        Dec.  7, 1978  M. Freni/K. Te Kanawa (A.) V. Luchetti (G.) P. Cappuccilli (S.) N. Ghiaurov/C. Siepi (F.)

                        Jan. 20, 1982  M. Freni (A.) Y. Marusin (G.) P. Cappuccilli (S.) N. Ghiaurov (F.) C. Abbado cond.

Modena      Comunale    Winter   1966  R. Orlandi-Malaspina (A.) G. Cecchele (G.) P. Glossop (S.) R. Ariè (F.) A. Erede cond.

Naples      San Carlo   Dec. 26, 1958  L. Gencer (A.) M. Picchi (G.) T. Gobbi (S.) F. Mazzoli (F.) M. Rossi cond.

                        Feb. 28, 1970  L. Maragliano (A.) B. Prevedi (G.) P. Cappuccilli (S.) N. Ghiaurov (F.) U. Rapalo cond.

                        Mar.  8, 1986  I. Cotrubas (A.) T. Ichihara (G.) R. Bruson (S.) C. Siepi (F.) G. Oetvös cond.

Palermo     Massimo     Jan. 25, 1951  C. Mancini (A.) R. Lagares (G.) T. Gobbi (S.) A. Mongelli (F.) F. Ghione cond.

                        Dec. 16, 1964  C. Parada (A.) R. Merolla (G.) G. Taddei (S.) R. Ariè (F.) F. Previtali cond.

|        |              | Jan. 2, 1969 | I. Ligabue (A.) G. Merighi (G.) G. Taddei (S.) R. Ariè (F.) O. De Fabritiis cond. |

Parma        Regio        Dec. 26, 1965  R. Orlandi-Malaspina (A.) G. Cecchele (G.) P. Glossop (S.) R. Ariè (F.) A. Erede cond.

Pisa         Verdi        Oct. 24, 1978  I. Ligabue (A.) N. Todisco (G.) G. Mastromei (S.) C. Cava (F.) F. M. Martini cond.

Ravenna      Rocca Bran-  July 28, 1984  J. Ligi (A.) C. Cossutta (G.) R.
             caleone                     Bruson (S.) C. Siepi (F.) Campori cond.

Rome         Opera        Mar. 23, 1949  O. Fineschi (A.) M. Picchi (G.) T. Gobbi (S.) C. Siepi (F.) T. Serafin cond.

                          Dec. 8, 1952   M. Caniglia (A.) M. Filipeschi (G.) T. Gobbi (S.) G. Neri (F.) V. Gui cond.

                          Jan. 8, 1957   M. Pobbe (A.) U. Borsò (G.) T. Gobbi (S.) B. Christoff (F.) G. Gavazzeni cond.

                          Apr. 24, 1969  L. Maragliano (A.) R. Cioni (G.) G. Guelfi (S.) R. Raimondi (F.) F. Previtali cond.

                          May 2, 1980    M. Parazzini (A.) G. Cecchele (G.) M. Manuguerra (S.) B. Christoff (F.) D. Oren cond.

                          Dec. 17, 1982  G. Savova (A.) G. Merighi (G.) L. Miller (S.) P. Thau (F.) G. Patanè cond.

                          Mar. 23, 1988  J. Omilian (A.) N. Martinucci (G.) R. Bruson (S.) N. Ghiuselev (F.) A. Erede cond.

Trieste      Verdi        Nov. 11, 1971  I. Merrigioli (A.) P. Cappuccilli (S.) G. Gavazzeni cond.

                          Nov. 12, 1985  S. Evstatieva (A.) C. Cossutta (G.) R. Bruson (S.) B. Giaiotti (F.) T. Pál cond.

Turin        Regio        Jan. 2, 1969   L. Maragliano (A.) R. Cioni (G.) G. Guelfi (S.) R. Raimondi (F.) G. Gavazzeni/Sabbioni cond.

                          Apr. 3, 1979   I. Ligabue (A.) V. Luchetti/G. Casellato-Lamberti (G.) A. Cassis (S.) G. Luccardi (F.) G. Gavazzeni cond.

Venice       La Fenice    Jan. 21, 1950  C. Mancini (A.) G. Penno/F. Ferrari (G.) C. Tagliabue (S.) B. Christoff (F.) O. De Fabritiis cond.

Feb. 13, 1964 O. Fineschi (A.) A. Mori (G.) G.
Taddei (S.) R. Ariè (F.) C. Franci
cond.

Mar. 26, 1970 M. Chiara (A.) N. Martinucci/A. Li-
viero (G.) M. Zanasi (S.) R. Raimon-
di (F.) A. Votto cond.

Verona        Arena        Aug.  3, 1973 K. Ricciarelli (A.) C. Cossutta (G.)
P. Cappuccilli (S.) B. Giaiotti (F.)
N. Sanzogno cond.

JAPAN[49]
Osaka                      Sep.    1982 M. Freni (A.) V. Luchetti (G.) P.
Cappuccilli (S.) N. Ghiaurov (F.) C.
Abbado cond.

Tokyo                      Sep. 23, 1977 K. Ricciarelli (A.) G. Merighi (G.)
P. Cappuccilli (S.) N. Ghiaurov (F.)
O. De Fabritiis cond.

Sep.  1, 1982 M. Freni (A.) V. Luchetti (G.) P.
Cappuccilli (S.) N. Ghiaurov (F.) C.
Abbado cond.

Yokohama                   Sep.    1982 M. Freni (A.) V. Luchetti (G.) P.
Cappuccilli (S.) N. Ghiaurov (F.) C.
Abbado cond.

JUGOSLAVIA
Dubrovnik     Main Square July 11, 1969 I. Ligabue (A.) B. Prevedi (G.) P.
Glossop (S.) A. Ferrin (F.) O. De
Fabritiis cond.[50]

MONACO
Monte Carlo   Lent         1961 A. M. Rovere (A.) A. Lo Forese (G.)
T. Gobbi (S.) R. Ariè (F.) M. Wolf-
Ferrari cond.

NETHERLANDS
Amsterdam                  1960-61 A. Tiemessen (A.) A. Bartoli (G.) A.
Oppicelli (S.) U. Trama (F.) A. Do-
rati cond.

NORWAY
Oslo          Norwegian    Oct. 21, 1985 F. Klausberger/K. Ekeberg (A.) E.
Alvarez/L. Gentile (G.) K. Skram/T.
Stensvold (S.) O. Tennfjord/S. Carl-
sen (F.) M. Chung cond.

PORTUGAL
Lisbon        Sao Carlos   Mar. 17, 1968 R. Bakocevic (A.) F. Labò (G.) G.
Guelfi (S.) L. Roni (F.) O. De Fa-
britiis cond.

---

[49]. The Osaka, Tokyo and Yokohama performances in September 1982 were all by the company of the Teatro alla Scala, Milan.

[50]. By the company of the Teatro Massimo in Palermo. Due to rain, the performance had to be stopped after the prologue. It was concluded the next night (July 12).

RUSSIA
Moscow                              Summer ? 1958 V. Nestyagina (A.) I. Subbotin (G.)
                                                  J. Vutiras (S.) B. Shtokolov (F.)
                                                  (in Rus.)

                   Bolshoi         May  30, 1974 M. Freni (A.) Fr. Tagliavini (G.) P.
                                                 Cappuccilli (S.) N. Ghiaurov (F.) C.
                                                 Abbado cond. (in It.) (By the compa-
                                                 ny of the Teatro alla Scala, Milan)

SPAIN
Barcelona          Liceo           Dec. 20, 1970 L. Kelston (A.) R. Merolla (G.) C.
                                                 MacNeil (S.) B. Giaiotti (F.) I. Sa-
                                                 vini cond.

                                   Jan. 13, 1977 S. Del Grande (A.) R. Francesconi
                                                 (G.) P. Cappuccilli (S.) D. Petkov
                                                 (F.) G. Morelli cond.

                                   Dec. 30, 1985 M. Freni (A.) J. Carreras (G.) J.
                                                 Pons (S.) N. Ghiaurov/F. Furlanetto
                                                 (F.) R. Abbado cond.

Bilbao             Coliseo         Sep. 12, 1960 G. Tucci (A.) L. Ottolini (G.) G.
                   Alba                          Taddei (S.) B. Giaiotti (F.) M.
                                                 Wolf-Ferrari cond.

Madrid             Zarzuela               1982

Valencia           Principal       Apr.  2, 1979 M. Zampieri (A.) M. Alexander (G.)
                                                 F. Bordoni (S.) B. Giaiotti (F.)

SWITZERLAND
Geneva             Grand           Nov. 24, 1966 G. Davy (A.) J. Thomas (G.) C. Marsh
                                                 (S.) J. Van Dam (F.) N. Santi cond.

Zürich             Stadt           Oct. 18, 1975 A. Sgourda (A.) B. Prevedi (G.) N.
                                                 Mittelmann (S.) B. Giaiotti (F.) N.
                                                 Santi cond.

UNITED STATES
Atlanta            Fox             May   7, 1960 M. Curtis-Verna (A.) R. Tucker (G.)
                                                 F. Guarrera (S.) G. Tozzi (F.) N.
                                                 Verchi cond.

                   Civic           May   6, 1985 A. Millo (A.) V. Moldoveanu (G.) S.
                   Center                        Milnes (S.) P. Plishka (F.) N. Santi
                                                 cond.

Boston             Metro-          Apr. 23, 1960 Z. Milanov (A.) W. Olvis (G.) A.
                   politan                       Colzani (S.) G. Tozzi (F.) D. Mitro-
                                                 poulos cond.

                   Wang Center Apr. 26, 1985 A. Millo (A.) V. Moldoveanu (G.) S.
                                                 Milnes (S.) P. Plishka (F.) N. Santi
                                                 cond.

Chicago            Lyric           Oct. 23, 1959 M. Roberti (A.) R. Tucker (G.) T.
                                                 Gobbi (S.) F. Mazzoli (F.) G. Gavaz-
                                                 zeni cond.

                                   Nov. 30, 1960 R. Tebaldi (A.) R. Tucker (G.) T.
                                                 Gobbi (S.) F. Mazzoli (F.) G. Gavaz-
                                                 zeni cond.

|  |  | Oct. 11, 1965 | I. Ligabue (A.) R. Cioni (G.) T. Gobbi (S.) R. Ariè (F.) B. Bartoletti cond. |
|--|--|--|--|
|  |  | Sep. 20, 1974 | M. Arroyo (A.) C. Cossutta (G.) P. Cappuccilli (S.) R. Raimondi (F.) B. Bartoletti cond. |
|  |  | Nov. 3, 1979 | E. Shade (A.) C. Cossutta (G.) S. Milnes (S.) B. Bartoletti cond. |
| Cincinnati | Music Hall | May 30, 1981 | M. Arroyo (A.) C. Bini (G.) C. Mac-Neil (S.) D. Kavrakos (F.) |
| Cleveland | Auditorium | Apr. 30, 1960 | M. Curtis-Verna (A.) R. Tucker (G.) F. Guarrera (S.) G. Tozzi (F.) D. Mitropoulos cond. |
|  | State | May 2, 1985 | A. Millo (A.) V. Moldoveanu (G.) S. Milnes (S.) P. Plishka (F.) N. Santi cond. |
| Detroit | Masonic Temple | May 23, 1960 | M. Curtis-Verna (A.) R. Tucker (G.) A. Colzani (S.) G. Tozzi (F.) N. Verchi cond. |
|  |  | May 23, 1985 | A. Millo (A.) V. Moldoveanu (G.) S. Milnes (S.) P. Plishka (F.) N. Santi cond. |
| Houston | Grand Opera | Mar. 29, 1984 | M. Nicolescu (A.) P. Visconti (G.) L. Nucci (S.) C. Siepi (F.) M. Gomez Martinez cond. |
| Los Angeles | Auditorium | Oct. 20, 1956 | R. Tebaldi (A.) R. Turrini (G.) L. Warren (S.) B. Christoff (F.) O. De Fabritiis cond. |
|  |  | Oct. 29, 1960 | Cavalli (A.) G. Zampieri (G.) T. Gobbi (S.) G. Tozzi (F.) L. Ludwig cond. |
| Minneapolis | Auditorium | May 20, 1960 | Z. Milanov (A.) R. Tucker (G.) A. Colzani (S.) G. Tozzi (F.) N. Verchi cond. |
|  |  | May 31, 1985 | A. Millo (A.) V. Moldoveanu (G.) S. Milnes (S.) P. Plishka (F.) N. Santi cond. |
| New York | Metro-politan | Nov. 28, 1949 | A. Varnay/S. Roman (A.) R. Tucker (G.) L. Warren/A. Sved (S.) M. Szekely/L. Vichegonov (F.) F. Stiedry cond. |
|  |  | Mar. 1, 1960 | M. Curtis-Verna/Z. Milanov/R. Tebaldi (A.) R. Tucker/C. Bergonzi (G.) L. Warren/F. Guarrera/A. Colzani (S.) G. Tozzi/J. Hines (F.) D. Mitropoulos cond. |

Dec. 19, 1960 R. Tebaldi/Z. Milanov (A.) R. Tuc-
ker/ W. Olvis (G.) F. Guarrera/A.
Colzani (S.) G. Tozzi/C. Siepi (F.)
N. Verchi cond.

Dec. 9, 1964 R. Tebaldi/Z. Milanov (A.) G. Shir-
ley/G. Campora/R. Tucker (G.) A.
Colzani/C. MacNeil (S.) G. Tozzi/J.
Hines/C. Siepi (F.) F. Cleva cond.

Oct. 17, 1968 R. Orlandi-Malaspina (A.) R. Tucker/
B. Prevedi (G.) C. MacNeil (S.) S.
Milnes (P.) N. Ghiaurov (F.) P.
Plishka (Pi.) F. Molinari-Pradelli
cond.

Dec. 1, 1973 A. Maliponte (A.) R. Tucker/W. Lewis
(G.) I. Wixell (S.) G. Tozzi (F.) S.
Ehrling cond.

Nov. 23, 1984 A. Tomova-Sintow/A. Millo (A.) V.
Moldoveanu/V. Popov (G.) S. Milnes/
P. Glossop (S.) P. Plishka /F. Fur-
lanetto (F.) J. Levine cond.

Philadelphia                  Apr. 11, 1960 Z. Milanov (A.) C. Bergonzi (G.) A.
Colzani (S.) G. Tozzi (F.) D. Mitro-
poulos cond.

Ac. of Mus. Nov. 2, 1972 H. T'Hézan (A.) M. Maievsky (G.) G.
Mastromei (S.) B. Giaiotti (F.) A.
Guadagno cond.

San Diego      Opera      June 23, 1984 M. Arroyo (A.) A. Van Limpt (G.) S.
Milnes (S.) N. Ghiuselev (F.) E.
Müller cond.

San Francisco Opera      Oct. 9, 1956 R. Tebaldi (A.) R. Turrini (G.) L.
Warren (S.) B. Christoff (F.) O. De
Fabritiis cond.

Sep. 27, 1960 L. Amara (A.) G. Zampieri (G.) T.
Gobbi (S.) G. Tozzi (F.) L. Ludwig
cond.

Sep. 23, 1975 K. Te Kanawa (A.) G. Merighi (G.) I.
Wixell (S.) M. Talvela (F.) P. Pelo-
so cond.

Sep. 6, 1980 M. Price (A.) G. Casselato-Lamberti
(G.) R. Bruson (S.) C. Siepi (F.) L.
Gardelli cond.

Washington     Kennedy     Sep. 13, 1976 R. Kabaivanska/M. Freni (A.) V. Lu-
               Center      chetti (G.) P. Cappuccilli/S. Carro-
li (S.) R. Raimondi (F.) C. Abbado
cond. (By the company of the Teatro
alla Scala, Milan)

May 31, 1985 A. Millo (A.) V. Moldoveanu (G.) S.
Milnes (S.) P. Plishka (F.) N. Santi
cond.

22. AROLDO-*Melodramma* in three acts
Rimini-Teatro Nuovo-Aug. 16, 1857
Libretto by Francesco Maria Piave

Mina (M.)                              Marcellina Lotti Della Santa sop.
Aroldo (A.)                                      Emilio Pancani ten.
Egberto (E.)                                        Gaetano Ferri bar.
Briano (B.)                          Giovanni Battista Cornago bass
Godvino                                      Salvatore Poggiali ten.
Enrico                                       Napoleone Senigaglia ten.
Elena                                          Adelaide Panizza sop.

Conductor                                          Angelo Mariani
Director                                           Giuseppe Verdi


OTHER PRODUCTIONS-NINETEENTH CENTURY

ARGENTINA
Buenos Aires   Ant. Colón   Nov. 15, 1860 C. Manzini (M.) E. Ballerini (A.) G.
                                          Bertolini (E.) C. Castagneri cond.

               Mar. 13, 1870 G. Gasc (M.) L. Lelmi (A.) A. Celes-
                                          tino (E.)

AUSTRIA
Vienna         Kärntnertor May   5, 1858 B. Steffenone (M.) E. Pancani (A.)
                                          G. Ferri (E.)

BRAZIL
Rio de         Lirico        Dec.  2, 1864 I. Alba (M.) G. Mazzi (A.) M. Pa-
  Janeiro      Fluminense                 dilla (E.)

CHILE
Santiago       Municipal     Aug. 31, 1865 A. Bazzurri (M.) E. Ballerini (A.)

Valparaiso     Victoria      Feb. 14, 1867 M. Mollo (M.) E. Ballerini (A.) A.
                                          Rossi-Ghelli (E.)

CUBA
Havana         Tacon         Feb. 12, 1862 E. Kenneth (M.) G. Tombesi (A.) G.
                                          Ferri (E.) E. Muzio cond.

FRANCE
Ajaccio        San           Dec.    1864 G. Ottonelli-Bresciani (M.) A. Boet-
               Gabriele                   ti (A.) A. Pantaleoni (E.)

Nice           Regio         Oct. 25, 1860 E. Berini (M.) F. Pozzo (A.) S. Bi-
                                          naghi (E.)

GREECE
Athens         Royal         Oct.    1862 A. Murio-Celli (M.) L. Guglielmini
                                          (A.) A. Garcia (E.) Bolognini cond.

ITALY[51]
Alessandria    Municipale    Oct.    1860 E. Poinsot (M.) G. De Antoni (A.) V.
                                          Collini (E.) O. Maini (B.)

---

[51]. *Aroldo* was also given in Catanzaro in 1862, Foggia in 1869, Gubbio in 1862, Novi in 1880, Rieti in 1865, Sassari in 1872, Trani in 1866 and Trapani in 1863.

| Ancona | Muse | May | 1, | 1864 | T. Cotta-Morandini (M.) E. Barbacini (A.) G. Giori/V. Quintili-Leoni (E.) |
|---|---|---|---|---|---|
| Ascoli Piceno | Ventidio Basso | Autumn | | 1860 | F. Capuani (M.) De Benedetti (A.) A. Mazzanti (E.) P. Medini (B.) |
| Bari | Piccinni | Feb. | | 1860 | C. Peccia (M.) V. Sabattini (A.) G. Sansone (E.) |
| Bergamo | Riccardi | Dec. | 26, | 1870 | C. Bolla (M.) F. Toni-Nazari (A.) F. Sutter (E.) L. Lombardelli (B.) G. Zavaglio cond. |
| Bologna | Comunale | Oct. | 3, | 1857 | A. Basseggio (M.) R. Mirate (A.) L. Merly (E.) A. Selva (B.) G. Manetti cond. |
| Brescia | Grande | July | 31, | 1861 | E. Berini (M.) G. Tombesi (A.) R. Pizzigati (E.) G. B. Cornago (B.) |
| Cagliari | Civico | Sep. | 21, | 1867 | N. Dunord (M.) E. Concordia (A.) F. Bertolini (E.) G. Devasini cond. |
| Chieti | Marrucino | Apr. | 21 | 1860 | E. Sutton-Ruta (M.) E. Concordia (A.) F. Pandolfini (E.) |
| Como | Sociale | Dec. | 26, | 1866 | S. Norsa (M.) E. Biondini (A.) S. Otto (E.) |
| Crema | Sociale | Dec. | 26, | 1882 | Variglia (M.) L. Dal Passo (A.) Bacchetta (E.) |
| Cremona | Concordia | Jan. | | 1858 | L. Ponti dall'Armi (M.) A. Dall'Armi (A.) P. Baraldi (E.) G. C. Nerini (B.) |
| Fermo | Aquila | Aug. | 29, | 1860 | A. Ortolani-Brignoli (M.) F. Mazzoleni (A.) C. Boccolini (E.) |
| Ferrara | Comunale | Apr. | | 1860 | I. Galletti-Gianoli (M.) F. Mazzoleni (A.) G. Giori/M. Zacchi (E.) |
| Fiume | Civico | Mar. | 26, | 1859 | L. Ponti dall'Armi (M.) A. Dall'Armi (A.) P. Baraldi (E.) |
| Florence | Pergola | Feb. | 28, | 1858 | C. Carozzi-Zucchi (M.) G. Musiani (A.) L. Giraldoni (E.) F. Fiorani (B.) |
| | Pagliano | Nov. | 19, | 1861 | L. Ruggero-Antonioli (M.) F. Mazzoleni (A.) A. Mazzanti (E.) A. Garcia (B.) |
| Genoa | Carlo Felice | Mar. | 19, | 1859 | E. Parepa-Rosa (M.) A. Agresti (A.) R. Pizzigati (E.) H. von Rokitansky (B.) A. Mariani cond. |
| | | Feb. | 9, | 1860 | L. Ponti dall'Armi (M.) C. Vincentelli (A.) A. Mazzanti (E.) |
| Jesi | Concordia | Sep. | 1, | 1861 | E. Weisser (M.) P. Bignardi (A.) A. Mazzanti (E.) |
| Mantua | Sociale | Jan.? | | 1868 | |

Messina        Vittorio       Feb. 28, 1866 S. Casimir-Ney (M.)  G.  Petrovich
               Emanuele                     (A.) F. Giannini (E.)

Milan          Carcano        Dec. 31, 1861 S. Della Valle (M.)  C.  Fabris/E.
                                            Irfré (A.) F. Gnone (E.) P. Poli-
                                            Lenzi (B.)

               Politeama      Apr.?    1871 L. Banti (M.) P. Tagliazucchi (A.)
                                            I. Viganotti (E.) S. Mazza (B.)

Modena         Comunale       May   9, 1859 S. Vera-Lorini (M.)  F.  Mazzoleni
                                            (A.) C. Visai (E.) M. Ghini (B.) A.
                                            Sighicelli cond.

               Dec. 25, 1866 M. Majo (M.)  V. Belardi' (A.)  G.
                                            Boretti (E.) P. Mazzarini (B.) I.
                                            Manni cond.

Monza          Sociale        Autumn   1864 T. Cotta-Morandini (M.) G. Ghislan-
                                            zoni (A.) G. Valle (E.)

Naples         San Carlo      Nov. 28, 1859 M. Spezia-Aldighieri (M.) F. Mazzo-
                                            leni (A.) R. Pizzigati (E.) A. Fa-
                                            relli cond.

Novara         Antico         Dec. 26, 1870 M. De Zorzi (M.) E. Biondini (A.) G.
                                            Gambetti (E.) G. B. Del Fabbro (B.)
                                            A. Buzzi cond.

Padua          Concordi       Jan. 15? 1868 S. Bellot (M.) G. Gambetti (A.) D.
                                            Mazzoli (E.)

Palermo        Carolino       Nov. 22, 1860 E. Boccherini (M.) F. Mazzoleni (A.)
                                            R. Pizzigati (E.)

Parma          Regio          Dec. 26, 1857 A. Basseggio (M.) V. Sarti (A.) D.
                                            Squarcia (E.) G. De Dominicis (B.)
                                            G. C. Ferrarini cond.

Pavia          Civico         Dec. 26, 1865 R. Vielli-Villa (M.) T. Villa (A.)
                                            D. Baldassari (E.) B. Donato (B.)

Piacenza       Comunale       Dec. 26, 1858 R. Gariboldi-Bassi (M.) E. Barba-
                                            cini (A.) G. Fiori (E.) L. Vecchi
                                            (B.)

Ravenna        Alighieri      May  14, 1859 F. Salvini-Donatelli (M.) V. Sarti
                                            (A.) L. Giraldoni (E.)

Reggio Emilia Municipale      May  21, 1862 M. Lotti Della Santa (M.) V. Sarti
                                            (A.) E. Fagotti (E.) H. Brémond (B.)

Rome           Apollo         Jan. 31, 1858 C. Carozzi-Zucchi (M.) G. Musiani
                                            (A.) L. Giraldoni (E.) C. Bossi (B.)
                                            E. Angelini cond.

               Nov. 12, 1859 G. Monti (M.) V. Sarti (A.) E. Fa-
                                            gotti (E.) C. Bossi (B.)

Sinigaglia     Comunale       July 17, 1858 I. Galletti-Gianoli (M.) V. Sarti
                                            (A.) E. Fagotti (E.) G. Sarti (B.)

Terni          Comunale       Feb.     1859 C. Peccia (M.) G. Valentini-Cris-
                                            tiani (A.) L. Spellini (E.)

Treviso        Sociale        Oct.      1857  V. Boccabadati (M.) G. Landi (A.) E.
                                              Delle Sedie (E.)

Trieste        Grande         Mar. 10,  1860  I. Galletti-Gianoli (M.) G. Tombesi
                                              (A.) F. Monari-Rocca (E.) G. A. Sca-
                                              ramelli cond.

Turin          Carignano      Oct.  1,  1857  R. Gariboldi-Bassi (M.) C. Negrini
                                              (A.) L. Giraldoni (E.) G. B. Cornago
                                              (B.)

               Vittorio       Apr.  2,  1864  M. Majo (M.) E. Mariani (A.) G. Fer-
               Emanuele                       ri (E.) O. Maini (B.)

Venice         La Fenice      Jan. 20,  1858  L. Bendazzi-Secchi (M.) E. Pancani
                                              (A.) G. Ferri (E.)

               Apollo         Oct.      1858  L. Abbadia (M.) A. Oliva-Pavani (A.)
                                              F. Bellini (E.) G. De Dominicis (B.)

               San            Dec. 26,  1860  A. Basseggio (M.) G. Ghislanzoni/A.
               Benedetto                      Dall'Armi (A.) A. Vitti (E.)

                              Oct. 29,  1870  C. Noel-Guidi (M.) A. Boetti (A.) G.
                                              Spallazzi/A. Parboni (E.) L. Lombar-
                                              delli (B.)

Verona         Nuovo          Oct. 31,  1857  E. Weisser (M.) A. Dall'Armi (A.) P.
                                              Baraldi (E.)

               Ristori        Apr.      1864  C. Rosavalle (M.) Toffanari (A.) R.
                                              Massiani (E.) F. Fiorani (B.)

JUGOSLAVIA
Zara           Nobile         Nov. 13,  1873  I. Kottas (M.) A. Boetti (A.) G.
                                              Tagliapietra (E.)

MALTA
La Valletta    Manoel         Oct.      1858  V. Lucci-Feralli (M.) A. Marchetti
                                              (A.) C. Bartolucci (E.) C. Leonar-
                                              dis (B.)

                              Nov. 10?  1867  A. Bianchi (M.) F. Toni-Nazzari (A.)
                                              A. Burgio (E.) L. Del Riccio (B.)

MEXICO
Mexico City    Nacional       Sep. 23,  1864  A. Ortolani-Brignole (M.) F. Mazzo-
                                              leni (A.) A. Ottaviani (E.) E. Del-
                                              gado cond.

PORTUGAL
Lisbon         Sao Carlos     Nov. 25,  1860  M. Gazzaniga (M.) A. Agresti (A.) E.
                                              Fagotti (E.)

                              Mar. 10,  1864  L. Banti (M.) G. Capponi (A.) F.
                                              Pandolfini (E.)

Oporto         Sao Joao       Feb. 10,  1859  N. De Roissi (M.) G. De Vecchi (A.)
                                              V. Morelli-Bartolami (E.) A. Rossi
                                              (B.)

ROMANIA
Bucharest      Nacional       Feb.      1860  E. Berini (M.) E. Barbacini (A.) F.
                                              Steller (E.)

|  |  | Jan. | 1864 | R. Gianfredi (M.) V. Sarti (A.) V. Collini (E.) |
|--|--|--|--|--|

**RUSSIA**

| Odessa | Municipal | Feb.? | 1859 | G. Marra (E.) |
|--|--|--|--|--|
| Tbilisi | Imperial | Mar.? | 1868 | C. Castelli (M.) F. Pozzi (A.) E. Storti-Gaggi (E.) N. Bassi cond. |

**SPAIN**

| Alicante | Principal | Oct. 4, | 1864 | C. Cattinari (M.) E. Irfré (A.) V. Prattico (E.) |
|--|--|--|--|--|
| Barcelona | Liceo | Dec. 4, | 1872 | L. Ponti dall'Armi (M.) C. Vincentelli (A.) G. Toledo (E.) A. Rodas (B.) N. Bassi cond. |
| Bilbao | Viejo | June 6, | 1868 | F. Gordosa (M.) E. Irfré (A.) V. Morelli-Bartolami (E.) A. Rodas (B.) |
| La Corugna | Principal | Autumn | 1859 | C. Briol (M.) |
| Madrid | Real | Dec. 7, | 1869 | A. D'Este/ M. D'Altona (M.) E. Tamberlick (A.) D. Squarcia (E.) |
| Palma de Mallorca | Princesa | Jan. | 1863 | G. Naglia (M.) E. Irfré (A.) P. Varvaro (E.) |
|  |  | Nov. | 1863 | L. Chiaromonte (M.) E. Irfré (A.) F. Gnone (E.) |
| Puerto Mahon | Coliseo |  | 1859-60 | G. Rusticelli (A.) G. Crotti (E.) |
|  |  | Oct. | 1884 | G. Bardelli-Corotti (M.) R. Osvaldella (A.) L. Valentini (E.) |
| Seville | San Fernando | Dec. | 1858 | S. Peruzzi (M.) G. Landi (A.) |
| Valencia | Principal | Feb. | 1863 | M. Pirola (M.) E. Nicolini (A.) A. Mazzanti (E.) P. Poli-Lenzi (B.) |
|  |  | Oct. 29, | 1869 | L. Ponti dall'Armi (M.) P. Bignardi (A.) P. Varvaro (E.) |
| Valladolid | Lope de Vega | Dec. 14, | 1865 | L. Ruggero-Antonioli (M.) E. Mariani (A.) V. Morelli-Bartolami (E.) E. Rodas (B.) |
| Zaragozza | Principal | Apr. | 1865 | E. Julienne-Dejean (M.) E. Irfré (A.) V. Prattico (E.) |
|  |  | Oct. | 1865 | L. Ruggero-Antonioli (M.) E. Mariani (A.) V. Morelli-Bartolami (E.) |

**UNITED STATES**

| New York | Ac. of Mus. | May 4, | 1863 | A. Ortolani-Brignole (M.) F. Mazzoleni (A.) D. Bellini (E.) J. Nuno cond. |
|--|--|--|--|--|

**URUGUAY**

| Montevideo | Solis | Jan. 24, | 1861 | C. Manzini (M.) E. Ballerini (A.) G. Bertolini (E.) |
|--|--|--|--|--|

OTHER PRODUCTIONS-1900-1945

ITALY
Rome            Sala RAI    Oct.   1, 1939 M.  Pedrini  (M.)  P.  Civil  (A.)  A.
                                           Reali   (E.)   G.   Pasetti   (B.)   F.
                                           Capuana cond.


OTHER PRODUCTIONS-POST-WORLD WAR II

GERMANY[52]
Hamburg         Stadt       Feb. 10, 1954 A.  Bollinger (M.)  P.  Anders (A.)  J.
                                          Metternich  (E.)  H.  G.  Ratjen cond.
                                          (in Ger.)

GREAT BRITAIN
London          St. Pancras Feb. 25, 1964 A.  Edwards  (M.)  N.  Petroff  (A.)  M.
                                          Maurel  (E.)  N.  Mangin  (B.)  G.  Gover
                                          cond.

IRELAND
Wexford         Th. Royal   Oct. 25? 1959 M.  Angioletti  (M.)  N.  Nicolov  (A.)
                                          A.  Protti  (E.)  C.  Mackerras cond.

ITALY
Florence        Comunale    June   3, 1953 A.  Stella  (M.)  G.  Penno  (A.)  A.
                                          Protti  (E.)  U.  Novelli  (B.)  T.
                                          Serafin cond.

Milan           Sala RAI    Nov. 17, 1975 A.  Gulin  (M.)  G.  Cecchele  (A.)  L.
                                          Montefusco  (E.)  A.  Zanazzo  (B.)  M.
                                          Rinaldi cond.

Trieste         Grande      Dec.     1954 A. M. Rovere (M.)  R.  Turrini (A.)  U.
                                          Savarese  (E.)  F.  Capuana cond.

Turin           Sala RAI    Oct. 24, 1951 M.  Vitale (M.)  V.  Campagnano (A.)  R.
                                          Panerai  (E.)  G.  De Manuelli  (B.)  E.
                                          Basile cond.

Venice          La Fenice   Jan.   1, 1986 S.  Pacetti/L.  Aliberti  (M.)  J.  Pinto
                                          (A.)  A.  Salvadori  (E.)  E.  Inbal
                                          cond.

SWITZERLAND
Zürich          Stadt                1954

UNITED STATES
New York        Amato Op.   Mar.     1961 G.  Shirley (A.)  A.  Amato cond.

                Carnegie    Apr.   8, 1979 M.  Caballé (M.)  G.  Cecchele (A.)  J.
                Hall                       Pons  (E.)  L.  Lebherz  (B.)  E.  Queler
                                          cond.

Sarasota        Op. House   Feb. 24, 1990

---

[52]. *Aroldo* was also given in Karlsruhe in 1954 and in Wuppertal in 1955.

23. UN BALLO IN MASCHERA-Melodramma in three acts
Rome-Teatro Apollo-Feb. 17, 1859
Libretto by Antonio Somma

| | |
|---|---|
| Amelia (A.) | Eugenie Julienne-Dejean sop. |
| Oscar (O.) | Pamela Scotti sop. |
| Ulrica (U.) | Zelinda Sbriscia mez. |
| Riccardo (R.) | Gaetano Fraschini ten. |
| Renato (Re.) | Leone Giraldoni bar. |
| Samuel (S.) | Cesare Bossi bass |
| Tom | Giovanni Bernardoni bass |
| Un Servo d'Amelia | Luigi Fossi ten. |
| Un Giudice | Giuseppe Bazzoli ten. |
| Silvano | Stefano Santucci bass |
| | |
| Conductor | Emilio Angelini |
| Director | Giuseppe Verdi |

OTHER PREMIERES

ARGENTINA
Buenos Aires   Ant. Colón   Oct.  4, 1862 T. Parodi (A.) G. Altieri (O.) M.
                                         Giovanelli (U.) G. Mazzi (R.) L.
                                         Walter (Re.) W. Fumi cond.

               Colón        May  31, 1913 C. Gagliardi (A.) I. M. Ferraris
                                         (O.) L. Garibaldi (U.) R. Grassi
                                         (R.) R. Stracciari (Re.) L. Manci-
                                         nelli cond.

AUSTRALIA
Adelaide       Th. Royal    Mar. 19, 1872 M. Zenoni (A.) G. Tamburini-Coy (O.)
                                         L. Polli (U.) F. Rosnati (R.) F. Co-
                                         liva (Re.) E. Dondi (S.)

Brisbane       Queensland   Apr.  3, 1875 Baldassari (A.) G. Tamburini-Coy
                                         (O.) A. Magi (U.) F. Rosnati (R.)
                                         Baldassari (Re.) E. Dondi (S.)

Melbourne      Haymarket    Jan. 29, 1868 L. Escott (A.) I. Vitali (O.) G.
                                         Hodson (U.) U. Devoti (R.) G. Ber-
                                         tolini (Re.) P. De Antoni (S.)

Sydney         Prince       June  1, 1868 L. Escott (A.) G. Warden (O.) A.
               of Wales                  King (U.) U. Devoti (R.) G. Berto-
                                         lini (Re.) P. De Antoni (S.)

AUSTRIA
Vienna         Kärntnertor  Apr.  1, 1864 M. Lotti Della Santa (A.) E. Volpini
                                         (O.) S. Ciaschetti (U.) L. Graziani
                                         (R.) O. Bartolini (Re.) G. B. Corna-
                                         go (S.) (in It.)

                            Nov. 19, 1866 M. Dustmann (A.) I. Di Murska (O.)
                                         K. Bettelheim (U.) G. Walter (R.) J.
                                         N. Beck (Re.) (in Ger.)

BELGIUM
Brussels       Cirque       Apr.  9, 1864 C. Poch (A.) C. Guerrabella (O.) De
                                         Ponti (U.) G. Musiani (R.) M. Zacchi
                                         (Re.) (in It.)

|  |  |  |  |  |
|--|--|--|--|--|

La Monnaie  Mar.  5, 1872 M. Roze (A.) Nordet (O.) P. Von Edelsberg (U.) Warot (R.) J. Lassalle (Re.) Singelée cond. (in Fr.)

Ghent       Grand       Apr. 10, 1864 C. Poch (A.) G. Musiani (R.) M. Zacchi (Re.) (in It.)

Nov. 22, 1871 (in Fr.)

Liège       Grand       Apr. 20, 1864 C. Poch (A.) G. Musiani (R.) M. Zacchi (Re.) (In It.)

BRAZIL
Rio de      Lirico      May  22, 1862 M. De Gianni-Vivez (A.) M. Palmieri
Janeiro     Fluminense                (O.) A. Alessandri (U.) T. Palmieri (R.) F. Briani (Re.) C. Bosoni cond.

Pedro II    July  8, 1871 A. Pasi (A.) I. Martinez de Escalante (O.) Perrotti (U.) E. Ballerini (R.) Mazzoni (Re.)

Municipal   Sep. 28, 1918 R. Raisa (A.) G. Besanzoni (U.) A. Pertile (R.) G. Rimini (Re.) R. Franciioli cond.

Sao Paulo   Provisorio  May  16, 1875 E. Pezzoli (A.) A. Cortesi (O.) St. Clair (U.) G. Limberti (R.) L. Barcena (Re.) G. Mirandola (S.)

Sao José    Nov. 13, 1879 A. Conti-Foroni (A.) S. Springer (O.) R. Vercolini-Tay (U.) F. Giannini (R.) V. Cottone (Re.) G. Mirabella (S.)

Municipal   Jan. 16, 1929 A. Conti (A.) L. Alessandrini (O.) A. Bertola (U.) A. Cingolani (R.) C. Cavallini (Re.) G. Picco cond.

BULGARIA
Sofia       Luxembourg  July      1895 G. Badarocco (R.) (in It.)

National    Oct. 22, 1926 (in Bulg.)

CANADA
Edmonton    Opera       Oct. 28, 1971 P. Tinsley (A.) R. Turofsky (O.) M. Forrester (U.) N. Di Virgilio (R.) C. Ludgin (Re.) A. Drake (S.) M. Bernardi cond.

Montreal    Ac. de Mus. Feb. 23, 1889 (in Eng.)

His         Mar. 30, 1910 N. Bari (R.) (in It.)
Majesty's

Toronto     Grand       Feb.  9, 1889 L. Natali (A.) C. Bassett (R.) R. Alonzo (Re.) (in Eng.)

Vancouver   Opera       Apr. 30, 1970 P. Tinsley (A.) R. Turofsky (O.) A. Glass (U.) M. Molese (R.) L. Quilico (Re.) M. Brown (S.) M. Bernardi cond.

Winnipeg    Manitoba    Jan.      1977 M. Galvany (A.) R. Bondino (R.) L.
            Opera                       Quilico (Re.)

CHILE
Santiago        Municipal   Aug. ?  1864 C. Manzini (A.) I. Vitali (C.) E.
                                         Ballerini (R.) G. Bertolini (Re.)

Valparaiso      Victoria    Mar. 11, 1864 C. Manzini (A.) I. Vitali (O.) Co-
                                         lombo (U.) E. Ballerini (R.) G. Ber-
                                         tolini (Re.)

CHINA
Shanghai        Lyceum      Jan. 21, 1880 R. Genolini (A.) B. Genolini (O.) F.
                                         Mancini (U.) E. Sbriscia (R.) G.
                                         Bergamaschi (Re.)

COLOMBIA
Bogota          Teatro      Sep. 27, 1869

CUBA
Havana          Tacon       Dec. 21, 1861 A. Basseggio (A.) E. Kenneth (O.) E.
                                         Masson (U.) G. Tombesi (R.) G. Ferri
                                         (Re.)

Santiago                    Feb.     1862

CZECHOSLOVAKIA
Bratislava      Stadt                1891-92

Brno            Stadt       Mar.  2, 1872 (in Ger.)

Prag            Ständisches Aug. 14, 1866 (in Ger.)

                Provisional June 30, 1869 (in Czech)

                Neues       May      1901 M. De Macchi (A.) F. Signorini (R.)
                Deutsches                 V. Brombara (Re.) V. Arimondi (S.)
                                         (in It.)

DENMARK
Copenhagen      Casino      May 18, 1867 A. Sarolta (A.) G. Bennati (O.) A.
                                         Ferlesi (U.) N. Andreef (R.) M.
                                         Padilla (Re.) P. Dérivis (S.) (in
                                         It.)

                Royal       Apr. 20, 1928 I. Rinolfi (A.) L. Allesandrini (O.)
                                         S. De Mette (U.) G. Taccani (R.) C.
                                         Morelli (Re.) L. Donaggio (S.) E.
                                         Tango cond. (in It.)

                            Sep. 25, 1935 E. Schott (A.) I. Steffensen (U.) M.
                                         Jacobsen (R.) H. Bruusgaard (Re.)
                                         (in Dan.)

EGYPT
Alexandria      Rossini     Jan.     1864 E. Leonpietra (A.) L. Corbari (U.)
                                         C. Liverani (R.) P. Poli-Lenzi (Re.)

Cairo           Khedivial   Jan.     1870 B. Merson-Ferrucci (A.) E. Grossi
                                         (U.) E. Naudin (R.) C. Boccolini
                                         (Re.) E. Muzio cond.

FINLAND
Helsinki        Nya         June  6, 1879 Engdahl (A.) Hofer (Re.) (in Swed.)

|  | Alexanders | Jan. 15, 1881 | A. Spaak (A.) Bottarelli (O.) Bettini (U.) A. Brunetti (R.) M. Danisi (Re.) (in It.) |
|---|---|---|---|
|  | National | Apr. 26, 1922 | (in Fin.) |

FRANCE

| Bordeaux | Grand | 1862-63 | I. Rey-Balla (A.) Jaulain (R.) Meric (Re.) (in Fr.) |
|---|---|---|---|
| Lyon | Grand | Mar. 26, 1873 | M. Roze (A.) Chelli (R.) (in Fr.) |
|  |  | June 6, 1873 | Lamare (A.) Peretti (O.) L. Caracciolo (U.) Chelli (R.) A. Strozzi (Re.) Aguirre cond. (in It.) |
| Marseille | Grand | Mar.? 1864 | Ecarlat (A.) Dumestre (U.) Morère (R.) Dumestre (Re.) (in Fr.) |
|  | Alhambra | May 9, 1897 | A. Gabbi (A.) Cesarini (O.) Saruggia (U.) L. Signoretti (R.) Moro (Re.) (in It.) |
| Nice | Regio | Feb.? 1861 | E. Berini (A.) C. Marini (O.) G. Sanchioli (U.) A. Corsi (R.) S. Binaghi (Re.) |
| Paris | Italien | Jan. 31, 1861 | R. Penco (A.) M. Battu (O.) M. Alboni (U.) Mario (R.) F. Graziani (Re.) V. Bonetti cond. (in It.) |
|  | Lyrique | Nov. 17, 1869 | Meillet (A.) Daram (O.) Borghese (U.) Massy (R.) Lutz (Re.) Pasdeloup cond. (in Fr.) |
|  | Opéra | July 1, 1951 | D. Martini (A.) A. Noni (O.) E. Stignani (U.) F. Tagliavini (R.) P. Silveri (Re.) I. Tajo (S.) G. Santini cond. (By the company of the Teatro San Carlo, Naples) |

GERMANY

| Baden | Festspielhaus | Sep. 1863 | A. Charton-Demeur (A.) M. Battu (O.) E. De Meric (U.) E. Naudin (R.) E. Delle Sedie (Re.) |
|---|---|---|---|
| Berlin | Hofoper | Nov. 23, 1861 | C. Marchisio (A.) M. Brunetti (O.) Z. Trebelli (U.) E. Pancani (R.) M. Zacchi (Re.) L. Agnesi (S.) (in It.) |
|  |  | Feb. 12, 1873 | V. von Voggenhuber (A.) Grossi (O.) Assmann (U.) A. Niemann (R.) F. Betz (Re.) (in Ger.) |
|  | Deutsche | Dec. 13, 1974 | C. Ligendza (A.) C. Cossutta (R.) I. Wixell (Re.) L. Maazel cond. |
| Braunschweig | Hoftheater | Nov. 29, 1868 | (in Ger.) |
| Breslau | Stadt | July 1873 | (in Ger.) |
| Cologne | Stadt | Nov. 24, 1876 | M. Lehmann (A.) Monhaupt (O.) Keller (U.) F. Diener (R.) Krückl (Re.) Kotz (S.) (in Ger.) |

Darmstadt      Hoftheater    Oct. 16, 1898 (in Ger.)

Dresden        Hofoper       Mar. 29, 1868 (in Ger.)

                             Apr. 13, 1874 D. Artôt (A.) M. Padilla (Re.) J.
                                           Goula cond. (in It.)

Frankfurt      Stadt         Oct. 21, 1872 Hofmeister (A.) Prohaska (O.) Oppen-
                                           heimer (U.) Richard (R.) Pichler
                                           (Re.) Cassio (S.) (in Ger.)

                             Feb. 24, 1873 D. Artôt (A.) M. Vidal (R.) M. Pa-
                                           dilla (Re.) J. Goula cond. (in It.)

Hamburg        Stadt         Nov. 29, 1862 (in Ger.)

Hannover       Hoftheater    Jan. 24, 1897 (in Ger.)

Kassel         Hoftheater    Oct. 30, 1884 (in Ger.)

Leipzig        Stadt         Nov. 21, 1880 Hofmeister (A.) Korbel (O.) Riegler
                                           (U.) Broulik (R.) Schelper (Re.) (in
                                           Ger.)

Mainz          Stadt         Mar.     1863 (in Ger.)

Munich         Hoftheater    Mar. 11, 1879 I. Cristofani (A.) G. Pasqua (U.) A.
                                           Celada (R.) G. Vaselli (Re.) (in
                                           It.)

                             Feb. 22, 1880 (in Ger.)

Nürnberg       Stadt         Apr. 14, 1871 (in Ger.)

Stuttgart      Hofoper       Mar.  6, 1862 (in Ger.)

                             Jan.   3? 1874 T. Friderici (A.) M. Dérivis (O.) A.
                                           Franchini (R.) T. Sterbini (Re.) (in
                                           It.)

Weimar         Hoftheater    Oct. 16, 1913 (in Ger.)

GREAT BRITAIN
Belfast        Th. Royal     Sep. 24, 1877 C. Salla (A.) M. Rodani (O.) E. De
                                           Meric (U.) F. Runcio (R.) A.
                                           Faentini-Galassi (Re.) F. Rialp
                                           cond. (in It.)

Birmingham     Prince        June 26? 1867 F. Lancia (A.) W. Parkinson (R.) C.
               of Wales                    Durand (Re.) (in Eng.)

Edinburgh      Operetta      Jan. 17, 1868 I. Gilliess (A.) F. Heywood (O.) E.
               House                       Heywood (U.) H. Bond (R.) H. Corri
                                           (Re.) Ha. Corri (S.) J. W. Pew cond.
                                           (in Eng.)

               Th. Royal     Oct.  6, 1910 Castellano (A.) Licette (O.) Defral
                                           (U.) Barbato (R.) Catini (Re.) (in
                                           It.)

Glasgow        Prince of     June 19, 1868 Haigh-Dyer (A.) F. Leng (O.) A.
               Wales                       Alessandri (U.) H. Haigh (R.) G.
                                           Cooke cond. (in Eng.)

|           | Th. Royal       | Nov. 6, 1875   | M. Bulli-Paoli (A.) Bianchi (O.) Ghiotti (U.) A. Oliva-Pavani (R.) N. Medica (Re.) A. Vianesi cond. (in It.) |
|-----------|-----------------|----------------|-------------------------------------------------------------------------------------------------------------|
| Leeds     | Amphi-theatre   | Sep. 25, 1867  | F. Lancia (A.) C. Zerbini (U.) W. Parkinson (R.) C. Durand (Re.) (in Eng.) |
| Liverpool | Saint James Hall | Oct. 28, 1867 | I. Gilliess (A.) F. Heywood (O.) E. Heywood (U.) H. Bond (R.) H. Corri (Re.) (in Eng.) |
|           | Royal Alexandra | Nov. 25, 1875  | M. Bulli-Paoli (A.) Bianchi (O.) Ghiotti (U.) A. Oliva-Pavani (R.) V. Maurel (Re.) A. Vianesi cond. (in It.) |
| London    | Lyceum          | June 15, 1861  | T. Tietiens (A.) J. Gassier (O.) M. Alboni (U.) A. Giuglini (R.) E. Delle Sedie (Re.) L. Gassier (S.) L. Arditi cond. |
|           | Covent Garden   | June 27, 1861  | R. Penco (A.) M. Miolan-Carvalho (O.) C. Nantier-Didiée (U.) Mario (R.) F. Graziani (Re.) M. Costa cond. |
| Manchester | Comedy         | Oct. 28, 1892  | M. D'Alcourt (A.) M. Titiens (O.) L. Mowbray (U.) I. St. Austel (R.) A. Rousbey (Re.) (in Eng.) |
|           | Gaiety          | Mar. 10, 1910  | (in It.) |
| Newcastle | Th. Royal       | July 24, 1868  | Haigh-Dyer (A.) H. Haigh (R.) |
| GREECE Athens | Real        | Jan.?  1865    | Alfano (A.) M. Plodowska (O.) Trucco (U.) A. Altavilla (R.) L. Buti (Re.) |
| Corfu     | San Giacomo     | Mar.?  1862    | Alvisi (R.) Ortolani (Re.) |
| GUATEMALA Guatemala City | Colón |      1876       | V. Potentini (A.) |
| HONG KONG Hong Kong | Th. Royal | Nov. 27, 1879 | R. Genolini (A.) E. Sbriscia (R.) G. Bergamaschi (Re.) |
| HUNGARY Budapest | Deutsches | Dec. 18, 1863  | I. Di Murska (O.) F. Steger (R.) Robinson (Re.) (in Ger.) |
|           | Nemzeti Szinház | Jan. 16, 1864  | A. Carina (A.) M. Rabatinsky (O.) S. Hofbaur (U.) L. Ceresa (R.) G. Simon (Re.) K. Köszeghy (S.) (in Hung.) |
|           |                 | Apr. 18, 1869  | A. Pozzoni (A.) S. Anastasi (R.) (in It.) |
|           | Operaház        | Nov. 13, 1884  | E. Turolla (A.) M. Kordin (O.) V. Bartolucci (U.) G. Perotti (R.) L. Odry (Re.) G. Erkel cond. (in Hung.) |

INDIA
Bombay        Grant Rd.    Dec.  7, 1878 R. Genolini (A.) G. Tamburini-Coy
                                        (O.) Brusa (U.) L. Coy (R.) G. Ber-
                                        gamaschi (Re.) Salvarani (S.)

Calcutta      Royal Th.    Dec. 21, 1866 R. Vielli-Villa (A.) Longhena (O.)
                                        A. Rasori (U.) T. Villa (R.) A.
                                        Grandi (Re.) F. Fiorani (S.) A. Zel-
                                        man cond.

INDONESIA
Batavia       T. Batavie   Aug. 6,  1869 R. Vielli-Villa (A.) C. Ghirlanda-
                                        Tortolini (O.) G. Ferrari-Pocoleri
                                        (U.) T. Villa (R.) L. Magnani (Re.)
                                        E. Gasperini (S.)

IRELAND
Cork          Th. Royal    Jan.  6, 1868 F. Lancia (A.) B. Cole (O.) C. Zer-
                                        bini (U.) W. Parkinson (R.) C. Du-
                                        rand (Re.) (in Eng.)

Dublin        Th. Royal    Sep. 25, 1861 T. Tietiens (A.) A. Whitty (O.) G.
                                        Lemaire (U.) A. Giuglini (R.) E.
                                        Delle Sedie (Re.) C. Bossi (S.) L.
                                        Arditi cond. (in It.)

ISRAEL
Tel Aviv      Auditorium   July 14, 1959 L. Udovick (A.) E. Tobin (R.) K.
                                        Paskalis (Re.) N. Sonzogno cond.

ITALY
Alessandria   Municipale   Oct. 12, 1861 A. Moro (A.) A. Bernardelli (O.) G.
                                        Visconti (U.) Fabris (R.) I. Viga-
                                        notti (Re.) E. Daneri (S.)

Ancona        Muse         May 14,  1861 E. Weisser (A.) Cambardi (O.) E.
                                        Barlani-Dini (U.) G. Bettini (R.)
                                        Morelli (Re.)

Ascoli        Ventidio     Oct.     1865 G. Borsi de Leurie (A.) Bacigalupi
Piceno        Basso                     lupi (O.) Cellini (U.) V. Sarti (R.)
                                        A. Carboni (Re.)

Bari          Piccinni     Feb.     1863 L. Banti (A.) E. Puerari (O.) De
                                        Rossi (U.) V. Massini (R.) L. Spel-
                                        lini (S.)

              Petruzzelli  Dec. 23, 1906 E. Mazzoleni (A.) N. Zanatti (O.) R.
                                        Agozzino (U.) A. Gamba (R.) A. An-
                                        ceschi (R.) G. Bavagnoli cond.

Bergamo       Riccardi     Aug. 11, 1864 P. Veneri (A.) G. Limberti (R.) S.
                                        Cappelli (Re.) E. Pelletti (S.) V.
                                        Petrali cond.

Bologna       Comunale     Oct.  4, 1860 C. Barbot (A.) E. Leonpietra (O.) L.
                                        Giry (U.) L. Graziani (R.) M. Ghini
                                        (S.) A. Mariani cond.

Brescia       Grande       Aug.?    1863 L. Bendazzi-Secchi (A.) G. Flory
                                        (U.) G. Pardini (R.) G. Guicciardi
                                        (Re.) S. Cesarò (S.)

Bussetto      Verdi         Sep.       1868 E. Berini (A.) Peroni (O.) Gaggiotti
                                            (U.) A. Prudenza (R.) Z. Bertolasi
                                            (Re.)

Cagliari      Civico        Oct.  4,   1862 Franchi (A.) A. Mazzetti (O.) A.
                                            Mazzucco (U.) F. Piccioni (R.) E.
                                            Corti (Re.)

Catania       Comunale      Dec.  7,   1861 A. Ortolani-Brignole (A.) M. Mancusi
                                            (O.) F. De Ruggero (R.) L. Rossi
                                            (Re.) Mangiulli cond.

              Bellini       Jan. 14,   1928 F. Franchi (A.) A. M. Laudisa (O.)
                                            S. Blanco Sadun (U.) N. Del Ry (R.)
                                            E. Frigerio (Re.) C. Benvenuti cond.

Cesena        Comunale      Aug. 19,   1865 T. Stolz (A.) C. Lefranc (R.) F.
                                            Pandolfini (Re.) A. Mariani cond.

Chieti        Marrucino     Apr.  2,   1864 M. Pancaldi (A.) E. Pezzoli (O.) E.
                                            Bernaroli (U.) G. Serri-Chiesi (R.)
                                            D. Baldassari (Re.) V. Boccabianca
                                            cond.

Cremona       Concordia     Dec.?      1861 C. Noel-Guidi (A.) E. De Baillou
                                            (O.) C. Soroldoni (U.) A. Prudenza
                                            (R.) F. Bacchi-Perego (Re.) G. Coll
                                            (S.) A. Cremaschi cond.

Fermo         Aquila        Aug.       1865 M. Velasco-Rocco (A.) L. Banti (O.)
                                            S. Tamanti (U.) V. Belardi (R.) C.
                                            Boccolini (Re.) G. Marchetti (S.) F.
                                            Cellini cond.

Ferrara       Comunale      May  13,   1863 V. Pozzi-Brazanti (A.) E. Cortesi
                                            (O.) G. Sanchioli (U.) A. Oliva-
                                            Pavani (R.) G. B. Bencich (Re.)
                                            Maccani (S.)

Fiume         Civico        Mar. 14,   1863 C. Lanzi (A.) R. Feltri-Spalla (U.)
                                            Giusti (R.) Dal Negro (Re.)

Florence      Pergola       Sep.       1861 M. Lotti Della Santa (A.) L. Aran-
                                            cio-Guerrini (O.) S. Marini-Testa
                                            (U.) L. Graziani (R.) L. Buti (Re.)
                                            F. Cuturi (S.)

Forli         Comunale      May        1867 Stella (A.) G. Zacometti (R.) G.
                                            Valle (Re.)

Genoa         Carlo         Apr. 10,   1861 C. Barbot (A.) C. Lanzi (O.) C. Acs
              Felice             (U.) G. Zacometti (R.) D. Squarcia
                                            (Re.) C. Bossi (S.) A. Mariani cond.

Livorno       Rossini       Feb. 13,   1862 S. Vera-Lorini (A.) Torricelli (O.)
                                            Ciotti (U.) V. Sarti (R.) L. Buti
                                            (Re.)

Lucca         Giglio        Aug. 28,   1862 S. Vera-Lorini (A.) Torricelli (O.)
                                            V. Sarti (R.) L. Buti (Re.)

Lugo          Rossini       Aug. 30,   1863 A. Ortolani-Tiberini (A.) N. Dario
                                            (O.) F. Basso (U.) M. Tiberini (R.)
                                            L. Buti (Re.) P. Milesi (S.)

Macerata      Condomini     Aug. 12? 1864 M. Palmieri (A.) S. Bottelli (O.) A.
                                          Falconi (U.) S. Perozzi (R.) F.
                                          Cresci (Re.)

Mantua        Sociale       Nov. 16, 1866 G. Bellini (A.) G. Ligi (O.) S.
                                          Scalchi (U.) A. Caramelli (R.) L.
                                          Buti (Re.) G. Bailini (S.) G. Luppi
                                          cond.

Messina       Vittorio      Mar. 24, 1863 L. Gavetti-Reggiani (A.) Ferrari
              Emanuele                    (U.) C. Liverani (R.) V. Prattico
                                          (Re.)

Milan         La Scala      Jan.  8, 1862 R. Csillag (A.) L. Arancio-Guerrini
                                          (O.) C. Acs (U.) L. Graziani (R.) F.
                                          Morelli-Ponti (Re.) A. Fiorini (S.)

Modena        Comunale      Feb.  2, 1862 M. Zenoni (A.) C. Lanzi (O.) A. Lan-
                                          franco (U.) E. Nicolini (R.) R. Piz-
                                          zigati (Re.) S. Cesarò (S.) A. Si-
                                          ghicelli cond.

Naples        San Carlo     Feb. 18, 1862 M. Lotti Della Santa (A.) A. Sarolta
                                          (O.) E. Grossi (U.) M. Tiberini (R.)
                                          G. Aldighieri (Re.)

Padua         Concordi      Dec. 26, 1865 M. De Zorzi (A.) M. Mazzoni Delle
                                          Sedie (O.) F. Basso (U.) G. Piccin-
                                          nini (R.) G. Orsini (Re.) G. Sam-
                                          pieri (S.)

Palermo       Carolino      Feb. 24, 1862 M. Gazzaniga (A.) M. Winter (O.) A.
                                          Orlandi (U.) A. Malagola (R.) G. Ci-
                                          ma (Re.) R. Marconi (S.) A. Lo Casto
                                          cond.

              Massimo       Apr. 29, 1908 E. Druetti (A.) P. Zweifel (O.) E.
                                          Petri (U.) I. Calleja (R.) C. Galef-
                                          fi (Re.) O. Luppi (S.) G. Marinuzzi
                                          cond.

Parma         Regio         Dec. 25, 1860 E. Poinsot (A.) A. Tagliani (O.) G.
                                          Flory (U.) P. Bignardi (R.) L. Buti
                                          (Re.) G. Romanelli (S.) G. C. Ferra-
                                          rini cond.

Pavia         Condominio    Jan.  ?  1864 L. Ruggero-Antonioli (A.) A. Ruggero
                                          (O.) C. De Caroli (U.) C. Baroni
                                          (R.) D. Baldassari (Re.) G. Dalbesio
                                          (S.)

Perugia       Morlacchi     Carn. 1863-64 Z. Papini (A.) M. Panseri (R.)

Pesaro        Rossini       Dec. 26? 1861 A. Jackson (A.) C. Noel (O.) M.
                                          Mallknecht (U.) L. Ceresa R.) E.
                                          Mari-Cornia (Re.) A. Adoni (S.)

Piacenza      Municipale    Dec. 26? 1861 L. Ruggero-Antonioli (A.) G. Viscon-
                                          ti (U.) G. Limberti (R.) G. Colombo
                                          (Re.) P. Milesi (S.) G. Jona cond.

Pisa          Ravvivati     Oct. 24, 1863 Binaghi (A.) L. Coy (R.) F. Proni
                                          (Re.) G. Manotti cond.

Ravenna        Alighieri    May    3, 1862 S. Vera-Lorini (A.) G. Limberti (R.)
                                           D. Squarcia (Re.)

Reggio Emilia Municipale   Apr. 25, 1861 S. Vera-Lorini (A.) G. Flory (U.) R.
                                           Mirate (R.) G. F. Beneventano (Re.)
                                           G. Tebaldi cond.

Rome           Costanzi     Nov. 19, 1885 A. Cattaneo (A.) E. Colonnese (O.)
                                           G. De Luttickau (U.) G. Sani (R.) M.
                                           Battistini (Re.) E. Masceroni cond.

Rovigo         Sociale      Oct. 17, 1868 G. Monti (A.) A. Giannetti (O.) E.
                                           Antonelli (U.) G. Sani (R.) A. Car-
                                           boni (Re.)

Siena          Rinnovati    Aug.     1863 F. Salvini-Donatelli (A.) A. Pozzo-
                                           lini (R.) F. Proni (Re.)

Sinigaglia     Comunale     Fiera    1861 I. Edelvira (A.) L. Arancio-Guerrini
                                           (O.) C. Acs (U.) P. Malagola (R.) E.
                                           Fagotti (Re.) Baccelli (S.)

Spoleto        Nuovo        Aug.     1865 Bellini (A.) F. Guillemin (O.) V.
                                           Falconi (U.) S. Perozzi (R.) C. Len-
                                           ghi (Re.) A. Fiorini (S.)

Trento         Sociale      June?    1869 B. Blume (A.) Rossetti (O.) Borotti
                                           (U.) E. Barbacini (R.) V. Quintili-
                                           Leoni (Re.) M. Della Torre (S.)

Treviso        Societa      Autumn   1866 T. Stolz (A.) F. Patierno (R.) F.
                                           Coliva (Re.)

Trieste        Grande       Oct. 20, 1861 L. Bendazzi-Secchi (A.) E. Leon-
                                           pietra (O.) G. Flory (U.) C. Negrini
                                           (R.) D. Squarcia (Re.) E. Colomberti
                                           (S.) G. A. Scaramelli cond.

Turin          Regio        Dec. 25, 1860 C. Barbot (A.) L. Stramesi (O.) E.
                                           Barlani-Dini (U.) V. Sarti (R.) G.
                                           Guicciardi (Re.) F. Reduzzi (S.) F.
                                           Bianchi cond.

Udine          Sociale      Nov. 14, 1866 C. Bianchi-Biffi (A.) De Ponte (O.)
                                           Perotti (U.) E. Giusti (R.) G. Spal-
                                           lazzi (Re.)

Venice         San          Dec. 26, 1861 A. Rubini-Zangheri (A.) A. Tagliani
               Benedetto                   (O.) R. Feltri-Spalla (U.) A. Zenna-
                                           ri (R.) G. Orsini (Re.) E. Anselmi
                                           (S.)

               La Fenice    Oct. 31, 1866 T. De Giuli-Borsi (A.) G. Caruzzi-
                                           Bedogni (O.) M. Antonietti (U.) C.
                                           Vincentelli (R.) A. De Antoni (Re.)
                                           E. Muzio cond.

Verona         Filarmonico Dec. 26, 1866 C. Ferlotti (A.) N. Dario (O.) S.
                                           Scalchi (U.) G. Musiani (R.) E. Fa-
                                           gotti (Re.)

|              | Arena       | July 31, 1932 G. Arangi-Lombardi (A.) M. Carosio (O.) N. Giani (U.) A. Pertile (R.) B. Franci (Re.) A. Righetti (S.) S. Failoni cond. |

Vicenza       Eretenio     Aug.      1868 T. Stolz (A.) L. Vanda-Miller (O.) G. Gavotti (U.) E. Barbacini (R.) F. Pandolfini (Re.)

Viterbo       Unione       July 12, 1864 G. Giovannoni-Zacchi (A.) Nizza (O.) Latini (U.) Pieraccini (R.) Bonetti (Re.)

JAPAN
Tokyo         Imperial     Mar. 26, 1927

JUGOSLAVIA
Ljubljana     National               1880 (in Ger.)

                           Nov. 26, 1897 (in Slov.)

Zagreb        National     Mar. 29, 1869 Z. Papini (A.) Brusa (O.) Borghi (U.) L. Abrugnedo (R.) G. Del Puente (Re.) G. Kaschmann (S.)

Zara          Nuovo        Oct.  7, 1865 L. Tencajoli (A.) F. Guillemin (O.) Castellani (U.) C. Baroni (R.) E. Storti-Gaggi (Re.) Wagner (S.) A. Ravasio cond.

LATVIA
Riga          National     May 14, 1927 T. Reiters cond. (in Let.)

LITHUANIA
Kaunas        National     Oct. 30, 1926 (in Lith.)

Vilnius       Municipal    Mar. 19? 1900 L. Montanari (A.) C. Zawner (U.) F. De Grandi (R.) Pompa (Re.) (in It.)

MALTA
La Valletta   Manoel       May       1862 A. Bazzuri (A.) Mercanti (R.) T. Sterbini (Re.)

MEXICO
Guadalajara   Degollado    July  5, 1868 E. Tomassi (A.) A. Boetti (R.)

Mexico City   Nacional     Aug. 17, 1864 A. Murio-Celli (A.) E. Tomassi (O.) H. Sulzer (U.) F. Mazzoleni (R.) A. Ottaviani (Re.)

MONACO
Monte Carlo   Salle        Jan. 19, 1884 C. Salla (A.) Mansour (O.) G. Novel-
              Garnier                   li (U.) E. Vergnet (R.) F. Pandolfi-
                                        ni (Re.) R. Accursi cond.

NETHERLANDS
Amsterdam     Stads        Jan. 29, 1863 E. Leonpietra (A.) Bijwater (O.) A. Phillips (U.) B. Danieli (R.) M. Zacchi (Re.)

NEW ZEALAND
Auckland      Prince       Nov. 10, 1871 M. Zenoni (A.) G. Tamburini-Coy (O.)
              of Wales                  E. Polli (U.) F. Rosnati (R.) F. Co-
                                        liva (Re.) E. Dondi (S.)

Dunedin        Queen's      Jan. 16, 1873 E. Bosisio (A.) T. Riboldi (U.) F.
                                          Rosnati (R.) F. Coliva (Re.) E.
                                          Dondi (S.)

Wellington     Th. Royal    Jan.  4, 1878 A. Guadagnini (A.) M. Caranti-Vita
                                          (O.) M. Venosta (U.) P. Paladini
                                          (R.) G. Gambetti (Re.)

NORWAY
Oslo           Christiana   May  12, 1868 M. Calisto (A.) G. Bennati (O.) A.
                                          L. Cary (U.) G. Bentami (R.) A. Pan-
                                          taleoni (Re.)

PANAMA
Panama City    Nacional     Nov. 12, 1908 L. De Benedetto (A.) A. Scalabrini
                                          (R.) G. Pimazzoni (Re.) A. Mauceri
                                          (S.)

PERU
Lima           Principal    Summer?  1863 A. Bazzurri (A.) O. Sconcia (O.) B.
                                          De Filatoff (U.) F. Bicchielli (R.)
                                          A. Rossi-Ghelli (Re.) N. Bergamaschi
                                          (S.)

PHILIPPINES
Manila         Principe     July?    1868 M. Bouché (A.) Povoleri (U.) V. Sa-
               Alfonso                    batini (R.) Pellico (Re.)[53]

POLAND
Lwov           Szarbek      May      1867 G. Ronzi-Checchi (A.) R. Cash-Pol-
                                          lini (U.) G. Sbriglia (R.) V. Cotto-
                                          ne (Re.) C. Dalla Costa (S.) (in
                                          It.)

Warsaw         Wielki       Oct. 22, 1865 G. Giovannoni-Zacchi (A.) Caselli
                                          (O.) Z. Trebelli (U.) A. De Antoni
                                          (R.) M. Zacchi (Re.) L. Vecchi (S.)
                                          (in It.)

PORTUGAL
Lisbon         Sao Carlos   Apr. 15, 1860 M. Lotti Della Santa (A.) E. Hensler
                                          (O.) F. Lustani (U.) G. Fraschini
                                          (R.) O. Bartolini (Re.)

Oporto         Sao Joao     Apr.?    1861 C. Briol (A.) Persini (O.) Viale
                                          (U.) P. Tagliazucchi (R.) V. Prat-
                                          tico (Re.) Marcucci (S.)

PUERTO RICO
Ponce          La Perla     Dec.     1880 C. Bossi (A.) V. Arnoldi (O.) G.
                                          Cavalleri (U.) I. Viganotti (Re.)

San Juan       Municipal    Mar.?    1881 C. Bossi (A.) G. Cavalleri (U.) A.
                                          De Sanctis (R.) I. Viganotti (Re.)

ROMANIA
Bucharest      Nacional     Dec.     1863 R. Gianfredi (A.) R. Cash-Pollini
                                          (U.) V. Sarti (R.) E. Mari-Cornia
                                          (Re.)

---

[53]. Since there were only two prima donnas in the company, the role of Oscar was shared by Bouché and Povoleri.

Apr.      1923 (in Rum.)

| Iasi | Teatrul | Oct. 28? | 1864 | S. De Montelio (A.) De Fanti (U.) E. Marelli (R.) F. Proni (Re.) |

RUSSIA
Kharkov        Municipal    May?       1864 C. Noel-Guidi (A.) A. Gottardi (R.)

Kiev           Imperial     Nov.?      1864 E. De Martini (A.) G. René (R.)

Moscow         Bolshoi      Nov. 20, 1862 A. Fricci (A.) D. Fortuna (O.) Hono-
                                            ré (U.) E. Pancani (R.) F. Steller
                                            (Re.)

Odessa         Municipal    Jan.       1862 C. Briol (A.) Sermattei (O.) G. Tati
                                            (U.) C. Vincentelli (R.) F. Coliva
                                            (Re.)

St.            Imperial     Nov. 29, 1861 E. Fioretti (A.) Bernardi (O.) C.
Petersburg                                 Nantier-Didiée (U.) E. Tamberlick
                                            (R.) F. Graziani (Re.) E. Baveri
                                            cond.

Tbilisi        Imperial     June       1862

SOUTH AFRICA
Capetown       Th. Royal    Dec. 10, 1875 A. Brambilla (A.) Setragni (O.) Neri
                                            (U.) Cosmi (R.) Greco (Re.)

SPAIN
Alicante       Principal    Apr. 22, 1863 C. Poch (A.) Ferlotti (U.) E. Irfré
                                            (R.) V. Morelli-Bartolami (Re.)

Barcelona      Liceo        Jan. 31, 1861 C. Carozzi-Zucchi (A.) C. Más-Por-
                                            cell (O.) E. Brambilla (U.) E.
                                            Naudin (R.) G. B. Bencich (Re.) A.
                                            Ardavani (S.)

Bilbao         Viejo        Feb.       1862 L. Chiaromonte (A.) A. Zamboni (O.)
                                            Marini (U.) F. Pozzi (R.) V.
                                            Prattico (Re.)

Cadiz          Principal    Jan.?      1862 C. Poch (A.) C. Martelli (O.) G. De
                                            Antoni (R.) G. B. Bencich (Re.)

Granada                     June       1863 L. Ponti dall'Armi (A.) A. Dall'Armi
                                            (R.) P. Giorgi-Pacini (Re.)

Madrid         Real         Mar. 5, 1861 E. Julienne-Dejean (A.) A. Sarolta
                                            (O.) E. De Meric (U.) G. Fraschini
                                            (R.) L. Giraldoni (Re.) S. L. Bouché
                                            (S.) J. Skoczdopole cond.

Malaga         Principe     Jan.?      1863 A. Albertini (A.) M. Plodowska (O.)
               Alfonso                      L. Marelli (R.) Magnani (Re.)

Palma de       Principal    Oct. 8, 1861 N. De Roissi (A.) Buzzi (O.) G. Za-
Mallorca                                    Zacometti (R.) S. Binaghi (Re.)

Santander      Principal    Apr.       1862 C. Noel-Guidi (A.) Berti (O.) C.
                                            Lumley (U.) A. Prudenza (R.) F.
                                            Bachi-Perego (Re.) A. Garcia (S.)

Seville        San          May       1862 E. Julienne-Dejean (A.) C. Mongini
               Fernando                    (O.) B. Bellocchio (U.) G. De Antoni
                                           (R.) G. B. Bencich (Re.)

Valencia       Principal    Nov.      1861 I. Edelvira (A.) C. Forti-Babacci
                                           (O.) Ghedini (U.) G. Piccinnini (R.)
                                           V. Morelli-Bartolami (Re.) G. Segri-
                                           Segarra (S.)

Valladolid     Lope         Jan.?     1866 L. Ruggero-Antonioli (A.) E. Mariani
               de Vega                     (R.) V. Morelli-Bartolami (Re.) A.
                                           Agostini cond.

Zaragozza      Principal    Nov.  2, 1862 I. Edelvira (A.) Ferlotti (U.) G.
                                           Piccinnini (R.) V. Morelli-Bartolami
                                           (Re.)

SWEDEN
Gotheborg                   Mar. 29, 1869 E. Tomassi (A.) M. Marimon (O.) Al-
                                           dini (U.) V. Sabatini (R.) L. Gua-
                                           dagnini (Re.) A. Garcia (S.) (in
                                           It.)

Stockholm      Mindre       Dec.  5, 1868 E. Tomassi (A.) Z. Dalti (O.) A. L.
                                           Cary (U.) G. Bentami (R.) G. Mendio-
                                           roz (Re.) T. Coulon (S.) (in It.)

               Royal        Feb. 12, 1927 G. Söderman (A.) K. Rydqvist-Alfheim
                                           (O.) K. Thorborg (U.) D. Stockman
                                           (R.) E. Larson (Re.) C. Molin (S.)
                                           G. Bergman cond. (in Swed.)

SWITZERLAND
Basel          Stadt        Dec.  2, 1887 (in Ger.)

Lugano         Sociale      Oct.      1873 C. Poloni-Coppa (A.) Fiorentini (O.)
                                           Levini (U.) Cosmi (R.) Valchieri
                                           (Re.)

Zürich         Stadt        Mar.  2, 1876 (in Ger.)

                            June 20, 1920 G. Russ (A.) Donatello (O.) Famadas
                                           (R.) M. Battistini (Re.) (in It.)

TURKEY
Constan-       Naum         Oct. 18, 1862 C. Cattinari (A.) G. Visconti (U.)
  tinople                                  L. Ceresa (R.) E. Mari-Cornia (Re.)

Smyrna         Cammarano    Nov.      1864 C. Rosavalle (A.) Bertoletti (O.)
                                           Alberti (U.) F. Rosnati (R.) Carmeli
                                           (Re.)

UNITED STATES
Baltimore      Holliday     Apr. 27, 1863 S. Vera-Lorini (A.) A. Cordier (O.)
               Street                      Morensi (U.) P. Brignoli (R.) A. A-
                                           modio (Re.) E. Muzio cond.

Boston         Boston Th.   Mar. 15, 1861 P. Colson (A.) I. Hinckley (O.) A.
                                           Phillips (U.) P. Brignoli (R.) G.
                                           Ferri (Re.) E. Muzio cond.

Chicago        McVicker's   June 29, 1863 S. Vera-Lorini (A.) A. Cordier (O.)
                                           K. Morensi (U.) P. Brignoli (R.) A.
                                           Amodio (Re.) E. Muzio cond.

Auditorium  Apr. 28, 1890 L. Lehmann (A.) F. Kaschowska (O.)
C. Huhn (U.) G. Perotti (R.) T.
Reichmann (Re.) J. Arden (S.) W.
Damrosch cond. (in Ger.)

Apr. 14, 1903 J. Gadski (A.) F. Scheff (O.) L. Homer (U.) E. De Marchi (R.) G. Campa-
nari (Re.) E. De Reszke (S.) L. Mancinelli cond. (in It.)

Lyric       Nov. 29, 1955 A. Cerqueti (A.) P. Bonini (O.) C.
Turner (U.) J. Bjoerling (R.) T.
Gobbi (Re.) W. Wildermann (S.) N.
Rescigno cond.

Cincinnati   Pike's      June 6, 1863 S. Vera-Lorini (A.) A. Cordier (O.)
K. Morensi (U.) P. Brignoli (R.) A.
Amodio (Re.) E. Muzio cond.

Opera       July 21, 1931 B. Saroya (A.) H. Freund (O.) C.
Eberhart (U.) F. Lamont (R.) M. Ros-
si (Re.) N. Cervi (S.) I. Van Grove
cond.

Cleveland    Ac. of Mus. Apr. 13, 1864 S. Vera-Lorini (A.) P. Castri (O.)
K. Morensi (U.) L. Stefani (R.) A.
Amodio (Re.) E. Muzio cond.

Dallas       Opera       Nov. 23, 1963 A. Stella (A.) M. Guglielmi (O.) B.
Berini (U.) G. Di Stefano (R.) M.
Sereni (Re.) N. Treigle (S.) N. Res-
cigno cond.

Detroit      Op. House   Feb. 1, 1889 L. Natali (A.) C. Poole (U.) C.
Bassett (R.) A. Stoddard (Re.) (in
Eng.)

Houston      Auditorium  Oct. 31, 1919 E. Destinn (A.) M. Sharlow (O.) L.
Eubanks (U.) A. Bonci (R.) G. Bakla-
noff (Re.) V. Arimondi (S.) T. De
Angelis cond.

Grand Opera Dec. 3, 1964 E. Ross (A.) V. Boselli (O.) I. Kra-
marich (U.) J. Vickers (R.) L. Qui-
lico (Re.) W. Herbert cond.

Los Angeles  Theatre     Oct. 13, 1897 L. Montanari (A.) C. Vicini (O.) B.
Franco (U.) F. Collenz (R.) L. Fran-
cisconi (Re.)

Louisville   Theatre     Apr. 8, 1864 S. Vera-Lorini (A.) P. Castri (O.)
K. Morensi (U.) L. Stefani (R.) F.
Morelli-Ponti (Re.) N. Barili (S.)
E. Muzio cond.

New Orleans  Opéra       Jan. 25, 1866 C. Ghioni (A.) P. Canissa (O.) A.
Patti-Strakosch (U.) A. Macaferri
(R.) G. Marra (Re.)

New York     Ac. of Mus. Feb. 11, 1861 P. Colson (A.) I. Hinckley (O.) A.
Phillips (U.) P. Brignoli (R.) G.
Ferri (Re.) D. Coletti (S.) E. Muzio
cond.

|  |  |  |  |
|--|--|--|--|
| | Metro-<br>politan | Dec. 11, 1889 | L. Lehmann (A.) B. Frank (O.) E.<br>Sonntag-Uhl (U.) G. Perotti (R.) T.<br>Reichmann (Re.) J. Arden (S.) A.<br>Seidl cond. (in Ger.) |
| | | Feb. 23, 1903 | J. Gadski (A.) F. Scheff (O.) L. Ho-<br>mer (U.) E. De Marchi (R.) G. Campa-<br>nari (Re.) E. De Reszke (S.) L. Man-<br>cinelli cond. (in It.) |
| Philadelphia | Ac. of Mus. | Apr. 18, 1861 | P. Colson (A.) I. Hinckley (O.) A.<br>Phillips (U.) P. Brignoli (R.) A.<br>Ardavani (Re.) E. Muzio cond. |
| St. Louis | Theatre | Feb. 22, 1864 | S. Vera-Lorini (A.) P. Castri (O.)<br>K. Morensi (U.) L. Stefani (R.) F.<br>Morelli-Ponti (Re.) E. Muzio cond. |
| San Francisco | Maguire's | May 25, 1865 | O. Sconcia (A.) Fleury (O.) A.<br>Phillips (U.) G. Sbriglia (R.) D.<br>Orlandini (Re.) |
| | Opera | Sep. 19, 1931 | E. Rethberg (A.) A. Farncroft (O.)<br>L. Silva (U.) G. Martinelli (R.) G.<br>Danise (Re.) L. D'Angelo (S.) P.<br>Cimini cond. |
| Washington | Theatre | Apr. 20, 1863 | S. Vera-Lorini (A.) A. Cordier (O.)<br>K. Morensi (U.) P. Brignoli (R.) A.<br>Amodio (Re.) E. Muzio cond. |
| URUGUAY<br>Montevideo | Solis | Sep. 19, 1862 | T. Parodi (A.) G. Altieri (O.) Gio-<br>vanelli (U.) G. Mazzi (R.) L. Walter<br>(Re.) |
| VENEZUELA<br>Caracas | Teatro | Jan. 16, 1878 | E. Savelli (A.) G. Toressi (R.) F.<br>Bertolini (Re.) |
| | Municipal | Jan. 9, 1881 | M. Lucchesi (A.) T. Mestres (U.) F.<br>Giannini (R.) D. Farina (Re.) R.<br>Mancini (S.) |

24. LA FORZA DEL DESTINO-*Opera* in four acts
St. Petersburg-Imperial Theatre-Nov. 10, 1862
Libretto by Francesco Maria Piave

| | |
|---|---|
| Leonora (L.) | Caroline Barbot sop. |
| Preziosilla (P.) | Constance Nantier-Didiée mez. |
| Don Alvaro (A.) | Enrico Tamberlick ten. |
| Don Carlo (C.) | Francesco Graziani bar. |
| Fra Melitone (M.) | Achille De Bassini bar. |
| Padre Guardiano (G.) | Gian Francesco Angelini bass |
| Curra | Legramanti sec. |
| Trabucco | Alessandro Bettini ten. |
| Marchese di Calatrava | Meo bass |
| Un Alcade | Marini bass |
| Un Chirurgo | Alessandro Polonini bass |
| | |
| Conductor | Eduardo Baveri |
| Director | Giuseppe Verdi |

OTHER PRODUCTIONS-FIRST VERSION-NINETEENTH CENTURY

ARGENTINA
Buenos Aires    Ant. Colón    June  6, 1866  C. Briol (L.) T. Moreno (P.) L. Lel-
                                             mi (A.) A. Celestino (C.) E. Bonetti
                                             (G.) F. Nicolai cond.

                              Feb. 24, 1867  C. Briol (L.) L. Lelmi (A.) A. Ce-
                                             lestino (C.) G. C. Nerini (G.) F.
                                             Nicolai cond.

                              Nov. 19, 1868  A. Pasi (L.) A. Uberti (P.) L. Lelmi
                                             (A.) L. Rossi de Ruggero (C.) A. Ce-
                                             lestino (M.) G. Segri-Segarra (G.)
                                             V. Fumi cond.

AUSTRIA
Vienna          Kärntnertor   May  2, 1865   I. Galletti-Gianoli (L.) A. Volpini
                                             (P.) L. Graziani (A.) F. Pandolfini
                                             (C.) P. Milesi (G.)

GREAT BRITAIN
London          Her           June 22, 1867  T. Tietiens (L.) Z. Trebelli (P.) P.
                Majesty's                    Mongini (A.) C. Santley (C.) H. von
                                             Rokitansky (G.)

ITALY
Florence        Pergola       Mar. 14, 1865  A. Ortolani-Tiberini (L.) B. Marchi-
                                             sio (P.) M. Tiberini (A.) L. Giral-
                                             doni (C.) H. Brémond (G.)

Genoa           Carlo         Apr.  3, 1866  C. Cattinari (L.) L. Caracciolo (P.)
                Felice                       F. Patierno (A.) G. Cima (C.) E.
                                             Corti (M.) C. Dalla Costa (G.)

Reggio Emilia Municipale      Apr. 25, 1863  I. Galletti-Gianoli (L.) M. Boscag-
                                             lia (P.) A. Prudenza (A.) L. Sacco-
                                             manno (C.) S. Ronconi (M.) H. Bré-
                                             mond (G.) G. Tebaldi cond.

Rome            Apollo        Feb.  7, 1863  C. Marchisio (L.) B. Marchisio (P.)
                                             L. Graziani (A.) D. Squarcia (C.) G.
                                             Ramoni (M.) C. Dalla Costa (G.) E.
                                             Angelini cond.

Jan. 30, 1864 A. Ortolani-Tiberini (L.) E. Grossi
(P.) M. Tiberini (A.) M. Zacchi (C.)
G. Cima (M.) E. Angelini cond.

Jan. 13, 1866 A. Ortolani-Tiberini (L.) L. Caracciolo (P.) M. Tiberini (A.) F. Pan
dolfini (C.) E. Corti (M.) G. F. Beneventano (G.) E. Angelini cond.

Jan. 23, 1869 C. Barbot/A. Ortolani-Tiberini (L.)
R. Vercolini-Tay (P.) G. F. Beneven-
tano (G.) R. Kuon cond.

Feb. 24, 1870 V. Pozzi-Brazanti (L.) C. Dory (P.)
A. Prudenza (A.) F. Pandolfini (C.)
A. Mazzoli (M.) G. Petit (G.) R.
Kuon cond.

| | | |
|---|---|---|
| Sinigaglia | Comunale | July 18, 1863 I. Galletti-Gianoli (L.) G. Sanchi-<br>oli (P.) A. Prudenza (A.) L. Sac-<br>comanno (C.) S. Ronconi (M.) A. Fio-<br>rini (G.) R. Sarti cond. |
| Trieste | Grande | Sep. 23, 1863 L. Bendazzi-Secchi (L.) C. Gavotti<br>(P.) L. Graziani (A.) D. Squarcia<br>(C.) L. Mazzoni-Osti (M.) A. Fiorini<br>(G.) A. Cremaschi cond. |

RUSSIA
St.            Imperial     Nov.  2, 1863 C. Barbot (L.) C. Nantier-Didiée
Petersburg                 (P.) E. Tamberlick (A.) F. Graziani
(C.) G. F. Angelini (G.) E. Baveri
cond.

Nov. 25, 1864 C. Barbot (L.) C. Nantier-Didiée
(P.) E. Tamberlick (A.) F. Graziani
(C.) G. F. Angelini (G.) E. Baveri
cond.

SPAIN
Madrid         Real         Feb. 21, 1863 A. De la Grange (L.) E. De Meric
(P.) G. Fraschini (A.) L. Giraldoni
(C.) A. Cotogni (M.) S. L. Bouché
(G.) J. Skoczdopole cond. G. Verdi
dir.

Mar.  1, 1864 A. De la Grange (L.) A. Borghi-Mamo
(P.) G. Fraschini (A.) L. Giraldoni
(C.) G. Guicciardi (M.) S. L. Bouché
(G.) J. Skoczdopole cond.

Oct.  4, 1866 C. Marchisio (L.) B. Marchisio (P.)
G. Fraschini (A.) E. Storti-Gaggi
(C.) A. De Bassini (M.) P. Medini
(G.) V. Bonetti cond.

UNITED STATES
Baltimore      Holliday     Apr.  3, 1865 C. Carozzi-Zucchi (L.) K. Morensi
Street                     (P.) B. Massimiliani (A.) D. Bellini
(C.) A. Susini (G.)

Brooklyn       Ac. of Mus. Mar. 14, 1865 C. Carozzi-Zucchi (L.) K. Morensi
(P.) B. Massimiliani (A.) D. Bellini
(C.) A. Susini (G.)

Chicago        Crosby's    June 13, 1865 C.  Carozzi-Zucchi  (L.)  K.  Morensi
                                         (P.)  B. Massimiliani (A.)  D.  Bellini
                                         (C.)  A. Susini (G.)

Cincinnati     Pike's      May  29, 1865 C.  Carozzi-Zucchi  (L.)  K.  Morensi
                                         (P.)  B. Massimiliani (A.)  D.  Bellini
                                         (C.)  A. Susini (G.)

New York       Ac. of Mus. Feb. 24, 1865 C.  Carozzi-Zucchi  (L.)  K.  Morensi
                                         (P.)  B. Massimiliani (A.)  D.  Bellini
                                         (C.)  Dubreuil (M.)  A. Susini (G.)  C.
                                         Bergmann cond.

Philadelphia   Ac. of Mus. Mar. 24, 1865 C.  Carozzi-Zucchi  (L.)  K.  Morensi
                                         (P.)  B. Massimiliani (A.)  D.  Bellini
                                         (C.)  A. Susini (G.)

Washington     Ford's      Mar. 27, 1865 C.  Carozzi-Zucchi  (L.)  K.  Morensi
                                         (P.)  B. Massimiliani (A.)  D.  Bellini
                                         (C.)  A. Susini (G.)

URUGUAY
Montevideo     Solis       May  23, 1867 C.  Briol (L.) M. Mollo (P.) L. Lelmi
                                         (A.)  A.  Celestino  (C.)  L.  Walter
                                         (G.)


OTHER PRODUCTIONS-ORIGINAL VERSION-POST-WORLD WAR II

GREAT BRITAIN
London         BBC         Aug.  8, 1981 M.  Arroyo (L.)  J.  Coster (P.)  K.
                                         Collins (A.)  P. Glossop (C.)  D. Gar-
                                         rard (G.)  J. Matheson cond.

UNITED STATES
Irvine, Cal.   Fine Arts   Apr. 22, 1980 C.  Vaness (L.)  C. Clarey  (P.)  H.
               Village                   Howell (A.)  J. Gardner (C.)  D. Ham-
                                         mond-Stroud (M.) B. Carmeli (G.)


Revised Version
Milan-Teatro alla Scala-Feb. 27, 1869

Leonora (L.)                                      Teresa Stolz sop.
Preziosilla (P.)                                    Ida Benza mez.
Don Alvaro (A.)                                  Mario Tiberini ten.
Don Carlo (C.)                                  Luigi Colonnese bar.
Melitone (M.)                                     Giacomo Rota bar.
Padre Guardiano (G.)                               Marcel Junca bass
Curra                                               Ester Neri sec.
Trabucco                                          Antonio Tasso ten.
Marchese di Calatrava                            Giuseppe Vecchi bass
Un Alcade                                      Luigi Alessandrini bass
Un Chirurgo                                    Vincenzo Paraboschi ten.

Conductor                                          Eugenio Terziani
Director                                            Giuseppe Verdi

OTHER PREMIERES-REVISED VERSION

ALGERIA
Algiers                     Apr. 23, 1890

ARGENTINA
Buenos Aires   Ant. Colón   Mar. 14, 1869   A. Pasi (L.) A. Uberti (P.) L. Lelmi
                                            (A.) L. Rossi de Ruggero (C.) G.
                                            Segri-Segarra (G.) V. Fumi cond.[54]

              Colón        July 16, 1921   C. Muzio (L.) L. Bertana (P.) G.
                                            Crimi (A.) V. Ballester (C.) G.
                                            Azzolini (M.) A. Didur (G.) G. Po-
                                            lacco cond.

AUSTRALIA
Adelaide       Th. Royal    Feb.  7, 1883   R. Pala-Graziosi (L.) C. Prampolini
                                            (P.) A. Castelli (A.) I. Viganotti
                                            (C.) F. Graziosi (G.) F. Ziliani
                                            cond.

Melbourne      Op. House    June 10, 1878   A. Guadagnini (L.) L. Parodi Fabris
                                            (P.) F. Rosnati (A.) G. Gambetti
                                            (C.) T. B. Browning (M.) G. Cesari
                                            (G.) M. Simonsen cond.

Sydney         Her          July  2, 1970   F. Como (L.) M. Beaton (P.) D. Smith
               Majesty's                     (A.) R. Allman (C.) R. Maconaghie
                                            (M.) N. Warren-Smith (G.) C. F. Cil-
                                            lario cond.

AUSTRIA
Vienna         Staatsoper   Nov.  2, 1926   M. Angerer (L.) R. Anday (P.) A.
                                            Piccaver (A.) E. Schipper (C.) R.
                                            Mayr (G.) Schalk cond. (in Ger.)

BELGIUM
Antwerp        Royal        Mar. 14, 1883   (in Fr.)

Brussels       Monnaie      Oct. 24, 1931   E. Deulin (L.) Y. Andry (P.) F. Ans-
                                            seau (A.) L. Richard (C.) M. Demou-
                                            lin (G.) L. Molle cond. (in Fr.)

Ghent          Grand        Jan. 31? 1909   M. Alexina (L.) Galan (P.) L. De
                                            Colli (A.) S. Arrighetti (C.) Pompa
                                            (G.) G. Wehils cond. (in It.)

BRAZIL
Rio de         Pedro II     July 22, 1871   A. Pasi (L.) I. Martinez de Escalan-
Janeiro                                      te (P.) L. Lelmi (A.) C. Marziali
                                            (C.) J. Ordinas (G.)

              Municipal    Aug. 21, 1924   C. Muzio (L.) A. Gramegna (P.) G.
                                            Crimi (A.) J. Segura-Tallien (C.) T.
                                            Pasero (G.)

Sao Paulo      Sao José     Nov.  1, 1879   A. Conti-Foroni (L.) R. Vercolini-
                                            Tay (P.) F. Giannini (A.) V. Cottone
                                            (C.) G. Mirabella (G.)

              Municipal    Jan.  2, 1929   A. Conti (L.) A. Franceschini (P.)
                                            A. Cingolani (A.) A. Lima (C.) B.
                                            Carmassi (G.)

---

[54]. Since the score of the revised version arrived in Buenos Aires in the middle of the
season, both versions of *La Forza del Destino* were given during the long 1868-69 season, with
the same cast.

BULGARIA
Sofia           Louxembourg  Aug. 14, 1895 A. Bottero (L.) G. Badarocco (A.)

                National     Feb. 21, 1934 (in Bulg.)

CANADA
Montreal        His          Sep. 15, 1920 B. Freeman (L.)  S. De Mette (P.) G.
                Majesty's                  Agostini (A.) V. Ballester (C.) P.
                                           De Biasi (G.)

Toronto         O'Keefe      Autumn   1969 M. Krilovici (L.)  M. Dunn (P.)  S.
                Center                     Novoa (A.) B. Rayson (C.) D. Garrard
                                           (G.)

Winnipeg        Walker       Apr.  6, 1921 B. Freeman (L.)  S. De Mette (P.) G.
                                           Inzerillo (A.) M. Valle (C.) P. De
                                           Biasi (G.)

CHILE
Santiago        Municipal    July 16, 1873 L.  Corsi  (L.)  S.  Lorini  (P.)  L.
                                           Lelmi (A.) E. Carnili (C.) D. Dal
                                           Negro (G.)

Valparaiso      Victoria     Jan.  1, 1874 L.  Corsi  (L.)  S.  Lorini  (P.)  L.
                                           Lelmi (A.) E. Carnili (C.) D. Dal
                                           Negro (G.)

CHINA
Shanghai        Lyceum       Jan. 15, 1881 R. Genolini (L.) A. Cobianchi (P.)
                                           F. Boganini (A.) G. Bergamaschi (C.)
                                           A. Bagagiolo (G.)

COLOMBIA
Bogota          Colón        July 27, 1891 R. Aimo (L.) A. Orlandi (P.) A. Ra-
                                           vagli (A.) A. Alberti (C.) E. Fucili
                                           (G.)

CUBA
Havana          Peyret       Nov. 30? 1878 L.  Drog  (L.)  A.  Pascalis  (P.)  A.
                                           Aramburo (A.) M. Ciapini (C.) G.
                                           Maffei (G.)

CZECHOSLOVAKIA
Bratislava      National     Jan. 21, 1928 M. Sponárová (L.) Chorovic (A.) G.
                                           Fiserovi (C.) Z. Folprecht cond. (in
                                           Czech)

Prague          Neues        Dec. 12, 1926 F. Reich-Dörich (L.) O. Barco (P.)
                Deutsches                  M. Adrian (A.) J. Hagen (C.) H. Hor-
                                           ner (G.) Steinberg cond.

                National     Apr. 13, 1937 (in Czech)

DENMARK
Copenhagen      Royal        Mar.  6, 1937 (in Dan.)

EGYPT
Alexandria      Zizinia      Jan. 21, 1879 M. Barbieri (L.) De Luca (A.) C.
                                           Castello (C.) A. Bettarini (G.)

Cairo          Khedivial    Feb. 13, 1873 A. Pozzoni (L.) C. Smeroschi (P.) C.
                                          Carpi (A.) V. Cottone (C.) F. Stel-
                                          ler (M.) P. Medini (G.) G. Bottesini
                                          cond.

FRANCE
Lyon           Opéra        Jan. 16, 1981 M. Zschau (L.) K. Szostek-Radkowa
                                          (P.) E. Mauro (A.) F. Bordoni (C.)
                                          D. Kavrakos (G.) M. Arena cond.

Marseille      Alhambra     Apr. 10, 1897 N. Gabbi (L.) O. Mettler (P.) L.
                                          Signoretti (A.) Moro (C.) F. Vecchi-
                                          oni (G.)

Nice           Municipal    Mar.  9, 1873 C. Scarati-Bresciani (L.) E. Treves
                                          (P.) T. Villa (A.) P. Silenzi (C.)
                                          F. Cresci (M.) A. Fiorini (G.)

Paris          Italien      Oct. 31, 1876 E. Borghi-Mamo (L.) E. Parsi (P.) A.
                                          Aramburo (A.) F. Pandolfini (C.) R.
                                          Nannetti (G.)

               Opéra        May   2, 1975 M. Arroyo (L.) F. Cossotto (P.) P.
                                          Domingo (A.) N. Mittelmann (C.) G.
                                          Bacquier (M.) M. Talvela (G.) J.
                                          Bastin cond.

GERMANY
Berlin         Kroll        Oct. 12, 1878 E. Saurel (L.) M. Bianchi-Fiorio
                                          (P.) G. De Sanctis-Marianecci (A.)
                                          G. Sweet (C.) P. Povoleri (G.) O.
                                          Bimboni cond. (in It.)

               Staatsoper   Apr. 30, 1927 G. Bindernagel (L.) T. Pattiera (A.)
                                          H. Schlussnuss (C.) L. Schützendorf
                                          (M.) E. List (G.) L. Blech cond. (in
                                          Ger.)

               Deutsche     June  2, 1970 H. Janku (L.) R. Sarfaty (P.) B.
                                          Prevedi (A.) I. Wixell (C.) M. Tal-
                                          vela (G.) L. Maazel cond. (in It.)

Cologne        Opernhaus    Nov.  9, 1927 H. Trundt (L.) J. Kalenberg (A.) (in
                                          Ger.)

Dresden        Staatsoper   Mar. 20, 1926 M. Seinemeyer (L.) T. Pattiera (A.)
                                          R. Burg (C.) F. Plaschke (G.) (in
                                          Ger.)

Frankfurt      Opernhaus    Nov. 24, 1927 V. Ursuleac (L.) J. Gläser (A.) (in
                                          Ger.)

Hamburg        Volksoper    Sep. 20, 1913 J. Heinrich (L.) G. Göhler cond. (in
                                          Ger.)

               Stadt        Apr. 25, 1928 D. Giannini (L.) C. Günther (A.) R.
                                          Bockelmann (C.) (in Ger.)

Leipzig        Neues        Sep. 18, 1926 F. Cleve (L.) W. Zilken (A.) M.
                                          Spilcker (C.) G. Sebastian cond. (in
                                          Ger.)

Munich        National      Nov. 11, 1926 F. Hüni-Mihacsek (L.) Jelmar (P.) F.
                                          Krauss (A.) H. Rehkemper (C.) B.
                                          Sterneck (M.) J. Gless (G.) K. Böhm
                                          cond. (in Ger.)

Stuttgart     Opernhaus     Dec. 30, 1926 (in Ger.)

GREAT BRITAIN
Belfast       Grand         Dec. 16, 1909 G. Vania (L.) D. Woodall (P.) E.
                                          Davies (A.) A. Turner (C.) A.
                                          Winckworth (G.) (in Eng.)

Glasgow       Grand         Mar. 14, 1910 G. Vania (L.) W. Wheatley (A.) A.
                                          Winckworth (G.) (in Eng.)

London        Her           June 19, 1880 M. L. Swift (L.) Z. Trebelli (P.) I.
              Majesty's                   Campanini (A.) A. Faentini-Galassi
                                          (C.) G. Del Puente (M.) C. Behrens
                                          (G.) L. Arditi cond.

              Covent        June  1, 1931 R. Ponselle (L.)  G. Pederzini  (P.)
              Garden                      A. Pertile (A.) B. Franci (C.) T.
                                          Pasero (G.) T. Serafin cond.

Manchester    Th. Royal     Nov. 25, 1909 G. Vania (L.) D. Woodall (P.) E. Da-
                                          vies (A.) A. Turner (C.) A. Winck-
                                          worth (G.) (in Eng.)

Newcastle     Palace        Feb. 18, 1910 I. Hill (L.) W. Wheatley (A.) A.
                                          Turner (C.) A. Winckworth (G.) (in
                                          Eng.)

GREECE
Athens        Falero        July 15? 1876 Caselli (L.) Bianchi (P.) Avagnini
                                          (A.) A. Navari (C.) R. Mancini (G.)

Corfu         San Giacomo Oct. 28, 1873 B. Remondini (L.) Frontoni (G.)

GUATEMALA
Guatemala     Colón         Dec. 29? 1877 T. Rastelli (L.) T. Riboldi (P.)  G.
City                                      Ferrari (A.) F. Bacchi-Perego (C.)
                                          A. Furlan (G.)

HONG KONG
Hong Kong     Th. Royal     Dec. 15, 1880 R. Genolini (L.) A. Cobianchi (P.)
                                          F. Boganini (A.) G. Bergamaschi (C.)
                                          A. Bagagiolo (G.)

HUNGARY
Budapest      Nemzeti       Nov.  9, 1875 I. Benza (L.) R. Szabó (P.)  J. Ell-
              Szinház                     inger (A.) F. Láng (C.) K. Köszeghi
                                          (M.) L. Odry (G.) (in Hung.)

INDIA
Calcutta      Op. House     Nov.  2, 1874 R. Genolini (L.) De Dominici (P.) L.
                                          Gallo (A.) F. Trapani-Buono (C.) A.
                                          Marucco (M.) N. Rebottaro (G.) G.
                                          Mack cond.

INDONESIA
Batavia       T. Batavie    Oct. 22, 1880 R. Genolini (L.) F. Boganini (A.) G.
                                          Bergamaschi (C.)

Soerebaya     Theatre      Sep. 24, 1889 M.  Balzofiore  (L.)  L.  Balzofiore
                                         (A.)  A.  Falciai  (C.)  F.  Zavaschi
                                         (G.)  G.  Serrao  cond.

IRELAND
Dublin        Gaiety       Dec.  3, 1909 G.  Vania  (L.)  D.  Woodall  (P.)  E.
                                         Davies  (A.)  A.  Turner  (C.)  A.  Winck-
                                         worth  (G.)  (in Eng.)

ITALY
Alessandria   Municipale   Oct.     1876 M.  Mantilla  (L.)  C.  Mantilla  De
                                         Lopes  (P.)  A.  Marini  (A.)  G.  Val-
                                         cheri  (C.)  C.  Bedogni  (G.)

Ancona        Muse         Jan. 19, 1878 L.  Mosconi-Alba  (L.)  G.  Caldani-Kuon
                                         (A.)  G.  Sweet  (C.)  G.  Gialdini  cond.

Bari          Piccinni     Dec. 23? 1872 A.  Moro  (L.)  Guidotti  (P.)  E.  Irfré
                                         (A.)  E.  Carnili  (C.)  D.  Dal  Negro
                                         (G.)

Bergamo       Riccardi     Sep.  4, 1876 M.  Mantilla  (L.)  Carpi  (P.)  A.  Aram-
                                         buro  (A.)

Bologna       Comunale     Oct. 27, 1870 A.  Fricci  (L.)  L.  Pitarch  (P.)  G.
                                         Fraschini  (A.)  E.  Storti  (C.)  A.
                                         Pantaleoni  (M.)  S.  Cesarò  (G.)

Brescia       Grande       Aug. 10, 1872 T.  Stolz  (L.)  M.  Waldmann  (P.)  G.
                                         Fancelli  (A.)  F.  Pandolfini  (C.)  M.
                                         Junca  (G.)  F.  Faccio  cond.

Cagliari      Civico       Oct. 13, 1874 O.  Legramenti  (L.)  M.  Marrani  (P.)
                                         A.  Marubini  (A.)  A.  Borella  (C.)  A.
                                         Pinto  (G.)

Catania       Comunale     Dec. 26, 1874 L.  Pitarch  (L.)  Orlando  (P.)  O.
                                         Tasca  di  Cappello  (A.)  G.  Capocci
                                         (C.)  S.  Cesarò  (G.)  R.  Spedalieri
                                         cond.

              Bellini      Mar.  7, 1900 M.  D'Arneyro  (L.)  E.  Marcomini  (P.)
                                         G.  Vilalta  (A.)  G.  Giani  (C.)  F.
                                         Vecchioni  (G.)  V.  Pintorno  cond.

Chieti        Marrucino    May  11, 1884 S.  Lezzi  (L.)  C.  Prampolini  (P.)  G.
                                         Procacci  (A.)  A.  Gnaccarini  (C.)  G.
                                         Belletti  (M.)  V.  Masini  (G.)  G.
                                         Dell'Orefice  cond.

Cremona       Concordia    Dec. 26, 1877 E.  Naldi  (L.)  E.  Beloff  (P.)  E.  Vi-
                                         cini  (A.)  R.  Coppola  cond.

Faenza        Comunale     Aug. 11, 1875 A.  Bianchi-Montaldo  (L.)  L.  Carac-
                                         ciolo  (P.)  A.  Aramburo  (A.)  A.
                                         Faentini-Galassi  (C.)  E.  Gasperini
                                         (G.)  G.  Li  Calsi  cond.

Fermo         Aquila       Fiera     1887 A.  Garbini  (L.)  G.  Novelli  (P.)  F.
                                         Signorini  (A.)

Ferrara       Comunale     May  30, 1874 R.  Skelding  (L.)  L.  Bagenova  (P.)  F.
                                         Tamagno  (A.)  E.  Utto  (C.)  L.  Vecchi
                                         (G.)

Fiume          Civico        Mar.        1880 M. Stolzmann (L.) G. Chastel (P.) A.
                                              Franchini (A.) U. Forapan (C.) T. S.
                                              Terzi (G.)

Florence       Pergola       Dec. 28, 1873 C. De Baciocchi (L.) C. Dory (P.) G.
                                              Fraschini (A.) E. Storti (C.) L.
                                              Vecchi (G.)

Foligno        Apollo        Sep. 13? 1872 A. Bianchi-Montaldo (L.) L. Carac-
                                              ciolo (P.) A. Masini (A.) V. Quinti-
                                              li-Leoni (C.) A. Fiorini (G.) E.
                                              Usiglio cond.

Forli          Comunale      May         1873 V. Potentini (L.) E. Treves (P.) T.
                                              Villa (A.) A. De Antoni (C.) R.
                                              Mailini (G.)

Genoa          Carlo         Dec. 26, 1874 F. Vogri (L.) C. Blenio (P.) A. Ce-
               Felice                         lada (A.) M. Ciapini (C.) V. Carpi
                                              (M.) C. Ulloa (G.) G. Rossi cond.

Livorno        Avvalorati    Dec. 26, 1872 C. De Baciocchi (L.) E. Werner (P.)
                                              G. Bardi (A.) G. Ardeliano (C.) E.
                                              Daneri (G.)

Lucca          Giglio        Aug.        1873 V. Potentini (L.) E. Treves (P.) A.
                                              Masini (A.) A. Pantaleoni (C.) R.
                                              Mailini (G.)

Lugo           Rossini       Sep.  7, 1878 Luchessi (L.) P. Rambelli (P.) F.
                                              Devillier (A.) L. Lalloni (C.) L.
                                              Miller (G.) A. Pomé cond.

Macerata       Condomini     Aug. 14, 1872 B. Blume (L.) M. De Gourieff (P.) L.
                                              Bolis (A.) G. Aldighieri (C.) G.
                                              Maffei (G.) Dall'Argine cond.

Mantua         Sociale       Dec. 27, 1873 R. Carozzi-Zucchi (L.) Cottino (P.)
                                              G. Villena (A.) G. Cima (C.) G. C.
                                              Nerini (G.)

Messina        Vittorio      Mar. 30, 1874 R. Skelding (L.) I. Melloni (P.) G.
               Emanuele                       Vanzan (A.) A. Burgio (C.)

Modena         Municipale    Dec. 25, 1876 E. Ciuti (L.) V. Falconis (P.) G.
                                              Ferrari (A.) E. Pogliani (C.) E.
                                              Cazzola (M.) A. Furlan (G.) A. Pomè
                                              cond.

Naples         San Carlo     Dec. 21, 1876 A. Bianchi-Montaldo (L.) G. Pasqua
                                              (P.) G. Capponi (A.) L. Colonnese
                                              (C.) G. Belletti (M.) E. Gasperini
                                              (G.) P. Serrao cond.

Novara                       Dec. 26, 1878 Q. Gianoli-Lorenzini (L.) Razzani
                                              (P.) A. Stucci (A.) Tadini (C.) E.
                                              Jorda (G.) Ricci cond.

Padua          Nuovo         June 28, 1874 A. Fricci (L.) E. Barlani-Dini (P.)
                                              F. Patierno (A.) F. Pandolfini (C.)
                                              P. Medini (G.)

Palermo         Bellini       Mar. 24, 1873 G. De Giuli-Borsi (L.) F. Vogri (P.)
                                             A. Masini (A.) A. De Antoni (C.) A.
                                             Augier (G.) L. Alfano cond.

                Massimo       Mar. 19, 1932 L. Bruna Rasa (L.) G. Galli (P.) A.
                                             Bagnariol (A.) V. Guicciardi (C.) E.
                                             Dominici (G.) G. Bavagnoli cond.

Parma           Regio         Apr. 22, 1873 M. Mariani-Masi (L.) S. Bonheur (P.)
                                             C. Carpi (A.) F. Pandolfini (C.) G.
                                             Toledo (M.) E. Barberat (G.) G.
                                             Rossi cond.

Pavia           Fraschini     Dec. 26, 1875 C. Mocoroa (L.) Razzani (P.) G.
                                             Carrion (A.) G. Valcheri (C.)

Perugia                       Dec. 26, 1877 T. Boccabianca (L.) I. Pergolani
                                             (P.) B. Massimiliani (A.) Ciolli
                                             (C.) Rinaldo (G.) Corticelli cond.

Pesaro          Rossini       Carn. 1880-81 A. Borgani (L.) T. Boccabianca (P.)
                                             P. Rossetti-Pellagalli (A.) G. Tamo-
                                             glia (C.) S. Aldovrandi cond.

Piacenza        Municipale    Dec. 26? 1872 I. Kottas (L.) R. Foà (P.) G. Fra-
                                             polli (A.) A. Parolini (C.) E. Retz
                                             (G.) P. Montaguti cond.

Pisa            Verdi         Jan.  1, 1878 C. Mocoroa (L.) G. Novelli (P.) V.
                                             Belardi (A.) G. Bolli (C.) G. Gal-
                                             locci (M.) T. Lamponi (G.) L. Quer-
                                             cioli cond.

Ravenna         Alighieri     May  23, 1874 C. De Baciocchi (L.) V. Donati (P.)
                                             G. Vanzan (A.) A. Parboni (C.) A.
                                             Pifferi (G.) C. Lovati-Cazzulani
                                             cond.

Reggio Emilia   Municipale    Aug. 26, 1876 E. Borghi-Mamo (L.) S. Barton (P.)
                                             A. Celada (A.) M. Ciapini (C.) D.
                                             Maiocchi (M.) A. De Giuli (G.) L.
                                             Mancinelli cond.

Rome            Argentina     Oct. 20, 1870 G. De Giuli-Borsi (L.) L. Corsi (P.)
                                             Grillo (A.) D. Squarcia (C.) Vecchi
                                             (G.) R. Kuon cond.

                Apollo        Dec. 30, 1874 V. Potentini (L.) E. Bedetti (P.) G.
                                             Capponi (A.) V. Collini (C.) S. Spa-
                                             rapani (M.) O. Maini (G.) E. Terzi-
                                             ani cond.

                Costanzi      June 11, 1881 A. Fossa (L.) G. Novelli (P.) G.
                                             Sani (A.) M. Ciapini (C.) G. Mira-
                                             bella (G.)

Rovereto        Sociale       Sep. 15, 1872 G. De Giuli-Borsi (L.) L. Corsi (P.)
                                             A. Prudenza (A.) F. Pandolfini (C.)
                                             M. Junca (G.)

Rovigo          Sociale       Oct. 18, 1873 E. Boronat (L.) A. Tancioni (P.) E.
                                             Pizzorni (A.) I. De Anna (C.) T.
                                             Campello (G.)

Siena          Rinnovati    Dec. 26? 1879 L. Seghini (L.) T. Bertini (A.) A.
                                          Falciai (C.) V. Coda (G.)

Spoleto        Nuovo        Aug.     1896 E. Bianchini-Cappelli (L.) M. Sigal-
                                          di (A.)

Trento         Sociale      June     1876 A. Conti-Foroni (L.) G. Tiozzo (P.)
                                          G. Villena (A.) N. Verger (C.) A.
                                          Castelmary (G.)

Treviso        Comunale     Oct. 12, 1873 V. Potentini (L.) S. Barton (P.) G.
                                          Villena (A.) A. Pantaleoni (C.) R.
                                          Mailini (G.)

Trieste        Grande       Nov.  5, 1873 M. Mariani-Masi (L.) S. Bonheur (P.)
                                          G. Capponi (A.) F. Pandolfini (C.)
                                          O. Maini (G.) F. Faccio cond.

Turin          Regio        Feb.  9, 1873 V. Potentini (L.) S. Bonheur (P.) G.
                                          Capponi (A.) A. Pantaleoni (C.) A.
                                          Brogi (M.) E. Barberat (G.) C. Pe-
                                          drotti cond.

Udine          Sociale      Aug.     1876 R. Pantaleoni (L.) S. Bonheur (P.)
                                          G. Villena (A.) G. Cima (C.) I. Vi-
                                          ganotti (M.) A. Castelmary (G.) E.
                                          Usiglio cond.

Venice         Rossini      Apr. 22, 1876 E. Borghi-Mamo (L.) E. Parsi (P.) F.
                                          Patierno (A.) A. Pantaleoni (C.) G.
                                          Kaschmann (M.) R. Nannetti (G.) F.
                                          Faccio cond.

               La Fenice    Dec. 31, 1943 C. Castellani (L.) M. Falliani (P.)
                                          G. Momo (A.) E. Mascherini (C.) D.
                                          Baronti (G.) F. Ghione cond.

Verona         Nuovo        Dec. 26, 1872 Brambilla (L.) Montigani (P.) L. Del
                                          Passo (A.) A. Souvestre (C.) Cesari
                                          (G.)

               Arena        Aug.  6, 1930 B. Scacciati (L.) G. Pederzini (P.)
                                          F. Merli (A.) C. Tagliabue (C.) E.
                                          Badini (M.) E. Pinza (G.) G. Del
                                          Campo cond.

Vicenza        Eretenio     Aug.     1869 T. Stolz (L.) E. Spitzer (P.) G.
                                          Fraschini (A.) V. Collini (C.) S.
                                          Sparapani (M.) G. Capponi (G.) A.
                                          Mariani cond.

JUGOSLAVIA
Ljubljana      National     Oct. 30, 1930

Zagreb         National     Feb. 11, 1882 E. Dotti (L.) Kramberger (P.) G. B.
                                          De Negri (A.) Vespasiani (C.) Ter-
                                          cuzzi (G.)

Zara           Nuovo        May  24, 1883 L. Morandi (L.) Mora (P.) N. Loren-
                                          zini (A.) Bacchetta (C.) Sampieri
                                          (G.)

LATVIA
Riga           National     Dec. 13, 1931 (in Let.)

MALTA
La Valletta    Real         May    5, 1873 A. Conti-Foroni (L.) Magi (P.) G.
                                           Villena (A.) C. Lenghi (C.) A.
                                           Padovani (G.)

MEXICO
Mexico City    Nacional     Sep. 18, 1872 C. Castelli (L.) G. Galassi (P.) F.
                                          Pozzo (A.) F. Bertolini (C.) G. Gia-
                                          nolli (G.) D. Antonietti cond.

NETHERLANDS
Amsterdam      Palais v.    Nov.   1, 1897 Caratelli (L.) I. Sambo (P.) L. Co-
               Volksvligt                  Colazza (A.) V. Morghen (C.) F.
                                           Spangher (G.)

Den Haag       Gebouw v.    Oct. 29, 1897 Caratelli (L.) I. Sambo (P.) L. Co-
               Kunst                      Colazza (A.) V. Morghen (C.) F.
                                          Spangher (G.)

PERU
Lima           Principal    Sept.?  1874 C. Carozzi-Zucchi (L.) G. Toressi
                                         (A.) A. Rossi-Ghelli (G.)

PHILIPPINES
Manila         Del Tondo    Jan.   2, 1887 E. Ancarani (L.) A. Silini (P.) A.
                                           Castelli (A.) G. Ciocci (C.) E.
                                           Vilelmi (G.) G. Branca cond.

POLAND
Lwov                                1929 (in Pol.)

Warsaw         Wielki       Jan. 28, 1875 F. Mariani De Angelis (L.) Mecocci
                                          (P.) A. De Sanctis (A.) A. Souvestre
                                          (C.) Greco (M.) E. Gasperini (G.) C.
                                          Trombini cond.

PORTUGAL
Lisbon         Sao Carlos   Mar. 15, 1873 A. Fricci (L.) G. Fancelli (A.) F.
                                          Pandolfini (C.) A. Castelmary (G.)

Oporto         Sao Joao     Mar.   8, 1876 C. Ferni (L.) G. Vanzan (A.) L. Gi-
                                           raldoni (C.) A. Buzzi (G.)

PUERTO RICO
San Juan       Municipal    Feb. 19, 1881 C. Bossi (L.) G. Cavelleri (P.) A.
                                          De Sanctis (A.) I. Viganotti (C.)

ROMANIA
Bucharest      Nacional     Jan. 28, 1880 M. Mantilla (L.) E. Theodorini (P.)
                                          T. Villa (A.) E. Pogliani (C.) P.
                                          Povoleri (G.)

RUSSIA
Leningrad                   Jan.    1935 (in Rus.)

Odessa         Municipal    Oct.   9, 1872 Angeleri (L.) M. Biancolini (P.) G.
                                           Toressi (A.) Belletti (C.) Melzi
                                           (G.)

St.            Imperial     Jan. 26, 1877 T. Stolz (L.) A. L. Cary (P.) A. Ma-
  Petersburg                              sini (A.) M. Padilla (C.) G. Capponi
                                          (G.)

|  | Conser-<br>vatoire | Feb. 7, 1901 | S. Kruszelnicka (L.) G. Fabbri (P.)<br>L. Longobardi (A.) M. Battistini<br>(C.) V. Arimondi (G.) |
|--|--|--|--|
| Tbilisi | Imperial | Mar. 1878 | C. Bossi (L.) Bignami (P.) R. Pe-<br>trovich (A.) E. Masi (C.) R. Mancini<br>(G.) |

SOUTH AFRICA

| Capetown | Nico Malan | Dec. 12, 1981 | M. Napier (L.) E. Dalberg (P.) K.<br>Collins (A.) L. Folley (C.) M. Fuger<br>(G.) F. Ferraris cond. |
|--|--|--|--|
| Johannesburg |  | Autumn 1975 | M. L. Cioni (L.) S. Mazzeri (P.) B.<br>Prevedi (A.) L. Folley (C.) N. Zac-<br>caria (G.) L. Quayle cond. |

SPAIN

| Alicante | Principal | Mar. 1879 | B. Remondini (L.) L. Signoretti (A.)<br>F. Amodio (C.) |
|--|--|--|--|
| Barcelona | Liceo | Dec. 21, 1872 | L. Ponti dall'Armi (L.) T. Ferni<br>(P.) C. Vincentelli (A.) G. Toledo<br>(C.) M. Junca (G.) N. Bassi cond. |
| Cadiz | Principal | Jan. 30? 1874 | C. Noel-Guidi (L.) C. Pisani (P.) G.<br>Frapolli (A.) C. Lenghi (C.) Monti<br>(G.) |
| Madrid | Real | Oct. 9, 1881 | C. Bernau (L.) M. Verati (P.) A.<br>Aramburo (A.) V. Cottone (C.) A.<br>Vidal (G.) |
| Seville | San<br>Fernando | May 3, 1876 | C. Ferni (L.) T. Ferni (P.) G. Van-<br>zan (A.) A. Parboni (C.) A. Buzzi<br>(G.) |
| Valencia | Principal | Jan. 20, 1876 | R. Pantaleoni (L.) Guidotti (P.) G.<br>Frapolli (A.) M. Ciapini (C.) A.<br>Fiorini (G.) Dell'Argine cond. |
| Valladolid | Calderon | Apr. 17, 1879 | B. Remondini (L.) Magi-Trapani (P.)<br>L. Signoretti (A.) F. Amodio (C.) J.<br>Petit (G.) |
| Zaragozza | Principal | Mar. 23? 1883 | R. Aimo (L.) Rossi (P.) C. Pizzorni<br>(A.) A. Gnaccarini (C.) G. Belletti<br>(G.) |

SWEDEN

| Stockholm | Royal | Jan. 21, 1928 | B. Hertzberg (L.) M. Mandahl (P.) D.<br>Stockman (A.) E. Larson (C.) E.<br>Stiebel (M.) A. Wallgren (G.) L.<br>Blech cond. (in Swed.) |
|--|--|--|--|

SWITZERLAND

| Basel | Stadt | Sep. 2, 1927 | (in Ger.) |
|--|--|--|--|
| Geneva | Grand | Mar. 24, 1884 | Strassi (L.) Guérin (P.) A. Guille<br>(A.) Bonnefond (C.) Labarre (G.) (in<br>Fr.) |

Lugano          Apollo        Apr. 22? 1905 E. Santa Marina (L.) E. Marenzi (P.)
                                            G. Graglia (A.) E. Fiorentini (C.)
                                            P. De Biasi (G.) Lombardi-Gonzales
                                            cond.

Zürich          Stadt         Feb. 25, 1927 Hoch (L.) M. Mülkens (P.) Depfer
                                            (A.) von Akacs (C.) Hiller (G.)
                                            Conrad cond. (in Ger.)

                              June 12, 1935 G. Cigna (L.) J. De Gaviria (A.) A.
                                            Borgioli (C.) A. Marone (G.) (in
                                            It.)

TUNISIA
Tunis                         Apr. 26, 1923 E. Pucci (L.) I. Righi-Briani (A.)
                                            G. Lazzarini (C.) C. Ulivi (G.)

TURKEY
Constan-        Varietées     Dec.  6, 1876 Gerli (L.) M. Verati (P.) A. Gottar-
  tinople                                   di (A.) Cesari (C.) Morelli (G.)

Smyrna          Cammarano     Oct.     1879 Fochi (L.) Margoni (P.) Cosmi (A.)
                                            R. De Giorgi (C.)

UNITED STATES
Baltimore       Lyric         May   4, 1921 L. Taylor (L.) S. De Mette (P.) G.
                                            Inzerillo (A.) G. Montanelli (C.) P.
                                            De Biasi (G.)

Boston          Op. House     Nov. 10, 1921 B. Saroya (L.) G. Tomassini (A.) J.
                                            Royer (C.) P. De Biasi (G.)

Buffalo         Teck          Dec. 26, 1922 Buckley (L.) S. De Mette (P.) E.
                                            Salazar (A.) M. Valle (C.) P. De
                                            Biasi (G.)

Chicago         Auditorium    Dec. 14, 1929 C. Muzio (L.) A. Paggi (P.) C. Mar-
                                            shall (A.) C. Formichi (C.) D. De-
                                            frère (M.) C. Baromeo (G.) E. Cooper
                                            cond.

                Lyric         Nov.  8, 1956 R. Tebaldi (L.) G. Simionato (P.) R.
                                            Tucker (A.) E. Bastianini (C.) N.
                                            Rossi-Lemeni (G.) G. Solti cond.

Cincinnati      Opera         Aug.  1, 1932 M. Sharlow (L.) L. Dozier (P.) M.
                                            Duca (A.) J. Royer (C.) I. Picchi
                                            (G.) I. Van Grove cond.

Cleveland       Schubert      Apr. 26, 1920 B. R. Shull (L.) S. De Mette (P.) E.
                                            Salazar (A.) V. Ballester (C.) P. De
                                            Biasi (G.) G. Merola cond.

Dallas          Opera         Dec. 15, 1983 M. Arroyo (L.) K. Ciesinski (P.) G.
                                            Giacomini (A.) M. Manuguerra (C.) D.
                                            Kavrakos (G.) N. Rescigno cond.

Detroit         Schubert      Oct. 31, 1919 L. Darve (L.) S. De Mette (P.) E.
                                            Salazar (A.) V. Ballester (C.) P. De
                                            Biasi (G.) G. Merola cond.

Houston         Grand Opera   Apr.  3, 1973 C. Carson (L.) S. Marsee (P.) S. No-
                                            voa (A.) L. Quilico (C.) E. Flagello
                                            (G.) Rosekrans cond.

Kansas City    Schubert     Mar. 31, 1920 B. R. Shull (L.) A. Paggi (P.) E.
                                           Salazar (A.) V. Ballester (C.)

Los Angeles    Mason        Feb. 29, 1920 A. Gentle (L.) A. Paggi (P.) R. Bos-
                                           cacci (A.) V. Ballester (C.) P. De
                                           Biasi (G.)

New Orleans    Jerusalem    Dec. 15, 1920 B. Freeman (L.) S. De Mette (P.) G.
               Temple                      Inzerillo (A.) V. Ballester (C.)

New York       Ac. of Mus.  Mar. 23, 1880 M. L. Swift (L.) A. L. Cary (P.) I.
                                           Campanini (A.) A. Faentini-Galassi
                                           (C.) G. Del Puente (M.) C. Behrens
                                           (G.) L. Arditi cond.

               Metro-        Nov. 15, 1918 R. Ponselle (L.) A. Gentle (P.) E.
               politan                     Caruso (A.) G. De Luca (C.) T. Chal-
                                           mers (M.) J. Mardones (G.) G. Papi
                                           cond.

Philadelphia   Ac. of Mus.  Mar. 30, 1920 R. Ponselle (L.) J. Gordon (P.) E.
                                           Caruso (A.) P. Amato (C.) T. Chal-
                                           mers (M.) J. Mardones (G.) G. Papi
                                           cond.

Pittsburgh     Syria        Apr. 19, 1920 B. R. Shull (L.) S. De Mette (P.) E.
               Mosque                      Salazar (A.) V. Ballester (C.) P. De
                                           Biase (G.)

St. Louis      Odeon        Apr.  7, 1920 B. R. Shull (L.) S. De Mette (P.) E.
                                           Salazar (A.) V. Ballester (C.) P. De
                                           Biasi (G.)

San Francisco  Grand        July 19, 1881 A. Bianchi-Montaldo (L.) G. Tiozzo
                                           (P.) G. Roig (A.) F. Lafontaine (C.)
                                           A. Parolini (M.) G. Paoletti (G.)

               Opera        Dec.  1, 1933 C. Muzio (L.) M. Leonard (P.) G.
                                           Martinelli (A.) R. Bonelli (C.) E.
                                           Pinza (G.) G. Merola cond.

Washington     Belasco      May   6, 1920 B. R. Shull (L.) S. De Mette (P.) E.
                                           Salazar (A.) A. Ordognez (C.) G.
                                           Merola cond.

URUGUAY
Montevideo     Solis        June 19, 1869 C. Carozzi-Zucchi (L.) Zacconi (P.)
                                           E. Irfré (A.) Bonetti (C.) E. Corti
                                           (G.)

VENEZUELA
Caracas        Municipal    Nov. 15, 1891

25. DON CARLOS-*Opera* in five acts
Paris-Academie Royale de Musique (Opéra)-Mar. 11, 1867
Libretto by Joseph Méry and Camille du Locle.

| | |
|---|---|
| Elizabeth de Valois (E.) | Marie Sasse sop. |
| Eboli (Eb.) | Pauline Guyemard-Lauters mez. |
| Don Carlos (C.) | A. Morère ten. |
| Rodrigue (R.) | Jean Baptiste Fauré bar. |
| Philippe II (F.) | Louis Henri Obin bass |
| Le Grand Inquisiteur (I.) | Joseph David bass |
| Un Moine | Armand Castelmary bass |
| Thibault | Leonia Levielly sop. |
| Comtesse Aremberg | Dominique mime |
| Comte de Lerme | Gaspard ten. |
| Un Hérault Royal | Mermant ten. |

Conductor
Director                                                    Giuseppe Verdi

OTHER PRODUCTIONS-FIRST VERSION

ARGENTINA
Buenos Aires    Opera         June 17, 1873 G. Marziali-Passerini (E.) R. Verco-
                                            lini-Tay (Eb.) C. Bulterini (C.) M.
                                            Ciapini (R.) G. Maffei (F.) O. Bim-
                                            boni cond.

                Ant. Colón    July  5, 1879 A. Bruschi-Chiatti (E.) M. Biancoli-
                                            ni (Eb.) F. Tamagno (C.) A. Brogi
                                            (R.) E. Dondi (F.) N. Bassi cond.

BELGIUM
Brussels        La Monnaie    Mar. 11, 1868 Erembert (E.) Sallard (Eb.) Dulau-
                                            rens (C.) Dumestre (R.) Vidal (F.)
                                            J. Jamet (I.) C. L. Hanssens cond.
                                            (in Fr.)

BRAZIL
Rio de          Pedro II      Aug. 29, 1879 A. Bruschi-Chiatti (E.) G. Prandi
Janeiro                                     (Eb.) F. Tamagno (C.) A. Brogi (R.)
                                            E. Dondi (F.) N. Bassi cond.

CHILE
Santiago        Municipal     July 11, 1883 M. Stolzmann (E.) E. Wiziak (Eb.) A.
                                            Aramburo/G. Santinelli (C.) E. Pog-
                                            liani (R.) E. Marcassa (F.) R. Man-
                                            cini (I.) D. Antonietti cond.

CZECHOSLOVAKIA
Prague          Ständisches   Oct. 13, 1870 Loewe (E.) M. Perechon (Eb.) V.
                                            Vecko (C.) A. Schebesta (R.) Chandon
                                            (F.) (in Ger.)

GERMANY
Darmstadt       Hoftheater    Mar. 29, 1868 Peschka (E.) Leutner (Eb.) F. Nach-
                                            bauer (C.)

GREAT BRITAIN
London          Covent        June  4, 1867 P. Lucca/H. Lemmens-Sherrington (E.)
                Garden                      A. Fricci (Eb.) E. Naudin (C.) F.
                                            Graziani (R.) J. Petit (F.) J. Ta-
                                            gliafico (I.) M. Costa cond.

Apr.  2, 1868 A. Fricci (E.) H. Lemmens-Sherring-
ton (Eb.) E. Naudin (C.) F. Graziani
(R.) J. Petit (F.) G. Capponi (I.)
M. Costa cond.

GREECE
Corfu           San Giacomo Nov.   1880 L. Allegri (E.) A. Leoni (Eb.) Gar-
cia (C.) Fedini (R.) G. Narberti
(F.) F. Sangiorgi cond.

HUNGARY
Budapest        Nemzeti     Mar. 14, 1868 A. Neszdava (E.) I. Kotsis (Eb.) J.
                Szinház                   Ellinger (C.) K. Köszeghi (F.) (in
                                          Hung.)

                            Apr. 25, 1871 G. Giovannoni-Zacchi (E.) M. Bianco-
                                          lini (Eb.) F. Steger (C.) F. Pandol-
                                          fini (R.) P. Medini (F.) (in It.)

ITALY
Bologna         Comunale    Oct. 26, 1867 T. Stolz (E.) A. Fricci (Eb.) G.
                                          Stigelli (C.) A. Cotogni (R.) G.
                                          Capponi (F.) L. Rossi (I.) A. Ma-
                                          riani cond.

                            Oct. 30, 1878 R. Pantaleoni (E.) A. Fricci (Eb.)
                                          R. Petrovich (C.) G. Kaschmann (R.)
                                          E. Dondi (F.) E. De Sereni (I.) F.
                                          Faccio cond.

Brescia         Grande      Aug.     1882 A. Bruschi-Chiatti (E.) A. Mazzoli-
                                          Orsini (Eb.) G. Sani (C.) G. Kasch-
                                          mann (R.) A. Silvestri (F.) L. Lom-
                                          bardelli (I.) F. Faccio cond.

Cagliari        Civico      Oct. 25, 1879 G. Casali-Bavagnoli (E.) M. Verati
                                          (Eb.) G. Gozzolini (C.) Fedini (R.)
                                          Panari (F.)

Cremona         Concordia   Sep.     1874 T. Stolz (E.) R. Vercolini-Tay (Eb.)
                                          G. Capponi (C.) N. Verger (R.) P.
                                          Medini (F.) C. Ulloa (I.) C. Trombi-
                                          ni cond.

Florence        Pagliano    Apr. 22, 1869 A. Ortolani-Tiberini (E.) M. Destin
                                          (Eb.) M. Tiberini (C.) L. Colonnese
                                          (R.) L. Vecchi (F.) S. Cesarò (I.)

Livorno         Avvalorati  Jan. 20, 1876 A. Creny (E.) A. Magi-Trapani (Eb.)
                                          L. Signoretti (C.) P. Silenzi (R.)
                                          E. Dondi (F.) U. Gianelli cond.

Milan           La Scala    Mar. 25, 1868 T. Stolz (E.) M. Destin (Eb.) G.
                                          Fancelli/G. Capponi (C.) V. Collini
                                          (R.) M. Junca (F.) L. Miller (I.) A.
                                          Mazzucato cond.

                            Dec. 26, 1868 T. Stolz (E.) I. Benza (Eb.) E. Bar-
                                          bacini/P. Mongini (C.) L. Colonnese
                                          (R.) M. Junca (F.) S. Cesarò (I.) E.
                                          Terziani cond.

Dec. 26, 1878 A. D'Angeri (E.) E. Turolla (Eb.) F.
Tamagno (C.) G. Kaschmann/L. Lalloni
(R.) J. Jamet/L. Miller (F.) R.
D'Ottavi (I.) F. Faccio cond.

Naples       San Carlo    Mar.  6, 1871 M. Palmieri (E.) R. Vercolini-Tay/M.
Waldmann (Eb.) E. Barbacini (C.) V.
Maurel (R.) P. Vecchi (F.) O. Lari
(I.) P. Serrao cond.

Dec.  2, 1872 T. Stolz (E.) M. Waldmann (Eb.) F.
Patierno (C.) V. Collini (R.) L.
Miller (F.) S. Cesarò (I.) G. Puzone
cond. G. Verdi dir.[55]

Padua        Nuovo        July 10, 1869 T. Stolz (E.) M. Destinn (Eb.) G.
Capponi (C.) G. Rota (R.) L. Vecchi
(F.) S. Cesarò (I.) E. Terziani
cond.

Palermo      Bellini      Mar. 25, 1874 L. Levielli (E.) R. Di Salvo (Eb.)
C. Vincentelli (C.) A. Parboni (R.)
T. Coloni (F.) E. Daneri (I.) L.
Alfano cond.

Parma        Regio        Apr. 24, 1869 T. Stolz (E.) M. Biancolini (Eb.) P.
Bignardi (C.) F. Bellini (R.) M.
Junca (F.) F. Rigo (I.) G. C. Ferra-
rini cond.

Pavia        Fraschini    Dec. 26? 1879 Reduzzi (E.) Ferrari (Eb.) Mozzi
(C.) Taurone (R.) Corrizzi (F.)

Piacenza     Municipale   Dec. 26? 1880 E. Giunti-Barbera (E.) Preziosi
(Eb.) C. Bulterini (C.) E. Pogliani
(R.) F. Vecchioni (F.) E. Villelmi
(I.) G. Bolzoni cond.

Reggio Emilia Municipale  May 14, 1874 A. Link (E.) A. Fricci (Eb.) S. Ana-
stasi (C.) A. Pantaleoni (R.) A.
Buzzi (F.) G. Roveri (I.) L. Arditi
cond.

Rome         Apollo       Feb.  9, 1868 T. Stolz (E.) P. Vaneri (Eb.) A.
Prudenza (C.) T. Sterbini (R.) H.
Brémond (F.) G. Vecchi (I.) E. Ange-
lini cond.

Nov. 20, 1872 R. Pantaleoni (E.) R. Giovannoni-
Zacchi (Eb.) G. Sani (C.) V. Maurel
(R.) R. Nannetti (F.) C. Morroto
(I.) E. Terziani cond.

Mar. 23, 1881 M. L. Durand (E.) G. Novelli (Eb.)
E. Barbacini (C.) G. Moriami (R.) E.
Cherubini (F.) R. D'Ottavi (I.) L.
Mancinelli cond.

---

[55]. This production, while still in five acts, constitutes a partial revision of the original version.

Sinigaglia    Comunale    Summer    1870 T. Stolz (E.) M. Destin (Eb.) G.
                                          Capponi (C.) F. Bellini (R.) C. Zuc-
                                          chelli (F.) G. Maffei (I.) A. Mari-
                                          ani cond.

Trieste       Grande      Oct. 31, 1868 M. Palmieri (E.) A. Pozzoni-Anastasi
                                          (Eb.) G. Capponi (C.) L. Colonnese
                                          (R.) L. Vecchi (F.) A. Cremaschi
                                          cond.

                          Sep.      1869 T. Stolz (E.) M. Waldmann (Eb.) E.
                                          Barbacini (C.) P. Medini (F.) R.
                                          Laterza (I.) A. Cremaschi cond.

                          Mar.      1877 E. Wiziak (E.) A. Fidi-Azzolini
                                          (Eb.) G. Marini (C.) L. Giraldoni
                                          (R.) E. Dondi (F.) G. Gialdini cond.

Turin         Regio       Dec. 25, 1867 E. Galli (E.) A. Fricci (Eb.) G.
                                          Capponi (C.) A. Cotogni/L. Brignole
                                          (R.) F. Coletti (F.) A. Fiorini (I.)

                          Jan. 22, 1870 T. Stolz (E.) E. Wiziak (Eb.) G.
                                          Fancelli (C.) A. Cotogni/Z. Bertola-
                                          si (R.) L. Vecchi (F.) G. Mafffei
                                          (I.) C. Pedrotti cond.

                          Dec. 26, 1877 E. Mecocci (E.) P. von Edelsberg
                                          (Eb.) G. Fancelli (C.) G. Mendioroz
                                          (R.) E. Dondi (F.) G. Roveri (I.) C.
                                          Pedrotti cond.

Venice        La Fenice   Mar. 11, 1869 B. Blume (E.) I. Galletti-Gianoli
                                          (Eb.) G. Villani (C.) V. Collini
                                          (R.) P. Medini (F.) F. Feitlinger
                                          (I.) C. Castagneri cond.

                          Dec. 26, 1870 T. Stolz (E.) A. Contarini (Eb.) G.
                                          Fancelli (C.) A. Cotogni (R.) G. F.
                                          Angelini (F.) R. Nannetti (I.) C.
                                          Castagneri cond.

Verona        Filarmonico Dec. 26? 1877 H. De Vasco (E.) D. Boetti (Eb.) T.
                                          Villa (C.) D. Belardi/Z. Bertolasi
                                          (R.) P. Milesi (F.) A. Pomè cond.

Vicenza       Eretenio    Aug. 24, 1872 A. Pascalis (E.) C. Smeroschi (Eb.)
                                          E. Barbacini (C.) G. Rota (R.) A.
                                          Castelmary (F.) T. Costa (I.)

MALTA
La Valletta   Manoel      Apr.      1869 E. Cortesi (E.) A. Moro (Eb.) R.
                                          Bertolini (C.) F. Bertolini (R.) I.
                                          Tasty (F.)

              Real        Oct. 15, 1881 A. Picchi/A. Giannetti (E.) L.
                                          Ferrara (Eb.) A. Passetti (C.) U.
                                          Forapan (R.) A. Bettarini (F.) L.
                                          Buti (I.)

POLAND
Lwov          Szarbek     Jan.  8, 1878 A. Gabbi (E.) (in It. and Pol.)

Warsaw          Wielki        Apr.  5, 1872 G. Giovannoni-Zacchi (E.) G. Pasqua
                                            (Eb.) L. Bolis (C.) E. Storti (R.)
                                            R. Nannetti (F.) C. Trombini cond.

                              Feb. 12, 1873 M. Mariani-Masi (E.) S. Barton (Eb.)
                                            A. Oliva-Pavani (C.) E. Storti (R.)
                                            R. Nannetti (F.) C. Trombini cond.

                              Feb. 28, 1874 F. Mariani De Angelis (E.) G. Pasqua
                                            (Eb.) A. Oliva-Pavani (C.) A. Sou-
                                            vestre (R.) E. Gasperini (F.) F.
                                            Feitlinger (I.) C. Trombini cond.

                              Feb. 15, 1875 F. Mariani De Angelis (E.) E. Mecoc-
                                            ci (Eb.) A. De Sanctis (C.) A. Sou-
                                            vestre (R.) E. Gasperini (F.) C.
                                            Trombini cond.

PORTUGAL
Lisbon          Sao Carlos    Dec. 21, 1871 A. Fricci (E.) E. Galli (Eb.) C.
                                            Carpi (C.) A. Cotogni (R.) L. Miller
                                            (F.) E. Gasperini (I.)

                              Nov. 26, 1880 R. Pantaleoni (E.) O. Synnerberg
                                            (Eb.) G. Fancelli (C.) F. Pandolfini
                                            (R.) R. Nannetti (F.)

Oporto          Palácio       Feb. 18, 1870 C. Cattinari (E.) M. Fustini (Eb.)
                de Cristal                  A. Arrigotti (C.) S. Orsi (R.)

ROMANIA
Iasi            Teatrul       Mar.     1874 E. Capozzi (E.) L. Caroselli (C.)

RUSSIA
Moscow          Bolshoi       Nov. 14, 1876 T. Stolz (E.) A. L. Cary (Eb.) A.
                                            Marin (C.) M. Padilla (R.) J. Jamet
                                            (F.)

Odessa          Municipal     Feb. 25, 1869 A. Bianchi-Montaldo (E.) E. Berini
                                            (Eb.) P. Bignardi (C.) F. Bachi-Pe-
                                            rego (R.) O. Maini (F.) G. Zambelli-
                                            ni (I.) D. Antonietti cond.

                              Jan.  3, 1870 A. Pascalis (E.) M. Destin (Eb.) G.
                                            Piccioli (C.) G. Moriami (R.) D. An-
                                            tonietti cond.

St.             Imperial      Jan.  1, 1869 A. Fricci (E.) E. Galli (Eb.) R.
  Petersburg                                Stagno (C.) F. Graziani (R.) G. F.
                                            Angelini (F.) E. Bagagiolo (I.) A.
                                            Vianesi cond.

                              Jan.  2, 1870 A. Fricci (E.) G. Capponi (C.) F.
                                            Graziani (R.) A. Vianesi cond.

                              Dec. 28, 1876 T. Stolz (E.) D. Artôt (Eb.) A. Ma-
                                            rin (C.) A. Cotogni (R.)

Tbilisi         Imperial      Feb.  8, 1869 L. Arancio Guerrini (E.) A. Colombo
                                            (Eb.) G. De Antoni (C.) E. Storti-
                                            Gaggi (R.) E. Manfredi (F.) N. Bassi
                                            cond.

SPAIN
Barcelona    Liceo        Jan. 27, 1870 C. Noel-Guidi (E.) R. Vercolini-Tay
                                        (Eb.) R. Bertolini (C.) V. Quintili-
                                        Leoni (R.) G. Capponi (F.)

                          Apr. 22, 1870 B. Blume (E.) R. Vercolini-Tay (Eb.)
                                        A. Oliva-Pavani (C.) V. Quintili-
                                        Leoni (R.) L. Vecchi (F.)

                          Feb. 19, 1873 L. Ponti dall'Armi (E.) C. Ferni
                                        (Eb.) C. Vincentelli (C.) L. Giral-
                                        doni (R.) M. Junca (F.) N. Bassi
                                        cond.

                          Oct. 14, 1876 R. Pantaleoni (E.) R. Vercolini-Tay
                                        (Eb.) F. Tamagno (C.) M. Ciapini
                                        (R.) P. Milesi (F.) E. Dalmau cond.

                          Apr. 18, 1880 Pichi (E.) R. Vercolini-Tay (Eb.) E.
                                        Barbacini (C.) V. Quintili-Leoni
                                        (R.) O. Maini (F.)

Madrid       Principe     June 15, 1872 V. Potentini (E.)    M. Biancolini
             Alfonso                    (Eb.) F. Steger (C.) V. Collini (R.)
                                        G. David (F.) E. Terziani cond.

UNITED STATES
New York     Ac. of Mus. Apr. 12, 1877 M. Palmieri (E.) P. Rambelli (Eb.)
                                        A. Celada (C.) Z. Bertolasi (R.) D.
                                        Dal Negro (F.) M. Maretzek cond.


First revision-in four acts
Milan-Teatro alla Scala-Jan. 10, 1884
Libretto in French by Camille du Locle; translated by Angelo Zanardini

Elizabetta di Valois (E.)              Abigaille Bruschi-Chiatti sop.
Eboli (Eb.)                              Giuseppina Pasqua mez.
Don Carlo (C.)                          Francesco Tamagno ten.
Rodrigo (R.)                                 Paolo Lhérie bar.
Filippo II (F.)                      Alessandro Silvestri bass
Il Grande Inquisitore (I.)            Francesco Navarini bass
Un Frate                               Leopoldo Cromberg bass
Tebaldo                                   Amelia Garten sop.
Conte di Lerma                        Angelo Fiorentino ten.
Un Araldo Reale                       Angelo Fiorentino ten.

Conductor                                    Franco Faccio
Director                                   Giuseppe Verdi

Second revision-in five acts
Modena-Teatro Municipale-Dec. 26, 1886

| | |
|---|---|
| Elizabetta di Valois (E.) | Maria Peri sop. |
| Eboli (Eb.) | Eugenia Mantelli mez. |
| Don Carlo (C.) | Francesco Signorini ten. |
| Rodrigo (R.) | Agostino Gnaccarini bar. |
| Filippo II (F.) | Alfonso Mariani bass |
| Il Grande Inquisitore (I.) | Eugenio Barberat bass |
| Un Frate | Vittorio Navarini bass |
| Tebaldo | Amalia Raschi sop. |
| Conte di Lerma | Gusmano Barbieri ten. |
| | |
| Conductor | Guglielmo Zuelli |
| Director | Guglielmo Zuelli |

OTHER PRODUCTIONS-REVISED VERSION-1884-1945

ARGENTINA
Buenos Aires    Opera         July 15, 1890 A. Gabbi (E.) E. Leonardi (Eb.) F.
                                            Tamagno (C.) G. Kaschmann (R.) F.
                                            Navarini (F.) M. Mancinelli cond.

                              July 21, 1892 A. Gini-Pizzorni (E.) E. Borlinetto
                                            (Eb.) M. Mariacher (C.) A. Scotti
                                            (R.) M. Mancinelli cond.

                              July 21, 1907 S. Kruszelnicka (E.) M. Claessens
                                            (Eb.) C. Rousselière (C.) G. De Luca
                                            (R.) A. Didur (F.) R. Ferrari cond.

                Colón         July  1, 1911 A. Agostinelli (E.) L. Garibaldi
                                            (Eb.) F. Constantino (C.) T. Ruffo
                                            (R.) N. De Angelis (F.) P. Ludikar
                                            (I.) E. Vitale cond.

                              May 27, 1930 C. Jacobo (E.) L. Bertana (Eb.) G.
                                            Thill (C.) C. Galeffi (R.) T. Pasero
                                            (F.) C. Walter (I.) E. Panizza cond.

                Coliseo       May 14, 1913 J. Capella (E.) R. Alvarez (Eb.) J.
                                            Palet (C.) G. De Luca (R.) G. Cirino
                                            (F.) G. Marinuzzi cond.

AUSTRIA
Graz            Stadt         Oct. 10, 1913 (in Ger.)

Vienna          Staatsoper    May 10, 1932 V. Ursuleac (E.) G. Runge (Eb.) F.
                                            Voelker (C.) E. Schipper (R.) J. von
                                            Manowarda (F.) A. Jerger (I.) C.
                                            Krauss cond. (in Ger.)

BELGIUM
Brussels        La Monnaie    Jan. 10, 1936 E. Deulin (E.) D. Pauwels (Eb.) J.
                                            Lens (C.) L. Richard (R.) L. Van
                                            Obbergh (F.) Molle cond.

Ghent           Grand         Nov. 22, 1937

BRAZIL
Rio de          Pedro II      Aug. 14, 1889 M. Peri (E.) A. Mazzoli-Orsini (Eb.)
  Janeiro                                   F. Cardinali (C.) F. Bartolomasi
                                            (R.) E. Serbolini (F.)

Municipal    May    9, 1913 J. Capella (E.) E. Casazza (Eb.) J.
                             Palet (C.) G. De Luca (R.) G. Cirino
                             (F.) G. Marinuzzi cond.

             July 23, 1926 B. Scacciati (E.) G. Zinetti (Eb.)
                             F. Merli (C.) C. Galeffi (R.) N. De
                             Angelis (F.) C. Sabat (I.) L. Ricci
                             cond.

Sao Paulo    Sao José    Oct.   1, 1892 A. Gini-Pizzorni (E.) E. Borlinetto
                             (Eb.) M. Mariacher (C.) A. Scotti
                             (R.) R. Ercolani (F.) E. Borucchia
                             (I.)

             Municipal    Aug. 21, 1926 B. Scacciati (E.) G. Zinetti (Eb.)
                             F. Merli (C.) C. Galeffi (R.) N. De
                             Angelis (F.) C. Sabat (I.)

BULGARIA
Sofia        National    Dec. 28, 1936 (in Bulg.)

CHILE
Santiago     Municipal    Aug. 23, 1916 E. Galeazzi (E.) E. Casazza (Eb.) J.
                             Palet (C.) J. Segura-Tallien (R.) L.
                             Nicoletti-Kormann (F.)

CZECHOSLOVAKIA
Bratislava   National    Mar. 23, 1938

Prague       Neues       Apr.     1921 F. Jokl (E.) B. Kleng (Eb.) Eisen-
             Deutsches              berg (C.) M. Klein (R.) Ludwig (F.)

             National    Jan. 21, 1931 (in Czech)

DENMARK
Copenhagen   Royal       Mar.   2, 1930 (in Dan.)

EGYPT
Cairo        Khedivial   Dec. 16? 1910 M. Viscardi (E.) L. Del Lungo (Eb.)
                             L. Zinovieff (C.) M. Ancona (R.) L.
                             Nicoletti-Kormann (F.)

             Jan.   1, 1926 A. D'Urbino (E.) R. Agozzino (Eb.)
                             E. Papania (C.) L. Montesanto (R.)
                             G. Lanskoy (F.)

FINLAND
Helsinki     National    Jan. 14, 1932 (in Fin.)

FRANCE
Paris        Gaité       June  2, 1911 Z. Brozia (E.) Olchanski (Eb.) F.
                             Fazzini (C.) R. Stracciari (R.) F.
                             Chaliapin (F.) M. Bouvet (I.) A.
                             Pomé cond. (in It.)

GERMANY
Berlin       Hofoper     Apr.   9, 1907 J. Lindsay (E.) Z. Brozia (Eb.) C.
                             Rousselière (C.) M. Renaud (R.) F.
                             Chaliapin (F.) M. Bouvet (I.) A.
                             Pomé cond. (in Fr.)

Oct. 11, 1913 L. Hafgren (E.) M. Arndt-Ober (Eb.)
H. Jadlowker (C.) C. Bronsgeest (R.)
P. Knüpfer (F.) Schwegler (I.) von
Strauss cond. (in Ger.)

Staatsoper Sep. 19, 1928 E. Julich (E.) S. Onegin (Eb.) C. M.
Oehmann (C.) Gottman (R.) A. Kipnis
(F.) L. Hoffmann (I.) G. Sebastian
cond.

Oct. 21, 1936 T. Lemnitz/Dobay (E.) M. Klose (Eb.)
F. Voelker (C.) H. Schlussnuss (R.)
J. von Manowarda (F.) W. Grossmann
(I.) W. Egk cond.

Cologne      Opernhaus   Jan. 19, 1924 F. Cleve (E.) Niggemeier (C.) Frese
(R.)

Dresden      Hoftheater  Jan. 31, 1885 L. Reuther (E.) M. Wittich (Eb.) L.
Riese (C.) P. Bulss (R.) E. Fischer
(F.) E. De Carli (I.) (in Ger.)

Frankfurt    Opernhaus   Oct.  9, 1913 M. van Dresser (E.) E. Clairmont
(Eb.) R. Hutt (C.) R. Breitenfeld
(R.) J. Föns (F.) K. Martin cond.

Hamburg      Stadt       Apr. 16, 1926 E. Land (E.) S. Kalter (Eb.) C. Günther (C.) J. Degler (R.) H. Marowski
(F.)

Munich       National    Dec.  4, 1937 T. Ralf (C.) A. Sved (R.) C. Krauss
cond.

Stuttgart    Opernhaus   Jan. 13, 1934 R. Krauss cond. (in Ger.)

GREAT BRITAIN
London       Covent      June  1, 1933 G. Cigna (E.) N. Giani (Eb.) U. Lap-
Garden                     pas (C.) G. Rimini (R.) F. Autori
(F.) G. Tomei (I.) T. Beecham cond.

Sadler's   Dec.  6, 1938 (in Eng.)
Wells

HUNGARY
Budapest     Operaház    Mar. 29, 1934 E. Bodó/A. Báthy (E.) E. Némethy
(Eb.) J. Halmos (C.) I. Palló (R.)
M. Székely (F.) (in Hung.)

June 16, 1936 G. Cigna (E.) F. Merli (C.)

ITALY
Ascoli       Ventidio    Nov. 12? 1910 T. Chelotti (E.) T. Alasia (Eb.) G.
Piceno       Basso                     Dimitrescu (C.) V. Romano (R.) G.
Sorgi (F.)

Bari         Piccinni    Jan.  5, 1899 G. Francescatti-Paganini (E.) M. Ma-
sula (Eb.) F. Runcio (C.) A. Arcan-
geli (R.) E. Borucchia (F.) U. Ceccarelli (I.) M. Palminteri cond.

Petrucelli Feb. 27, 1921 O. Turchetti (E.) R. Agozzini (Eb.)
F. Corbetta (C.) D. Viglione-Bor-
ghese (R.) G. Lanskoi (F.) A. Mongelli (I.) E. Mascheroni cond.

Bologna     Comunale     Nov. 21, 1912 J. Capella (E.) N. Frascani (Eb.) E.
                                       Johnson (C.) L. Montesanto (R.) C.
                                       Walter (F.) E. Liani Benazzo (I.) G.
                                       Marinuzzi cond.

                         Nov. 26, 1935 G. Cigna/E. Druetti (E.) E. Stignani
                                       (Eb.) F. Merli (C.) G. Rimini/M. Ba-
                                       siola (R.) T. Pasero (F.) D. Baronti
                                       (I.) A. Guarnieri cond.

Brescia     Grande       Aug.    1910 M. Viscardi (E.) N. Frascani (Eb.)
                                       F. Fazzini (C.) C. Formichi (R.) A.
                                       Masini-Pieralli (F.)

Florence    Politeama    May   2? 1914 J. Capella (E.) M. P. Bertolucci
                                       (Eb.) E. Johnson (C.) L. Montesanto
                                       (R.) C. Walter (F.)

Milan       La Scala     Feb.  6, 1897 C. Bonaplata-Bau (E.) M. Giudice
                                       (Eb.) F. Signorini (C.) E. Camera
                                       (R.) G. Scarneo (F.) L. Spivacchini
                                       (I.) V. M. Vanzo cond.

                         Oct. 26, 1912 G. Russ (E.) E. Magliulo (Eb.) B. De
                                       Muro (C.) C. Galeffi (R.) N. De An-
                                       gelis (F.) B. Berardi (I.) T. Sera-
                                       fin cond.

                         Nov. 14, 1926 B. Scacciati (E.) G. Cobelli/E.
                                       Stignani (Eb.) V. Trantoul (C.) C.
                                       Galeffi (R.) T. Pasero (F.) Marone/
                                       Sdanovski (I.) A. Toscanini/A. Votto
                                       cond.

                         Apr. 19, 1928 B. Scacciati (E.) E. Stignani (Eb.)
                                       V. Trantoul (C.) C. Galeffi (R.) T.
                                       Pasero (F.) C. Walter (I.) A. Tosca-
                                       nini cond.

Naples      San Carlo    Dec. 21, 1887 A. Gabbi (E.) G. Novelli/E. Mantelli
                                       (Eb.) G. Oxilia (C.) G. Kaschmann
                                       (R.) A. Boudouresque/E. Lorrain (F.)
                                       A. Mariani (I.) G. Gialdini/C. De
                                       Nardis cond.

                         Jan. 14, 1910 A. Agostinelli (E.) E. De Cisneros
                                       (Eb.) F. Vignas (C.) R. Stracciari
                                       (R.) V. Arimondi (F.) B. Berardi
                                       (I.) C. Campanini cond.

Padua       Verdi        June 12, 1886 M. Borelli (E.) G. Novelli (Eb.) G.
                                       Oxilia (C.) G. Kaschmann (R.) E.
                                       Jorda (F.) R. Drigo cond.

Palermo     Massimo      Dec. 22, 1910 M. Llacer (E.) L. Garibaldi (Eb.)
                                       C. Rousselière/G. Serranò (C.) G. De
                                       Luca/G. Kaschmann (R.) A. Ricceri
                                       (F.) V. Dammacco (I.) L. Mugnone
                                       cond.

Feb. 27, 1915 J. Capella/M. Cantoni (E.) M. P.
Bartolucci (Eb.) A. Lolia (C.) L.
Montesanto (R.) A. Masini-Pieralli
(F.) A. Galli (I.) G. Bavagnoli
cond.

Apr. 18, 1923 A. Zola (E.) A. Masetti (Eb.) G. Ci-
ràulo (C.) G. Noto (R.) A. Righetti
(F.) G. Tomei (I.) G. Armani cond.

Parma    Regio    Dec. 25, 1889 N. Gabbi (E.) E. Leonardi (Eb.) F.
Signorini (C.) G. Kaschmann (R.) G.
Beltrami (F.) V. Coda (I.) A. Conti
cond.

Oct. 5, 1913 G. Russ (E.) E. De Cisneros (Eb.) A.
Bassi (C.) G. Danise (R.) A. Masini-
Pieralli (F.) E. Benasso Liani (I.)
C. Campanini cond.

Rome    Apollo    Apr. 26, 1887 M. Borelli (E.) G. Novelli (Eb.) F.
Marconi (C.) M. Battistini (R.) E.
Lorrain (F.) G. Scarneo (I.) E. Mas-
cheroni cond.

Costanzi    Jan. 29, 1910 G. Russ (E.) L. Garibaldi (Eb.) A.
Bassi/F. Signorini (C.) G. De Luca/
G. Kaschmann (R.) C. Walter (F.) S.
Cirotto (I.) P. Mascagni cond.

Jan. 4, 1913 J. Capella/ E. Galeazzi (E.) L. Ga-
ribaldi (Eb.) E. Johnson/G. Taccani
(C.) M. Battistini/R. Stracciari
(R.) N. De Angelis/G. Cirino (F.) S.
Cirotto (I.) E. Vitale cond.

Dec. 21, 1918 G. Russ (E.) M. Blanco Sadun (Eb.)
A. Bassi (C.) C. Galeffi (R.) G. Cirino (F.) P. Argentini (I.) G. Mari-
nuzzi/T. De Angelis cond.

Jan. 2, 1926 B. Scacciati (E.) F. Perini (Eb.) F.
Merli (C.) C. Galeffi (R.) T. Pasero
(F.) C. Sabat (I.) G. Falconi cond.

Reale    Jan. 19, 1935 I. Pacetti/E. Druetti (E.) G. Peder-
zini (Eb.) F. Merli (C.) C. Galeffi/
M. Basiola (R.) G. Vaghi (F.) F. Au-
tori/E. Dominici (I.) T. Serafin
cond.

Oct. 14, 1941 G. Cigna/I. Pacetti (E.) C. Elmo/M.
Radev (Eb.) F. Beval (C.) T. Gobbi
(R.) T. Pasero (F.) G. Neri/G. Tomei
(I.) T. Serafin cond.

Adriano    Nov. 16? 1910 A. D'Albert (E.) F. Signorini (C.)
D. Viglione-Borghese (R.) G. Quinzi-
Tapergi (F.)

Sala RAI       May  16, 1931 M.  Serra-Massara  (E.)  B.  Bianchi
                            (Eb.) A. Facchini (C.) G. Castello
                            (R.) F. Belli (F.) G. Avanzini (I.)
                            R. Santarelli cond.

               Sep. 12, 1937 G.  Cigna  (E.)  E.  Stignani  (Eb.)  F.
                            Merli (C.) M. Basiola (R.) T. Pasero
                            (F.) N. Moscona (I.) G. Marinuzzi
                            cond.

Trieste   Grande        Dec. 26, 1895 M. De Macchi (E.) C. Mas (Eb.) F.
                            Signorini (C.) E. Camera (R.) G.
                            Scarneo (F.) G. Cimini cond.

Turin     Regio         Jan. 16, 1913 E.  Ruszkowska  (E.)  N.  Frascani/F.
                            Perini (Eb.) A. Scampini (C.) G. De
                            Luca/G. Danise (R.) L. Nicoletti-
                            Kormann (F.) G. Mansueto (I.) E.
                            Panizza cond.

               Jan. 30, 1923 A.  M.  Turchetti  (E.)  M.  Capuana
                            (Eb.) R. Grassi (C.) L. Almodovar/L.
                            Montesanto (R.) G. Mansueto (F.) E.
                            Dominici (I.) G. Marinuzzi cond.

          Sala RAI      May  31, 1934 G. Cigna (E.) N. Giani (Eb.) A. Me-
                            landri (C.) M. Basiola (R.) T. Pase-
                            ro (F.) D. Baronti (I.) F. Capuana
                            cond.

Venice    La Fenice     May   1, 1912 E.  Mazzoleni  (E.)  M.  P.  Bertolucci
                            (Eb.) J. Palet (C.) C. Galeffi (R.)
                            G. Quinzi-Tapergi (F.) L. Contini
                            (I.) R. Ferrari cond.

               Apr. 21, 1938 M. Grandi/I. Pacetti (E.) M. Bene-
                            detti (Eb.) F. Merli (C.) F. Valen-
                            tino (R.) G. Vaghi/ A. Righetti (F.)
                            A. Righetti/B. Sbalchiero (I.) A.
                            Guarnieri cond.

JUGOSLAVIA
Zagreb    National      May  20, 1939

MEXICO
Mexico City   Nacional  Nov. 13, 1886 R.  Aimo  (E.)  P.  Rambelli  (Eb.)  V.
                            Quintili-Leoni (R.) P. De Bengardi
                            (F.)

MONACO
Monte Carlo   Salle     Mar. 15, 1906 G. Farrar (E.) Z. Brozia (Eb.) E. De
              Garnier       Marchi (C.) M. Renaud (R.) F. Cha-
                            liapin (F.) M. Bouvet (I.) F. Bru-
                            netto cond.

               Mar. 26, 1907 J.  Lindsay  (E.)  Z.  Brozia  (Eb.)  C.
                            Rousselière (C.) M. Renaud (R.) F.
                            Chaliapin (F.) M. Bouvet (I.) A.
                            Pomé cond.

PHILIPPINES
Manila    Del Tondo     Mar. 27, 1887 E. Ancarani (E.) A. Silini (Eb.) A.
                            Castelli (C.) G. Ciocci (R.) E. Vil-
                            lelmi(F.) G. Branca cond.

PORTUGAL
Lisbon        Sao Carlos   Feb. 20, 1885 M. Borelli (E.) G. Novelli (Eb.) G.
                                          Ortisi (C.) S. Sparapani (R.) R.
                                          Nannetti (F.)

Oporto        Sao Joao     Jan. 13, 1906 T. Poli-Randaccio (E.) A. Cucini
                                          (Eb.) J. Garcia (C.) G. Kaschmann
                                          (R.) G. Rossi (F.)

RUSSIA
St.           Conser-      Feb. 18, 1903 E. Bianchini-Cappelli (E.) C. Mar-
Petersburg    vatoire                    chesini (Eb.) P. Cecchi (C.) G.
                                          Kaschmann (R.) V. Arimondi (F.)
SPAIN
Barcelona     Liceo        Nov. 21, 1897 C. Bordalba (E.) E. Borlinetto (Eb.)
                                          M. Sigaldi (C.) G. Kaschmann (R.) F.
                                          Navarini (F.)

Bilbao        Arriaga      June  5? 1919 G. Taccani (C.) C. Galeffi (R.) G.
                                          Cirino (F.)

Madrid        Real         Feb. 20, 1912 C. Gagliardi (E.) V. Guerrini (Eb.)
                                          L. Zinovieff (C.) E. Nani (R.) A.
                                          Masini-Pieralli (F.) G. Marinuzzi
                                          cond.

                           Jan. 21, 1913 C. Gagliardi (E.) V. Guerrini (Eb.)
                                          J. Palet (C.) T. Ruffo (R.) A. Masi-
                                          ni-Pieralli (F.) G. Zuccani cond.

                           Dec.  1, 1914 J. Capella (E.) R. Agozzino (Eb.) A.
                                          Scampini (C.) L. Montesanto (R.) G.
                                          Mansueto (F.)

SWEDEN
Stockholm     Royal        Nov.  2, 1933 B. Hertzberg (E.) G. Pälsson-Wetter-
                                          gren (Eb.) E. Beyron (C.) E. Larson
                                          (R.) J. Berglund (F.) C. Richter
                                          (I.) N. Grevillius cond.

SWITZERLAND
Basel         Stadt        Mar. 16, 1934 (in Ger.)

Zürich        Stadt        Apr.  3, 1911 Kriwitz (E.) Krüger (Eb.) Bernardi
                                          (C.) Bockholt (R.) Engel (F.) Wach-
                                          ter (I.) Conrad cond. (in Ger.)

TURKEY
Constan-      Concordia    Sep. 20, 1886
tinople

UNITED STATES
New York      Metro-       Dec. 23, 1920 R. Ponselle (E.) M. Matzenauer/J.
              politan                    Gordon (Eb.) G. Martinelli (C.) G.
                                          De Luca (R.) A. Didur (F.) L. D'An-
                                          gelo/V. Reschiglian (I.) G. Papi
                                          cond.

                           Jan. 18, 1922 R. Ponselle/F. Peralta (E.) J. Gor-
                                          don (Eb.) G. De Luca/G. Danise (R.)
                                          A. Didur (F.) L. D'Angelo (I.) G.
                                          Papi cond.

Dec.  2, 1922 F. Peralta (E.) J. Gordon (Eb.) G.
              Martinelli (C.) G. De Luca (R.) F.
              Chaliapin (F.) L. Rothier (I.) G.
              Papi cond.

Philadelphia  Metro-      Feb.  7, 1922 R. Ponselle (E.) M. Matzenauer (Eb.)
              politan                   G. Crimi (C.) G. De Luca (R.) A. Di-
                                        dur (F.) L. D'Angelo (I.) G. Papi
                                        cond.

URUGUAY
Montevideo    Solis       Aug. 28, 1892 A. Gini-Pizzorni (E.) E. Borlinetto
                                        (Eb.) M. Mariacher (C.) A. Scotti
                                        (R.)

SELECTED PRODUCTIONS-POST-WORLD WAR II[56]

ARGENTINA
Buenos Aires  Colón       July  7, 1953 P. Martorell/H. De Rosa (E.) E. Sti-
                                        gnani/M. Dois (Eb.) C. Bergonzi/M.
                                        Cubas (C.) R. Cesari/R. Catena (R.)
                                        J. Hines/H. González Alisedo (F.) J.
                                        Zanin (I.) F. Calusio/R. Zamboni
                                        cond.

                          Aug. 31, 1962 G. Brouwenstijn (E.) R. Resnik (Eb.)
                                        G. Zampieri (C.) A. Protti (R.) J.
                                        Hines (F.) W. Wildermann/H. Hotter
                                        (I.) F. Previtali cond.

                          June  9, 1967 G. Jones (E.) F. Cossotto (Eb.) C.
                                        Craig (C.) G. Bacquier (R.) J. Hines
                                        (F.) W. Wildermann (I.) O. de Fabri-
                                        tiis cond.

                          May  16, 1971 R. Orlandi-Malaspina (E.) M. Parutto
                                        (Eb.) P. Lavirgen (C.) P. Cappuccil-
                                        li (R.) N. Ghiaurov (F.) G. Foiani
                                        (I.) G. Gavazzeni cond.

                          July     1978 G. Dimitrova (E.) I. Bogachova (Eb.)
                                        N. Martinucci (C.) M. Manuguerra
                                        (R.) N. Ghiuselev (F.) W. Wildermann
                                        (I.) F. Molinari-Pradelli cond.

AUSTRALIA
Adelaide      Her         Mar.  8, 1968 R. Gordon (E.) L. Elms (Eb.) R.
              Majesty's                 Byers (C.) A. Major (R.) N. Warren-
                                        Smith (F.) R. Feist cond.

---

[56]. It is beyond the scope of this study to try to identify which version of *Don Carlos* was used in a given production, especially since the work usually contained slightly different music each time it was performed. (See Andrew Porter, Preamble to a new "Don Carlos", *Opera*, Aug. 1974, p. 665.) After Mr. Porter rediscovered the cuts made by Verdi before the Paris première, there were several performances of this original "ur-version". These are listed in a separate section. In addition, other productions of *Don Carlos* occasionally reinstated parts of the rediscovered music, in some cases (such as Venice, 1974) grafting them on to the opera's final version. Since it would be impossible to indicate all of these with any degree of accuracy, no attempt will be made to do so.

| | | | |
|---|---|---|---|
| Melbourne | | Apr. 18, 1968 | R. Gordon (E.) L. Elms (Eb.) R. Byers (C.) A. Major (R.) N. Warren-Smith (F.) R. Feist cond. |
| Sydney | | June 13, 1968 | R. Gordon (E.) L. Elms (Eb.) R. Byers (C.) A. Major (R.) N. Warren-Smith (F.) R. Feist cond. |

AUSTRIA

Salzburg    Felsen-      July 26, 1958 S. Jurinac (E.) G. Simionato/C. Lud-
            reitschule                 wig (Eb.) E. Fernandi (C.) E. Bas-
                                       tianini (R.) C. Siepi (F.) M. Stefa-
                                       noni (I.) H. von Karajan cond. (in
                                       It.)

            Aug.  1, 1960 S. Jurinac (E.) R. Resnik/C. Ludwig
                          (Eb.) E. Fernandi (C.) E. Bastianini
                          (R.) B. Christoff (F.) R. Ariè (I.)
                          N. Santi cond.

            Fest-        Aug. 11, 1975 M. Freni (E.) C. Ludwig/E. Randova
            spielhaus                  (Eb.) P. Domingo (C.) P. Cappuccilli
                                       (R.) N. Ghiaurov (F.) G. Crasnaru
                                       (I.) H. von Karajan cond.

            July 26, 1976 M. Freni (E.) F. Cossotto/E. Randova
                          (Eb.) J. Carreras (C.) P. Cappuccil-
                          li (R.) N. Ghiaurov (F.) J. Bastin
                          (I.) H. von Karajan cond.

            July 30, 1977 M. Freni (E.) F. Cossotto (Eb.) P.
                          Domingo/J. Carreras (C.) P. Cappuc-
                          cilli (R.) N. Ghiaurov (F.) J. Bas-
                          tin (I.) H. von Karajan cond.

            July 29, 1978 M. Freni (E.) E. Obraztsova/E. Ran-
                          dova (Eb.) J. Carreras (C.) P. Cap-
                          puccilli (R.) N. Ghiaurov/R. Raimon-
                          di (F.) J. Bastin (I.) H. von Kara-
                          jan cond.

            Apr.  8, 1979 M. Freni (E.) A. Baltsa (Eb.) J.
                          Carreras (C.) P. Cappuccilli (R.) N.
                          Ghiaurov (F.) J. Bastin (I.) H. von
                          Karajan cond.

            May   9, 1980 M. Freni (E.) A. Balsta (Eb.) J.
                          Carreras (C.) P. Cappuccilli (R.) N.
                          Ghiaurov (F.) J. Van Dam (I.) H. von
                          Karajan cond.

            Mar. 22, 1986 F. Izzo d'Amico (E.) A. Balsta (Eb.)
                          J. Carreras (C.) P. Cappuccilli (R.)
                          F. Furlanetto/J. Van Dam (F.) M.
                          Salminen (I.) H. von Karajan cond.

Vienna      Staatsoper Mar. 18, 1956 M. Reining (E.) E. Höngen (Eb.) K.
                          Friedrich (C.) E. Wächter (R.) J.
                          Greindl (F.) K. Dönch (I.) Rossi
                          cond. (in Ger.)

            Sep. 19, 1958 (in It.)

Oct. 25, 1970 G. Janowitz (E.) S. Verrett (Eb.) F.
Corelli (C.) E. Wächter (R.) N. Ghi-
aurov/M. Talvela (F.) M. Talvela/?
(I.) H. Stein cond.

Sep.  1, 1976 M. Caballé (E.) J. Veasey (Eb.) G.
Aragall (C.) P. Cappuccilli (R.) N.
Ghiaurov (F.) B. Rundgren (I.) M.
Gomez-Martinez cond.

Oct.  3, 1978 M. Freni (E.) N. Denize (Eb.) G.
Aragall (C.)P. Cappuccilli (R.) N.
Ghiaurov (F.) H. von Karajan cond.

May   6, 1979 M. Freni (E.) A. Baltsa (Eb.) J.
Carreras (C.)  P. Cappuccilli (R.)
R. Raimondi (F.) H. von Karajan
cond.

May  11, 1980 M. Freni (E.) A. Baltsa (Eb.) J.
Carreras (C.) P. Cappuccilli (R.) N.
Ghiaurov (F.) J. van Dam (I.) H. von
Karajan cond.

BELGIUM
Brussels      Monnaie      Jan.      1974 E.  Marton  (E.)  K.  Szostek-Radkova
(Eb.) R. Francesconi (C.) L. Monte-
fusco (R.) F. Voutsinos (F.) L. Hen-
drikx (I.) E. Boncompagni cond. (in
It.)

Jan.      1974 E.  Brunner  (E.)  I.  d'Ares  (Eb.)  M.
Maievsky (C.) N. Christou (F.) L.
Hendrikx (I.) E. Boncompagni cond.
(in Fr.)

Nov. 10, 1981 H. Doese (E.) L. Budai (Eb.) C. Bini
(C.) B. Luxon (R.) J. Van Dam (F.)
J. Pritchard cond. (in It.)

Nov. 13, 1983 H. Doese (E.) L. Budai (Eb.) G. Aragall (C.) B. Luxon (R.) S. Ramey
(F.)

BRAZIL
Rio de        Municipal    Sep.  6, 1951 E. Barbato (E.)  E. Nicolai (Eb.) M.
Janeiro                                  Picchi (C.) E. Mascherini (R.) B.
Christoff (F.) A. Votto cond.

BULGARIA
Sofia         National     May  29, 1984 G. Dimitrova (E.)

CANADA
Montreal                   Jan. 20, 1956 M. Lavergne (E.) F. Chiocchio (Eb.)
L. Roney (C.) R. Savoie (R.) J. Rou-
leau (F.) E. Cooper cond.

Toronto       O'Keefe      Sep. 14, 1977 C. Carson (E.)  T. Troyanos (Eb.) E.
Center                                   Mauro (C.) V. Braun (R.) P. Plishka
(F.) D. Garrard (I.) R. Giovaninetti
cond. (in Fr.)

Oct. 11, 1988 L. Mitchell (E.) C. Powell (Eb.) S. Algieri (C.) G. Laperrière (R.) K. Langan (F.) C. S. Kellogg cond.

Vancouver        Opera         Oct. 25, 1973 P. Tinsley (E.) G. Lavigne (Eb.) R. Moulson (C.) C. Opthof (R.) R. Cross (F.) J. Morris (I.) A. Guadagno cond.

DENMARK
Copenhagen       Falkoner      Feb. 16, 1967 C. Parada (E.) G. Lane (Eb.) D. An-
                 Center        tonioli (C.) D. Dondi (R.) B. Christ-
                               toff (F.) O. Ziino cond. (By the
                               company of the Teatro Comunale,
                               Bologna)

FINLAND
Helsinki         Exposition    May 24, 1986 N. Troitskaya (E.) B. Baglioni (Eb.)
                 Hall          L. Lima (C.) J. Hynninen (R.) M.
                               Salminen (F.) J. Ryhänen (I.) C.
                               Trailescu cond.

Savonlinna       Festival      July 12, 1979 R. Auvinen (E.) A. Takala (Eb.) K.
                               Koskinen (C.) J. Hynninen (R.) M.
                               Talvela (F.) R. Lauanne (I.) L.
                               Segerstam cond. (in Fin.)

                               Aug. 24, 1979 R. Auvinen/ M. Häggander (E.) L. Bu-
                               dai (Eb.) P. Lindroos (C.) W. Grön-
                               roos (R.) G. Pappas (I.) K. Lahtinen
                               L. Segerstam cond. (in It.)

FRANCE
Marseille        Opéra         Nov. 11, 1969 S. Sarroca (E.) M. Vilma (Eb.) C.
                               Cossutta (C.) R. Massard (R.) D.
                               Petkov (F.) J. Trik cond.

                               June  1, 1980 G. Dimitrova (E.) G. Aragall (C.) G.
                               Zancanaro (R.) B. Giasiotti (F.) L.
                               Roni (I.)

Nice             Municipal     Jan.  9, 1976 M. Caballé (E.) J. Coster (Eb.) G.
                               Aragall (C.) R. Blanc (R.) G. Howell
                               (F.) G. Masini cond.

                               Feb.  2, 1979 M. Caballé (E.) M. Vilma (Eb.) J.
                               Carreras (C.) M. Manuguerra (R.) J.
                               Van Dam (F.) Marco cond.

Orange                         June 13, 1984 M. Caballé (E.) G. Bumbry (Eb.) G.
                               Aragall (C.) R. Bruson (R.) S. Estes
                               (F.) L. Roni (I.) T. Fulton cond.

Paris            Opéra         Mar.  8, 1963 S. Sarroca (E.) A. La Morena (C.) L.
                               Quilico (R.) N. Zaccaria (F.) P.
                               Dervaux cond. (in Fr.)

                               June 15, 1964 F. Corelli (C.) N. Ghiaurov (F.) (in
                               It.)

                               Dec.  9, 1966 S. Sarocca (E.) J. Rhodes (Eb.) B.
                               Prevedi (C.) L. Quilico (R.) B.
                               Christoff (F.) J. Mars (I.) G. Se-
                               bastian cond.

Feb. 13, 1975 S. Sarocca (E.) F. Cossotto (Eb.) V.
Luchetti (C.) L. Montefusco (R.) N.
Ghiaurov (F.) J. Bastin (I.) G.
Prêtre cond.

Oct.     1986 M. Lagrange (E.) A. Milcheva (Eb.)
J. Dupouy (C.) T. Allen (R.) A. Muff
(F.) P. Thau (I.) G. Prêtre cond.
(in Fr.)

Mar. 16, 1987 S. Sweet (E.) G. Bumbry (Eb.) A. Ordonez (C.) A. Fondary (R.) R. Lloyd
(F.) L. Zagrosek cond.

Toulon                    Feb.  6, 1979 M. Caballé (E.) M. Vilma (Eb.) J.
Carreras (C.) M. Manuguerra (R.)

GERMANY
Berlin        Deutsche    Dec. 12, 1964 P. Lorengar (E.) P. Johnson (Eb.) J.
King (C.) D. Fischer-Dieskau (R.) M.
Talvela (F.) W. Sawallisch cond.

Apr. 22, 1970 G. Jones (E.) J. Veasey (Eb.) C.
Cossutta (C.) P. Glossop (R.) D.
Ward (F.) G. Solti cond. (in It.)
(By the company of the Royal Opera,
Covent Garden, London)

Feb.  1, 1976 A. Alexieva (E.) P. Johnson (Eb.) C.
Cossutta (C.) R. Kerns (R.) J. van
Dam (F.) G. Feldhoff (I.)

Cologne       Stadt       Feb. 22, 1974 S. Jurinac (E.) J. Coster (Eb.) R.
Ilosfalvy (C.) W. Janulako (R.) H.
Stamm (F.) T. Okamura (I.)

East Berlin   Staatsoper  Oct. 11, 1960 L. Dvorakova (E.)  H. Müller (Eb.)
M. Ritzmann (C.) R. Jedlicka (R.) T.
Adam (F.) G. Frei (I.) F. Konwitsch-
ny cond. (in Ger.)

Frankfurt                 Apr. 28, 1975 M. Caballé (E.) M. L. Nave (Eb.) B.
Christoff (F.)

Hamburg       Stadt       Jan. 18, 1979 E. Marton (E.) M. L. Nave (Eb.) V.
Moldoveanu (C.) L. Nucci (R.) R.
Raimondi (F.) O. De Fabritiis cond.

June  1, 1979 M. Freni (E.) S. Toczyska (Eb.) J.
Lloveras (C.) P. Cappuccilli (R.) P.
Plishka (F.) M. Gomez-Martinez cond.

Jan. 17, 1980 M. Freni (E.) T. Troyanos (Eb.) G.
Aragall (C.) Y. Mazurok (R.) N. Ghiaurov (F.) M. Gomez-Martinez cond.

Mar. 23, 1983 E. Marton (E.) E. Obraztsova (Eb.)
C. Murgu (C.) S. Milnes (R.) R.
Raimondi (F.) W. Steinberg cond.

Munich        National    May  6, 1970 G. Jones (E.) J. Veasey (Eb.) C.
Cossutta (C.) P. Glossop (R.) D.
Ward (F.) J. Rouleau (I.) E. Downes
cond. (in It.)

        July 15, 1975 K. Ricciarelli (E.) B. Fassbaender
            (Eb.) C. Cossutta (C.) E. Wächter
            (R.) R. Raimondi (F.) L. Roni (I.)
            G. Prêtre cond.

GREAT BRITAIN
Bristol   Hippodrome Oct. 26, 1973

Cardiff   New    May 15, 1973 J. Barstow (E.) J. Coster (Eb.) K.
            Erwen (C.) T. Sharpe (R.) F. Robin-
            son (F.) D. Gwynne (I.) R. Armstrong
            cond. (in Eng.)

         Oct. 2, 1973 E. Brunner (E.) J. Coster (Eb.) K.
            Erwen (C.) T. Sharpe (R.) F. Robin-
            son (F.) D. Gwynne (I.) R. Armstrong
            cond.

London   Sadler's  Jan. 16, 1951 J. Hammond (E.) A. Shuard (Eb.) J.
      Wells       Johnston (C.) T. Sharp (R.) Clarkson
            (F.) H. Alan (I.) M. Mudie cond.

      Covent   May 9, 1958 G. Brouwenstijn (E.) F. Barbieri
      Garden      (Eb.) J. Vickers (C.) T. Gobbi (R.)
            B. Christoff (F.) C. M. Giulini
            cond. (in It.)

         Apr. 22, 1959 G. Brouwenstijn (E.) G. Hoffman
            (Eb.) J. Vickers (C.) G. Evans/J.
            Shaw (R.) B. Christoff (F.) M.
            Langdon (I.) C. M. Giulini cond. (in
            It.)

         Apr. 6, 1963 M. Collier (E.) G. Bumbry (Eb.) R.
            Ulfung (C.) T. Gobbi (R.) B. Chris-
            toff (F.) N. Zaccaria (I.) J. Prit-
            chard cond. (in It.)

         Nov. 4, 1963 G. Brouwenstijn (E.) F. Cossotto
            (Eb.) R. Ulfung (C.) P. Glossop (R.)
            N. Ghiaurov (F.) D. Ward (I.) E.
            Downes cond. (in It.)

        June 10, 1966 G. Jones (E.) R. Gorr (Eb.) B. Pre-
            vedi (C.) P. Glossop (R.) B. Chris-
            toff (F.) D. Ward (I.) E. Downes
            cond. (in It.)

        June 19, 1968 G. Jones (E.) S. Verrett (Eb.) C.
            Cossutta (C.) P. Glossop (R.) D.
            Ward (F.) G. Fioiani (I.) C. Abbado
            cond. (in It.)

         Feb. 4, 1970 G. Jones/I. Ligabue (E.) J. Veasey
            (Eb.) C. Cossutta (C.) P. Glossop
            (R.) D. Ward (F.) M. Langdon (I.) G.
            Solti cond. (in It.)

         Apr. 21, 1972 J. Barker/M. Arroyo (E.) J. Veasey
            (Eb.) C. Cossutta (C.) V. Braun (R.)
            D. Ward (F.) M. Langdon (I.) J.
            Pritchard cond. (in It.)

|  |  | Oct. 7, 1977 | K. Ricciarelli (E.) G. Bumbry (Eb.) J. Carreras (C.) Y. Masurok (R.) N. Ghiaurov (F.) G. Howell (I.) M. Gomez-Martinez cond. (in It.) |
|  |  | Mar. 27, 1979 | S. Sass/G. Jones/M. Arroyo (E.) E. Connell (Eb.) V. Moldoveanu (C.) R. Bruson (R.) B. Christoff (F.) G. Howell (I.) J. Conlon cond. (in It.) |
|  |  | Mar. 31, 1983 | S. Evstatieva (E.) L. Budai (Eb.) P. Garazzi (C.) T. Allen (R.) R. Lloyd (F.) J. Rouleau (I.) B. Haitink cond. (in Fr.) |
|  |  | Apr. 12, 1985 | I. Cotrubas (E.) B. Baglioni (Eb.) L. Lima (C.) G. Zancanaro (R.) R. Lloyd (F.) J. Rouleau (I.) B. Haitink cond. (in It.) |
|  | Fairfield Hall | June 4, 1971 | R. Lloyd (F.) (in Fr.) |
|  | Coliseum | Aug. 21, 1974 | M. Curphey (E.) K. Pring (Eb.) J. Gabriels (C.) B. Luxon (R.) C. Grant (F.) R. Van Allen (I.) C. Mackerras cond. (in Eng.) |
| Swansea | Grand | May 22, 1973 |  |
| IRELAND Dublin | Gaiety | Apr. 10, 1985 | W. Donati (C.) L. Montefusco (R.) C. Cava (F.) A. Caforio (I.) |
| ITALY Bologna | Comunale | Dec. 4, 1953 | C. Mancini (E.) E. Stignani (Eb.) M. Picchi (C.) E. Mascherini (R.) B. Christoff (F.) M. Stefanoni (I.) A. Questa cond. |
|  |  | Nov. 30, 1962 | L. Gencer/C. Ferrario (E.) N. Rankin (Eb.) B. Prevedi (C.) D. Dondi (R.) N. Zaccaria (F.) C. Cava (I.) T. Serafin cond. |
|  |  | Apr. 1, 1988 | A. Millo (E.) G. Casolla (Eb.) A. Ordóñez (C.) P. Coni (R.) R. Raimondi (F.) J. Garcia (I.) M. Wung-Chung cond. |
| Florence | Comunale | May 27, 1950 | M. Caniglia (E.) E. Stignani (Eb.) M. Picchi (C.) P. Silveri (R.) B. Christoff (F.) G. Neri (I.) T. Serafin cond. |
|  |  | June 16, 1956 | A. Cerqueti (E.) F. Barbieri (Eb.) A. Lo Forese (C.) E. Bastianini (R.) C. Siepi (F.) G. Neri (I.) A. Votto cond. |
|  |  | May 8, 1961 | C. Rubio (E.) O. Dominguerz (Eb.) G. Gibin (C.) M. Zanasi (R.) M. Changalovich (F.) P. Washington (I.) V. Gui cond. |

                          May   2, 1985 M. Freni/I. Cotrubas (E.) G. Casolla
                                        (Eb.) L. Lima (C.) P. Cappuccilli
                                        (R.) S. Estes (F.) P. Washington
                                        (I.) J. Conlon cond.

Genoa        Carlo        Mar.  6, 1953 M. Pedrini (E.) F. Barbieri (Eb.) M.
             Felice                     Picchi (C.) E. Mascherini (R.) N.
                                        Rossi-Lemeni (F.) R. Morisani (I.)
                                        F. Capuana cond.

             Margherita   Feb.  7, 1959 T. Apolei (E.) B. Bortoluzzi (Eb.)
                                        R. Lagares (C.) P. Cappuccilli (R.)
                                        G. Montano (F.) E. Casolari (I.) L.
                                        Gavarini cond.

Macerata     Arena        Aug.  2, 1983 M. Caballé (E.) G. Bumbry (Eb.) G.
                                        Giacomini (C.) G. Zancanaro (R.) C.
                                        Siepi (F.) C. Cava (I.) M. Veltri
                                        cond.

Milan        La Scala     Mar. 29, 1947 M. Pedrini (E.) E. Nicolai (Eb.) T.
                                        Mazaroff (C.) C. Tagliabue (R.) T.
                                        Pasero (F.) C. Siepi (I.) F. Previ-
                                        tali cond.

                          May  22, 1952 Martinis (E.) E. Stignani (Eb.) G.
                                        Penno (C.) P. Silveri (R.) N. Rossi-
                                        Lemeni (F.) M. Stefanoni (I.) A.
                                        Votto cond.

                          Apr. 12, 1954 M. Callas (E.) E. Stignani (Eb.) M.
                                        Ortica (C.) E. Mascherini (R.) N.
                                        Rossi-Lemeni (F.) M. Stefanoni (I.)
                                        A. Votto cond.

                          Dec. 13, 1960 A. Stella/L. Gencer (E.) G. Simiona-
                                        to/C. Ludwig (Eb.)  F. Labò (C.) E.
                                        Bastiannini/T. Gobbi (R.) B. Chris-
                                        toff (F.) N. Ghiaurov (I.) G. Santi-
                                        ni cond.

                          Dec.  8, 1963 L. Gencer (E.) F. Cossotto (Eb.) B.
                                        Prevedi (C.) N. Ghiaurov (F.) M.
                                        Talvela (I.) G. Santini cond.

                          Dec.  7, 1968 R. Orlandi-Malaspina (E.) F. Cossot-
                                        to (Eb.) B. Prevedi (C.) P. Cappuc-
                                        cilli (R.) N. Ghiaurov (F.) C. Abba-
                                        do cond.

                          Apr. 13? 1970 R. Orlandi-Malaspina (E.) S. Verrett
                                        (Eb.) P. Domingo (C.) P. Cappuccilli
                                        (R.) N. Ghiaurov (F.) M. Talvela
                                        (I.) C. Abbado cond.

Naples       San Carlo    Mar. 15, 1946 M. Pedrini (E.) E. Nicolai (Eb.) F.
                                        Merli (C.) C. Galeffi (R.) I. Tajo
                                        (F.) A. Romani (I.) F. Ghione cond.

                          Dec. 20, 1950 M. Pedrini (E.) E. Stignani (Eb.) M.
                                        Picchi (C.) T. Gobbi (R.) I. Tajo
                                        (F.) G. Neri (I.) T. Serafin cond.

Dec.  2, 1961  M. Roberti (E.) N. Rankin (Eb.) A.
               La Morena (C.) T. Gobbi (R.) B.
               Christoff (F.) B. Ladysz (I.) M.
               Rossi cond.

Dec.  7, 1976  R. Kabaivanska (E.) F. Cossotto
               (Eb.) G. Casellato Lamberti (C.) R.
               Bruson (R.) C. Siepi/C. Cava (F.) B.
               Rundgren (I.) O. De Fabritiis cond.

Feb.  7, 1983  G. Dimitrova/I. Tokody (E.) G. Ca-
               solla (Eb.) G. Aragall (C.) R. Bru-
               son/G. Zancanaro (R.) N. Ghiuselev
               (F.) G. Nikolskij (I.) D. Oren cond.

Parma       Regio      Oct. 14, 1951  P. Martorell (E.) E. Nicolai (Eb.)
                                      K. Neate (C.) C. Taglabue (R.) C.
                                      Siepi/I. Tajo (F.) F. Capuana cond.

                       Dec. 26, 1961  G. Barrera (E.) A. M. Rota (Eb.) A.
                                      La Morena (C.) A. Protti (R.) C.
                                      Siepi (F.) B. Ladysz (I.) A. Basile
                                      cond.

                       Jan.  5, 1982  G. Dimitrova (E.) S. Toczyska (Eb.)
                                      V. Moldoveanu (C.) R. Bruson (R.) B.
                                      Christoff (F.) L. Roni (I.) G. Neu-
                                      hold cond.

Rome        Opera      Jan.  2, 1951  M. Pedrini (E.) E. Stignani (Eb.) M.
                                      Picchi (C.) T. Gobbi (R.) N. Rossi-
                                      Lemeni (F.) G. Neri (I.) T. Serafin
                                      cond.

                       Jan. 20, 1953  C. Mancini (E.) E. Nicolai (Eb.) M.
                                      Filipeschi (C.) T. Gobbi (R.) B.
                                      Christoff (F.) G. Neri (I.) G. San-
                                      tini cond.

                       Mar.  4, 1954  C. Mancini (E.) E. Nicolai (Eb.) F.
                                      Corelli (C.) T. Gobbi (R.) B. Chris-
                                      toff (F.) G. Neri (I.) G. Santini
                                      cond.

                       Jan. 23, 1958  A. Stella/M. Coleva (E.) C. Mancini
                                      (Eb.) F. Corelli (C.) T. Gobbi (R.)
                                      M. Petri (F.) G. Neri (I.) G. San-
                                      tini cond.

                       Nov. 20, 1965  S. Sarocca (E.) M. Parutto (Eb.) G.
                                      Cecchele/A. Bottion (C.) K. Paskalis
                                      (R.) C. Siepi (F.) M. Talvela (I.)
                                      C. M. Giulini cond.

                       Apr. 22, 1968  L. Gencer (E.) F. Cossotto (Eb.) B.
                                      Prevedi (C.) S. Bruscantini/M. Zana-
                                      si (R.) N. Ghiaurov (F.) L. Roni
                                      (I.) F. Previtali cond.

                       June  1, 1974  M. Arroyo (E.) G. Bumbry (Eb.) G.
                                      Cecchele (C.) A. Romero (R.) C. Sie-
                                      pi (F.) C. Cava (I.) T. Schippers
                                      cond.

Mar. 19, 1987 K. Ricciarelli (E.) D. Vejzovic
(Eb.) G. Aragall/L. Lima (C.) R.
Bruson (R.) N. Ghiuselev (F.) D.
Stantchev (I.) G. Kuhn cond.

Sala RAI    Nov. 20, 1951 M. Caniglia (E.) E. Stignani (Eb.)
M. Picchi (C.) P. Silveri (R.) N.
Rossi-Lemeni (F.) G. Neri (I.) F.
Previtali cond.

June 10, 1969 T. Zylis-Gara (E.) F. Cossotto (Eb.)
B. Prevedi (C.) P. Cappuccilli (R.)
N. Ghiaurov (F.) D. Petkov (I.) T.
Schippers cond.

Trieste    Verdi       Dec.  6, 1946 M. Pedrini (E.) F. Barbieri (Eb.) G.
Momo (C.) D. Checchi (R.) N. Rossi-
Lemeni (F.) A. Lucon cond.

Nov. 14, 1970 R. Orlandi-Malaspina (E.) L. Nave
(Eb.) C. Cossutta (C.) R. Bruson
(R.) B. Giaiotti (F.) A. Zerbini
(I.) O. De Fabritiis cond.

Turin    Nuovo       Apr. 29, 1952 P. Martorell (E.) E. Stignani (Eb.)
K. Neate (C.) P. Silveri/C. Taglia-
bue (R.) I. Tajo (F.) R. Morisani
(I.) O. De Fabritiis cond.

Sala RAI    June 30, 1954 A. Stella (E.) O. Dominguez (Eb.) M.
Picchi (C.) E. Mascherini (R.) C.
Siepi (F.) M. Stefanoni (I.) M.
Rossi cond.

May   5, 1961 M. Roberti (E.) A. M. Rota (Eb.) L.
Ottolini (C.) E. Bastianini (R.) B.
Christoff (F.) F. Mazzoli (I.) M.
Rossi cond.

Regio       Jan. 25, 1967 I. Ligabue (E.) F. Mattiucci (Eb.)
F. Labò (C.) S. Bruscantini (R.) R.
Ariè (F.) B. Marangoni (I.) V. Gui
cond.

Jan. 13, 1975 R. Orlandi-Malaspina/S. Del Grande
(E.) F. Cossotto/M. L. Nave (Eb.) G.
Casellato-Lamberti (C.) R. Bruson
(R.) B. Christoff (F.) G. Casarini/
L. Roni (I.) B. Bartoletti cond.

Venice    La Fenice   Jan.  7, 1954 A. Stella (E.) E. Stignani (Eb.) K.
Neate (C.) E. Mascherini (R.) B.
Christoff (F.) G. Neri/M. Stefanoni
(I.) F. Capuana cond.

Dec. 18, 1962 O. Fineschi (E.) S. Warfield (Eb.)
L. Ottolini (C.) D. Dondi (R.) B.
Christoff (F.) B. Marangoni (I.) F.
Molinari-Pradelli cond.

Apr.  3, 1969 M. Candida (E.) M. Parutto (Eb.) J.
Oncina (C.) M. Petri (R.) B. Chris-
toff (F.) F. Pugliese (I.) C. Franci
cond.

                                  Nov. 22, 1973 K.  Ricciarelli  (E.)  F.  Cossotto
                                                (Eb.) V. Luchetti (C.) P. Cappuccil-
                                                li (R.) N. Ghiaurov (F.) G. Casarini
                                                (I.) G. Prêtre cond.

Verona        Arena           Aug.  2, 1869 M. Caballé (E.) F. Cossotto (Eb.) P.
                                                Domingo (C.) P. Cappuccilli (R.) D.
                                                Petkov (F.) G. Fioiani (I.) E. Inbal
                                                cond.

JAPAN
Tokyo         Bunka           Sep.  2, 1967 G. Jones (E.) B. Cvejic (Eb.) S. Ko-
              Saikan                           nya (C.) S. Bruscantini (R.) N. Ros-
                                                si-Lemeni (F.) A. Zerbini (I.) O. De
                                                Fabritiis cond.

KOREA
Seoul         National        Nov. 22, 1988 E. Jung/K. Lee (E.) E. Park cond.
                                                (in Kor.)

MEXICO
Mexico City   Bellas          Aug. 22, 1961 M. Roberti  (E.)  O. Dominguez (Eb.)
              Artes                            U. Borso (C.) M. Ausensi (R.) C.
                                                Siepi (F.) N. Moscona (I.) A. Gua-
                                                dagno cond.

MONACO
Monte Carlo   Salle           Mar.  9, 1979 M. Krilovici (E.)  F. Cossotto (Eb.)
              Garnier                          V. Luchetti (C.) R. Bruson (R.) N.
                                                Ghiuselev (F.) I. Vinco (I.)

NETHERLANDS
Amsterdam                     Oct. 15, 1961 A. Tiemessen (E.)   A. Delorie (Eb.)
                                                J. van der Zalm (C.) J. Walters (R.)
                                                G. Litassy (F.) P. van den Berg (I.)
                                                A. Guarnieri cond.

                              June 28, 1966 G. Brouwenstijn (E.) M. Aarden (Eb.)
                                                A. Sergi (C.) H. Beresford (R.) N.
                                                Gyuselev (F.) G. Hoekman (I.) B.
                                                Haitink cond.

NORWAY
Oslo          Royal           Nov. 20, 1975 M. L. Isberg/M. Dancuo (E.) V. Hans-
                                                sen/E. Thallaug (Eb.) J. Blanc/R.
                                                Björling (C.) J. Sodal (R.) A. Heg-
                                                gen (F.) O. Tennfjord (I.) L. Mar-
                                                telli/P. A. Anderson cond.

POLAND
Poznan                             1970 K. Kujawinska (E.) A. Imalska (Eb.)
                                                S. Romanski (C.) J. Czekay (R.) H.
                                                Lukaszek (F.) M. Nowakowski cond.

PORTUGAL
Lisbon        Sao Carlos      Mar. 29, 1951 M. Caniglia (E.) E. Stignani (Eb.)
                                                M. Picchi (C.) E. Mascherini (R.) I.
                                                Tajo (F.) G. Neri (I.) A. Votto
                                                cond.

                              Apr. 22, 1954 E. Barbato (E.) G. Simionato (Eb.)
                                                M. Picchi (C.) T. Gobbi (R.) I. Tajo
                                                (F.) O. De Fabritiis cond.

Feb. 27, 1977 M. Zampieri (E.) V. Cortez (Eb.) G.
Cianella (C.) M. Zanasi (R.) C. Sie-
pi (F.) N. Verchi cond.

SPAIN
Barcelona    Liceo       Nov.  6, 1952 M. Pedrini (E.) M. Benedetti (Eb.)
M. Fillipeschi (C.) E. Mascherini
(R.) I. Tajo (F.) G. Neri (I.) A.
Questa cond.

Dec. 26, 1971 M. Caballé (E.) S. Verrett (Eb.) B.
Prevedi (C.) V. Sardinero (R.) B.
Giaiotti (F.) G. Gusmeroli (I.) A.
Guadagno cond.

Dec. 28, 1975 M. Caballé (E.) M. L. Nave (Eb.) G.
Aragall (C.) V. Sardinero (R.) G.
Howell (F.) A. Zerbini (I.) C. Suppa
cond.

June 17, 1982 M. Caballé (E.) E. Obraztsova (Eb.)
J. Carreras (C.) B. Weikl (R.) N.
Ghiuselev (F.) C. Vanderzand cond.

Nov. 11, 1982 M. Caballé (E.) E. Obraztsova (Eb.)
J. Carreras/E. Veronelli (C.) V.
Sardinero (R.) M. Talvela (F.) M.
Salminen (I.) R. Abbado cond.

Bilbao       Coliseo     Sep. 13, 1961 L. Serafini (E.) A. M. Rota (Eb.) L.
Alba                    Ottolini (C.) C. MacNeil (R.) G.
Modesti (F.) B. Giaiotti (I.) M.
Wolf-Ferrari cond.

Sep.  3, 1977 K. Ricciarelli (E.) F. Cossotto
(Eb.) J. Carreras (C.) P. Cappuccil-
li (R.) R. Raimondi (F.) L. Roni
(I.) M. Arena cond.

Sep.  2, 1982 M. Freni (E.) V. Cortez (Eb.) G.
Aragall (C.) N. Ghiaurov (F.) L.
Roni (I.) G. Rivoli cond.

Madrid       Zarzuela         1985 R. Stilwell (R.) N. Ghiuselev (F.)

Oviedo       Campoamor   Sep. 19, 1961 L. Serafini (E.) A. M. Rota (Eb.) U.
Borso (C.) C. MacNeil (R.) G. Modes-
ti (F.) B. Giaiotti (I.) M. Wolf-
Ferrari cond.

Sep. 15, 1977 K. Ricciarelli (E.) F. Cossotto
(Eb.) V. Luchetti (C.) V. Sardinero
(R.) R. Raimondi (F.) L. Roni (I.)
M. Arena cond.

Sep. 23, 1982 N. Troitskaya (E.) E. Gorojowskaia
(Eb.) G. Aragall (C.) J. Pons/L.
Saccomani (R.) J. Diaz (F.) L. Roni
(I.) G. Rivoli cond.

SWITZERLAND
Geneva       Casino      Dec. 11, 1959

                  Grand         Dec. 10, 1962 S. Sarocca (E.) C. Rubio (Eb.) A. La
                                            Morena (C.)   G. Bacquier (R.) R.
                                            Ariè (F.) C. Vöchting cond. (in Fr.)

                                June 24, 1988 R. Plowwright (E.) A. Balsta (Eb.)
                                            N. Shicoff (C.) H. Hakegard (R.) S.
                                            Ramey (F.) R. Armstrong cond. (in
                                            It.)

Lausanne        Beaulieu      Oct.     1969 M. Caballé (E.) F. Mattiucci (Eb.)
                                            L. Ottolini (C.) M. Zanasi (R.) C.
                                            Cava (F.) O. De Fabritiis cond. (By
                                            the company of the Teatro Comunale,
                                            Bologna)

Zürich          Opernhaus     Dec.  1, 1979 M. Chiara (E.) E. Randova (Eb.) L.
                                            Lima/J. Carreras (C.) G. Zancanaro/
                                            W. Brendel (R.) S. Estes/C. Siepi
                                            (F.) M. Salminen (I.) N. Santi cond.

                                June 14, 1980 M. Price (E.) E. Obraztsova (Eb.) N.
                                            Martinucci (C.) R. Bruson (R.) Y.
                                            Nesterenko (F.) M. Salminen (I.) N.
                                            Santi cond.

                                June  8, 1981 M. Price (E.) A. Baltsa (Eb.) L.
                                            Lima (C.)   G. Zancanaro (R.)   B.
                                            Christoff (F.) M. Salminen (I.) N.
                                            Santi cond.

UNITED STATES
Atlanta         Civic         May    4, 1979 G. Cruz-Romo (E.) N. Denize (Eb.) V.
                Center                       Moldeveanu (C.) S. Milnes (R.) P.
                                            Plishka (F.) J. Morris (I.) J. Le-
                                            vine cond.

Bloomington                   May    8, 1951 D. Rigal (E.) B. Thebom (Eb.) R.
                                            Tucker (C.) F. Valentino (R.) C.
                                            Siepi (F.) J. Hines (I.) F. Stiedry
                                            cond.

Boston                        Apr. 13, 1951 D. Rigal (E.) B. Thebom (Eb.) R.
                                            Tucker (C.) F. Valentino (R.) C.
                                            Siepi (F.) J. Hines (I.) F. Stiedry
                                            cond.

                                Apr. 27, 1979 G. Cruz-Romo (E.) N. Denize (Eb.) V.
                                            Moldeveanu (C.) S. Milnes (R.) P.
                                            Plishka (F.) J. Morris (I.) J. Le-
                                            vine cond.

Chicago         Lyric         Nov. 22, 1957 A. Cerqueti (E.) N. Rankin (Eb.) B.
                                            Sullivan/J. Bjoerling (C.) T. Gobbi
                                            (R.) B. Christoff (F.) W. Wildermann
                                            (I.) G. Solti cond.

                                Oct. 14, 1960 M. Roberti (E.) G. Simionato (Eb.)
                                            R. Tucker (C.) T. Gobbi (R.) B.
                                            Christoff (F.) F. Mazzoli (I.) A.
                                            Votto cond.

Oct. 28, 1964 L. Gencer (E.) G. Bumbry/F. Cossotto
(Eb.) R. Tucker (C.) T. Gobbi (R.)
N. Ghiaurov (F.) B. Marangoni (I.)
B. Bartoletti cond.

Nov. 3, 1971 P. Lorengar (E.) F. Cossotto (Eb.)
C. Cossutta (C.) S. Milnes (R.) N.
Ghiaurov (F.) H. Sotin (I.) B. Bar-
toletti cond.

Cincinnati      Opera       July 19, 1984 E. Shade (E.) B. Berini (Eb.) R. Dominguez (C.) B. Ellis (R.) P. Plish-
ka (F.) A. Voketaitis (I.) J. Rudel
cond.

Cleveland                   Apr. 13, 1951 D. Rigal (E.) B. Thebom (Eb.) R.
Tucker (C.) F. Valentino (R.) C.
Siepi (F.) J. Hines (I.) F. Stiedry
cond.

Dallas                      Apr. 28, 1951 D. Rigal (E.) B. Thebom (Eb.) R.
Tucker (C.) F. Valentino (R.) C.
Siepi (F.) J. Hines (I.) F. Stiedry
cond.

                Opera       Nov. 3, 1988 S. Dunn (E.) T. Troyanos (Eb.) K.
Johannsson (C.) T. Noble (R.) P.
Plishka (F.) J. Hines (I.) N. Res-
cigno cond.

Detroit         Masonic     May 26, 1979 G. Cruz-Romo (E.) N. Denize (Eb.) V.
                Temple      Moldeveanu (C.) S. Milnes (R.) J.
Hines (F.) J. Morris (I.) J. Levine
cond.

Hartford        Bushnell    Nov. 4, 1965 M. Collier (E.) N. Rankin (Eb.) D.
Barioni (C.) L. Quilico (R.) J. Hi-
nes (F.) L. Sgarro (I.) F. Patanè
cond.

Houston         Grand       Feb. 4, 1969 R. Kabaivanska (E.) B. Wolff (Eb.)
P. Domingo (C.) C. Meliciani (R.) A.
Saciuk (F.) M. Smith (I.) W. Herbert
cond.

                            Mar. 21, 1982 M. Freni (E.) G. Bumbry (Eb.) J.
Lloveras (C.) G. Zancanaro (R.) N.
Ghiaurov (F.) M. Gomez-Martinez
cond.

Miami           Opera       Jan. 15, 1979 M. Krilovici (E.) T. Troyanos (Eb.)
P. Visconti (C.) R. Edwards (R.) M.
Talvela (F.) W. Wildermann (I.) E.
Buckley cond.

Minneapolis     Auditorium  May 18, 1979 G. Cruz-Romo (E.) N. Denize (Eb.) V.
Moldeveanu (C.) S. Milnes (R.) P.
Plishka (F.) J. Morris (I.) J. Le-
vine cond.

New York      Metro-      Nov.  6, 1950 D. Rigal/E. Steber (E.) F. Barbieri/
              politan                   B. Thebom (Eb.) J. Bjoerling/R. Tuc-
                                        ker (C.) R. Merrill/P. Silveri (R.)
                                        C. Siepi/J. Hines (F.) J. Hines/ H.
                                        Hotter (I.) F. Stiedry cond.

              Mar. 21, 1952 D. Rigal/E. Steber (E.) F. Barbieri/
                            R. Resnik (Eb.) J. Bjoerling/R. Tuc-
                            ker (C.) P. Silveri/R. Merrill (R.)
                            C. Siepi/J. Hines (F.) H. Hotter/N.
                            Moscona (I.) F. Stiedry/R. Cellini
                            cond.

              Dec.  2, 1952 D. Rigal (E.) F. Barbieri/B. Thebom
                            (Eb.) R. Tucker (C.) R. Merrill (R.)
                            J. Hines/C. Siepi (F.) P. Schoeff-
                            ler/D. Ernster/J. Hines (I.) A. Ere-
                            de cond.

              Dec. 18, 1954 E. Steber/D. Rigal (E.) B. Thebom/N.
                            Rankin (Eb.) R. Tucker (C.) R. Mer-
                            rill/E. Bastianini (R.) C. Siepi/J.
                            Hines (F.) P. Schoeffler/N. Moscona
                            (I.) F. Stiedry/K. Adler cond.

              Mar. 16, 1957 D. Rigal/A. Stella (E.) I. Dalis
                            (Eb.) J. Bjoerling (C.) E. Bastiani-
                            ni/R. Merrill (R.) C. Siepi/J. Hines
                            (F.) H. Uhde/N. Moscona (I.) F.
                            Stiedry cond.

              Mar. 14, 1959 L. Rysanek/M. Curtis-Verna (E.) N.
                            Rankin/B. Thebom (Eb.) E. Fernandi/
                            G. Gari (C.) R. Merrill/M. Sereni
                            (R.) C. Siepi/J. Hines/G. Tozzi (F.)
                            H. Uhde/W. Wildermann (I.) F. Cleva
                            cond.

              Mar. 16, 1961 M. Curtis-Verna/L. Rysanek (E.) I.
                            Dalis/N. Rankin (Eb.) E. Fernandi/L.
                            Corelli (C.) R. Merrill/F. Guarrera/
                            M. Sereni (R.) G. Tozzi/J. Hines
                            (F.) W. Wildermann/H. Uhde (I.) N.
                            Verchi cond.

              Oct. 31, 1963 R. Kabaivanska/M. Curtis-Verna (E.)
                            R. Gorr/I. Dalis/B. Cvejik (Eb.) R.
                            Tucker/F. Labò (C.) R. Merrill (R.)
                            J. Hines/C. Siepi/G. Tozzi (F.) P.
                            Schoeffler/D. Ernster/D. Ward (I.)
                            G. Solti/K. Adler cond.

              Oct   7, 1965 R. Kabaivanska/M. Arroyo/M. Curtis-
                            Verna (E.) G. Bumbry/B. Cvejik/I.
                            Dalis (Eb.) B. Prevedi/R. Tucker
                            (C.) E. Bastianini/R. Merrill (R.)
                            J. Hines/C. Siepi/B. Giaiotti/N.
                            Ghiaurov/E. Flagello (F.) J. Diaz/D.
                            Ward/W. Dooley (I.) T. Schippers
                            cond.

Oct.  7, 1968 G. Tucci/R. Orlandi/R. Kabaivanska
(E.) I. Dalis/F. Cossotto/S. Verrett
(Eb.) B. Prevedi/R. Tucker (C.) R.
Merrill/M. Sereni (R.) N. Ghiaurov/
G. Tozzi/B. Giaiotti (F.) M. Talvela
(I.) C. Abbado/G. Schick cond.

Feb. 10, 1970 R. Kabaivanska/M. Lippert (E.) G.
Bumbry/F. Cossotto (Eb.) F. Corelli/
R. Tucker/S. Konya (C.) R. Merrill/
M. Sereni (R.) G. Tozzi/C. Siepi/B.
Giaiotti (F.) J. Macurdy/R. Mick-
ulsky (I.) K. Adler cond.

Sep. 20, 1971 M. Arroyo/R. Kabaivanska/M. Caballé
(E.) G. Bumbry/M. Dunn (Eb.) P. Do-
mingo/B. Morrell/ F. Corelli (C.) S.
Milnes/R. Merrill (R.) C. Siepi/G.
Tozzi (F.) J. Macurdy (I.) F.
Molinari-Pradelli cond.

June  6, 1972 G. Tucci/E. Ross (E.) F. Cossotto/N.
Rankin (Eb.) F. Corelli (C.) R. Mer-
rill (R.) G. Tozzi (F.) J. Macurdy
(I.) F. Molinari-Pradelli cond.

Feb.  5, 1979 R. Scotto/R. Hazzan (E.) M. Horne
(Eb.) G. Giacomini/V. Moldeveanu
(C.) S. Milnes/A. Boyagian (R.) N.
Ghiaurov/P. Plishka (F.) J. Morris/
D. Kavrakos (I.) J. Levine cond.

Feb. 14, 1980 R. Scotto/G. Cruz-Romo (E.) T. Troy-
anos/B. Baglioni (Eb.) V. Moldevea-
nu/ G. Giacomini (C.) S. Milnes (R.)
P. Plishka/J. Hines/N. Ghiaurov (F.)
J. Hines/F. Furlanetto (I.) J. Levine cond.

Feb. 28, 1983 M. Freni (E.) G. Bumbry/B. Berini
(Eb.) E. Mauro/P. Domingo (C.) L.
Quilico/A. Monk (R.) N. Ghiaurov
(F.) J. Hines/F. Furlanetto (I.) J.
Levine cond.

Mar. 31, 1986 M. Zampieri/A. Millo (E.) S. Ver-
rett/B. Berini/G. Casolla (Eb.) G.
Cianella (C.) L. Nucci (R.) J. Morris (F.) D. Kavrakos (I.) D. Stiven-
der/B. Bartoletti cond.

Jan. 27, 1989 M. Price/A. Millo (E.) T. Troyanos/
Ciurca (Eb.) N. Shicoff/E. Mauro
(C.) B. Weikl/B. Schexnayder (R.) R.
Raimondi/P. Plishka (F.) J. Levine/
M. Epstein cond.

Philadelphia  Ac. of Mus. Nov. 28, 1950 D. Rigal (E.) F. Barbieri (Eb.) J.
Bjoerling (C.) R. Merrill (R.) C.
Siepi (F.) H. Hotter (I.) F. Stiedry
cond.

|                  |              | Oct. 25, 1966 R. Kabaivanska (E.) O. Dominguez (Eb.) F. Corelli (C.) L. Quilico (R.) N. Ghiaurov (F.) N. Ghiuselev (I.) A. Guadagno cond. |

San Antonio                    Apr.  6, 1968 R. Kabaivanska (E.) M. Horne (Eb.) A. Turp (C.) C. MacNeil (R.) D. Gramm (F.) A. Berberian (I.) V. Allesandro cond.

San Francisco Opera            Sep. 16, 1958 L. Gencer (E.) I. Dalis (Eb.) P. Miranda Ferraro (C.) F. Guarrera (R.) G. Tozzi (F.) G. Modesti (I.) G. Sebastian cond.

                               Sep. 18, 1962 C. Rubio (E.) I. Dalis (Eb.) S. Konya (C.) T. Stewart (R.) G. Tozzi (F.) M. Langdon (I.) F. Molinari-Pradelli cond.

                               Sep. 27, 1966 C. Watson (E.) M. Horne (Eb.) J. Vickers (C.) P. Glossop (R.) G. Tozzi (F.) C. Ludgin (I.) F. Molinari-Pradelli cond.

                               Nov.  8, 1973 G. Jones (E.) J. Veasey (Eb.) A. Remedios (C.) N. Mittelmann (R.) M. Talvela (F.) S. Varviso cond.

                               Oct.  5, 1979 A. Tomova-Sintov (E.) L. Budai (Eb.) G. Aragall (C.) W. Brendel (R.) Y. Nesterenko (F.) S. Varviso cond.

                               Sep.  5, 1986 P. Lorengar (E.) S. Toczyska (Eb.) N. Shicoff (C.) A. Titus (R.) R. Lloyd (F.) J. Pritchard cond. (in Fr.)

Seattle      Opera             Mar.  6, 1971 E. Ross (E.) F. Cossotto (Eb.) B. Morell (C.) R. Torigi (R.) M. Smith (F.) M. Veltri cond.

Vienna, Va.  Wolf Trap         June  8, 1979 G. Cruz-Romo (E.) N. Denize (Eb.) V. Moldeveanu (C.) R. Edwards (R.) J. Hines (F.) J. Morris (I.) J. Levine cond.

VENEZUELA
Caracas      Municipal         May 16, 1975

Original   Version-in five acts, with music cut before the Paris premiere.
Boston-Opera Company of Boston-May 22, 1973

Elizabeth de Valois (E.)                          Edith Tremblay sop.
Eboli (Eb.)                                       Michèle Vilma mez.
Don Carlos (C.)                                   John Alexander ten.
Rodrigue (R.)                                     William Dooley bar.
Philippe II (F.)                                  Donald Gramm bass
Le Grand Inquisiteur (I.)

Conductor                                         Sarah Caldwell

OTHER PRODUCTIONS-ORIGINAL VERSION

GERMANY
| Hamburg | Stadt | Mar. 12, 1978 S. Sass (E.) G. Bumbry (Eb.) V. Mol-doveanu (C.) B. Weikl (R.) S. Estes (F.) K. Moll (I.) R. Kubelik cond. |

GREAT BRITAIN
| London | BBC | June 10, 1973 E. Tremblay (E.) M. Vilma (Eb.) A. Turp (C.) R. Savoie (R.) J. Rouleau (F.) J. Matheson cond. |

ITALY
| Milan | La Scala | Dec. 7, 1977 M. Freni/M. Price/M. Zampieri (E.) E. Obratzsova/N. Denize (Eb.) J. Carreras/P. Domingo/F. Tenzi (C.) P. Cappuccilli/R. Bruson/L. Decorato (R.) N. Ghiaurov/Y. Nesterenko (F.) B. Rundgren/L. Roni (I.) C. Abbado cond. |
| | | Dec. 17, 1978 M. Freni (E.) V. Cortez (Eb.) J. Carreras (C.) R. Bruson (R.) R. Raimondi (F.) M. Salminen (I.) C. Abbado cond. |

26. AIDA-*Opera* in four acts
Cairo-Khedivial Theatre-Dec. 24, 1871
Libretto by Antonio Ghislanzoni

| | |
|---|---|
| Aida (A.) | Antonietta Pozzoni-Anastasi sop. |
| Amneris (Am.) | Eleonora Grossi mez. |
| Radames (R.) | Pietro Mongini ten. |
| Amonasro (Ao.) | Francesco Steller bar. |
| Ramfis (Ra.) | Paolo Medini bass |
| Il Re | Tommaso Costa bass |
| Grande Sacerdotessa | Marietta Allievi sop. |
| Messagiero | Luigi Stecchi-Bottardi ten. |
| Conductor | Giovanni Bottesini |

OTHER PREMIERES

ARGENTINA
| Buenos Aires | Ant. Colón | Oct. 4, 1873 A. Pozzoni-Anastasi (A.) E. Stoika (Am.) S. Anastasi (R.) L. Colonnese (Ao.) M. Junca (Ra.) O. Bimboni cond. |
| | Colón | May 28, 1908 L. Crestani (A.) M. Verger (Am.) A. Bassi (R.) G. Bellantoni (Ao.) V. Arimondi (Ra.) L. Mancinelli cond. (Inauguration of the theatre) |
| Cordoba | Progresso | June 1888 C. Bevilaqua (A.) G. Gabrielescu (R.) |
| Rosario | Olimpo | June 1885 M. Peri (A.) I. Martinez de Escalante (Am.) A. De Sanctis (R.) E. De Bernis (Ao.) A. Buzzi (Ra.) |

AUSTRALIA
Adelaide        Th. Royal      Sep. 30, 1879 A. Link (A.) A. Palma (Am.) P. Pala-
                                             dini (R.) G. Verdi (Ao.) C. H. Tem-
                                             pleton (Ra.) A. Zelman cond.

Melbourne       Op. House      Sep.  6, 1877 A. Guadagnini (A.) M. Venosta (Am.)
                                             E. Camera (R.) G. Gambetti (Ao.) G.
                                             Cesari (Ra.) P. Giorza cond.

Sydney          Victoria       July 16, 1879 A. Link (A.) A. Palma (Am.) P. Pala-
                                             dini (R.) G. Verdi (Ao.) C. H. Tem-
                                             pleton (Ra.) A. Zelman cond.

AUSTRIA
Graz            Stadt          Oct. 12, 1878 (in Ger.)

Linz            Landes         Mar. 24, 1881 J. Czerwinska (A.) A. Tausig (Am.)
                                             A. Oberländer (R.) (in Ger.)

Salzburg                       Mar. 29, 1899 L. Ehrenstein (A.) (in It.)

Vienna          Hofoper        Apr. 29, 1874 M. Wilt (A.) A. Materna (Am.) G.
                                             Müller (R.) J. N. Beck (Ao.) H. von
                                             Rokitansky (Ra.) J. Herbeck cond.
                                             (in Ger.)

                               June 19, 1875 T. Stolz (A.) M. Waldmann (Am.) A.
                                             Masini (R.) L. Bignio (Ao.) P. Medi-
                                             ni (Ra.) G. Verdi cond. (in It.)

BELGIUM
Antwerp         Royal          Mar. 12, 1877 R. Mézeray (A.) Riff (Am.) Dofia
                                             (R.) Monier (Ao.) Boyer (Ra.) (in
                                             Fr.)

                               July 24, 1905 A. Agostinelli (A.) Gorretta (Am.)
                                             N. Zerola (R.) F. Vecchioni (Ra.)
                                             (in It.)

Brussels        Monnaie        Jan. 15, 1877 E. Fursch-Madi (A.) A. Bernardi
                                             (Am.) G. Tournié (R.) J. Devoyod
                                             (Ao.) Montfort (Ra.) J. Dupont cond.
                                             (in Fr.)

Ghent           Grand          Sep.  5, 1881 All'Davi (A.) (in Fr.)

                               Oct.  2, 1908 M. Alexina (A.) R. Galan (Am.) L. De
                                             Colli (R.) E. Pignataro (Ao.) (in
                                             It.)

Liége           Grand          Mar.  3, 1879 Guerin (A.) Vidal (Am.) Mazurini
                                             (R.) Elté (Ao.) Miranda (Ra.) (in
                                             Fr.)

BRAZIL
Rio de          Pedro II       Oct.  2, 1876 E. Wiziak (A.) E. Sanz (Am.) J.
Janeiro                                      Gayarre (R.) E. Storti (Ao.) G. Atry
                                             (Ra.) N. Bassi cond.

                Municipal      July 20, 1910 C. Gagliardi (A.) V. Guerrini (Am.)
                                             G. De Tura (R.) C. Galeffi (Ao.) G.
                                             Baroni cond.

| Sao Paulo | Sao José | Oct. 30, 1879 | A. Garbini (A.) R. Vercolini-Tay (Am.) F. Giannini (R.) V. Cottone (Ao.) G. Mirabella (Ra.) |
|-----------|----------|----------------|-------------------------------------------------------------------------------------------------|
|           | Municipal | July 30, 1912 | E. Rakowska (A.) R. Alvarez (Am.) G. Taccani (R.) E. Faticanti (Ao.) C. Walter (Ra.) |

**BULGARIA**

| Sofia | Luxembourg | Aug. 15. 1895 | A. Bottero (A.) (in It.) |
|-------|-----------|----------------|----------------------------|
|       | National  | May 19, 1914  | (in Bulg.) |

**CANADA**

| Edmonton | Empress | Jan. 20, 1919 | E. Amsden (A.) D. Fernanda (Am.) E. Salazar (R.) J. Royer (Ao.) |
|----------|---------|----------------|--------------------------------------------------------------------|
| Montreal | Ac. de Mus. | Feb. 27, 1879 | C. L. Kellogg (A.) A. L. Cary (Am.) C. Adams (R.) A. Pantaleoni (Ao.) |
| Toronto | Grand | Mar. 3, 1879 | C. L. Kellogg (A.) A. L. Cary (Am.) C. Adams (R.) A. Pantaleoni (Ao.) |
| Vancouver | Avenue | Jan. 8, 1920 | B. Freeman (A.) S. De Mette (Am.) E. Salazar (R.) M. Valle (Ao.) |
| Winnnipeg | Walker | Feb. 2, 1914 | J. Brola (A.) E. Thornton (Am.) M. D'Olsly (R.) Samuell (Ao.) (in Eng.) |
|          |        | Dec. 18, 1916 | D. Kaestner (A.) M. Correno (Am.) E. Salazar (R.) G. Battistini (Ao.) P. De Biasi (Ra.) (in It.) |

**CHILE**

| Santiago | Municipal | Oct. 26, 1881 | M. Ricci (A.) P. Rambelli (Am.) T. Bertini (R.) L. Lalloni (Ao.) A. Buzzi (Ra.) E. Contrucci cond. |
|----------|-----------|----------------|------------------------------------------------------------------------------------------------------|
| Valparaiso | Victoria | Aug. 12, 1885 | A. Gabbi (A.) A. Mazzoli-Orsini (Am.) H. Prevost (R.) E. Sivori (Ao.) V. Arimondi (Ra.) E. Contrucci cond. |

**CHINA**

| Shanghai | Victoria | Jan. 20, 1915 | F. Impallomeni (A.) L. Da Gradi (R.) A. Mauceri (Ra.) G. Gonsalez cond. |
|----------|----------|----------------|---------------------------------------------------------------------------|

**COLOMBIA**

| Bogota | Municipal | May 1, 1890 | I. Poli (A.) Sartini (Am.) E. Guardenti (R.) C. Ferri (Ao.) E. Lambardi (Ra.) |
|--------|-----------|--------------|---------------------------------------------------------------------------------|

**CUBA**

| Havana | Tacon | Jan. 23, 1878 | E. Volpini (A.) Bernardoni (Am.) A. Marin (R.) E. Storti (Ao.) A. Pinto (Ra.) |
|--------|-------|----------------|---------------------------------------------------------------------------------|
| Santiago |     | Nov. 1879 | A. Peralta (A.) Zipelli (Am.) E. Camero (R.) Astori (Ao.) G. Reina (Ra.) |

**CZECHOSLOVAKIA**

| Bratislava | Theatre | 1891-92 | |
|------------|---------|---------|---|

Brno            Interims     Feb. 26, 1880 (in Ger.)

Prague          Deutsches    Dec. 11, 1875 M. von Steinitz-Moser (A.) H. Buren-
                Landes Th.                  ne (Am.) S. Hájos(R.) A. Schebesta
                                            (Ao.) L. Slansky cond. (in Ger.)

                Neustädter   Aug.      1882 A. Adini (A.) A. Pascalis (Am.) A.
                                            Aramburo (R.) G. Vaselli (Ao.) E.
                                            Gasperini (Ra.) (in It.)

                National     Feb. 15, 1884 E. Turolla (A.) (in Czech)

DENMARK
Copenhagen      Royal        Oct.  4, 1885 Keller (A.) Dons (Am.) Torsleff (R.)
                                            N. J. Simonsen (Ao.) (in Dan.)

                             Apr. 15, 1928 I. Rinolfi (A.) S. De Mette (Am.) G.
                                            Taccani (R.) C. Morelli (Ao.) L.
                                            Donaggio (Ra.) E. Tango cond. (in
                                            It.)

EGYPT
Alexandria      Zizinia      Mar. 10? 1887 S. Bodrilla (A.) A. Orlandi (Am.) N.
                                            Carbini (R.) A. Alberti (Ao.) E.
                                            Dondi (Ra.)

Gizeh           Pyramids     Mar.  2, 1912 T. Desana (A.) R. Alvarez (Am.) J.
                                            Garcia (R.) B. Dadone (Ao.)

FINLAND
Helsinki        Alexanders   Sep. 17, 1896 A. Bruno (A.) Schaw (Am.) O. Delle
                                            Fornacci (R.) G. Pimazzoni (Ao.)
                                            Gandolfi (Ra.) (in It.)

                National     Apr. 17, 1916 (in Fin.)

FRANCE
Lyon            Grand        Dec. 17, 1879 Baux (A.) Bernardi (Am.) Tournié
                                            (R.) Delrat (Ao.) (in Fr.)

Marseille       Grand        Jan. 31, 1877 de Stucklé (A.) Perlat (Am.) W.
                                            Mierzswinski (R.) Dumestre (Ao.)
                                            Echetto (Ra.) C. Solié cond. (in
                                            Fr.)

                Gymnase      May 12? 1905 A. Agostinelli (A.) Gorretta (Am.)
                                            N. Zerola (R.) S. Arrighetti (Ao.)
                                            F. Vecchioni (Ra.) (in It.)

Nice            Municipal    Mar.  8, 1879 E. Ciuti (A.) Donati (Am.) Santinel-
                                            li (R.) V. De Pasqualis (Ao.) A.
                                            Buzzi (Ra.) (in It.)

Paris           Italien      Apr. 22, 1876 T. Stolz (A.) M. Waldmann (Am.) A.
                                            Masini (R.) F. Pandolfini (Ao.) P.
                                            Medini (Ra.) G. Verdi cond. (in It.)

                Ventadour    Aug.  1, 1878 E. Ambre (A.) Bernardi (Am.) O. Nou-
                                            velli (R.) Aubert (Ao.) Luigini
                                            cond. (in Fr.)

|            | Opéra      | Mar. 22, 1880 | G. Krauss (A.) R. Bloch (Am.) H. Sellier (R.) V. Maurel (Ao.) A. Boudouresque (Ra.) G. Verdi cond. (in Fr.) |
|------------|------------|---------------|-------------------------------------------------------------------------------------------------------------|
| Rouen      | des Arts   | Mar. 5, 1884  | Baux (A.) E. Leavington (Am.) Devilliers (R.) Manoury (Ao.) A. Ponsard (Ra.) Luigini cond. (in Fr.)         |

GERMANY

| Berlin       | Hofoper    | Apr. 20, 1874 | M. Mallinger (A.) M. Brandt (Am.) A. Niemann (R.) F. Betz (Ao.) Fricke (Ra.) C. Eckert cond. (in Ger.) |
|--------------|------------|---------------|--------------------------------------------------------------------------------------------------------|
|              | Kroll      | May 7, 1902   | M. De Macchi (A.) V. Guerrini (Am.) F. Signorini (R.) V. Brombara (Ao.) V. Arimondi (Ra.) (in It.)     |
|              | Deutsche   | Sep. 29, 1961 | G. Davy (A.) C. Ludwig (Am.) J. Thomas (R.) W. Berry (Ao.) J. Greindl (Ra.) K. Böhm cond.               |
| Braunschweig | Hoftheater | Apr. 24, 1875 | (in Ger.)                                                                                              |
| Breslau      | Stadt      | May 19, 1876  | M. Lehmann (A.) M. Borée (Am.) G. Perotti (R.) Siehr (Ao.) Krükl (Ra.) Hock cond. (in Ger.)            |
| Cologne      | Stadt      | Nov. 2, 1875  | Wilde (A.) Keller (Am.) F. Diener (R.) O. Schelper (Ao.) T. Petzer (Ra.) (in Ger.)                     |
| Darmstadt    | Hoftheater | Nov. 29, 1874 | (in Ger.)                                                                                              |
| Dresden      | Hoftheater | Dec. 8, 1876  | C. Kainz-Prause (A.) M. Nanitz (Am.) L. Riese (R.) Bulas (Ao.) E. Decarli (Ra.)                        |
| Frankfurt    | Opernhaus  | Nov. 17, 1880 | M. Wilt (A.) F. Moran-Olden (Am.) W. Candidus (R.) J. Beck (Ao.) O. Dessoff cond.                      |
| Hamburg      | Stadt      | Apr. 20, 1876 | E. Von Bretfeld (A.) H. Burenne (Am.) F. Nachbaur (R.) F. Krükl (Ao.) J. Kögel (Ra.) H. Seidel cond.   |
| Hannover     | Hoftheater | Apr. 1, 1879  | (in Ger.)                                                                                              |
| Kassel       | Hoftheater | Mar. 22, 1879 | (in Ger.)                                                                                              |
| Leipzig      | Carl       | Apr. 28, 1875 | (in Ger.)                                                                                              |
|              | Stadt      | Sep. 9, 1876  | O. Parsch (A.) Bernstein (Am.) G. Perotti (R.) Schelper (Ao.) Förster cond. (in Ger.)                  |
| Mainz        | Stadt      | Mar. 17, 1875 | (in Ger.)                                                                                              |
| Munich       | Hoftheater | May 13, 1877  | M. Weckerlin (A.) J. Schefsky (Am.) F. Nachbaur (R.) T. Reichmann (Ao.) A. Kindermann (Ra.) (in Ger.)  |

Mar.  2, 1879 I.  Cristofani  (A.)  G.  Pasqua  (Am.)
              A.  Celada  (R.)  G.  Vaselli  (Ao.)  W.
              Seidemann (Ra.) (in It.)

Nürnberg      Stadt         Feb.  6, 1876 (in Ger.)

Stuttgart     Hoftheater    Mar.  6, 1875 M.  Schröder-Hanfstaengl  (A.)  Lutte-
                                          rotti (Am.) L. Ucko (R.) H. Bertram
                                          (Ao.) Schütky (Ra.) Albert cond.

Weimar        Hoftheater    Apr.  8, 1889 (in Ger.)

GREAT BRITAIN
Belfast       Th. Royal     Sep. 14, 1892 E.  Russel  (A.)  L.  Meislinger  (Am.)
                                          B.  M'Guckin  (R.)  M.  Eugene (Ao.) B.
                                          Ralston (Ra.) (in Eng.)

Birmingham    Th. Royal     Nov. 26, 1888 E.  Russel  (A.)  J.  De Vigne (Am.) L.
                                          Ravelli  (R.)  F.  D'Andrade  (Ao.)  A.
                                          Foli (Ra.) L. Arditi cond. (in It.)

                            May  29, 1893 E.  Russel  (A.)  L.  Meislinger  (Am.)
                                          B.  M'Guckin  (R.)  M.  Eugene  (Ao.)  R.
                                          Lewis (Ra.) (in Eng.)

Bristol       Prince's      Sep. 12, 1892 E.  Russel  (A.)  L.  Meislinger  (Am.)
                                          B.  M'Guckin  (R.)  M.  Eugene  (Ao.)  (in
                                          Eng.)

Edinburgh     Royal         May  18, 1892 E.  Stewart  (A.)  L.  Lablache  (Am.)  G.
              Lyceum                      Dimitrescu  (R.)  L.  Crotty  (Ao.)  B.
                                          Ralston (Ra.) E. Goossens cond. (in
                                          Eng.)

Glasgow       Th. Royal     May   2, 1892 E.  Stewart  (A.)  L.  Lablache  (Am.)  G.
                                          Dimitrescu  (R.)  L.  Crotty  (Ao.)  B.
                                          Ralston (Ra.) E. Goossens cond. (in
                                          Eng.)

Leeds         Grand         Oct. 31, 1892 E.  Russel  (A.)  L.  Meislinger  (Am.)
                                          C.  Hedmondt  (R.)  M.  Eugene  (Ao.)  B.
                                          Ralston (Ra.) E. Goossens cond. (in
                                          Eng.)

Liverpool     Royal Court   Nov. 19, 1888 E.  Russel  (A.)  S.  Scalchi  (Am.)  L.
                                          Ravelli  (R.)  F.  D'Andrade  (Ao.)  A.
                                          Foli (Ra.) L. Arditi cond. (in It.)

                            Feb.  4, 1892 M.  Roze  (A.)  L.  Lablache  (Am.)  G.
                                          Dimitrescu  (R.)  L.  Crotty  (Ao.)  B.
                                          Ralston (Ra.) (in Eng.)

London        Covent        July 10, 1876 A.  Patti  (A.)  E.  Gindele  (Am.)  E.
              Garden                      Nicolini  (R.)  F.  Graziani  (Ao.)  G.
                                          Capponi (Ra.) E. Bevignani cond.

              Her           Feb. 19, 1880 M.  Hauk  (A.)  J.  Yorke  (Am.)  J.  Maas
              Majesty's                   (R.)  W.  Ludwig  (Ao.)  A.  Randegger
                                          cond. (in Eng.)

Manchester    Th. Royal     Dec.  3, 1888 E.  Russel  (A.)  J.  De Vigne (Am.) L.
                                          Ravelli  (R.)  F.  D'Andrade  (Ao.)  A.
                                          Abramoff  (Ra.)  L.  Arditi  cond.  (in
                                          It.)

                        Mar. 13, 1892 E. Palliser (A.) L. Lablache (Am.)
                                      J. Dimitrescu (R.) L. Crotty (Ao.)
                                      B. Ralston (Ra.) E. Goossens cond.
                                      (in Eng.)

GREECE
Athens          Olympic     June  5, 1882 N. Martinez (A.) M. Pia (Am.) A.
                                          Brunetti (R.) R. De Giorgi (Ra.) N.
                                          Giommi (Ra.)

Corfu           San Giacomo Jan. 27? 1884 F. Savio (A.) L. Caracciolo (Am.) G.
                                          Migliori (R.) E. Massini (Ao.)

Salonica                    Apr.  3? 1886 C. Bottarelli (A.) E. Parsi (Am.) A.
                                          Passetti (R.) E. Massini (Ao.) N.
                                          Giommi (Ra.)

GUATEMALA
Guatemala       Colón       Mar. 25, 1883 Q. Lorenzini-Gianoli (A.) F. Guidot-
City                                      ti (Am.) A. Celada (R.) E. De Bernis
                                          (Ao.)

HAWAII
Honolulu        Royal       Mar.  8, 1913 E. Adaberto (A.) B. Fox (Am.) E.
                Hawaiian                  Folco (R.) F. Nicoletti (Ao.) G.
                                          Martino (Ra.)

HUNGARY
Budapest        Nemzeti     Apr. 10, 1875 M. Hauk (A.) R. Szabó (Am.) J. El-
                Szinház                   linger (R.) F. Láng (Ao.) K. KÖsze-
                                          ghy (Ra.) S. Erkel cond. (in Hung.)

                Operaház    Apr. 12, 1885 E. Turolla (A.)

INDIA
Bombay          Excelsior   Apr.  6, 1916 A. De Revers (A.) N. Russ (Am.) L.
                                          Da Gradi (R.) G. Cacciali (Ra.) G.
                                          Gonsalez cond.

Calcutta        Grand Op.   Jan. 26, 1916 A. De Revers (A.) N. Russ (Am.) B.
                                          Capelli (R.) I. Belloni (Ao.) G.
                                          Cacciali (Ra.) G. Gonsalez cond.

INDONESIA
Batavia         T. Batavie  Apr.  3, 1882 M. Bulli-Paoli (A.) Renaut (Am.) A.
                                          Castelli (R.) I. Viganotti (Ao.) F.
                                          Bay (Ra.)

Soerebaya       Theatre     June 16, 1882 M. Bulli-Paoli (A.) Renaut (Am.) A.
                                          Castelli (R.)

IRELAND
Cork            Th. Royal   Aug. 12, 1892 E. Russel (A.) L. Meislinger (Am.)
                                          B. M'Guckin (R.) M. Eugene (Ao.) B.
                                          Ralston (Ra.) (in Eng.)

Dublin          Gaiety      Nov. 13, 1888 E. Russel (A.) S. Scalchi (Am.) L.
                                          Ravelli (R.) F. D'Andrade (Ao.) A.
                                          J. Foli (Ra.) L. Arditi cond. (in
                                          It.)

                            Aug. 18, 1892 E. Russel (A.) L. Meislinger (Am.)
                                          B. M'Guckin (R.) M. Eugene (Ao.) B.
                                          Ralston (Ra.) (in Eng.)

ISRAEL
Tel Aviv                           Nov. 20, 1924 (in Heb.)

                      National     June 18, 1960 L. Lafayette (A.) R. Samsonov (Am.)
                                   Y. Roden (R.) E. Menkes (Ao.) J.
                                   Pollak (Ra.) E. Paldi cond. (in
                                   Heb.)

ITALY
Alessandria   Municipale   Oct. 11, 1877 E. Tati (A.) C. Calash (Am.) T. Vil-
                                   la (R.) D. Belardi (Ao.) V. Petit
                                   (Ra.) A. Pomé cond.

Ancona        Muse         May  5, 1873 T. Stolz (A.) M. Waldmann (Am.) G.
                                   Capponi (R.) A. Pantaleoni (Ao.) O.
                                   Maini (Ra.) E. Usiglio cond.

Bari          Piccinni     Dec. 31, 1877 A. Spaak (A.) Garulli (Am.) Marini
                                   (R.) L. Borgioli (Ao.) G. Capriles
                                   (Ra.)

              Petruzzelli Apr. 16, 1903 A. Matini (A.) A. Degli Abbati (Am.)
                                   Albiach (R.) E. Moreo (Ao.) A. Ric-
                                   ceri (Ra.) G. Zinetti cond.

Bergamo       Donizetti    Aug. 15, 1882 E. Crosmond (A.) T. Maccaferri (Am.)
                                   A. Patierno (R.) E. Rubirato (Ao.)
                                   T. De Alba (Ra.) E. Usiglio cond.

Bologna       Comunale     Oct.  4, 1877 M. L. Durand (A.) G. Pasqua (Am.) A.
                                   De Sanctis (R.) G. Moriami (Ao.) F.
                                   Novara (Ra.) M. Mancinelli cond.

Brescia       Grande       Aug. 17? 1875 T. Singer (A.) A. Pozzoni-Anastasi
                                   (Am.) A. Masini (R.) G. Aldighieri
                                   (Ao.) M. Junca (Ra.) G. Rossi cond

Cagliari      Civico       Oct.  3, 1882 E. Aviera (A.) M. Bianchi-Fiorio
                                   (Am.) A. Anton (R.) A. Acconci (Ao.)
                                   L. Megia (Ra.)

Catania       Bellini      June 16, 1890 E. Leroux (A.) G. Novelli (Am.) F.
                                   Giannini (R.) E. Camera (Ao.) C.
                                   Fiegna (Ra.) C. Rossi cond.

Chieti        Maruccino    Apr. 29, 1872 G. De Giuli-Borsi (A.) S. De Sparta
                                   (Am.) A. Patierno (R.) E. Carnili
                                   (Ao.) A. Padovani (Ra.) C. Lovati-
                                   Cazzulani cond.

Cremona       Concordia    Sep. 10, 1881 I. Cristofani (A.) G. Novelli (Am.)
                                   E. Guardenti (R.) T. Wilmant (Ao.)
                                   A. Fradelloni (Ra.) E. Bernardi
                                   cond.

Ferrara       Comunale     May 12, 1875 T. Singer (A.) A. Pozzoni-Anastasi
                                   (Am.) F. Patierno (R.) G. Aldighieri
                                   (Ao.) R. Nannetti (Ra.) E. Usiglio
                                   cond.

Fiume         Comunale     Oct.  4, 1885 M. Borelli (A.) C. Sartori (Am.) T.
                                   Bertini (R.) G. Caruson (Ao.)

| | | | |
|---|---|---|---|
| Florence | Pagliano | Oct. 6, 1874 | T. Singer (A.) R. Vercolini-Tay (Am.) A. Masini (R.) P. Silenzi (Ao.) R. Nannetti (Ra.) E. Usiglio cond. |
| Genoa | Carlo Felice | Dec. 26, 1875 | T. Brambilla-Ponchielli (A.) P. von Edelsberg (Am.) A. Celada (R.) G. Villani (Ao.) A. Zesevich (Ra.) G. Rossi cond. |
| La Spezia | Politeama | Aug. 1, 1889 | E. Theodorini (A.) G. Casali-Bavagnoli (Am.) E. Guardenti (R.) G. Vaselli (Ao.) C. Bedogni (Ra.) E. Usiglio cond. |
| Livorno | Avvalorati | Dec. 26, 1878 | E. Tati (A.) C. Dory (Am.) A. Brunetti (R.) I. De Anna (Ao.) U. Gianelli cond. |
| Lucca | Giglio | Aug. 28, 1886 | T. Singer (A.) G. De Giuli-Borsi (Am.) E. Durot (R.) G. Moriami (Ao.) P. Povoleri (Ra.) E. Usiglio cond. |
| Lugo | Rossini | Aug.? 1880 | T. Singer (A.) G. Pasqua (Am.) C. Carpi (R.) Giacomelli (Ao.) G. Roveri (Ra.) L. Mancinelli cond. |
| Mantua | Sociale | Dec. 26, 1874 | C. Scarati-Bresciani (A.) L. Proch (Am.) L. Filippi-Bresciani (R.) A. Faentini-Galassi (Ao.) W. Seidemann (Ra.) C. Lovati-Cazzullani cond. |
| Messina | Vittorio Emanuele | Dec. 20, 1877 | A. Bruschi-Chiatti (A.) G. Casaglia (Am.) G. Ortisi (R.) G. Toledo (Ao.) F. Cherubini (Ra.) |
| Milan | La Scala | Feb. 8, 1872 | T. Stolz (A.) M. Waldmann (Am.) G. Fancelli (R.) F. Pandolfini (Ao.) O. Maini (Ra.) F. Faccio cond. G. Verdi dir. |
| Modena | Comunale | Jan. 19, 1881 | I. Cristofani (A.) S. De Sparta (Am.) E. Guardenti (R.) L. Giraldoni (Ao.) A. Fradelloni (Ra.) E. Usiglio cond. |
| Naples | San Carlo | Mar. 30, 1873 | T. Stolz (A.) M. Waldmann (Am.) F. Patierno (R.) V. Collini (Ao.) L. Miller (Ra.) P. Serrao cond. G. Verdi dir. |
| Novara | Coccia | Jan. 12? 1888 | E. Boronat (A.) C. Sartori (Am.) Rubella (R.) E. Sivori (Ao.) L. Rossato (Ra.) A. Toscanini cond. |
| Padua | Nuovo | July 3, 1872 | T. Stolz (A.) M. Waldmann (Am.) G. Capponi (R.) F. Pandolfini (Ao.) O. Maini (Ra.) F. Faccio cond. |
| Palermo | Politeama | Mar. 28, 1881 | T. Singer (A.) A. Pozzoni-Anastasi (Am.) A. Celada (R.) E. Barbieri (Ao.) G. Rapp (Ra.) G. Gialdini cond. |

Parma          Regio         Apr. 20, 1872 T. Stolz (A.) M. Waldmann (Am.) G.
                                           Capponi (R.) A. Pantaleoni (Ao.) R.
                                           Angiolini (Ra.) G. Rossi cond. G.
                                           Verdi dir.

Perugia        Morlacchi     Aug.  8, 1874 A. Pozzoni-Anastasi (A.) M. Waldmann
                                           (Am.) S. Anastasi (R.) G. Moriami
                                           (Ao.) O. Maini (Ra.) E. Usiglio
                                           cond.

Piacenza       Municipale    Dec. 25, 1877 N. Bonal (A.) M. Riccardi (Am.) L.
                                           Giraud (R.) E. De Bernis (Ao.) A.
                                           Rossi-Castagnola (Ra.) G. Bolzoni
                                           cond.

Pisa           Nuovo         Mar. 11, 1876 F. Tabacchi (A.) M. Destin (Am.) E.
                                           Barbacini (R.) L. Borgioli (Ao.) R.
                                           Mailini (Ra.) E. Contrucci cond.

Ravenna        Alighieri     June 24, 1876 T. Friderici (A.) G. Pasqua (Am.)
                                           A. Celada (R.) G. Moriami (Ao.) C.
                                           Bedogni (Ra.) L. Mancinelli cond.

Reggio Emilia Municipale     Dec. 27, 1885 L. Peydro (A.) G. Zeppilli-Villani
                                           (Am.) T. Fenaroli (R.) G. Villani
                                           (Ao.) U. Peroni (Ra.) M. Bavagnoli
                                           cond.

Rome           Apollo        Feb. 17, 1875 T. Stolz (A.) A. Pozzoni-Anastasi
                                           (Am.) E. Nicolini (R.) G. Aldighieri
                                           (Ao.) R. Nannetti (Ra.) E. Usiglio
                                           cond.

               Costanzi      Oct.  8, 1881 T. Singer (A.) G. Novelli (Am.) G.
                                           Sani (R.) S. Caldani-Athos (Ao.) G.
                                           Mirabella (Ra.) A. Pomé cond.

Siena          Rinnovati     Jan. 21? 1898 V. Petrilli-Sulli (A.) T. Alasia
                                           (Am.) Sarcoli (R.) F. Cattadori
                                           (Ao.) A. Brondi (Ra.)

Trento         Sociale       June 12? 1880 A. Gabbi (A.) E. Theodorini (Am.) E.
                                           Guardenti (R.) M. Battistini (Ao.)
                                           C. Bedogni (Ra.) D'Alessio cond.

Treviso        Sociale       Oct. 19, 1878 E. Tati (A.) Albini (Am.) C. Vincen-
                                           telli (R.) L. Guadagnini (Ao.) A.
                                           Marcassa (Ra.) C. Lovati-Cazzulani
                                           cond.

Trieste        Grande        Oct.  4, 1873 M. Mariani-Masi (A.) A. Fricci (Am.)
                                           G. Capponi (R.) F. Pandolfini (Ao.)
                                           O. Maini (Ra.) F. Faccio cond.

Turin          Regio         Dec. 26, 1874 T. Singer (A.) R. Vercolini-Tay
                                           (Am.) F. Patierno (R.) G. Moriami
                                           (Ao.) E. Barberat (Ra.) C. Pedrotti
                                           cond.

Udine          Minerva       Aug.  8, 1878 A. Bruschi-Chiatti (A.) C. Calash
                                           (Am.) A. Celada (R.) A. Pantaleoni
                                           (Ao.) A. Tamburlini (R.) G. Gialdini
                                           cond.

Venice        Malibran     July 11, 1876 M.  Mariani-Masi  (A.)  M.  Waldmann
                                         (Am.)  A.  Masini  (R.)  A.  Pantaleoni
                                         (Ao.)  P.  Medini  (Ra.)  F.  Faccio
                                         cond.

              La Fenice    Sep. 11, 1881 E.  Turolla  (A.)  G.  Pasqua  (Am.)  G.
                                         Sani  (R.)  G.  Aldighieri  (Ao.)  E.
                                         Serbolini (Ra.)

Verona        Filarmonico Dec. 26, 1876 T.  Friderici  (A.)  E.  Parsi  (Am.)  I.
                                         D'Avanzo  (R.)  G.  Villani  (Ao.)  A.
                                         Bettarini (Ra.) E. Bernardi cond.

              Arena        Aug. 10, 1913 E.  Mazzoleni  (A.)  M.  Gay  (Am.)  G.
                                         Zenatello  (R.)  A.  Passuello  (Ao.)  G.
                                         Mansueto (Ra.) T. Serafin cond.

Vicenza       Eretenio     Feb. 21? 1878 N.  Bonal  (A.)  M.  Riccardi  (Am.)  G.
                                         Santinelli (R.) S. Caltagirone (Ao.)
                                         P. Povoleri (Ra.) R. Drigo cond.

JAMAICA
Kingston      Th. Royal    Feb.  5, 1901 M.  Peri  (A.)  Longhi  (Am.)  L.  Otta-
                                         viani  (R.)  S.  Vinci  (Ao.)  I.  Picchi
                                         (Ra.)

JUGOSLAVIA
Ljubljana     Nobile                1880 (in Ger.)

              National     Sep. 29, 1898

Zagreb        National     Oct.  1, 1881 E.  Dotti  (A.)  Lesic  (Am.)  G.  B.  De
                                         Negri  (R.)  Prandi  (Ao.)  Vespasiani
                                         (Ra.)

LATVIA
Riga          Municipal    Jan. 21, 1882 (in Ger.)

                           Spring    1900 Pompa (Ao.) (in It.)

              National     Sep.  9, 1922 (in Let.)

LITHUANIA
Kaunas        Imperial     Nov.      1909 (in It.)

              National     Nov. 10, 1927 (in Lith.)

Vilnius       Municipal    Mar.  6, 1898 De Livron (A.) Pagnoni (Am.) G. Or-
                                         tisi (R.) Cattadori (Ao.) (in It.)

MALTA
La Valletta   Real         Oct. 15, 1877 M. D'Altenburg (A.) E. Dotti (Am.)
                                         Al. De Bassini (R.) T. Noto (Ao.) G.
                                         Zambellini (Ra.)

MEXICO
Guadalajara   Degollado    July  7, 1881 A. Peralta (A.)

Mexico City   Nacional     Sep.  1, 1877 A.  Peralta  (A.)  F.  Natali-Testa
                                         (Am.)  A.  Celada  (R.)  G.  Villani
                                         (Ao.) E. Barberat (Ra.)

MONACO
Monte Carlo    Salle        Mar. 11, 1884 F. Devries (A.)   G. Novelli (Am.) W.
               Garnier                    Mierzwinski (R.) F. Pandolfini (Ao.)
                                          A. Castelmary (Ra.) R. Accursi cond.


NETHERLANDS
Amsterdam      Palais v.    Oct. 15, 1886 A. Mielke (A.) Jaide (Am.) Ucko (R.)
               Volksvligt                 von Bengardt (Ao.) C. Behrens (Ra.)
                                          (in Ger.)

               Jan. 23, 1898 G. Carnielli (A.) I. Sambo (Am.) L.
                                          Colazza (R.)  G. Lunardi (Ao.)  F.
                                          Spangher (Ra.) (in It.)

               Stads        Dec.  7, 1886 Millie  (A.)  Zerder  (Am.)  Lourent
                                          (R.) Tricot (Ao.) (in Fr.)

                            Dec. 19, 1903 (in Dut.)

Den Haag       Royal        Jan. 23, 1878 Linse  (A.)  Defossez  (Am.)  Cholti
                                          (R.) Brégal (Ao.) Dartes (Ra.) (in
                                          Fr.)

               Gebouw v.    Jan. 18, 1898 Guasconi (A.) I. Sambo (Am.)  L. Co-
               Kunst                      lazza (R.) G. Lunardi (Ao.) F. Span-
                                          gher (Ra.) (in It.)

Rotterdam      Groote            1886 (in Ger.)

                            Jan. 29, 1898 (in It.)


NEW ZEALAND
Auckland       Th. Royal    Feb.  8, 1878 A. Guadagnini (A.) M. Venosta (Am.)
                                          E. Camera (R.) G. Gambetti (Ao.) G.
                                          Cesari (Ra.)

Dunedin        Th. Royal    Nov. 19, 1877 A. Guadagnini (A.) M. Venosta (Am.)
                                          E. Camera (R.) G. Gambetti (Ao.) G.
                                          Cesari (Ra.)

Wellington     Th. Royal    Jan. 11, 1878 A. Guadagnini (A.) M. Venosta (Am.)
                                          E. Camera (R.) G. Gambetti (Ao.) G.
                                          Cesari (Ra.)


NORWAY
Oslo           Royal        Nov.  6, 1909 (in Norw.)


PANAMA
Panama City    Nacional     Oct. 22, 1908 L. De Benedetto (A.) Milesi (Am.) A.
                                          Scalabrini (R.)  G.  Pimazzoni (Ao.)
                                          P. Wulmann (Ra.)


PERU
Lima           Politeama    Nov. 27, 1897 A. Barducci (A.) G. Prandi (Am.) G.
                                          Badarocco (R.)


PHILIPPINES
Manila         Del Tondo    Apr. 17, 1888 M. Balzofiore (A.) Knubel (Am.) L.
                                          Balzofiore (R.) A. Falciai (Ao.) V.
                                          Pozzi-Camola (Ra.)


POLAND
Lwov           Szarbek      Oct. 26, 1876 A. Gabbi (A.) Dobrzanska (Am.) Zo-
                                          kuski (R.)

Warsaw          Wielki        Nov. 23, 1875 C. De Cepeda (A.) Doniakowska (Am.)
                                            F. Cazeaux (R.) A. Souvestre (Ao.)
                                            E. Gasperini (Ra.) C. Trombini cond.
                                            (in It.)

PORTUGAL
Lisbon          Sao Carlos    Feb.  6, 1878 C. De Cepeda (A.) M. Biancolini
                                            (Am.) L. Bolis (R.) G. Aldighieri
                                            (Ao.) T. Costa (Ra.) R. Kuon cond.

Oporto          Sao Joao      May 30, 1880 R. Pantaleoni (A.) M. Biancolini
                                            (Am.) A. Celada (R.) E. Pogliani
                                            (Ao.) I. Sbordoni (Ra.)

PUERTO RICO
Ponce           La Perla      Feb.  9, 1887 M. Bulli-Paoli (A.) G. Tiozzo (Am.)
                                            G. Migliori (R.) F. Cavazza (Ao.) G.
                                            B. Del Fabbro (Ra.) R. Bracale cond.

San Juan        Municipal     Mar. 24, 1887 M. Bulli-Paoli (A.) G. Tiozzo (Am.)
                                            G. Migliori (R.) F. Cavazza (Ao.) N.
                                            Pozzi (Ra.) R. Bracale cond.

ROMANIA
Bucharest       Nacional      Nov.  8, 1876 A. Spaak (A.) V. Passigli (Am.) T.
                                            De Azula (Am.) E. Carnili (Ao.) A.
                                            Fiorini (Ra.)

                              Sep.     1920 (in Rum.)

RUSSIA
Moscow          Bolshoi       Jan.  1, 1876 T. Stolz (A.) D. Artôt (Am.) A. Ma-
                                            rin (R.) M. Padilla (Ao.) J. Jamet
                                            (Ra.) E. Bevignani cond. (in It.)

Odessa          Municipal     Jan.  2? 1881 A. Fossa (A.) A. Pascalis (Am.) O.
                                            Cappelletti (R.) G. Nolli (Ao.) P.
                                            Purarelli (Ra.) (in It.)

St.             Imperial      Dec.  1, 1875 T. Stolz (A.) A. L. Cary (Am.) E.
  Petersburg                                Nicolini (R.) A. Cotogni (Ao.) G.
                                            Capponi (Ra.) J. Goula cond. (in
                                            It.)

                Mariensky     Apr. 12, 1877 Menshikoff (A.) Kamensky (Am.) Or-
                                            loff (R.) Korstoff (Ao.) Strawinsky
                                            (Ra.) (in Russ.)

Tbilisi         Imperial      Jan. 18, 1877 C. Scarati-Bresciani (A.) C. Dory
                                            (Am.) T. Villa (R.) S. Sparapani
                                            (Ao.) Saccardi (Ra.) D. Antonietti
                                            cond. (in It.)

SINGAPORE
Singapore       Palladium     June  8, 1915 F. Impallomeni (A.) L. Da Gradi (R.)

SOUTH AFRICA
Capetown        Op. House     Feb. 29, 1912 A. Nicholls (A.) E. Thornton (Am.)
                                            J. Coates (R.) (in Eng.)

Johannesburg    Standard      Mar.  8, 1912 J. Brola (A.) E. Thornton (Am) J.
                                            Coates (R.) W. J. Samuell (Ao.) A.
                                            Hinckley (Ra.) T. Voghera cond. (in
                                            Eng.)

SPAIN
Alicante        Principal    Mar. 15, 1882 I. Kottas (A.) G. Casali-Bavagnoli
                                          (Am.) G. Ugolini (R.) E. Laban (Ao.)

Barcelona       Principal    Apr. 16, 1876 T. Singer (A.) R. Vercolini-Tay
                                          (Am.) L. Abrugnedo (R.) C. Boccolini
                                          (Ao.) E. Gasperini (Ra.) J. Goula
                                          cond.

                Liceo        Feb. 25, 1877 C. De Cepeda (A.) R. Vercolini-Tay
                                          (Am.) F. Tamagno (R.) M. Ciapini
                                          (Ao.) F. Uetam (Ra.) J. Baudouin
                                          cond.

Bilbao          Viejo        June  7, 1881 A. Conti-Foroni (A.) E. Treves (Am.)
                                          T. Fenaroli (R.) E. Laban (Ao.) C.
                                          Ulloa (Ra.) N. Guerrera cond.

Madrid          Real         Dec. 12, 1874 A. Fossa (A.) L. Vanda-Miller (Am.)
                                          E. Tamberlick (R.) C. Boccolini
                                          (Ao.) J. David (Ra.) J. Skoczdopole
                                          cond.

Malaga          Cervantes    Dec. 22, 1882 M. Mantilla (A.) E. Tamberlick (R.)
                                          A. Verdini (Ao.) C. Bosoni cond.

Seville         San          Apr. 30, 1875 A. Fossa (A.) M. Cortes (Am.) E.
                Fernando                   Tamberlick (R.) C. Boccolini (Ao.)
                                          A. Padovani (Ra.) J. Skoczdopole
                                          cond.

Valencia        Principal    June 22, 1876 T. Singer (A.) R. Vercolini-Tay
                                          (Am.) L. Abrugnedo (R.) S. Athos-
                                          Caldani (Ao.) F. Uetam (Ra.) J.
                                          Goula cond.

Valladolid      Calderon     Apr. 19, 1882 M. Mantilla (A.) I. Lumley (Am.) E.
                                          Tamberlick (R.) A. Verdini (Ao.)

Zaragozza       Principal    May  11, 1881 A. Conti-Foroni (A.) E. Treves (Am.)
                                          T. Fenaroli (R.) E. Laban (Ao.) F.
                                          Uetam (Ra.) N. Guerrera cond.

SWEDEN
Stockholm       Royal        Feb. 16, 1880 S. Ek (A.) D. Niehoff (Am.) O. Ar-
                                          noldson (R.) C. F. Lundqvist (Ao.)
                                          H. Häkansson (Ra.)

SWITZERLAND
Basel           Stadt        Sep. 28, 1888 (in Ger.)

Geneva          Grand        Mar. 15, 1881 J. Fouquet (A.) Strassi (Am.) Warot
                                          (R.) Couturier (Ao.) Guillabert
                                          (Ra.) (in Fr.)

Lugano          Apollo       Apr. 15, 1922 M. Aicardi (A.) M. Valverde (Am.) A.
                                          Baroggi (R.) G. Lazzarini (Ao.) G.
                                          Olaizola (Ra.) U. Tansini cond.

Zürich          Stadt        Mar.  5, 1883 (in Ger.)

                             May  23, 1916 I. Abry (A.) E. Rubadi (Am.) E.
                                          Arensen (R.) E. Giraldoni (Ao.) G.
                                          Armani cond. (in It.)

TURKEY
| | | | |
|---|---|---|---|
| Constanti-<br>nople | Petit<br>Champs | Oct. 5, 1882 | N. Martinez (A.) V. Galimberti (Am.) J. Manfrini (R.) R. De Giorgio (Ao.) N. Giommi (Ra.) F. Micci-Labruna cond. (in It.) |
| Smyrna | Alhambra | July 19, 1881 | Bottarelli (A.) De Marchi (Am.) A. Brunetti (R.) M. Danisi (Ao.) N. Giommi (Ra.) F. Micci-Labruna cond. (in It.) |

UNITED STATES
| | | | |
|---|---|---|---|
| Baltimore | Ac. of Mus. | Jan. 15, 1875 | A. Maresi (A.) A. L. Cary (Am.) C. Carpi (R.) G. Del Puente (Ao.) A. Fiorini (Ra.) E. Muzio cond. (in It.) |
| | | Feb. 26, 1881 | O. Torriani (A.) L. Annandale (Am.) A. Byron (R.) W. Carleton (Ao.) G. Conly (Ra.) (in Eng.) |
| Boston | Boston Th. | Feb. 5, 1874 | O. Torriani (A.) A. L. Cary (Am.) I. Campanini (R.) G. Del Puente (Ao.) R. Nannetti (Ra.) E. Muzio cond. (in It.) |
| | Globe | Nov. 8, 1880 | M. Roze (A.) S. Barton (Am.) A. Byron (R.) W. Carleton (Ao.) G. Conly (Ra.) (in Eng.) |
| Brooklyn | Ac. of Mus. | Mar. 12, 1874 | O. Torriani (A.) A. L. Cary (Am.) I. Campanini (R.) E. Muzio cond. |
| Chicago | McVicker's | Jan. 16, 1874 | O. Torriani (A.) A. L. Cary (Am.) I. Campanini (R.) G. Del Puente (Ao.) R. Nannetti (Ra.) E. Muzio cond. |
| | Haverly's | Dec. 8, 1880 | M. Roze (A.) S. Barton (Am.) A. Byron (R.) W. Carleton (Ao.) G. Conly (Ra.) (in Eng.) |
| | Auditorium | Dec. 16, 1889 | L. Nordica (A.) H. Synnerberg (Am.) F. Tamagno (R.) N Zardo (Ao.) F. Novara (Ra.) L. Arditi cond. |
| | Lyric | Nov. 1, 1855 | R. Tebaldi (A.) A. Varnay (Am.) D. Antonioli (R.) T. Gobbi (Ao.) W. Wildermann (Ra.) T. Serafin cond. |
| Cincinnati | Pike's | May 20, 1874 | A. Maresi (A.) A. L. Cary (Am.) V. Capoul (R.) G. Del Puente (Ao.) R. Nannetti (Ra.) E. Muzio cond. |
| | | Dec. 27, 1880 | M. Roze (A.) S. Barton (Am.) A. Byron (R.) W. Carleton (Ao.) G. Conly (Ra.) (in Eng.) |
| | Opera | July 17, 1921 | J. Barondess (A.) H. Wakefield (Am.) R. Boscacci (R.) G. Evans (Ao.) I. Picchi (Ra.) R. Lyford cond. |
| Cleveland | Euclid Ave. | Feb. 13, 1880 | E. Ambre (A.) A. L. Cary (Am.) I. Campanini (R.) A. Faentini-Galassi (Ao.) C. Behrens (Ra.) (in It.) |

|  |  |  |  |
|---|---|---|---|
|  | Ac. of Mus. | Apr. 28, 1881 | O. Torriani (A.) S. Barton (Am.) A. Byron (R.) L. G. Gottschalk (Ao.) G. Conly (Ra.) (in Eng.) |
| Dallas | Op. House | Jan. 24, 1910 | E. Adaberto (A.) D. Frau (Am.) A. Scalabrini (R.) |
|  | Opera | Nov. 1, 1969 | E. Suliotis (A.) S. Verrett (Am.) A. Zambon (R.) G. Guelfi (Ao.) L. Roni (Ra.) N. Rescigno cond. |
| Detroit | Whitney's | Mar. 12, 1879 | C. L. Kellogg (A.) A. L. Cary (Am.) C. Adams (R.) A. Pantaleoni (Ao.) S. Behrens cond. |
| Galveston | Tremont | Feb. 2, 1881 | O. Torriani (A.) L. Annandale (Am.) A. Byron (R.) W. Carleton (Ao.) (in Eng.) |
| Houston | Auditorium | Oct. 30, 1919 | R. Raisa (A.) L. Eubanks (Am.) A. Dolci (R.) G. Rimini (Ao.) V. Lazzari (Ra.) V. De Angelis cond. |
|  | Grand Opera | Jan. 31, 1958 | M. Novich (A.) N. Rankin (Am.) R. Cassilly (R.) C. Bardelli (Ao.) Y. Sze (Ra.) W. Herbert cond. |
| Indianapolis | Grand | Feb. 25, 1878 | C. L. Kellogg (A.) A. L. Cary (Am.) J. Graff (R.) G. Verdi (Ao.) G. Conly (Ra.) S. Behrens cond. (in It.) |
|  | Dickson's | Dec. 21, 1880 | M. Roze (A.) S. Barton (Am.) A. Byron (R.) G. Conly (Ra.) (in Eng.) |
| Kansas City | Coates | Feb. 9, 1881 | M. Roze (A.) L. Annandale (Am.) A. Byron (R.) W. Carleton (Ao.) G. Conly (Ra.) (in Eng.) |
| Los Angeles | Pavillion | May 19, 1887 | B. Pierson (A.) C. Van Zanten (Am.) W. Candidus (R.) W. Ludwig (Ao.) Stoddard (Ra.) (in Eng.) |
|  | Auditorium | Nov. 8, 1906 | E. Adaberto (A.) M. Campofiore (Am.) F. D'Ottavi (R.) C. Bacchetta (Ao.) V. Lombardi (Ra.) (in It.) |
| Louisville | Op. House | Dec. 24, 1880 | O. Torriani (A.) S. Barton (Am.) A. Byron (R.) W. Carleton (Ao.) (in Eng.) |
| Milwaukee | Ac. of Mus. | Jan. 27, 1874 | O. Torriani (A.) A. L. Cary (Am.) I. Campanini (R.) G. Del Puente (Ao.) R. Nannetti (Ra.) E. Muzio cond. (in It.) |
|  | Op. House | Apr. 7, 1881 | O. Torriani (A.) (in Eng.) |
| New Orleans | Opéra | Dec. 5, 1879 | T. Singer (A.) A. De Belocca (Am.) R. Petrovich (R.) E. Storti (Ao.) A. Castelmary (Ra.) (in It.) |
|  | St. Charles | Jan. 26, 1881 | M. Roze (A.) L. Annandale (Am.) A. Byron (R.) W. Carleton (Ao.) G. Conly (Ra.) (in Eng.) |

New York       Ac. of Mus. Nov. 26, 1873 O. Torriani (A.) A. L. Cary (Am.) I.
                                         Campanini (R.) V. Maurel (Ao.) R.
                                         Nannetti (Ra.) E. Muzio cond.

               Fifth Ave.  Mar.  9, 1881 O. Torriani (A.) L. Annandale (Am.)
                                         A. Byron (R.) W. Carleton (Ao.) G.
                                         Conly (Ra.) (in Eng.)

               Metro-      Nov. 12, 1886 T. Herbert-Förster (A.) M. Brandt
               politan                   (Am.) C. Zobel (R.) A. Robinson
                                         (Ao.) E. Fischer (Ra.) A. Seidl
                                         cond. (in Ger.)

                           Dec. 28, 1891 L. Lehmann (A.) G. Ravogli (Am.) J.
                                         De Reszke (R.) A. Magini-Coletti
                                         (Ao.) E. Serbolini (Ra.) L. Saar
                                         cond. (in It.)

Philadelphia  Ac. of Mus. Dec. 12, 1873 A. Maresi (A.) A. L. Cary (Am.) I.
                                         Campanini (R.) V. Maurel (Ao.) R.
                                         Nannetti (Ra.) E. Muzio cond.

               Chestnut    Nov. 22, 1880 M. Roze (A.) S. Barton (Am.) A. By-
               Street                    ron (R.) W. Carleton (Ao.) G. Conly
                                         (Ra.) (in Eng.)

Pittsburgh     Libr. Hall  Jan. 30, 1878 C. L. Kellogg (A.) A. L. Cary (Am.)
                                         G. Graff (R.) G. Verdi (Ao.) G. Con-
                                         ly (Ra.) (in Eng.)

St. Louis      De Bar's    Jan.  9, 1874 O. Torriani (A.) A. L. Cary (Am.) I.
                                         Campanini (R.) G. Del Puente (Ao.)
                                         R. Nannetti (Ra.) E. Muzio cond.

               Grand       Jan.  3, 1881 M. Roze (A.) L. Annandale (Am.) A.
                                         Byron (R.) W. Carleton (Ao.) G. Con-
                                         ly (Ra.)

San Francisco Baldwin      Oct. 17, 1877 C. L. Kellogg (A.) A. L. Cary (Am.)
                                         J. Graff (R.) G. Verdi (Ao.) G. Con-
                                         ly (Ra.) S. Behrens cond. (in It.)

               Grand       Apr. 19, 1887 B. Pierson (A.) C. Van Zanten (Am.)
                                         W. Candidus (R.) W. Ludwig (Ao.) M.
                                         Whitney (Ra.) (in Eng.)

               Opera       Oct.  3, 1925 C. Muzio (A.) M. D'Alvarez (Am.) A.
                                         Cortis (R.) C. Formichi (Ao.) M.
                                         Journet (Ra.) G. Merola cond.

Washington     National    Apr. 10, 1874 O. Torriani (A.) A. L. Cary (Am.) I.
                                         Campanini (R.) G. Del Puente (Ao.)
                                         R. Nannetti (Ra.) E. Muzio cond.

URUGUAY
Montevideo     Solis       July 14, 1877 V. Potentini (A.) Felix (Am.) E.
                                         Lestellier (R.) L. Lalloni (Ao.) G.
                                         Monti (Ra.) O. Bimboni cond.

VENEZUELA
Caracas        Municipal   Mar. 10, 1882 A. Conti-Foroni (A.) R. Cavalleri
                                         (Am.) L. Abrugnedo (R.) I. De Anna
                                         (Ao.) R. D'Ottavi (Ra.)

27. OTELLO-*Dramma lirico* in four acts
Milan-Teatro alla Scala-Feb. 5, 1887
Libretto by Arrigo Boito

| | |
|---|---|
| Desdemona (D.) | Romilda Pantaleoni sop. |
| Otello (O.) | Francesco Tamagno ten. |
| Iago (I.) | Victor Maurel bar. |
| Emilia | Ginevra Petrovich mez. |
| Cassio | Giovanni Paroli ten. |
| Rodrigo | Vincenzo Fornari ten. |
| Lodovico | Francesco Navarini bass |
| Montano | Napoleone Limonta bass |
| Un Araldo | Angelo Lagomarsino bass |
| | |
| Conductor | Franco Faccio |
| Director | Giuseppe Verdi |

OTHER PREMIERES

ARGENTINA
Buenos Aires  Politeama   June 12, 1888 R. Pantaleoni (D.) R. Stagno (O.) D.
                                        Menotti (I.) C. Campanini cond.

              Ant. Colón  July  6, 1888 M.  Kupfer-Berger  (D.)  F.  Tamagno
                                        (O.) J. Devoyod (I.) M. Mancinelli
                                        cond.

              Colón       July  1, 1908 M.  Farneti  (D.)  A.  Paoli  (O.)  T.
                                        Ruffo (I.) L. Mancinelli cond.

Cordoba       Progresso   July  6? 1889 L. Cerne (D.) E. Galli (O.) A. Gnac-
                                        carini (I.)

Rosario       Olimpo      June 12? 1889 L. Cerne (D.) E. Galli (O.) A. Gnac-
                                        carini (I.)

AUSTRALIA
Melbourne     Her         Nov. 23, 1901 C.  De Vere Sapio  (D.)  V.  Larizza
              Majesty's                 (O.) I. Bozzoli (I.) R. Hazon cond.

Sydney        Her         Sep.  7, 1901 D. Bassich (D.)  V. Larizza (O.)  F.
              Majesty's                 Cattadori (I.) R. Hazon cond.

AUSTRIA
Graz          Stadt       Nov.  6, 1900 (in Ger.)

                          June 16, 1904 M.  Winternitz-Dorda  (D.)  A.  Paoli
                                        (O.) F. M. Bonini (I.) (in It.)

Linz          Landes      Mar. 31, 1903 (in Ger.)

Vienna        Hofoper     Mar. 14, 1888 A. Schläger (D.) H. Winkelmann (O.)
                                        T. Reichmann (I.) (in Ger.)

                          Oct. 22, 1909 L.  Weidt  (D.)  L.  Slezak  (O.)  L.
                                        Demuth (I.) (in It.)

BELGIUM
Antwerp       Royal       July 26? 1905 Dumedi   (D.)   N.   Zerola   (O.)   S.
                                        Arrighetti (I.) (in It.)

Brussels        Monnaie       Feb. 22, 1902 C. Friché (D.) I. De la Tour (O.) H.
                                            Albers (I.) (in Fr.)

Ghent           Grand         Feb. 10, 1909 E. Adaberto (D.) L. De Colli (O.) S.
                                            Arrighetti (I.) (in It.)

BRAZIL
Rio de          Pedro II      Aug. 24, 1889 T. Singer (D.) F. Cardinali (O.) F.
Janeiro                                     Bartolomasi (I.) R. Bonicioli cond.

                Municipal     Sep. 17, 1919 G. Dalla Rizza (D.) A. Paoli (O.) L.
                                            Montesanto (I.) V. Bellezza cond.

Sao Paulo       Sao José      Nov.  6, 1889 M. Peri (D.) F. Cardinali (O.) F.
                                            Bartolomasi (I.)

                Municipal     July     1933 C. Gomes (D.) E. Reis e Silva (O.)
                                            A. Lima (I.)

BULGARIA
Sofia           Alhambra      Sep.  2? 1906 M. Pizzagalli (D.) A. Guasco (O.) D.
                                            Carnevali (I.) (in It.)

                National      May  17, 1922 (in Bulg.)

CANADA
Edmonton        Opera         Nov. 27, 1980 G. Cruz-Romo (D.) R. Cassilly (O.)
                                            R. Edwards (I.) A. Guadagno cond.

Montreal        His           Nov.  3, 1904 G. Rennyson (D.) J. Sheehan (O.) W.
                Majesty's                   Goff (I.) (in Eng.)

                              Jan.  1, 1914 L. Villani (D.) L. Slezak (O.) J.
                                            Segura-Tallien (I.) (in It.)

Toronto         Royal         Oct.     1960 M. Des Jardins (D.) N. Harper (O.)
                Alexandra                   L. Quilico (I.)

Vancouver       Opera         Aug.  1, 1981 C. Carson (D.) W. Johns (O.) R. Ed-
                                            wards (I.) A. Guadagno cond.

Winnipeg        Opera         Apr.     1983 W. Johns (O.) R. Edwards (I.)

CHILE
Santiago        Municipal     Sep.  1, 1894 T. Maragliano (D.) A. Querzé (O.) G.
                                            Pacini (I.)

Valparaiso      Victoria      Oct. 31, 1894 T. Maragliano (D.) A. Querzé (O.) G.
                                            Pacini (I.)

CHINA
Shanghai        Victoria      Jan. 20, 1915 E. Gonsalez (D.) V. Artino (O.) I.
                                            Belloni (I.)

COLOMBIA
Bogota          Municipal     July 19, 1893

CUBA
Havana          Tacon         Jan. 10, 1889 A. Gini-Pizzorni (D.) C. Pizzorni
                                            (O.) E. Pogliani (I.)

CZECHOSLOVAKIA
Bratislava      National      Sep. 10, 1925 Simánová (D.) Hübner (O.) Z. Otava
                                            (I.) (in Czech)

Brno            Stadt           Mar. 10, 1888 S. Kollar (D.) K. Zobel (O.) A.
                                              Fischer (I.) (in Ger.)

Prag            National        Jan. 7, 1888 B. Foerster-Lauterer (D.) W. Flor-
                                             jansky (O.) B. Benoni (I.) (in
                                             Czech)

                Neues           Dec. 20, 1911 (in Ger.)
                Deutsches

DENMARK
Copenhagen      Royal           Apr. 20, 1898 E. Dons (D.) Bruns (O.) N. J. Simon-
                                              sen (I.)

EGYPT
Alexandria      Zizinia         Jan.    1895 G. Carnielli (D.) V. Larizza (O.) S.
                                             Vinci (I.)

Cairo           Khedivial       Nov. 20, 1897 V. Mendioroz (D.) A. Angioletti (O.)
                                              D. Menotti (I.)

FINLAND
Helsinki        Societets       Feb. 12, 1897 O. Delle Fornaci (O.)

FRANCE
Lyon            Grand           July 11, 1914 F. Solari (D.) I. Righi-Briani (O.)
                                              E. Faticanti (I.) (in It.)

Marseille       Grand           Mar. 9, 1911 Garchery (D.) Lemaire (O.) Roselli
                                             (I.) (in Fr.)

Nice            Casino          Feb. 19, 1891 A. Musiani (D.) F. Tamagno (O.) V.
                                              Maurel (I.) (in It.)

                Municipal       Mar. 16, 1896 F. Strakosch (D.) F. Tamagno (O.) P.
                                              Ceste (I.)

Paris           Opéra           Oct. 10, 1894 R. Caron (D.) A. Saleza (O.) V.
                                              Maurel (I.) P. Taffanell cond. G.
                                              Verdi dir. (in Fr.)

                                Apr. 13, 1897 R. Caron (D.) F. Tamagno (O.) F.
                                              Delmas (I.) (in It.)

Rouen           des Arts        Feb. 1, 1895 Bonvoisin (D.) Soubeyran (O.) Illy
                                             (I.) (in Fr.)

GERMANY
Berlin          Hofoper         Feb. 1, 1890 E. Leisinger (D.) E. Sylva (O.) P.
                                             Bulss (I.) J. Sucher cond. (in Ger.)

                Kroll           May 24, 1892 M. De Macchi (D.) F. Signorini (O.)
                                             G. M. Sammarco (I.) (in It.)

                Deutsche        Sep. 1, 1962 R. Tebaldi (D.) W. Dooley (I.) G.
                                             Patané cond.

Braunschweig    Hoftheater      Feb. 18, 1900 (in Ger.)

Breslau         Stadt           Feb. 20, 1893 K. Rosen (D.) M. Schlaffenberg (O.)
                                              K. Somer (I.) (in Ger.)

Cologne         Stadt           Apr. 2, 1888 Röthgen (D.) A. von Bandrowski (O.)
                                             K. Mayer (I.) Kiessel cond.

Darmstadt     Stadt        Nov. 14, 1915 (in Ger.)

Dresden       Hoftheater   Nov. 13, 1898 (in Ger.)

Frankfurt     Stadt        Sep. 29, 1888 A. Jäger (D.) de Grach (O.) Heine
                                         (I.) Dessoff cond. (in Ger.)

Hamburg       Stadt        Jan. 31, 1888 R. Sucher (D.) A. Stritt (O.) F.
                                         Lissmann (I.) J. Sucher cond. (in
                                         Ger.)

Hannover      Hoftheater   Apr. 19, 1890 (in Ger.)

Kassel        Hoftheater   Apr. 30, 1908 (in Ger.)

Leipzig       Stadt        Mar. 20, 1891 (in Ger.)

Munich        Hoftheater   Feb.  5, 1888 P. Schöller (D.) H. Vogl (O.) E. Gu-
                                         ra (I.)

Nürnberg      Stadt        Dec. 26, 1897 (in Ger.)

Stuttgart     Hoftheater   Oct. 31, 1897 (in Ger.)

Weimar        Hoftheater   Mar.  8, 1908 (in Ger.)

GREAT BRITAIN
Belfast       Th. Royal    Sep. 15, 1893 M. Duma (D.) B. M'Guckin (O.) A.
                                         Marsh (I.) C. Jacquinot cond. (in
                                         Eng.)

Birmingham    Th. Royal    May 31, 1893 Z. De Lussan (D.) B. M'Guckin (O.)
                                         A. Marsh (I.) (in Eng.)

Bristol       Prince's     Oct. 13, 1893 B. M'Guckin (O.)

Edinburgh     Lyceum       Nov. 29, 1892 Z. De Lussan (D.) B. M'Guckin (O.)
                                         A. Marsh (I.) (in Eng.)

Glasgow       Th. Royal    Nov. 15, 1892 Z. De Lussan (D.) B. M'Guckin (O.)
                                         A. Marsh (I.) (in Eng.)

Leeds         Grand        Nov.  5, 1892 Z. De Lussan (D.) B. M'Guckin (O.)
                                         A. Marsh (I.) (in Eng.)

Liverpool     Royal Court  Jan. 24, 1893 Z. De Lussan (D.) B. M'Guckin (O.)
                                         A. Marsh (I.) E. Goossens cond. (in
                                         Eng.)

London        Lyceum       July  5, 1889 A. Cataneo (D.) F. Tamagno (O.) V.
                                         Maurel (I.) F. Faccio cond.

              Covent       July 15, 1891 E. Albani (D.)  J. De Reszke (O.) V.
              Garden                      Maurel (I.) L. Mancinelli cond.

Manchester    Prince's     Oct.  8, 1892 Z. De Lussan (D.) B. M'Guckin (O.)
                                         A. Marsh (I.) (in Eng.)

GREECE
Athens        Falero       Aug.     1898 F. Gambardella (O.) (Production
                                         announced, unconfirmed)

Corfu         San Giacomo  Oct. 24, 1892 N. Mazzi (D.) A. Baggetto (O.) G.
                                         Ferrari (I.)

GUATEMALA
Guatemala      Colón        Mar.        1893 B. D'Aponte (D.) F. Gambardella (O.)
City                                         S. Carobbi (I.)

HONG KONG
Hong Kong      Th. Royal    Feb. 23, 1915 E. Gonsalez (D.) V. Artino (O.) I.
                                             Belloni (I.)

HUNGARY
Budapest       Operaház     Dec.  8, 1887 G. Bellincioni (D.) G. Perotti (O.)
                                           L. Odry (I.)

INDIA
Calcutta       Grand        Feb. 18, 1916 E. Gonsalez (D.) L. Da Gradi (O.) I.
                                           Belloni (I.) G. Gonsalez cond.

INDONESIA
Batavia        Stads        June 25, 1915 E. Gonsalez (D.) V. Artino (O.) I.
                                           Belloni (I.)

IRELAND
Dublin         Gaiety       Sep.  2, 1893 M. Duma (D.) B. M'Guckin (O.) A.
                                           Marsh (I.) (in Eng.)

ISRAEL
Jerusalem                   Apr. 27, 1925 (in Heb.)

ITALY
Alessandria    Municipale   May  27? 1893 V. Mendioroz (D.) G. B. De Negri
                                           (O.) A. Gnaccarini (I.) A. Pomè
                                           cond.

Ancona         Muse         Nov.  8, 1908 G. Baldassare-Tedeschi (D.) O. Delle
                                           Fornaci (O.) A. Gregoretti (I.) F.
                                           Guerrieri cond.

Bari           Piccinni     Jan.        1898 L. Cerne (D.) A. Ceppi (O.) M. De
                                             Padova (I.)

               Petruzzelli July 31, 1904 E. Corsi (D.) F. Cardinali (O.) G.
                                           Pacini (I.) V. Lombardi cond.

Bergamo        Donizetti    Aug. 23, 1890 L. Cerne (D.) M. Mariacher (O.) E.
                                           Camera (I.) N. Bassi cond.

Bologna        Comunale     Oct. 27, 1888 E. Borghi-Mamo (D.) G. Oxilia (O.)
                                           V. Maurel (I.) F. Faccio cond.

Brescia        Grande       Aug. 10, 1887 A. Gabbi (D.) G. Oxilia (O.) P. Lhé-
                                           rie (I.) F. Faccio cond.

Cagliari       Civico       Dec. 25, 1898 A. Cruz (D.) P. Nobilini (O.) M. De
                                           Padova (I.) L. Molajoli cond.

Catania        Bellini      July 15? 1896 E. Zilli (D.) F. Avedano (O.) D. Me-
                                           notti (I.) O. Anselmi cond.

Chieti         Marrucino    May   3, 1900 E. Angelini (D.) E. Durot (O.) A.
                                           Arcangeli (I.) G. Armani cond.

Cremona        Concordia    Dec. 25, 1892 G. Vitali-Augusti (D.) F. Runcio
                                           (O.) E. Camera (I.) N. Bassi cond.

Verdi

Fermo        Aquila      Aug. 14, 1888 V. Mendioroz (D.)  G.  B.  De Negri
                                       (O.)  L.  Fumagalli  (I.)  G.  Cimini
                                       cond.

Ferrara      Comunale    Dec. 22? 1894 O. Litvinoff (D.) G. Piccaluga (O.)
                                       A.  Magini-Coletti  (I.)  A.  Vigna
                                       cond.

Fiume        Comunale    Apr. 10? 1893 F. Strakosch (D.)  G.  B.  De Negri
                                       (O.)  P.  Lhérie  (I.)

Florence     Pagliano    Apr. 24, 1888 A.  Gabbi  (D.)  G.  Oxilia  (O.)  G.
                                       Kaschmann (I.) E. Usiglio cond.

             Pergola     Dec. 26, 1903 F.  Labia  (D.)  A.  Paoli  (O.)  M.
                                       Hédiger (I.) G. Gialdini cond.

Forli        Comunale    Dec.     1913 I. Rinolfi (D.) I. Righi-Briani (O.)
                                       E. Faticanti (I.) A. Toni cond.

Genoa        Carlo       Nov. 24, 1888 V. Mendioroz (D.)  G.  B.  De Negri
             Felice                    (O.)  S.  Sparapani  (I.)  G.  Cimini
                                       cond.

Livorno      Avvalorati  Mar.     1899 E. Corsi (E.) E. Galli (O.) T. Wil-
                                       mant (I.)

Lucca        Giglio      Sep.  2, 1889 M.  Baux  (D.)  E.  Durot  (O.)  E. Du-
                                       friche (I.) E. Usiglio cond.

Lugo         Rossini     Aug.?    1901 G.  De Michelis  (D.)  O.  Cosentino
                                       (O.)  D.  Menotti  (I.)  V.  M.  Vanzo
                                       cond.

Mantua       Sociale     Dec. 26? 1890 R. Giovannoni-Zacchi (D.) F. Gianni-
                                       ni (O.) E. Camera (I.) G. Pomè Penna
                                       cond.

Messina      Vittorio    Nov. 17, 1888 L. Cerne (D.)  F. Giannini  (O.)  L.
             Emanuele                  Fumagalli (I.) C. Rossi cond.

Modena       Municipale  Jan. 11, 1888 I. Meyer (D.) E. Durot (O.) S. Spa-
                                       rapani (I.) E. Usiglio cond.

Naples       San Carlo   Feb.  4, 1888 A.  Gabbi  (D.)  F.  Tamagno  (O.)  G.
                                       Kaschmann (I.) G. Gialdini cond.

Padua        Verdi       June 12, 1890 E.  Zilli  (D.)  A.  Brogi  (O.)  D.
                                       Menotti (I.)

Palermo      Politeama   Dec. 23, 1888 T. Angeloni (D.) I. Warmouth (O.) G.
                                       Bianchi (I.) N. Bassi cond.

Parma        Regio       Sep. 13, 1887 A. Gabbi (D.) G. Oxilia (O.) P. Lhé-
                                       rie (I.) F. Faccio cond.

Piacenza     Municipale  Dec. 26? 1893 G. Cesareo (D.) F. Avedano (O.) G.
                                       Salassa (I.) P. Bandini cond.

Pisa         Verdi       Feb.     1894 E.  Corsi  (D.)  F.  Avedano  (O.)  G.
                                       Salassi (I.) A. Toscanini cond.

Ravenna      Alighieri   May 14, 1892 C.  Ferrani  (D.)  E.  Durot  (O.)  R.
                                       Blanchart (I.) V. M. Vanzo cond.

Reggio Emilia Municipale Dec. 25, 1903 L. Siebanech (D.) E. Galli (O.) G. Albinolo (I.) P. Cimini cond.

Rome          Costanzi     Apr. 17, 1887 A. Gabbi (D.) F. Tamagno (O.) V. Maurel (I.) F. Faccio cond.

Rovigo        Sociale      Oct. 17, 1897 F. Gregagnin (D.) O. Cosentino (O.) F. Aldobrandi (I.) A. Palmintieri cond.

Trento        Sociale      June 9, 1888 V. Mendioroz (D.) F. Giannini (O.) L. Fumagalli (I.) G. Cimini cond.

Treviso       Sociale      Oct. 13, 1888 V. Mendioroz (D.) G. B. De Negri (O.) L. Fumagalli (I.) G. Cimini cond.

Trieste       Verdi        Mar. 25, 1889 R. Giovannoni-Zacchi (D.) G. B. De Negri (O.) P. Lhérie (I.) G. Gialdini cond.

Turin         Regio        Dec. 26, 1887 E. Colonnese (D.) G. B. De Negri (O.) O. Beltrami (I.) G. Bolzoni cond.

Udine         Sociale      Aug. 10, 1889 I. Meyer (D.) A. Brogi (O.) L. Fumagalli (I.)

Venice        La Fenice    May 17, 1887 A. Gabbi (D.) F. Tamagno (O.) V. Maurel (I.) F. Faccio cond.

Verona        Filarmonico Apr. 30, 1892 R. Giovannoni-Zacchi (D.) A. Brogi (O.) D. Menotti (I.)

              Arena        Aug. 8, 1936 P. Tassinari (D.) F. Merli (O.) M. Basiola (I.) T. Serafin cond.

JAPAN
Tokyo         Imperial     Mar. 17, 1925 L. Ambroso (D.) V. Artino (O.) V. Scamuzzi (I.)

JUGOSLAVIA
Ljubljana     National     Oct. 6, 1903 (in Slov.)

Zagreb        National     Oct. 10, 1899 A. Alloro (D.) E. Cammarota (O.) B. Vulakovic (I.) N. Faller cond.

Zara          Nuovo        May       1897 E. Zilli (D.) P. Nobilini (O.) G. Tessari (I.)

LATVIA
Riga          National     May 13, 1926 (in Let.)

LITHUANIA
Kaunas        National     June 15, 1938 (in Lith.)

Vilnius       Municipal    Mar. 17, 1900 L. Montanari (D.) F. De Grandi (O.) G. Pimazzoni (I.) (in It.)

MALTA
La Valletta   Reale        Mar. 30? 1897 A. M. Rossini (D.) G. Peirani (O.) G. Lunardi (I.) A. Bovi cond.

MEXICO
Mexico City    Nacional    Nov. 18, 1887 L. Cerne (D.) F. Giannini (O.) J.
                                         Aragò (I.)[57]

                           Oct. 17, 1888 A. Gini-Pizzorni (D.) C. Pizzorni
                                         (O.) E. Pogliani (I.)

MONACO
Monte Carlo    Salle       Jan. 20, 1894 F. Saville (D.) F. Tamagno (O.) G.
               Garnier                   Soulacroix (I.) L. Jehin cond.

NETHERLANDS
Amsterdam      Park        Mar. 10, 1888 (in Dut.)

               Palais v.   Dec.  2, 1898 A. M. Rossini (D.) H. Prevost (O.)
               Volksvligt                G. Lunardi (I.) (in It.)

Den Haag       Gebouw v.   Dec. 16, 1898 Borghi (D.) H. Prevost (O.) G. Arma-
               Kunst                     ni cond. (in It.)

Rotterdam                        1889 (in Ger.)

               Groote      Dec.  3? 1898 A. M. Rossini (D.) H. Prevost (O.)
                                         G. Lunardi (I.) (in It.)

PERU
Lima           Principal   Aug. 19, 1898 A. Gabbi (D.) O. Delle Fornaci (O.)
                                         A. Moro (I.)

PHILIPPINES
Manila         Grand       Mar. 28, 1915

POLAND
Warsaw         Wielki      Oct.  3, 1893 L. Drog (D.) E. Durot (O.) Chodakow-
                                         ski (I.)

PORTUGAL
Lisbon         Sao Carlos  Mar. 23, 1889 E. Tetrazzini (D.) A. Brogi (O.) M.
                                         Battistini (I.) C. Campanini cond.

Oporto         Sao Joao    Dec. 20, 1893 S. Othon (D.) F. Cardinali (O.) A.
                                         Moro (I.)

PUERTO RICO
San Juan       Municipal   Feb.  2, 1917 J. Barondess (D.) G. Vogliotti (O.)
                                         M. Aineto (I.) I. del Castillo cond.

ROMANIA
Braila                     Jan.?    1889 G. Villa (D.) G. Gordoni (O.) E. Ga-
                                         lassi (I.) F. Micci-Labruna cond.

Bucharest      Boulevard   Aug.?    1889 G. Villa (D.) F. Guarini (I.) F.
                                         Micci-Labruna cond.

               National    Nov. 10, 1893 L. Cerne (D.) F. Signorini (O.) G.
                                         M. Sammarco (I.)

                           Dec.     1937 (in Rum.)

Galati                     Feb. 17, 1889 G. Villa (D.) G. Gordini (O.)

---

[57]. Given in a pirated version, with the orchestral score being falsified by a local
professor. The correct score was given on Oct. 17, 1888.

Iasi             Teatrul       July?     1889 G. Villa (D.)

RUSSIA
Moscow           Privé         Apr.  5? 1889 A. Soffriti (D.) N. Figner (O.) S.
                                             Sparapani (I.) (in It.)

Odessa           Municipal     Jan. 28, 1890 V. Damerini (D.) F. Giannini (O.) L.
                                             Pignalosa (I.)

St.              Imperial      Dec.  8, 1887 Paulowskaya (D.) N. Figner (O.) Cer-
 Petersburg                                  noff (I.) (in Russ.)

                 Panaieff      Nov. 15, 1890 Angeloni (D.) G. B. De Negri (O.) G.
                                             Kaschmann (I.) (in It.)

Tbilisi          Imperial      Nov.      1893 Papajeff (D.) Agullini (O.) Ferrari
                                             (I.)

SINGAPORE
Singapore        Palladium     May  29, 1915 E. Gonsalez (D.) V. Artino (O.) I.
                                             Belloni (I.) G. Gonsalez cond.

SPAIN
Alicante         Principal     Apr.  1, 1899 R. Calligaris-Marty (D.) F. Cardina-
                                             li (O.) A. Arcangeli (I.)

Barcelona        Liceo         Nov. 19, 1890 M. Kupfer-Berger (D.) F. Cardinali
                                             (O.) E. Laban (I.)

Bilbao           Arriaga       May   3? 1900 L. Di Benedetto (D.) E. Galli (O.)
                                             R. Blanchart (I.) (First production
                                             traced)

Madrid           Real          Oct.  9, 1890 E. Tetrazzini (D.) E. Durot (O.) M.
                                             Battistini (I.) L. Mancinelli cond.

Malaga           Principal     Feb.     1902 F. Cardinali (O.) I. Tabuyo (I.) G.
                                             Wehils cond.

Seville          San           Apr.  6, 1893 E. Tetrazzini  (D.)  F. Tamagno (O.)
                 Fernando                    D. Menotti (I.) C. Campanini cond.

Valencia         Principal     Jan. 23, 1893 E. Colonnese (D.) F. Tamagno (O.) I.
                                             Tabuyo (I.)

SWITZERLAND
Basel            Stadt         Jan. 18, 1901

Geneva           Grand         Feb.  2, 1938 L. Vifquain (D.) H. St. Criq (O.) J.
                                             Beckmans (I.) E. De Vecchi cond.

Lugano           Apollo        Apr.     1929 A. Massei (D.) Brunet (O.) (in It.)

Zürich           Stadt         Dec.  5, 1898 Triebel  (D.)  Lederer  (O.)  Fitzau
                                             (I.) (in Ger.)

                               June 18, 1938 M. Caniglia (D.) A. Pertile (O.) P.
                                             Biasini (I.) (in It.)

TURKEY
Constan-         Concordia     Aug. 24, 1888 G. Villa (D.) Di Napoli (O.)  L. Ta-
 tinople                                     vecchia (I.)

UNITED STATES

| | | | |
|---|---|---|---|
| Baltimore | Ac. of Mus. | Feb. 19, 1895 | E. Eames (D.) F. Tamagno (O.) V. Maurel (I.) L. Mancinelli cond. |
| | Lyric | Dec. 14, 1904 | G. Rennyson (D.) J. Sheehan (O.) W. Goff (I.) (in Eng.) |
| Boston | Grand | Apr. 30, 1888 | E. Tetrazzini (D.) I. Campanini (O.) A. Faentini-Galassi (I.) C. Campanini cond. (in It.) |
| | Tremont | Nov. 2, 1903 | G. Rennyson (D.) J. Sheehan (O.) W. Goff (I.) N. B. Emanuel cond. (in Eng.) |
| Brooklyn | Ac. of Mus. | Oct. 6, 1903 | G. Rennyson (D.) J. Sheehan (O.) W. Goff (I.) N. B. Emanuel cond. (in Eng.) |
| Chicago | Auditorium | Jan. 2, 1890 | E. Albani (D.) F. Tamagno (O.) G. Del Puente (I.) L. Arditi cond. |
| | Studebaker | Nov. 16, 1903 | G. Rennyson (D.) J. Sheehan (O.) W. Goff (I.) N. B. Emanuel cond. (in Eng.) |
| | Lyric | Oct. 11, 1957 | R. Tebaldi (D.) M. Del Monaco (O.) T. Gobbi (I.) T. Serafin cond. |
| Cincinnati | Grand | Dec. 12, 1904 | G. Rennyson (D.) J. Sheehan (O.) W. Goff (I.) N. B. Emanuel cond. (in Eng.) |
| | Opera | July 3, 1921 | J. Barondess (D.) R. Boscacci (O.) G. Evans (I.) R. Lyford cond. |
| Dallas | Opera | Nov. 20, 1962 | I. Ligabue (D.) M. Del Monaco (O.) R. Vinay (I.) N. Rescigno cond. |
| Denver | | Feb. 28, 1890 | E. Albani (D.) F. Tamagno (O.) G. Del Puente (I.) L. Arditi cond. (in It.) |
| Detroit | Op. House | Apr. 25, 1904 | G. Rennyson (D.) J. Sheehan (O.) W. Goff (I.) N. B. Emanuel cond. (in Eng.) |
| Houston | Houston Th. | Feb. 14, 1905 | G. Rennyson (D.) J. Sheehan (O.) W. Goff (I.) (in Eng.) |
| | Auditorium | Feb. 14, 1914 | L. Slezak (O.) (in It.) |
| | Grand Opera | Jan. 16, 1964 | N. Tatum (D.) J. MacCracken (O.) W. Dooley (I.) W. Herbert cond. |
| Indianapolis | | Mar. 21, 1904 | G. Rennyson (D.) J. Sheehan (O.) W. Goff (I.) (in Eng.) |
| Los Angeles | L. A. Th. | Oct. 18, 1897 | L. Montanari (D.) F. Collenz (O.) C. Cioni (I.) (in It.) |
| Louisville | | Mar. 3, 1890 | E. Albani (D.) F. Tamagno (O.) G. Del Puente (I.) L. Arditi cond. (in It.) |

New Orleans   Tulane       Jan. 22, 1905 G. Rennyson (D.) J. Sheehan (O.) W.
                                         Goff (I.) (in Eng.)

New York      Ac. of Mus. Apr. 16, 1888 E. Tetrazzini (D.) F. Marconi (O.)
                                         A. Faentini-Galassi (I.) C. Campa-
                                         nini cond.

              West End     Dec. 21, 1903 G. Rennyson (D.) J. Sheehan (O.) W.
                                         Goff (I.) N. B. Emanuel cond. (in
                                         Eng.)

              Metro-       Mar. 24, 1890 E. Albani (D.) F. Tamagno (O.) G.
              politan                    Del Puente (I.) L. Arditi cond.[58]

                           Jan. 11, 1892 E. Albani (D.) J. De Reszke (O.) E.
                                         Camera (I.) L. Saar cond.

Pasadena                   Mar. 31, 1966 M. Pobbe (D.) G. Di Stefano (O.) T.
                                         Gobbi (I.)

Philadelphia  Ac. of Mus. May  4, 1888 E. Tetrazzini (D.) I. Campanini (O.)
                                         A. Faentini-Galassi (I.) C. Campani-
                                         ni cond.

St. Louis     Music Hall  Apr.  2, 1895 E. Eames (D.) F. Tamagno (O.) V.
                                         Maurel (I.) L. Mancinelli cond. (in
                                         It.)

San Francisco Grand        Feb. 12, 1890 E. Albani (D.) F. Tamagno (O.) G.
                                         Del Puente (I.) L. Arditi cond.

              Opera        Dec.  5, 1934 E. Rethberg (D.) L. Melchior (O.) R.
                                         Bonelli (I.) G. Merola cond.

Washington    Grand        Feb. 22, 1895 E. Eames (D.) F. Tamagno (O.) V.
                                         Maurel (I.) L. Mancinelli cond. (in
                                         It.)

URUGUAY
Montevideo    Solis        Aug.  4, 1888 R. Pantaleoni (D.) R. Stagno (O.) D.
                                         Menotti (I.) A. Conti cond.

VENEZUELA
Caracas       Municipal    May 27? 1894 P. Roluti-Salto (D.) G. Ortisi (O.)
                                         L. Casini (I.)

---

[58]. This performance was not by the regular company. *Otello* was given by the regular
company two years later, on Jan. 11, 1892, as indicated below.

28. FALSTAFF-*Commedia lirica* in three acts
Milan-Teatro alla Scala-Feb. 9, 1893
Libretto by Arrigo Boito

| | |
|---|---|
| Nanetta (N.) | Adelina Stehle sop. |
| Alice Ford (A.) | Emma Zilli sop. |
| Mrs. Quickly (Q.) | Giuseppina Pasqua mez. |
| Mrs. Meg Page (M.) | Virginia Guerrini mez. |
| Fenton (Fe.) | Edoardo Garbin ten. |
| Sir John Falstaff (F.) | Victor Maurel bar. |
| Ford (Fo.) | Antonio Pini-Corsi bar. |
| Pistola (P.) | Vittorio Arimondi bass |
| Bardolfo | Paolo Pelagalli-Rossetti ten. |
| Dr. Cajus | Giovanni Paroli ten. |
| | |
| Conductor | Edoardo Mascheroni |
| Director | Giuseppe Verdi |

OTHER PREMIERES

ARGENTINA
Buenos Aires   Opera        July  8, 1893 L. Brambilla (N.) E. Tetrazzini (A.)
                                          M. Giudice (Q.) I. Rappini (M.) G.
                                          Cremonini (Fe.) A. Scotti (F.) A.
                                          Moro (Fo.) L. Cromberg (P.) C. Cam-
                                          panini cond.

               Colón        July 25, 1912 L. Bori (N.) C. Bonaplata-Bau (A.)
                                          L. Garibaldi (Q.) F. Perini (M.) R.
                                          Grassi (Fe.) P. Amato (F.) V. Bet-
                                          toni (P.) A. Toscanini cond.

AUSTRALIA
Adelaide       Th. Royal    May   5, 1962 P. Baird (A.) A. Matters (F.) A.
                                          Light (Fo.)

Melbourne      Palais       May  14, 1962 R. Keene (N.) P. Baird (A.) F. Broz-
                                          zesi (Fe.) N. Foster (F.) A. Light
                                          (Fo.) W. Loibner cond.

Sydney         Elizabethan July  6, 1962 R. Keene (N.) F. Brozzesi (Fe.) N.
                                          Foster (F.) A. Light (Fo.) C. Mac-
                                          kerras cond.

AUSTRIA
Graz           Stadt        Dec. 12, 1903

Salzburg       Fest-        July 29, 1935 E. Mason (N.) M. Caniglia (A.) A.
               spielhaus                  Cravcenco (Q.) M. Vasari (M.) D.
                                          Borgioli (Fe.) M. Stabile (F.) P.
                                          Biasini (Fo.) A. Toscanini cond.

Vienna         Hofoper      May  21, 1893 A. Stehle (N.) E. Zilli (A.) G. Pas-
                                          qua (Q.) V. Guerrini (M.) E. Garbin
                                          (Fe.) V. Maurel (F.) A. Pini-Corsi
                                          (Fo.) E. Mascheroni cond. (in It.)

               May   3, 1904 (in Ger.)

BELGIUM
Antwerp                      Feb. 15, 1930 (in Flem.)

Brussels      Monnaie      Dec. 17, 1920 E. Luart (N.) R. Heilbronner (A.) A.
                                        Richardson (Q.) L. Terka (M.) P.
                                        Razavet (Fe.) A. Huberty (F.) C.
                                        Charmat (Fo.) Maudier (P.) De Thoran
                                        cond. (in Fr.)

BRAZIL
Rio de        Lirico       July 29, 1893 O. Boronat (N.) A. Gabbi (A.) E.
Janeiro                                  Colli (Fe.) E. Camera (F.) E. Sotto-
                                         lana (Fo.) G. De Grazia (P.) M. Man-
                                         cinelli cond.

              Sao Pedro    July 29, 1893 C. Ferrani (N.) E. Tetrazzini (A.)
                                         G. Da Costa (Q.) I. Rappini (M.) G.
                                         Cremonini (Fe.) A. Scotti (F.) A.
                                         Moro (Fo.) L. Cromberg (P.) C. Cam-
                                         panini cond.

              Municipal    Sep. 11, 1916 N. Vallin (N.) R. Raisa (A.) G. Ber-
                                         tazzoli (Q.) A. Roessinger (M.) T.
                                         Schipa (Fe.) G. Rimini (F.) A. Crab-
                                         bé (Fo.) G. Mansueto (P.) G. Baroni
                                         cond.

Sao Paulo     Sao José     Aug. 24, 1893 C. Ferrani (N.) E. Tetrazzini (A.)
                                         G. da Costa (Q.) I. Rappini (M.) G.
                                         Cremonini (Fe.) A. Scotti (F.) A.
                                         Moro (Fo.) L. Cromberg (P.) C. Cam-
                                         panini cond.

              Municipal    Oct.  3, 1916 N. Vallin (N.) R. Raisa (A.) G. Ber-
                                         tazzoli (Q.) A. Roessinger (M.) T.
                                         Schipa (Fe.) G. Rimini (F.) A. Crab-
                                         bé (Fo.) G. Mansueto (P.) G. Baroni
                                         cond.

CANADA
Montreal                   Jan. 17, 1958 M. Tessier (N.) M. Novich (A.) M.
                                         Mayer (Q.) R. Kuhlmann (M.) A. Turp
                                         (Fe.) R. Savoie (F.)   N. Bisson
                                         (Fo.) E. Cooper cond.

Toronto                    May   6, 1953 P. Snell (N.) E. Benson Guy (A.) N.
                                         Smith (Q.) J. M. Scott (M.) R. Dou-
                                         cet (Fe.) J. Milligan (Fo.)

CHILE
Santiago      Municipal    Aug. 18, 1896 J. Huguet (N.) E. Tetrazzini (A.) S.
                                         Collamarini (Q.) L. Garavaglia (M.)
                                         L. Rosati (Fe.) A. Magini-Coletti
                                         (F.) F. Aldobrandi (Fo.) C. Campani-
                                         ni cond.

Valparaiso    Victoria     Aug. 17, 1898 A. Marchesini (N.) E. Zilli (A.) S.
                                         Mastrobuono (Fe.) A. Scotti (F.) G.
                                         Polese (Fo.)

CUBA
Havana        Tacon        Winter   1894 A. Cruz (A.)

CZECHOSLOVAKIA
Bratislava    National     Dec. 20, 1932 (in Czech)

Brno                                1913 (in Ger.)

Prague          National      Nov. 16, 1893 (in Czech)

                              May  20, 1894 (in Ger.)

DENMARK
Copenhagen      Royal         Jan. 16, 1895 (in Dan.)

EGYPT
Alexandria      Zizinia       Feb. 14, 1896 O. Mettler (N.) L. Gabbi (A.) A.
                              Cucini (Q.) S. Mastrobuono (Fe.) V.
                              Brombara (F.) Broglio (Fo.)

Cairo           Khedivial     Jan.?    1911 M. Viscardi (A.) S. Ponzano (Q.) M.
                              Ancona (F.) R. Minolfi (Fo.)

FRANCE
Lyon            Grand         Feb. 28, 1919

Marseille       Grand         Nov. 25, 1951 A. Hauth (A.) J. Oncina (Fe.) M.
                              Cortis (F.) V. Blouse (Fo.) J. Trik
                              cond.

Paris           Op. Comique Apr. 18, 1894 L. Landouzy (N.) L. Grandjean (A.)
                              M. Delna (Q.) E. Chevalier (M.) E.
                              Clement (Fe.) V. Maurel (F.) G. Sou-
                              lacroix (Fo.) J. Danbé cond. (in
                              Fr.)

                Châtelet      June  3, 1910 F. Alda (N.) B. Alten (A.) L. Homer
                              (Q.) J. Maubourg (M.) H. Jadlowker
                              (Fe.) A. Scotti (F.) G. Campanari
                              (Fo.) A. Toscanini cond. (in It.)
                              (Tour of the Metropolitan Opera Com-
                              pany, New York)

                Opéra         Apr.  3, 1922 J. Laval (N.) A. Allix (A.) K. La-
                              peyrette (Q.) M. L. Arne (M.) E.
                              Rambaud (Fe.) A. Huberty (F.) M. Du-
                              clos (Fo.) L. Narçon (P.) A. Vigna
                              cond. (in Fr.)

                              July  4, 1935 I. Alfani-Tellini (N.) P. Tassinari
                              (A.) I. Minghini-Cattaneo (Q.) V.
                              Palombini (M.) N. Ederle (Fe.) M.
                              Stabile (F.) E. Badini (Fo.) V.
                              Lazzari (P.) T. Serafin cond. (in
                              It.)

GERMANY
Berlin          Hofoper       June  1, 1893 A. Stehle (N.) E. Zilli (A.) G. Pas-
                              qua (Q.) V. Guerrini (M.) E. Garbin
                              (Fe.) R. Blanchart (F.) A. Pini-
                              Corsi (Fo.) E. Mascheroni cond. (in
                              It.)

                              Mar.  6, 1894 F. Betz (F.) (in Ger.)

                Deutsche      Dec. 11, 1977 C. Malone (N.) L. Peacock (A.) M.
                              Szirmay (Q.) C. Wyatt (M.) R. Wohler
                              (Fe.) R. Kerns (F.) W. Murray (Fo.)
                              M. Gielen cond. (in It.)

Braunschweig                  June 30, 1932 (in Ger.)

Breslau        Stadt        Jan. 30, 1900 (in Ger.)

Darmstadt      Stadt        Nov.  9, 1923 (in Ger.)

Dresden        Hoftheater   Nov. 17, 1894 H.  Schacko  (N.)  Ralph  (A.)  Weber
                                          (Q.) Braun (Fe.) Wendorf (F.) E.
                                          Nawiasky (Fo.) (in Ger.)

Frankfurt      Opernhaus    Jan. 12, 1896 R. Pröll (F.) (in Ger.)

Hamburg        Stadt        Jan.  2, 1894 (in Ger.)

Hannover       Hoftheater   Oct. 29, 1905 (in Ger.)

Kassel         Hoftheater   Nov. 23, 1915 (in Ger.)

Leipzig        Stadt        Apr. 30, 1894 Karnic (N.) E. Baumann (A.) Beuer
                                          (Q.) R. Merkel (Fe.) O. Schelper
                                          (F.) L. Demuth (Fo.) Panzner cond.
                                          (in Ger.)

Mainz          Stadt        Jan. 31, 1926 (in Ger.)

Munich         Hoftheater   Mar.  2, 1894 (in Ger.)

Stuttgart      Hoftheater   Sep. 10, 1893 A. Sutter (N.) L. Mulder (A.) Müller
                                          (Fe.) R. Pröll (F.) A. Hromada (Fo.)
                                          (in Ger.)

Weimar         Hoftheater   Apr.  8, 1894 (in Ger.)

GREAT BRITAIN
Belfast        Th. Royal    Oct. 21, 1894 S.  Ravogli  (N.)  A.  Kitzù  (A.)  G.
                                          Ravogli (Q.) P. Joran (M.) P. Pella-
                                          galli-Rossetti (Fe.) D. Bispham (F.)
                                          A.  Pini-Corsi  (Fo.)  A.  Seppilli
                                          cond.

Blackpool      Th. Royal    Aug. 31, 1894 S.  Ravogli  (N.)  A.  Kitzù  (A.)  G.
                                          Ravogli (Q.) P. Joran (M.) P. Pella-
                                          galli-Rossetti (Fe.) D. Bispham (F.)
                                          A.  Pini-Corsi  (Fo.)  A.  Seppilli
                                          cond.

Bristol        Prince's     Nov. 18, 1894

Edinburgh      Lyceum       Sep. 11, 1894 S. Ravogli (N.) A. Kitzù (A.) G. Ra-
                                          vogli  (Q.)  P.  Joran  (M.)  P.  Pella-
                                          galli-Rossetti (Fe.) D. Bispham (F.)
                                          A.  Pini-Corsi  (Fo.)  A.  Seppilli
                                          cond.

Glasgow        Th. Royal    Sep. 17, 1894 S. Ravogli (N.) A. Kitzù (A.) G. Ra-
                                          vogli  (Q.)  P.  Joran  (M.)  P.  Pella-
                                          galli-Rossetti (Fe.) D. Bispham (F.)
                                          A.  Pini-Corsi  (Fo.)  A.  Seppilli
                                          cond.

Liverpool      Royal Court  Oct. 28, 1894 S.  Ravogli  (N.)  A.  Kitzù  (A.)  G.
                                          Ravogli (Q.) P. Joran (M.) P. Pella-
                                          galli-Rossetti (Fe.) D. Bispham (F.)
                                          A.  Pini-Corsi  (Fo.)  A.  Seppilli
                                          cond.

| London | Covent Garden | May 20, 1894 | O. Olghina (N.) E. Zilli (A.) G. Ravogli (Q.) A. Kitzù (M.) W. Beduschi (Fe.) A. Pessina (F.) A. Pini-Corsi (Fo.) L. Mancinelli cond. |
|---|---|---|---|
|  | Lyceum | Dec. 11, 1896 | A. H. Nicholls (N.) E. Jones (A.) M. Foster (Q.) M. J. Williams (M.) L. Zaguty (Fe.) J. M. Lewis (F.) R. E. Davies (Fo.) C. V. Stanford cond. (in Eng.) |
| Manchester | Th. Royal | Nov. 12, 1894 | S. Ravogli (N.) A. Kitzù (A.) G. Ravogli (Q.) P. Joran (M.) J. O'Mara (Fe.) D. Bispham (F.) A. Pini-Corsi (Fo.) A. Seppilli cond. |
| Newcastle | Tyne | Sep. 6, 1894 | S. Ravogli (N.) A. Kitzù (A.) G. Ravogli (Q.) P. Joran (M.) P. Pellagalli-Rossetti (Fe.) D. Bispham (F.) A. Pini-Corsi (Fo.) A. Seppilli cond. |
| HUNGARY Budapest | Operaház | May 12, 1927 | G. Halász (A.) D. Bársony (Q.) I. Palló (F.) S. Farkas (Fo.) A. Fleischer cond. |
| IRELAND Cork | Th. Royal | Oct. 14, 1894 | |
| Dublin | Gaiety | Oct. 1, 1894 | G. Ravogli (N.) A. Kitzù (A.) G. Ravogli (Q.) P. Joran (M.) P. Pellagalli-Rossetti (Fe.) D. Bispham (F.) A. Pini-Corsi (Fo.) A. Seppilli cond. |
| ISRAEL Tel Aviv | National? | Apr.? 1958 | M. Adani (N.) I. Ligabue (A.) M. Spina (Fe.) F. Corena (F.) W. Monaschesi (Fo.) C. M. Giulini cond. |
| ITALY Ancona | Muse | Mar. 10, 1923 | L. Paikin (N.) L. Canetti (A.) I. Menghini-Cattaneo (Q.) F. Tuminello (Fe.) F. M. Bonini (F.) C. Patino (Fo.) V. Bellezza cond. |
| Bari | Petruzzelli | Feb. 12, 1925 | C. Floria (N.) G. Rosini (A.) R. Brunetti (Q.) S. Bruschi (M.) A. Bendinelli (Fe.) F. M. Bonini (F.) F. Federici (Fo.) A. Padovani cond. |
| Bergamo | Donizetti | Sep.? 1913 | C. Toschi (N.) G. Baldassare-Tedeschi (A.) E. Bruno (Q.) E. Giaconia (M.) G. Di Bernardo (Fe.) T. Parvis (F.) R. Tegani (Fo.) V. Arimondi (P.) L. Mugnone cond. |
| Bologna | Comunale | Nov. 15, 1894 | C. Vicini (N.) E. De Marzi (A.) E. Borlinetto (Q.) A. Belloni (M.) F. Giraud (Fe.) R. Blanchart (F.) A. Modesti (Fo.) G. Berenzone (P.) |

Brescia        Grande       Aug.        1893 A. Stehle (N.) E. Zilli (A.) V.
                                             Guerrini (Q.) V. Ferranti (M.) E.
                                             Garbin (Fe.) A. Pessina (F.) A.
                                             Pini-Corsi (Fo.) V. Arimondi (P.)

Cagliari       Civico       Dec.        1937 A. Damonte (N.) A. Sassone-Soster
                                             (A.) E. Casazza (Q.) E. Ticozzi (M.)
                                             P. Montanari (Fe.) M. Stabile (F.)
                                             C. Tagliani (Fo.) P. Fabbroni cond.

Catania        Bellini      Feb. 24, 1923 A. Gargiulo (N.) O. Giordano (A.) V.
                                             Ferluga (Q.) M. Galeffi (M.) L.
                                             Bergamini (Fe.) M. Stabile (F.) L.
                                             Paci (Fo.) Menni (P.) G. Falconi
                                             cond.

Cremona        Ponchielli   Feb.  3, 1923 L. Paikin (N.) C. Carpi-Toschi (A.)
                                             I. Menghini-Cattaneo (Q.) M. Vasari
                                             (M.) F. Tuminello (Fe.) A. Rossi
                                             (F.) R. Tegani (Fo.) F. Paolantonio
                                             cond.

Ferrara        Comunale     Jan. 11? 1895 O. Litvinoff (N.) L. Gabbi (A.) E.
                                             Bruno (Q.) M. Bastia (M.) Longone
                                             (Fe.) A. Magini-Coletti (F.) F. Cor-
                                             radetti (Fo.)

Fiume          Verdi        Apr. 21, 1923 R. Bardelli (N.) S. Dandolo (A.) C.
                                             Rota (Q.) L. Cecil (Fe.) P. Amato
                                             (F.) F. Federici (Fo.) E. Mascheroni
                                             cond.

Florence       Pagliano     Apr. 19, 1894 A. Occhiolini (N.) E. De Marzi (A.)
                                             E. Ceresoli (Q.) G. Borgatti (Fe.)
                                             R. Blanchart (F.) V. Arimondi (P.)

               Pergola      May  10, 1897 A. Sedelmayer (A.) E. Camera (F.) A.
                                             Pini-Corsi (Fo.)

Genoa          Carlo        Apr.  6, 1893 A. Stehle (N.) E. Zilli (A.) G. Pas-
               Felice                        qua (Q.) V. Guerrini (M.) E. Garbin
                                             (Fe.) V. Maurel (F.) A. Pini-Corsi
                                             (Fo.) E. Mascheroni cond.

Mantua         Sociale      Jan.  3, 1900 I. Timroth (N.) L. Iribarne (Fe.) M.
                                             De Padova (F.) E. Tango cond.

Modena         Municipale   Carn. 1894-95 A. Pane (N.) E. Zilli (A.) E. Cere-
                                             soli (Q.) A. Facco (M.) A. Stampa-
                                             noni (Fe.) A. Moro (F.) G. Marri
                                             (Fo.) L. Cromberg (P.) G. Gialdini
                                             cond.

Naples         San Carlo    Mar. 10, 1894 T. Maragliano (N.) E. Tetrazzini
                                             (A.) E. Borlinetto (Q.) E. Marcomini
                                             (M.) G. Moretti (Fe.) A. Pessina
                                             (F.) E. Sottolana (Fo.) G. Tisci-
                                             Rubini (P.) C. Campanini cond.

Palermo        Massimo      May  16, 1897 F. Ricci de Paz (N.) E. Petri (A.)
                                             E. Borlinetto (Q.) M. Paolicchi-Mug-
                                             none (M.) A. Sthele (Fe.) A. Pessina
                                             (F.) E. Sottolana (Fo.) R. Galli
                                             (P.) L. Mugnone cond.

Parma          Regio        Jan. 25, 1896 M. Martelli (N.) E. Bianchini-Cap-
                                         pelli (A.) G. Villani-Zeppini (Q.)
                                         M. Bastia (M.) A. Bonci (Fe.) S.
                                         Carobbi (F.) L. Bellagamba (Fo.) L.
                                         Rossini (P.) R. Bracale cond.

Piacenza       Municipale   Feb.?   1922 O. Perugino (N.) L. Cannetti (A.) I.
                                         Minghini-Cattaneo (Q.) R. D'Alessio
                                         (Fe.) M. Stabile (F.) G. Falconi
                                         cond.

Pisa           Nuovo        Mar.  7, 1895 C. Vicini (N.) E. De Marzi (A.) E.
                                         Borlinetto (Q.) A. Belloni (M.) F.
                                         Giraud (Fe.) R. Blanchart (F.) A.
                                         Modesti (Fo.) V. Arimondi (P.) A.
                                         Toscanini cond.

Ravenna        Alighieri    May  18? 1923 Romanelli (N.) L. Canetti (A.) I.
                                         Menghini-Cattaneo (Q.) M. Galeffi
                                         (M.) M. Govoni (Fe.) M. Stabile (F.)
                                         R. Tegani (Fo.) A. Vigna cond.

Reggio Emilia Municipale   Mar. 21, 1957 L. Marimpietri (N.) M. Mas (A.) G.
                                         Pederzini (Q.) L. Pedretti (M.) A.
                                         Kraus (Fe.) G. Taddei (F.) R. Cesari
                                         (Fo.) G. Neri (P.) F. Ghione cond.

Rome           Costanzi     Apr. 15, 1893 A. Stehle (N.) E. Zilli (A.) G. Pas-
                                         qua (Q.) V. Guerrini (M.) E. Garbin
                                         (Fe.) V. Maurel (F.) A. Pini-Corsi
                                         (Fo.) V. Arimondi (P.) E. Mascheroni
                                         cond.

Trento         Sociale      June    1894 E. De Marzi (A.) E. Borlinetto (Q.)
                                         R. Blanchart (F.) A. Modesti (Fo.)

Treviso        Comunale     Oct. 10, 1894 C. Vicini (N.) E. De Marzi (A.) E.
                                         Borlinetto (Q.) A. Belloni (M.) C.
                                         Cartica (Fe.) R. Blanchart (F.) A.
                                         Modesti (Fo.) G. Berenzone (P.) A.
                                         Toscanini cond.

Trieste        Grande       May  11, 1893 A. Stehle (N.) E. Zilli (A.) G. Pas-
                                         qua (Q.) V. Guerrini (M.) E. Garbin
                                         (Fe.) V. Maurel (F.) A. Pini-Corsi
                                         (Fo.) E. Mascheroni cond.

Turin          Regio        Dec. 23, 1893 F. Strakosch (N.) M. Petri (A.) E.
                                         Ceresoli (Q.) L. Iribarne (Fe.) R.
                                         Blanchart (F.) R. Angelini-Fornari
                                         (Fo.) A. Conti cond.

Venice         Fenice       May   2, 1893 A. Stehle (N.) E. Zilli (A.) G. Pas-
                                         qua (Q.) V. Guerrini (M.) E. Garbin
                                         (Fe.) V. Maurel (F.) A. Pini-Corsi
                                         (Fo.) E. Mascheroni cond.

Verona         Filarmonico Mar. 12? 1924 M. Stabile (F.) V. Bellezza cond.

JUGOSLAVIA
Ljubljana      National     Apr. 22, 1939 (in Slov.)

Zagreb          National      Nov.  6, 1937 N. Toncic (N.) V. Nozinic (A.) N.
                                            Sterle (Fe.) D. Hrzic (F.) L. Mir-
                                            kovic (Fo.) (in Croat.)

MALTA
La Valletta     Real          Nov. 23, 1929 T. Alcaide (Fe.) M. Stabile (F.)
                                             Mastronardi (Fo.)

MEXICO
Mexico City     Nacional      Oct.  7, 1893 A. Pettigiani (N.) A. Cruz (A.) M.
                                            Franchini (Q.) M. Svetade (M.) G.
                                            Moretti (Fe.) P. Ughetto (F.) A.
                                            Modesti (Fo.) A. Nicolini (P.)

MONACO
Monte Carlo     Salle         Mar. 29, 1919 L. Bori (N.) A. Zeppilli (A.) N.
                Garnier                     Lollini (Q.) De Angelo (M.) L. Ber-
                                            gamini (Fe.) E. Nani (F.) E. Badini
                                            (Fo.) V. Chalmin (P.) V. De Sabata
                                            cond.

NETHERLANDS
Amsterdam       Carré         Nov. 24, 1931 E. Alberti (N.) S. Scuderi (A.) N.
                                            Covaceva (Q.) P. Civil (Fe.) M. Sta-
                                            bile (F.) L. Piccioli (Fo.)

La Haye         Gebouw v.     Nov. 19, 1931 E. Alberti (N.) S. Scuderi (A.) N.
                Kunst                       Covaceva (Q.) P. Civil (Fe.) M. Sta-
                                            bile (F.) L. Piccioli (Fo.)

Rotterdam       Groote        Nov. 21, 1931 E. Alberti (N.) S. Scuderi (A.) N.
                                            Covaceva (Q.) P. Civil (Fe.) M. Sta-
                                            bile (F.) L. Piccioli (Fo.)

PORTUGAL
Lisbon          Sao Carlos    Feb. 27, 1894 V. Mendioroz (N.) A. Carrera (A.) V.
                                            Guerrini (Q.) A. Cucini (M.) A. To-
                                            mei (Fe.) V. Maurel (F.) M. Scara-
                                            mella (Fo.) A. Sabellico (P.)

ROMANIA
Bucharest       National      Mar. 29, 1939 P. Stefanescu-Goanga (F.) (in Rum.)

RUSSIA
Moscow          Bolshoi       Mar. 16, 1897 R. Pacini (N.) R. Storchio (A.) A.
                                            Cucini (Q.) G. Bayo (Fe.) S. Carobbi
                                            (F.) G. M. Sammarco (Fo.) (in It.)

Odessa          Municipal     Mar.  4, 1899 A. Sedelmayer (A.) L. Monti-Brunner
                                            (Q.) A. Stampanoni (Fe.) G. M. Sam-
                                            marco (F.) S. Vinci (Fo.) (in It.)

St.             Imperial      Jan. 29, 1894 (in Russ.)
  Petersburg

SPAIN
Barcelona       Liceo         Apr. 18, 1896 E. Tetrazzini (A.) G. Fabbri (Q.) R.
                                            Blanchart (F.) R. Angelini-Fornari
                                            (Fo.) C. Campanini cond.

Madrid          Real          Feb. 10, 1894 J. Huguet (N.) T. Arkel (A.) M. Giu-
                                            dice (Q.) L. Iribarne (Fe.) D. Me-
                                            notti (F.) A. Pini-Corsi (Fo.) J.
                                            Goula cond.

SWEDEN
Stockholm    Svenska      Nov. 16, 1896  P. Frödin (N.) C. Östberg (A.) A.
                                         Almati-Rundberg (Q.) A. Karlsohn
                                         (M.) O. Lemon (Fe.) C. F. Lundqvist
                                         (F.) C. A. Söderman (Fo.) R. Henne-
                                         berg cond. (in Swed.)

SWITZERLAND
Geneva       Grand        Sep. 26, 1936  C. Valobra (N.) M. Caniglia (A.) E.
                                         Casazza (Q.) E. Ticozzi (M.) M. Sta-
                                         bile (F.) L. Piccioli (Fo.) V. Bet-
                                         toni (P.) A. Votto cond.

Zurich       Stadt        Apr.  8, 1901  (in Ger.)

UNITED STATES
Atlanta      Auditorium   Apr. 21, 1925  F. Alda (N.) L. Bori (A.) M. Telva
                                         (Q.) K. Howard (M.) A. Tokaytan
                                         (Fe.) A. Scotti (F.) L. Tibbett
                                         (Fo.) A. Didur (P.) T. Serafin cond.

Baltimore    Harris'      Mar.  4, 1896  L. Beeth (N.) F. Saville (A.) S.
             Academy                     Scalchi (Q.) A. Kitzù (M.) G. Cre-
                                         monini (Fe.) V. Maurel (F.) G. Cam-
                                         panari (Fo.) V. Arimondi (P.) A.
                                         Seppilli cond.

Boston       Boston Th.   Feb. 28, 1895  Z. De Lussan (N.) E. Eames (A.) S.
                                         Scalchi (Q.) J. De Vigne (M.) G.
                                         Russitano (Fe.) V. Maurel (F.) G.
                                         Campanari (Fo.) L. Mancinelli cond.

Brooklyn     Ac. of Mus.  Jan. 28, 1896  L. Beeth (N.) F. Saville (A.) S.
                                         Scalchi (Q.) A. Kitzù (M.) G. Cre-
                                         monini (Fe.) V. Maurel (F.) G. Cam-
                                         panari (Fo.) V. Arimondi (P.) A.
                                         Seppilli cond.

Chicago      Auditorium   Mar. 23, 1895  Z. De Lussan (N.) E. Eames (A.) S.
                                         Scalchi (Q.) J. De Vigne (M.) G.
                                         Mauguière (Fe.) V. Maurel (F.) G.
                                         Campanari (Fo.) L. Mancinelli cond.

Cincinnati   Opera        Aug.  2, 1926  J. Ruth (N.) M. Sherwood (A.) K.
                                         Browne (Q.) E. Cornor (M.) G. Georgi
                                         (Fe.) R. Ringling (F.) E. Torti
                                         (Fo.) L. J. Johnen (P.) I. Van Grove
                                         cond.

Cleveland    Public Hall  Apr. 30, 1925  Q. Mario (N.) L. Bori (A.) M. Telva
                                         (Q.) K. Howard (M.) A. Tokaytan
                                         (Fe.) A. Scotti (F.) L. Tibbett
                                         (Fo.) A. Didur (P.) T. Serafin cond.

Detroit      Coliseum     Mar. 21, 1896  L. Beeth (N.) F. Saville (A.) S.
                                         Scalchi (Q.) A. Kitzù (M.) G. Cre-
                                         monini (Fe.) V. Maurel (F.) G. Cam-
                                         panari (Fo.) V. Arimondi (P.) A.
                                         Seppilli cond.

Houston      Grand Opera  Feb.  6, 1968  H. Thomson (N.) R. Kabaivanska (A.)
                                         C. Turner (Q.) D. Krebill (M.) K.
                                         Riegel (Fe.) G. Evans (F.) E. Sor-
                                         dello (Fo.) W. Herbert cond.

Los Angeles    Auditorium   Nov.    4, 1944  L. Albanese (N.) B. Landi (Fe.)

New York       Metro-       Feb.    4, 1895  Z. De Lussan (N.)  E. Eames  (A.) S.
               politan                       Scalchi (Q.) J. De Vigne (M.) G.
                                             Russitano (Fe.) V. Maurel (F.) G.
                                             Campanari (Fo.) L. Mancinelli cond.

Philadelphia   Ac. of Mus.  Feb.    7, 1895  Z. De Lussan (N.) E. Eames  (A.) S.
                                             Scalchi (Q.) J. De Vigne (M.) G.
                                             Russitano (Fe.) V. Maurel (F.) G.
                                             Campanari (Fo.) L. Mancinelli cond.

Rochester      Eastman      May     6, 1925  Q. Mario (N.) L. Bori (A.) M. Telva
                                             (Q.) K. Howard (M.) A. Tokaytan
                                             (Fe.) A. Scotti (F.) L. Tibbett
                                             (Fo.) A. Didur (P.) T. Serafin cond.

St. Louis      Music Hall   Apr.    6, 1895  Z. De Lussan (N.) E. Eames  (A.) S.
                                             Scalchi (Q.) J. De Vigne (M.) G.
                                             Russitano (Fe.) V. Maurel (F.) G.
                                             Campanari (Fo.) L. Mancinelli cond.

San Francisco  Opera        Sep. 27, 1927  M. Donnelly (N.) F. Peralta (A.) I.
                                             Bourskaya (Q.) E. Marlo (M.) A.
                                             Tokaytan (Fe.) A. Scotti (F.) L.
                                             Tibbett (Fo.) G. Merola cond.

Washington     Allen's      Mar.    7, 1896  L. Beeth (N.) F. Saville (A.) S.
                                             Scalchi (Q.) A. Kitzù (M.) G. Cre-
                                             monini (Fe.) V. Maurel (F.) G. Cam-
                                             panari (Fo.) V. Arimondi (P.) A.
                                             Seppilli cond.

URUGUAY
Montevideo     Solis        Aug. 21, 1894  S. Othon (N.) M. Petri (A.) M. Giu-
                                             dice (Q.) C. Zawner (M.) G. Cremoni-
                                             ni (Fe.) A. Scotti (F.) G. Caruson
                                             (Fo.)

VENEZUELA
Caracas        Municipal    June 27, 1975

## MISCELLANEOUS AND MULTIPLE COMPOSERS

This section is intended to provide some documentation for performances of
the most successful works by minor composers who, for one reason or another,
were not important enough to warrant separate entries in this study. Since
this section will essentially be limited to opera seria, some of the most
successful buffo operas of the mid and late nineteenth century could not be
included. Operas by multiple composers will also be included here. In the
case of works by the two Ricci brothers (Federico and Luigi), only the casts
of the world premieres will be indicated at this point; it is planned to
provide full details in a later volume.

1. IL COLONNELLO-*Melodramma* in two acts
Naples-Teatro del Fondo-March 24, 1835
Music by Federico and Luigi Ricci; Libretto by Giacomo Ferretti

| | |
|---|---|
| Adele | Alexandrine Duprez sop. |
| Elisa | Carolina Ungher sop. |
| Adolfo | Gilbert Louis Duprez ten. |
| Ser Faccenda | Francesco Pedrazzi ten. |
| Il Colonnello | Carlo Ottorino Porto bass |
| Michelina | Sacchi sec. |
| Carlo | Domenico Raffaelli bass |
| Ernesto | Achille Balestracci ten. |
| Paolo | Teofilo Rossi ten. |
| Dispetto | Francesco Salvetti bass |

2. IL DISERTORE PER AMORE-*Opera semiseria* in two acts
Naples-Teatro del Fondo-Feb. 16, 1836
Music by Federico and Luigi Ricci; Libretto by Giacomo Ferretti

| | |
|---|---|
| Luisa | Fanny Persiani sop. |
| Enrico | Giorgio Ronconi bar. |
| Giovannina | Amalia Zacconi sec. |
| Farfallino | Francesco Salvetti bass |
| Bernardo | Domenico Raffaelli bass |
| Cric | Teofilo Rossi ten. |

3. LA MARESCIALLA D'ANCRE-*Melodramma* in two acts
Padua-Teatro Nuovo-July 23, 1839
Music by Alessandro Nini; Libretto by G. Prati

| | |
|---|---|
| La Marescialla d'Ancre (M.) | Adelaide Kemble sop. |
| Isabella Monti (I.) | Fanny Goldberg sop. |
| Concino (C.) | Giovanni Battista Verger ten. |
| Michele Borgia (B.) | Orazio Cartagenova bar. |
| Il Conte de Luynes | |
| Armando | |

OTHER PRODUCTIONS

ARGENTINA
Buenos Aires  Argentino   July 20, 1855 I. Edelvira (M.) M. Eboli (I.) L.
Guglielmini (C.)

BRAZIL
| Rio de Janeiro | Sao Pedro | July 22, 1850 | I. Edelvira (M.) A. Candiani (I.) F. Tati (C.) C. Capurri (B.) |

CHILE
| Valparaiso | Victoria | Jan. 8, 1857 | I. Edelvira (M.) G. Amei (I.) G. C. Casanova (B.) |

ITALY
| Asti | Civico | May 1843 | G. Montuchielli (M.) L. Remorini (I.) A. Castellan (C.) G. B. Righini (B.) |
| Bergamo | Sociale | Jan. 22, 1851 | M. Anselmi (M.) C. Riva Fossati (I.) C. Carisio (C.) G. Zambellini (B.) |
| Cagliari | Civico | Feb. 7, 1844 | C. Lusignani (M.) A. Tassini (I.) C. Mugnai (C.) E. Mazzotti (B.) |
| Cuneo | Civico | Dec. 26? 1841 | R. Basso-Borio (M.) Marconi (I.) F. Tati (C.) G. B. Righini (B.) |
| Este | Sociale | Autumn 1842 | T. Tavola (M.) E. Zmyoschi (I.) G. B. Milesi (C.) Torre (B.) |
| Florence | Nuovo | Apr.? 1840 | A. Castellan (M.) F. Goldberg (I.) Gianpietro (C.) |
| Genoa | Carlo Felice | Dec. 31, 1839 | E. Tadolini (M.) L. Assandri (I.) I. Pasini (C.) F. Varesi (B.) G. Serra cond. |
| Livorno | Avvalorati | July? 1841 | J. De Mery (M.) G. B. Milesi (C.) |
| Novara | Nuovo | Jan.? 1845 | E. Dielitz (M.) G. Celini (I.) L. Bottagisi (C.) L. Walter (B.) |
| Rome | Argentina | Nov. 21, 1840 | |
| Trento | Sociale | June 1842 | T. Tavola (M.) G. B. Milesi (C.) G. Torre (B.) |
| Trieste | Grande | Dec. 26, 1841 | O. Malvani (M.) C. Gramaglia (I.) G. B. Verger (C.) M. Alberti (B.) A. Scaramelli cond. |
| Turin | Carignano | Aug. 1841 | O. Malvani (M.) C. Gramaglia (I.) G. B. Verger (C.) M. Alberti (B.) |
| Udine | Minerva | Aug. 20, 1842 | T. Tavola (M.) G. B. Milesi (C.) O. Bartolini (B.) |
| Venice | La Fenice | May 29, 1842 | T. Tavola (M.) G. B. Milesi (C.) G. Torri (B.) |
| | Apollo | Oct.? 1844 | A. De la Grange (M.) G. Ricci (C.) S. Scappini (B.) |
| Verona | Filarmonico | Feb. 8, 1843 | F. Goldberg (M.) G. B. Milesi (C.) V. Meini (B.) |

JUGOSLAVIA
Zara            Nobile        Mar. 28, 1842 E. Ranzi (M.) A. Tantalora (I.) F.
                                            Personi (C.) G. C. Casanova (B.) L.
                                            Garbato cond.

PORTUGAL
Lisbon          Sao Carlos    Apr. 4, 1845 G. Rossi-Caccia (M.) E. Carmini (I.)
                                           G. Zoboli (C.) E. Santi (B.)

Oporto          Sao Joao      Apr. 2, 1851 L. Abbadia (M.) G. Gamboggi (C.) V.
                                           Prattico (B.)

SPAIN
Barcelona       Principal     Aug. 5, 1843 E. Goggi (M.) V. Gaziello Brambilla
                                           (I.) G. B. Verger (C.) M. Alberti
                                           (B.)


4. VIRGINIA-*Dramma lirico* in three acts
Genoa-Teatro Carlo Felice-Feb. 21, 1843
Music by Alessandro Nini; Libretto by Domenico Bancalari

Virginia (V.)                                      Clara Novello sop.
Icilio (I.)                                        Giacomo Roppa ten.
Appio Claudio (A.)                                 Filippo Colini bar.
Virginio (Vo.)                                 Francesco Leonardi bass
Emilia                                            Luigia Olivieri sec.
Marco                                        Giovanni Garibaldi bass

Conductor                                          Giovanni Serra

OTHER PRODUCTIONS

ITALY
Bergamo         Sociale       Dec. 26, 1872 Curzi (V.) Grupello (I.) Notini (A.)
                                            Ardelliano (Vo.)

Cagliari        Civico        Dec.?    1844 A. Lasagna (V.) V. Jacobelli (I.) G.
                                            Solari (A.)

Cuneo           Civico        Jan. 13, 1844 A. Gambaro (V.) S. Lavia (I.) G. Do-
                                            nelli (A.) L. Walter (Vo.)

Genoa           Carlo         Apr. 6, 1844 S. Loewe (V.) G. Roppa (I.) G. Bian-
                Felice                     chi (A.) P. Dérivis (Vo.)

                              June 14, 1859 L. Lesniewska (V.) C. Negrini (I.)
                                            A. Rossi-Ghelli (A.) C. Dalla Costa
                                            (Vo.) A. Mariani cond.

Livorno         Avvalorati    Aug.     1843 T. Brambilla (V.) G. Roppa (I.) S.
                                            Ronconi (A.)

Rome            Apollo        Sep. 19, 1843 T. Brambilla (V.) G. Roppa (I.) S.
                                            Ronconi (A.) F. Fallar (Vo.) G. Nos-
                                            tini cond.

Venice          Apollo        May      1855 C. Crémont (V.) L. Saccomanno (I.)
                                            L. Guadagnini (A.)

Vicenza        Eretenio      July 25, 1843 F. Pixis (V.) G. B. Milesi (I.) R.
                                          Ferlotti (A.)

PORTUGAL
Lisbon         Sao Carlos    Apr.  8, 1844 G. Rossi-Caccia (V.) L. Flavio (I.)
                                          F. Botelli (A.)

Oporto         Sao Joao      Aug.?   1844 G. Rossi-Caccia (V.) L. Flavio (I.)
                                          F. Botelli (A.)

5. ANNA LA PRIE-*Tragedia lirica* in three acts
Naples-Teatro San Carlo-Mar. 28, 1843
Music by Vincenzo Battista; Libretto by Nicola Leone Cavallo

Anna La Prie (A.)                              Carlotta Gruitz sop.
Conte Adolfo La Prie (C.)                     Enrico Tamberlick ten.
Duca Federico Alboix (D.)                     Gaetano Fraschini ten.
Marchese Vouban (M.)              Giuseppe Federico Beneventano bar.
Elisa                                           Anna Salvetti sop.
Enrico Dulcy                            Giuseppe Benedetti bass

Conductor                                         Antonio Farelli

OTHER PRODUCTIONS

BRAZIL
Rio de         San           Jan.  1, 1852 G. Zecchini (A.)  D. Labocetta  (C.)
  Janeiro      Januario                    L. Di Lauro (M.)

ITALY
Catania        Comunale      Dec. 15, 1852 E. Lipparini (A.) L. Ferrari Stella
                                          (C.)  A.  Pagnoni  (D.)  L.  Pacifico
                                          (M.) M. Pappalardo cond.

Chieti         San           May  11, 1853 E. Delle Sedie (M.)
               Ferdinando

Naples         San Carlo     Dec. 27, 1843 C. Gruitz (A.) E. Tamberlick (C.) G.
                                          Fraschini  (D.)  G.  F.  Beneventano
                                          (M.)

                             July 22, 1855 G. Beltramelli (A.) P. Mongini (C.)
                                          P. Cecchi (D.) L. Brignole (M.) A.
                                          Farelli cond.

               Nuovo         Oct.  2, 1852 C. Mauri-Ventura  (A.)  L.  Bianchi
                                          (C.) G. Valentini-Cristiani (D.) R.
                                          Mastriani (M.)

MALTA
La Valletta    Manoel        Oct.  1, 1846 E. Servoli (A.) G. Ramoni (C.) L.
                                          Del Riccio (M.)

PORTUGAL
Lisbon         Sao Carlos    Apr.  4, 1848 T. Bovay (A.) A. Volpini (C.) R.
                                          Pizzigati (M.)

Oporto         Sao Joao      Mar.     1853 L. Giordani (A.) L. Ceresa (C.)

SPAIN
Barcelona      Principal     Apr. 17, 1847 C. Cattinari (A.) E. Tamberlick (C.)
                                           E. Barili (M.)

Madrid         Circo         Jan. 23, 1846 C. Gruitz (A.) E. Tamberlick (C.) R.
                                           Ferlotti (M.)


6. LUISA STROZZI-*Dramma tragico* in three acts
Parma-Teatro Regio-May 27, 1846
Music by Gualtiero Sanelli; Libretto by Pietro Martini

Luisa Strozzi (L.)                              Sofia Loewe sop.
Luigi Capponi (C.)                         Francesco Ciaffei ten.
Alessandro dei Medici (A.)                      Gaetano Ferri bar.
Filippo Strozzi                              Cesare Castelli bass
Matilde                                  Annetta Pochi-Riga sec.
Ser Maurizio                                 Luigi Loriani bass
Giomo                                      Angelo Calderani ten.
Lapo                                     Adriano Filippini bass

Conductor                                    Nicola De Giovanni


OTHER PRODUCTIONS

CHILE
Santiago       Principal     June 15, 1850 T. Rossi (L.) A. Zambaiti (C.) G.
                                           Bastoggi (A.) R. Pantanelli cond.

               Republica     May   6, 1852 T. Rossi (L.) G. Ubaldi (C.) G. Bas-
                                           toggi (A.) R. Pantanelli cond.

Valparaiso     Victoria      June 20, 1850 T. Rossi (L.) G. Ubaldi (C.) L. Ca-
                                           vedagni (A.) R. Pantanelli cond.

               Dec.  7, 1851 T. Rossi (L.) G. Ubaldi (C.) G. Bas-
                                           toggi (A.) R. Pantanelli cond.

FRANCE
Ajaccio        San           Oct.?   1854 C. Guerra (L.) F. Banti (C.)   Benti-
               Gabriele                    voglio (A.)

GREECE
Corfu          San Giacomo Oct.      1858 E. Devrient (L.) Minocchi (C.) G.
                                           Giotti (A.)

ITALY
Alessandria    Municipale    Sep.  3, 1847 R. Gariboldi-Bassi (L.) D. Mecksa
                                           (C.) C. Massera (A.)

Bologna        Comunale      Oct. 28, 1846 I. Fabre (L.) G. Baldanza (C.) L.
                                           Montemerli (F.) G. Manetti cond.

Cremona        Concordi      May   8, 1847 T. Bovay (L.) D. Mecksa (C.) G. C.
                                           Casanova (A.) G. Sanelli dir.

Florence       Pergola       Nov. 15, 1846 L. Assandri (L.) F. Borioni (C.) G.
                                           Ferri (A.)

| Genoa | Carlo Felice | Dec. 26, 1846 | M. Gazzaniga (L.) F. Borioni (C.) G. Ferri (A.) |
|---|---|---|---|
| | Andrea Doria | July 29, 1856 | G. Casali-Campagna (L.) |
| Livorno | Avvalorati | Mar.? 1846 | H. Nissen (L.) L. Graziani (C.) L. Della Santa (A.) |
| | | Sep. 27, 1846 | S. Loewe (L.) L. Bernabei (C.) G. Ferri (A.) |
| Padua | Nuovo | Nov. 1847 | E. Cuzzani (L.) E. Naudin (C.) |
| Pavia | Civico | Apr. 1847 | A. Bertucat (L.) V. Jacobelli (C.) T. Santi-Silva (A.) |
| Piacenza | Municipale | Spring 1847 | G. Leva (L.) D. Lorini (C.) L. Valli (A.) G. Jona cond. |
| Trieste | Mauroner | June? 1847 | A. Tirelli (L.) R. Dei (C.) Massard (A.) |
| Vercelli | Civico | Jan. 20? 1848 | D. Mecksa (C.) A. Olivari (A.) |
| Verona | Filarmonico | Dec. 26, 1846 | E. Parepa-Archibugi (L.) V. Ferrari-Stella (C.) L. Rinaldini (A.) |
| Vicenza | Eretenio | Dec. 26? 1846 | L. Ponti dall'Armi (L.) E. Naudin (C.) A. Tomasi (A.) |
| PERU Lima | Principal | Aug. 18, 1853 | T. Cailly (L.) D. Lorini (C.) F. Leonardi (A.) |
| PORTUGAL Lisbon | Sao Carlos | Oct. 22, 1848 | I. Secci-Corsi (L.) G. Baldanza (C.) G. Zucchini (A.) |
| ROMANIA Bucharest | National | Feb. 18, 1848 | C. Griffini (L.) A. Landi (C.) D. Marchelli (A.) |
| SPAIN Madrid | Circo | Aug. 18, 1847 | A. Bosio (L.) G. B. Milesi (C.) F. Morelli-Ponti (A.) |
| URUGUAY Montevideo | Solis | Nov. 22, 1856 | G. Cima (A.) |

7. L'AMANTE DI RICHIAMO-*Melodramma giocosa* in three acts
Turin-Teatro d'Angennes-June 13, 1846
Music by Federico and Luigi Ricci; Libretto by F. Dall'Ongaro

| | |
|---|---|
| Adele, Contessa di Valbianca | Adelina Rossetti-Rebussini sop. |
| Rita | Rita Gabussi De Bassini sop. |
| Giacinto | Giovanni Pancani ten. |
| Il Visconte | Antonio Superchi bar. |
| Bernardo | Stefano Scappini buf. |
| Vafrino | Faustino Lonati ten. |
| Frosina | Marietta Laghi sec. |
| Cavaliere Gustavo | Gioachino Luchesi sec. |


8. CRISPINO E LA COMARE-*Melodramma fantastico-giocoso* in four acts
Venice-Teatro San Benedetto-Feb. 28, 1850
Music by Federico and Luigi Ricci; Libretto by Francesco Maria Piave

| | |
|---|---|
| Annetta | Giovannina Pecorini sop. |
| La Comare | Giovannina Bordoni mez. |
| Contino del Fiore | Giuseppe Pasi ten. |
| Fabrizio | Luigi Rinaldini bar. |
| Mirabolano | Luigi Ciardi buf. |
| Crispino Tacchetto | Carlo Cambiaggio buf. |
| Lisetta | Paolina Prinetti mez. |
| Bortolo | Not named |
| Don Asrubale | Angelo Guglielmini bass |


9. IL SINDACO BABBEO-*Opera comica* in three acts
Milan-Teatro Santa Radegonda-Mar. 3, 1851
Music by Amilcare Ponchielli, Domenico Cagnoni, A. Curcio and G. Marcora;
Libretto by G. Giachetti

| | |
|---|---|
| | Giuseppina Morra sop. |
| | Luigi Guglielmini ten. |
| | Orazio Bonafous bar. |
| Sindaco Babbeo | Cesare Soares buf. |


10. IL FORNARETTO-*Dramma seria* in three acts
Parma-Teatro Regio-Mar. 24, 1851
Music by Gualtiero Sanelli; Libretto by Andrea Codebò

| | |
|---|---|
| Clemenza (C.) | Fanny Salvini-Donatelli sop. |
| Nella (N.) | Carolina Ghedini mez. |
| Pietro (P.) | Giovanni Battista Milesi ten. |
| Marco Tasca (M.) | Antonio Superchi bar. |
| Lorenzo Barbo (L.) | Domenico Maggi bass |
| Giovanni | Angelo Calderani ten. |
| Boundumier | Cesare Castelli ten. |
| Il Bravo | Federico Ghedini sec. |
| Conductor | Nicola De Giovanni |

OTHER PRODUCTIONS

ARGENTINA
Buenos Aires   Ant. Colon   May    8, 1858 C. Castigneri cond.

CHILE
Santiago       Republica    Oct. 23, 1853 T. Bayetti (C.)

                            Sep. 21, 1854 T. Bayetti (C.)

Valparaiso     Victoria     Jan. 15, 1854 T. Bayetti (C.) A. Pantanelli (N.)
                                          L. Cavedagni (P.) G. Bastoggi (M.)
                                          Borsotti (L.)

ITALY
Cagliari       Civico       Oct. 20, 1863 G. Ottonelli-Bresciani (C.)

Cremona        Concordia    Carn. 1867-68

Florence       Pergola      Mar.      1855 M. Piccolomini (C.) I. Secci-Corsi
                                          (N.) E. Naudin (P.) G. B. Bencich
                                          (M.) L. Domenech (L.)

Genoa          Anfiteatro   July 23, 1870 L. Pitarch (C.) L. Corsi (N.) E. De
                                          Serini (P.)

               Andrea       May  14, 1874 E. Montalba (C.) M. Venosta (N.) G.
               Doria                      Gozzolini (P.) E. Corte (M.) A. Pa-
                                          dovani (L.)

Parma          Regio        Mar.  9, 1870 E. Ciuti (C.) E. Serazzi (P.) I. Vi-
                                          ganotti (M.) R. Mailini (L.) G. C.
                                          Ferrarini cond.

Trieste        Grande       Dec. 12, 1851 R. Penco (C.) G. Mazzi (P.) F. Pons
                                          (L.) G. A. Scaramelli cond.

Venice         Apollo       Apr.      1855 C. Crémont (C.) L. Saccomanno (P.)

MALTA
La Valletta    Real         Dec.      1866

PERU
Lima           Principal    July  4, 1856 T. Bayetti (C.) L. Cavedagni (P.) G.
                                          Mirandola (L.)

SPAIN
Barcelona      Liceo        Nov. 27, 1859 C. Carozzi-Zucchi (C.) C. Doy (N.)
                                          T. Palmieri (P.) F. Bellini (M.) A.
                                          Rodas (L.)

URUGUAY
Montevideo     Solis        Aug.  7, 1858 T. Bayetti (C.) L. Lelmi (P.)

11. LA VERGINE DI KERMO-*Opera seria* in three acts
Cremona-Teatro Concordia-Feb. 16, 1870
Music by Antonio Cagnoni, Francesco Cortesi, Fiori, Jacopo Foroni, Ruggero
Manna, Alberto Mazzucato, Giovanni Pacini, Carlo Pedrotti, Amilcare Ponchi-
elli, Federico Ricci, Lauro Rossi; Libretto by Francesco Guidi

| | |
|---|---:|
| Maria | Giuseppina Caruzzi-Bedogni sop. |
| Penouel | Luigi Gulli ten. |
| Il Marchese di Lorcy | Erasmo Carnili bar. |
| Kerouan | Raffaele D'Ottavi bass |
| Il Cavaliere di Montesson | Lino Conti buf. |
| L'Ombra della Madre di Maria | |
| Il Podestà di Kermo | |
| Un Famigliere | |
| Un Ostiere | |

Conductor                                               Amilcare Ponchielli

12. IL CONTE VERDE-*Dramma lirico* in four acts
Rome-Teatro Apollo-Apr. 5, 1873
Music by Giuseppe Libani; Libretto by Carlo D'Ormeville

| | |
|---|---:|
| Gilberta (G.) | Emma Wiziak sop. |
| Laura (L.) | Giuseppina Ugolini-Rizzini mez. |
| Amedeo VI (A.) | Julian Gayarre ten. |
| Filippo (F.) | Gottardo Aldighieri bar. |
| Conte Della Torre (C.) | Antonio Faberi bass |
| David (D.) | Carlo Morroto bass |
| Maestro del Campo | Nazzareno Camporesi sec. |
| Monaca | C. Petrini sec. |
| Paggio | Raffaele Tamanti ten. |

Conductor                                               Eugenio Terziani

OTHER PRODUCTIONS

ITALY

| Cagliari | Civico | Feb. 11? 1885 | E. Callery-Viviani (G.) I. D'Avanzo (A.) A. Falciai (F.) |
|---|---|---|---|
| Carpi | Comunale | Aug. 19? 1875 | V. Potentini (G.) G. Machvitz (L.) F. Tamagno (A.) G. Belletti (F.) C. Bedogni (D.) A. Gori cond. G. Libani dir. |
| Fiume | Comunale | Mar. 3, 1877 | C. Mocoroa (G.) G. De Sanctis-Mari-anecci (A.) A. Navary (F.) |
| Padua | Concordi | Dec. 26? 1875 | V. Pozzi-Ferrari (G.) E. Ronconi (A.) A. Navari (F.) |
| Parma | Regio | Jan. 30, 1875 | C. Mocoroa (G.) E. Ronconi (A.) A. Pifferi (F.) G. Tanzini (C.) V. Paraboschi (D.) |
| Ravenna | Alighieri | Carn. 1875-76 | M. Boy-Gilbert (G.) C. Roussel (A.) V. Quintili-Leoni (F.) A. Moreschi cond. |

| Treviso | Sociale | Jan. 20, 1877 | R. Montanari (G.) V. Bacci (A.) O. Cresci (F.) N. Pozzi (D.) R. Furlotti cond. |
|---------|---------|---------------|--------------------------------|
|         |         | Oct. 29, 1879 | I. Martinez De Escalante (G.) G. Ortisi (A.) U. Gianelli cond. |
| Turin | Vittorio Emanuele | Nov. 30, 1874 | L. Mosconi (G.) A. Franchini (A.) G. Valcheri (F.) G. Libani dir. |
| Verona | Nuovo | Nov.? 1877 | L. Mosconi (G.) M. Verati (L.) G. B. De Negri (A.) Adolfi (F.) Favi cond. |
| Vicenza | Eretenio | Dec. 26, 1876 | M. Mantilla (G.) E. Ronconi (A.) E. Vanden (F.) |
| Viterbo | Unione | Aug. 1875 | Pogliaghi (G.) F. Guidotti (L.) A. Franchini (A.) G. Valle (F.) E. Terziani cond. G. Libani dir. |

13. I GOTI-*Tragedia lirica* in four acts
Bologna-Teatro Comunale-Nov. 30, 1873
Music by Stefano Gobatti; Libretto by Stefano Interdonato

| | |
|---|---|
| Amalasunta (A.) | Leonia Levielli Coloni sop. |
| Gualtiero (G.) | Laura Simoncelli mez. |
| Sveno (S.) | Luigi Bolis ten. |
| Teodato (T.) | Silvio Rossi-Rumiati bar. |
| Lausco (L.) | Numa Giommi bass |
| Svarano | Roberto Dazzi bass |

| Conductor | Agostino Mercuri |
|---|---|

OTHER PRODUCTIONS

ITALY

| Brescia | Grande | Aug. 11, 1874 | T. Singer (A.) L. Bolis (S.) F. Pandolfini (T.) O. Maini (L.) G. Zavaglio cond. S. Gobatti dir. |
|---------|--------|---------------|--------------------------------|
| Florence | Pergola | Mar. 24, 1874 | C. De Baciocchi (A.) I. Paul-Donati (G.) L. Abrugnedo (S.) E. Storti (T.) C. Ulloa (L.) |
| Genoa | Carlo Felice | Feb. 11, 1874 | R. Pantaleoni (A.) G. Tiozzo (G.) L. Filippi Bresciani (S.) G. Belletti (T.) Gi. Galvani (L.) G. Rossi cond. |
| Padua | Nuovo | July 18, 1874 | A. Fricci (A.) E. Barlani-Dini (G.) F. Patierno (S.) F. Pandolfini (T.) P. Medini (L.) |
| Parma | Regio | Feb. 4, 1874 | B. Montesini (A.) A. Veratti (G.) S. Anastasi (S.) L. Giraldoni (T.) G. Wagner (L.) E. Neri cond. |
| Rome | Apollo | Feb. 10, 1874 | A. Creny (A.) G. Capponi (S.) V. Collini (T.) O. Maini (L.) E. Terziani cond. |

Turin         Regio        Mar.   7, 1874 G. Giovannoni-Zacchi (A.) L. Manfre-
                                          di (G.) F. Patierno (S.) A. Panta-
                                          leoni (T.) A. Augier (L.) C. Pedrot-
                                          ti cond.


Revised Bologna-Politeama d'Azeglio-Aug. 27, 1898

Amalasunta (A.)                                          Emma Angelini sop.
Sveno (S.)                                            Luigi Longobardi ten.
Teodato (T.)                                              Bortolomasi bar.
Lausco (L.)                                       Giovanni Balisardi bass
Svarano                                                       Salotti bar.

Conductor                                                 Gaetano Zinetti
Director                                                  Stefano Gobatti

OTHER PRODUCTIONS

ITALY
Messina       Vittorio     Feb. 11, 1899 E. Angelini  (A.)  G. Villalta  (S.)
              Emanuele                   Bozzoli (T.) A. Didur (L.) Martini
                                         cond.


14. LA CONTESSA DI MONS-*Melodramma* in four acts
Turin-Teatro Regio-Jan. 31, 1874
Music by Lauro Rossi; Libretto by Marco D'Arienzo

Isabella (I.)                                 Ginevra Giovannoni-Zacchi sop.
Carlo (C.)                                          Filippo Patierno ten.
Uberto di Ligne (U.)                             Adriano Pantaleoni bar.
Il Prevosta                                          Antonio Bonori bass
Il Duca d'Alba (D.)                              Alfredo Giraudet bass
Del Rio                                              Luigi Manfredi ten.
Gibelta                                          Benedettina Dani sec.

Conductor                                                 Carlo Pedrotti
Director                                                  Carlo Pedrotti

OTHER PRODUCTIONS

ITALY
Cagliari      Civico       Jan.       1877 Rubini (I.) F. Barbieri (U.) Panari
                                           (D.)

Como          Sociale      Jan.       1877 C. Caselli (I.) G. Bassini (C.) G.
                                           Santini (U.) F. Caselli (D.) G. B.
                                           Caldera cond.

Correggio                  Oct.       1874 C. Scarati-Bresciani (I.) L. Filippi
                                           Bresciani (C.) L. Borgioli (U.) Del
                                           Fabbro (D.) G. Rossi cond. L. Rossi
                                           dir.

Ferrara       Comunale     Feb.    3? 1877 Robiati (I.) Avagnini (C.) De Giorgi
                                           (U.)

Genoa         Paganini     Oct. 22, 1881 T. Restelli (I.) Al. De Bassini (C.)

| Livorno | Avvalorati | Dec. 26? 1875 | V. Passigli (I.) L. Giraud (C.) G. Cima (U.) U. Gianolli cond. |
|---------|-----------|---------------|---------|
| Macerata | Lauro Rossi | Aug. 11? 1875 | F. Vogri (I.) G. Sani (C.) S. Sparapani (U.) R. D'Ottavi (D.) L. Mancinelli cond. L. Rosssi dir. |
| Milan | La Scala | Jan. 9, 1877 | Negroni (I.) P. Augusti (C.) A. Pantaleoni (U.) C. Bedogni (D.) |
| Parma | Regio | Dec. 26, 1874 | C. Mocoroa (I.) E. Ronconi (C.) A. Pifferi (U.) G. Tanzini (D.) G. Foschini cond. |
| Perugia | | Dec. 26? 1876 | O. Legramenti (I.) G. Caldani-Kuon (C.) Marchiani (U.) Amadei cond. |
| Rome | Apollo | Apr. 7, 1875 | A. Pozzoni-Anastasi (I.) S. Anastasi (C.) Z. Bertolasi (U.) R. Nannetti (D.) E. Usiglio cond. |
| Trieste | Grande | Nov. 18, 1874 | G. Giovannoni-Zacchi (I.) F. Patierno (C.) G. Aldighieri (U.) G. Atry (D.) E. Bernardi cond. L. Rossi dir. |
| Turin | Vittorio Emanuele | Oct. 2, 1875 | Mariani (I.) G. Sani (C.) Z. Bertolasi (U.) A. Furlan (D.) |
| Venice | La Fenice | Dec. 26, 1875 | C. Scarati-Bresciani (I.) L. Filippi Bresciani (C.) Z. Bertolasi (U.) G. Monti (D.) E. Usiglio cond. |
| Vicenza | Eretenio | Jan.? 1876 | A. Pantaleoni (U.) R. Kuon cond. |

15. DOLORES-*Dramma lirico* in four parts
Florence-Teatro della Pergola-Feb. 23, 1875
Music by Salvatore Auteri-Manzocchi; Libretto by M. Auteri-Pomàr

| | |
|---|---|
| Dolores (D.) | Isabella Galletti-Gianoli sop. |
| Lia (L.) | Ida Cristofani sop. |
| Ildebrando (I.) | Virginia Ferni-Germano mez. |
| Manfredi (M.) | Luigi Rampini-Boncori ten. |
| Fulco (F.) | Augusto Brogi bar. |
| Un Eremito (E.) | Andrea Zesevich bass |
| Ubaldo | |
| | |
| Conductor | Teodulo Mabellini |

OTHER PRODUCTIONS

ITALY

| Ancona | Muse | Feb. 6? 1886 | V. Ferni (D.) E. Milanesi (L.) Basset (M.) Garbini (F.) |
|--------|------|--------------|---------|
| Bologna | Comunale | Oct. 12, 1876 | I. Galletti-Gianoli (D.) A. Garbini (L.) C. Castiglioni (I.) A. Rossetti (M.) A. Brogi (F.) A. Silvestri (E.) M. Mancinelli cond. |

Brescia        Grande       Aug.       1876  I. Galletti-Gianoli (D.) C. De Mona-
                                             le (L.) G. Celega (I.) E. Barbacini
                                             (M.) V. Cottone (F.) G. David (E.)
                                             R. Kuon cond.

Cagliari       Civico       Dec. 26?  1880  Garulli (D.) Pasquali (M.)

Como           Sociale      Carn. 1883-84

Correggio                   Oct. 20?  1875  Berini-Maini (D.) B. Tati (L.) M.
                                             Chini (G.) E. Barbacini (M.) P. Si-
                                             lenzi (F.) I. Sbordoni (E.) Olivieri
                                             cond.

Florence       Pagliano     Nov. 26,  1876  I. Galletti-Gianoli (D.) C. De Mona-
                                             le (L.) G. Novelli (I.) A. Rossetti
                                             (M.) P. Silenzi (F.) Roncagli cond.

Milan          Dal Verme    June 23,  1875  I. Galletti-Gianoli (D.) I. Cristo-
                                             fani (L.) E. Barbacini (M.) L. Lal-
                                             loni (F.) A. Silvestri (E.) E. Ber-
                                             nardi cond.

                            May  24,  1876  I. Galletti-Gianoli (D.) L. Mecocci
                                             (L.) A. Rossetti (M.) S. Sparapani
                                             (F.) W. Seidemann (E.) R. Kuon cond.

               La Scala     Jan. 11,  1879  R. Vercolini-Tay/I. Galletti-Gianoli
                                             (D.) Rossini (L.) C. Prandi (I.) A.
                                             Rossetti (M.) L. Lalloni (F.) A.
                                             Pinto (E.)

Padua          Nuovo        June      1876  A. Fricci (D.) A. Franchini (M.) A.
                                             Strozzi (F.) E. Barberat (E.) R.
                                             Drigo cond.

Palermo        Circo        Jan. 27,  1875  I. Galletti-Gianoli (D.) M. Paolini
                                             (L.) G. Celega (I.) J. Gayarre (M.)
                                             L. Lalloni (F.) G. Mirabella (E.) F.
                                             Nicolao cond.

Parma          Regio        Dec. 25,  1875  E. Berini (D.) M. Porta (L.) A. Len-
                                             zi/M. Ghini (I.) A. Franchini (M.)
                                             G. De Veiga/G. Belletti (F.) G. Tan-
                                             zini (E.) G. Foschini cond.

Pisa           Verdi        Jan. 20,  1885  M. L. Paolicchi-Mugnone (D.) E. Mon-
                                             terey (L.) M. Massimi (F.) G. Monti
                                             (E.) L. Mugnone cond.

Rome           Apollo       Jan. 27,  1876  I. Galletti-Gianoli (D.) A. Garbini
                                             (L.) G. Celega (I.) I. Campanini
                                             (M.) V. Quintili-Leoni (F.) G. Mira-
                                             bella (E.) L. Mancinelli cond.

               Argentina    Nov. 14,  1880  I. Galletti-Gianoli (D.) A. Rossetti
                                             (M.)

Turin          Regio        Feb. 24,  1877  I. Galletti-Gianoli (D.) C. De Mona-
                                             le (L.) C. Castiglioni (I.) I. Cam-
                                             panini (M.) G. Kaschmann (F.) A.
                                             Silvestri (E.) C. Pedrotti cond.

16. FRANCESCA DA RIMINI-*Tragedia* in four acts
Turin-Teatro Regio-Feb. 19, 1878
Music by Antonio Cagnoni; Libretto by Antonio Ghislanzoni

Francesca (F.)                          Palmira Missorta sop.
Silvio (S.)                        Augusta Fidi-Azzalini sop.
Paolo (P.)               Lorenzo Abrugnedo/Victor Clodio ten.
Lanciotto (L.)                          Erasmo Carnili bar.
Fra Bonaventura (B.)                    Gaetano Roveri bass
Alberigo (A.)                      Alessandro Polonini bass
Guido                              Federico Becheri bass

Conductor                                    Carlo Pedrotti

OTHER PRODUCTIONS

ITALY
Asti          Alfieri      Nov. 26? 1889 E. Piave (F.) A. Volebele (P.) Fari
                                        (L.) E. Faff (A.) G. Foschini cond.

Bergamo       Donizetti    Jan. 15, 1891 V. Checchi (F.) A. Baggetto (P.) G.
                                        Pagnoni (L.) F. Romei cond.

Ferrara       Comunale     Feb.  8? 1888 C. Di Monale (F.) V. Ghilardini (P.)
                                        R. Bolcioni (L.)

Genoa         Politeama    July  8, 1889 E. Boronat (F.) G. Rizzini (P.) E.
                                        Sottolana (L.) V. Coda (B.) G. Pag-
                                        noni (A.) A. Toscanini cond.

              May  2, 1891 C. Di Monale (F.) A. Antonietti As-
                                        santi (S.) F. Avedano (P.) V. Brom-
                                        bara (L.)

Milan         Dal Verme    Nov. 19, 1888 E. Boronat (F.) V. Ghilardini (P.)
                                        G. Favi (L.) V. Arimondi (B.) E.
                                        Sivori (A.) A. Toscanini cond.

Rovigo        Sociale      Oct. 13, 1889 C. Di Monale (F.) O. Emiliani (P.)
                                        V. Brombara (L.) L. Contini (B.) E.
                                        Camera (A.) E. Usiglio cond.

Verona        Ristori      Nov. 17, 1889 C. Di Monale (F.) Bianco (P.) V.
                                        Brombara (L.) E. Camera (A.)

SPAIN
Barcelona     Liceo        Nov.  3, 1889 D. Barberini (F.) A. Del Bruno (S.)
                                        E. De Marchi (P.) E. Laban (L.) J.
                                        Goula cond.

17. ERO E LEANDRO-*Tragedia lirica* in three acts
Madrid-Teatro Real-Nov. 30, 1897
Music by Luigi Mancinelli; Libretto by Arrigo Boito

| Ero (E.) | Ericlea Darclée sop. |
|---|---|
| Il Prologo (P.) | Virginia Guerrini mez. |
| Leandro (L.) | Emilio De Marchi ten. |
| Ariofarne (A.) | Giovanni Scarneo bass |
| Voce de la Mare | |

Conductor                                                    Luigi Mancinelli

OTHER PRODUCTIONS

BRAZIL

| Rio de Janeiro | Lirico | Sep. 2, 1905 | M. De Lerma (E.) R. Verger (P.) F. Giraud (L.) G. Mansueto (A.) L. Mancinelli cond. |
|---|---|---|---|

GREAT BRITAIN

| London | Covent Garden | July 11, 1898 | E. Eames (E.) E. Schumann-Heink (P.) A. Saléza (L.) P. Plançon (A.) L. Mancinelli cond. |
|---|---|---|---|
| | | June 20, 1899 | F. Strakosch (E.) L. Homer (P.) A. Saléza (L.) P. Plançon (A.) L. Mancinelli cond. |
| Norwich | Festival | Oct. 8, 1896 | E. Albani (E.) E. Lloyd (L.) (in Eng.)[58] |

ITALY

| Genoa | Carlo Felice | Jan. 26, 1899 | F. Strakosch (E.) E. Bruno (P.) G. Anastasi (L.) D. Menotti (A.) O. Anselmi cond. |
|---|---|---|---|
| Naples | San Carlo | Apr. 24, 1900 | A. Karola (E.) A. Berti Cecchini (P.) A. Bassi (L.) C. Nicolay (A.) E. Perosio cond. |
| Rome | Costanzi | Feb. 27, 1904 | A. Karola (E.) E. Bruno (P.) F. Giraud (L.) L. Rossato (A.) L. Mancinelli cond. |
| Turin | Regio | Jan. 1, 1898 | C. Ferrani (E.) G. Zeppilli-Villani (P.) P. Zeni (L.) A. Lanzoni/G. Scarneo (A.) A. Toscanini cond. |
| Venice | La Fenice | Jan. 15, 1898 | A. Santarelli (E.) G. Apostolu (L.) V. Arimondi (A.) L. Mancinelli cond. |

POLAND

| Warsaw | Wielki | Nov. 23, 1902 | S. Kruszelnicka (E.) G. Anselmi (L.) |
|---|---|---|---|

PORTUGAL

| Lisbon | Sao Carlos | Mar. 8, 1902 | A. Stehle (E.) C. Marchesini (P.) G. Anselmi (L.) O. Luppi (A.) L. Mancinelli cond. |
|---|---|---|---|

---

[58]. Given as a cantata in concert form before its premiere as an opera.

SPAIN
Barcelona        Liceo        Apr. 10, 1913  C. Gagliardi  (E.)  V. Guerrini  (P.)
                                            L. Botta  (L.)  D. Biglione-Borghese
                                            (A.)

UNITED STATES
Boston           Boston Th.   Apr.  6, 1899  E. Eames   (E.)   E. Mantelli  (P.) A.
                                            Saléza  (L.)  P. Plançon  (A.)  L. Man-
                                            cinelli cond.

New York         Metro-       Mar. 10, 1899  E. Eames   (E.)   E. Mantelli  (P.) A.
                 politan                    Saléza  (L.)  P. Plançon  (A.)  L. Man-
                                            cinelli cond.

                              Mar.  4, 1903  J. Gadski  (E.)  E. Schumann-Heink
                                            (P.) E. De Marchi  (L.)  E. de Reszke
                                            (A.)  L. Mancinelli cond.

BIBLIOGRAPHY

Books, Dissertations and Manuscripts

Aiolfi, Renzo: *Il Teatro a Savona 1583/1984*-Savona, 1984

Allodi, Ivo: *I Teatri di Parma dal Farnese al Regio*-Milan, 1969

Alonso Cortes, Narciso: *El Teatro de Valladolid Siglo XIX*-Valladolid, 1947

Amadei, Giuseppe: *I Centocinquant Anni nella Storia dei Teatri di Mantova*-Mantua, 1973

Anker, Oyvind: *Christiana Theater's Repertoire 1827-99*-Oslo, 1956

*Annales du Théâtre Royal d'Anvers*-Antwerp, 1866-1884

Armstrong, W. G.: *A Record of the Opera in Philadelphia*-Philadelphia, 1884

Arnaudiès, Fernand: *Histoire de l'Opéra d'Alger*-Algiers, n.d.

Arrones Peon, Luis: *Historia de la Opera en Oviedo*-Oviedo, 1981-1987, 3 vols.

Artis, Jose: *El Gran Teatro del Liceo*-Barcelona, 1946

Aumont, Arthur and Edgar Collin: *Det Danske Nationalteater 1748-1889*-Copenhagen, 1897, 2 vols.

Ayesterán, Lauro: *La Musica en el Uruguay*-Montevideo, 1953

Baroncelli, J. G.: *Le Théâtre Francais a la Nlle Orléans 1791-1906*-New Orleans, 1906

Bartels, Adolf: *Chronik des Weimarischen Hoftheaters 1817-1907*-Weimar, 1908

Bartos, Josef: *Prozatimni Divadlo a Jeho Opera*-Prague, 1938

Battaglia, Fernando: *L'Arte del Canto in Romagna*-Bologna, 1979

Bauer, Anton: *Opern und Operetten in Wien*-Graz, 1955

Beetz, Wilhelm: *Das Wiener Opernhaus 1869-1945*-Vienna, 1949

Berutto, Guglielmo:*I Cantanti Piemontesi*-Turin, 1972

Bilbao, Jose: *Teatro Real Recuerdos de las Cinco Temporadas de Empresario Arana*-Madrid, n.d.

Bing, Anton: *Rückblicke auf die Geschichte des Frankfurter Stadttheaters von dessen Selbständigkeit (1792) bis zur Gegenwart*-Frankfurt am Main, 1892-1896, 2 vols.

Bishop, Cardell: *San Carlo Opera Company of America*-Santa Monica, 1980-81, 2 vols.

Bishop, Cardell: *Boston National Opera Company and Boston Theatre Opera Company*-Santa Monica, 1981

Blanc, T.: *Christiana Theater's Historie 1827-1877*-Oslo, 1899

Bloomfield, Arthur: *50 Years of the San Francisco Opera*-San Francisco, 1972

Bondi, Gustav: *Fünfundzwanzig Jahre Eigenregie-Geschichte des Brunner Stadttheaters 1882-1907*-Brunn, 1907

Bondi, Gustav: *Geschichte des Brunner Deutschen Theaters 1600-1924*-Brunn, 1924

Bosch, Mariano G.: *Historia de la Opera en Buenos Aires*-Buenos Aires, 1905

Bottenheim, Salomon: *De Opera in Nederland*-Amsterdam, 1983

Bouquet, Maria-Thérèse, Valeria Gualerzi and Alberto Testa: *Storia del Teatro Regio di Torino-Cronologie*-Turin, 1988

Branetti, Assunta: *Teatri di Viterbo*-Viterbo, 1980

Brewer, Francis Campbell: *The Drama and Music in New South Wales*-Sydney, 1892

Broadbent, R. J.: *The Annals of the Liverpool Stage*-Liverpool, 1908

Burada, T. T.: *Istoria Teatrului in Moldova*-Bucharest, 1975

Caamano, Roberto: *La Historia del Teatro Colón 1908-1968*-Buenos Aires, 1969, 3 vols.

Cambiasi, Pompeo: *Rappresentazioni date nei Reali Teatri di Milano*-Milan, 1872

Cametti, Alberto: *Il Teatro di Tordinona poi di Apollo*-Tivoli, 1938, 2 vols.

Canepa Guzman, Mario: *La Opera en Chile (1839-1930)*-Santiago, 1976

Carmena y Millan, Luis: *Cronica de la Opera Italiana en Madrid Desde el Ano 1738 Hasta Nuestros Dias*-Madrid, 1878

Carson, William G. B.: *St. Louis Goes to the Opera*-St. Louis, 1946

Cassidy, Claudia: *Lyric Opera in Chicago*-Chicago, 1979

Cella, Franca: *Leyla Gencer Romanzo Vero di una Primadonna*-Venice, 1986

Cellamare, Daniele: *Teatro Umberto Giordano-Cronistoria degli Spettacoli di 140 Anni (1828-1968)*-Rome, 1969

Cernicchiaro, Vincenzo: *Storia della Musica nel Brasile*-Milano, 1926

Cervetti, Valerio, and Claudio Del Monte: *Cronologia degli Spettacoli Lirici*-Parma, 1979-1982, 4 vols.

Chorley, Henry F.: *Thirty Years Musical Recollections*-New York and London, 1926

Christian, Hans, and Harald Hoyer: *Wiener Staatsoper 1945-1980*-Vienna, n.d.

Chusid, Martin: *A Catalog of Verdi's Operas*-Hackensack, N. J., 1974

Chusid, Martin: *Apropos Aroldo, Stiffelio and Le Pasteur, with a list of 19th Century Performances of Aroldo*-Verdi Newsletter No. 14, New York, 1986

Chusid, Martin: *Casts for the Verdi Premieres in London*-Verdi Newsletters 5 and 6, New York, 1978-79

Chusid, Martin: *Casts for the Verdi Premieres in the U.S.*-Verdi Newsletters 2 and 3, New York, 1976-77

Chusid, Martin, and Thomas Kaufman: *The First Three Years of Trovatore: A List of Stagings from 19 January 1853 to 18 January 1856*-Verdi Newsletter No. 15, New York, 1987

Cinelli, C.: *Memorie Cronistoriche del Teatro di Pesaro dall'anno 1637 al 1897*-Pesaro, 1898

Claeys, Prosper: *Histoire du Théâtre a Gand*-Ghent, 1892, 3 vols.

Clapp, William W.: *Record of the Boston Stage*-Boston, 1853

Clément, Felix and Pierre Larousse: *Dictionnaire des Opéras*-Paris, 1905

Clerico, Cesare: *Italo Tajo La Parte del Basso*-Turin, 1985

Clerico, Cesare: *Tancredi Pasero Voce Verdiana*-Turin, n.d.

Combarnous, Victor: *L'Histoire du Grand Théâtre de Marseille-Notes et Souvenirs*-Marseille, 1922

Comune di Brisighella: *Maria Pedrini-Celebre Soprano do Brisighella*-Brisighella, 1985

Conati, Marcello: *A Chronology of the First Performances of Rigoletto*-Bolletino 9 of the Istituto di Studi Verdiani, Parma, 1982

Conati, Marcello: *Prime Rappresentazioni di Ernani 1844-1846*-Bolletino 10 of the Istituto di Studi Verdiani, Parma, 1987

Conati, Marcello: *Stagings of Aida from 1871 to 1881*-Quaderno 4 of the Istituto di Studi Verdiani, Parma, 1971

Cone, John Frederick: *First Rival of the Metropolitan Opera*-New York, 1983

Cone, John Frederick: *Oscar Hammerstein's Manhattan Opera Company*-Norman, Okla., 1966

Cooper, Dorith Rachel: *Opera in Montreal and Toronto: A Study of Performance Traditions and Repertoire 1783-1980*-Ph.D. Thesis, Univ. of Toronto, 1983, 4 vols.

Covoes, Ricardo: *Os 50 Anos do Coliseu de Recreios*-Lisbon, 1940

Cox, Rev. T. C.: *Musical Recollections of the Last Half Century*-London, 1872

Danzuso, Domenico and Giovanni Idonea: *Musica, Musicisti e Teatri a Catania*-Palermo, 1985

Davis, Ronald: *Opera in Chicago*-New York, 1966

De Andrade, Ayres: *Francisco Manuel da Silva e seu Tempo*-Rio de Janeiro, 1967, 2 vols.

De Angelis, Marcello: *La Musica del Granduca*-Florence, 1978

De Brito Chaves, Edgard, Jr.: *Memorias e Glorias de un Teatro*-Rio de Janeiro, 1971

De Candolle, Roger: *Histoire du Théâtre de Genève*-Geneva, 1978

De Franceschi, Bruno, and Pier Fernando Mondini: *Ebe Stignani Una Vove e il suo Mondo*-Imola, 1980

Degani, Giannino, and Mara Grotto: *Il Teatro Municipale di Reggio Emilia, Opere in Musica 1857-1976*-Reggio Emilia, 1976

Dell'Ira, Gino: *Il Firmamento Lirico Pisano*-Pisa, 1983

Dell'Ira, Gino: *I Teatri di Pisa (1773-1986)*-Pisa, 1987

Del Pino, Enrique: *Historia del Teatro en Malaga durante el Siglo XIX*-Malaga, 1985

De Oliveira Castro Cerquera, Paulo: *Um Seculo de Opera em Sao Paulo*-Sao Paulo, 1954

De Silvestri, Lodovico: *Civico Teatro Fraschini di Pavia*-Pavia, 1938

Domanski, Piotr Jerzy: *Repertuar Teatrow Warszawskich 1901-1906*-Warsaw, 1976

Domanski, Piotr Jerzy: *Repertuar Teatrow Warszawskich 1907-1910*-Warsaw, 1977

Drake, James A.: *Richard Tucker*-New York, 1984

Dupêchez, Charles: *Histoire de l'Opéra de Paris 1875-1980*-Paris, 1984
Eaton, Quaintance: *The Boston Opera Company*-New York, 1965
Eaton, Quaintance: *Opera Caravan*-New York, 1957
Fabbri, Paolo, and Roberto Verti: *Due Secoli di Teatro per Musica a Reggio Emilia*-Reggio Emilia, 1987
Fawkes, Richard: *Welsh National Opera*-London, 1986
Fernandez, Roberto: *Los Primeiros Teatros en Valparaiso y el Desarollo General de Nuestros Espectaculos Publicos*-Valparaiso, 1928
Fernandez Serrano, D. Baldomer: *Annales del Teatro Cervantes de Malaga*-Malaga, 1903
Fioravanti, Roberto: *La Musica a Prato dal Duecento al Novocento*-Prato, 1973
Fiorda Kelly, Alfredo: *Cronologia de las Operas, Dramas Liricos, Oratorios, Himnos, etc. Cantados en Buenos Aires*-Buenos Aires, 1934
Fischer, Georg: *Musik in Hannover*-Hannover, 1903
Florimo, Francesco: *La Scuola Musicale di Napoli e i suoi Conservatori*-Naples, 1880-1882
Fonseca Benevides, Francisco da: *O Real Theatro de S. Carlos de Lisboa*-Lisbon, 1883
Fonseca Benevides, Francisco da: *O Real Theatro di S. Carlos de Lisboa-Memorias 1883-1902*-Lisbon, 1902
Forlani, Maria Giovanna: *Il Teatro Municipale di Piacenza (1804-1984)*-Piacenza, 1985
Formenton, Francesco D.: *Storia del Teatro Eretenio di Vicenza*-Vicenza, 1868
Fouque, Octave: *Histoire du Théâtre Ventadour*-Paris, 1881
Frajese, Vittorio: *Dal Constanzi all'Opera*-Rome, 1978, 4 vols.
Frassoni, Edilio: *Due Secoli di Lirica a Genova*-Genoa, 1980, 2 vols.
Fuentes Matons, Laureano: *Las Artes en Santiago de Cuba*-Havana, 1981
Gandini, Alessandro: *Cronistoria dei Teatri di Modena dal 1539 al 1871*-Modena, 1873
Gatti, Carlo: *Il Teatro alla Scala nella Storia e nell'arte*-Milan, 1964, 2 vols.
Geispitz, Henri: *Histoire du Théâtre des Arts de Rouen 1882-1913*-Rouen, 1913
Geispitz, Henri: *Histoire du Théâtre des Arts de Rouen 1913-1940*-Rouen, 1951
Gheusi, Jacques: *Histoire du Théâtre des Italiens de Paris*-Paris, L'Avant Scéne-Opéra Issues 55-65, 1983-1984
Ghirpelli, Giuseppe: *I Teatri di Modena*-Modena, 1988
Giovine, Alfredo: *Il Teatro Alfieri di Asti*-Bari, 1989
Giovine, Alfredo: *Il Teatro Piccinni di Bari*-Bari, 1970
Giovine, Alfredo: *Il Teatro Petruzzelli di Bari*-Bari, 1983
Gonzàlez, Jorge Antonio: *La Composicion Operistica en Cuba*-Havana, 1986
Got, Jerzy: *Das Oesterreichische Theater in Krakau im 18. und 19. Jahrhundert*-Vienna, 1884
Gualerzi, Giorgio, and Carlo Marinelli-Roscioni: *50 Anni di Opera Lirica alla RAI 1931-1980*-Turin, 1981
Gutierrez, Beniamino: *Il Teatro Carcano (1803-1914)*-Milan, 1914
Harris, Claude: *Opéra a Marseille 1685-1987*-Marseille, 1987
Hidalgo, Aurelio: *El Teatro Degollado 1866-1896*-Guadalajara, 1966
Hiller, Carl H.: *Vom Quatermarkt zum Offenbachplatz 400 Jahre Musiktheater in Köln*-Cologne, 1986
Hixon, Don L.: *Verdi in San Francisco 1851-1899*-San Francisco, 1980
Hortschansky, Klaus: *Die Herausbildung eines Deutsch-sprächigen Verdi-Repertoires*-Analecta Musicologica, Vol. 11
Hoza, Stefan: *Opera na Slovensku*-Bratislava, 1953, 2 vols.
Hughes, Spike: *A History of the Festival Opera Glyndebourne*-London, 1981
Hurst, Maurice: *Music and the Stage in New Zealand-A Century of Entertainment 1840-1943*-Auckland, 1943
Huwe, Gisela: *Die Deutsche Oper, Berlin*-Ludwigsburg, 1984
Isnardon, Jacques: *Théâtre de la Monnaie*-Brussels, 1890
Kapp, Julius: *Geschichte der Staatsoper Berlin*-Berlin, 1938
Kaufman, Thomas G.: *Italian Performances in Vienna 1835-1859*-Donizetti Society Journal 4, London, 1980
Kaut, Josef: *Die Salzburger Festspiele*-Salzburg, 1982
Kilian, Eugen: *Beiträge zur Geschichte des Karlsruher Hoftheaters unter Eduard Devrient*-Karlsruhe, 1893

Kmen, Henry A.: *Music in New Orleans-The Formative Years 1791-1841*-New Orleans, 1966
Kutsch, K. J., and Leo Riemens: *Grosses Sängerlexicon*-Bern and Stuttgart, 1987
Lawrence, Vera Brodsky: *Strong on Music-The New York Scene in the Days of George Templeton Strong, 1836-1975-Vol. I Resonances 1836-1850*-New York and London, 1988
Leicht, George, and Marianne Hallar: *Det Kongelige Teaters Repertoire 1889-1975*-Copenhagen, 1977
Lenotti, Tullio: *Il Teatro di Verona*-Verona, 1949
Leone, Guido: *L'Opera a Palermo dal 1653 al 1987*-Palermo, 1988, 2 vols.
Levey, Richard N., and J. O'Rourke: *Annals of the Theatre Royal, Dublin*-Dublin, 1880
Levi, Vito, Guido Botteri, and Ireneo Bremini,: *Il Comunale di Trieste*-Udine, 1962
Lewis, Kevin: *Memories of Wexford Festival Opera*-Wexford, 1984
Loewenberg, Alfred: *Annals of Opera, 1597-1940, 3rd Edition*-Totowa, N. J., and London, 1978
Longo, Giorgio, Sandro Dalla Libera and others: *La Fenice*-Milan, 1972
Love, Harold: *The Golden Age of Australian Opera-W. S. Lyster and His Companies*-Sydney, 1981
Lumley, Benjamin: *Reminiscences of the Opera*-London, 1864 and New York, 1976
Major, Norma: *Joan Sutherland*-London, 1987
Manferrari, Umberto: *Dizionario delle Opere Melodrammatiche*-Florence, n.d., 3 vols.
Maria y Campos, Armando de: *Una Temporada de Opera Italiana en Oaxaca*-Mexico City, 1939
Marinelli Roscioni, Carlo: *Cronologia del Teatro Comunale di Treviso*-Udine, 1962
Marinelli Roscioni, Carlo: *Il Teatro di San Carlo: Cronologie*-Naples, 1987
Martiny, Jules: *Histoire du Théâtre de Liège Depuis son Origine Jusqu'a nos Jours*-Liège, 1887
Massoff, Ioan: *Teatrul Romanesc*-Bucharest, 1961-1981, 8 vols.
Masui, Keiji: *Nihon no Opera*-Orien, Japan, 1984, 2 vols.
Mattfeld, Julius: *A Handbook of American Operatic Premieres*-Detroit, 1963
Mattfeld, Julius: *A Hundred Years of Grand Opera in New York 1825-1925*-New York, 1927
Mestres y Calvet, Juan: *El Gran Teatro del Liceo Viste por su Empresario*-Barcelona, n.d.
Mikulan, Marta: *Centenario del Teatro Municipal de Caracas*-Caracas, 1980
Mohr, Albert Richard: *Das Frankfurter Opernhaus 1880-1980*-Frankfurt, 1980
Moore, Edward C.: *Forty Years of Opera in Chicago*-New York, 1930
Moreau, Mário: *Cantores de Opera Portugueses*-Lisbon, 1981 and 1987, 2 vols.
Morini, Ugo: *La Re Accademia degli Immobili ed il suo Teatro La Pergola*-Pisa, 1926
Mueller, Georg Hermann: *Das Stadt Theater in Leipzig 1862-1887*-Leipzig, 1887
Nejedly, Zdenek: *Dejiny Opera-Narodniho Divadla*-Prague, 1949, 2 vols.
Odell, George C.: *Annals of the New York Stage*-New York, 1927-1931, 15 vols.
Olavarria y Ferrari, Enrique de: *Reseña Historico del Teatro en Mexico 1538-1911*-Mexico City, 1961, 6 vols.
Pacini, Giovanni: *Le mie Memorie Artistiche*-Florence, 1875
Palermo, Santo: *Saverio Mercadante*-Fasano di Puglia, 1985
Pallerotti, Antonio: *Spettacoli Melodrammatici e Coriografici Rappresentati in Padova nei Teatri Obizzi, Nuovo e del Prato Della Valle, dal 1751 al 1892*-Padua, 1892
Paoli Catelani, Bice: *Il Teatro Comunale del "Giglio" di Lucca*-Pescia, 1941
Pasarell, Emilio J.: *Origenes y Desarollo de la Aficion Teatral en Puerto Rico*-Santurce, 1970
Pavan, Giuseppe: *Teatri Musicali Veneziani-Il Teatro San Benedetto (Ora Rossini)*-Ataneo Veneto, Venice, 1916-17
Perdomo Escobar, Jose Ignazio: *La Opera en Colombia*-Bogota, 1979
Peth, Jacob: *Geschichte des Theaters und der Musik zu Mainz*-Mainz, 1879
Pichler, Anton: *Chronik des Grosherzöglichen Hof und National Theaters in Mannheim*-Mannheim, 1879

Pinzauti, Leonardo: *Il Maggio Musicale Fiorentino*-Florence, 1957
Portomastro, Giuseppe: *Cronistoria sul Teatro di Trani*-Trani, 1899
Prölls, Robert: *Geschichte des Hoftheater's zu Dresden-von seinem Anfängen bis zum Jahre 1862*-Dresden, 1878
Pulido Granata, Francisco Ramon: *La Tradicion Operatistica en la Ciudad de Mexico (Siglo XIX)*-Mexico City, 1970
Pulido Granata, Francisco Ramon: *La Tradicion Operatistica en la Ciudad de Mexico (1900-1911)*-Mexico City, 1981
Radiciotti, Giuseppe: *Teatro, Musica e Musichisti in Recanati*-Recanati, 1905
Radiciotti, Giuseppe: *Teatro, Musica e Musichisti in Sinigaglia*-Bologna, 1973
Radiciotti, Giuseppe: *Teatro e Musica in Roma 1825-1850*-Rome, 1905
Raffaelli, Michele: *Il Teatro Comunale di Forli nella Vita Musicale Italiana (1776-1944)*-Forli, 1982
Raggi, A. and L.: *Il Teatro Comunale di Cesena*-Cesena, 1906
Ralf, Klas: *Kungliga Teatern Repertoar 1773-1973*-Stockholm, 1974
Ramirez, Serafin: *La Habana Artistica Apuntes Historicos*-Havana, 1891
Ramos Perez, Vincente: *El Teatro Principal en la Historia de Alicante*-Alicante, 1965
Ravaldini, Gaetano: *Spettacoli nei Teatri e in altri Luoghi di Ravenna (1555-1977)*-Bologna, 1978
Ribera, Salvador A., and Luis Alberto Aguila: *La Opera*-Santiago, 1895
Rille, Albert: *Die Geschichte des Brunner Stadttheaters (1734-1844)*-Brunn, 1885
Rinaldi, Mario: *Due Secoli di Musica al Teatro Argentina*-Florence, 1978
Rolandi, Uldrico: *Musica e Musicisti in Malta*-Livorno, 1932
Rosenthal, Harold: *The Mapleson Memoirs*-New York, 1966
Rosenthal, Harold: *Two Centuries of Opera at Covent Garden*-London, 1958
Rossi, Michele: *Cronistoria del Teatro di Lugo*-Imola, 1970
Rubboli, Daniele: *Gino Bechi Il Palcoscenico e la Vita*-Bologna, 1988
Rudolph, Moritz: *Rigaer Theater und Tonkünstler Lexicon*-Riga, 1890
Ruffo, Titta: *La mia Parabola Memorie*-Rome, 1977
Rundberg, Alfred: *Svensk Operakonst-Kultur och From*-Stockholm, 1952
Salas, Carlos, and Eduardo Feo Calcano: *Sesquicentenario de la Opera en Caracas*-Caracas, 1960
Sallés, Antoine: *L'Opéra Italien et Allemand a Lyon au XIXe Siècle (1805-1882)*-Paris, 1906
Schepelern, Gerhard: *Italierne paa Hofteateret*-Copenhagen, 1976
Schiavo, Remo: *Luci sull'Eretenio*-Vicenza, 1978
Schiavo, Remo: *Il Teatro Eretenio tra Cronaca e Storia*-Vicenza, 1983
Secomska, Henryka: *Repertuar Warszawskich Teatrow Rzadowych 1863-1890*-Warsaw, 1976
Seltsam, William H.: *Metropolitan Opera Annals*-New York, 1947
Sittenfeld, Ludwig: *Geschichte des Breslauer Theaters von 1841 bis 1900*-Breslau, 1909
Sivec, Joze: *Opera v Stanovskem Gledaliscu v Ljubljani*-Ljubljana, 1967
Sokol, Martin L.: *The New York City Opera*-New York, 1981
Subira, Jose: *Historia y Anecdotaria del Teatro Real*-Madrid, 1949
Subira, Jose: *La Opera en los Teatros de Barcelona*-Barcelona, 1946, 2 vols.
Swietlicka, Halina: *Repertuar Teatrow Warszawskich 1832-1862*-Warsaw, 1976
Tardini, Vincenzo: *I Teatri di Modena*-Modena, 1899-1902, 3 vols.
Teuber, Oskar: *Geschichte des Praguer Theaters*-Prague, 1888, 3 vols.
Tolon, Edwin Teurbe, and Jorge Antonio Gonzalez: *Historia del Teatro en la Habana*-Santa Clara, Cuba, 1961
Tompkins, Eugene: *History of the Boston Stage*-Boston, 1908
Tosi, Bruno: *Pertile, una Voce, un Mito*-Venice, 1985
Traniello, Leobaldo, and Luigi Stocco: *Il Teatro Sociale*-Rovigo, 1970
Uccello, Giuseppe: *Lo Spettacolo nei Secoli a Messina*-Palermo, 1986
Upton, George P.: *Musical Memories-My Recollections of Celebrities of the Half Century 1850-1950*-Chicago, 1908
Valenti-Ferro, Enzo: *Las Voces Teatro Colón 1908-1982*-Buenos Aires, 1983
Vallaut, Jean Jacques Hanine: *Giulietta Simionato Come Cenerentola Divenne Regina*-Parma, 1987
Various Authors: *Amilcare Ponchielli*-Milan, 1985

Various Authors: *Amilcare Ponchielli 1834-1886*-Casalmorano, 1984
Various Authors: *A Budapesti Operaház 100 Eve*-Budapest, 1984
Various Authors: *A Nemzeti Szinház 150 Eve*-Budapest, 1987
Various Authors: *Die Oper in Stuttgart 75 Jahre Littmann-Bau*-Stuttgart, 1987
Various Authors: *Opéra de Nice 1885-1985-D'Un Siécle a l'Autre*-Nice, 1985
Various Authors: *Slovenskeho Narodneho Divadlo*-Bratislava, 1960
Várnai, Peter: *Verdi Magyarországon*-Budapest, 1975
Vasquez, Rafael: *Historia de la Musica en Guatemala*-Guatemala, 1950
Vetro, Gaspare Nello: *Giovanni Bottesini 1821-1889*-Parma, 1989
Virella Cassanes, Francisco: *La Opera en Barcelona, Estudio Historico-Critico*-Barcelona, 1888
Vol'f, A. I.: *Khronika Petersburgski Teatrov*-St. Petersburg, 1877, 2 vols.
Vol'f, A. I.: *Khronika Petersburgski Teatrov 1855-1881*-St. Petersburg, 1884
Vuillermez, G.: *Cent Ans d'Opéra a Lyon*-Lyon, 1932
Wagner, Hans: *200 Jahre Münchner Theater Chronik 1750-1950*-Munich, 1958
Watmough, David: *The Unlikely Pioneer: Building Opera from the Pacific through the Prairies*-Oakville, Ont., 1986
Wearing, J. P.: *The London Stage 1890-1899: A Calendar of Plays and Players*-Metuchen, N. J., 1976, 2 vols.
Weaver, William, and Martin Chusid: *The Verdi Companion*-New York and London, 1979
Weisert, John Jacob: *A Large and Fashionable Audience: A Checklist of Performances at the Louisville Theatre 1846-1866*-Louisville, 1955
Weisert, John Jacob: *Mozart Hall 1851-1866*-Louisville, 1962
Weiss, Fritz: *Das Basler Stadttheater 1834-1934*-Basel, 1934
Wenzel, Joachim: *Geschichte der Hamburger Oper 1678-1978*-Hamburg, 1978
Wimmer, Heinrich: *Das Linzer Landestheater 1803-1958*-Linz, 1958
Wolff, Stèphane: *L'Opéra au Palais Garnier 1875-1962*-Paris, n.d.
Wolz, Larry Robert: *Opera in Cincinnati: The Years Before the Zoo, 1801-1920*-Ph.D. Dissertation, University of Cincinnati, 1983
Zecchinato, Amedeo: *Il Teatro Filarmonico di Verona*-Verona, 1956
Zenger, Max: *Geschichte der Münchener Oper*-Munich, 1923
Zuccarini, Mario: *Il Teatro di Chieti dalle Origini ai Giorni Nostri*-Chieti, 1976

Political Newspapers

Aftonbladet, Stockholm, Sweden
Alta California, San Francisco, Cal.
The Argus, Melbourne, Australia
Baltimore Sun, Baltimore, Md.
Basler Nachrichten, Basel, Switzerland
Bataviaasch Nieuwsblad, Jakarta, Indonesia
Belfast News Letter, Belfast, Northern Ireland
Boletin Mercantil de Puerto Rico, San Juan, Puerto Rico
Boston Evening Transcript, Boston, Mass.
Boston Globe, Boston, Mass.
Cape Argus, Capetown, South Africa
Cape Times, Capetown, South Africa
Chicago Tribune, Chicago, Ill.
China Mail, Hong Kong
Cincinnati Enquirer, Cincinnati, Ohio
Cleveland Plain Dealer, Cleveland, Ohio
El Comercio, Lima, Peru
El Comercio, Manila, Philippines
El Comercio del Plata, Buenos Aires, Argentina
Courier Journal, Louisville, Ky.
Cork Examiner, Cork, Ireland
Dagblad, Den Hague, The Netherlands
Daily News-Advertiser, Vancouver, B. C., Canada

Daily Picayune, New Orleans, La.
Daily Southern Cross, Auckland, N. Z.
Dallas Morning Herald, Dallas, Tex.
La Democrazia, San Juan, Puerto Rico
Detroit Free Press, Detroit, Mich.
El Dia, Montevideo, Uruguay
Diario de la Marina, Havana, Cuba
Diario de Centro America, Guatemala City, Guatemala
Edmonton Journal, Edmonton, Alberta, Canada
Egyptian Gazette, Alexandria and Cairo, Egypt
The Englishman, Calcutta, India
La Epoca, Madrid, Spain
O Estado do Sao Paulo, Sao Paulo, Brazil
Evening Post, Wellington, N. Z.
Evening Star, Washington, D. C.
El Ferrocaril, Santiago, Chile
Le Figaro, Paris, France
Frankfurter Zeitung, Frankfurt, Germany
Freeman's Journal, Dublin, Ireland
Glasgow Herald, Glasgow, Scotland
Globe, Toronto, Ont., Canada
Golos, St. Petersburg, Russia
El Guatemalteco, Guatemala City, Guatemala
Haagsche Courant, Den Haag, The Netherlands
El Herlado, Bogota, Colombia
Houston Post, Houston, Tex.
Hufvudstadsbladet, Helsinki, Finland
El Imparcial, Cairo, Egypt
Independance Belge, Brussels, Belgium
Japan Advertiser, Tokyo, Japan
Java Bode, Djakarta, Indonesia
Jornal do Comercio, Lisbon, Portugal
Jornal do Comercio, Rio de Janeiro, Brazil
Journal des Débats, Paris, France
Kölnische Zeitung, Cologne, Germany
Leeds Mercury, Leeds, England
Levant Herald, Constantinople, Turkey
Liverpool Mercury, Liverpool, England
Liverpool Post, Liverpool, England
Los Angeles Times, Los Angeles, Cal.
Manchester Guardian, Manchester, England
Manitoba Free Press, Winnipeg, Man., Canada
El Mercurio, Santiago, Chile
El Mercurio, Valparaiso, Chile
La Minerve, Montreal, Canada
Le Moniteur Universel, Paris, France
Montreal Gazette, Montreal, Quebec, Canada
Montreal Herald, Montreal, Canada
Morgenbladet, Oslo, Norway
Morning Chronicle, Quebec, Que., Canada
Moskovskaia Viedomosti, Moscow, Russia
El Nacional Argentino, Buenos Aires, Argentina
Nacion Argentino, Buenos Aires, Argentina
Neue Freie Presse, Vienna, Austria
Neue Preussische Zeitung, Berlin, Germany
Neue Zürcher Zeitung, Zürich, Switzerland
New Zealand Herald, Auckland, N. Z.
Nieuwe Amsterdamsche Courant, Amsterdam, The Netherlands
Nieuwe Rotterdamsche Courant, Rotterdam, The Netherlands
North China Daily News, Shanghai, China
Novoe Vremia, St. Petersburg, Russia
Otago Daily Times, Dunedin, N. Z.
Pittsburgh Post, Pittsburgh, Pa.
Politiken, Copenhagen, Denmark

Prager Presse, Prague, Czechoslovakia
La Prensa, Buenos Aires, Argentina
El Progresso, Santiago, Chile
Rand Daily Mail, Johannesburg, South Africa
Rech', St. Petersburg, Russia
La Reforma Pacifica, Buenos Aires, Argentina
Russkiia Viedomosti, Moscow, Russia
St. Louis Globe-Democrat, St. Louis, Mo.
Sanktpetersburgskiia Viedomosti, St. Petersburg, Russia
The Scotsman, Edinburgh, Scotland
Severnaia Pchela, St. Petersburg, Russia
El Siglo Diez y Nueve, Mexico City, Mexico
El Sol, Madrid, Spain
Soerabaiasch Handelsblad, Surabaja, Indonesia
South Australian Register, Adelaide, Australia
Staats und Gelehrte Zeitung, Hamburg, Germany
Stamboul, Constantinople, Turkey
Standard and Digger's News, Johannesburg, South Africa
Statesman and Friend of India, Calcutta, India
Straits Times, Singapore
Sydney Morning Herald, Sydney, Australia
Le Temps, Paris, France
El Tiempo, Bogota, Colombia
Times, London, England
Times of India, Bombay, India
El Universal, Mexico City, Mexico
Wiener Zeitung, Vienna, Austria

## Theatrical, Musical and Literary Periodicals

Allgemeine Musikalische Zeitung, Leipzig, Germany
Allgemeine Wiener Musik-Zeitung, Vienna, Austria
Buon Gusto, Florence, Italy
Cosmorama Pittorico, Milan, Italy
Dwight's Journal of Music, Boston, Mass.
The Era, London, England
La Fama, Milan, Italy
La France Musicale, Paris, France
Gazzetta de'Teatri, Milan, Italy
Gazzetta Musicale di Firenze, Florence, Italy
Gazzetta Musicale di Milano, Milan, Italy
Gazzetta Musicale di Napoli, Naples, Italy
Italia Musicale, Milan, Italy
Le Guide Musicale, Brussels, Belgium
Mondo Artistico, Milan, Italy
Musical America, New York, N. Y.
Musical World, London, England
Napoli Musicale, Naples, Italy
Neue Berliner Musik Zeitung, Berlin, Germany
Neue Wiener Musik Zeitung, Vienna, Austria
Opera, London, England
Opera International, Paris, France
Opera News, New York, N. Y.
Il Pirata, Milan and Turin, Italy
Rassegna Melodrammatica, Milan, Italy
Revue et Gazette Musicale, Paris, France
Rivista Teatrale Melodrammatica, Milan, Italy
Signale für die Musikalische Welt, Leipzig, Germany
Il Sistro, Florence, Italy
Teatri, Arte e Letteratura, Bologna, Italy
Il Trovatore, Turin and Milan, Italy

INDEX

| | | | |
|---|---|---|---|
| Adelchi | 1 | Edmea | 34 |
| Aida | 527 | Elda | 31 |
| Ali Baba | 29 | Elena da Feltre | 78 |
| Allan Cameron | 145 | Elena di Tolosa | 186 |
| Alzira | 327 | Enrico II | 111 |
| L'Amante di Richiamo | 571 | Ernani | 293 |
| Amleto | 45 | Ero e Leandro (Bottesini) | 29 |
| Un Amour en Baviere | 28 | Ero e Leandro (Mancinelli) | 579 |
| Anna la Prie | 568 | L'Espiazione | 177 |
| Aroldo | 460 | Estella | 259 |
| L'Assedio di Firenze | 27 | Ester d'Engaddi (Pacini) | 145 |
| L'Assedio di Leida (Pacini) | 147 | Ester d'Engaddi (Peri) | 169 |
| L'Assedio di Leida (Petrella) | 193 | La Falce | 31 |
| Attila | 328 | Falstaff | 555 |
| Babele | 30 | Il Favorito | 168 |
| Un Ballo in Maschera | 466 | La Fidanzata Corsa | 128 |
| La Battaglia di Legnano | 366 | I Fidanzati | 171 |
| Belfegor | 152 | La Figlia dell'Arciere | 155 |
| Berta di Varnol | 153 | Il Figliuol Prodigo | 244 |
| Bertrando da Bornio | 226 | Fiorina | 156 |
| Bianca Orsini | 219 | Une Folie à Rome | 261 |
| Bondelmonte | 137 | Il Folletto di Gresy | 206 |
| Il Bravo | 81 | Il Fornaretto | 571 |
| I Briganti | 11 | La Forza del Destino | 482 |
| Carmelita | 152 | Fosca | 53 |
| Caterina Howard | 215 | Francesca da Rimini | 578 |
| Cedar | 29 | Furio Camillo | 117 |
| Celinda | 214 | Gelmina | 159 |
| Il Cid | 147 | Genoveffa del Brabante | 160 |
| La Cimodocea | 179 | Gentile da Varano | 61 |
| Clara di Mailand | 155 | Gianni di Nisida | 151 |
| Claudia | 109 | Gildippe e Odoardo | 116 |
| Colón en Cuba | 27 | La Gioconda | 230 |
| Il Colonnello | 565 | Il Giorno delle Nozze | 179 |
| Condor | 60 | Un Giorno di Regno | 265 |
| Il Conte Verde | 573 | Giovanna d'Arco | 320 |
| Il Conte di Königsmarck | 10 | Giovanna la Pazza | 109 |
| La Contessa d'Amalfi | 207 | Giovanna II di Napoli | 215 |
| La Contessa di Mons | 575 | Giuditta | 176 |
| Corrado di Altamura | 254 | I Goti | 574 |
| Il Corsaro | 364 | Griselda | 259 |
| Crispino e la Comare | 571 | Il Guarany | 48 |
| Dejanice | 32 | Guerra in Quattro | 166 |
| La Demente | 61 | Gulnara | 11 |
| Diana | 220 | Gustavo Wasa (Apolloni) | 10 |
| Il Diavolo Color di Rosa | 179 | Gustavo Wasa (Marchetti) | 75 |
| Il Diavolo della Notte | 28 | Isabella d'Aragona | 163 |
| Dirce | 170 | Isabella de'Medici | 258 |
| Il Disertore per Amore | 565 | Jérusalem | 361 |
| Le Docteur Rose | 262 | Joana de Flandres | 47 |
| Dolores | 576 | Jone | 196 |
| Don Carlos | 497 | Leonora | 97 |
| Don Diego di Mendoza | 152 | Lina (Pedrotti) | 155 |
| Don Giovanni d'Austria | 76 | Lina (Ponchielli) | 227 |
| La Donna delle Isole | 148 | I Lituani | 228 |
| Il Duca d'Alba | 127 | I Lombardi | 283 |
| Il Duca di Scilla | 205 | Loreley | 35 |
| I Due Foscari | 311 | Lorenzino de'Medici | 135 |
| I Due Ritratti | 260 | Luigi Rolla | 253 |
| Le Due Illustri Rivali | 77 | Luisa Miller | 369 |
| Le Due Regine | 110 | Luisa Strozzi | 569 |
| Un Duello Sotto Richelieu | 252 | Luisetta | 134 |
| L'Ebrea | 134 | Macbeth | 341 |
| L'Ebreo | 1 | | |

| | | | | |
|---|---|---|---|---|
| Malvina di Scozia | 146 | La Punizione | 148 |
| Manfredo | 219 | Il Reggente | 95 |
| Marco Visconti | 188 | La Regina del Nepal | 30 |
| La Marescialla d'Ancre | 565 | La Regina di Cipro | 143 |
| Margherita Pusterla | 148 | Rienzi | 178 |
| Maria Tudor | 58 | Rigoletto | 382 |
| Maria, Regina d'Inghilterra | 130 | Roderico Re dei Goti | 227 |
| Marion Delorme (Bottesini) | 28 | Rodrigo di Valenza | 147 |
| Marion de Lorme (Pedrotti) | 167 | Romea di Montfort | 156 |
| Marion Delorme (Ponchielli) | 245 | Romeo e Giulietta | 62 |
| Il Marito e l'Amante | 260 | Romilda di Provenza | 147 |
| I Masnadieri | 352 | Ruy Blas | 63 |
| Matilde | 155 | Saffo | 117 |
| Mazeppa | 167 | Il Saltimbanco | 149 |
| Medea (Mercadante) | 106 | Salvator Rosa | 55 |
| Medea (Pacini) | 131 | La Savoiarda | 227 |
| Mefistofele | 13 | La Schiava Saracena | 105 |
| Merope | 144 | Lo Schiavo | 59 |
| Le Miniere di Freinberg | 180 | Lo Scroccone | 179 |
| Monsieur de Chalumeaux | 247 | Simon Boccanegra | 443 |
| I Mori di Valenza | 246 | Il Sindacco Babbeo | 571 |
| Morosina | 205 | La Solitaria delle Asturie | 94 |
| Il Mulattiere di Toledo | 151 | Il Solitario | 169 |
| Nabucco | 266 | La Sorrentina | 110 |
| Nerina | 30 | La Spia | 11 |
| Nerone | 23 | Statira | 106 |
| Nicolo de'Lapi | 153 | La Stella del Monte | 227 |
| A Noite do Castelo | 47 | Stella di Napoli | 142 |
| Oberto, Conte di San Bonifacio | 263 | Stiffelio | 380 |
| Olema la Schiava | 168 | Tancreda | 170 |
| Orazi e Curiazi | 103 | Il Templario | 111 |
| L'Orfana Svizzera | 146 | La Traviata | 416 |
| Orfano e Diavolo | 171 | Il Trovatore | 398 |
| Otello | 544 | Tutti in Maschera | 160 |
| Il Paniere d'Amore | 261 | L'Uomo del Mistero | 127 |
| Il Paria | 61 | Vallombra | 258 |
| Il Parlatore Eterno | 228 | Il Vascello di Gama | 102 |
| Pelagio | 107 | Les Vêpres Siciliennes | 429 |
| Il Perucchiere della Reggenza | 159 | La Vergine di Kermo | 573 |
| Pietro d'Abano | 10 | La Vestale | 87 |
| I Pirati Spagnuoli | 180 | Vinciguerra il Bandito | 28 |
| I Portoghesi nel Brasile | 149 | Violetta | 106 |
| Le Precauzioni | 181 | Virginia (Mercadante) | 108 |
| La Prigione di Edimburgo | 247 | Virginia (Nini) | 567 |
| I Profughi Fiamminghi | 45 | Virginia (Petrella) | 207 |
| I Promessi Sposi (Petrella) | 216 | Una Visita a Bedlam | 169 |
| I Promessi Sposi (Ponchielli) | 221 | Vittor Pisani | 172 |
| Il Proscritto (Mercadante) | 95 | La Wally | 39 |
| Il Proscritto (Nicolai) | 116 | Zaffira | 146 |